GERMAN CULTURE IN AMERICA

1600–1900

German Culture in America

PHILOSOPHICAL AND LITERARY INFLUENCES

1600-1900

HENRY A. POCHMANN

With the assistance of ARTHUR R. SCHULTZ *and others*

THE UNIVERSITY OF WISCONSIN PRESS

Madison, 1961

Published by The University of Wisconsin Press

430 Sterling Court, Madison 6, Wisconsin

First Printing, 1957
Second Printing, 1961

Library of Congress Catalog Card Number 55–6791

Preface

A patent and irremediable fault of this book (and most books of its kind) is that its very nature makes it one-sided, or at least makes it appear one-sided. While I have tried to appraise German philosophical, educational, and literary influences in America against influences in these areas from other countries, I seldom found it possible to present any detailed comparative analysis, but had to content myself with what I consider a fair statement of the extent of *Germanic* influence. There will be time enough for a final synthesis and evaluation of the foreign *versus* the native elements in American culture once all the foreign impacts have been assessed. Findings in these and other spheres of comparative cultural relations will inevitably modify my conclusions and put them in a perspective now impossible. It is much to be desired that investigations in parallel areas may be pushed vigorously; for, as I see it, the study of literary culture in the United States has reached a point beyond which it cannot proceed effectively unless and until the several foreign accretions are segregated from one another and from the native ingredients and all of them are appraised in terms of each other and the final product.

A second fault is that while I constantly employ the terms *German* and *American*, I have not found it possible anywhere precisely to define those terms, or even to distinguish between what might be termed German *Geist* and American spirit. All formulations of *Nationalgeist* that I attempted turned out to be so vague as to be meaningless or so narrow as to be useless or so comprehensive as to be self-contradictory. In the end I came up with little more than such obvious distinctions as can be made in terms of persons, themes, ideas, forms—in terms of time and place. I can only hope that the cumulative evidence presented in the following pages of how a Kant inspired an Emerson to establish a *Prima Philosophia* in Boston, or the German tale influenced the American short story, or *Faust* supplied motifs for *The Golden Legend* will speak for itself and be interesting and illuminating in both directions. The time to answer the larger, more difficult questions regarding how German culture as a whole modified the course of American culture as a whole is not yet; at all events, it is not for me.

In the interest of economy, the manuscript of this book was subjected to two drastic condensations and complete rewritings by which its length was reduced from 2,800 to 1,800 to 1,000 typewritten pages. In the process three chapters were eliminated altogether: (1) German educational influences, (2) German-American radicalism in the Midwest, and (3) German-American writings (in German) in the United States. A goodly amount of material was transferred from the text to footnotes, and much more was omitted altogether. Documentation not absolutely essential was deleted. At several points in the text, notably in the chapter on Emerson, I have indicated that I shall be happy to supply such information for students desirous of having it. In order to make these materials more readily available for consultation or microfilming, I have deposited in the University of Wisconsin Library a copy of the first version of the manuscript. Since the arrangement or ordering of material (except for the omitted sections) is substantially the same as that of the printed version, it should not be too difficult to find what is wanted.

During the twenty-five years that I devoted to this study, I had the advantage, largely through the generosity of the Research Committee of the University of Wisconsin, of help from competent research assistants—among them Calvin V. Huenemann, Lucille Hein, Louise H. Johnson, Eleanor Coswell, Louis Budd, and Arthur R. Schultz. Dr. Schultz, during a two-year appointment as post-doctorate fellow, did much of the spade work on the vogue of German literature in the United States, on George Ripley, Theodore Parker, and Margaret Fuller, and on the introduction of German philosophy into American colleges and universities. In addition to the grants and research leaves from the University of Wisconsin, I have enjoyed fellowship appointments from the Henry E. Huntington Library and from the Rockefeller Foundation. The latter enabled me to consult materials in the larger depositories in Germany, the British Museum, and the more important stores of German-Americana in American libraries.

I cannot possibly detail in this foreword the extent of my indebtedness to earlier investigators in the field of German-American cultural exchange, but I have sought scrupulously to indicate in the notes my reliance on prior findings.

H. A. P.

January, 1954

Table of Contents

Book One

GERMAN THOUGHT IN AMERICA

Early Interest in German Culture

Table of Contents

Thought Currents of the Nineteenth Century

The Transcendentalist Writers

The Spread of Interest in German Philosophy

Table of Contents

Book Two

GERMAN LITERARY INFLUENCE

Some Areas and Lines of Influence

Germanic Materials and Motifs in the Short Story

Table of Contents

Nineteenth-Century Poets, Novelists, and Critics

Table of Contents

NOTES

LIST OF TABLES

INTRODUCTION

Introduction

Whether one Tyrker who accompanied Leif Ericson was a German, and whether Captain John Smith's settlement at Jamestown did indeed include some Germans are matters for the determination of which some antiquarians appear prepared to barter the promise of eternal bliss. Heated arguments revolve around the exact number of German immigrants who came to America at specific times, the precise location of their settlements, the details of their migrations, and the number of their descendants. Others seem ready to shed their heart's blood if, by so doing, they could establish as fact the old story that the German language missed becoming the official language of the United States by the margin of one vote of a Congressional committee, or authenticate the legend that Abraham Lincoln (Linkhorn?) was of German extraction.

Questions whether three or four families comprised the party that moved from New Orleans in a certain year to settle on the Red River are important, but for the matter in hand, what is more significant is whether the "German Coast" in Louisiana represented merely another racial or cultural "island," or whether the Germans of lower Louisiana were of a type to exert a cultural influence beyond their own little communal limits and racial sphere. It is not necessary to retell the circumstantial history of the first permanent German settlements in Pennsylvania (1683) and New York (1709), their phenomenally rapid growth and spread southward and westward, and the numerous accessions to their numbers direct from Germany. These matters have been treated adequately for our purposes (though not exhaustively) in a number of histories.[1] In all of these works the emphasis is on what the authors agree in calling "the German element," by which is meant the immigration, settlement, and distribution of the Germans in America, together with such concrete contributions as lie on the surface. The point of view is historical or biographical. Several are little more than a directory or a "Who's Who" of Germans and German-Americans in the United States—recounting the careers of notable individuals, their business successes, their participation in American wars, and the like. While further investigations into these areas of inquiry are worth while, the study of the more significantly cultural influences of Germany upon America needs not wait until all the data on the German element in America are recorded.

However late they were in making their entry into the United States, few important men, movements, or ideas of modern Germany failed, in one way or another, to impress themselves upon American cultural development. Kantian transcendentalism played havoc in the United States with Congregational and Unitarian theology just about the time that Hegelian and post-Hegelian criticisms were breaking up the empire of Kantian idealism in Germany. Hegel's philosophy of history arrived in this country with decided force after Marx and Engels had turned Hegelianism upside down in the fatherland, and a later generation of Americans took seriously Marxian materialism just at the moment when Mannheim was shooting it full of holes at home. But however belatedly Germanic influences made themselves felt in the United States, they have made—or are making—themselves forces in American civilization that cannot be disregarded.[2]

Considering the tremendous body of material that has been printed on the general subject of Germanic influences, one is at a loss to understand why the more strictly *cultural* influences—philosophical, political, religious, literary, and artistic—have received so little attention. Except for a few studies of limited scope, all of which will be particularized in their proper places in the sequel, nothing comprehensive has been done to segregate and evaluate Germanic influences of thought and art in the tradition of American cultural development. Professor Faust's two-volume work, by all odds the best in the field, was written nearly a half-century ago. The second volume, partially devoted to Germanic influences in American agriculture, industry, politics, education, religion, and the arts, is panoramic in its point of view and subject matter; but, as the author himself pointed out, it had necessarily to be less definitive than illustrative and suggestive of what subsequent investigations, following his efforts, might yield.[3]

For the process, now definitely beyond its initial stages, of rewriting the history of American culture, especially as it manifests itself in American thought and letters, the findings of Professor Faust and his coworkers have been useful; but the undertaking has now proceeded to a point where further analyses of foreign (including Germanic) contributions to American life need to be made before the larger work of reinterpreting American civilization can proceed satisfactorily.

The facts presented by Professors Faust and Wittke and a host of investigators of more special or local subjects provide an indispensable frame of reference. The historian of German cultural influences in America needs to remember Benjamin Franklin's estimate in 1766 that one-third of the population of Pennsylvania was Germanic and Crèvecœur's definition of an American as "a new man . . . an European, or the descendant of an European . . . whose grandfather was an Englishman, whose wife was Dutch, whose son married a French woman, and whose present four sons have now four wives of different nations." He must bear in mind that Germans and their descendants in the American colonies in 1775 numbered approximately 225,000; that by 1790, the year of the first census, the number had increased to 250,000; and that by 1900, it was some 18,400,000; but he must not lose sight of the relation of this last figure to others in the following estimate (also for 1900) of the relative strength of the more important European blood strains in America:

English element	20,400,000
German element	18,400,000
Irish and Scotch elements	13,900,000
All others	14,290,000
Total white population in 1900	66,990,000

The study of any foreign strain in America involves the necessity of bearing in mind the fact that the United States is a land in which the experience of Frederick Jackson Turner, the historian of the American frontier, is duplicated a thousandfold. He described his home town, Portage, Wisconsin, in these terms:

The town was a mixture of raftsmen from the "pineries"—of Irish (in the "bloody first" ward), Pomeranian immigrants (we stoned each other), in old country garbs, driving their cows to their own "Common"; of Scotch, with "Caledonia" near by; of Welsh (with "Cambria" adjacent); of Germans, some of them university trained (the bierhall of Carl Haertel was the town club house); of Yankees from Vermont and Maine and Connecticut chiefly; of New York Yankees; of Southerners (a few relatively); a few negroes; many Norwegians and Swiss; some Englishmen; and one or two Italians.[5]

It would be too much to expect the rapid completion of the already numerous studies of immigration, the interpretation of the voluminous census data, the elaborate ethnographical surveys, and the intricate history of races and nationalities in the United States; and it would be foolish to insist that the writing of the more strictly cultural history of the United States must wait until the historians, statisticians, and cartographers have done. There is no good reason why both cannot advance together, mutually supporting each other. Nor is it to be presumed that the task of re-evaluating and rewriting the history of American civilization will be accomplished in short order, or, indeed, that it will ever be completed to the satisfaction of everybody; but there appears to be no good reason why any future moment should be more propitious than the present for making a beginning. As a matter of fact, the critical study of American literary culture, beginning about twenty-five years ago, has already made appreciable progress. The reinterpretation of American literature has proceeded boldly and on the whole successfully from the presupposition that American letters are the composite result of the interplay between a foreign tradition and a native environment. Starting from the assumption that the interactions of foreign and indigenous forces comprise the essentials that demand analysis before any real study of American literature can be initiated, several students of American letters, during the twenties, voiced their disapproval of the prevailing methods and the status of American literary history and criticism.[6] Since then, American literature as the subject of academic study has made what, at least in some quarters, amounts to a conquest of academic curricula. Despite some over-enthusiastic professions of faith and some mushroom growth, the critical interpretation of American literature has proceeded in measures and degrees which would make the subject unrecognizable by the few brave men of the first two decades of this century who dared profess themselves professors of American literature. Bibliographical works, on a hitherto unprecedented scale, have been compiled; authoritative biographies of major American authors have appeared; definitive texts are in the making. Several multiform collaborative histories of American literature have been published, and other co-operative plans of study are under consideration or in process of execution. Meanwhile several departments have been generally overlooked. Since the appearance of Professor Jones's book on French cultural influence in America, little more than piece-work has been done on the very fundamental problem of segregating, analyzing, and appraising the several foreign influences that have infiltrated the very fabric of American culture during the three and one-half centuries of its growth.

That is to say, what we have grown accustomed to call the critical reinterpretation of American culture has been so uncritical as to overlook the necessity of keeping constantly in mind the basic definitions and the fundamental assumption that what we are studying is the result of the interaction between foreign backgrounds and native conditioning. We have paid scant attention to the elements that are British, or Germanic, or French, or classical, or otherwise. In short, we are proceeding without having in hand anything more than the most superficial ideas regarding what is American at all. Unless definition and analysis proceed a good deal further than they have gone so far, we may find that some of our most ambitious undertakings are ill-conceived, and that some of our proudest achievements are premature syntheses based on questionable premises and incomplete evidence.

All departments of comparative cultural study are complex, and that which includes America as one of its component elements of comparison is especially hazardous by reason of the complexity of American civilization. Derivative and eclectic, American culture is deeply indebted to the French, to the Germans, most signally to the British, and in lesser degrees to other nations, past and present; but it cannot fairly be said that any European nation, or indeed, all of them jointly, ever succeeded in reducing America to a mere cultural province. The point of view which regards American civilization as nothing more than a transplantation of European culture disregards the fact that from the moment of its transplantation, a native American environment began the process of remaking it into something as distinctly different from its European origins as the Declaration of Independence is different from the Magna Carta. To be sure there are degrees and stages by which America's Coming of Age can be traced, and it is not easy to see precisely when American writings, for instance, ceased being colonial and became American. Yet whoever reads will understand that a remarkable revolution took place between the dates that mark the publication of Captain John Smith's *True Travels* and Mark Twain's *Innocents Abroad*. For Smith's writings are truly a part of the great library of English renaissance travel literature, while Mark Twain's Innocents in the Old World, or William Dean Howells' Laphams in the New, cannot, by any stretch of the imagination, be regarded as European, although neither can be understood without reference to European backgrounds.

While, then, American literature is not a mere extension, or re-establishment, of European literary culture within new geographical limits, and American ideas and their expression are no mere iteration of European thought, American culture must be viewed in relation to its heritage from abroad. To understand this heritage is at once to deepen our understanding of the forces that have molded our civilization in the past and to illumine the process of acculturation that we see going on round about us.

Preliminary, therefore, to a critical revaluation, it would seem that we shall have'to investigate the several foreign influences in a manner involving some such program as this: (1) to differentiate among the varied impulses which have gone into and are still in process of going into that peculiarly eclectic hodgepodge which we call American culture; (2) to determine which of the elements thus analyzed are imported and which are indigenous; (3) to determine, if possible, what these foreign and native elements have contributed toward the making of this thing of rags and tags into a fabric showing some pattern or design; and (4) to reintegrate, or suggest a way toward the reintegration of, these various and sometimes mutually repellent particles, so that we may at least feel we understand what we are and why we are so, though we may still not have at our command the means of knowing how to proceed most wisely in sloughing off what is worst and cleaving to what is best.

Our progress in these essential considerations is far from having reached a point at which we can say anything definite about which of the several foreign impacts have been the most pervasive or effective. Quite possibly these questions will never be finally settled, although, for practical purposes, it may be assumed that the British influence has been the most profound. This assumption, based on obvious considerations, has been so generally accepted that it has led to many facile, oversimplified, and sometimes exaggerated conclusions.

Periodically the cry goes up from one or another of the several racial or national groups represented in the United States that historians have neglected to credit its particular constituents with this or that cultural contribution to which they lay claim. Historians representing the Germans, the French, the Italians, the Jews, the Norwegians, and several others have not been modest. So stoutly have the protagonists, defenders, and apologists of all descriptions argued their claims that if all claims were allowed, little would remain that could be credited to English influence, and nothing whatever that could be ascribed to what, in the final analysis, is of primary concern for the historian of American culture—namely, the motivating influence of native American conditioning. Among the several groups contending for the lion's share of the credit in making the United States what she is, none has been more denunciatory in attacking American historians for allegedly slighting their particular share or for reputedly falsifying the record to the disfavor of their particular party than those who have argued the claims of the Germans and German-Americans. Much of their attack has centered on what they maintain are the overrepresentations of the Scotch-Irish, who have not, themselves, been timorous in pushing their claims. Whatever may be said regarding the justice or injustice which the German element has received at the hands of American historians of whatever description, it cannot fairly be said (in view of thousands of items comprising the bibliography which forms the companion-piece of this study) that the Germans themselves have tamely submitted to what some of them call discrimination. Indeed, the Germans share with the Scotch-Irish a remarkable ability for surviving in the world of modern historiography, as they shared resourcefulness and pertinacity with their Scotch-Irish neighbors of the eighteenth century in pushing the farmer's frontier up the interior valleys, through the mountain gaps to the West, down the river courses to the Mississippi, and subsequently, beyond. Less able than the Scotch-Irish to make good their claims in certain departments of American life—public and political life, for example—they outshone them in others. For instance, in the realm of philology, no other department of comparative studies, as it impinges on European-American relations, has half as many solid and comprehensive bibliographical tools upon which to

proceed to further study. The thoroughness and indefatigibility of the bibliographers who have engaged in this spadework are remarkable. Even the study of British-American cultural relations lags far behind in these fundamental bibliographical matters.[7]

In the more restricted areas, such as Pennsylvania-German culture, the work shows even higher stages of development. Whoever looks into Dr. Emil Meynen's 7,858 numbered items in a stout volume of 636 closely-printed, double-columned pages, entitled *Bibliography on German Settlements in Colonial North America, Especially on the Pennsylvania Germans and Their Descendants 1683–1933* (Leipzig, 1937) will be struck with the advanced stage to which Pennsylvania Germans have brought the study of their cultural traditions. Dr. Meynen might easily have extended the number of his items two- or threefold and still fallen short of making his compilation truly comprehensive,[8] though it is to be doubted that its value would have been increased proportionally. What is to be inferred is that the Pennsylvania Germans have not fared ill at the hands of historians, and that they are not lacking in the sentiments that lie this side of *Ehrgeiz*. Professional genealogists regard the Germans of Pennsylvania as in no way behind the proud descendants of the Mayflower Pilgrims in the matter of recording their history.

Similarly, in the field of more comprehensive surveys of foreign elements in the United States, the investigations of the Germanic element exceed all others in number and scope. In this wider field, however, the historians of Germanic influence exhibit failings in degrees seldom matched by students of comparable areas for other nationalities. Too many of them, sometimes doubtless unwittingly, have been more intent upon German than upon American culture. This point of view, in its proper place is both valuable and valid, but for the reinterpretation of American culture it has little utility.[9] To be sure, we dare not overlook anything that falls under the broad head of German culture—be it Goethe or Kant or Mozart, *Gemütlichkeit, Gesang,* or *Biergarten,* Wallenstein, Hansel und Gretel, Baron von Munchhausen or the Katzenjammer Kids—either for its own sake or for its value to the world. But the student of German cultural influence in America, if he is intent on contributing anything of value to our understanding of American civilization, must adopt a straightforward course—must consider his study one of influence going from Germany to America. The reciprocal view by which *deutsche Kultur,* becoming a primary or sole object, is regarded as an all-conquering imperialism seeking, through the vulnerability of American receptivity, to make of America a cultural colony or province of Germany, is little to his purpose. American receptiveness to the radiation of German ideas, modes, and forms puts America in the place of the debtor nation but hardly in the position of the conquered.

That is to say, the vogue and influence of Goethe in America considered in relation to Goethe's stature as a German or as a world poet is one thing; his vogue and influence in America as a motivating and modifying force upon the course of American thought and art is another. Again, the confusion between one and the other point of view results in minute studies of Kotzebue or Schiller on the stages of various American cities, but never a hint as to why they were found acceptable in America during the early years of the nineteenth century, nor a suggestion concerning their effect upon the early development of the American drama and stage, nor even a clue to the reasons why they went into an eclipse when they did.

The investigator of German-American cultural influences needs to guard against adding new difficulties in an area already bristling with problems and confusions inherent in the intricacy of the subject. For instance, there is the problem of defining the influencing factor. What is meant by German culture, by German literature, by German philosophy, by a German ideal? How shall one conceive of Goethe: the Goethe of *Werther* and *Goetz* or the Goethe of *Meister* and *Faust II,* Goethe the man or Goethe the scientist? Which is the typically German motif: Lessing's thesis in *Nathan der Weise* of tolerance and cosmopolitanism, or Körner's celebration, in *Leier und Schwert,* of a Teutonic God and the glories of the Fatherland, or the Hitlerian concept of these themes? What constitutes German transcendentalism? Kantian criticism as it reputedly affected New England Transcendentalists during the thirties and forties of the last century, or Hegelian absolutism as it acted upon the St. Louis philosophers three or four decades later? What, moreover, is meant by a Germanic idea? "The history of ideas," remarks Professor Howard M. Jones, "cannot be a bloodless dance of categories; ideas must have been put to work; they must have contributed historical effects. But what constitutes an effective idea? . . . What shall we say of the creation of American scientific laboratories on European models, with all their far-reaching intellectual consequences?"[10] How shall we treat the techniques and ideas that lie behind an art movement, even when it is clear and precise, as it almost never is, and how can we evaluate its effects?

To take another example, how is Charles Sealsfield (Carl Postl) to be classified? Born an Austrian subject, in Bohemia, he eventually became an American citizen. In the United States he gathered materials for a series of books on American themes, which he published, then and afterwards, in the German language in Germany and Switzerland, and sometimes almost simultaneously in England and America, either in the original or in translation, or both. His books were translated into many languages, and he acquired international fame; but in America he had no great vogue, except among German-American groups, where his language presented no obstacles. Considering the fact that he acquired American citizenship, is he an American or a German writer? Without stretching the facts, he may be treated (1) as a German who was profoundly influenced by America; (2) as an American who had a tremendous vogue in Germany and in other European countries, and materially affected immigration to America; and (3) as a German-American who enjoyed a considerable vogue among other German-Americans and with an occasional Anglo-American, like Longfellow, who enjoyed his books and was influenced by them. In a study of this sort, where some analysis is in order, is he to be regarded as a German, an American, or a German-American? As a writer of books in German about American subjects, did he exercise any real influence upon Americans in the broader sense? The failure to see Sealsfield in proper perspective and relationships has led to some highly exaggerated claims for him, not only for his intrinsic worth as an artist but also for his influence in America.[11]

Complicating matters still more is a motive that for want of a better word may be called *Ehrgeiz*. Americans have, at various times, come under the spell of it; our terms for it have been nationalism, 100 per cent patriotism, or chauvinism. A militant form of it was abroad in Hitler's Germany, fostering the idea (and this applies as much to some German academicians as to German propagandists) that the Germans are a superior race, and that German culture is as good as the best and better than most. Such extremist nationalism, coupled with a sense of the high destiny of Teutonia, makes some German and German-American students attribute all the better elements in what we call "America's Coming of Age" to Germanic origins, meanwhile ascribing the less estimable ones to British, French, Spanish, and other influences. Altogether too many studies in the field are vitiated by this type of bias.

The relatively few objectively scholarly works which the field shows have been torn apart and reinterpreted by plagiarists, popularizers, and propagandists, who have twisted the facts and misapplied the sober conclusions of such a book as Faust's *German Element in the United States* in a manner and to a degree that they are unrecognizable by their author. The excuse given for much of this poaching and popularizing is that it is done to promote an enlightened internationalism—to effect better understanding and co-operation among races and nations; but in much of it the conclusion is inescapable that the real reason lies in a desire to advance German *Kultur* as we understood the word before 1914.[12] An examination of the piles upon piles of German propagandist literature circulated in this country, notably between 1900 and 1917, often under sober, academic titles, suggests that the Germans have had no near rival either in the scope of their activity in this field or in the unimaginativeness, not to say clumsiness, of their efforts. Then, as in more recent years, this kind of material was disseminated mainly among Americans of German extraction; it had little appeal beyond these circles; and most of it fell flat even among them.

Among treatises emanating from Germany that treat German literary influence upon the major American authors—and there is at least one each for Irving, Bryant, Poe, Hawthorne, Longfellow, Lowell, Emerson, Whitman, Lanier, and Mark Twain—there are few that do not suffer either from certain preoccupations of what is to be "proved" or from a failure to grasp the American angles of the problem posed. Their reliability as to fact is seldom to be questioned, but the marshaling of fact is often inept or misleading. Generalizations and conclusions offered, when checked against significant factors not taken into account, often turn out to be untenable. Strong on the accumulation and compilation of data, often unrelated or unassimilated, they are devoid of imagination, direction, interpretation. They have the unity of a dictionary and the coherence of an encyclopedia.

Without implying that our German colleagues' industrious gathering of facts is worthless, it may yet be suggested that in some departments we already have a staggering mass of facts—more than we shall ever know what to do with. So far as the evaluation of German intellectual and literary influence in the United States is concerned, we already have in hand the essentials for the project undertaken in this book (1) about the immigration, settlement, and distribution of Germans in the United States, (2) about the history of a number of restricted spheres of German-American social influence as these can be observed by following the history of German-American communities, and (3) about translations of German literature into English and about the accessibility of German literature, both in translation and in the original, in America.[13]

It is not to be urged, of course, that we should all, individually or collectively, fall to writing syntheses on the basis of the evidence accumulated. Before that can be done with a reasonable assurance of success, ground must be broken in areas as yet untouched. We need first to investigate hitherto unexplored fields of Germanic influence, to prosecute fundamental inquiries into Spanish, Italian, Scandinavian, Slavic, classical, and oriental influences, and to undertake comprehensive investigation into the one subject which is most important, but which shows little beyond a few restricted efforts—British influence in America.

As far as the progress of German-American cultural studies is concerned, there are several hopeful signs. The organization, in 1932, of the Anglo-German Literary Relations Group of the Modern Language Association of America provides a kind of clearinghouse for people interested in and engaged upon problems concerning the interrelations in language, literature, and thought between Germany and the English-speaking countries. Thus far, its programs have been devoted to German > American influences rather than the reciprocal relationship or German-British interrelations. Aside from its annual meetings, which have afforded opportunities for people with mutual or related interests to consult with one another, the most noteworthy work of the Group is the compilation of an annual list, published in the *Journal of English and Germanic Philology* (since 1941, in the *American-German Review*), first, of published books and articles in the field, and second, of projects of research in progress and unpublished studies, theses, and dissertations. The first seven installments (1934–1940, inclusive) list more than a thousand printed items and a third as many unpublished studies, many of them dissertations and monographs by mature scholars, in varying stages of completion. Of these many items, more than half deal with German-American literary and intellectual relations. It would seem that there is little cause for despairing of a field which engages some six or seven hundred students, many of them seasoned, reputable scholars.

But there are as yet few signs to indicate that this host of workers knows whither it is headed, or, indeed, that it cares very much. The Group has done little more than to listen, once a year, to several of its members who had particularly cogent subjects to present for the consideration of the members. The Committee on Bibliography has undertaken little more than to take notice of what is being done here, there, and yonder, and occasionally to pass cryptic judgment on an item that seemed especially good or notoriously bad. If the Group could be transformed into an effective steering body, the value of its work would be enhanced; but thus far this body has been no more successful than other subdivisions of the Modern Language Association in the much desired objective of giving unity and cohesion to its work.

In the meantime the Carl Schurz Memorial Foundation, under the leadership of its executive secretary, Wilbur K. Thomas (retired in 1947 and succeeded by Howard W. Elkinton), has taken initial steps to perfect a plan of organization that promises eventually to put the study of German-American cultural relations in a favored position as an effective, co-operative enterprise. During 1936–1937, Dr. Heinz Kloss undertook, at the direction of the Foundation, a preliminary survey of the status of research in German-American cultural relations. His "Report on the Possibilities for Research Work of an American-German Institute," comprising 238 typewritten pages, has been filed with the officers of the Foundation, and may well serve as an excellent point of departure for a program of research when the Foundation is prepared to proceed.

More than this, the Foundation has published since 1934 the *American-German Review*, a bi-monthly of high quality. In 1941, it secured permanent quarters in the Old Custom House at 420 Chestnut Street in Philadelphia. A capable director of research was appointed, and basic work was begun, including the compilation of a union catalog of German-Americana, until World War II interrupted the program.

An attempt is made in the Introduction to the *Bibliography*, which forms a part of this study, to list (1) the leading depositories of German-Americana, (2) German-American research associations, and (3) co-operating European organizations and institutes, and to give some indication of the location and contents of European libraries and archives of most immediate value for the prosecution of German-American cultural and historical investigations. Although my survey indicates that the amount and variety of material preserved is considerable, its state of preservation and, more especially, the inaccessibility of much of it balk the investigator at every turn. It is hoped that the *Bibliography* presented with this study will facilitate research, but it is too much to hope that really efficient work on a large scale can be done until comprehensive guides to archives, check lists of periodicals, indexes to the more important journals, and a union catalog of all printed materials become available. Until then the investigator will inevitably find himself forced often to rely on instinct and chance instead of scientifically accurate guides to locate the materials most pertinent to his study.[14]

Any attempt on the part of an individual to analyze and appraise so large and complex a field as German-American cultural relations is necessarily hazardous. Yet I should feel that I were side-stepping one of the problems of real importance if, after devoting years to compiling a bibliography and weighing the relative merits of thousands of the items surveyed, I should allow the hazards involved to deter me from setting down, however tentatively, my observations regarding (1) the areas of this general subject of investigation that have been treated with some degree of finality and (2) such fields as seem still to be relatively untilled. Such judgments as I shall venture to make can be checked against the *Bibliography*, to which, it is hoped, the cross-referenced index may provide a handy guide.

Enough has already been said on the score of purely historical studies of the influx of Germans into this country. Barring completion of many investigations small in scope and of the above-mentioned projects (e.g., the interrupted plans of the Carl Schurz Memorial Foundation), it would seem extravagant to expect immediately anything definitive on this head. Lacking numerous studies paralleling Rudolf L. Biesele's *History of German Settlements in Texas* (Austin, 1930) and John A. Russell's *The Germanic Element in the Making of Michigan* (Detroit, 1927), it is questionable whether anything designed to supersede the books by Professors Faust and Wittke could accomplish its purpose in a manner to justify the effort.

Before a synthesis of German "social" and "folk" influence upon American community life can be considered possible, many more individual and local studies need to be made of German customs, folk beliefs, popular lore, superstitions, handcrafts, etc. Linguistic and dialectal factors, economic and agricultural elements, educational and ethnographical considerations, as these affect the German and other national contingents in the United States, will have to be analyzed and squared against one another before anything comprehensive can emerge.

Among the more puzzling problems toward the solution of which many small investigations and at least two general treatments have already given partial answers is that regarding the importance in American society and the influence upon political, social, and economic theory in America of the many German communities—socialistic, communistic, and otherwise—which once dotted the American landscape. One should like to know whether these communities were socialistic or communistic, whence they derived their ideas, and what connections they had, if any, with such Anglo-American communities as Brook Farm, Fruitlands, and Economy. Ephrata, Amana, Zoar, the Nassau Adelsverein, and the rest are individually and collectively the subjects of books, but one is left to conclude, from the failure of their historians to tell us much about origins and connections, that, like Topsy, these communal experiments in living "just growed," that they existed in isolation for some years, and then suddenly or gradually ceased to be, leaving no appreciable influence behind them beyond sites upon which sentimental descendants or historical societies have erected markers or shrines for the edification of tourists.

For the purpose of the historian, the external data relating to German and German-American participation in the public and political life of America have already led to some significant conclusions, most notable progress on this head having been made under the auspices of Turner's theories about the frontier. Yet nothing more exhaustive has been attempted than occasional chapters in histories of particular sections or areas and in such works as Clifton J. Child's *German-Americans in Politics, 1914–1917* (Madison, 1939) and the two books by Professors Wittke and Zucker on the Forty-eighters. Charles B. Robson's University of North Carolina dissertation of 1930 on "The Influence of German Thought on the Political Theory in the United States in the Nineteenth Century" (a portion of which has appeared in print) is the best analysis available in its field. For the further study of German-American political influence in America, Dr. Heinz Kloss's *Um die Einigung des Deutschamerikanertums* (Berlin, 1937) is provocative and helpful. This history of the oft-attempted unification of German-Americanism, far from complete or final, is a mine of information for every kind of investigation utilizing historical facts and statistical data concerning German-American organizations, combinations, and associations—local, national, and international. The book is of especial significance for the future historian of German-American religious movements and of German religious influence in the United States, since many of the efforts to unite German-American groups had a religious or denominational orientation. Of German church history in America—Lutheran, Reformed, Mennonite, Moravian, and the others—there is a tremendous body of published material, but much of it is uncritical in method, and all of it is limited in scope, heterogeneous and incoherent. There is as yet no approximation toward a history of all German-American churches in America, and virtually no effort to consider their influence upon the broader stream of American religious thought. On the basis of materials already assembled covering individual churches, congregations, synods, conferences, and denominations, a historian able to see beyond the infinite minutiae in which the subject lies submerged should be able to make a notable contribution to the history of religion in the United States. Such a history should put us in a favored position to consider, next, questions regarding (1) how extensive and pervasive German religious influences were and are, beyond the circle of German-American communicants, (2) how these German church bodies were modified by the non-German religious groups surrounding them, and (3) how significant they are in the American religious tradition.

Some attempts are made at various points in the following pages to indicate how theological speculation filtered into American religious thought directly from Germany. For example, attention is directed toward the impact of German theological researches upon influential American ministers—Calvinists like Moses Stuart at Andover, who read the German Biblical investigations sympathetically and availed himself of the tools of German theological research; Unitarians like Andrews Norton, who read the German theologians, even though mainly to refute them; or later transcendental theologians like Theodore Parker, whose journals, sermons, pamphlets, and books bristle with the names of Tholuck, Hengstenberg, Jacobi, Schleiermacher, Herder, Strauss, and the "higher critics" of German Biblical research. Obviously the history of these infiltrations cannot be complete until the course of German-American religious movements has been traced and their influence evaluated.[15]

In the area of scientific influence from Germany (often closely related to that of philosophical and theological influence) basic work is currently being completed by my colleague, Professor Harry Hayden Clark.

Until quite recently it has been generally assumed and often flatly said that Americans were innocent of any knowledge of German thought until it was brought over in the heads and trunks of the generation of young Americans (Ticknor, Bancroft, Everett, *et al.*) who studied in the German universities during the second and third decades of the last century. On closer examination of the records left by earlier generations, we find a lively interchange on philosophical and more general intellectual matters that goes back, in an almost unbroken continuity and tradition, to Nathaniel Ward, John Winthrop II, Robert Child, and Cotton Mather. But when we come to such fundamental questions as how, when, and where German philosophy was introduced into our academic halls, we are constrained to turn the brittle pages of old college and university catalogs and bulletins.[16]

I have tried to clarify the issues, insofar as they involve Germanic influences, of the highly controversial questions (1) whether or not New England Transcendentalism was merely the natural and integral development out of native traditions, including Puritan idealism and Unitarian rationalism, (2) whether, if it was not mainly indigenous, it derived from Greek or German or French philosophy, or all three, and others as well, and (3) if so, how much and in what particular respects. And I have tried to sketch the history of how Emersonian Transcendentalism migrated westward to join forces with St. Louis Hegelianism, and how the Hegelians from St. Louis, Quincy, and Jacksonville, in turn, brought the current of idealistic thought full circle by joining in the activities of the Concord School of Philosophy in ways and degrees that threatened to wrest the sceptre from Alcott and Emerson. The emergence of pragmatism, personalism, behaviorism, and experimental psychology affords other examples of later forms of Germanic influence that await intensive study before the relations can become clear.

In the area of literary influence, the considerable body of exploratory, and in some instances definitive, studies provides a relatively greater and safer degree of guidance, although the special pleading and exaggerated claims characteristic of some of them create problems of their own. German-American literary relations of the seventeenth and eighteenth centuries—virgin territory until Professor Jantz published his preliminary survey in the *Journal of English and Germanic Philology* for January, 1942—promises the most immediately fruitful rewards. The study of poetry, drama, and prose fiction produced in German by Germans and German-Americans is still in its rudimentary stages.[17] The subject is not one of primary concern in the ensuing pages, except that I have endeavored to include in the *Bibliography* the authors and titles of greatest import. The brief summary chapter on German-American writings with which this book originally concluded had to be sacrificed to save space. The literary productivity (in the English language) of Americans of German descent is another subject which has received little attention. Besides writers like Henry Timrod and Joaquin Miller, there are hundreds of others —from Henry L. Mencken and Theodore Dreiser to Thomas Mann and L. Lewisohn —who might profitably engage the attention of the historian of German-American literary influences.

Literary influence is a broad subject, with many ramifications. It can be traced most readily in terms of men or of literary genres; but often associated departments, such as the stage, dramatic criticism, journalism and printing, eloquence and oratory, are of real importance because of the way they affect the literary development of a people. Thus eloquence, whether in the pulpit or on the lecture platform, exerted throughout Emerson's lifetime an effect which we have hardly begun to divine.[18] On first thought, it would seem that little in this respect could have come from Germany; and yet, when the significance of German university education in America is considered, we begin to see connections.

Certainly the people who heard Edward Everett soon after his return from Göttingen were quick to detect a new force in the man, his scholarship, and his lectures. There was wide divergence of opinion about his effectiveness: some thought him eloquent, others pedantic, but all agreed that he had something, in both matter and manner, that distinguished him from the homebred scholar and man of letters.

The history of the German periodical press in America, of German printing in this country, and of Germans in that business are other subjects which invite investigation. Seidensticker's monumental bibliography of German printing in America stops with 1830; bibliographies prepared by Flory, Bender, Reichard, Raunick, and others are all restricted to special subjects or to limited areas and periods. On the history of the German periodical press in America we have little beyond a few monographs and articles, such as Miller's early studies of German-American newspapers and magazines in Pennsylvania and those by Keidel on German newspapers in Maryland. The recent survey made by Dr. Felix Reichmann (Carl Schurz Mem. Found.) of the German periodicals that appeared in Baltimore during the last century and a half reveals at once interesting facts regarding their history, their circulation, and their influence that are of significance to the historian of American culture whether he is interested in Germanic influences or not. Similar investigations for such German centers as Philadelphia, New York, St. Louis, Cincinnati, Chicago, and San Antonio are in order.

Obviously, the gaps are numerous and broad. It is not my purpose to point out all of them, much less to fill them in. It would be more to the point to say briefly what this study purports to do, for an enumeration of what has not been done by others and of what is not undertaken here would be endless.

On that score I need perhaps to say no

more than to avow frankly that because I am a professor of American literature, I profess to the study of that subject, and have selected areas of investigation most germane to it. Accordingly I have undertaken to treat chiefly three aspects of Germanic influence in America—the philosophical, the educational, and the literary— which, in the first place, I felt I could treat with some degree of success, and which, in the second place, I believe to be of particular relevance to the progress of the history of American literary culture at this time, as forming a fairly unified and coherent body of material. I particularly regret my inability to treat the German influence in the other arts—notably music, the area in which German influence has been most pervasive and profound. There will be no lack of questions why this or that other subject was omitted, or why some phase of the three areas chosen was neglected. I have no defense except the knowledge that I possess all the common human frailties, that I have no assurance of longevity, that I am not omniscient, and that publishers still prescribe certain limits. I can only express the hope that my failures and omissions will stimulate, or irk, other laborers to help in the gathering of a rich, ripe harvest.

Book One

German Thought
in America

Early Interest in German Culture

THE SEVENTEENTH CENTURY

Points of View

The accepted view of colonial Americans as a singularly provincial people, isolated from the great cosmopolitan traditions of the world, is gradually being revised as investigation progresses into the cultural heritage of America. Among European influences felt in colonial times, those emanating from Germany have been consistently underestimated. The tradition persists that Americans were content to remain ignorant of Germany until the early nineteenth century when, so the legend goes, a group of young Harvard men, suddenly fired by Madame de Staël's account of the great German universities, journeyed thither and brought back with them the weapons wherewith to effect a Teutonic conquest of American learning, literature, and thought. The story is too pat to be credible, and recent investigations[1] lead to the inescapable conclusion that there was, almost from the date of the first settlement in New England, a lively and rather steadily mounting interest in Germany.[2]

The conventional account of early German-American relationships[3] takes cognizance of the work of Francis Daniel Pastorius as the founder of Germantown about 1683 and mentions the stream of German books that issued from the Saur and Ephrata presses, but it finds little else to record save the correspondence that Cotton Mather is known to have carried on with August Hermann Francke[4] of Halle until a century later—so the story runs—when Madame de

Staël's *De l'Allemagne* (London, 1813; Paris, 1814; New York, 1814) opened bright young men's eyes to the dazzling splendors of German libraries and to the unparalleled advantages of a German university education; whereupon Ticknor, Bancroft, Everett, and a few others set out at once to learn the language, only to meet the formidable obstacle of finding no German books available in all Boston.[5] Andrew Preston Peabody, recalling Dr. Carl Follen's introduction, in 1825, of German as a regular subject of instruction at Harvard, relates how he joined the first class of eight volunteers and how they encountered similar difficulties until Dr. Follen prepared a "German Reader for Beginners' . . . furnished to the class in single sheets as . . . needed and printed in Roman type, there being no German type within easy reach."[6]

Lowell, reminiscing in 1890 over a span of almost half a century, helped to give currency to this tradition by asserting, "Mr. George Bancroft told me that he learned German of Professor Sydney Willard, who, himself self-taught, had no notion of its pronunciation."[7] And Moses Stuart, who himself taught philosophy and theology of a sufficiently Germanic cast as early as 1810 to put the heresy hunters on his trail, recalled in 1841 how "for years together" he was "almost alone in the study of German," adding that "the late J. S. Buckminster, of Brattle Street Church, was the only man among the Literati of this region, who at that time had any other knowledge of German than what belonged

19

to the mere tyro."[8] Stuart's reference to Buckminster leads us back to Ticknor, who was on terms of intimacy with Buckminster as early as 1810, the year when Ticknor was admitted to the Anthology Club.[9] Obviously Ticknor's memory, trying to span fifty-five years, tricked him; for close as he was to Buckminster, he could hardly have been unaware of his friend's wholehearted devotion to German studies nor of the choice collection of German books which he had begun to acquire long before the publication of M. Villers' or of Madame de Staël's books.

The unanimity of testimony appearing in these reminiscences, which launched and kept afloat this myth, is hardly to be explained unless it is assumed either that these several individuals who undertook to study or to promote the study of German were so far separated from each other as not to be aware of their several efforts (an assumption hardly tenable for those who belonged to the Boston-Cambridge community), or that by the late nineteenth century these several pioneers[10] were, perhaps unconsciously, glorifying the role they had played in introducing a study that had attained a high respectability in the meantime.

Anglo-German Backgrounds

Early German-American intellectual interrelations cannot be appraised until sixteenth- and seventeenth-century German-English relations are studied more exhaustively. Such investigations as have been made are indicative of the influence which became increasingly significant, especially just before and during the period of the Thirty Years' War. These contacts can be traced in terms of British interest (1) in the German Reformation and subsequent religious developments in Germany and central Europe, (2) in German classical, scientific, and theological scholarship, and (3) in the dominance of German book-mak-

ers and printers in the preservation of learning and publication generally. The semi-annual Frankfurt Book Mart became the mecca of scholars and the clearinghouse of learning for all Europe.

Early Anglo-German relationships were reciprocal. There were settlements of English Puritans in Frankfurt, Zürich, and other German cities; English acting companies freely trouped through the German countries; and noted English savants and travelers (among them Roger Ascham, John Dee, Robert Fludd, John Pell, Henry Wotton, and John Durie) traveled, resided, and sometimes published their works in Germany.[11] There were also German savants, as well as political and religious refugees of various kinds who came to England, notably London, early in the seventeenth century, and who left behind a deposit of reform ideas that were found acceptable among groups of Puritans and Separatists from whom the New England colonists were recruited.

The outlines of these relationships, sometimes circuitous but often direct, begin to emerge with some degree of precision. For example, there was Johann Valentin Andreae, that interesting professor, theologian, scientist, mystic, and litterateur, whose Lutheranism readily absorbed Calvinistic principles, and whose interests in science did not preclude his enunciating ideas upon which the order of Rosicrucians was reputedly founded. What is of more importance is that Andreae was the author of a utopian work entitled *Christianopolis* (1619), the product at once of Tübingen Lutheranism and Genevan Calvinism, which exerted a considerable influence in England through such intermediaries as Comenius, Durie, Hartlib, Figulus, Hübner, and Haak.[12]

Andreae was one of the moving spirits behind several utopian and educational movements which came to the attention of New Englanders before they embarked for America, through the agency of Germans residing in London and of Palatine refugees. Thus some of the underlying ideas for the founding of a self-governing commonwealth in the new world, as it took shape in the minds of the Pilgrims and the founders of the Massachusetts Bay Company, were based partly upon German utopian ideas, whose prime source was the cosmopolitan circle that came within the Andreaen orbit of influence. Aside from Durie, Hartlib, and others in London who interested themselves in Andreae's ideas, there was a group of Palatine refugees of the 1620's in London and Dorchester who seem to have served as intermediaries and to have accentuated, at just the right time, certain Germanic ideas for which the ground had been prepared by English dissenting doctrine. We know that John White of Dorchester, the moving spirit for a "New England" (though he never went thither) opened his home to a number of them—Johann Nicholas Ruzilius (Reuliss), Johann Kaspar Hopff, and Theodor Haak, among others.[13] So did John Cotton, while he still lived at Old Boston in England.[14] The full substantiation of definite personal relations connecting Andreae's group, the Anglo-Germans in London, the leaders among the several trading and settlement companies, and the Pilgrim and Puritan fathers (an undertaking which Professor Jantz has set for himself) awaits the examination in detail of certain English documents and records; but already enough evidence has appeared to show that streams of thought emanating from men like Luther, Andreae, and Althusius were not unheeded by early English Separatists and Puritans. Quite possibly, when all the facts are in hand, a reorientation of the accepted history of how the earliest New England commonwealths were constituted will be in order.

Lutheranism

How far Luther and Lutheranism influenced colonial Americans poses other provocative questions. The complexity of the problem is aggravated by the fact that various sectarians, among them Anabaptists, Mennonites, Moravians, Amish, Dunkers, and Schwenkfelders, made their way to America by various routes. The influence of some of them can be traced with a fairer degree of surety than that of the parental movement from which most of them stem— namely, Lutheranism. The principles and implications of Luther's revolt, or "protest," in the new land became volatile forces readily adaptable and supplementary to the indigenous political liberalism in New England that attacked and eventually helped destroy the old theocratic absolutisms of church and state. The gunpowder packed away in Luther's doctrine of the priesthood of all believers and the right of every man to interpret his own Bible was capable of making breaches in political and social as readily as in theological ramparts, although the demonstration of how this was done in specific instances presents difficulties.

Puritanism in America developed from the first two broad tendencies, fundamentally opposed to each other: the one strict, the other liberal. The Puritans of Massachusetts Bay, who leaned most in the direction of Calvin, and who are often referred to indiscriminately as Calvinists, went most often to Geneva for their principles, but they often looked also in the direction of Zürich, Heidelberg, Wittenberg, Herborn, Franeker, and Leyden. Separatists, as represented by Plymouth, while ostensibly Calvinistic in their profession, oftener sought guidance in Luther's "protests" than in Calvin's *Institutes*. Two noteworthy facts uniformly overlooked are (1) that Calvin's *Institutes* are to be found very infrequently among early New England inventories, Luther *On the Galatians* alone appearing quite as often,[15] and (2) that German theological works of all kinds are listed with remarkable frequency.[16] The New England settlers were not in the strict sense of the word Calvinists. The designation of Calvinists is one that is attached to early American Pilgrims and Puritans because nineteenth- and twentieth-century American historians have fastened it on them. They regarded themselves as purifiers or reformers, not as Calvinists; nor were they content to stop where Calvin had stopped. They never admitted that Calvin had discovered the whole of religious truth.[17]

It is to be borne in mind, in the next place, that there were in the Colonies a great many schismatics—Anabaptists, Seekers, Congregationalists of various kinds, Antinomians, Mennonites, Dunkers, etc.—who, though differing among themselves. were united in the common purpose of breaking down social restrictions, theological uniformitarianism, and political absolutism. Under whatever name they went, or in whatever colony they agitated their reforms, they all represented a form of separatism that refused to abide by such Institutes as Calvin had imposed upon the Lutheran Protest. As the left wing of the Reform movement, they were bent on carrying through to logical conclusions the revolutionary premises upon which the Reformation was based. Like the New England Puritans, they had resolved to put into practice Luther's advice that where "constrained defence" fails against governors who are enemies of God and of God's word, it behooves God's children to sell or forsake all and go to a new land where they will be free to worship, "as Christ commandeth." Theirs was also, as Parrington has suggested, "the final expression of the disintegrating gospel of individualism implicit in the doctrine of the priesthood of all believers."[18]

The reaction which set in in Germany even during Luther's lifetime—indeed, in the older Luther himself—against the extreme liberalism which this doctrine incited may be represented as receiving codification at the hands of Calvin. Luther had been more mystical than rational, drawing his inspiration primarily from the New Testa-

ment, finding the creative source of the Christian life in the spiritual union of the soul with Christ, and inclining to tolerate differences of opinion among believers that did not involve fundamental matters of doctrine; Calvin was more austerely logical, drawing inspiration mainly from the Old Testament, exalting righteousness above love, following the Hebraic code, and laying emphasis upon an authoritarian system.[19] Neither developed a wholly consistent polity, but Calvin's training in jurisprudence and government enabled him to produce the more coherent system of the two. It has been said that the principal difference between Lutheranism and Calvinism is owing to the fact that Luther began life as a monk and Calvin as a lawyer. Calvinism was not only a creed but a system of government, the State serving as the protector of the Church; while Lutheranism developed (whatever it became later) under circumstances in Germany whereby religion was recognized as occupying a separate sphere from that of the State.[20]

Calvinism developed differently in different countries. In the case of Lutheranism, the differences were even more pronounced, for Lutheranism lacked an equally consistent body of political theory, and it early developed, as a consequence of social conditions in Germany, a schism as regards the relation of Church to State. Moreover, a distinction has to be made between the Luther before the Peasants' War of 1525 and the Luther after that date. The younger Luther recognized the tyranny of nobles and petty princes and was in accord with the "Twelve Articles" that formed the charter of the peasants' revolt, but the excesses of the uprising prompted him to call upon the nobles to crush the revolt at whatever cost. This change of front had the significant effect of tying him and his followers to the princes. While insuring his own safety and that of Lutheranism, this protection was won at the expense of liberty, and from that time forward Lutheranism in Germany became more and more a department of State.[21]

Luther's action had another important result. It led to a split that divided the German Reformation into two camps. "The Lutheran Reformation which had started as a national movement, now became middle-class in its orientation, while the peasant movement tended to break up into many fragments, all gathered under the general name of Anabaptist."[22] By the later sixteenth century there were a score or more of "Anabaptist" sects representing a great variety of religious and political opinions. Most of them came later to be more or less closely identified with either the Mennonites or some form of Halle or Herrnhut pietism, which in the beginning represented a movement within Lutheranism itself. Thus it came to pass that Lutheranism in Germany, instead of developing logically, as it might have, the democratic spirit implicit in Luther's "protests," became identified with a state system of religion, while the Anabaptists and pietists carried on the tradition of individualism and freedom. That is to say, when we speak of the influence of Luther among New England colonists, we refer less to Lutheranism as it developed into a state church in Germany than to the spirit of the younger Luther as it was exemplified first in the Protest and later in the Lutheran and Reformed schismatics, among them Anabaptists, Mennonites, Moravians, Dunkers, and Schwenkfelders.[23]

To return, now, to the original principles of Luther, we may set down as a fundamental tenet his proclamation that the only requisites for Christian life are conscionable righteousness and individual liberty.[24] "Neither pope nor bishop nor any other man has the right to impose a single syllable of law upon a Christian man without his consent; and if he does, it is done in the spirit of tyranny."[25] "A Christian man is a perfectly free lord of all, and subject to none. A Christian man is a perfectly dutiful servant of all, and subject to all."[26] These doctrines involve (1) a spirit of uncompromising individualism in church and state that leads to the overthrow of theocracy and autocracy, and (2) an advocacy of a doctrine of faith that is inimical to the Calvinistic doctrines of predestination, election, imputation, justification, sanctification, and works.[27].

In Calvin's system there was no room for such Christian liberty and freedom. The Genevan was more logician than philosopher—"a rigorous system-maker and dogmatist who knotted every argument and tied every strand securely into its fellows, till there was no escape from the net unless one broke through the mesh."[28]

But there is ample evidence to show that not all men and women who came to New England during the seventeenth century readily submitted themselves and their consciences to Calvin's strait-laced prescriptions. The proportionate fealty of Puritan attitudes toward Luther and Calvin is a matter than can be determined only in relative terms. If either of them had achieved a true and full Reformation, there would have been no occasion for the New England Puritans to desire further clarification of the Scriptures or of an extended purification of the Church. They understood that it did not begin with Luther, nor end with Calvin. John Cotton, for example, regarded the efforts of Petrus Waldus, John Huss, and Savanarola as inaugurating three eras of reformation, so that by 1500 "the Regions were white and ready for the harvest, else *Luther* had not found such good success in his Ministry"; yet Cotton grieved that "the pregnant strength and glorious lustre of many heroical and excellent gifts of Luther had bin so idolized that many and great Nations followed him in some notorious errors of his way instead of setting themselves to perfect what they [reformers like Luther] left defective."[29] That being so, various types or factions of Puritans found in various ones of their predecessors varying

degrees of guidance. Many set greatest
store by Calvin, even while admitting that
he was only one among many "judicious
and pious" reformers.[30] Others, especially
those most intent upon breaking the institutional power of church and state, found
in Luther their guide, for he had been the
first effectively to batter down the institutional forms and restrictions imposed upon
individualism. Accordingly the conven-
tional-minded leaned toward Calvin's "institutes"; the liberal-minded, seeking further liberalizations in their creed, government, and social arrangements, tended toward an extension of Luther's "protests."
As a group, they thought of themselves as
belonging to an eclectic and progressive
wing of the general Reformed church, and
accordingly when they consulted continental reformers, they esteemed the works of
the irenicist David Pareus of Heidelberg no
less than those of Calvin of Geneva or Luther of Wittenberg; while the efforts of John
Durie toward a Luther-Reformed union met
with the formal approval of the entire New
England Synod.[31] Altogether there was a
greater theoretical liberalism among the
Puritans than their practical conduct of
affairs leads one to believe.

Separatism

The earliest group to come to New England, the Separatists of Plymouth, steadfastly maintained their "separatism" and
escaped for some time the worst entanglements in Calvinistic meshes by the for-
tuitous circumstance of distance which
separated them from Boston. It would be
too much to suggest that Luther was principally responsible for their uncompromising individualism; no definite statements
of indebtedness to Luther for their separatism appear in the writings of those Pilgrims who came to New England. Yet it
seems altogether likely that during their
sojourn in Holland their contacts with Lutheranism predisposed them to embody in

their covenant the principle of separation
of church and state, one of Luther's cardinal tenets. Certainly their chief spokesman,
the Rev. John Robinson, who was with
them throughout their exile, incorporated
a number of Lutheran principles in his
writings, though he chose to differ from
Luther on consubstantiation, baptism, and
details of church discipline. When he bade
his parishioners farewell (he was destined
never to follow them to America), he ad-
monished them to this effect:

I cannot sufficiently bewail the condition
of the reformed churches, who are come to
a *period* in religion . . . The Lutherans cannot be drawn to go beyond what Luther
saw; whatever part of his will our good God
has imparted and revealed to Calvin, they
will rather die than embrace it. And the
Calvinists, they will stick fast where they
were left by that great man of God who yet
saw not all things. This is a misery to be
lamented; for though they were "burning
and shining lights" in their times, yet they
penetrated not into the "whole counsel of
God"; . . . I beseech you to remember it: it
is an article of your Church-covenant, "That
you will be ready to receive whatever shall
be made known unto you from the written
word of God."[32]

A second group, represented by Thomas
Hooker and congregations like those at
Newtown, Dorchester, and Watertown, who
opposed certain oligarchical forms of Puritan church polity, and who sought to introduce a modicum of democracy in both
church and state, only half succeeded in
their designs by breaking away from Massachusetts Bay and settling at Hartford and
elsewhere to the west. Here they achieved
a partial separation of church and state,
and by means of a set of Fundamental Orders, in the nature of a constitution, put
restrictions on "magisterial autocracy,"
placed authority in "the free consent of the
people," removed some property qualifications and religious tests for the franchise,
and declared the admission of freemen a
political matter to be left to the several
township democracies.

A third group, represented by antinomians like Anne Hutchinson and John Wheelwright, whose ideas were derived ultimately from Johann Agricola[33] and thus more or less closely allied with Lutheranism, chose to suffer expulsion rather than relinquish their heretical, "Germanic" principles.[34]

The worst offender on the score of nonconformity, except Samuel Gorton, was Roger Williams, who, in the eyes of the orthodox, was no better than a Seeker and only slightly less reprehensible than an Episcopalian wastrel like Thomas Morton. It is known that he read Luther, although we cannot be certain when—possibly in the library of Sir Edward Coke, or as a student at Cambridge, possibly also later. That he was familiar with Luther's treatises on civil liberty is indicated by his frequent references to Luther and his several writings on the subject.[35] By 1635 he came out in favor of the Lutheran principle of separation of church and state, and while in Salem he questioned certain theocratic dispositions of lands and civil rights, thus getting himself involved in difficulties with the authorities that led to his banishment. He proceeded soon to insist on complete autonomy of secular government, agreeing with Luther: "No temporal matter shall be taken to Rome . . . A pope shall have no authority over the emperor . . ."[36] He was in full accord also with Luther in preaching justification by faith alone, without priest or visible church organization, and he insisted upon the church as a purely spiritual entity, a communion of believers. Except for his dislike of Luther's reactionary modification of his earlier views, he held that Luther led the way to the true pattern of Christianity with "a spark of true Light," and consistently preferred Luther's doctrines to those of Calvin.[37] In his espousal of Separatist-Leveler ideas he proceeded on the basis of Luther's desire for neither autocracy or mobocracy, but for lawocracy or booklaw, that is, constitutional government, to a position that has won for him, from historians like Parrington and Ernst, the title of father of American democracy.[38]

Williams' reforms in religion were hardly less potent than they were in politics. He sought to secularize the church on its institutional side, according to six theses;[39] he endeavored, at the same time, to vitalize its spiritual nature by preaching, in conformity with Lutheran principles, the covenant of grace—the doctrine that man is justified by faith, and that he receives forgiveness of sins "in and for the merits of the Lord Jesus imputed and given to us." He rejected what he called the "hellish doctrine of Sanctification" and insisted on modifying the Calvinist Covenant of Works, substituting for it the principle that man receives "a pardon and justification freely . . . without desert."[40] For Calvinistic determinism and predestination he substituted Lutheran conditional election based on God's mercy, Christ's atonement, and spiritual regeneration, or New Birth.[41] Thus, in his two-fold aim at reformation—the separation of church and state and salvation by repentence and faith—Roger Williams followed in the steps of Luther rather than Calvin.

Samuel Gorton (*ca.* 1592-1677), involuntary founder of the "Gortonites," was a brother-in-iniquity of Roger Williams in the eyes of the orthodox in Massachusetts Bay.[42] The "heretical" principles which kept him in trouble, and which he boldly proclaimed, orally as well as in a series of pamphlets that culminated in his *Simplicities Defence against Seven-Headed Policy* (London, 1646), included the following: (1) he discounted the trinitarian doctrine; (2) he denounced a "hireling ministry," denying the fitness of men who were paid, and claiming that every man should be his own priest; (3) he wanted to abolish all outward ordinances; (4) he taught a conditional immortality depending on individual character; (5) he denounced the doctrine of imputed sin and righteousness; (6) he held

that by union with Christ one partook of
the perfection of God; and (7) he denied the
actual existence of heaven and hell. These
tenets bear the stamp of radical Protestant
doctrine as promulgated by Agricola, Luther, and their followers. The question of
precisely when and by what means Gorton
came by his principles presents problems
that await further investigation, but it may
be presumed, since he was "more than ordinarily skilled in the languages" and was
judged in Rhode Island as next in learning
to Roger Williams, that his "ample" library
did not lack the requisite facilities to put
him in touch with German religious
thought.[43]

Subsequent Pietistic, Mennonite, Anabaptist, and other quietistic or mystical
movements—sometimes allied with, sometimes opposed to, Lutheran trends—are
considerations that will engage our attention later. In the meantime we shall have
to survey other, more general, intellectual
relationships that obtained between Germany and America during the seventeenth
century.

German Books in the Colonies

Early American interest in Germany was
often neither philosophical nor literary but
general, reflecting a desire to keep abreast
of German advancements represented by
books in the realms of history, geography,
astronomy and related sciences, printing,
commerce, political theory, linguistics,
grammar, dictionary- and encyclopedia-
making. Often this interest was without
specific reference to Germany, for of Germany in the modern sense of the word there
was then no semblance. Oftener than not
during the seventeenth century the books
that engaged the attention of the well-read
in America were in Latin rather than in
German. By far the majority of books in
the libraries of educated New Englanders
were English books, of course; but of the
continental books in the collections of men

like Nathaniel Ward, Robert Child, Governor Winthrop the Younger, his son and his
grandson, Increase, Cotton, and Samuel
Mather, books written by Germans, printed
in Germany in either Latin or the vernacu-
lar, were decidedly in the majority, with
Dutch books next, followed by French,
Italian, and Spanish books in the order
named.[44]

Inventories of estates, however sporadic
and incomplete, indicate that German books
were not uncommon in Plymouth house-
holds from 1620 onward.[45] In the Massachusetts Bay settlements there were even
more German books. As early as the first
year of the colony, its official library included, besides two French works (Calvin's
Institutes and a Molerus), sixteen books by
Germans, including Johann Gerhard, Martin von Chemnitz, Johann Piscator, David
Pareus, and Johann Buxtorf[46]—all favorite
theological scholars whose names occur in
many private collections owned by New
England leaders. When in 1638 John Harvard presented Harvard College with his
library of 329 titles, aggregating about four
hundred volumes, the gift included twenty-
five titles (forty-five volumes) of books by
Germans—more than the French, Italian,
and Dutch combined.[47]

Early Enthusiasts for German Learning

THE WINTHROPS

German learning enjoyed an auspicious
introduction into America by no less a person than John Winthrop, Jr. (1606–1676),
who, after being well educated at Trinity
College, Dublin, and admitted a barrister
of the Inner Temple, London (1625), traveled in Italy and Holland, and followed his
father to Boston in 1631, where he became
at once one of the leading men in the colonies, one of the founders of Ipswich and
Connecticut, and governor of the latter colony (first elected in 1657 and annually from
1659 to his death in 1676). A man of gentle-
manly tastes and sound learning, the ear-

liest American Fellow of the Royal Society (elected January 1, 1662), first scientist in America, industrialist, ambitious promoter of projects to tap American natural resources, most widely traveled colonist of his day, he was also perhaps the best-loved man in all the colonies.

He not only possessed many German books but carried on an extended correspondence with German scholars and tried to keep abreast of scientific advances in Germany. His published correspondence contains many allusions to German titles, inquiries about German authors, and requests of friends to send him German books or scientific and literary intelligences about or from Germany.[48]

The library of John Winthrop, Jr., which his father mentioned December 15, 1640, as comprising "above a thousand" volumes,[49] has been dispersed.[50] The sources of some of Winthrop's German books have been established by Professor Jantz. Several, for example, a heavily annotated Paracelsus volume, came to Winthrop from the library of the famous scientist and mystic John Dee; a volume by Basilius Valentinus came from the Dutch scientist Cornelius Drebbel, the reputed inventor of the thermometer; and certainly some of them came into Winthrop's possession from Robert Child, whose mercurial career in New England came to an untimely, and, for him, unprofitable, termination in 1647 by what amounted to deportation.[51]

Volumes of primarily literary interest include that delightful composite of mining, homily, folk song, and wit, *Serapta oder Bergpostilla* (Nürnberg, 1564) of Johann Matthesius (Matthiae), the well-known pastor of Joachimsthal and the biographer of Luther (Nürnberg, 1570). Several of the volumes are entirely in German verse; others contain good and bad verses scattered through them. One large volume, composed mainly of Heidelberg theological disputations of the 1580's, contains a verse satire, *Der Schwäbische Uhu* (1588), and a pamphlet on the Spanish Armada. Conrad Gesner's *Mithridates, sive de differentiis linguarum observationes* (Zürich, 1555), one of the earliest essays on comparative philology by this famous Swiss scientist, whose works were not unknown to other colonial Americans,[52] attests Winthrop's interest in languages.[53]

Nine early Rosicrucian tracts in Winthrop's library form one of the most remarkable items in American colonial libraries. These include not only Johann Valentin Andreae's *Chymische Hochzeit Christiani Rosencreutz Anno 1549* (1616), of which only one copy is known to be in America, but also the even rarer tracts of 1614 and 1615, together with two pages of manuscript, written in Latin and giving the rules of this projected German scientific order (not to be confused with the modern Rosicrucians). Marginal notes, some of them in Winthrop's handwriting, together with the evidence contained in a letter from Child to Winthrop, dated May 13, 1648,[54] suggest that both Child and Winthrop were interested in the Rosicrucian society.

Several of Winthrop's scientific papers were published in the early volumes of the Royal Society;[55] others were lost in transit; still others, described as "a Barrell of Papers," were 'Burnt in a warehouse in Boston" about 1800.[56] The marginalia which Winthrop made in his German books, his correct use of German scientific terms in a letter to Slegelius (Nov. 10, 1650), and other German notations in his handwriting, all suggest that the German element was an active one in his thought processes, the precise extent of which awaits investigation by students of the progress of science in New England.

SAMUEL LEE

Another seventeenth-century library, next in size to that of the Mathers and in scientific content second only to Winthrop's, was the collection owned by Samuel Lee (1625–1691). When it was offered for sale in

1693, Wait Still Winthrop, as well as the Mathers, bought a number of the Lee volumes to add to their family collections. Not many of the Lee holdings were in German, but they included the Latin books by the usual German theologians and schoolmen, as well as a small but notable group of historical works, among them Rhenanus' *De Rebus Germanicis*.[57]

JOSHUA MOODY—DANIEL GOOKIN—MICHAEL WIGGLESWORTH—EBENEZER PEMBERTON

Among other collections of the seventeenth century are those of Joshua Moody (1635–1681) and Daniel Gookin (1612–1687), and with these may be considered those of Michael Wigglesworth (1631–1705) and Ebenezer Pemberton (1671–1717). In 1718, when the collections of Joshua Moody and of Daniel Gookin came up for sale together, they contained the best of the old German scholarly works, including a fine copy of Pistorius' *Illustrium Veterum Scriptorum de Rebus Germanicis Collectio*, besides an English book of travels through Germany and *An Account of Switzerland Written in the Year 1714*. The library of the author of *The Day of Doom*, though relatively smaller than those mentioned, contained several standard German scientific works besides the usual theologians. It may be that the latter were used to good advantage in the preparation of the elaborate Biblical references that adorn the margins of his fearful poem on the day of judgment. Ebenezer Pemberton's library, when it was sold shortly after its owner's death, included several of the standard scholarly German compends, a few of the better scientific works by Germans, and such newer books as Pufendorf's *Dissertationes*, Francke's popular *Manuductio ad Lectionem Scripturae Sacrae*, and Toland's *Account of the Courts of Prussia and Hanover*.[58]

ROBERT CHILD

The collections of the Mather dynasty, of Thomas Prince (1687–1758), Benjamin Colman (1673–1747), and Jonathan Edwards (1703–1758) belong to a later day. Before turning to these, we must retrace our steps to the age of John Winthrop, Jr., whose friend Robert Child (1613–1654) played a prominent part in the introduction of German learning, especially as it related to early American scientific efforts.[59] He and Winthrop supported each other's interest in German scientific works, and their exchange of lists of scientific books which each possessed indicates that they had in mind, and possibly effected, a satisfactory plan of exchange by which their libraries were made to supplement each other. Child's list of his chemical books, made in 1641, starts with fifteen German titles, continues with six Italian, twelve French, some English, and such important German works in Latin as Georg Agricola's *De Re Metallica* (1561).[60] Child's heading his list with his "libri . . . Germanici" indicates, perhaps, that, as in the case of Winthrop, his German library was not only the greatest in number but also the most highly prized.

GEORGE STIRK

Closely associated with Winthrop and Child, during the few years he spent in America, was George Stirk (or Starkey), B.A., Harvard, 1646, M.A., 1649. He appears to have received his introduction to chemistry and metallurgy chiefly from Child and Winthrop, the latter placing his books at Stirk's disposal. But he soon departed for England, where he became one of Child's group closely associated with Samuel Hartlib, Robert Boyle, John French, the translator of Agrippa's *Three Books of Occult Philosophy* (dedicated to Robert Child); he became a prominent alchemist, traveled in Germany, and achieved the distinction of being the first American-educated scientist to have a number of his works translated into German.[61]

JOHN DAVENPORT—JOHN WILSON—
NATHANIEL WARD

Other friends and associates of Governor Winthrop of Connecticut knew the German language, and many more were well acquainted with German scholarship through the media of Latin or English translation. Among the older generation was John Davenport (1597–1670), minister at New Haven, who received, about 1661, German mystical and religious books from John Durie, then traveling in Germany.[62] John Wilson (1588–1667), educated for the law at Cambridge, a Puritan minister, heretic hunter in America, and author of several poems, owned at least one of the famous volumes of German renaissance literature— the dramas of Nicodemus Frischlin. But the most important wit among the first generation of Puritans in America who cultivated German letters was Winthrop's friend and one-time neighbor and pastor at Ipswich— Nathaniel Ward (1578–1652),[63] the Simple Cobler of Aggawam, who promised to "mend his Native Country lamentably tattered, both in upper-Leather and sole," and to do it both gratis and merrily, however earnestly. His *Simple Cobler of Aggawam* (1647) contains numerous references to Germany and German matters—many of them doubtless reminiscent of his earlier sojourn in Germany. Among them are allusions to Paracelsus, Frederick Duke of Saxony, Prince Rupert, German Anabaptists, Theosophists, the Rosicrucians, David Pareus, and the state of the German churches. There is little external evidence regarding Ward's familiarity with German literature on the strength of which one might connect him with Hans Sachs beyond the striking parallel between the German cobbler poet and his American counterpart and the possibility that the *Knittelverse* of the Nürnberg wit may have suggested to the Simple Cobler of Aggawam the distichs with which he adorned the pages of his prose tract.

Harvard College

Although the scientific training of men like Winthrop and Child was acquired outside Harvard College, seventeenth-century Harvard was not as destitute of scientific learning as has often been supposed, in either the amount or the variety that was taught in the classroom or that was available in the library. One of the most prolific and popular German textbook writers of the early seventeenth century, Bartholomaeus Keckermann, was prominently represented by his logic, his mathematics, and his physics.[64] Professor Morison brackets with Keckermann and Peter Ramus, Johann Heinrich Alsted as the "favorite authors" for students' use. Among works of reference analogous to the general use to which the *Encyclopaedia Britannica* is put nowadays was Alsted's *Encyclopaedia*.[65] Other popular texts and works of reference of Germanic origin include books by Johannes Magirus, especially his physics (perhaps the most frequently used German textbook at Harvard), Wollebius' compendium or digest of theology, Johann Piscator's analysis of the New Testament, Johann Buxtorf's Hebrew grammar, Wolfgang Musculus' commentary on Matthew, Marcus Friedrich Wendelin's physics and his logic, and Martin Trost's Syriac New Testament.[66] As studies of seventeenth-century Harvard proceed, we find increasingly not only that education there embraced a wide range of subjects but also that German works in use covered almost every field of learning,[67] not excluding belles-lettres.[68]

Through gifts and donations,[69] the Harvard library soon acquired duplicate copies of a number of titles, which were disposed of by sale beginning about 1682.[70] The lists of these duplicates afford some indication of what books were popularly used. The money thus derived made possible the direct purchase of books in 1698, and it is a matter of some significance that the first accessions made with these resources were the German *Ephemerides*[71] of Nürnberg and the *Acta Eruditorum* of Leipzig,[72] both highly reputed learned periodicals of their day.

The first catalog of the Harvard library, published in 1723, reflects a strong predilection for German books throughout the seventeenth century that was superseded during the eighteenth by a tendency to acquire more Dutch and French works,[73] although for the entire period up to 1723 German works exceed in number the Dutch and at least equal the French works.[74]

The Colonial Book Trade

The general book trade as it was carried on in the late seventeenth-century in New England did not overlook German books, either, although Latin and English translations were more frequently imported than books in German.[75] There are the old standard scholarly works and also a few new ones, such as Johann Christian Sturm's compends on mathematics, architecture, and mechanics, which were used for collegiate instruction until the mid-eighteenth century.[76] German folk books in English translation appear especially often in the order invoices of the time. For example, John Usher, Boston bookseller, imported between 1682 and 1685 six copies each of *Reynard the Fox* and *Fortunatus*, twelve copies of *Seven Wise Masters*, and sixty-six copies of *Dr. John Faustus*, only Bibles, Psalm books, and a few school books appearing oftener and in greater numbers than *Dr. Faustus.*[77]

Forty-eight copies of *Dr. Faustus* received by Usher during 1683-1684 were apparently disposed of handily, for in 1685 he ordered six more. The popularity of the old Faustus story at exactly the time when Increase Mather was preparing his *Illustrious Providences* (1684) leads to conjectures about the possible influence of the book, not only on Mather but on the people generally, in preparing the ground for the hysteria that culminated in the Salem trials of 1692. The taste in New England for the marvelous and the magical did not pass immediately following the revulsion of feeling engendered by the witchcraft delusions. Although *Dr. Faustus* appeared less frequently in the invoices after the Salem tragedies, German books on related subjects continued popular, as indicated by the order placed by Michael Perry, another Boston bookseller, in 1700 for five copies of *Fortunatus* and three of the *Seven Wise Masters.*[78] Thus German literary productions early became associated in the popular mind with the mystical, the mysterious, the diabolical, and the bizarre. The vogue which this kind of literature maintained throughout the eighteenth century helps explain in some measure the attitudes toward it at the beginning of the nineteenth, when, under romantic auspices, it made a new bid for recognition and acceptance in America.

Prominent German-Americans

The vogue of German lore in early New England is all the more striking because there were then in the region comparatively few Germans who might have propagated it. Thus far we know of only a dozen or so Germans of sufficient importance to exert any considerable influence, although there must have been others. Among this number, the six who appear to have been most influential were, significantly, all physicians. The first appears to have been Dr. Felix Christian Spöri (Spörri) of Zürich, who except for a successful operation performed on the son of Governor William Brenton of Newport, R.I., did little more than visit in New England in 1661 and again between 1662 and 1665, despite very persuasive efforts that were made to induce him to settle permanently in the New World. But his experiences provoked him to write his *Amerikanische Reise-Beschreibung* (Zürich, 1677), which may have had its repercussions later in terms of the immigrant movement. The next was John Lederer, who, after exploring the Appalachians of Virginia and the Carolinas, went to Connecticut, where he performed chemical experiment with Governor Winthrop at Hartford, and then practiced medicine at Stratford and Stamford about 1674–1675.[79] The next two came in the 1680's: Dr. Heinrich Burchstead Birkstead, Birksted),[80] who settled first at Nahant and then moved to Lynn Town; and Dr. Johannes Kaspar Richter von Kronenscheldt,[81] who settled at Spring or Lynn Pond about 1684 but soon removed to Salem, where he became the progenitor of the famous mercantile family of Crowninshields. A few decades later Dr. Francis Grahtmann became a respected physician and citizen of Salem.[82] The sixth and best known was Christian Lodowick (Ludwig) of Leipzig, who, after completing his medical studies at the University of Leipzig, came to Newport in 1684, aged twenty-four. His Quaker leanings made him acceptable to the Newport Friends, in whose meeting house he taught school presumably until 1691, when his entrance into the Quaker controversy on the side of Cotton Mather and against George Keith[83] led to his closer association with notables of Boston like Mather, Samuel Sewall, James Oliver, and Thomas Brattle. Although his movements immediately after 1692 are not clear, about 1694 he seems to have made his home in Boston, where Sewall mentions meeting him.[84] Here he published his *New England Almanac for 1695*, interesting chiefly because of its critical prefatory essay directed against certain types of astrological predictions customarily printed in almanacs and suggesting that Lodowick's wit may have had a part in shaping the form which the *Old Farmer's Almanac* was to take in colonial America. Toward the end of 1695 he began what turned out to be an adventuresome journey to Europe. After a sojourn in France, England, and possibly Holland, he returned to Germany, settling at Leipzig as

a translator and teacher of English and serving actively as a linguistic and literary mediator between the German- and the English-speaking peoples. His English grammar was standard in its day, and his English-German dictionary in numerous editions from 1716 onward was widely used in America as well as in Europe. He was remembered with great respect long after he left America.[85] "All in all, Lodowick probably ranks second only to Pastorius among the distinguished seventeenth-century Germans in America." He and John Lederer appear to be the only German authors in America before 1700.[86]

Quakers, Quietists, and Pietists

A tantalizing problem is presented by the influence, direct and indirect, which the Quakers of Rhode Island, Nantucket, Pennsylvania, and elsewhere exerted in spreading German religious and philosophical ideas in colonial America. That close relationships were maintained by the Quakers and several like-minded German sects is a well-known fact, and historians of the Friends' movement freely acknowledge the parallelism of their doctrines with those of certain German mystics and pietists, as well as the strong probability of Germanic influence, especially from Jacob Boehme.[87] Before these problems can be resolved, historians of American religious thought need to investigate the extent and appraise the effect of Quaker doctrines on colonial American thought. The question of Boehme's direct influence in America is another unexplored field.

The introduction into America of ideas like those of Boehme's was not dependent upon Quaker intermediaries. Boehme's works had some circulation even during the seventeenth century. The Harvard library had a set of Boehme's works before 1723,[88] and a number of individuals possessed works of his[89] or books of a related mystical or quietistic nature.[90]

During the eighteenth century the German pietistic influence increased rather than diminished, not only through books but through direct contact with sectarians of a mystical or pietistic persuasion. Indeed, as the eighteenth century got under way, the avenues by which Germanic influences came to America were multiplied. During the earlier century, Germanic intellectual influences in America were, in the absence of personal media, dependent almost solely upon books and transatlantic correspondence; but during the next century, while the vogue of the German schoolmen (as represented by their encyclopedias, compends, textbooks, and periodicals) decreased,[91] German religious and philosophical ideas received accelerated dissemination and currency through the increasingly larger contingents of German pietists and mystics who came to America. In the meantime the old German schoolmen continued to be consulted and quoted; seventeenth-century libraries, often with relatively large Germanic contents, descended through successive hands, thus becoming agencies of transmission in the perpetuation of Germanic influences from the seventeenth to the eighteenth century, the two most notable examples being the Winthrop and the Mather collections.

THE EIGHTEENTH CENTURY

Before turning to the Mathers and, with them, to the eighteenth century, another word about the seventeenth is in order. The account of German contacts as given in the preceding pages is necessarily sketchy. It neglects many individuals and overlooks entire sections of the country. One should like to know more than is known about German travelers, traders, merchants, adventurers, and professional men in the middle and southern colonies, notably in New York, Pennsylvania, Maryland, and Virginia, and about their contacts with the Anglo-American portion of the colonial population. Particularly intriguing are questions regarding the precise position which Pastorius held among Pennsylvania colonists at large, i.e., his sphere of influence outside the settlement of Germantown. Similarly, there are Kelpius, Köster, Falckner, Seelig, Matthai, and the colony of millenial mystics who settled first at Germantown and later on the Wissahickon.[92] After Pastorius, Kelpius was probably the most influential individual in bringing to America the Arndt-Andreae-Spener complex of mystical religious ideas. Questions regarding his precise relations with Penn and the Quakers generally remain unexplored.

And then there were the Dunkards (Dunkers, Tunkers) who came early in the eighteenth century to settle at various places in Pennsylvania, many of them ultimately fanning out into Virginia, while others congregated at Ephrata. At Ephrata they established a community in which they strove for earthly self-sufficiency and heavenly salvation. Beissel and others among the gifted leadership provided for their communal requirements—spiritual, intellectual, and artistic—creating, for example, a body of song and music unequaled elsewhere in the American colonies. Christopher Saur (Sauer), one of the most successful of the group, did their printing until they set up their own press. How they affected their neighbors and what influence they exerted through correspondence and the distribution of their books in Pennsylvania and beyond Pennsylvania remain open questions. Our knowledge concerning the early Schwenkfelder, Moravian, and Trappist groups remains about where Professor Faust left it four decades ago. One wishes also to know more about William Penn's relations with the Germans who settled in his province and about the interactions between Penn's Quakers and Pastorius' pietists. Where, for instance, did the

German Friends stand on the Keithian controversy, and what were James Logan's connections with the early German settlers in the colony of Pennsylvania?

For New York the situation is no better. Professor Dieter Cunz's recent work is adding to our knowledge of early Germans in colonial Maryland, but in Virginia, the Carolinas, and Georgia existing studies leave us to infer that there were few or no German contacts during the seventeenth century. By and large, we are no better off so far as our knowledge of eighteenth-century German-American relations goes. The extension of knowledge in these areas is beset by a number of peculiarly difficult problems, not the least of which are the inaccessibility of the scanty and fragmentary materials and the equivocal promise of returns commensurate with the time and energy demanded by these ground-breaking investigations. There is little likelihood that our knowledge of German-American interrelations during the colonial period will be much enlarged until Professor Jantz completes his fundamental researches. That being so, the ensuing chapter has the same fault of incompleteness as the first chapter. For the nineteenth century, where, of course, our chief interest lies, we are in a more favorable position.

Interchange of Ideas

THE MATHERS

But to return to the Mather family—notably Increase and Cotton—we have to do with an unbroken family tradition of learning extending from Richard of the early seventeenth through Samuel of the late eighteenth century. There was no interruption or break in the German interests of later members of the family as in the case of the Winthrops. Moreover, in the case of Increase and Cotton, the son outlived the father by only five years, so that their periods of activity were almost coincident. Both drew largely upon the same store of books; both were active before 1700 but equally so after that date; their learning and their libraries therefore serve admirably to demonstrate the transition from the seventeenth to the eighteenth century.

Although Richard Mather had already concerned himself with German literary and theological productions, Increase was the first of the clan to take a prominent interest in German literature. He and his son Cotton, together with the Winthrops, were among the leading perpetuators of the seventeenth-century tradition of colonial learning. They were also the chief agents in New England at the turn of the century by whom German religious and intellectual currents, as represented by August Hermann Francke, Anthon Wilhelm Boehm, and Bartholomaeus Ziegenbalg, were promulgated, before the efforts of Whitefield, the Wesleys, and Jonathan Edwards gave them greater and more popular currency.

Increase Mather's interest in German learning may be judged in part by the contents of his library, large portions of which, together with additions made by Cotton, are preserved in the American Antiquarian Society and the Massachusetts Historical Society.[93] According to the catalog of 1664, Mather's library was similar to other noted colonial collections, only much larger. German works exceeded in number the books by French, Dutch, and Italian authors combined.[94]

The use to which the Mathers put the Germanic scholarly resources of their libraries in their prodigious labors involve investigations beyond the scope that I could undertake; but until these sources are thoroughly examined, as Professor Murdock has done for portions of their works,[95] the critical study of the Mathers can hardly be said to have begun. A list of the Germans referred to, or quoted, in text or footnote, by Cotton Mather alone is to present in outline the history of German scholarship and learning, holy and profane. Such a list would begin with Melchior Adam, Heinrich

Cornelius Agrippa, Johann Heinrich Alsted, Heinrich Alting, Johannes Arndt, A. W. Boehm, Johannes Brandmüller, Johann Buxtorf, Philip Camerarius, Johann Cloppenburg, Johann Coler, proceed through Wolfgang Franz and Paulus Freherus, Johann Gerhard and Conrad Gesner, and so on through the alphabet to Zwinger's *Theatrum Humanae Vitae* and his *Morum Philosophia Poetica*. It would aggregate several hundred names and titles.[96]

A preliminary survey indicates that the kinds of German works most attractive to Cotton Mather's foraging mind fall into the following categories (arranged roughly in descending order of importance, although exhaustive research may alter the order): (1) general reference works of an encyclopaedic nature;[97] (2) theological writings, (3) classical scholarship; (4) the occult, demonology, and witchcraft, notably during the years when all New England was absorbed in these subjects; (5) the sciences, with less emphasis on chemistry and metallurgy than among the Winthrops but with greater attention to astronomy, geology, and biology; (6) German charitable and missionary endeavors, involving often childhood training and educational methods; and (7) pietistic religion.

Among Germans upon whom Cotton Mather drew for much of his scientific and generally antiquarian lore, the following figure very prominently: Athanasius Kircher, the Jesuit antiquarian; Martin Weiller, a geographer and traveler; Peter Lambech, the historian; Otto von Guericke, the scientist; Johann Carl Rosenberg and Johann Jacob Waldschmidt, both physicians; Johannes Arndt, Johann Jacob Coler, and Johann Conrad Danhawer, the theologians; and Alsted, especially his *Theologia Naturalis*.[98] Often the source is veiled in some general attribution such as "A pious German scholar says" or "A famous German Doctor of Philosophy declares." Such references, when run down, usually lead to the two learned periodicals which seem to have

served Mather as his most constant source book, especially for curious lore—the Leipzig *Acta Eruditorum* and the oft-mentioned "German Ephemerides" of Nuremberg.[99] Cotton Mather's learning was uncommonly ostentatious, if for no other reason than that it is ostentatiously universal in its derivation. Although he knew little more than the names and titles of hundreds of his references, there still remains a solid residue which argues that he possessed a wide knowledge of authors and books and had at his fingers' tips a fund of bibliographical information that is encyclopaedic in variety and scope, even though it cannot be rated as profound.

Cotton Mather's extended correspondence forms an important chapter in early American-European cultural relationships. Among of his most interesting exchanges, covering the years from 1711 to 1724, was that with August Hermann Francke, one of the leaders in the German Pietistic movement of Halle, and with Francke's friends and colleagues, Anthon Wilhelm Boehm (1673–1722) and Bartholomaeus Ziegenbalg (1683–1719).[100] These letters illustrate the eagerness with which Mather, "tho' a sorry and obscure creature," seized upon the opportunity to exchange intelligences with the learned men of Halle ("my friends in the Frederician University"), thus giving him, as he modestly added, "a Name among ye great men of ye Earth" (*Diary*, Mar. 7, 1716). The discourses and books which they sent him were to him "as cool waters to a Thirsty soul" (letter to Boehm, June 6, 1716). That he was profoundly affected by what he called Francke's "*True, Real, Vital Piety*" and "*Glorious* Revival of the *Primitive*" religion appears at once in his professions to his "Frederician friends" and in his writings designed to acquaint his own countrymen with the numerous works of Francke and his extraordinary success as a teacher and missionary.[101]

The Francke-Mather correspondence and Mather's notes concerning it make it plain that the chief intermediary between Mather and Francke was Anthon Wilhelm Boehm,[102] the very active Lutheran court chaplain in London at the time, the chief promotor of German pietism in England, in contact with both German and American scholars, and an active transmitter in both directions. In him Mather found what Winthrop had found earlier in Hartlib, Haak, and Oldenburg. Boehm produced many pietistic tracts and discourses in English, which were distributed by the Society for the Promotion of Christian Knowledge and thus given wide circulation in America. He translated from the German the *Nachrichten* of the Orphan House and other institutions at Halle, together with several volumes of Francke's sermons, including Francke's long Latin letter to Mather, for the London *Pietas Hallensis* (Vol. III, London, 1716). The one labor of his that appears to have been most immediately influential was his translation of Johann Arndt's *Wahres Christenthum* and his *Paradies Gärtlein*,[103] both of which were put to good use by Cotton Mather in *The Christian Philosopher*.[104] He also influenced Americans directly through his voluminous correspondence—much of it in connection with the work of the Society for the Promotion of Christian Knowledge—which he carried on with Americans as well as Germans. His own works also had widespread currency in the American colonies. It is significant, for example, that Jonathan Edwards, a tutor at Yale, put down on the first page of his booklist,[105] Boehm's *Doctrine of Original Sin*; and it may well be, as investigation proceeds, that his *Great Christian Doctrine of Original Sin Defended* (written about 1757), on its positive side, may be as much the product of Boehm's influence as, on its negative side, it is a refutation of John Taylor's *Scripture-Doctrine of Original Sin* (1738).

Another correspondent of Mather's was Ziegenbalg, a pioneer in philological studies (particularly the Hindu language) that bore fruit a century later not only in German linguistic studies but also in romantic literature and philosophy. Collections of Ziegenbalg's letters and reports circulated freely in England from 1709 onward, being several times reprinted, once at least in Boston in 1813. Cotton Mather exchanged letters and gifts of books with him, ordinarily through Francke or Boehm. One letter from Ziegenbalg to Mather (now apparently lost) seems to have contained a very detailed account of his missionary efforts at Tranquebar in Malabar. For his part, Mather was inspired by this letter to write his *India Christiana* (Boston, 1721), in one section of which ("Unio Fidelium. Communications between Western and Eastern India") he printed his own letter to Ziegenbalg (dated Dec. 31, 1717, Latin and English on opposite pages, double pages 62–74). Mather's letter did not reach Tranquebar until after Ziegenbalg's death in 1719, when his fellow-pastor, Johann Ernest Grundler, sent a reply (reprinted in *India Christiana*, double pages 75–87), together with Ziegenbalg's translation of the New Testament in Damulic and several of his small books on Christianity. Mather donated all these materials to the Harvard library.[106]

The side of Cotton Mather that was attracted to German pietism is one that has been obscured by students who have dwelt too much on the harshness and dogmatism of Mather the Calvinist; for assuredly he saw in "Frederician vital pietism," in its "glorious intentions," and in its "*Miraculous*" achievements, means to counteract the "*Lifeless Religion*" that he believed New England to be suffering from. He considered Francke's training of children in piety and religious self-expression, as exemplified in the Orphanage at Halle and in the missions in far-away India, evidences of the "*True, Real, Vital Piety*" that would reinstitute "a *Glorious* Revival of the *Primitive* . . . Christianity."[107] Whatever the forces may have been that contributed to his adopting this point of view—whether he came to it by conviction from within or by pressure from without—the last years of his life demonstrate the softening process which granitic Puritanism underwent, even during the twenties, and that is symptomatic, in some sense, of the emotionalism and fervor that accelerated the spread of revivalism during the forties. It is safe to say that when this whole movement is exhaustively studied, Germanic factors will be found not merely contributory but conditioning forces that not only prepared the way but helped direct the course.

Samuel Mather (1706–1785), in whom the theocratic light of the earlier Mathers flickered low, was nevertheless a man of parts and of industry. His learning was nearly equal to his father's, and he carried on the German interests of his father. In 1733 Samuel Mather published and dedicated to Harvard worthies his *Vita B. Augustus Hermanni Franckii*, including a Latin translation of Francke's autobiography (supplied by Gotthilf A. Francke), a list of Francke's Latin[108] publications, and a chronicle of "memorables" in the history of the German churches. In 1736 young Francke sent several of his father's books, which Samuel gave to Harvard in 1744.[109] There is also evidence that Samuel Mather continued to use the German books which he inherited,[110] though with less "straining for far-fetched and dear-bought hints" and, as the last of the Mathers, with less visible effectiveness.

JONATHAN BELCHER

The career of Governor Jonathan Belcher suggests that interest in German pietism was not confined to Bostonians. On October 25, 1718, Cotton Mather wrote: "For my remittance to ye Orphan-house at Glaucha, I gathered eight pounds of our money for which Mr. Belcher generously furnished me with a Bill of Ten pounds Sterling." If this is a reference to Jonathan Belcher, who in 1730 became governor of Massachusetts and afterwards of New Jer-

sey, then one of the first patrons of the College of New Jersey was also early a benefactor of Francke's and had some knowledge of the famous institutions at Halle long before Princeton was founded as the seat of evangelical Christianity in America.[111]

BENJAMIN COLMAN

Benjamin Colman (1673–1747), the first pastor of the liberal Brattle Street Church, took a considerable interest in German intellectual matters. In William Bentley's opinion, he had "great advantages over every other Minister in his day from his early visits to Europe" and because of the European correspondence which he maintained.[112] He was active in the Society for the Promotion of Christian Knowledge, becoming a commissioner of the society in 1730. He kept in close touch with pietistic activities in Germany, England, and the American colonies, notably those in Georgia.[113] He urged the establishment of charity schools in Boston, Indian missions, and other enterprises in the spirit of the pietists. In the quarrel over emotional religion as initiated by Edwards, he sided with the innovators until the Great Awakening ran into what he considered "excesses."

THOMAS PRINCE

Another of the notable eighteenth-century Americans interested in Germany was the Rev. Thomas Prince (1687–1758), who collected a fine historical library at Old South Church in Boston in preparation for his elaborate history of New England. He acquired not merely Americana but also European works of all kinds that shed light on the thought and action of the New England fathers. The collection included many German works: some rare early English Protestant books printed in German cities, English translations of books by German Protestant reformers, German editions of the classics, the German theologians, and a good collection of German historians, including many volumes of that important source book, the Cologne periodical called the *Mercurius Gallobelgicus*.[114]

THE YALE COLLEGE LIBRARY

The history of Harvard during the seventeenth and eighteenth centuries is relatively complete in comparison with the paucity of authentic information and historical detail available regarding the early history of Yale (founded in 1701). While the Yale library did not at once overcome the advantage of sixty-odd years of growth which Harvard enjoyed over its rival at New Haven, the textbooks and reference works commonly used at Harvard were also those that were used at Yale.[115] For example, the reading list of Jonathan Edwards, who entered Yale in 1720, contains some of the same titles that we find in similar records left by contemporaries of his at Cambridge—among them Keckermann, Alsted's *Geometry* and his *Metaphysics*, and Wollebius.[116]

JONATHAN EDWARDS

Jonathan Edwards not only included Boehm's *Doctrine of Original Sin* on his reading list but appears to have read rather widely among German authors—certainly Luther, Pufendorf, Alsted, Wollebius, Keckermann, Stapfer's *Institutiones Theologicae Polemicae* (1743–1747), and Francke's *Letter Concerning the Most Useful Way of Preaching*.[117]

The Methodist Revival

GERMAN PIETISM AND METHODISM

The Wesleys' and Whitefield's activities in America provided the most important means by which German pietistic tendencies, already set in motion by individuals like the Mathers, gained widespread currency. John Wesley, accompanied by his brother Charles, made his first trip to America during the winter of 1735–1736 in company with eighty Salzburgers and twenty-seven Moravians going to Georgia.

His attraction to their pietistic faith, put to proof during a storm at sea, his learning German, the impact upon him even before this of Lutheran principles, and subsequently, the influence of his travels in Germany and his sojourn in Herrnhut—all form a story that is well known.[118] What is not so well known is that these contacts with German pietism were not only contributory but decisive influences in John Wesley's religious development,[119] and, through him and his co-workers, on the development of evangelical religion in England and in America.

Although German pietism, English Wesleyanism, and the Great Awakening in America, strictly speaking, started independently of each other, in their inner essence as well as in their outward characteristics they had affinities which, in the course of time, brought them into close harmony and in some instances almost identity.[120] Pietism in Germany antedates both Wesleyanism in England and the Great Awakening in America. Its rise is bound up with the work of Jacob Spener (1635–1705) and August Hermann Francke (1663–1727) and beyond them, Arndt and Andreae. More immediately, it grew out of the social and religious paralysis of Germany following the Thirty Years' War, especially as it affected the lower and middle classes. Pietism in Germany and Methodism in England were alike in that they became a powerful leaven in strengthening the moral fiber and self-consciousness of the "Bürger" class.[121] Conditions in America were naturally very different from those in Germany and England, but everywhere religious leaders were pointing to a falling-off in religion. In America the general indifference to religion in the Middle and Southern colonies was matched by the formalism of religion in New England.[122] Thus the ground was prepared for the quickening process which the country was to feel under the impetus of the Great Awakening, the most pervasive intellectual and emotional agitation experienced in the colonies before the Revolution.

The initiation of this movement is usually ascribed to Jonathan Edwards, in whose church at Northampton he held a notable revival as early as 1734. But he was not for long a sole laborer. The Tennents of New Jersey were not far behind him. Moreover, Edwards' *Narrative of Surprising Conversions* (1736) profoundly moved John Wesley, so that he, his brother Charles, George Whitefield, and others of the "Holy Club" soon joined Edwards in America and enlarged the movement to proportions such as Edwards could hardly have envisaged, and in a manner that soon took the leadership away from him.[123]

Although they had heard and read about Francke and the Halle *Stiftungen*, the Wesleys got their first real contact with German pietism on that memorable trip to Georgia, Oct. 14, 1735 – Feb. 5, 1736.[124] Two years were to pass before John attained peace of mind regarding his faith, but his observations of the Moravians' simple worship, their complete reliance on God and self-possessed calm in the face of adversity, together with questions put to him upon his arrival by August Gottlieb Spangenberg whether he had a witness within himself—whether he had a subjective experience of conversion— all helped put Wesley on the right track.

During his four months in Georgia in 1738 George Whitefield was profoundly affected by Arndt's *Wahres Christenthum*,[125] which, coupled with his earlier reading of Francke's *Fear of Man*, led him to accept the essential principles of pietistic religion as professed and portrayed by the Georgia Salzburgers. Henceforth the main theme of all his preaching was that of "regeneration."[126] A visit to the Orphan-House at Ebenezer inspired him to found, on his next trip, Bethesda College and an Orphan-House in Georgia. The latter, widely publicized through his extensive travels, was modeled upon Francke's institutions at

Halle, and formed one of the more tangible, direct German pietistic influences during the early history of American evangelism.[127]

During the winter of 1738–1739 the Wesleys became regular attendants at the Moravians' religious exercises in Fetter Lane (London). Peter Böhler (1712–1775), sent by Zinzendorf to Georgia, stopped in London and became their instructor in the doctrines: (1) that faith is the free gift of God, given instantaneously; (2) that a trust in and reliance on Christ is man's sole justification, redemption, and sanctification; and (3) that true faith in Christ is inseparably attended by dominion over sin and by constant peace arising from a sense of forgiveness and "the witness of the Spirit." On May 24, 1738, while attending a reading of Luther's preface to the Epistle to the Romans, in which Luther teaches what faith is and that faith alone justifies, Wesley felt himself "a Partaker of the Divine nature," and on June 11 he preached his famous sermon at Oxford on the text, "By grace are ye saved, through faith."[128]

The doctrines that conversion and regeneration are the work of the Holy Spirit, that justification is by faith, and that the convert must give a satisfactory account of his religious "experience"—these staples of personal or "experimental" religion the Methodist leaders learned from Peter Böhler and his associates. The philanthropic and charitable enterprises and the organization which they found most effective for the propagation of Methodism had been perfected by the Pietists of Halle and the Moravians of Herrnhut. From them Wesley and Whitfield derived both the forms and the doctrines that revitalized religion and that fixed the character of Protestant Christianity for the next century or more.[129]

GERMAN HYMNODY

Another Germanic influence attending the Great Awakening was the promotion of a new psalmody in America. Charles Wesley had been impressed, as early as 1737, by the angelic singing of the Moravian Society in London, and both John Wesley and George Whitefield were quick to see the value of hymn-singing as a means to further the social intention of the Gospel, as well as a check upon the time-hallowed opposition to "mere human composures" as infringements on the exclusive authority and sufficiency of the Scriptures. John Wesley's first literary effort in America was the publication in 1737 of his *Collection of Psalms and Hymns*, a book that marks an epoch in the history of English hymnody.[130] Successive English editions appeared in 1738, 1739, 1740, and 1742, in which the number of translations from German grew from five to thirty-five—all still in use today, not only among Methodists but incorporated in not fewer than a hundred important Protestant collections. A search for the authorship of these hymns and chorals leads at once to German pietism, for Wesley found his originals in Zinzendorf's *Gesangbuch der Gemeine in Herrn-Huth* and in Freylinghausen's *Neues geistreiches Gesang-Buch*.[131]

In the furtherance of this new hymnody no one labored more earnestly or successfully than Charles Wesley, for he possessed an unparalleled gift of sacred song. In more than forty publications he sent forth, between 1738 and 1785, some 4,100 hymns, and at his death two thousand more remained in manuscript. Thus he provided the readiest vehicle for the expression of the hopes, fears, beliefs, and aspirations of the people, in terms certainly more intimate and possibly more forceful than the thunderous sermons of Whitefield or the superlative church organization supplied by John Wesley.[132]

The character of these hymns is as sharply distinguished from the militant battle cries of Luther's "A Mighty Fortress is Our God" as from the austerely literal Puritan psalms. The aggressive spirit of the Reformation was lost, and the threadbare doggerel of the *Bay Psalm Book* gave way to poetry. The Wesleyan hymns are the pious outpourings of individual souls, longing cries for a mystic union with the divine, songs of praise and thanksgiving, or prayers and petitions for divine assistance—all pervaded by an unswerving optimism regarding the goodness and wisdom of an overruling Providence. The quickening effect of these new songs on a generation unaccustomed to thinking that the praises of God could be sung in any other strains than those of Sternhold and Hopkins or of the *Bay Psalm Book* can hardly be estimated today, but the impression produced by turning from the old "composures" to "Jesus, Lover of My Soul" must have been profound. This much seems clear: the modern hymn came to be an index of joyous faith and a spontaneous vehicle of heartfelt worship to the vast congregations assembled by the revivalists. It became an eloquent and fervent expression of the whole visible church, and being generally adopted by evangelical churches, came in time to supply, in a large measure, both liturgy and creed; it became a potent force to keep alive a vivid sense of the spiritual in the human soul, in the common consciousness of which all shared in a manner tending to level distinctions and differences, social as well as ecclesiastical.[133]

Thus, working through the medium of evangelical and experimental religionists, Germanic influences supplied much of the motivation that freed American religion from the strait jacket of Calvinism, while preserving feelingful piety. From the neo-Lutheranism of the German pietists and Moravians was derived a good part of the impetus that led to the formulation in American churches of a sense of duty owing to the poor, the aged, the weak, and the neglected.[134] From the "Pietas Hallensis," no less than from the London Society for the Promotion of Christian Knowledge, emanated a spirit that inspired the American churches to encircle the globe with a chain of missions and to attempt the evangelization of the entire earth. Finally, these same pious influences contributed to the creation of a new psalmody and church music that not only made over the church service but insinuated itself into the very heart of American spiritual life; while the impulse given by the moral literary productions of Gellert, Gessner, Bodmer, Klopstock, and Wieland reinforced and supplemented the essentially puritanic literary consciousness of eighteenth-century moralism and didacticism, the end of which is not yet, nor likely to be soon.

The Wave of German Immigration

The great wave of German immigration did not come until the nineteenth century when the accession of thousands upon thousands of German Lutherans, Mennonites, Moravians, and German Reformed exerted a powerful effect upon American religious life, not only in the Atlantic states from New York to Georgia but especially in the middle-western states, where they concentrated in ever-increasing numbers, so that by 1900 a city like Chicago contained as many communicants in the Lutheran church as in the Episcopal, Presbyterian, Baptist, and Methodist churches combined.[135] In cities like Buffalo, Cleveland, Detroit, Milwaukee, Minneapolis, and St. Louis the Lutheran church stands first in number of members. Only fourth in size among denominations in the whole of the United States about 1900,[136] and far from presenting a unified front (for of Lutherans in America there were in 1900 no less than seventeen varieties), the German sectarians have nevertheless exerted a modifying influence in American religious life and thought commensurate with their relative numbers. However, the effort to evaluate so-called German religious influences by denominations, or as a whole, presents insurmountable obstacles, for the sectarian and denominational threads have become so inextricably interwoven that it is vir-

tually impossible to trace them, or to speak of denominations once distinctively German as still being so. There are large numbers of Germans and German-Americans in the Catholic church; there are very large contingents in the Methodist and Baptist churches; others have become Presbyterians or Episcopalians or Congregationalists or Unitarians. Churches once conducted wholly in the German language have adopted the English language; and other interrelations have come into existence that make the effort to point to anything more than general tendencies hazardous.[137] Until much more piecework is done, it seems useless to try to say much more about the influence on American religion of German church organizations than to point to the total membership of the several Germanic sects and to suggest that so large a number of church members attending German churches necessarily exerted a leavening effect on American church life.

For the earlier periods of our history, when our social relations were less complex, and national groups had a greater tendency than now to keep their identity, the attempt to trace their interrelations presents fewer problems. In the beginning, German immigration left New England virtually untouched,[138] while the Middle and Southern colonies began to receive ever-increasing migrations of Germans. These were not always received with equanimity, either in the Middle or Southern colonies or, for that matter, in New England. For example, while the plight of the Salzburgers in Georgia and of the early Palatine redemptioners in New York often moved New Englanders to pity them, reports of quietistic, "Quakerish," or "extremist" doctrines among Dunkers, Mennonites, Moravians, and other Germanic sectarians moved others to alarm. The greatest apprehension seems to have been provoked in some quarters by the efforts of Zinzendorf to unite not only the Moravians and Lutherans but "all Protestant churches," for which purpose he sent out invitations to all sects to meet in Germantown on January 1, 1742.[139]

Unwilling as most of the German sectarians were to give up anything or to yield a point to the proposed "Congregation of God in the Spirit," Zinzendorf's plan came to naught, except that it aroused non-German Protestants to what they sensed as dangerous elements in both the doctrines and the organization of these churches, especially the Herrnhuter Moravians of the Zinzendorf variety. Forced as most of the orthodox churches were to make concessions to "experimental" religion (intrinsically as much Moravian as Wesleyan), they nevertheless conceded no more than they had to, meanwhile setting themselves to combat the gentle, quietistic doctrines of the Herrnhuter Moravians and Mennonite pietists as inimical to the strict and rational plan of salvation which they had striven hard and long to establish and opposing strenuously Zinzendorf's and all other attempts toward Protestant union.[140]

In the meantime industrial development, land speculation, and shipping companies co-operated in encouraging more and more Germans to come to the Middle colonies, while in the Southern colonies large landowners like Colonel William Byrd of Virginia made repeated efforts to attract Swiss and South Germans to settle on his broad acres in western Virginia.[141] Throughout the eighteenth century Germans in America tended to keep to themselves, to migrate and settle in groups, and thus to form cultural islands. Often this exclusiveness was viewed with alarm, even in cities like Philadelphia, whose cosmopolitanism seemed to Franklin, for example, in danger of being destroyed by the Germans. In 1753 he expressed the fear that the Germans would soon "so outnumber us that the advantages we have will, in my opinion, be not able to preserve our language, and even our government will become precarious."[142]

The alarm proved unfounded for Philadelphia, where the close propinquity of Germantown to the more multi-racial Philadelphia prevented the German language, culture, and customs from prevailing as exclusively as in some of the valleys of interior Pennsylvania, New York, and Virginia. Indeed, subsequent events have demonstrated that usually those German localities which showed themselves most adaptable to the cultural ways of their non-Germanic neighbors eventually exerted the more effective and profound influence in America. But throughout most of the eighteenth century the prevailing tendency among them was to maintain their cultural autonomy. They often pointed to the fact that the reigning monarchs of Britain themselves were men who spoke Hanoverian German far more fluently than English, and many of them refused to become bilingual or to adapt their habits to Anglo-American customs. Many actively worked for the Teutonization of the colonies; but the more farsighted saw that such aims were shortsighted, that a refusal to learn English would only diminish their sphere of influence, and that an uncompromising insistence upon Germanic folkways would alienate them from the common business of American life.

German-American Leaders

Hence it does not follow that the regions which contained the greater number of Germans and German-Americans always exerted the stronger cultural influence. Sometimes more was owing to the leadership among these groups than to their numbers. In Philadelphia, for example, the fact that Germantown was under the sagacious leadership of Pastorius from the beginning was a matter of prime importance in making the Germans a real factor that had to be reckoned with in every public question that arose. Under similar circumstances, other men—the Mühlenbergs, for instance, or the Saurs—not only unified the Germans within their sphere of influence but, as the spokesmen and visible embodiment of their national or racial constituency, became influential far beyond the possibility of anything to which they could have attained without such connections. In virtually all instances where Germans exerted any direct or pervasive influence during colonial days, it was because they were willing, through their leaders, to weld themselves integrally into the common life and traditions of America.

FRANCIS DANIEL PASTORIUS

Francis Daniel Pastorius (1651–1719) was the first of those leaders among the German groups whose influence went beyond his immediate locality and people. Educated in law and theology in the universities at Altdorf, Strassburg, Basel, and Jena, a polylinguist who wrote down his thoughts in his commonplace book in eight languages, acquainted with most of the cultured countries of his time, he was, in James Truslow Adams' opinion, "the most learned man of his day in America—not forgetting Cotton Mather."[143] On intimate terms with William Penn and Thomas Lloyd (president of the provincial council from 1684 to 1691), he was not merely the leader of Germantown but a member of the legislative assembly of the colony from 1687 to 1691, a teacher of German in the English Quaker schools of Philadelphia from 1698 to 1700, and thereafter headmaster of the first school in Germantown—a position which he held until his death in 1719. His *New Primmer* (1698) was the first school book published in the province of Pennsylvania. The first formal protest, in the form of a petition, against slavery to be made in the American colonies was the work of Pastorius' pen in 1688. Except for the effect of his writings, notably his reader, the influence of Pastorius was primarily personal through his political, educational, and social activities.[144]

CHRISTOPHER DOCK AND OTHER NOTABLE TEACHERS

Christopher Dock became a worthy successor to Pastorius in the Germantown Mennonite school, where he labored devotedly from 1714 to 1771. He is credited with being the first to substitute the rule of love for the rule of rod in American education; he introduced the blackboard and demonstration method for primary instruction; and in 1750 he published his *Schulordnung*, the first pedagogical work to be produced in America.[145] In recognition of these services, he is often called the German-American Pestalozzi.

Virtually every German sect established its schools. The Schwenkfelders were particularly active in their educational efforts, and the Moravians were hardly less so. They established schools of grammar grade (at Nazareth, Lititz, and Bethlehem) and young ladies' seminaries and academies, one of which (at Bethlehem, founded in 1749) is still doing service and claims to be the oldest of its kind in existence.[146] The Lutherans and German Reformed (the most numerous among the German groups) established schools early, but definite facts relating to them can be traced only from 1720. Among their most capable teachers were Johann Phillip Boehm (of Whitpain, Montgomery Co.), Georg Michael Weiss (a graduate of Heidelberg), Georg Stiefel (Tulpehocken, Berks Co.), and Johann Jacob Hock and Kaspar Leutbecker (of Tulpehocken)—all of whom served between 1720 and the middle of the century.[147] Later Mühlenberg among the Lutherans and Schlatter among the Reformed became great educational leaders, while the printing presses of Saur and of Franklin aided appreciably the movement toward more and better schools among the Germans.

JACOB LEISLER—PETER AND ANNA ZENGER

Among the earliest of the German colonials to win a patriot's name was Jacob

Leisler, who led the revolt in 1689–1690 in New York against Tory hirelings and British exploiters of the colonies, and suffered martyrdom for his pains in 1691. Peter and Anna Zenger led a triumphant fight against arbitrary governmental authority and for liberty of the press in the same colony during 1734–1735. By the time of the Stamp Act and the Lexington-Concord fight, all three had become enshrined in the popular consciousness as patriots and opponents of European domination and oppression.

THE MÜHLENBERGS

Even more generally popular and more immediately effective were the several members of the Mühlenberg family, which supplied clergymen, soldiers, statesmen, and scientists to our colonial society. The careers of the Mühlenbergs became legendary and helped raise their race in the popular estimation. Heinrich Melchior Mühlenberg (1711–1787) was the scholar preacher of Pennsylvania, able to speak in Latin, Dutch, English, or German as the occasion demanded. As one of the first students to enroll in the University of Göttingen, in March, 1735, it was he and his three sons, rather than Ticknor, Bancroft, Everett, and Cogswell, who first brought Germanic scholarship and educational methods to America. His sons, John Peter Gabriel (1746–1807), Frederick Augustus Conrad (1750–1801), and Gotthilf Henry Ernst (1753–1807) were all sent to Halle in 1763 to receive seven years of education in the best German schools. John Peter Gabriel settled at Woodstock, in northern Virginia, and from there he was elected to the Virginia House of Burgesses in 1774. He supported Patrick Henry eloquently in his resolution, closed his last sermon with the comment, "There is a time for preaching and praying, but also a time for battle," and, throwing off his clerical robes, presented himself to his congregation in the uniform of a colonel in the Continental Army.

Three hundred recruits were taken into his regiment on the spot; and the next day, with the number increased to over four hundred, Mühlenberg's regiment marched to war. He was Representative at Large in the First Congress during 1789–1791, and again in the Third and Sixth Congresses. In 1801 he was sent to the United States Senate from Virginia. Frederick Augustus Conrad was first Speaker of the Pennsylvania state legislature, member of the first four sessions of the United States Congress, and Speaker of the First and Third Congresses. The youngest, Gotthilf Henry Ernst (who usually wrote his name simply "Henry E. Muhlenberg"), was a scholar and scientist, said to have been as thoroughly in command of Greek, Latin, and Hebrew as of English, German, and French. As a publisher of several botanical works in both Latin and German he won high renown, and in 1787 was called to the presidency of Franklin College (later Franklin and Marshall College).[148]

JOHANN DAVID SCHOEPF

No less influential than the Mühlenbergs was Dr. Johann David Schoepf (1752–1800), who came to America with the German mercenary soldiers but remained after the Revolution and became an enthusiast for America and a prolific recorder of his scientific observation in the colonies.[149] At a time when the typical attitude of Europeans was one of condescension, he wrote appreciatively of the new world in his popular *Travels in . . . the United North American States* saying, "America has her genius as much as the old countries, and eventually the former will take the measure of the latter."[150] His special reports, together with his *Travels*, form so considerable a body of work that Schoepf is of importance not merely as one who told Europeans a great deal about the new world but as one who is entitled, on his own account, to a place in the intellectual history of America.

CHRISTIAN GOTTLIEB PRIBER

One of the most colorful of the earlier German adventurers in the Southern colonies was Christian Gottlieb Priber.[151] A native of Saxony, he enjoyed excellent educational advantages, but becoming indoctrinated with the radical utopian ideas of the time, suffered banishment, first to France, then to England, and finally to America, where he arrived in 1753. After spending two years at Amelia, S.C., he became objectionable to the authorities for his "subversive" agitation for "natural rights." Divesting himself of the superfluities of civilization and armed only with the weapons of the philosopher, he set forth on an exotic mission to the Indians.[152]

He chose as the base of operations the town of Great Tellico on the Tellico River, about 500 miles from Charleston by trading route, and soon became deeply involved in the struggle between the French and the English for the Indian trade, urging the Indians to look to their interests against the sharp trading practices of French and English alike. In 1739 the Assembly of South Carolina appropriated 402 pounds currency for the expenses of an expedition against him. Despite valiant attempts of Priber's Indian friends, the military mission sent to seize him succeeded in 1743. Charged with scheming "a confederation among the Southern Indians" against all whites,[153] he was summarily convicted. He spent his remaining few years in the Charleston prison. A utopian philosopher, linguist, scholar, friend of peace, of progress, and the Indian, he deserved a better fate than befell him. He is uniquely interesting as a forerunner of German "radicals" making similar efforts in other parts of the country a hundred years later.

There were other Germans in South Carolina, in Georgia, and notably in Virginia whose careers merit closer attention than they have received. In South Carolina, for example, there was Michael Kalteisen from Württemberg, founder of the German Friendly Society in 1766; there was Jeremiah Theus, who established himself in Charleston in 1739 and became "one of the very best of the colonial painters"; and there was an engineer named Von Brahm whose geographical book and map of South Carolina and Georgia were the first of their kind. By the beginning of the nineteenth century the Germans in Charleston had become prosperous enough to inspire the quip that the city was owned by the Germans, ruled by the Irish, and enjoyed by the Negroes. David Duncan Wallace names a number of prominent Germans in South Carolina during the eighteenth century, and an extended search of definitive histories of others of the Southern and Middle Atlantic provinces and colonies will yield many more.[154]

Benjamin Franklin's Position

Perhaps no American of his time was more actively interested in the Germans than Benjamin Franklin. Finding them omnipresent in and around Philadelphia, he regarded them variously. When they opposed him, as they sometimes did, he could be severely critical; when they could be of service to his purpose and made to support what he considered good political or public causes, he neither overlooked nor underestimated them. As early as 1730 he printed the first German-American book for them— the hymn book of the Ephrata Cloister. He had profitable printing contracts from them, and printed a number of German works, including hymnals, a prayer book, several textbooks, and a German catechism. As early as 1732 he proposed to print, and probably did issue several numbers of, the *Philadelphische Zeitung*, the first German newspaper in America.[155] After 1738, when Saur set up his famous printing press, Franklin's German business fell off. But in 1757 he joined with Anton Armbrüster in publishing a German weekly. Indeed, he kept in constant and close contact with the Germans and often found them staunch allies in his numerous enterprises, public and private.

Franklin's several educational ventures brought him in contact with institutions of higher learning in both Germany and America. His organization of the Junto Club in 1732, its enlargement into the Philosophical Society in 1743, and the part this society played in 1749 in the establishment of the Public Academy of the City of Philadelphia (eventually to become the University of Pennsylvania) are well known. Franklin himself planned the curriculum and recommended instruction in both French and German—the first instance of German being introduced into an American school above the grammar-school level. In 1753 the Academy became the College of Philadelphia, and the following year Wilhelm Krämer (Creamer) was appointed professor of the French and German languages. He served until 1775 and never had occasion to complain for want of students.

In 1764 Franklin went to England to represent Pennsylvania in the several colonial controversies, and in 1766 he made his first direct contact with Germany. An incident in his German tour that has been generally overlooked was his visit to Göttingen, by which he became the first prominent Anglo-American to visit and investigate a German university. The accounts of this "travel of discovery" are fragmentary and vague, and the reasons for his going are not clear;[156] but the 170th number of the *Göttingische gelehrte Anzeigen*, of September 13, 1766, referring to the sessions of the Royal Society of Sciences, held on the nineteenth of the preceding July, reported: "The two famous English scholars, the royal physician, Mr. Pringle, and Mr. Benjamin Franklin, from Pennsylvania, who happened to be at that time in Göttingen . . . took their seats as members of the Society."[157] The published reports of Franklin's visit to Göttingen record his conversation at the meeting of the Royal Society, and outside of it, on English colonial affairs and on other subjects relating to America, but make no mention of his interest in the University of Göttingen as a possible model for an American university; yet Johann Stephen Pütter, whom Franklin and Pringle also visited, says pointedly that Franklin was at that time working on the plan for an American university, and that his reason for coming to Göttingen was to inspect that institution. Pütter adds that Franklin, though unable at that time to read German easily, seemed very glad to get a copy of Pütter's history of the University, and that they discussed the book, as well as the University, at some length.[158] Pütter's testimony is of a nature deserving credence. In the light of Franklin's previous and subsequent interest in the Germans, it seems reasonable. It is altogether possible that the transformation of the College of the City of Philadelphia into the University of Pennsylvania and the provision for a "German Institute" within the University, effected soon after Franklin's return from Germany, were in some degree owing to Franklin's journey to Göttingen.

When, in 1779, the college was rechartered and the six strongest denominations in the city[159] were represented on the board of government, two of the most prominent German ministers in Philadelphia were named trustees, namely Johann Christoph Kunze and Kaspar Weiberg. Owing to the influence of these two men, aided doubtless by Franklin, the following remarkable resolution was passed on January 10, 1780: "A German professor of philosophy shall be appointed, whose duty it shall be to teach Latin and Greek by means of the German language in the academy as well as in the present university." Kunze, then one of the most eminent teachers of the classical languages in America, was appointed to fill the post, where he labored until 1784 to make the new university the Göttingen of America.[160]

When Kunze resigned in 1784 to become professor of oriental languages in King's (Columbia) College, he was succeeded by the Rev. Justus H. C. Helmuth, who could boast an increased enrollment to the number of sixty the next year. But his success was short-lived. Division among the Germans themselves led to agitation for another German college; and on March 10, 1787, an act was passed by the Pennsylvania Assembly incorporating and endowing the German College and Charity School in the borough and county of Lancaster "for the instruction of youth in German, English, Latin, Greek, and other learned languages, in theology, and in the useful arts, sciences, and literature." Franklin enthusiastically supported this new venture, contributed the largest single sum for its endowment ($ 1,000, a sizable gift for that day), and himself journeyed to Lancaster to lay the cornerstone,[161] in consideration for all of which the institution was named Franklin College. Unfortunately, however, neither the zeal of Helmuth nor the support of Franklin prevented the diminution of instruction in German at the University of Pennsylvania. By 1787 Helmuth's class had shrunk to six; and although he was retained as Professor of German, the German Institute was abolished.

One of the chief reasons why the progress of German instruction suffered so decided an interruption toward the closing years of the century was the general disrupting influence of the struggle for independence, which did not really come to an end until after the War of 1812. Many colleges (among them Columbia, from 1776 to 1784) closed for longer or shorter periods; others were abandoned altogether. Kunze's German Seminary in Philadelphia was among those swept away; Franklin College at Lancaster lost its distinctive character as a German institution. The alliance with France, the services of Lafayette, and the general pre-eminence which French ideas gained provide other reasons why Germanism re-ceived a setback. The hatred of Hessians was another contributory element, and so was the decrease in immigration from Germany. The war resulted in blockaded harbors, and it was only after 1817 that immigration on a scale at all commensurate with pre-Revolutionary days was revived. Meanwhile, various measures intended to Americanize America overnight were viewed as oppressive by Germans already here and as repulsive by many who contemplated coming.

German Learning in America

However, German intellectual influences, notably such as came through the medium of the printed word, did not come to a complete halt, although they often came by way of England or France. German scholarship and the tradition of German books did not enjoy the same importance as they had during the seventeenth century; for as the eighteenth-century Americans prepared for the struggle against British political and economic dominion, the colonies tended to find inspiration and support less in Germanic authorities than in the newer and more immediately applicable forms of radicalism emanating from Locke and Rousseau, chiefly because they were more readily available and because they were adequate for the purpose.[162]

PUFENDORF—LEIBNITZ

Meanwhile some of the late seventeenth- and early eighteenth-century German scholars were not neglected. Pufendorf (1632–1694) was unquestionably the best known of political theorists. Among his most popular works were *De Jure Naturae et Gentium* (1672), *De Officio Hominis et Civis* (1673), and *De Statu Republicae Germanicae*.[163] The first of these, translated by Basil Kennett in 1703, became one of the chief sources of eighteenth-century conceptions of natural law. The reputation of Pufendorf in colonial America may be judged by the fact that in 1721 Cotton Mather used and acknowledged *De Jure Naturae et Gentium* as the source for many of the supporting illustrations for his *Christian Philosopher*, Mather's attempt, in his way, to reconcile religion with science; and that when, in 1717, John Wise argued the cause of independency and autonomy of the separate congregations in his *Vindication of the Government of New-England Churches* against the proponents of unification, he professed (in Chapter II: "Of the Civil Being of Man"), "I shall Principally take Baron Pufendorf for my Chief Guide and Spokes-man." Pufendorf served admirably the purposes of liberal theologians and political theorists of the stamp of John Barnard and Jonathan Mayhew; while the prominence which Mather and Wise gave Pufendorf in their widely current and influential books enhanced his reputation among colonial religious and political polemicists.

Leibnitz (1646–1716) is another who was not unknown. Very probably Jonathan Edwards was acquainted with his work,[164] and another Yale man, Samuel Johnson, afterwards president of King's College, noted in 1727–1728 that he read Dr. Clark "His Papers between him and Leibnitz."[165] There are also references to Leibnitz' pupil Christian Wolf.

The Influence of Political Events

Political and historical events, too, had their effect. The accession of the Hanoverians to the throne of England in 1714 proved a stimulus to interest Americans in Germany. The question of Catholic versus Protestant succession itself was a matter of great concern in the colonies, and numerous sermons were preached lauding the Protestant Hanoverians and denouncing the Catholic Stuarts. A well-known example is Benjamin Colman's *Fidelity to Christ and to the Protestant Succession in the Illustrious House of Hanover*, delivered in Boston,

August 9, 1727, on the accession of George II. New England towns, sometimes without any German inhabitants whatever, were given German names like Hanover and Berlin. The importance of the German language in the English court and increasingly profitable commercial relations with Germany, notably Hamburg, made the acquisition of German desirable in both England and the colonies; and several books appeared designed to promote the study of the language. The earliest appears to have been the *German-English Dictionary* by Christian Ludwig (Lodowick) in Leipzig in 1716.[166] By the middle of the century Bailey's *English-German Dictionary* (revised edition by Theo. Arnold, Leipzig, 1752) seems gradually to have displaced the older Ludwig or Lodowick. In 1751 appeared John James Backmair's *German Grammar* in London, long the book in most common use for the acquisition of German. It seems to have been standard equipment in colonial libraries, in either English or American editions.[167]

Paths of Influence after the Revolution

LITERARY RELATIONSHIPS

By the seventies these influences, together with the long-sustained Hanoverian tradition and the rise of the University of Göttingen to pre-eminence, brought about the acceleration of scholarly interest—a half century before Madame de Staël's glowing account inspired the young men of Harvard to go to Göttingen. Among the earliest Göttingen publications to gain a popular reputation in America was Albrecht von Haller's *Physiologia* (1751), which remained standard far into the nineteenth century. The *Institutionum Historiae Ecclesiasticae* of Johann Lorenz von Mosheim (Helmstädt, 1755) translated by Archibald Maclaine in 1764, republished in Philadelphia in 1797 and many times thereafter, also reached a wide audience. These were followed by Johann David Michaelis' theological works and Anton Friedrich Büsching's comprehensive *Erdbeschreibung* (1754). When, in 1773, Harvard issued a select catalog of books in the Library in frequent use, the list included not only Mosheim and Büsching but also such works as the Dutchman Gerhardt Brandt's *History of the Reformation* (1668–1704), the journal of the Royal Scientific Society of Göttingen (4 vols.), three of Michaelis' works, three of Pufendorf's, and Christian Wolf's *Elementa Matheseos Universae* (5 vols., 1713–1715).[168] Again, one is reminded that the conventional account of the scarcity of German books in the vicinity of Boston in the second decade of the next century fails to take into consideration certain obvious facts regarding the contents of the Harvard Library.

Outside the staid walls of Harvard, a number of more spicy German books or memoirs, such as those of Baron Tott and Baron Trenck, enjoyed a sensational vogue. These, together with English books of travel in Germany, added detail and definiteness to the picture which many Americans had formed of German lands, German people, and German culture.[169] The catalog of the Boston booksellers, Cox and Berry, for 1772, lists other titles; while Harvard added many of the newer scholarly German productions, as well as such other works as Cramer's *Art of Assaying* and Winckelmann's *Reflections on the Painting and Sculpture of the Greeks*.

This accelerating interest in German literary productivity was reinforced by a stream of religious and moralistic books (already mentioned), which, in turn, led to curiosity about types of books requiring greater catholicity of taste. The unusual interest in Gessner's *Death of Abel* was followed by an almost equal relish for everything by "the divine Gessner," particularly his idylls, which were frequently reprinted in American newspapers and magazines.[170] Lavater's *Physiognomy*, in a British translation, was imported in large

numbers during the last half of the century, the bulk of the book evidently deterring American printers until 1803, when an abridgment of the Holcroft translation was published in Boston, but his *Aphorisms* was thrice printed in 1790 (in Philadelphia, Boston, and New York) and in 1793 at Newburyport,[171] while the periodical press found the reproduction of the *Maxims*, as well as his *Aphorisms*, especially well adapted to its purposes.[172] From Gessner's *Abel*, Wieland's *Abraham*, and Klopstock's *Messias* it was natural that the taste should turn to such works as Zimmermann's sentimentally romantic *Thoughts on the Influence of Solitude on the Heart*, which ran through ten editions between 1793 and 1819, to raise Zimmermann to first rank among German authors in American opinion.[173] With the rise of sentimentalism the public seized upon the German *Familienroman*[174] and naturally came soon to like a stronger and more sensational fare, such as Goethe's *Werther*[175] and Schiller's *Ghostseer*.[176] These and dozens of similar fictional works that followed in their wake gave rise to a flood of variants, imitations, adaptations, and translations that literally glutted the market;[177] while in the drama Goethe's *Goetz von Berlichingen* and Schiller's *Robbers* spawned a similar progeny during the last two decades of the eighteenth century that continued unabated until the Kotzebue craze ran its murky course under Dunlap in the early nineteenth.[178]

PETER WILL

Bobbing up repeatedly in this unusual literary ferment that centered upon the wilder productions of German romanticism and *Sturm und Drang* about the turn of the century is the name of Peter Will (1764–1839). He was a translator of exceptional ability[179] as well as industry,[180] who, according to the testimony of Dr. John W. Francis (1789–1861), an oracle on matters pertaining to old New York, lived in New York City during 1799 while furnishing translations from the German for the John Street Theatre.[181] We are still much in the dark about many of Will's activities in America, except that the yellow-fever epidemic in New York during the late summer of 1803 endangered his wife's health, so that he returned to London to continue his preaching there and to go on with his work of translating. About 1823 he went to Darmstadt, and continued active in the work of introducing German authors to the English-reading world. Engaged as he was in many literary undertakings, one should like to know whether, while he resided in New York, he moved in the same circle with Charles B. Brown, how intimately he was associated with Dunlap, the New York theatre, and the Kotzebue vogue in America, and what else he did during his year or two in this country. Apparently he did not himself see any of his books through the American presses, though several of them were published here, in cities ranging from Boston to Baltimore. It is certain that his reputation as the translator of current bestsellers in the realms of German piety, sentiment, and horror preceded his arrival. The *London Museum* (1799–1801), in which a large proportion of his contributions were initialed "P. W.," was promptly selected by American editors of journals as fit to plunder, with or without acknowledgment. Even the Phi Beta Kappa associates of Boston, when they published their *Literary Miscellany* during 1804–1806, appropriated Will's contributions on "Deutsche Literatur und Wissenschaft."[182] And Samuel Miller, while preparing his *Brief Retrospect*, found Will an equally acceptable authority for what became the first critical discussion of the whole of German intellectual life and literary activity available in the United States.

But in following the vogue of German pious, sentimental, and sensational literary productions in America, we have gone beyond the limits of the eighteenth century. We return now to the 1770's to resume our story.

POLITICAL AND DIPLOMATIC RELATIONS

While the Revolutionary War slowed down all literary and intellectual interchange with foreign countries—with Germany as much as with other European countries—in some respects the war contributed toward the establishment of closer contacts than had obtained earlier. Hessians were cordially despised, of course; but informed people did not mistake Hessian hirelings for German scholars and literary men,[183] while all could and did distinguish between mercenary soldiers and individuals like Frederick the Great, whose military prowess and private virtues had begun to interest American editors as early as 1758.[184] With the change of relations between England and Germany during the sixties, interest in Frederick cooled;[185] but when the German king was the first representative of any foreign power to recognize the political independence of the United States and to sign a commercial treaty, the old monarch's character, his idiosyncrasies, and his military achievements combined to make him a very popular subject for sketch and anecdote for nearly a century after his death.[186]

GERMAN-AMERICAN PATRIOTS AND MERCHANTS

Other paths of influence, relatively unimportant before the Revolution, came now to be of real significance. One was the increasingly closer, more frequent, and more sympathetic contacts fostered between Anglo-Americans and prominent German patriots like the Mühlenbergs, the Rittenhouse family, Baron von Kalb, and Baron von Steuben.[187] This growing feeling of mutual respect is reflected in Dr. Benjamin Rush's *Account of the Manners of the German Inhabitants of Pennsylvania* (1789). A second was the increasing number and prominence of German merchants in Philadelphia, Boston, and elsewhere—such, for example, as the great merchant family of

Crowninshield (Kronenscheldt), who, by reason of their combined civic enterprise, learning, philanthropy, and mercantile interests, came to be highly reputed.[188] German merchants and consuls in Hamburg (for example, Samuel Williams and Joseph Pitcairn) and in other ports, as well as ship captains—many of them, as we shall see, with keen cultural interests—came to form links effecting close German-American intellectual relations. A third means serving to promote nearer interrelations was established by travelers and diplomats, among them John Quincy Adams, John Trumbull, and Joel Barlow.

JOHN QUINCY ADAMS

John Quincy Adams' stay in Berlin as U.S. Minister Plenipotentiary to Prussia from 1797 to 1801 was important (1) in preparing for the significant role that he was to play later in supporting Follen, Ticknor, and other enthusiasts for German learning and literature, (2) in inspiring him to write for the *Port Folio* forty-four letters descriptive of Germany, and (3) in prompting him to translate Wieland's *Oberon* (during the period of his German residence)—a really excellent work which has only recently been edited and published.[189] Sotheby's translation of 1798 won Wieland's approbation, whereupon Adams modestly withdrew his version; but Professor Faust's recent edition, resurrected from the Adams Family Archives, makes it abundantly evident that it is not only the first *complete* translation of *Oberon* in the English language but also a performance in no way inferior to Sotheby's. The whole is distinctly more than an episode in the life of the sixth President of the United States, and future historians and critics of American culture will take more than passing note of John Quincy Adams' efforts as an enthusiast and translator of German literature fifteen years before Madame de Staël published her epoch-making *De l'Allemagne*.[190]

BENJAMIN SMITH BARTON

The part that Benjamin Smith Barton (1768–1815) played in the early German-American cultural exchange has not been appraised. After studying medicine at Edinburgh and London, Barton went (according to the biographical sketch by his nephew, W. P. C. Barton) to Göttingen in the fall of 1788 and took the M.D. degree there in 1789. A search of the official lists of matriculated students and of the archives of the medical department at Göttingen has failed to substantiate the story, but it may be that Barton studied at some other German university. In any case, the prominence of Barton as a botanist, as professor of medicine at the College of Philadelphia (after 1791, the University of Pennsylvania), and as the associate and eventually the successor of Dr. Benjamin Rush is such that his reputed travel and study in Germany are worthy of further examination.

JOHN TRUMBULL

Less well known but better authenticated than Barton's are the Rhineland travels of John Trumbull, the painter, in 1786, 1795, and 1797. His notes on the journey down the Rhine from Worms to the Netherlands are full of firsthand observations and pencil sketches well worth reproducing, not only as being probably the first of the Rhine made by an American but also because they are excellent in their kind.[191] His subsequent trips were made primarily to Stuttgart, where Müller was engaged on the engraving of Trumbull's famous picture of Bunker Hill.

THE VAUGHANS

Another intermediary agency—there must have been others like it—was the English family of Vaughans. Active sumpathizers with the colonies during the Revolution, they came to New England soon after the peace. They brought with them "fine libraries, containing German books, literary and

scholarly, to which they kept adding."
Many of the books of Benjamin and Samuel
Vaughan are now at Bowdoin, Harvard,
and other institutions; some are still in family possession. It was from one of the
Vaughans that William Bentley in 1786 obtained his first "View of the German Writers."[192] Indeed, the Vaughans, through
their correspondence and personal contacts,
served as connecting links among widely
separated individuals like William Bentley
of Salem, Daniel Ebeling of Hamburg, and
Joel Barlow of Connecticut and France,
thus bringing to a focus earlier German-
American relationships and providing a
substantial basis upon which the interchange of ideas between Germany and the
United States proceeded unabated during
the nineteenth century.[193]

The Ebeling-Bentley Relationship

CHRISTOPHER DANIEL EBELING

Christopher Daniel Ebeling, born in 1741
at Garmissen, Hanover, and educated at
Göttingen (1763–1767), where belles-lettres,
history, and geography with special reference to America already formed his central interests, became a teacher in the Hamburg Handelsakademie in 1769, and soon
after, its director. In 1784 he was made
Professor of History and Greek Language
in the Gymnasium, and in 1799 Hamburg
city librarian as well. Already bilingual, he
developed his strong interest in America
and especially his republican predilections
to a point that the geographical and institutional history of America became his
dominant interest, most notably demonstrated during the earlier period of his productivity by four numbers of the *Amerikanische Bibliothek* (1777–1778), the first German periodical devoted solely to America.[194]
In the meantime he had already undertaken an elaborate *Erdbeschreibung und
Geschichte von Amerika*, projected in many
volumes and comprehensive in scope. In
1793 appeared the first volume of this

systematically encyclopaedic survey of the
new world by states, territories, provinces,
and nations, beginning with New Hampshire in the north. He persevered with un-
remitting energy in the colossal task of
extracting from the letters of his numerous
correspondents and from the books they
sent him the data for the successive volumes. In 1816 he published Volume VII, on
Virginia, the southernmost state treated.
His death in 1817 terminated the ambitious
undertaking to which he devoted more than
forty years of his life.[195]

Although Ebeling never visited America,
he developed, in the course of his long
labors, an extensive correspondence with
Englishmen and notably with Americans of
prominence. For example, President Ezra
Stiles of Yale was one of his chief informants on Connecticut. Crèvecœur, a personal friend, supplied him with information
on the middle colonies, first, through his
Letters from an American Farmer (1782), and
later, through conversation while Crèvecœur resided near Hamburg during 1795–
1796. Another first-hand source was Aaron
Burr, whom he knew in Hamburg in 1810.[196]
Thereafter a steady stream of American
travelers and students visited Ebeling in
Hamburg, among them Ticknor, Everett,
Cogswell, and Thorndike.

American consuls in Hamburg likewise
supplied him with data. During 1796–1798
Samuel Williams helped him by soliciting
the aid of Timothy Pickering, Secretary
of State, in the procurement of information not available from any other sources.
Pickering, in turn, enlisted the help of
friends in America to send the information
and books most needed by the German
geographer-historian for his gigantic undertaking. Joseph Pitcairn, successor to
Williams as consul in Hamburg (1798–
1802), was similarly helpful then and later
when he established himself as a merchant
in Hamburg. Upon Ebeling's death in 1817,
it was the firm of Pitcairn and Brodie that
represented Edward Everett and Augustus

Thorndike as agents in the purchase of Ebeling's great library of 35,000 volumes besides manuscripts, maps, and charts for Israel Thorndike, by whom the collection (which cost him $65,000) was given to Harvard in 1818.

This incident signalizes the entrance of the American upon the German book market. The purchase of the Ebeling library was the forerunner of the *Bücherwanderung* which subsequently brought to America such famous collections as those of Bopp, Bluntschli, Zarncke, Scherer, Bechstein, Hildebrand, Weinhold, Goertz, Trendelenburg, and Bernays. The fact that the acquisition of German libraries followed hard upon the migration of American students to Germany is noteworthy. That so notable a library as the Ebeling collection should have gone to raw America, and that it was acquired against the competitive bidding of European royalty created comment not only in Europe but particularly in America.[197]

German merchants who lived or traveled in the United States provided other means by which Ebeling secured his data and kept alive contacts with his American correspondents. For example, there was the well-known and prosperous Hamburg merchant, Georg Heinrich Sieveking, one-time student of Ebeling's at the Handelsakademie, who improved the opportunities of his career to visit Bentley and others of Ebeling's learned correspondents in 1811 and 1812, and who remained to the end one of Ebeling's most helpful allies in the procurement of Americana.[198] Among other German merchants who helped Ebeling were some who settled in America. As early as 1794 Matthias Müller and Jeremiah Kähler were well-established merchants in Boston. The latter was received in Boston society; and as the friend and neighbor of Jeremy Belknap he prepared the way for the establishment of cordial relations between the German scholar and the founders and leaders of the Massachusetts Historical Society, the

American Antiquarian Society, and the New York Historical Society, in all of which Ebeling was elected to membership upon Bentley's proposal. The importance of merchants of the stamp of Sieveking, Müller, Kähler, and the Crowninshields in the establishment of early cultural interrelations is greater than has been recognized. Often they went to considerable trouble, outside the line of purely mercantile duty, to promote an exchange of ideas as well as of goods. The importance to William Bentley of the comings and goings of shipmasters and merchants had a special significance because of his relative isolation in Salem.

Ebeling exchanged intelligences on almost every conceivable subject of interest to a learned man with his transatlantic friends. To some of them he sent long lists of "Books I wish the most for" or "Lists of Maps and books which I desire most to procure in behalf of my American Geography,"[199] together with requests that his friends bear in mind his needs. And because they heeded his requirements and supplied them handsomely, he acquired the remarkable library of Americana that outshone anything America herself had to offer, and that put the Harvard Library into the undisputed position of leadership when it acquired the Ebeling collection. His queries and requests were often numerous and specific, so that they sometimes taxed the ability and energy of his correspondents;[200] but his demands upon them were easily overbalanced by his own prodigality in supplying answers to their questions, even to sending unsolicited information. He was, moreover, a most generous donor of books to the several historical societies to which he belonged, and his letters to his friends seldom reached their destination unaccompanied by a book, a monograph, a journal, a chart, or a pamphlet, so that he often repaid manifold what he received.[201]

Madame de Staël's eloquent appraisal of Göttingen, of German scholarship, and of

German literature might have fallen on deaf ears a decade later if Ebeling's detailed accounts and shipments of books and periodicals, circulated widely among his correspondents and reported, often circumstantially, in Bentley's column in the *Salem Gazette* (1794–1796) and the *Impartial Register* (1800–1819), had not prepared the way among the influential men of Bentley's circle.

WILLIAM BENTLEY

Ebeling's chief American correspondent, William Bentley, was born in Boston in 1759 and educated at Harvard (1773–1777). After teaching for several terms in various Boston schools, he became pastor of the East Church of Salem in 1783. Here he served until his death in 1819, refusing to leave either to assume the chaplaincy of Congress or to become, upon his friend Jefferson's solicitation, president of the University of Virginia. Almost fabulously learned, master of twenty-one tongues (including real facility in German, French, Dutch, Spanish, Italian, Slovenian, Latin, Greek, Arabic, and Persian), he made all learned subjects his province and set about collecting a remarkable scholar's library of some four thousand volumes, which became, in its day, second only to that of Jefferson.[202]

From first to last, Bentley's primary scholarly interest was the history of America,[203] but he early formed also a real enthusiasm for German scholarship, so that, next to his American antiquarian interests, German learning became his most absorbing intellectual concern. His fondness for German books goes back at least thirteen years before he received his first letter from Ebeling in 1795, for he began collecting such items as Buxtorf's works and Mosheim's ecclesiastical history—books available in Boston—as early as 1782.[204] By May 20, 1787, he was ordering, through Captain Benjamin Hodges, Müller's *Sammlung russischer Geschichten*, Gellert's works,

Müller's *Journal of Petersburg*, and German periodicals—all of which, together with French, German, Latin, and Russian dictionaries, were delivered to him by Captain Hodges on October 23, 1787.[205]

The manner in which Bentley put his German studies to use is indicated in various ways. They enabled him to attack successfully Noah Webster ("that literary quack," as Bentley called him) and to correct some of Webster's wilder theories on the origin of the English language,[206] but most especially they proved useful to him in his journalistic career, launched about 1794, when he began to contribute freely to the *Salem Gazette* and, from 1800 to 1819, to the semi-weekly *Impartial Register*, of which he soon became editor in all but name. His column in these two papers appeared for a quarter of a century under the head of "Summary." It was a digest of foreign and domestic news, chronicling not only political, military, and commercial events, but dealing also with everything new and noteworthy in philosophy, theology, astronomy, meteorology, geology, scholarship, literature, art, and so forth. To his desk came all the important American periodicals, which he subsequently sent to Ebeling,[207] who dutifully repaid him in kind. Thus his "Summary" became what was the best digest in America of foreign intelligence, raising the *Register* to a position hardly to be expected of a paper issued in Salem, and subscribed for by many prominent Americans in all parts of the country. In 1816, John Pintard, the virtual founder and long the secretary of the New York Historical Society, rated the "Summary" as "without compliment or flattery . . . the best brief chronicle of the times in this or perhaps the European world."[208]

From reports on Ebeling's works on America which Bentley printed in his "Summary," and in which he compared the critical methods of Ebeling with the superficialities of Morse and other American geographers and historiographers, Bentley soon enlarged his "summaries" to include German belles-lettres and virtually every other subject of intellectual interest regarding Germany. By 1796 the contagion had spread sufficiently among his friends for Thaddeus Mason Harris to undertake an abridgment of Zollikofer's *Exercises of Piety*.[209] In 1797, while visiting in Dorchester, he was entertained by a Mr. Schweizer from Zürich with accounts of Lavater, a relative of Schweizer's wife. By this time he began to be sought out by students ambitious to learn German. In August, 1797, William Jenks, a brilliant young tutor at Harvard, wrote him to say: "The German language pleases me much. I am at present engaged in a poetic translation of Klopstock's *Messiah*, which occupies much of my time. It is a heavenly work." Bentley lent Jenks books, and himself borrowed several from Jenks's slender library.[210]

An episode that did much to call popular attention to Bentley and to Ebeling as scholars of the first order, and that first spread among large groups of Americans the importance of German scholarship came as a result of the stir created in this country during 1798–1799 by the Illuminati. This passing phase of the bitter rivalry between England and France for ideological dominance in the United States was brought to a head by John Robison's *Proofs of a Conspiracy against all the Religions and Governments of Europe Carried on in the Secret Meetings of Free Masons, Illuminati, and Reading Societies* (Edinburgh, 1797; first American edition, Philadelphia, 1798). This inflammatory book and the numerous spawn that followed its wake, charged that America was in imminent danger of conquest by the powers of subversion. Robison, whose knowledge of Germany, of German secret societies, and of German was in inverse proportion to his credulity, saw a German Illuminatus lurking in every corner. Before long even some of the more sober of American stalwarts were aroused —among them Jedidiah Morse, Professors

Tappan and Pearson of Harvard, and President Dwight of Yale. New England was prepared to indulge in another orgy of witch-hunting that threatened to revive the delusions of a century before and to get as much out of hand.[211]

Bentley, an influential Mason, at once engaged Ebeling in correspondence on the matter and received from him a long letter, dated March 13, 1799, in which Ebeling, disclaiming membership in the Order of Illuminati as well as in the Masonic Lodge, proceeded step by step, and point by point, to give Robison the lie and to demonstrate that Robison "knows a little of all and nothing exact."[212] By this time the American anti-Illuminati had made themselves pitifully vulnerable by their sweeping assertions and violent accusations, so that Bentley and his friends, armed with the scholarly, documented arguments of Ebeling regarding the true nature of German secret societies, overwhelmed their opponents. Their rout became complete when Ebeling's letter itself appeared in November, 1799 (thereafter often reprinted, extracted, or summarized by newspaper editors), and for several years only Morse dared show his head—not indeed on the main points of the controversy, but on quibbles.

The issues of this controversy themselves proved to be negligible, and the effect of the entire ferment was mainly negative. One positive result was the wide currency which Ebeling's letter gained in America, but what was still more important was the really detailed account of German religious and intellectual history from Francke of Halle to Kant of Königsberg which the letter presented. Bentley especially enjoyed to the full the advantage he had over his adversaries, and he improved every opportunity, from 1800 onward, to heap confusion upon their heads (even after the controversy had run its course) by excerpting and enlarging upon the points of Ebeling's letter, the bibliographical richness of which supplied him with endless opportunities to deny the charge that German philosophy was inimical to religion and to assert that German literature represents the truly "golden age" of modern literary achievement.

The controversy seems also to have had its immediate effect upon Bentley. The utility of German learning in such a controversy as he had just passed through set him now more energetically than ever to build up a first-class library of German periodicals, of Biblical and classical scholarship, and of German writers from Klopstock to Schiller.[213] His interest in and knowledge of German thought and art grew steadily during the years,[214] and with them his reputation and influence. His relationships with famous men included five presidents—John Adams, John Quincy Adams, Thomas Jefferson, James Madison, and James Monroe.

Toward the end of his long and fruitful career, the intellectual atmosphere was turning increasingly in favor of the kind of learning he advocated, and even Professor Norton was compelled to admit, in his inaugural address (1819), that a knowledge of German was requisite to thorough scholarship. Recognition and honors came to Bentley from many quarters: not only from the Middle Atlantic and Southern states but also, now less reservedly, from nearer home—even from Harvard, which, under its new president, John Thornton Kirkland, was undergoing a change of heart with respect to German learning and letters. Edward Everett's funeral oration was an eloquent eulogy, in which Bentley was represented as a courageous pioneer seeking newer and broader intellectual spheres.[215]

Thus the relationship that seems at first glance to have been little more than an unusual correspondence between a German geographer and an American divine was in reality much more. In the course of the quarter century during which Bentley and Ebeling exchanged letters, their contacts and influence spread to include several scores of men, especially among the circle of Bentley's friends, the ramifications and interrelations of which invite further study. For example, during 1804–1805, when Ebeling's former pupil, Alexander von Humboldt, was in Washington, he became acquainted with Bentley's friend, the far-traveled Jacob Crowninshield, and with Samuel Latham Mitchill, who was on intimate terms with both Bentley and Crowninshield. It was the latter who sent Bentley the silhouette of von Humboldt which found a prominent place among portraits of other famous men—among them Ebeling, Gellert, Michaelis, Mosheim, Klopstock, and Luther.

By this time, too, the Phi Beta Kappa Society at Harvard evinced an interest in German literature. *The Literary Miscellany*, which the society published quarterly during 1804–1806, contained a contribution from William Jenks in the form of a series of articles on Swiss history, an essay by Francis Dana Channing entitled "A Brief Review of the Progress of Literature in Germany" (abridged from the London *German Museum* for 1800–1801), a review of Daniel Appleton White on the *Memoirs of Salomon Gessner*, and a review by Joseph Stevens Buckminster of Samuel Miller's *Brief Retrospect of the Eighteenth Century*, which included a long section on German developments. Another member of this same group, Sidney Willard, translated Eichhorn's life of Semler from the German, and published it in the *General Repository and Review* for 1812.

Bentley and his colleagues prompted and encouraged many of the younger generation to turn, during the first decades of the nineteenth century, to German arts and sciences. Thus young Joseph Buckminster and Samuel C. Thatcher were persuaded to include Germany in their European itinerary. Both brought back with them in 1807 many German books.[216] The next year Thatcher was installed as librarian at Harvard. In 1808, when Bentley visited Cambridge and was shown "every attention from Mr. [Levi] Hedge P[rofessor] of Logic," he was also pleased by Thatcher's active concern to increase the Germanic content of the college library. As pastor of the Brattle Street Church in Boston, Buckminster was in a favored position to promote the cause of German theological and classical scholarship. In 1809 he saw through the press an American edition of Griesbach's New Testament.[217] In preparation for the Dexter Lectureship of Biblical Criticism at Harvard he earnestly studied German theological books; and although he died shortly after his appointment in 1812, he had already won for himself an enviable reputation as a scholar. Among the liberal-minded and forward-looking clergy, he was regarded as a pioneer in the introduction of Germanic Biblical research methods. When his library was sold at auction in 1812, his German books provoked the most spirited bidding and brought the highest prices.

Another group with which Bentley and his associates had more than cursory connections formed the Anthology Club, several members of which (besides Buckminster) began actively to agitate the importance of German methods and models for American theology, classical scholarship, and letters. For example, George Ticknor reviewed Wieland's *Oberon* for the club on August 14, 1810, and published this review, together with a biographical sketch, in the club's journal, the *Monthly Anthology and Boston Review* for September, 1810.[218] He was soon to investigate German universities in person. Thus something like a tendency or movement came into being and gathered momentum;[219] and when the peace of 1815 facilitated travel and removed other inconveniences of cultural exchange, and Madame de Staël's book accentuated the long tradition that had been building since the earliest days of the colonies, the young Harvard men were ready to embrace the opportunities which, according to thor-

oughly publicized report, the German universities were reputed to present.

Early American Lexicography

Meanwhile, Noah Webster (1758–1843) and James Gates Percival (1790–1856), in the course of their linguistic studies, had interested themselves in German. Taking a cue from John Horne Tooke, Webster came to the conclusion that English was a Teutonic, not a Latin language as was generally held, and that an investigation of its principles depended upon a study of all the German dialects. Accordingly, in preparation for the *Compendious Dictionary* (1806), he added German to his store of twelve languages. When he resumed work on his unabridged dictionary, he found it necessary to acquaint himself also with the early English and Teutonic dialects, so that by 1813 he had acquired twenty languages, and had become not only America's first eminent lexicographer but also her first comparative philologist. After completing two letters of the alphabet, he turned aside to prepare a synopsis of the affinities of these twenty languages, with the view to study word relationships and root meanings. Unfortunately he did not search deeply enough the literatures of the languages involved, and at times erred because he adopted a dictionary definition without taking account of the subtle nuances which literature supplies. Also he worked independently and failed to avail himself of the morphological studies of Rask and Grimm.

While the work was nearing completion, Percival came to lend a hand, first as proofreader and eventually as critic and collaborator. Percival, who had studied the findings of Bopp, Grimm, and other German philologists, called numerous errors to Webster's attention—so much so that his meticulous criticisms came to try Webster sorely. Percival counseled holding up publication until every etomology was correct; but Webster, seeing the sand run out of the glass, believed that perfection was impossible. Although Webster had his way with the publication, Percival, feeling himself better fitted to see the work through the press, clung with his post as he clung to no other. He belonged to the new order of philologists whose work was piling up new proofs of the relationships of languages, but their incomplete investigations had not yet progressed far enough to upset Webster's conclusions.[220] Thus it was that Percival's contributions, inspired by German morphological science (while they immeasurably enriched the accuracy of the dictionary) remain mainly hidden and indistinguishable from the work of Webster, but they signalize the entry of German linguistic methods into American philological study.

To CONSIDER the American publication in 1814 of Madame de Staël's book on Germany as marking an epoch before which Germany was only a "geographical conception," and after which German literature and thought quickly conquered America is to neglect the facts adduced in the preceding pages. They serve to demonstrate the fact that there was by 1800 already a well-defined tradition and a history extending back nearly two centuries. Madame de Staël's book was less initiatory than climactic in its effect.

It was primarily Bentley and the group about him who brought to a head, as it were, American concern with German lore at the end of the eighteenth century. When the younger generation—Ticknor, Bancroft, Everett, Cogswell, *et al.*—left for Germany, Bentley supplied them with books, with advice, and with letters of introduction and recommendation; while Ebeling, for his part, introduced them to his friends among the professors at Göttingen, received them in his home at Hamburg, inquired after their welfare, and otherwise interested himself in their behalf. After their return, Ticknor, Everett, Lyman, and Peabody visited Bentley during his last months and told him about their German experiences and studies.[221] Thus it came to pass that their activities bridged the gap between the concern with Germany which the seventeenth and eighteenth centuries had fostered and the closer and deeper preoccupation with German belles-lettres and critical philosophy which characterized the nineteenth. So far from being a sensational or revolutionary development, this shift was perfectly orderly and natural. It was a long, slowly-developing, indigenous coming-to-fuller-consciousness of a vital set of cultural and intellectual tendencies which had long been nurtured and with which many Americans were already thoroughly familiar.

Thought Currents
of the Nineteenth Century

THE GROWTH OF INTEREST IN GERMANY

The Colleges and the Clergy

The nineteenth century got under way with no immediately discernible changes in American intellectual interests or developments. Philosophical inquiry remained, as in earlier eras, the concern primarily of the colleges, of the clergy, and of occasional individuals. In the universities new winds of doctrine had begun to stir the dead air of tradition throughout the preceding century without accomplishing any marked revolution. But after the turn of the century the phenomenal increase in the number and variety of institutions,[1] spread over a wide geographical area, necessarily encouraged a greater scope of interests, including an ever-widening awareness of what was happening abroad. But what particularly operated in liberalizing and humanizing the mechanically rigid regimen of traditionalism was the advent of more liberal and enlightened college presidents, such as Joseph Caldwell at North Carolina (from 1796 to 1835), Eliphalet Nott at Union (1804–1859), Horace Holley at Transylvania (1818–1827,) James Marsh at Vermont (1826–1833), Mark Hopkins at Williams (1836–1872), and Josiah Quincy at Harvard (1829–1845). While the famous Yale Report of 1827, drawn primarily by President Jeremiah Day, made short shrift of visionary innovations and much prolonged the *status quo*, protests against the collegiate treadmill and gerund-grinding could not be stifled forever, and under men like Philip Lindsey (president of the University of Nashville, 1825–1850), Francis Wayland (Brown, 1827–1855), Henry P. Tappan (Michigan, 1853–1863), and Frederick Barnard (Columbia, 1864–1889) the work of liberalization was carried forward, until the generation of university presidents represented by Andrew D. White (Cornell, 1867–1885), Daniel C. Gilman (Hopkins, 1876–1902), and Charles W. Eliot (Harvard, 1869–1909) saw the revolution completed.

Although some philosophical instruction was given throughout the four years of the college course at Harvard and at several other institutions, it was generally concentrated in the senior year, and in most cases entrusted to, or at least supervised by, the president of the college. In the hands of such men as have just been mentioned, philosophy took on a new meaning. To many undergraduates it became the high spot of their college career. Loosely organized though it still was under the head of moral philosophy, its core of ethics was leavened by some instruction in logic at the same time that it embraced also whatever literary criteria, political economy, and psychological data (usually derived from the old Aristotelian categories), and religious doctrine the institution wished to give its charges before sending them forth into the world. A topping-off course of this kind, with its virtually limitless content, afforded almost boundless opportunities for ingenious and gifted teachers—opportunities which, as we shall have occasion to observe, several of the nineteenth-century preceptors were adept at utilizing.

Samuel Miller and Joseph Buckminster

The other chief area of philosophical activity was among the clergy, who remained traditionally orthodox and were generally opposed to new or foreign ideas. But even as early as 1800 these guardians of orthodoxy were not wholly unaware of German currents of thought. For example, it was directly out of a sermon by the Rev. Samuel Miller (1769-1850), one of the most influential of the Presbyterian stalwarts, on the first day of January of the new century that he expanded his now nearly forgotten but once widely read two-volume *Brief Retrospect of the Eighteenth Century* (N.Y., 1803).[2] At once one of the earliest and most extended considerations of German achievements in learning, philosophy, and the arts and sciences, it is already typical in its reservations and suspicion of German philosophy expressed in many American comments of a later day. Admittedly derived, often at second or third hand, Miller's presentation is rather severe on the transcendental philosophers, especially Kant, against whom he repeats the accusations as he found them in his British sources.[3] Kant is charged with having brought forth nothing new, nothing definite. His enigmatic language, instead of promoting human progress, serves only "to delude, bewilder, and to shed a baneful influence on the true interests of man." So much for blame. Leaving, now, the castigations of his British authority, Miller adds what his sense of fairness appears to have dictated:

The system of Kant had found numerous friends and commentators, particularly in Germany, who contend that it sets limits, on the one hand, to the scepticism of Hume; while, on the other, it refutes and overturns materialism, fatalism, and atheism, as well as fanaticism and infidelity. [II,ii]

Despite the insuperable difficulties reputedly involved in grasping Kant or in attempting a résumé of his thought,[4] he proceeds to do just that. Following his British expositor in the London *Monthly Review*, he devotes two and one-half pages to a simplified explanation of Kant on space and time, analytical and synthetical judgments, reason and understanding, pure and practical reason, and the categories. The account concludes with a list of advocates of Kant (Reinhold, Schultze, Jacobi, Will, Reimarus, and Adelung), while Herder, Plattner, and Selle are classified as opponents of the Critical Philosophy.[5]

What is more important in the *Retrospect* than Miller's judgment on this or that German is the extraordinary comprehensiveness of his report. His summary embraces at least twenty-four German philosophers, twenty classical scholars, nineteen Hebrew scholars and nine engaged in scholarly pursuits of a more general nature, eighteen poets, eleven historians, thirty physicians, fourteen chemists, eighteen zoologists, fourteen botanists, and a host of other representatives of German learning.[6]

Miller's main source of information on German literary and learned achievement was Peter Will's "Historical Account of the Rise and Progress of Literature in Germany" printed in the London *German Museum* for 1800 and 1801, which he contented himself with paraphrasing in some instances and copying in others, at the same time that he followed his model also in the arrangement and organization of materials. His dependence on Will is most marked in the earlier portion of his survey of German literature, less so for the later sections and for the more scattered references in other sections of the work, for Miller was no slavish copyist. For example, his section on German philosophy is markedly different from Will's treatment, and his favorable opinion of Schiller departs radically from Will's judgment.[7]

Emphasized by Miller as the distinctive achievements of Germany during the preceding century are (1) the development of the German language;[8] (2) the progress in "Natural and Mechanical Philosophy" as typified by Leibnitz, Wolff, von Humboldt, Werner, and seventy-two others; (3) the rise to prominence of German historians, such as Meusel, Müller, Ebeling, and Schiller; (4) the flowering of German romances and novels and the various forms of poetry; (5) the advance in classical learning; (6) the development of oriental studies;[9] (7) the extraordinarily large number of professional writers (15,000) and the accompanying generally prevalent taste for reading, numerous printing presses, and the incredible number (6,000–7,000) of books published annually; (8) the great Leipzig and Frankfurt books fairs; (9) the general encouragement to literary and artistic productivity given by princes and lesser noblemen, so that "the residence of many a petty prince is more fertile in literary productions, than some large cities in England and France," where the concentration of literary centers is said to be inimical to similar literary progress; (10) the resulting decentralization of the book trade, which is beneficent for the general diffusion of literary culture; (11) the "incredible . . . zeal and enterprise of German booksellers," whose "agents and correspondents in every part of Europe" promote literary intercourse among the nations, whence it often happens that the originals and the translations are offered at the same time; (12) the thirty-nine German universities, contrasted with seven in the British Isles—each a "grand focus from which the rays of light are thrown over the whole adjacent country . . . bringing the means of knowledge to almost every door"; (13) the emphasis in German education upon the modern foreign languages; and (14) the multiplication of public libraries and literary and scientific societies.[10]

Aside from the three sections devoted to an organized treatment of philosophy, language, and literature, numerous other achievements are particularized at appro-

priate places in the survey.[11] Several observations and judgments take on particular significance in the light of German-American relations of the day. While Miller deplores the "pernicious moral tendency" of some of the more sensational German dramas, he believes the German playwrights performed a notable service in the creation of a "more distinct and national" drama in America by supplying the native dramatists with materials to free the stage of a cramping British domination (II, 482–83). Besides seeing special significance in the German influence on the American book trade, he often calls attention to the accomplishments of Germans in America, particularly the fine typography of the Saur Bible (II, 506), the establishment of Franklin College, especially by and for the Germans of Pennsylvania (II, 502), the missionary work of the Moravians in America (I, 535), and the unusual prominence of Germans in the early development of American botanical studies (I, 142; II, 370, 402).

Miller lays no claim to firsthand knowledge of the entire range of men and books surveyed, but his work is decidedly more than a superficial throwing together of heterogeneous materials from the compends of the time.[12] It is a matter of some moment that a New York clergyman of the conservative kind should have prepared the first comprehensive and well-organized survey of German classical literature, antedating Madame de Staël's book by more than a decade, and preparing many thoughtful readers for the message to which the Frenchwoman subsequently gave further emphasis and currency.[13]

Imposing as Miller's *Retrospect* is, it is quite likely, so far as the spreading of popular information about German scholarship goes, that less pretentious essays in the periodicals and, even more notably, the work of individuals like Bentley and Buckminster were more immediately effective. Yet it seems that it was precisely Miller's *Retrospect* that aroused Buckminster's interest in Germany, at the same time inspiring him to write his first published essay, a review of Miller's *Retrospect*, for the *Literary Miscellany* for 1805 (I, 82–92). After a tour of England, Holland, Germany, and Switzerland, Buckminster returned to Boston in 1806, bringing with him upwards of three thousand books, many of them German. In 1808 he collaborated with William Wells in the preparation and publication, under the patronage of Harvard College, of Griesbach's *Greek Testament* (1809), and himself wrote four articles for the *Monthly Anthology* for 1808, 1809, and 1811 in which he defended Griesbach's scholarly methods as the only adequate means for dealing with technical problems of Biblical exegesis. His Phi Beta Kappa address of 1809 "On the Dangers and Duties of Men of Letters" included an eloquent plea for a sound American scholarship modeled on that of Germany. His proposal to prepare a critical edition (in translation) of Griesbach's *Prolegomena* came to naught by his untimely death.[14] His career was meteoric, but it was sufficiently profound to lead young Emerson, a decade after Buckminster's death, to read his sermons and addresses and to honor him as a brilliant pioneer in the cause of Transcendentalism.[15] Moreover, Buckminster was the first New England minister to study German specifically for the purposes of Biblical research and to champion German scholarship as indispensable for the progress of American theological learning.[16] His example was emulated soon after by Moses Stuart at Andover; while nearer at home, George Ticknor, who was with Buckminster to the last, and who was intrusted with his papers and subsequently had a hand in preparing the "Memoir" incorporated into the volume of Buckminster's *Sermons*, was influenced to turn his attention to Germany.[17] The influence spread through Ticknor to Bancroft, Everett, Cogswell, Harvard College, New England, and beyond.

In New York City, meanwhile, young

Elihu Hubbard Smith (1771–1798), having become an enthusiastic student of German as early as 1796, played a similar role by communicating his interest to the members of the Friendly Club, which included Samuel Miller, Charles Brockden Brown, and William Dunlap.

Journals and Journalistic Exchange

In the meantime, writers for American periodicals, who included both clergymen and professors, were beginning to introduce to their readers the more notable names of German scholars, men of letters, and philosophers. Kant's name was mentioned as early as July, 1797, in the *New York Magazine* (VIII, 365), in a brief "Explanation and Vindication of the Kantian Tenets," with special reference to the Categorical Imperative, quoted largely from Nitsch's *View of Kantian Principles* (London, 1797). During the next year the *Philadelphia Monthly Magazine*[18] published what appears to be the first notice of Kant that was more than perfunctory. The writer seems to have relied for his information upon Lange's note on Kant appended to his German translation of Stewart's *Elements*. With so little to draw on, he naturally misunderstood Kant on some points and misinterpreted him on others. He identified Kant's pure and practical reason with objective and subjective knowledge and bridged the gap too handily between mind and the *Ding an sich*. Kant's great contribution is, however, correctly stated to be a criticism of philosophical methodology.[19]

References to German philosophers at first are scattered, indicating little more than ephemeral interest. Jacobi is noticed as early as 1798 in the *Philadelphia Monthly Magazine* (I, iii, 205), but he is not again mentioned until three years later, when John Quincy Adams' *Journal of a Tour through Silesia* (first published in 1801 in the form of letters in the Philadelpia *Port*

Folio in forty-four installments) brought a good deal of information on German philosophy in general and on Garve, Wolff, and Kant in particular. Adams expressed a "preference of Garve for Kant," preferring "that philosophy which is easily applied to the purposes of life" to "that which is merely speculative."[20] On January 21, 1801, William Bentley in the Salem *Impartial Register*, already a prominent periodical, reproduced passages from Fichte to refute the charge of atheism directed against him "in some newspapers."[21] The twenty-fifth number of the *Port Folio* (June 20, 1801) presented another series of "Letters of an American, Resident Abroad, on Various Topics of Foreign Literature," in which are mentioned Kant, Lessing, and Fichte (I, 197). The next year the *New England Quarterly Magazine* (II, 135) of Boston published a notice on Christian Gottlieb Heyne, and later in the same year (III, 26–28), a two-page essay entitled "Observations on the Philosophy of Kant," signed by the initials "A. B."

Insofar as American periodicals provide an index, this early sporadic interest in German philosophy dropped off to almost nothing during the first decade of the century,[22] while concern with German theology and with literature, particularly literature with a pietistic or moralistic cast, became more marked. Meanwhile there was discernible a steadily mounting interest in the polite literature of Germany; and when, in 1814, the *Analectic Magazine* of Philadelphia (III, 284–308) and the New York *Quarterly Review* (X, 355–409) printed essays of twenty-four and fifty-four pages, respectively, on Madame de Staël's *De l'Allemagne*, the preliminary phase of concern on the part of the American review-reading public was past and a new epoch had begun. Each year brought more articles and new allies among the journals, not the least of which was the newly founded and immediately influential *North American Review*.[23] In 1815, too, George Ticknor and

Edward Everett left for the University of Göttingen. In 1816 Everett contributed the first of his letters on Germany to the *North American Review*,[24] and the year following George Bancroft, another of the young Americans studying in Germany, published the first of his essays designed to awaken Americans to the significance of the new spirit abroad in Germany.[25] Henceforth, especially after this first group of Harvard men returned from Germany and took academic posts in strategically located American educational institutions, the work of disseminating information about Germany was in the care of native Americans who had seen and heard at first hand, and who spoke with authority and conviction. Their primary concern was according to their predilections: one was interested primarily in belles-lettres, another in German historiography, still another in German classical scholarship, in German educational advances, or in theological investigations. None made it his main business to instruct Americans on the score of German philosophy more than on any other subject; but incidentally much information regarding German metaphysics in general and regarding men like Kant in particular got into their reviews, essays, and lectures. By the early twenties the "German craze," as it came to be known in Boston and vicinity, had fairly begun. The educated and well-read no longer cared or dared to confess themselves ignorant of the latest literary intelligences from Germany, the country which it had become the fashion to acknowledge "the most advanced intellectually on the face of the earth," and even John Adams, in one of his almost endless exchanges of letters with the sage of Monticello, claimed to be a "diligent student of many books" entirely unknown to Jefferson and fully informed "on the controversies in Germany and the learned researches of universities and professors."[26]

Even before the work of Ticknor's associates could make itself felt, another force or influence, hitherto overlooked[27] by students of comparative literary relations, had got under way. According to Peter S. Du Ponceau, a prime mover in the affair, a kind of "conspiracy" to promote a close cultural alliance with Germany was formed among his associates in Philadelphia at the time when Harvard first sent her graduates to Germany. The motivation had its origin in a growing literary self-consciousness after the War of 1812, when, says Du Ponceau, "some patriotic gentlemen of Philadelphia and New York," finding "that our weak efforts were derided by British critics," determined that as Americans had sought alliances abroad to secure political independence of Great Britain, so, to secure cultural autonomy, they must now "seek literary friends on the continent of Europe . . . . We began with Germany."

Two journals were established, one in English in New York, under the title of *The German Correspondent* and another in German, at Philadelphia, under that of *Views of America (Amerikanische Ansichten)* . . . . At the same time there appeared in Leipzick another periodical publication entirely devoted to this country and tending to the same end with the other two, entitled *America described by herself (Amerika dargestellt durch sich selbst)*. These three periodicals lasted little more than a year; the last, however, was followed by another, entitled *Atlantis*, also published at Leipzick, by a gentleman who is now a respectable member of the medical profession of this city (Dr. Eduard Florens Rivinus), and went through two octavo volumes. These works produced the desired effect.[28]

Thus it happened, says Du Ponceau, that the two contending parties, the Anglophiles and the Gallophiles, found themselves challenged by a third party, the Germanophiles, whose general effect was to inject a healthy leavening influence from Germany into what had been too exclusively an Anglo-French competition for cultural supremacy in the young nation.

The third of the periodicals mentioned by Du Ponceau, but actually the first in the field, was *Amerika dargestellt durch sich selbst*, published by Georg Joachim Göschen of Leipzig and running through three volumes of 56, 96, and 96 numbers, respectively, for the years 1818–1820. This semi-weekly paper, normally in four-page numbers with occasional supplements, was the organ in Germany of an "Institute" just as *The German Correspondent* was in America.[29] According to the "Prospectus" issued with the first number, the "Institute" has for its purpose the dissemination of four kinds of information: (1) intelligences on all political developments: (2) reports on cultural progress, including spiritual, ethical, religious, literary, artistic, educational, and scientific matters, and anecdotes taken from the lives of famous and representative men illustrative of the traditions of both countries; (3) full accounts of industry, agriculture, commerce, ship schedules, population, comfort, entertainments, etc.; and (4) reports on unusual happenings, remarkable observations in nature, the heavens, and the earth, oddities in peace and war, etc. Already the information in hand is so abundant that nice editorial care in the selection of materials is required.[30]

As the "Prospectus" suggests, this periodical was truly a miscellany, dividing its materials in its three volumes about equally between general information and current news. By the end of 1820, however, the Leipzig editor found that his semi-weekly could no longer compete on equal terms with the London newspapers in reporting current American affairs in Germany.[31] Accordingly the editor announced a change of policy in the last number (Dec., 1820): *Amerika* will appear henceforth in the form of annals, which, properly edited and shorn of irrelevances and partisanship, will bring to German readers reliable reports in the realms of learning, art, literature, and the moral and political life of America. With this change of policy the project lost its distinctive features and was soon swallowed up in the welter of books on America that issued from German presses.

In the meantime the founding of *The German Correspondent* in New York, the American counterpart of the Leipzig *Amerika*, had been delayed until January 31, 1820, when an anonymous editor who signed himself "Hermann" (probably the Rev. Eduard C. Schäffer) published the first number.[32] In his introductory remarks "to the Public," the editor, stating the editorial policy in terms often identical with those used by Göschen, his Leipzig collaborator, dedicates himself to correcting the false opinions of Germany which Americans derive from French and English accounts. The pages of *The German Correspondent*, "while they shall merit the attention of the general reader, will be entitled to the notice of the philosopher and the Christian." In exhibiting the German character, "Hermann" says he proposes "to refute the calumnies, with which the land of his forefathers is assailed," but he hastens to add that while he "feels happy in being descended from German ancestors," he considers it "one of the greatest earthly privileges to be a native citizen of America." A true miscellany,[33] this paper came to an abrupt, unexplained termination in January, 1821, having run just a year.

Meanwhile one of the German periodicals published in America distinguished itself from the numerous other German-language periodicals of the day by going beyond the purpose of informing Germans about America and Americans about Germany. It adopted the added purpose of promoting cordial relations between German-American and Anglo-American groups. This journal, entitled *Amerikanische Ansichten*,[34] grew out of the Mosheimsche Gesellschaft in Philadelphia, founded in 1804, by a group of young unmarried men who originally aimed through union to advance piety among their number and to perfect themselves in the use of the German language, which they hoped to preserve in its purity,

unaffected by the Pennsylvania-Dutch dialects and by Americanisms. By 1810, when the Society was incorporated, it had forty resident members and a number elsewhere, for whenever a member withdrew for as much as five miles from the city, he became a corresponding member. Composed largely of young ministers, teachers, artists, and merchants (and some learned corresponding members in Europe), its aims soon grew to embrace the general objectives of other learned societies of the time. Ten years after incorporation, the Society established the monthly *Ansichten*,[35] which ran for ten issues (to October, 1820), when the editor related the difficulties involved in editing the *Ansichten*, expressing doubt of his ability to prepare the promised annual volume, and announcing the decision to postpone the November and December numbers, in the hope that meanwhile the subscribers might be increased beyond the 300 now on the list, so that the publication could be resumed in January. These hopes were evidently not realized, for no more numbers appear to have been published.

The publication during 1818–1820 of two journals in America (one in German and one in English) and another in Germany, all designed to encourage cultural exchange, through the agency of men like Du Ponceau (who was active in many directions, and who maintained contacts with men as variously situated as Bentley of Salem, Buckminster and Follen at Harvard, Stuart at Andover, and Marsh at Vermont), exerted more than a passing influence in disseminating knowledge of Germany in America before the work was taken over by the more firmly established American reviews and the Harvard graduates who had studied in Germany.

This work, carried forward apparently successfully during 1818–1820 and then interrupted, was revived a few years later through the establishment by C. N. Röding of Hamburg of a monthly entitled *Columbus: Amerikanische Miscellen*[36] and of the quarterly *Atlantis*[37] by Eduard Florens Rivinus[38] of Philadelphia. The first of these, both larger and more informative on the more strictly artistic and cultural matters than its predecessors, maintained itself throughout 1825-1832 in Hamburg and was sold in Vienna, London, and Paris.[39] The *Atlantis* (1826-1827), too, was a more considerable journal than its predecessors of 1818-1820. Its editor, Rivinus (1802-1873), an accomplished man, a prominent physician and botanist, long resident in Philadelphia, and widely traveled, could speak with greater assurance regarding America than earlier editors of periodicals that circulated in Germany. But he, too, labored under difficulties. His residence in Philadelphia necessitated long delays while his manuscript was transmitted to Leipzig for publication—sometimes as long as four months. As a result he had to minimize current news in favor of materials of more enduring informational value, such as official acts, laws, proclamations, statistical reports, and general accounts. Eventually he found the competition of Röding's *Columbus* insuperable.[40]

Although these early journalistic ventures shrink in importance when compared with the more significant roles played a decade or two later by such American periodicals as the *Christian Examiner*, they performed a distinctive service for their day. Their position again illustrates what becomes increasingly apparent as researches are pushed forward, namely, that the stream of Germanic influence was relatively steady, and that the activity of Ticknor, Everett, Bancroft, and their associates represents less a sudden wave than an invigorated flow in the continuous current of influence from earlier days. Du Ponceau's "conspiracy," the efforts of editors and publishers in Philadelphia, New York, Hamburg, and Leipzig, and the preparation and plans which had of necessity to precede the establishment of these journals are all currents of a stream of cultural interchange that had already acquired some momentum when Madame de Staël's book had not yet become popular in America, and while Ticknor and his friends were still reputedly ransacking libraries and bookshops in and about Boston in search of a German dictionary.

American Students in Germany

Recent investigations dealing with the first generation of Americans who went to study in German universities make it unnecessary to relate in detail what is readily available elsewhere regarding their tours, studies, and subsequent influence.[41] Altogether they exerted more effort and were more effective as literary intermediaries than as proponents of German philosophy; yet several of them—notably Ticknor, Everett, Cogswell, and Hedge—served, in one way or another, repeatedly to call American attention to German intellectual matters other than the merely literary, so that for the sake of completeness and some degree of proportion, the more important relations must be rehearsed, however briefly.

GEORGE TICKNOR

George Ticknor (1791-1871) was the first of this group to be inspired—in his case principally by Madame de Staël's *Germany* and Charles de Villers' sketch of the University of Göttingen—to complete his education in the land where Madame de Staël had found a university at virtually every crossroad.[42] He spent nearly two of his four years abroad (1815-1819) at Göttingen, where he found himself from the first heartily welcomed by the most prominent professors. His primary interest being classical scholarship, he heard the lectures of Eichhorn, Schultze, Heeren, and Dissen, but he also attended the lectures of Saalfeld on modern European history, of Bouterwek on aesthetics, and of Blumenbach on natural history, while Benecke, the professor of

English literature, taught him German. His letters to Jefferson and others of his American correspondents leave no doubt that he readily adjusted himself to the tempo of the German university system, and that he profited tremendously by the instruction he received.[43]

Ticknor's call, during 1816–1817, to the Smith Professorship of the French and Spanish Languages and Literatures at Harvard necessitated his removal to Paris.[44] Following sojourns in Switzerland, Italy, France, Spain, England, and Scotland, he returned to Boston on June 6, 1819, and his formal inauguration took place two months later.

During the sixteen years that he served at Harvard he devoted his time principally to French and Spanish literatures, and until 1825, when Karl Follen joined the Harvard faculty, he seems to have done little more than to "discourse on German literary history at large," undertaking "simply to teach a few young men every year to *read* German and to know what German books they may afterwards read by themselves."[45] But when Follen came to Boston, he was quick to recognize Follen's worth and utility for his own educational objectives, and was instrumental in securing his appointment as the first regularly appointed instructor of German at Harvard.[46]

Ticknor preferred his philosophy in moderate doses, and seems to have cared little for German philosophy as such. Indeed, he did not know much about it. In his letters from Germany he occasionally referred to the extraordinary advance of philosophy among the Germans, never, however, without some qualification, usually with reference to its extremely theoretical nature.[47] Yet he was not averse to all philosophy and clearly recognized the advantages of what he called the "philosophical" approach of German scholarship. He and Everett undertook, in the fall of 1816, a tour "for the express purpose of seeing all the universities and schools of considerable name" and some of the more famous preparatory schools, notably those at Meissen and Schulpforta. Writing to Jefferson, to whom he reported his observations, he enlarged upon "the liberal spirit of German scholarship," and particularly praised the Germans for pursuing the arts as well as the sciences philosophically, adding that he wanted to see this method, together with the attendant tradition of academic freedom of inquiry, "transplanted to the U. States."[48] Although he declined Jefferson's several invitations to join the faculty of the new university at Charlottesville, he assisted him by sending "a list of the principal German works in literary History and of the best belles-lettres writers" for the library; he advised him in the selection of five professors from abroad, including Dr. Blaettermann, who taught German; he forwarded to Jefferson syllabi of his own courses in Cambridge; and he counselled him regarding the organization, discipline, and methods of instruction for the new Virginia institution.[49] But when Jefferson asked for a copy of the regulations governing Harvard, Ticknor refused to furnish it because he considered the rules at Harvard "one of the most cumbrous and awkward systems"[50] and sent instead the prospectus of the famous Round Hill School established at Northampton, Mass., by his friends Joseph Cogswell and George Bancroft. In the same letter he gave an outline of his own general plan of reform at Harvard for which he had been laboring since the summer of 1821 in the face of inertia and entrenched opposition bred of provincial tradition. His plans included a revision of the organization and administration of the departments, more freedom in the choice of studies, especially for students not pursuing work towards a degree, a separation of students into divisions according to proficiency, improvement in the quality of instruction, and a general expansion of the scope and function of the institution.[51]

In his own department he successfully carried out his reforms. Indeed, his views on innovations were adopted by the Corporation of Overseers in June, 1825, but the faculty persistently balked at his efforts, so that in 1827 his ideas were modified and virtually abandoned, except in his own department.[52] Discouragement at his failure to make Harvard over into an institution of university grade partly prompted his resignation in 1835. Most of the next three years he spent in Germany and Austria, where he was received with great acclaim in the highest circles of officials, scholars, and literary men, and he met virtually everyone of importance.[53] Upon his return, he devoted ten years to the preparation of his *History of Spanish Literature* (3 vols., 1849), the work upon which his reputation as a scholar principally rests.

Impressed by the central position occupied in the German universities by their great libraries, he became, in 1852, the chief founder of the Boston Public Library, the first of its kind in the United States. In June, 1856, he made a third trip to Europe, chiefly to confer with prominent European librarians and to purchase books in Italy, France, Germany, and England. Active in many directions, he was until his death in 1871 one of the most influential figures in the social and intellectual life of Boston and of his country; along with Everett and Bancroft, he formed the earliest group of American-born savants to represent the German-trained scholars in the United States who gave the German spirit in letters and learning a savory reputation in America.

EDWARD EVERETT

Closely associated with Ticknor was Edward Everett (1794–1865),[54] who sailed with Ticknor in the spring of 1815 and returned in the autumn of 1819, after almost five years in Europe, nearly half of which he spent with Ticknor at Göttingen. Except for a brief excursion to see his brother Alexander in Holland, Everett was inseparable from Ticknor throughout their period of residence at Göttingen. They lived at the same house, the home of Professor Bouterwek, attended many of the same classes and lectures, and traveled together during their vacations. Everett was by far the more assiduous student of the two. Ticknor declared that his friend required only six hours of sleep, and that his capacity for work was "prodigious, unequalled."[55]

Everett's primary interest was, of course, Greek under Dissen, but he also heard the lectures of Heeren on modern history and of Hugo on civil law. He received private instruction from Eichhorn in Hebrew and Arabic, devoted considerable time to the study of the modern languages, receiving two hours of private instruction weekly from Eichhorn in German, and found special delight in reading Winckelmann, Klopstock,[56] Schiller, and Voss's *Luise*. Reading Schiller led him to Kant: "He [Schiller] was a high Kantiner, as they call it. We are going to take Kant by the horns."[57] His initiation into Goethe came through *Torquato Tasso*, followed by *Dichtung und Wahrheit*. After a year at Göttingen his unfulfilled promise to send contributions to William Tudor, editor of the *North American Review*, began to trouble his conscience. The result was a forty-five–page review of Goethe's autobiography, published in the January, 1817, number of the *Review*, the first significant paper on Goethe published in an American journal.

Armed with letters from Professor Wolff and from Mr. and Mrs. Sartorius, he and Ticknor visited Goethe on October 25, 1816. Everett's judgment of Goethe was far more critical than Ticknor's; and though he was pleased several days after their visit to find that a letter from Goethe to the Professor of Mineralogy recommending them to membership in the Jena Mineralogical Society had preceded them, he wondered whether this was not merely Goethe's way of asking them to send him a box of American minerals. Nevertheless, in September, 1817, he followed up his acquaintanceship with Goethe by giving his young Harvard friend, Theodore Lyman, a letter of introduction to Goethe, together with a copy of Byron's *Lament of Tasso* and a request that Goethe autograph "any volume" of his writings for the Harvard Library and also Everett's own copy of *Hermann und Dorothea*.[58]

Here are the beginnings of the negotiations that ultimately led, through the more direct instrumentality of Cogswell, to Goethe's giving a twenty-volume set of his writings to the Harvard Library. Soon he began to carry out his commission, assigned to him by act of the Harvard Corporation, to purchase five hundred dollars' worth of books for the college library.[59] Subsequently he aided Cogswell in perfecting the negotiations by which Israel Thorndike of Boston purchased and presented to Harvard the famous library of the Hamburg geographer-historian C. D. Ebeling.[60] On September 17, 1817, he realized his ambition to become, as he said at the time, "the first American, and as far as I know, Englishman" to receive the degree of Doctor of Philosophy from Göttingen.[61]

The manner in which he was welcomed at Harvard in 1819 is indicated by Emerson, then beginning his third year, who expected "all the good of his lectures" during the next term, only to find that he was not eligible "to profit by him" until his senior year, when he was permitted to enroll in Everett's class.[62] Of even greater significance than his classroom teaching,[63] in Emerson's estimation, were Everett's numerous lectures on the public and lyceum platforms.[64] During the years of his professorship he wrote for the *North American Review* (of which he was editor during 1820–1823) six long reviews[65] of various German books, and an extended essay on "University Training,"[66] in which he commended Jefferson's plan of organization and instruction in Virginia, reviewed the history of university education in Europe, and pleaded for a more liberal policy and more

enlightened methods of higher education in America. Among educators, he corresponded with several of his former professors at Göttingen and, on this side, with Jefferson chiefly, sending him copies of his textbooks. When he saw his name reported among those who had criticized Jefferson for importing professors from abroad, he wrote to his friend at Monticello:

. . . having myself gone (at a period, when most men regard themselves as emancipated from academic restraints) and plunged into the cells of a German university, and used all my influence . . . tho ineffectually —to induce our Trustees to import a German Professor in my own department, I may claim not to be suspected of so ridiculous . . . a sentiment, as crept into some of our newspapers, on the arrival of your teachers from abroad.[67]

Jefferson replied assuring him that no explanation was necessary, at the same time inviting him to pay a visit to Charlottesville and soliciting the benefit of Everett's criticism based on his extensive European experience.[68]

But Everett needed to make no journey to Virginia to find objects of criticism. He found enough at Harvard that he would change. Like Ticknor, he found his plans and desires continually frustrated by tradition or authority;[69] unlike Ticknor, his resolution to quit his post was soon made. He longed for a larger sphere of activity and opportunity. Elected to Congress in 1824, he "quit coldly," to use Emerson's phrase, "the splendid career which opened before him" and took "the road to Washington . . . attracted by the vulgar prizes of politics."[70] Except for the years from 1846 to 1849, when he returned to Harvard as president, his distinguished political career was continuous until his retirement from public life in 1854. No longer actively engaged in scholarship, he nevertheless continued to exchange letters with some of his friends in Germany,[71] found pleasure in reading German literary works, and encouraged the extension of German educational methods in American institutions. In 1837, when called upon to speak at the Williams College Commencement exercises, he prepared an address on "The Influence of German Thought on the Contemporary Literature of England and America."[72] His address, entitled "University Education," delivered on his inauguration as president of Harvard, on April 30, 1846, and inspired by his own experiences in Germany, was thoroughly imbued with German educational ideas, notably those of Herder.[73] As an administrator he turned out, contrary to expectations, rather conservative in his attitude toward curricular changes and at times even hostile to the liberalizing tendencies of foreign universities. On educational reform, men of Longfellow's generation stood now where Everett himself had stood in 1820; but twenty-five years had elapsed, and Everett would have none (or little) of innovation. Longfellow wrote dolefully: "The whole system of college studies is now undergoing revision. Everett wants to bring things to something like the old order of things."[74] His administration at Harvard was fraught with difficulties and was notably brief.[75] His long public career overshadowed, in the popular estimation, his earlier scholarly activity; but it is to be doubted that his active life as a politician exerted the same abiding influence as did the stamp which he helped impress on the intellectual character of the young nation.

JOSEPH COGSWELL

Joseph Cogswell (1786–1871), graduate of Harvard in 1806, lawyer for a year, tutor of Latin for two years at Harvard, and traveler for some more, in 1816 decided to go to Göttingen. He sailed in September, having under his charge Augustus Thorndike, a young Harvard graduate who was to complete his education in Europe. In the beginning Cogswell found himself at a disadvantage, for he had not, like Ticknor, read *Werther* nor, like Everett, studied

Herder's *Theologische Briefe* before leaving for Germany. Already thirty years of age, he found university routine in general and the difficulties of the German language in particular irksome, but he soon learned to recite lessons, construe words, and submit to correction "with as much docility [he confessed] as if I had never known what it was to be myself a teacher and a governor."[76] His program of studious activity, which he himself deemed "respectable," his friends Ticknor and Everett agreed in calling "prodigious."[77] He grew restive under the strict attention he was required to give to philology, history, and politics, and he came to look upon these disciplines merely as supplementary to his main purpose of preparing for the career of a scientific explorer—to which end he concentrated on scientific subjects, especially geology, mineralogy, and botany.

During his first vacation period Cogswell undertook a tour of Prussia and Saxony, as Ticknor and Everett had done the year before, devoting special attention to the famous schools at Schulpforta, Meissen, and Grimma, thus already foreshadowing an interest later to be developed in his and Bancroft's educational venture at Northampton, Massachusetts. Although he expected "a repulsive reception," he was charmed by the manner in which Goethe received him at Jena and conducted him on a tour of the mineralogical collections.[78]

Upon his return to Göttingen in May, he set really to work. To Ticknor, then in Paris, he wrote on May 23, 1817:

I go on very regularly, rising at four, study till six, then hear Hausmann on Geognosy . . . At 7 Schrader . . . at 8 Welcker . . . . From 9 to 11 I am at liberty to study—11. hear Hausmann privatissime in Mineralogy . . . . From 12 to 1, free,—1 to 2 in Botanic Garden or Library; 2, Heeren who lectures well; 3, with Reck; 4 Saalfeld in Northern History; 5, Blumenbach; 6, Benecke . . . . At 7 comes my drill sergeant and so ends the day as do the lectures I hear. At 8 I give Augustus [Thorndike] one in Italian, and study as much afterwards, before 12, as . . . circumstances allow . . . . Saturday I make excursions with Schrader, and Sunday with Hausmann, who makes nothing of carrying us a round of 15 or 20 miles.[79]

Small wonder that Bancroft said, "Mr. Cogswell behaved like an absolute mad man. He studied and became sick, and studied and became almost dead, and yet studied. Mr. Everett behaved more like a Christian."[80]

In this varied and heavy program of work nothing appealed to Cogswell more than the library training that he received, at Bancroft's suggestion, from Professor Georg Benecke, who explained to him the system of organization and administration of the library at Göttingen, and instructed him in the methods of classifying, cataloguing, and arranging the books. In his future travels Cogswell never neglected to inspect university and public libraries, thus acquiring information later turned to excellent use in reorganizing the Harvard Library and in planning and organizing the Astor (later New York Public) Library.

After a tour including Hamburg, Bremen, Kassel, and the Harz region, during June, 1817, in the company of Everett and Thorndike, Cogswell returned to his studies, only to grow more restless and dissatisfied at finding, as he put it, that "at this period of my life . . . I knew nothing." Deciding that he had "grasped too much," and that he could not at this late date bring his mind "to new habits," he tried to reconcile himself to the idea that he must be content to remain ignorant and adopt, instead of an academic career, his natural calling as "a bird of passage."[81]

On September 6, 1817, he left for Munich, where he enjoyed knowing Sömmering, famous for his anatomical discoveries, Schilling, and others of the Royal Academy of Science, of which society he was elected a corresponding member in March, 1818.[82] From Munich, he proceeded by way of Vienna and the Tyrol to Rome, where he

met Bancroft, who viewed with alarm the "perfect fanaticism" with which Cogswell pursued his mineralogical studies.[83] The following spring and summer were spent in Switzerland, where he covered 1700 miles afoot in pursuit of mineralogical and botanical specimens, but he also took time to visit Fellenberg at Hofwyl and Pestalozzi at Yverdun. He talked with both and noted carefully their methods, thus adding to his store of educational theory acquired earlier at Schulpforta, Meissen, and Grimma, put to use later when he and Bancroft established the Round Hill School.

Following a period in Paris, he turned to England and Scotland, and in the spring of 1819 returned to Germany with his protégé Thorndike. They spent varying periods of time in Dresden, Hamburg, Göttingen, and elsewhere, fraternizing with scientists, forming new acquaintanceships among scholars and literary men, or renewing old friendships.[84] The most interesting chapter in the history of Cogswell's second residence in Germany pertains to his relations with Goethe, whom he had met at Jena in 1817, and to whom he had sent several American scientific publications in the interim. Cogswell called on Goethe again in May, 1819, and again in August, being graciously entertained on both occasions.[85] While Everett had furnished the original suggestion, it was Cogswell who finally induced Goethe to execute his idea of sending his books to Harvard. He turned to Cogswell for specific directions for transmitting his gifts and utilized Cogswell as the official intermediary between himself and the Harvard authorities. "America owes to Cogswell," says Professor Long, "a debt of gratitude for aiding in establishing friendly relations between Germany's greatest poet and our oldest seat of learning."[86]

In September, 1819, Cogswell left Germany for Switzerland, where at Yverdun he again visited Pestalozzi (whose system he did not consider nearly so good as Fellenberg's) and after a winter in France and the following summer in the British Isles, he returned to America in October, 1821. The following January he accepted an appointment as Professor of Mineralogy and Librarian at Harvard. He set at once systematically to reform the library, classifying, cataloguing, and rearranging all the books according to the methods employed at Göttingen. So it came about that the oldest American university library was organized on the German plan—a circumstance which, in the end, had far-reaching effects upon American education and learning.[87]

But Cogswell shared the experience of Ticknor, Everett, and Bancroft in finding Harvard unwilling to adapt herself rapidly to Göttingen methods. With George Bancroft, who was equally dissatisfied with his position as tutor of Greek,[88] he pooled resources and information on European schools, and together they opened in 1823 the Round Hill School at Northhampton, Mass., on principles avowedly copied from German and Swiss models and embodying the theories of Fellenberg, Pestalozzi, and Schleiermacher.[89] Considering the manifold handicaps under which Cogswell and Bancroft proceeded, their school prospered admirably. It enrolled, during the first eight years of its existence, 293 pupils, drawn from nineteen states and four foreign countries. But after five years of "entire devotedness to one object," which offered little or no intellectual gratification," Cogswell's mercurial temperament again asserted itself, and he felt, by March 23, 1830, "There must be a change ere long or I die."[91] His purchase of Bancroft's interest in March, 1830, and his subsequent single-handed management of the school gave him a temporarily renewed interest in the work, but the end of the school in the spring of 1834 could have been foreseen long before.

More or less at loose ends for several years,[93] he purchased, in 1838, an interest in the *New York Review*, and from 1839 to 1842 found himself sole owner and editor. During these years the journal took a prom-inent position by way of introducing German literature and thought to its readers and in championing the German system of secondary and university education as superior to all others.[92]

His New York associations led to a friendship with John Jacob Astor, whom he assisted and advised in collecting books, and to whom, when Astor sought a worthy enterprise upon which to bestow "three or four hundred thousand dollars," Cogswell suggested founding the Astor Library. He settled "all the points which arose during the progress of the affair," went to Europe repeatedly to inspect important collections and to purchase books, and in 1843 became the superintendent and first librarian of what is now the New York Public Library. He was responsible for every detail of its organization: he formulated the cataloguing, classification, and numbering systems which it still retains in all essentials, and which have since been widely adopted and recognized as among the best in use in America. He also prepared the first published catalog of the Astor Library, in four volumes. He wrote his name indelibly into the history of American library science and scholarship; for when, on January 9, 1854, he threw open the doors of the Astor Library (says Dr. H. M. Leyenberg, carefully choosing his words) Cogswell "set before the public the first collection of books ever made in this country primarily for the scholar and the research worker."[93] Thus in all his activities—as teacher, scientist, editor, and librarian—Cogswell is another of the pioneers who, while not a philosopher or even greatly interested in philosophy, yet labored effectively in this country to make prevail principles and practices which originated in German philosophical systems, and which ultimately aided signally to advance American learning.

GEORGE BANCROFT

George Bancroft (1800–1891), the fourth

of the young Harvard men to go to Göttingen, had graduated with distinction in the classics in 1817 and remained for graduate studies until the Harvard Corporation sent him to Germany for three years, on a scholarship with an annual stipend of $700, to become, as President Kirkland hoped, "an accomplished philologian and Biblical critic, able to expound and defend the Revelation of God." With him sailed, on June 27, 1818, Frederic Henry Hedge, the son of Levi Hedge, in whose home Bancroft had lived while a student at Harvard. They arrived in Göttingen on August 14, in the midst of a particularly violent town-and-gown riot, which caused Bancroft to feel "proud of home and the good discipline that reigns there." Within a few days they were comfortably established in the home of Bouterwek, where Ticknor and Everett, too, had resided.[94]

He formally matriculated on September 22, and heard the lectures of Eichhorn in the New Testament, Köster in Hebrew, Welcker in Latin, and Dissen in Greek. The next year he added historical studies under Planck and Heeren and Syriac under Eichhorn.[95] Professing to know already "enough theology for use in America" and considering Göttingen "no place to study the subject," he assured President Kirkland, "I have nothing to do with it [German theology], except so far as it is merely *critical*. Of their infidel systems I hear not a word."[96]

By the following winter Bancroft became critical of the foul weather and the rude society of Göttingen, but sought recompense in the fact that "in Göttingen are assembled the choicest instructors and all good books of all ages and tongues." However, the students were vulgar and their linen dirty; professors were "neither polished in their manners nor elevated in their ways of thinking, nor even agreeable, witty, or interesting in their conversation." He complained that learning at Göttingen is not "the companion of public life, nor the

beautifier of retirement, nor the friend and comforter in affliction," but is "attended to as a trade, is cultivated merely because one can get a living by it."[97] The theologians as a group he found especially rude, indecent, even blasphemous.[98] These strictures, made in letters to Kirkland, Norton, Stephen Higginson, S. A. Eliot, and others,[99] did much to give currency to what came to be common charges of the infidelity and atheism of German theology. Coming from a brilliant young scholar who had been sent to Germany specifically to gather what would enable him to advance the cause of true Christianity upon his return, Bancroft's accusations had a devastatingly disillusioning effect upon his patrons and sponsors.

Among these Harvard correspondents, Norton was at the time the best informed on Germany. Sensing in Bancroft's animadversions a degree of exaggeration, Norton questioned some of his criticisms, and Bancroft replied loftily defending his veracity and repeating his charges.[100] The truth of the matter was, as they discovered even before Bancroft returned to Cambridge, that he had acquired a critical, not to say supercilious attitude, which he expressed more or less unconsciously when he wrote to Norton that he found "one place nearly as bad as another."[101] Norton detected a degree of affectation and a certain captiousness, so that he reminded Bancroft of the state of society in Cambridge and of the American dislike of "ostentation or vanity, anything *outré* or *bizarre*."[102] But when he strode forward to welcome his young friend home, Bancroft accosted him in the European manner by kissing him on both cheeks —whereupon followed a serious breach between the two.[103] While they came eventually to make allowances, some of the odium of his charges against German theology lingered. Bancroft alone could not have been responsible, but it is more than a mere coincidence that henceforth, for fifty years to come, the accusations launched by him against German scholars and theologians are identical with those so widely repeated in the American press afterwards.[104]

Bancroft never suggested that learning at Göttingen was not earnestly pursued. He charged that it was done too earnestly, that the scholar was too diligent, that Germany made too much of science and too little of the scientist, that the whole process was too coldly calculating and impersonal. On leaving Göttingen, on September 19, 1820, to go to Berlin, he again leveled his charges of uncouthness at the city and the professors' manners, saying, "I go from Göttingen without regret"; but he also added what bespeaks a real appreciation of the intellectual stimulation which Göttingen had given him during his two years there, "Farewell, oh! Georgia Augusta, and mayst thou long continue to bring forth offspring worthy of thy present glory."[105]

Berlin he found more satisfactory.[106] He pursued his philological studies under Boeckh, Hirt, and Wolf, and attended Hegel's course in philosophy and Schleiermacher's lectures on education.[107] Berlin offered other attractions. He reveled in the city life which he had missed in Göttingen. He especially appreciated the frequent opportunities he had to be a guest in the homes of Schleiermacher, Savigny, and W. von Humboldt. With Savigny and Humboldt he discussed Shakespeare, Milton, Goethe, Schiller, the Schlegels, and German literature in general, and with Schleiermacher, German educational methods and their applicability in America.[108] When his five months in Berlin were up, he left reluctantly. He visited Goethe twice, on March 7 and 17, at Weimar, and found himself received graciously. His comments on Goethe at the time exhibit nothing of the venom that he later displayed in his essay on Goethe. From Weimar, he proceeded to Stuttgart, Frankfurt, Darmstadt, and Heidelberg, where he spent a month in the company of university scholars and attended the lectures of Schlosser the historian. He arrived in Paris in time to meet A. W.

Schlegel, then preparing to leave for Bonn, and soon established contacts with Alexander von Humboldt, Cuvier, Lafayette, Baron de Staël, Irving, Gallatin, and many other notables. Three months in Paris and three weeks in London were followed by a walking tour through Switzerland, a winter chiefly in Rome and Naples, and a visit to Byron at Monte Nero in the spring. He embarked from Marseilles in June and landed in New York on August 3, 1822.[109]

Yielding to his father's wishes, he was licensed to preach. While he preached for several years, it was without much satisfaction to himself or his auditors, and he soon came to prefer the lecture room to the pulpit. He applied unsuccessfully for permission to deliver lectures on history at Harvard, and then accepted a tutorship in Greek. Bedeviled by students who failed to appreciate either his parts or his methods, he soon found college "a sickening and wearisome place . . . nothing but trouble, trouble, trouble." Constantly under correction or criticism of his elders, who, he complained, "do not understand my character . . . have not taken any pains to consider it,"[110] he threw up his post and joined Cogswell in establishing the gymnasium at Northampton.[111] Because of differences between his and Cogswell's temperaments and views concerning methods of teaching and the management of the school, Bancroft sold his interest in the school to Cogswell in August, 1831, but remained a year longer as a salaried instructor. Thereafter he devoted himself to literary and historical scholarship and to political pursuits.

Besides some early, very Byronic verses, some miscellaneous essays, and texts for his classes,[112] he published in 1828 a translation of Heeren's *Ideen über die Politik, den Verkehr und den Handel . . . der alten Welt*. During his years at Northampton he wrote several important essays and review articles on German subjects, especially for the *North American Review* and the *American Quarterly Review*.[113] His *History of the*

United States, in ten volumes, appeared at varying intervals over a period of forty years (1834–1874). His career as Secretary of the Navy (1845–1846), as minister to England (1846–1849), and as minister to Berlin (1867–1874) is well known. During the critical years while the kingdom of Prussia was transformed into the North German Confederation and finally into the German Empire, Bancroft's former experience in Germany enabled him to represent his country tactfully and effectively in the German capital.

Throughout his career Bancroft injected a strong leaven of German culture into the manifold roles that he played.[114] Like Ticknor, Everett, and Cogswell, his main interest was not philosophy; but, as in their cases, his championship and exemplification of German scholarship made him at once a pathfinder in American learned endeavor and an effective agent for the reception which German philosophy was accorded by later generations of Americans. More particularly, his historical writings, inspired chiefly by Heeren's methodology and Hegel's philosophy of history,[115] set the fashion for American historiography—in fact, created it. While every successive volume of his *History of the United States* was, as it were "another vote for Jackson," Bancroft's historical writings were the first notable examples in America embodying the German concept by which historical writing was related to and given orientation in philosophical concepts and enveloping movements. If it is true that "his position as Father of American History is as unshaken as is that of Herodotus among the Greeks,"[116] then Bancroft's influence on what John Spencer Basset called the Middle Group of American Historians is more readily understood. Later historians, however (e.g., Henry Adams), did not regard Bancroft's methodology sufficiently scientific or "Germanic."

HERE we interrupt the account of the Har-vard graduates who went to Göttingen, before proceeding to Motley, by a brief review of the historical work of Prescott and Parkman, who stood between Bancroft and Motley; for it is to be observed that neither Bancroft nor his Harvard associates were solely responsible for leading American historiography in the direction of the scientific, or philosophical, method of the Germans.

In 1821 William Hickling Prescott (1796–1859) began his lifelong association with the *North American Review* and with its editor, Edward Everett, whose sympathy for Germany was manifesting itself in the *Review* to the extent that some of the older subscribers and contributors complained that it was "becoming too partial to the German at the expense of our worthy brethren, the English."[117] More than that, George Ticknor came to exert a leading influence on Prescott, so that when Prescott found the poor state of his eyes preventing his continued study of German, it was Ticknor (who had been at Göttingen at the time when German interest in Spain was at its height) who turned Prescott in the direction of Spanish subjects.[118]

His essays written for the *North American Review* between 1823 and 1839 on critical subjects indicate that he was being initiated into what was called at the time the "modern historical literary criticism" coming out of Germany.[119] Having formed a high opinion of German scholarship, it was natural, once he had chosen to study the history of the conquest of Mexico, that he should consult A. von Humboldt's writings on Mexico.[120] In preparing for *Philip II* (1855–1858), he not only read Schiller's *Geschichte des Abfalls der vereinigten Niederlande von der spanischen Regierung* but studied most intently Ranke's *Spanish Empire*, while both Humboldt and Ranke assisted him in the procuring of materials from the public offices and libraries of Tuscany, Austria, Prussia, and Gotha.[121]

Prescott still relied in large measure upon

British models, such as Robertson, Gibbon, and Scott, and upon Mably's *De l'étude de l'histoire;* that is, in attempting to see the record of history as time had left it, he was not following exclusively German models. His method of hunting out original sources was well established, even by American precedent. Nor did he follow the objective critical method of the Germans sufficiently to satisfy Theodore Parker, who observed that Prescott often referred events to Providence which other men would be content with ascribing to human agency.[122] In his way, however, Prescott, like Bancroft before him, while still regarding history as a branch of polite literature, sought to emulate German models and in so doing expedited the tendency toward following the methodology of German historiography.

Francis Parkman, too, belongs still basically to the school of literary historians, but in the care with which he examined historical evidence and in his emphasis upon the rational rather than the inspirational aspect of writing, his practice is allied to that of the German school. Also, he was meticulous about going to firsthand sources and supplying full documentation, but there is little more to connect him with the German school.[123]

JOHN LOTHROP MOTLEY

Turning to John Lothrop Motley, we return to the Harvard-Göttingen men and more distinctively Germanic influence.[124] Association with Cogswell and Bancroft at Round Hill and with Dr. Follen at Harvard led him to sail for Europe in April, 1832, for three years of travel and study. Not unnaturally he proceeded directly to Göttingen, where his first task was to improve his German under the tuition of Benecke.[125] The first fruits of his study in Germany appeared in two excellent articles on Goethe in the *New York Review* for October, 1838, and July, 1839; and in December of the next year he published in the *New World* an acceptable translation of Tieck's five-act

drama *Bluebeard.* In the meantime he had written and published *Morton's Hope* (1839), a kind of counterpart of Longfellow's *Hyperion,* in which he pictured, in novelized form, his early life, his love of languages, literature, and history, and his aspirations. His friend Bismarck, "the mad Junker," is thinly disguised as Otto von Rabenmarck.[126] Only after the failure of this loosely-constructed autobiographical novel did Motley turn seriously to history.

By the time Motley began his work as a historian, Ranke had already sent forth from his seminar in Berlin groups of gifted students imbued with the desire to subject the sources of history to severe criticism and had himself illustrated, in a series of brilliant works, the principles on which the internal criticism of sources was to proceed. The movement thus initiated was accentuated by the work of Guizot in Paris as well as by several Dutch and Belgian historians, so that by 1851, when Motley had done his preparatory work for *The Rise of the Dutch Republic* and set sail for Europe to investigate the primary sources, the new historical science had already produced a school of historians. What is more, the groundwork of making available collections of documents bearing on Motley's subject had been done so that the subject was ripe for a well-equipped scholar to make the synthesis.[127] Having set out with little conception of the requirements of the new historical science, Motley did what he could with the materials available in Boston, but in 1851 it became apparent to him that he must visit Germany and Holland. The result was that he wrote this, his first major historical work, practically three times—once in the United States, a second time in Germany, and a third time in Holland.[128] While omitting formal bibliographies and still using the cryptic, or clipped, form of footnotes in vogue during Irving's day, Motley's *Dutch Republic* (1856) is based on painstaking, methodical research and a careful criticism of all the available sources in a way to identify his method of work with that of the new scientific school, while in his manner of writing he remained still close to the tradition of the "literary" historians.[129]

The preceding sketch of American educators, men of letters, and scholars who sought inspiration at Göttingen is representative but incomplete. Another who was profoundly influenced in his life and his writings by residence in Germany was Longfellow, who might be considered along with Ticknor, Everett, Cogswell, and Bancroft; but since his period of residence in Germany came some years later and his work was distinctively more literary than theirs, a discussion of his career falls more logically into the section of this study that deals with the more strictly literary influences.

OTHER AMERICANS IN GERMANY

Among others who ought to be mentioned in this connection is Robert Bridges Patton (1794–1839), the one-man audience that applauded when Bancroft made the American eagle scream in his Fourth-of-July oration at Göttingen in 1820.[130] George Henry Calvert (1803–1889), the great-grandson of the founder of the colony of Maryland, was at Göttingen during 1824–1825;[131] and William Emerson (1801–1868), the older brother of Ralph Waldo, and a fellow-student of Calvert's, studied theology at Göttingen, and later turned to the law.[132]

The earliest American at the University of Berlin was Henry Edwin Dwight, son of "Pope" Dwight of Yale, who was registered in the philosophical faculty from November 9, 1825, to June 26, 1826, and whose *Travels in the North of Germany* (1829) had a wide circulation at precisely the time when Americans were becoming greatly interested in Germany.[133] During the thirties and forties, the generation represented by Henry Boynton Smith and James Elliot Cabot, following the example of Bancroft and Cogswell, included more than one German university in their itinerary. Göttingen remained the most popular, but Berlin, Halle, and Leipzig were definitely on the circuit, and by 1850 there was no German university that did not have its American colony. Something of the force of this movement can be gained from the following figures: from 1820 to 1830, an average of 5 students were registered annually; by 1840, there were 9; by 1850, 11; by 1860, 77; by 1880, 173; by 1890, 446; by 1900, well over 500. When it is considered that by 1900 upwards of ten thousand Americans had studied in Germany,[134] and that of the first 225 of these, 137 became professors in American colleges and universities,[135] it will be seen that the movement set afoot by Ticknor and Everett in 1815[136] had effects the full import and detailed ramifications of which are hard to estimate.

Aside from the Harvard graduates who made a breach in the wall of ignorance and insularity that separated Germany from the rest of the world, there were younger men like Hedge and Thorndike, who began to go thither either for their secondary education or, as in the case of Thorndike (who already held the Harvard baccalaureate degree), less to take advanced degrees in preparation for learned professions than to complete their education, as the phrase ran. Another important group, to be taken into account later, were the German exiles—men like Follen, Beck, and Lieber—who labored to promote educational reforms in the land of their adoption. Finally, there was an ever-growing number of travelers and observers who went to Germany (either on their own responsibility or because they were commissioned to go on a special assignment), many of whom published formal reports or informal essays on their return. Soon the idea became current that a visit to Germany promised more stimulation and profit than a tour of any other European country.

German Influences on American Colleges

In the meantime a general movement toward educational reform had gained momentum. Students like Ticknor, Bancroft, and Longfellow were joined by observers, mainly teachers and school supervisors or administrators who sought firsthand information about educational theory and practice in Germany. One of the first and most influential among this group, which included Wm. C. Woodbridge, Calvin S. Stowe, Alexander D. Bache, the Rev. Charles Brooks, Horace Mann, and Henry Barnard, was John Griscom (1744–1852), a respected teacher in New York City, who spent the year 1818–1819 studying European universities and charitable institutions.[137] Griscom's influence was exerted mainly in New York and New England, but it made itself felt even in Virginia, where Jefferson pronounced the book the best report on European literary and public institutions that he had read; at the same time he acknowledged that he had incorporated in his plan for the University of Virginia (which he was then engaged in establishing) as many of Griscom's suggestions as seemed practicable.

Jefferson's plan, adopted by the Virginia Legislature in 1819, shows the marks of many influences. Among others, it is said to have been affected by Alexander von Humboldt's views of education. This alleged influence does not lend itself readily to verification, but it is certain that Humboldt was the guest of Jefferson in Washington, that a long correspondence and exchange of books ensued, and that consequently Jefferson may have been led by Humboldt, who had definite views on the form and function of universities, to substitute for the "French Academy"[138] that he had projected earlier, his later plans for a "State University." What is clearer is that the German system of elective studies in general and of Ticknor's counsel in particular (possibly also von Humboldt's and Griscom's) decided Jefferson in favor of the system.[139] Another of the plans that Jefferson derived from German practice was to make the department of languages and literatures the core of the university.[140]

Follen's appointment at Harvard followed closely upon Blaettermann's at Charlottesville. By this time, too, Moses Stuart was vexing the ecclesiactically orthodox by introducing his students to the findings of German theological investigators and urging the adoption of methods of German Biblical research; while in another quarter James Marsh was busying himself with remaking the University of Vermont on Coleridge's plan, editing Coleridge's *Aids to Reflection*, and spreading a new philosophical gospel soon to be denominated "Transcendentalism."

Thus teachers in public and private schools, professors in colleges and presidents of universities, theologians in seminaries, and observant travelers contributed to provoke similar or allied tendencies that soon fomented a movement of recognizable proportions, and that prepared the groundwork upon which the New England Transcendentalists could build. Thus, too, was perpetuated a tradition of veneration for German scholarship which, on being introduced by men like Bentley and Buckminster, was established by Ticknor and his colleagues. It was carried forward by various agencies and persons (including the Ticknor-Longfellow-Lowell succession at Harvard, the Transcendental ferment, and the steadily mounting interest on the part of the Unitarian theologians in German Biblical criticism) until it carried through the century and beyond. Professor Bliss Perry,[141] speaking for a later day and accounting for the reasons that led him and his friends to the German universities, tells us: "That Germany possessed the sole secret of scholarship was no more doubted by us young fellows in the eighteen-eighties than it had been doubted by George Ticknor and Edward Everett when they sailed from Boston, bound for Göttingen, in 1814 [1815]."

NEW ENGLAND TRANSCENDENTALISM

Character of the Movement

Although since its efflorescence more than a century has elapsed, New England Transcendentalism remains still desperately vague. It has been variously regarded as a philosophical system, a reform movement, a religion in revolt, a mental or spiritual attitude. It had its connections with philosophy and theology, with literature and sociology, with economics and politics. It was at once theoretical and practical. Its origins were both native and foreign: its sources lie in American democracy, in New England Unitarianism, in ancient Greece, in England, in France, in Germany, in the Orient. While this is neither the time nor the place to attempt a history of Transcendentalism, an examination of possible Germanic influence on Transcendentalism suggests the need for attempting a definition or description.

Emerson tried to define the term in his lecture on Transcendentalism in 1842:

The first thing we have to say respecting what are called *new views* here in New England, at the present time, is that they are not new, but the very oldest thoughts cast into the mold of these times . . . . What is properly called Transcendentalism among us is Idealism; Idealism as it appears in 1842.

The idealist . . . reckons the world an appearance . . . Mind is the only reality . . . . Nature, literature, history, are only subjective phenomena . . . .

It is well known to my audience that the Idealism of the present day acquires the name Transcendentalism from the use of that term by Immanuel Kant, of Königsberg, who replied to the skeptical philosophy of Locke, which insisted that there is nothing in the intellect which was not previously in the experience of the senses, by showing that there was a very important class of ideas or imperative forms, which did not come by experience, but through which experience was acquired; that these were intuitions of the mind itself; and he denominated them *Transcendental* forms.

The extraordinary profoundness and precision of that man's thinking have given vogue to his nomenclature . . . to that extent that whatever belongs to the class of intuitive thought is popularly called at the present day *Transcendental*.

Almost as if he were afraid of having spoken too definitely, Emerson went on to make certain circumspect qualifications:

The Transcendentalist adopts the whole connection of spiritual doctrine. He believes in miracles, in the perpetual openness of the human mind to new influx of light and power; he believes in inspiration, and in ecstasy . . . .

This way of thinking, falling on Roman times, made Stoic philosophers; falling on despotic times, made protestants and ascetic monks . . . ; on prelatical times, made Puritans and Quakers; and falling on Unitarian times, makes the peculiar shades of idealism which we know.

Obviously this is no narrow policy and represents no exclusive party.

You will see by this sketch that there is no such thing as a Transcendental *party*; that there is no pure Transcendentalist; that we know of none but prophets and heralds of such a philosophy . . . .

This seems rather to enlarge than to define the meaning of Transcendentalism. This much, however, Emerson does indicate, namely, that among the many sources and affinities of Transcendentalism, three are paramount: the idealism of Plato, the Unitarianism of America, and the critical transcendentalism of Germany. The three chief influences on New England Transcendentalism are (1) Hellenic, (2) American, and (3) Germanic.[142]

Frothingham, the historian and one-time disciple of the movement, says unequivocally, "Transcendentalism was a distinct philosophical system," only to add in the next sentence, "Practically it was an assertion of the inalienable worth of man; the-

oretically it was an assertion of the immanence of divinity in instinct, the transference
of supernatural attributes to the natural
constitution of mankind."[143] Subsequently
it appears that so far from being a distinct
philosophical system, with both theoretical
and practical aspects, it was also a religion;
for, says Frothingham, while "Transcendentalism is usually spoken of as a philosophy, it is more justly regarded as a gospel.[144] As a philosophy it is abstract and
difficult . . . inexact and inconclusive; so
far from uniform in its structure, that it
may rather be considered several systems
in one."[145] Later we learn that it is little
more than a state of mind, an inspiration, a
certain temperament—"an enthusiasm, a
wave of sentiment, a breath of mind that
caught up such as were prepared to receive
it, elated them, transported them, and
passed on,—no man knowing whither it
went."[146] Next, Transcendentalism was a
challenge; it immediately took the offensive. "The problem of transcendental philosophy," declared Parker, "is no less than
this, to revise the experience of mankind
and try its teachings by the nature of mankind; to test ethics by conscience, science
by reason; to try the creeds of the churches,
the constitutions of the states, by the constitution of the universe."[147] This was an
offensive on a broad front. The Unitarians,
no less promptly than the Congregationalists and Presbyterians, accepted the
challenge. In the beginning the controversy
was engaged in chiefly by clergymen and
fought primarily on religious grounds.[148]
Emerson's *Nature* of 1836 and his *American
Scholar* of the year following, although both
were as radical as anything he published
later, were allowed to pass, but the Divinity
School address (1838) put the fat in the fire.
At the request of the Alumni Association
of the Cambridge Theological School, the
Rev. Andrews Norton wrote a vigorous
attack on the new intuitional philosophy
under the title, *A Discourse on the Latest
Form of Infidelity* (1839), which provoked

Ripley's spirited reply and successive
counterblasts from both sides. Two years
later Parker declared open war in his South
Boston sermon on *The Transient and Permanent in Christianity*. The periodicals joined
in spiritedly. The *Dial* set forth the claims
of Transcendentalism as an outgrowth of
Unitarianism[149] at the same time attacking
the traditionalism of Unitarianism. The
result was that Unitarians found themselves in the dilemma of having to choose
between adopting the Transcendentalists,
thus lending color to the old charge that
Unitarianism was merely the halfway house
on the road to infidelity, or expelling
them from their midst, thereby abandoning
the very principles for which they had
fought all along.

The *Biblical Repertory and Princeton
Review*, the orthodox Presbyterian organ,
felt it to be "a solemn duty" to warn its
readers against "this German atheism,
which the spirit of darkness is employing
ministers of the gospel to smuggle among
us under false pretenses."[150] In the *Christian
Examiner*, a Unitarian organ of liberal
tendencies, the argument waxed especially
hot—symptomatic of the internal dissen-
sion and civil warfare that it provoked. The
controversy was carried on so vigorously,
and it touched so many important persons
and groups, that the temptation is strong
to regard religion as not only fundamental
but all-embracing for the movement. So to
view it, however, would be to mistake a part
for the whole.

Nor do these points of view exhaust the
angles from which Transcendentalism must
be considered. "The Transcendentalist,"
says Frothingham, "was by nature a reformer. He could not be satisfied with men
as they are. His doctrine of the capacities
of men . . . kindled to enthusiasm his hope
of change. However his disgust may have
kept him aloof for a time, his sympathy
soon brought him back, and his faith sent
him to the front of battle."[151] The times
were propitious for the reformer; dissent

and agitation were in the air; and every cause—mad, insignificant, worthy—had its hearing and its following.[152]

If anything emerges from this account, it is that the framing of a definition of the Newness or the New Views, as Transcendentalism was originally called, is no slight task. Frothingham, by and large the best commentator on the movement, tried drawing distinctions but never kept them clear. Nothing is gained by corralling all the Transcendental views, ideas, reforms, currents, and eddies under such a heading as the New England Renaissance. It adds a name, but it clarifies nothing. When the term *Transcendentalism* is pressed into service and made to stand for all the manifestations of the quickening spirit felt in New England during the forties, it definitely goes beyond what Emerson, for example, or Parker thought it was. Transcendentalism was a part of the so-called Renaissance of New England, but not the whole of it.[153] Two more quotations and we shall be done with definitions. Professor Henry D. Gray offers this statement:

New England Transcendentalism was produced by the deliberate importing of certain imperfectly understood elements of German idealism into American Unitarianism; . . . it became a creative force in American life and letters; but . . . as a philosophy it was merely a sort of mystical idealism built on pragmatic premises.[154]

Harold C. Goddard puts it in the following terms:

Transcendentalism was a part of the thought currents of its own day, and . . . like those currents themselves, it was linked with the thought of earlier times. . . . Hence it is that transcendentalism seems from one point of view a gradual outgrowth and culmination of Unitarianism; that it connects at a score of points with French Revolutionary influences; that it is almost an offshoot of German philosophical idealism; that it is intimately bound up with the growth of the scientific spirit; that it is by no means unaffected by contemporary currents of social unrest.[155]

While these statements do not define Transcendentalism, they do afford suggestions for tracing its origins, pointing out its affinities, and analyzing its tenets, and thus help us to an understanding of it.

It has been argued that Transcendentalism was essentially indigenous,[156] that in its simplest analysis it was little more than Unitarianism in the process of "getting religion."[157] This last observation is particularly pertinent and contains more than a germ of truth; for as Unitarianism had opened the New England mind and removed from it some of its more rigorous dogmas, so Transcendentalism carried forward this process of liberalization. The chief exponent of this idea is George Willis Cooke, whose opinion, considering his association with the later Transcendentalists, might well be considered authoritative if it were not based on disputable terms and questionable generalizations. Cooke's argument runs as follows: Transcendentalism "has always been indigenous to New England *in some form.*[158] In the earliest days in Boston it was accepted under the form of Antinomianism by John Cotton, Anne Hutchinson, and Sir Henry Vane. By the Friends it was preached with eagerness, and it was notably exemplified by William Penn . . . . No one had more of its true spirit than John Woolman, though he taught it in the form in which it was promulgated by George Fox."[159] John Wise, as he appears in the *Churches' Quarrel Espoused* (1707) and his *Vindication of the Government of New-England Churches* (1717), and Jonathan Edwards as the instigator of the Great Awakening, the theological teachings of Samuel Hopkins, the sermons of Jonathan Mayhew, the teachings of Professor Andrews Norton and Dr. Henry Ware, and lastly the preaching of Dr. Channing are paraded in review by Cooke, in the order named, with a view to illustrate the continuity of Transcendentalism from John Cotton to Emerson—from 1636 to 1836.

It is not necessary to repeat Cooke's

argument of twelve pages. Obviously, in the case of every man named except Dr. Channing, the term *Transcendentalist* cannot properly be applied. All had leanings in the direction either of mysticism or idealism, but therefore to identify them as Transcendentalists seems an unwarrantable procedure. All Cooke succeeds in doing is to trace an element of liberal thought in New England from Puritanical to Transcendental days, but he does not thereby establish the origin and descent of Transcendentalism. It may be observed, however, that while only one of the persons named by Cooke closely approached Transcendentalism as formulated by Emerson, together they did facilitate its coming. Without their preparation of the ground, it seems certain, not that Transcendentalism would necessarily have been impossible, but that it might have been long delayed. To claim much more requires better proof than Cooke has advanced. Without this native stock of idealism, the Newness might not have succeeded in making itself articulate as early as 1836; and insofar as this is so, Transcendentalism may be said to be indigenous; for its basic ingredient was idealism. But this is not to say that native idealism, unassisted by influences from the outside, would or could have engendered the Transcendentalism of 1836.

The first clear indications that a new philosophy was abroad in New England were rumblings within the Unitarian Church. Begun as a revolutionary attack on Calvinism, Unitarianism remained primarily a negative movement. While it could point to something like a continuity of circumstances to explain its rise—from 1785, when King's Chapel became Unitarian by the revision of its Trinitarian liturgy, to 1819, when Dr. Channing preached his famous sermon on "Unitarian Christianity"—it really had no internal history of growth or development. It remained, as it had begun, critical in orientation and incapable of developing a distinctly positive program.[160]

Among the academic philosophers the situation was even worse, for they were completely under the domination of the Scotch common-sense system of Stewart, Brown, and Hamilton. There was no help to be derived from that quarter. Native idealism was helpless to proceed; while Unitarianism itself, whether of the theologian or the academician, did not have within itself the necessary life; it was, by its very nature, static.

When the necessary impetus came, it came from abroad. It was inevitable that the intense fervor and new ideals of Europe—among them the revolutionary ideas of France, the romantic literature of England, and the transcendental philosophy of Germany—should invade America;[161] it was equally inevitable that with the arrival of these foreign commodities, there should be young people, imbued with liberal and idealistic yearnings, ready to embrace them.[162] Thus it would seem that native idealism, acted upon by certain energizing impulses from Europe, brought to a logical completion, in the form of Transcendentalism, the revolt against Calvinism that Unitarianism had begun. For as Dr. Channing admitted somewhat sorrowfully to Elizabeth Peabody, "This Unitarianism which so many people think is the last word . . . is only the vestibule.[163]

Transitional and Intermediary Figures

Channing, at once the greatest of the Unitarians and the first of the Transcendentalists, early rejected the Calvinistic belief in the depravity of human nature and soon went on to adopt what Emerson called his "one sublime idea"—the divinity of man—which became the cardinal tenet of Transcendentalism. As early as 1820 Channing had voiced his dissatisfaction with current Unitarianism:

I wish to see among Unitarians a development of imagination and poetical enthusi-asm, as well as of the rational and critical power . . . . Unitarianism has suffered from union with a heart-withering philoso-phy . . . it has suffered also from a too ex-clusive application of its advocates to Biblical criticism and theological contro-versy, in other words, from a too partial culture of the mind. I fear that we must look to other schools for the thoughts which thrill us, which touch our most inward springs, and disclose to us the depth of our souls.[164]

The phrases, "other schools" and "thoughts which thrill," when combined with Emerson's derogatory remark about the "pale negations of Boston Unitarian-ism" are fraught with meaning. So far as Channing was concerned, he had already found the thoughts that thrill in other schools, as we shall see presently.

About 1840, recalling his college years, he confided to Miss Peabody: "Only three books that I read at that time were of any moment to me: one was Ferguson on 'Civil Liberty,' one Hutcheson's 'Moral Philosophy,' and one was Price's 'Disserta-tions.'"[165] About the same time, while read-ing Jouffroy, he said to Miss Peabody:

I have found here a fact which interests me personally very much. Jouffroy says that Dr. Price's Dissertations were trans-lated into German at the time of their first appearance, and produced a much greater impression there than they did in England; and he thinks they were the first movers of the German mind in the transcendental direction. Now, I read Price when I was in college. Price saved me from Locke's Phi-losophy. He gave me the doctrine of ideas, and during my life I have written the words Love, Right, &c., with a capital. The book probably moulded my philosophy into the form it has always retained, and opened my mind into the *transcendental depth*. And I always have found in the accounts I have of German philosophy in Madame de Staël, and in these later times, that it was cognate to my own. I cannot say that I have ever conceived a new idea from it; and the cause obvious, if Price was alike the father of and of *mine*.[166]

This avowal, whatever the historian of

philosophy may think of Channing's ex-planation of how Kant came by his think-ing, is interesting, first, as an admission that Channing regarded his philosophy as "tran-scendental," and second, in its implied denial that he derived anything from the Germans, or, indeed, that he ever read them. He suggests also that what he knew of Kant, Fichte, and Schelling was derived from Madame de Staël and, "in these later times," from such commentators as Cole-ridge, Carlyle, Cousin, and Jouffroy.[167] As will appear in the sequel, the name of one other teacher of Channing must be added to the list—that of Carl Follen.

Now, Madame de Staël, although she wrote wittily on many subjects, did not always write very clearly about the German idealists; but Channing was not dependent solely on her, for Coleridge had attempted an exposition of the Kantian terminology in his *Biographia Literaria* (1817), and his *Aids to Reflection* and *The Friend* reiterated the significance of the Kantian contribu-tions. Meanwhile Channing had come in contact with transcendental ways of thought as represented by De Gerando and Cousin. While Miss Peabody copied fifty sermons of his for him, he translated for her "the whole of De Gerando's 'Du Perfec-tionnement Morale,'"[168] and subsequently she read to him translations of Cousin's *Introduction to Philosophy*[169] and his *Exam-ination of Locke*.[170] If he did not make the acquaintance of Jouffroy through Ripley's *Philosophical Miscellanies* of 1838, his nephew's translation, in 1840, of the *Intro-duction to Ethics* directed his attention to Jouffroy. Yet most of his "acquaintance with the master minds of Germany" that gave him such "intense delight" came through the medium of Madame de Staël and especially of Coleridge and Carlyle. Through them (and through such transla-tions as were available) he also learned something about Goethe, Schiller, Herder, and Richter. In all this reading he found ideas "cognate" with his own; he found his own ideas "quickened," but would not admit that he "ever received a new idea from it."[171]

Despite Channing's disclaimers of dependence upon others for his ideas, his contemporaries were right in observing, "Dr. Channing is a great moralist and the best kind of religious genius, but *no philosopher*."[172] His was not an acutely original or speculative mind, and his relations with Dr. Follen indicate pretty clearly that he had much to learn from Follen about metaphysics in general and about the German philosophers in particular.

Introduced under most favorable circumstances into the Cambridge-Boston community, Follen made his way easily to intimacy with the most notable men of that group. The meeting between Channing and Follen took place in the autumn of 1826 at one of the informal discussion group meetings at Dr. Channing's. The subject was the significance of the death of Christ. Channing turned to Follen with the idea of drawing him out. As Follen spoke, Channing became "entirely absorbed, his countenance growing brighter at every word. He saw he had struck a mine . . . . From that moment was cemented a friendship that never had a shadow of misunderstanding fall upon it, but was a perfect mutual respect and tender love."[173] After some deliberation, Follen acceded to Channing's urging to become a Unitarian minister, and until Follen's untimely death in 1840, they remained on most intimate terms.[174] Follen exerted a powerful influence upon him, although this does not mean that he remade or radically altered Channing's thinking; but we cannot be far wrong if we agree with John White Chadwick, who observed: "I have seemed to find in Channing's later thought more of Follen's than of any other personal influence. Those tendencies in his preaching which were deplored as transcendental were quite surely, in some measure, developments of germs which fell into his own from Follen's fruitful mind."[175]

Channing's basic faith in man's moral nature as instinct with divinity hints the paternity of the German idealists, but he espoused and proclaimed this idea long before he knew much about German philosophy. We may take him at his word when he declared that he arrived at it by himself, but was pleased when, later, he found corroboration for his view among the German transcendentalists. After 1826 Follen was available to give him expert instruction in the Kantian epistemology, but there is nothing to indicate that Channing cared much for precise and abstract forms of metaphysics. He employed the Kantian nomenclature, including Understanding, pure and practical Reason, and Categorical Imperative, but without benefit of any sharply defined analytic. Follen's explanation of the terms appears to have satisfied him. Indeed, it is pretty clear that he adopted, as agreeable to his own way of thinking, Follen's modification of the rigor of the Kantian categorical imperative, and that, like Follen, he objected to the tendency of Kant to regard the moral principle as the sole foundation of religion. Kant's "demands of duty" appeared to leave too little room for the "grounds of religious faith." He sided rather with Follen's explanation of Schiller's doctrine of freedom and happiness, allowing for a measure of natural desire, enthusiasm, and affection.

The point at which Channing comes closest to Follen is in his view of morality as the direction of the mind toward the happiness that results from a striving after the greatest efficiency, after perfection, and of religion as the direction of the mind toward the happiness which results from the desire and belief that the world is so constituted and governed as to make possible this greatest perfection. The attainment of this perfection depends not solely upon man but partly upon Providence—upon the power which has created the universe in such a way that man is aided in his striving after it. These elements, which Follen took over from Fries, were expounded in detail in Follen's *Moral Lectures*, and we may be sure that they formed the subject of extensive discussion between him and Channing.

Finally, there are striking parallels between Channing's and Schleiermacher's views of religion, and again Follen is the intermediary. This view of religion is posited on Kant's denial of the possibility of knowing God by means of cognition. It regards religion as an essential element of human nature—as indispensable to the development of the inner life of man. But it does not seek, like metaphysics, to explain the universe, nor, like morals, to advance and perfect the world by the free will of man. Instead, the finite individual's pious contemplation of the order and majesty of the external universe raises in him a consciousness of his oneness with the infinite All. The Christian Church becomes an association of pious men. This involves a sharp differentiation between dogma and religion, the repudiation of all irrational devotion to creed, the concept of religion as consisting at once of feeling, piety, and reverent contemplation of God, the sublime work of nature and art as the expression of an immanent Deity—as a symbol through which the mind and heart are directed toward the one eternal God; and the Christian Church as an association of pious men for mutual aid and the cultivation of a closer relation with God. Thus Schleiermacher, Follen, and Channing alike emphasize the social nature of religion, quite apart from the old Puritanic concept of "Works" or the deistic notion of merely utilitarian "service to man." Thus, too, Channing freed his Unitarian beliefs from the "heart-withering" philosophy of John Locke without abandoning his ambition to keep his religion

philosophical and his philosophy religious. Thus he stimulated and accelerated a way of thinking that made him, in the eyes of Transcendentalists like Emerson, "our Bishop."

Channing stands a transitional figure, first, in the manner in which he straddled Unitarianism and Transcendentalism, and second, in that he marks the point beyond which the indigenous influences recede and the foreign importations gain in importance; for in proportion as the Transcendentalists went beyond the position of Channing, in so far, usually, did they go to foreign sources for those advances.

At this point it becomes necessary to consider the ways and means by which German ideas made their way to America. The chronology of how they gained vogue and influence in the United States is, roughly, as follows: first, through the discipleship of German transcendental views among English writers like Coleridge and Carlyle; second, through the adaptation of German transcendental ways of thought by such eclectic French thinkers as Cousin and Jouffroy, whose restatements gained currency in America; and third, through the domestication which German philosophy attained at the hands of those who got their information more directly from Germany herself. Among the last named group are to be distinguished (1) German *émigrés* like Beck, Follen, and Lieber, who labored conscientiously to translate the thought of their homeland into the land of their adoption, and (2) native Americans like Stuart, Marsh, and Hedge, who initiated inquiries on their own account and sought to spread the gospel until the major Transcendentalists— Emerson, Parker, *et al.*—took over.

AVENUES OF TRANSMISSION

German Philosophy in England

Although it has been shown that German transcendental ideas began to filter through

English insularity as early as 1793,[176] Kant was introduced into England only slowly, partly because of the difficulties of the language and the failure of Kant's first proponents (Nitsch, Willich, and Richardson) to attract attention, but more particularly because of the opposition of the prevailing Scottish philosophy.[177] While on the Continent Kant's *Critique of Pure Reason* called forth some three hundred books and articles during the first ten years following its publication, the first English book on Kant, written by Friederich August Nitsch,[178] did not appear until 1795. It met with an indifferent reception, as did the second, two years later, by Anthony Florian Willich.[179] Meanwhile, in 1797, had appeared the first translation, a very free one, in which Kant's *Ding-an-sich* was rejected and his fundamental distinction between *Begriff* and *Anschauung* modified, by John Richardson.[180] In 1798 and 1799 appeared two volumes, presumably Richardson's work,[181] entitled *Essays and Treatises on Moral, Political and various Philosophical Subjects by E. Kant. From the German by the Translator of the Principles of Critical Philosophy* (2 vols., London, 1798, 1799). This was followed by Kant's *Metaphysic of Morals, together with a Sketch of Kant's Life* (London, 1799). All this seeming activity with Kant's works about the end of the century belies the facts, for the combined influence of these early books appears to have been, with four notable exceptions, negligible. The first exception is that Coleridge possessed a copy of Willich's *Elements*, which he annotated copiously. In the second place, Samuel Miller used the book in preparing his *Brief Retrospect of the Eighteenth Century* (1803), which gave many Americans their first glimpse of the new German philosophy. Third, the Harvard library listed in its catalog for 1830 a copy of Willich's *Elements*, but by that time it had also the two *Critiques* and several other works of Kant, all in the original. The fourth case is A. Bronson Alcott's reading, toward the end of 1833, both Nitsch's *General View* and Willich's *Elements*. He covered fifty-seven pages of his journal with extracts from the former and worked carefully through the latter, but

apparently neither radically changed the essentially intuitive cast of his mind. These isolated cases suggest that there were probably others in America who read these early books. What is odd is that no clues appear to indicate that Richardson's several books on Kant were known in America. Emerson possessed the Hayward translation of Kant's first *Critique* (London, 1838), but we do not know when it was acquired.[182]

DUGALD STEWART

We may pass by the ephemeral work of Franz von Baader and of Berthold Georg Niebuhr; that of Thomas Brown, in 1803, as the first professional philosopher in England to take notice, slight though it was, of German transcendental philosophy;[183] and the ridicule and diatribe in William Drummond's *Academical Questions*. The first important fact in the history of Kant in England, and in America, is the notice which the high priest of Scottish philosophy, Dugald Stewart, himself deigned to take of Kant,[184] in 1822, in his *General View of the Progress of Metaphysical, Ethical, and Practical Philosophy Since the Revival of Letters in Europe in Two Dissertations* (or two parts, London, 1815, 1822; Boston 1822). This work is important (1) as being among the first in time to bring information about Kant to America, Emerson, for example, reading it attentively in 1822, and (2) as being incomparably bad as a commentary on Kant. Stewart's ignorance of German prevented his reading either Kant or the lucid exposition of the Kantian philosophy by Carl Leonhard Reinhold, a copy of whose works Dr. Samuel Parr had given him,[185] but it does not explain why he did not profit by the relatively adequate *Abstract of the Critical Philosophy* by Thomas Wirgman, a manuscript copy of which the author had sent to Stewart in 1813.[186]

As to Kant's works [he confessed], I must acknowledge that although I have frequently attempted to read them in the Latin edition [tr. by F. G. Born, 4 vols., Leipzig, 1796–1798], I have always been forced to abandon the undertaking in despair, partly from the scholastic barbarism of the style, and partly from my inability to unriddle the author's meaning. Wherever I have happened to obtain a momentary glimpse of light, I have derived it, not from Kant himself, but from my previous acquaintance with those opinions of Leibnitz, Berkeley, Hume, Reid, and others, which he has endeavored to appropriate to himself under the deep disguise of a new phraseology.[187]

This confession of bias, together with the evidence which his footnotes afford of his complete reliance upon secondary sources of questionable value,[188] explains his success at misinterpreting Kant in the twenty-odd pages that he devoted to him. After quoting a half-dozen commentators on Kant's philosophical aims, he attacks Kant's distinction between the sensitive faculty and the understanding as merely a revival of Locke's distinction between perception and intuition, which Reid had effectively exploded.[189] Missing altogether Kant's distinction between Understanding and Reason, he insists that Kant has been anticipated in this, as in practically every other part of his thought, by French thinkers, by Dr. Price, and by the Cambridge Platonists, but especially by the "immortal Cudworth," who is "far superior to the German metaphysician, both in point of perspicuity and of precision."[190] Indeed, Kant is really not worth an Englishman's attention. The inimitable De Gerando is quoted to the effect that even in Germany, at present, a pure Kantian is scarcely to be found, except such as have so much exhausted their minds deciphering the intricacies of Kant that they have not enough energy left to deny him and to embrace a true faith.[191] "In fine, the *Critique of Pure Reason*, announced with pomp, received with fanaticism, disputed with fury, after having accomplished the overthrow of the doctrine taught by Leibnitz and Wolff, could no longer support itself

upon its own foundations, and has produced no permanent result, but divisions and enmities, and a general disgust at all systematical creeds." With this, Stewart leaves Kant for dead and proceeds to Fichte, who gets two pages of comment à la Madame de Staël and De Gerando, and to Schelling, who gets one.[192]

This, be it remembered, is the thin fare that Emerson, late in 1833, said "saves you a world of reading . . . . It is a beautiful and instructive abridgment of the thousand volumes of Locke, Leibnitz, Voltaire, Bayle, Kant, and the rest."[193]

SIR WILLIAM HAMILTON

Sir William Hamilton was the first of the British professional philosophers to appreciate the historical magnitude of Kant's intellectual reform and to comprehend the Kantian distinctions between Understanding and Reason and his deduction of the categories.[194] He agreed with Kant, also, in his view of the synthetic powers of the mind without, however, accepting the transcendental apperception in the Kantian sense. His declaration that a comprehension of Kant "is now a matter of necessity to all who would be supposed to have crossed the threshold of philosophy"[195] bore weight, and his appointment, in 1836, to the Professorship of Logic at Edinburgh marks a date in the history of English thought since which every British philosopher has had to take a stand for or against Kant.

The first eleven pages of Hamilton's essay in the *Edinburgh Review* of Cousin's *Cours de Philosophie* present a clear-headed summary of Cousin's system, ending with the conclusion: "it is manifest that the whole doctrine of M. Cousin is involved in the proposition,—*that the Unconditioned, the Absolute, the Infinite, is immediately known in consciousness, and this by difference, plurality, and relation.*"[196] For Cousin, the condition and end of philosophy is the recognition of the Absolute as a constitutive[197] principle of intelligence. This is followed by a section of twenty-seven pages, of which three are devoted to philosophical tenets which Hamilton himself holds true, four to an exposition of Kant's position, four more to what the author considers unwarrantable extensions of Kantian thought by his followers, notably Schelling, and sixteen to Cousin and a criticism of Cousin's Absolute.[198]

While Hamilton approached nearer than any of his British predecessors to an understanding of Kant, even to adopting some of his ideas, he was no disciple. His interpretation and use of the Kantian doctrine is opposed to the more logical application adopted by the post-Kantians in Germany —Fichte, Schelling, and most notably, Hegel;[199] for Hamilton regarded the *Critique of Pure Reason* as having raised insuperable barriers between the human mind and its knowledge of the Absolute. Entrenched as he already was in agnosticism, he embraced and perhaps exaggerated the negative aspects of Kant's criticism as lending support to his own views, and consequently became one of the chief retarding influences toward the domestication of German philosophy from Kant through Hegel in the English-speaking world.[200]

Ultimately, however, a serious study of Kant led to a consideration of Hegel. During the fifties, Ferrier in his essays on Schelling and Hegel sought conscientiously to understand and to present the meaning and significance for contemporary thought of the philosophy of the absolute;[201] and in the early sixties Frederick Denison Maurice led the way by pointing out that De Quincey's notion of Kant as the "Alles-zermalmende" was exaggerated, and that Hamilton's emphasis on Kant's negations was essentially wrong.[202] Finally, James Hutchison Stirling, powerfully stirred by *Sartor Resartus*, was led, in 1856, to study at Heidelberg, where he came to a realization that only through Kant could Hegel be reached. A firsthand study of the former led, in 1860, to a period of eight years of intensive study devoted to Hegel. The first fruit of this labor was *The Secret of Hegel: being the Hegelian System in Origin, Form, and Matter* (2 vols., London, 1865).[203] This work, which articulated the significance of Fichte and Schelling in the succession from Kant to Hegel, marks at once the full arrival of German idealism in England and a new departure in English philosophy, T. H. Green declaring that Stirling's book "contrasted with everything else that has been published as sense with nonsense." Jowett, Carlyle, and German Hegelians agreed that Stirling had truly assimilated Hegel's thought;[204] while in America Emerson hailed the book as "the most competent and compulsive of modern British books on metaphysics" and carried it with him on a prolonged lecture tour of the West. By the thirties, however, the work of Coleridge, De Quincey,[205] and Carlyle had made Kant known in circles beyond the "learned" and the "academic," and had popularized the names of Fichte, Schelling, and Hegel, especially Schelling.

SAMUEL TAYLOR COLERIDGE

Samuel Taylor Coleridge's knowledge of German philosophy was acquired independently of the work of his British predecessors, partly during his residence in Germany and more particularly about 1801 when he studiously read the German philosophers and Kant especially, as he says, "took possession of me with a giant's hand."[206] Coleridge's important intermediary position between German and American transcendentalists and the reliability of his interpretation of the critical philosophy have occasioned much inconclusive argument[207] until recent years when a thorough examination[208] of the extant German philosophical works in Coleridge's possession,[209] plus his illuminating annotations of these volumes[210] and the evidence furnished by Coleridge's several unfinished metaphysical manuscripts,[211] lead Professor Muirhead to the considered conclusion that Coleridge's ideas form a "far more important . . . and coherent body of philosophical thought than he has been anywhere credited with."[212] This thorough consideration of Coleridge as a philosopher by a philosopher stresses (1) Coleridge's sensitiveness to current philosophical currents and eddies, (2) his recognition of the fundamental problem that had to be formulated and the inadequacy of regnant methodologies for solving it, or for interpreting the rich and varied spiritual movements of the age, and (3) his positive contributions to the discussion of the problem as it appeared in the several fields of logic, metaphysics, ethics, religion, politics, aesthetics, and natural science.[213]

The crisis in Coleridge's philosophical development came in 1801, when (March 16) he declared to Tom Poole: "*I have not only extricated the notions of time and space*, but have overthrown the doctrine of association . . . and with it all the irreligious metaphysics . . . especially the doctrine of necessity."[214] A week later he professed to having found the underlying fallacy of the whole Newtonian philosophy, namely, that the mind is merely "a lazy *looker-on* on an external world."[215] His making these discoveries coincides with his "most intense study" of Kant, under whose influence he frankly avows himself in the *Biographia Literaria*:

The writings of the illustrious sage of Koenigsberg . . . more than any other . . . at once invigorated and disciplined my understanding . . . . After fifteen years' familiarity with him, I still read . . . his . . . productions with undiminished delight and increasing admiration. The few passages [in the first *Critique*] that remained obscure to me, after due efforts of thought (as the chapter on original apperception) and the apparent contradictions which occur, I soon found were hints and insinuations referring to ideas, which Kant either did not think it prudent to avow, or which he considered as consistently *left behind*, in a pure analysis, not of human nature *in toto*, but of the speculative intellect alone. Here

therefore he was constrained to commence at the point of reflection, or natural consciousness; while in his *moral* system he was permitted to assume a higher ground (the autonomy of the will) as a postulate deducible from the unconditioned command, or (in the technical language of his school) the categorical imperative, of the conscience.[216]

After voicing his refusal to believe that Kant "meant no more by his *Noumenon*, or Thing in itself, than his mere words express,"[217] and repeating substantially Schelling's objection to Kant's "matter without form" as having the effect of making "all conceptions of cause and effect arise in our mind,"[218] Coleridge proceeds to Fichte, whose *Wissenschaftslehre*, besides giving the "mortal blow to Spinozism . . . supplied the *idea*" of a truly metaphysical system, "i.e., one having its spring and principle within itself." Unfortunately Fichte allowed "this fundamental idea to be overbuilt with a heavy mass of mere *notions*" so that his philosophy degenerated into "a crude *egoismus*," involving a "boastful and hyperstoic hostility to Nature," a godless religion, and an ascetic ethicism demanding an unnatural denial of all "the natural passions and desires."[219]

Schelling was much more congenial to his way of thinking. Indeed, at the time he was writing the *Biographia Literaria*, parts of Schelling's system harmonized so well with his own thought that he translated, or adapted, and incorporated into his manuscript whole portions of Schelling,[220] meanwhile risking his reputation on a blanket avowal of obligation prefaced by these words: "In Schelling's *Natur-Philosophie* and the *System des transcendentalen Idealismus*, I first found a genial coincidence with much that I had toiled out for myself, and a powerful assistance in what I had yet to do."[221] The reader of the very long paragraph that follows cannot escape feeling that Coleridge doth protest too much. But what is more important for our purpose than the degree of plagiarism is that Chapters VII, VIII, IX, and XII of the *Biographia* brought to American readers a rather accurate account of Schelling's philosophy of nature and of his system of transcendental idealism.

This much seems clear: however satisfied Coleridge had been with his new-found philosophy based on a Kantian terminology, about the time he was engaged on the *Biographia*, he faltered sufficiently in his self-confidence to come under the spell of Schelling. How passing a phase Schelling's influence represents is hard to determine and of no great importance for our purpose. That it did pass seems certain from his own criticism of the *Biographia*, which, considering that it was uttered within a month of his death, has someting of a testamentary deposition:

> The metaphysical disquisition at the end of the first volume of the "Biographia Literaria" is unformed and immature; it contains the fragments of the truth, but it is not fully thought out. It is wonderful to myself to think how infinitely more profound my views now are, and yet how much clearer they are withal.[222]

Coleridge did not live to give final expression to a completed system, but Professor Muirhead's skillful work in equating the unfinished manuscripts with the published works substantiates his conclusion that Coleridge's thinking was far from unprecise and unsystematic—in short, that his final thought presents a remarkably harmonious body of doctrine. As basic to such a system Coleridge set out to construct a "Logic." This "propaedeutic" or "introductory to a *system*" he projected even before he realized the full significance of what Kant had done in that direction. An abstract of the *Logic* or the *Opus Maximum*, or both, is beyond the limits of this inquiry, nor is it necessary, first, because the combined work of Professors Snyder, Muirhead, and Wellek has done this admirably, and second, because, as far as Americans are concerned, these works could not have influenced them less if they had been non-

existent. But they are significant because they offer evidence to show that whatever Coleridge's understanding of German critical philosophy may have lacked in 1809–1810, when *The Friend* was published,[223] and however much he may have been under the spell of Schelling about 1816–1817, when the *Biographia Literaria* was written,[224] he had, by 1825,[225] when *Aids to Reflection* was published, arrived at a complete and unmixed understanding of the Kantian system and had proceeded, independently of Hegel, to make the same effort which Hegel was making to achieve a higher synthesis, although neither the methods nor the results were the same.

Whatever changes his philosophy underwent, one thing remained constant—the necessity of reaching a view of the world from which it could be grasped as the manifestation of a single principle. By the time he wrote the *Aids*, he had found that point of view in the distinction between Understanding and Reason. It had become a fixed frame of reference which he applied to every object that came within the range of his thought. But a merely casual perusal of his published works is not sufficient to show that this is so. Although he censured Bacon and even his favorite Leighton for using philosophic terms like Reason and Understanding indiscriminately and thus running into difficulties out of which they sought to extricate themselves by sustituting fantastical and mystical phrases, only to find themselves worse involved than before,[226] Coleridge himself is not entirely guiltless on this score, though in his case the dilemma proceeds not from ignorance but rather from the necessity under which he felt himself to "write down" to the level of the general reader. For example, in a passage in which he prefers charges against his favorites, Bacon and Leighton, he compounds rather than clarifies their mistake when he says: ". . . by reason Leighton means the human understanding . . . namely, 'the faculty judging according to sense.'"[227]

With this definition we have cause to find fault, but before passing judgment, it is pertinent to bear in mind the circumstances and purposes which led him to prepare *Aids to Reflection*. Writing for the general reader, he allowed, perhaps forced, himself to write popularly and often with less terminological precision than he did in the *Logic*. The effort to avoid abstruseness is everywhere apparent. Failure on the part of the reader to comprehend the *Aids to Reflection* would have been a grim jest indeed on the purpose avowed in the title. But he appears not to have been sufficiently aware of the equally great danger of leaning too far in the opposite direction. Thus, in defining Understanding as the "faculty judging according to sense," he carried simplification too far. He translated quite correctly from the Transcendental Analytic (Bk. I, Ch. I, sec. i) Kant's definition of Understanding as the "faculty of judging," but this effort to simplify and at the same time to synthesize the elaborate analysis of sensation in the preceding Transcendental Aesthetic—full of passages suggesting and in a manner justifying Coleridge's qualifying phrase "according to sense"[228]—led him to qualify and limit the sphere of the Understanding too severely. American readers, unfamiliar with the Kantian anallysis, could easily be led to conclude (as Emerson, indeed, did) that the Understanding is prevented from going beyond the sphere of sensuous data, that it can proceed *a posteriori* only. This view led some of the Transcendentalists to conceive of the Understanding as being at some points opposed, and at others inferior, to the Reason. Since they found this limited and erroneous view of the Understanding corroborated in Carlyle's essays, the misconception gained currency.

Another difficulty, especially among those who find Coleridge inconclusive, arises when detached statements are taken literally or out of their context. The very definition just adduced has been singled out

as evidence of his blundering efforts to follow Kant. But the point is that this definition is but a preliminary statement to a section of twenty-six closely-printed pages in the *Aids*[229] solely and specifically devoted to the further elucidation of the meaning of Understanding in relation to Reason and Sensation, in the course of which the Kantian meaning appears clearly enough—as clearly perhaps as such meaning can appear without quoting the entire section of the Kantian text itself.[230] Intent on popularizing the thought of Kant, Coleridge avoids technical explanations, presumably because he feared that too many minutiae might explain the meaning quite away for the general reader.[231]

Another tantalizing problem that has troubled students of Coleridge is how nearly Coleridge's Reason approaches Jacobi's *Gefühl*; whether Coleridge does not, indeed, forsake Kant's Pure Reason and by gradual transition through the medium of Schelling's "intellectual intuition," arrive finally at Jacobi's philosophy of pure faith. Coleridge's injection of "Revelation as the essence of religion" into the argument which finds the moral grounds of religion in the Kantian reason is confusing, so much so that Dr. Wellek offers the opinion that "on the whole the *Aids to Reflection* seems . . . like an attempt at a reconstruction of Kant for the purposes of a philosophy of faith."[232] The point is important, for if Dr. Wellek can so interpret Coleridge, it is all the more likely that Emerson and his American disciples might have thus interpreted him.

Shortly after Dr. Wellek raised the question, it was cleared up by Professor Julian I. Lindsay [233] by examining various marginalia which Coleridge wrote into his copy of Jacobi. They demonstrate beyond the possibility of any doubt that he understood precisely what the controversial issues were between Jacobi and Kant. His comments show that he reread Schelling and checked Jacobi against Schelling, and both against Kant, and concluded that Jacobi's role was one of stupidity and Schelling's one of cowardice in attacking "the Herculean intellect of Kant."[234]

If Coleridge's reason seems sometimes to act with the immediacy of intuition, the intuitiveness is always an intellectual one, and that makes all the difference; for it means that however immediate the act may seem, it is penetrated by a light which it owes to the organizing power of thought. In short, two philosophies can hardly diverge more radically in tendency than those of Coleridge and Jacobi. On the basis of his "reason," Jacobi could know by intuition *that* God and soul are, but never what they are; they must remain, so far as his philosophy is concerned, forever ungrounded possibilities. Coleridge, on the other hand, was led by his conception of reason to become absorbed in the great questions of morality, including the freedom of will and of moral evil, and to seek a purely metaphysical interpretation even of the doctrine of Trinity. Thus the whole trend of Coleridge's metaphysical labors is in conflict with the method of Jacobi's mysticism. Coleridge's marginalia illustrate abundantly that his temporary concern with Jacobi was no more than a moment in a lifelong war that he waged within himself in the effort to restrain his sensibility and susceptibility to feeling by sound principles grounded on reason—"to make," as he said, "the reason spread light over the feelings, to make our feelings diffuse vital warmth over the reason." After *The Friend* Coleridge never again mentioned Jacobi in his writings.

This advance beyond Jacobi's position is pertinent to our inquiry of how the American disciples of Coleridge interpreted Kant. It is significant that James Marsh, as the American editor of Coleridge and the first so-called Coleridgean in America, in preparing the first American edition of *The Friend*, felt it incumbent upon himself to point out that Coleridge's qualification of Jacobi's definition of reason represents a complete transcendence of the German's meaning.[235]

It does not follow that Emerson, for example, read Coleridge correctly, but it does suggest that if he read Coleridge as Marsh tried to explain him (first, in his edition of *The Friend* and, second, in his long Preliminary Essay and the elaborate Notes to the *Aids* in 1829), he should have got what is essentially the Kantian sense of understanding and of reason.[236] Again, this is not to imply that the American Transcendentalists, following Marsh and Coleridge, grasped the whole of Kant. For the philosophy of Coleridge, as it came to America in his popular works, combined elements of Fichte, of Schelling, and of others superimposed upon Kant's basic distinctions. Nor does it mean that the American Transcendentalists always kept clearly before them the Kantian distinctions either between understanding and reason or between the pure and the practical reason. But the fact remains that nothing goes deeper in the life or philosophy of Coleridge than the meaning and significance that he attached to these distinctions. Whether he discussed religion, morals, the state, art, or metaphysics, he invariably based his judgments upon these distinctions and seemed incapable of thinking except in terms of them.

But he was as unwilling to stop with Kant's negations of pure reason as he had been discontent to rest in sensationalism or utilitarianism. A philosophy that failed to justify and satisfy his inmost spiritual aspirations was for him inadequate. Irrefutable as he recognized the rigor of Kant's logic on the speculative side to be, he was quick to grasp Kant's practical reason, as it operated in the realms of morality and religion, in order to assert his faith in God, immortality, and freedom, and to harmonize his religion with his philosophy. Whenever he speaks of reason in the highest sense, he means always the practical reason. The primacy of the practical over the speculative reason is a constant with him. Actually, the distinction between pure and practical reason is with Coleridge far more important than that between understanding and reason; and it is the failure to recognize this basic fact that led Carlyle to throw off his clever but shallow quip about Coleridge's "sublime secret of believing by the reason what the understanding had been obliged to fling out as incredible." Such a verdict overlooks a very pointed statement like the following, taken from the *Aids* (of which a dozen more can be adduced):

> The Practical Reason alone is Reason in the full and substantive sense. It is Reason in its own sphere of perfect freedom; as the source of ideas, which ideas, in their conversion to the responsible Will, become ultimate ends. On the other hand, Theoretic Reason, as the ground of the universal and absolute in all logical conclusion, is rather the light of Reason in the Understanding and known to be such by its contrasts with the contingency and particularity which characterize all the proper and indigenous growths of the Understanding.[237]

In some of his phrasings Coleridge asserted more than Kant dared affirm, although it does not follow therefore that Kant was right and Coleridge wrong—not until a greater philosopher arise than has yet appeared, to demonstrate greater validity for the pure than for the practical reason or to establish the superiority of philosophy over religion.

Coleridge accepted the Kantian distinctions gratefully but passed over whatever of the Kantian system he could not use. Thus he tacitly minimized the restrictions to which the pure reason seemed forever subject, and forthrightly rejected Kant's critical position by which noumena could never mean more than the mere word suggested. But Kant's postulates of the practical reason, which he found more in accord with the irresistible spiritual yearnings within him for union with reality, he elevated into the "truths of reason." Fundamentally, he agreed with Kant that the supersensuous convictions of the soul are not objects of logical or syllogistic reasoning,

and he refused to believe the neo-Platonic mystics that there were pure intuitions.[238]

On one point he steadfastly refused to follow Kant—that is, in subjecting his feelings completely to the rigor of logic. Instead, he wanted "to make the reason spread light over the feelings, to make our feelings, with their vital warmth, to actualize our reason—these are my objects, these are my subjects."[239] That being so, he found it impossible to accept what he called Kant's "false, unnatural, even immoral" stoic principle, by which he treats the affections "as indifferent . . . in ethics, and would persuade us that a man who disliking, and without any feeling of love for virtue, yet acts virtuously, because and only because of his duty, is more worthy of our esteem than a man whose *affections* are aidant to and congruous with his conscience."[240] This insistence upon the value of the feelings in morals represents the chief point of his departure from the position of Kant, differentiating the emotionalism of Coleridge from the rationalism of Kant. It was this fondness for the affections that moved him to modify Kant's connotation of reason so as to make it a means of contact with objects which Kant had banished to the limbo of noumena.[241] It was the predilection of the romanticist—of one who "prayed with drops of agony on my brow, trembling not only before the justice of my Maker, but even more before the mercy of my Redeemer"—that differentiated his position from the coldly logical criticism of Kant. But it was also this that raised Coleridge above the position of a mere translator of Kant—a mere ape of other men's thought—and provides that element of originality that entitles him to be taken seriously as a philosopher at all. Although it led him to push beyond the limits of practical reason as defined by the cautious logic of Kant, it was precisely this reinvestment of philosophy with an emotional-spiritual content that marked his characteristic and significant contribution to his and succeeding generations. Kant's thought, in passing through Coleridge's mind, issued a Coleridgean-Kantian product, in which the Coleridgean element was dominant. Although Kant's critical method early took hold of him with a "giant's hand," as he confessed, it was the hopes that Kant's practical reason offered that appealed to Coleridge. On the practical reason he was ready to stake all:

Let the believer never be alarmed by objections wholly speculative, however plausible on speculative grounds such objections may appear, if he can but satisfy himself, that the result is repugnant to the dictates of conscience, and irreconcilable with the interests of morality.[242]

This principle is a constant in his thinking, at least from 1820 onward, when he advised a friend in terms leaving no doubt (1) that he understood precisely the limitations placed by Kant on the pure reason in its strictly regulative functions as against the "affirmations" of the practical reason as constitutive and (2) that, despite Kant's warnings, Coleridge knew what he was about.

I by no means recommend an extension of your philosophic researches beyond Kant. In him is contained all that can be *learned*, and as to the results, you have a firm faith in God, the responsible will of Man and Immortality; and Kant will demonstrate to you, that this faith is acquiesced in, indeed, nay confirmed by the Reason and Understanding, but grounded on Postulates authorized and substantiated solely by the *Moral* Being. They are likewise *mine*: and whether the Ideas are regulative only, as Aristotle and Kant teach, or constitutive and actual, as Pythagoras and Plato, is of living interest to the philosopher by profession alone. Both systems are equally true, if only the former abstain from denying *universally* what is denied individually. He, for whom Ideas are constitutive, will in effect be a Platonist; and in those for whom they are regulative only, Platonism is but a hollow affectation.[243]

In his attempted reconciliation of philosophy with religion, of knowledge with belief, four doctrines were of primary importance: (1) the existence of God, (2) immortality, (3) sin, and (4) redemption.[244] His determination of these four ideas is illuminating as showing his relation to Platonic thought, on the one hand, and to the Kantian criticism, on the other—often pushing beyond the circumspections of the cautious logic of Kant, who regarded the attempt to reduce the postulates of the practical reason to the terms of the understanding as nothing short of perilous. But following Kant in attributing to the practical reason the power of positing a reality beyond the limits of experience, Coleridge was impelled by his religious convictions to go further and to assert the unassertable, if not on the ground of reason, at least on the ground of conscience loosely identified, in its highest reaches of religious insight, with the categorical imperative. He made no attempt to reduce supersensible truths to logical terms, but he sought with spiritual zeal to stir the divine element in man to justify itself on its own terms.[245]

However strenuously Coleridge objected to Kant's unknowable *noumenon*, he accepted *in toto* his methodology—though, like Fichte and Schelling, he sought to close the gap in the Kantian dualism and "to make philosophy all of one piece." He gave Fichte his due as having substituted Act for Substance, or Thing, and of emphasizing the Dynamic principle in man. He accorded to Schelling full credit as "the most successful improver of the Dynamic System" in applying the Dynamic to Nature. To Schelling he bowed for having identified subject with object, thus closing the chasm between noumena and phenomena and preparing the way for the Schellingian synthesis, or trichotomy of subject-object-identity—a principle which he defended, with minor alterations, to the last. These acknowledgments he made, but not without realizing the wide divergence between Fichte and Schelling, and between both and Kant, nor without realizing that the true synthesis still remained to be made. The exaggerated

Egoism of Fichte and the thinly veiled Spinozism of Schelling[246] served but to show him the errors of any but the "Critical Way"; hence he returned to Kant, and set out, on the solid ground of Kant's Critiques, to make his own synthesis. This effort, in so far as it was successful, he made independently of Hegel (of whom he knew little at first hand) by combining, consciously and unconsciously, something of Fichte's Egoism and larger portions of Schelling's theory of the Dynamic and of his trichotomy with his own deep-rooted conviction about the reality (both natural and spiritual) of the creative activity of the human mind and of the principle of that activity as the *nisus* toward true Individualism. This last idea is the central principle in Coleridge, round which all the rest revolves. In the words of Professor Muirhead, it is this principle of "the true meaning and place of Individuality in the world both of nature and of man"[247] on the basis of which Coleridge sought the rational synthesis to solve the problems of the many and the one, matter and form, the actual and the ideal, the finite and the infinite.[248]

The Kantian elements in Coleridge, lengthy and involved though our analysis of them has been, need to be considered in any evaluation of Kantian influence on the American Transcendentalists, for their opinions of Kant were derived from the Coleridgean or some other restatement, and almost never from a firsthand study, of Kant.

WORDSWORTH—SOUTHEY—ROBINSON— HAZLITT—DE QUINCEY

William Wordsworth, lagging always some years behind Coleridge in his philosophical development, even during the period of their close association, dropped hopelessly behind him in his later years. Little inclined to philosophical pursuits and averse to abstruse research, ignorant, moreover, of German, he remained a poet while Coleridge turned more and more to strictly intellectual

activity. To Kant have been referred certain phrases and ideas in "Ode to Duty": "Stern Daughter of the Voice of God" as guide, law, and law-giver; the weariness of "chance-desires"; the wish to become a "Bondman" of Duty;[249] but they apply equally well to the Christian tradition. Emerson was quick to detect a transcendental note in Wordsworth's

> obstinate questionings
> Of sense and outward things,
> Fallings from us, vanishings,
> Blank misgivings of a Creature
> Moving about in worlds not realized,[250]

but they cannot be related directly to German transcendentalism. Similarly, passages such as Dr. Wellek mentions[251] are, as he himself suggests, more logically derived from Coleridge than from Kant. Asked whether the Wanderer's discourse in the *Excursion* (beginning Book IV, line 65: "And what are things eternal?") derived from Kant, Wordsworth said that he was "utterly ignorant of anything connected with Kant and his philosophy."[252] The answer seems sufficient.

Robert Southey's concern with German philosophy was confined almost entirely to the use he made of Kant's *Idea of a Universal History in a Cosmopolitan Plan*, as translated by De Quincey for the *London Magazine* of October, 1824, in an imaginary dialogue between Sir Thomas More and Montesinos—a work of limited circulation in America.

Henry Crabb Robinson had a real interest in and grasp of the essentials of critical idealism,[253] but his letters and several essays long remained buried either in the pages of forgotten reviews or in unpublished manuscript, so that in America his services as a disseminator of German ideas went for naught.[254]

The notice that William Hazlitt took of Kant illustrates how difficult it was for the British mind (though in this case it had been prepared by Coleridge and a prior rejection of Locke) to understand and accept German transcendentalism. Hazlitt penned two articles for the *Morning Chronicle* that deal with Kant, both occasioned by Madame de Staël's *De l'Allemagne*.[255] The second is the more considerable of the two. It presents an elaborate criticism of Kant, based almost solely on Willich and therefore poorly informed.[256] These essays are of little significance except that their appearance in the *Morning Chronicle* gave the misinformation with which they were packed some currency in both Britain and America.

Thomas De Quincey's concern with Kant, in point of time, was one of the longest among English romantics. His first published notice of Kant was in 1825, and the last preceded his death in 1859 by only a year.[257] The first article, in the *London Magazine* for July, 1823,[258] while abounding in generalities, is void of any effort to expound Kant's philosophy. The second, "Last Days of Immanuel Kant," in *Blackwood's Edinburgh Magazine* for February, 1827,[259] is wholly biographical and anecdotal; but in *Blackwood's* for August, 1850,[260] he promised to give an exposition of transcendental philosophy as outlined in "Kant's Miscellaneous Essays." However, he lived up to his declared purpose only to the extent of commenting briefly on five or six of Kant's minor works, and then proceeded to belabor Kant as an unlettered, uncouth German who "never read a book in his life," and who, as an "enemy of Christianity . . . shuffled, equivocated, in fact (it must be avowed) *lied*."[261] More substantial was his work of translating for the British periodical press of Kant's essays "On National Character, in Relation to the Sense of the Sublime and the Beautiful,"[262] "Abstract on Swedenborgianism,"[263] "Idea of a Universal History on a Cosmopolitan Plan,"[264] and "Age of the Earth."[265] But much of his work, except what appeared in the British journals that were widely read in America, left little mark on the American mind.[266]

THOMAS CARLYLE

Because Carlyle's writings, after those of Coleridge, were the main source of information from which Americans learned something about German thought, the relative success and failure of Carlyle as an expositor of German philosophy is a matter of importance. For our purposes Carlyle is most readily understood when he is viewed as the opponent, in his time, of the Lockean tradition, of hedonism, of atomism, of utilitarianism, and as the promulgator of the creative and the dynamic in literature, thought, and society.[267] For this program, Carlyle sought fresh concepts as well as new terms. He found both in the German writers.

Little interested in technical philosophy, he often handled metaphysical ideas with the licence of a dilettante, altering old concepts, employing ambiguous expressions, referring ideas to indefinite and sometimes wrong sources, going merrily on his way "appropriating, rejecting, transforming" and exercising a kind of royal prerogative to take his materials wherever he found them and to order them as best served his purposes.[268]

While much interested in thought, Carlyle, like his chief master, Goethe, "never thought about thought."[269] As a matter of fact, he was not abundantly endowed for the pursuit of speculative philosophy, although he loved, "especially when talking theology, to play with metaphysical language," not unlike the layman who "ventures on the terminology of lawyers and finds that he has implied far more than was in his mind." [270] "His distrust of speculative reason he found succinctly stated for him in Goethe, and elaborately justified—so he thought—in Kant's *Kritik der reinen Vernunft*. He sought the stimulating power of a great personality, and found it presented in Goethe himself, and its cultivation set forth in admirable detail in *Wilhelm Meister*. He had fought with the demons of skepticism and suicidal despair; and Schiller's triumph and Goethe's progress from *Werther* to the serenity of the *Wanderjahre* and the second part of *Faust* showed him that his problems had been other men's problems and had been solved. What he missed in current English and French thought—the dynamic element—he found in Fichte, and especially in Novalis."[271] His passion for history (which Hume, Gibbon, and Robertson left dissatisfied) fed on the theories of Schelling, Schiller, Novalis, and the Schlegel brothers; while his admiration of great men and the wish to account for them found a ready ally in Fichte's popular essays and in the romantic notion of the man of genius. In spite of his native Puritanism, he had a number of common interests with the German writers.[272]

Of all the Germans who helped shape Carlyle's thinking, the influence of Goethe is the greatest single one,[273] although Carlyle himself was inclined also to credit Kant with helping him to his fundamental convictions. Certainly Carlyle's knowledge of Goethe was wider and deeper than that of Kant and of equally long duration.[274]

What Goethe fundamentally taught him was faith in himself . . . Carlyle admired increasingly Goethe's union of the singer and the sage, his combination of the real and the ideal in *Werther, Meister,* and *Dichtung und Wahrheit,* his treatment of the actual as the raw materials of the ideal, his conception of renunciation as the preliminary act of true living, his reverence for sorrow, his pantheism—so far as it was present in his teaching—his wise silence on the unseen. Goethe's serenity, breadth, and tolerance, achieved after heroic struggle, gave significance to Carlyle's own problems. Long after the novelty had worn off the doctrines of Kant, Fichte, Schelling, and Novalis, and Carlyle had ceased to ponder the speculative enigmas of the philosophers, Goethe remained the permanent and vitalizing power in his thinking.

Indeed, concludes Professor Harrold, "all other German writers had relevance for Carlyle only as they elaborated or confirmed

the principles he had derived from Goethe. It is difficult to imagine how he would have interpreted Fichte's doctrine of the hero, Novalis' doctrine of *Selbsttötung*, of Schelling's doctrine of organism, had he not found in Goethe himself an example of a hero, in *Entsagen* an ideal comparable to 'self-annihilation,' and in Goethe's general philosophy an expression of the organic character of Nature."[275]

One gathers from Carlyle's numerous references to Kant, beginning as early as 1820, that he was thoroughly conversant with Kant. As a matter of fact, he privately confessed but an incomplete comprehension of "Kant, Schelling, Fichte and all those worthies,"[276] but in his published works he usually spoke as if he were an authority on critical transcendentalism.[277] His reading of Kant was probably confined to a perusal of 150 pages of his edition of the *Kritik der reinen Vernunft*. On September 27, 1826, he reported:

I am at the 150th page of the *Kritik der reinen Vernunft*; not only reading but partially understanding, and full of projects for instructing my benighted countrymen on the true merits of this sublime system, at some more propitious season. To speak truth, however, one of Scott's Novels would suit me much better: last night I found Kant was getting rather abstruse; and in one or two points he puzzled me so, that today I have not once opened him.[278]

In the light of such interpretations of Kant as Carlyle incorporated in his writings, we may believe him when he confessed that he found Kant puzzling on "one or two points," for there is good evidence to indicate that he understood neither the Kantian explorations into the limits of human knowledge nor the significance of his conclusions. Without following in detail what has already been expertly examined by Miss Storrs, we may summarize her findings, which are (1) that Carlyle's conception of the ideality of Time and Space is quite divorced from the meaning of Kant, (2) that

Carlyle's and Kant's conceptions of the nature of Reason and Understanding, as well as their interpretations of the value of the distinction between these two faculties, are essentially at variance, (3) that Carlyle is opposed to Kant's whole explanation of the derivation and character of moral law, and (4) that, on the whole, the essence of critical idealism remained foreign to Carlyle.[279]

All this, however, did not prevent his attempting to instruct his "benighted countrymen in the true merits of his sublime system," for when he undertook his next work, *Wotton Reinfred*, he incorporated, in Chapters IV and V, relatively lengthy expositions of Kantian doctrine, put in the mouth of Dalbrook, who is undoubtedly Coleridge. While the hearers of Dalbrook's discourse readily recognize his sentiments as "Kantism! Kantism!" the reader today fails to find in Dalbrook's distinction between Reason and Understanding anything but the old dichotomy of the head and the heart; while Space and Time are said by Dalbrook to be "modes, not things; forms of our mind, not existence without us; the shapes in which the unseen bodies itself forth to our mortal sense; if we were not, they also would cease to be."[280] This represents a misconstruction that Carlyle never fully corrected.

By the autumn of 1827, when "The State of German Literature" was written, Carlyle had discovered that the "critical philosophers, whatever they may be, are not mystics . . . Kant, Fichte, and Schelling are men of cool judgment and determinate energetic character; men of science and profound universal investigation."[281] But he proceeds to discuss them *en masse* without making distinctions among them.[282] We learn further that the "ultimate aim of all philosophy must be to interpret appearances"; and the "first steps towards this, the aim of what may be called Primary or Critical Philosophy, must be to find some indubitable principle; to fix ourselves on

some unchangeable basis; to discover what the Germans call *Urwahr*, the Primitive Truth, the necessarily, absolutely *True*."[283] This the German idealists, with Kant as leader, are said "to seek by intuition in the deepest and purest nature of Man."[284]

All this one might get over, particularly since Carlyle's grouping together of Kant, Fichte, and Schelling allows him a certain latitude; but one begins to have real trouble with his peculiar interpretation of Reason as not being possessed by all men alike—and the resulting implication that the Reason is neither necessary nor universal.[285] He goes definitely beyond Kant in another respect, i.e., in limiting the Understanding too strictly while glorifying the Reason unqualifiedly. "Reason," says he, "discusses Truth itself, the absolutely and primitively *True*; while Understanding can discern only *relations* and cannot decide without *if*."[286] The Reason freely discerns the Ultimate, the Absolute, "not by logic and argument; . . . its domain lies in that higher region whither logic and argument cannot reach; in that holier region, where Poetry, and Virtue and Divinity abide, in whose presence Understanding wavers and recoils dazzled into utter darkness by that 'sea of light,' at once the fountain and the termination of all true knowledge."[287]

And with this we have arrived not only at a general misapprehension of Understanding and Reason but also at a confusion of Pure and Practical Reason. Entirely outside the area of Kant's careful analysis, we are back in the realm of the head versus the heart, of science versus religion, where knowledge and faith stand in irreconcilable opposition to each other.

In 1829 Carlyle produced his essay on Novalis, into which he incorporated a lengthy exposition of Kantism, the fundamental principle of which is "to deny the existence of Matter."[288] He goes on to argue triumphantly that since Time and Space are mere "forms" of the mind, Matter itself is annihilated:

If Time and Space have no absolute existence . . . out of our minds, it removes the stumbling-block from the very threshold of our Theology. For on this ground, when we say that the Deity is omnipresent and eternal, that with Him it is a universal Here and Now, we say nothing wonderful; nothing but that He also created Time and Space, that Time and Space are not laws of His being, but only of ours. Nay, to the Transcendentalist, clearly enough, the whole question of the origin and existence of Nature is at an end, for Matter is itself annihilated; and the black Spectre, Atheism, "with all its sickly dews," melts into nothingness forever.[289]

Even worse confused are Carlyle's conceptions of Reason and Understanding as they are represented in the essay on Novalis.[290] In the end, he comes to the conclusion that the "Teologia mistica" of Tasso, the "Mysticism" of Novalis, the "Faith" of Jacobi, and "generally all true Christian faith and Devotion appears, so far as we can see, more or less included in this doctrine of the Transcendentalists; under their several shapes, the essence of them all being what is here designated by the name Reason, and set forth as the true sovereign of man's mind."[291] Here, apparently, is no glimmer of comprehension of Kant's distinctions between Reason and Understanding or between speculative and practical reason.[292] *Sartor Resartus* contains no evidence that Carlyle had penetrated to a deeper or truer conception of Kant by 1830–1831, when this work was written except that he appears in the chapter entitled "The World Out of Clothes" to approach the Kantian interpretation of Time and Space, but he does not retract the idea that Kant's "annihilation" of Space and Time had also annihilated matter, or things-in-themselves. Indeed, this peculiarly Carlylean misconception of the Kantian notion of Time and Space becomes one of the cardinal doctrines in the Philosophy of Clothes.[293]

Nor do Carlyle's references to Kant after the thirties (i.e., after he "had happily got done" with all philosophy) reveal any advance in his comprehension of Kant. He thought of Kant, in 1841, as the means of deliverance "from the fatal incubus of Scotch or French philosophy, with its mechanisms and its Atheisms,"[294] but he never penetrated to the foundations upon which Kant based this deliverance. Twenty years later he repeated what had been the measure of Kant's worth to him throughout the years: "Kant taught me that I had a soul as well as a body."[295]

Seeking for weapons with which to do battle against what Dalbrook, in *Wotton Reinfred*[296] calls "atheism in religion, materialism in philosophy, utility of morals, and flaring, self-seeking mannerisms in art," Carlyle perceived the general effectiveness that certain of Kant's ideas would provide for the impending battle and boldly adopted them. He did not bother to learn the new technique required for wielding them most effectively and never achieved finesse in handling them, but laid about him, as was his wont, with a heavy cudgel to make prevail German idealism, or immaterialism generally. In this campaign he found the Kantian ideality of Time and Space,[297] a loosely interpreted distinction between Reason and Understanding, and above all, moral law (embracing Kant's Categorical Imperative as well as Goethe's doctrine of *Entsagen*) satisfactory war slogans in the crusade to re-open the road to faith. But in the process, his loose interpretation of critical terms did a great deal of harm,[298] as we shall observe later, to earnest people like Emerson, who, adopting Carlyle as a guide, found themselves involved in all kinds of perplexing epistemological difficulties.[299]

Carlyle was influenced, positively or negatively, by other German writers,[300] but for the purpose in hand we need to take note of those ideas only which he transmitted to his American readers— not always in purest form. He appropriated Fichte's practical philosophy, especially the broad implications of the Fichtean ego. He made little effort to comprehend Fichte's technical treatises, and remained unaware of any great incompatibilities between Fichte and Kant or, for that matter, between both of these and Goethe, but drew what he believed to be theoretical support from both (especially from Fichte) for practical doctrines already derived from Goethe. Among the more pivotal ideas that he found in Fichte (although his expression of them is often couched in the more figurative language of Goethe) are the following: (1) the world as physical in appearance but spiritual in significance and reality, (2) the perpetual outpouring of the Infinite into the many finites, the immanence of the Divine in the actual, and the divine symbolism of Nature, (3) the function of history as revelation of deity through progressive development and the alternation of periods of belief with periods of unbelief, (4) the divine mission of the hero as a superior vehicle of the divine idea, and (5) the moral doctrine of action, or work.[301]

Although Carlyle frequently mentioned Schelling, his reading probably extended little beyond the *Methode des akademischen Studiums*; [302] but it was sufficient to confirm (and to pass on to his American disciples) Schelling's views of the nature of history, of the universe as *"Offenbarung,"* of the world as an organism in process of "Becoming," and of Nature as the "vast Symbol of God," or "the garment of God." In the vivid and precise rendering of Novalis' *Fragmente* he found appealing and stimulating interpretations of many of the more abstract principles that he had encountered in Fichte,[303] Schelling,[304] Schiller, and Goethe; while his concern with Goethe's philosophy of *Entsagen* made him susceptible to the doctrine of *Selbsttötung* as he found it in Novalis. To Jean Paul he was indebted for (1) elements of style (such as memorable images or expressions the better to clothe abstractions derived from other writers), (2) the structure of *Sartor Resartus*, and (3) confirmation for the idea that the whole aim of philosophy as well as the meaning of life

should be grounded and sought in the ethical deed. Jean Paul's success, not unlike Goethe's and Schiller's, in working his way through sheer heroism from unhappiness, doubt, and despair to an affirmative philosophy of experience made a strong appeal. While the new concept of development as applied to history by Schelling and especially by Herder in his *Ideen* affected him negatively, Schiller's theory of history, in spite of its several highly theoretical and *a priori* elements and the prominent place it gave to "perfectibility" and the *Humanitätsideal* (which Carlyle's Calvinism rejected) was more to his liking.[305] From the Schlegels, Carlyle derived criteria regarding German belles-lettres, a new approach to the critical evaluation of literature, further support for his antagonism toward the Enlightenment, and, in the case of Friedrich Schlegel, the conception of Fantasy as "the organ of the God-like" and contributory ideas for his theory of the revelation in history.[306]

In all his German studies Carlyle's mind worked like a magnet picking a phrase here that expressed the essence of his notion or lifting an idea there that served his purpose.[307] Thus he went swashbuckling through German writers with the result that his philosophy, insofar as he developed it before 1834,[308] was a curiously eclectic, inharmonious product.[309] While he elucidated few abstract principles, his practical doctrines, often couched in "apoplectic" terms, were such as made young Emerson (even before he knew the name of Carlyle) recognize in him a "Germanick new-light writer" who "gives us all confidence in our principles."[310] As an expounder of the technical features of critical idealism, Carlyle failed dismally, but all Young America understood the lessons he taught on the practical side, and in this respect he brought a message from Germany more potent than the more adequately conceived and accurately phrased metaphysical exegesis that Coleridge offered to Emerson and his confreres.[311]

German Philosophy in France

MADAME DE STAËL

Some twenty years before Carlyle's influence was felt in America, German thought had gained some degree of notoriety, if nothing more, through the instrumentality of the French. Indeed, in some respects the most important, and in others, the first information concerning Germany to reach America came from Anne Germaine Necker, Baronne de Staël-Holstein, whose *De l'Allemagne*, published almost simultaneously in Paris and London in 1813, was reprinted (from the English edition) in New York the following year. The vogue which this book enjoyed in America was tremendous.[312] Many of its readers gathered from it their first information about Germany.[313] But while Madame de Staël was the first to tell Americans about the new German culture, much of the information that she spread is neither profound nor accurate.[314] Her lengthy discussions, as in the case of Schiller and Goethe, tend often to be vague and superficially facile; and what is true of her analyses of belles-lettres holds also for her feeble attempts to explain German metaphysics. Carlyle, after recovering from his first enthusiasm for her book, found her often "misty and inconsistent"[315] and, in the third book, which is devoted to German philosophy, "very mysterious, now and then quite absurd."[316]

Strongly biased as she is by religious prepossessions,[317] she is less concerned about explaining Kant's ideas than about generalizing upon the ethical and religious import of his doctrines. Regarding Kant's epistemological inquiries and his purely speculative problems, the reader learns little beyond the statement that Space and Time are "primitive intuitions" and that the categories, which are listed, are "the principles of reasoning."[318] She dwells at greater length on the piety of Kant. But—

So few minds are able to comprehend these reasonings, and those who are able

are disposed to combat each other, that it is rendering a great service to religious faith to banish metaphysics from all questions that relate to the existence of God, to free-will, to the origins of good and evil (p. 165).

Whatever others may think of the *Critique of Pure Reason*, Madame de Staël finds it "impossible not to read with respect" the *Critique of Practical Reason* "and the different works he has written on morals" (p. 173). Unfortunately "the style of Kant . . . deserves almost all the reproaches with which his adversaries have treated it" (p. 175), so that "no one in France will give himself the trouble of studying works so bristling with difficulties as those of Kant." This is the gist of the chapter of twenty-three pages on Kant. The four pages devoted to Fichte explain that he "makes the whole universe consist of the activity of mind" (p. 190); while Schelling, "like Fichte . . . [aims] to reduce existence to a single principle" (p. 195). But this is merely a return to Spinoza, with which observation Madame de Staël leaves the reader to his own thoughts on German transcendental philosophy while she goes into a lengthy discussion of pantheism (p. 195).[319] Too frequently her enthusiasm turns her away from objective exposition of German thought into subjective rhapsodies of her own, a passage on Jacobi (pp. 184–87) being a good case in point. Even on the subject of ethics, which represents her primary interest and to which she devotes fifty-six pages (pp. 231–86), she makes many words but says little.[320] Although she censures the French for making the principal end of their writing "not the subject they treat, but the effect they produce" (p. 146), she herself indulges her fondness for repeating anecdotes, literary gossip, and other tittle-tattle.[321] Madame de Staël had an abundance of wit of the sort that makes women of her type interesting, but of philosophical acumen, in the Kantian sense of the word, she had not a whit. Certainly no reader who sought to penetrate to the core of critical transcendentalism came away from a reading of her two volumes with much more than the recollection of some names, including those of Kant, Fichte, Schelling, and Jacobi—the first of whom somehow brought about a divorce between philosophy and religion (an effect the virtue of which Madame is not prepared to praise), the second representing a kind of stoic morality, the third a vague sort of pantheism, and the last somehow overshadowing all three. He came away, also, with a recollection of many details of German geography, manners, dress, customs, national feeling, educational methods and institutions, and a good deal of solid information on German literary people. But concerning the philosophy of the new Germany Madame de Staël had little to impart.

THE ECLECTICISM OF COUSIN AND
JOUFFROY

It was not long, however, before her countryman, Victor Cousin, came to her assistance in the effort to instruct the world on the subject of German philosophy. Although Americans of the early nineteenth century read French more readily than German, there is little indication that Cousin's writings were popularly read before they were translated in the early thirties, the first of such translations being Henning G. Linberg's rendition of Cousin's *Introduction à l'histoire de la philosophie* in 1832.[322] If any reader failed to grasp the point of view and significance of eclecticism as outlined in this work, the publication, two years later, of Caleb Sprague Henry's translation, with notes and appendices, of the *Elements of Psychology: Included in a Critical Examination of Locke's Essay on the Human Understanding*[323] left little room for misunderstanding either the eclectic philosophy or Kant and his merits and defects, that is, as Cousin conceived them. For Henry, conscious that Cousin "developed his philosophy rather in his applica-

tions, by history and criticism, than in any full and systematic exposition of its first principles," first called attention to Lectures IV, V, and VI of the *Introduction* as containing a concise "exposition of the fundamental principles"[324] of eclecticism, and then proceeded, in the following eighteen pages, to sketch, in laudably clear terms, both Cousin's psychology and his philosophy.[325] Since Henry's exegesis is of value not only as indicating what the American reader of the thirties and forties understood Cousin to stand for, but also what he understood Kant to teach, several quotations are reproduced. Says Henry:

In the psychological analysis of M. Cousin, all the facts of human consciousness are reduced to three classes,—sensible, voluntary, and rational.
The first and the last have the characteristic of necessity; those of the will alone are personal and imputable. Personality belongs solely to the will; and self is the centre of the intellectual sphere . . . . We perceive by the light which comes not from ourselves; for our personality is our will, and nothing more. All light comes from the reason, and it is the reason that perceives both itself, and the sensibility which envelops it, and the will also upon which it imposes obligation, though without constraining it. The element of cognition is, by its essence, rational; and consciousness, though composed of three integrant and inseparable elements, has its own most immediate foundation in reason, without which there would be no possible knowledge, and consequently no consciousness.[326]

In short, sensibility is the external condition of consciousness; will is the center; and reason is the light. The relation of these three elements—the intelligence, the activity, and the sensibility—is so intimate that when one is given, the other two enter into exercise. "Since the *me* cannot so much as perceive itself, and perceive the sensation, but by the reason, or intelligence, it follows that the exercise of reason is contemporaneous with the exercise of the personal activity and sensible impressions."[327] Hence the triplicity of consciousness (the three elements of which are distinct and cannot be reduced to each other) reduces itself to a single fact, a unity of consciousness, which exists only under condition of its triplicity.[328]

The most distinctive part of Cousin's system is his two-fold development of reason: the first, primitive, unreflective, instinctive; the second, ulterior, reflective, voluntary. The former he terms the spontaneous reason, spontaneity of reason, or simply spontaneity; the latter, reflective reason, reflection of reason, or simply reflection.[329] At this point Cousin comes to his criticism of Kant, who, along with Aristotle, "listed all the elements of reason" and "exhausted all the statistics of reason"; but he adds, "I am far from thinking that the reduction of these elements which they have made is the last boundary of analysis; nor that they have discerned the fundamental relations of these elements."[330] Kant erred in objectifying the laws of our thought, without arriving at any legitimate and veritable objectivity. He never got outside the realm of the subjective, and hence did not "legitimately arrive at any thing truly objective."[331]

Now, if the laws of human thought are purely subjective, we have no right to transfer them beyond the sphere of our consciousness; in their utmost reach they could engender only irresistible convictions, but never independent truth. For sensation and reflection begin in subjectivity and remain subjective.[332] Therefore, says Cousin, "the problem upon the solution of which this good man suffered shipwreck, modern philosophy still finds before it." However, all is not to be despaired of, for, claims Cousin, "I have myself, on a former occasion, given a solution of it, which time has not shaken."[333] This solution rests upon a fundamental fact: "we do not commence with science, but with faith; with faith in reason, for no other faith is given."[334] All this, of course, is referable to nothing more complex than the phenomenon of pure affir-

mation, the *faith* that God is represented in us by reason; whence it follows that if man "believes that he exists, he then believes that his thought—he believes that his existence—is worthy of faith; he therefore places faith in the principle of thought;—now, *there* is God. Because every thought contains faith in the principle of thought, therefore, according to my doctrine, every word pronounced with confidence, is nothing more than a profession of faith in reason itself, that is, in God. Every word is an act of faith."[335]

At this point Emerson may well be pardoned if he discovered what he believed to be "an optical illusion"[336] in Cousin and in eclecticism generally. Precisely what constituted this "optical illusion" he did not specify, but it requires no great philosophical astuteness to pick flaws in the eclectic practice of Cousin, for whom, as Mr. Van Wyck Brooks recently put it, "all systems were true in what they affirmed, false in what they denied."[337] A lesser man than Emerson might have seen, as indeed most American Transcendentalists eventually did see, that Cousin made everything too splendidly simple.[338]

Meanwhile eclecticism had already enjoyed a considerable vogue in America, especially during the thirties and forties. Cousin, available in the Linberg and Henry translations,[339] acquired added circulation in 1838 through Ripley's *Philosophical Miscellanies from the French of Cousin, Jouffroy, and Benjamin Constant*.[340] The periodicals, while not unanimous in welcoming Cousin and eclecticism, all devoted space to the new French thought tinged, as it was understood to be, with German transcendentalism. In 1829, A. H. Everett, in the *North American Review*, devoted some fifty pages to Cousin.[341] The *American Quarterly Review* for December, 1831,[342] discussed eclecticism, commented on its lack of "new truths" and its inability "to combine the fragments of old hypotheses into new unities," but upheld Cousin generally against Locke and praised him for re-establishing God on his throne; for "idealism is right, and sensationalism is wrong, as the Coleridges and the Cousins exist to show."[343] The *American Monthly Review*[344] for January, 1832, and the *North American Review*[345] for July of the same year agree upon Cousin's catholicity of spirit, his just respect for humanity, and his reverence for religion;[346] while the *Quarterly Christian Spectator* for March, 1835, paid tribute to S. C. Henry's translation of Cousin's *Elements of Psychology*.[347]

By 1836, Orestes Brownson, not yet a full-fledged Transcendentalist and still some years removed from his Catholicism, chimed in enthusiastically and expressed gratification over Cousin's attracting "considerable attention" and his exerting "no little influence on our philosophical speculations."[348] In November, 1837, Francis Bowen wrote on "Locke and the Transcendentalists" for the *Christian Examiner*. Brownson replied in the newly-founded *Boston Quarterly Review*. Presumably, said he, Bowen's article was prompted by a desire to vindicate Locke and to issue warnings to all right-thinking Christians against all Transcendentalists. He denies that American Transcendentalists exhibit any "overweening fondness for German literature or philosophy." Instead, he argues, *"The genius of our countrymen is for Eclecticism."*[349] Meanwhile the *Christian Review* found Cousin's doctrines to be based on error and their tendencies injurious to philosophy and religion; it hoped that this "poison of German Transcendentalism" might be expelled from the land.[350]

Emerson's Divinity School address provoked the Rev. James Waddel Alexander, editor of the *Princeton Review*, and his colleague Albert Baldwin Dod to utter a tremendous blast against what they called "the latest form of infidelity," reputedly inspired in part by Cousin, the translations of whose works by Linberg in 1832 and by Henry in 1834 they had read "upon their

first appearance." "But," they added, "we kept silence because we did not wish in any degree to draw public attention to them until evidence was afforded that they were read. We now have that evidence [presumably in Emerson's address], and have felt it our duty to be no longer silent."[351]

Their surmise as to the derivation of Emerson's ideas from Cousin was wrong,[352] for he had come to have serious doubts about Cousin and eclecticism at least a half-year before he delivered the address before the Divinity School; but of these dissatisfactions of Emerson with Cousin, Alexander and Dod, of course, were entirely unaware.

While it would appear, then, that about 1838–1839 Cousin was running onto the opposition of conservative clergymen like Alexander, Dod, and Norton and of such liberals as Emerson, there was no lack of support for him. Brownson came to his rescue with thunderous metaphysical arguments in the *Boston Quarterly Review*,[353] paying particular attention to the Reason *au* Cousin.[354] He distinguished between the objective and the subjective reason in the following terms:

By the objective reason we may understand the eternal Reason, the immaterial world, the world of necessary Truth . . . identical with the Logos of the Apostle and the Greek Fathers, the 'inner light' of the Quakers . . . . In this sense Reason is not mine, nor any man's. It is impersonal and absolute . . . . By the subjective reason we may understand . . . our general faculty of knowing, that by virtue of which we are intelligent beings, capable of intelligence . . . . But we apprehend that a careful analysis of the facts of consciousness would go far to identify this subjective reason with the objective reason, and so far at least as to prove that our reason must be in immediate relation with the impersonal reason—that it is, in fact, as it has been called, "a fragment of the Universal Reason."[355]

The ease with which Brownson shifts from Reason to Intelligence to Intuition to the Inner Light is a common characteristic among several of our American Transcendentalists, especially among the lesser lights. It often involves, as we shall see, a certain slackness not only in the use of terms but also in thinking. However that may be, the vogue of Cousin mounted. By the end of the thirties, eclecticism had spread to Wisconsin and the old frontier, where Calvin Stowe and the Beechers argued about it with Ephraim Peabody, J. F. Clarke, J. H. Perkins, and W. H. Channing.[356] By 1848 de Bow was running Linberg's translation of Cousin's *Introduction to the History of Philosophy* in installments in his *Commercial Review*.

From 1838, immediately following the publication of Ripley's *Philosophical Miscellanies . . . of Cousin, Jouffroy, and B. Constant*, and increasingly after 1840 (reflecting doubtless the effect of W. H. Channing's translation of Jouffroy's *Introduction to Ethics*),[357] Jouffroy is a matter of concern for reviewers and editors. Often he and Cousin are discussed together, Constant, in comparison, attracting little attention.

Ripley reported that his *Specimens of Foreign Standard Literature* were meeting "encouragement to a degree beyond the expectation of its proprietors." Meanwhile Brownson was proceeding, enthusiastically though unsuccessfully, to eschew the word *Transcendentalism* and to give currency instead to the term *Eclecticism*. In his opinion, the latter seemed better to fit the varied groups represented by the Newness, and he hoped it might avoid the connotation of foreign skepticism with which the word *Transcendentalism* had become associated. He hoped, too, that the adoption of eclecticism would act as a deterrent to the obscure terminology and the wild speculation to which some Transcendentalists seemed addicted. Brownson's praise of Cousin and Jouffroy as the high priests alike of Eclecticism and Transcendentalism did not fail to give both currency among the discipleship. By 1840, in Volume I of the *Dial*, there was rejoicing: "Few, if any,

living writers upon Ethical Philosophy stand so high in the estimation of those who have made this science a study" as Jouffroy.[358] The *Boston Quarterly Review*, in replying to Andrews Norton and the two articles in the *Princeton Review*, defended Cousin against all charges of atheism, pantheism, egoism, and fatalism;[359] while the *Christian Examiner*, after making a "comprehensive survey" of all moral systems, found that "no French writer has appeared whose labors can be so agreeable to English minds as those of Jouffroy," who combines with his "national enthusiasm . . . all the cautious logic of the Scotch school."[360] The *North American Review*, more reserved, while admitting that eclecticism had a great vogue in America, considered it a shallow system.[361]

By 1841 the indefatigible Brownson was constructing a complete system of philosophy based on Cousin, which was published in the *Democratic Review* for 1841, 1842, and 1843; while the *American Eclectic* presented a translation of the first of Cousin's series of essays in the *Revue des Deux Mondes*[362] on "Kant and His Philosophy."[363] In 1842, the Henry translation of Cousin's *Psychology* was prepared "for use in Colleges"; during the next year Jouffroy's *Prolégomènes au Droit Naturel*, in Channing's translation, was introduced as a textbook at Harvard by James Walker.[364]

The year 1842 appears to have been the high-water mark of Cousin's as well as of Jouffroy's popularity. The *North American* continued to express its doubts.[365] Brownson, who had by this time passed successively through Presbyterianism, Universalism, Socialism, and Unitarianism, besides coquetting for a while with Transcendentalism, finally coming to profess a real affection for Eclecticism, was already beginning to feel "dissatisfactions" even with it, and all but ready to embrace Catholicism. In an essay of 1843, entitled "Remarks on Universal History,"[366] he suspects Michelet of being a Manichean, inclined to fatalism

(p. 459), Jouffroy of holding a false view of human development (pp. 464–65); while Cousin's impersonal reason, borrowed from Hegel (whom, be it observed, Brownson professes not to be acquainted with at first hand), asserts the "impotency of humanity" and is in danger of annihilating it (pp. 267–74). In the second installment of this essay, which appeared in June, 1843, he vigorously defended the "providential theory" of history as enunciated by the Catholic Bossuet at the expense of Jouffroy and Cousin's eclectic pantheism, and improves the opportunity to attack also Friedrich Schlegel's and Herder's philosophies of history (pp. 579–80). He entered the Catholic Church in 1844. The first of his anti-Transcendental articles appeared in his new journal, *Brownson's Quarterly Review*, in May, 1844. In it he attacked Cousin's theory of knowledge and defended scholasticism against eclecticism. Jouffroy, whose Catholicism Cousin is accused of having perverted, is repudiated in January, 1845. With this, Brownson washed his hands of eclecticism. A few articles which follow in 1845 and subsequently add nothing new. Cousin and Jouffroy, forsaken by their chief American proponent, have had their brief day and disappear rapidly from the pages of American periodicals.

One is inclined to think that where there is much smoke, there should be some fire; but so far little evidence has appeared to indicate that the eclectics left any lasting marks on American thought. The problem of precisely how much influence French eclecticism had in America has been attacked by two French students, M. William Girard and M. Regis Michaud,[367] but the old study made by Dr. Walter L. Leighton of *French Philosophers and New-England Transcendentalism* (1908) remains still the best treatment of the subject. Leighton points out that eclecticism, popular though it was for a decade, never overshadowed other foreign influences, whether Greek, German, or British;[368] and in this conclu-

sion he is supported by the authoritative researches of Professor Howard M. Jones. However, Girard and Michaud serve to show that eclecticism made its appeal to American Transcendentalists as being nonpartisan, urbane, and rational in manner, clear and distinct in statement, democratic and religious in inspiration. Some of the Transcendentalists who found Kant unfathomable comprehended Cousin more readily. Kant was understood to have recovered the mind of man from sensationalism and materialism to reassert "the freedom of the moral will, the dignity of moral being, the nobility of existence, the persistency of the individual as a ground of continuous effort and far-reaching hope, the spirituality of man and his destiny."[369] And Cousin was understood to have taught the same doctrine. But the difficulties of the German language and the crabbedness of Kant's style deterred many from confirming their belief by a firsthand examination of the critical philosophy of Kant. For them, Cousin seemed a Kant to advantage dress'd —what Kant had thought but ne'er so well express'd. Moreover, Cousin established close personal connections with several Americans, carried on a voluminous correspondence with American translators and friends, and worked hard to effect cordial Franco-American relations.[370] That Cousin enjoyed an unparalleled vogue for a brief span of years, approximately from 1838 to 1842, is obvious; that he made a profound or lasting impression on American thinking does not follow. His was a vogue more than an influence, except in one important respect. For it is apparent from the numerous periodical references to Cousin's "Reason" that for a number of American idealists, particularly among the lesser Transcendentalists, Cousin's distinction between spontaneous and reflective reason was synonymous with the Kantian distinction between Reason and Understanding—an error which men like Hedge and Parker did not make. In proportion as the Transcendentalists were equipped with philosophical acumen and linguistic ability, they worked out their Kantian epistemology for themselves, or with the aid of reliable commentaries; the lesser lights meanwhile contented themselves with Kant as he came through the refractory rays of Madame de Staël, Cousin, and Jouffroy.

James Murdock—who was in an enviable position to know and whose candid *Sketches of Modern Philosophy Especially Among the Germans* is, considering its early date (1842), not only a good exposition of German idealism but also the first history of Transcendentalism in America—points out that the term *transcendental* as used by some of its American exponents would certainly have been repudiated by Kant, who would have denominated their method not "transcendental" but "transcendent" (pp. 167–68). After giving Coleridge his due as an expositor of transcendentalism, Murdock continues in a strain which, while it suggests oversimplification, is illuminating.

None of the Transcendentalists . . . are Philosophers by profession. Nearly all of them are clergymen, of the Unitarian school; . . . their aims are manifestly theological; . . . they give [no] proof that they have devoted very great attention to philosophy as a science . . . . So far as I can judge, they have taken up the philosophy of . . . Cousin, and after comparing it according to their opportunity with that of the more recent German schools, have modified a little some of its dicta, and applied them freely to scientific and practical theology . . . . They address us as if we all read and understood . . . Cousin, and were not ignorant of the speculations of the German pantheists (p. 177).

Now, Cousin, who adopts and uses at his own pleasure the peculiar tenets and phraseology of all systems, "causes his writings to exhibit not only great variety, but apparently, if not really, great inconsistency of terminology" (p. 178). Hence,

different persons, aiming to follow him as a guide, may easily mistake his meaning, they

may adopt different principles; or, if they adopt the same principles, they may express themselves in a very different manner. And, if we suppose the same persons, with only a moderate share of philosophic learning and philosophic tact, to attempt to reconstruct the philosophy of Cousin, by comparing it with the German systems from which it is taken, and at the same time to adopt Cousin's lax use of language; we may easily conceive what confusion of thought and obscurity of statement may appear on their pages. Now, the Transcendentalists, if I do not mistake, have thus followed Cousin. Of course, they differ considerably from one another; some following Cousin more closely, and others leaning more towards the German; some preferring one set of Cousin's terms, and others another, or coining new ones to suit their fancy. After all, Linberg's translation of Cousin's Introduction to the History of Philosophy may be considered as the great storehouse, from which most of them—e.g. Brownson, Emerson, Parker, &c.—have derived their peculiar philosophical opinions, their modes of reasoning, and their forms of thought and expression (pp. 178–79).

The last sentence is too sweeping. As will be indicated later, Murdock's contention does not hold true for Parker and Hedge; there is some doubt about its applicability to Emerson; it fails to allow for the widespread popularity and influence of Coleridge, years before Linberg's and Henry's translations appeared; nor does it recognize the vogue of Carlyle. More particularly, it does not take into account the lengthy discussions of German thought in the periodicals of the day.[371] Certainly Emerson, unless he is to be put down as not knowing his own mind, felt and said that in so far as New England Transcendentalism owed anything to foreign sources, it owed a debt to Kant. He never mentioned Cousin in this connection.

In short, eclecticism did not affect the basic thinking of the Transcendentalists except as some of the minor or peripheral figures were led to interpret the Kantian reason in terms of Cousin, so as to include in it the "unreflective apperception of truth," inspiration, revelation, spontaneous faith, and intuition.[372] Brownson, for example, raised no objections, before 1843, to the all-inclusiveness of Cousin's *spontaneous reason*, which amounted at times to clairvoyance, and which Cousin variously spoke of as "an instinctive perception of truth, an entirely instinctive development of thoughts," "the absolute affirmation of truth, without reflection,—inspiration,— veritable revelation," "an original, irresistible, and unreflective perception of truth," and "pure apperception and spontaneous faith."[373] For Brownson, perhaps, it was true, as Murdock says, that the "radical principle of the Transcendental philosophy, the corner stone of the whole edifice, is Cousin's doctrine that *Spontaneous Reason* acquaints us with the true and essential nature of things."[374] But, then, it must be recalled that Brownson was never fairly launched as a Transcendentalist: the Symposium had hardly begun its meetings when, as Dr. Hedge (whose name the club bore for a while) recorded, "Orestes Brownson met with us once or twice, but became unbearable, and was not afterward invited.[375]

Brownson's fervent sponsoring of eclecticism contrasts sharply with Emerson's reserved attitude. Following his acquaintance with De Gerando's *Histoire Comparée des Systèmes de Philosophie*[376] in 1830,[377] Emerson was led, in 1832, to take some cognizance of eclecticism,[378] and in 1833 he put down Cousin's translation of Tennemann's *Grundriss*[379] as a book to be read. The following June he heard Jouffroy lecture at the Sorbonne,[380] and then there is complete silence in his *Journals* on both Cousin and Jouffroy until March 4, 1838, at which time Ripley's *Philosophical Miscellanies* forced the French eclectics upon his attention. It was now almost a decade since he had become engrossed in Coleridge's interpretation of German critical metaphysics in *Aids to Reflection*,[381] the *Friend*,[382]

and the *Biographia Literaria*;[383] while Carlyle had been known to him since 1830[384] as the translator of *Wilhelm Meister* and, what is more to the purpose, since 1832[385] as the author of essays in a "Germanick" style on "new-light" subjects. He had approached Coleridge's philosophical works almost reverently, and had resolved to understand them;[386] while Carlyle served to give him "confidence" in his own principles.[387] Small wonder, therefore, that Cousin had no great appeal for him in 1838. After drinking the Coleridgean vintage, what Cousin had to offer was but new wine in old bottles, apt to put one's teeth on edge. Accordingly we find him recording Cousin's worth to him in 1838 as "a mere superficiality." What others considered Cousin's virtue—his clearness, his precision—Emerson considered his great fault, for he found these qualities in Cousin "but unluckily never an inspiration."[388] And when he delivered his oration on "Literary Ethics" at Dartmouth on June 24, 1838, he employed the occasion to say:

Take . . . the French eclecticism, which Cousin esteems so conclusive . . . . It avows great pretensions. It looks as if they had all Truth, in taking in all systems, and had nothing to do but sift and wash and strain, and the gold and diamonds would remain in the last colander. But Truth is such a fly-away, such a sly-boots, so untransportable and unbarrelable a commodity, that it is as bad to catch as light . . . . Translate, collate, distil all the systems, it steads you nothing; for truth will not be compelled in any mechanical manner (*Works*, I, 171).

Emerson's position here is noteworthy; for he agreed neither with Brownson, who accepted at face value Cousin's claim of having made the perfect synthesis of all existing philosophies nor with the orthodox for whom Cousin's arguments led into too many vagaries. Instead, he held that Cousin was not vague enough—that he was too precise, and that he made everything too beautifully simple. Himself able by now to make some headway reading German (though apparently he never read extensively in Kant), he did not agree with those who, unable to read German, found Cousin an acceptable substitute.[389]

THE CONTROVERSY OVER INFIDELITY

Aside from the linguistic difficulties which Kant and his German confreres in philosophy and theology presented to American readers, a potent cause for Cousin's popularity lay in the fact that the Transcendentalists, desirous of popularizing their unpopular creed, were hesitant about citing their German sources[390] because of the horror felt by the orthodox at the mention of the names of Kant, Fichte, Schelling Hegel, Schleiermacher, De Wette, and Strauss.[391] They often recommended Cousin's simplifications of German thought to those unskilled in the German language and in the critical methodology as a means both to get across their ideas and, if possible, to direct hostile attention away from the Germans and toward the relatively mild, compromising eclectics, who had not yet acquired the same infamous reputation. So far as orthodoxy was concerned, however, this was an idle gesture. For example, what Andrews Norton understood in 1839 to be the latest form of infidelity was represented not by Cousin (whom he does not so much as mention in his *Discourse on the Latest Form of Infidelity* or in his *Remarks* that followed) but by ideas enunciated by Emerson the year before in the Divinity School address and, more particularly, what lay behind them, namely, German philosophy and theology. The attack is upon the "modern German School of Infidelity,"[392] represented chiefly by Hegel, De Wette, Schleiermacher, and Strauss.[393] Norton's pamphlet defends the "Exclusive Principle" that "Miracles recorded in the New Testament are the only proof of the divine origin of Christianity," as against the "higher criticism" of the Germans. Norton's *Discourse* provoked Ripley's anonymous reply, *"The*

Latest Form of Infidelity" Examined. Heavily documented as this polemic is with citations of the Bible, classical authorities, and European as well as American theologians, Ripley does not get round to the French eclectics until the 129th page, where Cousin's and Jouffroy's opinions of Spinoza are discussed.[394] After this belated reference, neither is again mentioned. The emphasis throughout is on German theology, and especially upon a defence of Spinoza, Schleiermacher, and De Wette against Norton's charges.

Norton's reply, *Remarks on a Pamphlet Entitled "The Latest Form of Infidelity" Examined*, although the author was aware of his opponent's identity, is less free of names than the first *Discourse* and resolves itself into three parts, one each designed to substantiate his views (which Ripley had attacked) on Spinoza (pp. 11–27), on Schleiermacher (pp. 27–52), and on De Wette (pp. 52–70). Again there is the same meticulous care as in the *Discourse* to give sources and render translations strictly, but nowhere are the French eclectics mentioned.

Ripley had the last word in two more letters, one on Spinoza and another on Schleiermacher and De Wette.[395] Absorbed as he is, in these letters, in the central problem, he gives chapter and verse for every statement made, citing frequently the works of the men whose ideas are under debate, but never so much as mentioning Cousin.[396] Nor did the issues long remain beclouded for the layman once the editors, reviewers, and watchdogs of orthodox theology set out to instruct the general reading public on the sources of Transcendentalism and the evils to be apprehended from that quarter. It is noteworthy that while the Rev. James Waddel Alexander and Albert B. Dod placed at the head of their famous article on "Transcendentalism" in the *Princeton Review*[397] the titles of Cousin's *Introduction* and his *Elements* and of Emerson's Divinity School address (ostensibly intending to review these works), they did not get round to an examination of Cousin until they had first devoted twenty-nine pages to Kant, Fichte, Schelling, and Hegel as the originators of New England Transcendentalism.[398]

A year later Dr. Charles Hodge, the founder and moving spirit of the *Princeton Review*, lent his voice to the argument.[399] We know, he begins, that this latest form of infidelity "had its origin in German philosophy." Like Alexander and Dod, he was diverted from his intention of presenting a review of contemporary American publications bearing on the subject by launching an attack on atheism in Germany, as he understood it. Although he set out to review Norton's and Ripley's pamphlets, he shifted, at the very outset, to a castigation of Hegel,[400] Schleiermacher, Strauss, Gans, Meyen, Richter, and Marheineke.[401] Cousin is mentioned once in passing.[402] Andrew Preston Peabody, in his review of Norton's *Discourse*,[403] also slurs over Cousin. The fight, everybody understood, was over German idealism, not French eclecticism—over Kant, not Cousin. Transcendentalism, everybody understood, bore the mark "Made in Germany."[404] Only Brownson and the translators Linberg and Henry (who were not among the select circle of Transcendentalists), and to a lesser degree Ripley and W. H. Channing, cared anything about eclecticism *per se*, or about Cousin and Jouffroy. It was well known, also, that the French presented nothing better than a very diluted form[405] of what the Transcendentalists considered the true philosophy, and what the orthodox called the infidelity of Germany. Although Cousin and Jouffroy played a part in provoking the controversy, the fight itself vitally involved neither, but centered upon German philosophy and theology, where it was believed the American disciples were learning their "infidelity."

The influence of the theological principles of Herder, Schleiermacher, De Wette, and Strauss upon American theology is a matter

of more than passing moment but at present virtually unexplored. Portions of the works of the first three were translated by New Englanders and used by the Transcendentalists in their religious arguments, while the work of Strauss, especially *Das Leben Jesu* (1835), was by no means unknown in America. Ripley was enthusiastic in his *Letters* and his articles in the *Christian Examiner* about Herder, Schleiermacher, and De Wette.[406] George Bancroft, during his stay in Berlin, had been on intimate terms with Schleiermacher; and Carl Follen had worked in close association with De Wette at Basel before coming to America. Increasingly during the twenties and thirties, these German theologians were presented to the review-reading American public.

Herder's ideas were discussed as early as 1808[407] in the *Monthly Anthology and Boston Review*,[408] and the *Christian Disciple and Theological Review* for 1820–1821 printed a translation of *Briefe das Studium der Theologie betreffend*.[409] By 1822 even the *Religious Inquirer*[410] of Hartford was ready to take cognizance of Herder, and three years later Bancroft contributed his essay on Herder to the *North American Review*.[411] The next year the *New York Mirror*[412] published some translations, and by 1834 the *Knickerbocker*[413] joined in the work of making Herder known in America. The publication, the year before, by James Marsh of Herder's *Spirit of Hebrew Poetry*[414] inspired Ripley's enthusiastic "Life of Herder," of 56 pages, in the *Christian Examiner*.[415] This interest was well sustained[416] until 1841, when the New York reprint of the 1800 London edition of T. O. Churchill's translation of Herder's *Ideen* provoked interest in Herder beyond theological circles. Herder's idea of the organic in the history of man received a thorough airing in the magazines; while his religion, which he said was comprised in "the one theme" of preaching "the full humanity of human nature" and his philosophy, which taught "the philosophy of human nature" as enthusiastically as did Emerson, were welcomed by those who felt the stirrings within them of the Newness.[417]

The vogue which the works of Wilhelm Martin Lebrecht De Wette enjoyed in America is attributable mainly[418] to the inclusion of *Theodore; or, the Skeptic's Conversion*[419] and of *Human Life; or, Practical Ethics*[420] in Ripley's *Specimens*. The former elicited two long reviews, one by Barnas Sears in the *Christian Review* for December, 1841,[421] and the other by C. A. Bartol in the *Christian Examiner* for January, 1842.[422] Both temper their criticism with praise.[423] While De Wette provoked no great to-do in the literary journals, the theological reviews continued for years to make him a controversial subject. The American translations of *Theodore* and of *Human Life* went into second printings in 1856; and Parker's translation of De Wette's *Critical and Historical Introduction to the Canonical Scriptures of the Old Testament*[424] went through three editions by 1858. In that year Frederick Frothingham offered his translation of *An Historical-Critical Introduction to the Canonical Books of the New Testament*,[425] as a "monument in the history of New Testament literature," possessing a standard of "high authority and . . . a permanent interest and value" (p. iii). This statement went unchallenged. The general silence of the opposition on the appearance of these last two works suggests that by 1858 the opposition had become passive, and that the more liberal theologians were inclined to accept De Wette's researches and interpretations for what they were worth.[426]

Although parts of Schleiermacher's works were available in British translations,[427] and Ripley was his enthusiastic exponent (speaking of him as "the greatest thinker who ever undertook to fathom the philosophy of religion"[428]), Schleiermacher encountered strenuous opposition from first to last. Ripley's advocacy, for example, in his *Letters* to Norton and in his long reviews in

the *Christian Examiner*, was almost a single-handed one. While the threads may be exceedingly hard to run down, it is to be desired that students of American religious thought examine closely the effect which the widespread publicity attending the Norton-Ripley controversy gave to Schleiermacher. It does not seem fantastic to expect to find that the liberal theologians and the orthodox, by reaction, should have been influenced by the emphasis which Schleiermacher placed upon a spiritual Christianity without proselytism, priest, dogma, or intellectual limitation, upon the social elements of religion, and upon the right and duty of the individual to assert his true individualism in his religion.[429] He was never popularly known in America, nor even widely read by the clergy, so that he never exerted what might be termed either a popular vogue or a wave of influence among the laity.[430] But that he left his mark upon the Unitarian religious consciousness appears in several instances.[431]

Least apathetic was the American reception of *Das Leben Jesu* by David Friedrich Strauss. Published originally in 1835, it was noticed in American periodicals as early as April, 1837.[432] The most important review which the book inspired in America was one in the *Christian Examiner*[433] by Theodore Parker, whose résumé-critique served admirably in lieu of the book itself for those unable to read it in the original. In 1843, however, the first American edition appeared in New York, three years after the first French version[434] but three years before the first British translation.[435] Meanwhile Parker declared that the work "is valuable to every student of the Scriptures, who has sufficient sagacity to discern the true and the false; to any other it is dangerous, very dangerous, from its 'specious appearance.'"[436] A second edition was called for in 1845; and a new version, from the fourth German edition, was produced by Marian Evans in 1855, reprinted in 1860. By 1842, knowledge of Strauss's book was well disseminated, and the controversy which it provoked was so well under way that Ripley, writing in the *Dial* for April, 1842, predicted that "this book may be regarded as the forerunner of a theological controversy which, if once begun, will not be soon ended."[437] It goes without saying that the end is not yet, for although the name of Strauss is today seldom used in theological arguments, many of the questions raised by him are still argued on lines indicated by him in 1835. Many of the threads of the twentieth-century controversy of fundamentalism versus liberalism, if traced back, lead directly to Strauss, although they need not be considered as originating there. Most of the issues were latent in American theology long before Strauss's book became known, but he did serve to crystallize the opposition to conservatism and to make it articulate.[438]

A significant by-product, perhaps better regarded a parallel movement, of the theological ferment in New England during the thirties and forties was the rapidity with which the liberal-minded as well as a portion of the orthodox clergymen learned German. However widely they differed in their views with those advanced by the Germans, they felt increasingly the need for knowing the latest theories emanating from men like Niebuhr, Eichhorn, Hengstenberg, Herder, De Wette, Tholuck, and Strauss.[439] Increasingly one finds that the controversially-minded and review-writing clergy of New England not only read but studied, however disagreeable some of them found the principles they encountered, the German works which marked the progress of the "higher criticism."[440]

That some were more glib than profound in their knowledge is apparent; and that there was some lip service, springing from a desire to do what was being done by those who set the intellectual pace, is patent in some of the perfunctory reviews and superficial articles appearing in the periodicals. But among people who matter—people like Stuart, Marsh, Emerson, Ripley, Parker, and Margaret Fuller—there was no pretending. The group of young men who learned the language in Germany—Hedge, the two Everetts, Ticknor, Bancroft, Calvert, Cogswell, Motley, and Longfellow—were completely masters of the language; while people like Emerson, Ripley, Clarke, Parker, Dwight, and Margaret Fuller, although mainly self-taught, made no show of knowing what they did not know. All these became proficient as students of German, though several of them, notably Parker and Margaret Fuller, professed to have trouble interpreting Kant and Fichte—as who has not? Their professions are indicative rather of a sincere desire to read German literature in the original and to fathom German thought than of any reluctance to do so. If they had professed to comprehend completely the intricacies of German speculative idealism, we should be justified in doubting their proficiency. The inability to read German resided oftener among the opponents than the exponents of Transcendentalism, although there were, as has already been observed, a good number of theologians, editors, and critics among the orthodox who got their knowledge of German thought at first hand. That their attitude was not always one of uncompromising antagonism, or based on inadequate knowledge, is illustrated vividly in a little book of two hundred pages, entitled *Sketches of Modern Philosophy Especially Among the Germans*, published in 1842 by the Rev. James Murdock, a retired Congregational minister then residing in New Haven.[441]

MURDOCK'S *Moral Philosophy among the Germans*

Murdock's book is illustrative both of a thoroughness which entitles it to a greater importance in the history of American philosophy than has been recognized and of a method at once objective and unbiased in a degree relatively rare during the period.[442] After the introductory chapter, in which

Murdock distinguishes between two fundamental "modes of philosophizing," namely empirical and metaphysical, and a discussion, in Chapters II and III, of the exponents of these two methods, Chapter IV sketches German philosophy prior to Kant. The next four chapters (pp. 44–92) present a lucid exposition of Kant.[443] Among the Anti-Critical philosophers, who have sought to "bridge the *unpassable gulf* of Kant, which separates phenomena and noumena" p. 94), are mentioned Reinhold and Fichte. The latter's doctrine of Science (*Wissenschaftslehre*), based as it is on the self-evident equation, $A = A$, leads, says Murdock (following Tennemann), to Fichte's "annihilating, by his idealism, the evidence of the objectivity of any sensible world, leaving us only a system of empty images" (p. 100). Tennemann's *Grundriss* (the 5th Ger. ed., by A. Wendt, Leipzig, 1829), which Murdock had before him as he wrote, and which he often refers to (always giving accurate page citations), supplied his information on Fichte and Schelling, as well as for his briefer sketches of Bouterwek, Bardili, Eschenmayer, Wagner, and Krause.

Hegel's philosophy, which forms the subject of Chapter XI (pp. 118–28), Murdock professes to have studied earnestly only to find himself "after a fortnight's hard study . . . nearly as ignorant of the whole process, and of every part of it, as when I first sat down to examine it" (pp. 120–21). Accordingly, in his efforts to distinguish between Schelling and Hegel (p. 121), Murdock makes a slight attempt to draw upon his own reading of Hegel but comes soon to the easier alternative of quoting, for the remaining six pages given to Hegel, Krug's *Encyclopädisch-Philosophisches Lexikon* (ed. 1832–1838), although he is constrained to add that Krug handles Hegel "with too much severity" (p. 126). The issue of the controversy following Hegel's death in 1831 Murdock says he has no means of knowing.

Instinctive philosophy, with Jacobi as head, forms the subject of Chapter XII (pp. 129–40), the whole of which Murdock derived from Krug and, more particularly, from Tennemann. Although strictly derivative, the sketch is not inadequate. Chapter XIII (pp. 141–55), on French eclecticism, centers attention on Cousin, and recounts his focal principles as contained in Linberg's translation of the *Introduction to the History of Philosophy*. The next section (pp. 156–66) deals with Coleridge, especially his *Aids*, as an intermediary in transplanting idealism from Germany to America. The origin and radical principles of American Transcendentalism are discussed in Chapter XV (pp. 167–88), a portion of which has already been quoted; and the volume concludes with a chapter on the psychology of Friedrich A. Rauch (pp. 189–201).

Elementary and derivative though portions of Murdock's book are, it is, nonetheless, one of the various avenues through which German thought filtered into America. It is especially significant as indicating that by 1842, at least, critical transcendentalism received sometimes an unbiased hearing, even from people temperamentally opposed to the whole system of German idealistic thought and fearful of its consequences for orthodox theology.

While the last section aims to correct the impression that only the greater German metaphysicians exerted an influence on American thought by pointing out that men like Schleiermacher and De Wette also had their day, each in his way, it is necessary to reassert that the greater influence is, of course, attributable to the major German philosophers. Although their influence is not always readily discernible, they nevertheless left their mark on the American consciousness, for there was, before 1838, when the first English translation of Kant's first critique appeared,[444] a much deeper and more widely diffused knowledge of Kant and his associates than is commonly allowed. This is not to assume that either German philosophy or theology ever became a commodity for popular consumption, or

that the German metaphysicians and theologians ever found a large buying public in
Boston or elsewhere in America. Yet there
was in Boston and Cambridge, about 1830,
a definite predilection for things German.
Already in 1825, on Dr. Carl Follen's arrival
in Boston, he found there "much inclination" to study German; and before the year
was out, he had secured, through the intervention of Du Ponceau and Ticknor, an
appointment to teach German at Harvard.[445]
Only a decade earlier, Ticknor, in his efforts
to learn German, had found useful German
books hard to get in Boston.[446] Now the
picture had changed: the interest in German had gained so much that Lafayette
spoke of Boston and Cambridge as "la portion des Etats Unis où la littérature allemande est le plus en honneur."[447] "Before
Channing died, in 1842," says Barrett Wendell, "you could find in Boston few educated people who could not talk with glib delight about German philosophy, German
literature, and German music."[448]

EARLY EXPONENTS IN AMERICA

Among the earliest and more potent influences that brought about the "German
craze" in New England (for so it was called
by those who opposed "Germanism") was
the personal influence of Carl Beck and
Carl Follen, both native-born German university men, who, falling under political
suspicion in Germany, and finding every
avenue for academic or public advancement
closed to them there, came together to
America in 1824.

From Beck to Hedge

CARL BECK

Beck, younger than Follen by two years,
had enjoyed unusual educational advantages as the stepson of the theologian De
Wette, as a student at the universities of
Berlin, Heidelberg, and Tübingen, and as
docent at Basel. In America, he soon became associated, through the influence of
Ticknor, with Cogswell, then director of the
Round Hill School at Northampton, Massachusetts. He taught Latin at Round Hill,
developed a gymnasium there, and translated Jahn's Deutsche Turnkunst.[449] In
1830, with two others, he opened a school
at Philipstown on the Hudson, opposite
West Point. Here, as at Northampton, the
study of languages, especially German, was
emphasized. In 1832, he was elected professor of Latin at Harvard, in which capa-

city he served for eighteen years before
retiring. Conscientious, thorough, and independent after the German academic tradition, he did much to introduce German
scholarly and educational methods in the
United States,[450] and in this capacity as
well as through his active participation in
civic and political affairs,[451] wielded a
strong personal influence in and about Cambridge. On terms of familiarity with men
like Ticknor, Everett, Cogswell, and Bancroft—the first generation of American
students to study in Germany—Dr. Beck
and Dr. Follen were held up by them to the
younger generation as the ideal products of
the German university system, and both
did much to inspire ambitious young American students to study in Germany.

CARL FOLLEN

The career of Dr. Carl Follen was especially influential. Dismissed from his lectureship at Jena for his participation at Giessen
and at Jena in the so-called Burschen-
schaftsbewegung and charged with complic-
ity in Carl Sand's assassination of Kotzebue,
he was hounded out of Germany by the
reactionary authorities. Unable at once to
make satisfactory professional connections
in America, he and his fellow-exile Beck
were ready to turn to anything—farming or day-labor—when Lafayette came to
their rescue. Through him, Du Ponceau,

and Ticknor, Follen became, in 1825, the first instructor of German at Harvard College, giving at the same time lectures on civil law. Besides teaching German classes and lecturing on jurisprudence before selected audiences of Boston lawyers, he gave practical lessons on the new art of gymnastics with which the name of Jahn is associated, wrote his own textbooks,[452] besides philosophical and theological treatises,[453] organized a German club,[454] advocated Pestalozzian and Froebelian theories of education,[455] contributed essays to the critical reviews, preached occasionally in the Unitarian churches in and around Boston, lectured on German literature and philosophy, and in the fall of 1828 became instructor in ethics and ecclesiastical history in the Harvard Divinity School. His marriage the year before to Eliza Lee Cabot opened to him the circle of the socially elite in Boston, his intellectual versatility having already won for him an important place in intellectual circles.[456] By March, 1830, he acquired American citizenship,[457] and in August of the same year Harvard College elevated him to the position of Professor of German Literature.

Successful and respected in educational, as well as public, affairs, he was readily accepted by the several literary and educational groups of Cambridge and Boston and became at once their guide and interpreter of German culture.[458] His influence was not purely personal nor local. For example, with J. Q. Adams, who was an admirer of German literature, he carried on an animated correspondence, in which he acted in the capacity of guide and critic. To Thomas Tracey, the translator of Fouqué's *Undine*, he gave encouragement as well as much practical assistance by way of explaining obscure allusions and difficult passages; while both Marsh and Henry turned to him for advice in their efforts to make Kant and Coleridge intelligible to the American reading public.[459]

He became an ardent abolitionist, joining the New England Anti-Slavery Society in 1834. His "Address to the People of the United States Concerning the Problem of Slavery" contributed largely to his failure of re-election to the professorship of German at Harvard when the appointment for five years expired in August, 1835. His bold stand as an abolitionist also led to his resignation, in 1838, as pastor of the First Unitarian Church in New York City.[460] For the remaining five years of his life (after the termination of his Harvard connections), he taught German privately, contributed to periodicals, began a work on psychology, and served in several Unitarian pulpits, ardently battling against all forms of oppression that seemed to him to endanger democracy. At the age of forty-four he perished in the fire of the steamer *Lexington* while returning from an engagement in New York City, where he had delivered a course of lectures on German literature before the Merchants' Library Association.[461]

Follen's association with leaders of thought in New England did not stop with Channing, Marsh, and Henry. During the period covered by his diary and during the remainder of his life (devoted as it was in part to the Unitarian ministry), he associated with such men as Ware, Palfrey, Peabody, and Higginson and freely discussed with them theological, philosophical, and literary matters, at the same time stimulating their interest in his broad, enlightened views on religion and ethics.[462]

It is in connection with his ethical teachings in the Harvard Divinity School from 1828 to 1830 that we can best trace his influence, for his position brought him in close contact with prominent Unitarians outside the College circle as well as with the theological students who were afterwards to become the leaders in the Transcendental movement. It is in this connection, also, that we can best reconstruct his ethical teachings, for the subject matter, if not the form, of his lectures before his students[463] is preserved in his popular lectures on "Moral

Philosophy" delivered in the winter of 1830–1831[464] to a "large and appreciative audience" in Boston and subsequently printed to form the third volume of his collected *Works*.

As a representative of German idealism, which he considered "the system of fundamental and regulative principles of all the various branches of learning and knowledge,"[465] Follen utilized every means at his command to further the reception of it by informal discussion, by correspondence, and by lecture.[466] For him, German philosophy was no separate field sundered from literature, or education, or ethics, or religion. Each of these areas (and he labored in all four) was related by him to German idealism, grounded in Kantian transcendentalism.[467] For example, the system of ethics that he taught had its basis in the Kantian terminology and ideology, in which he had been schooled by his German university training. For him, Kant had laid the foundation for all modern intellectual life;[468] to the Kantian principles he referred all speculative questions, and by them he squared all his practical teachings. But he was no slavish follower of Kant. His course of fifteen lectures on Moral Philosophy demonstrates that while the entire fabric of his thought rests upon the Kantian epistemology, he had made himself master also of the leading systems of morals prior to, and of several since, Kant,[469] and that he boldly deviated and dissented from Kant's position in several important particulars.

What is especially noteworthy about Follen's presentation of Kant is that he in no wise initiated the practice that later became so common among New England Transcendentalists and Unitarians of the left wing, namely, to slur over the negative conclusions of the first Critique with regard to the inability of the Pure Reason to prove its Ideas true. On that head he said at the outset:

This theory of human knowledge, proposed by Kant, particularly in his great work, "The Critique of Pure Reason," must have proved unfavorable to the establish-

ment of moral and religious principles Kant had not assigned to reason another, practical function, which, in his own judgment, far surpassed its theoretical use. The highest function of reason consists in laying down the laws of morality.[470]

Follen's independence of the master appears most markedly in his rebellion against Kant's categorical imperative because Kant's rule of morality is "too general and too vague to serve as the supreme rule of conduct, or to enable us to deduce from it any practical duty."[471] But his greatest objection stems from Kant's definition of the categorical imperative in terms that lead to too "strange a disproportion between the grounds of faith and the demands of duty." "According to Kant religion is founded wholly and exclusively on morality,"[472] and this proposition Follen is neither prepared nor willing to admit.[473]

Follen's chief departure from Kant, then, arises from his objection to the rigor of the Kantian doctrine by which the moral principle becomes the sole foundation of religion. While holding with Kant, as with Fichte, that moral law is the utterance of reason, he sided with Schiller in rejecting Kant's doctrine that an act loses its moral character if it is performed for the sake of happiness or pleasure.[474] He agrees with Fries that moral action springs from conviction through reason, but disagrees with his demand that the conviction of the individual should necessarily coincide with that of the cultured man. Instead, Follen taught that every individual man must determine by his own reason in what his duty consists. His action, to be ethical, must proceed from choice, or free will, and from a desire for happiness. Since happiness increases as one advances toward perfection, the ultimate object of ethical conduct is perfection. In this respect religion and morality are alike, for the true element of religion, like that of morality, is the innate desire of man for the greatest happiness.[475] But this desire, he is at pains to point out, loes not identify religion with morality.[476] t does no more than indicate that both rest apon the same foundation.[477] "On the vhole," concludes Spindler, "Follen coniders religion not as a theological speculaion, not as a belief in dogmas, not as moral action, but as a pious contemplation of the aarmonious working of the universe; as a aatural impulse toward and a reverent eeling of dependence toward the Infinite Spirit in whom we live and move and have our being[478]—a view quite in harmony vith Schleiermacher."[479]

Schleiermacher and Follen alike followed Kant in distinguishing between pure and practical reason and in throwing aside the possibility of knowing God by means of cognition. With Schleiermacher, Follen held that religion is an essential element of human nature, indispensable to the development of the inner life of man; that it does aot seek, like metaphysics, to explain the universe, nor, like morals, to advance and perfect the world by the free will of man; but that the finite individual's pious contemplation of the order and majesy of the external universe raises in him a onsciousness of his oneness with the innite All and a feeling of dependence upon he Author of life.[480] Follen tells us that vhile he was still pursuing his studies in Germany, he felt "the inefficacy of the established forms of faith and worship,"[481] nd was led by Schleiermacher to envisage a universal church resting for foundation and support solely upon the natural interests of man in religion. This church of mankind was to be reared on the principles of freedom, intimate spiritual intercourse among men, and the tendency toward innite progress in human nature.

These ideas he brought with him from Germany. By 1835 he had developed them nto a grandly conceived plan of religious reform for the United States. On August 13 of that year he wrote to his old Giessen riend, Christian Sartorius, then resident in Mexico, about his plan by which he hoped

"to put an end forever to schisms, while in the one general church each sect shall appear merely as the representative of one of a number of confessions, all of which are important for the information of the whole church."[482] These and related ideas, derived chiefly from Schleiermacher, were reworked by Follen into a philosophy of religion independent of any American influence and long before he knew anything of the New England movement. In all likelihood, the close parallelism between the religious thought of the New England Transcendentalists and his own (and with that of Schleiermacher) is in some measure attributable to Follen himself. His forceful presentation of this religion, its social nature, its creedlessness, and its emphasis upon individualism found a ready hearing among Unitarians who were veering toward the left, toward the New Views. During the two years following 1828, when he began lecturing on ethics and ecclesiastical history in the Harvard Divinity School, he had unusual opportunities for sowing the seeds of his ideas among the young theological students who heard him. His broad, liberal interpretation of the New Testament, his doctrine of the fatherhood of God, the brotherhood of man, moral freedom, the dignity of human nature, and the incarnation of God in humanity which progresses constantly toward perfection, toward the divine life to come— these ideas made an impression on his students. Prepared to lend willing ears to a teacher of a religion that would liberate them alike from the bondage of a harsh Calvinism and from a torpid Unitarianism, the more liberal-minded among them were inspired by the sense of inner freedom which this Follenesque religion of Schleiermacher's offered;[483] and though they may have been unaware of its derivation from Schleiermacher, when they later went into the new religious movement, they brought to it a critical attitude toward theology strongly reminiscent of Schleiermacher.

Socio-religious minded as Follen was, it

would have been strange indeed if he had not formed definite political views. Follen was, from the time of his arrival in America, intensely interested in American politics; and, as we have already observed, his participation in public affairs cost him his professorship at Harvard. Thereafter, for the rest of his brief life, he was freer than ever to engage in public controversy. In the realm of political thought, Follen, along with Lieber, was among the first to add a third to the two main currents of thought upon which American political theory was developing—English utilitarianism and French socialism. The strain of German idealism which they added was at first insignificant in comparison with the older and more firmly entrenched philosophies, but from the first it provided a salutary leaven, and eventually it became a significant ingredient in the evolving theory of the young nation.[484]

Follen's political views are to be found primarily in his lectures on moral philosophy, his *Address to the People of the United States on the Subject of Slavery* (1834), and an article "On Peace and War."[485] Although he was familiar with the history of civil law and with the works of Niebuhr, Savigny, Hugo, and Loehr, he followed in the main the philosophical approach of Kant and the German natural-rights philosophers by deducing all political principles from man's nature as a moral and rational personality.[486] Man's moral and rational nature implies the right and duty of each man to employ his faculties in such a way that he and his fellowmen do justice to themselves in all their relations to nature, to their fellow men, and to God,[487] whence it follows that men have found it convenient to form themselves into "a society for maintaining the rights of all by common legislation and administration," for "this is the origin, the essence, and the object of the state."[488] Such a state, resting upon a contract, was, in Follen's opinion, no artificial contrivance but the natural state of

man, though it could have no existence as a personality having will, reason, or conscience apart from the men who compose it. To this end, a republic, in which the majority rule, is best adapted.[489]

Follen's argument against slavery is founded on the natural right of personal freedom based on morality and justice.[490] In that cause he was an energetic agitator from the first and one of the first to suffer for it. His political theory, inspired by a range of theorists including the Roman jurisconsults, Mably, Locke, Kant, Fichte, and Robespierre, the teaching of Jesus, and the principles of the Declaration of Independence, was calculated to appeal to men like Garrison and Sumner, with whom he maintained a shoulder-to-shoulder association in the agitation against slavery at the same time that he kept up a lively exchange of ideas with men like Channing and Parker on the more general topic of the nature and foundations of the state.[491]

The blending of ethics and politics is as old at least as Plato. Throughout the eighteenth and well into the nineteenth century political philosophy was commonly regarded as a branch of moral philosophy. But the unique conception of the relationship between the *rights* and the *duties* of the individual, which identifies the New England agitators with the German idealists while distinguishing them both from other groups, is not common to earlier schools of thought. Earlier theorists had often enough differentiated between political duties and political rights, but "the derivation of individual rights from individual duty and the peculiar conceptions of freedom and duty which made this possible had not been developed before the time of Kant."[492]

The New England and the German transcendentalists alike held that since man cannot become free by liberation from law, he was to be made free by subjection to the law of his own will. But such a solution could rest only upon a conception of individual man as the ultimate moral unit, capable of imposing upon himself a law emanating from his own will, but of a general character, for this moral capacity is identical in all men.[493] It was this capacity of man, this autonomous will, whose existence Kant had been at great pains to demonstrate, that Channing and his followers accepted intuitively on the evidence of their inner persuasion or conscience. Whether it be Kant's conception of "practical reason," of the "categorical imperative" resting on a "spontaneous, autonomous, universal, and free will," or Channing's idea that "Man's rights belong to him as a moral being, as capable of perceiving moral distinctions, as a subject of moral obligations," or Emerson's doctrine of the origin of all government in the moral identity of man,[494] the foundation is the same. "The superstructure of political and social theory is built in each case upon what Hegel designated 'Morality' (*Moralität*) as distinguished from 'abstract law' (*das abstrakte Recht*), on the one hand, and 'social ethics' (*Sittlichkeit*), on the other."[495]

Follen's doctrine was ideally adapted to the purposes of the New Englanders in protesting against the existing restrictions which hindered the growth of the individual to the full stature of his moral and rational nature and their advocacy of a self-reliant individualism. Yet there are indications to suggest that they caught only the broad implications of the Kantian moral-political philosophy without troubling themselves much about the details. For example, Dr. Channing, in his *Discourse Occasioned by the Death of the Rev. Dr. Follen* (1840), said:

His intellect . . . had one quality which, whether justly or not, prevented its extensive action on our community. It did not move fast enough for us. It was too deliberate, too regular, too methodical, too anxious to do full justice to a subject, for such an impatient people as we are. He did not dazzle men by sudden, bold, exaggerated conceptions. In his writings he seemed compelled to unfold a subject in its order; and sometimes insisted on what might have been left to the quick conception of the hearer.[496]

Channing's passage expresses a common attitude of the Transcendentalists toward the Germans. "Impatient" as they were to grasp the "sudden, bold, exaggerated conceptions," they caught the broad import of Kant's (in this case, Follen's) demonstration of the innate moral capacity of man in his political nature, but passed over the systematic demonstration itself, meanwhile turning to the French and English commentaries, supplied by Madame de Staël, Cousin, Coleridge, and Carlyle, as being more "dazzling." Kant's practical reason became by a "quick intuition" and with little regard for its epistemological foundations, the unlimited intuitive capacity of man. In politics and ethics, as truly as in the conception of God, they "took to Germany what they sought there."[497]

Circumstances of this kind make it difficult to ascertain the extent of Follen's influence upon the young men of the day, or to determine definitely the direct influence which he exerted on such students of German thought as Emerson, Alcott, Ripley, Parker, Clarke, W. H. Channing, and Margaret Fuller. Emerson, for example, was a resident in Divinity Hall at the time when Follen joined the Harvard staff, and again in 1828–1829.[498] Intimate as both he and Emerson were with Dr. Channing, they must have met, and Emerson must have become acquainted with Follen's religious views.[499] Considering, moreover, that Follen and Emerson became, in a manner, rival candidates to assist the Rev. Henry Ware, Jr., at Old North Church during the winter of 1828–1829, Emerson receiving 74 to Follen's 3 votes,[500] it is all the more likely that the two should have known each other: although Emerson's references to Follen are scant indeed. In the absence of stronger external evidence, the merely internal evidence is not sufficient to establish direct influence. One is tempted to read a special meaning into Cabot's assertion that Emerson's differences with his congregation on the Communion service were symptoms of deeper differences—questionings not so much about particular doctrines and observances as about their sanction and authority, and that they had begun to declare themselves when he was still in the Divinity School, "listening to the schemes of the Liberal Theologians."[501] Follen would qualify as one of these "Liberal Theologians" who set Emerson to dissenting. But we do not know that the young candidate heard Follen; we can only surmise that he should have; and surmises, in the case of Emerson, are hazardous.

One is tempted, also, to take such sermons as have been preserved from this early period of Emerson's ministry and relate them to Follen's utterances. The coincidences of thought are extensive and startling. Among them might be listed these: the same criticism of ecclesiastical authority as resting upon antiquity; the same insistence that every individual must test his religion for himself and for his own time; the same criticism of formal Christianity and the same repugnance for conventional prayer. Both define religion and ethics in like terms—the terms of Schleiermacher; and both appear to have reshaped the mental processes of man, as defined by Kant, in the terms of Schleiermacher to include under the "Reason" that "highest faculty of the soul, which never reasons, never proves; it simply perceives";[502] whence it follows that both agree with Schleiermacher that "that pious contemplation of the order and majesty of the external universe raises in the finite individual a consciousness of his oneness with the infinite All." To this parallelism between Emerson and Schleiermacher we shall have occasion to return later. Here it is enough to remark that it were a nice solution to the problem of how Emerson came by his views so like Schleiermacher's if Follen could definitely be put down as the intermediary, but the evidence to establish such a connection appears to be missing.

Indeed, such purely objective evidence

as is at hand suggests that Follen's enthusiasm for German thought and art left Emerson cold at this particular time. Certainly this much is certain: Emerson was not persuaded by Follen, as were Clarke, Parker, and Ripley, to take up the study of the German language, literature, theology, and philosophy. In 1824, he wrote to his brother William, then in Göttingen:

If you think it every way advisable, indisputably, absolutely important that I sh[oul]d do as you have done & go to G[öttingen] — & you can easily decide — why say it distinctly & I will make the sacrifice of time & take the risk of expense immediately. So of studying German . . . . Say particularly if German & Hebrew be worth reading; for tho' I hate to study them cordially I yet will the moment I can count my gains. Had I not better put on my hat & take ship for the Elbe?[503]

Here is no great reverence for anything that comes from "the paradise of dictionaries and critics."[504] Four years later, during Emerson's second residence at the Divinity Hall, Dr. Hedge "tried to interest him in German literature, but he laughingly said that as he was entirely ignorant of the subject, he should assume that it was not worth knowing."[505] This was at a time when Follen had already labored for three years at Harvard, though he had not yet begun his lectures in the Divinity School. Although Emerson had placed Madame de Staël's *Germany* on his list of "Books Inquirenda" as early as 1821[506] and professed, the next year, to be delighted by Stewart's "beautiful and instructive abridgment of the thousand volumes of Locke, Leibnitz, Voltaire, Boyle, Kant and the rest,"[507] his general attitude toward German art and learning in 1828 appears not to have been materially changed from what it was in 1822, when he said, in a letter to his friend William Withington of Andover, "I am delighted to hear there is such a profound studying of German and Hebrew, Parkhurst and Jahn, and such other names as the memory aches to think of, on foot at

Andover."[508] The very names one encountered in the German were an ache to the memory. In spite of the enthusiasm and energy of the new professor of German at his Alma Mater, German had as yet no great attractions for Emerson. The stimulation, when it came, beginning in 1829–1830, came mainly in consequence of his reading Coleridge and Carlyle, who gave him a desire to read Goethe in the original.[509] Simultaneously with his interest in Goethe and the intellectual ferment caused by his first acquaintance with German transcendental philosophy, as relayed by Coleridge and Carlyle, came a curiosity also to know more about Schiller. And at this point (about 1831–1832) Follen, who during Emerson's days in the Divinity School apparently meant little to him, entered to contribute his bit toward the unmaking and remaking of Emerson's mind.[510] In October, 1832, while he was groping for a philosophy by which to square his heart by his head, his reading of Carlyle's essay on Schiller in *Fraser's*[511] prompted the resolution to add Schiller to his list of Germans to be investigated further: "I propose to myself to read Schiller, of whom I hear much."[512] The words, "of whom I hear much," suggests Follen; for alive as Emerson was to the intellectual crosscurrents in Boston during the early thirties, and immersed as he was in the lyceum program and lecture courses,[513] he could hardly have overlooked Follen's eloquent lectures on Schiller during the winter of 1831–1832, nor his "Introduction" to the first edition of Carlyle's *Life of Schiller* (1833). Indeed, on April 30, 1835, he wrote at great length to persuade Carlyle that the ground was well prepared in and about Boston for the "worshipful Teufelsdroeck . . . to command all ears on whatever subject pleased him," but that lectures on Goethe and Schiller would be most enthusiastically received. Goethe's name, he felt, would stimulate the curiosity of scores of persons; while the missionary work which Dr. Follen had done with his

"lectures to a good class upon Schiller"[514] would make the latter equally attractive. Of course, by 1835 Emerson was studying German at first hand, as well as with the aid of Coleridge and Carlyle, Stuart and Marsh, so that Follen's help seemed no longer necessary. But what we should like to know is whether Emerson heard Follen's lectures on "Moral Philosophy" in the winter of 1830–1831 and, during the next winter, those on Schiller, with their elaborate analysis of Schiller's ethical system and its relation to German thought generally. That assurance would help to explain how Emerson, in the interval between 1830 and 1835, came to hold moral convictions so strongly reminiscent of Follen, of Schleiermacher, and of Schiller, and how the Unitarian preacher came to be the author of *Nature* (1836).

In passing from a consideration of the Follen-Emerson relationship to that of Follen's contacts with others of the Transcendentalists, we reach surer ground. The first impetus to set Ripley off on his long and ardent career as a student of German came in 1821, two years before he was graduated at Harvard at the head of his class. He found his "progress in the intricate mazes of metaphysics" facilitated by the guidance of "our learned Professor Hedge"; but the influence of Follen did not lag far behind. It is hard to determine precisely when he met Follen. Follen began teaching German at Harvard in 1825, but his lectures in the Divinity School did not begin until 1828. Meanwhile Ripley had left Cambridge in 1826, and was at once ordained pastor of the new meetinghouse on Purchase Street in Boston. But Ripley was acquainted with Dr. Channing as early as 1823, and later he became a member of Channing's circle of "Friends" (likened by Parker to a "Socratic meeting"). He and Follen doubtless became intimate either before Ripley left Harvard or during the early years of his ministry in Boston. Frothingham mentions Hedge's article on

Coleridge's literary character, his German metaphysics, and his theological views in the *Christian Examiner* for March, 1833 (which included a commendation of Kant, Fichte, and Schelling and a general recommendation of the intellectual influence of the transcendental philosophy), as a "potent influence in determining Ripley's mind."[515] True as this statement is, it should be pointed out that already in 1831, Ripley had taken careful notice of Follen's *Inaugural Address*, by all odds the best general account of German literature and philosophy that had appeared up to this time, and had published, in the *Examiner*,[516] a highly complimentary review of it. This is the fourth of a series of ten papers contributed to the *Examiner* between 1830 and 1837, all foreshadowing his later conclusions regarding German theology and philosophy as these appear in the Norton-Ripley controversy of 1839–1840, the *Specimens of Foreign Standard Literature* (1838–1842), and the other numerous works that issued from his study well stocked with German books. Follen's strong defense of the German theologians was doubtless of primary importance for the position which Ripley took in defending Schleiermacher and De Wette against the charges of Professor Andrews Norton.

Theodore Parker, the man of many languages, early felt the influence of Follen. Coming to Harvard in 1830, just when Follen was made Professor of German, Parker availed himself, in 1831, of Follen's help in teaching himself German, as he had already acquired French and Spanish, and as he was later to teach himself Italian, Portuguese, Dutch, Icelandic, Chaldaic, Arabic, Persian, Coptic, Swedish, Hebrew, Syriac, Anglo-Saxon, and Modern Greek.[517] The next year he fell under the spell of Convers Francis, who henceforth exerted the strongest influence upon Parker's extensive studies in German theology and philosophy,[518] but his contacts with Follen continued both then and later—as when,

in 1834, Parker entered the Cambridge Divinity School, when both he and Follen became members of Dr. Channing's Boston "Society of Friends of Progress,"[519] when the Transcendental Club began to hold its sessions, at which Follen was sometimes a visitor, or when they met in the infectious atmosphere of the Peabody book shop.[520]

Even the ethereal Alcott took kindly to the German scholar. When he went to Boston in 1828 to open his school and to seek out the "Minds" of Boston,[521] he found among such minds as he could appreciate that of Follen. With him Alcott discussed Pestalozzi, Froebel, and his own theories of education. He remained on intimate terms with Follen, whom he continued to meet at the Peabody bookstore, at Dr. Channing's, and sometimes within the hallowed circle of the Club, on the periphery of which both Channing and Follen hovered.[522]

According to James Freeman Clarke, who was himself a student of Follen's and the constant companion of Margaret Fuller during his Harvard years,[523] Margaret undertook the study of German in 1832, shortly after Carlyle's articles in the English reviews and Follen's *Inaugural Address* of 1831 and his lectures on Schiller drew her attention to German literature.[524] Encouraged and aided by Clarke, she could record in her diary "rapid progress."[525] Moving as she did in the same intellectual and social circles as did Follen, she very probably heard some of his discussions of Goethe and Schiller at Channing's or in the various reading circles in which Follen had been active since 1827. Under the combined stimulus of Carlyle and Follen, she read far enough by June, 1833, to know that she did not "like Goethe as well as Schiller now." His "perfect wisdom and merciless nature" seemed "cold" after Schiller's "seducing pictures of forms more beautiful than truth."[525] Later she was to modify her views, Goethe becoming an all-absorbing interest; but for the moment she was grateful to Carlyle and Follen for giving her this "pursuit of immediate importance" to which she would, and did, give her "undivided attention."

Follen's services in spreading the German gospel in America were especially significant because at the time when some of the Transcendentalists seemed to be more enthusiastic than thorough in their study of German, he encouraged them to look to first principles and provided them with the necessary tools. As a school, the Transcendentalists were all too content to get their metaphysics from secondary sources—for example, Coleridge, Carlyle, and Cousin. They were, for the most part, ministers, teachers, or men of letters, who, as Ripley put it, appeared to "care more for freethinking than for precise thinking."[527] Yet some of them were keenly conscious of their limitations and made intermittent, sometimes heroic, sometimes pathetic, attempts to remedy their shortcomings. Margaret Fuller, for example, said of herself in 1832:

When I was in Cambridge I got Fichte and Jacobi; I was much interrupted, but some time and earnest thought I devoted; Fichte I could not understand at all, though the treatise which I read was one intended to be popular, and which he says must compel to conviction. Jacobi I could understand in details, but not in system. It seemed to me that his mind must have been moulded by some other mind, with which I ought to be acquainted, in order to know him well — perhaps Spinoza's. Since I came home I have been consulting Buhle's and Tennemann's histories of philosophy, and dipping into Brown, Stewart, and that class of books.[528]

About the same time she wrote regarding her religion and philosophy of life:

I have not formed an opinion; I have determined not to form settled opinions at present; loving or feeble natures need a positive religion—a visible refuge, a protection—as much in the passionate season of youth as in those stages nearer to the grave. But mine is not such . . . . I believe in eternal progression; I believe in a God, a beauty and perfection, to which I am to strive all my life for assimilation. From these two principles of belief I draw the rules by which I strive to regulate my life.[529]

The tenor of all this is distinctly negative. She had no philosophy. Yet she was in a state of mind to accept the "cardinal truths" of a philosophy such as transcendentalism, without having the desire or the power to apprehend its metaphysical groundwork. If she had entertained a philosophical creed, it would doubtless have been that of Schelling, or one very like it. But she was no philosopher; she was content to be a stimulating conversationalist and an appreciative critic—a critic by gift rather than by training. In the final analysis, her creedlessness consisted in holding to her creed that her "genius" alone was her proper guide.

To take another representative, Theodore Parker, admitted by himself and by most of the fraternity to be the intellectual giant and the most indefatigible student among them all—Parker who, even in the Norton-Ripley controversy, sought to speak a "higher word" than either of the disputants had spoken, and to base the argument on "first principles, unobscured by personalities and irrelevancies"[530]—even he lamented the fact that he "was meant for a philosopher and the times called for a stump orator."[531] And then, after years of earnest labor as student and translator from the French and German, he was to find, upon his first visit to Europe, that he could not make himself understood in either language.[532] There is, of course, a difference between reading German and speaking the language; and in the case of men like Parker and Ripley, the inability to speak German in no way detracted from their understanding of a German treatise. Yet even for them it was definitely reassuring to have in their midst a man like Follen, who could expound a doctrine authoritatively or interpret a knotty passage satisfactorily.

Another contribution to the intellectual life of Boston and Cambridge made by such German scholars as Beck and Follen was the stimulation they gave to a broader and deeper study of all the other departments of knowledge: history, archaeology, biology, economics, and especially theology and philosophy—subjects in which, it was understood by the well-informed, German scholarship was supreme. The German universities of the early nineteenth century, more than any others, gave systematic training in the use of libraries and laboratories, inculcated the habit of independent thought and research, quickened the creative impulse, and engendered a spirit of freedom both in teaching and learning. Their ideal was the pursuit of truth; their aim, the emancipation of the human spirit. Accordingly, *Wissenschaft, Lernfreiheit,* and *Lehrfreiheit* were the ideals which Beck and Follen taught and illustrated; and in these ideals they were actively supported by the Harvard-Göttingen men, whom all New England pointed to with pride as products of the German university system. Together they helped break down the sterility and insularity of eighteenth-century collegiate education in America, thus preparing the way for the tremendous growth that American university education has since experienced.

GEORG BLÄTTERMAN

Another German scholar whose influence dates back to the twenties was Georg Blättermann, professor of German at the University of Virginia from 1825 to 1840. Apparently little interested in philosophy, he exerted his influence mainly in encouraging the study of German literature and advancing German educational methods in the United States.

FRIEDRICH LIST

A fourth German intellectual who came to America about the time of Beck, Follen, and Blättermann, although the full

force of his influence was not felt until later, was Friedrich List (1789–1846). After a stormy career in Germany, as university professor, legal counsellor, legislator, and publicist, he followed Lafayette to America in 1825.[533] Profoundly impressed by the accelerating economic development after the War of 1812, List set himself to thinking on the means by which the emerging American economy might meet British competition. He enlisted on the side of the protectionists and in 1827 proposed his "American System," which he called a "Declaration of Economic Independence." Allied with Charles J. Ingersoll, Mathew Carey, Pierre S. Du Ponceau, and Redwood Fisher, he became influential in the Pennsylvania Society for the Promotion of Manufactures and Mechanic Arts, and at the 1827 convention of this body in Harrisburg was one of the principal speakers. On the opening day of the meeting he published the last of a series of letters that comprised his first American book, *Outlines of American Political Economy*, of which the Society distributed many thousand copies. It systematized the principles that gained currency as the "American System," and that were written into law as the high-tariff program by Congress the next year. Next to Hamilton, List is the most influential advocate of American protectionism.[534]

After Germany herself, no nation was more profoundly stirred by List's teachings during the later years of the last century than the United States, where his principles were kept in a place of prominence by the writings and efforts of the school headed by Mathew Carey (1760–1839) and Henry C. Carey (1793–1879), soon to be reinforced by an ever-growing number of American students who returned from the German universities indoctrinated by List's ethico-economic theories.[535] Their efforts to formulate an ethical foundation for political economy represent not only (in Professor Gabriel's words) "the spirit of List returning to the United States,"[536] but also a union of American economic theory with the ethico-political theory of Francis Lieber, whose influence on American political scientists had grown markedly since the late thirties, and who, by the time of his death in 1872, had written his name indelibly into the intellectual history of the United States.

FRANCIS LIEBER

Francis Lieber came to America in 1827 (following a tempestuous career at home) on the invitation of Carl Follen to direct the Tremont Gymnasium in Boston, which had grown beyond the ability of Follen to supervise.[537] Finding his evenings free, Lieber became the American correspondent of a group of German newspapers; and when the winter months afforded still more leisure, he set himself to edit an encyclopaedia after the model of the Brockhaus *Conversations-Lexikon*, in the preparation of which he proceeded adroitly to make contacts with the most influential men in America, soliciting their favor and help. When the *Encyclopedia Americana* (later *Appleton's American Encyclopedia*), in fourteen volumes, appeared between 1829 and 1833, he had drawn advice and help from an imposing array of America's finest scholars. The venture was not only successful financially but brought him prominently before the public. Not since Tom Paine's day had an immigrant to these shores succeeded so promptly in winning the favor of influential Americans.[538]

Not the least service performed by Lieber was his giving America an encyclopedia which did not follow the pattern of those in common use at the time. For it is a matter of importance whether a people that does not possess an encyclopaedia of its own uses a British, a French, or a German one. His German birth and education accounted for an emphasis on German civilization that was lacking in earlier encyclopaedias. Indefinite and incalculable as the effect of this emphasis may have been, the wide circulation of this work served as a means by which a strong element of the German spirit was injected into the American mind, leading Americans to a fuller understanding and appreciation of German arts, sciences, and institutions.[539]

The encyclopaedia conferred a lasting benefit on Lieber himself. As editor of so comprehensive a work, he was forced to acquire a broad and accurate knowledge of American life and history, which, coupled with his excellent university training, prepared him for the writing of his significant books on political science.[540] His contributions to political theory marked the beginning of a new era in American ideas on the nature of the state. There had been anticipatory statements of the theory he advanced, but these had been fragmentary and unsystematic as compared with the organic system presented in his learned treatises. The publication between 1838 and 1853 of his three books on political ethics, on legal and political hermeneutics, and on civil liberty and self-government put him at the head of the new school of political thought, at the same time putting the then regnant theory of natural law to rout.[541]

A liberal idealist, unhampered by local ties or sectional loyalties, and instructed by his youthful European experience in the fatal weakness of disunited states, Lieber found the natural-rights theory flimsy and sought to substitute for it a government by law, in which liberty was to be guaranteed by the twin safeguards—the Federal Constitution and the Common Law. A historical evolutionist, he found the seeds of freedom in institutions, defined as the organic expressions of daily life and the customs of society which take spontaneous form from social needs. For natural law he substituted the idea, caught from Kant, of *rational* development as a broader and safer basis for the evolution of a consciousness of law. Similarly, for his *Manual of Political Ethics*, he derived his principles from his study of German ethics, notably the Kantian con-

cept of moral law. He accepted at the outset, as the basis of political relationships,
Kant's imperatives, and stated them in the
following terms:

Consider constantly and without exception the intelligent being as being its
own proper end and which can never become a simple means for the ends of another.
Act always in such a manner that the
immediate motive or maxim of thy will
may become a universal rule in an obligatory legislation for all intelligent beings.[542]

Both, Lieber and Kant abandoned the
utilitarian and eudaemonistic conceptions
as regards the legitimate objects of state
activity; and both rejected the paternalistic
government as injurious to the self-activity
and self-development of the individual.
Both regarded the insurance of justice in
all relationships as the chief function of the
state, arguing that if this protection were
adequately provided, civilization would be
advanced in other necessary particulars by
independent action.

Lieber's crowning work, *Civil Liberty and
Self-Government*, while it grew partly out of
his experiences with despotic princes and
his predisposition to glorify Anglo-Saxon
liberty, derived most particularly from his
early indoctrination in German idealism.
His subtle and unobtrusive application of
Kantian political philosophy and moral law
to American institutions gave a new turn to
American speculation on the origin and
nature of the political state. His conception
of the organic nature of the state and his
theory of an evolutionary freedom rooted
in the institutions of the people fell in with
the centralizing movement that followed in
the wake of the Civil War and prepared
later generations, in certain quarters (as we
shall observe later), for the acceptance of
Hegelian concepts of political theory.[543]

Lieber was the first scholar of note widely
to introduce the German scientific methods
of research into American colleges and universities.[544] Aside from the regimen of

method learned at Jena, he had demonstrated to him, during his residence in Rome
at the home of Niebuhr, the importance of
giving quotations, examples, and citations
fully and accurately so that the reader
could not only verify the truth of statements made on the authority of another,
but also be put in contact with the authorities on any particular subject, to the end of
initiating further investigations or independent researches.[545] This method, introduced
by Lieber and emphasized both by precept
as a teacher and by example as a writer, did
not, at first, appeal to American students,
and one continues to hear mumbled
grumblings among writers of doctoral dissertations and certain historians, biographers, and critics who seem to feel that
footnotes and bibliography detract from
the aesthetic appeal of the printed page;
but the system has prevailed and continues
in general use.[546]

Whether Lieber's labors in this area affected New England Transcendentalists and
the course of German philosophy in America is a question to which no exact answer
appears. It is safe to say, however, that
although the new methodology went largely unnoticed by Emerson, Alcott, Margaret Fuller, and others of the Transcendental hierarchy, it made its impression on
men like Hedge, Francis, Stuart, Parker,
Ripley, and later disciples, and strongly
seconded the parallel movement for reform
in educational and scholarly methods
which the Harvard-Göttingen men sought
to effect at Harvard and elsewhere. Eventually, the acceptance or non-acceptance of
this method of study and of writing spelled
the degree of success or failure which German critical transcendentalism attained in
its partial conquest of American thought;
for without attendance to close reading and
careful interpretation, to sources and comparative methods, to accuracy and precision, the domestication of German thought
in the United States could not prosper.
Indeed, in proportion as the early New

England Transcendentalists failed or refused to commit themselves to a thoroughgoing study of their sources, insofar did they fail to establish themselves upon sound philosophical grounds at all. Much of the inconclusiveness of their theorizing—Emerson's, for example—is attributable to their impatience with details, their unwillingness or inability to bring their minds to strict discipline—to think hard and straight.[547] This failing, more than any other, perhaps, accounts for the fact that New England Transcendentalism, philosophically considered, proves so evanescent when one seeks to evaluate its influence on the history of American thought.[548]

Another salutary effect to Lieber's credit is that he helped to dispel the prejudice current in England and America against Germany as the "paradise of dictionaries and critics," a land whence nothing original or inspired could come. Combining as he did an exacting scholarship with a keen interpretation of humanistic values, and representing at once the active and the passive life of the scholar at his best, he did much to break down the old idea that all German scholars are born pedants. Here at last was a scholar after Emerson's own prescription—a scholar at once Man Thinking and Man Acting;[549] and the extensive contacts that he made and maintained paved the way for an ever-widening sphere of influence.

During his long tenure from 1835 to 1856 as Professor of History and Political Economy at South Carolina College (later the University), Lieber established cordial relations with Southern leaders of thought. His removal, in 1857, to Columbia enlarged the compass of his friendships and influence even to being summoned (much as "brain-trusters" of the New Deal era were summoned) to Washington during and after the Civil War for consultations with the President, the Secretary of War, and others in high office. On a number of occasions he was drafted to execute important educational and governmental commissions, one of which, requisitioned by Lincoln and promulgated as General Order No. 100 of the War Department, was his *Instructions for the Government of Armies of the United States, in the Field* (Washington, D.C., 1863) —the starting point for more humane rules of warfare and the basis for similar codes adopted by the English, French, and Germans. It is not too much to say that this work constitutes the most important contribution which America made to the law of nations before the twentieth century.[550]

Throughout his long career he carried on an extensive correspondence, national and international in scope, that operated to promote cordial relations among the nations. Among his more famous foreign correspondents were De Toqueville, De Beaumont, Rolin-Jacquemyn, Pierantoni, Garelli, Heffter, von Mohl, von Helzendorff, Mittermeier, Bunsen, Niebuhr, Laboulaye, and Bluntschli.[551]

It remains to mention Lieber's remarkable success as a teacher in South Carolina and New York,[552] his personal influence among his many students, his success in illustrating and making prevail scholarly methods, and the widespread use of his books, both in college halls and among the first men of the land. But his most distinctive achievement remains his contribution to American political science,[553]—the direct result of the impact of his German philosophical theories upon his experience among the historical realities of Anglo-American liberty.

CHARLES SUMNER

A man who did much toward giving Lieber's political ideas currency in the United States was Charles Sumner (1811–1874). From 1834 until Lieber's death in 1872 (except for the years 1851–1861, when the slavery issue temporarily estranged them), they were in constant touch with each other. During the years that Lieber was in South Carolina he often availed himself of Sumner's friendly offices in negotiating with publishers in Boston and in bringing his works before the public. Sumner, on his side, found Lieber an excellent guide in the department of political ethics and philosophy, and often sought his views on questions of international and public law.[554]

As a thoughtful, studious youth, Sumner had enjoyed the best educational advantages of New England, including instruction in French and Spanish from Ticknor and German and civil law from Follen.[555] He went to Europe in 1837–1840 and again in 1857 and 1858, on each occasion visiting Germany. His European experience in 1837 constituted a turning point in his life.[556] His five weeks in Berlin were filled with unusual opportunities. Besides meeting the Crown Prince, he talked with Alexander von Humboldt, the historians Ranke and Raumer,[557] and he discussed his favorite subject, the codification of law, with Savigny. The same subject was considered also in 1840 with Thibaut at Heidelberg, where Sumner spent "five delightful weeks." Here he was also shown particular attentions by Mittermeier, with whom he had already had much correspondence upon legal matters before leaving America.[558]

During the period of his editorial connection with the *American Jurist* Sumner invited Mittermeier to write for the journal, and Mittermeier contributed several articles.[559] From time to time Mittermeier wrote directly to Sumner concerning prison discipline, capital punishment, penal jurisprudence, public administration, and codification, and Sumner kept him abreast of important American developments in these fields by sending him the latest publications.[560] Sumner performed a similar service for Dr. Julius, the Heidelberg criminologist and translator of Ticknor's *History of Spanish Literature*, whom he had met in the United States in 1835 and whom he visited in Berlin in 1857.[561]

Upon Sumner's return to the Senate in 1859, he became intimate with Rudolph Schleiden, Minister from the Hanseatic towns during 1853–1864. Although Schleiden had little sympathy for antislavery principles, Sumner placed a high value upon the opinions of this shrewd observer of world affairs, and together they discussed "American and foreign politics, as well as literature and art."[562] The effect of all these contacts was not to change radically Sumner's political views, which remained basically English in origin; but he was an important agent in disseminating among Americans information regarding the developments of political theory in Germany and in securing a hearing in America for Lieber's idealistic system of political science.

The course of German political theory in the United States beyond these early figures becomes complicated. It merits specialized analysis, and lies outside the province of this study. It has been charted briefly in an essay by Professors Thomas I. Cook and Arnaud B. Leavelle through Lieber, Whitman, the St. Louis Hegelians, O. A. Brownson, Elisha Mulford, Theodore D. Woolsey, John W. Burgess, W. W. Willoughby, Joseph A. Leighton, George Howison, Josiah Royce, and Wm. E. Hocking.[563] It is discussed at greater length by Professor Charles B. Robson[564] and Miss Anna Haddow.[565] We shall also have to forego a discussion of the historiographical influence of Germans like Möser, Heeren, Niebuhr, Ranke, Meinicke, Treitschke, Spengler, and others like Herder, Schlegel, and Hegel upon American historians from Bancroft to Turner;[566] and individuals like Eduard F. Rivinus, Johann Georg and Robert W. Wesselhoeft, Franz J. Grund, Franz W. Gräter, and August Konradin must be passed over while we turn to the more influential American-born scholars who bent their efforts to introducing German thought into America.

MOSES STUART

Among the first active workers falling into this category was Moses Stuart (1780–

1852), who in 1810 was called to the professorship of sacred literature in the newly established stronghold of Calvinism, the theological seminary at Andover, Mass. He speedily became dissatisfied not only with the state of American theological study at the time but equally with his own insufficient scholarship.[567] Recognizing the necessity of knowing somewhat of Hebrew, he consulted Schleissner's *Lexikon*, the German terms of which troubled him and aroused his desire to add German to his theological tools. After securing the necessary books, he professed having made enough progress in a fortnight to read the Gospel of St. John in the German. With the aid of a friend he secured Seiler's *Biblische Hermeneutik*, which supplied him with the suggestions and references necessary to collect for the seminary the best library of German Biblical literature in America at the time.[568] His search for books brought contacts with others who shared his interests, among them young Edward Everett, with whom he began corresponding in 1812. He urged Everett to make a translation of Herder's *Briefe das Studium der Theologie betreffend*, encouraged him in his ambition to study in Germany, and commissioned him to buy German books for him.[569] In 1829, when Follen visited Stuart, Follen reported finding "more German books in the library than elsewhere in the country."[570] Since Follen was, of course, thoroughly familiar with the contents of the library in Cambridge, Stuart must have been pleased by Follen's estimate, especially considering what it had been a decade earlier. But he was soon to learn that there were others less happy than Follen about his success in building up a good German theological library at Andover.

Having concluded that thoroughness was not to be attained without mastering, first the Hebrew texts and next the German commentaries, Stuart published, for the benefit of his own and of theological students generally, a *Grammer of the Hebrew*

Language, without Points (Andover, 1813) and a *Grammar of the Hebrew Language, with Points* (Andover, 1821).[571] He introduced Rosenmüller and De Wette in his classes; he translated and published a collection of *Dissertations on the Importance and Best Methods of Studying the Original Languages of the Bible, by Jahn and Others* (Andover, 1821); and he translated, for the use of his students, from the Latin of J. A. Ernesti, *The Elements of Interpretation . . . with Notes and Appendices* (Andover, 1822), which included extracts from Kiel, Beck, and Morus. But if he encountered difficulties teaching his students Hebrew and interesting them in German and the German theologians, he found it harder still to convince his colleagues of the need to emulate German methods. Nothing daunted, he battered against entrenched opposition with a series of some forty books and brochures, none of which failed, by direct statement or pointed implication, to champion the cause of German Biblical research. In the course of twenty years he succeeded in breaking down much of the opposition. But he found, before he had gone very far, that he had aroused the suspicion and enmity of many of his colleagues:

It was whispered that I was not only secretly gone over to the Germans, but was leading the Seminary over with me, and bringing up, or at least encouraging our young men to the study of the deistical "Rationalism"; and besides this, it was also whispered about, in a very significant way, that it was as much as the other professors could do to keep the Seminary from going over to Unitarianism.[572]

Well might they whisper, for it was common knowledge that the study of German was dangerous. Did not the Unitarians of Cambridge and Boston favor it? Now, it appeared, one from among their own fold stood ready to deliver the last stronghold of Calvinism in the country into the hands of the enemy. In 1825 Stuart was investigated by the trustees of the seminary, whose committee reported that "the unrestrained cultivation of German studies has evidently tended to chill the ardor of piety, to impair belief in the fundamentals of revealed religion, and even to induce, for the time, an approach to universal skepticism."[573] Stuart denied the charges against himself as teaching heretical doctrines and against the Germans as being conducive to irreligion, at the same time pointing out that if the Unitarians had been led into any errors, it was by their reading the English deistical writers and not by their German studies, for of a serious study of the latter, he claimed, the Unitarians were as yet entirely innocent.[574]

It is obvious that in this claim Stuart was unaware of, or was minimizing, the growing tendency among the Unitarians, notably at Harvard, to read German theologians like Tholuck, De Wette, Hengstenberg, Paulus, and Schleiermacher; but it is also clear that his German studies were not making a Unitarian of him. How little he was being led by the German scholars, chief among whom were Ewald, Rosenmüller, and Gesenius, in the direction of Unitarianism may be gauged by his zealous defense of Trinitarianism against Dr. Channing's attack.[575] Indeed, Stuart's spirited Letter to Dr. Channing Containing Remarks on His Sermon Recently Preached in Baltimore (Andover, 1819) laid the worst fears of some of his colleagues. The extraordinary interest which this pamphlet aroused,[576] coupled with Stuart's assertion that he could not have written it without the aid of his German studies, helped dispel some of the opprobrium then usually heaped on German theology. For assuredly, if German philological research and Biblical investigation could be thus effectively brought to the defense of "true" religion, then perhaps it was not altogether vicious. For his part, Stuart set himself with renewed energy to facilitate the study of exegetical science in America by publishing, in addition to the books already mentioned, the following: (1) Ernesti's Elements of Interpretation,[577] (2) Georg B. Winer's Greek Grammar of the New Testament,[578] (3) Hebrew Chrestomathy, Designed as a Course of Hebrew Study,[579] (4) Practical Rules for Greek Accents and Quantity,[580] (5) Grammar of the New Testament Dialect,[581] and (6) Hebrew Grammar of Gesenius, as Edited by E. Roediger, Translated with Additions and Also a Hebrew Chrestomathy.[582]

His first important original work on Biblical criticism, a Commentary on the Epistle to the Hebrews (2 vols., Andover, 1828–1829),[583] demonstrated the excellent use to which these German tools could be put. The work won high repute for him as a Biblical scholar in America, in England, and even among the German theologians.[584] During the next quarter century he established himself as the undisputed leader in American exegetical science by publishing commentaries upon Romans,[585] Revelation,[586] Daniel,[587] Ecclesiastes,[588] and Proverbs[589]—all demonstrating in detail how German scholarship had revolutionized the field of Biblical criticism.[590]

Stuart's letter to the editor of the Christian Review on "The Study of the German Language,"[591] in reply to Barnas Sears's attack on the irreligious character of German literature published in an earlier number of the same journal,[592] sets forth his position on the value of German for American students of theology and suggests at the same time the reason for his success in breaking down the prejudice on the part of American theologians against German theology; for he was among the first to point out the use to which German theological science could be put in combatting the evil which men like Norton and Sears feared. The letter concludes with the observation that "it is not [now] so much a matter of praise to be acquainted with it [German], as of shame to be ignorant of it."

This essay was written in 1841. Though the institutional vis inertiae of American colleges still operated against a broad extension of the study of German, and though an occasional father still forbade his son to study the language for fear of corrupting his Calvinism or Unitarianism, as the case might be, the battle was all but won. Eleven years later, in 1852, when Stuart died, the smoke had cleared away, and F. B. Sanborn, entering Harvard that year, noticed that "the prejudice against German had worn itself out," and that "many studied it."[593] Moses Stuart must have derived considerable satisfaction from the knowledge that his efforts had not been in vain.[594] What he may have known also was that his labors had earned for him the title of "Father of Biblical Learning in America."[595] What he could not have estimated was the full extent of his influence upon the fifteen hundred American clergymen and the seventy-odd professors and presidents of American colleges who learned their theology at his feet.[596] One of his students, however, he had the pleasure of seeing follow in his own footsteps—James Marsh, whose discipleship bade fair to outstrip the success of the master, until his untimely death in 1842 cut short his brilliant career.

JAMES MARSH

James Marsh (1794–1842) came under the influence of Stuart in 1817 when, after graduating from Dartmouth College,[597] he decided to prepare himself for the ministry at Andover. After one year at the seminary, he returned as tutor to Dartmouth to spend two formative years. During this second Dartmouth period he became dissatisfied with the philosophy and theology he had been taught.[598] He determined to go to Cambridge, where he believed the advantages offered would be greater than those at Andover. However, after a stay of less than two months, he was back at Andover, by November, 1820, apparently satisfied that Andover provided as good opportunities as did Harvard. After all, Andover had Moses Stuart; Harvard, only Andrews Norton. He

set about the task of completing his theological training. Falling under the spell of Stuart's enthusiasm for exegetical studies, he resolved to make a critical study of the Old and New Testaments under Stuart's direction and to study modern languages and literatures. By January 21, 1821, he was satisfied with his knowledge of German.[599]

In search of the true belief, which should replace the religion of the day and "keep alive the heart in the head," at the same time that it brought "unity to all his knowledge,"[600] he rediscovered Coleridge's *Biographia Literaria*.[601] Coleridge struck him as having been remarkably successful in effecting what his own heart yearned for, namely, to "satisfy the heart as well as the head." The phraseology used here is reminiscent of a passage in Chapter X of the *Biographia Literaria*, in which Coleridge gave credit to Kant for bringing unity out of the chaotic state of his mind when his "head was with Spinoza" while his "whole heart remained with Paul and John." Taking the obvious hint from Coleridge, he reread his Plato and reanalyzed St. Paul. Since both Madame de Staël and Coleridge recommended Kant highly, he secured a copy of the *Kritik der reinen Vernunft* and searched it for "the certain guiding light" which Coleridge professed to have found in that work.[602] Here, in 1821, it would seem, we come upon a very early direct contact between Kant and the New England Transcendentalists. A contact it unquestionably is, but one not to be taken too seriously, as will appear hereafter in a letter, written eight years after this date, as well as in others of Marsh's writings.

Prompted by Stuart's urging him to study the Germans, Marsh went foraging into German literature, philosophy, and theology. By 1822 he had become perhaps the most widely read American-born student of German in this country,[603] and he promptly set out on a career of instructing Americans on the subject of German religious and philosophical progress. In 1822, he undertook, with a friend, to translate and edit Bellermann's *Geography of the Scriptures* (completed December, 1823). The next year he went to Hampden-Sydney College as a teacher of ancient and modern languages. During his three-year residence in Virginia he began his translation of Herder's *Spirit of Hebrew Poetry*, the first sections of which were published periodically in the *Christian Repository* at Princeton, although the whole did not appear until 1833.[604]

Marsh's election to the presidency of the University of Vermont in October, 1826, greatly enlarged the sphere of his influence. It marks the beginning of the Vermont School of Transcendentalism, whence the gospel was carried first, to Concord and Boston and later, westward as far as St. Louis. Marsh's inaugural address was the first published utterance of the Transcendentalists in America.[605] It left no doubt in the minds of his auditors that the new president of the University (which a series of unfortunate circumstances had reduced to the status of a struggling and generally ineffectual college) possessed a dynamic personality and a head chockful of Coleridgean ideas. For those who understood his inaugural address he became at once the American Coleridge. We cannot pause here to trace the influence which Marsh exerted on American collegiate education generally,[606] or to detail the steps by which he wrought a reformation in the University of Vermont, transforming it from a provincial college into the first academic center in America of the new idealistic philosophy. He caused to be adopted a new course of study,[607] the revolutionary nature of which has been described in these terms:

If this course of study is carefully examined, it will be found to contain perhaps, what no other Collegiate study in the United States has so fully attempted. It seeks to give coherence to the various studies, in each department, so that its

several parts shall present, more or less, the unity, not of an aggregation, nor of a juxtaposition, nor of a merely logical arrangement, but of a *development and a growth*; and therefore, the study of it, rightly pursued, would be a growing and enlarging process, to the mind of the student.[608]

Here was a program based on ideas caught from Herder and Coleridge, as the American edition of Coleridge's *Aids to Reflection*, just published by Marsh, made abundantly plain to all who put two and two together. If they read on in the prospectus, they discovered that the courses offered were, indeed, designed to effect an "enlarging process" in the minds of the students. Marsh's own department, that of philosophy, cut across departmental lines with splendid audacity, aiming at a transcending synthesis—it was to be the integrated integration; for Marsh, like Bacon, was equal to taking all learning for his province. The whole was based on the all-important distinction between Understanding and Reason, the significance of which Marsh never wearied of reiterating. Thus was born, between 1826 and 1829, the first American university drawn after the transcendental pattern. It was Kant, Herder, Schlegel, and Coleridge, as much as Marsh, who reorganized the University of Vermont and made it the first asylum for transcendental idealism in America.

In 1833 Marsh voluntarily resigned as president to take over the chair of Moral and Intellectual Philosophy, but it was an open secret that he remained, as long as he lived, the power behind the throne. Relieved of administrative duties, he now turned to what had always been his first love—his philosophical teaching. In the course of the sixteen years which he devoted to teaching, he developed from various sources what became known, among his students, as "Marsh's philosophy," the general composition of which has already been noted.

In the meantime Marsh had contributed

to the *Christian Spectator* for March, 1829, a review of Stuart's *Commentary on the Epistle to the Hebrews.* This, his most technical theological piece of writing, bears strong resemblances in both vocabulary and ideas to Coleridge—similarities to which Marsh himself called attention in a letter to Coleridge.[609] Nor did Marsh rest here. His next act was to present to the American public one of the works of the master himself from whom he had learned most. He had long wanted to edit a volume of selections from his beloved seventeenth-century divines. Such a book, he believed, might be able to counteract the "materialism" of his age. Coleridge's *Aids*, with its long extracts from Archbishop Leighton and Dr. Henry More, seemed ideally suited for that purpose.[610] Accordingly he set to work upon an American edition. To it he prefixed a fifty-five–page "Preliminary Essay," which Professor Nicolson calls the first publication of American Transcendentalism.[611] Its exposition of Coleridgean doctrine, together with the accompanying text, Rufus W. Griswold credits with giving to the orthodox of New England their first serious shock.[612]

That Marsh, born a Vermonter, trained in a Calvinistic seminary, knew what he was about in going beyond even Unitarianism to sponsor the Transcendentalism of Coleridge, as presented in *Aids to Reflection*, appears in his opening remarks:

I must not be supposed ignorant of its bearing upon those questions which have so often been, and still are, the prevailing topics of theological controversy among us . . . . I have not attempted to disguise from myself, nor do I wish to disguise from the readers of this work, the inconsistency of some of its leading principles with much that is taught and received in our theological circles (pp. x–xi).

Candid as this statement is, his treatment of Coleridge's book and its significance is no less so. He wastes no words in getting to the main point that he wishes to make, namely,

that *"Christian faith is the perfection of human reason."*[613] This principle leads him at once to the fundamental and all-important distinction against which all philosophy and all theology must be squared—the distinction between Reason and Understanding.[614]

Marsh's argument regarding the momentous effect and far-reaching implications of this distinction need not be rehearsed here. More to our purpose is what is not easily determined, namely, his interpretation of the two terms, as it comes out incidentally in the "Essay" and more particularly in the Notes. Marsh, like Coleridge before him, has often been accused of inaccuracy and of inconsistency in the use of philosophic terms.[615] On this score, such evidence as the "Preliminary Essay" affords would seem to argue exactly the contrary. Indeed, the "Essay" exists chiefly to point out the current misconceptions regarding reason as they have grown out of the philosophy of Locke,[616] and according to which the reason, "considered as a thing differing in kind from the understanding, has no place in our popular metaphysics." "Thus we have only *understanding*, 'the faculty judging according to sense,' a faculty of abstracting and generalizing, of contrivance and forecast, as the highest of our intellectual powers."[617]

In this restriction of our common terminological and philosophical conceptions lie, says Marsh, the popular objections raised against Coleridge's "peculiarities of language" and "the unintelligibleness of his thoughts" (p. xlvii). The first is not a peculiarity referable solely to Coleridge, but arises from the common confusion of usage derived from Locke and the Scottish school. Should Coleridge, therefore, "still use these words indiscriminately, and either invent a new word, or mark the distinction by descriptive circumlocutions, or shall he assign a more distinctive and precise meaning to the words already used ?" The question is rhetorical.

The charge that Coleridge is unintelligible, he says, can be answered in only one way, namely, not to answer it at all; for the critics who bring this charge are either prejudiced against him or feel that his philosophy is "too deep for them"; whence we may conclude that they mean to insinuate, spite of all their professed love of truth, either that there are depths in philosophy "not worth exploring" or that they prefer "to sleep after dinner" (p. xlix). The simple truth is that Coleridge is in no wise to blame if his subject is one requiring "labour both of attention and of severe thinking." Indeed, among the four objectives aimed at in the book, his first and chief aim is "to direct the reader's attention to the Science of Words, their use and abuse, and the incalculable advantages attached to the habit of using them appropriately, and with a distinct knowledge of their primary, derivative, and metaphysical senses."[618] The success achieved by Coleridge in this respect is insisted upon by Marsh a number of times; and if the reader will bear in mind, says Marsh, that Coleridge uses terms like *reason, understanding, free will,* and *conscience* in a "precise, exclusive, and steadfast sense," the chief cause of his supposed obscurity will be removed.[619] Later he revised his high opinion of Coleridge's perspicuity. His biographer tells us that Marsh awaited impatiently the appearance of Coleridge's promised treatise on "Elements of Discourse," which went the way of so many of Coleridge's promised performances.[620]

In view of his well-established character for probity, Marsh's assertions that about 1829 he understood, or thought he understood, Coleridge's distinctions must be taken at face value. The problem therefore resolves itself into the questions of (1) whether Marsh failed, his belief to the contrary, in his understanding of Coleridge, or (2) whether Coleridge drew the distinctions correctly. Some doubt has been cast upon the trustworthiness of Coleridge as an expositor of Kant by reason of his apparent reliance, in some of his works, rather upon the seventeenth-century divines than upon Kant for his definitions.[621] Some support, too, may be given to this idea by Marsh's statement:

In most cases, where his language may at first seem wholly unauthorized, it will be found, that he derived it from those profound thinkers and unrivalled masters of language, the great English Philosophers and Divines of the Seventeenth Century.[622]

Here it may be observed, first, that one element—a very important one—in Marsh's thought which must never be overlooked is that of neo-Platonism, theologically interpreted; for Marsh found in the seventeenth-century Cambridge Platonists most of the important ideas which his own and the next generation felt were peculiar to German romanticism. Thus he was led by his fondness for the Cambridge Platonists to overemphasize Coleridge's making them major objects of reference in his *Aids,* and, in the absence of any exhaustive firsthand knowledge of Kant himself, to defer too much to Coleridge's interpretation of Kant and to overestimate the influence upon Coleridge of the Cambridge Platonists. What he seems to have overlooked is Coleridge's frank avowal in the *Biographia Literaria* that his studies in the mystics and neo-Platonists had done little more for him than "to keep alive the heart in the head," and thus prepared him for an understanding and acceptance of Kant, at the same time saving him from "irreligious Pantheism"; whereas Kant is credited with having drawn the all-important distinction between Understanding and Reason by which Coleridge professes to have equated his own thinking.[623] However, since Coleridge nowhere, in the *Aids,* specifically mentioned Kant as having originated the distinctions, but referred them also to Bacon and Leighton as having, in a measure, anticipated Kant by setting forth the essentials of these distinctions, Marsh was easily led to overstate the case. That it is an overstatement appears from the fact that Coleridge himself seldom cited Bacon and Leighton on Reason and Understanding without finding it necessary, in some detail, to correct their language in order to make it harmonize with the critical terminology of Kant.[624]

The precise relationship of thought between the Cambridge idealists and the German transcendentalists is still being debated. The correct answer doubtless depends on the degree and kind of parallelism insisted upon. Modern scholarship is coming to the conclusion that the differences are more apparent than real—that there is less difference in spirit than in letter—thus essentially substantiating what Coleridge seemed to imply and what Marsh asserted. Of a close coincidence or identity of thought it is impossible to speak (indeed, neither Coleridge nor Marsh went so far), for the terminological differences, to say nothing of the divergences of aims, between the seventeenth-century theologians at Cambridge and the critic of metaphysics at Königsberg are too obvious.[625]

For Marsh, the "New Movement" in Germany appears to have been not new so much as a necessary and right revival of the thought already implicit in his beloved English divines, although he did not emphasize, in his edition of Coleridge's *Aids*, the sharp differences between the spirit of German and English idealism, or, to put it more accurately, between native English thought and the thought of Coleridge as derived from the Germans.[626] Hence he held that *so far as its relation to theology was concerned*, the new philosophy of Germany, or, for that matter, Coleridge's interpretation of it, was not so much something apart from seventeenth-century British thought as an interesting parallel to and extension of it.

Another consideration to be borne in mind is that philosophy for Marsh was worth while chiefly as the handmaid in the development of a satisfactory theology.

Like the Cambridge Platonists, he was less interested in founding a new philosophy, apart from theology, than to bring the two into harmony. Like them, too, he was more vitally interested in ethics than metaphysics.[627] Hence, after he had grasped what he considered the correct distinction between Understanding and Reason, the theoretical argument of Kant's Critiques held little of vital interest for him; what was more to his liking was the wide and practical application to which the distinction could be put in theology and morality.[628] Thus it is extremely hard to determine precisely what Marsh's conception of the Kantian distinction was. Although he asserted, on the one hand, that all that was needful for a proper understanding of the terms was to grasp the interpretation of Bacon and of Leighton, yet in practice (e.g., in the "Preliminary Essay," as well as in the Notes and Appendices) he went beyond the meaning of the seventeenth-century writers by subscribing to definitions which, refurbished as they were by Coleridge in a Kantian terminology,[629] Bacon and Leighton would have had trouble identifying as their own. Marsh concurred completely with the Coleridgean interpretation as presented in the *Aids* and added numerous passages from others of Coleridge's works to elucidate the Coleridgean meaning.[630]

Nothing short of a close examination of all these commentaries by Marsh, together with a comparison of their import in Coleridge's text, suffices to determine how accurately Marsh followed Coleridge and, through him, Kant. Such a search substantiates abundantly the fact that Marsh, following Coleridge, is usually accurate in interpreting Kant in approximately the same degree that Coleridge is so. For example, following Coleridge, he is faithful to the letter in interpreting the Kantian Reason as a faculty above Understanding, grasping correctly Kant's direct statement: "All knowledge begins with the senses, proceeds thence to the understanding, and ends with reason";[631] although it is obvious that Kant had no intention of conveying quite the meaning which Marsh extracts from the statement, namely, that the Reason begins to function at the point where the Understanding leaves off.

Here it is worth remembering that Marsh was not only a sincere Christian but also an attentive reader of Aristotle, whose *Metaphysics* was always by him. John Dewey summarizes Marsh's philosophy as "an Aristotelian version of Kant made under the profound conviction of the inherent *moral* truths of the teaching of Christianity."[632] While this characterization is too summary, as Dewey himself admits, there is a large element of truth in what he says; for it was not only Fries[633] but also the Aristotelian tradition as well as contemporary scientific writers, notably the Schellingian physicist Oersted and the psychologist Carus, whose doctrines of natural development were responsible for Marsh's comparative neglect of Kant's phenomenalism and the subjective view of nature and for the equivocal manner in which Marsh dealt with the Understanding and Reason.[634]

What goes even deeper is Marsh's treatment of the relations of Sense to Understanding and of both to Reason. It should be said in extenuation of the too ready facility with which Marsh presents the Reason as based on the Understanding, and the Understanding as growing out of Sensation, that had he consulted Kant's first *Critique*, he could have found plenty of parallel passages to justify such a view; for Kant, in several instances, uses a phraseology which easily lent itself to such a construction.[635] The danger (of which Marsh seems not to have been aware, and concerning which Coleridge neglected to warn him)—the danger lies in taking an introductory statement of Kant at face value without considering the explanations, elucidations, and qualifications that follow. Another defect in Marsh's method appears to have been that he followed Coleridge rather uncritic-

ally and therefore failed to recognize in Coleridge certain oversights and certain liberties that Coleridge took with Kant's text, as when he defined the Understanding as the "faculty judging according to sense."[636] The errors which arise from such generalizations,[637] however, are not as detrimental as are those arising from another cause—the inability of the mind untrained in the critical methodology to keep the critical transcendental way throughout. This is illustrated in Marsh's failure to distinguish always clearly between *a posteriori* and *a priori* methods[638]— a distinction which Kant makes the very foundation of his criticism. Apparently Marsh failed to keep steadily in mind the point which Kant had enforced in the Introduction to his *Critique of Pure Reason*, namely, that "a priori knowledge" must be kept "*perfectly pure*," and that "Transcendental philosophy is the wisdom of pure speculative reason."[639] Marsh uses terms like *logical faculty, intuition, reflection,* and *reason* not only loosely but at times interchangeably for something which, in Kant's sense, none of them is.[640] Coleridge is not guiltless of a similarly loose use of terms. For example, when he says, "Reason indeed is far nearer *Sense* than Understanding: for Reason . . . is a direct aspect of Truth, an inward Beholding, having a similar relation to the Intelligible or Spiritual, as Sense has to the Material or Phenomenal," he is (1) saying what may lead the uninitiated to believe that he imputes to the Reason a direct, sensual, empirical, or *a posteriori* basis which Kant did not admit into the transcendental system in the first instance, or (2) ascribing to pure Reason the immediacy of vision and consequently either some mystical or constitutive power which Kant emphatically denied, or (3) transgressing the boundary of pure Reason and entering the domain of the practical Reason, or (4) attempting to say (and this we may credit as being his intention) that the pure Reason has a certain primacy or directness similar to that which sensibility enjoys in respect to its intuition. At all events, he has not said anything profoundly helpful to the novice, while his use of popular and variously interpreted terms tends merely to compound misconceptions in the mind of the general reader.

Finally, we suspect in Marsh, as in Coleridge, an all-too-ready transition in his thinking from the realm of speculative Reason to that of practical Reason, from metaphysics to ethics,[641] and consequently from transcendental to transcendant principles.[642] Religious-minded as both Coleridge and Marsh were, they were less patient to consider the severe limitations of the pure Reason than impatient to substantiate their faith in the three Ideas of the Reason (God, immortality, and freedom) by the so-called "proofs" of the practical Reason, without always heeding Kant's clear warning regarding the "brilliant pretensions of reason."[643] They were less interested in the "records and full details" of the "lawsuit"[644] which Kant brought against Reason to prove the insufficiency of transcendental philosophy, in its purely speculative applications, to establish the validity of its three Ideas beyond their existence as Ideas merely (however great its service might be, as Kant pointed out, "to correct our knowledge of them if they can be acquired from elsewhere")[645] than they were eager to follow the processes by which the practical Reason, starting from the moral order as a unity founded on the essence of freedom, "traces the design of nature to grounds which must be inseparably connected *a priori* with the internal possibility of things and leads thus to *transcendental theology*, which takes the ideal of the highest ontological perfection as the principle of systematical unity that connects all things according to general and necessary laws, as having their origin in the absolute necessity of the one original Being."[646] Their hearts intent primarily on the latter, and their main purpose to ground their theology in

philosophy, they readily made the unifying synthesis which Kant hinted at in the conclusion of his *Critique of Pure Reason* and came at once to the point where "practical and speculative Reason become united."[647] By a process natural to the romanticist, they relegated the pure Reason and its annoying negations to the realm of the forgotten, and spoke, whenever they spoke of the practical Reason simply as the Reason, usually without the prosaic adjective.[648] Thus Coleridge, in his popular works (although he drew the distinction clearly enough[649]) commonly failed, once he had drawn it,[650] to keep the distinctive terminology; while men of less acute philosophic understanding, coming after him, either failed to understand Coleridge or—if they did understand him—failed to make distinctions among terms. Thence arise some of the difficulties we encounter in attempting to reconstruct the speculative thinking of men like Marsh who seem, at several points, to waver in their meaning, chiefly because Coleridge, however dutifully they tried to follow him, had not sufficiently enforced the significance of such Kantian warnings as the following:

Thus we find that pure reason, which at first seemed to promise nothing less than extension of our knowledge beyond all limits of experience, contains, if properly understood, nothing but regulative principles, which indeed postulate greater unity than the empirical use of the understanding can achieve, but which, by the very fact that they place the goal which has to be reached at so great a distance, carry the argument of the understanding with itself by means of systematical unity to the highest possible degree; while, if they are misunderstood or mistaken for constitutive principles of transcendent knowledge, they produce, by a brilliant but deceptive illusion, some kind of persuasion and imaginary knowledge, but, at the same time, constant contradictions and disputes.[651]

While Marsh had begun to read the *Critique of Pure Reason* as early as 1821, there is little to indicate that he comprehended (if, indeed, he ever read thus far) the solemn warning of Kant's sentence, the torturous sinuosity of which, in the original German, even Max Müller's ability as a translator did not materially alleviate.

The word *regulative* in the passage just quoted from Kant suggests the cause of another error perpetrated by uncritical followers of Kant. On the point that the proper use of the pure reason permits only regulative, never constitutive, uses, Kant insists repeatedly.[652] That Marsh was acquainted with the distinctions between the terms *transcendent* and *transcendental* as they are used by Kant appears from Marsh's addition of a note,[653] based on his reading of Chapter XII of the *Biographia*. But we can understand why he encountered difficulties (in the absence of Coleridge's failure, in either the *Biographia* or the *Aids*, to emphasize the question whether the Ideas of the Pure Reason belong to the constitutive or the merely regulative order)[654] in his efforts to understand the speculative foundation work upon which (as he understood it) the Reason supports the mandates of religion. When we add to this the difficulties inherent in the problem of distinguishing consistently between *a priori* and *a posteriori*, between reason with *constitutive* and reason with merely *regulative* uses, and between the *practical* and the *pure* reason, we have sufficient reasons for surmising the causes that led Marsh to write to Coleridge, on March 29, 1829, in a tone suggesting that there were, indeed, "some things hard to understand," and that he should welcome a work from Coleridge in which these complexities would be "unfolded from first principles in a manner suited to the novice."[655] While he wrote thus to Coleridge, he had no doubt whatever that Coleridge had drawn the distinctions correctly. In spite, therefore, of such questions as he privately confessed, he proceeded publicly, eight months later, when his edition of the *Aids* was published, to avow his complete confidence in the principles which the book stressed.

To return, now, to the "Preliminary Essay," we observe that Marsh lists Coleridge's next great service (after his explanation of the all-important distinction between reason and understanding) to be the reconciliation which Coleridge effected between religion and philosophy.[656] This reconciliation, says Marsh, the system of thought currently dominant in New England can never hope to make, for Locke and the Scottish school can only establish and defend the essential difference between what is *natural* and what is *spiritual*; they can never find rational grounds for the feeling of moral obligation, let alone make religion and philosophy of a piece.[657] Coleridgean transcendentalism, on the other hand, supplies the philosophy which satisfies the understanding and does not contradict or offend the reason. It satisfies the thinking man who demands to rise above doubt and confusion to a conception of religion which his understanding can find acceptable at all points, and which his reason will, at the same time, verify.[658] Here again Marsh has transcended the realm of the pure reason to that of the practical. To Marsh, as seemingly to Coleridge also, this transition from the former with its limitations to the latter with its assurances was too inviting to resist; and men like Emerson, who followed one or the other, seem at times equally careless or unconscious of the necessity for keeping sufficiently distinct the several domains presided over by the theoretical reason and the moral will.[659]

Marsh's early death was not solely responsible for his leaving his later philosophical writings in a fragmentary state. Something of his inability to develop the desired consistently Kantian philosophy is owing to his failure to grasp clearly and unmistakably the Kantian terminology. Although his later writings contain evidence that in some particulars he attained after 1829 to a better understanding of the Kantian position with regard to the tripartite mind than he had before that time, there is also evidence to argue that even if he had been completely successful in this respect, he would no doubt have modified the critical philosophy to suit what he considered the "higher" ends of philosophy.

However that may be, we know that shortly after publishing his edition of the *Aids*, Marsh felt that all was not well with his understanding of Kant, for in a letter to Coleridge, already mentioned, he frankly admitted:

The German philosophers, Kant and his followers, are very little known in this country; and our young men who have visited Germany have paid little attention to that department of study while there. I cannot boast of being wiser than others in this respect; for though I have read a part of Kant, it was under many disadvantages, so that I am indebted to your writings for the ability to understand what I have read of his works, and am waiting with some impatience for that part of your works which will aid more directly in the study of those subjects of which he treats. The same views are generally entertained in this country as in Great Britain, respecting German literature; and Stewart's *History of Philosophy* especially has had an extensive influence in deterring students from the study of their philosophy. Whether any change in this respect is to take place remains to be seen. To me it seems a point of great importance, to awaken among our scholars a taste for a more manly and efficient mental discipline, and to recall into use those old writers, whose minds were formed by a higher standard.[660]

Both the date (March, 1829) and the contents of this letter are significant as indicating, first, that Marsh's study of Coleridge's prose works published before 1829 had not succeeded in clearing up for him all the knotty problems which he sensed as attaching to Kant, and second, that he still looked to Coleridge to supply his wants in this respect. According to Torrey, Marsh had set himself the "grand object to prepare himself by reading and reflection, for taking a comprehensive view of all the parts of knowledge, as constituting a connected and organic whole, and to understand the relations and relative importance of the several parts."[661] Four parts, at least, of this comprehensive work, begun in 1832, were these: (1) a sketch of the general architectonic of philosophy, in which psychology, logic, ethics, metaphysics, physics, mathematics, etc. were to be related, one to another, in a way to demonstrate the "unity of human knowledge"; (2) remarks on physiology; (3) a psychology, which, following the advice of Dr. Follen,[662] was to be the propaedeutic to the entire philosophical organon; and (4) a logic, which should aid in this design by laying the necessary groundwork.[663]

These philosophical fragments were not published until a year after the death of Marsh, when Joseph Torrey collected them, together with several theological discourses, under the head of *Remains of the Rev. James Marsh . . . with a Memoir of His Life.* It is doubtful, therefore, that in the printed form they exerted any considerable influence. They are significant, however, as demonstrating (1) what Marsh taught in his classes, (2) what the derivation of some of those teachings was, and consequently (3) what modifications he made while interpreting German critical philosophy.

His attempted general organization of human knowledge comprises twenty-four pages as edited by Professor Torrey.[664] It is entitled "Letter to an Advanced Student. A Fragment," and bears the subtitle, "Outlines of a Systematic Arrangement of the Departments of Knowledge, with a View to their Organic Relations to Each Other in a General System." It begins with pseudo-Kantian definitions of Space and Time[665] and a discussion of *a priori* and *a posteriori* principles, and proceeds to a discussion of Metaphysical Principles of Natural Philosophy and Organic Life, but it affords no conclusive evidence bearing on his interpretation of Understanding and Reason, although Kant is several times referred to in the text as well as in the footnotes, suggesting that he had read as far as page 293 of the particular edition of the *Kritik der reinen Vernunft* he possessed.[666]

The "Remarks on Physiology"[667] has no other importance for our purpose than that of presenting the main principles which Marsh regarded as lying at the basis of that important science. He was in the habit of commencing his course in philosophy with a presentation of the principles sketched in these "Remarks." They serve to illustrate the importance which he attached to correlating philosophy with science. His views are the same that are hinted at by Coleridge and more fully exhibited in the works of the German Carus.[668]

The fragment of the "Psychology"[669] is at once the longest and the most helpful in any attempt to determine the question of how nearly Marsh approached Kant. It consists of ten chapters and a fragment of the eleventh. The arrangement suggests that he proposed to write a psychology on Kantian terms. The first five chapters are devoted to Sensation, and the next five to Understanding. Both sections are drawn faithfully enough after Kant, although the explanation of the Understanding is given without utilizing the Kantian categories or their applications. For a psychological work not designed as a critique of psychology, these first two divisions are adequate. It is in the eleventh and last chapter, where the Reason is introduced, that we are primarily interested. Up to this point even a rigorous critic of the Kantian school might raise little more than minor objections to individual statements or details. The moment, however, that Marsh reaches the point at which he attempts a definition of Reason and an explanation of its attributes and functions, the critic experiences trouble commensurate with those which Marsh himself appears to have encountered. Significantly, only seven pages of this chapter (*ibid.*, pp. 360–67) were written, and here the "Psychology" abruptly ends.

A nearer examination of this fragmentary chapter reveals evidence that Marsh ran into a dilemma by which, when he sought to define Reason, it became either somewhat too much like a rarified form of Understanding or, when he attempted to use a freer terminology, too much a type of free intuition to accord with the meaning which he sensed Kant had given to it. The same difficulty that frustrated his efforts in distinguishing between Understanding and Reason in the *Aids* still dogged his steps. He still failed to see them as disparate faculties, and he still saw the former as supplying the materials for the latter to work on. Hence he encountered difficulties in his efforts to explain why the truths in the realm of the one are transferable to that of the other. Unwilling to circumscribe the Reason by the severe limitations with which Kant's *Critique* had hedged it round, but ambitious to ascribe to the Reason the establishment, upon grounds of undisputed validity, of its Ideas of God, immortality, and free will, he found in the end the same insuperable chasm between matter and mind that Emerson was to discover when he sought to graft upon his essay on *Nature* another to be entitled *Spirit*.

A letter written at the time hints at the great difficulty. In it he speaks of the "novelities in terminology necessary to a thorough scientific system."[670] This terminology was wanting; and wanting that, he found his epistemology inconclusive, and the continuance of his work impossible. "He was waiting," says his biographer, "in hopes of deriving some assistance in respect to language from Coleridge's promised 'Elements of Discourse,'"[671] which never appeared. Thus he died before he could realize the object to which so much laborious study and serious reflection had been devoted—still "waiting with impatience," as he had writen to Coleridge in 1829, "for that part of your works which will aid more directly in the study of those subjects of which he [Kant] treats." What is singular, in view of Marsh's personality, is that he relied so largely upon Coleridge to supply him with a short cut to Kant when he might have resumed his firsthand study of Kant and thus gotten for himself what he had little reason to expect from Coleridge, who had never acknowledged or replied to his letter of 1829.[672] The alternative is to assume that having read his Kant and made the discovery that the Kantian Reason was incapable of accomplishing what Marsh had concluded it must be made to accomplish, he had given up Kant (though this is unlikely in view of his repeated references to Kant as his authority) and was waiting for Coleridge, or a light from some other source, to supply what was lacking.

One other circumstance helps explain the inconclusiveness of Marsh's philosophizing. It arises from the fact that he had been led, by Follen, into too great an admiration for Fries, and that he appears not to have recognized the points at which Kant and Fries were at variance.[673] Any attempt to reconcile Kant with Fries and both with Coleridge could not produce anything but unsatisfactory results. These irreconcilable elements explain, as much as does Marsh's early death, the fragmentary nature of his philosophical accomplishments. The Friesian elements in his thinking, however, could have been communicated only to his students. His edition of the *Aids* was unaffected by them. Hence, so far as the general influence of Marsh on the Transcendentalists goes, we are more concerned with the Coleridgean than the Friesian version of Kant.

It is possible, of course, that there lies at bottom a deeper reason still for Marsh's incompleteness: that he purposely avoided identifying his thought, in his later efforts of thinking and writing, with Kant. It is hard to believe that Marsh's extraordinary fondness for Fries should have proceeded solely from Follen's enthusiasm for this neo-Kantian faith-philosopher. Marsh grew increasingly conservative during his later years. About 1836 the spirit of the times

had become displeasing to him, and many of his later comments represent the mind of a man who seeks criticism in theology less than piety in religion. It is possible, therefore, that the *pure faith of reason* which Fries offered appealed more strongly to him than the inadequacy of the Pure Reason of Kant, which was incapable of affirming anything concerning the soul's three great Ideas.

That Marsh had a vague sense of something lacking in Coleridge's metaphysics does not surprise us, who, after the lapse of more than a century, still find it difficult to interpret Coleridge satisfactorily on purely Kantian terms. It still requires the most attentive reading, together with careful research in Coleridge's unpublished manuscripts (all unavailable to Marsh), to understand that Coleridge not only grasped correctly the Kantian method of criticism but went beyond it in his attempt to make a higher synthesis, which may be likened to the similar and more successful attempt made by Hegel. Aside from Coleridge's too ready facility in shifting from the theoretical to the practical (and back again) and the terminological perplexities that he introduced, Coleridge nowhere, in a single work, developed a system of philosophy. His first American editor was left to piece it together as best he could. The works in which Coleridge planned to bring all into a central unity were never completed, and they remain to this day generally inaccessible manuscript fragments. What is more, he was not content merely to repeat and elucidate the Kantian aesthetic, analytic, and dialectic; he was ambitious to build, upon the basis of the Kantian analysis, a System of Pure Reason which Kant himself had preferred not to attempt. He was ambitious to go beyond Kant, yes, to correct him at certain points. With Fichte and with Schelling, he adopted the Kantian terminology and as much of the methodology as served his purpose; but like Fichte, he objected to Kant's unknown and unknowable *noumenon*, and like Schelling, he sought to close the gap in the Kantian dualism—to make philosophy all of one piece. The result was that his philosophy, as it came to his American disciples, combined, with the critical way of Kant, first, something of Fichte's Egoism, or Individuation, as Coleridge preferred to call it; second, larger portions of Schelling's theory of the Dynamic and of his trichotomy of subject-object-identity;[674] and third, his own deep-seated conviction regarding the true meaning and place of Individuality in the world both of nature and of man. In so far, therefore, as the American Transcendentalists of Vermont and Massachusetts derived their Kant from Coleridge, it was never a pure Kant, but always one with admixtures of Fichte, of Schelling, and of Coleridge himself.[675]

However inaccurately interpreted, Kantian idealism received through the medium of Coleridge and Marsh a considerable currency in America. Its effect was less dramatic than pervasive. Where Marsh's book failed to penetrate, the literary and theological journals carried the message in reviews and articles, for and against. During the ten years following the publication of Marsh's book, a great number of significant reviews appeared in the various American periodicals. Not to have an article, either laudatory or condemnatory, on Coleridge and German thought was to be behind the times. Among the earlier and more significant was one by Frederic Henry Hedge in the *Christian Examiner* for March, 1833;[676] among the later articles was one by Noah Porter in the *Bibliotheca Sacra* for February, 1847, on "Coleridge and his American Disciples." The latter indicates at once the influence of Coleridge and the growth of the Transcendental ferment. Porter's point of view is that of a theologian, in which capacity he finds much to object to in Coleridge, but he credits Coleridge with exerting a powerful influence in directing American thought.[677]

Marsh sought to reinforce the general influence of Coleridge in America by editing in 1830 *Selections from Old English Writers on Practical Theology*,[678] and by preparing a preface, in 1831, for the first American edition of *The Friend*.[679] Two years later appeared, in book form, Herder's *Spirit of Hebrew Poetry*[680] and four years later his translation of D. H. Hegewisch's *Introduction to Historical Chronology*.[681] In the last years of his life he returned to the "great work" which he had projected years before —the preparation of a comprehensive work on all forms of knowledge. His reorganization of the University of Vermont had been one step in this program; his edition of Coleridge, the article on Stuart's *Hebrews*, and his translation of Herder, three others; and now he set himself to write something fundamental on psychology and logic. These works were far from complete at his death in 1842.

When we reflect how heterodox Emerson's addresses before the Phi Beta Kappa Society and the Harvard Divinity School were considered by his comparatively liberal-minded Cambridge audience, we get some idea of the stir which Marsh must have provoked in Vermont ten years earlier. His success in carrying through his reforms of the University without a dissenting vote from his colleagues sufficiently emphasizes his forcefulness. The most effectual medium by which Marsh exerted his later influence was through his students. It is said that of the young men who attended his lectures, eighty-one became teachers, fourteen of them in colleges, and twelve became ministers—all of them distributed, according to an alumni report, in nearly every state of the union.[682] Twelve years after his death many of his former students gathered at their Alma Mater to celebrate the semi-centennial of the founding of the University. By 1864, when another alumni celebration was held, the center of Transcendentalism had swung to Concord and thence westward,[683] but the reports of the celebration leave no doubt that the students and alumni of the University of Vermont considered Marsh the originator and their university the fount of the movement which had, by that time, spread its influence throughout the land. No oration, poem, or address delivered on that occasion failed to pay tribute to Marsh's commanding personality, his Christian character, his literary achievements, his philosophical astuteness, his influence as a teacher, and his success in bringing the University into a prominent position of leadership.

CONVERS FRANCIS

With Convers Francis and Frederic Henry Hedge we reach firmer ground, for the evidence of their understanding of German thought and art is unequivocal, and their close contact with and influence upon the Transcendentalists is indisputable. In point of time, only Moses Stuart, among native Americans, anticipated them.

Older than the generation of Emerson and Parker, Convers Francis (1795–1863)[684] was revered by them as a student of the classics and of modern European literature. Scholarly and retiring, he was never conspicuous, nor was he regarded by the Transcendentalists as a representative apostle of the Newness; but, as being an "elder statesman," so to speak, he was accorded the honor of presiding at some of the meetings of the Transcendental Club. In this capacity, as well as through his essays and lectures, he contributed much toward a liberal reception of German thought in the United States. During the period of his active ministry he read widely and gained the reputation of being a veritable encyclopaedia of information on theological scholarship, particularly of German theology.[685] His interest in German was more that of the theologian than the philosopher. There is no indication that he read far into Kant's criticism or his followers' transcendental speculations. Like others of his generation, he was content to take on trust the gener-

ally current opinion among the progressive party that German transcendentalism had re-enthroned religion on a sound philosophical basis, without inquiring into the precise steps by which this re-enthronement had been effected.

Francis enjoyed a wide personal popularity both before and during the period of his teaching career at Harvard. When Parker went to Watertown in 1832, he found in Francis a man of liberal and undogmatic views who stood ready to help him in his ambition to acquire a knowledge of German thought both by teaching him and by lending him books from his well-stocked library.[686] As early as 1836 Francis prognosticated correctly that the recent pronouncements of men like Ripley, Brownson, Alcott, Furness, and Emerson indicated that the "spiritualists" were taking the offensive and carrying the field. Francis himself was on the side of the insurgents, the spiritualists, the German school, the Transcendentalists.[687] His successive classes of divinity students imbibed from him a stimulus and direction that carried them into the ranks of the Transcendentalists. This shaping influence is discernible in the life and work of such students of his as Samuel Johnson, Samuel Longfellow, and Thomas Wentworth Higginson. Yet he was a Transcendentalist with a difference. He was, on the whole, a gentleman scholar of the eighteenth-century stamp, a bibliophile, and an antiquarian, possessing a tolerant personality; he was too old to be aroused to flaming enthusiasm by the influx of romantic feeling. While he presided at the conclaves of the Transcendentalists, at once the confidant and adviser of a host of Emersonians, he retained the good will and friendship of conservatives like N. L. Frothingham and Andrews Norton. He actively participated in the Transcendental movement so long as it confined itself mainly to idealistic discussion, but when the plans for propagandism and schemes for social reorganization were agitated, he quietly withdrew, yet continued to follow closely the fortunes of his younger, enthusiastic friends. By temperament, he was less zealous than the younger men in the cause of insurgent idealism, but his sister once said to him what seems to sum up his position very neatly: "You have the highest peaks of your mind at least a little gilded with transcendentalism." "A conscientious natural eclectic," he revered Emerson and loved Parker as men, but he disagreed with the former on many points and regretted what seemed to him sarcastic, arrogant, derisive, and destructive in the work as well as the manner of the latter. Less dynamic than thoughtful, he contented himself with exercising an inspirational and shaping influence, rather than himself assuming, offensively or defensively, an active role in this latest idealistic crusade.[688]

FREDERIC HENRY HEDGE

A colleague who took a more energetic course, both practically and theoretically, and who delved relatively deeper into the intricacies of the German speculative science was Frederic Henry Hedge (1805–1890).[689] Educated as he was chiefly in Germany, he early became known as "Germanicus" Hedge, and was one of the principals in the great drama of progressive thought which the diverse and stimulating ideas from abroad helped to produce in New England during the fourth and fifth decades of the last century, for among the native sons of New England he was one of the few who could speak authoritatively on matters pertaining to German philosophy.[690] His sympathy with the spirit and ideas of Kant, Fichte, and Schelling, whom he continued to read, was a tendency of mind that displayed itself while he was still a student in the Harvard Divinity School, and it may well have been communicated to Emerson during their period of close association while fellow-students there. This enthusiasm for German thought he transmitted to Margaret Fuller, James F. Clarke, Theodore Parker, and George Ripley. Hedge's perso-

nal influence in communicating his knowledge of German philosophy to these thoughtful and earnest young people has never been evaluated. Higginson, one of the later generation of Transcendentalists, spoke of him as "a fountain of knowledge in the way of German," and "the best trained and most methodical of the early Transcendentalists." Obviously, they were not entirely without guidance in their efforts to grasp the new thoughts which Coleridge and Carlyle were praising and making some attempts to explain.[691]

As early as 1833, when Emerson first planned a "periodical paper," he thought well enough of Hedge to want his assistance.[692] By 1835, Hedge seems to have become the prime mover for the establishment of a journal on the plan of the *Dial*, which did not come into immediate existence, we may believe, mainly because Hedge was to be the editor, and because in that year the editor-elect was called from among his confreres to the ministerial charge at Bangor, Maine. In 1836, however, he attended the bicentennial celebration at Harvard. After the exercises, he fell into conversation with Emerson and Ripley regarding the state of thought and religion in the churches in general and the fate of the projected journal in particular. This was the preliminary meeting of the Transcendental Club, also variously called the Symposium, the Club, the Hedge Club, and Hedge's Club—in deference to his priority of knowledge of German philosophy, his arrival in town being an informal notification to the several subscribers to the Newness of another gathering to be held.[693] That the personal influence of Hedge had a good deal to do with popularizing German philosophy among the Transcendentalists may be surmised from his wide contacts with them. His essay on Coleridge was the first clear and specific exposition of Kant, Fichte, and Schelling published in the United States by a native-born American. The essay itself, comprising twenty-one pages, was occasioned by the American editions of the *Biographia Literaria* (1817), Marsh's editions of the *Aids* (1829) and *The Friend* (1831), and the three-volume London edition of Coleridge's *Poetical Works* (1829). "Coleridge's Literary Character" forms the subject of the first ten pages, near the end of which Coleridge's reflective and critical powers are assessed,[694] logically followed by a consideration of his stature as a philosopher and of his relation to German transcendentalism. Deploring Coleridge's failure to write more precisely when discussing the critical philosophy, Hedge proceeds to the main object of his essay— "a few explanatory remarks respecting German metaphysics, which seem . . . to be called for by the present state of feeling among literary men in relation to this subject."[695] The sequel demonstrates Hedge's firsthand knowledge of Kant's *Critiques*, of Fichte's *Wissenschaftslehre*, and of Schelling's *System des transcendentalen Idealismus*, quite independent of any reliance upon Coleridge or Carlyle.

Indeed, the next eight pages present as luminous and comprehensive an exposition of the basic tenets of Kant, Fichte, and Schelling, and of the general import of their systems as can easily be incorporated in so short a space. German philosophy, he says, is the expression of just such a tendency as characterizes the present age in this country, when, passing from a state of spontaneous production to a state of reflection, men are particularly disposed to inquire concerning themselves and their destination, the nature of their being, the evidence of their knowledge, and the ground of their faith—when they are "striving after information on subjects which have been usually considered as beyond the reach of human intelligence."[696]

But transcendental philosophy does not seek immediately to answer these questions: "It seeks not to explain the existence of God and creation, objectively considered, but to explain our knowledge of their

existence." Moreover, Kant did not himself create a system, but furnished the hints and materials from which all the systems of his followers have been formed." Kant, as the father of the critical philosophy, aimed to do no more than develop the preparatory or "propaedeutic" branches of the science,[697] leaving to Fichte, Schelling, and Hegel the creation of the system itself. Among them, there was developed a transcendental point of view as well as a philosophy which Hedge describes as one of "interior consciousness . . . of spirit and form, substance and life, free will and fate, God and eternity." Their attempt to test what is called "*a priori* knowledge" is only an inquiry "concerning themselves and their destination. . . a striving after information on subjects which have been usually considered as beyond the reach of human intelligence, an attempt to penetrate into the hidden mysteries of our being."[698] However synthetical the *method* of some of Kant's successors, the Kantian critical method itself is analytical; and the *result*, "the last step in the process, the keystone of the fabric, is the deduction of time, space, and variety, or . . . the establishing of a coincidence between the facts of ordinary experience and those which we have discovered within ourselves, and scientifically derived from our first fundamental position." And this, Hedge argues, "is not a skeptical philosophy; it seeks not to overthrow, but to build up; it wars not with the common opinions and general experience of mankind, but aims to place these on a scientific basis, and to verify them by scientific demonstration." After re-emphasizing the revolutionary significance of the Kantian search for *a priori* principles, Hedge points out that the followers of Kant did not long content themselves with the analytical method, with the merely epistemological problems, but soon adopted the "synthetical, proceeding from a given point, the lowest that can be found in consciousness, and deducing from that point 'the whole world of intelligences, with the whole system of their representations."[699]

This system, characterized in a manner to suggest that he had Schelling in mind, received its preparation at the hands of Fichte, who stood midway between Kant and Schelling. Already in Fichte there is "an alternation of synthesis and analysis." There follows a brief but precise statement of Fichte's demonstration of the "identity of consciousness" in the *Wissenschaftslehre* (pp. 122–23). But Fichte's tendency toward skepticism repels Hedge; Fichte's egoism, moreover, based on his axiom "I am I," whence he derived "I am all" (*Ich ist Alles*), was more than Hedge was prepared to accept. Fichte, he concludes, is "altogether too subjective" (p. 124).

The objective idealism of Schelling, as contrasted with the subjective idealism of Fichte, is more to Hedge's mind, Schelling's converse proposition by which "All is I" (*Alles ist Ich*) being more in the nature of objective universalization. Of all the Germans who have built upon the foundations of Kantian epistemology, Schelling, the "ontologist of the Kantian school" and the "projector of the *natural* philosophy," is the "most satisfactory."[700] "If Fichte confined himself too exclusively to the subjective, Schelling on the other hand treats principally of the object, and endeavors to show that the outward world is of the same essence with the thinking mind, both being different manifestations of the same divine principle." Going on to Schelling's *Transcendentaler Idealismus*, Hedge points out that "all knowledge, according to him, consists in an agreement between the object and the subject. In all science, therefore, there are these two elements or poles, subject and object, or nature and intelligence; and corresponding to these two poles there are two fundamental sciences, the one beginning with nature and proceeding upward to intelligence, the other beginning with intelligence and ending in nature. The first is natural philosophy; the second, transcendental philosophy."[701]

This passage in the *Christian Examiner* for March, 1833 (XIV, i 125), which Emerson found on his desk immediately upon his return from Europe, was something to his purpose for the book which he had begun aboard ship. In it he found stated, in terms the echoes of which are obvious in several sections of *Nature* (1836), the entire range of ideas which he soon set himself to elaborate in two essays—one on "Nature" and another on "Spirit," although the latter was never to be written and published in its projected form.

Hedge does not profess to more than he knows, and does not attempt to go beyond the three books before him: Kant's *Kritik der reinen Vernunft*, Fichte's *Wissenschaftslehre*, and Schelling's *Transcendentaler Idealismus*. While he admits that "the immediate, and if we may so speak, the incalculable results of their speculations . . . are chiefly under the head of method," yet there are to be mentioned also "the sharp and rigidly dividing lines that have been drawn within and around the kingdom of human knowledge; the strongly marked distinctions of subject and object, reason and understanding, phenomena and noumena;—the categories established by Kant; the moral liberty proclaimed by him as it had never been proclaimed by any before; the authority and evidence of law and duty as set forth by Fichte; the universal harmony illustrated by Schelling" (p. 126). These "direct results of the critical philosophy . . . by no means exhaust all that philosophy has done for liberty and truth," for the "excellence" which Germany has attained "in science, in history, or poetry is mainly owing to the influence of her philosophy . . . in a word to the transcendental method."[702] Its richness is immediately and noticeably evident in the theological writings of Coleridge, which President Marsh has labored so effectively to give currency. And thus Hedge closes with a tribute to Coleridge's "intellect of the highest order" and his success as an expositor of German philosophy—for, adds Hedge, "as a translator, he has not his equal in English literature" (p. 128).

Enthusiastically as he expresses himself for German philosophy, Hedge himself was neither Kantian nor Hegelian;[703] he studiously avoided identifying himself with any particular school, except that he could always be found on the side of the idealists and opposed to the sensationalists, experimentalists, and realists.[704] As a preacher, he was not mainly theological or speculative; he was mainly ethical, in which respect he was a follower of the Kantian basis for religion.[705] But again, he asserted his independence, for where Kant would combine what he called Physico-theology with Ethico-theology to arrive at an explanation of God, Hedge reinvested his proofs with something of Revelation.[706]

Hedge's *Prose Writers of Germany*, influential though it was in spreading among the popular American audience a knowledge of German literature and philosophy, is little to our immediate purpose; for by 1847, when it appeared, the leading Transcendentalists had progressed beyond the formative stages in developing their thought, and for such books as Emerson's *Nature* or his Divinity School address, it came a decade too late.[707] Moreover, as regards the German philosophers represented in the volume, the translations are by the hands of co-workers,[708] while the introductory sketches are either the work of helpers or, as in the cases of Jacobi, Fichte, and Schelling, though penned by Hedge, concerned with general or summary statements of the significance of their contributions rather than with a detailed explanation of their thought. One important feature of the book is that Hedge re-emphasized the distinctive differences between Kant and his followers that he had first pointed out in 1833. His success in grasping clearly these distinctions when almost everybody else in America missed them, betokens his perspicuity. He was also the first to use the term

transcendental in the sense in which it was understood by the better Transcendentalists; and he was quite correct in surmising that the word, as he understood it, would continue, in common usage, to signify both the method of Kant and the systems of his followers.

Although Hedge early formed an ambition, like another Milton, to sing "a song to generations," his poetic achievements were modest. A few of his hymns and lyrics have survived.[709] For the most part, his best creative work was done in his orations, notably the one on Luther, delivered *memoriter* in Boston in 1883, when Hedge was seventy-eight, on the occasion of the four hundredth anniversary of Luther's birth. As a lecturer he was popular from the thirties until well into the eighties, ever ready to pass on to successive generations of Americans the philosophy of idealism that had first inspired him as a youth in Germany. As late as 1881 he participated in the third session of the Concord School of Philosophy by lecturing on the founder of critical philosophy in commemoration of the centenary of Kant's *Critique of Pure Reason*.[710] Perhaps his most effective work was done as editor and translator.[711] His *Prose Writers of Germany* (1847), his numerous translations of German poems, the *Hours with German Classics* (1886),[712] and a translation of Chamisso's *Peter Schlemihl* (1848, 1889) were all notable achievements. But his many contributions, in the form of books and articles, to theology and philosophy also made a powerful impression in their day.[713] His appointment, in 1872, to the professorship of German at Harvard was a somewhat tardy recognition of his zeal and scholarship. Professor Gray observes quite correctly that "the introduction or rather domestication of German philosophy, which brought New England Transcendentalism itself into being, was the work, mainly, of Frederic Henry Hedge."[714] As time went on, able coadjutors joined him in the work, but he was the pioneer and the most accomplished leader of the German party in the Transcendental movement.

The Unitarian and Congregational Clergy

Before we turn to Emerson and a consideration of the role played by others of the major Transcendentalists in domesticating certain aspects of German culture in America, we must correct a common impression, namely, that Unitarians consistently and implacably opposed German ideas. Nothing can be further from the truth, for there were Unitarians and Unitarians. In the first place, the disciples of the New Views who espoused German thought and art were, or had been, almost without exception, Unitarians. Furthermore, in many areas, conservative Unitarian ministers, in good standing in the Association, prosecuted German studies quite as diligently as did the liberal left-wingers who went by the name of Transcendentalists. The columns of journals like the *Christian Examiner*, itself the recognized organ of Unitarianism, provided the chief arena in which the battle for and against Germanism was fought. Even the Presbyterian *Princeton Review* opened its pages to the German heresies, though, of course, its facilities were available principally for the defenders of the faith against "German skepticism" and "atheism." The German theologians provided the Unitarian clergymen with arguments for the maintenance of their position against Calvinism quite as often as the Transcendentalist ministers sought in them principles in support of their position against the conservative Unitarians. Often to be sure, the Unitarian clergy read German theology and philosophy not only to answer their gainsayers, whether Calvinist or Transcendentalist, but also to refute the Germans themselves. We have already seen how among the Unitarians a long succession of their leaders, from William Bentley to Frederic Henry Hedge,

were pioneers in this realm. Between the two, and forming a kind of succession, were W. E. Channing, Carl Follen, Convers Francis, and J. S. Buckminster. It will be recalled, also, that Emerson, Parker, Ripley Clarke, Furness, Cranch, Dwight, W. H. Channing, and even Brownson were basically Unitarians; while among the younger generation, Samuel Osgood, C. A. Bartol O. B. Frothingham, John Weiss, D. A Wasson, Moncure D. Conway, Samuel Longfellow, Samuel Johnson, and G. W Cooke, all started as Unitarian ministers. Apart from the notable work of W. E Channing in preparing the New England of Jonathan Edwards for the New England of Ralph Waldo Emerson, there were stalwarts in the Unitarian church—men like James Walker (1794–1874)—whose temperate pronouncements on Transcen dentalism bore especial weight.

Walker was one of the founders of the American Unitarian Association in 1825 editor of the *Christian Examiner* from 183 to 1839, Alford Professor of Natural Reli gion, Moral Philosophy, and Civil Polity a Harvard from 1839 to 1855, and Presiden of Harvard from 1853 to 1860. As early a 1834, that is, two years before *Nature* wa published, he declared himself in favor o "a better philosophy than the degradin sensualism, out of which most forms o modern infidelity have grown."[715] He wen on to assert that "to a rightly constitute and fully developed soul, moral and spiritu al truth will be revealed with a degree o intuitive clearness and certainty, equal a least to that of the objects of sense." Th young Transcendentalists seized immediate ly upon this statement as supporting thei position. Actually, however, Walker wa more the critic of Unitarianism than th proponent of Transcendentalism. What h aimed at was to repel skepticism by th argument that innate faculties exist in th soul for the apprehension of spiritual trutl He had not yet (indeed, he never) proceede much beyond the desire to transfer "th sanctions of authority from outward to inward, from external testimony to immediate consciousness, from the senses to the soul." In short, he was still largely under the influence of the Scottish realists. He never got from under their influence, and in 1849 he edited Dugald Stewart's *Philosophy of the Active and Moral Powers* and the next year Thomas Reid's *Essays on the Intellectual Powers of Man*.[716]

But when we have said all this, there remains the fact that his mind was not closed to the new thought. In 1840, for example, he declared, in a discourse before the Cambridge Divinity School, that "the return to a higher order of ideas, to a living faith in God, in Christ, and in the church" had been promoted by such men as Schleiermacher and De Wette. Voicing the conviction that the religious community had reason to look with distrust and dread on a philosophy which limits the ideas of the human mind to the information imparted by the senses, denying the existence of spiritual elements in the nature of man, he went on to welcome the philosophy taught in England by Butler, Reid, and Coleridge, in Germany by Kant, Jacobi, and Schleiermacher, and in France by Cousin, Jouffroy, and De Gerando. And he concluded by saying that "men may put down Transcendentalism if they can, but they must first deign to comprehend its principles."[717] Such words from the prominent expounder of the metaphysics of nineteenth-century Unitarianism caused even the most conservative to surmise that there might be something in transcendentalism worth inquiring into.

Quite aside from the several generations of Transcendentalists who began as Unitarian ministers and apart from other Unitarians (James Walker, for instance) who adopted a liberal attitude toward the transcendental philosophy of Germany, there were the dyed-in-the-wool Unitarians themselves who gave more than passing attention to German developments. The following Unitarian ministers represent in their attitudes toward German idealism all the varying stages from enthusiastic approbation to unqualified opposition; but whether they expressed themselves for or against German theologians, philosophers, and men of letters, none of them spoke without some knowledge of the subject. The list,[718] though far from complete, is imposing, including as it does the names of Joseph Henry Allen (1820–1898), William Bentley (1759–1819), Joseph Stevens Buckminster (1784–1812), Stephen Greenleaf Bulfinch (1809–1863), Frederick Frothingham (1825–1891), Nathaniel L. Frothingham (1793–1870), William Batchelder Greene (1819–1878), Thomas Wentworth Higginson (1823–1911), Andrews Norton (1786–1853), George R. Noyes (1798–1868), Andrew Preston Peabody (1811–1892), Ephraim Peabody (1807–1856), James H. Perkins (1810–1892), Palmer Putnam (1814–1872), Henry Ware, Jr.[719] (1794–1843), William Ware (1797–1852), and W. D. Wilson (1816–1900). That the Presbyterians were not far behind the Unitarians in a knowledge of what was transpiring in theologians' cells and philosophers' studies in Germany appears from the following list of clergymen who took a stand for or against Germanism: James Waddell Alexander (1804–1859), Daniel Dana (1771–1859), Henry Davis (1771–1852), Albert Baldwin Dod (1805–1845), Charles Hodge (1797–1878), James Marsh (1794–1842), Samuel Miller (1769–1850), James Murdock (1776–1856), Noah Porter (1811–1892), Henry Boynton Smith (1815–1877), and Moses Stuart (1780–1852). Among Baptists, Barnas Sears (1802–1880) was the most noted for his knowledge of German.

These lists include only the names of clergymen whose writings on the subject warrant consideration in a survey of this kind. Obviously the lists could be extended, but enough has been indicated to suggest that the Transcendentalists were not alone in considering German thought as having a bearing on American problems, for there were among the orthodox clergymen some who not only supported but topped the efforts of the "German party." Even when they stood at opposite poles in the controversy over the "Latest Form of Infidelity," as did the Transcendentalist Ripley and the Unitarian Norton, their efforts may be considered, from one point of view, as having eventually promoted the same ends. Perhaps no one brings this matter into sharper focus than the Rev. Andrews Norton, often thought of as the leading opponent of German philosophy because his several pamphlets on "German infidelity" and his refusal to permit his son to study German at Harvard lest it corrupt his Unitarian principles are emphasized out of all proportion to his general work and to the disparagement of his just reputation as a Biblical scholar.

Norton's long association with Harvard as Dexter Professor of Sacred Literature in the Divinity School (1819–1830)[720] and his substantial contributions[721] to Biblical criticism and controversial literature long maintained him at the head of the conservative Unitarian spokesmen. How he acquired his knowledge of German is not clear, but his contributions to the *General Repository and Review* (1812–1813), which he edited, to the *North American Review*, the *Christian Examiner*, the *Select Journal of Foreign Periodical Literature* (edited jointly by Norton and Charles Folsom; 4 vols., 1833–1834), and his tracts on the "latest form of infidelity," all serve to show that he was well enough read, particularly among the German theologians, to score telling blows against their principles, against the extension of their doctrine in America, and against Ripley and Emerson, reputedly their exponents. But these earlier essays were only preliminary exercises to his more substantial work *The Evidences of the Genuineness of the Gospels*, which he began as early as 1819, and the first volume of which was published in

1837,[722] at precisely the moment when it seemed to him the German heresies were making dangerous inroads upon "true" religion in America. The scope of Norton's indebtedness to the German theologians in this work is signalized in the "Introduction: Statement of the Case," at least five of the eleven pages being translations which he made from Eichhorn's *Einleitung in das neue Testament* (1804–1837), and much of what follows being a refutation of Eichhorn's *Urevangelium* hypothesis. Aside from his own investigations, he relied chiefly upon British theologians, notably Jones, Marsh, Kaye, Lardner, Paley, Pearson, and Wake, for the positive part of his argument; but the Germans whom he quoted, used, and misused are also prominent.[723] The French Biblical scholars run a poor third.[724]

Norton's summary condemnation of German philosophy and theology was, of course, displeasing to the Transcendentalists; and Brownson, in the newly-founded *Boston Quarterly Review*, was one of the first to oppose and twit Norton. Reviewing the first volume of the *Evidences* (1837) he observed that Norton's references to the German Credner, "a young man scarcely known in his own country," left one to infer that the author was widely read among the German theologians whom he so much abhorred.[725] Brownson also expressed, ironically, his disappointment that Norton's book does not lay the charges of infidelity brought against Norton by his friends and enemies. Considering Norton's reputation as a "first-rate theologian," Brownson finds it all the more disappointing to find Norton resting his case for the truth of Christianity on little more than his argument regarding the truth of the miracles. If he possessed much philosophical sagacity, he would not have fallen into the absurd position of citing Locke in support of the theory which rests the basis of Christianity upon the miraculous. Even Jonathan Edwards, say Brownson, was less blind in this respect than the learned Dexter Professor. The fac is, says Brownson, the Lockean system "embraced by our author is as fatal to all sound morality as it is to religious faith," and nothing is to be expected from either Norton or any other professor of Harvard, entangled as they are in the toils of Lockean sensationalism.[726]

To make a fairer representation of the controversy we should present the more moderate views of men like Barnas Sears and Francis Bowen, but enough has already been said to indicate that for every Norton who set his face against the inevitable there was a colleague who took a more tolerant view and sought to guide the new religious and theological impulses issuing from Germany into the "proper" channels. Regardless of the many varying attitudes assumed by the several defenders of the "right" and "true" religion, whether Congregational or Unitarian, it is clear that without the Unitarian tradition of "free inquiry" and without the active support of many individual Unitarians as well as Congregationalists, German ideas would have been much longer than they were in making their way into America. To come to a realization of how the attitude toward German thought changed, one needs only to compare the attitudes expressed during the thirties toward "Germanism" in such periodicals as the *Princeton Review* with the attitude explicit not only by direct statement but also in the proportion of articles devoted to German theological and philosophical subjects, as well as in the elaborate "Literary Intelligence" and "Notices of New Publications" from Germany that we find during the fifties in such a journal as the *Bibliotheca Sacra*.[727] And what became typical in conservative periodicals was multiplied manifold in more liberal journals like Parker's *Massachusetts Quarterly Review* and the *Radical*, the *Index*, and the *Open Court* of a later day.

HAVING defined our terms, traced the avenues by which German ideas came to America, and considered the agencies that prepared the way for their adoption and adaptation by New England Transcendentalism, we turn now to Emerson as the leading promulgator of the new philosophy in America.

The Transcendentalist Writers

RALPH WALDO EMERSON

Ralph Waldo Emerson (1803–1882) is by common consent at once the most original and the most influential of the New England Transcendentalists. He was their leader and their philosopher—not because he led them or because he gave them a distinct system of philosophy, but because he came so much nearer doing so than any other that his primacy went unchallenged in his day and later. But Emerson did not consider himself the head of a "school," he denied being a systematic philosopher,[1] and he blandly put off a would-be but questioning follower by saying, "Very well, I do not wish disciples."[2]

But all this is not equivalent to saying, as has been said too often by those who misquote and misinterpret Emerson's *bon mot* about a foolish consistency being the hobgoblin of little minds that his philosophy had neither unity nor cohesion; nor is it to imply, as is equally common, either that Emerson was incapable of thinking clearly or that he complacently contented himself with half-truths in religion and patent falsehoods in philosophy. It was rather that he was cautious about forcing his thoughts into set forms and rigid terms.[3] He had a profound distrust of all "systems" and all system-makers, even to the point of disliking preachers and preaching. "I hate preaching," he said, "whether in pulpits or in teachers' meeting. Preaching is a pledge, and I wish to say what I feel and think to-day, with the proviso that to-morrow perhaps I shall contradict it all. Freedom boundless I wish."[4] It was for the same

reason that he disliked being called a Transcendentalist—not because he disclaimed his beliefs or denied his associates, but because he believed people did not know the meaning of the word. He did not like labels which lent themselves too readily to misinterpretation. Hence he preferred the word *idealist*. Transcendentalism to him was idealism—"Idealism as it appears in 1842."

Idealism was nothing new in 1842. It was not new to him. In fact, it was instinctive. In 1841 he recalled how, as a mere child, he developed an attitude of mind that laid the groundwork for what, in 1835, he tried to formulate into a "First Philosophy."

I remember, when a child, in the pew on Sundays amusing myself with saying over common words as "black," "white," "board," etc., twenty or thirty times, until the word lost all meaning and fixedness, and I began to doubt which was the right name for the thing, when I saw that neither had any natural relation, but all were arbitrary.[5]

This experience he interpreted correctly as "a child's first lesson in idealism." And this, we may believe, was all that was needed to lead the curious mind of Emerson into the high road to Idealism.

Much has been made of the influence upon Emerson of Plato, of the neo-Platonists, of Oriental philosophy, of the Scottish philosophers, of German thinkers working through Carlyle and Coleridge, and of a score of others. The effect of one or all of these, considered as shaping influences, is easily overstated. The alleged influence of Plato on Emerson illustrates the point. An active reader of Plato from first to last, Emerson undoubtedly found in Platonic thought his most steady point of reference. But to relate the whole of Emerson's intellectual development to Platonism, as John S. Harrison tends to do in his otherwise excellent *Teachers of Emerson*, is obviously doing violence to the facts.[6] It fails to take sufficiently into account other influences; it neglects too much the native heritage of New England idealism and individualism,[7] of which Emerson was never unconscious; and it tends to overlook what must ever be put first in any accounting for Emerson's thought, namely, that strong element of originality and individuality without which Emerson would not have been Emerson. Too great an insistence upon "influences" runs counter to Emerson's oft-repeated principles of individualism, independence, and originality, and overlooks his saying that "the office of reading is wholly subordinate . . . I get thereby [only] a vocabulary for my ideas."[8] There can be no doubt about the correctness of Emerson's observation that he read mainly for the "lustres,[9] the quotables and memorabilia, and to get confirmation for his ideas. Books, asserted Emerson, are for the scholar's idle times; but since he added in the same breath, they "make my top spin,"[10] we infer that the stimulus derived from them sometimes went beyond the mere suggestiveness of single words or phrases. That he read for something more than a vocabulary is suggested by such a note as that made on August 20, 1837: "Carlyle and Wordsworth now act out of England on us,—Coleridge also,"[11] as well as by the arrangement he made of his reading in 1847, by which the writings of Goethe and Coleridge are put under the head of "Tonic Books," and Cousin, Madame de Staël, and Southey are listed under "Importers."[12]

And yet, while he refused, like Carlyle, to acknowledge discipleship to any master,

every page of his diary refutes the inference that he contemned studies. He kept constant company with books; no man kept company with better books, and few men kept better company with books.[13] Take out of his essays and lectures what is owing to his reading, and we should leave them poor, shrunken things indeed.

After the first exuberance of youthful individualism had worn off, Emerson, in 1855, made what appears to be a maturely considered general statement of indebtedness: "My best thoughts come from others."[14] This bald utterance provokes knowing winks and raised eyebrows among the influence-seekers and source-hunters, and sets them off on the old tack of pointing out parallels and tracking down coincidences, all of which are afterwards lumped under the head of "influences." But Emerson's observation is only another instance among many that must not be taken out of the context, for what he adds in the next breath suggest that he did, indeed, borrow, but with a difference: "I heard in their words my own meaning, but a deeper sense than they put into them; and could well and best express myself in other people's phrases, but to finer purposes than they knew."[15]

Books [he wrote on Christmas Day, 1831] are apt to turn reason out of doors. You find men talking everywhere from their memories, instead of from their understanding. If I stole this thought from Montaigne, as is very likely, I don't care. I should have said the same myself.[16]

Two weeks later he found a thought in Mendelssohn's *Phaedo* that pleased him, and that he wrote down on his blotter: "Little matters it to the simple lover of truth to whom he owes such and such a reasoning."[17] In his essay on Plato he said, "Out of Plato come all things that are still written and debated among men of thought. Great havoc makes he among our originalities . . . Plato is philosophy and philosophy is Plato"; but in his journal he was more chary: "My debt to Plato is a certain number of sentences; a like to Aristotle. A larger number, yet still a finite number, makes the worth of Milton and Shakespeare to me."[18]

All these statements, diverse as they are in the conclusions which they suggest, are yet consistent in the implication which they leave, namely, that Emerson read and read abundantly, though never to appropriate merely or to steal.[19] However, his good Yankee habit of storing up in his copious notebooks—the penny-savings bank of the lecturer and the stock-in-trade of the essayist—the "lustres" which he found in his readings suggests that they were designed to be put to use.[20] The several genetic studies that have been made of how these notebook materials went first into his lectures (sometimes into letters) and later into essays have made abundantly plain how this design was carried out. Always the memorabilia of his journals were metamorphosed into the finished discourses of his public utterances or writings by undergoing a transmutation, a selection and reordering, an assimilation and naturalization, a revision or reapplication. By contact with the genius within him, they came forth in a new synthetic form which was no longer Platonic or Kantian, Shakespearean or Goethean, Carlylean or Coleridgean—but Emersonian.

The Platonic Period (to 1830)

It is not necessary to suppose that Emerson, once he had learned "the child's first lesson in Idealism," required to appropriate much from Plato to become the idealist he became. Indeed, it is difficult to put a finger on a passage in his writings which he could not have come by even if he had never read Plato. It might be observed, also, that while there is in Emerson's essays between 1836 and 1838 hardly an idea in the expression of which he was not anticipated, either wholly or partly, by Carlyle (especially in Carlyle's earlier

essays),[21] yet it would be hard to find an idea in Emerson's essays of the period which he could not have thought of even if he had never discovered this "Germanick new-light writer,"[22] as he called him in 1832. Not that Emerson was original at all points, or that he learned nothing from Plato, or that he found nothing in Carlyle; but rather to suggest that it is all but impossible indisputably to relate this or that idea in Emerson directly to a similar or identical one to be found in either Plato or Carlyle. There are few thoughts in Emerson's writings which, in the light of his various reading, could not be related to several sources; and whoever is minded to seek them out will find a dozen coincidences with Plato, a like number with Kant, as many more with Coleridge or Schelling, and so on.

Another influence upon Emerson that has been overrated is that of Quakerism.[23] Entirely too much has been made of Emerson's saying, none too well authenticated, that he considered himself "more of a Quaker than anything else."[24] Emerson's Unitarian heritage made him forever suspicious of Quakerish enthusiasm.[25] To be sure, his "spiritual religion" is at some points similar to Quaker doctrine, notably in the matter of conscience or the inner light. But these are only particularizations of his doctrine of self-reliance, not referable to any creed or sect. Similarly, other points on which Emerson seems in agreement with the Quakers, such as the doctrines of the immanence of God, of obedience, and of individual responsibility, are all common ideals which Emerson doubtless learned at his mother's (or Aunt Mary's) knee.

Finally, as will appear in the sequel, Emerson did not rest content with a religion that relied as largely and unquestioningly as did the Quakers' on the mystical inner light. His most conscientious efforts were exerted to raise his belief into something approximating knowledge—to bring his heart and head into agreement. Conditioned as he was by the harsh discipline of Puritan dogmatism and Unitarian rationalism, his strong will and insistence upon understanding his religion constantly egged him on to rationalizing this inner light—to lift it out of the realm of mysticism into that of intelligibility.

The entire method of his reading, studying, thinking, and writing supports the view that insofar as Emerson's thought was derivative, it was eclectic. Systems of thought interested him little, but individual ideas he grasped eagerly, especially when they tallied with the genius for truth within him. The result was an eclecticism that developed, as all eclecticisms do, a number of mutually repellent particles, which the critics call inconsistencies. For him, fortunately, consistency and inconsistency were mainly quibbles on words. He neither loved the former nor feared the latter, and in the privacy of his journal he lustily damned both.[26] Not that he was unambitious to bring unity into his thinking, but that he objected to the subtle sophistries of critics who could not see the forest for the trees— who failed, in their worship of the great god Consistency, to see the larger truth for the smaller exceptions. Once he had grasped the three Ideas of Reason as truths, no apparent contradictions, whether bred of the Understanding or the speculative Reason, could shake his faith in them. For above all contrarities was the absolute Unity, by which the Many become the One, or the Over-Soul, in which subject and object, spirit and nature, ego and non-ego, merge into one.

Insofar, then, as it is possible to speak of Emerson's "body" or "system" of thought, students who made its resolution their object have found themselves involved in difficulties. The main components of his thought are clear enough, and they have been charted too often to require restatement here. Professor Henry David Gray's study is among the more succinct and satisfactory of these analyses. But while there remains little doubt about what Emerson thought, there is less certainty about how he came to hold such views. Although Professor Gray recognizes in Emerson the "material for a system," and is prompted to order and systematize it in a way to present Emerson's "final theory," he finds the necessity under which this plan puts him of translating Emerson's statements into precise metaphysical terms a hard and thankless task.[27] The reason for the difficulty is threefold. In 1869 Emerson confessed frankly: "I never could get beyond five steps in my enumeration of intellectual powers: say, Instinct, Perception, Imagination (including Fancy as a subaltern), Reasoning or Understanding."[28] Epistemologically, Emerson's mind was not richly equipped.

Another circumstance that threw obstacles into the path of Emerson's progress as an epistemologist was his thorough indoctrination, at the hands of his Harvard professors, Levi Hedge and Levi Frisbie, in the Scottish school—Stewart, Reid, Hamilton, and Brown—a philosophy which identified the intuitive moral sense with the highest reason.[29] Emerson never fully divested his mind of the tendency to make this easy identification; and when later he sought to define Kant's pure Reason, it often took on admixtures of meaning from the Scottish moralists.

A third cause for Emerson's incomprehensibility to himself and to us lies in the element of mysticism which was an innate part of his mental equipment. Wherever it rears its head, his philosophy ducks out of sight. All his efforts to the contrary, whenever he reached the highest point in his philosophical aspirations, he lapsed into a rapt, inspirational tone which belongs to that which is sacred and becomes often the attempt to utter the unutterable.[30] When he reaches this point, Emerson lapses from metaphysics into mysticism, which the philosopher endeavors vainly to resolve into propositions, for mysticism has no genealogy. Whenever we approach the point at which Emerson leaves off thinking and begins communing, we have to leave him to his devices. Yet we can attend him some distance on the way in his speculative efforts. It is certainly a mistake not to take Emerson's philosophical aspirations seriously. Professor Harry H. Clark's searching study of the extent of Emerson's early concern with natural philosophy and of his indebtedness to the sciences[31] is a very effective refutation to the conventional view which regards Emerson as a purely mystical and philosophically irresponsible traveler in the land of whim, blandly affirming an impossible optimism and enunciating inconsistent and untenable platitudes.

To be sure, Emerson once asked whether a sensible man ever looked twice into a metaphysical book, and he sometimes professed to share with Wordsworth a disgust for the scientific analyst; but these isolated statements are nullified by hundreds upon hundreds of references in his writings that belie this supposed disdain.[32] He defined philosophy as "the account which the human mind gives itself of the constitution of the world"; and, he went on to say, "Two cardinal facts lie forever at the base; the one and the two.—1. Unity, or Identity; and 2. Variety . . . Oneness and otherness. It is impossible to speak or to think without embracing both."[33] Nothing goes deeper toward explaining Emerson's mind than the recognition that the primary passion of his life was the reconciliation of this Unity and Variety, to find "for all that exists conditionally . . . a ground unconditioned and absolute";[34] in short, to find what he called the "First Philosophy." He approached religion philosophically: no religion that did not have its justification in the light of reason was acceptable to him, and no philosophy that did not include his religious prepossessions was possible for him; he could no more accept an irreligious philosophy than an unphilosophical religion.[35]

At this point we become aware of a fourth problem that aggravated Emerson's difficulties and that compounds our difficulty as we try to follow him through this period of uneasy and puzzled Platonism that preceded his German transcendental phase. Naturally inclined though he was to take an idealistic view of life (a view for which his delvings into Platonic thought during the twenties lent support), what he was taught at Harvard College and the Divinity School about Lockean sensationalism and Scottish common-sense seemed forever at odds with his idealism. Nearsighted though the Lockean empiricist undoubtedly was, Emerson had to admit that he was clear-sighted and not easily moved from his position by anything short of logic. However far he read in Platonic literature, he failed to find arguments with which to beat the Lockean rationalist on his own grounds or with his own weapons. And he was not himself a sufficiently astute psychologist or epistemologist to arbitrate, once and for all, between the widely disparate claims of the Lockean rationalist on the one hand and the Platonic intuitionalist on the other. Instinctively he sided with the Platonists, but he found no way, in any epistemology with which he was acquainted before 1830, to reduce Plato's two worlds to one, and no convincing logical argument by which to refute Locke. And so he continued to waver, inclining at one time toward intuitive divination, and the next toward logical understanding—knowing well enough that he preferred Plato to Locke, but never able to convince himself that Plato had the better of the argument.

Before inquiring into the epistemological difficulties which Emerson encountered, it is necessary to indicate the broad propositions upon which his practical philosophy rested—to indicate *what* he believed before we attempt an inquiry into *how* and *why* he could believe thus.

Emerson's speculation began with nature, and his first published work bore the title

Nature. "A noble doubt," he wrote in that book, "perpetually suggests itself whether . . . nature outwardly exists." This noble doubt, occasioned by "my utter impotence to test the authenticity of the report of my senses, to know whether the impressions they make on me correspond with outlying objects," he recurs to repeatedly; and in the end he concludes, "Be it what it may, it [Nature] is ideal to me so long as I cannot try the accuracy of my senses."[36]

Merry though the frivolous make themselves with the ideal theory of nature, the stability of nature is in no wise affected by her ideality. Indeed, "any distrust in the permanence of [the] laws [of Nature] would paralyze the faculties of man." However illusory, Nature has yet a very practical reality. But if Nature is illusory, what, we may ask, gives reality and permanence to her laws? The answer is simple, so simple that Emerson enjoys repeating the seeming fallacy: "Whilst we acquiesce entirely in the permanence of natural laws, the question of her absolute existence still remains open."[37]

The Kantian Phase (1830–1838)

Thus far Emerson could well have traveled for himself after having learned "the child's first lesson in Idealism." Thus far Berkeley, whom he read "in early youth" might readily have carried him.[38] But Berkeley alone could never have led to the conclusions he reached in the latter portions of *Nature.* Indeed, the combined heritages of Puritanism, of his early study of Plato and Berkeley, of Harvard College and the Divinity School and all they stood for, of Aunt Mary Moody Emerson, of marriage and death, of the joys and sorrows that acted upon the young man, potent as these were, all still left his mind beclouded and his tongue inarticulate—left both his religion and his philosophy incomplete and unsatisfactory. The impetus to go on, to extract an essential unity out of his inchoate prepossessions and half-substantiated ideas, did not come until he found the key in the Kantian threefold division of the mind. It is impossible to segregate and evaluate absolutely the several component influences that wrought this electrifying effect between 1830 and 1836. Whatever we attribute to the manifold influences of travel, to the personal contacts with Coleridge, Wordsworth, and Carlyle, and to his reading of their works, to the influence of men like Follen, Stuart, Marsh, Francis, Hedge, Channing, and the Göttingen men of Harvard and Boston, it all comes, in the end, to what is essentially the sum of all of them, namely, the distinction (derived from Kant through Carlyle and Coleridge) between Understanding and Reason.

No philosophy with which he was acquainted previous to 1830, whether of Greek or British or some other origin, seemed to supply the means for bridging the gap between what he called variously "spirit" or "mind" on the one hand and "nature" or "matter" on the other, or to supply what he felt would be a satisfactory metaphysical basis for the truths which he believed to be truths, but could not demonstrate to be so. Of the apparent dualism he was painfully aware; he could not bring mind and matter, spirit and nature, into correspondence. Although his genius for the truth within him told him he was right in denying the sensationalism of Locke and in insisting upon a tempering of Unitarian rationalism, he recognized the folly of a purely destructive criticism so long as he found nothing constructively consistent to replace what he proposed to take away. How to reconcile philosophically the dualism patent on the very surface of things? This remained an open question until he discovered Kant.

For "Nature is brute but as the soul quickens it; Nature always the effect, mind the flowing cause."[39] Yet the two must be shown to be one, and to the "marrying of

Nature and Mind"[40] he devoted his best efforts. The first extant notation, written in 1820, on his "Blotting-Book" is concerned with an attempt to define nature, mind, and God. Seldom thereafter, during the next ten years, does he make an entry or reflection without in some way reverting to this knotty problem of dualism,[41] until in the early thirties, it became a problem of all-absorbing proportions without the solution of which he felt all further speculation would be futile.

But as early as January 11, 1823, at least, he was in the clear regarding moral reality. Concerning it there never was any doubt in his mind:

There is one distinction amid these fading phenomena—one decided distinction which is real and eternal and which will survive nature—I mean the distinction of Right and Wrong. Your opinions upon all other topics, and your feelings with regard to this world, in childhood, youth, and age, perpetually change. Your perceptions of right and wrong never change . . . . The mind may lose its acquaintance with other minds and may abandon, without a sigh, this glorious universe; but it cannot part with its moral principle . . . . If there be anything real under heaven, or in heaven, the perception of right and wrong relates to that reality . . . It is the constitution of the mind to rely with firm . . . confidence upon the *moral principle,* and I reject at once the idea of a delusion in this. This is woven vitally into the thinking substance itself, so that it cannot be diminished or destroyed without dissipating forever that spirit which it inhabited. Upon the foundation of my *moral* sense I ground my faith in the immortality of the soul, in the existence and activity of good beings, and in the promise of rewards . . . .[42]

This, when reduced to essentials, will be recognized as Kant's practical philosophy, without analytic or dialectic. Yet in 1823, when this passage was written, Emerson was entirely innocent of any knowledge of Kant, nor had he read Coleridge and Carlyle. To be sure, he could have been helped to his view of moral reality by one of several impulses, among them his Puritan

and Unitarian heritages, the Quaker influence, the personal influences of his mother and Aunt Mary, his study of Plato and the English Platonists, or his careful reading of "Price on Morals" two years before.[43] Any one or all of these could have inspired this creed. But, as seems more likely—and the fervency of his expression indicates that he held it to be an irresistible *personal* persuasion—he worked it out for himself. At any rate, he felt it to be incontrovertibly true, though he had no guarantees for its validity other than the sanction of his innermost feelings. And to it he clung, without giving a jot, for the rest of his life; to it he held as fast before 1830, when it seemed to him without all philosophical corroboration whatever, as after that date, when Kant's metaphysics of morals gave him all the confirmation he could wish. Thus Emerson made, almost at the outset of his philosophical career, a moral synthesis, which, had he been a more systematic philosopher, he might have put off until he had probed more carefully the preliminary epistemological and metaphysical bases upon which such an ethical conclusion could, or should, rest.

Indeed, the record of his philosophical inquiries, as revealed in his diaries and letters of the next decade, demonstrates how, holding always to this moral fundament, he labored, step by step, to substantiate it. The course of these endeavors, circuitous though it was, must be plotted, for it goes to the very roots of Emerson's philosophy, and demonstrates most forcibly the influence of German transcendentalism upon him. Through him, it developed into the most fertile idealistic movement yet experienced by America. These endeavors led him back always to this starting point —the dualism of mind and matter.[44] By 1822 nothing more satisfactory had suggested itself to him than a vague sort of Platonic sense of communion, born of a "Sunday morn," by which he was enabled "at intervals . . . to depart from the pursuits and habits of men to hold conversation with the attributes of Deity, and, in the emphatic language of the Hebrew historian, *to walk with God.*"[45]

Satisfying though such intuitive communion may have been to the religious faith within his heart, his head, seeking always a more strictly reasoned approach, found it inadequate. In the final analysis, it rested on nothing more than faith and, in the particular form in which it presented itself to him, seemed dangerously near to Pantheism. He felt uncomfortable, for "to believe too much is dangerous, because it is the near neighbor of unbelief. Pantheism leads to Atheism."[46] He found that neither his strong-minded Aunt Mary[47] nor the "consecrated" Channing,[48] neither his uncle the Rev. Samuel Ripley[49] nor the "consistent Atheist" Murat,[50] with whom he fraternized in Florida, had anything to his purpose. He turned to books of the past and present. The *Journals* for the later twenties and early thirties record varying degrees of familiarity with the following: Zoroaster (26)[51] Confucius (27), Mohammed (12), the Scriptures, both canonical and apocryphal (38), the Church Fathers, both Catholic and Protestant (12), Thales (2), Anaximander (5), Pythagoras (13), Xenophanes (8), Anaximanes (2), Anacreon (1), Heraclitus (19), Anaxagoras (4), Democritus (3), Empedocles (4), Epicurus (4), Zeno (3), Lucretius (5), Plutarch (78), Epictetus (4), Socrates (20), Plato (168), Aristotle (27), the Neo-Platonists from Plotinus to Cudworth (60), Boethius (2), St. Augustine (17), Thomas à Kempis (9), Luther (53), Calvin (19), Knox (2), Fox (32), and the Quaker doctrine (36), Bacon (88), Galileo (12), Descartes (4), Milton (109), Hobbes (11), Locke (24), Newton (68), Leibnitz (16), Laplace (2), Shaftesbury (3), Whitefield (7), Hume (25), Berkeley (12), Hartley (2), Montaigne (61), Pascal (13), La Rochefoucauld (1), La Bruyère (3), Fénelon (17), Fontenelle (14), Le Clerc (2), Montesquieu (18), Voltaire (22), Buffon (5), Rousseau (19), Chateau-

briand (6), Madame de Staël (45), Wollaston (3), Sir Thomas Browne (13), Richard Hooker (6), Bishop Butler (8), Burnet (1), Clarke (3), Taylor (15), Paley (9), Price (3), Reid (4), Priestley (6), Bentham (15), Malthus (9), Adam Smith (7), Stewart (13), Burke (36), Gibbon (14), Mackintosh (23), Playfair (5), Jane Marcet's *Conversations on Chemistry* (1), Wm. Sherlock's *Sermon on Faith* (2), Mellen *On Divine Vengeance* (1), Forsyth's *Principles of Moral Science* (1), Thomas Browne's *Lectures on the Philosophy of the Human Mind* (3), Combe's *Constitution of Man* (4), Sampson Reed's *Growth of the Mind* (22), Swedenborg (118),[52] Herder (10), the German theologians (13),[53] Eichhorn (6), Mosheim's *Ecclesiastical History* (2), Alexander von Humboldt (25), Cotton Mather (6), Jonathan Edwards (3), and the sermons of W. E. Channing (17), J. S. Buckminster (4), Henry Ware, Jr. (2), and Nathaniel Frothingham (2).

This prodigious regimen of philosophical reading (consult also the reading lists given below), begun during the twenties and pursued with increasing intensity until the early thirties, when his interest in science began to overshadow his concern with philosophy, operated more to compound his problems than to resolve them. His fundamentally unshakable moral principles notwithstanding,[54] he was left to wonder whether the understanding was indeed "the ultimate determiner,"[55] as Price argued; and whether "Morals and Metaphysics, Cudworth and Locke, may both be true, and every system of religion yet offered to man wholly false."[56] This represents a groping state of mind, the vacillation of an agitated, half-believing, half-knowing, half-trusting, half-doubting young probationer, seeking guidance everywhere and finding it nowhere—approaching even to the despair of Carlyle's "Everlasting Nay" in several journal entries of 1826–1827.[57] He seemed forced to conclude: "The argument for Necessity can never be got the better of. It is like a goose which,—fight it down as much as you will,—always cackles of victory. It always turned on you as you retired."[58]

Troubled though he was, he had no desire to avoid the issues. Indeed, the very inscrutability of his problem, we may surmise, held him inexorably. Resolutely he concluded, on April 18, 1824, "I deliberately dedicate my time, my talents, and my hopes to the Church."[59] This he did knowing full well that in embracing theology, he was entering "from everlasting to everlasting 'debatable ground'"—knowing also that his "reasoning faculty" was "proportionally weak." But he was willing, then as later, to risk all upon what he correctly evaluated as his "strength of moral imagination." So he added, "In Divinity I hope to thrive."[60]

In the decision thus reached lie evidences of the best elements of both the Puritan and the Yankee that Emerson was. He was born self-reliant and tenacious of purpose. He would not temporize or compromise; he would follow the admonition to seek, and expect to find. Indeed, the very day on which he had reached what seemed an impasse and found himself powerless to answer the arguments either of Necessity or of Berkeleian Idealism, he discovered the word *Transcendentalism*, which, imperfectly understood though it was at the time, was the clue that led eventually to his bringing something like unity into his chaotic thoughts. Among the seven "Peculiarities of the Present Age," which Emerson jotted down on his blotter on that day (January 30[?], 1827), there stands, in fourth place, this one: "Transcendentalism. Metaphysics and Ethics look inwards—and France produces Mad. de Staël; England, Wordsworth; America, Sampson Reed; as well as Germany, Swedenborg."

A comparison of the names associated with Transcendentalism in 1827 with those which came, by 1837, to represent this new philosophy shows that he had not by 1827 proceeded far in his comprehension of what the new spirit abroad in Europe held for

the solution of his difficulties. Jouffroy and Cousin came later to occupy the place assigned in 1827 to Madame de Staël; Wordsworth sank into the background before the ascendancy of Coleridge and Carlyle; Channing, Marsh, Hedge, Margaret Fuller, Alcott and other disciples of the "Newness" came to occupy a place of honor alongside Sampson Reed; while, for Germany, Swedenborg seemed less representative than Kant, Fichte, Schelling, and the great German poets and philosophizing theologians. He had still to go through what we may call, if we make allowances for the differences between Carlyle and Emerson, the Centre of Indifference before he would find answers to his most pressing questions. Indeed, this first period of his philosophic development, which we may liken to the period when Carlyle tossed about disconsolately in the perplexities of the Everlasting Nay, was of considerable duration, and may be dated, in Emerson's case, from the winter of 1826–1827 to the end of 1829. The musings prompted by those "Dark Hours" in St. Augustine, Florida, whither he had gone to recoup his health, and whence he was not sure he would return alive, led to crises less turbulent, to be sure, than those encountered by Teufelsdröckh in the Slough of Despond; yet they were occasioned by similar causes, and nonetheless real. Despondingly the candidate for the Church and future exponent of self-reliance now asked himself:

What am I in the general system of being but an iota, an unregarded speck . . . . And what is the amount of all that is called religion in the world ? Who is he that has seen God of whom so much is known, or where is one that has risen from the dead ? Satisfy me beyond the possibility of doubt of the certainty of all that is told me concerning the other world, and I will fulfil the conditions on which my salvation is suspended. The believer tells me he has an evidence, historical and internal, which make the presumption so strong that it is almost certainty, that it rests on the highest probabilities. Yes; but change that imperfect to perfect evidence, and I too will be a Christian. But now it must be admitted I am not certain that any of these things are true. The nature of God may be different from what is represented. I never beheld him. I do not know that he exists.[61]

But once this outburst had given the overflowing soul relief, the worst was already over. Returning health brought renewed hopes[62] and a reaffirmation of his faith that he was "a moral agent of an indestructible nature, and designed to stand in sublime relations to God and to my fellow men."[63] While the inquiries and the puzzle-headed questionings (as revealed in the *Journals*) continue for some years longer, they become increasingly less frequent; the tone of his reflections loses all evidence of such turbulence of mind as was revealed during the Florida period. Eventually questions regarding the worth of man, the absolute validity of moral law, and the existence of God stop altogether. Meanwhile he begins to note correspondences, connections, interdependencies, compensations, and identities of various kinds and orders, as between "poor matters" and "rich ends,"[64] "greatness of destiny and lowness of lot," "contiguities between what is minute and what is magnificent,"[65] and what is most immediate to the all-important question, between matter and mind, man and God. The Centre of Indifference has not yet been passed, but there is already noticeable the steady effort to seek a positive meaning of life and to withstand its negations—all symptoms that the antidote is taking effect, that the poison is being dispelled, and that the patient's illness has reached a stage when medicine, if the right one can be prescribed, will effect a cure, though the period of convalescence may still be protracted.[66]

Among the first of the restoratives to facilitate the recovery was that effected by Madame de Staël, whose name, at least, had been known to him as early as June 10, 1821. In November, 1826, he had her book

on Germany in hand, and two months later he spoke of her as one of the more potent influences on the times.[67] Henceforth, for some years, *De l'Allemagne* was his chief guidebook or manual to the newly discovered land. Fortunately for his understanding of German art and thought, he eventually found more authoritative commentators to guide him.

A second and more immediately personal influence to direct his attention to Germany was that of his brother William, whose European travels and studies Emerson followed eagerly. He was sorely tempted to throw up school-keeping and hear at first hand some of the revelatory doctrines taught in Germany. William urged him repeatedly to study German and Hebrew and to join him at Göttingen. Between them they calculated the cost. Although Waldo acknowledged that William's "German advice must needs be weighty,"[68] he demanded that William commit himself flatly on the absolute necessity of studying in Germany.

If you think it is every way advisable, indisputably, absolutely important that I sh'd do as you have done & go to G—& you can easily decide—why say it distinctly & I will make the sacrifice of time & take the risk of expense, immediately. So of studying German . . . . Say particularly if German and Hebrew be worth reading for tho' I hate to study them cordially I yet will the moment I can count my gains. Had I not better put on my hat & take ship for the Elbe?[69]

Unless (he added) he could take the wings of morning for a packet and feed on wishes instead of dollars and be clothed with imagination for raiment, he must not expect to go.[70] Apparently William failed to send the necessary assurances, for on February 9, 1825, he took a room in Divinity Hall, deeming it wiser "to forswear Germany & go to the cheapest stall where education can be bought . . . an economy of time not to be despised by a hard handed American who reckons acquisitions by

dollars & cents, not by learning and skill."
"I tell you," he added, "your German
towns are Castles in the air to me."[71]

Although he did not regard a German
education as a positive requisite to his
professional career, at least not to the extent of journeying thither in person, he was
nevertheless prepared, by his brother's
experience and the strength of his advice,
to lend an attentive ear to the new thoughts
issuing thence. Indeed, the process by
which he was led to hold German learning
in high regard had begun during his undergraduate days upon the return of Everett,
Ticknor, and Bancroft from the German
universities. As a sophomore, he gleefully
recorded the news of Everett's expected
arrival, in August, 1819, expecting himself
and his classmates to have "all the good of
his lectures" during the next term, only to
find that the junior class were not permitted "to profit by him."[72] He heralded the
return of Ticknor and Bancroft in similar
terms and praised their perfect scholarship
and accomplished oratory.[73]

Sampson Reed's *Observations on the
Growth of the Mind* (1826) and Swedenborg's
doctrine of correspondences, which Reed
emphasized, acted further to make his
mind receptive to the new philosophical
doctrines from Germany, when they should
come; while the influence of Wordsworth's
nature poetry, although critically received
in 1819 as "the poetry of pigmies"[74] when
it first came to his attention,[75] came eventually (especially after he reinterpreted
Wordsworth in the light of Coleridge's
critical writings) operative in the same
general direction. Yet all these, individually
and collectively, were only milk-and-water
fare; what Emerson needed was strong
wine—strong intellectual and strong emotional stimulation.

When the stimulus came, it hit hard. It
hit twice, and very nearly together. The
first was purely intellectual—his reading,
toward the end of 1829, of Marsh's edition
of Coleridge's *Aids to Reflection*. (The

second, a crisis provoked by a series of
soul-stirring experiences, we shall come to
in due time.) What appears to have struck
him most forcibly in the book was what
Marsh had most emphasized in his Preliminary Essay—the Kantian distinction
between Understanding and Reason. It
inspired him to write to his Aunt Mary a
letter, the original of which is now lost, but
the contents of which we can divine because
in her reply she speaks of her nephew's
letter having satisfied her "craving for
Kantism for the day."[76] Two months later
he was reading *The Friend* "with great
interest" and finding Coleridge's philosophy comparable "much as astronomy [is
to] . . . other sciences, taking post at the
centre and, as from a specular mount, sending sovereign glances to the circumference
of things," at the same time expressing
wonder at his Aunt Mary's refusal to be as
enthusiastic as he. "What a living soul,
what a universal knowledge!" People might
wag their heads ever so much at Coleridge's
reputed obscurity. For himself, he thanked
God for Coleridge as being "one more
instance of . . . the restless human soul
bursting the narrow boundaries of antique
speculation and mad to know the secrets of
that unknown world."

I say a man so learned and so bold, has
a right to be heard, and I will take off my
hat the while and not make an impertinent
noise . . . . His theological speculations are,
at least, *God viewed from one position* . . . .
I love him that he is no utilitarian, no
necessarian, nor scoffer, nor *hoc genus omne*,
tucked away in the corner of a sentence of
Plato.[77]

At last here was a mind, an original mind,
Emerson believed, that promised to show
him the way to resolve, at long last, the
seemingly inexorable dualism to which
Plato had bound him for so many years.
Here was no man whose philosphy could be
tucked away in a phrase or two of Plato.
Coleridge boldly transcended the old
master. He would lend an attentive ear to

this new philosophy and see what it had for the purpose of reducing Platonic dualism to a monistic synthesis.[78]

This change of heart must be recognized as a repudiation, temporary at least, of Plato—a pivotal point in the progress of Emerson's intellectual development, which, odd though it be, has been generally overlooked. Important as is this rebellion against Plato (wrought by Coleridge's use of the weapons borrowed from Kant) for our understanding of the most fructuous period of Emerson's life and work, there is, in this questioning of the Platonic position, an effect of even greater significance. It represents the first effective shock transmitted by German critical transcendentalism to the incipient American Transcendentalism, by which, ere it dissipated its energies, it effected the most influential renaissance of American idealism since early Puritan days.[79]

During the years from 1830 to 1838 Kant rose as Plato sank in the scale by which Emerson judged a man's philosophical worth. Thereafter, until about 1850 (when his thinking underwent still another change), the order was reversed. In the meantime, however, he had published *Nature*, *The American Scholar*, and the Divinity School address, and had worked out, or phrased for lectures, practically all that was needful for the composition of "Self-Reliance," "Compensation," "Spiritual Laws," "Heroism," and all else that preceded or accompanied the *Essays* of 1841. In all these Kantian transcendentalism more than Platonic, or neo-Platonic, dualism is the mainspring.

To return to our problem, we must turn back to the years immediately preceding 1830, when Emerson was still under the influence of the Scottish school and far from realizing the significance which the Kantian distinction was eventually to have for him. Its full import did not dawn upon him until after his return from England and his settlement in Concord. Indeed, it pro-

duced no tangibly constructive effect on his mind or his writings before the end of 1834. One is inclined to believe, rather, that, coming as it did, when his mind was in a state of ferment at the complexity with which the affairs of his life were arranging themselves, the first effect of the Coleridge-Kantian philosophy was more to agitate than to assuage his troubles.

Only half-recovered from his strictures of the chest, and still undecided, upon his return from the South, whether he had not better give up altogether the ministry "on the score of ill health"[80] and turn author, yet going on to fill various pulpits, he found himself, in March, 1829, installed as pastor of the Second Church of Boston. In November of the year before he had been profoundly shaken when his brother Edward, "the admired, learned, eloquent, striving boy," was reduced by a mental derangement to the state of a maniac.[81] But by now there were indications of a more cheerful future. Earlier in the year he had met and fallen in love with Ellen Tucker. Edward made a rapid, though incomplete recovery. Emerson's own health was better than ever before; his professional career seemed assured, especially if he should accept the call to fill the pulpit of Henry Ware, Jr., who was going to the Harvard Divinity School. At last his life seemed to be regulating itself; it seemed too good to be true. Would this luck last? Apprehensive of "reverses always arising from success," he wrote early in 1829, a strange letter of dark foreboding to Aunt Mary.[82] Three weeks later his bride fell ill of tuberculosis, necessitating a postponement of the marriage until September. A year later he buried his wife.[83] The old doubts returned with renewed force. A new program of reading in scientific books, begun early in 1830, served merely to accentuate the troubled state of his mind. By June of 1832 he resolved to throw off cowl and frock; on September 8, he delivered his farewell sermon; and on January 2, 1833, he sailed for Europe.

The record, as it can be read in the *Journals*, leaves little to the imagination regarding the agitating influence of these events. Ill-health for himself; insanity in a beloved brother; exalted love for the woman whom he loved above all others, her threatened death of consumption, her recovery, their marriage, a brief respite of happiness, mocked shortly after by her death; growing scruples regarding religious forms and observances in the church to which he ministered; agony in consequence of his own irresolution; the mental and emotional excitement occasioned by the decision to unfrock himself and resign his ministerial charge; the resultant criticism from parishioners and colleagues; and worst of all, the agony of his own uncertainty whether he had done right or not—all these catapulting themselves into the life of the young minister during a brief span of years, conspired toward the end of 1832 so thoroughly to dishearten him that he determined to find surcease of sorrow and quiet for his troubled mind across the waters.

The death of his young wife produced a deeply humanizing distress. It was his profoundest emotional experience up to this time, and it is doubtful that he later experienced anything of comparable poignancy. He felt a "miserable apathy"; his grief left him dry; and questioningly he wondered: "Will the dead be restored to me ? . . . Shall I ever again be able to connect the face of outward nature, the mists of the morn, the star of eve, the flowers, and all poetry, with the heart and life of an enchanting friend ? No. There is one birth, and one baptism, and one first love, and the affections cannot keep their youth any more than man."[84] Ten days later he wrote what takes on added significance from the crisis he had just experienced:

The questions that come to me this morning are few and simple.
It is worth recording that Plotinus said, "Of the Unity of God, nothing can be predicted, neither being, nor essence, nor life, for it is| above all these." Grand is it to recognize the truth of this and every one of the first class of truths which are *necessary*. Thus, "Design proves a designer," "Like must know like," or "the same can only be known by the same," out of which come the propositions of ethics . . . and a thousand sayings more which have a *quasi* truth instantly to the ear, the real worth of which is this elementary fact in all, "like must know like." It would be well . . . to . . . make a catalogue of "necessary truths." They are scanned and approved by the Reason far above the understanding. They are the last facts by which we approximate metaphysically to God.[85]

Here for the first time the terms *Reason* and *Understanding* stand in juxtaposition in something like the sense in which he habitually used them several years later.[86] It had been something over a year since he had first read about the Kantian distinction between these mental faculties, but neither its importance nor its applicability to his own problems seems to have occurred to him until the first great sorrow of his life had heightened his perceptions and quickened his intuitions.

Here also, at the beginning of 1831, we may, if we wish to pursue further the analogy already suggested between Carlyle and Emerson, place the point at which Emerson passed into the phase designated by Carlyle as the Centre of Indifference, out of which was to emerge the affirmation of Carlyle's Everlasting Yea. Actually, however, the victory was not won in a day. While Emerson's mental agitations were perhaps less turbulent than those of Carlyle, who identified the point at which the light broke in upon Teufelsdröckh in the Rue Saint Thomas de l'Enfer with one June afternoon in 1821, as he went down Leith walk to bathe in the firth of Forth,[87] they were more prolonged. The spiritual crisis in Emerson assuredly did not come and go with the dramatic vividness described in *Sartor Resartus*. So far as the written records indicate, the final phases belong to the period between his return from Europe in September, 1833, and the completion of *Nature* three years later.

Meanwhile, between his first coming upon Coleridge's metaphysical aids and his first close contact with death, two or three purely intellectual influences worked steadily though unobtrusively to prepare his mind for the Kantian interpretation of Understanding and Reason and for the idealism enforced by Fichte, Schelling, Goethe, Schiller, and the other exponents of German art and thought whom he was soon to encounter.

Always a lover of manuals, handbooks, digests, compendia, and other short cuts to learning,[88] he hailed with delight Dugald "Stewart's last Dissertation"[89] in November, 1822, when his eyes first lighted on that book. Madame de Staël's book on Germany was similarly used and abused by him.[90] A sounder manual came to hand in 1829, in the form of De Gerando's *Histoire Comparée des Systèmes de Philosophie*,[91] which he set about seriously to read through in the spring and summer of 1830, even to making copious extracts (covering some fifteen pages of the printed *Journals*)[92] and sketching the entire sweep of ancient occidental[93] and oriental[94] thought. In January of 1832, when Cousin's *Introduction à l'histoire de la philosophie* was first translated and published in America by Linberg, Emerson fell upon this abridgment with similar though more short-lived avidity.[95]

Unquestionably the greatest single effect which De Gerando had on the mind of Emerson is discernible already in the first references which he made to the Frenchman. On October 27, 1830, Emerson began reading De Gerando and recorded the fact that he was led thereby "in the outset back to Bacon."[96] In De Gerando's tendency to search the foundations of science Emerson found the Frenchman strongly corroborated by his reading in Coleridge and in Bacon.[97] While he had discovered, as early as November 3, 1830, what he believed to

be the essential difference between the facts of science and the ideas of Reason,[98] he came to hold, four months later, what seemed a necessary corollary, vouched for by both Coleridge and De Gerando and by his own innermost conviction, namely, that "the religion that is afraid of science dishonors God and commits suicide. It acknowledges that it is not equal to the whole of truth, that it legislates, tyrannizes over a village of God's empire, but is not the immutable universal law."[99]

More and more impressed by the idea that Nature speaks in parables to man's spirit,[100] and that religion is thus revealed to man each hour and not only in past centuries,[101] he began to read books of science with keen interest and to make notes recording facts in support of this theory or belief.[102] De Gerando and Coleridge both sent him back to Bacon,[103] and thence he made his way, sometimes independently, oftener by the aid of encyclopaedias, manuals, and other aids to study, back to Bruno (5), Copernicus (11), Galen, *apud* Abernethy's Lectures (2), to Aristotle (27), and forward to Kepler (13), Galileo (12), Leibnitz (12), Dampier (1), Newton (68), Sir Thomas Browne (13), Scougal (10), Swedenborg (118), Kant (41), Pestalozzi (12), Herder (10), Goethe (172), Schelling (46), Hegel (38), Humboldt (25), Neander (3), Priestley (6), Buffon (5), Laplace (12), Thenard (2), Davy (12), Hunter (12), Abernethy (3), Faraday (14), Hutton (4), Wm. and John Herschel (16), Cuvier (16), Gay-Lussac (4), Jussieu (3), Biot (3), Arago (7), Jouffroy (6), Cousin (22), De Gerando (8), Amici (2), Jacob Perkins (4), Stevenson (1), James Hall (2), Gregory Watt (1), Adam Smith (7), Bentham (15), Malthus (9), Oberlin (1), Brougham's *Discourse upon the Advantages and Prospects of Science* (6), Basil Hall's *Voyages and Travels* (1), Mary Somerville's *Mechanism of the Heavens* (2), Gilbert· White's *Natural History and Antiquities of Selborne* (4), Daniell's *Meteorological Essays* (2), Huber's *Natural History of Ants* and *New*

Observations on . . . Bees (1), Sir George Bell's *Animal Mechanics* (1), Benjamin Silliman's Boston course of lectures on geology (1), Parry's *Voyages* (3), Turner's *Elements of Chemistry* (1), Condelle and Sprengel's *Elements of the Philosophy of Plants* (2), Knapp's *Journal of a Naturalist* (1), Kirby and Spence's *Introduction to Entomology* (2), Mawe's *Linnaean System of Conchology* (1), Bigelow's *Florula Bostoniensis* (2), Nuttal's *Ornithology* (2), and Audubon's *Ornithological Biography* (2).

Emerson's interest in science during 1831–1833 is so concentrated that it becomes remarkable. The list enumerated above[104] includes only the more important of the scientists and scientific writings that engaged his attention during the period. From 1833 to 1836, Erasmus Darwin (8), Lamarck (2), Linnaeus (20), and Lyell (12) are among the scientists who began to act significantly upon him. Thereafter, the list becomes quite extensive and includes the names of virtually all the scientists who attracted attention at all. A study of the all-important influence upon Emerson's thinking of such men as Saint-Hilaire (5), Robert Chambers (10), Asa Gray (8), Agassiz (51), Richard Owen (7), Michael Faraday (7), Charles Darwin (8),[105] and Thomas Huxley (4) remains still to be made.[106] The significant exploratory study of Professor Harry H. Clark ends with the year 1838.

If science, before 1830, had been only a secondary interest with Emerson, it became, during 1830–1833,[107] a passionate pursuit for facts to reinforce his religion and his philosophy.[108] Without being truly systematic or thorough, his knowledge of scientific thought was more extensive and his interest more prolonged[109] than that of most of his contemporaries. In the words of Burroughs, "Emerson went through the cabinet of the scientist as one goes through a bookstall to find an odd volume to a complete set . . . . He took what suited him";[110] yet the fact is worth recording that Agassiz remarked he preferred Emerson's

conversation on scientific subjects to that of any other man of his acquaintance.[111] While his approach to science smacks often of the dilettante, his end was nonetheless downright serious. He searched the sciences to find answers to questions which were to him matters of real moment. Oddities, to be sure, attracted him, but not as oddities —rather as eloquent refutations to the tendency which he deplored among the systematizers to make everything too beautifully but rigidly simple. His was no love of the spectacular for it own sake, but a desire to find help in his efforts to bring order into his thinking.

Although his concern with science was most intense during 1832–1833, it is a significant fact for the understanding of the maturer Emerson that this interest became an abiding one, displaying itself not only in an eager reading of scientific and pseudoscientific treatises but equally in grasping every available opportunity to visit museums of natural history, to view collections of various kinds, or to do a little independent botanizing for himself.[112] A correlation of the important passages in his journals of 1833–1835 that relate to his firsthand study of nature and to his reading of scientific lore[113] with his first public lectures and with such essays as *Nature*, "The Over-Soul," "Circles," and *The Natural History of Intellect* will indicate the extent to which the scientific influence contributed to his writings. As will be observed, by referring to the dates given in the note immediately preceding, the number of references to science in the journals tapers off soon after *Nature* was published. The subsequent diaries and the letters demonstrate a sustained interest but no longer an intense concern with the natural sciences, until about 1850, when they became (for reasons to be suggested later) once more all but a preoccupation. For while Emerson never asserted that science could discover the processes of God, he frequently suggested that science, when allied with ethics, could do much in that way.

A consideration of some importance in this study is the fact that the influence of German critical transcendentalism (imperfectly understood though it was by Emerson in 1832, when his scientific studies were most intense) and that of science were not mutually exclusive. Emerson's study of natural history in the light of preconceived abstract laws was encouraged by Kantian transcendentalism learned between 1829 and 1832 chiefly from Coleridge and, increasingly after 1832, from Carlyle, also.[114] "Transcendentalism," Emerson explained, "is Idealism"; however "the Idealist does not deny the sensuous fact: by no means; but he will not see that alone . . . . The Idealist takes his departure from his consciousness, and reckons the world an appearance." He values the data of the scientist as "a manifold symbol, illustrating with wonderful fidelity of detail the laws of being."[115] This is followed by passages in which Emerson refers the ethics of Transcendentalism directly to Fichte and Jacobi and refers its metaphysics to the "extraordinary profoundness and precision" of Kant's thinking.[116] Kant's distinction between Understanding and Reason became invaluable to Emerson, for, as he understood it, Kant had validated both the Ideas of the Reason and the data of the Understanding. Thus Kant laid the foundations upon which Goethe had opposed the science of his day. Writing in 1867 on the subject of "Life and Letters in New England" in the thirties, Emerson interpreted the effect of Kant on Goethe in the following terms:

Goethe declared war against the great name of Newton, proposed his own new and simple optics; in Botany, his simple theory of metamorphosis; — the eye of a leaf is all . . . . He extended this into anatomy and animal life, and his views were accepted. The revolt became a revolution. Schelling and Oken introduced their ideal natural philosophy, Hegel his metaphysics, and extended it to Civil History.[117]

Great as he considered the gain for the religionist, he felt the gain for the scientist no less great. At last it had been demonstrated that both the speculative and the practical thinker, both the metaphysician and the moralist, both philosopher and theologian, yes, both nature and God, had equal claims to validity—one in Understanding, the other in Reason. Thus ran Emerson's musings.

The relation between German speculation and Emerson's concern with science is further illustrated in the reinforcement which Emerson drew from Goethe's natural theories. Goethe was most influential upon Emerson between 1830 and 1840,[118] precisely during the most formative period of Emerson's intellectual life.[119] Emerson read both Goethe's belletristic[120] and scientific works. Of the latter he consulted with great interest the *Metamorphosis of Plants*,[121] the Introduction to *Morphology*,[122] as well as the *Theory of Colors*.[123] Qualified though his admiration of Goethe sometimes was,[124] he considered Goethe as having laid the speculative foundations of comparative morphology in both the animal and vegetable worlds. "Goethe," he said, "suggested the leading idea of modern botany, that a leaf, or the eye of a leaf, is the unit of botany"; and he quoted Goethe's doctrine that as "the tapeworm, the caterpillar, goes from knot to knot and closes with the head," so "man and higher animals are built up through vertebrae, the forces being concentrated in the head."[125] While he was struggling with the intricacies of his own theory, only imperfectly grasped in 1835–1836,[126] concerning the Each in All and the All in Each, he found in Goethe[127] what he described in his diary as "a comment and consent to my speculations on the All in Each in Nature."[128] Finally, in Goethe Emerson came upon Saint-Hilaire's theory regarding the unity of type and variety of form; in Goethe, also, he had access to the doctrine of a deity immanent in natural law. It seems probable, then, concludes Professor Clark, that Goethe was not the least influential among those who encouraged Emerson, in 1838, to define deity as "conscious, animated law."

In following the Goethe-Emerson relationship, we have got ahead of our story, and shall have to retrace our steps to the crucial year of 1832.

It is significant that Emerson's scientific inquiries, notably in physics and astronomy as relating most directly to the constitution of the universe, came to a head at precisely the time when he decided (unless he were permitted to dispense with the rites of the Lord's Supper) to resign his pastorate.[129] Prompted by his conviction that the immutable laws of physics translate, as it were, the laws of ethics, he set down in his diary on May 26, 1832, his conclusion that "astronomy . . . modifies all theology . . . . [It] proves theism, but disproves dogmatic theology."[130] The *next* entry, a week later, records "a week of moral excitement." These bare words, phrased almost laconically, are almost the only record which Emerson made in the journal of that most turbulent as well as epochal moral and intellectual crisis. Having decided that science modifies all theology, proving theism, but disproving dogmatic theology, he resolved to repudiate "an effete, superannuated Christianity" and "the dead forms of our forefathers."[131] Accordingly he proposed to his congregation the omission of certain rites. When they declined to sanction the change, Emerson was forced to decide between conforming and resigning. Following the example of Jesus in periods of trial, he withdrew to the mountains for self-communion, spiritual renewal, a reconsideration of life, and a re-examination of the grounds upon which he had proceeded thus far.[132] In the White Mountains, in July, 1832, he fought it out with himself. Though he knew "very well that it is a bad sign to be too conscientious and stick at gnats," the truths learned of science, on the one hand, and of German philosophy, on the other, held fast; and he concluded, "I can-

not go habitually to an institution [the Lord's Supper] which they [the congregation] esteem holiest with indifference or dislike."[133] On September 9, 1832, he delivered his farewell sermon, at the same time stating the ground of his dissent.[134]

Precisely how much Goethe contributed toward Emerson's dissatisfaction with the clerical profession and the determination to resign his pastorate are questions not hitherto considered. A letter of Emerson's to his Aunt Mary, dated August 19, 1832, suggests the strong probability that Goethe supplied the final impetus that caused him to quit the church. To her he reports "entering into acquaintance with Goethe who has just died"—Goethe, whom the Germans rate with Homer and Shakespeare, and whom he invites her to read with him. "We will try him whether he deserves his niche . . . . The Germans regard him as the restorer of Faith & Love after the desolations of Hume & the French, that he married Faith & Reason, for the world."[135] Directly to the point of the disagreement with his congregation (and it is significant that the date of this letter is August 19, less than a month before he preached his farewell sermon), he goes on to tell her: "[While] I have not yet come to any point with my people . . . I apprehend a separation." And the reason he gives is the dictum upon which Goethe had insisted so often, namely, of acting strictly according to one's own lights as far as they are given. "I can only do my work well by abjuring the opinions & customs of all others & adhering strictly to the divine plan a few inches of whose outline I faintly discern in my breast." "Is that," he asks significantly, "German enow? It is true."

The decision turned out to be a hard one; and the criticisms and whisperings among his colleagues subjected him to a trial equally severe. The death, the year before, of his wife, whose memory he commemorated daily by an early morning walk to her grave, the long battle with himself regarding his beliefs, and finally the resolution to renounce his profession, the resulting hubbub, together with hints that he had acted "Quakerish" and the "loud whispers of mental derangement,"[136] all conspired to break his spirits. His brother Charles wrote to Aunt Mary on November 26, 1832:

Waldo is sick. His spirits droop; he looks to the South, and thinks he should like to go away. I never saw him so disheartened. When a man would be a reformer, he wants to be strong. When a man has stepped out of the intrenchments of influence and station, he would feel his powers unimpaired and his hopes firm. One does not like to feel that there is any doom upon him or his race.[137]

Little though he realized it at the time, his battle was already won. He had been through a baptism of fire, and his newly achieved principles, compounded of a new scientific synthesis, a Goethean self-reliance, and a Kantian metaphysics (vaguely conceived though the last still was) had stood the test. Science had supported his Transcendentalism, and the transcendental division between Understanding and Reason had given meaning and validity to the cold facts of science, at the same time affirming the irresistible persuasion of his soul that he must be true to himself. Together they had enabled him to assert the Everlasting Yea of his inmost convictions—enabled him to have faith in himself in the face of all the opposition the world and men could marshal. Henceforth, although he was not yet fully cognizant of the victory he had gained, the denial and the doubt would present less formidable opposition to the affirmative principles of his soul. Having once spoken the Everlasting Yea, he felt the old trammels were broken. Meanwhile, however, he suffered from a temporary relapse, bred, we may be certain, largely of the cruel criticism showered upon him. The slurs and sly digs that came directly or were relayed to him cut deeply and upset him emotionally.

Considering he had made his decision and given his reasons as manfully as he could, he saw little to be gained by bandying words or replying tit for tat. Nine more years were to elapse before he wrote, in the essay, "Self-Reliance," "Nothing can bring you peace but yourself . . . nothing but the triumph of principles"; but already the truth of this principle seemed substantiated. He resolved to test it in the laboratory of life, applying the full flame to the crucible, to determine whether the residue were solid. Meanwhile, however, his body cried for rest and a change of scene, and his spirit longed to be away—to commune with those two or three who beckoned from Europe and promised clarification and confirmation of the ideas on which he had acted.

Disconsolately, yet with something of hope, too, he determined to meet Coleridge and Carlyle—the men by whom he had arrived at the principles which, together with the newly-learned insight inspired by science, had given him the courage to renounce his clerical robes as unbecoming to himself and inconsistent with his philosophy. Carlyle had exerted a bracing effect upon him even while his identity still remained hidden.[138] On October 1, 1832, less than a month after the farewell sermon, and at a time when he felt the brunt of criticism most keenly, he had written: "I am cheered and instructed by this paper on Corn Law Rhymes in the Edinburgh by my Germanick new-light writer, whoever he be. He gives us confidence in our principles."[139] Nineteen days later he discovered Carlyle's name.[140] Before the year was out, he was aboard ship headed for the Mediterranean; if it had not been a winter sailing, he would have gone directly to Scotland. Instead, he looked up first Landor, whose *Imaginary Conversations*, enforcing self-reliance and idealism, had attracted him.[141] He saw something of the remains of past ages and the accumulated treasures of art,[142] wandered about southern France, and then settled in Paris, where he was "not well pleased" either with the city or with himself.[143] At the end of six months in Europe he felt he had gained little by all his travel. Three weeks after arriving in Paris, he reflected: "A man who was no courtier, but loved men, went to Rome—and there lived with boys. He came to France, and in Paris lives alone, and in Paris seldom speaks. If he do not see Carlyle in Edinburgh, he may go to America without saying anything in earnest, except to Cranch and to Landor."[144] He resolved he would not neglect Carlyle and Coleridge.

Although Coleridge must always be given first place as influencing Emerson at this stage of his intellectual development (both because Emerson lighted on him first, and more particularly, because it was Coleridge who first supplied him with the idea without which the Transcendentalism that he later enunciated could never have been possible for him), it was Carlyle, rather than Coleridge, whom Emerson sought in Europe in 1833. Both, he believed, would be able to enlighten his mind on the score of Kantian transcendentalism, but he presumed that Carlyle would be the better expositor.[145]

During his undergraduate days Harvard had, of course, been innocent of all enthusiasm for or knowledge of German critical idealism.[146] Later, when he studied in the Theological School, he learned little about the German theologians, although Andrews Norton disparaged them, and Follen's close relation to the German Biblical scholars and his championship of their methods could not have escaped his attention altogether.[147] Madame de Staël's book had been something to the purpose since 1826.[148] Dr. Hedge, in 1828, pointedly suggested that he should learn German, but Emerson had not deemed it necessary to go further than to take some cursory note of the German theologians, whom he refers to several times, *en passant*, from 1826 onward.[149] However, reader of reviews that he was, the names of Herder, Schleiermacher, and De Wette came to be something more than mere names during the late twenties, when the American, as well as the British, literary and theological reviews began to take note of them and to bring intelligences concerning them. Of Herder, indeed, Emerson had known something since 1826; ten years later he had grasped the importance of Herder's great seminal ideas as they relate to history, language, and literature.[150] Meanwhile in 1834 Hedge had read to him "good things out of Schleiermacher" regarding physics and ethics, how "*all things* [are] *brought into the mind*," and how "*the mind* [goes] *into all things*,"[151] and had discussed with him "why I was I."[152] Steeped as Hedge was at he time in German metaphysical and theological speculation, we may presume that Emerson received rather pointed instruction on this score during the years from 1829 to 1837, when they were often together. Similarly, his contacts with Dr. Francis Convers, who shared with Hedge the distinction of being the first among the brotherhood to have a thorough command of the German language and a respectable knowledge of German theology and philosophy, might have transmitted to him information in a form more appealing than Emerson could possibly have found it in reviews or the ponderous German tomes themselves.

As far as the *Journals* and *Letters* indicate, Emerson did not then or later set himself avidly to reading Kant, Fichte, Schelling, Hegel, Jacobi, Oken, M(B)aader, De Wette, Schleiermacher, Strauss, Tholuck, Hengstenberg, and the rest. The first reference to Kant in the *Journals* is dated October 2, 1832;[153] Schelling had been noticed only the year before;[154] Hegel, in 1832;[155] and Fichte's name does not occur before 1834.[156] Schleiermacher, too, is mentioned in 1834,[157] but the names of Oken[158] and Strauss[159] do not appear before 1842; that of Baader[160] in 1846; Tholuck[161] first in 1848, and Jacobi[162] waited until 1853, although Emerson had borrowed one of

Jacobi's volumes from the Boston Athenaeum as early as March 24, 1837. While it does not follow that because Emerson fails to mention an author or book in his diaries or letters, he had no knowledge of him, yet it may be assumed, in view of his habit of referring often to the men who occupied his mind most, that the German theologians, by and large, were not of primary importance in his thinking. Nor can we be sure that Emerson knew nothing of these men and their works before the dates indicated, for there were such readily accessible intermediary sources as Madame de Staël, De Gerando, Tennemann, Coleridge, Carlyle, and Cousin. Indeed, there is plainly discernible after the first contact with Coleridge's and Carlyle's writings, a steadily growing tendency on the part of Emerson to forage among the hitherto neglected Germans. After his allegiance shifted from such handbooks as Madame de Staël's and De Gerando's, serving as little more than orientators, he found in Coleridge his best instructor in German philosophy, and in Carlyle his tutor in German literature. Both presented engaging glimpses of the German theologians, but his attention was not thereby focused upon them exclusively nor did he ever become deeply absorbed in them.

We return now to 1830, shortly after Emerson's first contact with Carlyle, when the latter's services as translator of Goethe's *Meister* came to his notice. It should be observed that at this time Emerson was impressed more by Goethe than by his translator; for while he was becoming acquainted, about 1830-1831, with German writers "through articles by Carlyle and others in *Fraser's Magazine*, the *Foreign Review*, and other sources," Carlyle himself meant nothing to him except as a translator and commentator. But once he discovered the identity of this new-found "Germanick, new-light" expositor of German literature, Carlyle's influence became all-powerful, especially after their meeting at Craigenputtock in August of 1833. As a result, many

a new German philosopher, theologian, scientist, and author swam into his ken or was reinvested with a new interest[163] —among them Lessing,[164] Schiller,[165] Goethe,[166] Novalis,[167] and A. W. Schlegel,[168] to be followed shortly after by Boehme,[169] Winckelmann,[170] Wieland, [171] Niebuhr,[172] Heeren,[173] von Ranke,[174] Fichte,[175] Schelling,[176] Hegel,[177] Jacobi,[178] Schleiermacher,[179] Friedrich Schlegel,[180] Spurzheim,[181] Leonhard Euler,[182] Lavater,[183] Jakob and Wilhelm Grimm,[184] Musaeus,[185] Jean Paul Friedrich Richter,[186] Tieck,[187] Jung-Stilling,[188] Pückler-Muskau,[189] Oegger,[190] Johann von Müller,[191] Merck,[192] Zelter,[193] Eckermann,[194] Karoline von Günderode,[195] Bettina von Arnim,[196] and Heine,[197] while Leibnitz,[198] F. A. Wolff,[199] Kant,[200] Herder,[201] Alexander von Humboldt,[202] Mendelssohn,[203] Neander,[204] Krummacher,[205] and Pestalozzi[206] received renewed attention and emphasis. His acquaintance with Varnhagen von Ense,[207] Hölderlin,[208] von Platen,[209] Mundt,[210] Tauler,[211] von Hammer-Purgstall,[212] Tholuck,[213] Baader,[214] Oken,[215] Strauss,[216] Gervinus,[217] Lieber,[218] Scherb,[219] Stallo,[220] Liebig,[221] Mülder,[222] Oersted,[223] Max Müller,[224] Karl G. Müller,[225] Friedrich M. Müller,[226] Friedrich[227] and Herman[228] Grimm, Berthold and August Auerbach,[229] Schopenhauer,[230] and Karl Marx,[231] among Germans who are prominently mentioned in the journals and letters, belongs to later years.[232]

The index which this array of men and books gives of Emerson's curiosity about German literature and philosophy after 1833 contrasts sharply with the inference to be drawn from his answer to Hedge's suggestion, five years earlier, that he should interest himself in German literature, when he "laughingly said that as he was entirely ignorant of the subject, he should assume that it was not worth knowing."[233] What happened between 1828 and 1833 was that he had made the acquaintance of Coleridge and Carlyle. Between them, they completely changed his evaluation of German art and thought. Emerson wrote truly, though somewhat tardily, when he inscribed on his blotter this notation: "August 20 [1837]. Carlyle and Wordsworth now act . . . on us,—Coleridge also."[234] This notation was made eight years after he had first read *Aids to Reflection*, seven years after being cheered and supported by this "Germanick new-light writer," and four years since he had seen both *vis-à-vis*. The insistence with which Coleridge[235] and Carlyle[236] had occupied his mind between these dates may be surmised from the diaries of the period. Reference to the dates given in the footnotes above indicates that in proportion as Emerson's concern with Coleridge decreased, after 1833, his interest in Carlyle increased, suggesting that after 1833 the philosophical influence of Coleridge was supplanted by the more immediate stimulus from Carlyle as affecting Emerson's ethical outlook, his literary interests, and his general view of life.

As between Coleridge's sinking and Carlyle's rising in the scale by which Emerson measured men's worth to him, he was affected by the very different impressions which they made on him when he met them face to face. His visit to Coleridge turned out to be "rather a spectacle than a conversation, of no use beyond the satisfaction of my curiosity."[237] It had been a great disillusionment. The man who had seemed three years before "a living soul," possessed of "universal knowledge . . . bursting the narrow bounds of antique speculation and mad to know the secrets of that unknown world" had turned out in fact to be only "a short thick old man with bright blue eyes, black suit and cane, and anything but what I had imagined,"[238] his mind ossified, hopelessly lost midst the mazes of metaphysics and Anglicanism, reduced to parroting the books he had written long ago.

However, a distinction must be made between Emerson's relative judgments of Coleridge and Carlyle as men and as thinkers. For though Coleridge the man failed

him dismally, Coleridge the critic-philosopher never did. The magnetism by which friendship for Carlyle drew him increasingly to the person of the lovable Scot during the years 1833–1838 did not alienate him from the ideas which he derived from Coleridge. Indeed, the journals for these years show him studying (where three years earlier he had only read) the books of Coleridge, and coming to a fuller appreciation than ever of the Coleridgean mind and the significance of his ideas for his own thinking. From Coleridge he derived at last a critical appreciation of Wordsworth, and upon him, in large measure, he built his own body of literary criteria.[239] Best of all, from Coleridge primarily he derived the Kantian distinction between Understanding and Reason—the most important single philosophical doctrine that ever came to him from without, or that could not readily have come to him from within himself. By it he learned to bring a semblance of unity into his confused thoughts and to compose the first four of his writings. By it, too, he arrived at a means to rid himself of Locke's "heart-withering" sensationalism, to discredit the old spectre Dualism, and to repudiate Platonism, as he had understood it. Between 1838 and 1841 the cyclic development of his mind passed into another phase, to be discussed later, by which the repudiation of Plato became less a denial than a reconciliation of Platonic with Transcendental idealism. This reconciliation contented him (except for some years of restlessness after he met the St. Louis Hegelians) for the remainder of his life. As a result of his association with the St. Louisans, his later formulation of his Transcendentalism took on certain admixtures from Schelling, Hegel, and Darwin, as will appear in what follows; but it remained more a Transcendental than a Platonic form of idealism.

But back in 1833, contemplating the great differences in the persons of Coleridge and Carlyle, he had no doubts regarding the relative worth of the two men. To be sure, Carlyle's mind, on some subjects, had already hardened into rigidity; and on others, they were as far apart as the poles; but Coleridge's mind was utterly lost. However wide Carlyle considered the cleft between his and Emerson's "ways of practically looking at the world"[240] in 1850, Emerson for his part having already put down Carlyle as *"Kleinstädlich"*[241] and as harboring "a large caprice,"[242] they both saw the point "where the rock-strata, miles deep, united again; and the two poor souls are at one."[243]

Dismal as August 5, 1833 (the day on which he had gone to Highgate Hill), had turned out, he put down August 25, 1833, as "a white day in my years," for on that day, he added, "I found the youth I sought in Scotland, and good and wise and pleasant he seems to me."[244] A week later, ready to sail from Liverpool, he set down this considered opinion:

I thank the Great God who has led me through this European scene, this last schoolroom in which he has pleased to instruct me . . . . He has shown me the men I wished to see,—Landor, Coleridge, Carlyle, Wordsworth; he has thereby comforted and confirmed me in my convictions. Many things I owe to the sight of these men . . . . To be sure not one of these is a mind of the very first class . . . . Especially are they all deficient, all these four,—in different degrees, but all deficient,—in insight into religious truth . . . . But Carlyle—Carlyle is so amiable that I love him.[245]

The next evening, still becalmed in Liverpool, he reflected: "Ah me! Mr. Thomas Carlyle, I would give a gold pound for your wise company this gloomy eve. Ah, we would speed the hour." But, he was constrained to add, "It occurs to me forcibly, yes, somewhat pathetically, that he who visits a man of genius out of admiration for his parts should treat him tenderly. 'Tis odds but he will be disappointed."[246] Reviewing his experiences and taking stock of the men he had sought out, he consider-

ed that to "an intelligent man, wholly a stranger to their names . . . they would be remembered as sensible, well-read, earnest men, not more . . . . They have no idea of that species of moral truth which I call the first philosophy. Peter Hunt[247] is as wise a talker as either of these men. Don't laugh."[248]

Was it distance that had lent enchantment, or was it merely that he was coming to himself? Rather the latter. He was comforted to know that even genius such as he had encountered had its limitations—even as he.

I shall judge more justly, less timidly, of wise men forever more . . . .
The comfort of meeting men of genius such as these is that they talk seriously, they feel themselves so rich that they are above the manners of pretending to knowledge which they have not . . . .[249]

Carlyle described Emerson as "the lonely wayfaring man" touring Europe in search of men possessing the key to life's riddles—and finding it in the talisman of self-sufficiency. Emerson found the object of his search in Carlyle more than in any other man. Not that Carlyle answered his questions, for that is precisely what he found his British friends could not do; Carlyle—and for that matter, Coleridge and Wordsworth and Landor, too—possessed the same defects which he found in himself, greater even than those he recognized in himself. All were old men with closed minds—all but Carlyle. But even he lacked religious insight as much as the others. They, the greatest among the great in his estimation, could give him no satisfactory answers. Coleridge had gushed religious and metaphysical nonsense; Wordsworth was sunk in hopeless orthodoxy; Landor had a closed mind; and Carlyle, even he, the best of them, beset by undeniable doubts and unanswerable questions, had roundly skirted his impassioned queries, put as they sat high up on the Craig, about the worth of Christianity and the belief in immortality, by a wave of the hand to Dunscore Kirk in the valley below and dashed off to help catch a pig that had got out. The rector's pig had got out of the sty and had to be caught; meanwhile Christianity and the immortal soul might wait. Emerson sensed at once Carlyle's reluctance and his inability to answer either question. Truly, these men had no preternatural endowments any more than he; indeed, they lacked some strengths that he possessed. This discovery hit him like an encouraging and reassuring slap on the back—back-handed though it was. 'Twas himself he had come three thousand miles and more to find.

He loved their very limitations; they gave him confidence in himself. 'Twas the great lesson of Self-Trust—this unfolding to him of the idea which had been struggling for years to find confirmation, now attested by his experiences with some of the wisest men on earth. Wordsworth was right, ever so right, in saying that a poet is merely "a man speaking to men." A genius, whether Coleridge or Carlyle, was no more than a man, endowed, to be sure, "with more lively sensibility, more enthusiasm and tenderness . . . and a more comprehensive soul, than are supposed to be common among mankind"—but in the final analysis, merely a man like himself.

This discovery had an electrifying effect. It gave him confidence in himself and led him to examine more minutely than ever before the mysteries of the Self that was his. Turning to his diary to set down what he had "seen and heard" during the four days that he had been detained in Liverpool, he recorded what takes on added significance in the light of his most recent discovery: "Really nothing external, so I must spin my thread from my own bowels."[250] There follow now in the diary passage after passage of self-examination and self-assertion, beginning on September 8, with "This is my charge plain and clear, to act faithfully upon my own faith, to live by it myself, and see what a hearty

obedience to it will do,"[251] and ending a week later, with what had become already, as he said, "the old string," namely, that "we are bound to be true to ourselves."[252] Turn to whatever subject he wished, he came always "back again to myself," whence he derived these important conclusions: "A man contains all that is needful to his government within himself. He is made a law unto himself. All good or evil that can befal[l] him must be from himself. Nothing can be given to him or taken from him but always there is a compensation."[253]

At this point he recalled the philosophical distinctions between mind and matter and between Reason and Understanding, imperfectly as he had grasped the latter from Kant through Coleridge during 1829. He now associated with them the lore derived from science during 1830–1832, namely, the correspondence between the laws of physics and those of ethics; and adding to these concepts his old persuasion regarding the validity of moral law, his belief in the divinity of man, and the new-found faith in self-reliance, he suddenly found the whole jig-saw puzzle coming round to fit in one piece. Self supplied the key piece, round which the others arranged themselves. All the parts assembled in their proper order spelled out the broad generalization that "there is a correspondence between the human soul and everything that exists in the world." Since "the purpose of life seems to be to acquaint a man with himself . . . he is not to live in the future as described to him, but to live in the real future by living in the real present," for "the highest revelation is that God is in every man."[254]

Never a system-maker or lover of systems, yet he was struck with what seemed so obviously simple and so simpy consistent that he could not but pay heed and give credence. It was remarkable how One led to the Many and the Many back to One; how from Self he arrived at God, and thence back from the all-encompassing Circle of God to the Centre of Self.

All this, be it observed, came suddenly to him, although the five individual parts of this synthesis had been previously considered, but never put together to form a whole. The passages just quoted were all written "At Sea on Sunday, September 8 [1833]"; and coming thus precipitously, they were less metaphysical analyses or syntheses than intuitive convictions. The metaphysical bases upon which to erect a philosophy embracing all five of his convictions were not yet worked out. They might wait, as, indeed, they did. Meanwhile he was content to grasp as a whole these gloom-dispelling principles, and willing to leave to God and the future what the present did not supply. Of more immediate concern was the problem expressed on September 8: "I wish I knew where and how I ought to live. God will show me. I am glad to be on my way home."[255]

He was already living in the real future by making the most of the present. Accordingly he thanked the Great God who had led him through this European scene, "this last great schoolroom," and had taught him (through Wordsworth, Coleridge, and Carlyle) the great lesson of Selfhood. Although it was the same "old string" on which Aunt Mary and even he himself had harped for years, it had now been revitalized, and it had acquired a new potency. Under its spell he began to write, and his first efforts pleased him sufficiently to record, in his diary, what is the first significant record in the life of Emerson the author: "I like my book about Nature."[256]

He reflected that he had seen somewhat of men, and read more in books; now he must turn from Man-thinking into Man-acting. The first step in this resolution had already been taken in setting down, in his blotting-book, the great seminal ideas out of which *Nature*, *The American Scholar*, the *Address* before the Divinity School, and *Self-Reliance* were to be compounded. What

he wrote at sea on September 8, 1833, although he could hardly have known it at the time, contained in embryo almost everything he was to write later. It was enough, for the time being, to grasp these great principles. Their justification might wait until a later day, when more reading, more thinking, and more living should supply what was still lacking completely to bring them all under the discipline of the Understanding and the Reason—to fill in the connecting links and to erect the philosophical buttresses.

Two significant facts emerge. First, his contact with the men whom he had gone to Europe to see brought him to the realization that by their side he was no dwarf—in some respects, indeed, he topped them all— whence he concluded that their high achievements were not entirely outside the pale of the possible for him. They surpassed him only in having lived longer and more abundantly; otherwise they possessed no mysterious powers that he did not have or could acquire. Second, being cheered by the confirmation drawn from their example, he became suddenly articulate. His journals, referred to as "my Savings Bank," had grown richer daily. The prolific deposits, fractions though they still were, were being added to others and "made integers by their addition."[257] He must combine and add them all up. He would write a book!

He began (in the process of getting at fundamentals) where he always began— with morality. Piqued by the challenge of a fellow-passenger aboard ship that he define what he meant by morals, he defined, as he lay in his bunk, ethics as "the science of the laws of human action as respects right and wrong." "Right," he concluded, "is conformity to the laws of nature as far as they are known to the human mind."[258] "What," he asked, "is this they say about wanting mathematical certainty for moral truths? I have always affirmed they had it. Yet they ask me whether I know the soul immortal. No. But do I not know the Now to be eternal?"[259]

It may be recalled at this point that ten years earlier Emerson had judged his "moral imagination" as strong, and his "reasoning faculty" as proportionally weak.[260] His strength in the former led him to formulate early what remained a constant throughout his life, namely, the faith that God (depersonalized though Emerson's Over-Soul was) is made manifest in "animated universal law," or, to put it another way, that the "celestial geometry . . . affirms the coincidence of science and virtue."[261]

Irresistibly persuaded though he might be of the validity of moral laws and their parallelism with scientific laws, and indignantly though he denied the need either for justifying the former on scientific grounds or of demonstrating the coincidence of the two, yet his own intellectual curiosity continued to pique him into doing just what he asserted to be unnecessary. After all, he was, in 1833, too good a scientist not to be struck by what seemed a fallacious prop in his argument, namely, of regarding something to be true simply because he asserted it to be so. The search for the demonstrability of moral in natural law was to be long and arduous, largely because of the weakness of his "reasoning faculty," or, as he put it on January 15, 1833, because "my comprehension of a question of technical metaphyics [is] very low."[262] The journals for 1833–1836, covering the time which elapsed between his visit to England and the publication of Nature, illustrate vividly the successive steps by which he progressed, and enable us to judge the relative success and failure which he attained.

The flush of excitement attending the composition of the first pages of Nature left him exhilarated to the point of telling himself that the book was already all but done.[263] If the initial passages literally wrote themselves, subsequent sections presented formidable difficulties. Originally

sketched during the first weeks of September, 1833,[264] the little book was three years getting itself down on paper—long years as Emerson impatiently reckoned time then and weighed his accomplishments against the passage of the years. On June 28, 1836, he reported to William:

My little book is nearly done. Its title is "Nature." Its contents will not exceed in bulk S. Reed's "Growth of the Mind." My design is to follow it by and by with another essay, "Spirit";[265] and the two shall make a decent volume.[266]

On August 8, he reported:

The book of Nature still lies on the table. *There is, as always, a crack in it not easy to be soldered or welded,* but if this week I should be left alone . . . I may finish it.[267]

Finally, on August 27, came the first proof sheet, and the booklet itself appeared in September, precisely three years after he had begun it.

The causes for the long delay in writing so slight a book are not hard to find. While, as Cabot remarks, the first five chapters, including the introduction and the four Uses of Nature, had been "for some time in hand,"[268] the section on Spirit, originally designed as a separate essay to balance or provide a counterpart for *Nature*, threw many a stumbling block into his way. Eventually the idea of a separate work was abandoned altogether, and what he had to say on the subject of Spirit became the seventh, the shortest, and the least satisfactory chapter of *Nature*, the preceding section on "Idealism" serving to make the transition between "Nature" and "Spirit." In these later chapters he sought to illustrate the interrelation between nature and spirit, between matter and mind—in short, to bridge the gap between science and philosophy. In the first five divisions he had merely to find and explain the theory of nature, which is science. But "philosophically considered," he went on to observe, "the universe is composed of Nature *and* Soul";[269]

and the theory of Soul, he was soon to find, presented far deeper problems for him than the theory of Nature. The last sections of *Nature*, in which he planned to demonstrate how "the axioms of physics translate the laws of ethics," involved several formidable difficulties, not the least of which was his lack of an epistemology adequate for the purpose.

Unlike Lucretius, who, upon determining to write on the Nature of Things, planted his footsteps firmly on the "imprinted marks" of his predecessor, Epicurus, Emerson, having another *De Rerum Natura* to write, was a long time choosing the right guide. As we shall see, it was only as he came to perceive the relatively greater soundness of Coleridge over Carlyle as a metaphysician that he found an adequate epistemological basis for his work in "the illustrious sage of Koenigsberg . . . the extraordinary profoundness and precision of whose thinking" he acknowledged publicly in 1842.[270]

The record of his struggle with his difficulties can be read in the journals. As has been intimated, he had, as early as 1832, confirmed his belief in the efficacy of science to deal with nature. Even earlier, at least as early as 1823, he had convinced himself of the absoluteness of the moral principle, woven so vitally into the thinking substance itself that it could not be diminished or destroyed without "dissipating forever the spirit which it inhabited."[271] Now that he came to the necessity of putting his thought on paper, to give definite expression to his ideas on these two realms and their correspondence, he encountered the need of something more than an intuitive feeling or inner conviction to supply the exactitude that words demand. Lover or no lover of metaphysics, he had, in the first place, to understand precisely his problem; in the second place, he had to solve it; and in the third place—and this seemed hardest—he had to set forth his solution in intelligible terms, which meant philosophical terms. It

became necessary now for the poet to turn philosopher—to turn from seeing and divining to articulating and defining; for if he aimed to say anything in this book of his, as he did, he must say it so that it would be understood.

This precisely is the task that Emerson set for himself when he wrote his first book. The means to perform this high undertaking (as he must have reflected when *Nature* was finally done) had lain in his hands since the day in February, 1831, when, while reading Coleridge's *Aids*, he first grasped the significance of Kant's distinction between Understanding and Reason.[272] But there, in Coleridge's book, it reposed until after the several deeply humanizing experiences of 1832–1833 and especially those of 1834–1836 quickened his perceptions sufficiently to rouse his philosophical intuitions into constructive action. The stimulating emotional crises and affairs in his personal life can hardly be overemphasized.

On October 18, 1834, he received the sad news of Edward's death, the effect of which can be surmised partly from the references that he subsequently made to him.[273] A year and a half later, he buried Charles—"my brother, my friend, my ornament, my joy and pride."[274] In the meantime he had moved into the Old Manse in Concord, the home built by his grandfather, to take what he felt at the time to be his proper place in the "quiet fields of my fathers!" He had the feeling that his coming hither was "not wholly unattended by supernatural friendship and favor." This consciousness, coupled with the inspiration drawn from "Coleridge's fine letter (in the London *Literary Gazette*, Sept. 13, 1834)," moved him to rededicate himself to self-reliance: "Be it so. Henceforth I design not to utter any speech, poem or book that is not entirely and peculiarly my work."[275] During the summer of 1835 he bought the house and plot of ground which was to be his home for the remainder of his days; thither he brought his bride a month later;

and there, a year later, he held his first child in his arms. Truly, life was running deep: it was both real and earnest, compounded of deep sorrows and abiding satisfactions.

It was almost as if this concatenation of stirring events were necessary to bring the slowly developing genius to fruition. For, though he had left the audience of his favorite British triumvirate full of high resolution to write, and though he had actually made a fair beginning, yet the remainder of 1833, the whole of 1834, and much of 1835 had gone by without his doing much toward developing his "Prima Philosophia"[276] or completing his book on Nature.

The editors of Emerson's *Journals* hesitatingly prefix to the passage in which Emerson first set down in black and white the elements of his "Prima Philosophia" this note: "The following, probably written in 1833, are from a smaller note-book."[277] They are unquestionably in error by two years or more. In the first place, Cabot dates this same passage specifically and unhesitatingly as belonging to June, 1835,[278] and full corroboration for such a dating is supplied by internal evidence. To place it in 1833 would be to put it at least a year ahead of the time when the Kantian distinction between Understanding and Reason began actively to occupy his mind. Except for this misdated passage, there are between September, 1833, when *Nature* was begun, and December, 1834, when he turned his attention intently upon the Kantian distinction, only two cursory allusions in the *Journals* and only one in his letters, either to the Kantian distinction or to the Coleridgean explanation. There is much concern with the antagonism of mind and matter and with the particulars of the science of nature, as these apply to the first five sections of the book, *Nature*; but there is no coming to grips with the basic principles of epistemology involved in his problems.[279] But after December 2, 1834,

his concern with the two Kantian terms becomes a passionate and all-absorbing study, by which all other matters are relegated to a place of secondary importance. The distinction between them, or the Coleridgean explanation of them, and the applications to be made in the development of the First Philosophy are specifically mentioned (sometimes at considerable length) thirty-six times between December 2, 1834, and September 2, 1836.[280]

On December 22, 1834, just two weeks after his first reference to the "divine light of everyman's Reason," he observed significantly, "Mr. Coleridge has thrown many new truths into circulation."[281] A notation on January 13, 1835, indicates that he had returned to a reconsideration of the *Aids to Reflection*,[282] and that he was also researching Cousin's *Introduction to the History of Philosophy* for whatever light could be derived thence.[283] In May of 1834, preparatory to delivering his lecture on "The Naturalist," he reread Coleridge's *Friend: A Series of Essays to Aid in the Formation of Fixed Principles in Politics, Morals, and Religion* with special attention to Coleridge's remarks on the extreme importance of "the Science of Method."[284] He noted carefully that for the supreme problem of philosophy, namely to find a ground unconditioned and absolute for all that exists conditionally, only a critical epistemology (i.e., the transcendental "method") can provide the necessary "copula." It alone, in Coleridgean phrase, provides "the link or *mordant* by which philosophy becomes scientific and science philosophical," and by which he hoped to show that "the axioms of physics translate the laws of ethics."[285]

In the meanwhile, it may be observed that if the application of the Understanding and the Reason to his problem of marrying Nature to Spirit had been as definitely in his mind as the passage misdated 1833 by the editors indicates, *Nature* should have been finished out of hand, and there would have been no occasion for Emerson's complaining, as late as August of 1836 about the persistent "crack" that prevented his finishing the book. Instead the journals indicate that the section on "Spirit" was not formulated with any degree of definiteness until after his removal to Concord, and that the chapter on "Idealism," designed as a link between "Nature and her Uses" and "Spirit," remained largely in outline form as late as March 17, 1836.[286]

Emerson came by the philosophy that went into these two chapters by the hardest way. No one every showed him a royal road to philosophy any more than he found it for himself, and he never felt himself truly initiated in the science.[287] Meanwhile however, he made a serious effort to understand the philosopher's jargon, and so far as he was able, to write it.

His first serious attack upon the epistemological problem which had to be solved goes back to May, 1834. It is coincident with his rereading Coleridge on "The Science of Method," in *The Friend*. Writing to Edward, he spoke of the accidental and phenomenal data of the Understanding and the eternal truths of the Reason, and then added, as much as to ask his brother, to help him, to confirm, deny, add to, or subtract from his conception of Kant's terms at the time:

Now that I have used the words, let me ask you do you draw the distinction of Milton, Coleridge, and the Germans between Reason and Understanding[?] I think it is philosophy itself, and like all truth, very practical . . . . Reason is the highest faculty of the soul—what we mean often by the soul itself; it never reasons, never proves, it simply perceives; it is vision.[288] The Understanding toils all the time, compares, contrives, adds, argues;[289] nearsighted but strong-sighted, dwelling in the present[,] the customary. Beasts have some understanding but no Reason.[290] Reason is potentially perfect in every man—Understanding in very different degrees of strength. The thoughts of youth, and "first thoughts," are revelations of Reason, the love of the beautiful and of Goodness as the highest beauty[,] the belief in the absolute and universal superiority of the Right and the True[.] But understanding[,] that wrinkled calculator[,] contradicts evermore these affirmations of Reason and points at custom and Interest and persuades one man that the declarations of Reason are false and another that they are at least practicable. Yet[,] by and by[,] after having denied our Master[,] we come back to see at the end of years or of life that he was the truth.[291] "Tell him," was the word sent by Posa to the Spanish prince, "when he is a man to reverence the dreams of his youth."[292] And it is observed that "our first and third thoughts usually coincide."[293] Religion[,] Poetry[,] Honor belong to the Reason; to the real[,] the absolute. These [(]the Understanding sticks to it[)] are chimeras[:] he can prove it. Can he, dear? The blind man in Rome said the streets were dark. Finally to end my quotations, Fen[elon] said, "O Reason! Reason! art thou not He whom I seek"—The manifold applications of the distinction to Literature[,] to the Church[,] to Life will show how good a key it is. So hallelujah to the Reason forevermore.

But glad should I be to hold academical questions with you here at Newton.[294]

What Edward might have added by way of correcting Emerson's understanding of critical idealism at this point is problematical; but it is clear that he could hardly have confused him more or led him further off the mark than he was already.[295] By June 20, 1834, he had proceeded no further in his analysis than to record that "the gestures of the Reason are graceful and majestic, those of the Understanding quick and mean."[296] Two months later he referred to the "discord" between Reason and Understanding,[297] and on December 2 of the same year he spoke again of the "instinct of the Understanding to contradict the Reason,"[298] thus following the interpretation of Madame de Staël[299] and especially of Carlyle more than that of Coleridge.

Emerson's thinking never changed, in the same degree as did Coleridge's, from a sensual to a spiritual system of speculation; consequently he never learned what with

Coleridge was basic and instinctive, namely, that the Understanding and Reason, since they move in separate spheres or on different planes, are less capable of contradicting than of supporting one another, especially as the latter many correct the former.[300] Instinct, to be sure, Coleridge considers as standing "in antithesis of Reason";[301] but there is in Coleridge never any desire to debase the Understanding in the sense in which Emerson in this passage (and Carlyle in his essays) sought to degrade it.[302]

But in December of 1834 Emerson was still following poorer expounders of Kant than Coleridge—among them de Staël, Cousin, and Carlyle. In the last passage adduced, in which the Understanding is endowed with the instinct eternally to contradict the Reason, Emerson is accurately quoting Carlyle, who in turn is quoting not Kant but Jacobi. In Carlyle's essay on Novalis, Emerson found this passage: "The elder Jacobi who indeed is no Kantist, says once, we remember: 'It is the instinct of the Understanding to *contradict* Reason.'"[303] Not only is Emerson here setting forth a distinction gotten at third hand—a quotation of a quotation—but he is definitely outside the pale of Kant, wandering in the misty realm of Jacobi and Faith.[304] Fortunately he was already turning back to Coleridge, whose *Table-Talk* lay on his desk.[305] Either in it or in his rereading of the *Aids* or the *Friend*,[306] he found what made him question Carlyle's oversimplified explanation, about which Carlyle himself seems to have had some qualms of conscience.[307] But before Emerson divested his mind of the misconceptions derived from Carlyle, a full year was to pass.[308] Meanwhile Cousin's eclecticism had been called to his attention at least as early as May 24, 1831, by which date he had read "7 or 8 lectures of Cousin—in the first three vols. of his Philosophy . . . .[309] 'Tis good reading—well worth the time."[310] The next year Linberg's translation brought Cousin still more forcibly to his attention.[311] But

the influence of the French eclectic was very evanescent. Although mentioned in the *Letters* as early as May 24, 1831, noticed in the *Journals* as early as January 20, 1832,[312] and referred to three more times in the course of the year,[313] by December 9, 1834, Emerson boldly questioned Cousin's contention that all men alike possess "the Divine Light of Reason." To the proposition, "Every man's Reason is sufficient to his guidance," Emerson was compelled to add, "*if used*." As Cousin would have it, "Every man's Reason can show him what is right. Therefore every man says what is right, whether he use his Reason or no." "I hate," added the Brahmin in Emerson, "this fallacy the more that it is, beside being dire nonsense, a profanation of the dearest truths."[314] Thus he speedily and thoroughly disabused his mind of Cousin and eclecticism before any serious damage was done. Four years later, when the publication of Volumes I and II of Ripley's *Specimens of Foreign Standard Literature* brought eclecticism once more prominently to the fore, Emerson felt called upon to renounce, once and for all, eclecticism as a "shallow" and "pompous" system.[315]

Thus was Cousin finished off. Carlyle, however, was not thus easily disposed of; and it may well be that Sir William Hamilton's generally prejudicial and oversimplified view of Kant contributed to Emerson's difficulties in arriving at an understanding of Kant,[316] at the same time predisposing him to follow Carlyle's, rather than Coleridge's, explanation. It is certain that it took Emerson several years to rid his mind of Carlyle's exposition of German metaphysics, and it is not unlikely that much of the difficulty he experienced is attributable to what must have seemed irreconcilable between Hamilton's half-hearted criticism of Kant and Carlyle's whole-hearted championship of him. For Carlyle was not to be summarily shunted aside. Aside from Carlyle's latest writings, there were those unforgettable personal relations and the reciprocal invitations and editings of each other's books. No, Carlyle had to be heard to the bitter end. It is questionable that Emerson ever completely divested his mind of the false ideas regarding Kant to which Carlyle (and Hamilton) predisposed him.

Talking German metaphysics and reading Schleiermacher with Hedge doubtless helped clarify his thinking on some points, but it seems not to have explained to him that in opposing the Understanding to the Reason, he was voicing a Carlylean and not a Kantian conception; for he continued to make, throughout 1835, antithetical statements regarding the one being unalterably opposed to the other.[317] For example:

The Reason is well enough convinced of its immortality. It knows itself immortal. But it cannot persuade its down-looking brother, the Understanding, of the same.[318]

He [the philosopher] speaks from the Reason, and being, of course, contradicted at every word by the Understanding, he stops, like a cog-wheel at every notch to explain. Let him say, I idealize, and let that be done once for all; or I sensualize, and then the Rationalist may stop his ears.[319]

The Understanding, the usurping understanding, the lieutenant of Reason, his hired man,—the moment the Master is gone, steps into his place; this usher commands, sets himself to finish what He has been doing, but instantly proceeds with his own dwarf architecture, and thoroughly cheats us, until presently for a moment Reason returns, and the slave obeys, and his work shrinks to tatters and cobwebs.[320]

Carlyle agreed with Coleridge that the Verstand-Vernunft distinction is "preeminently the Gradus ad Philosophiam"[321] as being "not only . . . true, but the foundation and essence of all other truth."[322] But he also understood the transcendental philosophy to teach that in "Reason (Vernunft) the pure, ultimate light[323] of our nature . . . lies the foundation of all Poetry, Virtue, Religion," and that "all true Christian Faith and Devotion" appear to be included in this Vernunft-über-Verstand

relationship.[324] At the same time he indicated that the Time-Space relativity and the principle underlying it provided a double premise for the conclusion that the Understanding can produce only relative truth—"true only for us, and if some other thing is true."[325] At the same time, also, "he appears to pass directly from the principle of Time-Space relativity to a resulting assurance of the permanent within the flux, over-leaping the Vernunft-Verstand distinction as implicit."[326] By November, 1831, he avowed the belief that man's conception of immortality depends on that of time, and indicated this conception of time to be at once a requisite of the deepest philosophy and the greatest single triumph of modern philosophy. The Time-Space relativity is indicated to be the only efficient reconciler of contradictions,[327] and as late as 1829 he professed to see a connection between Kant's definitions of Time and Space and his own faith in immortality.[328] In the beginning the Reason-Understanding distinction was to him all-important; later it became subordinate to the Time-Space relationship and in a sense sequent to it.[329]

There is nothing to indicate that Carlyle derived these ideas directly from Kant, or, indeed, that he considered them derived thence. He nowhere specifically related them to any precise source in Kant, but merely referred them to "Kantism."[330] The overemphasis upon the contrariety between Reason and Understanding, in both Carlyle and Emerson, proceeds generally from one cause: Carlyle (in his essays on "Novalis," the "State of German Literature," and "Characteristics") and Emerson (in the Journals for 1834–1836[331]) refer consistently to Reason and mean thereby the practical Reason, without, however, using the qualifying adjective. Emerson here simply fell into what in Carlyle is an habitual proceeding from ignorance, and what even in Coleridge is not unprecedented, although the latter knew well enough the difference between the relative validity of the Practical and the Pure Reason, and several times, in works Emerson was thoroughly conversant with, pointedly called attention to the difference,[332] without however himself being scrupulously or uniformly careful to use the adjectives *pure* and *practical*.

Thus it is that what to Carlyle, Marsh, and Emerson seemed the "momentous" distinction between Understanding and Reason resolves itself, for him who would reconstruct the epistemological steps by which they arrived at their conclusions, into a problem of distinguishing between Pure and Practical Reason (or between regulative and constitutive ideas), at one time, and between Understanding and Practical Reason, the next time—rather than the strictly Kantian distinctions as drawn in the first Critique.

It is significant that after July, 1835, there is only one more statement in the *Journals* that dwells upon these supposed contradictions and contrarieties between Understanding and Reason.[333] How much Coleridge contributed toward rectifying Emerson's thinking on this head is problematical, but it appears pretty clearly from Emerson's comments in the journals that as he progressed, during 1835, to a greater appreciation of Coleridge as a philosopher, his esteem of Carlyle as a thinker fell proportionally. On January 23, 1835, he expressed the opinion that Carlyle is "the best thinker of the age" only "since Coleridge is dead."[334] On August 13, in the midst of his period of greatest concern with the Understanding-Reason puzzle, he asked himself: "Who can read an analysis of the faculties [of the mind] by an acute psychologist like Coleridge, without becoming aware that this is proper study for him and that he must live ages to learn anything of so secular a science?"[335] On October 30, he remarked that "it will not do for Sharon Turner,[336] or any man not of Ideas, to make a System . . . . But Coleridge sets out to

idealize the actual, to make an epopoea out of English institutions, and it is replete with life."[337] A month later he recorded what he seems to have been overlong getting at:

Carlyle's talent, I think, lies more in his beautiful criticism, in seizing the idea of the man or the time, *than in original speculation*. He seems to me most limited in this chapter or speculation in which they regard him as most original and profound—*I mean in his religion and immortality from the removal of Time and Space.*[338]

He seems merely to work with a foreign thought, not to live in it himself.[339]

This judgment, be it observed, represents an accurate analysis of precisely the weak spot in Carlyle as an expounder of German critical thought; for however facilely Carlyle bandied about the words *Verstand* and *Vernunft*, it was at the very beginning of Kant's first *Critique*—in what Kant had to say about Space and Time—that Carlyle's misunderstanding began, when he concluded that because Kant treated of Space and Time as mere forms, he had thereby annihilated Matter.[340] However much inspiration Emerson drew from Carlyle for his purposes in the realm of practical ideas, Carlyle had inevitably to act upon him as a sterilizing agent in the domain of pure speculation. The truth of this was long coming to Emerson. When it did come, he set out, with divine optimism, to suggest, albeit somewhat obliquely, to Carlyle that he return to a consideration of "first principles." But Carlyle commented sneeringly upon Emerson's aspirations to establish the First Philosophy in Boston as "The Euthanasia of Metaphysic altogether." For himself, he added that he had happily discarded "innumerable sets of metaphysical spectacles," and now that he had got done with philosophy altogether, he hoped "one day actually to see a thing or two."[341] Emerson, on his side, grieved over the death of a philosophical brother, lost henceforth, in vitriolic scoffings and worship of power and a dead past, to the sweet uses of philosophic insight. "I always feel his limitations," he wrote in 1842, "and praise him as one who plays his part according to his light, as I praise the Clays and Websters. For Carlyle is worldly, and speaks not out of the celestial region of Milton and the angels."[342] Nine years later, he added, "I still feel, as of old, that the best service Carlyle has rendered is to Rhetoric or the art of writing."[343] Only the great barrier of the ocean that rolled between them preserved their friendship. Nearer association always provoked the sharpest risibilities in both men.[344]

By June, 1835, then, it was already amply apparent to Emerson that Carlyle's career as a philosopher was retrogressive, or at least, at a stand. Yet the false metaphysical lessons learned of that source continued for some time to plague him and to becloud the issues raised in the composition of *Nature*. And when, in June of 1835, he wrote, "I endeavor to announce the laws of the First Philosophy,"[345] he incorporated into them certain ideas which belong more to Carlyle than to Kant, or even to Coleridge. "It is the mark of these [laws]," he continued, "that their enunciation awakens the feelings of the moral sublime, and great men are they who believe in them. Every one of these propositions resembles a great circle in astronomy." This emphasis on sublime morals and the practical Reason, found as it is in both Coleridge and Carlyle, smacks, in its phraseology, more of Carlyle's rhapsodical language in the essay on "Novalis" (where a résumé of German transcendentalism is inserted) than of the more strictly reasoned discourses of Coleridge's *Aids*.

"The *first philosophy*, that of mind," Emerson goes on to say, "is the science of what *is*, in distinction from what *appears*. . . . Reason, seeing in objects their remote effects, affirms the effect as the permanent character. The Understanding, listening to Reason, on the one side, which says, *It is*, and to the senses on the other side, which

say *It is not*, takes middle ground and declares *It will be*."[346]

And here we appear to be once more within the realm of the Coleridgean explanation, for however indistinct Practical and Pure Reason are still left in the passage just quoted, there appears at least a recognition of Sense as distinguished from Understanding—a distinction which Carlyle did not bother to make. Indeed, the passage may well have been suggested by one in Coleridge's *Table Talk*, for this book, which lay on Emerson's study table at the time the passage was penned, contains this statement: "The Understanding suggests the materials of reasoning: the reason decides upon them. The first can only say,—This *is*, or *ought* to be so. The last says,—It *must* be so."[347]

But already in the next sentence Emerson is off again in pursuit of strange gods: "Heaven is the projection of the Ideas of Reason on the plane of the understanding."

Jesus Christ [he goes on] was a minister of the pure Reason. The beatitudes of the Sermon on the Mount are all utterances of the mind contemning the phenomenal world. 'Blessed are the righteous poor, for theirs is the kingdom of heaven. Blessed are ye when men revile you," etc. The Understanding can make nothing of it. 'Tis all nonsense. The Reason affirms its absolute verity.
Various terms are employed to indicate the counteraction of the Reason and the Understanding, with more or less precision according to the cultivation of the speaker. A clear perception of it is the key to all theology, and the theory of human life. St. Paul marks the distinction by the terms natural man and spiritual man.[348]

With the "absolute verity" of the affirmations of "Reason" and the attempt to make Christ and St. Paul speak the language of Kant we appear to have wandered far from the interpretation of Kant's critiques of both the Pure and the Practical Reason. The beatitudes of the Sermon on the Mount, as related to "[practical] Reason" are construed less in the manner of Kant's second

Critique than in the tone of Carlyle's "moral science as the highest development of purest and highest truth" and the "boundless importance of Religion," as he identifies these with Novalis.[349]

Indeed, the next paragraph in this first statement of Emerson's "Prima Philosophia" provides the clue for ascertaining the derivation of these ideas and their terminology. "When," writes Emerson, "Novalis says, 'It is the instinct of the understanding to contradict the Reason,' he only translates into a scientific formula the sentence of St. Paul, 'The Carnal mind is enmity against God.'"[350] This statement was available to Emerson in only one source in 1835, Jacobi, the originator of the statement, being as yet unknown to him except in the account of him as given by Madame de Staël, who did not use the statement. That source was Carlyle's essay on Novalis.[351] Emerson's finding it there and his quoting it from memory explain why the statement is erroneously attributed by him to Novalis rather than to Jacobi.

Closely associated with this extremely loose interpretation by which the voice of Reason becomes associated with the word of God, or with the authors of the Scriptures, is the similarly loose application to which the distinction between Understanding and Reason is put. Without attempting a nearer identification, it might be observed that many of the followers of Kant—among them Goethe[352] and Schiller[353]—were given to making applications of the Kantian distinction much in the same manner in which Emerson made them. In this respect Emerson was simply doing what is a natural inclination and common procedure among romantic idealists, particularly among the Germans who built on Kantian or pseudo-Kantian premises. All things, so long as they could be placed in antithetical relation to each other, were referred to the distinction in a manner against which Kant would certainly have remonstrated. From the distinction between the Ideas of Reason

and the factual data of Understanding, it seemed to Emerson but a short step to the distinction between mind and matter,[354] spirit and nature,[355] religion and science,[356] wisdom and knowledge,[357] right and wrong,[358] thought and thing,[359] reality and illusion,[360] the true and the false,[361] the divine and the human.[362] All these antipodal relationships and many more besides had been made commonplaces in German literature by the various followers and "improvers" of Kant. That Emerson was aware of the uses to which Kant had been put in Germany appears from a passage in the *Journals*, where, commenting on the distinction between the Real and the Apparent, he wrote on September 23, 1836 —precisely at the time when he was most concerned with the practical uses to which Kant might be put:

This came deepest and loudest out of Germany, where it is not the word of a few, but of all the wise. The professors of Germany, a secluded race, free to think, but not invited to action, poor and crowded, went back into the recesses of consciousness with Kant, and whilst his philosophy was popular, and by its striking nomenclature had imprinted itself on the memory, as that of phrenology does now, they analysed in its light the history of the past and present times which their encyclopædical study had explored. All geography, all statistics, all philology was read with Reason and Understanding in view, and hence the reflective and penetrating sight of their research. Niebuhr, Humboldt, Müller, Heeren, Herder, Schiller, Fichte, Schlegel.— *Journals*, IV, 93–94.

A comparison of the list of antitheses expounded by Emerson shows remarkable similarities with a similar list made from, say, Schiller's dissertation concerning the naive and the sentimental in poetry. Emerson's list and applications, set down in the order of their first occurrence in the journals, presents, besides those already mentioned, the following: the beautiful and the ugly,[363] strength and weakness,[364] inward religion and outward form,[365] moral philosophy and natural science,[366] the conscious and the unconscious,[367] love of God and love of self,[368] country and town,[369] ethics and physics,[370] moral law and physical law,[371] immortality and mortality,[372] saint and sinner,[373] idealist and sensualist,[374] the real and the apparent,[375] genius and talent,[376] self-reliance and dependence,[377] poetry and prose,[378] imagination and fancy,[379] wit and humor,[380] noumena and phenomena,[381] the eternal and the temporal,[382] unity and variety,[383] the whole and the part,[384] synthesis and analysis,[385] the universal and the particular[386]—yes, even Carlyle's strength of silence and weakness of speech.[387]

All these applications are the work of Emerson the poet, not the philosopher. They did little harm, and no good. Epistemologically and ontologically, they brought him no nearer the solution of the most difficult problem of philosophy than he had been when he first set to work on Nature in 1833. Thus far Carlyle proved more of a hindrance than a help. Always there remained the "crack" in his reasoning which neither Carlyle's definitions of Reason and Understanding nor his practical applications of them seemed capable of cementing. Fortunate for the metaphysical foundation-work upon which Nature finally came to rest was Emerson's turning back to Coleridge. On May 3, 1834, he sensed the fact that "Mr. Coleridge has written well on this matter of Theory in his Friend."[388] Gradually he discovered that Coleridge's elaborate analysis of science in The Friend[389] and the more strictly philosophical portions of the Aids on Reason and Understanding were deserving of closer attention. In preparation for the lecture on "The Naturalist," given before the Boston Natural History Society on May 8, he reread The Friend;[390] and thereafter, although he continued to draw the distinctions ad nauseam almost, the name of Coleridge is mentioned with rapidly mounting reverence.[391] Throughout 1835 and 1836, Coleridge won increasingly high regard from Emerson. The result of this changing of horses in midstream, as it were, can be studied in Nature, compounded, half of Carlyle's shallow metaphysics seeking refuge in capital letters, and half of Coleridge's more strictly reasoned, if still somewhat indefinitely phrased, philosophy.

There were times when Emerson agreed with Confucius in defining knowledge as knowing what was understood and admitting ignorance of all else; there were other times when, with Coleridge, he wanted to find the foundation in thought for everything in fact. At the time when Nature was composed, Carlyle had already passed to the position of Confucius; but Emerson was never more ambitious, than precisely at this time, to know all. In the opening passages of Nature he went so far as to declare, "undoubtly we have no questions to ask which are not unanswerable." No wonder, therefore, that he should turn from Carlyle, who held out little hope, to Coleridge, in whom he found stated again and again the principles: (1) that the "truths" of moral, or Practical, Reason take precedence over all others;[392] (2) that these "truths" contain their own sufficient evidence;[393] and (3) that, these things being so, philosophy, as the science of finding a ground "for all that exists conditionally" in the "unconditioned and absolute," becomes possible.[394] Thus it is that Nature emphasizes in language reminiscent of Coleridge (1) that philosophy is the science of grounding the conditional in the unconditioned and absolute, and (2) that "all science has one aim, namely, to find the theory of nature," which, when the true theory appears, "will be its own evidence." All this is prefaced by the naively and supremely optimistic assumption, derived from Coleridgean hypotheses and inferences, that we are justified in trusting "the perfection of the creation" so far as to believe that whatever curiosity the order of things arouses in our minds, "the order of things can satisfy"—whence we may conclude that there are no questions for which answers cannot be found.[395]

It is to be expected that Emerson would not be able to confine himself solely to the theory of nature in its purely scientific aspects. Already in the third and fourth sentences of *Nature* he expresses the wish that the modern man might recapture and enjoy his original relation to the universe by beholding "God and nature face to face," and thus he goes, at the very outset, far beyond the strictly scientific purpose of expounding "the theory of nature."

There follow some obvious definitions regarding the Soul and nature, the *me* and the *not-me* of the philosophers, and the distinctions within them, which (although their expression suggests Coleridge[396] and beyond Coleridge, the Germans Schelling, Fichte, and Kant, as giving fresh currency to the *me–not-me*, the ego–non-ego, relationship in philosophy) are commonplaces, and need not be referred to any specific source. The same holds true for the paragraph on the reverence inspired by the starry heavens. It suggests Kant's oft-quoted observation about the "ever-increasing admiration and awe" inspired by "the starry heavens above and the moral law within."[397] But again, the idea is a stock-in-trade of the philosophers, and Kant's expression is not unusually unique. Hence this paragraph and those which immediately follow concerning the kinship between the soul of man and outward nature could be related to Coleridge or Wordsworth and dozens of other sources quite as reasonably as to the German idealists. Certainly at the point where Emerson becomes "a transparent eyeball—part and parcel of God," aware of the Universal Being circulating through him, he transcends the position of German transcendentalism and passes, by a method common to philosopher-poets, from the doctrine of Transcendence to that of Immanence. In so doing, Emerson is not going beyond the possibilities suggested and seemingly approved by Carlyle,[398] but he is clearly outside the limits of Kantian

principles or of the Coleridgean explanation of them. As a poet's preface, the Introduction to *Nature* will do; as an introduction to a philosophic *Weltanschauung*, the scientist and philosopher justly object to its vague, confused point of view.

The violence here done to strict philosophical methodology is in a manner repaired in the succeeding chapters on Nature's uses. In Chapter II, Nature as Commodity is related to the useful arts and sciences in terms of Sensation and Understanding; and in Chapter III, Nature as Beauty is related to the fine arts in terms of Sensation, Understanding, and Reason.[399] In presenting a rather clearheaded exposition of the Time-Space relationship to Sensation,[400] the derivation of the knowledge of Understanding as based on the data of Sensation,[401] and the view of Beauty by which "it becomes an object of the intellect,[402] this section becomes, in the main, the most satisfactory part of *Nature*, considered from Kant's epistemological point of view. It is still, especially in the latter portion, a poet's version of Kant, with admixtures of Fichte and Schelling, all three seen through the eyes of Coleridge; but the distinctions are drawn essentially correctly and together they represent a succinct expression of transcendental idealism in practice on the several levels of Sensation, Understanding, and Reason.[403]

The next chapter, on Language, attempts to carry forward the triplicity of Sensation, Understanding, and Reason as related to the realm of language. The plan or pattern is unquestionably inspired by a hint caught from Coleridge in both the *Aids to Reflection* and the *Biographia Literaria*[404] regarding sphericity as manifest in the triplicity of unity, multeity, and totality—the several triads and trichotomies of the post-Kantians. The substance itself of the chapter on Language, in its emphasis on the derivation of words from nature and their philosophical import, strongly suggests a similar emphasis placed by Coleridge on these aspects of language in the Preface to his *Aids* and in the book itself. But again, it is safer to regard Coleridge and the Germans who stood behind him as supplying corroboration for ideas which Emerson doubtless came by of himself. Three propositions are advanced and discussed: (1) "Words are signs of natural facts"; (2) "Particular natural facts are symbols of particular spiritual facts"; and (3) "Nature is the symbol of spirit." A poetical version though these seem to be of Schelling's *Transcendentaler Idealismus*, as explained by Coleridge, they are perhaps best regarded simply as Emerson's.[405] Little more is involved than the familiar Emersonian doctrine of symbols (or of correspondences), phrased in terms of the transcendental epistemology.

An important point to notice in this chapter, as well as in the preceding one, is that Emerson made no effort here to repeat either the Reason-*supra*-Understanding or the Reason-*contra*-Understanding fallacies —no effort to elevate the one at the expense of the other. Natural facts as embodied into laws by the Understanding are neither inferior nor opposed to spiritual "facts" of [Practical] Reason; instead, they represent a reciprocal parallelism or symbolism.[406]

In the chapter on Discipline, with which Emerson should logically have closed his book on *Nature* (if the poet in him had permitted him to do so), he reaches the point at which he might have come to grips with his epistemological problem. For in discipline all the other uses of Nature are comprehended. Nature disciplines man by educating him through "both the Understanding and the Reason."[407] Indeed, "To this one end of Discipline, all parts of nature conspire."[408]

Emerson proceeds to say what bears evidence of having been derived from Coleridge's disquisition "On the Difference in Kind of Reason and Understanding" as set forth in the eighth of the "Aphorisms on Spiritual Religion Indeed" in *Aids*: "The Understanding divides, combines, measures,

and finds nutriment and room for its activity in this worthy scene"; while "Reason transfers all these lessons into its own world of thought, by perceiving the analogy that marries Matter and Mind."[409] At last we have arrived at the essential problem. Precisely how, we ask, is this marriage effected?

The answer is not given in the chapter on Discipline, which instead, consists of trenchantly phrased but essentially obvious observations on the means by which Nature, working through Understanding and Reason, disciplines the mind of man, that is, provides the moral education of man.[410] But the final teaching of the former by its "lessons of difference, of likeness, of order, of being and seeming, of progressive arrangement" is but "to instruct us that 'good thoughts are no better than good dreams, unless they are executed,'"[411] i.e., fulfill "the doctrine of Use";[412] while the ultimate teaching of the Reason is to show that underneath all variety lies a Unity as "the undergarment of Nature," betraying "its source in Universal Spirit."[413] This, whether it be called Reason, Moral Law, the Unconditioned and Absolute, or God, "lies at the centre of Nature and radiates to the circumference . . . it is the pith, the marrow of every substance, every relation and every process . . . . it is like a great circle, comprising all possible circles."[414] "Every particle is a microcosm, and faithfully renders the likeness of the world";[415] and "Every universal truth . . . implies or supposes every other truth."[416] In the final analysis, then, Nature and Goodness are but two aspects of the same thing, i.e., as they are contemplated by the Understanding and the Reason.

All this is asserted; nothing is proved, except as the "design of nature" is said to "hint and thunder to man the laws of right and wrong."[417] This might be loosely identified with the physico-theological argument advanced in Kant's dialectic as deserving of more respect (even though it can never be wholly and scientifically valid) than the ontological, cosmological, or any other argument. But since, when *Nature* was written, Emerson had not, as far as we know, any firsthand acquaintance with Kant's *Critiques*, it is more likely that these ideas, if they are to be related to external sources at all, were derived from Coleridge and from such an essay of Carlyle's as the one on Novalis. The latter contains, both in Carlyle's summing up of German idealism generally and in his lengthy quotations from Novalis, striking parallelisms, even to verbal identities, with Emersonian phrases.[418]

Having disposed of Emerson's four "Uses" of Nature, we look, next, into Chapter VI, on Idealism, for the metaphysics which shall identify subject and object; for here is reinforced the idea of the preceding chapter, namely, that "to this one end of Discipline, all parts of Nature conspire." Yet all is again left doubtful—nobly doubtful: "A noble doubt perpetually suggests itself,—whether this end be not the Final Cause of the Universe; and whether Nature outwardly exists."[419] "Man is . . . apprised that whilst the world is a spectacle, something in himself is stable."[420]

In his impotency "to test the authenticity of the report of [his] . . . senses," Emerson professes to be entirely unconcerned whether the stars are in their heaven or whether some god paints their images in the firmament of the soul. "Whether nature enjoy a substantial existence without, or is only an apocalypse of the mind, it is alike useful and alike venerable to me. Be it what it may, it is ideal to me so long as I cannot try the accuracy of my senses." Any other conclusion is unthinkable, because "any distrust in the permanence of laws would paralyze the faculties of man." Their permanence is sacredly respected, and man's faith in them is perfect.[421] With this conclusion we are again beyond the realm of the unknowables of Kant's Pure Reason and within that of the morally necessary persuasions of the Practical Reason. On the basis of the practical Reason, we may be irresistibly persuaded (even where we can not find proof) of the permanence of natural laws and their coincidence with moral laws; but on the basis of the speculative Reason, the question of the absolute existence of nature must forever remain open.[422]

The contradiction between affirmation in the realm of practice and denial in the realm of speculation is close enough, in all essential points, to Kant to indicate its derivation. What is un-Kantian is that Emerson is impelled to go on—in the realm of the practical Reason—to assert more than Kant deemed justifiable and against which he pointedly remonstrated. Thus Emerson wrote:

When the eye of [Practical] Reason opens, to outline and surface are at once added grace and expression. These proceed from imagination and affection, and abate somewhat of the angular distinctness of objects. If the [Practical] Reason is stimulated to more earnest visions, outlines and surfaces become transparent, and are no longer seen; causes and spirits are seen through them. The best moments of life are these delicious awakenings of the higher powers, and the reverential withdrawing of nature before its God.[423]

By the addition of imagination and affection to Reason, Emerson transforms the faculty of moral will into one of intuition. The doctrine of Transcendence becomes one of intuitional Immanence, seeking to make knowable what the purely critical transcendentalist must hold forever unknowable.[424]

But Emerson, so far from being content merely *to believe*, sought always *to know*—never more than at precisely this time. His problem was what Plato held to be the problem of philosophy: to ground all that exists conditionally in the unconditioned and absolute. And so he was prompted to peer through phenomenal nature and fasten his attention "upon immortal necessary uncreated natures, that is, upon Ideas," in whose presence "we feel that the outward circumstance is a dream and a shade."

We ascend into their region, and know that these are the thoughts of the Supreme Being. . . . we learn the difference between the absolute and the conditional or relative. We apprehend the absolute. . . . We become immortal, for we learn that time and space are relations of matter; that with a perception of truth or a virtuous will they have no affinity.[425]

While he went on to say that this "ideal theory" is "precisely that view which is most desirable to the mind—is, in fact the view which Reason, both speculative and practical, take,"[426] he realized that thus far he had offered no positive proof for his sweeping assertions. He knew very well that the five arguments for the ideal theory that he had just enumerated[427] were only "arguments"—possessing practical appeal but no absolute authority. Accordingly, in the next chapter, on "Spirit," he returned to his tantalizing problem, this time fronting it squarely by asking the three questions put by nature to the mind: "What is Matter? Whence is it? and Whereto?" Unfortunately idealism has an answer for only the first of these questions. "Idealism saith: matter is a phenomenon, not a substance. Idealism acquaints us with the total disparity between the evidence of our own being and the evidence of the world's being."[428] It has no answer for the second and third questions. He concludes by admitting himself defeated, for on purely speculative or absolute grounds, idealism is nothing more than "a hypothesis to account for nature by other principles than those of carpentry and chemistry." So far from laying the old Spectre Dualism by demonstrating the identity of matter and mind, idealism serves merely "to apprize us of the eternal distinction between the soul and the world."[429] All the protestations of Carlyle, Coleridge, and Marsh to the contrary, Emerson found the Kantian distinction between Understanding and Reason unequal to the task he had set for himself in Nature—except as he found quasi-answers to his questions in the "truths [that] arise

to us out of the recesses of consciousness," where Kant gave him no license to stray.[430]

The chapter on "Prospects" with which Emerson concludes Nature adds nothing to the philosophy advanced except to re-emphasize, in the long last paragraph, the idea of individualism, which, in view of the earlier statement that the individual is "part and parcel of God,"[431] provokes the disturbing question whether Emerson is not involving himself in a deep contradiction. That he was himself conscious of the danger of the point of view which sees the individual as part and parcel of God, and who is, therefore, no individual at all, appears most clearly in the essay on "Nominalist and Realist" of the Essays, Second Series (1844):

I wish to speak with all respect of persons, but . . . they melt so fast into each other . . . it needs an effort to treat them as individuals. . . . But this is flat rebellion. Nature will not be a Buddhist. . . . As man is a whole, so is he also a part; and it were partial not to see it . . . . You are one thing, but Nature is one thing *and the other thing*, in the same moment. She will not remain orbed in a thought, but rushes into persons.[432]

Thus we have, on the one hand, "that overpowering reality . . . that unity, that Over-Soul, within which every man's particular being is contained and made one with all other,"[433] and, on the other, a Nature which "rushes into persons," each of which possesses both true individuality and freedom. This involves an inconsistency that troubled Emerson. Writing down, in 1835,[434] the basic tenets of his philosophical creed, he observed:

Our compound nature differences us from God, but our Reason is not to be distinguished from the Divine Essence. To call it 'ours' or 'Human' seems an impertinence, so absolute and unconfined it is. . . .[435] Time and space are below its sphere; it considers things according to more intimate properties; it beholds their essence, wherein is seen what they can produce. It [the Divine Essence, or Reason] is in all men, even the worst, and constitutes them men.

In bad men it is dormant, in the good, efficient; but it is perfect and identical in all, underneath the peculiarities, the vices, and the errors of the individual.

In this explanation is involved man's threefold nature: (1) in its lowest form is man's sensory organism, which, as a part of nature, never loses hold of the reality of which it is only the effect; (2) above it, and in a sense springing from it, is the understanding, "the executive faculty" or "the hand of the mind," which "mediates between the soul and inert matter"; and (3) above both is the Reason, not to be distinguished from the Divine Essence, ready to surrender its freedom and return to the great reality from which it came to dwell in the soul of man. This much is clear. All is roughly within the pale of German transcendentalism, even if Reason, as used by Emerson, is almost always the Practical Reason put to extraordinary uses, i.e., more than strictly Kantian uses. This position represents Emerson's highest reach in the realm of transcendental epistemology, modeled on a Kantian-Coleridgean base. Its best expression is found in *Nature*.

But like Schelling, and like Coleridge, Emerson sought to go beyond this "first philosophy," which, as he came to look back upon it, was, after all, far from satisfactory in all points. The philosophy enunciated in *Nature*, so far from establishing the identity of subject and object, left unanswered two of the three big questions. The marriage of mind and matter remained uncelebrated. At its best, the thesis advanced in *Nature* was mere theory. Epistemologically considered, it was only a nettling possibility; it defied all proof. Accordingly the transcendental idealism of *Nature* is put down as being, "in the present state of our knowledge," only an hypothesis—a "useful introductory hypothesis, serving to apprize us of the eternal distinction between the soul and the world."[436] More than this, Emerson has to admit, it is impossible to claim for it.

Whether he comprehended Kant's differentiation between pure and practical reason and his demonstration of the failure of the pure reason to prove its Ideas and of the inefficacy of the practical reason to establish indisputably the Ideas of God, freedom, and immortality, Emerson sensed that his own demonstration of the marriage of mind and matter, as well as of the perfect identity of moral and natural law, had failed. If he had read Kant's pointed statement in the Preface to the second edition of his *Critique of Pure Reason*, "I have found it necessary to deny any *knowledge* of God, freedom, and immortality, in order to find a place for faith," it is possible that Emerson might have saved himself a good deal of trouble; but it is more likely that even if he had read this statement of Kant's, he would still have gone through the steps of his attempted proof, if only to satisfy his own mind.

The phrase "in the present state of our knowledge" suggests three things: (1) that in 1836 he was far from satisfied with his results, (2) that the final synthesis needed still to be made, and (3) that in making it, he would need, perhaps, to draw more than he had upon analysis—upon the knowledge bred of science. Two avenues of approach to the problem presented themselves: he could proceed intuitively or synthetically, or he could retrace his steps to 1832 (back to where he had left science) and proceed rationally and analytically. Emerson would not have been Emerson if he had not attempted first the former alternative. While he was about it, however, he did not entirely lose sight of the gains of science which he had noted in his studies before *Nature* was undertaken. Far from espousing scientific evolution, Emerson does avow already in *Nature* a belief in "a certain occult recognition and sympathy in regard to the most unwieldy and eccentric forms of beast, fish, and insect,"[437] a belief in a "progressive development"[438] and in a "principle of growth,"[439] for "it is essential to a true theory of nature and of man that it should contain *somewhat progressive.*"[440] Widely though this differs from Darwinism,[441] there are in Emerson, side by side as it were, two tendencies: one seeks to push the philosophy of intuition to the limit of its capacity, and the other inquires of science the means to establish the absolute identity. Both tendencies are discernible before 1836, and they continue to engage his mind after he became more clearly aware of the inadequacy of transcendentalism as expressed in *Nature*; but the emphasis varies with the years. From 1836 to 1839, approximately, the emphasis is upon the theory of emanation, the concern with science being secondary; thereafter, especially after 1850, Emerson concentrates more and more upon the theory of evolution, while the doctrine of emanation and the intuitional approach become gradually subsidiary.

While Emerson speaks in *Nature* of "an occult relation between man and the vegetable"[442] that demands "somewhat progressive,"[443] the motto which stood at the head of the book in 1836 was a sentence from Plotinus to the effect that "Nature is but an image or imitation of wisdom, the last thing of the soul."[444] This must be recognized as being more appropriate to the thesis of the book than the verses which were substituted in 1849, ending,

And striving to be man, the worm
Mounts through all the spires of form.

The latter motto represents an afterthought, put there thirteen years after the work was done, and reflecting a new stage in the author's thinking. In 1836 he was far from such a position.[445]

The Neo-Platonic Interlude (1838–1850)

Emerson's choice of Plotinus to furnish the motto for the first edition of Nature is a matter of some moment. It supplies the cue to the next step in the thinking of Emerson, which thus far had gone through three phases: first, the Lockean sensationalism learned at college; next, a loosely conceived Platonic idealism, viewed as dualistic, which served to discredit Locke; third, a revolt against the "spectre dualism" by an attempted adherence, from about 1830 to 1838, to German transcendentalism. When this, in turn, failed to effect the identity of subject and object, it was only natural that he should proceed to the next step (instinctive in the mystic) by which reason becomes intuition.

The journals between 1836 and 1841 (between the publication dates of *Nature* and the *Essays, First Series*) illustrate how earnestly, though futilely, Emerson sought, at one moment, to reason his way through to a complete and consistent whole and, at the next, to grasp the mystical intuitions of truth.[446] Idealism pure and simple (as he looked back upon *Nature*) presented him with the dilemma by which man remains a mere "idea"; evolution, as he grasped it at the time, accounted for man as merely the product of a great evolving reality—not an established unit, but merely an evolving, partial phase of that reality or unity.[447] Both problems occupied him equally and simultaneously throughout 1836 and 1837. The journals of these years indicate the steps by which he was prepared to grasp neo-Platonism, notably the emanation theory of Plotinus,[448] in an effort to effect a reconciliation.

By the end of 1837, the Kantian Understanding and Reason, hailed a short time before with great delight and looked to for glorious results, have shrunk to "Common-Sense" and "Vision," respectively.[449] "The Intellect always ponders"; it is no longer the high Reason which it was represented to be in *Nature*. It never participates. "It is always [merely] the observer."[450] Yet Emerson feels himself "continually impelled by the influx of the higher principle to abstract himself from all effects, and dwell with causes," to dwell "in the region of laws," in the "native air of the human soul." He seldom finds himself able to climb so high; but "the child lives with God, as a dweller in the higher sphere, that of the Absolute Truth."[451] "This infinite nature bursts through at last into the affirmation of real being; I am."[452] "Long prior to the age of reflection is the thinking of the mind. Out of darkness it comes insensibly into the marvellous light of today." "God enters by a private door into every individual."[453] Here is a man all ready to forsake metaphysics for mysticism—Kant and criticism and transcendence for Plotinus, intuition, and emanation.

The result of this transfer of allegiance can be read in the essay on "The Over-Soul," composed between 1836 and 1838,[454] and especially in what presents perhaps the best exposition of this phase of Emerson's philosophic development—the remarkable lecture on "The Method of Nature" (1841). That Plotinus' doctrine of perpetual emanation and return, however hard Emerson struggled with the doctrine,[455] would give him no final satisfaction could have been put down as a foregone conclusion. A minute examination of what Emerson derived from Plotinus and the neo-Platonists generally in the doctrines of emanation, archetypes, soul intuition, the One and the Many, microcosm, and related ideas involves matters foreign to our immediate purpose. Moreover, the studies of Professors Harrison, Carpenter, Christy, and Hotson do just that, and do it admirably.

So long as Emerson stuck to his intention to find and explain in the Absolute the ground for all that exists in the conditional world—and fundamentally he did not waver in the intention, however far afield the effort led him—there could be for him no final resting place in mysticism and sheer intuitionalism. Neither the intellectual demand to establish the identity of subject and object nor the personal urge, which would not down, to find a philosophic certainty for the Individual as distinguished from the all-absorbing Totality could be satisfied by the theories emanating from Asia. Eventually it was inevitable that he should endeavor to equate his inherited idealism with the theory of evolution. The latter forced itself upon his attention with increasing insistence. Though he never wholly gave up his belief that "nature proceeds from above" and that man is part of the godly order, there is traceable throughout his work a growing faith in evolution. Hostile though it was to his earlier idealism, it finally forced him, even while he was immersed in the most unscientific stage of his thinking—in the occultism of the East—to pay ever more heed to the accumulated data of the scientists, at the same time that he suspended, more or less unconsciously at first, the intuitionalism and faith of his earlier position.

Thus it came to pass that even while he was phrasing, about 1838 to 1841, the brilliantly mystical intuitions and giving utterance to his reveries and communings in "Intellect" and "The Over-Soul," he was re-searching his mind for the scientific lore which he had made his own in the thirties and seeking to integrate it with what the newer scientific books told him. But during the years from 1841 to 1849 he seems to have called a halt to his philosophizing.[456] Of metaphysics pure and simple the works of this decade are signally free. His thinking, in so far as it can be traced in his published writings and public utterances, appears to have reached a plateau; that is, the decade of the forties was devoted chiefly to the philosophy of use, or to more purely literary concerns, either critical or creative. They were years during which he produced his essays on "practice"—essays like "Experience," "Character," "Manners," "Gifts," "Politics," "New England Reformers," and the book on *Representative Men.* They were also the years during which he gathered most of the matter that later went into *English*

Traits, Conduct of Life, and *Society and Solitude.* This does not mean that philosophy no longer engaged his mind, or that the high intellectual undertaking of his youth no longer interested him. It means that he preferred to express himself publicly on practical matters, while privately he sought as avidly as ever for a new theory, a new metaphysics, a reintegrated philosophy. Twice at least he had thrust before the public theories which he had had, in a measure, to repudiate (or modify) later. Before he spoke again as a philosopher, it might be well to make sure of his philosophic, i.e., epistemological, grounds. He planned not again to go off half-cocked.[457]

Generally quiet as the published works of the decade from 1840 to 1850 are on the subject of technical philosophy, his journals show him struggling as actively as ever to achieve a new metaphysical synthesis. But, except for the challenging idea of sphericity, formulated about 1840 for the essay on "Circles," he made no real progress until 1849,[458] when he came upon a book the tremendous significance of which in the development of Emerson's last stand in philosophy has never been evaluated.[459] This book was entitled *General Principles of the Philosophy of Nature: With an Outline of Some of its Recent Developments among the Germans, Embracing the Philosophical Systems of Schelling and Hegel, and Oken's System of Nature,* by J. B. Stallo, A.M., lately Professor of Analytical Mathematics, Natural Philosophy, and Chemistry, in St. John's College, N.Y. (Boston, 1848).[460] To Stallo's book belongs the credit, first, for bringing home to Emerson with compelling force how far science had advanced beyond the position of the scientists that he had studied in the thirties, and second, for giving him a more detailed and accurate account of post-Kantian metaphysics than he had hitherto found in any single source.[461] From this reading of Stallo forward,[462] he referred to Oken,[463] Saint-Hilaire,[464] and other scientific evolutionists, including Charles Darwin, and to Schelling and Hegel as evolutionary philosophers with increasing frequency. It is not too much to say that Stallo, more than any other, is responsible for what became about 1850 a serious effort, far more prolonged and more thoroughgoing than the earlier one, to understand what was going on among the evolutionary naturalists, on the one side, and among the philosophic theorists, on the other.

It was something more than mere chance that Emerson copied into his journal, in 1849, from Stallo the sentence expressing the idea that "the development of all individual forms will be spiral," and that he substituted, in the same year, for the motto in the 1836 edition of *Nature* (which he had derived from Plotinus) the verses describing the spiral ascent of the worm to the form of man.[465]

Another factor not to be overlooked in accounting for Emerson's revival of interest in science is his meeting, during his second visit to Europe, the leading British scientists. His letters of 1848 voice his delight in the companionship of these eminent men, of dining with them, or hearing them lecture. He particularly enjoyed his contacts with Robert Chambers, Charles Lyell, Michael Faraday, Richard Owen, William Buckland, Edward Forbes, Robert Brown, "the great Botanist," William Spence, "the entomologist," George Combe, and Sir William Hamilton.[466] That personal contact with these men should have stimulated him to a renewed interest in science was natural.

Important and interesting as these considerations of a scientific nature are, it is more particularly to philosophers and philosophy that we must turn our attention. Yet even while we do so, we shall constantly have to revert to science and scientists, for Stallo led Emerson to return not only to a more intense re-examination of German thought than even Coleridge had been able to arouse in him twenty years earlier, but also to evolution and science generally (which had gone into a decline in his thinking since 1836). Perhaps it would be more accurate to say that Emerson was more or less naturally impelled by reason of his dissatisfaction with his own philosophy of mystical and intuitional neo-Platonism during the forties, to come round full circle in his thinking to approximately the same approach which he had followed and then forsaken during the late thirties. Then he had studied science and the German thinkers as co-ordinate sources from which to extract his *prima philosophia*. Now he returned to what is essentially the same positon, except that the philosophic experience of the intervening years had disabused his mind of several ideologies as either false or sterile for his purposes. Truly might Madame de Staël, echoing Goethe, observe of the mind of man, "It is always advancing, but in spiral line." What is to Stallo's credit primarily is that he most directly influenced Emerson to make this spiral return, whence, as Emerson grasped with increasing surety the true import of evolution, he was to attempt another philosophical synthesis, this time with Schelling and Hegel as guides. That he turned with searching attention to these two rather than some others, the times and Emerson's own bent of mind about 1849 made inevitable.

At the time when Emerson was most interested in Kant, his ideas were available to Emerson only at second hand. Sometime after 1838, however, he acquired a copy of Francis Haywood's translation of the *Critique of Pure Reason* (London, 1838); but since there are few marks in the book, and since the index which Emerson habitually made of the books which he read includes, in this instance, only three entries or heads, namely "Locke and Hume," "Immortality," and "Oblate Sphericity," we cannot be sure that he read the volume either attentively or entirely. There is no indication of the date on which the book came into Emerson's possession.

But these are matters of little moment

in view of the fact that Kant never after 1838 held an important place in Emerson's thinking, although he did hold firmly on to an ethical philosophy that is, from first to last, essentially the same as Kant's in practice, though not necessarily derived thence. Not that Emerson dismissed Kant completely from his mind. The references to Kant in the later journals and writings continue, even with accelerated frequency; but they are often references of a general nature, and there is nothing to suggest that he returned to a serious consideration, or reconsideration, of Kant.[467] Instead, he sought to grasp Kant's significance for evolutionary philosophy, and honored him as initiating the point of view by which science and philosophy were to be equated. More to the later Emerson's taste than the epistemological abstractions and metaphysical analyses of Kant were the poetical vagaries of Schelling. The reasons for this deflection in Emerson's allegiance are fairly obvious to the student who follows Emerson through his neo-Platonic stage.

Emerson's interest in Fichte, if the journal references afford an indication, was even and prolonged, but never impassioned. There is not, in the published record, conclusive assurance that Emerson ever read Fichte either in the original or in translation, except the considerable portions of the first and third books of *The Destination of Man* printed in Hedge's *Prose Writers* of 1847.[468] Altogether, there are in the *Journals* eight references that warrant being noted: the first in 1834, the last in 1870, and several in between that refer to "the grand unalterableness of Fichte's morality,"[469] the "strength of his moral convictions" which form Fichte's "charm and character."[470] These characterizations are derived less from a firsthand knowledge than from a reading about Fichte in such secondary sources as Carlyle, who speaks of "the sublime stoicism" of Fichte's ethical sentiments in his essay on the "State of German Literature,"[471] and Madame de

Staël's *Germany*,[472] whence Carlyle himself appears to have drawn a good deal of his information about Fichte.

This being so, it is questionable whether the sweeping claims that have been made regarding the derivation from Fichte of Emerson's ethical theories are sustained by facts. What is more, Emerson could not, in 1847, have entertained appreciatively Fichte's strict determinism and necessity in Nature as described in *The Destination of Man*, however much the point of view and the aim, as expressed in Fichte's prefatory remarks, may have attracted him. Fichte's dictum that "Practical reason is the root of all reason" may well have struck a responsive chord, but that was something Emerson had held all along. If it could be established that Emerson read *The Destination of Man* before 1836, we should perhaps be justified in ascribing to Fichte large portions of *Nature*. By the same token we should be able to relate to Fichtean idealism the extreme egoism, optimistic self-reliance, and call to action of *The American Scholar* and the Divinity School address, but these are referable rather to other sources, as we have observed. Fichte, except as he came to Emerson at second hand, came too late to affect these utterances of 1836, 1837, and 1838. When, in 1847, Emerson did read Fichte's *Destination of Man*, it no longer held anything novel for him.[473] He himself had passed the state of mind which Fichte describes—that of "a mind just beginning to speculate on its own nature and destiny and the grounds of all being and knowing."[474]

If, on the other hand, Emerson had, in 1836, or even during the neo-Platonic stage of his thinking, come upon Fichte's Divine Will and Sublime Faith, as developed in *The Destination of Man*, he would undoubtedly have drawn confirmation from that source. But in 1847 he had advanced to the position which sought something more than Fichte's "Faith" to effect the epistemological reconciliation between Mind and Mat-

ter, Spirit and Nature, God and Man. Moreover, when, in 1847 Emerson encountered (in *The Destination of Man*) what Fichte called irresolvable Doubt and impossible Knowledge, he could not but be repelled by them; while the vague means by which Fichte's "sublime, living Will" effects the identity of the finite and the infinite could have given Emerson no substantial satisfaction. Already in 1837 he owned: "A believer in Unity, a Seer of Unity, I yet behold two." "Why," he cried, "cannot I conceive the Universe without contradiction?"[475] Although he was impelled at various times to assert the inscrutability of absolute truth, he never relinquished his search for it. He never gave up his desire *to know*. Fichte, on the other hand, said frankly in the treatise which Emerson read:

I will not attempt that which is denied to me by my finite nature, and which could avail me nothing. I desire not to know how thou art in thyself. . . . Thou workest in me the knowledge of my duty, of my destination in the series of rational beings. How? I do not know, and need not know. Thou knowest and perceivest what I think and will. How thou canst know it,—by what act thou bringest this consciousness to pass,—on that point I comprehend nothing.[476]

As philosophy, then, the popular works of Fichte held little for Emerson.[477] On the other hand, everything conspired to his giving Schelling's ideas a more favorable reception. Coleridge[478] had prepared the way, and there was available a good deal of other explanatory material on Schelling during the early period of Emerson's literary productivity. Yet he seems not to have availed himself of it, and a remark made in 1838 suggests what indicates that Schelling then had little to teach him: "Leave me alone; do not teach me out of Leibnitz and Schelling, and I shall find it all out myself."[479] Eight years later, he set down a conclusion, the exact import of which is hard to extract:

In Germany there still seems some hidden dreamer from whom this strange, genial, poetic, comprehensive philosophy comes, and from which the English and French get mere rumors and fragments, which are yet the best philosophy we know. One while we thought that this fontal German was Schelling; then Fichte, Novalis; then Oken; then it hovered about Schleiermacher, and settled for a time on Hegel. But *on producing authenticated books from each of these masters,*[480] we find them clever men, but nothing like so great and deep a poet sage as we looked for. And now we are still to seek for the lurking Behmen of modern Germany.[481]

It would seem that something transpired between 1838 and 1846 to direct Emerson's attention to Schelling. He had supplied himself between these years with some parts of Schelling's works, and considered himself by now sufficiently well read in post-Kantian speculation generally and in Schelling particularly to warrant his hazarding some rather sweeping generalizations. The letters made available in the Rusk collection, together with what is known about the general direction of Emerson's mind during the forties, afford fair indications of what happened, and enable us to sketch the steps by which he was led to appreciate Schelling.

First, the mystical intuitionalism, in which he dwelt following the collapse of his high hopes for the transcendentalism which he had expounded during the thirties, made him naturally susceptible to the mystical-religious philosophy of Schelling, all the more so because of Schelling's reinforcement of his own philosophy by poetry and religion. In Schelling the aesthetic reason served to harmonize religion and philosophy. Madame de Staël, Carlyle, and Coleridge all agreed on that point. Emerson doubtless recalled the high esteem in which Coleridge had held the *Identitätslehre* of Schelling.

Thus prepared, Emerson entered the second phase of his enthusiasm for Schelling. In November, 1842, Charles Stearns Wheeler began sending him reports from Heidelberg of "German universities and

scholars"—reports which Emerson decided to print in the *Dial.*[482] He professed at this time to be especially interested in Schelling because of the "grandeur" of the attempt in which Schelling and Oken combined "to unite natural and moral philosophy."[483] Wheeler next sent *Schelling's erste Vorlesung,* which Emerson promptly forwarded to Hedge to be translated for the *Dial,*[484] where it appeared in the January, 1843, number. Yet nothing substantial came of this burst of enthusiasm until James E. Cabot sent him, in February of 1844, an article on Kant for the *Dial,*[485] and himself came to Concord a year later "to comfort the dry land with a little philosophy," as Emerson whimsically reported.[486] Emerson's account to Elizabeth Hoar of this first visit indicates the antiphilosophic cast of his mind at the time. He asked her not to charge him with "levity and the old aloofness"; he professed to revolve as truly as ever, but with "humble docility and desire, the world-old problems." Steeped in neo-Platonic mysticism, he viewed the philosophy of the professionals as no more than "the poetry of the Understanding, the mirage of Sahara"; for himself, he added, "I worship the real, I hate the critical and Athwart."[487]

But the indefatigible Cabot gave him no rest. In the summer of 1845 he sent Emerson his "Essay on Freedom," a translation of Schelling's "Philosophische Untersuchung über das Wesen der menschlichen Freiheit." At last Emerson's interest was truly aroused. To Cabot he wrote:

This admirable Schelling, which I have never fairly engaged with until last week, demands the 'lamp' and the 'lonely tower' and a lustrum of silence. I delight in his steady inevitable eye, and the breath of his march including and disposing of so many objects of mark. . . . I cannot for the present let any Miss Peabody or other person have the book [Cabot's translation], which has, I am sure, come just to the right reader for the present. Whenever you choose to print it, which is the best thing to do with it, or, as soon as my good will to philosophic readers overpowers my desire to understand and appropriate it, I shall send it back.[488]

A month later he reported that while "Schelling continues to interest me . . . I am so ill a reader of these subtle dialectics, that I let them lie a long time near me."[489] Thus he kept the manuscript a year and then felt obliged to ask Cabot's forgiveness, at the same time passing on to Cabot his final estimate of the work:

The Schelling I have only now concluded to let alone. I wish you might some day feel disposed to print it, that it might go magnetising about to search for the souls now unknown that belong to it. Yet that were hazardous, since it is one of the books, like my Alexandrian Platonists, which seem to require a race of more longevity and leisure than mankind, to sound all these depths which yet do not pretend to be the sea, but only the swimming school. But again I should like to have you print it . . . .[490]

His intercessions with Munroe to publish the work came to naught,[491] and his interest in Schelling appears soon to have waned. The conclusion seems to be that this remarkable burst of enthusiasm had been impelled less from within than from without by enthusiasts like Heath, Wheeler, Hedge, and Cabot. In any case, the difficulties of Schelling's dialectics soon cooled his ardor. The chief significance of the episode is that it kept his moderate interest in natural philosophy from subsiding altogether and, what is more important, that his reading of Schelling and his contacts with Hedge, Cabot, and soon after, Stallo eventually brought Hegel prominently to his attention. When he next undertook to review ideas emanating from the post-Kantians, it was less Schelling than Hegel who interested him; and it is in connection with his view of the latter that we shall revert to his attitude toward the former.

The Hegelian-Darwinian Period (after 1850)

Of Hegel Emerson knew little more than the name prior to 1846, when he observed:

Hegel's philosopheme, blazoned by Cousin, that an idea always conquers, and, in all history, victory had ever fallen on the right side (a doctrine which Carlyle had, as usual, found a fine idiom for, that Right and Might go together), was a specimen of this Teutonism. Something of it there is in Schelling; more in his quoted Baader; something in Goethe, who is Catholic and poetic. Swedenborg had much; Novalis had good sentences; Kant nothing of it.[492]

Apparently repulsed at first by Hegel, Emerson was slow coming to him. The notes on his reading show him less interested during the forties in Hegelian than in the Schellingian kind of mystical naturalism as represented by Oken, Maader, and Boehme on the one hand and the mystical neo-Platonists, Iamblichus, Proclus, and Porphyry on the other. First impelled, about 1850, by Stallo to re-search the scientific bases of his thinking, Emerson made little progress in that direction between 1850 and 1855, when his observations in his diary show a vacillating state of mind between faith and knowledge, intuition and logic—the intuitional and the scientific methods striving against each other. Indeed, about this time he went so far as to remark that in Germany and in German philosophy he had "no interest . . . since the death of Goethe,"[493] to whom he still attributed "preternatural size,"[494] and whom he called "the pivotal man of the old and new times."[495] As for the German philosophers' having "found the profoundly secret pass that leads from Fate to Freedom," he professed, as late as 1855, to have grave doubts:

'Tis like that crooked hollow log through which the farmer's pig found access to the field; the farmer moved the log that the pig, in returning to the hole, and passing through, found himself to his astonishment, still on the outside of the field: he tried again, and was still outside; then he fled away, and would never go near it again. Whatever transcendant [sic] abilities Fichte, Kant, Schelling, and Hegel have shown, I think they lack the confirmation of having given piggy a transit to the field. The log is crooked, but still leaves grumpy on the same side of the fence he was before. If they had made the transit, common fame would have found it out. So I abide by my rule of not reading the book, until I hear of it through the newspaper.[496]

Yet unable to leave metaphysics alone altogether, he confessed, somewhat apologetically, "I write metaphysics, but my method is purely expectant."[497] One day he depreciated the results and significance of German speculation and scientific research, and on the next he paid them homage, as when he imputed to Edward Everett "an immense advantage in being the first American who sat in the German universities."[498] Moreover, Stallo and Hegel soon received a powerful ally in the person of Emmanuel V. Scherb, a German patriot and exile who came to Concord in 1849, precisely when Emerson professed to have little interest in any German since the death of Goethe. On hearing Scherb, Emerson said, "Mr. Scherb attempted last night to unfold Hegel for me, and I caught somewhat that seemed cheerful and large, and that might, and probably did come by Hindoo suggestion."[499] Still, he was far from converted to Hegelianism by Scherb's first effort, for, added Emerson:

But all abstract philosophy is easily anticipated,—it is so structural, or necessitated by the human mind. Schelling said, 'the Absolute is the union of the Ideal and the Real.'[500]

All in all, Stallo's *General Principles of the Philosophy of Nature* was the most persistent influence to keep Emerson's mind occupied with German thought. Already in November of 1849, he had set himself to copying out extracts.[501] A year and a half

later he paid a glowing tribute to Scherb and his "masterly" lectures as "a most gratifying monument to culture . . . such a regnant good sense, so sane, so catholic, so true to religion and reason."[502] His concern with the German philosophers and scientists became increasingly more frequent and sympathetic. During 1855 he made one more extended excursion into the neo-Platonists,[503] but after that year his active occupation with the thought of the near- and far-East was over; and even the bequest of Thoreau's oriental books (which came to him in May of 1862) seems not to have again actively aroused his interest.[504] Instead, he accorded, in 1856, the German philosophers and scientists his highest praise:

I think the Germans have an integrity of mind which sets their science above all other. They have not this science in scraps, this science on stilts. They have posed certain philosophical facts on which all is built, the doctrine of *immanence*, as it is called, by which everything is the cause of itself, or stands there for its own, and repeats in its own all other; 'the ground of everything is immanent in that thing.' Everything is organic, freedom also, not to add, but to grow and unfold.

They purify, they sweeten, they warm and ennoble, by seeing the heart to be indispensable, not in scraps, not on stilts.

In music, it was once the doctrine. The text is nothing, the score is all . . . but Wagner said the text must be fixed to the score and from the first; must be inspired with the score.

So in chemistry, Mülder said, — For a good chemist, the first condition is, he shall know nothing of philosophy; but Oersted and Humboldt saw and said that chemistry must be the handmaid of moral science. . . .[505]

Henceforth, to the end of his career, he clung to the idea he had grasped during the early thirties, but which he had temporarily forsaken a decade later—namely, the "identity of law, perfect order of physics, perfect parallelism between the laws of Nature and the laws of thought."[506] Stallo's principles of the philosophy of nature served to reinforce the ideas of ascending advance and development, rhythm, law, polarity, centrality, and identity. For the formulation, or reformu.'ation, of these principles Stallo provided the impetus, while Darwin, Schelling, and notably Hegel lent confirmation. "The iterations or rhymes of Nature," Emerson wrote in 1849, "are already an idea or principle of science, and a guide."[507] In Stallo he found these ideas of Schelling and Hegel, among others, which he thought worth copying into his journal for future reference:

Geologic strata whose supraposition in space is a sufficient warrant for their succession in time.
The configurations of Nature are more than a symbol, they are the gesticular expression of Nature's inner life.[508]
Whatever exists, exists only in virtue of the life of which it is an expression. [Stallo] p. 35.[509]
Every individual existence is but a living history.[510]
The development of all forms will be spiral.[511]
Matter is only by its relativity. The quantitative and qualitative existence of matter is an uninterrupted flight from itself, a never terminating whirl of evanescence. Stallo. p. 93.[512]
Animals are irregular men.[513]
Animals are but foetal forms of man.[514]
The limbs are emancipated ribs.[515]
Extension is petrified succession, or space is dead time.[516]

Immediately following these memorabilia from Stallo, and partly based on them, Emerson set down his generalization regarding cycles or eras in the history of man's attitude toward nature:

I easily distinguish three eras.
1. The Greek: when man deified Nature...
2. The Christian: when the soul became pronounced, and craved a heaven out of Nature and above it,—looking on Nature now as evil . . . .
3. The Modern: when the too idealistic tendencies of the Christian period running into the disease of cant, monachism, and a

church . . . forced men to retrace their steps, and rally again on Nature; but now the tendency is to marry mind to Nature, and to put Nature under the mind, convert the world into the instrument of Right Reason. Man goes forth to the dominion of the world by commerce, by science, and by philosophy.[517]

"Man goes forth to conquer the world by commerce, by science, and by philosophy"; and, Emerson might have added at the time, "the greatest of these is philosophy," for only when science is grounded upon philosophy is it capable of reaching the degree of perfection to which the Germans have developed it.[518]

Intertwined as science and philosophy are in this last phase of Emerson's intellectual development, leading eventually to a point which Emerson believed to be essentially Hegelian, we can yet trace with some degree of precision the steps by which, following the suggestions of Stallo, he advanced by regular gradations through Chambers, Lyell, Schelling, Oken, Humboldt, Saint-Hilaire, Agassiz, and finally Darwin, Huxley, and J. H. Stirling,[519] to a point where he felt "the supreme delight with the laws of Nature and its own law of life."[520] This he called the "universal law of Identity and Centrality,"[521] and to Hegel he ascribed the glory of having formulated it most clearly. For the acceptance of this doctrine he had been prepared by a principle grasped and accepted much earlier— that of sphericity. The direct impetus which lent most to his acceptance of the idea of Centrality was Schelling's *Identitätslehre* as Stallo explained it.[522] Three propositions (the first two from Schelling and the last from Hegel) from which Emerson appears to have derived most help and satisfaction at this time he found in Stallo's book, namely: (1) "The absolute is the union of the Ideal and the Real,"[523] (2) "All difference is quantitative,"[524] and (3) "Liberty is the spirit's realization of itself."[525]

Emerson himself did not rank the philosophical scientists whom he read at the time, and it is virtually impossible to do more than speculate on which were the more influential in shaping his thought during the fifties, except as the frequency with which he recurs to them and the tone of his comments on them give some indications. Darwin, apparently, did not at once interest him very vitally. Although he appears to have understood the general significance of *On the Origin of Species* shortly after its appearance, the first conclusive evidence now available strongly suggests that a careful consideration of the volume was delayed for some years. In 1869 Emerson speaks of having read Owen, Tyndall, and Darwin more than their compeer, Huxley; and in 1873 he observed significantly that while Darwin's *Origin of Species* was published in 1859, Stallo had anticipated him by a decade when he wrote, "Animals are but foetal forms of man."[526] The wording here and that in the passage which precedes it are such as to imply that Chambers (from whom he appears to have learned the phrase "arrested and progressive development"[527]), Lyell, Saint-Hilaire, Oken, and notably Stallo had taught him all he cared for in Darwin's doctrine of species, selection, and evolution.[528] Not that he rejected Darwin's theory of evolution. He simply asserted the Emersonian prerogative of not troubling his mind with the minutiae upon which the theory was based. Darwin's detailed explanations and specific demonstrations were merely welcome confirmatory evidence for a doctrine which he had grasped as a whole and accepted long before. That he had been impressed by the idea of evolutionary development as early as 1849 the *Journals* for that year illustrate; while the essay on "Poetry and Imagination" (substantially in the form in 1854 in which it is today) leaves little room for doubt that Darwin had little to offer Emerson in 1859 that he felt he had not long known. A few passages from that essay will suffice for illustrative purposes:

Nature is not final. First innuendoes, then broad hints, then smart taps are given, suggesting that nothing stands still in Nature; that the creation is on wheels, in transit,[529] always passing into something else, streaming into something higher; that matter is not what appears;[530] that chemistry can blow it all into gas . . . . The noble house of Nature we inhabit has temporary uses, and we can afford to leave it in one day. The ends are moral, and therefore the beginnings are such . . . . Everything [is] undressing and stealing away from its old into new form, and nothing [is] fast but those invisible cords which we call laws, on which all is strung . . .

All multiplicity rushes to be resolved into unity. Anatomy, osteology, exhibit arrested and progressive development in each kind; the lower pointing to the higher forms, the higher to the highest, from the fluid in an elastic sack, from radiate, mollusk, articulate, vertebrate, up to man; as if the whole animal world were only a Hunterian museum to exhibit the genesis of mankind . . . .

Each animal or vegetable remembers the next inferior and predicts the next higher.[531]

Here we recognize the advance which Emerson made in his scientific and philosophic thinking during the twenty-year interim which separates these passages from those in his first published work, by which he tried, in 1836, to explain "the theory of nature." In *Nature* he had sought after a similar idea, but it succeeded always in just eluding his grasp. The journals from 1850 on demonstrate, on nearly every page, how eagerly he set once more to groping about among the dead bones of zoology in an effort to reanimate a philosophy which had lapsed into so hopeless an intuitionalism that it stood in danger of sinking into fatalistic mysticism altogether.

But even the strictly "evolutionary" theory of science (not to be confused with the earlier graduated-scale or chain-of-being theory) would have been useless for his purposes without the philosophical concept which Emerson speaks of next, that of polarity and identity of thought. Thought, he says, taking the idea from Hegel *apud* Stallo—"Thought has its own polarity . . . . Identity of law, perfect order in physics, perfect parallelism between the laws of Nature and the laws of thought exist."[532] Here are two ideas perfectly companionable and congruent for Emerson, whom everything had conspired to prepare for Darwinian evolution and Hegelian idealism. Just as it was inevitable that in science he should pass from the old chain-of-being to the more organic evolutionary theory, so it was natural that in philosophy he should turn his back upon the hopeless dualism (which threatened to put man in a cave guarded by the twin monster Fate-Necessity) and to entertain the doctrine of organic centrality and absolute identity. The latter completed the former, and was reached by gradual, almost imperceptible, stages. This transition from the eighteenth-century concept of development to that of nineteenth-century evolution and from Platonic and neo-Platonic dualism to Hegelian absolutism is what chiefly distinguishes the mature from the younger Emerson. Contact with Hegelian thought is what chiefly accounts for the difference.[533]

Hegel appealed to Emerson because he seemed to put Nature and Spirit, matter and mind, in right relation—a relationship which Stallo repeatedly emphasized as being central to both Hegel's and Schelling's philosophy of nature. This was precisely the relationship which Emerson had endeavored to establish all along. There was another reason: Hegel's form of speculation (more accurately, the results of it) appealed to Emerson because there he found room not only for the concept of the organic but also for his sense of Nature's process of "unfolding"—an unfolding or flowering of nature from the mind. This was a favorite idea for which he had failed successively to find a completely satisfactory metaphysical confirmation. This metaphysics Hegel seemed to supply.

But Emerson did not proceed immediately from organic evolutionism to Hegelian absolutism, natural though such a step might have been. Stallo's agency in preparing him for the step has already been noted. Even more directly to the purpose was the position of Schelling as an agency by which Emerson came to accept Hegelianism, or (shall we say?) those portions of the Hegelian philosophy that he understood and liked.

The conclusion of *Nature* indicates that in 1836 all was not well with the epistemological groundwork of Emerson's philosophy. The ideal theory as enunciated in that book and as based on the Kantian distinction between Understanding and Reason he had had to put down as being at best only a "useful introductory hypothesis"—not a proved fact. Three years later, although he still found within him the "invincible tendency of the mind to unify," self-analysis and conversations with F. H. Hedge left him no alternative but to conclude that something in his metaphysics was askew. Hedge, arguing that "the world is not a dualism, is not a bipolar unity," accused Emerson of "overlooking great facts in stating the absolute laws of the soul.[534] The criticism disturbed Emerson.

For a decade, from 1839 to 1849, Emerson was in a dilemma: he was unable quite to establish or, for that matter, to accept a purely monistic universe; he was equally unable entirely to repudiate the dualism which he sought to transcend. The best he could do in 1839 was to assert that "there are degrees in idealism."[535] In this state of indecision and vacillation he languished until Stallo called his attention to Schelling's philosophy of identity by which "the Absolute is [explained as] the union of the Ideal and the real," and "all difference is merely quantitative."[536] The philosophic distinction between quantity and quality as Schelling had drawn it struck him forcibly, and in his journals he reverted to it again and again. One instance will illustrate.

Amount and Quality. Schelling's distinction, 'Some minds speak about things, some minds speak the things themselves,'[537] remains by far the most important intellectual distinction, as the *moral distinction,* or the *quality,* is the important moral distinction. Quality and Amount. Searching tests these![538]

Twenty years later he still regarded Schelling's idea of Identity as all-important. Under the head of *Identity,* he wrote:

The best identity is the practical one . . . . Steffens relates that he went into Schelling's lecture room at Jena(?). Schelling said, 'Gentlemen, think of the wall.' All the class at once took attitudes of thought; some stiffened themselves; some shut their eyes; all concentrated themselves. After a time, he said, 'Gentlemen, think of that which thought the wall.' Then there was trouble in all the camp.[539]

Variations of the themes which he found in Schelling, and which he preserved in his daybooks include the following (none of them in the printed *Journals*):

'Every growth in nature has but one moment of perfect beauty.' Schelling.[540]
'That is free which only acts conformably to the laws of its beauty.' Schelling.[541]
That effort of identity between the conscious and the unconscious activities that Schelling calls the sole privilege of genius. 'The infinite (or perfect) presented as the finite is Beauty.'—*Continental Review,* No. 1, p. 59.[542]

As these memorabilia indicate, what in Schelling appealed to Emerson was the possibility he provided for integrating with the philosophy of the Absolute the doctrine of the Organic, for by now he had caught hold firmly of the principle that "everything is organic, not to add but to grow and unfold."[543] This last doctrine he found best expressed by Hegel, for the reception of whose ideas Schelling had prepared him.[544] Thus we find Emerson recording from Hegel, presumably on the basis of his reading in Varnhagen von Ense's *Tagebücher* and Hoefer's *Nouvelle Biographie Géné-*

rale,[545] these thoughts (none of them in the printed *Journals*):

'Liberty is the spirit's realization of itself.' Hegel.[546]
'The man is what he does.' Hegel.
See passages from Hegel's Encyclopedia, Thl. II p. 461 and p. 84 cited in Varnhagen Vol. XI p. 43.[547]
Before Hegel, Heraclitus said, 'Nothing is, everything becomes.' See article, 'Hegel' in Biographie Generale.[548]

Just as he contented himself with secondary sources on Schelling, so he relied on expounders and historians of philosophy for what he wished to know of Hegel. Stallo was of primary importance in directing him to Hegel, but almost as influential were Hoefer's biographical dictionary and especially James Hutchison Stirling's *Secret of Hegel,* although the former did not reach his hands before 1862, while the latter he got hot from the press in 1865. Later he consulted such works as Schwegler's *History of Philosophy*[549] and Thomas Stanley's *Lives of the Philosophers*[550] and *History of Philosophy.*[551] Hardly less important, although the influence came later, were the *Tagebücher* of Varnhagen von Ense, through most or all of which he seems to have thumbed between 1870 and 1876.[552]

The receipt in September, 1865, of Stirling's *Secret of Hegel* (published in the same year) set him anew to praising Hegel.[553] He carried the two-volume work with him on a lecture tour of the West the following January; and reading it of nights, in dingy, cheerless hotel rooms, he found it a "good book," one offering "some lasting knowledge." He declared it a book that invited him to "purer, loftier service," that lifted him "quite out of prosaic surroundings."[554] Whether or not he followed Hegel's technical arguments, Emerson saw in Stirling's *Secret of Hegel* what T. H. Green professed to see in it: the full articulation of the significance of German philosophy in the succession from Kant to Hegel,[555] in such a way that Stirling's book "contrasted with everything else that has been published as sense with nonsense." Emerson hailed it as "the most competent and compulsive of modern British books on metaphysics," and characterized Stirling as "a more subtle metaphysician than any other" on the British Isles.[556]

Meanwhile something of Hegel came to him through Hedge, with whom he continued to hold high philosophical talk, particularly during the sixties.[557] But the final impetus that led Emerson to give Hegel a sympathetic hearing was supplied by William Torrey Harris. Stallo, Hedge, and Cabot had, each in his way, repeatedly induced him to consider the Hegelian system; but until Harris entered upon the scene, Hegel had elicited from him only half-hearted attention. Thus, while he expressed this thanks to Cabot, in 1855, for having lent him some volumes of Hegel, he felt impelled to add: "I did not find my way into Hegel as readily as I hoped, nor was I as richly rewarded as probably better scholars have been."[558] A decade later he had met Harris in St. Louis, then engaged in organizing the Hegelian school of thought in the West—a philosophy which Harris took pains to explain should be an extension of Emersonian idealism. In letters written at the time Emerson's enthusiasm for Harris and his Hegelian confreres appears genuine. He introduced Harris to Cabot and Hedge as a "sharp sighted philosopher . . . an intelligent, faithful student, using his own eyes on a pretty wide range of facts."[559] He accepted the St. Louisans' invitation to speak before their Philosophical Society and urged Henry James, Sr., who had been prevented from accepting a similar invitation, to grasp the next opportunity. For himself, he reported to James: "It was a true gratification to see Harris at St. Louis amidst the German atheists, and to share his pleasure in that, though he had begun alone, he now counted . . . nineteen young men as spiritual and affirmative philosophers, and could rely on them as active prop-

agandists."[560] He appears to have lectured before the Philosophical Society in February, in March, and probably again in December of 1867.[561] He became an "auxiliary"[562] member of the Society and a reader of the *Journal of Speculative Philosophy* from the first, Harris supplying him with advance sheets of the first numbers, which were especially detailed in setting forth the aims of the St. Louis School and abundant in Hegelian materials, both translation and explanation. He complimented Harris upon his "brave undertaking," and added:

I shall think better than ever of my countrymen if they shall sustain it. I mean that you shall make me acquainted in it with the true value and performance of Hegel, who, at first sight is not engaging nor at second sight satisfying. But his immense fame cannot be mistaken, and I shall read and wait.[563]

Henceforth, until Harris himself settled in Concord in 1879, there was a steady interchange of letters and opinions between Emerson and Harris. They borrowed each other's books and pooled their efforts and influence to secure literary and academic advancement for J. H. Stirling.[564] They consulted each other regarding contributions and editorial policies for the *Journal*. Emerson steadily encouraged Harris' journalistic venture and paid for his copy of the *Journal*, although Harris had sent it *gratis*.[565] Apparently Harris confided to Emerson, as early as 1870, his ambition to bring Hegel to Concord, for Emerson wrote, on March 3, 1870:

We have no news yet to give you of real progress in speculative Philosophy in Mass^tts. It is a good sign surely of the courage of our new President at Cambridge in establishing University Lectures; and he is this year making a direct attempt to bring Mr Stirling from Edinburgh. I think it is good that Mr J. E. Cabot reads lectures in these weeks on Kant. The class are very small. It was a mistake to make the price of admission too high.[566] I have put my three vols. of the 'Journal' to be bound and mean to read them much in the next month. Thanks especially for Hegel in No 12, and for Mr Davidson's 'Parmenides.' This last is a wonderful piece of Greek precocity.[567]

The "Hegel in No 12" for which Emerson thanked Harris is doubtless a reference to the latter's translation, in Number 1 of Volume IV,[568] from Hegel's "Philosophische Propaedeutik," which the translator entitled "The Science of Rights, Morals, and Religion." Lacking decisive evidence regarding how long Emerson continued to read Harris' publication, we are unable to conjecture how closely he studied Hegel's system as revealed in this source. If he read no further than Volume IV, number 1 (March, 1870) he became exposed to more than a smattering of German speculation; if he continued to read, and to comprehend, subsequent numbers, he stood an excellent chance to become one of the best informed men of his time on the subject of Hegelianism. That he became thus informed is improbable.[569]

In the absence of precise evidence demonstrating the influence of these materials on Emerson's subsequent thinking and writing, the conclusion must be that while he may have made good his resolution, his reading the *Journal of Speculative Philosophy* did not affect him vitally. Much of it was highly technical, and quite possibly his old aversion for the technicalities of philosophy revived. The conclusion seems to be that now, as earlier, he divined the general import of Hegel and his compeers, but that he contented himself with grasping the general significance of Hegelianism without plumbing the metaphysical depths requisite for a detailed comprehension and complete assimilation.

In 1879 the Concord School of Philosophy was established, with Alcott the titular, and Harris the real, head. Henceforth there was an abundance of talk in Concord about Hegel, with Harris most assiduous about doing the work of the master, but Alcott, too, lending a hand occasionally, as when

he took an active part in the Kant centennial of the third session.[570] Emerson joined the School. Though he did not talk about Hegel, he delivered two lectures—one on "Aristocracy" and the other, ironically enough, on "Memory." By this time Emerson's memory was failing, and his mind was beginning to wander. Whatever their impact on others may have been, or was to become, Harris and his Western Hegelians settled in Concord too late to be of much use to Emerson.

In the light of what has been recorded regarding the ways and means by which Emerson came by his knowledge of Hegel, it is apparent that, lacking a firsthand acquaintance with the German's works, he never mastered the metaphysical logic and dialectic of the Hegelians. Stirling's *Secret*, if Emerson succeeded in extracting it, and the columns of the *Journal of Speculative Philosophy* served his purpose.

As he said in 1840, when Scherb first tried to unfold Hegel to him, he caught "somewhat that seemed cheerful and large" in Hegelian thought; but the technical groundwork upon which Hegel's Identity and Absolute rested did not much concern Emerson. He was ready to take the word of those who told him that Hegel had, by means of his doctrine of opposites and the triadic dialectic of thesis, antithesis, and synthesis, reconciled the finite and the infinite, and established the Absolute as that Identity by which "One law consumes all diversity"[571]—by which subject and object become one, nature and mind are merged in the Absolute, and liberty (freedom) becomes "the *spirit's realization* of 'itself.'"[572] The propositions, arguments, and proofs Emerson was willing now, as formerly, to leave to those who had seen them. His metaphysics, he reaffirmed before the Harvard students of philosophy who came to hear him lecture in 1870, were "to the end of use."[573] And so he continued to speak lightly of metaphysical books, even to saying, "Dreary to me are the names and number of volumes of Hegel and the Hegelians . . . . I want not the metaphysics, but only the literature of them."[574] About the same time he declared:

The reason of a new philosophy or philosopher is ever that a man of thought finds that he cannot read in the older books. I can't read Hegel, or Schelling, or find interest in what is told me from them, so I persist in my own idle and easy way, and write down my thoughts, and find presently that there are congenial persons who like them, so I persist, until some sort of outline or system grows. 'Tis the common course: ever a new bias. It happened to each of these, Heraclitus, or Hegel, or whosoever.[575]

The intimation, conscious or unconscious, seems plain enough. Again, he wrote:

Bacon or Kant, or Hegel, propound some maxim which is the keynote of philosophy thenceforth; but I am more interested to know, that, when at last they hurled their deep word, it is only some familiar experience of every man in the street.[576]

Yet, while he belittled metaphysics and metaphysical books, the metaphysicians themselves—Kant, Schelling, and Hegel, singly and collectively—he uniformly apostrophized during this later period. They are "grand masters"[577] and "architects" building "our inward heaven,"[578]—"the foremost scholars in all history."[579] Hegel's is "a superior mind," and Schelling is spoken of as "another great genius."[580] The questionings whether the German idealists had solved their philosophical problems cease about 1856. Henceforth he has nothing but praise for them, singly and together— British and American thinkers, by comparison, being often depreciated:

In England and America there is the widest difference of altitude between their scholars and that of the Germans, and here in America a nation of Germans living with the Organon of Hegel in their hands, which makes the discoveries and thinking of the English and Americans look of a Chinese narrowness, and yet good easy dunces that we are, we never suspect our inferiority.[581]

THE QUESTION of precisely to what extent Emerson was indebted to philosophy generally and to German philosophy specifically remains, in some respects, an open one. Within limits, however, certain conclusions may be drawn.

First, Emerson was not a philosophic anarchist repudiating tradition and law. Rather, he sought from first to last—and few men more fervently—a unified philosophical religion and a consistent religious philosophy.

Second, Emerson made at least four rather closely defined attempts at philosophical synthesis—each time on a new epistemological base. These are, if we exclude the Lockean sensationalism and Scottish common sense in which his Unitarian heritage and Harvard schooling had given him a thorough indoctrination— these are (1) Platonic dualism up to about 1830, (2) Kantian transcendentalism (à la Coleridge and Carlyle) roughly from 1830 to 1840, (3) mystical intuitionalism from 1840 to 1850, and (4) an eclectic philosophy composed primarily of Hegelian idealism and Darwinian evolution to produce what the mature Emerson believed to be his nearest approach to a perfect system of thought for him.

Third, Emerson represents the developing rather than the static type of thinker whose entire career demonstrates one consistent and coherent point of view. Except for holding fast to some form of ethical idealism, Emerson's theorizing changed as often as his epistemological hypotheses changed. During two of these phases he was dominantly under the influence of Germanic epistemologies, once under British, and twice under systems derived mainly from Greek thought. It may be found, when these variations in Emerson's epistemological allegiance are scrutinized in their relation to his more practical thinking, that the gross inconsistencies of which he stands accused are not so much inconsistencies as changing conclusions drawn from shifting epistemological bases.

Fourth, Emerson not only dwelt longer under what was a prevailingly Hegelian influence than under any other, but he published the bulk of his work while under that influence. Including *Nature*, he published before 1850 only five full-length books; after that date, which marks the point at which Hegel began to exert a noticeable effect, appeared ten more.

Finally, it is worth observing that during the Kantian period, Emerson produced *Nature, The American Scholar,* the *Address . . . before the Divinity College,* and the bulk of *Essays, First Series.* These four works, under the impetus of Kantian idealism, signalize Emerson's finding himself, and to the general reading public they remain his best known and most influential works. Quite possibly, if the matter were determinable or measurable, it would be found that German thought gained through these four books of Emerson's its most effective means of diffusion in America, for the manner and means by which Emersonian idealism insinuated itself into the intellectual consciousness of America were as subtle as they were various and pervasive.

OTHER EARLY TRANSCENDENTALISTS

George Ripley (1802–1880)

Among the Transcendentalists grouped about Emerson, the more influential of those who made philosophy a major concern were Ripley, Parker, and Alcott, although lesser lights like Clarke and the Channings had their own spheres of activity and influence. George Ripley, never as fiery an agitator in any cause as Theodore Parker, was nonetheless in the thick of the controversy raging about Transcendentalism, Germanism, infidelity, and the attendant innovations that were debated during the first half of the nineteenth century. His position as manager of the Brook Farm Association for Education and Agriculture necessarily kept him in the public eye even after the termination of his rather mediocre ministerial career. Subsequently he forsook religious controversy, philosophical disputation, and social reform altogether for a humdrum but calm editorial career; but before he passed from the scene of activity, he had, both by what he said and by what he did, affected the lives of many of those who helped foment and further the "Newness" between 1830 and 1850. Germanic influences were admittedly of primary importance in directing his thought and action. The examination of these influences as determining factors in Ripley's career resolves itself into three parts, according to Ripley's three major interests before his retirement: (1) as student and disseminator of Germanic thought, (2) as defender of German theology, and (3) as social reformer.

Under the tutelage of F. H. Hedge, Ripley early displayed a keen interest in German thought. Impressed even more than was Emerson at about the same time by the precept and example of Hedge, Everett, Ticknor, and Follen regarding the utility of studying in Germany, Ripley, having graduated at the head of the Harvard class of 1823, would have devoted several years to residence at the German universities except that his lack of funds forced him, like Emerson, "to forswear Germany and go to the cheapest stall where education can be bought"—the Harvard Divinity School.[582] He took up ministerial duties as pastor in the meetinghouse at Purchase and Pearl streets in Boston. During the fourteen years of his service there he kept up his study of philosophy and theology, at the same time acquiring a fine library that included many German and French works.[583] Throughout his ministerial career Ripley, as an eager champion of the new liberal religion, published a series of articles, mainly reviews of German and French theological works, which, together, proved to be an important source of information and interpretation during the early thirties of the new "spiritual" Christianity of the post-Kantians and the French eclectics.

His article on "Degerando and Self-Education" (1830)[584] strikes the keynote of that whole series which culminated in the papers of the Norton-Ripley controversy by making an earnest plea for a profounder appreciation of the inward truths of religion as revealed by intuition in preference to the doctrine of miraculous revelation.[585] His article on "Religion in France" (July, 1831),[586] reinforces his high opinion of the intuitive religious movement abroad in Europe. His essay on Pestalozzi of January, 1832,[587] indicates that he is thoroughly familiar with the writings of Pestalozzi; while his discussion of Carl Follen's inaugural address at Harvard, in the same number of the Examiner, is so replete with intelligent comments on German literature and philosophy as to make untenable the assumption that his knowledge was superficial.[588]

Neither in 1832 nor later did Ripley espouse a single philosophical system or attempt to rear, for himself or others, a systematically philosophical credo. His effort was always to find an essentially spiritual, intuitional base for the higher truths of Christianity, divorced from dogmatic narrowness. Accordingly he was never a close follower of Kant. But this is not to imply that Ripley, either during the thirties and forties or later, failed to comprehend the Kantian criticism or to grasp the distinctions between understanding and reason, the regulative and constitutive aspects of reason, the categories, and the other technicalities of the critical system.[589] It means simply that he deliberately chose to rest his faith on intuitive persuasion in realms where Kant had demonstrated the inability of man to attain to knowledge. Religion he defined as "a gift from heaven," and Christianity as a "divine communica-

tion to man." He constantly called Christ "Saviour" and spoke of him as "the highest of all the soul's prophets"—though as synonymous with moral Truth rather than with Divinity.[590] A curious combination of detached thinker and zealous Christian reformer, he had none of the pedantry or vanity of the recluse scholar but used his library to find support and guidance toward that purer religion that he envisioned.[591]

The article of May, 1835, on Marsh's translation of Herder's Spirit of Hebrew Poetry is indicative at once of his great admiration for Herder and his appreciation and defense of German literary and theological writing,[592] as well as of his command of the German language. He shows himself competent in pointing out minute errors of translation in Marsh's book and in making penetrating criticisms of Marsh's rendition of the text.

Although Herder hardly more than made a beginning at constructing a positive critical and metaphysical basis for idealism, he appealed to Ripley because he expressed with poetic fervor the spirit of the modern intuitional school. "He formed," says Ripley, "a connecting link between the old school of Lutheran orthodoxy and the modern school of Rational divines. The progress of his own mind seems . . . to mark the progress of theological opinion; and in his voluminous writings may be found the germ of most of the important thoughts which have since produced such a mighty revolution in the prevalent conception of religion."[593] That the religious tenets of Herder (and Schleiermacher) were of some influence in shaping Ripley's own thought is not to be doubted, for, like his German preceptors, he sought an intuitive basis for religion. Though he admired Kant, he felt that Kant's system left too little room for the irrational and supernatural.[594] However, his desire to preserve part of the irrational domain of religion did not prevent his enthusiastic championship of German historical and philosophical study of the Scriptures.[595]

Ripley prefixed a sketch of the history of religious thought in Germany to his second article on Herder (November, 1835).[596] Here he placed Herder squarely in the new tradition of Biblical criticism, identifying him with those who assert the efficacy of continual immanent revelation as opposed to a literalist's strict dependence on the holy word. History, he pointed out, was to Herder the account of the spiritual development of man. In his article of March, 1836, on the theological writings of Gieseler, Lücke, Mitzsch, and the memoirs of Schleiermacher, Ripley again revealed his sympathy with those who wanted to "save the validity of religion against science" and to "make a harmony between philosophy and theology" by putting the emphasis "on the religious consciousness of human nature."[597] In the same year he embodied this point of view in a simple and persuasive pamphlet, *Discourses on the Philosophy of Religion, Addressed to Doubters Who Wish to Believe*, and in a review of Martineau's *Rationale of Religious Enquiry* he incorporated a moving plea for the development of a truly spiritual religious science.[598] What this science of divinity ought to be is defined more closely in his evaluation of Professor Ullmann's *Theological Aphorisms*, printed in the *Examiner* for January, 1837.[599] Here he asserts his allegiance to Herder, Schleiermacher, and De Wette as having produced "a higher life, of more consummate beauty, and of more divine energy, in religion, theology, and society" than had obtained earlier (pp. 385–86).

Thus Ripley acquired during the thirties the knowledge and facility to use that knowledge in the controversy with Norton and with entrenched Unitarianism that was to come.[600] So far his opinions, derived though they were from Germany, escaped the charge of heresy; his championship of German philosophy and theology aroused no great animosity. Thus far he had done no more than exercise the right which every Unitarian minister claimed—to make

free inquiry into the Scriptures, even when such an inquiry led to keeping company with suspect persons like the German critics. It was only after Emerson attacked the citadel of Unitarian orthodoxy itself and Ripley rushed to his defense against Norton that his "Unitarianism" became odious. Thereafter he was put down as a Transcendentalist and an Infidel. Soon after 1840, when he resigned from the Unitarian Association, quit the pulpit, turned to farming, and later, to editorial work, the Defenders of the Faith lost interest in him. However, between the time of Emerson's *Address* before the Divinity School (1838) and Parker's sermon on *The Transient and Permanent in Christianity* (1841), he was as lustily belabored as ever were Emerson and Parker.

The Norton-Ripley controversy was a natural and inevitable culmination of events that can be traced backward a century or more, and that had been coming to a head during the two decades immediately preceding.[601] It was a peculiar compound of native critical developments, scientific influences, and German importations, which, as they progressed (first under the banner of Unitarianism and afterwards under the auspices of Transcendentalism), brought upon the Unitarians the uncomfortable accusation that theirs was "a halfway house to infidelity," and that Unitarianism was merely a temporary stage in the decline from true religion to infidelity.[602] The orthodox pointed the finger of scorn not only at the Transcendentalists but also at the Unitarians for having hatched such a brood; while the Unitarians, attacked on both sides, were at a loss to know whether to defend themselves against the one or the other, or both at once.

The three chief apostates, by their own confession in articles, sermons, and addresses, were Emerson, Ripley, and Parker. Their defection seemed to the Unitarians nothing less than treachery within their own ranks. Besides finding themselves in a dilemma that seemed of their own making, the Unitarians were confronted with the necessity of making a hard choice. To continue association with men like Ripley and Parker was to lend confirmation to the old, now vociferously renewed, charge by the orthodox that Unitarianism was, as they had always foretold, merely the portal to infidelity and complete skepticism; to expel them was to abandon the principles of free inquiry and an "open house," principles for which they had long fought, and which they still cherished.[603]

Emerson's "infidelity" (or "atheism") was not easily related to specific sources. To be sure, he had kept several terms in the Harvard Divinity College, but he had also traveled to Europe specifically to learn at first hand the questionable principles of Coleridge and Carlyle. Clearly, Harvard might wash her hands of any responsibility for Emerson's opinions. What was more, Emerson's resignation six years before he delivered his offensive address to the divinity class at Harvard in 1838 had put him effectively beyond the reach of Unitarians and Calvinists alike. Both groups might damn him roundly, but obviously no one need assume any responsibility for a man who had unfrocked himself, and who had, by his own confession, left the church with a yawn.

Parker's case was different. His opinions seemed clearly traceable to his Unitarian training under Andrews Norton of Harvard, under whom he had studied as late as 1834–1836. So said many. So said Noah Porter, recently elected Professor of Metaphysics and Moral Philosophy at Yale College, who in summing up the whole ugly business, asked pointedly: "Where learned Mr. Parker his philosophical system? Where did he discover that man himself might be so inspired, that his God could give him no added inspiration? . . . Mr. Norton will start up with his accustomed promptness, and reply: 'Not from me—not from me.'"[604]

Mr. Norton did just that. Endeavoring to anticipate the charges and trying to defend Unitarianism *and* himself, he shifted the blame to the German metaphysicians, or to the adoption, on the part of addlepates like Emerson and Parker, of every latest heresy issuing from the cells of theological and philosophical professors of Germany. "The latest form of infidelity," he took care to say, with great emphasis, in his pamphlet by that title (1838), was bred in Germany, not at Harvard; Kant is responsible, not Norton.

But Norton's pamphlet turned out to be a boomerang. Far from clarifying the issues, it served only to set the stage for the entrance of the third of the renegades. George Ripley, another of Norton's erstwhile fledglings, had been suspected of mild apostasy since 1830, when his articles on Coleridge, the French eclectics, and the German transcendental theologians had begun to appear in the *Examiner*. Now that Ripley came to the defense of Emerson with a reply to Norton, entitled *"The Latest Form of Infidelity" Examined* (1839), there was left little room for further doubt; and when the controversy thus provoked ran through a series of replies and counterreplies, Ripley, refusing to yield to Norton the last word, was put down by all right-thinking Unitarians as one of the chief of the inglorious fallen.

The controversy added nothing essentially new or significant to the arguments up to date, and the result was virtually a stalemate. So far as Ripley was concerned, it yielded nothing to his solution of the problems involved and added little to his stature as a philosopher or a theologian. Indeed, Parker felt that "Pope" Norton's "steel-cold intelligence" was driving Ripley into a position which made it hard to make out a case for the Germans as believers in a personal God and immortality or the trustworthiness of Herder, Schleiermacher, and De Wette as guides in Biblical studies. The situation, he said, called for "a higher word,"[605] and he prepared to say it in *The*

Previous Question between Mr. Andrews Norton and His Alumni Moved and Handled in a Letter to All Those Gentlemen, by Levi Blodgett (Boston, 1840). In it he reached the conclusion which, as Noah Porter observed, marked Parker as "a consistent and logical thinker [who] . . . has carried them [the principles and modes of thinking peculiar to liberal Christians of the Germanic persuasion] to no unnatural conclusions."[606] Parker's impatience with halfway measures led him to shift the argument to a broader base by asserting that neither Christ's divinity nor the authenticity of miracles was necessary to true religion. For all he cared, all might go by the board— Old Testament, New Testament, miracles, ordinances, and formularies. Planting himself on the ground that man has a spiritual nature endowed with original capacity to apprehend primary religious truth directly, without mediation of sacrament, creed, or Bible, he stood outside and above the controversy, while his enemies declared that he had "done Transcendentalism up."

Needless to say, Parker's position went beyond that which Ripley was prepared to embrace, though, like Parker, he found himself far from done with Transcendentalism or religious problems. In the transition from Unitarianism to Transcendental theology, Ripley occupied a position approximately midway. He was more the son of Channing than the brother of Parker. Unable, on the one hand, to proceed with the rigor of Kantian logic, and unwilling, on the other, to lose himself in transcendent mysteries, he was poorly equipped for theology, however good a religionist he may have been. He went too far to please the Unitarians, and he did not go far enough to satisfy the Transcendentalists. His association with the latter and his management of Brook Farm kept him for some years more in the midst of the theological and philosophical quabbles of the times, but it was not by choice. If he had had his way, he would have given up theorizing altogether. The resignation of his ministerial charge in 1840 and his assumption of the managership of the Brook Farm community immediately thereafter are indicative at once of his dissatisfaction with speculation and controversy and the recognition that his abilities in both fields were mediocre and of his resolution to turn from theory to practice. If, in 1840, he applied to himself what Emerson was just then saying about the Knower, Sayer, and Doer, he may have considered that he had now passed, not entirely satisfactorily to himself, through the phases of life designated, in Emersonian phraseology, by the terms, Knower and Sayer, and that the was ready to turn Doer.

While 1840 was a climactic year in Ripley's career, his resolution to give up the pulpit and turn farmer was not reached overnight. Impassioned and full of strong religious conviction though he was, Ripley had little gift for pulpit oratory. This inability appears to have been one of the basic causes why his congregation, in the course of his fourteen years among them, lost many of its members, although the general deterioration of that part of the city was certainly a contributing factor. Even more important was the rift between his thinking and that of his parishioners—all set down, as Ripley himself says, with "great plainness of speech" in the second of the three letters which he addressed to his congregation during 1840. As in Emerson's experience eight years earlier, "a profound feeling of incompatibility" had grown up between the pastor and his flock. As in Emerson's case, too, Ripley set forth his position in a formal statement, which made his avowal of "the principles of Transcendental philosophy" so plain that there was but one possible termination. Ripley's offered resignation was accepted three months later.[607] Ripley's letter to his congregation makes abundantly obvious that his studies in the transcendental religion as developed by Herder, Schleiermacher, and De Wette—"now taught," says Ripley, "in every Protestant university on the Continent of Europe . . . [as] the common creed of the most enlightened nations"—supplied the fundamental reason why he preferred to resign his pulpit rather than continue to occupy it under restraint of being prevented, by congregational opinion, from freely preaching those principles. Like Emerson, he left the church feeling that as a minister he had failed; unlike Emerson, he never, in any form, resumed the ministry, or re-entered the pulpit, except to deliver the "Address to the People" at the ordination of his successor, J. I. T. Coolidge, on February 9, 1842. But he was not therefore unconcerned about religion or about the ministerial profession.[608] Among the first things he wrote after his release from the ministry was his "Letter to a Theological Student," published in the second number of the *Dial*. In it he exhorted the young probationer to attend faithfully to the new methods and teachings and to follow Herder above all others.

Ripley's papers contributed to the Norton-Ripley controversy are a neat summation of how his Unitarian theology was modified into a mild form of transcendental religion by the German theologians. Never willing to follow them to a purely scientific interpretation of the Scriptures, such as Strauss for example reached, he nevertheless borrowed from them the tools that enabled him candidly and expertly to handle a limited phase of the argument provoked by Norton. These letters also demonstrate, more succinctly than do any of his other writings, that he was a confirmed believer in German idealism and in the German method of Biblical criticism. He found his faith strengthened instead of weakened by his German studies, and though he never credited himself or any other theorist with having found strict philosophical confirmation for religious "truths," he confidently believed that he had shifted the arguments for Christianity to a firmer, because more practical, basis than that upon which they had rested before.

Ripley's strong sense for the need of social reform, or what he termed "the practice of religion," was not a sudden inspiration that came to him about the time the Brook Farm experiment was planned. As early as 1832, in one of his articles in the *Christian Examiner*, he paid tribute to the achievements of Pestalozzi as a pioneer in the realm of social as well as educational reform. Ripley was well acquainted with the Neuhof experiment eight years before he organized Brook Farm, where were combined Yankee agricultural methods with larger portions of Pestalozzian educational methods than are generally recognized. He underwrote Pestalozzi's manner of teaching as "a return to the dictates of nature and good sense,"[609] and expressed the hope that the Pestalozzian revolution might have far-reaching social effects. Ripley was not espousing any thoroughgoing socialism; he was arguing, on a simple humanitarian ground, for the greater benefits to come to the lower classes of society by means of a better education. When the Brook Farm Institute of Agriculture and Education was formed, the articles of incorporation combined specific stipulations regarding education, agriculture, and common business principles.[610] But there was not a breath about "socialism" in the then accepted sense of the word, or of "communism." Little effort was made to win proselytes and of course there was no thought of setting up an international organization. George Ripley was not one to agree with his wife Sophia—somewhat more volatile than himself—when on one occasion she rebuked Theodore Parker for not "shrieking at wrongs," though, like her, he did not want to lose "humanity in abstractions."[6...] Farmer Ripley was no visionary, either in the management of the affairs of the Farm or in his educational theories. But he did insist that it were well for all American teachers to study the philosophical bases of their educational procedure with the view to square their aims with social objectives

He interpreted the system of Pestalozzi not as a means for the sudden regeneration of mankind but as a step toward the amelioration of social ills.[612] It was Ripley's strong idealistic turn of mind, his faith in practical Christianity, or what was synonymous with it in his mind, socialized religion—not at all his personal interest—that led him to turn his energies to organizing Brook Farm, even to sacrificing his personal feelings in pushing the enterprise. The manner in which Christian idealism impelled men like Ripley to experiment with the practical reformation of society is described by Ripley himself in the *Harbinger*,[613] and in 1846, writing an article on Fichte, he described explicitly the easy transition in his mind from the position of a religionist to that of a practical reformer:

The study of German philosophy is more attractive in an historical point of view than for the positive, scientific results to which it has arrived . . . . It has failed to solve the mighty problems of Divine Providence and Human Destiny . . . It presents nothing to the scientific inquirer . . . [except] cautions against error . . . and noble aspirations after the spiritual dignity and excellence . . . .
The ultimate tendency of . . . [Fichte's] philosophy is to enkindle a holy enthusiasm for the progress of man toward the fulfilment of his earthly destiny. The exercise of the pure intellect leads only to scepticism and despair; the last result of the Infinite can never be fathomed by the finite understanding . . . . But the nature of man comprises higher elements than the power of abstract thought. His most important convictions are not the fruit of speculation. He lives also in a world of moral emotions and ideas. He finds within the depths of his own soul an instinctive sense of justice, duty, universal sympathy and unity. An interior voice calls upon him to shape his life in accordance with these principles. Hence, the world presents him a field of moral action; and to realise these truths in all material relations is the earthly destiny of man. The transition is not difficult from these views, to the doctrine of social harmony as set forth in the writings of Fourier. And to the philosophic mind, the study of

Fichte, in his most remote abstractions, is an admirable preparation for the broader and more commanding synthesis of the great expounder of social sciences.—*Harbinger*, II (Apr. 18, 1846), 297.

These passages, written after the best days of Brook Farm were already over, are significant as indicating that except for Fichte, whose practical tendency he admired, he had grown dissatisfied with the extreme abstraction of the German metaphysicians. They express also a certain disillusionment, possibly with such efforts at social reform as had been tried at Brook Farm, certainly with some of the philosophical theories that had prompted these reforms.[614] In the end he turned even upon his beloved Schleiermacher, not, it may be presumed, because he came to consider him false, but simply because he regarded the abstruse speculations of transcendental theologians and metaphysicians alike as relatively inconsequential. Urged by Parker to publish a translation which Ripley had made earlier of one of Schleiermacher's works, he replied, January 31, 1852, that he would not (1) because no one would read the work, and (2) because he had lost all "immediate interest in that line of speculation."[615]

His disillusionment with speculative philosophy in general and with German metaphysics in particular was no sudden development. It will be recalled that Brook Farm, where Ripley was the guiding resident spirit, was abreast of Boston in the interest taken in German thought and literature, and well ahead of any community in the country in the appreciation of German music. Ripley's library was at hand in the "Eyrie" for all who cared to read. The *Harbinger*, under Ripley's editorship, contained many reviews of German books, translation of German poetry, and Dwight's column devoted to music, including long discussions of German music. Ripley himself taught Spinoza, Kant, and Cousin in the school at Brook Farm. Nowhere on the

American continent was there a more concentrated effort to absorb German art and thought. But as the debts mounted, and as the course of the Farm moved steadily downward, Ripley had cause to reflect upon the inefficacy of transcendental philosophy to solve the practical problems of living. The failure of the enterprise swallowed up everything he possessed, including his library. He had literally given his all, and it had availed him nothing. When he moved to New York City to begin life anew, in his forty-seventh year, he broke off all active association with Boston Transcendentalism beyond the maintenance of a friendship and correspondence with some of his old colleagues, such as Dwight and Parker.

During his last years, as assistant editor of the New York *Tribune*, reader for *Harper's*, and contributor to numerous magazines, his primary interests were literary. While he established himself as "the father of literary criticism in the American press," he left the fields of theological and philosophical controversy far behind him. In 1866 he and his second wife, who was German-born, made a long-deferred trip to Europe, and the visit was repeated and greatly extended in 1869. While he entered enthusiastically upon these tours that led to many of the places for which he had yearned in his youth, the opportunities came too late to leave any more visible effects upon him than such as can be read in the travel sketches which he sent back to the *Tribune*. The rest of his life was devoted to journalistic work and the making of encyclopedias.

After Brook Farm, Ripley's growth in philosophical and theological speculation, while not reaching a positive period, went into a decline. In reviewing such books as came across his desk, he continued to write interestingly about the Germans whom he had studied in his younger days; he did some book reviews of German authors who were new to him; occasionally he re-emphasized the worth of the transcendental

school generally and Kant particularly;[616] and to a friend who expressed surprise at Ripley's facility in throwing off an article on Goethe, he said, "It is not wonderful, seeing that I have been fifty years about it."[617] But, by and large, his enthusiasm for Kant and for Goethe belonged to his earlier career as idealist and reformer. The principles for which he had striven appeared to be defeated. The socialization of Christianity as Herder, Schleiermacher, and Ronge had formulated it, and as he had sought to propagate it, had failed. While his hatred of slavery and his accounts of the social conditions in Europe, especially in his reports of the Prussian War of 1866 and the Franco-Prussian War, manifest his continued interest in social progress, his erstwhile zeal was gone. He wrote as a reporter, not as a participator. Something may have been owing to his second marriage, to a woman thirty years his junior, who took him out into New York society; something, to the substantial increase of his income from the editorship of the *New American Encyclopedia*; more, to his disillusionment based on personal experience.[618] His own ambitions as a minister had come to naught when, after fourteen years of earnest endeavor, both his matter and his manner had failed to satisfy. It seems clear, too, that not the least important result of his long theological career, during which he never felt what he called "firm ground under his feet,"[619] was the melancholy conclusion that his own theology was unsatisfactory to himself. Convinced though he was that his efforts as the editor of the French eclectics, his numerous essays on German theology, and his letters to Andrews Norton helped to shift the bases of Christianity to firmer ground than that on which they had rested, they were not, after all, secure enough. Unable to subscribe to a thoroughgoing rationalism and unwilling to follow uncritically a "transcendent" mysticism, he sought to find ground midway between the two in "the inward truths of religion" as revealed by the intuitions of the moral man, only to find that the "truths" still escaped him. Like Emerson, he found theology "from everlasting to everlasting debatable ground"; like Emerson, too, he gave up the profession of the theologian; for trying, as he did, to steer a middle course between two extremes, he approached neither, and he failed to satisfy even himself. About all that can be said with certainty is that he was never, between 1820 and 1850, a Unitarian of Norton's kind nor a Transcendentalist of Parker's. Nor was he then or afterwards an infidel. After abandoning the religious beliefs of his "transcendental" period, he never returned to them, never deplored their loss; and on his deathbed, if he could have had his way, he would have had in attendance neither a Unitarian nor a Transcendental minister, but Father Hecker.[620] Except Orestes A. Brownson, none of the Transcendentalists illustrates better than Ripley the difficulty that beset Emersonian idealists who sought, like their master, to find in German philosophy the means to square their head by their heart—to make their religion philosophical and their philosophy religious. Ripley's failure was no greater than that of many another, more richly endowed than he, who found it equally impossible to reconcile faith with knowledge.

Theodore Parker (1810–1860)

Theodore Parker was eight years younger than Ripley and seven years the junior of Emerson. Beginning his studies a decade after Ripley and Emerson, he was in a better position than they to discover early the richness of German literature and scholarship and to make them a central part of his studies. He began these studies a little before the year 1832, which, as we have seen in connection with Emerson, Hedge, and Ripley, was en epochal one for the introduction of German studies in Boston. Parker, more than any other of his generation, was

the one who sought, in the phrase of John Weiss, "to invoice the lot" of freight from Germany that was dumped on the Boston wharves, despite the warning of the older generation that German was "the natural language of infidelity and spiritual despair," and that none could associate with freethinkers of the Germanic cast without losing his homebred piety. He did not read far before he concluded that his elders did not know enough of the proscribed literature even to misrepresent it effectively. Their antagonism seemed to him prompted by no more than languorous laziness, timid fear, or dogmatic orthodoxy. Before he would condemn, he would see for himself.

Already during his year of teaching in Boston (1831) he had added German to his French and Spanish, and had acquired some facility in writing the language. While preparing for the Harvard Divinity School during 1830–1834, he plunged into the deepest waters of German philosophy and theological criticism, and often found himself in depths over his head; yet what he read he liked well enough to begin laying the foundations for his great library of scholarly works in the diverse fields in which he was interested. He was introduced to a good deal of this material by Dr. Convers Francis of Watertown, at the time when Parker was conducting a private school there (1832). The older man gave him free run of his large theological library, in which German books were especially prominent. Here were "*Dogmatik, Metaphysik,* and *Hermeneutik* for Theodore, with a competent guide to hold the clue for him. The two years spent with these advantages were always gratefully remembered by him. Theodore's questions accumulated frightfully when he found such a hospitable ear for them."[621] His reading during the Watertown period included the Greek and Latin classics, some metaphysics, including Hegel and Kant, besides Cousin and the new school of French philosophers, the poets Goethe, Schiller, and Klopstock, and Coleridge's *Aids to*

Reflection.[622] Here was enough revolutionary idealism to entice any young mind from the path of orthodox sensationalism. The rapidity of his progress toward the transcendental position is indicated by the record of his studious activity while in the Divinity School during 1834–1836. He undertook to study eleven languages (in addition to those he had already acquired), to translate parts of Eichhorn's *Urgeschichte*, Paulus' *Handbuch*, Ammon's *Fortbildung des Christenthums*, and other smaller works, to give tutoring lessons in Hebrew, Greek, and German, and to read in fourteen months a parcel of over three hundred volumes of literary and critical books, at the same time that he clarified his own position on the important questions of revelation and prophecy as raised by such German theologians as De Wette and Astruc. Even at this early date he took a stand "in advance of the average Unitarian of the time."[623] That he was ahead of orthodox Unitarians, although he himself was hardly able at the time to define just where he stood, or whither his reading was leading him, is revealed in his report of a conversation with Professor Andrews Norton concerning the value of Biblical research among the Germans. Having read in 1836 such books as Ackermann's *Das Christliche in Plato*, Schelling's *Lectures on Academic Study*, and De Wette's *Introduction to the Old Testament*, he came to Norton "bursting with enthusiasm for German scholarship . . . but Professor Norton assured him coldly that all the Germans were 'raw' and inaccurate, unfitted for the refinements of metaphysics. They made good dictionaries and grammars, he admitted, but even these were so large one could not use them. Parker was considerably dashed, and that night he confided to his journal that Norton was a bigot."[624]

To round out his knowledge of philosophy and literature, he read carefully during his stay at the Divinity School in such authors as Coleridge (notably *Table-Talk*

and *Aids to Reflection*), Wegscheider, Stäudlin, Storr, Schmidt, the English Platonists Cudworth and More, as well as Descartes, Leibnitz, Lessing, Schelling, Cousin, Constant, Kant, the Gnostics, and the medieval mystics. It was at the Divinity School, too, between August, 1836, and May, 1837, that he began to translate De Wette's *Einleitung*.[625]

During the period of his ministry at West Roxbury (1837–1847) much of Parker's extra time was spent in the preparation of the monumental set of notes and commentaries which went into his edition of De Wette's *Critical and Historical Introduction to the Canonical Scriptures of the Old Testament*. Published in two volumes in 1843, this work was Parker's offering on the altar of scholarship—an imposing, accurate, clearly organized, and shrewd digest of all that the world had accumulated on the subject of the Old Testament Canon. To prepare it, he bought and read hundreds of German works, consulted the libraries of Francis and Ripley, studied history, philology, comparative religion, and oriental literatures, with an intense zeal and absorption.[626] The book received little acclaim from American reviewers and turned out a bad financial loss for the author, but it remains a testimony to the genuine sincerity and enthusiasm which Parker brought to the profoundest questions of theological study.[627]

During the years of his pastorate at West Roxbury Parker's time was still largely devoted to pastoral duties and theological studies—not, as later, much taken up with agitation and reform. He could spend long hours in discussion with his neighbors, the Russells, or with the congenial spirits of Brook Farm, within walking distance. His circle at the time was occupied with Bettina von Arnim and Goethe, Fourier, Emerson's lecture in the Divinity School and the controversy stirred up by it over the Latest Form of Infidelity, and "all Kosmic questions."[628] Following the example of his beloved German scholars, Parker was determined to put his studious efforts on the broadest possible foundations—to collect and read the best that had been said in his own field and in all related fields. Accordingly he soon owned a collection of books that was considered one of the marvels of American scholarship during the fermentation period of Transcendentalism, and even those who were not enthusiastic about the study of the German theologians conceded it to be "the richest and most varied library in the whole of New England." At his death in 1860 the library contained some 16,000 volumes, three-fourths of them in foreign languages, German heavily predominant.[629]

During the West Roxbury period Parker wrote his exhaustive critical reviews of German scholarly works for the *Christian Examiner* and the *Boston Quarterly* and his articles for the *Dial*. As a critic, his judgments were independent and penetrating, his study of each work thorough and complete, in avowed imitation of the "depth, philosophic grounding, and all-sidedness" of the Germans.[630] So he bewildered his readers by flinging at them the names of scores of unheard-of German writers, astounding them with the sharpness and clarity of his judgments, his easy, comprehensive grasp of so many strange, new fields of study.

The first of this series was a review of Ackermann's *Das Christliche in Plato*.[631] In April, 1840, appeared his long and somewhat condemnatory appraisal of Strauss's *Leben Jesu*.[632] In the light of Parker's later position, both of these reviews may be considered unduly conservative. He was by no means willing to underwrite all the startling conclusions of Strauss about miracles and prophecy, and he denied what Strauss asserted, namely, that Biblical history is nothing more than the record of myths and popular ideas without basis in fact. At the point of reducing the story of Jesus to sheer myth Parker balked, though twenty years later he expressed a more favorable opinion of Strauss.[633]

In 1840 Parker was still deep within the career of a dutiful pastor. His controversial period had not yet begun; few suspected as yet the future great heresiarch. But his ponderings upon the theses and arguments of Strauss and more particularly his intensive historical, analytical, and critical work on De Wette's *Introduction to the Old Testament* were conditioning him for the position that is foreshadowed in his sermon on *The Transient and Permanent in Christianity* (1841) and that is more explicitly expressed in his discourse on *The Relation of Jesus to His Age and the Ages* (1845). The steps by which he progressed from the relatively orthodox position of his Unitarian colleagues in 1840 to that which he held ultimately regarding the nature of Jesus can be traced in his sermons and published tracts. Strauss was the major factor, though he never wholly agreed with Strauss.

One important result of his preoccupation with Strauss before 1840 was to increase Parker's suspicion that the New Testament as well as the Old had a mythology (though he would never go to the extreme of Strauss and claim that it was all myth), and that the evidence on which miracles rested was in all cases insufficient to establish their claim.[634] Despite his thorough preparatory work and his complete familiarity with Strauss's book and its background, his review is disappointing. Its point of view is confused, and the conclusions are equivocal.[635]

The review of Menzel's *German Literature* printed in the *Dial* for January, 1841, was a similarly overwhelming exhibition of erudition.[636] In the biographical essay on his friend Follen (printed in the *Dial* for January, 1843), Parker tells the stirring life-story of this champion of freedom, who found refuge at Harvard and there introduced the study of German literature. Parker's address on "The American Scholar"[637] is an analysis of the relation of literature and scholarship to general culture, with special reference to the advance of learning in Germany.

His study of Schleiermacher, Strauss, and De Wette was followed by numerous references in the journal to indicate the growth in Parker of a skeptical attitude, first most notably apparent in connection with the Norton-Ripley controversy. In 1838 Emerson had made his statement regarding transcendental religion in his address before the Divinity School; he was promptly answered by Norton in *The Latest Form of Infidelity*. Thereupon Ripley undertook the vindication of Spinoza, Schleiermacher, and De Wette against Norton's charge of irreligion and atheism, and in an anonymous pamphlet sought to combat the doctrine that miracles are the only evidence of revelation. Impatient of what he considered halfway measures, Parker entered the fray at this point and sought to shift the argument to a much broader base. While Ripley affirmed the divine mission of Christ and his belief that the miracles related in the Gospels were actually wrought by Jesus, Parker set out to show that neither Christ's divinity nor faith in miracles was necessary to true religion.[638] He believed that Norton's "steel-cold intelligence"[639] had driven Ripley into a position that made it difficult for Ripley to make out a case for the Germans as believers in a personal God and in immortality. He felt himself called to extricate Ripley from a weak position, and accordingly announced that since Ripley, in his forthcoming reply to Norton, would "not say all that I wish might be said," he intended to say "a higher word." He had concluded that he might as well face the issue squarely and have it out once and for all. His Germans would help him, and so he set about saying his "higher word" in an anonymous pamphlet, *The Previous Question between Mr. Andrews Norton and his Alumni Moved and Handled in a Letter to All Those Gentlemen*, by Levi Blodgett. This was his reply to those of the lay brethren who believed that

Mr. Norton had laid Transcendentalism low. Planting himself on the ground that that man has a spiritual nature endowed with original capacity to apprehend primary religious truth directly, without meditation of sacrament, creed, or Bible, he stood outside and above the controversy that raged about him. His faith, he argued, was unassailable by either historical skepticism or literary criticism. For all he cared, all might go by the board—scriptures, miracles, ordinances, forms, usages. He was safe. Here was Transcendental religion full blown.

In 1841 Parker came on the scene again with his sensational sermon on *The Transient and Permanent in Christianity*, the title itself being taken from one of Strauss's essays. Parker's knowledge of German Biblical inquires and especially of Strauss's theories regarding mythology and history had destroyed for him his belief in the inspiration of the New as well as of the Old Testament, so that in this ordination sermon he ranged the miracles, the prophecies, the story of Jesus himself among the "transient" elements of religion, affirming on the other hand a warm and enthusiastic preference for the undying religious spirit, divorced from all theological and ritualistic forms. As a result Parker was henceforth assailed as "infidel," "scorner," and "blasphemer,"[640] and he found it increasingly difficult thereafter to receive invitations for exchange sermons with his Unitarian brethren.

The year 1841 also saw the composition of Parker's first group of collected lectures, entitled *Discourse of Matters Pertaining to Religion* and published the following year. With imposing scholarly documentation[641] and great clarity and forcefulness, Parker set forth his views of religious doctrine and religious history in this book, which he looked upon as a sermon on the transient and permanent "writ large." Original in plan and development, the work defines the main articles of the Transcendental point of view, denying much of Christian orthodoxy that still adhered to the New England Protestant position, at the same time attempting a positive statement of the bases of belief for enlightened, scientific, rational inquirers in his age. The book could hardly have been written without the aid of the scholarly German works referred to so frequently in the footnotes on his pages. Despite its many innovations in doctrine, the text of the book itself is written in a clear, simple language, the erudite and technical terminology being kept to a minimum. Parker obviously aimed at reaching the popular audience,[642] and the fact that three editions were distributed during the year indicates that in this aim at least he was successful.

In the first book, Chapter II, "Of the Sentiment, Idea, and Conception of God," and in Chapter IV, on "The Idea of Religion Connected with Science and Life," he employs a distinctly Kantian terminology in his division of religion into the speculative and the practical.[643] He also cites Kant to show that all purely philosophical arguments for the existence of God are inadequate,[644] and in his definition of religion employs a phraseology obviously derived from Kant.[645]

But Parker's independence of any single philosophical system is clearly revealed in a footnote, wherein he sets side by side the definitions of a host of thinkers: Plato, John Smith, Kant, Schelling, Fichte, Hegel, Schleiermacher, Hase, Wollaston, and Jeremy Taylor. He does not waste time on Kant's fruitless speculation, on the ground of pure Reason, regarding the three ideas of the Reason. He is content to regard Kant's antinomies as valid and to accept the Kantian pure Reason as impotent to prove God, immortality, and freedom. Instead, he readily adopts the intuition of the post-Kantians, "the instinctive intuition of the divine, the consciousness that there is a God,"[646] which is universal and primary in the soul of man, the necessary basis for all religious forms.[647]

Leibnitz and Hegel likewise engaged Parker's attention during the West Roxbury period and later. After having begun the study of Leibnitz in 1836,[648] he came to employ certain Leibnitzian terms in his discussion of the problem of evil. On some occasions he calls the soul the "primitive monad,"[649] and he argues very much in the manner of Leibnitz on the question of the infinite God in the universe. However much Parker was tortured by the outward signs of evil, pain, and misery in the world (and it was this that lay at the bottom of his strong reformist sympathies), he had an unshakable conviction that in the totality of the universe all apparent evil is resolved in a higher good, with a prospect of future infinite progress toward perfection, in which all created things, animal as well as human, could in the after-life attain to a state of ever-increasing felicity and harmony.[650] There is not enough evidence definitely to link these ideas to Leibnitz; yet what there is is highly suggestive that he read Leibnitz to good purpose. It may represent no more than the conscious reaction, shared by others of his contemporaries, against orthodox Protestant views of sin. Though Parker had not yet finished struggling with this question, he is here approaching the position that ultimately became his settled conviction on the subject.[651]

Toward Hegel, he remained unsympathetic on several counts. As early as 1841 he attacked Hegel's identity of *Sein* and *Nicht-Sein* in God. In general, he rejected the "fruitless subtleness" of the modern metaphysical schools,[652] and deplored the fact that Hegel had to resort to such very intricate reasoning to preserve the divinity of Christ; he felt it far more expedient to abandon the attempt altogether. Parker was content to rest his case with Kant; he expected no one (indeed, wanted no one) to prove the existence of God—to tell us "the metaphysics, and the physics, too, of God." He classified Hegel's philosophy as an idealistic monism, a "spiritual pantheism," which denies the perfection of God. Hegel gives us "a variable God, who learns by experience, and who grows with the growth and strengthens with the strength and growth of the universe itself . . . for their [the pantheists'] God knows nothing until it is either a fact of observation in finite nature—in the material world,—or else a fact of consciousness in finite spirit—in some man; he knows nothing till it is shown him. That is the fatal error with Hegel and his followers in England and America."[653]

But it was not only the theology of Germany that interested Parker. From his earliest years he read the leading literary writers of that country and constantly recorded his criticism or appreciation of them in his journal. Most frequently his attention turned to Goethe, whose works he read in their entirety (except for the *Grand-Cophta*, which alone he found uninteresting). Even more than Emerson, however, he found Goethe not commendable in all points. He did not, like Emerson, search him assiduously for support for either his own philosophy or theology; certainly he did not find as much in Goethe as did Emerson. Goethe's morality he found "commonplace," but his language "exceedingly graceful . . . its richness, clearness, and beauty . . . above all praise."[654]

Besides Luther and Schiller (whose poetry Parker heartily disliked),[655] Heine attracted his attention, and he once planned an article on the poet. In his later years especially he read a good deal of him; though, as might be expected, he did not relish all of Heine, for "Heine has a good deal of the Devil in him, mixed with a deal of genius.[656]

All in all, however, the poets and romancers of Germany meant little compared with the significance to him of the philosophers and theologians. Parker's thinking, even more than Emerson's, was rooted in religion. In Emerson the tendency generally is to accord religion a primacy over philosophy, but often he rates the two domains as more or less on a par, and always he seeks to reconcile one with the other. In Parker, the tendency is rather to show the great disparity between the two. Religious truth is consistently held to be not only distinct from but superior to philosophic truth. Whenever philosophical reason and religious intuition clash, the former is summarily denied. This tendency he developed relatively early in his career, and he consistently propounded it from pulpit and platform. Yet he accorded philosophy an honored place. Looking back on the days of his early wrestlings with these problems, he said near the end of his life that although he had "studied assiduously the metaphysics and psychology of religion," as well as Locke, Hobbes, Berkeley, Hume, Paley, and the French Materialists, Reid and Stewart, Clarke and Butler, Cudworth and Barrow, and Cousin, he "found most help in the works of Immanuel Kant, one of the profoundest thinkers in the world, though one of the worst writers." "He gave me the true method, and put me on the right road."[657] This is followed by a brief statement of his three-point "instinctively intuitive" philosophy by which he is assured of God, moral law, and immortality. This he called a system of "absolute theism," "the foundation of all religion, laid in human nature itself."[658]

The contribution of German idealism to Parker's "absolute theism" is to be found, first of all, in the insistence on the function of "instinctive intuition" as the ground of our knowledge of God—the belief that the existence and nature of God cannot be ascertained by the finite understanding, since it is an idea of Reason not constitutive, but regulative. In this negative aspect of Kant's first *Critique*, Parker is in full accord with Kant. Further, we recognize in Parker's insistence on the efficacy of an inner moral law something akin to Kant's imperative—the all-important principle on which God, freedom, and immortality are postulated. But the fundamental nature of the "proofs" on which these ideas are based by Parker and by Kant are as far apart as the two poles; for with Kant moral law is a categorical imperative, and with Parker it is a compound of Christian piety, instinctive intuition, and the still small voice. It is likely that Parker's acquaintance with Jacobi, however little he said in appreciation or criticism of him, and with Schleiermacher, whom he mentioned often, helped him to formulate his ideas on the function of intuition; though considering Parker's innate sense of piety, it is not necessary to assume that the influence of either was requisite for such a formulation. Similarly, the emphasis on man's feeling of dependence, which for Parker is the basis of his consciousness of God, is traceable to the Christian tradition generally, but, so far as his dependence on books goes, seems closest to Schleiermacher and De Wette. There was no system in Europe or America which represented in its entirety the kind of "absolute theism" preached by Parker although, as Parker himself admitted, De Wette came "nearest to it."[659]

Parker's formulation of his religious creed was not a result, as with Emerson, of a long struggle between conflicting positions. "The new philosophy commended itself to Parker at once . . . . Religion had always been a spiritual thing with him from childhood, never a formal or doctrinal thing."[660] His lack of interest in the finer points of metaphysical argumentation is revealed by the fact that he often resorted to modes of thinking foreign to the transcendental method.[661] But insofar as the New Thought confirmed and strengthened his belief in his personal religion, Parker drew on the great German thinkers and theologians at every turn. From the German scholars he learned about critical discipline, and, following them, he set a standard of responsible and thorough research such as had not been seen in American theology up to his time. His interest in the interpretation of history in terms of the *Mythos* was undoubtedly excited by his study of Herder and Strauss;

similarly, his great respect for the philological tools as used by Biblical scholars, and his argumentation from the new discoveries of archaeology and oriental history are modes of working adopted from his German mentors.[662] His prodigious talent for the organization of huge masses of knowledge, which is convincingly displayed in his preparatory notes for a great projected history of religion, was developed under the tutelage of German historians in the tradition of Herder, Eichhorn, Schlosser, and Gervinus. But Parker had never time enough to devote his whole mind to these scholarly pursuits. In the end he emerged not so much a thinker or scholar as a pulpit orator and a popular moralist. Least of all did he give evidence of being fitted for strictly speculative philosophy. Even in the sphere of his reformist activities, he was spurred on by the example of the German liberals. Just as George Ripley received encouragement from watching the attempts of Ronge to introduce a type of Christian Associationism in Germany, so Parker was interested in Ronge's projects.[663] Writing to Ronge in 1854, he professed to draw support from Ronge's example for his own project of "liberalizing" America.[664] And finally, he received no little comfort and moral support from the knowledge that the European reformers and democrats as well as the young German exiles in America joined with him in the great cause to which he dedicated the larger part of his life.[665]

It was not until 1844, when he was well along in his ministerial career, and had published many books of sermons, lectures, articles, and the great commentary on De Wette, that he found the opportunity to go to Europe. He saw Italy, France, Germany, and England, and made full use of his opportunities to visit the cathedrals and art centers. His notebooks record relatively little comment about art and music, but much on manners, education, religion, and social conditions; for these things, together with his interviews with men of letters and scholars, engaged his liveliest interest. In Germany he made it a point to visit the university towns, and he made a determined effort to seek out many of the great scholars and philosophers whose books he had come to know so well. He attended the lectures of Schelling at Berlin, met Tholuck, Gervinus, Ullman, and Ewald at Halle, and visited De Wette at Basel. He heard the scientist Oken at Zürich, met Carlyle in London, and Martineau in Liverpool. His visit to Wittenberg was a pilgrimage to the scenes of Martin Luther's historic rebellion against Rome. Wherever he went, he collected local statistics on population, wealth, crops, flora and fauna. Of course, he sometimes came away from his interviews with professors disappointed or disillusioned; they did not always measure up to his preconceived pictures of them, but he managed, despite the language difficulties,[666] to establish some lasting friendships and to learn a good deal about the state of Biblical criticism and philosophical discussion in the Europe of the forties. And he learned, how some professors could be nothing less than ridiculous, when, with their pompous metaphysical apparatus, they attempted feats of reasoning which any man's common sense knew to be unreasonable.[667]

Following his trip to Europe he was on intimate terms with many German theologians and teachers, and especially from about 1847 on, his works began to be translated and noticed in Germany. His *Discourse* was published in 1847 at Kiel in a translation by Archdeacon Wolf, who in that year sent a copy to the author. During the years 1854–1861, Parker's *Sämmtliche Werke* (tr. by Dr. Johannes Ziethen, 5 vols.) appeared in Leipzig. He was much heartened to read the favorable reviews as they came to him from time to time.[668]

Parker's career was that of a publicist, moralist, and rationalistic critic of the conservative order; he was a reformer, teacher, and agitator for the fulfilment of the demo-cratic promise of America. He was not an outstanding speculative philosopher, nor a real appreciator of literary art, but rather a practical Yankee leader, with a penchant for law and polemics almost as strong as for preaching. His great service was to bring his pious worship of an infinitely good and wise Creator—without the ritualistic and formalistic limitations of American Protestantism—to millions of Americans who were drifting out of the denominational churches. Without the instruments of *Wissenschaft* and *Kritik*, with which he was able to cull out of Protestantism many of those ingrained inconsistencies that he felt hampered its development, he could never have carried through the revolt which he undertook. From German scholarship and philosophy he borrowed heavily because these were fashioned to his purposes. He was not in a position to add much to the rapidly expanding knowledge of Biblical criticism; his contribution lay primarily in the practical application that he made of German scholarship and criticism to contemporary American religious problems. To the Germans he was indebted also for something positive—for revealing to him in strong, impassioned, poetic terms the universal human basis of man's consciousness of the eternal and the infinite; they gave him a vision, not anywhere else so clearly and beautifully drawn, of the "pure" or permanent values that reside in the Christian movement. And the success which he attained in revealing that vision to the Americans of his generation virtually summarizes the worth of Parker in the tradition of American culture.

James Freeman Clarke (1810–1888)

James Freeman Clarke, born the same year as Parker, took a much less radical stand than Parker on questions that separated the Transcendentalists from the orthodox. He preceded Parker by some years at the Harvard Divinity School and was repelled less than Parker by the prevailing theological doctrines of Ware and Norton. For example, he felt that the Rev. Henry Ware exerted the strongest pedagogical influence that came to him during his college years. But, as in others of his class, the famous Class of 1829, his reading in Carlyle,[669] Coleridge,[670] Goethe,[671] and Jacobi[672] soon raised doubts regarding the "wooden philosophy of John Locke."[673]

He came utterly to reject sensationalism and went over to the camp of the intuitionalists. He came, like others of his classmates, to consider the distinction between reason and understanding, as sketched by Coleridge, the crucial discovery of modern philosophy. He became a professing Transcendentalist, or, as he put it, a "pure idealist, sure of the real presence of God . . . sure that society was to be made over again within fifty years."[674]

Though a member of the Transcendental Club and throughout the period of his ministry in the West in close touch with the transcendental rebels of Boston, Clarke exhibited a "philanthropic comprehensiveness" that precluded partisanship and doctrinal narrowness.[675] Because of his disinclination to preach about the different points of the divinity of Christ, revelation of the New Testament, and damnation and ultimate restoration, he was looked upon as best fitted to represent the Unitarians as a group: he took a judicious middle ground, and refused to be badgered into any semblance of a creed or dogma, and accordingly his writings have come to be regarded as the most nearly authoritative statement of the essential Unitarian belief.[676]

Clarke's education, like that of all the more advanced Unitarians of his generation, included a considerable training in German theology and a fair acquaintance with German literature. During part of the time that he was a student at Harvard, Emerson was living in Divinity Hall, and it is recorded that the two discussed the writings of Goethe. He formed a friendship with F. H.

Hedge, and W. H. Channing had been his intimate friend since his Latin School days. Clarke took up the study of German in 1832, and from that time on Goethe and Schiller ranked very high in his list of favorite authors. Soon his interest was extended to include Tieck, Novalis, Jean Paul, and Lessing.[677] The *Memoirs* of Margaret Fuller, edited in part by Clarke, bear testimony of the great admiration for German literature shared between them in the years 1832–1833 and after.[678]

In the course of a half-century Clarke produced a great many translations from the German, some of which appeared at various times in periodicals and anthologies. While most of them remain unprinted, the best of them were published in 1876 under the title of *Exotics, a Collection of Translations in Verse*. Some of these "exotics" are from Latin, French, and Persian (the last chiefly retranslations of German versions), but the great majority are from the German.

Already in 1836, at the age of twenty-six, Clarke wrote to Margaret that he saw no "use of Metaphysics,"[679] and there is no evidence to indicate that he read seriously in German philosophy either then or later. But his interest in German literature was stimulated all the more, while his professional studies put him in close touch with German theology. Thus he was being prepared for the articles he was soon to write for the *Western Messenger*.

The *Messenger*, established in 1835 in Cincinnati, contains Clarke's first contributions to the literature of Transcendentalism. This magazine, which he established and edited with the support of Wm. G. Eliot, Ephraim Peabody, C. P. Cranch, and others, foreshadows in many ways the aims and achievements of the later *Dial*. It was as definitely Transcendentalist in tone as the latter, and at least ten of its contributors later wrote for the *Dial*.[680] It defended Emerson against Norton in the controversy over American "infidelity," French eclecticism, and German theology; and it gave a good deal of prominence to German literature, both in review and translation.[681]

Clarke's contribution to the crusade designed to spread the gospel of idealism, as promulgated in German literature and theology, through the columns of the *Western Messenger* include the following more considerable offerings: extensive excerpts from De Wette's *Theodor* in translation,[682] a translation of Schiller's *Philosophische Briefe*,[683] an adaptation of Jean Paul's *Ein toller Vorbericht der Zukunft*,[684] a highly laudatory review of Carlyle's essays on German literature,[685] and a good appreciative review of John S. Dwight's *Select Minor Poems of Goethe and Schiller*.[686]

The ready reception of parts of *Theodor, oder die Weihe des Zweiflers*, which he had Englished for the *Messenger* under the title of "Theodore, or the Skeptic's Progress to Belief," induced Clarke to undertake a translation of the complete work. It appeared in 1841 in two volumes. In the Translator's Preface, he explained that De Wette represents the "average condition of German theology," and that, since he is neither extremely radical nor extremely conservative, his book should serve as a good introduction to German theology.[687] Although he recognized *Theodore* to be a book for popular consumption—of less intrinsic merit as a fundamental work, for example, than Parker's translation of De Wette's *Introduction to the Old Testament*— he nevertheless felt it a work excellently calculated to suit the needs of the times.[688]

In his later years as professor at the Harvard Divinity School (he was appointed in 1867) and as an author of semi-popular books on the Unitarian doctrine and the history of religion, he made use again and again of his knowledge of German theology.[689] His influence at Harvard was brought to bear on the reorganization of the educational system toward a closer approximation of the continental plan. He urged such reforms as greater emphasis on modern languages, the admission of women to medical studies after the example of the University of Zürich, the introduction of the elective system, and the broadening of the scope of the Divinity School.[690] Throughout his life he retained a measure of transcendental fervor and idealism, and he remained a staunch opponent of the skepticism and materialism which he saw growing around him.[691]

Amos Bronson Alcott (1799–1888)

Alcott, like Emerson, learned his philosophy first from nature. No school of philosophy, no institute of theology, could have taught Alcott of Spindle Hill what Emerson learned at Roxbury about meeting with God in the bush. Yet, like Emerson, Alcott all his life found a pure nature philosophy inadequate; both searched constantly, though more or less unsystematically, in books for that something more which neither external nature nor their own inner nature seemed able to supply. Their own assertions to the contrary, they did not find in themselves their own sufficient guides, although Alcott, perhaps more steadily than Emerson, found in the mystic inner light a unifying and guiding voice.[692]

From young manhood to old age Alcott read insatiably, throwing himself sometimes upon books "with a passion amounting to monomania."[693] More neglectful of history than Emerson, he came to be, especially after his Germantown period, very nearly as well-read in the natural sciences and in philosophy as Emerson; but on the whole he stuck more consistently than did Emerson to the "intuitional" thinkers. His reading of Coleridge's *Aids to Reflection* and *The Friend* in 1832 marked, he said, a "new era in my mental and psychological life."[694] Swedenborg fascinated but never quite convinced him. Jacob Boehme's mysticism he found basically harmonious with his own thinking. Hindu literature, particularly the *Bhagavad-Gita*, his hospitable mind readily domesticated. Aristotle, Plato (in the stimulating but inaccurate paraphrases of Thomas Taylor), Plotinus, Proclus, and Bacon filled his thoughts with "majestic and cloudy conjectures."[695] Yet all these and others,[696] "bright and glorious as they are," seemed to Alcott "lost in the transcendent radiance of the Gospel of Jesus," whom he regarded as "the exponent of human nature," and whose "theory of Life and Being" he considered "a sublime synthesis of Infinite and Absolute."[697] On March 28, 1850, he wrote with a note of deliberation that betokens a certain finality:

> My debt to Plato is greater, perhaps, than to any [other] mind—greater than to Christ, I sometimes think, whose spirit is an element of humanity but whose genius I did not entertain and comprehend till Plato unsealed my eyes and led me to the study of his fair performance. . . . Plato and Christ interpreted each other and the mind of mankind.[698]

That being so, German critical philosophy could have only a secondary importance for Alcott. Though he read, from first to last, in the writings of many Germans, he usually found in them little more than supplementary notions or complementary affirmations of ideas either his own or derived from Platonic tradition or Christ's example. In a few instances, however, the German complement was of real signifiance, so that an account of his indebtedness from that quarter is in order.

On the basis of available records it would seem that Alcott's introduction to German came during the early twenties—during one of his peddling circuits, when he read Locke's *Essay on Human Understanding* and Lavater's *Physiognomy* and found the former as uncongenial as the latter was congenial to his thinking.[699] He remained interested in physiognomy all his life, consistently maintaining that "the body is a type of the soul."[700] We do not know what books fell in his way during the spring and summer of 1825 when he was "reading widely in philosophical literature, and helping to edit the *Churchman's Magazine*,"[701] but during the four consecutive terms of school-teaching that followed, while he was master of the Centre Cheshire School in Cheshire, Connecticut, he earned the right to be called "The Pestalozzi of America." Bronson Alcott did not derive from Arminius, Rousseau, Wordsworth, Pestalozzi, or any other bookish source his conviction that childhood is essentially innocent, nor did he ask John Calvin or Jonathan Edwards whether children, like men, are essentially depraved; he simply looked at the children who sat daily before him and drew his own conclusions. But in formulating his practical educational procedure, he did have recourse to books, notably two little books, written by men who had been closely associated with Pestalozzi: Joseph Neef's *Sketch of a Plan and Method of Education* (Philadelphia, 1808)[702] and Hermann Krüsi's *Coup-D'Oeil on the General Means of Education* (Yverdon, 1818). More than that (says Professor Shepard):

> William Alcott[703] . . . was a friend and associate of the Rev. Wm. C. Woodbridge of Hartford, who had spent some time in Hofwyl, Switzerland, in the School founded by Fellenberg, one of Pestalozzi's assistants. Dr. J. M. Keagy, a Swiss physician, who was conducting a Pestalozzian school at Harrisburg, wrote to Alcott about the principles and methods of his master in April, 1826. Eight months later there came a long epistle on the same topic from William Maclure,[704] a wealthy philanthropist, geologist, and President of the Philadelphia Academy of Natural Science, who was at that time managing a Pestalozzian school at New Harmony, Indiana. In July, 1826, Alcott read a little book called *Hints to Parents . . . in the Spirit of Pestalozzi's Method*, from which alone it would have been easy for him to secure a clear knowledge of the system. Upon the whole, therefore, he was not making a vague and boastful reference to matters of which he was really ignorant when he entitled the first volume of his Journals 'The Cheshire Pestalozzian School.'

But this was not all. At Philadelphia, in May 1828, Alcott got from the famous bookseller Matthew Carey a Pestalozzian pamphlet entitled *Exposition of the Principles of Conducting Infant Education*, written by J. P. Greaves—a man, then unknown to him, who was to have a deep effect upon his later life and thought. Early in 1829 Alcott compiled for William Russell's *Journal [of Education]* an article on "Pestalozzi's Principles and Methods of Education." Two years later he was reading with close attention an admirable book by Dr. E. Biber entitled *Henry Pestalozzi*, then just published in London.[705]

"And so," observed Professor Shepard "one might continue to tedious length; but these citations are enough to show that Bronson Alcott was far from ignorant of the theories and practices evolved by the foremost educational genius of his time. During the second and third decades of the nineteenth century, Pestalozzi's teaching was inescapable anywhere in Europe, England, or America.[706] Before he had been many months in Cheshire he certainly knew the chief Pestalozzian principles, which taught that education ought to be: moral and religious; organic, harmonious, and complete; not mechanical but designed to penetrate and regulate the entire being; free, natural, and individual; based upon intuition rather than upon memory and the lower reason; gradual and progressive and linked, like a chain; social and domestic, and closely related to life. All this sounds like Alcott. It actually is Pestalozzi."[707]

During his Germantown period (1830–1834) Alcott read "fast and far and deeply, at first under the guidance of William Russell and then under Dr. Channing,"[708] who spent part of 1833 in Philadelphia. During the summer of 1835 Alcott left his family in Germantown and took an attic room in Liberty Street in order to be near the Philadelphia and Loganian libraries. There he shut himself up for months to read, in a sort of frenzy. Innately inclined toward Platonic philosophy, he now went right through Plato and Coleridge and

goodly portions of Plotinus, Proclus, Boehme, Bacon, Berkeley, and Kant.[709] Besides British romantic poetry, he read the *Biographia Literaria*[710] and Marsh's edition of *Aids to Reflection*, some Swedenborg, Carlyle's *Sartor Resartus*,[711] his translation of *Wilhelm Meister*, and everything else of Carlyle's available in the British reviews.[712] The next year Coleridge's *Essay on Method* moved him deeply.[713] During 1834, too, he gained some acquaintance with Schlegel's history of literature, with the writings of Richter, Herder, Lessing, Schiller, and Goethe (always in translation).[714] In these works, which he identified with "whatever comes from the higher order of minds in Germany," he found "Imagination and Reason blended in one Whole, and the human spirit . . . led onward by their mutual aid." "How long," he exclaimed, "it has taken me to make the discovery!"[715]

Coleridge assisted me in the beginning, Wordsworth too exerted a genial influence, and by these and my own innate tendency to pure ideality and a life of intellectual pursuits, I was led to a full view of things. Herder, Schiller, Richter, Goethe—and even Bulwer and Carlyle, though Englishmen yet German in education and in spirit —were understood and believed. Before this, however, Channing had spoken intelligently to me, and I had sympathized with the spirit of Plato, perused Plotinus, and found the depths of Aristotle, Bacon, Locke and Kant. With these last I was dissatisfied.[716]

What in Aristotle, Bacon, Locke, and Kant dissatisfied him is clear enough from his explanation that they "narrowed the range of human faculties, retarded the progress of discovery by insisting on the supremacy of the senses, and shut the soul up in the cave of the Understanding."[717] Obviously he did not interpret Kant as Emerson interpreted him at the time, for Emerson asserted Kant's great service to have been precisely the opposite—widening the range of human faculties, insisting on the supremacy of the Reason, and freeing the soul from the cave of the Understanding. Of course, Alcott had not yet met Emerson, but had made his own interpretation of Kant, which was, in the end, no more correct than Emerson's, though it had the merit at least of being his own. Where Emerson failed to distinguish between the negations of the *Critique of Pure Reason* and the affirmations of the *Critique of Practical Reason* (while asserting for the *pure* reason what Kant had limited to the realm of the *practical* reason), Alcott apparently did not, then or later, get beyond the restrictions which Kant hedged about the pure reason. There is nothing to show that Alcott ever seriously considered the practical validity of the reason as interpreted in Kant's second *Critique*. The Kant who became available to Alcott in 1834 was precisely what would lead Alcott to the conclusion he reached. He read, toward the end of 1833, Friedrich A. Nitsch's *General View of Kant's Principles* (London, 1895) and A. F. M. Willich's *Elements of Critical Philosophy* (London, 1898). It may be, as Professor Shepard observes, that Nitsch had been "one of Kant's pupils and professional associates,"[718] but it is clear that he had not been one of Kant's star pupils, and that his professional association had not been very close. Nitsch's book is noteworthy only for its superficiality. Although Alcott copied "no less than fifty-seven pages" from it and carefully worked through Willich's book, equally unsatisfactory as an organized, lucid exposition of Kant, he did not get from either any clearer idea of Kant than he got from Cousin's *History of Philosophy*, which he read in 1831, and which left him equally dissatisfied.[719] What he did get was the conviction that Kant, à la Nitsch and Willich, was not for him. He never acquired facility in the German language, and he did not later avail himself of such opportunities as more accurate commentaries on Kant offered. Consequently he remained all his

life faithful to his own "Spiritual instincts"[720] and suspiciously wary of Kantian critical philosophy.

More nearly harmonious to his way of thinking were such books as Zimmermann's *Einsamkeit*, which he read about 1837, in a poor translation then in its twentieth American edition.[721] By this time, too, he was rereading annually the famous twelfth chapter of the *Biographia Literaria* with its glorification of Schelling's idealism.[722] Both Schelling and Kant were often in his mind and doubtless contributed something to his thinking during those crucial years of 1833 and 1834 when he was undergoing the radical transformation from the philosophy of Sense and the Baconian method to that of Transcendentalism.[723] But neither of them, then or later, influenced him as profoundly as did the philosophy of Jesus, Plato, and Coleridge.[724] He understood the general import of Kantian transcendentalism to be in support of idealism and *a priori* knowledge;[725] and, following the lead of Coleridge, he gave both a place of honor—but below the place assigned to his "Master" Coleridge and the "Sublime" Plato.[726] Antagonistic to the method of the critical transcendentalists, Alcott sometimes found in them corroborative support but never much germinal or inspirational value.

Alcott's change of thought was completed during his Germantown period and before he knew Emerson. With his introduction to Emerson in 1835 and his participation in the Symposium the next year, he learned much about other Germans, such as Fichte and Schleiermacher, from men like Francis, Hedge, Parker, and Ripley. Thus stimulated, Alcott's knowledge of German literature increased rapidly during the next few years, but there is little to suggest that, so far as German philosophy is concerned, he read much beyond some of the more popular works of Schelling, Fichte's *Destination of Man*, and the mystical aphorisms of Novalis. By October of 1838 he recorded his dissatisfaction with French eclecticism as "not deep enough for us,"[727] and in December he was urging that Confucius, Zoroaster, Paracelsus, Galen, Plato, Bruno, Boehme, Plotinus, More, Swedenborg, and "others of the sublime school" should be put into the hands of English readers.[728] By 1840, in the midst of much concern with More, Cudworth, Iamblichus, and Porphyry,[729] he was turning from the more literary works of various Germans to more specialized books like Goethe's *Theory of Colors*.[730] Among fifty-five titles of books which he purchased in London in 1842 there were, according to his own memoranda, "Fichte's Vernunft, Fichte's Bestimmung, Schelling's Bruno, Novalis Schriften, 2 vols., Theosophia Revelata of Behmen, with Life, and Behmen's Life by Okely."[731] At Fruitlands, while Mrs. Alcott asked for "one day of practical philosophy," which would be "worth a century of speculation and discussion,"[732] Alcott's love for books did not abate.[733]

Alcott had first run upon Boehme, the theosophical shoemaker of Görlitz, in the form of Francis Okely's *Life of Jacob Behmen*, in Philadelphia during the summer of 1833, at the same time that Swedenborg's *Treatise on the Nature of Influx* first fascinated him.[734] But nothing definite came of this first contact, for his miscellaneous readings at the time in the Puritan fathers, the French revolutionists, the Greek idealists, Jesus, Bacon, Locke, Kant, and the mystics generally would not mix until the next year when Coleridge's *Essay on Method* supplied the solvent[735] by which he segregated from the disciples of Sense and Understanding those with "Spiritual instincts"—Plato, the neo-Platonists, Law, Leibnitz, Oken, Schelling, Goethe, Baader, Coleridge, Swedenborg, and Boehme. He bought Boehme's works in 1842 and read and reread them.[736] Apostrophizing Boehme as "the subtilest thinker on Genesis since Moses,"[737] he derived thence his theory of temperaments, which involved the doctrine of man's soul as "lapsing out

of innocency" and the four chambers or complexions;[738] but he disagreed (by the right asserted by all mystics when they interpret symbols) with Boehme on the fall of man and the symbolism of the serpent.[739] In an essay on Boehme (first published in the *Radical* for 1870 and reprinted in *Concord Days*, 1872), he praised Boehme's teeming genius as "the mother of numberless theories since delivered," and suggested that Law, Leibnitz, Oken, Schelling, Goethe, and Baader all depended on him.[740] As late as 1882, he founded, with Sanborn and Harris and a few other choice theosophically-minded spirits, a "Mystic Club," chiefly for the reading of Boehme.[741] He repeatedly and publically espoused Boehme's doctrines of temperament and lapse and even attempted to apply the former to his own family relationships. That is, he sought several times ingeniously but unsuccessfully to explain Abigail May Alcott's occasional tartness of mind and harshness of tongue in terms of Boehme's declaration that persons of dark complexion are of "demonic" origin. In the end, however, he was relieved to find a more natural explanation of his wife's dark complexion in a geneaological book which traced the Mays back to Portuguese origins.[742]

Associated with his liking for Boehme was his interest in Lorenz Oken, the speculative scientist, whom Alcott discussed with Emerson on August 5, 1849: "All day discussing the endless and infinite theme in the study and while walking, the late revelation leading all the rest—Oken, Goethe, Swedenborg, subordinated and sunk in their theories of the Creation as they seemed and were."[743] The "infinite theme," "late revelation," and "my late experiences and their fruits" all refer to Alcott's theory of Genesis, now first formulated though not yet fully elaborated or expressed. Goethe, Swedenborg, the neo-Platonists, Baader, and Stallo all contributed something to it,[744] but apparently it was Oken who brought on, during the summer of 1849, the intensive period of illumination, or what Alcott called "introversion,"[745] that resulted in the "late revelation" of Genesis. A remarkable passage in his journals attempts to describe the "ecstatic moment" induced by his submersion in Swedenborg and Oken, during which he had a vision that included, besides "a goblin or two," an image of "the entire universe as one vast spinal column."[746] "This [adds Professor Shepard], he sensibly decided, was going too far. Urged thereto by his wife—who again thought that he must be losing his reason and that he was going to die—he went to Concord for a fortnight's rest."[747] There and then it was that he had the long discussions with Emerson already noted. Besides Boehme, Goethe, Oken, and Oegger, they talked about Emerson's *Representative Men*, notably "Swedenborg"; and Emerson read to him "the introductory paper to his *Representative Men*, now nearly ready for the press."[748] These circumstances help to explain a portion of Emerson's essay on Swedenborg, in which, immediately after the passage that refers obviously to Goethe's morphology of the leaf, he speaks of "a poetic anatomist, in our day" (who could be Alcott or Oegger or Oken), "who teaches that a snake, being a horizontal line, and man, being an erect one, constitute a right angle; and between the lines of this mystical quadrant all animated beings find their place."[749]

With this idea of man and serpent forming a right angle, other animals filling the quadrant, Emerson had been familiar since July of 1835, when Elizabeth P. Peabody lent him the manuscript of a translation of a portion of Guillaume C. L. Oegger's *La Vraie Messie* (Paris, 1829), which she published later in the same year as *The True Messiah*. "I find good things in this manuscript of Oegger [wrote Emerson at the time], and I am taken with the design of his work."[750] From the manuscript he copied "many pages of extracts," of which only "a few" are reproduced in the publish-ed *Journals*, among them the one referred to.[751] In "Swedenborg" Emerson details a similar theory, obviously derived from Oken *apud* Alcott:

Nature puts out smaller spines as arms; at the end of the arms, new spines, as hands; at the other end, she repeats the process, as legs and feet. At the top of the column she puts out another spine, which couples or loops itself over, as a span-worm, into a ball, and forms the skull, with extremities again: the hands being now the upper jaw, the feet the lower jaw, the fingers and toes being represented this time by upper and lower teeth.[752]

This and what immediately follows paraphrase a passage in the Tulk translation of Oken's *Physiophilosophy* that ends with "The Mouth is the stomach in the head, the nose the lung, the jaws the arms and feet."[753] The same idea finds expression in Alcott's theory of Genesis.[754]

These passages illustrate at once something of the manner in which Alcott came upon some of his mystical ideas of Genesis and Lapse, the means by which the curious lore from men like Boehme, Oken, Swedenborg, and Oegger, after transmutation by Alcott, found its way into Emerson's published writings, and finally, the manner in which Emerson and Alcott served mutually to inspire and influence each other. They are indicative of the uses to which Alcott put the neo-Platonists, theosophists, physiophilosophers, and scientists in the derivation of his peculiar doctrines. The strong attraction which the mystics exerted on his mind was conducive to his pondering also upon the Schellingian philosophy of nature and related scientific and pseudo-scientific theories that could be combined with his unique divinations. It is not unnatural, therefore, that the concern with theorists like Oken should have led in Alcott's case, as it did in Emerson's, to a renewed interest, during the fifties, in scientific books, to a re-examination of the dynamic transcendentalism of Fichte and

Schelling, and ultimately to a consideration of Hegel. And so it was also in the natural course of events, after 1859, when Alcott encountered Harris' Hegelians in St. Louis, that he should find it impossible not to take cognizance of Hegel, whom Harris' "young men" knew so well and he knew not at all.[755] As soon as he returned to Concord, he procured some simplified expositions of the philosophy of Hegel, but he could make little of them. Anyway, the war and its disturbances, as well as his duties as the newly appointed Superintendent of the Concord Public Schools, soon pushed Hegel into the background.[756]

Yet, between 1859 and 1866, his first and second visits to St. Louis, there kept recurring to Alcott memories of the remarkable men of St. Louis and of their more remarkable performances, executed in the name of the Hegelian "system." He had seen enough of both to be disturbed by the feeling that in shutting his mind resolutely to Hegelianism and to systematized thought he might be missing something. To be sure, these Hegelians were not an altogether likable lot. For one thing, they were aggressive, in a Western sort of way. When he had read them some of his "Orphic Sayings," they had wanted to know precisely what each term meant. They had much to say about "dialectic" and "method," and they got results by their sinuous circumlocutions. It left a man to wonder whether his own methods did not stand in need of reexamination. "Examine myself," he wrote in his *Journals* on October 26, 1861. "A deplorable lack of early discipline in expression that leaves me lame at last." There was nothing fundamentally wrong with his ideas, he concluded; he was merely having dialectical difficulties. He recalled an unhappy evening at Emerson's, back in the forties, when Emerson had invited in some people whom he wanted to make acquainted with the Orphic Sage—so that they might "know what a rare fellow he is." Among them had been Theodore Parker, of

the "steel-cold intelligence," sharpened on German metaphysics. The evening had been a humiliating failure, for when Alcott's intuitions clashed with Parker's reason, Parker (says Emerson) "wound himself around Alcott like an anaconda; you could hear poor Alcott's bones crunch."[757] He recalled the bad moments he had suffered in the "hard logical" grip of Brokmeyer, "who was far more like an anaconda than Theodore Parker had been when it came to the crunching of transcendental bones."[758] His memories gave him food for thought. Foreigners like Brokmeyer could be in error; but surely Harris, a New Englander by birth and one of his own disciples, could not be deluded by a philosophy that did not have something to it. So he set himself to reading Hegel's *Philosophy of History*, which the St. Louisans told him was the key to Hegel and to the universe. Glorifying the "state" and "institutions," as they did during their earlier period (quite in contrast with Alcott's emphasis on the "individual"), they had told him that nothing could be understood except in terms of history, in terms of the "world spirit" and "world progress." To Alcott, who knew scarcely any history, this was all very perplexing. Humbly, he set about reading Hegel on history. But this first direct contact with an utterly new point of view left him beaten as his first encounter with Brokmeyer had left him cowed.

I look into Hegel's *Philosophy of History*, Sibree's translation, published by Bohn, 1857. I find the book much too dry and crabbed for my taste, as I have found nearly all books claiming the merits of system; but it contains valuable information and repays perusal. Hegel has the advantage of writing later than his masters, and of drawing largely from them all . . . and I think without due acknowledgment. I do not find anything better than Plato and Behmen have for me, and read best at first hand what I wish to find, being more sure of falling upon it in the pages of these masters.[759]

But Alcott was never one to turn tail

where a matter of principle was involved. Once the war was over, he set forth again to "exchange views" with the men who were coming to be known as the St. Louis Philosophers.[760] This time he was better prepared for the West and the Westerners. The war years had given him an appreciation of the "slovenly greatness" of the West, after all as much a part of the "united" States as his own beloved, little New England.[761] Brokmeyer especially intrigued him—this German immigrant, bootblack, shoemaker, iron puddler, hermit, huntsman, politician, spellbinder, lawyer, speculator, entrepreneur, soldier, philosopher, mayor of St. Louis, legislator, and soon-to-be governor of the state of Missouri. Constantly busy in a dozen activities, Brokmeyer had remained an impassioned student of Hegel and an inspired interpreter of Goethe. He had completed a translation of Hegel's *Logic* with characteristic indifference to the niceties of English idiom. Whatever else he was not, Brokmeyer was clearly a man cast in a large mold.

On the second occasion (1866), Alcott remained four weeks among Harris and his colleagues in St. Louis—amazed to find such a company encamped there on the edge of the wilderness and going deeper into German philosophy than he or the Eastern academicians cared, or dared, to go. "Brokmeyer—at any rate when he was not idly whittling sticks or spinning tall tales—was a perfect tornado of intellectual force and speed. Harris had a precision and delicacy of metaphysical thought to which Alcott never pretended and the like of which he had never before seen. Dr. Watters, a physician, had been thinking out for some years, it seemed, precisely Alcott's own favorite doctrine of 'Genesis.' He had perfected it by the campfires of the Union Army, and meant to publish his results as soon as he could get free from political work. Kroeger, primarily a student of Fichte rather than of Hegel, was Treasurer of the City and a man of many affairs.

Howison had a surprising erudition in many fields. Young Denton Snider, although not a man of any deep thoughtfulness, had an audacious and irreverent wit that sometimes made one uncomfortable."[762] Snider adored Brokmeyer and worshipped Shakespeare—neither of whom Alcott could appreciate. Tom Davidson, the unpredictable, was an Aristotelian of no mean ability. Amateurs, they met at Harris' house for "musical evenings," and played Beethoven, Mozart, Schumann, and Mendelssohn like professionals; he heard them discuss aesthetics, the likes of which he never dreamed possible outside the sacred halls of Harvard. Their clubs, associations, and societies—philosophical, artistical, musical, educational, literary—were enough to make one's head whirl.

He did not come away from his second visit without receiving several severe jolts, notably from Brokmeyer and Snider, and he was not sure that he had met fully the expectations of this exacting group;[763] but, on the whole, they pleased him in spite of their forthrightness and tough-mindedness; while they, professing to see in him some hopeful hints and gleams of Hegelianism, seemed inclined to accept him.[764] What worried him a good deal was that they should detect in his philosophy certain ideas of their beloved Hegel. He knew not how they got there. But Harris, already with an eye on Concord, assured Alcott that he was "a Hegelian in spirit"; and the Philosophical Society, under Harris' prompting, seemed disposed to claim him "as of their master's school."[765] Who was he to gainsay "so competent a judge as Harris"?[766] So he let it pass. After all, it seemed a good deal easier to agree rather than argue with these Hegelians. When he got home in March, he found Concord and its less strenuous life and thought "good and enjoyable." Still, the inevitable comparisons between New England Transcendentalism and Midwestern Hegelianism disturbed his peace of mind. He went to compare notes with Emerson, who also had just returned from "those wild parts." Emerson doubted that systematic thinking was superior to the intuitive affirmations of Concordian Transcendentalism, but Emerson's assurances did nc' allay all the doubts of Alcott, who had tested the matter at first hand. His delicate intuitive divinations had made a rather poor showing against Brokmeyer's bludgeoning logic. He was beginning to develop a new respect for systematic thinking.[767]

It is claimed [he reflected] for Hegel that his dialectic is an organism of the spirit, like the mathematics of nature, completing for mind what Plato and Aristotle attempted in their way. Certainly the uses to which Harris and Brockmeyer [sic] put it were surprising to me, and almost persuaded me that Hegel's claims are valid.[768]

As a preliminary to reducing his own philosophical thought to a system, he set to reading Stirling's *Secret of Hegel*,[769] but it does not appear that he made much progress with his own "system," or that Hegel proved of much assistance, though it is clear that the example of Harris in St. Louis, Jones in Jacksonville, and others in Dubuque, Quincy, Rockford,[770] and elsewhere revived within him the old ambition to form at Concord a philosophical "school." In his *Journals* he makes comparisons between East and West and begins to find in Boston and vicinity too much "exclusiveness and reservedness." He begins, also, to dream of "founders of schools" who, "complementing the defects of the teaching at the schools," might correct the eclipse that New England has undergone.[771] Why should not he do at Concord what had been done so brilliantly by Harris in the wild West?

The beginning was made with an informal meeting of Weiss, Wasson, and Alcott at Emerson's. James E. Cabot and others were to be invited for "future meetings . . . at Emerson's or at my house."[772] But the "school," first called the Free Religious

Club,[773] became the Radical Club[774] after a year, and soon languished. His "system-making" fared no better. In November, 1869, he started westward again, with St. Louis as his destination, but planning several stops on the way.[775] Between 1852 and 1882 he made ten "conversational tours" of the West, speaking, from first to last, in about a hundred towns in New York, Ohio, Indiana, Illinois, Wisconsin, Iowa, Kansas, and Missouri. He met with varying degrees of success—at all events with sufficient encouragement to entertain ambitions, even after he had passed three score and ten, of going all the way to the Pacific Coast, "belting the hemisphere with ideas."[776] In some towns he appeared repeatedly, notably in Bloomington, Peoria, Dubuque, Evanston, Chicago, Rockford, Quincy, Jacksonville, Beloit, Janesville, Cleveland, and St. Louis. During the seventies he grew accustomed to being called "the American Plato," "The Sage of Concord," yes, even "Emerson's Master."[777] He took his honors lightly, but the thought of setting up a school of philosophy in Concord with himself at its head was constantly with him after the trip of 1869–1870.[778] Throughout the seventies, therefore, he went adroitly about recruiting a "Faculty" and drumming up "students" for the Concord School. As early as May 3, 1870, he had a tentative plan of organization: "With Sanborn and Harris as neighbors, what might I not hope for! My cup would overflow. Concord is the proper seat for an Academy of Philosophy, Literature, and Religion."[779] Before the decade was out, his plan had materialized. He had not only Sanborn from Springfield; he had Emery from Quincy; he had, also, Harris from St. Louis, and Hiram K. Jones from Jacksonville. Harris, to be sure, was a bit "too Hegelian" and Jones was "too Platonic,"[780] but there were compensations: besides forming the nucleus of his "Faculty," each brought with him a class of students.

So it came to pass that his visions of a Concord School of Philosophy materialized. The School ran through nine successive summer sessions, from 1879 until the year of his death. It was a dignified, wholly beneficent, though somewhat Victorian institution. Its success was made possible less by Alcott's contributions than by "the frequently brilliant lectures of William T. Harris, Ednah Dow Cheney, Professor Benjamin Peirce, Thomas Davidson, Denton J. Snider, Frederic Hedge, E. P. Peabody, Noah Porter, Emerson, and Dr. Hiram K. Jones." But the school was "Mr. Alcott's," and the Boston papers reported its activities respectfully, while all Concord was agape at the two thousand or more persons who were attracted to its sessions between 1879 and 1887.[781]

He experienced some trouble keeping the debates between Harris and Jones,[782] between Snider and Sanborn,[783] and later between Harris and William James,[784] from getting out of hand; but he was ambitious to have thought discussed "freely," and therefore took philosophically the tiffs that developed. As the school progressed, he saw how impossible it was for his several professors to get together on fundamentals. As the debates went on, Alcott himself, always bent on preserving unity and peace, sometimes had a hard time of it. On one occasion, when Harris and Jones waxed particularly warm, he began to deprecate the apparent misunderstanding by suggesting a higher ground upon which the two disputants might find a common footing, only to have both turn upon him with exclamations that they did not understand what he meant. As the worthy Dean subsided into his seat, he muttered, "Well, I don't know as I know what I mean myself," adding, as the audience tittered, "I am a 'mystic,' you know."[785] Gradually he learned that his own attempted systematization of Plato and Hegel was hopeless. Try as he would, he never got much beyond his position recorded on July 18, 1871, while Harris was again in Concord:

Emerson calls on Harris, and we have conversation for the moment, sitting in my arbor on the hilltop.—We are at his library in the evening and have further discourse on the Hegelian thesis of Being. Emerson's categories are those of the imagination, not of pure reason. The Hegelian logic is strange and unintelligible to him, as it is to myself; but I see what marvels it performs in the hands of a master like Harris, and owe it a deep respect.[786]

He tried repeatedly afterwards to follow Harris' dialectic[787] and to regularize his own thinking by it,[788] but in the end he concluded, "I am not philosopher enough to know whether I am a philosopher in the strictest sense of pursuing a methodical habit of thinking."[789]

I confess full faith in Mr. Harris' logic but am incapable of following the steps leading to his conclusion . . . . At the 'Orchard' with Emery, Harris, Dr. Jones, Dr. Kedney and McClure, discussing the Hegelian Idea and methods. I find my thinking ideal, my method analogical rather than logical, and thus reaching the conclusion by concrete symbols. Accepting Personality as the Prime of things, I aim at exhibiting this alike to imagination, reason, and the conscience in its three-fold attributes as one and entire, thus speaking to the reason and faith at once.[790]

In 1882, within three months of the time when he terminated his journals, he wrote what takes on a confident tone:

I confess less interest in the philosophic methods of German thinkers than in the more familiar English methods of treatment. With difficulty I follow even Harris in his interpretations of Hegel, Fichte, Schelling and others. I find nothing of this in Dr. Jones' methods. I fancy my method is of a subtler and more salient type than either, and implies an active and sprightly imagination inflaming the reason and divining the truths it seeks. The philosopher who finds the pure truth is also the poet, interblending imagination and reason by the alchemy of his genius.[791]

It becomes therefore all the more ironic that the last time he wrote in his *Journals* he had to admit his method incapable of making his beloved philosophy comprehensible to his most devoted disciple: "Harris comes and takes me to tea at the 'Orchard House.' . . . We have much discussion of The Lapse. I do not succeed in showing them the place of this in my theory of Genesis, or of the Renovation of men from the ruins of sin."[792]

Constitutionally incapable of entertaining German critical transcendentalism, Alcott was able to absorb few positive doctrines from the Germans directly. But indirectly, even while his method of philosophizing remained incomprehensible to men following more precise methods, he wielded a powerful influence by perpetuating the idealistic tradition of thinking in America. To him perhaps more than to anybody else belongs the credit of having kept alive and finally of drawing together, near the end of the century, the numerous and sometimes divergent idealistic "schools" which the earlier Transcendentalism had engendered. Alcott was the main influence in the intellectual awakening of W. T. Harris, who in his turn—as editor of the *Journal of Speculative Philosophy* and, later, as Commissioner of Education—spread Hegelian idealism throughout the country. Without Alcott's numerous western tours and his Concord School, Harris, in all likelihood, would never have reached Washington. Without Alcott's inspiration, he might never have gone to St. Louis in the first place. From this point of view, Alcott, as much as any other individual, can be accounted responsible for the fact that by 1900 the regnant philosophy in American colleges and universities became Hegelian[793]—a philosophy which he himself had never been quite able to fathom.

Orestes Augustus Brownson (1803–1876)

In sharp contrast with the consistent career of Alcott is that of Orestes A. Brownson (1803–1876), who changed his basic views a half-dozen times, at each stage explaining the error of his earlier position and arguing that this time he could not be wrong. From the Calvinism in which he was reared, he turned to the Presbyterian Church, and thence veered toward agnosticism and Universalism. By 1830, however, he revolted against the extreme Universalist views and began to approach the Unitarians in his sympathies and until 1840 allied himself with Boston Unitarianism, though he was never in complete agreement with either the conservatives or the Transcendentalists.[794]

At first only tentatively accepting the name of Transcendentalist, he soon identified himself with the group, although he realized that they were not united on any single program, either philosophical or social; while they, for their part, found him too outspoken and belligerent. Hedge considered him "unbearable," and after two or three meetings of the Transcendental Club, he was not again invited.[795] But, writing continuously and vigorously, he put himself before the public as one of the most aggressive proponents of the Newness. For the promulgation of his ideas of social reform, which had been shaped through his reading of Saint-Simon,[796] he organized the Society for Christian Union and Progress,[797] and in the same year (1836) published his first book, *New Views of Christianity, Society and the Church*, in which, with all the fervor of the inspired prophet, he announced the necessity of a bold radicalism in social organization and a revitalized conception of practical religion. The three articles of his Society were "intellectual liberty, social progress, and a more spiritual morality than animated the ministers who took care not to offend State Street."[798] The ideas set forth in *New Views* came, according to his own testimony, mainly from French eclectic sources, supported however by Heine's *De l'Allemagne*, Schleiermacher, and Dr. Follen's treatise on Religion and the

Church.[799] In Brownson's view Cousin was "if not the first, one of the first philosophers of the age,"[800] who settled in a satisfactory manner the controversy over *a priori* knowledge raised by Kant. In his long critical articles on modern philosophy published in the *Boston Quarterly Review* for 1838–1842 he set forth with skill and precision a defense of Cousin much more closely reasoned and logically tenable than anything that previously appeared in America on the subject. Undertaking the conduct of the *Boston Quarterly Review* in January, 1838, he dedicated it to the presentation of new views on a great variety of subjects. Himself an indefatigible writer, he accepted outside contributions only occasionally.[801] He was outspoken, vigorous, thorough, presenting in five volumes of the journal several long analyses of philosophy, much political discussion in favor of a thoroughgoing democratic national policy, and many important reviews of current publications.

His allegiance to Cousin is apparent from the "Introductory Remarks" in the first number, where he announced his intention to appeal from tradition and authority to the "Universal Reason, a ray of which shines into the heart of every man that cometh into the world,"[802] for it was Cousin's doctrine of impersonal reason on which he based his whole position. Later, in the same number, in an article on "Locke and the Transcendentalists" (an answer to a piece on Locke in the *Christian Examiner*[803]), he again apostrophized impersonal Reason (not the limited *Vernunft* of Kant) as the "true light" which "enlighteneth every man who cometh into the world."[804] Brownson denied Cousin's dependence on any German since Kant, and, while praising Kant's experimental method, maintained that the German failed in "the application of his method to the phenomena which a profound psychology detects." While Kant had taught that there exists "no objective rational principle above the understanding," Cousin obtained "the objective by a

process at once simple and legitimate," by "detecting in the fact of intelligence the presence of an element which escapes our control, and which determines our judgments."[805] This conclusion, subtly argued and skillfully presented, is Brownson's interpretation of Cousin's epistemological discovery.

By the time he was writing the final number of the *Boston Quarterly Review* in 1842, Brownson was revising his theological views and beginning to move away from Transcendentalism. Feeling that regenerate Unitarianism lacked the necessary grounding of deep piety and all-embracing warmth, he began defending the Roman Catholic position, read Aristotle, the Fathers and Schoolmen, and renounced the political liberalism exhibited in his writings during the campaign year of 1840. Running thus almost the complete cycle of possible thought, Brownson might be suspected of sophistry or insincerity if the earnestness of his writings, at each successive stage, did not argue convincingly to the contrary.

The pages of the first volume of *Brownson's Quarterly Review* (1844) show how far out of the Transcendental current he had moved. His review of Margaret Fuller's *Woman of the Nineteenth Century* (1845) shows how stubbornly and bitterly he was opposed to feminism and to reform generally. The error of Margaret Fuller and of all other so-called modernists is that they think "the true moral and social state is to be introduced by the free, full, and harmonious development of human nature," to which end natural nature becomes an object of worship. But nature, says Brownson, in the fullness of his conviction that the world and all that it contains is of Satan, does not suffice, cannot be trusted, is rotten and accursed. The earth is a "prison house," and no amount of earnest human effort to improve it will ever turn out according to the plans of projected reforms.[806] Transcendentalism represents by now for Brownson the summation of all the erroneous doctrines abroad in the world. He traces out its effect in current publications. While the Transcendentalists in particular are the objects of his attack,[807] his incipient Catholicism is already at war with all forms of Protestantism.[808]

Brownson's influence was directed against all forms of idealism in thought and liberalism in politics and religion. His hope of meliorating the status of the common man had been shattered by the bitter experience of the campaign of 1840, when the Whigs, using every trick to discredit the serious aims of the Democrats, established again the party of capitalism, vested interests, and power in the White House. In his disillusioned state of mind he came to believe that only "Conservatism" is the "condition of Reform"; and in philosophy he took refuge in the doctrine of Aristotelian order and stability as the only true basis of human society.[809]

But before Brownson could enter the Roman church, he had to put his philosophic house in order. To do so, he felt he had to disprove Kant's contention regarding the impossibility of reaching absolute truth on the plane of pure reason.[810] While editing the *Boston Quarterly Review* from 1838 to 1842, he had made long excursions into Kant's Critiques and had enthusiastically seconded Cousin's contention that there was, after all, a way of reaching absolute truth in terms of reason. Obviously the newly espoused Catholicism would require a reorientation of this doctrine.

In spite of his frequent shifts and changes in religious associations, Brownson was, from first to last, the most persistent and most consistent epistemologist of all the disciples of the Newness—that is, after he had once repudiated Universalism and Unitarianism. Before 1836 he was as unwilling as Emerson, Parker, Ripley, or Hecker to rest his faith in sheer intuition, and as eager as any of them to substitute knowledge for faith. It is a mistake to consider the Transcendentalists as a group

to have adopted easily any shallow form of intuitionalism, and Brownson is no exception.[811] Brownson's difficulties were no less serious and prolonged than those of his associates. The chief point at which he is to be distinguished in this respect from the rest is that once he was started in the direction that he finally went, he proceeded more steadfastly and more assuredly than any of the others toward that goal. It can be said, too, that more than any of the others, he systematically examined the epistemological bases upon which he reached his decisions, and that among them all he alone made a really thorough examination of Kant's actual text, in the original, before he made up his mind. That done, he repudiated Kant and espoused a form of intuitive faith without further qualms. In this respect he and Hecker were unique.

Before and during the period of his conversion he came at several stages to several conclusions and positions that seem sometimes irreconcilable with each other. For an understanding of these developments his numerous contributions to the periodical literature of the day provide an index and record.

Beginning in 1834, that is, during his Unitarian ministry, when he undertook to read German, he enthusiastically recommended the German theologians from Herder to Schleiermacher, especially the latter, as effecting a "meeting of inspiration and philosophy" and as exhibiting at once "remarkable warmth of feeling and coolness of thought."[812] By 1839[813] he was espousing Cousin's "impersonal Reason" above all other human faculties and comparing it with Kant's "pure Reason" to the discredit of the latter.[814] Already he made objections to Kant's denial of any objective rational principle above understanding, even while admitting, as he was always ready to admit, Kant's "masterly skill and wonderful exactness" of method and his "analysis of Reason" as "complete and final."[815] As against Kant's severe limitations placed on the pure Reason, he preferred Cousin's epistemological conclusions,[816] though even here he wished to make emendations. In his essay on "Eclecticism—Ontology" for April, 1839, he suggested:

Perhaps it would not be amiss to divide the Reason into objective reason and subjective reason. By the objective reason we may understand the eternal reason, the immaterial world, the world of necessary Truth which overshadows us, underlies us, and constitutes the ground of our intelligence,—identical with the Logos of the Apostles and the Greek Fathers, the inner light of the Quakers. . . . In this sense Reason is not mine, nor any man's. It is impersonal and absolute. . . .
By the subjective reason we may understand . . . our general faculty of knowing, that by virtue of which we are intelligent beings, capable of intelligence . . . . But we apprehend that a careful analysis of the facts of consciousness would go far to identify subjective reason with the objective reason; so far at least as to prove that our reason must be in immediate relation with the impersonal Reason—that it is, in fact, as it has been called, 'a fragment of the Universal Reason.'[817]

This passage, with its obvious departures from Kantian definitions, be it observed, was written five years before he turned his attention more closely and intently on the text of Kant. It represents Brownson's general position about 1838–1839, when he took part of Kant and more of Cousin to get an eclectic epistemology which contributed to the collapse of transcendentalism altogether, as far as he was concerned, in 1844. But it is to be noted that even in 1839 he was already clearly opposed to the negative aspects of the Kantian epistemology, and that by 1842 he explicitly rejected rational idealism.

The refutation of Kant and Fichte, and therefore of all Idealism, Egoism, and skepticism, whether atheistic or pantheistic, is in the simple fact . . . that the *object-element of thought is always not me*. The error of Kant and the error which led astray his whole school and all others, is the assumption that the *me* does or may develop as pure subject, or, in other words, be its own object, and therefore at once subject and object. Kant assumes that the *me* develops itself, without a foreign object, in cognition; hence he infers that all knowing is purely subjective, and asserts the impotency of reason to carry us out of the sphere of the *me*.[818]

But Brownson was cognizant of the fact that this statement did not present Kant adequately, for he added a note saying:

We know very well that this was not the real doctrine of Kant, that it was only demonstrated by him to be the result, to which all philosophy must come, that *is based on pure reason*. He himself relied on practical reason, that is to say, on plain common sense, and his purpose of writing critiques of pure reason was to demonstrate the unsatisfactory character of all purely metaphysical speculations. A wise man, after all, was that same Emanuel Kant.[819]

Yet it is clear, both from his use of the term "common sense" as identical with practical reason in this essay[820] and from another essay of the next year, that this partial retraction of his objections to Kant still rested in part upon oversimplification or misconception, and that he was subsequently to criticize the whole critical philosophy too severely on the basis of the *Critique of Pure Reason* alone, i.e., without taking into account Kant's other treatises. But in 1844 he set to work anew on the *Kritik der reinen Vernunft*, this time studying the text intently for several months, translating much of it for his own use, and writing a long analysis of it.[821] The result of all this labor was that he rejected the entire argument, because (as he believed) he laid bare Kant's "capital blunder at the outset," namely the logical difficulty involved in the very statement of Kant's problem; for, says Brownson, "To ask if the human mind is capable of science [knowledge of reality] is absurd; for we have only the human mind with which to answer the question."[822] Looking back on his intellectual wanderings of the previous years, Brownson recounted, in the first pages of the new *Quarterly*, his adventures among the philosophers in terms of a gradual approach out of night into light—as a constant progression in the direction of Aristotelian dogmatics. He explained his interest in Cousin as a "state of transition from Naturalism to Supernaturalism," and asserted, while making a clean breast of his former defections that might seem to stand in the way of his becoming a good Catholic, that the Germans (except Kant) had never won his approval for long. Kant's "eminent analytic ability" he was still prepared to acknowledge, but his philosophy as a whole he now considered "fundamentally false and mischievous . . . an inextricable maze of error."[823]

But it appears that Kant was not, after all, thus summarily disposed of, for immediately after writing this blanket disavowal, he busied himself with the careful analysis of the *Kritik der reinen Vernunft* already mentioned. The result was three closely reasoned essays,[824] which served the dual purpose of filling a considerable portion of the first volume of the new *Quarterly* and of laying low the worst dragon of modern philosophy, so that henceforth he could, with good conscience, devote his time to the Aristotelians, ancient and modern.

Thus Kant was to Brownson from first to last an acute technical analyst of purely logical and epistemological matters, but Kant's general tendency and conclusions were essentially repugnant to him, at least after 1842, when he avowed his objectivism and anti-Cartesianism.[825] His tendency to neglect Kant's teachings except in the first *Critique* and his oversimplification of Kantian doctrine represent Brownson's greatest single error in his interpretation of Kant, though it may be understood in the light of his drift toward Catholicism after 1838 and his avowed Romanism after 1844. Yet it is worth noting that his position among the Transcendentalists is unique in this respect: they were all but unanimous in their glorification, conscious and unconscious, of what they conceived to have been Kant's great service in establishing the "proofs" of religion upon the basis of the "Reason"; he steadily maintained that that was precisely what Kant had not done.

In view of Brownson's professed objectivism and his general disavowal of German philosophy, we are already prepared to surmise what his attitude toward Fichte was. Fichte, he says, in an article written in 1842, represents the *reductio ad absurdum* of subjective idealism. He "fell into the absurdity of representing all ideas as the products of the *me*, and even went so far as to tell his disciples how it is that man makes God." While aware of Fichte's later speculative as well as more practical writings, he felt that these did not sufficiently mitigate his earlier "speculative errors," and he did not change his views of Fichteism as an "egoistic philosophy."[826] In 1864 he saw a direct Cartesian-Kantian-Fichtean descent of iniquity that terminated in the Fichtean assertion that God and the external world are only the soul projecting itself. This he considered the logical heretical deduction from Kantian premises, as derived from Descartes.[827]

Schelling's more objective idealism and his *Naturphilosophie* temporarily struck a responsive chord in Brownson during the period when he was most closely associated with the Transcendentalists. The Schellingian philosophy seemed to him in 1836 "a magnificent poem"; but even while he believed it "to be mainly true," he concluded that it is "nevertheless no philosophy, and can in no degree solve the difficulty stated by Hume."[828] After his conversion he saw Schelling as an atheist and Spinozist who "maintains the identity of subject and object, and thus asserts, from the subjective point of view, the Egoism of Fichte and, under the objective point of view, the Pantheism of Spinoza, while under both he denies the intention and even the possibility of science."[829]

Of Hegel, Brownson is the only one of the disciples of the Newness early to have any distinct views. In an essay of 1843 he objected to Hegel on two grounds—philosophical and political. On the first head, besides rejecting the whole deductive method, Brownson raises ontological objections: he cannot admit that "the system of a universe is only a system of logic," and that the "Ideal and Eternal, idea and being" are identical.[830] Moreover, Hegel's method "claims for man, confessedly finite, absolute knowledge, which would imply that he himself is absolute, and therefore not finite, but infinite"—obviously a "vain" boast.[831] Aside from rejecting the Hegelian pretense to absolute knowledge, Brownson's Yankeeism is outraged by what he considered Hegel's political absolutism, and he sees something profoundly funny in the view that "the infinite God and all his works, through all the past, have been engaged expressly in preparing and founding the Prussian monarchy" as if "his gracious majesty Frederick Wilhelm" were "the last word of creation and progress."[832] After entering the Roman Catholic Church, Brownson throws off the bantering tone and lashes out bitterly against Hegel as nothing less than "a reproduction of the old French atheism."[833]

Except for occasional references, the smaller fry among the German transcendentalists were beneath Brownson's notice. Having finished with the "four horsemen," he was quit of all and could conclude in 1857, "Germany has produced no philosophical system not already exploded, and no philosophers to compare with Vico, Galluppi, Rosmini, Gioberti and Balmes."[834] Among all of those not in the Catholic communion, Leibnitz seemed to Brownson the "greatest of all modern philosophers," for "his refutation of the Cartesian doctrine that the essence of substance is extension"

and his "rejection of the atomic" in favor of "the dynamic theory of matter" were for Brownson invaluable contributions. Yet he found even Leibnitz "the veritable father of German Rationalism" as well as a "mistaken believer in the ontological argument and the priority of the possible before the real."[835]

Except for the brief period from about 1836 to 1842 when he was close to the New England Transcendentalists, and except for his life-long admiration of Kant's proficiency as an analyst, German philosophy was for Brownson a regrettable episode in his earlier life. His significance for the history of German philosophy in America was in the nature of an episode before his entry into the Catholic church, but a highly influential one as long as it lasted. After his conversion, his full influence was exerted against any further acclimatization of German thought in America. Still active though he was during the decades when the Germanization of philosophical instruction in American colleges and universities went on apace, his Catholic withdrawal left him relatively powerless to do much about it; while among the Catholics who formed his chief reading clientele, there was no particular need for his thundering against German skepticism and "atheism."

Isaac Thomas Hecker (1819–1886)

Another whose Transcendentalism was as short-lived as Brownson's (largely for the same reasons), and whose addiction to German philosophy was brief yet influential in directing the course of his life, was Isaac Thomas Hecker. The youngest son of immigrants from Prussia, he enjoyed few educational advantages in his native New York. At the age of eleven he went to work in his brother's bakery, but his hunger for an education and for a tenable religious faith were such that, in the words of his biographer, the boy in his teens could be seen "at his kneading trough with Kant's

Critique of Pure Reason fastened up on the wall before him, so that he might lose no time in merely manual work. Fichte and Hegel succeeded Kant, all of them philosophers whose mother-tongue was likewise his own";[836] but they merely combined to perplex him all the more in his efforts to reach a religious position grounded in philosophy.

The stimulation to consult the German philosophers in the first place appears to have come from Orestes A. Brownson, sixteen years his senior, whom Hecker met in the fall of 1834, when he was not yet fifteen. From Brownson, too, he imbibed an enthusiastic humanitarianism; he accepted unquestioningly the perfectionism of Brownson's social philosophy at the time, joined the Workingman's Party, and made numerous political speeches, while still in his teens.[837] But his naturally mystical and ascetic nature soon turned from political to religious subjects. Unable by himself to make satisfactory headway in the solution of his religio-philosophical problems, and suffering from "a certain singular intensification of disquiet with himself and his surroundings"[838] in 1842, he followed Brownson's advice to join Brook Farm, where he arrived in January, 1843.[839] He hoped to profit by the fullness of a varied activity and the opportunity for that contemplative calm that were denied him at his home and that were reputedly to be had at Brook Farm. In the midst of his struggle to attain certainty with regard to the nature and extent of the Christian revelation, he enrolled in Ripley's classes in "Spinoza, Kant, Cousin, and their compeers," but got little help from that quarter. While he spoke, many years later, of Ripley as "a great man, a wonderful man,"[840] he was unable to put philosophy ahead of religion, as Ripley suggested and as the philosophical method demanded. Philosophy could never be more for him than the handmaid of religion. He was never truly a member of the inner community of whose aspirations and convictions the farm was intended to

be the embodiment. Then and later he smiled good-naturedly at the singularities he observed at Brook Farm, but he was a "general favorite," his "charming amiability" and earnestness endearing him to all. George Willis Curtis called him "Ernest the Seeker," after the title of the story of mental unrest which W. H. Channing was then publishing in the *Dial*.[841]

For more than a year he earnestly sought help from the Transcendentalists. He consulted Emerson in Concord. He went to hear Parker preach in the Unitarian church in the neighboring village of Roxbury, he consulted Brownson in Boston, and on April 18, 1843, Easter Sunday, he went to the Catholic church in West Roxbury, and found the "sanctified atmosphere" inspiring "awe" in him.[842] On July 11, he hopefully joined Alcott at Fruitlands only to be speedily disillusioned because Alcott's experiment left out of account "the Eternal" and made mere "human perfection" the goal.[843] Two weeks later he resolved to seek his own salvation and to seek it elsewhere. After a brief visit to his friends at Brook Farm, he returned to the home of his parents. But after less than a year with his family and the bakeshop, his asceticism reasserted itself, and he spent April, May, and June of 1844 in study and contemplation in Concord, where he lived with the Thoreau family.[844] When Henry D. Thoreau, then preparing to make his experiment in individual living at Walden Pond, discovered Hecker's drift toward Catholicism, he tried to rally Hecker, saying, "What's the use of your joining the Catholic Church? Can't you get along without hanging on to her skirts?" "I suppose [says Hecker] Emerson found it out from Thoreau, so he tried his best to get me out of the notion." Emerson was disturbed by this first defection from the ranks of the Transcendentalists. On June 13, two days after Hecker had gone to Boston to inquire of Bishop Fenwick about "the necessary preliminaries for one who wishes to be united to the Church," Emerson invited Hecker to tea and endeavored repeatedly but unsuccessfully to draw him out. The next day he took Hecker on a two-day visit to the Shaker community at Harvard, Massachusetts.

All the way there and back [says Hecker] he was fishing for my reasons, with the plain purpose of dissuading me. . . . Then Alcott and he arranged matters so that they cornered me in a sort of interview, and Alcott frankly developed the subject. I finally said, 'Mr. Alcott, I deny your inquisitorial right in this matter,' and so they let it drop.[845]

The next day Hecker went to Boston to put himself under the instruction of Bishop Fenwick. That night he poured out his heart in his diary: "My soul is clothed in brightness; its youth is restored. O blessed, ever-blessed, unfathomable, divine faith! O faith of apostles, martyrs, confessors and saints! Holy Mother of Jesus, thou art my mother. . . . Bless me, Virgin Mother of Jesus."[846]

Thus Emerson, Thoreau, and Alcott, far from preventing his entry into the Catholic church, badgered him into taking the step which he had resisted for years, and which he did not take until he had long considered both Transcendentalism and the Episcopal church, not to mention the claims of "pantheism, subjectivism, idealism, and all the other systems."[847] After his baptism on August 1, 1844, he saw less and less of Emerson and his associates,[848] but went on to an influential career in the Catholic church, first as a Redemptorist priest among the steadily increasing number of German immigrants in New York, and, after 1857, as the founder and superior of the Missionary Priests of St. Paul the Apostle, or the Paulist Order.

Possessed as Hecker was of a natural linguistic faculty to read the German philosophers and theologians, he read them eagerly for several years; but lacking the philosophic urge or the metaphysical prowess of a Brownson, he appears not to have followed them far in their epistemological involutions and theological convolutions. The Germanic influence upon him was primarily a negative one. The only thing of a positive nature that he derived from German transcendentalism or its American complement was a confident democratic faith in individualism which inspired him and Brownson alike to harmonize Catholic doctrine and spirituality with the American democratic faith and liberty.[849]

William Henry Channing
(1810–1884)

William Henry Channing, though principally known as a spiritual leader, exhibited less interest in the purely speculative problems of the movement than did his contemporaries. On the other hand, he formed, along with Margaret Fuller, a link between the theological and the aesthetical phases of Transcendentalism.

Despite the leadership of his uncle William Ellery, of Emerson, and of Parker in going to German sources for the foundations of their transcendental faith, Channing hardly approached the important questions with philosophic inquiry until he was forced to do so by the violent eruptions in the Unitarian ranks of 1840. Meanwhile he had been preaching a very emotional, spiritualized kind of Christianity based on the assumption of the priority of transcendental over the sensualistic epistemology of the old school. Traveling in Italy in 1835–1836, he came to appreciate the beauties of Roman ritual and tradition and was strongly attracted to Romanism. This tendency is reflected in *Ernest the Seeker*, which appeared in the 1840 volume of the *Dial*. The plan of *Ernest* involves taking a hero through a series of religious experiences in the various denominations until he finally arrives at a kind of "spiritual" or "higher" religion which takes on the best features of all. The structure is obviously based on the pattern of the *Bildungsroman*, such as were well known in New England, notably Goethe's *Wilhelm Meister*, Novalis *Heinrich von Ofterdingen*, and Pestalozzi's *Lienhard und Gertrud*; but the immediate suggestion probably came from De Wette's *Theodor*, a translation of which Clarke was preparing when Channing was with him in Louisville in 1839–1840.[850] Channing's translation of Jouffroy's *Introduction to Ethics* (1840) was his only excursion into the study of fundamental philosophical questions.[851]

William Henry Furness (1802–1896)

William Henry Furness was one of the older generation of Unitarians who, like Parker, went over to the Transcendentalists early in his ministerial career. His special theological study was the life of Jesus, on which subject he wrote much. Disagreeing violently with the myth-theory of Strauss, Furness argued that the story of Jesus' life and the miracles were not legend but fact, and that this fact is the primary source of religious faith and inspiration in modern times.[852] He contributed to the knowledge of German theology by publishing in 1866 a translation of Daniel Schenkels' *Character of Jesus Portrayed* (Philadelphia, 1866).[853]

The first flush of excitement over German thought began to fade in men of the generation of Transcendentalists like W. H. Channing and W. H. Furness. In others of the group—Margeret Fuller, Henry David Thoreau, Christopher P. Cranch, and John Sullivan Dwight, for example—attention centered more steadily upon German literary and broadly aesthetic than upon theological and philosophical matters. A discussion of their contributions is therefore deferred to a later section of this study, where they will find treatment along with Bayard Taylor, T. W. Higginson, and others of this later group of Germanists. Here it remains to consider now a group of so-called second generation Transcendentalists in whom something of the earlier attachment to German philosophy lived on—among them Osgood, Bartol, Frothingham, Weiss, Wasson, Conway, Samuel Longfellow, Johnson, and Cabot.

THE LATER TRANSCENDENTALISTS

Conflicting Points of View

The leaders in Transcendental theology, among them Emerson, Parker, Ripley, and Clarke, performed the useful service of establishing rational Biblical criticism as acceptable in American seminaries and pulpits; but as soon as they had enunciated their principles, there was established *ipso facto* an American body of authority that was as respectable, or reprehensible, as the foreign in the opinion of their successors. Henceforth, when the orthodox vented their wrath against transcendental philosophy or theology, they oftener attacked Emersonianism or Parkerism (notably the latter) than Kantian or Tübingen criticism. For example, when Joseph Cook delivered

the popular Boston Monday Lectures for 1877,[854] he singled out Parker as the real author of "what calls itself Free Religion in Boston."[855] It is true, says Cook, that Boston, Cambridge, and especially Concord "once listened to Germany"; and even now "Cambridge cannot show at the foot of her text-book pages five English names where she can show ten German,"[856] but the "right wing and center" of a "great movement" like Transcendentalism must not be confused with the "left wing," its "erratic side," which "broke with Christianity, and which now is variously denominated the Free Religious Movement or the Religion of Humanity. It was Parker who led these schismatics; since his death, his mantle has fallen on O. B. Frothingham, who has the shamelessness proudly to confess his succession. Parker had the misfortune of grasping too early, too eagerly, and too imperfectly the principles of the Tübingen school; for subsequent developments have shown that what Parker espoused was in Germany herself only a reactionary eddy."[857] Similarly, Emerson "made pantheism the logical outcome of Fichte's teaching," but Fichte's own son has shown that German "philosophical discussion, beginning with Leibnitz, running through Kant, and so coming to Lotze . . . had never broken with Christianity, nor been drawn into either the Charybdis of materialism or the Scylla of pantheism (Applause)."[858] "Ethical theism is now master of the situation" in Germany, where "the naturalistic theory was swallowed by the mythical theory, and the mythical by the tendency theory, and the tendency by the legendary theory, and each of the four by time (Applause). Strauss laughs at Paulus, Baur at Strauss, Renen at Baur, the hour-glass at all (Applause)."[859] Joseph Cook, like other orthodox apologists of the time,[860] regarded the German tradition of "sound philosophy" from "Leibnitz and Kant to Lotze" as his ally rather than his antagonist in the fight.

After the Civil War the theological journals continued to carry notices of new German publications, but not in as great a number as formerly; and the reviews were not the lengthy analytical articles which the periodicals of the thirties and forties presented.[861] Meanwhile the defenders of orthodoxy themselves often turned to German theological authority for help in combating the views and influence of heterodoxy as represented by the several forms of Transcendentalism, the Young Men's Christian Union (after 1857),[862] the Free Religious Association (after 1867), the Boston Radical Club,[863] the various types of free-thinkers and Freie-Gemeinden, the "godless Hegelians of St. Louis," and all those who, from whatever source they drew

their inspiration, and with whatever groups they fraternized, adhered to what was called, after Comte's phrase, the Religion of Humanity.[864]

At the center stood the Free Religious Association, which, in New England, found expression (notably during the seventies) through the Boston Radical Club and its annual *Proceedings*, as well as through the columns of the *Tribune*, the *Index*, and the *Radical*.

The Boston Radical Club met on the first Monday of each month, usually at the home of the Rev. John T. Sargent in Chestnut Street, to conduct a forum for "the freest investigation of all forms of religious thought and inquiry." According to Mrs. Sargent, who prepared a volume of memoranda for the club, it grew from thirty persons, present at the first meeting in 1867, to nearly two hundred at the closing sessions in 1880. The communicants considered themselves the heirs and perpetuators of the Transcendental Movement of an earlier day, although some of their number insisted on carrying their radicalism far beyond anything that would have been countenanced by Emerson's generation.

In the beginning the decorous rooms of the Sargents provided a proper setting where "conservatives," "liberals," and "radicals" might expound their views.

Here on one occasion Thomas W. Higginson and D. A. Wasson led the assault of the liberals upon the well-fortified position held by Calvin and Harriet Beecher Stowe. On another occasion, one day in October, 1871, Charles Sumner . . . dropped in to discuss 'The Function of the Heart in Religion' . . . John Fiske and Wendell Phillips also joined in the melee of that day. At a November meeting of the same year the aged Alcott came to hear . . . Julia Ward Howe's paper on 'Moral Trigonometry.' The author of the famous battle hymn . . . had been pained by the destructive logic emanating from the trenches of the radicals. Determined to turn their own weapons upon them, Mrs. Howe wheeled her mathematical artillery into position and laid down upon her adversaries a withering barrage of moral sines and cosines.[865]

Hither came men and women of little and great renown, of all complexions of creed, and visitors from all sections, though the core of the group remained solidly Bostonian and decidedly genteel. There never was any doubt who was a member and who was a visitor. Social and intellectual decadence was already in the air; the death of Sargent provided a convenient excuse for closing the house and terminating the meetings in 1880; New England reticences, on the one hand, and free scientific inquiry, on the other, had done their work.[866]

The injection of Darwinian principles into the program caused some of the members to conclude that the reputation which the Club had abroad as "the jumping-off place of all belief into negation"[867] was not altogether undeserved. Some of the stouter-hearted, intent on checking the scientific tendency, remained within the Club; others withdrew and eventually joined forces with the more orthodox. A rival series of lectures was conducted, during 1870, 1871, and 1872, by the General Association of Congregational Churches of Massachusetts, acting through the Committee of Congregational Pastors of Boston, on "philosophical subjects," "themes of Biblical criticism," and "internal evidences of Christianity.' These lectures, published annually as *Boston Lectures: Christianity and Skepticism*, were delivered by the most influential worthies, clergymen, and professors of divinity that could be drawn, chiefly, from Bowdoin, Bangor, Boston, Andover, Harvard, Amherst, Brown, and Yale. They presented the conservative, or orthodox, point of view; but it is to be noted that they, no less than those who spoke on Radical Club forums, drew upon German Biblical scholars for the arguments with which to confound what the German exegetical and historical critics were credited with having generated in America in the first place.

The origins of the several liberal or radical religions lay in numerous, not always compatible, sources and forces, among them (1) native idealism, a heritage that traced a direct descent through various transformations from Puritanism, (2) German transcendentalism, critical and intuitive, as imbibed by the left-wing Unitarians of the thirties and forties, and as it became transmogrified into the New Views in New England, (3) German exegetical and historical research in the Scriptures, (4) rationalism as fostered by sensationalism, deism, and Unitarianism, (5) New England Transcendentalism itself, (6) Comtean positivism, and (7) Darwinian and Haeckelian science. The result was a welter of dissent various enough to embrace O. B. Frothingham and F. B. Sanborn as well as Andrew D. White of Cornell and, some said, Robert Green Ingersoll himself.[868] Some adhered to Kant, some to Hegel, others to Feuerbach, still others to nobody. Some repudiated Comte, others damned Spencer; but all agreed in defining religion as the direct effort of man to perfect himself. Freedom and unity were the watchwords: (1) freedom from the bondage of sect, creed, and dogma, (2) the right to follow the new humanism whether by the avenue of scientific evolution or of historical criticism of the Scriptures, and (3) liberty for all living religions to unite into a universal religion of humanity.

Cast into a milieu so complex, the later Transcendentalists were even more diverse in the systems of thought toward which they leaned than were their predecessors of the prewar era. They made less claim to being Kantians or post-Kantians than did Emerson and his associates. Some of them, like Weiss and Wasson, were well enough read in German metaphysics to write discriminating philosophical essays which took up the epistemological questions raised by Kant; many of them, trained in the liberal atmosphere of Harvard in the forties and fifties and guided by men like Hedge and

Francis, gained a firsthand acquaintance with German theological criticism and, becoming familiar with it early, took it as a matter of course. Although the Germans may ultimately have meant as much in their intellectual development as they did to the earlier men, their coming upon the Germans was not nearly as much in the nature of a discovery as it had been for the older generation.

Throughout the nineteenth century, of course, the German influence exerted on American students who studied in Germany grew steadily stronger. Important as it was for the development of the natural sciences, the evolution of literary and critical theory, the study of history, and the cultivation of philosophy generally, German academic training could not contribute much to the growth of American transcendental philosophy, principally because Germany herself, in those later decades, had ceased to teach the faith-philosophy of Schleiermacher and De Wette and had gone over to the side of the positivists, materialists, and evolutionists, who were all ranged on the opposite side of the philosophic battleground, and who eventually hoped to discredit idealism rather than support it.

In a world of thought dominated by the new Darwinian science, while literary taste was undergoing slow but sure atrophy under the auspices of the genteel tradition, few of the later Transcendentalists adhered with complete fidelity to the idealism advocated by W. H. Channing and Margaret Fuller. Some continued on the road taken by Parker when he sought for a substantiation of his faith in the scientific deductive method, and others emphasized extreme rationalism or skepticism and continued to fight both the supernaturalism of the old school as well as the vague faith-philosophy of some of the earlier Transcendentalists. In their philosophical and religious differences the later group can be distinguished most readily from the older generation by comparing Emerson and Margaret Fuller's

Dial or Parker's *Quarterly* with Morse's *Radical* and Abbot's *Index*. The *Index* owes its significance principally to its opposition to, and criticism of, the idealism of an earlier day. This tendency can be seen in Abbot's essay on "The Scientific Method of Religion,"[869] his "Free Religion versus Transcendentalism,"[870] and the resulting controversy[871] between the "intuitional free-religionists" and the "free free-religionists." Emerson and Parker were deferred to as authorities, sometimes by both sides, for there were some who believed that Emerson and Parker were essentially in harmony and therefore agreed with Edwin D. Mead when he declared that "Emerson was Parker writing books; Parker was Emerson's truth in the pulpit."[872] But most of the Free Religious Associationists saw in Emerson and Parker deep and fundamental differences regarding their philosophical methods and therefore their religious tendency. Emerson represented intuitive idealism; Parker, historical criticism.[873] To be sure, Emerson had attacked conventional Christianity in the Divinity School itself, but he had of his own accord scratched his name off the roll of the Unitarian Church, though he maintained a pew for his family and himself occasionally attended. But Parker, after daring to draw the line between the Permanent and the Transient in Christianity, had been virtually excommunicated by the Church herself, yet had pursued, to the day of his death, his uncompromising criticism of the holy books. Whereas Emerson's general tendency had been to attempt a reconciliation of mysticism with criticism, Parker had steadily pursued the methods learned of the German rational school, and the whole tendency of his work was interpreted as illustrating the disparity between religion and philosophy.

They took sides accordingly and divided themselves into the Emersonians and the Parkerites. In the end B. F. Underwood, the junior editor of the *Index* during its last years, tried to sum up the whole controversy in an editorial bearing the significant title "Transcendentalism at Bay"[874] by observing that few members of the Newness were left, and that he regarded the intuitionalism and sensationalism defended by their respective adherents in his youth as now absorbed in a "deeper synthesis," in which the error of either (or both) was lost in a synthesis "entirely consistent with evolution" as promulgated by Spencer.

Thomas Wentworth Higginson made a last "Transcendentalist's Plea for Life."[875] He confessed his own belief in evolution—but the evolution of Darwin, not that of Spencer—maintaining at the same time that transcendentalism and agnosticism were both legitimate forms of Free Religion. While this controversy did little to settle the issues, one conclusion emerges pretty clearly, namely, that Samuel Johnson was correct when he said that it had been a "prevailing habit" to call the Transcendental movement a halfway step, a school outgrown, good and needed in its day, but belonging to the past. The Newness was no longer new. "In allying itself with each intellectual protest that was made in America during the later nineteenth century, Transcendentalism finally completed the circle, and turned against itself when it showed itself friendly to the protest of science."[876]

While ideologically the unity of the "Emersonidae" dissipated itself in the later years of the century by breaking up under the stress of new times and new forces, the later Transcendentalists remained as unitedly sympathetic with the proponents of social reform as their predecessors had been, even though this meant that they had on occasions to strike peculiar alignments with atheists and materialists. Thus it happens that some of the extreme freethinkers, writing in the columns of the *Radical* (a journal set up by men who generally are to be classed as Transcendentalists), actually welcomed the rise of extreme German radicalism on American soil and for a time

considered a political alliance between the adherents of Karl Heinzen and themselves.[877] In 1876 the *Index* printed a long letter from Heinzen wherein he discussed the possibility of a political merger between the German-American radicals and the liberal groups within the Unitarian church. Almost patronizingly he extended to them an invitation to join with him in his program, though he bluntly told them that he felt his brand of radicalism would be too strenuous for them to stomach.[878] That the eastern group was at least on friendly terms with these German-Americans of the intellectual vanguard in the Middle West is indicated by the fact that from time to time the *Index* printed communications from member bodies of the Union of German-Amercan Liberal Societies.[879] It likewise printed appeals for aid on behalf of German liberals suffering persecution under the Prussian government.[880] Boston, with the presence of W. Wesselhoeft, Eduard Schläger, and later, Karl Heinzen, was one of the outposts of the movement toward unification of all German political forces, which culminated in the Philadelphia and Wheeling Congresses of 1851 and 1852. The Boston liberal press, ever since the days of the *Harbinger*, had followed the career of John Ronge with interest; and in their ambitious plans for a world union of German revolutionaries the Boston German-American radicals achieved, if for a short time only, a direct alliance with their sympathizers in London.[881] The Schiller Celebration of 1860, at which the Transcendentalist Furness of Philadelphia was the principal speaker, was a project conceived and planned by the liberal Forty-eighters, including Schurz, Hecker, and Douai. When the Germans of Boston met in Faneuil Hall on July, 1870, it was Frederic H. Hedge who addressed them in these terms:

Your country in one sense is also mine. It is the fatherland of my mind. It was there I first drew the breath of intellectual life; it was there I imbibed my first ideas of poetry and philosophy; it was in German that I made my first essays in prose and verse. All that I am intellectually I owe to your country . . . .

The body of the speech, reprinted in the *Index* for August 27, 1870,[882] is epitomized in his statement, "Unreservedly I side with Prussia in her struggles against France (Applause)." Circumstances and statements such as these unified sympathies and solidified friendships between Eastern Anglo-American liberals and Midwestern German-American radicals.

The *Radical* and *Index* illustrate how fast Transcendentalism was being diluted and dissipated. Both periodicals carried broadside attacks on the old-fashioned idealism. Though they printed occasionally articles like those by Cram in defense of Spinoza,[883] the preponderance of space went to discussions of the St. Louis Hegelian school[884] and of post-Hegelians. In subtle, indirect ways the center of gravity shifted from New England to the radical Midwest. Though they printed accounts of the Goethe course of lectures at the Concord School of Philosophy, they indicated, too, that the "transcendental" theorizings of some of the speakers there amounted to a "too exclusive veneration" for the German writers.[885] Instead of the long interpretative articles on Goethe, Richter, De Wette, and Schleiermacher that appeared in the Transcendental organs of an earlier day, we find in the periodicals of 1855–1870 a scattering of undistinguished translations of prose tales, novels, and lyrics. Political events, the Franco-Prussian War, the insurgence of free religionists like Ronge—these are noticed in some of the magazines; but before the appearance of the *Journal of Speculative Philosophy* (1867–1888 [1893]) there is much less concern with philosophy than had prevailed in the days of Emerson, Ripley, and Parker. Many of the later Transcendentalists turned journalists and essayists in the genteel tradition, and the greatest literary reputations as interpreters

of German literature were held by such essentially uncreative literati as Charles T. Brooks and Bayard Taylor. Men of talent, not genius, they often divided their energies and were profound in no single field. As a group they belonged to the class of whom Emerson asked, "Of what use is genius if its focus be a little too short or a little too long?"[886]

Of the later group of Unitarian clergymen associated with the Transcendentalists, Samuel Osgood and Cyrus Augustus Bartol were the oldest. Both deviated from the tradition of Parker in important respects, and from others of their predecessors in other matters; together with W. H. Channing and W. H. Furness, they illustrate the gradual transition from the position of the older to that of the younger Transcendentalists.

Samuel Osgood

Osgood (1812–1888) was old enough to write voluminously for the *Western Messenger* during its brief existence. An earnest student of German, he contributed a mass of articles and reviews[887] to the *Messenger*, as well as a translation of Krug's *Atonement*[888] and a shortened version of Hermann Olshausen's *History of Our Lord's Passion*[889] (also published in book form in Boston in 1839).

In the *Christian Examiner* he published articles such as the one on "De Wette's *Views of Theology*,"[890] showing no thoroughgoing penetration into German metaphysics, but sincere, enthusiastic appreciation of the "faith philosophy" of Germany as it was understood by his group. His most important contribution toward the domestication of German ideas in America was his translation of De Wette's *Human Life; or Practical Ethics*, published in 1842 as Volumes XII and XIII of Ripley's *Specimens of Foreign Standard Literature*. In 1856 he brought out still another German book, this time a series of drawings by Overbeck representing events in the life of Christ.[891]

How far Osgood's reading and editing of the liberal German theologians contributed toward his own liberalism is hard to determine. He remained untouched by what he would have called the "destructive" elements of the German, or, for that matter, of American, criticism.[892] Typical of his attitude is his essay on "The Schleiermacher Centennial and Its Lesson," published in 1869.[893] Without subscribing to all of Schleiermacher's opinions, Osgood sees him as playing a most important role in the resurgence of faith. He was a "restorer of faith in the nineteenth century, as Voltaire stood at the head of its assailants in the eighteenth century."[894] Schleiermacher's *Christian Faith* is "the most memorable theological work since the 'Institutes of Calvin!'"[895] But the "evangelical order of Unitarians," with whom Osgood now identifies himself, no longer stand in any direct relation to German theology, however much they recognize its importance as a liberalizing agent in the earlier decades of the century. And in a later article, Osgood shows an even stronger tendency to minimize the significance of German importations. He takes issue with Frothingham and endeavors to show that the growth of Transcendentalism in America can be understood as stemming from the English and native traditions.[896] Writing from the vantage point of this late date, Osgood is inclined to believe that idealism will have to undergo a metamorphosis in order to be preserved at all. In the past the Transcendentalists (with whom he says he would not want to break) have been "too exclusively idealists"; they have been "meditative, lonely, introversial, and separatists" when they should have been doing more practical missionary work, forming themselves into a more united, militant body.[897] This is the answer of Osgood and, we may add, of his brethren of the later generation when forced to meet the challenge of the rising materialism and evolutionism. His statement of adherence to the Transcendentalist faith is almost the last to be found—the last expression of the hope that the revolt of the forties will not find its energies depleted in the face of new conditons and new forces.

Cyrus Augustus Bartol

Bartol (1813–1900) graduated from Harvard Divinity School in 1835, and in 1837 settled in the West Church of Boston. He was a liberal and independent theologian, in his early years closely associated with the members of the Transcendental Club, who sometimes met at his house. Nevertheless, he held himself a little apart from the movement, being more mystical in his faith than Parker and anxious to preserve some of Parker's "transient" elements of Christianity.[898] In 1842, at the height of the transcendental enthusiasm for German theology, Bartol took the relatively conservative position that the German idealism prevalent in Boston is not altogether good for the development of an American faith.[899]

Like so many others in the Boston liberal tradition, Bartol shared the common enthusiasm for German literature. Though he wrote little on the subject in his earlier years, he contributed an important essay on "Goethe and Schiller" to the 1885 volume of Concord lectures. He sets Goethe far above Schiller, at the same time that he defends Goethe against typical earlier American charges of moral laxity and social indifference.[900] The lecture revises American critical opinion of Goethe, while preserving down to this late date, characteristic transcendentalist appreciation of Goethe's nature-philosophy and Spinozism. In Bartol we see the original liberalizing impulse of the Newness still at work seeking to emancipate American thought from its narrow provincial bonds.

Octavius Brooks Frothingham

Frothingham (1822–1895) grew up under the influence of a father, who, albeit a member of the conservative group of the Unitarian church, was a thorough student of German literature.[901] While studying at the Divinity School, Frothingham was influenced by Longfellow, Felton, Beck, Francis, and the German tutor Roelker to read a good deal among the less "dangerous" of the German Biblical scholars, by now in good repute among the Unitarian professors of divinity. Though he admired Emerson, he did not count himself a Transcendentalist until he made the acquaintance of Parker and as a result, underwent a "crisis in belief" that ended in his adopting a thoroughly critical attitude toward all conventional forms of theism. Under Parker's influence he read the theologians of the Tübingen school.[902] He left his Salem parish, to which he had gone in 1847, to travel in Europe, and finally, in 1855, resumed his ministerial work in Jersey City with a group of liberal Unitarians. In 1859 he moved to the Congregational Unitarian Society of New York, where he remained for twenty years, preaching first in Lyric Hall and, after 1875, in the Masonic Temple.

Frothingham's theological position was further from traditional Christianity than Parker's; and in his later years, while yet the close associate of many younger Transcendentalists, he opened his mind more and more to rational scientific skepticism and became known as a leading evolutionist.[903] He kept in close touch with current theological criticism of Europe and America, and besides occasionally writing reviews of new German works,[904] incorporated many of the latest findings of German Biblical research in his sermons.[905] Despite his alleged skepticism, he was a man of real spiritual powers, to whom the Transcendentalism of Emerson and Parker had been "balm and elixir" until German historical criticism cast doubt upon Emerson's too exalted concept of nature, and Darwinian science robbed him of his "absolute faith" in the mysticism of New England Transcenden-

talism generally.[906] Though "the sunset flush [of Transcendental idealism] continued a long time after the orb of day had disappeared," a new age and new forces demanded a reinterpretation that could not overlook the claims of science and the positivistic progressivism by which a mystical Emersonian Over-Soul could be given content, meaning, and force.

Frothingham's new religion of humanity abandoned conventional theism, together with its traditional affirmation that God is still actively working in the world.[907] His congregation on Sixth Avenue in New York heard with increasing regularity sermons on "The Despotism of Faith," "Authority and Religion," "Letter and Spirit," "Secular Religion," "Reasonable Religion," "The Larger View of Christianity," and "The Proper Treatment of the Infidel Tendencies of Our Day."[908] This congregation, numbering between six and nine hundred, included George Ripley, now a journalist and professional literary critic, George C. Barrett, the jurist, Calvert Vaux, the architect, E. C. Stedman, the broker-poet,[909] Henry Peters Gray, the artist, Sanford G. Gifford, the painter, and C. P. Cranch, the poet. Frothingham himself characterized his flock as having ceased long ago to be a Unitarian Congregation. "These were people of Catholic training, many of Protestant training, some of no religious training whatever, materialists, atheists, secularists, positivists—always thinking people, with their minds uppermost. It was a church of the unchurched."[910]

Frothingham's numerous theological discourses were widely circulated in pamphlet and book form, and his biographies of Theodore Parker (1874), Gerritt Smith (1878), George Ripley (1883), and W. H. Channing (1886), together with his histories of Boston Unitarianism (1890) and of Transcendentalism in New England (1876), established him as a notable theologian, biographer, historian, and critic. Much of his influence was exerted through the columns of the *Index*.[911] During the seventeen years of its existence, it remained the organ of the Free Religious Association, printing again and again the "Fifty Affirmations" of the movement.

Religion [proclaimed the *Index*] is the effort of man to perfect himself. Its root lies in universal human nature; because of this common root, historical religions are all one. Free religion is emancipation from the outward law, and is voluntary obedience to the inward fundamental law. Its moving power is faith in man as a progressive being. Its objective is the perfection or complete development of man, the race serving the individual, and the individual the race. Its practical work is to humanize the world, to make the individual nobler here and now and 'to convert the human race into a vast Co-operative Union devoted to universal ends.'[912]

Much of this has a strongly positivist tone and may, indeed, have derived from Comte, who gained some American readers after 1853 through Harriet Martineau's free translations and condensations and through such works as David Goldman Croly's *Positivist Primer* (1871), dedicated to "the only supreme being man can ever know, the great but imperfect Humanity, in whose image all other gods were made, and for whose service all other gods exist, and to whom all the children of men owe labor, love, and worship."[913]

But this book, as well as the Positivist Society, organized in New York in 1871, came too late to have vital influence on Frothingham,[914] who had developed his religion of humanity as early as 1858, the year before he moved to New York City, and about a decade before he organized the Free Religious Association in Boston. There were many natural causes why Comtean positivism was very slow to win a following in the United States.[915] Eventually positivism made a strong contribution to the movement of progressive humanism, but evolution and the advance of science generally had a long head start in this country and consequently

made more effective contributions earlier. Basically the religion of humanity was an American movement growing out of native needs, the greatest of which was the desire for intellectual freedom. As far as Frothingham was concerned, he sensed the importance of science as a creative instrument for his purposes and used it accordingly, just as, during the eighties, positivism was used by the disciples of the new humanism. First and foremost for his purposes in freeing the American mind from the grip of orthodoxy was the native tradition of rational criticism implicit in Unitarianism, which goes back to the rationalism of the Englightenment. Frothingham himself had been a Unitarian minister, and he had watched the ineffectual efforts of the Unitarians to effect a humanistic revolution long enough to know that Unitarian orthodoxy and traditionalism would not surrender to the spirit of criticism from within the church. Emerson, Parker, Ripley, Clarke—all of the first generation Transcendentalists—bore testimony that American Transcendentalism as they had conceived and promulgated it, on idealistic ground, was unequal to the task. Neither Kantian nor Hegelian idealism sufficed.[916] To shake American Christianity free of popular lethargy and the ecclesiastical strait jacket, strong methods were wanted. These he found in Baur, Schwegler, the Tübingen *Theologische Jahrbücher*, and the criticism of the Tübingen school generally. Without these he could hardly have been more successful than his predecessors in uprooting the deeply imbedded traditionalism. With them, aided by the times and the steadily mounting importance of science and positivistic progressivism, he battered away until he became, in the eyes of his orthodox contemporaries, the arch-infidel—as fearful in this later day as Parker had been in his. By their aid, too, he exerted an influence that extended into the Midwest, where, his religious humanism, in all its social and political implications, joined forces with freethinking, radicalism, and the democratic spirit as these were bred and spread among various radical groups of German-Americans on the frontier.

John Weiss

One of the most serious students and active translators of German among the younger Transcendentalists was John Weiss (1818–1879). Born in Boston, he represented the third generation in America of a family of German Jewish refugees who originally made their living by giving lessons in the language. In 1837 Weiss graduated from Harvard College, and in 1840 from the Divinity School. During 1842–1843 he studied in Heidelberg, and upon his return became pastor of the church in Watertown, succeeding Convers Francis. Like so many liberal Unitarians before him, he found that the ministerial duties did not well suit his talents, and accordingly he left his pastorate for writing and lecturing. He wrote on a wide range of subjects—history, religion, literature, reform—and always exhibited great mental power and often startling brilliance.[917]

At first a confirmed Transcendentalist and a thorough student of German metaphysics and theology, in the tradition of Theodore Parker,[918] he turned later toward a position of extreme radicalism, espoused the new evolutionism, and propounded an "animalistic conception of immortality."[919] This later position, charged with all the warmth of feeling and optimistic faith characteristic of the Transcendentalists, is set forth in his book of 1871, *American Religion*, in which he treads the borderland between religion and science, recognizing the claims of both, and bringing to their adjustment as fine intellectual scales as any of his contemporaries. His central idea is the harmony of religious conceptions with the law of progressive development in the domain of science, the facts of genera, species, strata, epochs, and transitions expressing our mental recognition of the principle of pro-

gressive evolution of religious themes "in just such a manner and under such conditions as the individualism and freedom of America are best fitted to promote."[920] Thus Weiss provided one of the strongest impulses which led later Transcendentalists away from their idealism toward the scientific rationalism so prominently espoused by the *Index* and the *Radical*.[921]

Weiss's energies were drawn equally toward literature and polemics. Some of his colleagues adjudged him more poet than thinker.[922] His translation of Schiller's *Philosophical and Aesthetic Letters and Essays* (1845)[923] was one of the most difficult and demanding of all translation projects in German undertaken up to that time in America. In the Preface he treats the relation of Schiller to Kant and Fichte with remarkable accuracy and finesse. That he was definitely interested in the metaphysical criticism of the German authors is evident in the circumstance that he edited and translated works by Novalis, Fichte, Schiller, and others as early as 1841.[924] In the next year he edited an anonymous translation of *Heinrich von Ofterdingen* and furnished the translations of the poems contained in the work. In 1846 he edited, with a preface, William Smith's *Memoir of Fichte*, and the next year he contributed his translation of Schiller's *Über naive und sentimentalische Dichtung* to Hedge's *Prose Writers of Germany*, thus bringing before the American public one of the most important theoretical essays of the modern period of German literary theory. The publication in 1877 of Weiss's translation of Goethe's *West-östlicher Divan* marks the first translation by an American of this group of Goethe's lyrics, and is recognized as one of the two best versions that have ever been made of them.

David A. Wasson

David A. Wasson (1823–1887) was a brilliant essayist and erstwhile Unitarian minister who was "converted" to Transcendentalism under the influence of Carlyle, Hedge, and Emerson.[925] A student of German at first hand,[926] he read more widely among German literary authors than among the philosophers, though his acute mind was well equipped for metaphysical analysis, and he had enough independence of spirit to make penetrating judgments on many current problems.[927] His essays are distinguished for vigorous and rigorous thought, for sharp judgment, and for a quaint but forceful simplicity of style.

A decided rationalist, a friend and defender of Parker, a sympathizer with the Free Religious Association, a shining light of the Radical Club, a frequent contributor to the *Radical* and the *Index*, as well as the *New Englander*, *North American Review*, *Atlantic Monthly*, and *Unitarian Review*, a thoroughgoing individualist, Wasson pursued his solitary, defiant way, upholding at once the Free Religious Associationists and the intuitive faith-disciples of Emerson's generation. He was almost holily jealous of the influence of Comtism and of men like Spencer, Mill, Bain, and the latest school of experimental psychologists. The essence of his doctrine, particularly as it relates to the objective or material system, is closely stated in his essay on the "Nature of Religion," published by the Free Religious Association in a volume entitled *Freedom and Fellowship in Religion* (Boston, 1875), as well as in his essay on "The Adequacy of Natural Religion" in the *Radical* for March, 1866.[928]

Samuel Longfellow, George Willis Cooke, Samuel Johnson

Most of the remaining Transcendentalists of the later decades—men like Samuel Longfellow, George Willis Cooke, and Samuel Johnson[929]—show little immediate dependence either on contemporary German thought or on the great tradition of post-Kantian idealism. The older generation had been thrilled by the discovery of each new German author who appeared on their horizon. These authors were now established classics, and most of the younger generation took them for granted. Many of the younger group felt that enthusiasm for German literature was on the wane.

Samuel Johnson's career in this respect is typical. After an undergraduate education at Harvard, where he enthusiastically read Cousin and Jouffroy under Walker's tutelage, he included Germany in his tour of Europe but showed little interest in either German universities or German philosophy. Upon his return, he entered the Harvard Divinity School and soon allied himself with Parker's cause. While espousing Baur's theology and welcoming the work of the Tübingen school,[930] he did not follow Parker's example of reading widely in German theological literature. Early identified with the group that contributed to the *Radical* and *Index*, he found (like others of the Free Religious Associationists) more immediately important authorities than Kant, De Wette, and those other Germans who had been vital for the first generation of Transcendentalists. His essay on "Transcendentalism,"[931] aside from a stock quotation from Kant[932] and another reference to Kant and Fichte,[933] contains nothing to indicate that German philosophical speculation or theological investigation touched him vitally.

Moncure Daniel Conway

Only Conway and Cabot were actively interested in Germanism in anything like the manner in which earlier Transcendentalists had been.

Moncure Daniel Conway (1832–1907) was inspired by Emerson's enthusiasm and by Longfellow's lectures on Goethe at Harvard in 1853 to appreciate Goethe.[934] While he felt that "the Goethean cult at Cambridge and Concord had cooled,"[935] he studied Goethe intently; and during his years as a

Unitarian minister in Washington and Cincinnati he frequently derived the texts for his sermons from Goethe, notably *Wilhelm Meister*.[936]

In Cincinnati Conway made an unsuccessful attempt to establish a new Transcendental monthly under the resurrected name, *Dial*. It ran for a year (1860), printing such items as poems by Emerson and translations of oriental verse from the German, but had not enough vitality to establish itself firmly.[937] In 1864 Conway visited Germany and became acquainted with a host of famous writers, teachers, and theologians, making special efforts to consult Strauss at Heilbronn and Gervinus at Heidelberg.[938] While in Germany he wrote popular sketches and essays on German life and literature.[939] In Cincinnati he associated himself with various German-American radical and liberal movements and knew intimately Johann B. Stallo and August Willich, editor of the *Republikaner*. He was an enthusiast for the Free Religious movement, the friend of every liberal German thinker and reformer, and a disciple of the new science and the positivist philosophy. His voluminous writings as foreign correspondent for the *New York World*, together with his numerous contributions to radical periodicals such as the *Index* and the *Radical*, interpreted these new tendencies for the American public.

James Elliot Cabot

Finally, there was James Elliot Cabot (1821–1903), who, among all the later "Emersonidae," was the most faithful to the ideals of the earlier Transcendentalists. As the scribe of Emerson during the later years of Concord's sage, and Emerson's appointed biographer, he was closer to the master than the others. More thoroughly schooled in Kant, Schelling, and Hegel than they (not excepting even Hedge, for Cabot, when he studied at Heidelberg, Berlin, and Göttingen, was no longer a lad in his early teens as Hedge had been when he went to Germany), Cabot espoused the idealistic absolutism of Germany that had been popular among the Transcendentalists before the Civil War and set his face resolutely against the progressivism and relativism that had come into vogue under the auspices of the Boston Radicals, the Free Religious Associationists, and the National Liberal Leaguers. Outliving the nineteenth century and feeling, with his fellows, the full impact of the new science, he nevertheless refused to let evolution and the exclusively inductive method shake his faith in Kantian epistemology and Hegelian logic, and as a consequence came to be regarded by his fellows as anachronistic even while they deferred to him as the authority among them on German philosophy generally.[940]

Cabot returned from Europe in 1843, enrolled in the Harvard Law School, and took his degree two years later.[941] Not greatly interested in the law (nor later, in architecture, when he became his brother's partner in an architectural firm), he indulged his literary and philosophical tastes by consorting with the Transcendentalists. While still in Harvard Law School, he prepared the admirable essay on Kant that was altogether the best single exposition of Kantian criticism to appear in the *Dial*.[942] During 1844–1845 Cabot was often in Concord. Emerson, whose first bout with Kantian epistemology had not been altogether successful, and who had by now developed an antimetaphysical animus, reported whimsically that Cabot came "to comfort the dry land with a little philosophy."[943] In the summer of 1845 he sent Emerson his "Essay on Freedom," a translation of Schelling's *Philosophische Untersuchung über das Wesen der menschlichen Freiheit*, which Emerson gratefully acknowledged,[944] and which he appears to have studied attentively for a while, only to report, a year later, "the Schelling [translation] I have only now concluded to let alone,"[945] though he urged Cabot to seek a publisher for it, and himself sought to persuade Munroe to print it. To this period also belong Cabot's translations of the portions of Kant's *Critique of Judgment* and of *Zum ewigen Frieden*, as well as the "Introductory Remarks" on Kant and the translation of Schelling's lecture *On the Relation of the Plastic Arts to Nature* which Hedge printed in his *Prose Writers of America* (1847).

When, in May of 1847, Parker assembled a group of fourteen at Emerson's home to discuss ways and means for founding a new journal that was to be a successor to the *Dial* (only more *"Tremendous"*—"a *Dial* with a Beard"), it was natural that Cabot should have been present. While Emerson consented "rather weakly" to aid in the project, Cabot (whom Parker had put down in his notebook as "Certain and Valuable," along with John Weiss and W. H. Channing) agreed to act as corresponding secretary and business manager.[946]

Already in the first contribution to the new journal (a notice of George P. Marsh's Phi Beta Kappa address) Cabot announced his attitude toward German philosophy when he reported, with apparent approval, Marsh's view of the prospect of American literature as bright because "the American intellect combines the speculative propensities of the German with the practical tendencies of the English mind."[947] His position with regard to German metaphysics became more explicit in his essay on "The Inductive System," a review article of J. S. Mill's *System of Logic*, in which Kant and Hegel are cited as authorities to refute what Cabot considers the too strictly inductive philosophy of Mill. Of special interest is Cabot's review of J. B. Stallo's *General Principles of the Philosophy of Nature: with an Outline of some of its Recent Developments among the Germans, embracing the Philosophical Systems of Schelling and Hegel, and Oken's System of Nature* (Boston, 1848). Professing inability to do justice to the book in anything short of "a regularly

projected article," Cabot calls it "altogether the best thing upon the profound subjects to which it relates that has yet appeared ... a most intelligible and thorough analysis of the modern Identity-system of the Germans," discriminating "most sharply and successfully the true story of Development from that bold, popular generalization which first appeared in the 'Vestiges.' Its analysis of the German systems from Kant to Oken is just, clear, and comprehensive—just the thing for our meridian."[948] It is not impossible that this enthusiastic review in the second number of the new journal, for which Emerson wrote the "Editors Address," may have led him to consult Stallo's book in the first place. We have already considered the immediate influence of this book on Emerson, as it can be traced in his journals, in the poem that he prefixed to the 1849 edition of *Nature*, and in the new resolve which it inspired in him to make one more attempt to equate his religion with his philosophy, this time in terms of Hegelian synthesis and Darwinian evolution.[949]

After his trip to Lake Superior with Agassiz in 1850, Cabot settled in Brookline, married Elizabeth Dwight in 1857, became active in various civic and cultural enterprises, participated mildly in reform movements, including abolition, revisited Europe in 1857 and 1885, indulged his fondness for sketching and water-color landscapes, gave a series of lectures on Kant at Harvard (1869–1870), and acted as Instuctor of Logic for a time.[950] About 1875 he became the volunteer secretary for Emerson, and upon Emerson's death wrote his *Memoirs*, by the wish of the family—a work so well done that it remained until very recently the best biography of Emerson.

For the rest, he sent occasional contributions to the magazines, including the *North American Review*[951] and the *Journal of Speculative Philosophy*.[952] He was on friendly terms with W. T. Harris and other individuals of the St. Louis and Concord schools, but did not take a prominent part in the ten Concord summer sessions.

The Hegel essay in the *North American Review* for April 1868, is indicative at once of his attitude toward Hegelian idealism and of the reason why he withdrew more and more from the enthusiasms and movements of the day, pursuing instead his favorite studies, following the quieter pursuits of art and literature, and adjusting himself to an attitude that recognized, while it acquiesced in, the fact that he was in a manner superseded by the newer, rising generation. He knew that he was setting himself against the current of the time which regarded his philosophy of idealism anachronistic, but he believed that it was only momentarily so, and accordingly he quietly maintained his own faith, only occasionally taking the trouble gracefully to reiterate his point of view, which, modernity to the contrary, he believed would prevail in the end. Hence he saw all the less reason for getting excited or angry about it, though occasionally he employed a tone of gentle raillery or irony to call the attention of the younger generation to a position which he believed they stood in danger of forgetting. Thus the essay on Hegel begins with a frank avowal of his love for metaphysics as against those who say that "metaphysics is exploded, obsolete."[953]

Here, then, from among the Eastern Transcendentalists themselves, is a belated statement and attempted vindication of a philosophical point of view of idealism that had been dominant during the forties, but that was rapidly falling before the advance of evolution, induction, and positivism. Yet, while his voice is that of a bygone day, its insistence upon the Hegelian logic and methodology, which should make provision within the Hegelian synthesis for the new science, forms a link between the Emersonian idealism as it was expounded in the East in an earlier day and the Hegelian absolutism of the St. Louisans in the West. At the same time, it left the door open for the catholicism expressed in the Concord School of Philosophy and did not absolutely shut it in the face of the anti-idealistic, pro-scientific Radicals and Free Religionists.

The Spread
of Interest in German Philosophy

THE ST. LOUIS MOVEMENT

History of the Movement

Among the more easily discernible avenues by which Emersonian idealism spread were two associated movements: (1) the St. Louis Movement in Philosophy, Psychology, Literature, Art, and Education, and what was eventually merged with it, (2) the Concord School of Philosophy. The relations between New England Transcendentalism and these two later movements are clearer than are those contacts which Emerson and his cohorts formed with individual clergymen, editors, writers, and auditors inside and outside New England, and to whom they communicated elements of Transcendental thought. The conversations, lectures, articles, and books that attended the Newness wrought powerfully upon successive generations of students who came to Boston and Cambridge, and who, in turn, went thence into the highways and byways of the country to spread the gospel of idealism. We have sporadic reports and occasional attestations of how a Follen or Hedge, a Marsh or Emerson, a Parker or Ripley inspired some young man to hold aloft the torch of "plain-living and high-thinking" or to search for the "permanent" among the "transient" elements of religion. But the influence of individuals was soon dissipated unless they happened to congregate, as they did, for example, in Louisville, Kentucky, where J. F. Clarke, W. G. Eliot, and Ephraim Peabody published the *Western Messenger* from 1835 to 1841, or somewhat

later, in Cincinnati, where M. D. Conway, assisted by O. B. Frothingham and C. A. Bartol, sought to spread the doctrine of Transcendentalism under the aegis of the western *Dial* (1860).

More precise is the connection between New England Transcendentalism of the thirties and forties and the St. Louis Movement, dated by Denton J. Snider (the last survivor of the founders and the historian of the movement) as beginning in 1865 and ending in 1885. The St. Louis Movement was regarded by its promoters and adherents, and was in fact, the second phase and, in a way, the result of the Newness in New England. Its members—although most of them never wearied of paying tribute to Emerson, Alcott, Thoreau, Parker, and other revoltees of New England[1]—felt that the New England idealists had contented themselves too readily with mere iconoclasm, a negative program of attack. To break down formalism, topple authority from the throne, and liberate the individualistic spirit were accomplishments worth while but good only as far as they went. What was wanted was a positive, progressive program, to which end a broad philosophy based on first principles seemed necessary. As the St. Louisans contemplated the philosophical pretensions of the Concordians, they smiled indulgently at the New Englanders' ready contentment with German philosophy got for the most part at second hand. For themselves, nothing less would do but to trace Transcendentalism to its fountainhead—in Kant, Fichte, and, notably, Hegel. Writing from the retrospective point of view of half a century, Snider recalled that

the time was calling loudly for First Principles. The Civil War had just concluded, in which we all had in some way participated, and we were still overwhelmed, even dazed partially by the grand historic appearance. What does it all mean? was quite the universal question. . . . Naturally our set sought in philosophy the solution, that is, in Hegel as taught by our leaders. A great world-historical deed had been done with enormous labor and other panoramic pageantry. . . . We began to grope after the everlasting verities, the eternal principles, the pure Essences (*reine Wesenheiten*) as they are called by our philosophic authority. These transcendent energies of men and of the world were said to be collected and ordered in one book— Hegel's Logic.[2]

In their effort to formulate a philosophy for the times, Henry Conrad Brokmeyer, William Torrey Harris, Denton J. Snider, and other knights-errant of thought and deed seized upon Emersonian Transcendentalism and Hegelian idealism as their chief weapons. But they did not stop with theorizing; they were ambitious to translate thought into action, and accordingly they attacked and sought to reform every realm of practice—literature, the arts, education, politics, religion, economics, social institutions. Philosophy, they felt, had a high public service to perform. They all combined thought and action; they were, all of them, teachers—many of them professional teachers. Most of them spent their lives in class- and lecture-rooms.[3]

Although Harris chose for his *Journal of Speculative Philosophy* the motto (from Novalis' *Blütenstaub*), "Philosophy can bake no bread, but she can procure for us God, Freedom, and Immortality," the associated philosophers were no cloistered academicians. In their clubs and schools they seriously propounded and tried to solve the intricacies of the Hegelian logic,

and in the *Journal* their discussions often turned technical; but they were not content to be merely "knowers" but sought to follow the Emersonian command to be "sayers" and "doers" as well, and they were eminently successful in all three capacities. Henry Conrad Brokmeyer[4] (1826–1906) translated Hegel's *Larger Logic*, published two plays and a diary, besides writing some verses, and he rose politically to govern his state. W. T. Harris' list of publications approximates five hundred titles,[5] while his active life embraced educational posts from the lowest to the highest in the country, besides editorships of school books, philosophical series, encyclopedias and dictionaries, a long succession of lectureships, and numerous special reports and commissions. Denton J. Snider (1841–1925), the self-styled Writer of Books, has fifty titles to his credit, including novels, poems, dramas, translations, literary and art criticism, educational treatises, psychology and philosophy, religion, biography, and history. He was, in addition, the head of the Communal University and an indefatigable lecturer in many places and before many groups. Thomas Davidson (1840–1900) wrote upon educational problems of democracy and was, among other things, a recognized authority on Greek art, the founder of summer schools at Farmington, Connecticut, and Glenmore, New York, and the editor of *The Western: Review of Education, Science, Literature, and Art* (1872–1874). Adolph Ernst Kroeger (1837–1882) translated several works of Fichte and a collection of German lyrics, aided Harris in establishing the *Journal of Speculative Philosophy*, and contributed extensively to other periodicals.[6] John Gabriel Woerner (1826–1901) wrote a novel, two German plays, and two famous works on law, all admittedly motivated by Hegelian and "Sniderian" philosophy.[7] William McKendree Bryant (1843–1909) published books on American education, on Goethe, Hegel,

Dante, landscape painting, ethics, psychology, and religion. James Kendall Hosmer (1834–1927) turned from the Unitarian ministry to teaching, first at Antioch, next in the University of Missouri, and finally in Washington University, and published a number of literary and historical works, one of which, *A Short History of German Literature*, was the first history of merit by an American of German literature. Frank Louis Soldan (1842–1908) wrote on education and published several German text books. Horace Hills Morgan (1839–1893) devoted ten volumes to literary research, notably on Shakespeare, and to education. In 1875 he succeeded Davidson as editor of *The Western*, which bore henceforth the subtitle: *A Journal of Literature, Education, and Art* (1875–1881). Susan Blow (1843–1916) and Anna C. Brackett (1836–1911) wrote numerous educational tracts, participated in several schools (such as the Concord School of Philosophy), and headed the kindergarten movement in the West. George H. Howison (1834–1916), first vice-president of the Philosophical Society and a teacher of philosophy in various universities and finally at the University of California (1884–1909), which he raised to the western center of philosophical studies, wrote extensively and drew a number of brilliant younger men into philosophical pursuits.[8] Louis (Lewis) J. Block (1851–1927) published a dozen volumes of dramatic sketches and poems. Charles F. Childs (1831–1866) wrote essays on educational and generally cultural subjects. Britton Armstrong Hill (1818–1888) wrote extensively in legal, economic, and politic areas. John Calvin Learned (1834–1893), one of the few theologians associated with the movement, wrote numerous pamphlets and books on religion, ethics, and social criticism. A half-dozen others contented themselves with contributing to Harris' *Journal* or Davidson's *Western*, or both. All of them were articulate. No similar group, before or

since, has remotely approached their published output.[9] All members of the group subscribed to their leader's doctrine of "self activity" and followed his injunction: "If you have any thoughts to give to the world which you consider of value, get them printed; disseminate them."[10]

Begun as an intellectual movement which seized upon Hegel's philosophy as the most effective weapon with which to combat what seemed to this young group of western idealists an engulfing materialism and invidious agnosticism, the St. Louis School nevertheless drew inspiration from the frontier milieu, with its optimistic faith in materialistic progress, its expansive ambitions, its grandiose schemes. In his history of the early phases of the movement Snider speaks of a deep-seated dualism of which he and his confreres themselves were not aware at the time—their devotion, on the one hand, to the life of pure thought and the search for "the eternal principles, the pure Essences," and, on the other, their enthusiastic and uncritical faith in the Great Illusion of the time that St. Louis was the Future Great City of the World. A remarkable energy, a unique cultural outburst, unbounded aspiration of individuals, along with grandiose civic ambition, were felt throbbing throughout the community. When Snider came to St. Louis in March of 1864, he felt at once the electrifying "city soul" and recognized it as an "all dominating psychical trait," which, says he "I soon caught, and then it caught me."[11]

When the census of 1880 shattered the Grand Illusion and demonstrated that the "wicked Sodom" to the north had withstood the Wrath of God (visited on Chicago in the form of the great fire) and had actually outstripped the "world's coming Metropolis" in the race for size, wealth, power, and splendor—even then many clung to their illusion and declared the United States Bureau of Census in league with the forces of evil to subvert the good and the beautiful. The best mathematician of Washington University was engaged to check the names and the arithmetic of the census tabulations and to give the official census-taker the lie. Faith in the approaching triumph of the Great Continental Capital had for so long been axiomatic in every mouth and on every street corner that it took some time for the bare, cold fact of Chicago's supremacy to dispel the illusion. Snider makes 1885 the terminal date of the movement; it coincides with the date by which the Grand Illusion finally made way before the Grand Disillusion. Meanwhile, the twenty years between 1865 and 1885 sufficed to combine a pregnant idea with a powerful *Zeitgeist* and to revive the most energetic and pervasive idealistic movement that the United States of America had felt up to that time.

There were other forces at work too, not the least of which was the peculiar combination in St. Louis of a very strong Germanic strain and the Hegelian idea of Teutonic destiny. Many of those comprising the "little German world that arose in the West with St. Louis as its heart"[12] were intellectual idealists of 1848—trained in the philosophical modes of German thought from Kant to Hegel and exiled from Germany because of their protest against bureaucracy and militarism. Nearly all of them had received military training in the Fatherland: they represented virtually a standing army equipped to step from peaceful to military pursuits on a moment's notice. Although they had fled from militarism in Europe, they saw in the issues of the Civil War a call to take up arms once more. In a day's time they were mobilized under Francis Preston Blair, and the next day they struck at Camp Jackson. This was the first decisive fight for Federal union: universal history pivoted momentarily on St. Louis. At Camp Jackson was performed, says Snider, "The First Great St. Louis Deed."[13] Both Grant and Sherman were in St. Louis at the time—spectators, not participants. A month later both had cast

off indecision and were colonels in the Union Army.

The German regiments were in the thick of the fight all the way, and when they returned—victorious, confident, assertive —they demanded and got their share of the spoils. Already when Snider reached St. Louis in 1864, he found the Germans in possession of the "city's control, material and spiritual."[14] Soon the muster of the city council read like the roll of the Reichstag. The German language was introduced into the public schools, and a bilingual citizenry was stoutly advocated. The constitutional convention of 1864–1865 chose a German for its president, and that of 1875 was completely dominated by Brokmeyer and his German supporters, including Pulitzer, who had risen to prominence by Brokmeyer's assistance, and who was now editor and owner of the *Post-Dispatch*. When Finkelnburg was sent to Congress, and Schurz was elected U.S. Senator, the victory was complete. The capture of Washington and the transfer of the nation's capital to St. Louis seemed assured. St. Louis was Teutonizing, and the Hegelian sense of Teutonic destiny ran subtly but powerfully through the entire population.[15]

Another vehicle of this inter-Teutonism at the time was the surprising circulation of German literature, in periodical and book form. Snider found in St. Louis "three considerable book-stores, well-stocked and doing good business . . . not to speak of lesser shops ever ready to send orders to Leipzig and Berlin for old and new volumes. All these places were manned with a trained German book-seller, known over the entire globe as the unparalleled of his kind, and as the main pillar of the vast German book-trade, being found in Asiatic Tiflis and African Timbuctoo as well as in our Western cowboy town of Hardscrapple."[16]

Though of native or local origin, the movement was propagated chiefly by men who migrated to St. Louis. "I do not recall," says Snider, "a single born St. Louisan in the set, though nearly all of us were Americans. Still the movement was not immigrant, but indigenous; . . . it originated on the soil of St. Louis, and . . . was begotten of the city's unique spirit of that time."[17] Thus it came to pass that Snider felt his destiny wrapped up in the West. During his period of participation in the Concord School later he refused to be "colonialized," though Emery gravitated between the East and the West, and Harris' thoughts seem never to have dwelt far apart from New England. There was all but an open clash. The St. Louisans were considered "borderers" in Concord, and the New Englanders "immigrants" in St. Louis. Paradoxically, the only real immigrant among the leading spirits was Brokmeyer;[18] and among them all, he turned out to be the truest son of the West. Of his kind, i.e., of immigrants from Europe, there were several sorts in St. Louis. Predominantly Germanic though the movement was, both in principles and in membership, all persons of Germanic origin were not therefore welcome. The several radical groups of St. Louis—socialistic, communistic, anarchistic—were excluded; so were the immigrant laborer, the untutored, the boorish. Not that the workingman was excluded because he was a laborer. Quite the contrary. He was as welcome as any other, but he had to demonstrate his eligibility to participate in the life of pure thought. Proselyting was not carried on in the saloons, on the river front, or in the factories. All conversions were effected in Philosopher's Row[19]—itself humble enough in external appearance; but within burned the pure light of the Absolute. The members demanded of their fellows what Shelley asked of his mate: the ability "to feel poetry and understand philosophy."

Whatever aspects the more popular phases of the movement bore, the members of the Philosophical Society kept their eyes steadily on America. All the members sought to deepen their own thinking and to equate it with the German thought which Brokmeyer proclaimed, but they cared little for Germany as such. It was America that they kept constantly in mind. So, too, their president. In leaving Germany as a youth, Brokmeyer had forsaken it for all time. He wasted no time romanticizing a lost Fatherland or indulging in escapist fantasies. In this respect Brokmeyer and the idealistic movement that he engendered are to be sharply distinguished from many another that began, continued, and soon ended as a Germanic *tour de force*, restricted to an exclusive German point of view, and consequently destined to exert little influence beyond the sphere of its peculiarly restricted cultural "island" of Germans and German-Americans. The St. Louis Movement was thoroughly American in everything but inspiration.

Given (1) the dramatic episodes of the struggle for national unity, (2) a strong German contingent dedicated to humanitarian and political reform, and (3) a boundless West to which St. Louis was the gateway, it was perhaps inevitable that St. Louis should seize upon the romantic features of Hegelian thought by which to bring order out of the chaos of the Civil War and to give interpretation and purpose to the role that St. Louis was to play in a frontier society. Hegel was the philosopher of progress, of advance. He was also the proponent of the absolute, pure, free thought. Above all, he was the reconciler of opposites. The young men of St. Louis seized upon him as pointing the way to reconcile materialism and idealism, faith and knowledge, individual statehood and federal unionism, rights and duties, and a dozen other conflicts of the time. Viewed in the light of American civilization as a whole, the St. Louis Movement is a phase of the conflict between naturalism and supernaturalism that characterized the nineteenth century generally—a phase of that long crisis, partly religious, when many a thoughtful man saw but one choice: to avow himself either a medieval man and a Christian or a modern man and a skeptic.[20]

The men of St. Louis were distinguished more for their aloofness from churches than for their adherence to religious creeds. Emerson, when he first met the group, half jocularly but approvingly called them Harris' "German atheists." But they were, to a man, profoundly serious and thoughtful. They were philosophers whose philosophy impinged at every point on religion. They professed themselves to be, and were, the disciples of the Kantian reason and the Hegelian logic, but they denied the capacity of understanding and pure reason alone to solve all of man's problems. With certain tendencies of twentieth-century philosophic inquiry they would have had little sympathy—for instance, with the aspiration to be strictly scientific, in the sense in which physics and geology are scientific, in areas apparently not belonging solely to the scientific realm. The "pure essences," they contended, were not discoverable by any *one* of man's mental faculties or by such a procedure as the scientific agnostic employed. Truth, Beauty, and Goodness were not to be analyzed by chemical techniques or measured in physical terms. Nor were they mystics, content with soul-satisfying but fundamentally irrational intuitions. On the first page of the first number of their *Journal*, Harris expressed their dissatisfaction alike with pure naturalism and with pure mysticism. He explained that while he and his associates would not accept tradition unmodified, neither would they break with it altogether. They regarded the old truths as still true, not because they were old, but old because they were true. Nourished on Christian concepts, they were men who sought a philosophy that would enable them, without sacrificing their intellectual integrity, to accept both the measurable facts of science and the immeasurable concepts of the heart and soul.

Harris, whose philosophic course is most consistently straightforward, set his face against the Atomists, the Sophists, the Brahminists, the Eleatics, against Spinoza, Hamilton, Hume, Rousseau, Mill, Comte, Cousin, Spencer, and all others whose teachings led, in his opinion, to mechanism, materialism, pantheism, agnosticism, atheism. In conformity with Hegelian precept and example, Harris fought less against any one or all of these than against the presumption of any one of them to be the only true system. He studied all systems, even the various oriental mysticisms, for what they held that might be of value in making the final synthesis, but he consistently denied that they, individually or collectively, represented the whole truth any more than Occidental modes of thought. For him, one was thesis; the other, antithesis; what was wanted was a proper synthesis, a "correlation of forces," a reconciliation of opposites, neither one of which was wholly true or false but merely, in and of itself, inadequate. In short, he sought in the speculative the point at which "the two are one."

These Hegelian concepts, which the average American, if he considers them at all, treats lightly, were amazingly useful in the practical situation with which the St. Louisans were confronted. Harris saw, on taking a second look, what others have seen—namely, that the involved dialectic of Hegel is simply the philosopher's queer statement of principles which the average successful American knows and applies almost instinctively, and to which he owes a large measure of his practical success. That Hegel helped the leaders of the St. Louis Movement out of the dilemma which the times presented is not be doubted. Hegel's doctrine, that for a man to understand anything at all he must see it in its relations, held a large meaning. The American way of life is a continuous compromise. Success in America, whether in business, family, church, or government, requires a constant willingness to conciliate opposing interests. All American experience seemed to substantiate the Hegelian doctrine that all that is finite is provisional, that no antagonisms are final, and that all objects and institutions are but phases of a process referable to the dialectic of thesis, antithesis, and synthesis. These Hegelian principles and their implications struck a bewildered group of young intellectuals groping about in a chaos compounded of disunion, war, and reconstruction in a "border" state with compelling force. Ambitious to get the whole lesson, the leaders sought to master the intricacies of Hegel's abstruse dialectic, and some of them succeeded markedly. The lesser lights, content with being practical idealists, accepted Brokmeyer's or Harris' explanations. Hegel's involved logic and dialectical subtleties they regarded as merely the professional philosopher's jargon for those principles which every practical man knows and applies without triadic mental gymnastics. Hegelian thought, at all events, its practical applications and implications, fitted the men and the times of St. Louis.

Circumstances such as these suggest but do not entirely explain why the St. Louis Movement occurred in St. Louis instead of one or several of a half-dozen other cities in the Mississippi Valley. They hint no reason why Harris, for example, left Yale at the end of two and a half years to teach Pitman's shorthand in St. Louis rather than in Chicago or Milwaukee, why Brokmeyer walked out of the woods into St. Louis rather than Cincinnati or Detroit, nor why, shortly before Appomattox, Snider, a graduate of Oberlin, engaged himself by letter to teach in a Catholic College in St. Louis—all at about the same time. It has been said that the best explanation is that winds of doctrine from Germany and similar winds from New England crossed each other's path in St. Louis and caused a rotary motion which whirled a goodly

portion of the population up into the empyrean.[21]

The St. Louis Movement itself was about as unorganized and formless as it could be and remain a movement at all. Like New England Transcendentalism, it found its *modus operandi* in a club, denominated the Philosophical Society (organized in January, 1866); but even more than its New England predecessor, its meetings and business were left to inspiration or occasion. It had a titular president, Brokmeyer, characterized by Snider as "the primal Titanic demiurge of our Movement."[22] Harris was the acknowledged secretary, but instead of keeping minutes, he saw his chief duty the editing of the *Journal of Speculative Philosophy*—surely more important work, but hardly calculated to perfect and preserve the organization. Both ardent disciples of Hegel, president and secretary mutually encouraged and supported each other; they led the talk and steered the symposium, but they formed no constituted hierarchy. When Brokmeyer was drawn into active pursuits, Harris simply carried on until Brokmeyer left St. Louis altogether, whereupon the mantle fell on the shoulders of Harris, who bore it lightly. When Harris himself, and Davidson and Snider, too, left about 1880, the club as a club simply ceased to be.[23]

There were within the limits of St. Louis three other philosophical clubs—the Kant Club,[24] the Hegel Club,[25] and the Aristotle Society[26]—not to mention such organizations as the Art Society, the Society of Pedagogy, the Shakespeare Society, and a dozen other literary or musical clubs. There were, besides, several others in neighboring cities and states, among all of which there was kept up a continual interchange of visitations by the associated members. Most prominent among these were (1) a philosophical club at Quincy, Illinois, under the direction of Samuel Emery, (2) another at Osceola, Missouri, under the guidance of Thomas M. Johnson, (3) the Plato Club of

Jacksonville, Illinois, under the leadership of Dr. Hiram K. Jones, and (4) the Kant and Hegel clubs of Chicago, founded by the Rev. Robert A. Holland, not to mention the several schools organized later by Harris and the cc..1munal universities directed by Snider in Chicago, Cincinnati, Milwaukee, and elsewhere, or Davidson's retreats in the Adirondacks, or the educational mission of Brokmeyer among the Indians of the Oklahoma Indian Territory.

All this activity betokens a considerable amount of enthusiasm. That out of it all emerged so substantial an achievement as the twenty-two volumes of the most distinguished philosophical journal produced in this country during the nineteenth century bespeaks also the fact that the membership possessed something more than ebullition. Considering that the multiplication of organizations invited divergent points of view and divided energies, their extraordinary tenacity of purpose is all the more remarkable. The stage was all set for them to dissipate their energies in talk; but they followed their leader's command *to do* and, above all, *to publish*.

The failure of the Philosophical Society to achieve anything like a close organization appears, on first consideration, all the more odd because, unlike the Transcendental Club (which grew out of very informal discussions and never rallied round anything so definite as a great book or a single saint, but revered a whole galaxy of high priests from Confucius to Emerson himself), the St. Louis Movement acknowledged its "original source and inspiration" to have been "in Brokmeyer's translation of Hegel's Logic."[27] Yet this book came to be a veritable "Book of Fate, destined to stay unborn in the unprinted underworld during the whole life of the St. Louis Movement."[28] The great Bible of the movement remained "in the voluble and expansive genius of Brokmeyer," whence neither his own heroic exertions nor the combined and almost

cabalistic efforts of his friends succeeded in extracting anything like a printable draft. So long as he, "a thinker," in Harris' estimation, "of the same order of mind as Hegel,"[29] remained among them, he was both Hegel and Hegel's *Logic* for them. So long as Brokmeyer's genius, "equal to that of Hegel and more poetical" (says Snider) stood by, they needed no Canonical Book. Time and again, Brokmeyer would, by "one lightning flash of his consuming dialectic," resolve their doubts and explain their queries.[30] In him they found a certain unity that held them together even while such individualists among them as Davidson and Kroeger chafed at the bit. When he left, however, without having given them the great Bible by which to chart their course, the several individuals asserted their individualism. That commandment of their master's they had learned complete.[31] Brokmeyer himself set the example of self-determinism. Like another Thoreau, the primary passion of his life was to be himself, to go his own way. An idealistic exile, journeyman, steel worker, huntsman, soldier, lawyer, and philosopher, he next turned statesman and finally hermit. An egoist, and idealist, he was never an organizer.

The mild-mannered but nonetheless individualistic Snider was the next to strike out on his own path. As soon as he had mastered Hegel, he put philosophy behind him, and carefully husbanding his talents, prepared for his Super-Vocation. His years (1865-1871) of devotion to his eighteen volumes of Hegel—although he recognized this period of intense study as "not without influence" on his future career—he soon came to view as basically nothing more than "a time of pure acquisition." "I was still repeating, not creating, though possibly getting ready for the latter."[32] This "German Era," during which he "not only thought Hegel, but lived Hegel, was Hegel," was to what he spoke of as his 'Life's Central Node" only a "German

Overture"[33] that "graved upon me certain lines, which have continued to run through my whole career."[34] They led directly to "Life's Central Node," which meant for him a life dedicated to literature—the pursuit of his Super-Vocation as a "Writer of Books," though it meant keeping close company with "Chum Poverty."[35] He side-stepped every opportunity and refused every offer that might have led him astray, even when it promised sure pecuniary gain, or influence, or power. He was a "talented and lovable man, but he had to be a free lance: he would not submit to being edited and consequently had to publish his work himself; he would not accept administrative responsibilities or tie himself down to an academic position."[36]

Davidson, "a jolly drifter and a general free fighter," delighted much more to kick over the traces than help pull the load.[37] Howison, whatever capabilities he later developed, did not show any remarkable administrative ability while he remained in St. Louis. Miss Blow was a very intelligent and energetic woman, but she was a woman and therefore never in the inner circle of the original group. Moreover, if Snider's picture of her is accurate, she was poorly adjusted to her social environment and incapable of assuming a leadership requiring pliability, forbearance, and tact.[38] That left Harris to keep some semblance of organization. Harris showed himself efficient in many ways, notably as an editor and an educator. In the latter capacity he was particularly effective; but the broad boundaries of all his educational endeavors were already staked out. He was superb as a co-ordinator of details within the framework of an organization, both in the public schools and later in the office of the Bureau of Education;[39] but the work of founding and organizing was not his forte. His greatest success in this respect was his establishment of the *Journal of Speculative Philosophy*, through which he made himself, for a time, the voice of the Movement.

He could publish a magazine in which his associates could air their views: he could arrange publication for them, could get them speaking engagements, could provide them with chances to earn a livelihood. He could, and did, keep the community stirred up over philosophy. For moments at a time he could sway and mould and lead.[40] He could lead his hearers to a view of the Eternal City from the rarefied atmosphere of the delectable heights of pure thought; some were moved beyond the capacity of their understanding. But fundamentally Snider was correct in denying that Harris was a philosopher *par excellence*. Indeed, Harris never claimed pre-eminence as an original thinker but contented himself with making "Hegel talk English."[41] His return East to help found the Concord School was prompted less by a desire to rear an original Amerian philosophy than to further the cause of Emersonian Transcendentalism by leading it into Hegelian channels—to "hitch the two horses, Concord and St. Louis, to his philosophic chariot,"[42] as Snider put it. If Snider had had his way, he would not have tried "to capture and reconstruct" New England Transcendentalism, but would have started anew and built from the ground up. He questioned Harris' wisdom in going East at all, and foretold his failure.[43] His misgivings did not prevent his participating in five of the first seven sessions; but when he heard Sanborn berated as "a Yankee renegade for his part in foisting the Western set of philosophers upon Emerson's Concord,"[44] he was sure there would be trouble. As for himself, he knew he lacked the necessary "coloniality."[45] He felt that Emery, nominally the Director of the School, would not stick, as indeed he did not. Moreover, F. B. Sanborn, officially the Secretary and actually the chief journalistic spirit of the enterprise, puzzled him from the first. He was soon to learn that behind Sanborn's "mellifluous" voice and "winsome" smiles there was "concealed a stinger which he knew how to flesh upon occasions."[46] Hiram K. Jones's Platonism and W. T. Harris' Hegelianism seemed forever to provoke arguments which even the philosophic serenity and sepulchral voice of the presiding Alcott could not always assuage;[47] and when the disturbing subject of psychology, as promulgated by William James,[48] reared its head, and Tom Davidson's learned sneer and paradoxical sardonicism[49] confounded the confusion, he foresaw the end. In 1882 Emerson died, and Alcott was stricken with apoplexy. Snider rated the third session the best; henceforth, he felt, the course would be downward. He went fishing to Walden Pond and interpreted his failure to get even a nibble as a sign that the St. Louisans were not destined to make any "great haul of philosophical fishes" in Concord. "No," he told himself, "the Mississippi cannot be made to flow eastward through New England."[50] He could only shake his head over the way things were going. He feared that Harris would not be able to maintain his intellectual primacy over Sanborn, "the unparalleled man of publicity," ever eager to start a new order. The failure of Harris' high-minded effort, he reflected, was inevitable; and so he was not surprised when, after laboring in Concord for a decade, Harris fell back into his old pedagogy—"lapsed," says Snider, "into the national Bureau of Education and almost quit philosophy." The contrarieties in the times, yes, in Harris himself, were too great.[51]

Finally, there was from first to last a strong contingent of dissent. There was Thomas Davidson, a lively and ingenious Scotchman, a veritable free lance, who usually upheld Aristotle against Hegel, and the Greek world against the Christian. He possessed both erudition and spirit but loved nothing better than a good fight in open meeting. Another of the brethren who often kicked over the traces was Kroeger, stout defender of Kant against Hegel and translator of Fichte. Soldan remained usually neutral, but he really preferred Spinoza to any of the Germans. Finally, Snider, one of the triune leadership, was himself something of an apostate. The six hundred pages of his history explain, whatever else they do not clarify, that all his earnest early efforts to understand Hegel and to follow the Hegelian path eventually came to little. The subjects of his "Literary Bibles" were Homer, Dante, Shakespeare, Goethe. He was "a writer of books," not a philosopher. St. Louis Hegelianism, like New England Transcendentalism, embraced a number of inharmonious elements, and neither bred a leader capable of organizing and controlling the several "individuals" who comprised it. There were bickerings and jealousies the moment Brokmeyer relinquished the leadership to devote his time and energies to politics. Snider himself protests his own forbearance and magnanimity too much, as in the case of his tiff with Miss Blow, who had remained in St. Louis, and who, on his return, seemed inclined to dispute the leadership with him.[52] And there were deep-seated differences that grew out of the opposition of East to West, of the native to the foreign. Brokmeyer was of foreign birth; he adopted St. Louis as a temporary scene of his activity; but whether he dwelt in the mansion of the Governor of Missouri or pitched his tent among the Creek Indians of the Oklahoma territory was all one to him. He was no native, no true son of St. Louis. Harris was suspected from the start as a New Englander at heart; "underneath all his enthusiasm for the West lay an exile's longing for New England." For a while Snider wondered "why Harris should so often bring to us the aged Alcott to say over again what the repeating sayer of the said had already better said, and why he could be so assiduous in admiration of what he had often sufficiently admired." In 1879, when Harris went to Concord, Snider saw the light: Harris had been preparing the time and manner of his "great Departure from the St. Louis Public Schools to a new career purely philosophical." But Snider doubted that "it was the part of wisdom in Harris to make this change." For himself, says he, "my goal remained in the West, even when I was compelled to quit St. Louis. I had no Mayflower tradition to chain me to Plymouth Rock or to any other piece of stone."[53] Aside from these antithetical elements, there was the irrepressible individualism of the several personalities. Brokmeyer demonstrated it less by what he said than by what he did when he turned his back upon the civilization for which he had planned so much, and went to live among the savages. For some years, while the time was right and the enthusiasm rife, the Hegelian triadic thought processes served to effect something like a unified movement; but as the times changed, the political scenes shifted, the individualities asserted themselves, the abstruse Hegelian dialectic fell apart, and the movement split in a number of tangential directions.

At the time when Brokmeyer first agitated the minds of his friends, the practical social and political situation had fully prepared them to receive his message. For the fact needs to be emphasized that in the beginning the movement was more practical than theoretical; its center of gravity was political, not scholastic.[54] "There was an urgent social *milieu* in which the flint of Brokmeyer struck fire"; he could not have hit upon "a solvent theory to bring order out of chaos or a systematic defense of his faith more to the point than Hegel's."[55] When the first meetings in Old Philosophers' Row were held, three of the group— Brokmeyer and the two judges, Jones and Woerner—were already actively engaged in politics. Together they considered the dialectic of politics, political parties, and impending problems. Of most basic concern was the relation of the Federal government to the individual states that comprised it, and the means to prevent each from

devouring the other. The uncontrolled desire of both to do just that had resulted in the debacle of war, from the consequences of which the men of their generation were trying to extricate themselves. They studied political theories; they delved into the Constitution of the United States; they planned a philosophical work on the subject that never materialized, unless we accept Judge Woerner's *Rebel's Daughter*, a novel with an elaborate presentation of political points of view and arguments; but especially did they pore over Hegel's philosophy of the state and its applicability to the United States in the sixties.

It seems paradoxical that the men who fled from Prussian tyranny should have chosen for their guide Hegel, nowadays credited with having been the creator and glorifier of the Prussian state. But the paradox is more apparent than real: it rests upon a misalliance between Hegelian theory and subsequent historical events by which what happened in 1848 and later is imputed to Hegel as if he had willed it.[56] However much power Hegel came to surrender to monarchy, and whatever uses his philosophy was put to in Prussia, the essence of his political theory was, from beginning to end, his dictum that "the history of the world is the unfolding of liberty."

Thus the St. Louisans understood him, and the *Journal of Speculative Philosophy* repeatedly enforced this interpretation. It is discussed at length in the sixth volume (1872) under the head, "Hegel, Prussia, and the Philosophy of Right,"[57] where it is argued that it was Hegel's drastic criticism of the radical student corps that first gave him the erroneous reputation of being antidemocratic, but that he "did not become false in Prussia to that conception . . . of the fully developed rational state . . . [which he had] earlier advocated at Jena,"[58] and that the Hegelian state remains the most rational, and the expression which it attained in Hegel's presentation, the most beautiful.[59]

To the political philosophers of St. Louis nothing was clearer than that Hegel was the prophet of a reunited nation after it had suffered the terrible "dialectic" of civil war. The Southern position, Brokmeyer explained, was what Hegel termed "abstract right"; the Northern, that of an equally "abstract morality"; while the Union represented what Hegel called the "ethical state." This interpretation is clearly stated, though not exactly in these terms, by Harris in his prefatory remarks in the first number of the *Journal*. At once faithful to the Hegelian principle that the history of the world is the progress of liberty, and obedient to the letter, as well as the spirit, of the master, the St. Louis disciples did not shrink from the conflict, but met it, confident that no real synthesis in history is possible except through the tragic process of the dialectic of events.

These circumstances explain the rumble of the Hegelian traidic movement throughout the written record of these Hegel-intoxicated men and women. They vied with each other in applying the fixed formula of Hegel to every phase of the gigantic struggle. Thus, Fort Sumter was the "thesis," Camp Jackson the "antithesis," and the declaration of war the "synthesis."[60] The great real-estate boom, or "illusion," in St. Louis is the "thesis," the founding of the Philosophical Society is the "antithesis," and the building of the Eads Bridge is the "synthesis."[61] The Hegelian dogma was applied even to the rivalry between St. Louis and Chicago. The rise of the latter was in "antithesis" to St. Louis. Unshamefacedly they hailed the Great Fire of Chicago as the conclusion of the "phase," following which St. Louis would be free to establish the hoped-for "synthesis." In 1890, Harris recalled that they used the Hegelian dialectic to solve "all problems connected with school-teaching and school management," and that "even the hunting of turkeys and squirrels was the occasion for the use of philosophy."[62] He empha-

sized the applicability and significance of this dialectic again and again in the *Journal*. While Judge Johann G. Woerner refrained from putting it as baldly as did Snider and Harris, nevertheless the idea of *The Rebel's Daughter: A Story of Love, Politics, and War*, involving, as it does the clash of Southern and Northern issues, turns upon the same development of thought;[63] and Anna C. Brackett early enshrined the Hegelian triad in some verses entitled "Comprehension," which conclude that

only when the one is twain,
And where the two are one again,
Will truth no more be sought in vain.[64]

For the matter before us several approaches are possible. We may consider the movement in its several relations to religion, politics, philosophy, education, and art, or we may consider it from the point of view of the chief participants. For the sake of economy, a combination of the two methods may serve.

Since the movement was not primarily religious, what has been said on that score may be deemed sufficient, except for such incidental observations as will be made in connection with individuals to be discussed hereafter. The political activity of the group has been sketched.[65] It is best viewed in relation to Brokmeyer, who was most prominent in politics. Our examination of Harris will provide numerous opportunities to consider the educational activities of the group, although he had many assistants whose careers merit individual attention. The philosophical endeavors were shared alike by all members, although Brokmeyer and Harris took the lead. To Harris, as editor of the *Journal* and as a prime mover in the Concord School, belongs the primacy, the twenty-two volumes of the *Journal* and his books on *Hegel's Logic* and the *Psychologic Foundations of Education* affording an objective body of data for evaluation. In Snider are concentrated the literary ambitions of the movement, although he, too, had numerous assistants, as well as other interests.

Brokmeyer and the Translation of Hegel's *Logic*

To resume, then, we turn to Brokmeyer, whose career remains vague partly because of his quixotic manner of living in retirement, partly because historians and biographers have unaccountably overlooked him.[66] It is not known precisely when and by what means Brokmeyer came by his knowledge of Hegel. He appears generally to have given the impression that he was born "a full-fledged Hegelian."[67] In his revolt against society and his headlong measures to achieve "universalized emancipation," he seemed to his friends the perfect embodiment of the daemonic and titanic in Nature, as elemental as Nature herself. It came, therefore, as a great surprise to Snider when in 1904, while talking over old times, Brokmeyer confessed his spiritual evolution to have grown out of the orthodox Lutheranism of Germany and the hidebound fundamentalism of the Bible belt of the United States. During his stay in Mississippi he had been a member in good standing of the Baptist Church, and by letters of transfer from the church had won admittance to Georgetown University. But while there, Brokmeyer went on to confess, "I got to reading on the outside and slowly began drifting away from my former moorings."[68] He gave little further intimation of any other influence that led him to Hegel except that in Providence he came to know Dr. Hedge, and that he drew from Hedge's *Prose Writers of Germany* his first conception of Hegel's philosophy. This conception must have been faint, for Hedge's book contains little that is pivotal in Hegel's system; although Hedge himself may have supplemented, by way of personal explication, what his book failed to supply.

Another important result of Brokmeyer's

sojourn at Brown University was that there he discovered New England Transcendentalism. He greedily appropriated the ideas of the Newness, carrying Transcendental notions of individualism, originality, and worship of nature to their extreme conclusions. His flight from the established social order to the backwoods of Missouri was nothing plaintive like Emerson's bidding good-bye to a "proud world." The Yankee experiments in living, at Brook Farm, Fruitlands, and elsewhere, were diminutive compared with the way of life he adopted for himself in Missouri and the colonization scheme which he promoted in Illinois about 1856.[69] Thoreau's famed flight into his shanty on Walden Pond was an inconsequential lark compared to Brokmeyer's life in the primeval forest, in defiance of Family, Church, State, and Society. He transcended Transcendentalism.

A Mechanic's Diary makes it clear that the main lines of his thought were already graved on his mind by 1856. Hegel was already his god,[70] while Kant and Aristotle contended for second place.[71] When Harris and Brokmeyer first chanced to meet in 1858, the latter (although already a self-confessed Hegelian and ready to answer questions by the book) was still not fully emancipated from his quixotic romanticism. He had just returned to St. Louis for one of his brief periodic trips to earn from society the money necessary to keep up his anti-social life in the woods.[72] Shortly after their meeting, he disappeared. A year later, Harris, George Stedman, and Dr. J. H. Watters found him in his wild retreat nearly dead from a congestive attack. Rescued from his hermitage, and restored to health, he was persuaded by his benefactors to give up his primitive life and to settle down in the city to purely intellectual pursuits.[73] Themselves poor, they staked him to food and established him in the attic of an old lodging house in South Market Street, Brokmeyer for his part agreeing to translate and thus to make available to them the wonder-working truths of Hegel's *Wissenschaft der Logik* (after the 1841 Henning edition).

Meanwhile Harris had drummed up a small group of "respectable vagabonds," who formed themselves into a loose organization known as the Kant Club, not to be confused with the more formal organization by the same name founded by Harris in 1874. Of these "fifty-eighters" little is known. Snider, the historian of the movement, did not meet with the group until 1865. Dr. J. H. Watters of McDowell's Medical College and George Stedman were two, and Ira Divoll and Dr. R. A. Holland were probably two others of the group. The members were few; they met informally, their several boarding-house rooms being the place for their more-or-less chance meetings. Harris at this time knew little more of Hegel than the name; he was still immersed in Kant. While Brokmeyer proclaimed Hegel's *Logic* to be "the book to tackle," he approved their study of Kant as good preparation for Hegel, whom he hoped they would be ready to receive when his translation would be done. Meanwhile he set blithely to work to "make Hegel talk English," as ironically enough, Harris found it necessary, many years later, to attempt doing all over again.[74]

Brokmeyer lived the life of a medieval ascetic during 1859–1860, preparing his own meals and sleeping on a pallet on the floor, wrestling with the abstrusities of Hegel, the confusing nomenclature, and his own difficulties with the English medium.[75] Although it was planned to have the translation published at once, what steps, if any, were taken at the time cannot now be ascertained. Soon the plan was obscured by the more pressing events of the Civil War, in the prosecution of which Brokmeyer himself led the way, swapping off his Hegel for Hardie's *Infantry Tactics* and sporting soon an eagle on his shoulder straps.

Shortly after the end of the war, the *Journal* was founded. In view of the fact that Harris found room in it for several translations at least as long as Brokmeyer's, his failure to publish what he and Brokmeyer agreed to be the greatest philosophical book takes on added significance. Snider's implied criticisms of Harris and the associated members for their failure to perform their "first duty" of revising and printing "this central work" explain little. The simple conclusion of any disinterested student who takes the trouble to examine Brokmeyer's manuscript (and there is no good evidence to show that it has been looked at by anyone since the Missouri Historical Society acquired it in 1921) is that Brokmeyer's best efforts left it unprintable.[76]

But it would be a mistake to assume that since Brokmeyer failed in his efforts to translate Hegel in writing that he failed also in expounding him verbally. Everyone who heard him discourse testifies to the pungency and clarity of his exposition of Hegel— among them Snider and Harris, both of whom possessed intellectual integrity and some philosophical perspicacity. Certainly Harris can be trusted. Moreover, there are Brokmeyer's nine "Letters on Faust,"[77] which form an intelligent application of Hegelian dialectic to Goethe's poem, and there is *A Mechanic's Diary*, which demonstrates Brokmeyer's ability to write a clear, crisp, straightforward sentence. His main difficulty with the *Logic* appears to have been that having made an ultraliteral translation, he was unable to recast it into English idiom.

The failure to get Hegel's *Logic* printed was, in Snider's opinion, a serious defection of the members of the Philosophical Society. "The publication of the Logic . . . would have anchored our movement, which because of this capital deficiency has shown itself unsteady, aimless, and vanishing."[78] Snider's observation appears sound because the school did eventually disintegrate, but it is to be remembered (1) that the strong individualism—"self-activity" was their word for it—of all the members would have defeated any effort at long-sustained and concerted effort anyway, and (2) that while the movement split into several constituent parts, each of the scattered members became a co-ordinating center in its own right and situation, thus affecting perhaps more people and spreading its influence over a wider area than would have been possible for a movement, however close-knit and unified, that remained localized in St. Louis. Before we can follow these later developments, we shall have to consider Brokmeyer's crowning achievement for the movement, namely, his organization of the Philosophical Society, its membership, and its work.

During the war Harris had remained in St. Louis and had kept the home-fires burning. Brokmeyer returned shortly after Appomattox. Snider met him less than a year later at the Pension Française of Pierre Guilloz on Walnut Street, and was at first rebuffed by the daemonic in this "backwoods philosopher," but their paths crossed again during the early fall of 1865 when he accompanied his friends J. G. Woerner and Dr. J. Z. Hall to a small gathering at Harris' house in Salisbury Street.[79] Following other preliminary meetings, the formal organization was effected on January 22, 1866. A constitution was adopted and Brokmeyer was elected President; Howison and Watters, Vice-Presidents; Hill, Treasurer; and Harris, Secretary. There were three classes of members: Directors (or full members), Associates, and Auxiliaries, the last being mainly philosophers and scientists not resident in St. Louis. There were no dues, and minutes were not regularly kept. A roll of the membership can be reconstructed today only by patching together stray bits of information.[80]

The establishment of the Philosophical Society welded into a visible body the Hegelians of the West and set the stage upon which Harris decided early in 1866 to show off his friend from "back East,—

Amos Bronson Alcott, the Plato of Concord." Nothing was further from Harris' design or Alcott's wish than that this stage should provoke an open clash between East and West, but neither as yet knew Brokmeyer well enough to know that the only thing about him that could be predicted with certainty was his unpredictability.

Alcott and Brokmeyer had met earlier, back in 1859, when Alcott came to "converse" with the first, pre-war group of philosophers. But on that occasion Brokmeyer had kept the peace. He was not yet the high and mighty commander of men. So he contented himself with damning his friend, William Hyde of the *Missouri Republican*, for persuading him to give up an evening with his beloved books to go hear this wise man from the East, who had turned out to be an "unmitigated charlatan" parading about in the nineteenth century in the cast-off rags and tags of second- and third-rate neo-Platonists. The rest of his steam he let off harmlessly in his diary, by calling Alcott mild names, such as "peddler of infantile asininities of mummy wrappage," the result of having "burrowed round until he hit upon the works of Iamblichus and Plotinus."[81]

On Alcott's second visit, things were different. In the first place, Harris had, in a measure, mismanaged the affair; certainly he had not exercised his usual circumspection. The Society had been formed on January 22, ostensibly to gather support for the publication of Brokmeyer's translation of Hegel's *Logic*. President Brokmeyer had been asked to institute the programs of the Society by presenting his exegesis of *Faust*. Then it developed that apparently Harris had hurried up the organization of the Society to have it in readiness to receive Alcott. Brokmeyer had delivered only the first of his discourses on *Faust*. Brokmeyer did not like the looks of things. Still he contented himself, during the first of Alcott's lectures, with sniffing audibly, and once he observed that he had difficulty in following Alcott's theory of "lapse," or emanation, by which he could derive, through some process of reasoning incomprehensible to Brokmeyer, from the indestructible, unsayable One any resultant at all, thus making a reduction from an irreducible and unknown Godhead to a known atom. For himself, he said, he cared not a fig for divining as against reasoning. It was at the seventh meeting that Brokmeyer's daemon overpowered him.

On this occasion some twenty men had gathered "into a kind of circle before the new Orpheus," who read in a "sepulchral tone" from slips of paper, which, as he finished with them, he threw down in an annoying manner as if to say, "There, gentlemen, what say you to that?" Directly in front of the prophet sat Brokmeyer, eyes alert and mischievous, ready to act both as chief interpreter and hierophant. Soon Alcott began to suspect that as a mouthpiece Brokmeyer was not altogether trustworthy. To some of his oracles Brokmeyer gave "an easy sober signifiance, which all understood, but others he seemed to turn inside out and then shiver into smithereens." Finally he picked up one that had just been read, and "at the fiery touch of his dialectics, set off with his Mephistophelean chuckle, he simply exploded it into mist with a sort of detonation, as if it were a soap bubble filled with explosive gas." At this point Alcott began to realize that, by some Hegelian process which he did not understand, his oracles were being made to contradict themselves. He grew testy, as a man well might; then he lost his temper; and finally, turning upon Brokmeyer, said: "Mr. Brokmeyer, you confuse us with the multiplicity of your words and the profusion of your fancy." "This," says Snider, "was the first wholly intelligible saying of Orpheus that evening." Brokmeyer, visibly restraining himself and recollecting that he was Mr. Alcott's host, replied calmly, "Perhaps I do"; but it was evident to the men trained in Hegelian logic at "Brok-

meyer University" that if it ever came to a serious intellectual tussle between this "poor old man, thin in thews and in thought," and their Titanic president, the New Englander would leave hardly "a philosophic grease spot."[82]

Other eastern luminaries came to St. Louis to shed or reflect light, but of them all only Emerson created any great stir in Old Philosophers' Row, when, the winter following Alcott's ill-starred visit of 1866, Harris imported the chief of the Transcendental diviners. On their side, the St. Louisans instantly recognized Emerson as made of firmer metal than Alcott; for the moment the introductory formalities were over, Snider observed, he took the offensive by "whipping out his rapier and giving sly but very courtly digs at our Teutonic idol." He observed plaintively that he could find in Hegel "no pithy saying or memorable metaphor": "When I fish in Hegel, I cannot get a bite." Snider sighed for Brokmeyer, who would have given Emerson "some of his much-desired pithy sentences . . . enwrapped in a metaphorical tornado which would have whirled him off his feet." But Brokmeyer had enough of Concordians and kept his distance; so Snider mustered enough audacity to lecture Emerson "with some degree of ardor" on the virtues of systematic thought. In his youthful self-conceit and ardent devotion to Hegel, Snider did not realize that Emerson knew all that—had known it ever since the early thirties when he had tried to give order to his thoughts in *Nature*; nor did Snider then know that Emerson had given up the method as unsatisfactory, had lapsed back into an intuitional phase, and was only recently coming round to something approaching, though still far from identical with, the method which Snider was championing.[83]

Little is known about the rest of Emerson's stay in St. Louis, which seems not to have extended beyond a day or two. Yet he continued to demonstrate some enthusiasm for "Harris and his men," maintained an auxiliary membership in the Philosophical Society, subscribed for the *Journal*, and before the year was out was twice more in St. Louis, on at least one of which occasions he lectured before the Society.[84]

Others came to St. Louis, but only Alcott returned repeatedly, "to repeat again," says Snider, "what had been already too oft repeated." For the rest of the time, the days passed uneventfully enough. Harris saw to it that the members worked industriously. The translations from Hegel, Schelling, Fichte, Kant, and a half-dozen other thinkers proceeded satisfactorily, and many of them found their way into print in the *Journal*. The Society continued to meet regularly.[85]

The first serious defection from the ranks came in 1868 with Brokmeyer, the "high-throned Olympian" who might have excelled even Hegel if, as Snider thought, he had stuck to philosophy instead of allowing his daemon (and Frank Blair) to turn him into political pursuits.[86] Brokmeyer explained that he was only temporarily forsaking his true vocation "to work out his world-view of philosophy, in literature, in poetry—and become a Writer of Books," in order, first, to devote himself to those human institutions that needed reforming. Thirty years later he returned to his earlier vocation, only to discover that he was now incapable of doing what, as a man of forty, he might have disciplined himself to do.

Even though he failed to get himself in hand and failed in his ambition to give every American the opportunity to read Hegel in English, Brokmeyer performed two notable services: (1) he put into circulation several copies of his manuscript translation—no one knows how many, and (2) he inspired Harris to carry on in a fashion that never won Brokmeyer's wholehearted approval, but that was doubtless more effective than Brokmeyer's own plans could have been if they had been realizable.

On the first score it was long assumed that the fragment of Brokmeyer's transla-

tion in the Missouri Historical Library was the only one in existence. While there were conjectures that other copies existed, none came to light until Professor Paul Russell Anderson found a complete copy in Jacksonville, Illinois. That discovery led to clues concerning still another complete draft presumably stored somewhere in Quincy, Illinois, but not yet located, and to an earlier draft, dating back to 1859–1861, part of which was found in the possession of Miss Edith Davidson Harris, daughter of W. T. Harris.[87]

How these manuscripts came into being and how they circulated is part of the story of Hegel's introduction in America. In the Preface to his book, *Hegel's Logic*, Harris intimates that Brokmeyer's first translation was made in longhand; he speaks of copying every word of it. Actually, it seems that Brokmeyer dictated part of it to Harris, who took it down in Pitman shorthand.[88] In conformity with the original plan, Harris copy was submitted in 1861 to the publisher Henry Bohn, who rejected it because he considered it unpublishable unless first "revised by a fluent English scholar," though he doubted that even then it would prove salable. Harris' copy circulated among the members of the Philosophical Society, who were commissioned to study and revise it. Brokmeyer himself was active in the revision and gave portions of the original draft to Snider and C. F. Childs for correction.[89] Harris, too, was busy, apparently making a completely new copy in 1866. How many complete copies and parts of copies came into existence during the sixties and later can only be guessed at today.

In 1875 a manuscript, comprising twenty-seven sections in large folders, was sent to S. H. Emery, Jr., of Quincy, Illinois, at his own request. Miss Sally Williams, copied it for him, and the original was returned in 1876.[90] Two years later Emery had a copy of his copy made for Dr. Hiram K. Jones of Jacksonville (at Jones's request). The latter, bound in three volumes, is today in the Illinois College Library.[91] About 1882 another copy was struck off by Meeds Tuthill for the use of the Hegel Club of Chicago, organized about this time by R. A. Holland. The several St. Louis copies underwent various vicissitudes. Harris took at least one of them when he went East; others appear to be irretrievably lost. About 1890 Brokmeyer began a new revision, some of which was typed by his daughter before she eloped in July, 1894. He continued to make alterations. Finally he decided to add extensive notes. In this manner he continued until 1902, but at his death in 1906 he remained still dissatisfied with his work.[92]

What is more important than the fate of Brokmeyer's translation is that what Brokmeyer gave his associates was accurate, however literal and crabbed in style. It was no attempted restatement or popularization of Hegel in Brokmeyer's terms, as was Coleridge's exegesis of Kant and Schelling. It was Hegel as nearly as Brokmeyer could render him in English. Of equal importance is the fact that a number of copies were in circulation. Harris carried one (or several) with him to Concord and later to Washington.[93] Samuel Emery and Edward McClure showed up with another copy (in three bound volumes) at the Concord summer sessions. What the precise influence of Brokmeyer's translation may have been upon the younger, or for that matter on the older, generation of Transcendentalists who partook of the philosophical repasts in Concord during the eighties remains largely conjectural; but it is safe to say that the influence, impossible as it is today to trace the various journeyings of the several manuscripts, was pervasive. But Brokmeyer's most notable achievement lay in his inspiring Harris to promulgate Hegelianism far and wide. He kept the Society together for some years longer, at least until 1880, when he went to Concord. The twenty-two volumes of his philosophical

Journal, his position as the virtual head of the Concord School, and later his influential career as U.S. Commissioner of Education, together with his half-thousand books, articles, and addresses, spread Hegelianism into all the departments of life—public and private—that his multiform activities touched.

Harris and the *Journal of Speculative Philosophy*

The development of Harris' philosophic personality began in a prolonged, almost quixotic, search, for which he found little help in the formal educational facilities of his native New England. Following a preparatory-school education that included a year each in five academies, he entered Yale; but his peripatetic training, his restlessness, and his dissatisfaction with the college curriculum (which did not satisfy his impatience to study the "three moderns—modern science, modern literature, and modern history") caused him to leave in the middle of his junior year for the West in pursuit of vaguely defined goals of self-realization.[94] Several years earlier he had encountered Emerson's essays and, like other young men of his generation, taken to heart, as confirmatory evidence of his own vague convictions and aspirations, Emerson's advice to oppose formalism, authority, and orthodoxy. His revolution became complete when he met Alcott, who came to New Haven to hold "Conversations" during the first two weeks of March, 1857. Alcott disabused his mind of the phrenological psychology and convinced him of the "doctrine of pre-existence and of the primordial power of the soul." In Alcott he saw Idealism personified—"a living commanding personality" illustrating "the supremacy of the soul and the ideality of the material world." This he later called his "Aufklärung," his progression from an epoch of "negation" to "the attitude of insight and reliance on reason." Alcott saved him from the worst vagaries of spiritualism and led him upon his *Lehrjahre*, as he later came to think of his development in terms of Wilhelm Meister's *Lehrjahre, Wanderjahre*, and *Meisterschaft*.[95]

Soon after Harris showed up in St. Louis in 1857, ostensibly to teach the new Pitman shorthand in the Franklin School, he found himself teaching a half-dozen subjects besides and serving also as assistant principal. Promotions followed rapidly: he became principal of the Clay School in 1858, assistant superintendent of the city school system in 1867, and superintendent a year later—a position which he held until 1880, when he left St. Louis for Concord. These cumulative responsibilities soon made of the young man a solid citizen, nonetheless eager than formerly to learn but less given to chasing will-o'-the-wisps.

During his first year in St. Louis he read "an eloquent essay by Theodore Parker on German literature" which spoke of the high "German achievements in philology and history, in theology and philosophy" and of the ascent of "four philosophical lights—Kant, Fichte, Schelling, and Hegel." About the same time, he discovered *Wilhelm Meister*, a book that turned him from "books of protest" to "constructive books." "On the frontier," he observed, "man becomes a builder of civilization and has no time to criticize it." He took to heart the lesson he saw running "like a continuous thread" through *Wilhelm Meister*—Goethe's gospel of culture, "finally culminating in the nobler aim of building up the institutions of humanity."[96] The better to prepare for his *Lehrjahre*, he turned back to philosophy. He recalled Parker's recommendation of Kant, Fichte, Schelling, and Hegel. Brokmeyer, who had just then come into Harris' orbit, enthusiastically seconded the recommendation.

Harris was twenty-three when, in 1858, he chanced to meet Brokmeyer, then an iron-worker, at a meeting in the old Mercantile Library, where the conversation turned upon theosophy, mesmerism, and phrenology—from the toils of which Harris had just extricated himself. Brokmeyer singled out Harris as the one sane person in the assemblage, accosted him on leaving, engaged him in talk, and began to question him as they walked along. When the name of Cousin, one of Harris' late divinities, came up, Brokmeyer undertook to show his companion that the French eclectic "contradicted himself on every page," and to make the demonstration, he went with Harris to his quarters. "This," says Brokmeyer, "was the beginning of our friendship, and the nucleus of the group of students who soon gathered together." This is also the beginning of the first Kant class in America, the inspiration of the first American translations of Fichte and Schelling, and the initiation of the first systematic study of Hegel in America.[97]

Harris had possessed a copy of Kant's first *Kritik* since 1857. When the new preceptor appeared, he had already spent a year making "repeated attacks upon the work, reading a few pages at a time and turning back to the beginning again," only to find Kant's style "so difficult" that he "did not seem to understand one page of it all." He professed not to be "particularly discouraged by all this," because he found, to his great delight, that he was acquiring "a power of reading other works which formerly had been very heavy and dull." However, under Brokmeyer's tutelage, he broke through the shell and began to reach the kernel of Kant's critical philosophy. This experience he interpreted as forming "a real epoch" in his life.[98]

By 1859 Harris felt himself prepared to grapple with Fichte, Schelling, and Hegel. Fichte and Hegel at first proved much harder to follow in their systematic expositions than anything he had encountered in Kant. Fichte he soon relegated to a second, and Schelling to a third, place after Hegel, in two of whose books he found all he wanted at the time and more than he could digest. These were the *Wissenschaft der Logik* and *Philosophie der Geschichte*—"the two works of Hegel," he said in 1887, "that made and still make on me a deeper impression than all other books." Of the former he could make little before 1866, when Brokmeyer returned from the war and resumed his tutorship; with the latter he had better success because he saw the immediacy of its political application to the war-torn era in which he lived. Meanwhile the main lines of his thinking during the war years seem to have been worked out by himself:

In 1863 I arrived at the insight which Hegel has expressed in his *Für-sich-seyn* or Being-for-itself, which I called and still call 'independent being.' I did not obtain this insight by study of Hegel's logic, however, but rather by following out the lines of thought begun in 1858.

The next year he arrived at "an insight into the logical subordination of fate to freedom": the idea that the totality of conditions cannot have a fate outside it, but must be spontaneous in itself and self-determined; and hence that all fate and all changes not spontaneous must be secondary and derivative from a higher source that is free.[99]

Harris defined philosophy from the epistemological point of view as a science that aims to discover the first principles by the intellect. Lest such a philosophy be considered abstract, he repeatedly iterates his contention that "the test of any system of philosophy is the account it gives of the institutions of civilization," whence it follows, because Hegel "is pre-eminently the thinker that explains and justifies institutions," that Hegel is the guide to be hearkened to.[100] But "thought alone," he concluded, "makes life valuable, and has power to protect and preserve us."[101] Thus he held firmly to the conviction of the idealist that spiritual life determines the material, and accepted Kant's *a priori* possessions of the mind as conditioning the world. Time and

Space are two of these possessions, the necessary presuppositions of the extension and multiplicity of objects. But a deeper principle than space and time is Causality. It is their logical condition. "Causality implies both Time and Space . . . [which] are in a certain sense included in causality as a higher unity." The principle of causality is as "deep and logical a condition of experience as . . . time and space are themselves." No act of experience is complete without all three.[102]

In any series of causes we see each cause presupposing a preceding cause; but a real cause requires no cause behind it. It is independent, absolute, self-caused. Hence there is Cause and Self-Cause;[103] that is, there are two classes of beings in the world —dependent and independent.[104] The latter are their own causality; they are free and morally responsible, endowed with causal energy, hence with power to build themselves. While they are not *fully realized*, they are *potentially realizable*. The presupposition of man as a developing free and independent individual is "the perfect individuality of the Absolute Reason, or God."[105]

Self-Cause, or Self-Activity, had many stages or degrees of realization, depending on the use made of sensation, understanding, and reason. Harris proceeds, in Kantian terms, to distinguish among (1) men of "common sense," who see the world as a number of real and independent objects,[106] (2) men of understanding (or reflection), to whom relativity is the highest category of thought,[107] and (3) men of pure reason, who represent the highest manifestation of self-activity in man.[108] Upon this "psychologic system" as outlined in some detail in his *Psychologic Foundations of Education*,[109] Harris proceeds to construct his views on freedom, immortality, and God.[110] The multiform applications and implications of these premises, together with the extent of his reliance upon Kant, Fichte, Schelling and most notably, Hegel, are beyond the possibility of representation here. This object had been satisfactorily achieved by the ingenious and meticulous work of Marietta Kies in her *Introduction to the Study of Philosophy Comprising Passages from his* [W. T. Harris'] *Writings* (New York, 1889), which comprises quoted passages from his writings, selected and arranged, with commentary and illustrations (with Harris' "full consent and approval"), in a very logical order.

Lest Harris be regarded as an American mouthpiece of Hegel, a mere echo of German philosophy, sight must not be lost of his assertion in 1868 (repeated many times thereafter) that what was wanted was not "American *thought* as much as American thinkers."[111] However much he derived from Hegel, his concern with Plato, Aristotle, Leibnitz, Kant, Fichte, and Schelling,[112] as well as with the oriental philosophers,[113] is not to be minimized in the development of his philosophic individuality.

His interest in oriental thought, by which he meant Indian philosophy, antedated by two years his acquaintance with Hegel, but he did not attain real familiarity with it until 1861. He had only a slight knowledge of Sanskrit, but provided himself with the best translations available.[114] By the time he launched the *Journal*, he was as apt to insert a discussion of Vedantic or Buddhistic concepts into an article on kindergarten methods as into an outline of the history of philosophy or, later, into a government report on educational procedure.[115] But he remained too uncompromisingly American and Christian to admit the validity of the fundamental ideas of Indian philosophy. Individual oriental concepts appealed to him, and he recognized the value of Hindu thought for western culture, but on the whole he interpreted it as abstractionism or nihilism.[116] Dedicated to a progressive and enterprising America, he could not accept what he deemed an essentially negative or static creed. Schooled as he was in Hegelian dialectics, he found

in it the contrasts and opposites to American ideas that moved his dialectical thought processes.

Harris' unbounded faith in the verbal inspiration of gospel truth according to Hegel and his eagerness to lead his friends to the same glimpses of rarefied pure thought that he was experiencing about the time of the end of the Civil War, and which significantly coincided with Brokmeyer's return to St. Louis, led to the formation of the Philosophical Society in January, 1866. Snider, who had come to St. Louis the year before, found Harris already possessed of Hegel's works in the original and bent on forming an "inner group who might become agitators and promulgators." Always methodical, Harris made the rounds, helped them with their studies, and kept them at their tasks.[117] For himself, he set to the severe task of copying Brokmeyer's translation of the *Logic*, correcting it, and preparing a draft for publication when the opportunity should arise.

The matter of publication presented difficulties. None knew it better than Harris. He never acquired a nice ear for style; he could write clearly, but never with the distinction of a stylist. His best efforts —represented at this time by an essay in which he attacked the "materialism" and "agnosticism" of Herbert Spencer—had come back to him repeatedly, most recently from the *North American Review*, together with a critical letter from the co-editor, Charles Eliot Norton. The refusal of this article provided the last or direct impetus that called into being the *Journal of Speculative Philosophy*. Although Brokmeyer had earlier suggested the idea of a periodical, and Harris himself had consulted Alcott and Emerson on the advisability of founding a "Speculative Journal," nothing had come of it, except that Harris had kept the plan in mind. Shortly after receiving Norton's rebuff, he brought with him to one of the meetings of the Society a tin box, which he deposited with the declaration: "We are going to have a German philosophical magazine." When Howison asked who was going to supply the necessary money, Harris replied, "We don't propose to print it. We are going to make papers and read them here, and put them away in this tin box." Then he proceeded to read Norton's letter to the group assembled in Brokmeyer's office, stopping to make "sarcastic comments which made all laugh." The reading concluded, he "jumped up, clenched his fist and brought it down defiantly upon the empty air, saying, 'Now I am going to start a Journal myself.' This he did at once [and] the first number appeared in January, 1867,"[118] the condemned article on Spencer leading others resurrected from the little tin box, among them also Brokmeyer's "Letters on Faust."[119]

The historian of the St. Louis Movement suggested in the title of his book the relative importance of philosophy, literature, education, and art, in the order named. The following analysis of the contents of the 9,254 pages comprising the twenty-two volumes of the *Journal* substantiates this rating and indicates that the *Journal* is a faithful mirror of the movement.

PHILOSOPHY: *Total pages, 7,411*

TRANSLATIONS, HISTORY, CRITICISM: 5,632 *pages*

ANCIENT PHILOSOPHY: 308 *pages*

Trismegistus	83
Sanhyka Karika	4
Zoroaster	11
Parmenides	16
Plato	86
Aristotle	81
Porphyry	28

MEDIEVAL PHILOSOPHY: 56 *pages*

Bonaventura	36
Aquinas	20

MODERN PHILOSOPHY: 4,278 *pages*

French: 146 *pages*

Descartes	91
Lachelier	55

Philosophy: Modern, (continued)

Dutch: Spinoza — 60

German: 3,400 *pages*

Leibnitz		127
Kant		938
Fichte		401
Schelling		133
Hegel		1,244
Goeschel		159
Schopenhauer		136
Minor figures		218
Baeder	2	
Bayrhoffer	19	
Delff	12	
Herbart	49	
Jacobi	10	
Lambert	12	
Lotze	14	
Michelet	22	
Noire	18	
Preyer	30	
Scheffler	7	
Zeller	15	
General Essay		44

English: 501 *pages*

Berkeley		42
Spencer		117
Bradley		70
Buckle		64
Minor figures		104
Boole	11	
DeMorgan	9	
Green	19	
Martineau, J.	32	
Oliphant	23	
Tyndall	10	

American: 45 *pages*

Edwards	21
Emerson	8
Alcott	4
James, Henry, Sr.	8
James, Wm.	4

Polish: Trentowski — 52

Swedish: Swedenborg — 42

Italian: Rosmini — 22

PHILOSOPHY OF SCIENCE: 122 *pages*

General	81
Darwin	41

PHILOSOPHY OF MATHEMATICS: 58 *pages*

Philosophy, Modern, (continued)

EDITORIALS, COMMENTS, ETC.: 820 *pages*

Correspondence, notes, discussion	460
Book notices	169
Book reviews[120]	190

ORIGINAL SPECULATION:[121] 1,779 *pages*

Abbott, Francis	14
Alcott, A. B.	62
Anderson, Jos. G.	12
Bayrhoffer, C. T.	13
Blood, Benj. P.	53
Boulting, Wm.	10
Brinton, D. G.	3
Burns-Gibson, J.	10
Cabot, J. E.	12
Caird, Edward	19
Day, H. N.	33
D'Orielli, A.	7
Dewey, John	20
Eliot, J. E.	6
Fullerton, Geo. S.	30
Gulliver, Julia S.	15
Hall, G. Stanley	6
Halsted, Geo. B.	7
Harris, W. T.[122]	229
Hazard, R. G.	22
Hebbard, S. S.	38
Henkle, W. D.	19
Henry, Francis A.	128
Hickok, Laurens P.	8
Hodgson, S. H.	20
Holland, R. A.	50
James, William	96
Jones, Hiram K.	65
Kapp, Ernest	11
Kimball, Wm, H.	76
(*pseud.* Theron Gray)	
Kroeger, A. E.	7
Lutoslawski, W.	5
Morgan, H. H.	7
Mitchell, Ellen M.	8
Patten, Simon N.	10
Peabody, Eliz. P.	19
Peirce, C. S.	45
Randolph, Richard	11
Rigg, J. M.	16
Salter, W. M.	31
Sewall, May W.	12
Sheldon, W. L.	14
Spence, Payton	83
Stearns, F. P.	9
Stirling, James H.	79
Thompson, John C.	17
Tuthill, Meeds	106
Vera, A.	100
Ward, James	31

Philosophy: Modern, Original Speculation (continued)

Watson, John	40
Weiss, John	19
Woerner, J. G.	13
Anonymous	3

LITERATURE: *Total pages,* 1,178

CRITICISM AND HISTORY: 1,066 *pages*

Homer	115
Bion	8
Dante	222
Shakespeare	286
Milton	4
Coleridge	12
Shelley	68
Goethe	323
Schiller	20
Turgenieff	8

ORIGINAL VERSE: 112 *pages*

EDUCATION (includes Educational Psychology):[123] *Total pages,* 281

ART: *Total pages,* 229

ARTISTS: 82 *pages*

Leonardo da Vinci	9
Michael Angelo	27
Raphael	28
Turner	18

HISTORY OF ART: 58 *pages*

CRITICISM: 89 *pages*

Grimm, Herman	82
Winckelmann	7

MUSIC: *Total pages,* 67

COMPOSERS: 30 *pages*

Beethoven	18
Mendelssohn	6
Schumann	6

HISTORY AND CRITICISM: 37 *pages*

MISCELLANEOUS: *Total pages,* 88

Sanskrit	5
Grammar	14
Japanese Character	43
Library Science	
(classification of books)	14
Friendship, Essay on	11

Thus, the 9,254 pages classified are distributed as follows:

Philosophy	7,411 pages, or	80.1%
Literature	1,178	12.7
Education	281	3.0
Art	229	2.5
Music	67	.7
Miscellaneous	88	.9

That the *Journal* would devote more space to German philosophy than to any other is to be expected. The 4,576 pages[124] devoted to translations from or the history and criticism of philosophical writings are distributed as follows:

German	3,400 pages, or	74.3%
English	501	10.9
Ancient	308	6.7
French	146	3.2
Dutch	60	1.3
Polish	52	1.1
American	45	1.0
Swedish	42	0.9
Italian	22	0.5

Among the Germans, Hegel, of course, gets the greater share of attention. A further breaking down of the 3,400 pages devoted to German philosophers shows the following distribution:

Hegel	1,244 pages, or	36.6%
Kant	932	27.6
Fichte	401	11.8
Goeschel	159	4.7
Schopenhauer	136	4.0
Schelling	133	4.0
Leibnitz	127	3.7
All others[125]	262	7.7

Several observations are in order. First, while Hegel, Fichte, Kant, and Schelling among the transcendentalists were of prime interest, the concern was not merely with these four; thirteen lesser figures received enough attention to justify the conclusion that the St. Louis philosophers read not only deeply in a few German critical transcendentel philosophers but also widely among their disciples and commentators.

Second, the remarkable interest in Goeschel is not as odd as it may appear when it is recalled that Goeschel among the post-Hegelians led those who sought to connect the theistic idea of God with the Hegelian concept of divinity.[126]

Third, the 127 pages devoted to Leibnitz indicate a real interest in the author of the *Monadology*, represented particularly by translations made by F. H. Hedge and A. E. Kroeger, which seek to demonstrate that "God alone is the primitive unity," the "Pre-established Harmony."[127]

Fourth, the extraordinary concern of Brokmeyer's men with Schopenhauer, while never intense, was reasonably well sustained—much more so, for instance, than concern with Spencer, the other of their chief aversions among nineteenth-century thinkers. Schopenhauer is represented by translations or discussions in 1867, 1871, 1874, 1875, 1877, 1879, and 1883. J. H. Stirling's fifty-page article on Schopenhauer's relation to Kant—so severe as to be just short of scurrilous in its attack—was used by Harris as the leading article in the 1879 volume. The inference is inescapable that Schopenhauer was read mainly to be refuted.[128]

Fifth, Kant throughout is praised as having established the basis upon which Hegel was able to make his supreme synthesis. Represented by 938 pages in the *Journal* (123 of which represent A. E. Kroeger's translations from the *Metaphysics of Rights* and *Prolegomena* and the entire *Anthropology*), Kant attracted more attention and from a greater number of students than any philosopher save Hegel.

It is easy to overemphasize the uniformity in point of view and purpose of the *Journal*. One of the greatest services performed by Harris for the future of American philosophy was that his periodical became the outlet for many of the younger generation of philosophers to air their views. G. Stanley Hall, G. H. Howison, George S. Morris, Charles S. Peirce, William James, Josiah Royce, and John Dewey, already developing divergent tendencies, nevertheless found in Harris and his *Journal* both patron and patronage.

Harris' influential career as an educator belongs to the history of education in the United States.[129] His educational philosophy appears in broad outline in the studies of John S. Roberts and Merle Curti.[130] As U.S. Commissioner of Education, his greatest achievement was the organization of the American public school system into a unit. He did his work so well that, as Nicholas Murray Butler remarked in 1929, his service is already almost forgotten. The fixed and absolute principles upon which he proceeded in his organization, correlation, and conservation of educational forces in the United States were destined eventually to fall before the onslaughts of the New Education. The first indication that his dogma of formal discipline and educational principles of Hegelian absolutism were under fire as early as 1895 is Dr. B. A. Hinsdale's epoch-making paper read before the National Council of Education at Asbury Park. The following year at Cleveland, before the Department of Superintendence, Charles DeGarmo and the two McMurrays bounded into the arena with new weapons drawn from the armory of Herbart and Rein of Jena to debate the really great paper of Dr. Harris on the Hegelian Correlation of Studies. There came a time when G. Stanley Hall, with his brilliant platform method, preached eloquently the gospel of a wholly different psychology from that taught by Harris; and eventually the forces of James, Dewey, *et al.* overwhelmed Hegelian absolutism in American education, leaving only a few die-hards like President Butler to proclaim Harris "the one truly philosophical mind which has yet appeared in the western continent," and to assert, all appearances to the contrary, that the spirit of Harris still marches on.

Harris' participation in the Concord School of Philosophy is reserved for discussion later. We turn now to Snider, the last of the triumvirate.

Snider and the Literary Schools

As Brokmeyer was the philosopher of the St. Louis Movement, and Harris its educator, so Denton J. Snider was its litterateur, though, like the others, he was much in evidence in other fields besides. All three alike had nothing but disgust for narrow specialization; yet each followed his own bent—pursued, as Snider put it, his "Super-Vocation." Through Snider's literary and educational efforts many people became interested in Great Books, notably those of Homer, Dante, Shakespeare, and Goethe. In the prosecution of his purposes he wrote fifty books, conducted many classes, and gained a following that expressed its appreciation by forming in his name an association for universal culture and by making, as late as 1936, an annual pilgrimage to his grave.

Nurtured as Snider had been in the tight little Puritanic community of Oberlin College, he was hardly prepared for the catholicity of thought and action that he found among the St. Louisans when he first came among them. In his autobiography he described his herculean efforts "to master abstract Thought." When he finally achieved what he called a "disentanglement from that vortical labyrinth of ever-spinning and interlacing triplets of categories" and felt that he could spin them better than they could spin him, he terminated his epoch of concentrated "acquisition" and turned his whole-hearted attention to "creation." Freely acknowledging that Hegel "graved" upon him "certain life lines," of which he remained acutely conscious, he nevertheless followed henceforth his super-vocation as "a Writer of Books."[131]

He took the first step in 1872 when he printed in the *Inland Magazine* his youthful poetical drama, *Clarence*. To earn a livelihood, he had become a teacher of philosophy in the high school in which Morgan was the principal and over which Harris presided as superintendent.[132] During the latter years of his "decennium" in the high school (1867–1877) he added to his already remarkably comprehensive program a course in Shakespeare for seniors. To this ambitious regimen of teaching he devoted himself wholeheartedly until administrative work, in the form of an assistant superintendency, threatened to divert him from the main business; then he threw up a promising educational career to return to his beloved books.[133]

In the meantime two conceptions, "twinned in origin yet different in character," had been crystallizing in his mind. His ruminations on Hegel's political theory and on the Hegelian aesthetic had resulted in series of essays (beginning about 1871) on the American state and on Shakespeare. A half-century later, as he looked back upon these early literary efforts, he still saw the fundamentally unifying conception that resulted in these two so apparently disparate books: *The American State* and *The System of the Shakespearean Drama*.

The deepest and most distinctive thing in them . . . was my persistent effort to grasp the World-Spirit . . . Philosophically I had wrestled with the pure Idea of it for years, all the way from Plato to Hegel . . . and to unfold it as the ultimate vital factor in our American political system. . . . At the same psychological moment . . . was born the imperative push to trace this elusive but super-eminent World-Spirit, the presiding Genius of History, in Great Literature, especially in Greatest Shakespeare, who must have the highest if he be the highest.[134]

The American State was inspired by the discussions held by the St. Louis philosophers as they contemplated the results of the struggle that had been occasioned by "the attempt of the Single-State to destroy the Union." Although they had fought for the Union and had rejoiced in the victory, "now a few years' turn brought just the opposite danger: the victorious Union, grown insolent in its triumph, was threatening to undo the Single-State, by which

deed, if successful, it would simply undo itself." This whole subject, says Snider, "I threshed over to the limit of my powers." The result was a series of essays, first published in *The Western* and afterwards collected in a booklet, in which a theory of the state is unfolded on strictly Hegelian terms.[135]

But by now Snider was getting weary of his too "excessive immersion in Hegel." Moreover, philosophy had delivered its message, or as much of it as he could assimilate. He longed for a new intellectual exercise that might afford a new expression of himself and of the universe, "less abstract, more living and concrete." When he was asked to add Shakespeare to his courses of instruction, he says, "I seized with all my might the opportunity to change my masters . . . to pass from Hegel the philosopher to Shakespeare the poet."[136] But he had been too long organizing "all branches fo instruction upon a basic principle of the Hegelian philosophy"[137] to break away at once and altogether:

It must not be thought that I flung away philosophy entirely and forever; I could not. On the contrary, I took it over with me into Shakespeare, who also has his philosophic substrate . . . I hold that he would not be the supreme poet that he is unless he were in his way at the same time the supreme philosopher. Thus in my case my Hegel was the forecast and the preparation for my Shakespeare.[138]

The first play which he undertook to study with his pupils was *Julius Caesar*. In it he immediately recognized Shakespeare "grappling with the loftiest world-historical character of all time at one of History's supreme nodes." In it he saw Shakespeare's "sublimest, his most ideal conception and characterization, that of the World-Spirit itself, the immortal soul of History, incarnate in a poor mortal, who sinks to death in its conflict."[139] Snider's analysis of *Julius Caesar*, first published in the *Journal* for July, 1872, is sufficiently Hegelian to satisfy the most devout disciple: all the forces in the play are brought to stand in typical Hegelian thesis-antithesis-synthesis relationship to each other. The play is interpreted in three "moments," each incarnate in one of the three leading characters: Cassius representing the political, Brutus the moral, and Caesar the world-historical point of view. The struggle presents "a complete cyclus of characterization." In stabbing Caesar, Cassius and Brutus triumph momentarily, but thesis and antithesis serve only to negate each other, and in the end the synthesis is effected: for though Caesar is slain, the Caesarian movement is vindicated in the triumph of Anthony.[140]

In like manner Snider continued to publish his analyses of nine more of Shakespeare's plays in the next five volumes of the *Journal*.[141] In each of them appears the familiar three-fold movement. The neatness with which the individual plays fell into this mold led him to "a very thorough study of Hegel's three large volumes of Aesthetic," and that, in turn, inspired him to search for the key to the Shakespearean pattern or system—"to organize them [the Shakespearean plays] internally and then unite them externally into groups according to what seemed to me their deepest principle." This is the idea that was to result in his two-volume *System of Shakespearean Drama* (1877).[142]

By now the love of systematizing had a secure hold in Snider. His autobiography explains how this propensity led him next to consider *Faust*, which Brokmeyer declared to be the world's greatest poem, and which Snider now felt needed "reconstructing" upon what he had come to believe "a complete standard of interpreting a world poem."[143]

Shakespeare to my mind could not help calling up his fellow-giants of the World's Literature, of whom I then had begun to see the huge outlines of three more— Homer, Dante, Goethe. . . . I felt myself unprepared for this Gigantomachia . . . .

At first I skulked out of the fight, but I could not escape the ever-haunting idea. I must go to Europe and there speak and hear spoken the mother-tongue of Italian Dante and even of old Greek Homer.[144]

After his European journey (1877–1879), which took him to England, Germany, Italy, and Greece (the homes of his four poet-gods), the remaining three parts of his grand commentary on the "four Bibles" dutifully appeared: Goethe's *Faust* (2 vols., 1886), Dante's *Divine Comedy* (3 vols., 1892–1893), and Homer's *Iliad* and *Odyssey* (2 vols., 1895–1897). All of them are animated by what Snider calls "my ideal lifelong friend, the World-Spirit," the systematizing and unifying principle by which he sought to synthesize the universe. All of them bear the mark of the Hegelian dialectic. Together, they represent the most unique, if not the most profound, case of literary influence exerted by Hegel in America.

The man of the twentieth century smiles indulgently at Snider's confessed ambition to become the "organizer of the thought-world,"[145] and the modern literary critic takes philosophically Snider's "philosophic" method of pressing the world's great poems into Hegelian categories. He finds the involved analogies, sweeping generalizations, and cosmic symbolisms, couched as they often are in ornate, rhetorical terms, overdone. But even where Snider's style becomes prolix and his argument sinuous, as they do, for example, when he endeavors to point the analogy between *Faust* (especially in Part II[146]) and the dialectical movement of Hegel's logic, there remains no doubt about his ability as a dialectician or his enthusiastic and sympathetic critical faculty. All in all, his commentaries on the "Literary Bibles" form, whatever else they may or may not be, the most ambitious attempt made in America to organize and explain, from one consistent philosophic point of view, the works of four of the greatest writers the world has known.

While vigorously prosecuting his own several educational ventures, Snider also participated in five of the nine Concord programs by lecturing like an Hegelian on Shakespeare, Homer,[147] and Goethe,[148] but refusing "to spout pure Hegel,"[149] and trying to avoid all involvement in the factions engendered by Harris' Hegelianism, Jones's Platonism, Davidson's Aristotelianism, and James's Pragmatism. From the first he deplored the great emphasis placed on philosophy in the Concord School. He felt that Harris' "heaviest philosophic bombardment," however profound, was neither what was most wanted nor what was best suited to the capacities of the students. When, about 1885–1886, the School turned its attention to Goethe and Dante, it pleased him to think that his lectures on Shakespeare and Goethe had been partly responsible for turning the emphasis from metaphysics to literature.[150]

Aside from his participation in the Concord School, Snider was active, during the remainder of his diversified career, mainly in three directions: (1) in supporting the kindergarten movement, (2) in the formation of "communal universities," and (3) in the creation of what he called a "psychological renaissance."

That he should have become ambitious to create "communal universities" was a natural outgrowth of circumstances that followed upon his return from Europe in 1879. With Brokmeyer away in Oklahoma and Harris in Concord, the several currents and eddies in and about St. Louis flowed around Snider. He directed his first efforts toward the establishment of the "home-grown university" in the West, to be kept distinct from the Europeanized American university.[151] Soon the small, informal groups grew in size and number so that before long he had classes going simultaneously in all the four Bibles. His journeyings to the East to participate in the Concord sessions spread his reputation, taught him something about the organization of schools, and encouraged him to spread the gospel according to Homer, Dante, Shakespeare, and Goethe.

The first venture in which he participated as more than a mere lecturer was the Goethe School in Milwaukee in August, 1886, immediately after the conclusion of the Concord session devoted to Dante. While this school was engineered mainly by residents of Milwaukee, it fell to the lot of Harris and Snider jointly to arrange the program. It was decided to reassemble the great triumvirate—"Harris from the far East, Brokmeyer from the far West, and Snider from the Midland somewhere between."[152] Harris was enthusiastic. He saw in the Milwaukee Goethe School an opportunity to extend the influence of the Concord School into the West.[153] Snider looked upon it as an opportunity to effect the return of Harris to the West, where, in Snider's opinion, lay the best opportunity for striking an effective blow for Hegelian idealism. Brokmeyer, too, signalized his enthusiasm by his ready acceptance of the invitation. But it turned out that the decision to have Brokmeyer was ill-advised. His behavior was little short of outrageous.[154] He delivered his address in *Faust* with "a backwoods informality of speech and manner which stamped him at once as aboriginal, if not original," and he interlarded his remarks with Creek-Indian expressions which he claimed had no English equivalents. Worst of all, in view of his former glorification of *Faust* as the world's sublimest poem and in consideration of his Goethe-worshipping audience, he turned *Faust* upside down by interpreting the life of "the ever-striving Faust" as leading to an utterly "negative outcome." He appeared to take a kind of sardonic pleasure in turning "a very unconventional somersault right in the presence of fastidious Lady Convention herself"—though, in Snider's estimation, his unconventionality was not as painful as his repudiation of *Faust*. The latter symbolized for Snider "a kind of Adam's fall of the man whom I loved." Only Harris' masterful tact kept the Milwaukee School together and brought it to a successful conclusion. Neither Harris nor Snider could account for Brokmeyer's unseemly conduct, but they were in complete accord on two points: (1) "Milwaukee, in spite of the city's loyal and generous co-operation, had to be given up, though the same management talked of having another session the following year," and (2) Brokmeyer could not be invited again. Not that Brokmeyer cared; he had come to prefer Indian society to either a literary circle in Milwaukee or a philosophical school in Concord.

Snider, for his part, resolved upon four additional points: (1) the Literary School must go on in the West, for even under bad local handling and Brokmeyer's bombshell, the Milwaukee experience had proved that "it could not only live but thrive in the West"—thrive to the point of paying the lecturers double and treble as much as had ever been possible at Concord; (2) henceforth he would "take the Literary School into his own hands, especially as regards program, lectures, and the conduct of exercises," for a local committee could be trusted only with such matters as finance, attendance, and procurement of halls; (3) Harris must be secured as his "main prop" in all future schools; and (4) since Homer, Dante, Shakespeare, and Goethe are "a sort of breviary of all lettered excellence, veritably the central Organon of all Literature," the Literary School must be built closely around these central figures.[155]

These resolutions bore good fruit, and as the sequel proves, Snider exercised good judgment in seeking to evolve out of the philosophical school of the East (then already showing signs of decline) the literary school of the West.[156] Between 1884 and 1897, a period which Snider reckoned the busiest of his life, and which he called his "Epoch of Propagation,"[157] he ranged from Boston, New York, and Washington along the Atlantic Coast to Omaha and Minneapolis in the West. In Ohio, his native state, he appeared in three cities—Cleveland, Columbus, and Cincinnati;[158] but Oberlin, his Alma Mater, steadfastly refused to invite this evangelist of the new Bibles, until 1894, when she conferred "upon her greatest scholar"[159] the honorary doctorate. Mason and Dixon's old line, too, was tightly drawn against him, and he never penetrated deeper into the South than Baltimore on the eastern and Omaha on the western borderland.[160] But it was no longer St. Louis that held him: the old ties were all broken, his former colleagues had gone, and the Future Great City of the World seemed to him, in 1885, only a husk of her former enterprising self.

In the autumn of 1884 he gave his first course of lectures in Chicago, on Homer, to a small and miscellaneous audience in a schoolroom. The course was so well received that it ran for five weeks. There followed requests for a number of similar classes on others of the Literary Bibles. Chicago was experiencing a cultural outburst such as he had witnessed in St. Louis twenty years earlier. Seeing that he had staunch friends and promoters, mainly "people who had been either at Concord or at St. Louis" (in the latter case chiefly kindergartners like Elizabeth Harrison, who had studied with Miss Susan Blow), he plunged into the civic and cultural "maelstrom that was Chicago" and adopted it as the "Center of Propagation."[161] Chicago had the great advantage over St. Louis of being nearer to the center of his wider activities, for Illinois and Indiana remained, year after year, his "main seed-fields."[162] Something like a circuit formed itself for him in this territory, with Chicago as the base of operations.

In Chicago itself he had, by 1887, a rather pretentious Dante School in progress in the Art Institute.[163] He made especially elaborate preparations for the Goethe School of 1888. He organized numerous small classes for the study of various ones of Goethe's works, conducted lecture courses for a more general audience, and thus drummed up a clientele.[164] In all this he was ably assisted by his kindergartners, recruited fom St. Louis but also from among native Chicagoans who were becoming enthusiastic about the kindergarten movement. Thus the stage was set for the Goethe School in December, 1888, at the Madison Street Theater. Eight of the lectures were given by Harris, Davidson, and Snider, and one each by Mrs. Caroline K. Sherman (whom Snider called the Margaret Fuller of Chicago) and Professor Calvin Thomas of the University of Michigan.[165] The cycle was completed by a Shakespeare School in 1889 and a Homer School in 1890; then the whole cycle was repeated for the years 1891–92–93–94.[166]

In the meantime news concerning Snider's success in Chicago had got back to St. Louis, and he was invited to return to rouse that city from its "deepest lethargy and benightment of her Great Disillusion."[167] Three schools were held there under Snider's direction and with the assistance of Messrs. Harris, Holland, Soldan, and the Misses Mary E. Beedy and Susan Blow. But the old ardor was gone from the city.

Moreover, Miss Blow, assisted by Mary E. Beedy, Mary C. McCulloch, and other women, left leaderless by the departure of Brokmeyer, Harris, and Snider, had set up an independent cultural movement.[168] Miss Blow had her own ideas. Of a distinguished family, she had already at twenty (when Snider first came to St. Louis) acquired a reputation for erudition, including more than cursory acquaintance with German literature, philosophy, and education. Though her sex disqualified her for membership in the Philosophical Society, she was closely associated with all other activities of the group. Harris selected her as his special lieutenant to propagate the kindergarten in the public-school system of St. Louis. He also instructed her in metaphysics, particularly in

Hegel. She possessed real talent, abundant energy and a flair for organization and leadership.[169]

Miss Blow was not one to welcome the returning males without some mental reservations. She had no intention of surrendering to them her hard-won laurels. But she recognized in Snider a possible ally, bringing to St. Louis a fresh and inspiring message from Hellas. So she invited him to lecture on Sophocles to her advanced class of kindergartners. Having tested him, she engaged him the next year to lecture to the same class on the Greek historians, Herodotus and Thucydides; but she took care, says Snider, that "I was the teacher . . . she was the ruler." It soon developed that Snider was "too heathenish" for her, and she put an end to all further collaboration, thus dashing Snider's hopes of transforming what he called her "Calvinistic Regeneration" into a "Classical Renaissance." Henceforth she was his chief critic and gainsayer whenever he appeared in St. Louis—even to the point of setting up her own classes in Dante to save her fellow-townspeople from the "perversion" of Dante as interpreted by the "heathen backslider" Snider.[170]

While Snider's courses in the Greek historians in 1881 were, in his own opinion, "the culmination of the Greek Renaissance in St. Louis . . . and the beginning of its decline," he returned in several successive years to repeat the Schools held earlier in Chicago—notably in 1887, 1888, and 1889, and once (in 1908) to conduct the St. Louis Communal University on the Literary Bibles. But what he calls "the backflow to St. Louis" of the older generation of leaders was little more than a trickle.[171] Brokmeyer was impossible; Harris was getting ready to go to Washington; and he himself could not make headway against Miss Blow. The movement in the city was in younger hands.

Yet something of real importance for Snider came out of his contacts with Miss

Blow. Through her, he became interested in the kindergarten movement. Though too old himself to become a practical kindergartner, his enthusiasm for the kindergartners and their work carried over into his work in Chicago, where they became his chief stay in supporting his "Schools" and later his "University," while he, in turn, became their teacher. In 1886 he was a "Lecturer" and after 1891 a "Professor" in the Chicago Kindergarten College, established in 1886 at 10 Van Buren Street.

The final phase of Snider's career was a natural outgrowth of his Literary Schools and his Kindergarten College experiences. By 1891 his lectures in the latter institution began to broaden in scope so as to include the Philosophy of Literature, of Art, and of History. In 1894 he added the Philosophy of Psychology; in 1900, the Philosophy of Ethics; and in 1901, the Philosophy of Social Institutions.[172] In 1907, when his official connection with the Chicago Kindergarten College appears to have become nominal (although he continued to give occasional series of lectures there until 1913),[173] he was ready to start his own "University."

Snider's first Communal University was organized in St. Louis in 1908, but it soon shifted to Chicago. In St. Louis, the Communal University was created less, says Snider, by his own initiative than by the co-operative work of Professor Francis E. Cook, president of the Kant Club, and Miss Amelia D. Fruchte, president of the Society of Pedagogy.

The old Pedagogical Society, dating back to Harris' days in St. Louis, had been reorganized upon a plan of University Extension by Professor Wm. M. Bryant, who renamed it the Society of Pedagogy and built up its membership to 1500. Under Miss Fruchte's leadership the Society enrolled more than 2000 members and became one of the largest organizations of its kind in the West. When Snider reappeared among his friends in St. Louis, after his Chicago period, with the slogan "The Psychological Age is dawning," and set about organizing his first Communal University in St. Louis, in 1908, the Society supported him eagerly.[174]

Snider's interest in psychology had been forming slowly through the years since he had taught Hegelian "Mental Philosophy" to a class of seniors during his "high-school decennium." He had kept "in cold storage a pretty full manuscript" of that course. As a reader of the *Journal of Speculative Philosophy* he had become familiar with the name of Wundt, first mentioned in that periodical in 1878. Thereafter psychology had become a subject of some concern in the *Journal*.[175] Most important of all, William James, at Concord in 1883, had confirmed his faith in "the rise of Psychology to the forefront of the New Education."[176] When eventualities proved his faith well founded, Snider was ready.

While on the faculty of the Chicago Kindergarten College, he had already enlarged the scope of his lectures to incorporate psychology and its applications. Through the years he published a series of books that formed what he called a veritable "Psychological Organon." Arranged chronologically, the titles are these:

Psychology and Psychosis. 1896.
The Will and the World, Psychical and Ethical. 1899.
The Life of Frederick Froebel. 1900.
The Psychology of Froebel's Play-Gifts. 1900. (*Froebel's Mother Play-Songs, a Commentary*, had appeared in 1895.)
Social Institutions in Their Origin, Growth and Interconnection, Psychologically Treated. 1901.
The State, Especially the American State, Psychologically Treated. 1902.
Ancient European Philosophy; the History of Greek Philosophy Psychologically Treated. 1903.
Modern European Philosophy; the History of Modern Philosophy Psychologically Treated. 1904.
Feeling Psychologically Treated and Prolegomena to Psychology. 1905.

*Architecture as a Branch of Æsthetic
Psychologically Treated. 1905.
Music and the Fine Arts; a Psychology
of the Æsthetic. 1905.*[177]

In all this there is a recognizable Hegelian
organization and systemization of psychology so as to embrace education, ethics, aesthetics, social and political philosophy, and
even the history of philosophy. Thus, to use
Snider's own words, "the Psychological
Organon had completed itself as a written
work" for the "newborn association of
workers headed by Miss Fruchte and Professor Cook," who would provide readers
and hearers ready to receive the new doctrine.[178]

A beginning had been made in St. Louis
about 1900 by D. H. Harris and his wife,
who first started classes in their home in
psychology as promulgated by Snider's
Psychology and Psychosis (1896) and his *Will
and the World, Psychical and Ethical* (1899).
About 1902, the work was transferred from
Harris to Francis E. Cook, who continued
to instruct classes, at his home, in Snider's
psychological system. When, in 1905,
Snider's *Feeling Psychologically Treated*
became available, it formed a third text.
As the classes grew in size, they were moved
to the Public Library auditorium. When
Snider himself entered upon the scene in
1908, the stage was all set, and all he had
to do was to assume charge. The Communal
University enrolled, says Snider, "150, and
never fell below 100."[179] Snider participated
in several other "universities" and "schools"
in St. Louis after 1908, but their management appears to have been entrusted to
Cook, in programs embodying two-year
courses.[180]

In Chicago Snider had watched the phenomenal rise of the new University of Chicago at the same time that he witnessed the
demise of his Literary Schools. While the
"new university of the Rockefeller millions"
seemed to him "the best medicine for the
time and the place," it also seemed to him
too much like "a complete German univer-

sity, bought somewhat as if it were a valuable European book or picture or piece of
merchandise, with its full equipment of
men, material, and libraries . . . lifted out
of its homesoil . . . and set down in the
West along the Michigan lakeside . . . a
marvelous achievement—but still the hug-
est sudden dose of old-world traditionalism
that was ever administered to any mundane
patient." Feeling that his sustained attack
upon the "mighty fortress of ignorance and
philistinism called Chicago" had had some
share in preparing the cultural climate that
made the new university possible, he rejoiced in its establishment; but he also felt,
in his "autobiographical ego,"[181] that still
another antidote was needed to humanize
"this crude, ephemeral, vortical Chicago."[182]

By 1913, therefore, he had his Communal
University in full swing in Chicago. Most of
its students were recruited from the Kindergarten College, but there were also others
"not in touch with kindergarten work." That
there were some among Snider's students
(not among the kindergartners but among
the seekers of "mental improvement")
whose smiling appreciation on their countenances was no clear indication of real
comprehension within their heads goes without saying. That the adulation paid to the
lecturer, or lecturers, by their students was
often excessive is also clear from the reminiscences left by some of them.[183]   But
there is abundant evidence that Snider
never took himself too seriously, and that
he could have his little joke about himself,
as when he repeated with relish the bit of
badinage, tricked out in Hegelian terminology by a local wit, that he defined a hole
in one's coat as "the partial negation of the
totality of being on-and-around-itself (des
an-und-um sich Seyns)." The conclusion is
inescapable that Snider's Literary Schools
and Communal Universities were more than
literary feasts or philosophical banquets,
and that a good deal of honest work was
done.[184]

His failing health during the early twenties put an end to the Communal Universities, but upon his death in 1925 the Denton J. Snider Association for Universal Culture, an outgrowth of the Communal University, was formed with headquarters in St. Louis. It met regularly every Saturday afternoon at the Cabanne Branch Library and appears to have heard chiefly addresses from members, who followed set programs. As late as 1929, when W. F. Woerner, son of J. Gabriel Woerner, was president, the Association carried forward a program of organized study of Dante and Shakespeare of the type that Snider would have approved.[185]

Related Clubs and Movements in St. Louis

Other members of the St. Louis Movement deserve more attention than they can receive here—notably Thomas Davidson, Johann Gabriel Woerner, A. E. Kroeger, James Kendall Hosmer, William McKendree Bryant, Horace Hills Morgan, Francis E. Cook, Louis (Lewis) James Block, Anna Callender Brackett, Amelia Fruchte, and Susan E. Blow. Some of their activities that have a particular bearing upon Germanic aspects of the movement have already been noted; others will appear in the account that follows of the various clubs, societies, and associations that had connections with the St. Louis Movement in St. Louis, Chicago, Jacksonville, and elsewhere.

The prime mover of club life in St. Louis was Harris. He was especially active among the women, conducting classes on philosophy and on art at the homes of Mrs. Rebecca N. Hazard, Mrs. Beverly Allen, Mrs. Lackland, and others. In this way many of the women, though excluded from membership in the Philosophical Society, were in close touch with whatever agitated the minds of the St. Louis philosophers.

The Kant Club, organized by Harris in 1874, met every Saturday evening alternately in the north and south parts of the city. Francis E. Cook was the first and only president, but Harris, as expositor, interpreter, and inspirer, was the moving spirit. The Club began with the study of Kant; in 1875–1876 it took up to the *Smaller Logic* of Hegel, then the *Phenomenology* (in Brokmeyer's translation), and finally the second volume of the *Larger Logic*. Although Harris left St. Louis in 1880, he returned frequently to present his expositions of Hegel's *Logic* as he completed successive sections of his commentary. The Club flourished until 1887 and became defunct about 1890.[186]

Thomas Davidson, who arrived in St. Louis in 1867, became soon the center of a group who desired to study Plato and Aristotle, and who called themselves the Aristotle Club. It was organized in 1873 by Davidson, then teaching Greek and Latin in the St. Louis schools, as an antidote to what he considered a too-strict addiction of his friends to Hegelian logic. The group included about a dozen young men, none over forty, among them, Harris, Soldan, Pulitzer, C. A. Todd, Dr. D. V. Dean, and George Class.

Often closely associated with these philosophical clubs were several literary groups, the leading spirit behind which came to be Snider.[187] In these organizations the women found their special sphere of activity. Among the more long-lived was the Shakespeare Society, founded in 1870 by Amelia C. Fruchte. Originally a study club, dedicated to a consideration of Snider's Hegelian interpretation of Shakespeare, it became, after Mrs. Adeline Palmier Wagoner took over the management, more and more social in orientation.[188]

The arts were not neglected. Harris' "Musical Evenings," once a week, effected an introduction of classical German music in circles beyond the Germans and German-Americans in St. Louis. Himself a competent amateur, he gathered around him other accomplished performers on the piano, violin, and cello to play "Beethoven, Mozart, Schumann, and Mendelssohn and the entire galaxy of German genius"; but Beethoven, "in trio, quartettes, sonatas, and four-handed renditions," remained the favorite. That they were more than dilettanti in their appreciation and performance of the German masters is apparent in the essays they contributed to the early numbers of the *Journal*.[189]

Related Clubs and Movements Elsewhere

While these multiform activities within the city suggest the St. Louis Movement was local, the truth is that it was ambitious to become national in influence. It remained rooted in St. Louis, but wherever and whenever an occasion arose for a St. Louisan to carry the light into the provinces, east or west, he accepted the challenge. Not one of them was content to be a *Kleinwinkler*; all professed nothing less than a cosmic point of view. And when, in 1921, a commemorative meeting was held on the occasion of Snider's eightieth birthday, Louis J. Block said with justice that to call the movement the St. Louis Movement involved a diminution of its true scope and influence—that the movement belonged "organically and properly to the entire history of philosophic thought in the United States."

Aside from Snider's far-flung operations and Harris' numerous appearances in many cities, there were men resident in other cities and towns who organized philosophical societies of their own that came, in one way or another, eventually within the orbit of the St. Louis Movement.

The most influential of these in the West was the Plato Club founded by Dr. Hiram K. Jones at Jacksonville, Illinois, "The Athens of the West."[190] Jones (1818–1903) was omnipresent in the cultural and literary life of Jacksonville.[191] Already during his college years he had been inspired, by a reading of Emerson, to cultivate the sweet

uses of philosophy. He was led by natural stages from Emerson to Plato; in 1845 he published his *Plato Against the Atheists*, a running commentary on the tenth book of the *Laws*. Throughout the fifties he was busy establishing his practice and studying Plato and Swedenborg, and by 1860 he had won three converts to Plato—Miss Louise Fuller, Mrs. J. O. King, and Mrs. Elizur Wolcott. For five years they met once a week at various homes; in 1865, when Jones's study became the regular meeting place, the Plato Club was formally organized.

After the first influx of new members, recruited from the ranks of local teachers, a second group, also largely teachers, was admitted during the early seventies. These included David H. Harris, brother of W. T. Harris, and Louis J. Block, Superintendent of the Jacksonville Schools, whom Harris, imported to become principal of the high school. "With these two men, particularly with Block, a wave of Hegelian philosophy came in."[192] While their influence was never strong enough for the Hegelian point of view seriously to threaten the supremacy of Plato in the "Athens of the West," they added a leaven that prevented what might, without their influence, have developed into an esoteric Platonism.

As a matter of fact Jones himself was a man who read widely, and who constantly associated Platonic ideas with similar ones in Dante, Shakespeare, Hegel, Goethe, and others, intent upon drawing parallels in Christian, Hindu, Persian, Chinese, Greek, British, and German thought. The Club made no creedal, religious, or racial discriminations, and individual members maintained special preferences and allegiances of their own.

While the Plato Club remained largely a Jacksonville institution, it attracted visitors from such cities as Quincy, Decatur, Bloomington, and Chicago, Illinois; St. Louis and Osceola, Missouri; and Davenport, Iowa. Thomas M. Johnson of Osceola and Horace Hills Morgan, editor of *The Western*, came often; Snider talked to them on Hegel, Shakespeare, and Goethe; Thomas Davidson, on Aristotle; W. T. Harris, on Education and Hegel; and Alcott visited them repeatedly. So it came about that Jones and the Plato Club attained to more than merely local influence even before Jones went to Concord and before the Club began to reach out for a larger sphere of influence through its *Journal of the American Akademe*.

The Concord School, upon which Alcott had ruminated for forty years, became a reality in 1879. Without the encouragement of the flourishing Plato Club in Jacksonville and the Philosophical Society in St. Louis, it would not have materialized.[193] In July 1878, Jones, accompanied by eight or ten of his disciples, spent a fortnight with Alcott in Concord; before they left, it had been decided that the moment was propitious. When the school opened in 1879, its two chief attractions were Jones and Harris, both midwesterners, and S. H. Emery, Jr., leader of the Plato Club in Quincy, became the permanent director.[194]

Jones, a confirmed Platonist, carried on a continuous debate with Harris, equally confirmed in his Hegelianism. After the fourth session, when, according to Snider, Hegel's logic more or less overpowered Jones's less rigorous Platonic intuitionalism, Jones was persuaded by his associates from the West to insist that the School should be held in the West in alternate years. Disappointed when the vote went against them, Jones and his followers started the American Akademe in Jacksonville the following year. Jones never again appeared on any of the Concord programs.

The American Akademe was organized on July 2, 1883, at a meeting where Jones acted as president and Alexander Wilder of Newark, N. J. (whom Jones had met at Concord in 1881) as secretary.[195] While the Akademe found a unifying bond in Plato, it was a school rather than a sect in philosophy. Block, originally inspired by Hegel, often had difficulty squaring his earlier philosophy with his more recently acquired Platonism, and sometimes engaged Jones in disputes of a kind that Jones had found distasteful in Concord. But stout defender of the faith though he was, Jones was not the man to cut off discussion or to maintain a closed mind. Long before the influx of the St. Louis Hegelians—before even the Akademe had been founded—he had caused S. H. Emery, Jr. (who had a copy of Brokmeyer's translation of Hegel's *Logic*) to have a complete transcription of that bulky manuscript made for himself. It may be presumed that he did not pay to have a manuscript of some 2600 legal-cap pages copied without putting it to some use. Moreover, W. T. Harris himself was often on hand to expound Hegel authoritatively.[196]

Dr. Jones's professional practice, his teaching duties at Illinois College, the death of his wife in 1891, and his failing health were among the reasons why he decided, in 1892, that he could no longer shoulder the responsibility for the Akademe and the *Journal*. Another, less tangible but clearly deciding, factor was the naturalistic trend of the age. The Akademe felt its impact first in 1884, when Elizur Wolcott discoursed on "The Theory of Evolution." Although Jones and his stauncher disciples set themselves against this current of thought, Wolcott did not long need to fight single-handedly, and eventually the winds of new nineteenth-century doctrine helped sweep away, before the end of the century, the Akademe as it did the other schools of idealistic thought from St. Louis to Concord, together with their journals.

St. Louis and Jacksonville exerted spheres of influence that often diverged and then drew together again. Thus the St. Louis school projected itself most clearly (1) in the ferment which Snider and his colleagues created in Chicago, (2) in the Hegelian tinge that Harris succeeded in giving to the Concord School, and (3) in the effect that Harris exerted in places like Terre Haute, Indiana, and Kirksville, Missouri, where the normal school movement developed a distinctly Hegelian orientation. The Platonists of Jacksonville inspired smaller but no less enthusiastic groups of disciples in Osceola, Missouri, and Decatur, Bloomington, and Quincy, Illinois. In the Concord School of Philosophy (1879–1888) all the threads converged again.

The school at Osceola, under the leadership of Thomas M. Johnson, appears not to have achieved the closely unified organization that Jones's Akademe attained. Under Johnson's direction the members were less interested in following closely Plato or any other single philosopher than in the historical study of the Platonic and neo-Platonic traditions. Of the club itself little information is available today. Johnson's several publications exist, of course. They yield little to indicate that German philosophy was actively pursued by the Osceola group, so that, for our purposes, Johnson's activities are of interest primarily as part of the general philosophical ferment that was working throughout the body of American thought at the time and helped keep alive the tradition of idealism in America.

Quincy, like Jacksonville, early had a high institutional and educational development.[197] There was enough catholicity of thought and spirit in Quincy for Emerson and Alcott to appear without encountering any annoying hecklers or other untoward experiences.[198] In Quincy, as in Jacksonville, it was the intermittent visits of Emerson and Alcott, coupled with the work of local leaders (in this case Mrs. Sarah Denman and Samuel H. Emery, Jr.) that brought the movement to fruition. Although Emery was destined to become the head of the Quincy movement, back in 1866 he was only twenty-five, so that Mrs. Denman (1802–1882)[199] held the priority by reason of her wider experience and her following in the club life of the little city. By way of im-

plementing and providing organizational support to the feminist movement, she organized, in 1866, the Friends in Council (chartered 1869), one of the first women's clubs in the United States.[200]

In the beginning essentially a reading club, designed to prepare women for their legitimate rights and duties, the original twelve members met weekly for communal readings.[201] After an experimental period of three years, Friends in Council divided (in 1869) to enlarge its membership, while maintaining a maximum of thirty-five members. Along with this enlargement of membership came a diversity of interests. Plato as a sole or primary subject of study was given up for a more varied program, the club being divided into sections according to the interests of the several groups. Plato was never again the main concern except among a group organized by Mrs. Denman especially for the purpose. In the meantime a number of men, chief among whom was Samuel H. Emery, Jr.,[202] took over the philosophical department.

Early in the seventies Emery organized the Plato Club, a less formal organization than Jones's group in Jacksonville.[203] The combined efforts of Mrs. Denman and Dr. Jones (who made frequent and protracted trips to Quincy) were not enough to counteract the steady nourishment which Emery drew from the *Journal of Speculative Philosophy* and particularly from Harris, who maintained that Plato and the Greeks had failed to pursue philosophy as systematically as Hegel. If Emery had had his way, his club would have been called the Hegel Club rather than the Plato Club,[204] but his own feeling of incompetence and the interest of others offset his personal wishes. He bought Hegel's works in the original, but, unable to trust his own ability as a translator, borrowed from Harris the Brokmeyer translation of Hegel's *Logic* and had a copy prepared during 1875. By March, 1878, he had won over Dr. Jones, at whose request another copy was made.[205] When, the next year, Emery and McClure went east to study in the Harvard Law School[206] and to participate in the Concord School, they took their manuscript translation with them, used it to good purpose throughout the Concord sessions, and even sought to indoctrinate Boston and Cambridge by turning philosophical discussion toward Hegel and the idealistic tradition.[207]

The literary productivity of the Quincy group is meager in comparison with that of St. Louis, Concord, or Jacksonville.[208] The departure of Emery and McClure for Concord robbed Quincy of its dominant masculine figures, and Mrs. Denman's death two years later was another blow. When Emery and McClure returned in 1888, philosophy had lost its organizational stability, other interests having usurped its place. The men and women of Quincy had talked and lived philosophy, but they did not write it. Emery served as a link between Quincy and St. Louis, between Quincy and Jacksonville, and between all three and the Concord School, to which we shall turn after considering briefly the several schools instituted by Thomas Davidson in New York State and elsewhere.

Thomas Davidson (1840–1900), Scottish-born and educated, drew inspiration from the "University Brockmeyer" during the mid-sixties, but soon developed tangential interests, professing Aristotle in favor of Hegel,[209] berating modern Christianity while confessing himself a classic heathen, and playing to perfection the part of the *advocatus diaboli*, subsequently turning even upon Greek culture (with what Snider called "damnatory bitterness") in his essay on the Parthenon (London, 1882). Upon leaving St. Louis in 1875, he became, as the London *Spectator* called him, "the last of the Wandering Scholars," primarily interested in Greek and Roman antiquities, but returning often to the United States to take part in the schools held in Concord, Milwaukee, Chicago, and elsewhere.[210]

About 1888 he established, first, at Farmington, Connecticut, a summer school for his pupils; and then another, on a farm in the more remote region of Glenmore in the Adirondacks, near Keane, N.Y. Here, beginning in 1891, he provided for his young East-Siders (and for all cultists who cared to share his lavish hospitality) an extraordinary array of lecturers, including himself, Percival Chubb, Mary C. McCulloch, W. T. Harris, Amelia C. Fruchte (all with St. Louis connections) but also people like Henry N. Gardiner, Josiah Royce, William James, and John Dewey. Thither came, too, Platonists from Osceola and Hegelians from Chicago and several members of the Jacksonville Akademe to spend their vacations and to enjoy "good lectures, choice spirits, delightful conversation, superior wisdom, and a sprinkling of enthusiasts of various cults that gave spice and variety to the entertainment."[211]

Thus were brought together, in remote Glenmore, under the aegis of Aristotelian Tom Davidson, Jews and Gentiles, the Hegelians of St. Louis and the Platonists of Jacksonville, the Transcendentalists of Concord and the professional philosophers of the academic halls. What is more remarkable about all this is the extraordinary forbearance and mutual good will evidenced by all who heard the babble of sense and nonsense and witnessed the display of whim and eccentricity that passed current at Glenmore. Davidson's death in 1900 cut short his elaborate plans to insure the perpetuity of his "beautiful Akademe."

Meanwhile, back in St. Louis, the leadership had devolved on the shoulders of men like Kroeger and Woerner who had their business or profession to attend to, or upon women like Susan E. Blow and Amelia C. Fruchte who, for one reason or another, were unable to take over where Brokmeyer, Harris, and Snider had left off. Thus the Western movement as a movement lost force, even while the individuals who had once formed it went on with unabated vigor to prosecute its work, each one as he happened to conceive it and in whatever locality he found himself.

A gleam of hope that all might yet be saved appeared in the Concord School of Philosophy, and to it all turned about 1880. The Concord School is often rated as the most influential, as it probably was, of the idealistic movements of the late nineteenth century. It is also sometimes considered merely a recrudescence of Platonism on Puritanic soil, or simply a resurrection of earlier New England Transcendentalism. It was more than either, for without the Western Hegelians, the Concord institution could never have got beyond the conceptual stage in Alcott's mind.[212] Dean Alcott, without Emery, Jones, Harris, and the "students" they brought in their wake, would have had the title but little more. The entire movement is best viewed as a cyclic development, which, beginning in New England Transcendentalism in the thirties and forties, partially begot (or reinforced), during the next decades, the Hegelian movement in St. Louis; both combined to fructify the smaller outposts of idealistic thought in Jacksonville, Quincy, and Osceola in the West; finally, during the eighties, when all the Western groups— Platonic, Aristotelian, and Hegelian— converged toward Concord to join the Eastern idealists in the formation of the Concord School, the movement came round full circle.

The emphasis given to the conflicts and rivalries between St. Louis and Concord tends to obscure the mutually co-operative relationship that existed between Eastern Transcendentalism and Western Hegelianism, for it is clear that as the St. Louis Movement without inspiration from New England could not have developed as it did, just so the Concord School of Philosophy without Harris, Snider, Davidson, Emery, Jones, and the groups which each represented could not have materialized.

THE CONCORD SCHOOL OF PHILOSOPHY

The Nine Sessions

As early as 1840 Alcott had envisaged an "academe" or "university" in Concord with himself, Hedge, Ripley, Parker, and "one or two others . . . to make a puissant faculty."[213] But nothing constructive or practical was done until the summer of 1878, when Hiram K. Jones, accompanied by his wife, the Wolcotts of Jacksonville, the Denmans of Quincy, and two or three other Westerners visited Concord. After "a fortnight of glorious talk," Jones and his party returned home. "The Concord School was assured."[214]

It is significant that Dr. Jones the Platonist and not Dr. Harris the Hegelian was the co-founder of the school. Jones and Alcott originally conceived a Platonic institution; but once Harris was invited to participate, the die was cast. However much Jones gesticulated and Alcott regretted the "purely speculative," Hegel rose in repute in direct proportion as Harris gained control of the academy.

The school got off to an auspicious start. The several lieutenants in the various parts of the country whipped up enthusiasm for it. Though the school opened on July 15, 1879, "without funds," it almost paid its way even the first year.[215] Following Emery's "genial welcome" to the assembled scholars, Alcott gave "an outline of our method . . . and the spirit of our purpose," which was "to pursue the path of speculative philosophy . . . the lectures serving mainly as a text for discussion," though (as Alcott solemnly declared) "dispute and polemical debate" were to be avoided. Harris lost no time declaring the logically rational method the only one fitted to their undertaking, and that same evening he, Emery, Jones, McClure, and the Rev. Dr. J. S. Kedney discussed further "the Hegelian ideas and methods." Thus the Concord

School got off to a start under Hegelian auspices which Alcott, if he had had his way about it, would have modified in a way to make the method less speculative—in a way to treat "imagination, reason, and conscience in its threefold attributes as one and entire, thus speaking to the reason and faith at once." This method, he believed, would reach "the many," while the method of Harris would reach "but the few."

Accordingly Alcott lectured the next day on psychology as the key to all knowledge, taking care to make his discourse a "stairway" or introduction to Harris' subtle metaphysical method. The day following Dr. Jones initiated his series of ten lectures on Plato with a discourse on "the Platonic significance of ideas," in a manner to "provoke eager discussion;" but Alcott also observed that when in the afternoon Harris resumed "his exposition of the speculative method," his auditors admired "the subtlety of his expositions and are apparently persuaded of his holding the key to the absolute truth . . . . The faith he inspires is almost universal, though none, it may be comprehend [sic] his method completely." Between the two it was hard to choose. Jones's "allegorical genius" was "refreshing;" yet Alcott was forced "sometimes to question whether the Platonic ideas are not modified essentially by the Doctor's exposition." Then, too, such a remark as Higginson's, that "the defect of the Transcendental School is want of form," was a little disturbing.[216]

Moreover, Jones, though he had disciples who would have heard him all day, lacked the virtue of condensation; his lectures had virtually no terminal facilities.[217] What's more, the Illinois Platonist was used to holding the center of the stage and delivering his opinions *ex cathedra*. Harris, brought up in the school of Brokmeyer, was used to the give-and-take method of trading philosophic opinions. He might lecture formally for an hour or more, but his discourses inspired questions, and his manner encour-

aged animated discussion. As the meetings went on, Alcott continued to prefer the analogical method by which reason and imagination were brought into play jointly; yet he began to perceive also that though Jones was being heard with "deep interest," the attention inspired by Harris somehow seemed to have a more substantial quality. By July 25, Jones was lecturing on the "Apology of Socrates" to "a smaller but interested audience"; while Harris, speaking on "methods of study" and recommending "Kant's Critique of Pure Reason particularly" as a whetstone of the mind, held a "large" audience. Harris emerged from the first school having on the whole "the larger audience."[218]

The first Concord School, covering a wide range of human interests, was truly introductory. Subsequent sessions were more specialized. That of 1880 already showed some evidence of planned specialization, doubtless the result of Harris' influence.[219] The third session (1881) continued Harris and Jones as the protagonists, each with his customary ten lectures on Hegel and Plato, respectively. Two innovations are noteworthy. First, Snider's lectures on Shakespeare the preceding year had been so successful that he was asked to enlarge the literary content of the school by discoursing on "Greek Life and Literature," a subject on which he was primed so shortly after his return from Athens. Second, the centennial of Kant's *Critique of Pure Reason* was observed by seven lectures on Kant, August 2–6.[220]

After some preliminary discussion of the methods and results of Kantian philosophy, Alcott set forth his views of the distinction between pure and practical reason. His remarks demonstrate that some Transcendentalists had not yet divested their minds of the over-simplification under which the Kantian terms had gained currency among them forty years earlier. "In the first treatise," said Alcott, Kant tried "to explore the possibilities, the reach of the pure rea-

son, or the reason unilluminated by faith,
or by what he called the 'categorical imperative,' the conscience. So I will take
these two terms—reason and conscience—
as expressing, in a generalized form, the
two phases of Kant's thinking."[221] He went
on:

In the first treatise he [Kant] does not
seem to have taken into his thought what
he called the Practical Reason in the other;
he uses "reason" in two senses. But really
does he not mean faith, or the necessary
influence which the affections have upon
reason? He finds in the first treatise that
the reason cannot solve moral questions . . .
he becomes confused because he is seeking
to find depths of the pure reason which of
itself it cannot fathom. He finds he can
come to no conclusion, and he ends in the
unknowable, and must be classed as an
agnostic with Spencer and Huxley and all
that class. The Free Religionists largely,
and even Unitarians to some extent, appear
to have fallen into that error, and may
quote Kant as authority.[222]

Now, putting these two facts [sic] together—conscience and reason—and trying
to find a term which will express all that
can be thus received and conceived, we say
revelation. For, unless a revelation is made
to the heart, the love in us, and also to the
reason through the moral sentiment, revelation is incomplete; it is but a doctrine, a
dogma.[223]

Professing to treat Kant "with all hospitality," Alcott likens him to "a Columbus
exploring unknown regions":

Kant is an explorer; he goes on to unfold
relations, and tells us, with an absolute
honesty of conviction, what he saw, and no
more. When he saw anything, he has reported it to us; and when he put out his
sounding-lines and brought up nothing, he
said so. Is not that what he did, this Columbus? That is the man we are here celebrating in this chapel.

This is a perfect example of Alcott's
favorite kind of "analogical" reasoning—
"the pure truth of the poet interblending
imagination and reason by the alchemy of
his genius."[224]

Finally, with a flourish of inconsistency

not at all uncommon among the Transcendentalists, and forgetful of the fact that
he had, only a few minutes earlier, crowned
Kant as the high priest of the "Free-Religionists," "Unitarians," "agnostics . . . and
all that class," he concluded:

. . .here was a grand mind to whom all
are indebted; and we shall no longer go into
that realm where went the deists and that
class of people, and tried to solve the riddle
of the world through their senses. Kant
lifted us from that, and showed us that
there is something in our minds not derived
from the senses, that the senses can only
reflect what is in the mind. What a step
that was! to take us out of our senses and
show us that these can only reflect in images
the ideas in the mind; which are innate,
eternal; that we brought them with us at
birth as truth, justice, love, mercy, and
beauty, being all revelations and intuitions.[225]

Here Mr. Cohn, one of the "students,"
ventured to "offer a criticism" of the Dean's
interpretation, by emphasizing the difference between *Pure* and *Practical* Reason
and by relating the word *practical* to its
original meaning: "to do, to act, to make."
Cohn was not much concerned about how
"definite" or "true" Kant's conclusions
were; he was not concerned at all about
Kant's conclusions. What did interest him
was Kant's "method." His conclusion,
"The whole is a question of method," is one
that could hardly have harmonized with
Alcott's way of thinking.

At this point Harris took the floor. Although he was not scheduled for this part
of the program with a formal paper, what
he delivered has all the earmarks of having
been prepared in advance. He began by
taking up Alcott's metaphor of Kant as the
Columbus of speculation, but objected to
the assertion that Kant often "put out his
sounding-lines and brought up nothing."
After a passing reference of agreement to
Jones's point that neither Kant nor any
other philosopher had yet said "the last
word," he proceeded to a discussion of the
paper read the day before by George Syl-

vester Morris, formerly a lecturer on philosophy at Johns Hopkins, recently installed Professor of Philosophy at Michigan, the translator of Ueberweg, and now working on a critical exposition of Kant's first *Critique* (published the next year). Harris emphasized the natural process of development and, at the same time, the essential unity of thought that runs from Plato and Aristotle, through Kant, Fichte, and Schelling, to Hegel. In order to discover the "fundamental" and "central" principles of this essential unity that will give us "rational explanations and reduce the many to the one," it is necessary to take into account all "previous philosophers." Although Harris usually had scant praise for electicism and electic methods of the sort he advocated on this occasion, his recommendation was doubtless made in view of the need he felt for greater harmony than the remarks thus far had engendered. And on this note of harmony, the morning session of the Kant centennial closed.[226]

In the afternoon, President John Bascom read the principal paper, on "The Freedom of the Will, Empirically Considered," prefacing it "with some criticism of Kant, and also some remarks upon philosophical technique," in which he contended that philosophic terminology should be translatable into common language. Immediately following Bascom's address, Samuel Emery arose to say, "while somebody else is getting ready to speak," that he too had had some trouble with the Kantian time, space, and categories (if viewed as purely subjective), and that it might reasonably be doubted that Kant was being fairly interpreted by Dr. Bascom, who put a peculiarly individualistic construction upon Kant's view of the subjectivity of time and space. With Bascom's interpretation of Kant on free will and liberty, he agreed heartily.

By the time Emery had finished, Harris was ready. This time he spoke extemporaneously. He interpreted Bascom's criticism of philosophical terminology as directed at

him. While Bascom had seemed, in his prefatory remarks, to disparage the use of special terms, he had gone on to use technically philosophical words "derived from a good many systems," and had given them varying applications. Far from disparaging technique in speculation, Harris repeated his arguments for a more exactly technical nomenclature, at the same time calling upon President Bascom's "long experience in teaching philosophy" to bear out the principle that "the most fearful technique in philosophy is that of a person who uses a common term in a special sense and yet leaves the reader to think that he is using it in an ordinary sense."[227] Yes, Harris' mellifluous voice, too, concealed a stinger which he knew how to flesh on occasions.

At this point Sanborn, evidently anxious to avoid a squally session, suggested that all might find a harmonious common ground in Emerson, through whom more than "all other persons combined . . . the Kantian movement had affected America."[228] And Alcott, taking his cue from Sanborn, went on to deliver the valedictory upon the Kant centennial by reminding all that "human faculties are differently cast in different types . . . . Do not seek to put your minds, those of you who are not logical, into logical forms . . . neither shall I say to you who are logical, put your thoughts into poetic forms." Having delivered this "charge" to the scholars, the Dean went on to pronounce the benediction.

The beauty of this school is that we have those who speak from these different aspects . . . . We call it a School of Philosophy, it is true. Mr. Emerson puts his philosophy into warm tropes . . . but Hegel and that class of thinkers strip off the image and give us the pure, absolute truth as it lies in their minds. Mr. Emerson could not . . . do his work as Hegel did . . . . The poet and the philosopher work differently, but they do the same work.[229]

With this final word of wisdom the Concord Kant Centennial came to a triumphant and harmonious close.[230]

However often Alcott reminded his "faculty" of the virtues of tolerance and catholicity, there remained an undercurrent of rivalry between the Platonists and the Hegelians, the poets and the metaphysicians. It was decided that the fourth session should be arranged in such a way that the lines of methodology would be less sharply drawn. The leading lecturers were, as before, Harris, Jones, Alcott, Kedney, Sanborn, and Watson. Alcott was to go on, as before, to expound his own philosophy; but Harris' ten lectures were to be less strictly Hegelian and less abstruse than heretofore (five were to treat of the general history of philosophy, three of Fichte, and two of art); while Jones's eight lectures, instead of expounding Plato solely, were to deal, four of them, with Christian philosophy, three with Oriental thought, and only one with Plato.[231]

But Harris' lectures on the history of philosophy turned out to have a strongly Hegelian cast; those on Fichte presented Fichte in relation to Hegel; and his two discourses on art were pure Hegelian *Aesthetik*. And Jones, whether he was scheduled to lecture on Christ, Zoroaster, or the relation of science to philosophy, discoursed on Plato. He still remained one of the major attractions, but his position had grown progressively subordinate to that of Harris. Even Alcott found himself less and less drawn to the Jacksonville Platonist with his earnest but interminable Platonic expositions. Moreover, the influence of Harris, as a Concord resident, was more nearly present and compelling than that of Dr. Jones in faraway Illinois. Before the fourth school opened, Alcott wrote significantly in his *Journals*, "Sanborn and Harris are now taking warm and sweet places in my regard."[232] By the end of the 1882 session it was apparent to the Jacksonville contingent that unless the Concord "ring" of Hegelians could be broken up, Jones would not be able to maintain a position of respectable and co-ordinate leadership with Harris. The

Westerners held a caucus, whence they emerged with the decision, since so many of the students were from the Midwest, to ask that the next school be held there, and that thereafter it should alternate between the East and the West.

When the decision went against the petitioners, they were keenly disappointed, none more than Dr. Jones. Some of them, notably the St. Louisans, remained faithful and continued to attend; but others, especially those from Illinois, ceased going and joined efforts with Jones in the formation, the next year, of the American Akademe in Jacksonville. Jones maintained cordial personal relations with Alcott, Sanborn, Emery, Harris, and others of the Concord School, but he never again appeared on any of its programs or attended its meetings, thus making inevitable the eclipse of Plato by Hegel in Concord.

The withdrawal had other important effects. The departure of Jones and his colleagues meant not only the loss of a number of hitherto faithful attendants but also the loss of competition and consequently a diminution in the intensity of philosophical interest and discussion, thus preparing the way for the encroachment of the literary upon the more purely philosophical interests of the school.

This trend did not become immediately apparent. The program for 1883 included the usual course of lectures by Harris on Hegel and the philosophy of the absolute; Howison lectured on Hume and Kant; and Sanborn on Puritanic philosophy, Franklin, and Emerson; while the most distinctive feature was William James's three lectures on psychology.[233] But, as regards the general tendency of development in future years, the most noteworthy element of the 1883 school was the recall of Snider (absent during the preceding session, for he had become a bit obstreperous and not sufficiently mindful of the Concord reticences) to present four lectures on the second of his "Literary Bibles," namely, Homer.[234]

Snider considered the third session (1881) "the culmination of the School" and "its best and happiest year," because in later years he missed "the same up-swing . . . the same spontaneous overflow of enthusiasm."[235] But all the indications are that the best year, the climax, came about 1882. Emerson died in that year, and he had always been a powerful magnet drawing people to Concord, even though he cared little about schools of any kind and never took a prominent part in this one. Alcott's health grew progressively worse. But most destructive to the distinctly philosophical nature of the school was its increasingly literary character. The session of 1883 had already been deflected from its philosophical course; that of 1884 was devoted almost solely to Emerson, with considerable emphasis on his literary character;[236] the program for 1885 was dedicated to Goethe, nineteen of the lectures being devoted to him.[237]

The lectures on Goethe at the seventh Concord School (1885) represent a landmark in the history of Goethe's vogue and influence in the United States, and they provide an illuminating commentary on the state of American literary culture. They suggest also that the tradition of speculative thought in America was not yet strong enough to withstand dilution, for they indicate that a marked change had taken place in the school to deflect it from the original "paths of speculative philosophy."[238] Another change is signalized by the fact that the directors could no longer count on the same singleness of purpose, unanimity of interest, and general knowledge of their students, all of which they had taken for granted during the earlier years; for in 1885 they began to distribute in advance bibliographies and lists of readings for the better preparation of the students and to encourage their more general participation in the discussions following lectures.[239]

Estimates vary regarding the preparation of the students who came to Concord from 1879 to 1887. Denton Snider always spoke a little disdainfully of the intelligence of his hearers at Concord. By his own account, he could not always resist giving way to the imp of the perverse and spilling over into some *diablerie* at the expense of the Concordians, in a manner to shock or offend the gentry of "vacant face-long gravity" who sat before him.[240] He doubted that the "smiling appreciation" of the students was always synonymous with "adequate understanding" as "Harris talked his unmixed Hegel to that mixed crowd," and himself related with obvious satisfaction the story current that the erudite lectures could be tersely summed up as "What's mind? Never matter. What's matter? Never mind," as well as the report that the Concord faculty was much concerned with "the Whatness of the Howsoever" and "the Thingness of the Why." While he hastened to add, "I never heard such talk there,"[241] he often displayed an illiberal disposition when he compared the Concord School with his own schools in St. Louis, Milwaukee, Cincinnati, Chicago, and elsewhere.[242] That some who went to Concord were essentially Chautauqua-addicts is obvious; but it is equally clear, from the stature of many of the lecturers and the excellence of their lectures, that the intellectual fare at Concord was phenomenally good. Men of the caliber of Harris, Howison, Morris, Fiske, James, Royce, Porter, and Bascom would hardly have devoted their time and energy to sham philosophical and literary feasts.

The fact remains, however, that after 1885 the course of the Concord School went rapidly downward.[243] The inadequacy of its "scholars" cannot have been the only cause. The "faculty" remained, to the end, as distinguished as they had been during the earlier years, though some of them began to develop tangential interests. Harris, for example, was turning more toward practical educational matters and was soon to go to Washington as Commissioner of Education. Emery returned to the West. Alcott died in 1888. Some responsibility for the decline of the school must be attributed to the loss, beginning in 1883, of its speculative character. Following the Emerson school of 1884 and the Goethe school of 1885, the two weeks of the 1886 session were divided equally between Dante and Plato; while for the ninth and last session (1887) the directors returned to their original aim of pursuing "the path of speculative philosophy" by devoting the major part of the program to Aristotle. But Alcott's "university" was past saving and came to an end almost simultaneously with his own earthly existence.

Interrelations with Other Movements

Two general observations are in order. First, we may take note that American Transcendentalism, originating in the vicinity of Boston during the thirties and forties, migrated westward, or was carried thither by lectures, essays, reviews, books, by young ministers, editors, and New England pedagogues, who spread fanwise over the West. Here it did fruitful and practical work in a pioneer society, even while it became decentralized into groups, circles, and cults that exercised their own originality to such degrees that their common origin was sometimes hardly perceptible. The movements in Missouri and Illinois, wherever else they derived their nourishment, drew heavily on New England Transcendentalism; and though free lances like Snider and Jones believed their destiny lay in the West and therefore desired to declare their independence from Plymouth Rock, and others like Davidson denied allegiance to anybody and anything, all of them eventually gravitated toward the East. In the name of Alcott and under the direction of Harris, American idealism returned to its fountainhead. Finally, through efficient propagandists like Harris, it was given a wider and more practical applica-

tion, notably in the educational system (elementary, secondary, and collegiate) of the United States.

Second, German transcendentalism, beginning with Kantian epistemological and ontological techniques, was given applications in socialized religious forms by Schleiermacher and in ethico-political forms by Fichte, and received its final institutionalization in Hegel. In America a similar, though by no means identical, progression is discernible. American Transcendentalism, in Emerson's hands, originated a theory under the impetus of Kantian terminology, however widely Kant and Emerson differed at other points. In the hands of men like Ripley, Transcendentalism took on elements of Fichtean ethics and assimilated something of the socialization of religion as taught by Schleiermacher and Ronge; while in the West, Brokmeyer, Harris, and their colleagues, in their pursuit and practice of Hegelian principles, represented in some respects a complementary and in others an antithetical movement. Finally, in Concord all differences and opposites were drawn together and given something like a synchronization or synthesis. Hegelians like Harris and Snider could not fail to observe that the course of American idealism, as affected by German absolutism during the nineteenth century, was but another illustration of the Hegelian triadic dialectic of thesis, antithesis, and synthesis.

Undoubtedly the most lasting effect of the St. Louis Movement, as it can be traced today, lies not strictly within the realm of philosophy but in the work that Harris performed as Commissioner of Education in channelizing, systematizing, and standardizing the public-school system of the United States within the Hegelian framework. While the revolt against his principles and procedures grew steadily stronger from the mid-nineties onward, the disciples of the New Education never succeeded in undoing the work of the Great Conservator, so that even today the American public-school system remains so much the development of Harris' principles and the result of his labors that the product (especially in its fundamental organizational aspects) is indistinguishable from the principles that shaped it.

In most other respects the influence of the St. Louis Movement becomes elusive and evanescent when we try to appraise it in terms of the twentieth century. While Harris' multiform activities, Snider's widespread operations, Brokmeyer's great personal magnetism, Davidson's flittings hither and thither, and the great bulk of their published writings, all insinuated themselves in some degree into the life and sum-total of American culture, the movement as such dissipated itself without leaving many clearly recognizable tokens. The latest survivor was the Denton J. Snider Association for Universal Culture with headquarters in St. Louis until the depressed thirties sent it on the way that many such anachronistic relics went during that discouraging decade.

It may be that if Harris had adopted a more popular tone for the twenty-two volumes of his *Journal*, he might have won a larger audience among nineteenth-century Americans for his philosophy which offered so many conciliations in an age that was a compound of contradictions and oppositions. But that was not the way of William Torrey Harris. Persuaded by Brokmeyer that the only proper explanation of history lies in the Hegelian law of dialectical growth, he chose to move in the rarefied atmosphere of scholastic symbols, even to the point of subordinating Hegel's ethics and political works to the sixth and seventh places in a list of eight, in which the *Logic* is placed first.[244] The wonder is that, in his educational endeavors, he succeeded as well as he did in giving currency and cogency to his abstruse phrases and his fine-spun doctrines among the teachers and public-school administrators of his day. What's more, if he had addressed himself more largely to the popular audience, he would

have missed winning the academic allies who, as things turned out, provided the chief stronghold in which his type of thinking was fostered and perpetuated.

It may be that the St. Louisans would have been more successful if they had stuck more closely to the profession which bred them in the first place. Although most of them remained teachers in some sense of the word, many of them chose to work outside the common framework of teaching in the organized schools. Few of the original group were ambitious to take regularly appointed positions in established colleges and universities. Only G. H. Howison, the first vice-president of the Philosophical Society, was a regular academician, but eventually he demonstrated his "self-activity" by becoming virtually the founder of personalism. Something of the original Hegelian impulse was surely imparted to the successive generations of his students in California, but he veered more and more from the absolute idealism of Hegel in favor of a form of personal idealism or spiritual pluralism. Thus the great following that he built up became as much a dissipating as a perpetuating force, so far as the St. Louis Movement was concerned.[245]

One other who was more or less closely identified with various individuals of the St. Louis group, notably with Harris, was George S. Morris, though his enthusiasm for Kant and Hegel was acquired independently of the St. Louisans.[246] His influence is another example of the type of following and influence which the St. Louis Hegelians might have secured for themselves if, instead of expending their energies on semipopular groups, communal universities, summer schools, and philosophical clubs of various complexions, they had sought the stability of regular academic appointments. Certainly Harris and Kroeger, possibly Snider, and others of the many writers for the *Journal* possessed, or could readily have acquired, the requisite qualifications.

Looking back upon the late nineteenth

century as we can today, we have no difficulty seeing that while the media through
which the St. Louisans chose to work tended in the end to diffuse or dilute rather than
prolong and preserve the ideals for which
they strove, Hegel in more academic accoutrements conquered many of the philosophy departments in American colleges
and universities, and often those of history
and political science as well. The conquest
was in some instances short-lived; but while
it lasted, it was pretty general. The Hege-
lization of our universities was more the
result of the trek of American students to
the German universities than of direct connections with the semi-popular Hegelian
movement on native soil. Royce, for example, learned his absolute idealism in
Germany, where he studied with Lotze,
Wundt, and Windelband at Göttingen and
Leipzig. Peirce turned directly to Kant's
Critiques; as for Hegel, whose philosophy
he said "mine resuscitates, though in a
strange dress,"[247] he got something from
Morris at Hopkins and more from Augusto
Vera's commentaries in the *Journal of Speculative Philosophy* and still more from
Hegel's books themselves. Palmer acquired
his knowledge of German idealism partly in
Germany and (particularly as affects Hegel)
from the books of the Scottish Hegelians
Stirling and Caird, as well as from Hegel's
works. Bowne studied at Halle and Göttingen, and Creighton at Leipzig and Berlin.
James, too, studied in Germany, read the
Germans themselves, and consulted their
commentators. Hall, Ladd, Cattell, Baldwin, and Münsterberg imported experimental psychology directly from Germany.[248] Among the contributors to Harris'
Journal were Benjamin Rand, G. Stanley
Hall, Josiah Royce, Charles S. Peirce,
William James, and John Dewey, all of
whom became philosophers in their own
right and professors in American universities. To most of these the *Journal* was
more than an outlet for their first efforts at
philosophical writing, and all of them ac-

knowledged that German philosophy exerted a shaping influence on their own
philosophic personalities; but the greater
impetus directing them to a consideration
of German thought came from quarters
other than St. Louis. William James—even
while grudgingly acknowledging that Hegel's influence "remained always more or
less pronounced"—usually poked good-
natured fun at the St. Louis Hegelians.[249]
On the other hand, John Dewey, whose
primary sources of inspiration were obviously not St. Louis, and whose final position developed much beyond anything he
could have learned from Hegel, nevertheless
wrote to Harris on December 17, 1886:

When I was studying the German philosophers I read something of yours on them
of which one sentence has always remained
with me . . . you spoke of the 'great psychological movement from Kant to Hegel' . . . one thing I have attempted to do
is to translate a part at least of the significance of that movement into our present
psychologic movement.[250]

There was no dearth of personal contacts
among them. Even in Tom Davidson's quixotic retreat, Josiah Royce, William James,
and John Dewey found themselves eating
at the same table with the men from Jacksonville, Osceola, St. Louis, and Concord.
The Glenmore retreat, the communal
university movement, and the Concord
School all sought to effect the consummation of American idealism, but all were
swept aside by the times. The naturalistic
trend of a new age made headway, however
resolutely Jones opposed it at Jacksonville
or Alcott in Concord. It was no mere coincidence that the Plato Club, the American
Akademe, the Philosophical Society, the
Concord School, the *Journal of Speculative
Philosophy*, the *Journal of the American
Akademe*, and the *Bibliotheca Platonica* all
came to an end within the short period of
five years (1887–1892). The same years saw
the first appearance of the *Monist* (1890–
1936), the *International Journal of Ethics*

(1890), and the *Philosophical Review* (1892), which, together with the *Journal of Philosophy* (1904), remained until recently the chief periodicals for the publication and exchange of speculative opinion in the United States. The Western Philosophical Association was established in 1900, and the American Philosophical Association in 1901. All announced in unmistakable terms that a new era had begun, that the old dispensation, however much the new might be indebted to the old, was dead. In the search for a distinctively "American" philosophy, there were few who agreed with Walt Whitman that "Only Hegel is fit for America—is large enough and free enough . . . an essential and crowning justification of New World democracy."[251]

Struggling against hopeless odds, the half-dozen idealistic schools and movements—East and West—put up a stiff resistance from 1836 to the end of the century against what came increasingly to be called "the American philosophy." Time and again, especially after 1880, they were forced to retreat. In every counteroffensive that they launched, they moved under the banner of Plato or Kant or Hegel—or all three. But their best efforts were ineffectual. After the cycle from Concord to St. Louis, to Jacksonville, and back to Concord was once completed, it was not repeated, not only because the times were against absolute idealism of whatever kind but also because the idealists had neglected to train among the younger generation able successors to take over and carry forward the movements which had, in all instances, depended too much on individual leadership. The individualism of "self-activity," developed no less in New England Transcendentalism than in St. Louis Hegelianism, failed to breed the required community of effort and solidity of association to perpetuate either of them as a movement or as an institution.

However, while failing to change radically or even to deflect the direction of American thought, the several groups, taking them altogether, did assist significantly in the revitalization of the oft-dormant and equally oft-recurrent strain of idealism that has been a vital part of American consciousness from earliest Puritan days, and that, thanks to the nineteenth-century idealists, still runs deeply through the American mind. This they effected because they never surrendered or admitted themselves utterly routed, even while they bowed before the more strongly organized and compelling forces of naturalism and materialism.

Another important service which they performed was that in their insistence upon free inquiry they proved strong allies and supporters of the long line of liberal American academicians from James Marsh of Vermont and Henry Boyton Smith at Amherst to Josiah Royce at Harvard and J. E. Creighton at Cornell, who fought a slow but increasingly successful fight to liberate American philosophy from a too exclusive domination by Lockean sensationalism and Scottish common-sense. Emerson and Jones, Harris and Emery, no less than this succession of professors of philosophy, opposed academic tradition and professional prejudice: (1) the deepseated predilection in American universities for British empiricism, and (2) the prevalent prejudice against any brand of philosophy that emanated from Germany, whether critical or romantic. In these aims, however widely they differed in other particulars, the Platonic intuitionists of Concord and Jacksonville and the Hegelian rationalists of Quincy and St. Louis were united no less among themselves than were the professors of philosophy and of theology who were developing a sense of historicity and of criticism. Thus they helped prepare the way for twentieth-century freedom and objectivity that permitted the evolution of the pragmatic, or the "American" philosophy, which they opposed, and which, as things turned out, spelled the doom of their hope that idealism might become the prevailing American philosophy.

But while late nineteenth- and early twentieth-century winds of new doctrine swept all these early semi-popular currents before them, the academic halls remained places where the tradition of idealism from Kant to Hegel could find a domicile promising a degree of perpetuity. The significant shaping influence of German philosophy upon the idealism of Royce, the psychology of Münsterberg, the pragmatism of Peirce and James, and the educational philosophy of Dewey are later and transmuted manifestations of a long process of acculturation

that earlier conditioned New England Transcendentalism, that was carried forward by the St. Louisans and the Concordians, and that persists very markedly in current pragmatism, as well as in the current academic tradition of philosophical instruction in American colleges and universities. By such means and avenues, the several motifs of German philosophical idealism have become so deeply imbedded in the course of constructive thought in the United States that the termination of its influence cannot be envisaged unless American thinking itself should come to a period.

GERMAN PHILOSOPHY IN AMERICAN COLLEGES

The Early Teaching of Philosophy

The history of the introduction, vogue, and effect of German philosophy on the substance and methods of American collegiate instruction provides a relatively valid test of the degree of penetration that German thought attained in the United States. Since only acculturated materials ordinarily become the accepted objects of classroom treatment, it is important to note at what juncture and under what circumstances German philosophy was able to command the sanction of authorities in the American institutions of higher learning. Was the so-called "Germanization" of the American college system during the latter half of the nineteenth century confined to matters of external organization, or did the American university take over also something of the very spirit and ideological background from its continental models? What American teachers and writers of texts incorporated terms, points of view, and basic philosophic attitudes stemming from Germany in their thoughts? Only by inquiring into the genetic history of this process can approximate answers to these questions be given.

THE COMMON-SENSE TRADITION

The philosophical orientation of American colleges throughout the seventeenth century was Ramean or Aristotelian. Early in the eighteenth century the emphasis shifted to Locke, who was introduced at Yale in 1714 and at Harvard shortly after. His long hold on the American mind[252] fostered the firm establishment by the opening of the nineteenth century of the common-sense philosophy derived from the Scottish school.[253] Even deism and Berkeleian idealism nowhere gained a firm foothold in the college halls, and it was not until the 1840's, when the Transcendentalists began their agitation for German idealism, that any strong challenge was offered to the cautious and discreet treatment of philosophical problems prevalent in the leading institutions.[254]

GERMAN INFLUENCE BEFORE 1800

Insulated as the American college of the eighteenth century was against direct influence from the Continent, German thought had access in only a few minor instances. The schools of Pennsylvania, established by and for the preponderant German-

American element of that region, had on their faculties immigrant teachers who brought with them from Germany a knowledge of contemporary *Aufklärung* and of Kantian thought;[255] but because they used the German language almost exclusively and drew students chiefly from the immediate vicinity, their influence was limited. Perhaps none of the Mühlenbergs achieved fame much beyond German-American circles. Gotthilf Mühlenberg (1735–1815), who studied at Halle for seven years, was president of Franklin College after 1787 and a well-known preacher, scientist, and linguist. In Boston the Rev. Johann Christoph Hartwig (1714–1796), a German immigrant who endowed Hartwick College, exerted some influence in favor of German culture from 1784 to his death. In Columbia College Johann Daniel Gros, minister of the German Reformed Church and friend of Baron von Steuben, become the first German-born professor at one of the larger American colleges. In his teaching of moral philosophy from 1789 to 1795 he devoted some direct attention to German philosophy.[256] Thomas Cooper, teacher at the University of South Carolina and at Carlisle College, is the first, so far as is known, among American authors, to cite German higher criticism of the Bible in attacking the claims of the orthodox theologians.[257]

German Influence, 1800–1850

GERMAN THEOLOGY AT HARVARD, VERMONT, AND ANDOVER

Meantime the pioneering work of teachers of theology such as Moses Stuart at Andover, Joseph Buckminster at Harvard, and James Marsh at Vermont in directing attention to German Biblical criticism initiated an unbroken sequence of events which contributed to the Transcendentalist revolt of the thirties and forties. Such German-born teachers as Follen and Lieber reached large audiences with accounts of German philosophy and literature, and native Americans like Hedge in Maine,

Marsh at Vermont, and Francis of Harvard became active in the promulgation of German thought, seeking to demonstrate that German criticism and Biblical research could no longer be ignored in American seminaries. Though the broadly liberal tendencies of the German theologians were often violently denounced, there were always a few earnest students who made use of Ernesti, Semler, Baur, and later, Strauss. Even at Andover, in 1824, the interest in German philosophy and theology was sufficiently general for the authorities to investigate the unrestricted study of the "infidel" German writers.[258]

HENRY BOYNTON SMITH

The work of Henry Boynton Smith (1815–1877) at Amherst from 1847 to 1850 made that school, in close association with Andover, a center for one branch—the conservative "right"—of German theological doctrine. This famous Presbyterian teacher, converted from Unitarianism at Bowdoin, studied at Andover and Bangor, taught for a year at Bowdoin, and then on the advice of President Leonard Woods,[259] spent a year at Halle and Berlin (1837–1838).[260] Upon his return Smith became minister to a Congregational Society at West Amesbury and devoted part of his time teaching at Andover. Hedge engaged him, as a known authority on Hegel, to contribute several translations from Hegel to Hedge's *Prose Writers of Germany*.[261] Correspondence and visits kept Smith in close touch with the movements of thought in Germany. He prepared several translations of German theological treatises (chiefly from Twesten) for the *Bibliotheca Sacra*. His article, "A Sketch of German Philosophy,"[262] won for him the notice of Presidents Wayland of Brown and Sears of Newton College and Professors Torrey, Hitchcock, and Gibbs. The result was a call to Amherst, where he taught mental and moral philosophy. Here he changed the tenor of philosophical teaching, discarding the slavish use of texts, assigning special readings for subsequent open discussion in the classroom, and encouraging a profounder grappling with fundamental questions raised by the new Biblical criticism. In 1850 he moved to Union Theological Seminary, where he remained until 1874. His friendship for George S. Morris was perhaps the strongest guiding influence in the early work of that influential teacher, who, in a few years, was to bring German idealism to Michigan and Johns Hopkins.[263]

WILLIAM G. T. SHEDD

William Greenough Thayer Shedd (1820–1894), a Presbyterian student at Vermont strongly influenced by James Marsh to become an "ardent disciple of Coleridge, Kant, and Plato," is notable for his work of popularizing Transcendentalism of the Coleridgean type. After graduating from Andover Theological Seminary in 1843, Shedd taught at Vermont, Auburn Seminary, Andover, and finally Union Theological Seminary, where he remained for eleven years as successor to Henry Boynton Smith. Though in his later years he became a violent critic of the German Higher Criticism, before 1860 he was a champion of the type of idealism stemming from post-Kantian sources. Like Coleridge, he tended to equate the ideal with the supernatural, and looked upon the doctrines of the German orthodox theologians as an important source of truth for his generation.[264] Schleiermacher and the Tübingen school he rejected, and in the 1870's he felt constrained to warn American students against being "deluded by the phosphoric lights of schemes and schemers."[265] Like Smith and others who made use of German Biblical scholarship, Shedd was by no means fully conversant with the entire history of recent German philosophy, and he made use of it only to the extent that it could easily be assimilated by native theological principles and tenets. Shedd's most significant contributions were his

edition of Coleridge (1853) and his translations of several standard German theological works.[266]

FREDERICK AUGUSTUS RAUCH

The seminaries of the German Reformed Church produced a group of important professors of theology[267] who were generally more conversant with German thought than their colleagues in the secular colleges. One of them, Frederick Augustus Rauch (1806–1841),[268] was an enthusiastic disciple of Hegel and probably the first bearer of Hegel's teaching to America. His *Psychology* (1841) is the first book in English bearing the title "Psychology," and was designed by the author to "unite German and American mental philosophy." Dividing the field of psychology after the German fashion into Anthropology and Psychology, he presented a system of "Hegelian realism," intended to "give the science of man a direct bearing upon other sciences, and especially upon religion and theology."[269] The book received instant notice, among both Transcendentalists, like Brownson, and Unitarians, like Walker at Harvard. Its acceptance was, of course, not complete in every quarter, the orthodox being quick to label it as pantheistic in tendency; nevertheless, it was used as a text in some schools and colleges, reaching four editions by 1853.[270] Rauch was equally well informed on Kant and on Hegel: he drew strictly the Kantian distinction between understanding and reason, and was careful in selecting an adequate and intelligible terminology for the new Hegelian concepts. Dr. Haag remarks that with Rauch, Hegel spoke English.[271] He certainly impressed his native American successor, John Nevin, as having succeeded markedly in adapting himself and his German heritage to the needs and capacities of his American surroundings.[272]

PHILIP SCHAFF

Another early German-born teacher

whose influence reached beyond the limits of German groups was Philipp Schaff, a renowned teacher and scholar who was active for many years at the Union Theological Seminary in New York. He had studied at Tübingen, Halle, and Berlin from 1837 to 1840, and became *Privatdozent* at Berlin in 1842. Subsequently he was established at Mercersburg, whence he removed to New York. He was one of the best informed men in America to interpret the Biblical scholarship and points of view of such men as Neander, Edersheim, Gieseler, and Hagenbach.[273]

From 1850 to 1880: College Courses and Texts

From about 1850 to 1880 there was little outward change in the philosophical teaching, except that, on the whole, the increment of scientific courses in the college curriculum grew at the expense of courses in philosophy. Meanwhile "philosophy" split into three major components—natural, mental, and moral; and mental philosophy tended further to divide into two increasingly distinct fields—logic and psychology. A list of texts in use during the period reveals a considerable number of books reflecting a mounting direct influence, either through translation or commentary, of German philosophy.[274]

LOGIC

Textbooks in logic used most frequently were those by Levi Hedge (1816), Archbishop Whately (1826), John S. Mill (1843), Henry P. Tappan (1844), W. D. Wilson (1856), Henry C. Coppée (1858), Francis Bowen (1965), Charles Everett (1869), and R. H. Lotze (1887). Despite the general hostility to German idealism as a system, none of the writers after 1850 could disregard the contributions made by Kant,[275] and every one of the later American texts acknowledged a greater or lesser, direct or indirect, debt to German thought. Even

Bowen (1811–1890), instructor and later Alford Professor at Harvard, and a very outspoken critic of American Transcendentalism, recognized the changes wrought since the appearance of Whately's book. By 1842, when he published his *Critical Essays* (a book which, according to Dr. Haag, "marked Bowen as the best informed contemporary critic and expositor of the philosophy of the Germans in relation to American thought"), Bowen boasted of the extent to which European philosophy was being studied in the American colleges.[276]

The Elements of Logic (1844) of Henry P. Tappan (1805–1881), written some years before the author became chancellor of the University of Michigan, reflects more strongly than does Bowen's a dependence on Kant. In his earlier books on the will Tappan had struggled vainly to find a way out of the determinism of Edwards; he finally succeeded by adopting the Kantian threefold determination of the mental faculties.[277]

Charles C. Everett (1829–1900), a professor in the Harvard Divinity School from 1878 to 1900, had studied in Germany under Gabler, the disciple of Hegel. His *Science of Thought* (1869), as he explains in the Preface, is an adaptation of Hegelian logic, especially in "form." Everett made extensive forays into German philosophy, and in 1884 published a critical exposition of Fichte's *Science of Knowledge* in Griggs's influential series of "German Philosophical Classics," edited by George S. Morris.

The Laws of Discursive Thought (1870) by the Scottish-born James McCosh (President of Princeton from 1868 to 1888), while honoring Kant, emphasized the "errors" of the "new," or post-Kantian philosophers. McCosh, an able critic, spent much of his energy fighting Hegelianism. He was so successful, and his reputation in academic circles rose so high that he was generally credited with having raised Scottish realism to the position of being *the* American philosophy of the time.

Finally, it is to be noted that Lotze's *Outlines of Logic*, in George Trumbull Ladd's translation of 1887, was introduced in several institutions during the last decade of the century; Lotze's earnest religious tone appealed to conservative and "semi-theological" academicians.[278]

ETHICS

Until late in the nineteenth century the college course in ethics, usually taught by the president, was a conspicuous feature of the curriculum of the senior year. Under the title of Moral Philosophy, often in conjunction with courses on the Evidences of Christianity of Natural Theology, this important study embraced a broad range, from simple character building to an inquiry into the powers of the mind and their application to individual and social life.[279] Paley's *Principles of Moral and Political Philosophy* (1788) reached its tenth American edition in 1821. The texts of McBride (1796), Wayland (1835), Jouffroy (1842), Whewell (1847), Bowen (1855), Hickok (1856), Whately (1857), Metcalf (1860), Hopkins (1862), Calderwood (1874), and Andrew P. Peabody (1887) were the most extensively used, though there were others.[280]

At the time of the Transcendental ferment the teaching of ethics at Harvard was under the supervision of James Walker, who used Jouffroy's books as a text during the forties. Whatever its defects on the side of superficial, inconsistent eclecticism, it afforded many students their first glimpse of German thought. Walker, like Bowen, was a staunch Scottish realist, who, however, was thoroughly informed about the ethical theories of Kant, Schleiermacher, and Hegel; and in his edition of Stewart's *Philosophy of the Active and Moral Powers* (1849) he included them in a list of German treatises that "*must* be read" by anyone who wished to pursue the study.[281]

The *System of Moral Science* by President Hickok of Union College, quite as much as his general system, owes much to Kant. Hickok defined the individual soul as a supernatural force and a free agent. As Kant postulated freedom of the will and immortality as the necessary grounds for practical morality, so Hickok argued that the facts of the moral life require and demonstrate the reality of the individual soul. His ethical views were rigoristic in the Kantian manner.[282] The position of President Mark Hopkins of Williams was similarly close to Coleridge and Kant. Although he started from the common-sense philosophy, he later dissented from Paley's "doctrine of ends" and adopted instead a doctrine "of an ultimate right, as taught by Kant and Coleridge, making that the end."[283] This view, which has been called a kind of "sublimated utilitarianism," roused the vigorous opposition of McCosh and other conservatives.[284] Calderwood's *Handbook of Moral Philosophy* (1874) enjoyed some vogue in American schools and was in use at Indiana University in 1880. Because it assembled the ethical doctrines from a host of authorities, ancient and modern, continental and British, it gave a fair idea of recent German ethical thought. In such ways as these, directly and indirectly, the Kantian position was brought to and interpreted for the American student.

METAPHYSICS AND PSYCHOLOGY

Another large class of textbooks and corresponding college courses was devoted to metaphysics and psychology. Under the various titles of Intellectual Philosophy, Philosophy of Mind, and Mental Philosophy (later generally more sharply differentiated into metaphysics and psychology) these courses in their development followed the trend of philosophical speculation apparent throughout the century. The roots of the study of epistemology and the mental processes are to be found in the agnostic attitude of Hume and the speculations of Berkeley on the one hand, and in the

German Kantian and post-Kantian speculations on the other. On the whole, American teachers remained loyal to the Scottish
realists. Nevertheless, the new points of
view revealed in the agitation over Transcendentalism and Kantian skepticism is
described by Hall as having been "amazingly fructifying . . . from without." That
is to say, even the most unwilling of the
orthodox were forced to come to grips with
the questions posed by Emerson, Parker,
and company.[285]

An important innovator among writers
of texts[286] in this field was Thomas Upham
(1799–1872), a student at Andover under
Stuart and later professor at Bowdoin.
Beginning in 1827, Upham published his
large and carefully worked-out *Elements of
Mental Philosophy* (first entitled *Intellectual
Philosophy*) in a series of revisions. The
1831 edition contained for the first time the
very important tripartite division of the
faculties, which afterward was taken up in
most American textbooks.[287] Upham's text
was a very successful one, still widely used
as late as the eighties.

Another highly successful writer of philosophic textbooks was Francis Wayland
(1796–1865), President of Brown University
(1827–1855), whose *Moral Science* (1835),
Political Economy (1838), and *Intellectual
Philosophy* (1854) were very popular. In his
Intellectual Philosophy he cited Coleridge,
Cousin, Hamilton, together with other
Scottish and English writers as his authorities, and his *Political Economy* appears to
rely most directly on Fichte.[288]

Laurens Perseus Hickok (1798–1888)[289]
wrote between 1849 and 1875 a series of
philosophical texts and treatises embracing
the fields of psychology, "moral science,"
cosmology, and logic, elaborating a system
of "Constructive Realism" which he felt
would avoid the errors alike of idealism and
of naive realism. He felt he could make a
defense of Christian theology without
resorting to mysticism by putting it rather
on a firm and broad rational foundation.

The terms of his problem were set for him
by Kant's *Critique of Pure Reason*, whose
significance he understood better than did
his theological contemporaries.[290] His *Rational Psychology* (1842), a tome of seven
hundred pages, which reached a second
edition in 1861, was a reworking of Kantian
epistemology, wherein he attempted to
overcome Kant's negative conclusions by
setting up *a priori* principles free from the
subjectivity of the Kantian categories.
Hickok's ethics, as already indicated, were
grounded on the Kantian doctrines of
liberties and rights, and his *Rational Cosmology* (1858) expounded *a priori* principles
in the manner of Kant.[291] Hickok's *Empirical Psychology* (1854) employed the Kantian
division of the mental faculties. Revised
twenty-five years later by Julius H. Seelye,
the book long found adherents among
college teachers.[292]

Professor Joseph Haven (1816–1874),
student at Göttingen and Berlin in 1830
and translator of Heine's *Letters on Polite
Literature of Germany* (1836), is another of
the Amherst teachers who published a
textbook, *Mental Philosophy* (1857), and
whose tendency ran counter to the prevailing realist doctrine. Haven adopted Upham's threefold division of the mental
faculties and cited Cousin as his forerunner
"and previously still, Kant of Germany."
Among the first in America to interpret the
German aesthetic theories, his *Mental Philosophy* included a short historical sketch
of German aesthetic thought, as represented by Leibnitz, Winckelmann, Lessing,
Herder, Goethe, Kant, and Schiller.[293]

Asa Mahan (1799–1889), first president
of Oberlin College, published in 1845 his
System of Intellectual Philosophy, which, in
its original form at least, acknowledged the
significance of continental idealism and
brought together ideas from Locke, Reid,
Cousin, Coleridge, and Kant.[294] From
Cousin, especially, he absorbed much of
Fichte's teachings, which he stated accurately in the *Intellectual Philosophy* (1845),

as well as in his *Doctrine of the Will* (1847).

Noah Porter (1811–1892) was the author of *Human Intellect* (1868), and *Elements of Intellectual Science* (1871), two compendious works, which, coming somewhat after the violent outbursts against idealism had died down, gave relatively more space to the history of the subject. They treat of theories of sense-perception from Aristotle to Kant, and set forth the Hegelian doctrine of the Absolute. Porter had spent a year of travel and study in Europe in 1853–1854, during which time he attended the University of Berlin. Essentially a conservative, in his later years he became more tolerant and a decidedly better critic of German metaphysics. In 1886 he published his book on *Kant's Ethics* and wrote a section on American philosophy appended to G. S. Morris' translation of Ueberweg (1871–1873). Because of his prominence in educational circles (he was professor at Yale from 1846 to 1871 and president from 1871 to 1886) Porter wielded great authority and influence in his time.

President John Bascom (1827–1911) of the University of Wisconsin, author of textbooks in many philosophical branches, was a student and disciple of Hickok and used Hickok's texts in his classes. He firmly believed in Hickok's system of rational psychology as opposed to empirical psychology. His *Science of Method* (1881), while resisting the evolutionism of Spencer and Bain, made use of the genetic method and shows an awareness of the results of German psychology.[295]

Factors in the Development of Germanic Influence

A NEW TYPE OF UNIVERSITY

The introduction of the elective system on a widespread scale, the development of graduate studies and the seminar method, and the mushroom growth of the sciences made it impossible to keep all the old studies alongside the new. The classical languages were commonly made optional, modern languages were generally introduced, German and French being made compulsory; and the entire course, while still within prescribed limits, permitted a far higher degree of specialization than before. Philosophy was kept, often as a required course, but it weighed much less in proportion to the sum total of subject matter than it had in the earlier years of the century. Even so, there was a considerable increase in both professors and courses;[296] and with the increase in offerings, room was made in the program for the closer study of special problems, of individual philosophers or schools of philosophy, and for courses in the history of philosophy, the entire study of philosophy becoming comparable in scope to the German system.[297] The crucial innovation in the eighteen-seventies was the introduction of regular instruction in the domain of German philosophy. This occurred at Harvard in 1873–1874, when Professor Bowen for the first time conducted his course in modern German philosophy. Harvard's lead was followed in a few years by others of the larger schools.[298]

These developments are closely linked with the gradual victory of the so-called "German" principles of university education—elective studies, the seminar and lecture methods, and the support of scholarship and research activities. Not the older schools of the East, but the University of Michigan in the fifties introduced this ideal conception of the German university, under its enthusiastic Germanist, President Henry P. Tappan (1805–1881).[299] During the period of his presidency (1852–1863), he insisted on the important distinction between the College and the University, the College being the preparatory or trade school, fitting men for special practical careers, the University instead being "libraries, cabinets, apparatus, professors, and provision . . . where study may be extended without limit"—an assembly of gifted scholar-teachers and mature, responsible, well trained graduate students.[300] After a deliberate consideration of the claims of all types of higher education the world over, Tappan found the German practice most nearly approaching his ideal; and that is why, in his earlier writings on the subject and in his addresses and official duties as President or Chancellor of the University of Michigan, he constantly cited Prussian examples, even to the point of annoying and antagonizing local opinion in intensely democratic frontier Michigan with his Germanic enthusiasms.[301] In 1863 he was ousted by the combined forces of Protestant orthodoxy (fearing the rise of a state university as a threat to denominationalism) and of narrow, personal, and political partisanship.

Not long afterward, Tappan's famous colleague, Andrew Dickson White, was given the opportunity to organize Cornell University and thus to carry forward some of the principles first charted by Tappan.[302] Cornell, established in 1868, and Johns Hopkins, founded in 1876, both emphasized certain features of the German system, especially the cultivation of experimental science, the creation of great libraries, and the use of lecture and seminar methods. The story of their establishment and their debt to German example has been told too often to require further elaboration,[303] but none of the later exponents of the German idea defined the concept of the University quite in the liberal, broadly humanistic spirit of Tappan. In an era of scientific discovery it was not difficult for Johns Hopkins, Harvard, and soon afterward, the other larger schools vastly to increase the expenditures for libraries, laboratories, and scientific apparatus.

COLLEGE COURSES IN 1880

After 1875 college philosophy benefited under the new dispensation, and many features of accepted German practice in the teaching of that subject were introduced, especially in the larger institutions. As early as 1861 Tappan had outlined for Michigan a course of study for postgraduates entitled the History of Philosophy, though it seems not to have been immediately given. By 1886, however, there were offerings of fourteen different courses at Michigan, including psychology, logic, the history of philosophy, aesthetics, the philosophy of the state and of history, experimental psychology, ethics, the philosophy of Herbert Spencer, speculative philosophy, and seminars in Plato's *Republic*, in Hegel's *Logic*, and in Aristotle's *Ethics*.[304] At Hopkins, the graduate school offered in 1879–1880 and thereafter, the history of philosopy and ethics, the history of British philosophy, and in addition, private readings in ethics (using Kant's *Critique of Practical Reason*), in German philosophy (1880–1881), systematic ethics, and some phases of the history of American philosophy (1881–1882).[305] While more progressive schools welcomed the study of German philosophy, [306] the process was not generally spontaneous and easy elsewhere. The intellectual tone of the college did not change overnight from indifference to enthusiasm, and it was only by experimentation and piecemeal change that the principles of free electives, a wider range of studies, and the emancipation from the textbook were put into practice.[307] In the smaller denominational colleges and in some of the older or larger institutions like Princeton, Columbia, and Wisconsin, the philosophical faculty continued its warfare on idealism until the end of the century and beyond.[308] President McCosh of Princeton published numerous attacks on idealism as well as materialism from 1875 to 1894. He was convinced that the interest in German thought was an infatuation and delusion destined quickly to pass.[309]

RESISTANCE TO IDEALISM

In 1875 Princeton awarded a fellowship to J. P. K. Bryan for the study of philosophy in Europe, this being the first awarded in that branch, though others had gone before him to do work in the natural sciences. From the report of his work published by Bryan on his return, one gains the impression that he heard the German lecturers more to refute them than to be taught by them. His report was an attempted defense of the Scottish point of view and a summation of errors and weaknesses of the Germanic. McCosh's comments on Bryan's report and on the state of affairs in Germany amounts to this: Bryan, while attending Zeller's lectures, learned that

[Zeller's] system is Ideal-Real—whatever that may mean .... It is clear that the ideal philosophy is running to seed, and the adherents are giving us nothing of any value except histories of ancient and modern speculation. All over Germany there is an ominous reaction from it, and a strong tendency toward materialism.[310]

In 1882 McCosh continued the argument in a paper contrasting the Scottish philosophy with the German, at the same time conceding the practical necessity of making a judicious use of Kant and of the recent researches into psychology by Wundt and Lotze. So McCosh in a manner joins the Back-to-Kant movement, insisting, however, that German philosophy will not be transplanted into America "till there is a change to suit it to the climate." It must accommodate itself to us. In fact, McCosh in his later writings tended to reject sensationalism and to agree with the Concord School on the subject of the "divine Idea in the mind." Though he remained suspicious of "lofty systems," he wanted to be empirical and inductive in his method.[311] The attack came from other quarters, too. James Hervey Hyslop, Professor of Logic and Ethics at Columbia, ridiculed those who enter the "blue empyrean of transcendentalism,"[312] and President Bascom in 1881 feared idealism as conducive to atheism.[313]

The growth of interest in German philosophy continued despite these retarding forces—fostered in part by the influence of those Americans who received all or part of their academic training in German universities; for throughout the period under consideration a large proportion of America's most famous students and teachers of philosophy learned to know at first hand the German tradition of philosophic study and imported directly the methods and points of view of these centers of learning.[314] The presence of German-trained men in various technical and humanistic fields other than philosophy further facilitated the reception and vogue of German philosophy.[315]

INFLUENCE OF TRANSCENDENTALISTS AND HEGELIANS

Despite the oft-heard contention that academic teaching was little affected by either New England Transcendentalism or its later counterpart, the St. Louis Hegelian Movement, it is to be noted that men closely identified with these groups were given opportunities in several of the colleges and universities to present their views. At Harvard, R. W. Emerson and J. E. Cabot were among those appointed to participate in the University lecture course in philosophy in 1870–1871. The Transcendentalist Samuel Osgood was called to lecture on German literature and modern thought at Union College in 1876. Joseph Cook, a popular speaker on the Boston Monday Lecture Series, presented in 1876 a course of lectures at Mount Holyoke Seminary, including such subjects as "Decline of Rationalism in Germany," "Evolution," and "Materialism."[316] The Hegelian W. T. Harris presented series of lectures before many schools and institutes and, in 1882, gave a special course on the philosophy of education at Holyoke.[317] Students of the Massachusetts Institute of Technology heard not only Howison but were permitted during the seventies to attend the lectures of the Lowell Institute free of charge; and there, in 1874–1875, for example, they heard a course of eighteen lectures on modern philosophy, half of which were devoted to German thinkers since Leibnitz.[318]

Professors of Philosophy

Thus many factors conspired to make the last twenty years of the century the high point of Germanic influence in American philosophy. As idealism became dominant, even its opponents—including pragmatists, personalists, and realists—were profoundly influenced by the German classical and post-Hegelian philosophies. Aside from a host of influential professors trained in Germany under men like Lotze, Fechner, Windelband and the psychologists Hartmann, Helmholtz, and Wundt, more and more of our more influential universities came under the guidance of men like Andrew D. White, widely known for their interest in promulgating the German ideal of higher education in this country.[319] Furthermore, the influence of the St. Louis Philosophical Society, founded in 1866, together with the Kant Club and the *Journal of Speculative Philosophy*, expressing the views of the Hegelians Harris and Brokmeyer, formed a rallying point for a whole generation of rising young teachers—Peirce, Howison, Hall, Morris, James, Royce, and Dewey, all availing themselves of the pages of this journal to publish their early writings.[320]

CHARLES S. PEIRCE

The writings of Charles S. Peirce (1839–1914) are an important and oft-mentioned source of many points of view later developed by James, Royce, Dewey, and others. The son of Benjamin Peirce, the mathematician, the boy received a thorough scientific training in the Cambridge atmosphere then pervaded with German thought. Years later he recalled that of all the national schools, the German had the deepest influence on him.

The first strictly philosophical books that I read were of the classical German schools; and I became so deeply imbued with many of their ways of thinking that I have never been able to disabuse myself of them. Yet my attitude was always that of a dweller in a laboratory, eager only to learn what I did not yet know, and not that of philosophers bred in the theological seminaries, whose ruling impulse is to teach what they hold to be infallibly true. I devoted two hours a day to the study of Kant's *Critique of Pure Reason* for more than three years, until I almost knew the whole book by heart, and had critically examined every section of it. . . . The effect of these [studies] was that I came to hold the classical German philosophy to be, on its argumentative side, of little weight; although I esteem it, perhaps am too partial to it, as a rich mine of philosophical suggestions.[321]

Peirce's great contribution was the formulation of the concept of "pragmatism"—the doctrine that only through application to existence, to some future consequence, can any philosophic proposition be given meaning. The choice of the term rests upon Kant's distinction between "*praktisch*" and "*pragmatisch*,"[322] but Peirce was the first to insist on its wider significance. While Peirce's ideas are scattered in a number of fragmentary or special studies, his careful and independent study of the problems of cosmology and psychology may be considered to be in harmony with the Kantian point of view—even though certain Kantian ideas are discarded.[323] Professor Muirhead, in a summary statement of Kant's influence on Peirce, asserted that Kant's *Critique of Pure Reason*—"the textbook, as it might be said, of the philosophically wise of his generation"—furnished him with the doctrine of the "purposiveness of all activity, whether practical, theoretic, or aesthetic. It was the general view founded on the recognition of this purposiveness that, to distinguish it from pragmatism, he called pragmaticism . . . . In the second place, he learned from Kant the place of thought as the direction of intellectual and moral activity towards unity and organization in the 'matter of experience.'"[324] The third thing he learned from his study of Kant was the "impossibility of combining the belief in an intelligible thing-in-itself with the real teaching of the Critique."[325]

Peirce did not rule out the possibility of the final harmony of all reality in an absolute, and this makes it understandable why he could say, as he once did, "My philosophy resuscitates Hegel, though in a strange costume."[326] Following his avowed purpose of erecting "a philosophical edifice that shall outlast the vicissitudes of time," he found only one system, "the new Schelling-Hegel mansion," that "stands upon its own ground."[327] His mathematical conceptions were employed to support and modify this "Schelling-fashioned idealism" which emerged more and more in the later stages of his writing.[328] Like Hegel, Peirce was fond of formulating his thought in triadic forms;[329] and idealists like Royce were indebted to Peirce for insights and ideas which contributed to their idealist logic, and which they traced back to Hegel.[330] Thus, contrary to the impression conveyed by certain remarks of his in condemnation of Hegel,[331] Peirce on the whole, and especially in his later writings, did not remain entirely uninfluenced by the German idealists.

GEORGE S. MORRIS

During the time when Peirce was a lecturer on Logic at Hopkins (1879–1884), he was associated with George Sylvester Morris and G. Stanley Hall in the conduct of courses for advanced students. This group of three, all somewhat older than the group of idealists and pragmatists whose brilliant work was to raise the status of American philosophy in the succeeding years, is to be credited with inspiring and guiding the future development, not only by their own work but also by the work of their students, Royce and Dewey.[332] Peirce's original and penetrating studies contained the germ of many divergent ideas elaborated by the idealists, pragmatists, and realists alike. Hall was interested

mainly in furthering the study of experimental psychology, while Morris propounded Hegelianism.

Morris (1840–1889)[333] left comparatively little original writing to perpetuate his fame, but as a teacher in that critical period he was acknowledged to be a real influence in the dissemination of German philosophical points of view, laboring indefatigibly and effectively to make the department of philosophy an integrating force where science and ethical and religious knowledge could have a common meeting-ground,[334] and becoming widely known as a champion of Hegel and Kant and a co-worker with W. T. Harris. Even while nominally a professor of modern languages at Michigan, he undertook, during 1871–1873, the work of translating Friedrich Ueberweg's *History of Philosophy*, in the "Theological and Philosophical Library Series" edited by Henry B. Smith and Philip Schaff. A little later he assumed the editorship of a series of critical expositions of "German Philosophical Classics"—Leibnitz, Kant, Fichte, Schelling, and Hegel—in which series he himself published *Kant's Critique of Pure Reason, a Critical Exposition* (1882) and *Hegel's Philosophy of the State and of History* (1887).[335]

Ever the earnest and grateful disciple of Henry B. Smith, Morris was yet destined, mainly because he belonged to a younger generation, to find little solace in his teacher's reconciliation of faith and speculative thought. Coming from orthodox Presbyterian circles, he was depressed and troubled for a long time by this problem.[336] The British Hegelians, T. H. Green, the Caird brothers, and Adamson, were the first to aid Morris in constructing an idealistic view that overcame the dualism of science and faith.[337] He undertook an intensive study of Kant, Fichte, and Hegel only after 1877, at the time when he was preparing the critical expositions of Kant and Hegel for his series. These works are critical and expository, not an independent adjustment of the ideas of Kant and Hegel to American needs of the time. In later lectures and essays, Morris discussed the main doctrines of Protestant dogmatics in terms of "what may be loosely called Hegelianism of the extreme Right Wing."[338] He drifted toward speculative idealism, but lapsed into an ethical theism which constantly skirted the basic problems. There was in him to the end of his short life a large residue of Calvinistic moralism, individualism, and dualism.

GEORGE HOLMES HOWISON

While the interest of George Holmes Howison (1834–1916) in technical philosophy was first aroused by his personal contact with the St. Louis group of Hegelians, he later attacked the orthodox Hegelians for their metaphysical absolutism and pantheism, and took his stand in favor of spiritual pluralism and personal idealism.[339] At first a Hegelian "pure and simple,"[340] he took part in the *Symposia* of the absolutists and lectured before the Concord School of Philosophy. But by 1883 he had formulated an important objection to absolutism, on the basis of which he separated from the Hegelians ever afterward: he wished to reconcile the affirmation of the existence of the individual with Hegelianism. Going back to Plato and Aristotle, and reading more of Spinoza, Fichte, and Hegel, he moved closer to rational theism. But his doubting of Hegel continued, until he rejected the belief in impersonal ideas and, reading James and the English writer, F. C. S. Schiller, came to believe in objective causes analogous to the will.[341]

JOSIAH ROYCE

One contributing reason why philosophical idealism had so many devoted followers and exponents at the close of the last century was the challenge which the empirical and naturalistic science offered to religion. Evolutionism and radical empiricism had rendered the traditional concepts suspect, while idealism provided a reformation of religion without completely rejecting science. Josiah Royce (1855–1916), perhaps the most formidable of all the champions of idealism in the America of his day, was a student of Peirce and Morris at Johns Hopkins in 1878. But for two years before that he had studied at Göttingen and Leipzig under Lotze, Wundt, and Windelband. After a few years of teaching in California, he began his career at Harvard, where he remained until his death in 1916.

His total system contained features derived from many sources. Especially after being subjected to the criticisms of Howison in the "Great Debate" of 1898, Royce emphasized the voluntaristic aspect of his thought, derived mainly from James and Lotze.[342] From Peirce he learned the method of mathematical logic which he used in his later books. Professor Cohen suggests that he was strongly influenced by the Kantian doctrine of the primacy of the practical reason and by the whole metaphysic of the *Critique of Pure Reason*.[343] Other elements are traceable to Fichte, Schelling, Schopenhauer, and Hegel. "The creative Ego of Fichte and the Self of Hegel, the Ego as spectator of itself, as Royce expresses it, living on the spectacle of its birth and death; these are all found in his philosophy."[344] From Schopenhauer, perhaps, was derived his tendency to give prominence to the will,[345] while the emphasis on duty suggests Fichte.[346] According to Royce's own testimony, Hegel was not as important in his thought as the other Romantics.[347]

By such means he constructed a system which was so complex and inclusive that it harmonized with much of James's pragmatism, while providing a metaphysics and epistemology built on the foundations of Kant and presenting the problems of the relation of the American individual to his universe, physical and moral, in terms of an absolute idealism that is essentially Germanic. His community is one in which personal subordination is sublimated into identification of the self with the larger social world or whole. Thus he retained what he regards as true individualism. For the world of Royce is one in which there are objects to be attained and defects to be made good. And so the unique meaning of the individual life, the meaning of the differences between individuals, is retained. This emphasis on uniqueness, suggested to him most immediately by James, but developed also by others, ultimately recommended Royce's system to the American community, notably New England, while his pervasive and profound personal influence, in the years up to 1916, did much to uphold the reputation of idealism at a time when realism and instrumentalism were threatening to carry all before them.

GEORGE HERBERT PALMER

Professor George Herbert Palmer (1842–1933), beloved teacher of ethics at Harvard and translator of Homer, taught an idealistic theism which owed much to the Kantian formulation of the function of the Practical Reason. Absorbing less from the college courses at Andover and Harvard than from his independent reading, Palmer was drawn to German idealism as early as 1865–1866, when he read Coleridge and F. H. Maurice as well as Kant. His years at Tübingen (1867–1869) made him a confirmed follower of Kant, in whom he found his "liberator" from the "arbitrary limitations of English empiricism."[348] On the appearance in 1878 of the Scottish-Hegelian Caird's book on Kant, Palmer struck up a lasting friendship with the Scottish author, though he by no means subscribed to Hegel's system. In teaching his course in ethics Palmer acknowledged himself a follower of Jesus and Kant, setting the Kantian imperative (in simplified, generalized form) as the basis of morality.[349]

JAMES EDWIN CREIGHTON

James Edwin Creighton (1861–1924) was perhaps the strictest Hegelian of all the later idealists. He studied in Leipzig and Berlin in 1888, afterwards becoming instructor at Cornell and later being associated with the Sage School of Philosophy. He defended speculative idealism against absolute idealism, pragmatism, and realism. He rejected the tendency in Kant to center the philosophical universe in the subject and to set subject and object transcendentally opposed to one another. Instead of mentalism—whereby everything is defined as mental in character, of the content and substance of mind—he proposed speculative idealism, appealing to the principle of the concrete universal which recognizes that only the individual is real.[350] His translation of the writings of Wundt materially aided in the introduction of German philosophy into America.

JOHN DEWEY

Though John Dewey (1859–1952) was later to develop radical empiricism to greater lengths than any other American thinker of his generation, during his youth he was strongly influenced by the German idealists and particularly by Hegel.[351] Influenced also by Green and the Cairds, he made an intensive study of the works of Hegel, which left its mark on his subsequently developed thought principally in his opposition to dualisms of all sorts, "in his historical approach to all cultural life, his mastery of concrete material, and his extraordinarily acute perception of the continuities between matter and life, life and mind, and mind and society. . . . Even after he abandoned Hegelian idealism and its artificial schematicism, he honored Hegel's insight into the processes of change out of which the relative and shifting concretions of things emerge that provide the context of all discourse and action. He naturalized Hegel's historical approach by a biological theory of mind and an institutional analysis of social behavior."[352]

WILLIAM JAMES

The idealist systems proposed by Royce, Howison, and others, though they were successful in making a rationalistic union of science and religion and thus in preserving, in a sense, much of the view of life espoused by the genteel tradition against the continued strong attacks of realists and materialists, were found to be far from satisfactory to a number of typically American personalities. The absolute threatened to give a static, predetermined, intellectualistic picture of the world at a time when American thinkers wished to express in philosophy the opposite picture of practicality, change, flux, and meliorism, with full freedom for the individual will to alter the course of events. William James (1842–1910) was the one first vividly and effectively to present this view.

His father, "half-Swedenborgian, half-Hegelian," trained his sons in the methods of philosophical discourse and taught them a type of transcendentalism in their earliest years that William later partially rejected and partially revived.[353] After a period of eighteen months in Germany (1867–1868) he read widely in Comte, Spencer, Jouffroy, Schopenhauer, Kant, Schleiermacher, Fichte, and Renouvier,[354] besides a great deal of French and German literature, and in 1867, Hegel's and Cousin's lectures on Kant.[355] After publishing his *Principles of Psychology* in 1890, his books were mainly devoted to the statement of his pragmatism and his study of problems of religion.

Not a system-maker primarliy, but a man gifted in presenting imaginatively the philosophic structure of the American world here and now, James took Peirce's term *pragmatism* and made it, with simplifications and slight changes of emphasis, the central concept of his doctrine. Pragmatism for him became a theory of truth, not merely, as for Peirce, one of meaning. James, the student of fact-loving Agassiz and of Peirce, had an intense interest in and

respect for empirical facts; he would allow no abstraction to come between him and the hard, irregular, primal stuff of experience. But like so many romantics, he had moments and moods when the desire for a final merging of disparate individuals into one ultimate totality overcame all else. James "was not insensible to the Hegelian influence which really always remained more or less pronounced in his mind"; and, following Fechner, he approached at times a sympathy with Royce's idea of a vaster consciousness enveloping our own—though his method of reaching this absolute was concrete and hypothetical, not abstract and deductive as was that of his colleague.[356]

James's absorptive mind was nourished on a wide range of books, and the sources of his thought are manifold and sometimes remote. But the outstanding fact is that his friend and contemporary, Renouvier, offered him the necessary help at a critical juncture in 1870, so that he said in 1884, "My reasonings are almost wholly those of Renouvier."[357] While James protested "the circuitous and ponderous artificialities of Kant" and felt that the "true direction of philosophic progress lies . . . not so much *through* Kant as *round* him to the point where we now stand,"[358] Kant was not thus easily outflanked. For one thing, as Renouvier confessed himself "a continuer of Kant,"[359] so James recognized the fact that Renouvier started out with the acceptance of Kant's forms and categories and with his definition of phenomenon. Thus it was from ideas originating in Kant that the empiricism of James developed.[360] Seeing contemporary philosophies gravitating to the two extremes of Hegelian idealism and evolutionism, and concluding that the philosophy of the future would be "either that of Renouvier or that of Hegel," he unhesitatingly took sides with the French thinker, "determined to continue, in an even more radically empiristic fashion, the tradition of neo-criticism simultaneously with the tradition of men like Lotze and Sigwart."[361]

But James arrived at some of the same ideas through other channels. The system and temperament of Fechner were similar to those of Renouvier and were important to James in reinforcing his thinking. In 1908 James waxed enthusiastic over the German writer's *Zend-Avesta*, calling it "a wonderful book, by a wonderful genius. He has his vision and he knows how to discuss it, as no one's vision ever was discussed."[362] James's polytheism—his theory of the multiplicity of consciousness and his transcendentalist theory of the soul, whereby particular souls proceed from a single immense reservoir, an infinite thought or mother consciousness—were inspired by Fechner and his disciple Myers, rather than Renouvier.[363]

Lotze, another critic of Hegel, and Wundt, whose teachings were derived from both Fechner and Lotze, were recognized by James as those of contemporary German thinkers with whom he could feel most in sympathy.[364] Not only did James and Lotze agree on philosophical method and orientation, but James also derived some of his special arguments from his reading of Lotze. These are especially noteworthy in his *Psychology*. James used several of Lotze's books (in English translation) in his classes at Harvard.[365]

Inasmuch as James rejects most of Kant and is unsympathetic to the ways of thinking of the German idealists, he represents a force tending to discredit what had long been considered the main current of German philosophy. But he had close relations, some indirect, with some lesser-known German writers, and his debt to German teachers in another and quite separate field—psychophysics and experimental physiology and psychology—was very great.[366] The substance of his first book, the *Psychology* (1890), was in sympathy with and partly derivative from German experimental psychology. He had learned the experimental methods during his eighteen months in Germany in the sixties.[367] During his later years he concerned himself less and less with

experimental psychology, but kept up his close and friendly relations with German writers in the field,[368] and it was entirely through his efforts that Professor Hugo Münsterberg was induced, in 1892, to leave his laboratory at Freiburg and carry on his work at Harvard,[369] in co-operation with Palmer, Royce, and James.

THORSTEIN VEBLEN

The work of the independent, ironical, enigmatical Thorstein Veblen (1857–1929) is difficult to categorize because it belongs to several fields at once. In 1880 Veblen began his graduate studies at Johns Hopkins,[370] taking work in philosophy with Morris and Peirce. On the whole he was closer to Peirce's critical point of view than to Morris' attempts at constructing an idealism consonant with Christian theism. Earlier, Veblen had read W. T. Harris' *Philosophical Basis of Theism* and found himself unsympathetic with Hegel. Instead, he was more willing to align himself with the neo-Kantians and evolutionists, trusting that an extension of Kantian metaphysics would provide a basis for solid work in the contemporary scientific age. He continued his philosophical studies at Yale under the famous conservative Noah Porter. In preparing his dissertation on the "Ethical Grounds of a Doctrine of Retribution," he made a thorough study of Kant and the post-Kantians and, rejecting current utilitarianism and hedonistic ethical theories, replaced them with Kant's rigoristic ethics of duty. It is interesting to note that Harris' *Journal of Speculative Philosophy* in 1884 printed the first article of Veblen's to appear before the public—an analysis of Kant's *Critique of Judgment*.[371] Veblen's antagonism to Hegelianisms of all kinds—conservative or materialistic—dates from this period of his study of Peirce and Kant, and was a permanent safeguard against any tendency to accept Marxian socialist doctrine without close criticism and important revisions.

Although Veblen devoted his years of teaching and writing to the fields of economics and sociology, every book that he wrote was finally grounded on his individual philosophical approach to the problems of his day. Many, because of their ironic, iconoclastic attitude toward existing institutions, hide the author's positive beliefs under an almost impenetrable mask of indirection, wit, and cautious circumlocution. His last work in the field of philosophy proper was the translation he made for George Trumbull Ladd of the volumes of Lotze's *Dictata*.[372] On those rare occasions where Veblen presents a positive statement of his convictions, he returns to the neo-Kantian emphasis on an ethics of duty, on the centrality of morality. This is perhaps clearest in the *Instinct of Workmanship* and in his book on the *Nature of Peace*, in the Preface of which he cites Kant's late work, *Zum ewigen Frieden*.

BORDEN P. BOWNE

Contemporary with James was Borden P. Bowne (1847–1910), professor at Boston University, who constructed a transcendental empiricism or personalism with many features similar to those noted in James. Bowne studied at Halle and Göttingen from 1871 to 1873, under Lotze, Erdmann, and Ulrici. In his personal idealism he faced the same problems that Howison encountered: he differed from Royce by putting his system on a basis of the primacy of practical reason. Bowne defended the rights of the religious consciousness against positivism, materialism, and naturalism, following Lotze closely in his arguments but drawing also on Plato, Aristotle, Berkeley, Leibnitz, Kant, and Renouvier. With his emphasis on particular, concrete experience, and his suspicion of abstractions, his general receptivity to pragmatic positions makes him a personal idealist opposed to impersonalism or the Hegelian fondness for the abstract.[373]

GEORGE SANTAYANA

George Santayana (1863–1952), naturalist and materialist, was ever the enemy of the absolute idealists. In many forceful utterances he criticized the point of view of the whole German post-Kantian group of thinkers. Nevertheless, his period of study in Berlin under Paulsen, as well as under Palmer at Harvard, was fruitful. He enjoyed Paulsen's exposition of Greek ethics and his living sense of the historical spirit of the time. Fichte and Schopenhauer, he asserts, helped him formulate what he calls necessary radical transcendentalism, his doctrine of essences.[374]

Santayana in his time stood virtually alone in rejecting almost completely the work of the German classical idealists. For his colleagues, the discoveries of Kant and Hegel, if not of the post-Hegelians, together with recent writings on psychology and the history of philosophy, were so obviously in the direct line of the Western philosophical tradition that they could not afford to neglect them, either in formulating their own ideas or in their teaching.[375] Further evidence of the widespread adoption by the 1880's of the method and content of German philosophical study appears in the use of a large number and variety of German textbooks, some in the original[376] and others in translation.[377]

Experimental Psychology: G. Stanley Hall

American experimental psychology was imported from Germany during the seventies and eighties by such students as George Trumbull Ladd of Yale and G. Stanley Hall of Clark. Hall set up the first experimental psychological laboratory in America, patterned directly on those he had observed in Leipzig under Wundt's direction in 1879–1880. By 1895 the study was being carried on in "two-score of the best institutions" in this country.[378] Earlier widespread notice of the work of Lotze and Eduard von Hartmann's on the *Unconscious* (1869) undoubtedly facilitated the rapid spread of interest in the subject.

Hall spent nearly six of the twelve years between 1870 and 1882 in the lecture halls and laboratories of the German investigators.[379] The experience of complete intellectual freedom as afforded by the German university in contrast with the narrow limitations of American college life was refreshing and stimulating. The range of Hall's studies was so wide as to include the theological discourses of Dorner, Trendelenberg's seminary on Aristotle, Delitzsch's lectures on Biblical psychology, recent psychology by Pfleiderer, and much more in the fields of Hegelianism and Herbartianism, chemistry, biology, physiology, anatomy, neurology, and anthropology.

Aspects of German Culture (1881), Hall's first book, was a collection of foreign letters originally published in the *Nation* and other journals. For the most part a commentary on German theology, science, and philosophy, the essays embrace a fairly wide range of loosely related subjects, indicating the extent of Hall's immersion in German life and thought. In 1881-1882 he was invited to give a lecture course at Johns Hopkins, where Morris was lecturing on a similar appointment. Here he set up the first psychological laboratory in 1881; and his work ever afterward was devoted to experimental psychology, the study of childhood and adolescence, and related pedagogical subjects. John Dewey and James McKeen Cattell were students under him in Baltimore in 1882-1883. His call to the presidency of Clark University, with which school his name is closely associated, gave him his opportunity, as he termed it, to make Clark (in respect to its graduate studies in psychology and philosophy) an "offshoot of Johns Hopkins," where the methods and techniques of German research could be organized on his plan.[380]

The titles of courses in various schools in the 1880's point to a rapid introduction of experimental methods. At Cornell in 1878-1879, for instance, the course was labeled "nervous physiology in relation to mental phenomena." In 1890-1891 a special psychological laboratory was set up by William James at Harvard, although several years earlier James had introduced experimental features into his lecture courses. The study of the new psychology in all the larger schools dates from the early eighties. In 1892 Professor Münsterberg, who had been trained in the school of Wundt and had been invited to the University of Freiburg, took charge of the experimental work in psychology at Harvard.[381]

The History of Philosophy

Among the last but in some respects most important developments in American philosophical teaching was the remarkable acceleration of emphasis during the period from 1880 to 1900 on the history of philosophy after the German fashion. A beginning had been made much earlier—at first with little reference to German precedent,[382] but during the last quarter of the century the movement was in the hands of men enthusiastically sympathetic toward the German academic tradition, many of them having acquired a deep understanding of the language and the philosophy of Germany at first hand. Bowen's *History* of 1877 and Bascom's *History* of 1893 (each devoting a large amount of space to Germans from Kant to Lotze) represent significant concessions made by the entrenched realists to the new materials and modes of teaching. With the capitulation of the conservative Scottish realists the newer school may be fairly credited with a victory for their cause. Henceforth the teaching of philosophy was set squarely on the road it has traveled since. Eventualities during the period from 1880 to 1900 amount to a vindication of the aims of men like Seelye, Hickok, and Hall.

The year 1900 is in a sense an arbitrary

stopping-point in the history of American teaching of philosophy, for the situation as it developed through the eighties and nineties remained almost unchanged until the outbreak of the war of 1914. The German-trained professor still occupied the position of command over the body of American teachers in that branch. Nevertheless, the rise of the group of neo-realists and critical realists early in the twentieth century is symptomatic of that vigorous protest against all forms of idealism that has gained in strength up to the present time. Before that day there was no significant movement in American philosophy— with the possible exception of the radical empiricism of John Dewey—which did not look to German thinkers for important contributions to their systems. The school of naive realism represented by McCosh rapidly lost prestige after 1880 and made concessions to neo-Kantianism in an effort to save its system from complete bankruptcy; while the growing power of materialistic and positivistic thought facilitated the tendency, as administrators saw that it was better to defend faith by teaching a tenable idealism than to let all religion wither and die under the attacks of blatant mechanistic materialism. The idealists, led by Royce, were everywhere recognized as one of the most formidable groups; and the proponents of various forms of personalism, pragmatism, and realism—all acknowledging their debt either to German classical or to post-Hegelian writers—contended for supremacy in those places where idealism was not fully accepted.

WHILE no attempt to summarize the results of so complex a relationship as that obtaining between German and American thought is, at this stage of the inquiry, as yet in order, three or four observations may be made. The introduction of German philosophy was no isolated event, but a series in a chain that led Americans to examine all traditions of philosophic thought from ancient to contemporary times. In their effort to find a universal explanation of things, they not only became acquainted with ideas until then unfamiliar to them but achieved a rational maturity of their own. It is noteworthy that at precisely the time when this process of winning intellectual maturity was at its height, the acculturation of German philosophy was strongest.

Begun primarily as an effort to find a philosophic reorientation for religion and theology, the search for a comprehensive philosophy led, in the first place, to a redefinition of the place and meaning of philosophy in the whole of our intellectual life. Philosophy came to be not only logic and ethics but an attempt to find a more scientific method by which to solve the problems of religion, aesthetics, politics, and the sciences in terms of a sound epistemology and a comprehensive metaphysics. In the place of the older catechetical methods of instruction by which accepted dogma and sectarian doctrine in catenarian series were memorized, the basic definitions and concepts of German philosophy encouraged a spirit of free inquiry that eventually brought all arts and sciences, as well as religion, within the orbit of philosophy, and provoked a philosophic reorientation of all aspects of human thought and life, theoretical and practical, such as neither the older Calvinistic nor the later Common-Sense dispensations had deemed possible or permissible.

In this process nothing went deeper than the new bearings taken, under Kantian and Hegelian auspices, by which all religious experience and all theological speculation were subjected to the refining fires of rational investigation. Thus philosophy was raised from the rank of a dependent science to the status of a disinterested critic of the entire cosmic and human scene—to become the science of sciences, precisely as it was in Germany. This growing faith in the universal applicability of philosophy and the growing sense for the necessity of translating concept and theory into action and life made it come to pass, also, that the new philosophy should be applied to the political and social patterns of a democracy. In this respect Platonic as well as Christian precedent was re-enforced by the application of the speculative and practical reason of Kant in his Critiques as well as his other writings, by Fichte's addresses to the German nation, and by the Hegelian application of his dialectics to the philosophy of history, with its promises of inner unity in the face of outer disparities; and the return from Germany of the first group of Harvard men, supported by the examples of Follen and Lieber, signalized the advent in America of this idea, soon to be given further objectification by the New England Transcendentalists and the St. Louis Hegelians. In short, philosophy was made practical and was domesticated to the common political and social contingencies of the day.[383]

A second result accruing to American philosophy from this closer alliance with German thought was the acceptance of the methodology of the Germans, involving careful research, meticulous analysis, and a willingness to follow through to conclusions indicated by the data. It led to an objectivity hitherto unapproached by American scholarship, revolutionizing the methods of research, enlarging the scope of investigation, and involving a new attitude toward literary sources of philosophy and history, a re-evaluation of libraries, books, and periodicals for purposes of university instruction as well as of research, a remarkable increase in book and periodical publication, a rejection of the textbook method of teaching and the substitution therefor of the lecture and seminar methods, a reorientation of the teacher-pupil relationship by which the student was led or guided into the ways of the history of ideas to solve his own problems rather than instructed *ex cathedra*, a complete reformation of curricula and disciplines, and a tendency to develop a greater open-mindedness, tolerance, and universality in point of view.

Another and in some respects more immediately effective influence was exerted by the more precise ideas and concepts which American thought derived, or gained support for, from German sources. Among the more influential of these is the concept of development (variously called *das Werden* or *der Entwicklungsprozess*) as applied not only to science but also to the history of ideas. Long before the spirit of Buffon, Lamarck, Hutton, Lyell, Wallace, and Darwin profoundly affected Americans, Herder, Goethe, the Schlegels, and Hegel had boldly declared that ideas in the realms of literature and language, philosophy, and history itself, as well as forms of organic life, exhibit traceable forms of development or evolution. Zeller's and Heeren's studies of Greek civilization and the vast amount of German Biblical history, much of which was translated by Americans between 1830 and 1850, are other examples. Following these cues, thinking Americans were quick to conceive of reason in terms of organic unity—as incorporated in Kant's Critiques, as developed in Fichte and Schelling, and as it received its rational culmination in Hegel's phenomenology, logic, and dialectics. The thought of an active world-soul working in every area of human experience and achieving synthesis and objectivity in progress appealed to democratic Americans. The New England Transcendentalists vaguely grasped but boldly accepted this sense of movement, growth, and evolution. The St. Louis Hegelians, adopting the Hegelian triadic movement of thesis, antithesis, and synthesis, made it an integral part of their philosophy and applied it to the resolution of the conflicting forces and ideas of the postwar period. The academic and professional philosophers of the idealistic persuasion domesticated it by acclimatizing it to American conditions and incorporating it into what passes currently for the characteristic American philosophy. The conception of man's place at the center of the universal order of evolution is at once an illustration of the "irrefragable unity of all western thought"[384] and an indication of America's readiness to assume its place in the onward movement of thought and culture.[385] This concept provided a new sense of freedom and withal a sense of relatedness. Thus American philosophy early declared its independence by joining a philosophical process, the dependence upon which it has as yet shown little indication to throw off. This ready acceptance of the Hegelian doctrine of *Prozess* in the philosophy of history prepared the way for the acceptance of Darwin and did much to help thoughtful Americans over the baffling difficulties involved in the synthesis of the religious heritage with the newer evolutionary discoveries. But above all else, this view of evolution meant most for the development and expression of American philosophy, the progress of American education, and the historical concept of American destiny. The breadth, catholicity, and freedom from bigotry explicit in Kantian transcendentalism and its emphasis on human values powerfully impressed the American Transcendentalists from Channing through Frothingham; it directly influenced the "Religion of Humanity" promulgated by the Free Religious Associationists; and ultimately it was transmuted and utilized in the basically humanistic philosophy of Charles S. Peirce and William James, labeled Pragmatism. One of the seminal concepts that found recognition in American pragmatism, Instrumentalism, and Experimentalism is the basic distinction made by Kant between *das Praktische* and *das Pragmatische*, as adopted by Peirce. Finally, the philosophical concern with personality as accentuated by the German transcendentalists found exemplification and emphasis in American speculation that led to what is currently called Personalism, or Personal Idealism, as expressed by Howison, Bowne, Ladd, Calkins, and Brightman.

Fourth, and last, it is to be observed that while idealistic thought in America owed its first allegiance to English interpretations of Greek and Christian philosophy, it received a remarkable revivification from German idealism. The reaction against British thought that set in after the Revolutionary War and the dissatisfaction alike with French rationalism and Scottish common-sense led American idealists to Germany. Here they found two important ideas not an integral part of the earlier idealistic tradition in America: first, the concept of the activity of the mind as a part of the total cosmic process, and second, the emphasis upon mind as the active agent in the approximations to reality above the level of nature. The first is one growing out of Kantian transcendentalism, and the second, especially as it places emphasis upon the mind as creative, derived mainly from Hegel. These two became the cardinal principles of American idealism from Channing and Emerson through Henry Boynton Smith and William Torrey Harris to its more recent exponents, Creighton, Royce, and Hocking. By them and through the instrumentality of idealists among the professors of philosophy in American colleges and universities, idealism of a basically Germanic cast has been perpetuated in America despite numerous graftings upon the parent stem and offshoots in new directions, long beyond the time of its decline in other countries.

Book Two

German Literary Influence

Some Areas and Lines of Influence

THE VOGUE OF GERMAN LITERATURE—A SURVEY

From the Beginnings to 1810

EIGHTEENTH-CENTURY SENTIMENTAL
LITERATURE

As has been indicated earlier, scholars in Boston in the seventeenth century had kept in touch with the learning of Germany, a number of New England leaders acquiring for their libraries a considerable proportion of German treatises. There was some interest in the popular literature of Germany as well, though not as great as in England.[1] Pietistic and mystical religious literature and moralistic tracts furnished the bulk of German writing that appeared in translation between 1788 and 1810.[2] In the eighteenth century certain political events and a popular military figure aroused the earliest widespread American interest: e.g., the successes of Frederick the Great of Prussia, ally of England in 1758–1759 in his campaigns against France and Austria. There were numerous translations, adaptations, and imitations of his poems, especially "The Relaxation of War" (1752).[3] Acquaintance with literary figures as such was limited and was largely dependent on British example. Salomon Gessner, author of prose pastorals in a gentle, sentimental vein and of the *Death of Abel*, a prose epic in imitation of Klopstock's *Messias*, appeared frequently in American magazines and in book form between 1741 and 1804.[4] The *Messias* itself, in Collyer's indifferent translation, the fables of Christian Gellert and of Herder, and Sotheby's version of

Wieland's *Oberon* were known through translation and printings in the magazines,[5] and certain pieces of juvenile and humorous literature, notably the Baron Munchhausen tales, became widely popular.[6]

INTEREST IN *Sturm und Drang*

A new phase of interest was reached with the arrival of the *Sturm-und-Drang* writings of the young Goethe and Schiller, the *Lenore* of Bürger,[7] and the tales of Zschokke. These reinforced the growing interest in Gothicism and horror. The *Wertherfieber* struck America with the first printing of the novel in 1784 (to be followed by nine other printings by 1809), and in 1787 the *American Museum* carried the earliest of many poetical and dramatic adaptations of the story.[8] While *Werther* had much in common with the products of the sentimental school, its fascination lay in its challenge to existing ethical standards and in the forthrightness with which it treated an engrossing emotional conflict.[9] Schiller was first known for his novel of mystery and intrigue, *Der Geisterseher*, which was extensively extracted in the magazines in 1794 and after, and twice published in book form before 1801.[10] The appearance of Zschokke's horror tale of the bandit Abaellino, adapted for the American stage in 1792 and thrice reprinted before 1809, brought readers into the world of Schiller's epochal *Räuber*. Of *The Robbers* (in the British translation by Tytler) there were reprints in 1793, 1795, 1802, and 1808. A generation of readers found this story of

327

the high-minded outlaw and champion of pure justice against the venality of the social institutions extremely satisfying. The story underwent several of permutations in popular fiction and drama, and it enjoyed a moderate popularity on the stage from 1795 to 1815. Schiller's *Kabale und Liebe* appeared in 1795 and was reprinted in 1802 and 1813, and *Fiesco* and *Don Carlos*, together with Coleridge's translation of the *Piccolomini*, were reprinted from British translations between 1799 and 1805.[11] Lessing's *Miss Sara Sampson* was published in 1789 in a translation by David Rittenhouse; at the end of the century his *Emilia Galotti* appeared in book form and in a periodical.[12]

KOTZEBUE

The best known of German authors at the turn of the century, however, was not one of the classical writers but the dramatist Kotzebue. By virtue mainly of the work of William Dunlap, translator, adaptor, and theatrical entrepreneur, thirty of the plays of this prolific author were published in America between 1799 and 1820, the greater number before 1803.[13] London managers had discovered a few years before that Kotzebue provided fresh, sure-fire material for the popular stage, and Dunlap in his first venture hit upon Kotzebue's most famous and perhaps most characteristic work, *Menschenhass und Reue* (billed as *The Stranger*). Dunlap now perfected his German and undertook further translations, and in seven seasons between 1798 and 1805 the dramas of Kotzebue made up a substantial portion of his play list. Few critics, Dunlap least of all, read literary merit into these plays, but they were stageworthy, and they satisfied the tastes of the moment, mixing sentiment and heroics with shallow rationalism and exotic allure. Audiences were kept amused by what a contemporary critic called Kotzebue's "facility of invention," his "admi-

rable incidents," and even his "fine delineation of character."[14] The meretricious quality of Kotzebue was used by some critics, unfortunately, as the basis of attack on all German drama and the "Teutonic Muse" generally.[15] But on the whole American criticism in these years was preparing the way for a fuller understanding of German literary life by bringing a number of sketches of men like Bürger, Schiller, Klopstock, Wieland, and Gellert.[16] John Quincy Adams, Charles Brockden Brown, William Dunlap, and others contributed moderate, informative discussions on the subject.[17]

From 1810 to 1864

CLASSICAL AND ROMANTIC AUTHORS

The year 1810 marks the point of division between the first and second phases of American interest in German letters. German writers of the recent romantic schools then became of some importance to American readers and students, and soon afterward the first personal links were established between representative American literary men and some leading German authors. The first important event in this development was the printing of Madame de Staël's *Germany* in 1814 in New York and the subsequent discussion of her work in the periodicals.[18]

From 1815 to 1817 George Ticknor and Edward E. Everett were at Göttingen, absorbing German learning at its source. They and their many successors gave to German literature the prestige which only personal advocacy could give, and the results of their studies were soon afterwards appearing in the *North American Review* along with essays by George Bancroft.[19] The coming of that early refugee, Carl Follen, to Harvard in 1825 and the attendant publicity of his inaugural, the appearance of Carlyle's early trumpet-blasts in support of German thought and German *Poesie*—these events are further stages in the growth of German-American rapport, affecting at first, of course, only a small body of eager students but providing the impetus for the mounting interest of the next twenty years. The studies in German philosophy and belles-lettres made by such theological students as Joseph Buckminster, Convers Francis, Moses Stuart, and James Marsh likewise aided this development, encouraging many to study the language and to acquire libraries of German books, and making a wide circle of religious students conversant with German speculative thought in all its ramifications.

To such well-schooled and cultivated men as Ticknor, Everett, Bancroft, and Longfellow must go the credit for demonstrating that the recent classical and romantic German schools take precedence over the eighteenth-century sentimentalists, Gothicism, and *Sturm und Drang*. Their essays and reviews, based on the judgments of the professors whom they had heard at Göttingen, gave a more penetrating and a sounder analysis of German literary history than anything hitherto written by American critics.[20] In the next forty years there was an ever-widening stream of serious and appreciative reviews and articles. Within that time certain ingrained British–New England taboos were cast aside; Goethe, Jean Paul, and Schiller came to be cordially accepted—a result not of the efforts of the "Germanico" Transcendentalists alone, but of a more broadly based revolution in taste and feeling.[21] During the thirties the minds of Emerson, Margaret Fuller, J. F. Clarke, George Ripley, and Theodore Parker matured in an atmosphere "charged with an intense excitement over the newly-discovered German writers."[22] One editor commented in 1836:

Five years ago the name of Goethe was hardly known in England and America, except as the author of a 'silly book,' *Werter*, an incomprehensible drama, *Faust*, and a tedious novel, *Meister*. . . . But now

a revolution has taken place. Hardly a review or a magazine appears that has not something in it about Goethe, and people begin to find with amazement that a genius as original as Shakespeare and as widely influential as Voltaire, has been among us.[23]

The journals carried a vast amount of discussion—charges, countercharges, denunciations, and vindications—of the Germans and Germanism. Though journals like the *North American Review* and the *Christian Examiner* provided the principal battleground over German philosophy, virtually all periodicals in all sections opened their columns to reprints of German poetry and fiction in translation.[24] Furthermore, in the book trade a wide variety of collections and anthologies of German poetry and tales were issued, beginning with Carlyle's *German Romance* (London, 1827) and continuing throughout the period.[25] A number of volumes of literary history, commentary, or criticism were printed, notably C. C. Felton's translation of Wolfgang Menzel's *German Literature* (1840), Joseph Gostick's *German Literature* (1854), and G. H. Lewes' *Life and Works of Goethe* (1855).

RELATIVE STANDING OF VARIOUS GERMAN AUTHORS

As for the relative popularity of various authors and groups of authors, it is possible on the basis of accurately compiled data[26] to show that Schiller and Goethe were the best known German writers of the period. Almost a third of all the periodical items—translations, notices, reviews, critiques, sketches—carried in the journals to 1864 dealt with them. Among authors introduced before 1810 the following ranked in the order indicated: Goethe, Schiller, Jean Paul, Zschokke, Kotzebue, Herder, Luther, Lessing, Bürger, Klopstock, Wieland, and Gellert. Of those who became known after 1810, Körner, Uhland, Heine, Fouqué, Rückert, Tieck, the Schlegels, and Freiligrath reached such prominence as to rank alongside the older men.[27] For the period as a whole the older classics Herder and Lessing remained high on the list, though favored not as much as Jean Paul or Kotzebue. The appearance of so many romantic writers—poets and authors of *Novellen*—among the most popular is in accord with the romantic tastes and interests of the period. In the field of the lyric poem (counting the frequence with which individual poems were printed in the magazines or included in American collections) Schiller held slight precedence over Goethe; Körner, Geibel, Rückert, Uhland, Freiligrath, Heine, Bürger, and Klopstock followed next in frequency.[28]

The classicist Goethe was brought to American attention by Madame de Staël, Carlyle, and the Göttingen students. Before 1812 there had been nothing to alter the popular estimate of him as the author of a notorious *Werther* and an affecting ballad, the "Erlking." However, in 1812 the *American Review* came out with a review of the recent novel *Die Wahlverwandtschaften*, at the same time enlarging somewhat on the whole of Goethe's career to that moment.[29] This marks the beginning of the long history of mingled praise and censure, the note of acrid controversy that governs American comment on Goethe to 1864.[30] Considering how much Goethe's philosophy had in common with the regnant doctrine of Unitarianism, the history of his influence in America would have been quite otherwise than it was if he had been accepted by those who guided the literary taste and set the intellectual pace. During the early years he had only a few champions, such as Margaret Fuller, James F. Clarke, and George H. Calvert. The qualified approval, the hesitance of men like Emerson, Longfellow, Parker, and Motley, was as great an obstacle to general acceptance as the outright hostility of a Bancroft or Norton. In the stock comparison which the New England (and in many ways Puritan) conscience customarily made, namely of contrasting Goethe and Dante

(or Milton), the German poet was invariably worsted.

The printing of Goethe's *Memoirs* (*Dichtung und Wahrheit*) in 1824 and of *Wilhelm Meister* (1828), together with the translation of a number of poems, opened the way for comment on the private life of Goethe before the public had the opportunity to study his most characteristic longer poems and dramas. Madame de Staël had of course paid her respects to Goethe's greatness and genius, but at the same time she felt constrained to mention what appeared to her his moral shortcomings—his aloofness from politics, his retreat from the sphere of the practical or active life, his lack of sympathy, his coolness toward the creatures of his imagination—in short, his moral neutrality.[31] The important long reviews by Everett (1817) and Bancroft (1824)[32] repeated these charges. Carl Follen at Harvard deepened the lines of contrast between Goethe and Schiller, to the disadvantage of the former, and Professor Felton penned articles that illustrate his inability to reconcile his artistic and moral judgments. Felton's review of *Iphigenie* (1830) praised the author's genius, imagination, versatility, depth and power, and command of language, but when some years later he examined the *Elective Affinities* (*Wahlverwandtschaften*) from the standpoint of morals alone, he crossed it off as "licentious and detestable."[33]

One of the first of modern histories of German literature was the *Deutsche Literatur* (1827) of Wolfgang Menzel, a work inspired by a youthful spirit of rebellion against the "indifference" of Goethe. His genius was denied; he was accused of possessing nothing more than a talent for the gracious comforts of life, an aesthetic appreciation of sensual pleasures and delicate refinements. The overpowering image of the older writer appeared to Menzel's socially conscious *Jung Deutschland* generation as the symbol of the politically under-

developed and irresponsible German tradition that they were fighting. Menzel's
history, partisan and extreme as it was, was
selected by the Transcendentalist George
Ripley to be included in his *Specimens of
Foreign Standard Literature*, in a translation
by C. C. Felton (1840). It was not Ripley's
intent, by printing the work in his series, to
prejudice American opinion to the advantage of Schiller and the political poets;
nor was Felton willing to subscribe to all
that Menzel charged, feeling indeed that
Menzel was unfair to his subject.[34] Yet, the
years of the thirties and forties were
marked by bitter controversy, even vituperation. This vein was most extreme in
the writings of Andrews Norton and George
Bancroft, more temperate in reviews by
Leonard Woods, Jr., and J. L. Motley.[35]
By 1840 Hayward's *Faust* (prose) and
Margaret Fuller's translation of Eckermann's *Conversations with Goethe* (1839) had
appeared, and the next decade brought the
Faust by Anna Swanwick, the Schiller-
Goethe *Correspondence*, the *Essays on Art,
Iphigenie, Egmont*, and *Hermann und Dorothea*, all in American printings. Goethe's
general popularity as a lyric poet is evident
from the fact that after Schiller, poems by
him were most frequently included in
American collections.

Up to the appearance of the *Dial* and the
growth of Transcendentalist influence in
American criticism, the American critics
hardly knew how to explain, much less to
justify, the pre-eminence of Goethe. To
neutralize what they saw of the harmful
implications of his naturalistic philosophy,
they bound him with the threads of a
parochial and often illiberal ethical system.
Theodore Parker, Margaret Fuller, J. F.
Clarke and many of the younger Transcendentalists were temperamentally disposed to accept the Goethean point of view
fully. Their intense study of his works and
times equipped them to see that the subject
was far more complex than a reading of
Menzel or Heine would indicate. How far

they understood Goethe and in what respects they differed from him are matters
considered elsewhere in this study. Parker's
temperament was drawn to the more exclusively religious elements in German
literature; Margaret Fuller and her disciples
had perhaps a closer affinity with the
Romantic successors of Goethe than with
Goethe himself. Emerson treated Goethe
the writer in *Representative Men*, and, while
preserving his sense of a difference in *Weltanschauung*, created perhaps the greatest
single monument to Goethe yet produced
in American criticism. Longfellow's *Hyperion* approached the subject from the
point of view of nostalgic romanticism and
remains an interesting document of American romantic feeling toward Goethe. On
the whole the Transcendentalist critics were
willing to keep the categories of moral and
aesthetic judgment apart—to distinguish
between the moral character of the author
and the ethical teaching of his writings.[36]
One reviewer of 1846 argued that when
Goethe is considered as *"The Artist of His
Age* . . . the contradictions of his career
become plain; . . . his conduct as a man"
is justified. Goethe "saw in the issues and
tendencies of art, a universality and grandeur of development, which no man before
him had ever seen so clearly and no contemporary had so successfully embodied or
expressed."[37] This attitude was supported
by G. H. Lewes in his *Life of Goethe*
(Boston, 1856), which centered attention
on Goethe as artist and wise observer of
life. For its earnestness and high competence
the flood of Transcendentalist discussion of
Goethe is impressive, especially as it was
combined with so many noteworthy
pioneering efforts at the translation of his
later writings and his poetry. Dwight's
Select Minor Poems of Goethe and Schiller
(1838), Brooks's metrical version of *Faust I*
(1856), and Margaret Fuller's Englishing of
Eckermann's *Conversations* in 1839 are
among the most notable in a long list of
works which by 1864 had made most of the

major writings of Goethe (except *Faust II*) accessible to the English-reading public.[38] After 1850 American opinion gravitated toward a view of Goethe as a man of great gifts and of artistic integrity. In some circles, though not among the Fundamentalists who continued to be vocal, his name carried high repute and prestige.[39]

If Goethe ranked first in number of magazine articles and of books in English translations, his friend Schiller still led all German authors in the number of biographical studies devoted to him, and his poems were printed more frequently in American magazines than those of any other German author. In the absence of any significant controversy over him,[40] he of all German authors inspired the greatest admiration and affection in American readers. His stature as a wholesome moralist and expounder of Kantian idealism was recognized soon after Madame de Staël's opinions became current.[41] By 1850 Schiller had won the hearts of Americans in every section and of every philosophic persuasion. The centennial of his birth in 1859 was an occasion for elaborate festivals in his honor. By this time there were of course eloquent and enthusiastic transplanted Germans in all the larger cities of the East and Northwest, and they joined vigorously in paying homage to the German who they felt had lived and created in the spirit of the New World.[42]

Temporarily eclipsed, the older writers Herder and Lessing became relatively less prominent after 1810 than they had been earlier and were again to be later. Yet Herder was well known in the twenties for his *Letters Relating to the Study of Divinity*, his monumental *Ideen*, and his study in folk poetry and religion called *Vom Geist der ebräischen Poesie*, translated in 1832 by James Marsh. Herder was frequently treated in biographical reviews and studies throughout the period, and the American attitude toward him was one of admiration and reverence. Lessing's dramas had

occasionally been translated and played in the early years of the century. Afterward not much attention was paid to him, though in the forties appeared several studies and a new translation of *Minna von Barnhelm* (1849). Both *Minna* and *Emilia Galotti* were included in the "Select Library of the German Classics" instituted by the *Democratic Review* in 1848, a series that issued such universally admired works as Goethe's *Hermann und Dorothea*, *Iphigenie* (in part), and Schiller's *Taucher* (*The Diver*).[43]

The sudden great vogue of Jean Paul Friedrich Richter in the thirties marks the transition to a temporary ascendancy of the German romantics. A romantic a little before his time, a German Sterne or Fielding with a portion of whimsey and willfulness all his own, this contemporary of Goethe and Schiller had an amazingly strong hold on American interest in those years. Carlyle not only patterned a good deal of the manner of *Sartor Resartus* on Jean Paul's style but in his essay on the "State of German Literature" (1827) and elsewhere set him among the foremost of the august body of German writers. As a result of Carlyle's advocacy, Margaret Fuller in 1832 was talking in extravagant superlatives about this somewhat remote and difficult Jean Paul, defending him vigorously. As a teacher of second-year pupils in German literature at Alcott's Temple School, she guided the class through the whole of the interminable, rambling, and often brilliant *Titan*; and Charles Follen likewise influenced his students to devote long hours to the deciphering of Jean Paul's crabbed, elusive pages. The periodicals printed extracts and *sententiae* from him. As George Calvert put it, Jean Paul was loved for his German "truthfulness," religiosity, earnestness, "playfulness," mysticism, "warm affections and aptness to sympathy."[44] And then, to insure the perpetuation of his fame, Charles Timothy Brooks started his long task of putting a number of his novels into English, the last of which came out as late as 1884, thus prolonging Jean Paul's popularity well into the Genteel era. Jean Paul ranks third among all German authors for the number of magazine references devoted to him, and a total of forty-six books of his were issued in English translation after 1810, nearly half of them after 1864.[45]

Among contemporary German writers popular after 1810 were a number of the leading members of the Romantic schools and certain representatives of the *Jung-Deutschland* group as well: Theodor Körner, Ludwig Uhland, Heinrich Heine, Friedrich Rückert, Ludwig Tieck, and Ferdinand Freiligrath ranked among the first twenty Germans most frequently reviewed and translated in the periodicals, and Baron Fouqué, Adelbert Chamisso, E. T. A. Hoffmann, Justinus Kerner, Wilhelm Hauff, and J. H. D. Zschokke ranked among the first thirty. In general, America showed a warm interest in two genres: the lyric— simple, naive, expressive of the personal emotions, and drawing on the resources of the folksong; and the tale or *Novelle*, which exploited in prose the realms of legend, folklore, phantasy, and the supernatural. The popularity of the latter was in a sense an outgrowth of late eighteenth-century interest in the Gothic tale, and the line of division between Gothicism and Romanticism was not very precisely drawn by the American audience. In 1813 there had appeared a long article by Alexander Hill Everett on Musaeus, whimsical and fanciful storyteller who had collected his materials from the common folk. Musaeus himself was not much printed in America, but the demand for the kind of art that he discovered was to develop to large proportions and to influence the development of the short tale and short story in this country.[46] The year 1821 saw the British printing of Fouqué's *Undine*, and in 1824 both this work and Chamisso's famous *Peter Schlemihl* appeared in America. *Undine*, the

highly fantastic but essentially simple story of the love of a knight for a sea nymph, was one of the three or four most frequently reprinted of all German tales.[47] Zschokke's popularity likewise remained high. Out of a long list of titles, his *Hours of Devotion* (*Stunden der Andacht*), a far cry from the blood-curdling Gothicism of *Abaellino*, was translated in 1834 and went through several printings. The first notice of the brothers Grimm and their *Märchen* came in 1822; their book was to increase steadily in popular acceptance through the century. In the latter half of the period the shorter narratives of Gerstäcker (*Tales*), of Gutzkow (*Prince of Madagascar*, 1853), Storm (*Immensee*, 1863), Paul Heyse (*Novellen*, from 1857), Auerbach's *Schwarzwälder Dorfgeschichten*, and the stories of Ernst von Wildenbruch were well received,[48] along with a number of important items of children's literature that found a vast market in America.[49] However, the most important vehicle for the transmission of the *Novelle* and tale to America was the book of collections.[50] Though full-length novels were also being imported from Germany, the critics took to the shorter narratives in a kindlier way, finding as one critic put it that the "length and merit of German fictions" were in a "directly inverse ratio."[51]

Americans were warmly receptive to many of the contemporary German lyricists, both the poets of a distinctly Romantic persuasion, such as Rückert, Uhland, and Eichendorff, and those who combined the patriotic note or *Jung Deutschland* social criticism with their Romanticism, as did Heine, Grün, Herwegh, and Freiligrath. In general the American critics found the lyric superior to German writings in other genres. After Goethe and Schiller, those reprinted most frequently in American collections were Körner, Geibel, Uhland, Rückert, Heine, Bürger, and Grün. This group had not quite the high distinction and perfection of the art of the *Lied* that we find in Eichendorff, Platen, Novalis, and Wilhelm Müller (who enjoyed a moderate popularity later), but the simplicity, directness, and heartfelt warmth which characterized their work made it eminently successful here. The young Körner's "Prayer during Battle," from *Lyre and Sword*, was the most frequently printed German poem in America.[52] To 1848, Geibel, Uhland, Rückert, and Freiligrath retained an impressive popularity as they embodied in their songs the issues of the great movement toward popular representative government, American sympathy going out toward a man like Freiligrath who was exiled for the republican sentiments expressed in his writings. The older ballads and folk-song genres were of course not forgotten. *Lenore*, long a favorite, was translated anew by C. T. Brooks and Sarah Whitman in the thirties. In addition to many translations—good, bad, and indifferent—scattered among the periodicals, there was a good market for collections of German lyrics: Brooks's *Songs and Ballads of Uhland, etc.*; his *German Lyrics*; Longfellow's *Poets and Poetry of Europe*; W. H. Furness' *Song of the Bell and Other Poems and Ballads*; and others by J. C. Mangan, C. A. Dana, C. G. Leland, and Hermann Bokum. Heine made his bow in the twenties as a prose writer, author of the *Reisebilder*, and was known in the mid-thirties as a critic with a style and manner uniquely facile, penetrating, and witty. In general, American opinion regretted his sharp hostility to the romantic point of view and his irreverence toward the older classics;[53] but when the more appreciative estimates by George Eliot and Matthew Arnold were reprinted in 1856, the way was prepared for the more cordial reception of Heine that prevailed in later decades.[54]

Some novelists occupied high rank in the tabulation of translations and periodical items despite the fact that critical opinion was generally agreed that the German novel lacked humor and was overburdened with reflections on morality and tediously minute descriptions. In the category of *Unterhaltungsliteratur* the contemporary novel found its usefulness in America because there was a good market for great quantities of fiction.[55]

REPRESENTATIVE AMERICAN CRITICS

The translators, critics, and reviewers in all sections who guided American tastes toward the appreciation of particular authors and genres are too many to enumerate here. The Boston community, the Harvard faculty, and the body of Unitarian clergy provided a number of critics, among whom Nathaniel L. Frothingham (1793–1870) may be taken as typical. A Unitarian minister and man of cultivation and literary attainments, Frothingham was a student of the classics and of Goethe. He is represented in several collections of poems in translation, including a variety of poems from the German.[56] He was a conservative in a Boston where insurgent ideas and unorthodox philosophies were much in evidence. Characteristically he agreed with Professor Felton on the subject of Goethe and "greatly preferred Schiller to Goethe," but shared with the Transcendentalists their delight in a number of German authors. His "favorite language next to English was German, then came French, then Latin."[57] His opinions are representative of Bostonian taste. What was later to become the genteel tradition was already in process of formation in the forties among his wide and influential circle, which included Felton, Convers Francis, Parkman, Longfellow, Hilliard, Ticknor, and Prescott.[58]

Among authors of the Middle South, George Calvert (1803–1889) played a commanding role in the introduction of German literature. He was one of Goethe's visitors in Weimar, his admirer and defender, and his first American biographer.[59]

He made his debut as translator with a rendering of *Don Carlos* in blank verse (1834)—the first serious translation of a Schiller drama by an American.[60] His reviewing in 1836 and 1837 covered a wide range of German letters but emphasized Goethe, Jean Paul, A. W. Schlegel's lectures *Über dramatische Kunst und Literatur*;[61] and by 1845 he had published a translation of one half of the *Correspondence between Schiller and Goethe*. In the Preface to this work Calvert joined with Margaret Fuller to refute animadversions against Goethe then current.[62] Calvert the Southern gentleman revealed a more tolerant understanding of Goethe's life and character than did many New Englanders even after decades of controversy over the subject. He set the issue of Goethe's domestic morality in a fair light and, like Margaret Fuller, he answered the old charge of political indifference and conservatism in the older Goethe by pointing out that he needed aesthetic calm to carry out the "great things of his high calling."

From 1864 to 1900

The war period, a time of slackening in the book trade and of a diminution in the output of periodical literature generally, accentuates the line of cleavage between the "Romantic" and "Genteel" eras. A low point in the printing of translations was reached during 1860–1864.[63] Explanations of this falling off of interest in German literature are to be found in the turmoil of the Civil War period, the alterations of aesthetic standards, the receding of older interests, the shifts in critical evaluations, and the movement of German letters out of the position of leadership which they had enjoyed in the first half of the century. The romantic spirit as embodied by several successive groups of German lyricists and prose artists had been the most potent attracting force—the best appreciated element in the American

picture of German letters. The most widely enjoyed quality was the stress on spiritual freedom in a framework of high ethical purity. Consequently Schiller, unlike Jean Paul or Theodor Körner in literary intention, doctrine, or form of expression, was regarded as a fellow-warrior in the cause of idealism. Neither Goethe nor Heine, as we have observed, in spite of their obvious importance and genius, withstood the test of ideality, virtue, and nobility of spirit as successfully as did a host of lesser men.

American taste was not homogeneous or static at any time, and after 1860 the balance was apparently tipping slightly on the side of the "un-German" Germans. While Schiller continued to hold first place on many counts, the genius of Goethe was contending for more earnest attention, and though Heine perturbed many with the shocking directness of his wit in the *Reisebilder*, many readers began to recognize his brilliance. Schiller's strain began to seem empty rhetoric, lacking charm and beauty of natural forms—addressed to the conscience of the individual but silent on the absorbing modern questions of national and public life. So American criticism reached a kind of impasse with regard to German literature: many of the old favorites were gradually falling into neglect, and the public was finding few contemporary writers to fill the void.

During the seventies, on the broadest level of appreciation, fiction and romance dominated all else. Berthold Auerbach, Spielhagen, Gerstäcker, and a number of female novelists of the "Gartenlaube" type were published frequently and with great success in the American market. The shift in appreciation of the classics is indicated by the fact that in the seventies Goethe was more often represented in poetry collections than any other German writer, and the period 1865–1879 also marks the highest frequency in the printing of Heine's lyrics. The period was rich in translations of important works like the *Faust* and the lyrics of Heine. Lessing not only retained his modest popularity but even enjoyed something of a revival. Scholarly studies on the subject of German literature by American students, notably E. P. Evans, James K. Hosmer, Bayard Taylor, Helen S. Conant, and H. H. Boyesen, were becoming more numerous. In the last two decades recent fiction, largely of a second- or third-rate kind, dominated the popular journals. Comment and reprinting of such important contemporaries as Nietzsche and Schopenhauer, on the other hand, is very sparse, and thère was not much interest in the new naturalists Sudermann and Hauptmann.

LEADING CRITICS AND TRANSLATORS

Who were the critics and translators most active in transmitting German authors to American readers?[64] Among a host of occasional writers were a number of the later Transcendentalists of Boston and the Midwest, including W. H. Furness, Samuel Osgood, George Ripley, Moncure D. Conway, Cyrus A. Bartol, O. B. Frothingham, and that patriarch of the movement for the study of German letters in America, Frederic Henry Hedge. These were sometimes closely associated with those members of the evolutionary-scientific movement who wrote for the *Radical, Western,* and *Journal of Speculative Philosophy.* Brooks, Calvert, Bayard Taylor, and Leland devoted relatively the largest part of their talents to the introduction of German authors into America, and the fame of each rested in large measure on their labors as critics and translators. When we add the name of Nathaniel L. Frothingham, we have named the five most active and typical interpreters of German letters during the later nineteenth century—not the keenest or ablest critics of their time, nor the best equipped in scholarship, but on the whole the most devoted and most

influential American proponents of German literature. In addition to the host of more occasional contributors, many professors of German in the newer and older seats of learning now presented their views to a wide public in books and periodicals.[65]

RELATIVE POPULARITY OF GENRES, SCHOOLS, AUTHORS

A decided revival of interest was under way by 1870. Though the average length of notices was perhaps less than in early decades, there was a considerable over-all increase in space over the preceding period. Instead of directing their attention to a single writer or a particular school, reviewers now displayed an urbane though still not an altogether discriminating catholicity toward classics and new writers, romantics and post-romantics, the more serious as well as the ephemeral fiction writers. That certain older groups, such as the romantic lyricists, held their popularity well is evident from their high ranking in collections. Uhland was next in popularity after Goethe, Heine third, with Rückert, Schiller, Geibel, Lenau, Herder, and Freiligrath following next in order. The last fifteen years of the century especially showed an unparalleled high frequency of German poems in American collections. Despite the persistence of the old and inevitable Puritan bias, there was now sentiment for the absorption and acclimatizing of the best of German literature (along with music and philosophy) as an indispensable component of Western culture—a mark of genteel cultivation and good taste.[66]

The respect for German letters was enhanced by the military and political events that suddenly raised Germany into prominence among Western nations. She had been friendly to the Union in the Civil War, and in 1870 the Reich gave notice to the world that it had assumed a new status as a unified, prosperous, and victorious power. By this time influential colonies of German-Americans had established themselves throughout the nation, and now they tended to look upon this development with pride. The development of German language and literature study in schools and colleges, the high repute of German universities in scientific and scholarly pursuits, the influence of many educators who had studied there, and the emergence into prominence of so many German-American citizens of high cultural attainments and social respectability— all these combined to open the way to the steady and easy access to German culture, which for centuries had been the dark region of western Europe. The list of "Collected Works" of German authors grew rapidly. In the eighties such study groups as the Chautauqua, the Concord School, and the schools of the St. Louis group made German writers the object of zealous missionary effort. Most reviews took an interest in German letters for granted; they printed large numbers of notices and detailed reviews, even when the works were not available in English. It was no longer necessary to urge the study of the language, for the opportunities to learn it were nowhere far to seek.

From the famous 1870 translation of *Faust* by Bayard Taylor through the various sets of Goethe's works published in the later decades, the stream of works in English by and about Goethe was notably heavy.[67] Critical notes in the journals were correspondingly voluminous; fifty-two leading periodicals carried as many as 522 references in 162 journal volumes in the five years of 1885–1889.[68] *Faust* was the single work most frequently discussed,[69] and *Meister*, the lyric poems, *Werther*, *Goetz, Hermann und Dorothea, Iphigenie* and *Tasso*, the *Wahlverwandtschaften, Dichtung und Wahrheit, Egmont*, and *Reineke Fuchs* ranked next in frequency in the order named. If magazine references were most numerous about 1890, that was

owing in large measure to a combination of external factors. The periodicals found him "good copy" when they could report the opening of the Goethe-Houses at Frankfurt and Weimar, the examination of the archives, the discovery of important unpublished manuscripts, including the *Urfaust*, the founding of Goethe societies, and the erection of monuments to Goethe on both sides of the Atlantic. *Faust* as play and opera was being performed on the American stage, and prominent lecturers (in a day when the lecture was an important medium of cultural education) carried his name down the highways and byways of the East and Middle West.[70]

The prevailing opinion came to be that there were "impurities" in Goethe's writings, but these did not overweigh the value of his positive teaching. The American consciousness attached high value to "purity," moral elevation, and genteel propriety, and in these terms marked its difference with the catholicity, calm realism, and broad tolerance of the Goethean spirit.[71] Only by 1900 had a gradual change of tone in the hostile criticism upon Goethe taken place, so that even when writing on a topic such as the "Loves of Goethe," popular writers could temper their objections with the reflection: "from his myriad heart experiences and mind experiments we all profit."[72] Progress in the nineteenth century toward a full understanding of the poet of Weimar was painfully slow.

Schiller's rank in this period as fifth in frequency of representation in American collections (he had been first in the pre-war period) is indicative of a gradual falling-off of interest in him.[73] The general critical attitude was that he had little to say in the present age of modern optimism. As the *Literary World* put it in 1884, he was "the poet of idealism, in an age of realism." Of course there were those who hoped that the older fashion for the literature of instruction and ethical guidance would not die out, and the exemplary "purity" and "sweetness of his private life" recommended him to the adherents of the moderate "genteel" idealism that existed far down the century.[74] But by 1900 he was no longer the subject of attention from the periodical press, though he had by then become enshrined as a "classic" in the American high-school and college textbook.

It was in the sixties that Lessing came into his own. *Nathan, Minna,* and the famous essay *Laokoon* were newly translated, and the reviews carried several critical sketches, notably a long essay by Lowell (1867) and the translation by Edwin D. Mead of Eduard Zeller's essay "Lessing as a Theologian" (1878). Adolph Stahr's two-volume *Lessing. Sein Leben und seine Werke* was translated in 1866 by Professor E. P. Evans. The first American edition of the *Works,* albeit a very incomplete one, appeared in 1895, and to the end of the period appeared a number of competent sketches in the journals on his career and his historical position.[75]

For his saving grace of humor, Jean Paul continued to be read and praised. He was fondly remembered by Lowell and depicted by Boyesen as the "healthiest" of the romantics.[76] C. T. Brooks issued the lengthy *Levana* in 1866, and even as late as 1883 and 1884 was still adding new works to the series of translations from Richter.[77]

In point of frequency of translation, Heine earned a measure of popularity that sets his name next to Goethe's. Introduced during the preceding epoch, his *Reisebilder* and his book on the Romantic School (together with a good deal of his lyric poetry) were already well known. The *Reisebilder* went into the fifth edition by 1866,[78] and selections from the lyrics appeared in volumes by Emma Lazarus (1874), Leland (*Book of Songs,* 1864, 1868, 1874, and 1881), and others. The *Works* in twelve volumes (edited by Leland) began to appear in 1891, and Frances Hellman, F. Johnson, Kate Kroeker, and Martin and

Bowring issued volumes of his poetry after 1880. The main lines of criticism were the same as those established earlier. In 1863 Matthew Arnold had spoken for a large section of his Anglo-Saxon audience when he praised Heine's strictly literary abilities but declared that his work had only "a half-result, for want of moral balance, of nobleness of soul and character."[79] In 1866 E. I. Sears, and with him at about the same time, Ripley, Hedge, and Parker, granted him lyric grace but denounced his personal character, his shockingly brutal treatment of his friends in his writings. Lowell, Leland, and Howells expressed a greater delight in his wit and caprice, his brilliance and beauty.[80] Emma Lazarus pointed out the reflections of Jewish tradition in his work—his being at once Hebrew and Hellene.[81] Heine's criticism undoubtedly was an influence in shaping the American view of German literary history. His essays appeared to special advantage by virtue of the contrast in style between his concise, deft, and lucid exposition and the usual ponderousness of scholarly prose. In later years there was less moral condemnation than formerly, but Americans clung to the opinion that Heine should have been less the scoffer and more the champion "of the ideals of the existence of which he had spoken so fervently,"[82] even while most readers were entranced by the lightness and delicacy, tenderness and subtle pathos of his lyrics.

Heine's attacks, together with a swing of the pendulum away from the Transcendentalist intuitionism and idealism, put a halt to the growth of interest in such writers as Novalis, Tieck, and Hoffmann. Infrequently discussed in the journals, they were dismissed as "morbid," "hypermystic," "intensely egoistic," and "lacking in intellectual balance and symmetry."[83] The lyrics of Uhland, Lenau, Freiligrath, Geibel, Müller, and others continued to hold their place high on the list of lyricists most frequently represented in collections.

Rückert, admired for his facility in handling difficult forms and his easy didacticism, appeared with his *Weisheit des Brahmanen* (1882), a collection of lyrics in oriental style, in translation by Brooks, and there were new editions of Uhland's *Poems* in 1871 and 1899. The profoundly romantic *Taugenichts* of Eichendorff, translated in 1866 by Leland, was reviewed unfavorably. Late romantic *Dichtung* and drama received only sparse and sporadic publication: Gutzkow's *Uriel Acosta* in 1876; Grillparzer's *Sappho* (1876, translated by Ellen Frothingham); Geibel's *Brunhild* (1879) and *Loreley* (1872); Grün's *Letzter Ritter* (1871).[84] Scheffel's epic poem *Der Trompeter von Säckingen* was translated in 1887, and his *Gaudeamus*, a collection of lusty humorous verse, by Leland in 1872. The indefatigible Brooks introduced the poetry of Karl Kortum (1863 and 1867), Leopold Schefer (1867), and the comic cartoons of Wilhelm Busch, presenting two of the latter's works in the seventies.[85] Of contemporary drama, Freytag's fine comedy *Die Journalisten* appeared in 1888 and Hermann Sudermann's *Heimat* in 1896. Gerhart Hauptmann came to notice just before the close of the century, when his *Weber* and *Hanneles Himmelfahrt* were produced on the New York stage in English.[86]

THE GENTEEL TRADITION

During the first half of the century the public found few German novels to its taste, but with the rise of the popular magazines room was found for increasing numbers of stories by such good craftsmen as Freytag, Auerbach, Reuter, and Spielhagen as well as a whole army of second- and third-rate fiction writers. As one critic observed this development in 1869, he found that no genre "now has a sale so large, or so ready as this."[87] From 1864 to 1879 there were twenty American editions of twelve separate works of Berthold

Auerbach, in translation, by Brooks, Eliza Lee Follen, and others.[88] This author was at his best when portraying sturdy peasant life and rural scenes (though somewhat prettified to make them acceptable in the salon); his *Dorfgeschichten* had charm and interest, even if a didactic purpose lay just under their surface.[89] His village tales, best exemplified by the excellent *Black Forest Tales*, were regarded by American readers as a delightful and "new branch of literature."[90] Gustave Freytag's novel of middle-class life, *Debit and Credit*, had been available since 1858 and was preferred to *Die verlorene Handschrift* and *Die Ahnen* (introduced some years later). Freytag's not too searching realism was enjoyed by a public which insisted that its fiction treat the "more smiling aspects of life."[91] Friedrich Spielhagen wrote studies of contemporary life (*Hammer und Amboss, Problematische Naturen*, translated by Professor de Vere and others) that forcefully expressed the progressive political convictions of their author. Though a few reviewers welcomed his vigor, his down-to-earth portrayal of the modern industrial and metropolitan scene, America on the whole preferred the roseate coloring of an Auerbach or the pleasant remoteness of the historical romance.[92] Gerstäcker (for his *Germelshausen* especially), Zschokke (for his *Toter Gast* and other stories), Fouqué, and Heyse remained well known throughout the period. American readers accepted Fritz Reuter more readily than did the British. His long autobiographical novel *Ut mine Stromtid* was serialized in *Littell's* in 1871, and the charm and wit of this regional dialect humorist was increasingly popular through the years. His great Swiss contemporary Gottfried Keller, on the other hand, was not noticed until 1880 and then only occasionally mentioned by the critics, nor did these other masters of the short narrative, Conrad F. Meyer and Marie von Ebner-Eschenbach, attract notice. Viktor von Scheffel's massive historical novel of medieval life, *Ekkehard*, was given three printings between 1881 and 1895.

The great bulk of fiction throughout these years was supplied by a succession of long-lived and astonishingly productive female authors, most of whom were never prominent in German literary history and who are now quite forgotten. This large group of the "Gartenlaube" school (many of whom published under pseudonyms) is perhaps best typified in the work of "Luise Mühlbach" (Frau Klara Mundt). Twenty-three of her grandiose historical romances were introduced in the late sixties (but some had started in the late forties) to total twenty-seven printings by 1880 and to hold a vast audience down to the outbreak of World War I.[93] The market for these romances was cultivated by American publishers and fostered by large-scale promotion. They fed the same level of popular taste that supported the native domestic novels of Susan Warner, Maria Cummins, Mrs. E. D. E. N. Southworth, Caroline Lee Hentz, and others characterized by Hawthorne as a "damned mob of scribbling women." The firms of Leypoldt and Holt and Roberts Brothers vied with each other in publishing Auerbach. Appleton and Lippincott sponsored the female writers especially. For a time no amount of ridicule or condemnation could diminish the trade. Surprisingly enough, some critics gave their approval to the whole lot, professing to prefer them even to Auerbach, Hawthorne, Scott, or Turgeniev.[94] At bottom, the reason for their popularity was the fact that the life and manners depicted in these novels was enhanced and veiled over with a glow of romantic coloring. The books were not without incident and sensational climaxes; they drew out suspense in an elementary and obvious way, and the characters, though dull or unconvincing, were blessed with one virtue, as a reviewer remarked: they were never "gross." About 1890 the tide of interest ebbed noticeably, though

individual authors retained their following to 1914.[95]

American interest in German literature at the close of the century presented conspicuous gaps. Hauptmann and Sudermann, powerful exponents of a new naturalism, Nietzsche and Schopenhauer, caustic and merciless in their attacks on the moral bases of earlier thought—these did not gain even a foothold among any important groups of American readers or critics.[96] Further, those German writers and poets who themselves were discovered late and popularized but slowly in their own land remained virtually unknown here: the poets Hölderlin, Platen, Mörike, the dramatists Kleist, the later Grillparzer, Hebbel, and Otto Ludwig; the prose masters Stifter, Keller, Storm, Meyer, and Fontane.[97] In sheer volume of materials published in America, the juveniles and the novel together overshadowed almost all of the writers of higher literary standing.[98]

Any attempt to determine by quantitative count alone precisely what impact German books had on the minds and tastes of the elusive "average reader" must be inconclusive. In 1886 a critic writing in the Boston *Literary World* put the matter in the following extreme terms: German literature is not commonly studied; "its true character . . . has not become known." Far fewer German than French books are being purchased, and there is "the utmost ignorance of everything pertaining to German literature." The literature itself is at fault: it has "too great richness," it is "heavy food," "overflowing with 'Gehalt,'" but its "new and valuable ideas" are wasted. Regard for its authors is "reputation" only; they are universally accepted but "thought of by nobody."[99] This is at bottom a diagnosis of phenomena attendant on the growth of the Genteel tradition. The loss of ground on the part of the classical authors and the romantics is concomitant with the basic change in temper which took place after 1860, from an intense pre occupation with the idealistic striving so much a part of the great tradition in German letters, to an easy-going and, by comparison, undisciplined, vague, and unfocussed interest in "culture" per se. In a time when the gap between the specialist scholar and the public was widening, Americans no less than large groups of the reading public in Germany and elsewhere were not keeping alive the spiritual values that had produced their classics. The approach to Goethe, Heine, Lessing, or Schiller was for the average reader not an easy one, and the scholarly guides and erudite interpretations of these classics were not as helpful as they might have been if they had been more clearly and attractively written.[100]

After 1860 there ceased to exist the fervor and profound personal commitment that marked the enthusiasms of an earlier generation. Through teaching, lectures, and personal advocacy they had guided and shaped opinion, causing their insights to radiate through ever-widening circles. By raising German idealism to the status of an intellectual issue, the Transcendentalists had forced a reconciliation of the extremes of radical and traditional thought. By contrast, the St. Louis group (to use the clearest example) did not win the same hearing or respect from their contemporaries. The popular journals ignored the Hegelians or dismissed them with the stigma of "cult," and there was no such give-and-take as had agitated New England when the "Newness" first arrived. Not even the presence of large concentrations of German-Americans in the cities fostered any great degree of 'German-mindedness" in the public at large. It is interesting to note the opinion of Josiah Royce in connection with the study of Faust in America. In 1881 he noted the neglect of "important matters that used to be a good deal talked about."

The true end of life [he observed], the nature and grounds of human certitude, the problems of Goethe's Faust and of Kant's Critique—these disappear from the view of many representative men . . . only within twenty years has there been a general inattention to the study of the purposes and hopes of human life—a study that, embodied in German idealism, or in American Transcendentalism . . . had been filling men's thoughts since the outset of the Great Revolution.[101]

By 1850 the Transcendentalists had established a precarious balance between native standards of taste and propriety and a sense of membership in a cosmopolitan and international realm of letters. By 1900 progress toward the acceptance of a concept of *Weltliteratur* fell short of what a Margaret Fuller would have desired. Nevertheless, the sheer quantitative increase in the number of books imported from Germany in the later decades was keeping pace with the over-all growth of the book trade in this country. At the end of the period the vogue of German authors in America could be charted by these developments: the general veneration for many, especially older, German authors (though not in those quarters where Puritan and Fundamentalist sentiment prevailed); the broad familiarity with many of the major works of these authors; the ready acceptance of a century of German lyrics from Klopstock to Heyse; the incorporation of a number of children's book from Grimm's *Märchen* to *Heidi* into the body of standard American favorites; and the establishment of a continuing tradition of the study of German language and literature in our schools and colleges.

TABLE I

PERIODICAL ITEMS (1810–1864) IN AMERICAN JOURNALS*

Rank	Name	Number of Items	Rank	Name	Number of Items
1	Goethe	379	20	Freiligrath	18 (1844——)
2	Schiller	264	20	Fr. Schlegel	18 (1817–1849)
3	Jean Paul Richter	101	22	Matthison	17 (1831——)
4	Th. Körner	80 (1815——)†	23	Hauff	15 (1835——)
5	Uhland	73 (1835——)	23	E. T. A. Hoffmann	15 (1825–1852)
6	Zschokke	50	23	Lavater	15 (to 1839)
7	Heine	46 (1828——)	26	Auerbach	14 (1847——)
8	Kotzebue	43 (to 1845)**	27	J. Kerner	13 (1836–1862)
9	Herder	41	27	W. Menzel	13 (1817–1842)
10	Fouqué	36 (1818——)	27	Varnhagen v. Ense	13 (1839——)
10	Luther	36	30	Gessner	12 (to 1853)
12	Rückert	33 (1839——)	30	"Grün"	12 (1839——)
13	Lessing	27	32	Arndt	11 (1821——)
13	Tieck	27 (1818——)	32	Gerstäcker	11 (1847——)
15	Krummacher	26 (1818——)	32	Brothers Grimm	11 (1822——)
16	Bürger	25	32	J. H. Voss	11 (1816–1852)
17	A. W. Schlegel	24 (1812–1852)	36	Gellert	10
18	Klopstock	21	36	Novalis	10 (1810——)
19	Wieland	20 (to 1862)	38	W. Müller	9 (1828–52)††

* The table includes data on translations, notices, reviews, and critical articles on German literature, and biographical sketches on German authors. Based on Goodnight and Haertel.

† Omission of terminal dates indicates that the author appeared in the journals both before and after the period 1810–1864. The omission of the prior date signifies mention before 1810; of an end-date, after 1864.

** Forty of the forty-three items occurred before 1824.

†† In the remaining twelve places in a list of the fifty most frequently mentioned authors, the following would be added: G. Freytag, 8; I. v. Hahn-Hahn, 8; Geibel, 7; Gutzkow, 7; Pückler-Muskau, 7; Salis, 7; Bettina v. Arnim, 6; Claudius, 6; J. J. Engel, 6; Gleim, 6; Jung-Stilling, 6; Zimmermann, 6.

TABLE II

THE NUMBER OF POEMS BY GERMAN AUTHORS APPEARING IN TRANSLATIONS IN AMERICAN COLLECTIONS
1830–1899*

OVER-ALL RANK	NO. OF ITEMS	AUTHOR	1830–1864						1865–1899					
			30–39	40–49	50–59	60–64	RANK	TOTALS	65–69	70–79	80–89	90–99	RANK	TOTALS
1	312	Goethe	17	26	55	3	2	101	...	45	73	93	1	211
2	252	Schiller	20	18	85	...	1	123	...	41	37	51	5	129
2	252	Uhland	1	15	35	18	5	69	2	36	81	64	2	183
4	215	Rückert	7	21	40	1	5	69	38	46	33	29	4	146
5	201	Heine	...	7	15	12	8	34	8	42	51	66	3	167
6	154	Geibel	...	...	55	15	4	70	...	26	8	50	6	84
7	118	Körner	53	5	16	...	3	74	...	19	12	13	12	44
8	109	Freiligrath	...	20	18	...	7	38	4	42	10	15	9	71
9	93	Herder	3	6	1	6	16	16	22	30	4	21	8	77
10	83	Lenau	...	...	4	...	...	4	45	21	10	3	7	79
11	72	Luther	...	2	20	...	12	22	2	13	6	29	11	50
12	71	Chamisso	...	1	16	...	15	17	7	6	29	12	10	54
13	58	Bürger	10	5	12	...	9	27	...	8	8	15	18	31
14	56	"Grün"	...	5	17	2	11	24	2	17	8	5	17	32
15	52	Kerner	3	...	15	...	14	18	2	18	6	8	13	34
15	52	Klopstock	7	5	14	1	9	27	1	6	1	17	19	25
17	44	Müller	...	2	8	...	...	10	2	9	12	11	13	34
18	37	Gerhardt	...	5	16	...	13	21	7	6	3	...	...	16
18	37	Walther v.d. Vogelweide	...	...	3	...	...	3	...	28	6	...	13	34
20	36	Tieck	1	2	8	...	...	11	...	4	3	18	19	25
21	35	Hölty	7	...	6	...	25	13	...	7	7	8	24	22
22	33	Bodenstedt	...	...	...	...	...	...	...	...	5	28	16	33
23	32	Arndt	1	2	10	...	20	13	4	4	5	6	25	19
24	31	Eichendorff	...	...	6	...	...	6	1	2	8	14	21	25

OVER-ALL RANK	NO. OF ITEMS	AUTHOR	1830–1864						1865–1899					
			30-39	40-49	50-59	60-64	RANK	TOTALS	65-69	70-79	80-89	90-99	RANK	TOTALS
25	29	Claudius	2	4	6	1	20	13	1	3	5	7	..	16
26	27	Lessing	..	..	3	..	..	3	1	1	2	20	22	24
26	27	Platen	..	1	3	..	..	4	1	2	8	12	23	23
28	24	Fouqué	1	..	4	..	..	5	..	3	1	15	25	19
28	24	Gleim	3	4	5	..	25	12	..	5	7	..	..	12
28	24	Herwegh	..	6	5	4	17	15	..	3	1	5	..	9
28	24	Novalis	2	..	4	..	..	6	2	1	7	8	..	18
28	24	Wieland	..	1	6	..	..	7	..	1	2	14	..	17
33	23	Salis	2	4	5	..	..	11	..	2	7	3	..	12
34	20	Stolbergs	4	6	5	..	17	15	..	2	2	1	..	5
35	18	Fallersleben	..	3	11	..	19	14	..	..	3	1	..	4
35	18	Schlegels	..	..	2	..	..	2	..	..	..	16	..	16
35	18	Spitta	..	..	..	..	..	..	13	1	2	2	..	18
38	17	Dach	..	2	3	..	..	5	1	4	7	..	..	12
38	17	Gellert	1	1	11	..	20	13	1	1	2	..	..	4
40	16	Hebel	..	1	7	..	..	8	..	..	7	1	..	8
41	15	Heyse	..	..	..	..	..	..	..	..	..	15	..	15
42	14	Hauff	..	1	..	..	..	1	..	..	2	11	..	13
42	14	Krummacher	4	2	..	..	..	6	1	7	..	..	..	8
44	13	Dingelstedt	..	2	1	..	..	3	..	2	1	7	..	10
45	12	Mörike	..	..	2	..	..	2	..	1	3	6	..	10
...	169	Miscellaneous†	7	14	48	3	..	72	21	25	28	23	..	97
	3022	**TOTALS**	156	199	612	60		1027	189	540	523	743		1995

* Based on Morgan's Bibliography.

† Includes 27 poets, none with more than 11 items. Among these are Droste-Hülshoff, 1; Brentano, 11; Hölderlin, 7; Arnim, 2; Matthisson, 10; Schenken-dorf, 3; Schwab, 7; Hebbel, 7; Pfeffel, 7; Tersteegen, 9; Angelus Silesius, 8; Scheffel, 7; Storm, 9.

TABLE III

COUNTS OF TRANSLATIONS (BRITISH AND AMERICAN) OF THE WORKS OF
THE MOST FREQUENTLY TRANSLATED GERMAN AUTHORS, BY GENRES
AND PERIODS—1840–1864 AND 1860–1899 *

Rank	Author	No. of Items	1810–1864	1865–1899

Rank	Author	No. of Items	1810–1864	1865–1899
	"CLASSICS" AND EARLIER WRITERS			
1	Goethe	527	216	311
2	Schiller	294	187	107
3	Grimm Brothers (*Märchen*)	132	26	106
18	Lessing	56	15	41
18	Kotzebue	56	52	4
21	Jean Paul Richter...	46	24	22
26	Raspe (*Munchhausen*)	39	16	23
26	Luther	39	21	18
39	Klopstock	26	26	...
55	Gessner	19	18	1
...	J. G. Zimmermann (*On Solitude*)	13	12	1
...	Jung-Stilling	10	10	...
...	Wieland	9	9	...
...	Lavater	7	5	2
...	Frederick the Great	3	2	1
	ROMANTIC AUTHORS			
7	Fouqué	109	54	55
12	Heine	79	7	72
13	Zschokke	77	52	25
29	Fr. and A. W. Schlegel	37	24	13
32	Hauff	35	11	24
34	E. T. A. Hoffmann	30	8	22
43	Bürger	24	13	11
43	Chamisso	24	12	12
55	Musaeus	19	13	6
...	Pückler-Muskau	12	12	...
	POST-ROMANTIC AUTHORS			
4	R. Wagner	131	3	128
15	Auerbach	66	19	47
17	Gerstäcker	63	30	33
28	Heyse	38	4	34
29	Freytag	37	11	26
31	Sealsfield	36	25	11
43	W. Busch	24	...	24
47	Spielhagen	23	2	21
...	G. Hauptmann	8	...	8
...	H. Sudermann	8	...	8
...	F. Nietzsche	2	...	2

* Based on Chart II in B. Q. Morgan, *op. cit.*; pp. 15–17.

TABLE III (Continued)

Rank	Author	No. of Items	1810–1864	1865–1899
	LESSER FICTION AND PROSE WRITERS			
9	"E. Werner"	98	...	98
10	"L. Mühlbach"	97	19	78
11	G. Ebers	86	1	85
15	"E. Marlitt"	66	3	63
23	"W. Heimburg"	43	...	43
37	J. G. Kohl (Travels)	28	15	13
38	Ida Pfeiffer (Travels)	27	22	5
42	W. v. Hillern (Fiction)	25	...	25
43	Hackländer	24	10	14
48	I. v. Hahn-Hahn	22	15	7
52	O. Wildermuth	20	4	16
59	E. Eckstein	16	...	16
	JUVENILES AND RELIGIOUS INSTRUCTION			
5	Christopher Schmid	124	76	48
6	Wyss (*Swiss Family Robinson*)	119	27	92
14	Franz Hoffmann	73	15	58
20	Bogatzky (*Golden Treasury*)	47	21	26
21	C. G. Barth	46	34	12
	POPULAR DRAMA AND OPERETTA			
34	F. Zell	30	...	30
39	G. Moser	26	...	26
	PHILOSOPHY, HISTORY, SCIENCE			
8	A. v. Humboldt	108	79	29
24	Niebuhr (History)	41	36	5
25	Kant	40	9	31
33	Schopenhauer	31	3	28
36	D. F. Strauss (Theology)	29	14	15
39	Fichte	26	15	11
48	Lotze	22	...	22
48	Max Nordau (Popular Philosophy)	22	...	22
51	E. Curtius (History	21	3	18
52	Heeren (History)	20	20	...
52	Marx	20	3	17
55	Mommsen (History)	19	7	12

AMERICAN THEATER AND DRAMA

The Stage before 1800

DEPENDENCE ON BRITISH DRAMA

No event in the history of our Colonial stage points to any significant direct contact with German theater or German drama. Indeed, until William Dunlap came upon the New York scene in 1798, little seems to have been known of German practice that was not transmitted via British translation, adaptation, or previous performance on the British stage.[102] After 1790 the stages in New York, Philadelphia, and in many smaller cities as well, performed the same Restoration and eighteenth-century favorites as had held the boards in England: Otway, Addison, Farquhar, Shakespeare, Lillo, Vanbrugh, Cibber, Goldsmith, and Mrs. Inchbald. In the closing years of the century the condition of the British theater was such that directors went abroad to supplement the output of "Monk" Lewis, Holcroft, Colman, and Dibdin; and it took over countless works of every genre, musical and dramatic, that the Continental theater afforded. Many pieces attributed to British authors had as their source (whether acknowledged or not) French or German originals, which in turn were often borrowings from some remoter source in another language. France was the mediator for the transmission of much German material: both Schiller's *Robbers* and Kotzebue's *Stranger*, for example, reached London through French translations. After 1780 the British periodicals noticed contemporary German drama, and on the whole the public showed itself receptive to the sentimental, moralizing tone and even the *Sturm-und-Drang* violence of recent German drama. This drama, as reformed by Lessing and influenced by Shakespeare, was patently closer to English tradition than the French forms, and there arose in England such pro-German spokesmen as Henry

Mackenzie (with his famous lecture on the German drama in 1788), Alexander Tytler (original translator of the *Räuber*), William Taylor of Norwich (translator of Lessing's *Nathan* in 1791 and of Goethe's *Iphigenie* in 1783), and Matthew Gregory "Monk" Lewis (translator of Schiller's *Kabale und Liebe*).[103]

LESSING AND SCHILLER

The first German play on the New York stage was *The Robbers*, introduced on May 14, 1795, and repeated in the next three seasons.[104] In other respects the American stage showed few innovations over the British,[105] and German immigrants and Americans of German origin appear to have had little interest in the drama.[106] The notorious *Robbers*, even in its curtailed and diluted British versions, was recognized as the work of an original genius whose power, wealth of ideas, and floods of passion could hardly be contained in the bounds of his poetic product. On the surface the action is that of a family tragedy, but the play reveals deep perspectives of brooding on the structure of the moral cosmos and is the battleground of philosophical systems, among which a youthful pessimism of blackest hue gains the upper hand.[107] Too violent, pessimistic, and Satanic to please all American playgoers, it nevertheless enjoyed a long life owing to its essential power, strong situations, and splendid acting roles of Karl and Franz, and to the implicit sentimentalism that could be grafted onto the story of Amalia and Karl. It becomes doubly important in theater history because, along with Goethe's *Goetz* and certain examples of the German ballad and tale then current, it established the motifs of banditry and outlawry, the use of romantic natural scenery as background, and the themes of violence and mystery, in the manner of the Gothic horror tale.

The Vogue of Kotzebue, 1798–1804

With the arrival of the 1798–1799 season, the history of German influence on our stage becomes the account of the work of an outstanding manager, William Dunlap, who, following his unsuccessful production of Schiller's *Don Carlos* and *Kabale und Liebe*, in the last weeks of the season introduced with startling success the name of Kotzebue into our theatrical annals, thus rendering, as Dunlap put it, "Hamlet and Macbeth and all the glories of the drama for a time a dead letter."[108] Kotzebue's *Menschenhass und Reue*, as presented in a version fashioned by Dunlap and entitled *The Stranger*, with Thomas A. Cooper in the title role, took the town. It was given at least a dozen times in that season, incidentally relieving the acute financial distress in which the company found itself.[109] This, Kotzebue's earliest play, is a sentimental drama in the tradition of Lillo, Lessing, and Schiller's *Kabale und Liebe*, but spiced with equivocal moral rationalizations, excessive emotionalism, and the new doctrines of libertinism and democracy.[110] It was a play that exercised the moralists and nativists to thunder against foreign importations, but it held audiences enthralled for many seasons. To follow up his success, Dunlap set to perfecting his knowledge of German so as to be able to translate from the original.[111] His next offering was *Lovers' Vows* (from *Das Kind der Liebe*, 1791), another bourgeois drama, in a version prepared from a well-known English translation by Mrs. Anne Plumptree. The season saw eight performances, all enthusiastically received by the press. After a relative failure with *Count Benyowsky*, a heroic drama of Siberia, the season's final offering was Kotzebue's *Indians in England*, another failure. Out of a total of 93 performances in that season from December, 1798, to June, 1799, there were 28 performances of 6 German originals. This sudden Germani-zation of a leading American stage is a remarkable episode and quite as significant as that which obtained in England at the same time. The next season Dunlap had his weary, overworked, underpaid company study the parts of fourteen pieces by Kotzebue, all given in rapid succession between November, 1799, and June, 1800.[112]

Not every Kotzebue *première* became a hit, but the events of this crowded year established the fame of four great successes: the sentimental *Stranger* and *Lovers' Vows*, the spectacle *Pizarro*, and the farce *The Wild Goose Chace*. Out of a total of 94 recorded performances of plays of all types at the Park during the 1799–1800 season, 54 were German translations or adaptations.[113] As a consequence of the prestige gained through their acceptance in Britain, and because of their genuine effectiveness with the audience of the time, the majority of newspaper notices encouraged the growth of the Kotzebue fever.[114] Kotzebue's sensational and (to our taste) meretricious attractions were not in the Gothic style. *Pizarro* and *The Virgin of the Sun* made pathetic grand tragedy out of the conquest of Peru. Much of the success of these plays depended on costume and scenery[115] and on their appeal to the Rousseauistic sentimentalism toward the noble savage. Their emotional impact was not far different from that of the *Rührstück*. A contemporary reviewer spent fine words depicting the situations of *Pizarro*:

What can be more affecting to the female part of the audience than the picture presented at the opening of the 2d Act, a beautiful young creature playing with and caressing her infant while the fond father hangs over them in delight.... 3d Act... warriors returning from victory—the clangor of arms—the animating sound of numerous warlike instruments—the sight of Cora with her babe in search of her husband among the ranks, and almost inanimate with apprehension, enquiring... of Rolla and Ataliba and her lost Alonzo... as beautiful a collection and contrast of circumstance as ever was imagined.[116]

This was the piece that became the stand-by for virtually every season down to 1830 in New York and Philadelphia, a favorite vehicle of the great stars for decades thereafter—scoring a triumph on every considerable stage in the nation.[117] In its first forty years it was given approximately two hundred times; its nearest competitor, *The Stranger*, was given half as often.

Domestic comedy, represented by *Lovers' Vows* and *The Stranger*, was a type perhaps more characteristically Kotzebue's than any other. Both plays turn upon motives of remorse contrition, renunciation, and noble forgiveness. As George Odell observes:

There is something about the tone of *The Stranger* that exactly fitted the mood of the last three years of the 18th century. The melancholy and misanthropy of the mysterious stranger, who must have suffered horribly to have acquired that fine frown and far-away look and that fatal propensity to sit on stage banks under stage boughs, typified, no doubt . . . the essence of what we have since learned to call the romantic revival. It was very degenerate Rousseau and Werther. 'Neath melancholy boughs and afternoon sun always reminded of the grave. Tears wetted many handkerchiefs in the theater and in life.'[118]

The severest strictures upon the moral (or immoral) tendencies of *The Stranger* were expressed in the early years of its vogue. The immediate question was to decide whether Kotzebue was condoning marital inconstancy by permitting the restoration of his heroine to happiness after her self-confessed defection. While some, like Joseph Dennie ("Oliver Oldschool") condemned the author for subversive morality and for antiaristocratic and Jacobinical tendencies as well,[119] the play was staunchly defended by others. A writer in the *Port Folio* for 1802 (II, vi, 42) doubted

whether the censure . . . [was] altogether just . . . . [He was] strongly inclined to doubt the purity and justice of that morality, which would refuse our pity and forgiveness to one, whose fall was momentary, and who had attempted to repair her error by three years of solitary life and repentance.

At first Hodgkinson was preferred for the role of the Baron in *Lovers' Vows*,[120] and Mrs. Melmoth received the highest plaudits for her interpretation of Mrs. Haller in *The Stranger*. Leading stars of the American stage regularly chose it for their benefits.[121]

The nature of the Kotzebue fever can be shown most precisely by citing some statistics relating to the number of performances of German plays as compared with those of British, French, and native American origin (see Table IV).

The figures for the years 1798–1804 encompass the rise and fall of the first wave of enthusiasm for German drama. Kotzebue's significance in the over-all picture can be judged from the fact that of a total of 262 performances of German pieces in the two cities, 211 (over 84 per cent) were of his productions. In both cities the crest of the wave was reached in the phenomenal season of 1799–1800, when fifteen dramas by Kotzebue were produced. A reaction and falling off of interest soon after 1800 was probably inevitable, for the extravagant praise in newspapers and journals had gone far beyond what the pieces merited.[122] Even in 1799–1800, the New York company of actors rebelled against being forced to play the "Dutch stuff," and in Philadelphia Cooper, while bowing to popular demand by appearing in Kotzebuean roles, preferred to act Shakespearean parts.[123] In 1800 the *United States Gazette* expressed the hope that Cooper would "vindicate the insulted majesty of Shakespeare from the insolent usurpation of the play mongers";[124] yet Joseph Dennie's exultation, in 1801, "that, after an unaccountable run of popularity, the plays of Kotzebue are now sinking fast into oblivion . . . the reign of good taste again revives," was premature.[125]

TABLE IV

PERFORMANCES OF GERMAN PLAYS
AS COMPARED TO THOSE OF OTHER ORIGINS (1798–1804)

Season	All Plays Number of Perform- ances	Number of German Plays	Performances of German Plays		Kotzebue Plays	
			number	percentage	number	performances
In New York*						
1798–1799	93	6 (1)	28 (3)	30%	4	25
1799–1800	94	19	54	57	17	52
1800–1801	106	13 (1)	39	37	11	29
1801–1802	91	13 (6)	27 (16)	30	10	20
1802–1803	118	12 (5)	27 (5)	23	8	13
1803–1804	...†	4 (17)	7	...	2	5
In Philadelphia						
1798–1799	...	3	7	...	2	6
1799–1800	...	9	28	...	9	28
1800–1801	...	8	18	...	8	18
1801–1802	...	8	10	...	7	9
1802–1803	...	5	10	...	2	2
1803–1804	...	6	7	...	4	4

* Data compiled from Baker (*op. cit.*). Figures for Philadelphia are not as detailed as those for New York. The figures in parentheses in the third and fourth columns count plays which Baker described as doubtful; i.e., as reflecting possible but not definitely ascertainable German influence, or as dealing with German subject matter only. Data on the short summer seasons are here omitted.

† Data not available.

The introduction of new German works continued. Kotzebue was represented by *Fraternal Discord*, a five-act comedy, translated and adapted by Dunlap from *Die Versöhnung, oder der Bruderzwist* (1798), and first played on the New York stage on October 24, 1800. There had been seven performances in Philadelphia of Dibdin's version the previous season, and there followed scattered repetitions down to 1825–1826, for a total of 31 performances in that city. The New York version of Dunlap was even more popular, with seven performances in 1800–1801 and a total of 33 to 1828–1829.[126] The failure of *The Blind Boy* (from Kotzebue's *Das Epigramm*), premiered in New York in March, 1803, was warning to Dunlap that the vogue of Kotzebue was not completely secure. At

this juncture he turned to other Germans in search for materials. Only one of his several introductions in this category, Zschokke's *Abaellino*, can be called successful.[127] In December, 1800, Dunlap was already preparing it for the stage and publicizing it as superior to *The Robbers*, "in sublimity . . . and in its denouement" exceeding *The Stranger*.[128] Dunlap's, the earliest rendering into English, was published in 1802. Played nine times in 1801, it reappeared virtually every season until 1823–1824; it had 59 performances in New York and 39 in Philadelphia to 1828–1829. A good deal of the interest of the piece lies in its clever concealment of the identity of Abaellino—an anticipation of the stock device of the mystery play which was to become popular a century later.[129]

TABLE V

NUMBERS AND PERFORMANCES OF GERMAN PLAYS IN NEW YORK AND PHILADELPHIA, 1804–1829*

YEAR	GERMAN PLAYS				KOTZEBUE PLAYS			
	NUMBER	AVERAGE	PERFORMANCES	AVERAGE	NUMBER	AVERAGE	PERFORMANCES	AVERAGE
IN NEW YORK								
1804–1805	4	...	6	...	3	...	4	...
1805–1810	22	4.5	47	9.4	15	3.0	36	7.2
1810–1811	6	...	13	...	5	...	11	...
1811–1812	5	...	13	...	4	...	8	—
1812–1813	5	...	15	...	3	...	8	...
1813–1814 (2 theaters)	11	...	36	...	8	...	30	...
1814–1815	11	...	19	...	6	...	10	...
1815–1820	38	7.6	99	20.0	25	5.0	67	13.4
1820–1825 (2 theaters)	38	7.16	145	29.0	28	5.6	98	19.6
1825–1826 (3 theaters)	7	...	27	...	4	...	22	...
1826–1827 (4 theaters)	10	...	64	...	5	...	49	...
1827–1828	11	...	62	...	8	...	42	...
1828–1829	10	...	58	...	8	...	52	...
IN PHILADELPHIA								
1804–1805	7	...	11	...	6	...	10	...
1805–1810	29	5.8	35	7.0	18	3.6	25	5.0
1810–1815	42	8.4	90	18.0	29	5.8	64	12.8
1815–1821	38	7.6	60	12.0	28	5.6	50	10.0
1820–1824	41	8.2	169	33.8	30	6.0	142	28.4
1825–1829	29	7.3	92	23.0	22	5.5	69	17.5

* Translations or clearly recognizable and close adaptations of German originals only are here included. A count, if it were possible, of plays showing some influence of German romantic literature, or incidental bor-
manifold. Also excluded are works in the operatic form, though after 1823–1824 Mozart, Weber, and Beethoven were being performed in New York and Philadelphia.

From 1804 to 1830

The type of play which Dunlap had supplied so abundantly lost popularity after 1804. For a short period to about 1812 there were relatively few German importations. Thereafter followed a gradual increase of performances of German items, owing mainly to the revival and repetition of a small number of established dramas. The statistical counts, based on surviving records, are given in Table V.

Kotzebue continued to enjoy more and more performances until very nearly the end of the period, though only two new pieces by him were introduced after 1812–1813. Unfortunately there are no figures extant to show what proportion of the plays performed in any year after 1804–1805 were of German origin, but we may assume that the proportion was never again so high as in the remarkable season of 1799–1800, when 57 per cent of the plays produced in New York were German. While constituting an important portion of the theatrical fare available in America, German drama was never again so prominent as to be pre-eminent in the total picture.

THE SUCCESS OF NEWLY INTRODUCED PLAYS

For the succeeding years, noteworthy theatrical introductions include the following works of Kotzebue, Müllner, Fouqué, Wieland, and Goethe.

KOTZEBUE

La Pérouse, or the Desolate Island.—This "Grand Pantomimical Drama" was introduced in Philadelphia, December 26, 1804. It is a play with music prepared by the Englishman J. Fawcett, based on Kotzebue's *La Peyrouse, Schauspiel in zwei Aufzügen* (1798). The story is taken from the adventures of a well-known French explorer in Africa. Fawcett's version is a radical remaking of Kotzebue's plot. While the latter was indelicate enough, the dramatic problem posing the claims of two wives for the love of the same husband, Fawcett vulgarized it even further by introducing a chimpanzee as one of the main characters. La Perouse is about to be burned at the stake at the behest of a love-smitten but spurned native girl, but in this crisis he is rescued by a faithful chimpanzee, which earlier had been befriended by La Perouse. This elementary exercise in pantomime entertainment was relegated to the palaces of lighter amusements and seldom if ever played in the regular houses. It had 84 performances to 1830.

How to Die for Love.—This farce in two acts was prepared by an unknown translator from Kotzebue's *Blind Geladen* (1811). After its introduction in December, 1812, it had a total of 76 performances to 1830 in New York and Philadelphia.

The Poachers, or Guilty or Not Guilty.—Translated for the London stage from Kotzebue's *Der Rehbock, oder die schuldlosen Schuldbewussten* (1815), this comedy in three acts was premiered in October, 1827. By 1830 it had 19 performances in New York (sometimes billed as *The Roebuck*) and three in Philadelphia. It continued popular for some years after 1830.[130]

MÜLLNER

Guilt, or the Gipsey's Prophecy (*Die Schuld*, by A. G. A. Müllner).—A British blank-verse translation of this play, announced as a "German tragedy" in five acts, had two performances in 1820.

FOUQUÉ

Undine, or The Spirit of the Waters.—This melodramatic spectacle adapted by the Britisher G. Soane from the popular tale by Baron Fouqué was played nine times in Philadelphia in 1822. In 1823–1824 it enjoyed a run of 21 performances in the Park Theatre, New York. *Undine* exploited novel "water-effects" and exhibited such fascinating fantastic personages as Kuhleborn, the Water-King, the Rosicrucian Seer (protector of the quasi-mortal heroine), and a "goblin-spirit . . . who at his pleasure, is either mortal or a 'goblin-fiend.'"— *New York Mirror and Ladies' Literary Gazette*, I, xix (Dec. 6, 1823), 151.

WIELAND

Oberon, or the Charmed Horn.—Romantic fairy tale in two acts after Wieland's celebrated poem, written by James R. Planché with music selected from eminent composers by T. Cooke, was transported from London to New York in September, 1826. It enjoyed ten performances that season in New York and twelve in Philadelphia—a considerable success.

GOETHE

Faustus.—Also known as *The Devil and Dr. Faustus* this romantic drama was prepared by Soane, with original music by Bishop and Horn. It was introduced in New York in October, 1827, and was given 14 performances that season. Two seasons later it ran for 13 performances in Philadelphia. Reviewers, obviously unprejudiced by acquaintance with the original, recommended it enthusiastically: "It teaches that unbridled curiosity if mingled with enthusiasm of feeling and power of intellect, and directed by those mysteries which are too intricate and too vast for human understanding, must necessarily end in despair."—*New York Spy*, October 13, 1827; Baker, *op. cit.*, pp. 140 f. The plot is little more than a series of commands by Faust for indulgences in sensual pleasures, with hurried denouement wherein he is whisked off to the inferno. Musical numbers included a chorus of fishermen, "Home! there's a storm in the whistling blast"; chorus of hunters, "The wild Bird is rocking in his nest"; chorus of peasants, "Now for the Fireside's cheerful blaze"; chorus of fiends beneath the earth, "He comes! he comes!" etc.—C. F. Brede, *op. cit.*, pp. 291 f.[131]

The account of these introductions puts in relief the fact that romantic spectacle, usually with music (and thus in the nature of melodrama or of opera), was displacing the sentimental comedy of the type that had made Kotzebue supremely popular about 1800. The quality of the shallow sensationalism seems largely to have determined the selection of dramatic subjects from German authors. The theater reveled in exoticism of every sort: the primitive in *La Perouse*; the fantastic in *Undine, Oberon,* and *Faustus*; the Gothic in *Abaellino, Faustus,* and *Guilt*; the foreign, medieval, and remote in *Peter the Great* and *The Tournament.* By 1830 "German drama" came to be synonymous with the violent, exotic, and overstrained, and unbridled romantic. Kotzebue's peculiar type of sentimentalism combined with libertine motifs persisted most powerfully in the *Stranger, Lovers' Vows,* and *Fraternal Discord.* His most distinctive contribution to the American theater (a field in which he had no rival) was to develop the sentimental bourgeois drama to a point of highest finish. Schiller was not widely known for any but his first play, and this was appreciated as a unique mixture of the Gothic and the sentimental.

The genre of the melodrama (*mélodrame*), a superficially violent play with sensational effects, came into prominence after 1800. As is true of Gothicism and horror in the prose narrative, the type of the melodrama is in considerable measure of Germanic origin. From the beginnings British melodrama drew both plot and atmosphere from German balladry, folktales, fantastic romances, legends, and tales of outlawry. Lewis' *Castle Spectre* (1797) bears unmistakable marks of kinship with *The Robbers.*[132] *The Bleeding Nun* and *The Forest of Rosenwald*, both adapted from *The Monk*, share with that work certain features borrowed from Schiller's *Ghost-Seer.* Similar traces in plot, setting, and character and a fondness for German backgrounds[133] are evident in Lewis' *King Alfonso of Castille* (Philadelphia, from 1802–1803 on), in *Rugantino*, and in his *Adelmorn the Outlaw* (New York, 1801–1802, and Philadelphia, 1802–1803); and in many other works which had long runs on the nineteenth-century stage.[134] Ballad themes find echoes in *The Gnome King, or the Giant Mountains*, a legend of the Riesengebirge (1819–1820), and *The Wood Demon, or The Clock has Struck* (1807–1808 and thereafter). *The Flying Dutchman* was a melodrama founded on the familiar German theme, and the story of Faust was repeated in such pale imitations as *Melmouth* (New York, 1824–1825) and *The Harlequin Dr. Faustus*, a pantomime (Philadelphia, 1796–1808). A native production illustrating the affinity of melodrama with the Faust story is S. B. H. Judah's blank verse drama *Odofriede, the Outcast* (printed 1822).[135]

It has often been said that writers like Kotzebue, however popular, hardly outlived their little hour; but investigations into the American stage history demonstrate that Kotzebue's *Stranger* and other plays of Germanic origin were played regularly to within the memory of some persons living today, existing in the bills of the larger houses into the nineties. The tabulation of some scattered records from representative stages serve to sketch the course of that long trail which started in 1797 at the Park. The list of performances, in rough chronological order, based on studies available,[136] demonstrates a vitality often unsuspected and unknown.

Abaellino

New York: 1834–1843 (2 performances); 1857 (1 perf.)
Philadelphia: 1835 (3 perf.)
St. Louis: 1820 ("two or three nights," with the Ludlow Company)

The Robbers

(EXCLUSIVE OF PERFORMANCES IN GERMAN)

New York: 1850–1857 (7 perf.); 1857–1865 (5 perf.); 1865–1870 (8 perf.); 1870–1875 (4 perf.); 1875–1879 (2 perf.)
Philadelphia: 1842–1855 (43 perf.)
Chicago: 1849–1875 (31 perf.)
St. Louis: 1820–1839 (3 perf.)
Nashville: 1819 (1 perf.); another, June 20, 1832
Davenport: 1857, 1859
Boston: 1872 (with Mr. and Mrs. J. B. Booth)
New Orleans: Jan. 1, 1806; Nov. 9, 1859

Wilhelm Tell

(By Knowles and others; operas excluded)

New York: 1834–1843 (29 perf.); 1850–1857 (12 perf.); 1857–1865 (14 perf.); 1865–1870 (9 perf.); 1870–1875 (10 perf.); 1875–1879 (3 perf.); 1879–1882 (1 perf.); 1882–1885 (3 perf.)
Philadelphia: 1835–1855 (13 perf.)
Chicago: 1857–1870 (13 perf.)[137]
St. Louis: 1830–1839 (5 perf.)
Nashville: "William Tell, the Swiss Patriot," 1830–1838 (3 perf.)
Davenport: 1830–1838 (3 perf.)
Boston: 1856–1857 (Boston Theater, introduced by Edwin Forrest); repeated, 1861–1862
Houston: 1839 (in each of two theaters); 1839–1840 (Houston Theater, 2 perf.)

PLAYS ON THE STORY OF *Faust*

(After Goethe)

New York: Soane's *Faustus*, 1834–1843 (4 perf.); 1850–1857 (7 perf.); 1857–1865 (3 perf.); 1865–1870 (11 perf.); 1870–1875 (4 perf.) 1879–1882 (3 perf.); 1875–1879 (1 perf.); 1882–1885 (none); 1885–1888 (8 perf.)
———. *Faust, or the Demon of the Drachenfels*, 1842 (1 perf.); 1845–1846 (1 perf.)
———. *Faust and Marguerite*, 1857 (1 perf.); 1862 (1 perf.)
———. *Faustus and Mephistopheles*, 1854 (perf., Bowery Theater)
———. *Faust*, parody in French, 1870 (1 perf.)
———. *Faust*, burlesque, 1865–1870 (5 perf.)
———. *Faust*, ballet, 1857–1865 (10 perf.)
Philadelphia: Soane's "grand romantic spectacle," 1845–1851 (19 perf.)
Boston: 1886–1887 (Margaret Mather); 1887–1888 (Henry Irving, supported by Ellen Terry, run of 22 days); 1888–1889 (2 weeks' engagement of Lewis Morrison as Mephistopheles)
———. *Faust and Marguerite*, 1858–1859 (4 weeks' run, with Thomas Barry); 1866–1867 (J. B. Roberts)
———. *Faust*, ballet, 1857–1858 (in repertory of the Ronzani Ballet Troupe)

Undoubtedly these plays owe their long life largely to the fact that they were standard items in the repertories of the

TABLE VI

PERFORMANCES OF GERMAN GOTHIC AND ROMANTIC SPECTACLE PLAYS

PLAY	PHILADELPHIA		NEW YORK		ST. LOUIS
	PERFORMANCES	YEARS	PERFORMANCES	YEARS	YEARS
Of Age Tomorrow	18	1836–48	11	1834–40	...
How to Die for Love	10	1836–52	8	1834–50	...
Virgin of the Sun	...	...	3	1843–57	...
La Perouse	...	1847	...	1851	...
Rugantino	...	...	...	1857–65	1834
Birthday, or Reconciliation	...	...	...	...	1835
Lovers' Vows	...	...	...	...	1816, 1830
Rinaldo Rinaldini	5	1836–37	...	...	...
Ugolino	19	1835–54	...	...	...
Undine	14	1847–49	...	...	...

great stars, who in that day exercised imperious command over their choices of roles. *The Stranger* was used by Edwin Booth, Charlotte Cushman, and Julia Dean; the part of Karl von Moor by J. B. Booth; that of Faust by Henry Irving; Mephistopheles by Lewis Morrison; and Rolla by Edwin Forrest, Wyzeman Marshall, and John McCullough. Despite the long life of certain German favorites, the general trend of the mid-century was the gradual displacement of melodrama by the romantic drama in the grand style. However, some German Gothic and romantic spectacle plays continued to be given, as the data in Table VI indicate. Under the encouragement of such stars as Forrest, James Hackett, the Keans, J. B. Booth, W. C. Macready, and the Kembles, the preference shifted to a drama wherein the action was more unified, better motivated, and psychologically more subtle than in the melodrama. These actors were catholic in their tastes, playing Shakespeare, Restoration comedy and tragedy, eighteenth-century comedy, Hugo, and Dumas; but they ignored almost completely the post-Goethean German drama. By the time of the Civil War, the stream of exchange between the American and the German stage had fallen to its lowest ebb since 1795.

From 1830 to 1900

The period following 1830 shows no effort to present Germany's classical or contemporary dramatists in America, or to interpret the work of such outstanding experimenters as Kleist, Hebbel, Grillparzer, Ludwig, Freytag, or Geibel. Most of these were, of course, far from successful in their own country; in America their work was hardly noticed. In a few cases, American theatrical entrepreneurs took a risk on some adaptation or translation from a German stage success. The word "success" is some clue to the level of literary worth to which these stray recruits belonged. They were of the class of heavy romantic tragedy which had evolved out of the genres discussed above. Friederich Halm's *Ingomar, or the Son of the Wilderness*, introduced in the fifties and maintained as a standard acting vehicle until 1870 and beyond, is of the type. Translated by the Englishwoman Maria Lovell, this romantic drama in the grand style had as its theme the triumph of personal morality and love over uncontrolled primitive passion. It was performed in New York at least 28 times in 1850–1857 and 34 times in 1857–1870; in Philadelphia 45 times from 1851 to 1855; in Boston from 1854 to 1859 in the repertories of Julia

Dean, Mrs. Bowers, Kate Reignolds, and Mary Anderson. The latter brought the play to Boston annually from 1877 to 1882. This same role was used in 1887 by the great Julia Marlowe at her debut.

About the period of the Civil War the "stock system" of theater management (in centers outside New York City) showed signs of disintegration, and the practice of filling the gaps with performances of traveling stars was initiated. As a result more and more theatrical history was concentrated in the larger houses of New York City, whose managers in this way gained greater control over the theater than earlier managers had enjoyed. One of the most successful of these New York managers was Augustin Daly (1838–1899). The large group of German farces and comedies adapted from such contemporary popular writers as the Schönthans, Blumenthal, Mosenthal, Genée, Rosen, Kadelburg, and Benedix that the American public saw in the sixties and later is owing almost exclusively to the managerial work of Daly.[138]

Daly was not an actor but a writer of great skill in meeting the popular demands and an astute manager in the highly competitive field of commerical drama.[139] He began his career with an adaptation of Salomon Hermann von Mosenthal's melodrama *Deborah* (1850) under the title *Leah the Forsaken*, produced in Boston in 1862, with Kate Bateman in the title role, and brought to New York the next year.[140] In 1873 he scored another great success with his adaptation of Mosenthal's *Madeleine Morel*, a "tragedy bordering on the melodrama"[141] done on the pattern of French romantic tragedy after Dumas.[142] Among some ninety productions from the hand of Daly throughout his career, about a third are adaptations from such German writers as Gustav von Moser, Franz and Paul von Schönthan, and Julius Rosen, the others being altered or adapted from English and French theatrical literature, or from novels.

In almost all cases Daly altered the originals freely, transferring the action to this country and changing characters and situations to make them conform.[143]

Daly brought more plays to the American stage than did Dunlap, but his adaptations approached less closely the main line of the Germanic dramatic tradition than did Dunlap's. Because the authors he was interested in cultivated a broadly international type of light comedy, and because his adaptations thoroughly Americanized them,[144] these plays of Daly's were not known to audiences as of distinctively German origin or character. There was apparently no such critical discussion as in Dunlap's time over the pro's and con's of the "Dutch" or "Germanic" element in them. Their virtues were almost exclusively those of craftsmanship and easy mastery of technique, and in this respect they exactly fulfilled the function that was served by the facile Kotzebue seventy years earlier. Daly was always ready to admit that he chose his pieces because they lent themselves to easy alteration. On the whole, it cannot be said that Daly's adaptations deeply influenced or materially altered the course of the American dramatic tradition.

Many of the remaining plays on our list of adaptations from the German were introduced by or for the German-American actors or actresses who became prominent after 1860. From 1840 on, the German theater was a lively institution in several large centers, especially in New York.[145] The high cultural aspiration of the German-speaking theater in America, its extraordinary vitality and perseverence, and the general respect that it won among playgoers and critics even outside the German circles make it a considerable factor in the history of the American drama. If we look at its activities in New York, we gain some idea of its function in a dozen other cities where, while not as firmly entrenched, it was nevertheless well established through the second half of the century. Using a variety of halls, theaters, and places of amusement, the German theater in New York between 1840 and 1848 gave a total of 88 different plays in 149 performances.[146] Even in those early years, the literary level of these plays was considerably higher than that of the German drama in translation. They included *Tell*, *Die Räuber*, and *Kabale und Liebe* by Schiller, Heinrich v. Kleist's *Kätchen von Heilbronn*, Grillparzer's *Ahnfrau*, and Müllner's *Schuld*. After 1854 the German theater centered around the two famous *Stadttheater*: the *Altes Stadttheater*, in existence from 1854 to 1864, and the *Neues Stadttheater*, from 1864 to 1872. In the former from 1854 to 1864 Leuchs finds a total of 123 plays given 289 performances. Of this total, Shakespeare, Lessing, Schiller, and Goethe accounted for 48 performances, or 16 per cent, though the lesser comedy writers like Charlotte Birch-Pfeiffer and Benedix accounted for a large proportion, too.

Just as important as the maintenance of this large inclusive repertory was the introduction of German actors, many of whom very quickly gained fame outside the German-speaking populace. Occasionally an actor from the English theater attempted a performance in German for the German theater, but more frequently the situation was reversed.[147] Heinrich Moesinger of the New York Theater in 1869 performed *Huiko* in English, "a drama especially translated for him by Professor J. E. Frobischer."[148] The actress Methua-Scheller made her English debut in 1864 in an English version of Birch-Pfeiffer's *Dorf und Stadt* under the title of *Lorlie's Wedding*. It was given at the Winter Garden on March 28, 1864, and seems to have been seen in Boston two

weeks earlier, given there by the same actress, supported by John McCullough and Forrest's Company on March 2 and 5. This play traveled to Baltimore and Buffalo, and was given with Booth in the cast in 1866. For the season of 1865 we find a similar adaptation from Birch-Pfeiffer for Daniel Bandmann, for at Niblo's Garden in that year he played *The Beauforts* (based on Lytton's novel *Night and Morning*), as especially re-translated into English by Alfred Ayres. In 1867 arrived Fanny Janauschek, "the most distinguished of all German actresses to change from one language to the other." After two sensational seasons in the German theater, she changed in 1870–1871 to the English and achieved widespread renown in a number of roles. Her repertory included *Bleak House* (adapted from Dickens), *Macbeth*, *Deborah*, *Mary Stuart*, and *Brunhild*. The German-language theater enjoyed a healthy, uninterrupted existence until the outbreak of World War I.[149]

The production of Hauptmann and Sudermann in English in America began in the nineties, with considerable success; but this movement hardly got under way before 1900 and does not belong in the era under discussion. On the whole, the German contribution to the American theater was (first) to provide some effective Kotzebuean roles for a number of the greater guest stars and (second) to bring to our stage certain well-liked plays of the light comedy class. The foreign-language theater also exerted some influence in this way. Yet in the drama there is nothing comparable to the tremendous enrichment which Americans received from the hands of German musicians, composers, and orchestra leaders.

EARLY AMERICAN FICTION

The student of American literature finds little purely "literary" Germanic influence[150] until after the War of 1812, when a trend toward the development of a national

literature became marked. The seventeenth-century Puritan who read *Dr. Faustus* or the eighteenth-century scholar who consulted Pufendorf or Alsted or Keckermann was not indulging in a love for belles-lettres so much as his desire to acquire knowledge or to get a better understanding of his relation to his God. Even when the taste began to turn to Klopstock, Lavater, Gessner, and Wieland, it was principally their pious didacticism that attracted the American reader. But by the turn of the century we come upon isolated examples of American interest presaging a purely literary concern with German productions. Among the first is John Quincy Adams (1767–1848), who developed an abiding appreciation of the poems of Bürger, Goethe, and Schiller, and made, while he was U.S. Minister to Prussia, during 1797–1801, a verse translation of Wieland's *Oberon*. There were other isolated instances—even in remote Lexington, Kentucky, where we are told on the authority of James Lane Allen that the bookstores sold, along with Fielding, Smollett, Goldsmith, Paley, Butler, and Watts, the works of Lavater and Baron Trenck as early as 1800.[151] By the thirties, of course, there had developed a "German craze" in and about Boston, and people like James F. Clarke, Ephraim Peabody, Samuel Osgood, and Christopher P. Cranch were carrying their enthusiasm for Goethe and Schiller with them to Louisville and Cincinnati, where, through the columns of the *Western Messenger*, they disseminated it throughout the West, and where their efforts were soon seconded by those of the German intellectuals called the *Dreissiger* as well as the *Achtundvierziger*, and only a little later, by the far-flung efforts of the St. Louis disciples of Goethe and Hegel.

William Hill Brown

In the meantime the early American novelists had become infected by the fever of Wertherism and German *Sturm-und-Drang* sentimentalism generally. One of the earliest instances of infiltration occurs in William Hill Brown's Richardsonian novel, *The Power of Sympathy* (1789), generally regarded as the first American novel. Toward the end of the story, the hero (Harrington) is discovered, a suicide, and by his side is found *The Sorrows of Werther*. German productions of the *Werther*, *Goetz*, *Räuber*, and *Geisterseher* type spawned (as we have observed) a numerous progeny of English and American translations, adaptations, and imitations, in all imaginable forms, by second- and third-rate novelists, dramatists, and story-tellers who count for relatively little in the sum-total of the abiding American literary production. Of the seventy-odd American novels published between Brown's *Power of Sympathy* and Cooper's first success, *The Spy* (1821), only those of Charles Brockden Brown escaped oblivion and need detain us as exhibiting Germanic influences.[152]

Charles Brockden Brown

Gothic horror did not derive solely from Mrs. Radcliffe or "Monk" Lewis. German "romance," the common parent of both, subsisted alongside English Gothicism and found many avenues by which to insinuate itself into the American consciousnses about 1800 without benefit of any British (or other) intermediary, though often it came to America in guises and forms virtually indistinguishable from the British versions. Much of this was stuff of a sub-literary nature—not only Bürger's ballads and Goethe's and Schiller's *Sturm-und-Drang* productions but popular tales of banditry, plays based on the Illuminati and the *Fehmgericht*, and novels designed to teach lessons of social melioration as well as domestic virtue. Coincidentally with the time when Brown was preparing for a career as a writer of novels, the flood of this type of literature reached its crest.[153] Aside from Goethe's *Werther* (available in translation since 1779), Schiller's *Räuber* (translated in 1792), Goethe's *Goetz* (1795), Bürger's *Lenore* (1796), Kotzebue's *Pizarro* (1796) and *The Stranger* (1798), and Zschokke's *Abaellino* (1798), to say nothing of the numerous adaptations and imitations which they inspired, there appeared translations of a number of *Familienromane* and *Räubergeschichten*.[154] This is the sorry stuff on which Brown's fancy was nourished during his apprentice days.[155]

As early as 1793 Brown claimed familiarity with Gessner, Haller, and Leibnitz, but among all the German names, the one that stood above all others in his estimation was Wieland[156]—a circumstance that explains why, when he cast about for a title, characters, and background in which to invest his story of the supernatural, terror, religious fanaticism, spontaneous combustion, ventriloquism, transformation, and rational moralism, he should have chosen to identify his Wieland family with the German poet of the same name as descended from a common ancestor.[157] Not unnaturally Clara Wieland seeks distraction for her troubled thoughts in German ballads of chivalry,[158] her brother received from Germany a new tragedy by a Saxon poet, wherein "headlong passions are portrayed in wild numbers, with terrific energy,"[159] the Wielands and Pleyel rehearse a German verse tragedy,[160] the sweetheart of Pleyel is the Baroness Theresa de Stolberg,[161] Wieland's mother is a disciple of Zinzendorf,[162] virtually all the characters of the book have lived or have traveled in Germany, and all but Carwin are familiar with the language.[163] It would seem that Brown followed his own recommendation to the readers of the *Monthly Magazine and American Review* that they should become acquainted with the writings of Kotzebue, Gessner, Iffland, Wieland, Haller, Schiller, and Goethe as sources of "intellectual pleasure and improvement,"[164] and that German romance supplied more than a dash of seasoning for *Wieland*, for Brown's indebtedness goes deeper than a borrowing of externalities.

For example, *Wieland* exhibits what was a common and mutually interdependent characteristic of German and English tales of terror, of history, of adventure, of sentiment, and of purpose, differing only in national backgrounds. A subtle force arising from the Enlightenment gave special emphasis in Germany to a more thorough psychological investigation of character, largely for the purpose of combating superstition and other aberrations of the mind, and therefore also to a balanced, rational approach to life.[165] Not only Rousseau in France and Godwin in England but a hundred writers in Germany enforced lessons of the dangers and evils of following too strictly *one* of the mental faculties, and habitually illustrated and applied this theme to programs of social and political betterment, Utopian meliorism, institutional reform, the position of women, marriage, punishment for crime, and other advanced areas of social thinking.[166]

Brown adopted this motif of a reasoned approach to life. *Wieland, or the Transformation* presents a number of illustrations of the tragic effect, or transformations of humanity, that occur when human reason is overthrown by superstition or passion.[167] While this theme is not exclusively Germanic, when we find it repeatedly in conjunction with others that are obviously of German origin, the presumption is strong that there is a connection—that the German rational tale had at least a contributory effect. In both *Wieland* and *Ormond* we find characterizations that bear the unmistakable stamp "Made in Germany." Ludloe in *Carwin the Biloquist*, the sequel to *Wieland*, and Ormond are both members of secret societies "in Berlin" on the order of the Illuminati. Both "had met with schemers and reasoners who aimed at the new-modeling of the world, and the subversion of all that has hitherto been conceived elementary and fundamental in the constitution of man and of government."[168] They are bound by dreadful oaths of secrecy to this society, whose purpose, since it is to erect a "political structure" as "the growth of pure wisdom," is not evil, though the pursuit of it raises questions regarding whether the means adopted justify the end sought.[169]

Aside from these similarities in atmosphere and theme, there are, especially in *Wieland*, identities with other German productions. In 1900 F. H. Wilkins suggested that Brown borrowed part of *Wieland* from Schiller's *Geisterseher*,[170] and a decade later Walter Just found the whole plan of Brown's novel there.[171] He pointed out that the secret efforts by unknown persons (the Armenian—Carwin) are directed against a guileless youth (Prinz von ***—Theodore Wieland), and that in both cases the mysterious unknown foretells the death of a beloved one. What neither pointed out, but what is more to the point is that both the Prince and Wieland are susceptible to a species of religious fanaticism.[172] But it is Tschink's *Geisterseher* (or *The Victim of Magical Delusion*) that stands even closer to Brown's *Wieland*, especially in the lesson that is inculcated. Both turn upon identical themes. Both present victims of delusion (Wieland and Miguel) played upon by men (Carwin and the Unknown) who seem to possess supernatural powers. Both discuss with their victims the probability of supernatural manifestations in the same terms. The purpose of Tschink's *Victim* is explained in the Preface in words that Brown could readily have inserted *verbatim* almost anywhere among the arguments of *Wieland*:

If we . . . conceive an exclusive attachment to *one* of . . . the different Sources of Knowledge . . . or confine ourselves merely to sensation and experience, if we desire to *see* and to *feel* those things which cannot be perceived by the senses, but are known to us only through the medium of our understanding; if we, for example, are not satisfied with what the contemplation of nature and the gospel teach us of God, but desire to have an immediate, and physical communion with the invisible; we then cannot avoid the deviations of fanaticism, and are easily led to confound our *feelings* and *ideas* with external effects; the effects of our soul with effects produced by superior beings; we believe that we see, hear, and perceive what exists no where but in the imagination; we . . . are misled by the variety and strength of our feelings and mistake for *reality* what is *ideal*. . . . All pretended apparitions, every imaginary communication with superior beings, the belief in witches, sorcerers, and in the secret power of magical spells, owe their existence to this species of fanaticism (I, i–iv).

Just so, Theodore Wieland jumps too readily to the conclusion that the voice of the ventriloquist is of supernatural origin. His senses become "depraved" so that he becomes a religious maniac; Clara's equilibrium is overthrown by terror, Pleyel's by disgust. Only tragedy can restore the balance, and the speedy denouement after the murders enforces the moral: "This scene of havoc was produced by an illusion of the senses."[173] Carwin, the master mischief that occasioned all the delusions and their fearful consequences, resolves to write "a faithful narrative" of his life "as a lesson to mankind of the evils of credulity on the one hand, and of imposture on the other."[174] Brown's characters are exemplifications of precisely the errors against which Tschink's story and Schiller's had given warning. Wieland failed to take into account the common human experience in respect to man's moral duty and the common opinions of God's attributes—he violated all the fundamental rules of rational procedure and consequently ended according to the exact prescriptions of the *Geisterseher* of Schiller and of Tschink.[175]

It would seem, then, that Charles Brockden Brown, the first American writer of fiction whose work possesses more than ordinary merit, gave to American fiction at the very outset a Germanic coloring, and that he used Germanic sources in a measure which, considering his influence, acknowledged and unacknowledged, upon Irving, Cooper, Poe, Hawthorne, Melville, and Dana,[176] profoundly affected the development of the American novel and American fiction generally.

Elihu Hubbard Smith

Although none of Elihu Hubbard Smith's writings show more than modest accomplishment, his friendship for Charles Brockden Brown, William Dunlap, and the Rev. Samuel Miller, his connections with the Connecticut Wits, his interest in the progress of American literature, and his position as one of the well-known scientific writers of his day make him important despite his death at twenty-seven. His manuscript diary reveals that he studied German in 1796 and looked forward to the time when he would be able to make considerable use of his knowledge.[177] He and Brown were inseparable for years, and Smith communicated his enthusiasm for German thought and art to Brown as well as to Dunlap, who began in the year of Smith's death to present Kotzebue in his theater.[178] As a prime mover in the Friendly Club and adviser and collaborator of both Brown and Dunlap in their early literary endeavors, Smith served as a catalyst among his friends in New York during the last decade of the eighteenth century very much as Joseph S. Buckminster did in Boston during the early years of the next century.

James Fenimore Cooper

While the vogue and influence of Cooper in Germany is the more significant,[179] the reciprocal influence of Germany on Cooper is in several respects more important than has been recognized. For one thing, he made four trips to Germany or Switzerland instead of the two recorded by Lounsbury.[180] The first journey was made from Paris to Berne during July, 1828.[181] Except for

Italy, Switzerland appealed to Cooper more than any other European country, for here he found natural beauty heightened by an abundance of romantic tradition. Of all the traditions, legendary and authentic, the story of Wilhelm Tell had the greatest appeal for him,[182] and he gathered information on it from the guidebooks, the oral tradition, and Schiller's play.[183]

In Italy during 1829–1830, Cooper moved his family via the Tyrol and Munich to Dresden in May of 1830, where they remained until the July revolution attracted him to Paris, whither the family followed him in September. A third journey, in the nature of a circular tour from Paris, was taken the following summer through Belgium, the Rhineland, back to Paris. It was on this trip that Cooper was inspired by the Abbey of Limburg and the castle of Hartenburg, the Heidenmauer and the Teufelstein, all near Dürkheim, to write *The Heidenmauer* (1832).[184] The fourth trip was begun on July 18, 1832, in a *calèche* commodious enough to accommodate the entire family, plus two servants, one of them a Saxon girl hired in Germany.[185] These journeys, in and of themselves, would mean little if they had not provided the leading motifs for two of his books and formed the direct materials for two others. The latter use is best exemplified in *Sketches of Switzerland*, which appeared in two parts in two volumes each in 1836.[186] The first volume of Part One of these *Sketches* relates his excursion from Paris through Burgundy to Berne in 1828. Throughout Cooper shows himself a competent student of Swiss history and an alert traveler.[187] The second volume of Part I takes us to Lake Lucerne, the Tell country, thence through the upper regions of the Rhine, the Alpine passes, Berne, and finally to Milan. The whole is plentifully supplied with German phrases and tourist information from Ebel, anecdotes from Winckelmann, and statistics from Picot, plus much legendary and general antiquarian lore garnered from miscellaneous sources, including oral tradition.[188]

In Part II of *Sketches of Switzerland*[189] Cooper the antiquary comes to the fore even more prominently than in Part I. He pokes about in dusty corners and amid crumbling ruins, especially alert for literary lore, even to dragging into the book a circumstantial account of how, two years before in Dresden, he nearly made the acquaintance of Tieck.[190]

In the midst of the travels thus circumstantially described, Cooper began the second of his European trilogy, *The Heidenmauer*. In the Preface he describes substantially the same itinerary that is related in Part II of the *Sketches*, though an earlier Rhineland journey is merged with it, for the original inspiration for *The Heidenmauer* had come during the tour of 1831, when the illness of one of Cooper's entourage had necessitated a halt at Dürkheim. As the account in the novel has it, Cooper asks the host at the inn at the Sign of the Ox what of novelty the vicinity holds; he is directed to "a ruined abbey, and a ruined castle, too!" "Here," says Cooper, "is sufficient occupation for the rest of the day. An abbey and a castle!" And when the host tells him about the Heidenmauer and the Teufelstein, Cooper engages Christian Kinzel, a loquacious guide, and sets out on a tour of inspection.[191]

The Heidenmauer is the second of Cooper's European novels of social purpose. Where *The Bravo* enforces the moral that "the good in human nature will triumph over the evil in government," *The Heidenmauer* is a broader objectification of the process by which the "group mind of man" undergoes a transition "from medieval to modern social and religious ideas." Cooper draws an elaborate parallel between social changes that took place in the Palatinate following the Reformation and those of the group mind of his own day.[192] In thus illustrating the effect of Lutheranism in liberating the mind of man from superstition and the

social order from corruption, and in drawing the parallel to his own times by indicating the effect of the American ideal of liberating the modern mind from the corruption of a world controlled by the ancient regime, Cooper made a notable and altogether unique contribution to the American novel. As Professor Spiller has remarked, the final paragraph of the novel states the dominating motif not only of *The Heidenmauer* but also of several of Cooper's later books.[193] That being so, Cooper's rumination upon historical and legendary events of German intellectual and social life and his embodiment of his conclusions in *The Heidenmauer* mark a significant point in his development as novelist and thinker.

The last of the European trilogy, *The Headsman*, is a better story and less of a social document than the second. The moral, while less prominently displayed, is the same as that of *The Heidenmauer*. The conclusion of the book is that the American heritage is twofold: European tradition grants to America the culture and the sanity born of long experience, and American resources grant exemption from the evils attending a decadent European society. Like *The Heidenmauer*, *The Headsman* applies old Germanic institutions to American civilization in a manner to reveal the difference between them, and (as Cooper observed in *A Letter to His Countrymen*) to show that a direct imitation would be of the utmost danger to the integrity of the new country. Seen in this light, the influence upon Cooper of German and Swiss associations is far from trivial.

The Gothic Element

Even while the Gothic and Germanic motifs became the rage in periodical literature, spokesmen for the "American" tradition from Royall Tyler and Joseph Dennie onward strenuously opposed the introduction of foreign exoticism of all kinds. One of the most forceful proponents for the indigenous of a slightly later day was James Kirke Paulding.[194] Despite such opposition, Gothic mystery and Germanic horror long continued popular. The Gothic insinuated itself into American architecture of the late eighteenth century (and afterwards), and early in the nineteenth Washington Allston embodied some of its elements in his paintings. Freneau's "House of Night" (1779), Joseph Story's *Power of Solitude*, and Jonathan M. Scott's *Sorceress, or Salem Delivered* (1817) are exemplifications in verse before Whittier in his *Legends of New England, in Prose and Verse* (1831) and Poe, from 1827 onward, worked the same mine of romantic materials.[195]

The drama, of course, provided ample scope for the melodramatic, and after Dunlap's *Fontainville Abbey* (acted 1795, printed 1806), the Gothic play with or without German motifs of the *Faust-Werther-Robbers-Stranger* sort, produced a veritable flood that threatened to inundate the whole land and submerge every other style. Most of these were translations, adaptations, or bold plagiarisms. Among the more original in conception and style was the dramatic poem *Odofriede, the Outcast* (printed 1822) by Samuel B. H. Judah.[196] But the combined influences of *Faust*, *Manfred*, and *The Robbers* were not enough to raise this play or any other of the same type into the realm of literary excellence.

Only in fiction did Gothicism attain anything approaching distinction, partly because the earlier decades of the nineteenth century produced few authors of merit other than writers of fiction. Moreover, fiction permits what is forbidden by the inescapable realness of the stage, including a free imaginative range and the indefiniteness of effect so essential to the treatment of the weird. These circumstances help explain why the Gothic element is a primary ingredient of American fiction from the first. Its earliest exemplification is found in the first regular American novel—William Hill Brown's *Power of Sympathy*

(1789), in which one of the characters, in a Dantesque dream, visits the realm of departed sinners and is thrown into a paroxysm of fear and horror when he beholds the punishment that is meted out to one guilty of seduction, the blackest crime on the blotter of Hell. Just as he is seized by a demon, who thrusts him among the damned, he awakes, thus initiating the American fashion of explaining mysteries and supernatural happenings naturally or rationally.

But the distinction of writing the first Gothic novel and of channelizing the conventions which the *genre* was to follow in America (including the technique of rational explanation, its frank adaptation of the typical literary themes of German Gothicism, and its transfer of medieval European settings to contemporary America) belongs to Charles Brockden Brown, whose *Wieland* (1798) is the first full-blown flower of this exotic plant. The Americanization, or naturalization, of the Gothic theme and setting is carried forward in George Watterston's *Glencarn; or, the Disappointment of Youth* (1810) and Isaac Mitchell's *Asylum* (1811), and soon received its best illustration in some of Washington Irving's Hudson River legends.

The modern short story has long been regarded as the one literary *genre* that is distinctively American. The epic, the novel, the drama, and the others we have never laid claim to. "But the short story," we are in the habit of saying, "that is ours. We invented it, we developed it, we perfected it." And we point to Irving, Hawthorne, Poe, and their successors for proof.

But our patent to the short story has not gone unchallenged. Not long after the first specimens appeared in *The Sketch Book* (1819–1820), it was pointed out that one of the best of them, "Rip Van Winkle," was based on a German tale and could not, therefore, lay claim to absolute originality.[197] Succeeding tales by Irving drew from the critics the charge of plagiarism.

In a review of *Bracebridge Hall* (1822), a contributor to *Blackwood's* declared that "the great blemish of the work . . . is that it is drawn not from life, but from musty volumes."[198] When *Tales of a Traveller* appeared in 1824, English readers were disappointed that it was no *Sketch Book* of Germany, as Irving had led them to expect, and reviewers voiced their displeasure by charging him with "pilfering the materials of other men, working up old stories."[199]

Such were some of the comments elicited by America's first examples of this new *genre*, and similar charges followed Irving throughout his story-writing career. Nor did Irving's successors fare much better. Almost the first critical comment published on Poe's tales connected them with "Germanism,"[200] and Poe felt himself called upon to declare: "If in any of my productions terror has been the thesis, I maintain that terror is not of Germany, but of the soul."[201] And Poe himself was the first to accuse Hawthorne of plagiarizing the Germans when he professed to have found the secret of Hawthorne in Tieck.[202] Thus, from the beginning, the American short story has been coupled with the German tale. An examination of the basis for making these allegations is in order.

Germanic Materials and Motifs in the Short Story

WASHINGTON IRVING
(1783–1859)

Early German Interests

While Irving's earliest writings demonstrate his discipleship of the eighteenth-century literary tradition, *The Sketch Book* shows him striking out on a new course, utilizing certain German romantic materials in short prose tales instead of the conventional multi-volume novel of the eighteenth century. Irving's earliest contacts with things Germanic include the Gothic novel, the periodical literature (British and American) of the day,[1] and Dunlap's concoctions from Schiller and Kotzebue for the Park Theater, where Irving was an habitué throughout the years of his dandyhood in New York City.[2] In England during the latter half of the second decade of the nineteenth century, he moved agreeably in the infectiously romantic atmosphere of Murray's London drawing rooms, and a visit to Scott, whose "border-tales, witching-songs, and stories crowded" Irving's mind with "a world of ideas, images, and impressions" producing a "kind of delirium," supplied what was needed to direct, or re-direct, his attention to the literature of Germany.[3] Irving's visit to Abbotsford was followed by a wild effort to take German by storm. He bought a German grammar and fell to work on Rabenhorst's German dictionary as the

corridor to the inviting land of legendary lore and literary inspiration which Scott had described.[4] On May 19, 1818, he reported to his friend Brevoort that while learning German had proved "a severe task" requiring "hard study," he was "able to read and splutter a little," and that however great the labor, he believed that "the rich mine of German literature holds forth abundant rewards."[5]

The Sketch Book

In *The Sketch Book*, written mainly during 1818, we have some of these "abundant rewards." Composition formerly so halting, now proceeded readily, often spontaneously.[6] "Rip Van Winkle" is one of the pieces written "under direct inspiration"—a quaint but not altogether erroneous way of putting it when we observe Irving's close reliance in this so-called "first" American short story upon its source, the old German legend of Peter Klaus. The parallelism is worth considering in detail that the extent of Irving's borrowing may be known and that his technique in rewriting old materials may be observed and appraised. The German source is therefore reproduced entire, together with parallel passages from Irving's version.*

---

* The German tale of "Peter Klaus" (Otmar's *Volks-Sagen* (pp. 153–58)

"Peter Klaus, ein Ziegenhirt aus Sittendorf, der seine Heerde am Kyffhäuser weidete, pflegte sie am Abend auf einem mit altem

* The substance of Irving's "Rip Van Winkle"

Rip Van Winkle, a happy-go-lucky inhabitant of an old village on the Hudson, in company with his faithful dog, Wolf, clambers one day to

It is obvious that "the direct inspiration" lay open before Irving as he wrote his story about Rip Van Winkle,[7] and yet Irving's tale is more than an English version of Otmar's story. In spite of the extensive and precise debt to "Peter Klaus," "Rip Van Winkle" cannot fairly be assigned to any single source. Like Shakespeare, he lifted

Gemäuer umschlossenen Platze ausruhen zu lassen, wo er die Musterung über sie hielt.

"Seit einigen Tagen hatte er bemerkt, dass eine seiner schönsten Ziegen bald nachher, wenn er auf diesen Platz gekommen war, verschwand, und erst spät der Heerde nachkam. Er beobachtete sie genauer, und sahe, dass sie durch eine Spalte des Gemäuers durchschlüpfte. Er wand sich ihr nach, und traf sie in eine Höhlung, wo sie fröhlich die Hafenkörner auflas, die einzeln von der Decke herabfielen. Er blickte in die Höhe, schüttelte den Kopf über den Hafer-Regen, konnte aber durch alles Hinstarren nichts weiter entdecken. Endlich hörte er über sich das Wichern und Stampfen einiger mutigen Hengste, deren Krippe der Hafer entfallen musste.

"So stand der Ziegenhirt da staunend über die Pferde in einen ganz unbewohnten Berge. Da kam ein Knappe, und winkte schweigend, ihm zu folgen. Peter stieg einige Stufen in die Höhe, und kam, über einen ummauerten Hof, an eine Vertiefung, die ringsum von hohen Felsenwänden umschlossen war, in welche durch überhängende dickbelaubte Zweige einiges Dämmerlicht herab fiel. Hier fand er, auf einen gut-geebneten, kühlen Rasenplatz zwölf ernste Ritter-Männer, deren keiner ein Wort sprach, beim Kegelspiel. Peter wurde schweigend angestellt, um die Kegel aufzurichten.

"Anfangs that er dies mit schloddernden Knien, wenn er, mit halbverstohlnem Blick, die langen Bärte und die aufgeschlitzten Wämser der edelen Ritter betrachtete. Almählig aber machte die Gewohnung ihm dreister; er übersah alles um sich her mit immer festerm Blick, und wagte so endlich aus einer Kanne zu trinken, die neben ihm hingesetzt war, und aus welcher der Wein ihm lieblich entgegenduftete. Er fühlte sich wie neubelebt; und so oft er Ermüdung spürte, holte er sich aus der nie versiegenden Kanne neue Kräfte. Doch endlich übermannte ihn der Schlaf.

"Beim Erwachen fand er sich auf dem umschlossnen grünen Platz wieder, wo er seine Ziegen ausruhen zu lassen pflegte. Er rieb sich die Augen, konnte aber weder Hund noch Ziegen entdecken, staunte über die Sträucher und Bäume, die er vorher nie bemerkt hatte. Kopfschüttelnd ging er weiter, alle die Wege und Steige hindurch, die er täglich mit seiner Heerde zu durchirren pflegte; aber nirgends fand sich

eine Spur von seinen Ziegen. one of the highest parts of the Kaatskill mountains in pursuit of squirrels. About to descend, he hears his name called and perceives a man, strangely dressed, laboring under the load of a stout keg, which he is carrying up the mountainside. The stranger asks Rip to assist him, with which request Rip, though wondering at the oddity of the man and his task, promptly complies. Passing through a ravine, they come to "a hollow, like a small amphitheatre, surrounded by perpendicular precipices, over the brinks of which impending trees shoot their branches so that one catches only glimpses of the azure sky and the bright evening cloud.

"On entering the amphitheatre, new objects of wonder presented themselves. On a level spot in the centre was a company of odd-looking personages playing at nine-pins. . . . What seemed particularly odd to Rip was that though these folks were evidently amusing themselves, yet they maintained the gravest faces, the most mysterious silence. . . . As Rip and his companion approached them, they suddenly desisted from their play, and stared at them with such fixed, statue-like gaze, and such strange, uncouth, lack-lustre countenances, that his heart turned within him, and his knees smote together. . . . By degrees Rip's awe and apprehension subsided. He even ventured, when no eye was fixed upon him, to taste the beverage, which he found had much the flavor of excellent Hollands. One taste provoked another; and he reiterated his visits to the flagon so often that at length his senses were overpowered, his eyes swam in his head, his head gradually declined, and he fell into a deep sleep.

"On waking, he found himself on the green knoll whence he had first seen the old man of the glen. He rubbed his eyes—it was a bright morning. . . . He looked round for his gun, but in place of a clean well-oiled fowling-piece, he found an old firelock lying by him, the barrel incrusted with rust, the lock falling off, and the stock worm-eaten. . . ."

He calls for his dog, but no dog comes. The

a ready-made plot, but in subjecting the material to his own personality, his descriptive and narrative technique, made it his own.[8] His workmanship in "Rip Van Winkle" is typical of his manner of writing almost every other selection comprising *The Sketch Book*. None is without some incident, character, or motif gleaned by

---

Unter sich sah er Sittendorf, und endlich stieg er, mit beschleunigtem Schritt herab, um hier nach seiner Heerde zu fragen.

valley, every foot of which he had known for years, is a network of birch, sassafras, and witch-hazel. The night before, it had been a smooth meadowland.

". . . He again called for and whistled after his dog; he was only answered by the cawing of a flock of idle crows. . . . He shook his head, shouldered the rusty firelock, and with a heartful of anxiety, turned his steps homeward.

"As he approached the village, he met a number of people, but none whom he knew, which somewhat surprised him. . . . Their dress, too, was of a different fashion from that to which he was accustomed. They all stared at him with equal marks of surprise, and whenever they cast their eyes upon him, invariably stroked their chins. The constant recurrence of this gesture induced Rip, involuntarily, to do the same, when to his astonishment, he found his beard grown a foot long!

"His mind now misgave him; he began to doubt whether both he and the world around him were not bewitched. Surely this was his native village, which he had left but a day before! There stood the Kaatskill mountains — there ran the silver Hudson at a distance — there was every hill and dale precisely as it had always been."

"Die Leute die ihm vor dem Dorfe begegneten, waren ihm alle unbekannt, waren anders gekleidet, und sprachen nicht so, also seine Bekannten; auch starrten ihn alle an, wenn er nach seine Ziegen fragte, und fassten sich an das Kinn. Endlich that er fast unwilkürlich eben das, und fand, zu seiner Erstaunung, seinen Bart um einen Fuss verlängert. Er fing an, sich und die ganze Welt um sich her, für verzaubert zu halten; und doch kannte er den Berg, den er herabgestiegen war, wohl als den Kyffhäuser, auch waren ihm die Häuser mit ihren Gärten und Vorplätzen alle wohlbekannt. Auch nannten mehrere Knaben, auf die Frage eines Vorbeireisenden, den Namen: Sittendorf.

Rip believes himself still under the influence of the "wicked flagon." Shaking his head, he enters the village.

"It was with some difficulty that he found his way to his own house. . . . He found the house gone to decay — the roof fallen in, the windows shattered, and the doors off the hinges. A half-starved dog that looked like Wolf was skulking about it. Rip called him by name, but the cur snarled, showed his teeth, and passed on.

"He entered the house. . . . It was empty, forlorn, and apparently abandoned . . . he called loudly for his wife and children — the lonely chambers rang for a moment with his voice, and then all again was silence."

"Kopfschüttelnd ging er in das Dorf hinein und nach seiner Hütte. Er fand sie sehr verfallen, und vor ihr lag ein fremder Hirtenknabe in zerrissenen Kittel, neben einem abgezehrten Hunde, der ihn zähnefletschend angrinzte, als er ihm rief. Er ging durch die Öffnung, die sonst eine Thür verschloss, hinein, fand aber alles so wüste und leer dass er, einem Betrunkenen gleich, aus der Hinterpforte wieder hinaus wankte, und Frau und Kinder, bei ihren Namen rief. Aber keiner hörte, und keine Stimme antwortete ihm.

Unaware that a new nation has been born since he left, he goes to his favorite loafing place, the village inn; but instead of the quiet old Dutch inn, he finds a rickety wooden hotel, flying a flag which he does not recognize.

"The appearance of Rip, with his long grizzled beard, his rusty fowling piece, his uncouth dress, and the army of women and children at his heels, soon attracted the attention of the tavern politicians."

"Bald umdrängten den suchenden Mann mit dem langen eisgrauen Bart, Weiber und Kinder und fragten ihn um die Wette: Was er suche? Andre vor seinem eignen Hause nach seiner Frau oder seinen Kindern zu fragen, oder gar

himself, and none is without borrowings from other gleaners.[9] This circumstance may explain why Irving's note (obviously designed as Knickerbocker banter) misdirects the reader by referring the source of the story to "Emperor Frederick, *der Rothbart*," entombed with his army in the Kyffhäuser mountain. This story, as given in the collections by Otmar, Büsching, Grässe, and others, has little more in common with

---

nach sich selbst, schien ihm so sonderbar, dass er, um die Fragen los zu werden, die nächsten Namen nannte die ihm einfielen. 'Kurt Steffen!' Die meisten schwiegen und sahen sich an; endlich sagte eine bejahrte Frau: 'Seit zwölf Jahren wohnt der unter der Sachsenburg, dahin werdet ihr heute nicht kommen.' 'Velten Meier!' 'Gott habe ihn selig!' antwortete ein altes Mütterchen an der Krücke, 'der liegt schon seit fünfzehn Jahren in dem Hause das er nimmer verlässt.'

"Er erkannte zusammenschauernd seine plötzlich alt gewordene Nachbarin; aber, ihm war die Lust vergangen, weiter zu fragen.

"Da drängte sich durch die neugierigen Gaffer ein junges rasches Weib, mit einem einjährigen Knaben auf den Arm, und ein vierjähriges Mädchen an der Hand, die alle drei seiner Frau wie aus den Augen geschnitten waren. 'Wie heisst ihr?' fragte er erstaunend. 'Marie.' 'Und euer Vater?' 'Gott habe ihn selig! Peter Klaus; es sind nun zwanzig Jahre, dass wir ihn Tag und Nacht suchten auf den Kyffhäuser, da die Heerde ohne ihn zurück kam; ich war damals sieben Jahr alt.'

"Länger konnte sich der Ziegenhirt nicht halten. 'Ich bin Peter Klaus,' rief er, 'und kein anderer!' und nahm seine Tochter dem Knaben vom Arm. Alle standen, und noch eine Stimme rief: 'Ja, das ist Peter Klaus! Wilkommen Nachbar! nach zwanzig Jahren Wilkommen!'"

The strange old man is accused of being a spy or a runaway prisoner. Rip assures the crowd that he has merely returned to find some of his old friends and neighbors. They demand to know:

"'Well—who are they? — Name them.'

"Rip bethought himself a moment, and inquired, 'Where's Nicholas Vedder?'

"There was a silence for a little while, when an old man replied in a thin piping voice, 'Nicholas Vedder! Why, he is dead and gone these eighteen years. . . .'

"'Where's Brom Dutcher?'

"'Oh, he went to the army in the beginning of the war; some say he was killed at the storming of Stony Point — others say he was drowned in a squall at the foot of Antony's Nose. I don't know — he never came back again. . . .'

"Rip's heart died away at hearing of these sad changes. . . . He doubted his own identity, and whether he was himself or another man.

"At this critical moment a fresh comely woman pressed through the throng to get a peep at the gray-bearded man. She had a chubby child in her arms, which, frightened at his looks, began to cry. 'Hush, Rip,' cried she, 'hush, you little fool; the old man won't hurt you.' The name of the child, the air of the mother, the tone of her voice, all awakened a train of recollections in his mind. 'What is your name, my good woman?' he asked.

"'Judith Gardenier.'

"'And your father's name?'

"'Ah, poor man, Rip Van Winkle was his name, but it's twenty years since he went away from home with his gun, and never has been heard of since — his dog came home without him. . . . I was then but a little girl. . . .'

"The honest man could contain himself no longer. He caught his daughter and her child in his arms. 'I am your father!' cried he — 'Young Rip Van Winkle once — old Rip Van Winkle now! Does nobody know poor Rip Van Winkle?'

"All stood amazed until an old woman, tottering out from among the crowd, put her hand to her brow, and peering under it in his face for a moment, exclaimed, 'Sure enough! it is Rip Van Winkle — it is himself! Welcome home again, old neighbor — Why, where have you been these twenty long years?'"

"Peter Klaus" than that they are both laid in the same locality.[10] This misleading reference appears to have been deliberate. That it was a mere slip of the memory does not seem likely, for he recalled the details of the *Rothbart* story too precisely three years later in Germany to have made a mistake about it in 1819. Whatever the reason, we find Irving subjoining a note to "The Historian" in *Bracebridge Hall* (in a later undated edition of his works[11]), in which he defends himself, yet studiously avoids naming the real source:

In a note which follows that tale, I alluded to the superstition on which it is founded, and I thought a mere allusion was sufficient, as the tradition was so notorious as to be inserted in almost every collection of German legends. I had seen it myself in three. I could hardly have hoped, therefore, in the present age, when every ghost and goblin story is ransacked, that the origin of the tale would escape discovery. In fact I had considered popular traditions of the kind as fair foundations for authors of fiction to build upon, and made use of the one in question accordingly.[12]

And here we might as well let the matter rest. If he sought to cover his tracks, the critics gave him sufficient cause. What is important for our understanding of Irving's literary personality is that he "considered popular traditions . . . as fair foundations for authors of fiction to build upon," and that while he won a notable success in *The Sketch Book* by following this method, he recognized it as a dubious, dangerous procedure and accordingly developed an unhappy self-consciousness and hesitancy about working up like materials that he gathered for his later collections of stories.

Another of the short stories in *The Sketch Book* generally accepted as an authentic Knickerbocker tale—"The Legend of Sleepy Hollow"—also derives from the German. The introductory parts of the story relating to Ichabod, his school, his pupils, his aspirations, the Van Tassels, and their "quilting frolic" are all native; but the incidents which give the very point to the story are borrowed from the German legends about Rübezahl as recorded by Musaeus.[13] In this story Irving went to work very much as he did in "Rip Van Winkle." He transferred the scene from the Riesengebirge of Silesia to Sleepy Hollow on the Hudson. The characters he found ready to hand, having simply to draw upon his Dutch burghers of Knickerbocker notoriety, though Ichabod Crane himself may be a concoction of the Yankee pedagogue and various eighteenth-century English schoolmasters (notably those of Shenstone, Fielding, and Goldsmith), set in a Dutch-American community. The climax of the story, however, he borrowed from the fifth of the *Legenden von Rübezahl*.[14] The settings are identical: ghost-and-goblin-ridden localities, where old wives' tales abound.[15] The mind of Johann (who corresponds to Ichabod) has been infected by this fabulous lore. Finding himself in the famous resort of Rübezahl, all the stories rush to his head, and he wishes "with all his soul" that he had "never heard a syllable of the matter." Ichabod is equally susceptible and equally apprehensive.[16] Johann and Ichabod have the same fearful misgivings.[17] When the apparition appears to Johann, it is "a jet-black figure, of a size exceeding that of man"; Ichabod, in the same situation, beholds "something huge-misshapen, black and towering."[18] The maneuvers of the night-riders are identical. When Johann quickens his pace, so does "the figure"; whenever "Ichabod quickened his steed, the stranger quickened his horse to an equal pace"; when he fell into a walk, the other did the same.[19] Suddenly to both comes the terrible discovery that their adversary is headless.[20] Ichabod, like Johann, receives another shock, for the pursuer does not wear his head as normal people do. Johann's carries his under his arm, Ichabod's "on the pommel of the saddle."[21] Unable to outrun his headless adversary, Johann tries, as a last resort, a conjurer's word to drive away the ghost, but too late—the monster hurls his head at Johann and tumbles him headlong. Ichabod, too, is about to free himself of his unwelcome companion, by gaining the hallowed bridge, across which the ghostly rider cannot follow, when he turns and sees "the goblin rising in his stirrups in the very act of hurling his head at him." It encounters his cranium with "a tremendous crash," and Ichabod is "tumbled headlong into the dust."[22] In Irving's story, the fearful missile that fells Ichabod is a pumpkin; in Musaeus' story it turns out to be "an huge hollowed gourd filled with sand and stones, and worked up into a very grotesque figure, by the addition of a wooden nose, and a long flax beard."[23] The mystery is explained naturally in both stories. The goblin in *Rübezahl* is not Rübezahl at all, but a rival of Johann, who is motivated by revenge and robbery. In Irving's story the robbery motif is lacking, but all other details are closely parallel. Moreover, Johann's adversary is a big, strapping *Krauskopf* (Curly-pate, in the Beckford version), who fits pretty accurately the description of Brom Bones, and who uses the same methods in undoing his rival in love.[24]

The story of the inception of "Sleepy Hollow" can now be revised. Pierre M. Irving, the biographer, tells us:

The outline of this story had been sketched more than a year before at Birmingham [autumn, 1818], after a conversation with his brother-in-law, Van Wart, who had been dwelling upon some recollections of his early years in Tarrytown, and had touched upon a waggish fiction of one Brom Bones, a wild blade, who professed to fear nothing, and boasted of having once met the devil on a return from a nocturnal frolic, and run a race with him for a bowl of milk punch. The imagination of the author kindled over the recital, and in a few hours he had scribbled off the framework of this renowned story, and was reading it to his sister and her husband. He then threw it by until he went up to London, where he expanded it into the present legend [completed Dec. 29, 1819].[25]

It appears, as in the case of "Rip Van Winkle," that something had been lacking to complete the story. The framework, the setting, and the characters of the tale all came readily enough; all that was needed was an incident, together with a good motif, to provide a climax with a punch. This necessary impetus to complete the story Irving found in Johann's fearful ride as related by Musaeus in the Rübezahl legends.

The source of the third short story in *The Sketch Book*, a tale significantly entitled "The Spectre Bridegroom," Irving himself indicated when he had the Baron relate, at the wedding feast, "the history of the goblin horseman that carried away the fair Leonora,—a dreadful story, which has since been put into excellent verse, and is read and believed by all the world."[26] Bürger's *Lenore*, the ballad relating the ghastly ride of Lenore with her lover who has been slain in battle, and who returns to keep his love-tryst with her, is well known. Irving's tale begins with the young Count von Altenburg on his way to Castle Katzenellenbogen to wed the Count of Landshort's beautiful daughter, whom he has never seen. Near Würzburg he falls in with an old friend, Herman von Starkenfaust. In a thickly-wooded pass they are attacked by robbers, and von Altenburg is mortally wounded. With his dying breath he entreats his friend to proceed to Katzenellenbogen to explain the cause of his not keeping his appointment with the bride. Herman von Starkenfaust arrives at the castle some hours after the appointed time for the wedding, and, without being given an opportunity to say a word, is married to the blushing bride, who had all but despaired of having a wedding at all. He is hurried from the wedding ceremony to a banquet, and from one place to another without a chance to explain his imposition. Only when the wedding company assemble in the old armorial hall and begin to tell "wild tales and supernatural legends" does he get an opportunity. Old Landshort tells the tale of Leonora; Herman jumps up, announces that he must away, that he must be buried at midnight, that the grave is waiting for him; he jumps on his black charger and is lost in the whistling of the night blast. The company breaks up in consternation. Old Landshort is in a rage; the bride is in tears. On the night of the second day of her widowhood, however, she sees the spectre bridegroom at her window; and, although she faints from fright, she understands enough to be ready the next night to mount behind the goblin and gallop away with him. Katzenellenbogen is again in turmoil. But just as preparations are completed to scour the country for the goblin rider and the erring maid, they return, make explanations, and are forgiven on the spot. The old count is in transports of joy that his son-in-law is no wood demon, that his grandchildren will be Katzenellenbogen and not a brood of goblins. Finding the spectre-bridegroom substantial flesh and blood, he is perfectly satisfied; only the aunt of the bride is mortified that this marvelous story is thus marred, and that the only spectre she has ever seen should turn out a counterfeit. Irving's banter and pleasant ridicule of Bürger's ballad is too obvious to need further illustration. The story is one of the best examples of the sportive Gothic, a genre in which Irving has scarcely been surpassed.

Between Irving's saying in 1818, while at work on *The Sketch Book*, that he was learning "to read and splutter a little" in German on the promise that the "rich mine of German literature" held forth "abundant" rewards, and July 11, 1823, when he wrote his last entry in his Dresden diary, a good deal had taken place to change his literary personality. The Dresden notebook closes with a comment which, in its undoubted personal application, takes on added significance in the career of Irving as the romantic antiquary. He wrote: "Solitary miners of literature in Germany—men working hours and hours each day in dull little towns."[27] This observation, together with the fact that his first book of tales had drawn heavily on Germanic sources, and the further fact that as soon as the opportunity appeared, he paid a visit to Germany, suggests that the stories of Irving's subsequent volumes might be expected to show even greater Germanic influences than *The Sketch Book*.

Irving's German Tour

In passing from the period of *The Sketch Book* to that of *Tales of a Traveller*, we proceed from the first stage of Irving's development as a romanticist to that of the second. Of the intervening period the greater part of the years 1822 and 1823 were spent in Germany. He entered the Rhineland a lukewarm romanticist, with more interest in the grotesquely romantic than in the truly romantic; he returned from Dresden, two years later, an out-and-out romantic, prepared to write *Tales of a Traveller* (1824) and the *Alhambra* (1832), in which for the first time, as far as American prose fiction is concerned, the vein of romanticism is fully developed.[28]

He had hardly entered upon German soil, when rheumatism "tripped up his heels" in the Hôtel de Darmstadt in Mayence; but already he was inspired to start a new book, and then and there he wrote the Preface to *Tales of a Traveller*.[29]

I attempted to beguile the weary hours by studying German under the tuition of mine host's pretty daughter, Katrine; but I found even German had not the power to charm a languid ear, and that the conjugation of *ich liebe* might be powerless, however rosy the lips which uttered it.

I tried to read . . . I turned over volume after volume, but threw them by with distaste: "Well, then," said I at length, in despair, "if I cannot read a book, I will write one." Never was there a more lucky idea. . . . I rummaged my portfolio, and cast about, in my recollections, for those floating materials which a man naturally collects in travelling; and here I have arranged them in this little work. . . . I am an old traveller; I have read somewhat, heard and seen more, and dreamt more than all. My brain is filled, therefore, with all kinds of odds and ends. In travelling, these heterogeneous matters have become shaken up in my mind, as the articles are apt to be in an ill-packed travelling trunk; so that when I attempt to draw forth a fact, I cannot determine whether I have read, heard, or dreamt it; and I am always at a loss to know how much to believe of my own stories.

These remarks are at once symptomatic and prophetic of his manner of writing his next book, which he hoped to have ready for spring publication. The writing of that book was long delayed, but meanwhile he assiduously stored up and tried to assimilate a vast body of "floating materials" against a time when another "fit of scribbling" should hit hem.[30] As he proceeded into the upper Rhineland, he surrendered to romance as well as sentiment; in his reveries, the Hudson, the Rhine, and the Neckar were fused into one, the Odenwald mountains beckoning to him as once the Catskills had. At Heidelberg he intensified his study of German. As he progressed southward, he discovered that he liked best the smaller villages, as being quainter and richer in lore and color. At Ulm, Augsburg, and Blenheim his thoughts turned to mementous historical events that had taken place there.[31] On arriving at a town of any size, one of the first places he visited was its library.[32] After leaving Munich, he felt he was shaking off civilization, and as he approached Salzburg, anticipated getting into a veritable gnome- and pixie-land, where mountains still held entombed bewitched phantom armies. He rededicated himself to the purpose formed as early as 1817, back at Abbotsford, to create his own volume of German legends. At Salzburg he wrote down eight local legends, told him, it seems, by the *valet de place*.[33] Almost the first thing he did on arriving in Vienna was to explore the castle of Dürenstein, and as he walked the garden of Prince Lichtenstein

the thought struck him that he must prepare "a collection of tales of various countries made up of legends, etc., etc., etc."[34] Another vain wish. A month exhausted the possibilities of Vienna. Having regained his health, he decided to push on to Dresden for the winter. He chose Dresden as "a place of taste, intellect, and literary feeling," as "the best place to acquire the German language, which is nowhere so purely spoken as in Saxony," and as a place where he hoped to find congenial fellow-countrymen.[35]

From November 22, 1822, to the following July he made Dresden his home, finding especially delightful the company of Emily Foster, the oldest daughter of an English family, and spending much time in the Foster home studying German, French, and Italian, reading collections of German fairy-lore, and participating in amateur dramatic productions. Through the English Minister John P. Morier, an old friend of his days in Washington, he immediately found himself mingling freely with the diplomatic corps and moving agreeably in the court circle, where he was "in great favor with the old queen." He participated in the old Saxon ceremonies ranging from formal court parties (where he joined in dancing the "Grossvater") to the royal boar hunt. The old conventions and punctilious forms exemplified by the court, the retinue of huntsmen, the villagers, their costumes, the inns, and the very countryside seemed to rejuvenate his jaded imagination that had gone stale on English scenes.[36] The forty-seven friends listed by Irving in his Dresden journal suggest reasons why during this "most agreeable" winter's round of gaiety he did so little toward his projected book. Prominent among them was Dr. Karl Böttiger, a German antiquary and director of the Museum, who repeatedly gave him expert help in his folklore studies,[37] and Colonel Livius,[38] with whom he collaborated in translating German operas.[39] Throughout the Dresden period there were formal and informal occasions where he met German literary people. On Christmas day, at Count Knobelsdorf's house, the foremost American humorist of the day met the foremost German humorist, Jean Paul.[40] On May 3, he paid a visit to Kleist, with whom he had some "pleasant literary conversation."[41] Among the most stimulating of his literary connections in Dresden was his friendship with Tieck, who had come to Dresden in 1819, and was already the central literary figure of the little capital when Irving arrived.[42]

When he first arrived in Dresden, Irving still bemoaned his bad French and "worse German,"[43] but he soon took steps to alleviate this situation by devoting two hours a day, from seven to nine in the morning, to regular instruction from a German tutor.[44] What we know of Irving's love for the comforts of life argues that he would not have risen early every morning to take two hours of instruction in the language without learning at least to read it with ease, especially at a time when he was steeped in the study of languages, for in addition to studying German, he would go in the afternoon or in the evening to the Foster's, where Mrs. Foster taught him Italian, and Emily superintended his French exercises. Moreover, he kept up his German after he moved on to other interests, such as the Spanish, and kept coming back to his German books, notably Schiller and Goethe, and reading them.[45]

In thus conscientiously studying German while searching for legends and traditions and frequently committing them to paper, Irving consciously gathered what he termed "those floating materials which a man naturally collected in travelling."[46] But the distractions of Dresden, not the least of which was his unprosperous love affair with Emily Foster, kept him restless and unable to write. He found what consolation he could in telling himself: "I have *lived into* a great deal of amusing and characteristic information." Thus he acquired new ideas and a "variety of modes of expressing them"[47] (German, French, and Italian) if and when he should be able to get control of his pen. But he did not succeed in getting down to work on his German book for a year after he had torn himself away from Dresden and established himself at 89 Rue Richelieu in Paris in August of 1823.[48] A year later (September 4, 1824) he wrote what throws light on his manner of writing *Tales of a Traveller* and explains much about subsequent developments in his literary career.

I have been thinking over the German subjects.[49] It will take me a little time to get hold of them properly, as I must read a little[50] and digest the plan and nature of them in my mind. There are such quantities of these legendary and romantic tales now littering from the press both in England and Germany, that one must take care not to fall into the commonplace of the day. Scott's manner must likewise be widely avoided. In short, I must strike out some way of my own, suited to my own way of thinking and writing. I wish, in everything I do, to write in such a manner that my productions may have something more than the mere interest of narrative to recommend them, which is very evanescent; something, if I dare use the phrase, of classic merit, i.e. [,] depending upon style, &c., which gives a production some chance of duration beyond the mere whim and fashion of the day. I have my mind tolerably well supplied with German localities, manners, characters, &c., and when I once get to work, I trust I shall be able to spin them out very fluently.[51]

Other passages in the same letter show how anxious Irving was "to keep on steadily" until he could "scrape together enough" from all his "literary property to produce a regular income, however moderate" and thus become "independent of the world and its chances."[52]

Tales of a Traveller

The most likely thing for him to prepare speedily for the press, aside from the dramatic and operatic pieces on which he was engaged, was the unfinished story of "Buckthorne" (sometimes called "History of an Author"), which had been laid aside as the groundwork for a novel. He took it up but laid it by a fiftieth time, to try his hand anew at his "German subjects."[53] That did not prosper either; he changed plans a dozen times,[54] fagging on at this discouraging task until August 24, 1824, when *Tales of a Traveller* finally appeared. Although he always regarded portions of the book as the best of his writings, its inception was slow, its composition spasmodic, its final revision troublesome, and the result—a book of pieces ill-arranged, poorly classified, a disjointed, piece of patchwork.[55]

"Buckthorne and his Friends," which was begun first, had its inception in Paris at the suggestion of Tom Moore in the summer of 1821.[56] Designed originally as part of *Bracebridge Hall*, then as a separate work, it ultimately became Part II of *Tales of a Traveller*. The early portion, with its background of Longmans' dinner and Paternoster Row, has no connection with things German; but the latter portion, in which Buckthorne, no longer a free lance in London, becomes a strolling player and finally a theater manager and owner, is German inspired.[57] Like Wilhelm Meister, Buckthorne feels he has a theatrical mission. The latter part of "Buckthorne" is a German graft upon an English stem, growing from native roots, containing, as Irving's story does, shadowy sentimentalized elements drawn from his own career.

The parallelisms with *Wilhelm Meister* can be traced from the very beginning of the story, though it should be observed at the outset that whereas Goethe is serious and hesitates to ridicule the young apprentice, Irving is playfully sportive throughout. Both Wilhelm and Buckthorne, idealistic visionaries, are endowed with the poetical feeling and passion for the theater, so much so that both steal from their homes at night

to see the plays. Both are grossly misunderstood by very matter-of-fact fathers and coddled by indulgent mothers. Both are extremely sensitive to feminine beauty, and both have sentimental love affairs which result in broken hearts and contribute to their leaving home and throwing in their lot with a strolling theatrical company. Both are held spellbound by the wonders of the stage—the pageantry, the pantomime, the magical tricks of the conjurors, the distressed damsel, the fun of it all.[58] Both become fully initiated in the mysteries backstage, including the disorderly dressing-room of their dirty-muslined heroine—but the gay disarray and the merry informality of it convince both they are getting a glimpse into another planet.[59] Both become actor-folk quite unconsciously, naturally; though both tell themselves they are seeking only temporary gratification and indulgence of their humors, their genius.[60]

Our heroes drift along contentedly for a while, playing here and there, paying little heed to the world. But as they observe (in almost identical terms) the dissensions, petty jealousies, and quarrels that go on backstage,[61] their illusions about the happy gaiety of their actor-life suffer. As in *Wilhelm Meister*, so in "Buckthorne," the only thing on which all parties agree is to backbite the manager and to cabal against his rule. Then comes Buckthorne's unlucky love affair with Columbine, which may well be considered a burlesque of Wilhelm's sentimental connection with Marianne. Following this disillusioning experience, Buckthorne gives up his theatrical career. Unlike Goethe's hero, he has had enough.

Irving's story turns to other matters, and the similarities with *Wilhelm Meister* cease for a time, but in the last chapter of "Buckthorne," Mr. Flimsey, the great tragedian of the company, carries forward the role of Wilhelm Meister. Finding an unorganized, ungoverned, half-disbanded theatrical group, Flimsey, like Meister, invests his small capital in the company and becomes its manager. Irving's account of Flimsey's trials as manager exactly parallels Goethe's.[62] Worse still, Flimsey's wife is jealous, and like Frau Melina and Philine, she compounds the poor manager's troubles.[63] Learning that the playhouse in a neighboring town is vacant, Flimsey sees an opportunity to realize his life's ambition, even as Wilhelm Meister had conceived his mission. Flimsey engages the place, and like Wilhelm, reaches the very summit of his ambitions, only to discover, even as Wilhelm had, that his position is fraught with vexations and troubles, within and without—bickerings, jealousies, disputes, and finally, failure. In disgust both give up their theatrical careers.

Irving's story is a slight sketch, a loosely organized extravaganza, vastly different, of course, from Goethe's methodically planned and carefully executed *Kulturroman*—in several ways, the history of his own soul. But the one was undoubtedly largely motivated by the other.

In the "Strange Stories by a Nervous Gentleman," which form Part I in *Tales of a Traveller*, we have a group of tales set in a framework.[64] The framed tale is a device as old at least as Boccaccio, and Irving himself had used a similar device in *Bracebridge Hall*. But his scheme to get the stories related, the interruptions of the narratives, the critical comments on the tales by various members of the group, and the wit combats they engage in, all call to mind the motivating framework employed by Tieck in *Phantasus*, in which a group of men, dedicated to the spirit of "Fantasy," tell stories like "Der getreue Eckart," "Der Tannhäuser," "Der Runenberg," and "Die Elfen."[65]

"The Adventure of My Uncle," the first tale, is related by "the old gentleman with the haunted head." The narrator's uncle, an experienced traveler, on asking for a night's lodging at an ancient turreted castle in Normandy, was hospitably received by the Marquis and put into a chamber of the oldest, most venerable wing of the chateau. During the night the tread of approaching footsteps awakened him in time to see a stately female figure enter his room, warm itself at the fire in the grate, and glide softly out again. Questions addressed to the host the next morning cleared up the mystery. The Marquis, after much halting and stammering, explained that the lady's honor had one night been violated by an ancestor of his as she had sought hospitality in the chateau, that the deed had been perpetrated in the very room the uncle slept in, and that the night before had been the anniversary of the deed. Every year, on the night of the shameful crime, the outraged woman visits the chamber, warms herself, and quietly departs.

The lady dressed in white who haunts certain localities is a very common figure in many folk literatures. Grässe tells the stories of no less than a dozen "weisse Frauen."[66] Irving, who seems to have preferred ghost stories to all others, actively pursued the trail of "weisse Frauen" stories in Germany. One especially, "Die Edelfrau von Scharzfeld," resembles Irving's tale and may have suggested it. It is a story of deceitful hospitality and outraged virtue. The lady, after her death, becomes a *Burggeist* and haunts the wing of the castle where the deed was perpetrated. Every year, on the anniversary of the crime, she comes in a rush of wind, enters by way of the turret, and pays a visit to the same chamber.[67] Irving used the occasion of one of these annual visits as the central point in his story.[68]

"The Young Italian" is traceable to Schiller's *Räuber*.[69] The story, taken ostensibly from a manuscript, is the autobiography of the Mysterious Stranger, the subject of the preceding introductory sketch: A young Neapolitan nobleman, of sensitive and passionate nature, is placed, while still a boy, in a monastery. Here his melancholy nature is nurtured. A chance trip into the world arouses his dejected spirits. He escapes from the cloister and seeks out his father. His older brother urges the father to send the young man back to the monastery. He overhears their plans and leaves his home. In Genoa he falls in with a celebrated artist, under whose tutelage he becomes an inspired painter, especially adept in delineating the human countenance. By chance he sees the lovely Bianca, daughter of a noble Genoese house, who becomes his betrothed; but the relationship is kept secret because the young painter, nameless and exiled, has small hope of securing the consent of Bianca's proud guardian. News arrives from Naples that his older brother is dead, and that his father, old and ill, wishes his son to return to be restored to his home, title, and father. He leaves at once for Naples after making Fillipo, son of his patron, the confidant of his plans. To Fillipo is intrusted the charge of watching over the lovers' interests. He is also to forward their letters to each other. Finding his father very ill, the young painter remains at his bedside. Only upon the death of the old man, two years later, can he return to Genoa. He comes upon Bianca unexpectedly in the garden. After a convulsive embrace, she tears herself from his arms and reveals to him the fact that she is married to Fillipo. The whole dark plot of Fillipo is quickly discovered. He had intercepted the lovers' letters, persuaded Bianca that her lover had died, thrust himself into her confidence, and married her. Seeing Fillipo approaching, the young artist rushes forward, runs him through, and fearfully mangles the corpse. The shrieks of Bianca bring him to his senses. He looks with horror upon the scene, and like another Cain he flees. Restless wanderings and frenzied remorse drive him finally to Genoa where he surrenders himself to justice.

Intercepted and falsified letters, a betrayed bride, a lover's revenge are old and overworked themes, and not peculiar to Schiller's play. Moreover, the young painter is no Carl Moor, no banditti leader, no world reformer. Yet he has all the mental qualities of Schiller's hero—fine sensibilities, talent, dash, a romantic imagination, and a sense of a high mission in life. Finally, like Carl Moor, he surrenders to law and justice. Irving's story seems to be one of the numerous productions—dramas, poems, tales—that followed in the wake of *Die Räuber*,[70] drawing inspiration if not direct influence from Schiller's *Sturm-und-Drang* play.[71]

"The Bold Dragoon" reads like a veritable chapter from Jean Paul's *Schmelzles Reise* or Tieck's *Vogelscheuche*,[72] but the resemblances are only general, so that no direct borrowing seems to be involved. On the other hand, Irving's journals record his seeing in Prague, on November 25, 1822, "a tolerable piece in three acts called "Alps Röslein," and among undated memoranda this further notation:

> At Prague actor who played Almacrin— good scenes in mittelalter wars—young warrior flushed with wine—fiery—moustaches turn[e]d up—feather thrown back— staggering into house of sturdy burg[h]er— sitting down throwing out leg—slapping on thigh—trying to stick arms akimbo but staggerling—seizes burg[h]er's daughter.[73]

The description fits the bold dragoon, even to the phrasing employed; but as in the case of "The Adventure of My Aunt," Irving incorporated into the tale, in addition to its Germanic details, a jumble of his experiences on a tour of Holland and other general observations so that the tale has hardly any national character.[74]

The Italian Banditti tales, forming Part III of *Tales of a Traveller* and strung out over a hundred pages, make the least interesting reading in the volume. For these basically trivial robber stories, with their trite plots turning on hairbreadth escapes and pseudo-chivalrous adventure in the Appenines, a traveling man like Irving required little help from the outside

beyond the descriptive effects and atmosphere provided by Mrs. Radcliffe and other
commonplace fiction fashions of the day.

In Part IV, chiefly addenda for the book
and rifled from his inexhaustible Knickerbocker notes,[75] the only story (incidentally,
the best of the group) that owes anything
to Germany is "The Devil and Tom
Walker." It is a sort of comic New England
Faust,[76] which, in the happy blending of the
terrifying and the ludicrous, rivals "The
Legend of Sleepy Hollow." The setting is a
gloomy, snake-infested swamp. Here Tom
encounters the Devil and sells his soul in
exchange for pirate gold. After a career of
iniquity, he is whisked back to the swamp
on a black horse and is never seen again.

Significant as borrowings from the German are in individual stories, the whole is
not an honest body of German lore but
rather a "huddle of tales of all nations"—
emasculated German legends jostled by
Dutch-American lore, Italian backgrounds,
French anecdotes, and English travel experiences. Lacking the unified integrity of
Bracebridge Hall and the saturation of
Spanish lore in *The Alhambra, Tales of a
Traveller* reminds one, as Professor Williams has observed, of Irving's own characterization of the bastard wedded to the lady
of easy virtue as "nobody's son marrying
everybody's daughter." The entire volume
lacks cohesion, unity, concentration. Even,
in Part I, the portion for which Irving
relied most on his accumulation of German
materials, no story makes such direct,
effective use of Germanic stuff as does "Rip
Van Winkle," for example.[77] Fearing the
cry of "Stolen goods," he wrote camou-
flaged composites and succeeded in making
only diluted spectral stories that were no
more original or effective than any frank
reworkings of the kind he might have made
(with much less trouble to himself) of the
Märchen-lore reposing in his journals. It
was no German Sketch Book. It was a
Scrap Book.

Tales of a Traveller failed in England,
where he was anxious that it should succeed.
The truth of the matter is (and no one knew
it better than Irving) that even regarding
The Sketch Book, great as its popularity had
been, the critics had been right in designating many of its pieces as essentially "*Dorf-
schilderungen*," "new leaves on old trees."[78]
When his latest book turned out neither a
German Sketch Book nor a comic Knickerbocker's history of Germany, but a ragout
of miscellaneous pieces, the English were
disappointed. The notes and prefaces of
concealment, designed to throw the
hounds off the trail, only put the scent in
their noses. The critics wrote more ill-
naturedly than ever.[79] And there was little
he could do about it beyond defending himself obliquely among his friends by calling
the reviewers "crows" and "buzzards of
criticism."

The Alhambra

We pass now to *The Alhambra* (1832),
which most fully exemplifies Irving's
romanticism. Heretofore he had never
yielded to romance so completely as not to
be able to put his feet on solid ground at
any moment he chose.[80] But *The Alhambra*
contains no Knickerbocker capering; the
book is "an arabesque, as redolent of the
orient as the tales of Scheherazade."[81] His
surrender is complete because, as he put it,
"I gave myself up, during my sojourn in the
Alhambra, to all the romantic and fabulous
traditions connected with the pile . . . lived
in the midst of an Arabian tale, and shut
my eyes . . . to everything that called me
back to everyday life."[82] One might suppose
that German literature, so stimulating
during 1818–1824, would have continued
its influence during the Spanish period.
That seems not to be the case. *The Alhambra* contains only two instances of possible
Germanic inspiration. "The Legend of the
Moor's Legacy" and "The Legend of the
Two Discreet Sisters" are reminiscent in a
general way of Otmar's "Der Ritterkeller

auf dem Kyffhäuser" and "Die Dümburg," respectively. Yet buried treasure is common matter for folk material, and there is little ground for doubting Irving's assertions that he took the legends from Spanish sources. It may well be that he first caught the contagion for the romantic past of Spain from the enthusiasm rife among the German *Romantiker* while he lived among them,[83] but once the Spanish and Oriental influences began to work directly on him, they proceeded under their own power. The German influence, traceable from *The Sketch Book* through *Tales of a Traveller*, was important in Irving's development as a romanticist; without his prior contacts with German literature, *The Alhambra* is hardly conceivable. But the interest in German things suffered an abatement, and the Spanish influence, personal and literary, is directly responsible for the ripening of those romantic fruits which Scott had planted and German literature had nurtured.

Woolfert's Roost

Finally, there is a volume entitled *Wolfert's Roost* (short pieces written chiefly after 1832 and first collected in 1855), which contains, as a contemporary reviewer remarked, "representative" pieces of all of Irving's former works. One of the nine narratives in this volume—"Guests from Gibbet-Island"—rests on a German source, namely Grimm's "The Gallows' Guests."[84] Irving's method in adapting this tale from Grimm is very like his procedure in "Rip Van Winkle" and "The Legend of Sleepy Hollow." Giving the tale a local habitation in Communipaw, adding to the characterization, and turning the German tipplers into pirates, he made of it a Knickerbocker tale some ten times as long as the original and infinitely more entertaining.

Another story, "Don Juan: A Spectral Research," may well have received a suggestion from Gottschalck's "Der Seebürger See."[85] In both stories a dissolute young nobleman[86] and his companions determine to attack a convent. In Gottschalck's tale the villain succeeds and despoils his own sister, who, unknown to him, is a novice in the nunnery. He spends the remainder of his life in a cloister in expiation of his crimes. Irving's tale presents a similar situation except that the incestuous deed is not committed.[87] He is stopped in time by a stranger who cries, "Rash man, forbear! is it not enough to have violated all human ties ? Wouldst thou steal a bride from heaven!" Don Manuel turns, draws, runs the stranger through, and makes his escape. The next day he sees the funeral of a young man, who, he is told, is Don Manuel. He stops the funeral proceedings, declaring that there is an imposture, that Don Manuel is alive, that *he* is Don Manuel de Manara.

"Avaunt, rash youth!" cried the priest; "know that Don Manuel de Manara is dead! — is dead! — is dead! — and we are all souls from purgatory who are permitted to come here to pray for the repose of his soul."

Don Manuel falls down senseless. The next day he sends for a priest, confesses his crimes, enters a cloister, and like Count Isand in Gottschalck's story, spends the rest of his life doing penance for his sins.[88]

PERHAPS the greatest of Irving's numerous services to American literature is his robbing short prose fiction of its moral—making his first models of the American short story vehicles of entertainment, producing a pleasurable rather than a moral effect. Finding the eighteenth-century subjects "trite and commonplace," so much so that in *The Sketch Book* and in *Bracebridge Hall* he apologized for traveling "over beaten ground," he started a search for new subjects. These books already exhibit some of the fruits of that search, which was as much a new manner of treating old materials as a search for new materials—both exemplified in the stories of these early volumes which are borrowed from the

English Gothic and the German legendary stores. *Bracebridge Hall* proved less popular than *The Sketch Book* had been, and Irving realized that if he hoped to "develop a line of literature peculiar to himself," he must bow to his "desultory habits" and husband his slender talents by "writing when I can, not when I would . . . and occasionally shifting my residence, write whatever is suggested by objects before me."[89] His year in Germany represents such a change of residence in the effort to find subjects sufficiently congenial to activate his pen. *Tales of a Traveller* out of the way, he spent a miserable two years doing little more than chew his pen while casting about for material to make his wayward powers tractable, until the opportunity to shift his residence to Spain presented itself.

To be sure, in *Knickerbocker* he had shown a remarkable felicity in one genre of writing, and ten years later, a similar excellence in the short story. But everything after *The Sketch Book* was retrograde, as the critics told him so often that he feared he had written himself out. The effect was to make him more timorous than ever, and, except for *The Alhambra* and a few miscellaneous short pieces later, to settle upon history and biography as less demanding of originality than fiction. Thus was born (or rather, finally confirmed) Irving the biographer and historian. Beginning his career under the influence of Addison and Goldsmith, Sterne and Swift, he felt during the most creative period of his life the impact of English, then German, and finally Spanish romanticism, until he retreated to the comforting safety of historical fact and biographical detail. Under the influence of books from the beginning, he continued under their power to the end. Yet he succeeded in writing forty-five examples of what he was the first to produce—the American short story. Of this number about a third are traceable, wholly or in part, to Germanic sources. Thus the German tale from the very first brought a powerful influence to bear on the American short story. Irving was unquestionably the most influential native literary force during the early part of the nineteenth century in America, and his influence consciously or unconsciously directed the course that the short story was to pursue in its development.

Already in 1824 Irving wrote to his friend Brevoort: "Other writers have crowded into the same branch of literature [the short story], and I now begin to find myself elbowed by men who have followed my footsteps; but at any rate I have had the merit of adopting a line for myself instead of following others."[90] This being so, we turn to Hawthorne and Poe as Irving's more important successors (and admirers), in order to see whether the close connection between the German tale and the American short story as initiated by Irving was continued by them.

NATHANIEL HAWTHORNE
(1804–1864)

Allegations of German Influence

Almost as soon as critics began to notice Hawthorne's tales, they pointed out similarities with Tieck's works. A reviewer of *Twice-Told Tales* (1837, 1842), writing in the *Foreign and Colonial Quarterly* for October, 1843, found cause in Hawthorne's "fantasy," his "linking the seen to the unseen, the matter-of-fact to the imaginative," to be reminded of Tieck, despite "vast differences in the materials used by the two authors."[91] A few months later the *Democratic Review* designated Hawthorne "the Tieck of this American literature of ours (though the gayer fancy of the German is clouded in his case by a slight tinge of the gloom of puritanical New England)." The

London *Athenaeum* for August 8, 1845, in a review of *Mosses from an Old Manse* (1846), saw in Hawthorne and Tieck a like "power of translating the mysterious harmonies of Nature into articulate meaning." The next year came Poe's charge that Hawthorne "is *not* original in any sense" but only "peculiar," and that "those who speak of him as original mean nothing more than that he differs in his manner of tone, and in his choice of subjects, from any author of their acquaintance—their acquaintance not extending to the German Tieck, whose manner, in *some* of his work, is absolutely identical with that *habitual* to Hawthorne."[92] Following Poe's pronouncement, as critics became better acquainted with Hawthorne, the allegation of his indebtedness was made less often,[93] and so the notion gradually faded until more recently students reopened the question for the dual purpose of evaluating Poe's critical honesty and the degree of Hawthorne's alleged indebtedness.[94] The general conclusion, voiced by Miss Myrtle J. Joseph, is that "in style Hawthorne owes nothing to Tieck." Between Poe's and this later opinion there is a vast difference. As is common in such cases, we may expect to find the truth somewhere between the two extremes.

Influence of Tieck

While Hawthorne began to study German in 1838, at the instigation of Sophia Peabody, who became his wife in 1842, he appears to have made no phenomenal progress. During April, 1843, when he devoted several hours of four successive days to plodding through "the rugged and bewildering depths" of an unidentified tale of Tieck's, he succeeded only by constant references to his "phrase-book." While his references, on these same days, to his catching ideas "by the skirts" and "dimly shaping out scenes of a tale" are provocative, he found his task "slow work, and dull work, too!"[95] And there is nothing to

suggest that this one serious bout with German did not leave him content to let severely alone a language so bristling with difficulties.

But his lack of German was no insuperable barrier to becoming acquainted with the German romancers, for the English and American translators were busy making them available in books and periodicals.[96] One of Tieck's translated tales, "The Friends," appearing in the *Democratic Review* for May, 1845 (XVI, 496–501), is of particular importance as the probable occasion for Poe's criticism of Hawthorne as a borrower from Tieck. The story runs as follows:

On a beautiful spring morning Ludwig Wedel sets out for a distant village to see a friend who lies dangerously ill, and who wishes to see his friend just once more (p. 496). As Ludwig wanders through an idyllic country, his mind is turned to melancholy reflections by the voices of Nature and of Spring. Seating himself on the trunk of a fallen tree to reread his friend's letter, he falls into a trance.

"He forgot that it was Spring; that his friend was ill; he listened only to the wondrous melodies whose echoes flowed upon him from distant shores, the wildest tones blending with those most familiar, and his whole soul was changed. From the deep perspective of Memory, from the abysses of the Past, arose the images that once filled him with delight and anguish, those uncertain, formless phantoms, which so often flit around the brain, and overwhelm the senses with their perplexing voices. The sports and puppets of his childish days danced before him, covering the green sod, so that he no longer saw the flowers beneath his feet. His first love encircled him with the beamings of its early dawn, and caused its sparkling rainbows to fall upon his eyes; his first sorrow passed by and threatened at the end of life, to meet him in the self-same hope. Ludwig sought to detain these shifting fancies, in their magical enjoyment to remain conscious of himself, but in vain. Like the grotesque pictures in story books, suddenly opened and then in a moment closed again, these apparitions appeared to his soul, fleeting and unstable" (p. 497).

In this (Hawthornesque) dream, he continues his journey. He wonders that "the purple flush of evening had so soon over-spread the clouds," for evening appears to be drawing nigh. A shadowy, vaguely-remembered figure glides before him, and he is impelled to follow, while all Nature conspires, through myriad forces and influences, to effect a transformation by which he is led by subtle, almost imperceptible, steps into Fairyland (p. 498). In it stands the fairest of palaces, to which he is welcomed by noble female figures. Trembling, he draws near, and finds a veritable paradise, the fullest realization of his most ethereal imaginings.

Asked whether this life contents him, he replies that this "golden existence" fulfills all his anticipations and aspirations. In this land of ideality he lives on happily, though "at times it seemed as if the crowing of a cock was heard near by; and the whole place quivered and his companions grew suddenly pale" (p. 500). At such times Ludwig dimly remembered the world he had left behind, and his sick friend. Once he asked the Fairy ladies whether they can cure his friend by their arts; they replied, "Thy desire is already accomplished." Suspecting that his question betokens a lingering fondness for his former life, they ask whether he longs "for the earth," and he replies, "Nevermore." But having missed "friendship and love" in the "old world," he expresses some disappointment at not finding "both united in beautiful harmony" in this Fairyland. Given his choice between staying with the Fairies and returning to the earth, he chooses to remain. Wandering about one day, he meets a stranger, who salutes him with the words: "It is good to see thee once more. . . . I am thy sick friend."

"Impossible! thou art wholly a stranger to me," said Ludwig.

"Simply for the reason," said the Unknown, "because to-day, for the first time, thou seest me in my true shape. Hitherto thou hast found in me only a reflection of thyself. Thou dost right to remain here, where there is no friendship, no love; where all is illusion and show."

Ludwig sat down and wept. "Oh, let us go back to the dear, dear Earth," he cries, "where once again we may know each other, although in borrowed shape; where we may possess the sweet illusions of Friendship. What do I here?"

"What will it avail?" said the stranger.

"Thou wilt straightway wish thyself back again. The earth is not splendid enough for thee, its flowers are too little, its songs are inharmonious; not so richly does the light blend with the shadows; the flowers wither soon and fall; the birds are thinking of their death and sing but sorrowfully. But here all things are in fadeless beauty."

"Oh, I will be content," cried Ludwig, between hot gushing tears, "only return with me once more, my old friend—let us escape this desert, let us flee from this splendid exile" (pp. 500–501).

At this point Ludwig awakes from his dream to find his friend bending over him. He had unexpectedly recovered, and having received Ludwig's letter announcing his intended visit, had set out to meet him on the way and found him asleep in the forest. Ludwig asks his friend's forgiveness for having doubted his friendship, and after relating his strange dream experiences, wonders whether "after all, there are such things as Fairies."

"That such things exist," answered his friend, "there can be no doubt, but that is only a fiction which represents them as delighting to make men happy. Unconsciously to ourselves, they plant within our hearts those exaggerated fancies, those supernatural longings which prompt us to misanthropic musings, and to despise this beautiful earth with its rich blessings."

Ludwig answered him with a pressure of the hand (p. 501).

Even this summarized form of Tieck's tale illustrates the dozen points of similarity between it and Hawthorne's type of tale. The translator, whoever he was, succeeded in giving his version a decidedly Hawthorn-esque turn, not only in idea but especially in tone—so much so that Hawthorne himself (if he had been given to translating from the German) could hardly have made it more peculiarly like his own style. Nor is it the allegory only that suggests Hawthorne; it is also the psychology that underlies the story—the practical moral for the conduct of the soul—that makes the resemblance startling. How often in Hawthorne's stories and essays are we not warned against the extravagancies of fancy—against "those exaggerated fancies, those supernatural longings which prompt us to misanthropic musings and to despise this beautiful earth with all its rich blessings!'"[97]

Small wonder that Poe, who had already noticed in his 1842 review of *Twice-Told Tales* Hawthorne's lack of versatility or variety,[98] should have been struck by this thirteen-fold repetition in *Mosses from an Old Manse* of the same theme, developed in the same tone. A regular reader of the *Democratic Review*,[99] Poe, already prepared by previous reviewers to make his allegation,[100] reading Tieck's tale and readily finding striking similarities, concluded that the *manner* of this tale was "absolutely identical with that *habitual* to Hawthorne." And that seems to be all the mystery there is to this matter.[101]

The obvious similarities in style and analogical meaning, including the dream and fantasy motifs, have been cited as cause for regarding "The Celestial Railroad" as derived from "Die Freunde." Mention of such places as Vanity Fair, Enchanted Ground, and Delectable Mountains, of characters like Mr. Flimsey-faith, Mr. Scaly-conscience, Rev. Mr. Stumble-at-truth, Rev. Dr. Wind-of-doctrine, of Christian, and finally of Bunyan himself suggests *Pilgrim's Progress* rather than "Die Freunde." Moreover, the references to "volumes of French philosophy and German rationalism"[102] and the description of the "terrible Giant Transcendentalist of German birth," who dwells in a cave where he seizes "honest travellers" and fattens them for his table with "plentiful meals of smoke, mist, moonshine, raw potatoes, and sawdust,"[103] indicate that the immediate purpose for writing the story originated in Hawthorne's desire to satirize such free-and-easy ways of entering heaven as his neighbor Emerson and his associated Transcendentalists seemed to advocate.

It has been suggested that there are hints of "allegory in Tieck's 'Märchen'—which are far from being mere fairy tales—that remind one frequently of Hawthorne's

shadowy art in such stories as 'Ethan Brand,' or 'The Minister's Black Veil,' or 'The Great Carbuncle.'"[104] And so they do. But when these hints are pursued, they lead nowhere. There is, for example, "The Elves," in which a little girl in stepping across the footbridge over the brook that borders her father's garden finds herself in a magic land where she stays, as it seems to her, a few hours; but on returning home, she learns that she has been absent seven years. The story suggests Hawthorne's "Snow Image" and "Wakefield." But we know that the former was suggested by an incident in the Hawthorne household,[105] and that the latter was derived from a newspaper article.[106] Then there is "Der Runenberg," in which a youth, wandering into the mountains, receives from a sorceress a wondrous tablet set with gems of a mystic pattern; and years afterwards he wanders back into the mountains, in search of more jewels, only to return again to his village and friends, an old and broken-down man, bearing a sackful of worthless pebbles, which he regards as precious stones. Several of Hawthorne's stories immediately suggest themselves, among them "The Great Carbuncle" and "The Three-Fold Destiny." But we find their immediate sources in Hawthorne's *Note-Books*.[107] It would be fallacious to suppose that because one finds a passage in his notebooks from which a story is expanded, that therefore this story is entirely original with Hawthorne. We would need to inquire where and when he got the idea that he jotted down in his journal in the first place. Moreover, a number of Tieck's tales, including "The Elves" and "Der Runenberg," had been translated long before 1836-1837. Hawthorne could have drawn suggestions from them for his notebook memoranda. However, such a conclusion is not consistent with other known circumstances: (1) it was Hawthorne's habit to draw upon his own experience or observation for the materials of much of his writing;[108] (2) most of his suggestions that came to him from the outside are traceable to his Puritan inheritance and to his intimate knowledge of colonial history;[109] and (3) his stories all appear to have developed from within—the product of his brooding upon the ideas or morals illustrated in his stories.[110] Hence their genesis is oftener in an idea than in an incident or character derived from another writer.[111] Unlike the methods of Irving and of Poe, Hawthorne's procedure was not as much a matter of "looking about" as of "looking within" him for his materials.

Thus, such a story as "The Shaker Bridal," which has points of similarity with Tieck's "Der Pokal"[112] (for in each story there is a pair of lovers whose union is frustrated and postponed until they find that only the ghost, or memory, of their love is left to mock their youthful hopes), resolves itself, in the final analysis, to an expression of an idea brooded over in Hawthorne's mind ever since his visit, in the company of Emerson, to the Shaker community at Harvard, Massachusetts. Its primary source lies in Hawthorne's familiarity with his native New England.

"Der Pokal" reminds the reader of another story of Hawthorne—"Wakefield." In Tieck's tale, a man, believing his beloved untrue, withdraws from society and, though he continues to live near her, never again sees the lady. In Hawthorne's story, Wakefield, out of mere whim or perversity (Hawthorne does not clearly indicate which) goes by his own door one night and lodges in a neighboring house. The next night circumstances prevent his returning home, but with every recurring opportunity, he finds it harder to resume his place, and so twenty years pass before he returns to his wife. Hawthorne concludes with this moral:

Amid the seeming confusion of our mysterious world, individuals are so nicely adjusted to a system, and systems to one another and to a whole, that, by stepping aside for a moment, a man exposes himself

to a fearful risk of losing his place forever. Like Wakefield, he may become, as it were, the Outcast of the Universe.[113]

The difference between the two tales, despite the similarities, is easily found. Tieck has only a tale to tell; Hawthorne is interested primarily in the subconscious workings of Wakefield's mind, in the psychical reactions and interactions of husband and wife, and in the moral. Concerning the source of the story, he tells us, "In some old magazine or newspaper I recollect a story, told as truth, of a man—let us call him Wakefield—who absented himself for a long time from his wife."[114] It is unlikely that this account should have been a translation of Tieck's tale; even Poe admits that "Wakefield" is based on "a well-known incident," and adds, "Something of this kind actually happened in London."[115]

Still there remains the fact that Hawthorne read a tale of Tieck's, presumably to the bitter end; and it provokes us to attempt an identification of the tale and to inquire concerning possible influence. It has been plausibly argued that Tieck's "Vogelscheuche," a tale of 365 pages in Tieck's *Gesammelte Novellen*, is the story in question, and that its influence can be detected in Hawthorne's moralized story of the scarecrow, "Feathertop."[116] There are enough parallels to make the presumption strong that Hawthorne had this story in mind when he wrote "Feathertop," but there are several considerations that need to be weighed before that conclusion can be reached.

In the first place, Hawthorne's notebooks for 1840 contain this notation:

To make a story out of a scarecrow, giving it odd attributes. From different points of view, it should appear to change, —now an old man, now an old woman,—a gunner, a farmer, or Old Nick.[117]

Tieck's story was first published in 1835, but in the Berlin *Novellenkranz*, an annual with a very limited circulation, so that Hawthorne would hardly have seen it there. The story was not published in Tieck's works until 1842, two years after Hawthorne made his entry in the *Note-Books.* Nor were there any translations of the story before 1840. Hence, if the 1840 note is accepted as the source of "Feathertop," the probability of Hawthorne's indebtedness is lessened. But there is another note in Hawthorne's journals, written in 1849, which should be taken into account:

A modern magician to make the semblance of a human being, with two laths for legs, a pumpkin for a head, etc., of the most modest and meagre materials. Then a tailor helps him to finish his work, and transforms this scarecrow into quite a fashionable figure. At the end of the story, after deceiving the world for a long time, the spell should be broken, and the gay dandy be discovered to be nothing but a suit of clothes, with these few sticks inside of it. All through his seeming existence as a human being, there shall be some characteristics, some tokens, that, to the man of close observation and insight, betray him to be a mere thing of laths and clothes, without heart, soul, or intellect. And so this wretched thing shall become the symbol of a large class.[118]

It is hardly to be doubted that this note of 1849 is the direct source of "Feathertop," which was first published in the *International Magazine* for February-March, 1852. Yet it does not follow that we need to dismiss both the note of 1840 and Tieck's tale as supplying earlier suggestions. They may represent first and second steps toward the composition of the story, for Hawthorne habitually proceeded slowly and gradually developed his stories by a process of thoughtful evolution rather than by sudden inspiration.[119]

But perhaps the parallelism between the two tales involves little more than a peculiar *Geistesverwandtschaft* between the two authors. Consider this characterization of Tieck by an anonymous reviewer in *Blackwood's* for September, 1837 (XLII, 396):

Tieck, whatever . . . his merits, does not possess the power of that vivid creation of character, of conception, of incident which . . . great poets have possessed. . . . Tieck has not the vigorous imagination which, acting on the materials furnished by acute and penetrating observation of life . . . enables the poet to create new combinations. . . . A certain air of vagueness pervades his descriptions; his incidents rarely, if ever, excite our curiosity; if he has to deal with strong passions, we have them exhibited, not in action, but narration, and more frequently in their results than in their birth and growth. The charm of a delightful style, no doubt, carries the reader pleasantly along his prose tales, as the lulling music of his versification and the luxurious sweetness of his imagery do along his legends in verse. . . . We are seldom roused, moved, melted. Finally, not one of Tieck's novels ever causes a hearty laugh, even where, from the extravagance of his combinations, it appears to have been his intention to excite a feeling for the ludicrous; nor have we ever happened to meet with one who has dropped a natural tear over one of his delineations.

In the Preface to the second edition (1842) of *Twice-Told Tales,* Hawthorne used strikingly similar words in his remarkably accurate description of his own stories:

They have the pale tint of flowers that blossomed in too retired a shade,—the coolness of a meditative habit, which diffuses itself through the feeling and observation of every sketch. Instead of passion there is sentiment; and even in what purport to be pictures of actual life, we have allegory, not always so warmly dressed in its habiliments of flesh and blood as to be taken into the reader's mind without a shiver. Whether from lack of power, or an unconquerable reserve, the Author's touches have often an effect of tameness; the merriest man can hardly contrive to laugh at his broadest humor; the tenderest woman, one would suppose, will hardly shed warm tears at his deepest pathos. The book, if you would see anything in it, requires to be read in the clear, brown, twilight atmosphere in which it was written; if opened in the sunshine, it is apt to look exceedingly like a volume of blank pages.

Hoffmann and Chamisso

There are a few similarities between some of Hoffmann's tales and Hawthorne's stories. Hoffmann was more widely translated than Tieck,[120] and it is possible that Hawthorne knew more about Hoffmann than Tieck. *Die Elixiere des Teufels* (1816), translated and published in London, 1824, contains an account of a painter who is able by the subtlety of his art to make it appear that the features of his portraits can change and shift. While it is possible that Hawthorne drew a hint from this source for his "Prophetic Pictures," the manners and methods of the two authors vary considerably. Hoffmann's interest is primarily in the peculiarity of the phenomenon and the telling of his story; Hawthorne's is mainly in the moral to be deduced from the story. A second parallel is between Hoffman's "Des Vetters Eckfenster," in which a man stations himself at an upper-story window and observes the life below him in the street, making comments on people and events, and Hawthorne's "A Sunday at Home." Hawthorne was fond of this device of standing in some out-of-the-way place and describing what passed; he used it in "Sights from a Steeple," "The Toll-Gatherer's Day," "Night Sketches," and elsewhere. But it seems clear that what we have here constitutes parallelism rather than influence.

Lastly, there is Hoffmann's "Die Abenteuer der Sylvesternacht," the story of a man who loses his *Spiegelschatten*—which suggests Hawthorne's "Monsieur du Miroir." But since a similar idea is used by Chamisso in *Peter Schlemihl*, and since Hawthorne refers directly to Peter Schlemihl's shadow, he probably got the suggestion, if one was needed, from Chamisso's tale. [121] As in the case of Tieck and of Hoffmann, the similarities can easily be overemphasized. The influence of Chamisso and Hoffmann must be put down as negligible, and that of Tieck as questionable.

The Faust Motif

More considerable is Hawthorne's reliance for several of his more basic motifs upon Goethe's *Faust*, notably his use of the daemonic or inner urge that possesses some of his characters and of certain Mephistophelean and Faustian elements of characterization. Already in 1835 he presented in New England dress the story of a naive, trustful young man's initiation into the mysterious iniquities of life. At the beginning of his journey into the dark forest he meets a stranger who has "an indescribable air of one who knew the world"—the prototype of Goethe's all-accomplished Mephisto. Under his guidance, Young Goodman Brown's demon is developed until it drives him, against his will but irresistibly, deeper and deeper into the forest of fearful revelation that leads to his undoing.

The daemonic desire of man for perfection or for ultimates and absolutes forms the core of several of Hawthorne's stories. Aylmer, Rappaccini, Ethan Brand, Septimus Felton, even Chillingworth, while they derive from different pages, are all drawn from the same chapter of Goethe's book. In his numerous case histories of the nature of sin, of evil, of intellectual pride, of the devil in man, and of man's overweening ambition to make himself equal to God in knowledge—in writing this anatomy of the daemonic-titanic-promethean-faustian desire—Hawthorne pondered not only the Bible account of Adam's eating of the forbidden fruit and the Miltonic portrayal of Beelzebub but also the entire library of deviltry that the Puritan mind created in early New England, the diabolical creations of Marlowe, of Byron, and of the Gothic novelists. It would have been odd, indeed, if he had stopped short of Goethe's conception of Faust, concerning which almost everyone of Hawthorne's acquaintance at Brook Farm and in Concord was voluble.

To be sure, we need not presuppose that Goethe's particular conception of Faust was necessary for Hawthorne's portrayal of Aylmer, Rappaccini, Brand, and Chillingworth. They all meet the fate of Dr. Faustus of legendary fame as recorded in the old chapbooks, current in New England from the earliest days. The example of Marlowe alone would have sufficed. But *The Marble Faun* exists to demonstrate the fact that Hawthorne's probings into the nature of sin and its effects on man went deeper than the old allegory, drawn in unrelieved black and white, of a compact by which man barters his soul for sensual pleasure and ends by being whisked off to hell. In Donatello, Miriam, and Hilda, contact with sin does not lead to the spiritual death of Hawthorne's earlier egoistical sinners. The evil they do, or witness, contributes toward the perfection, rather than the utter destruction, of their humanity. This is more nearly in accord with Goethe's view of man's ceaseless striving as leading, despite errors and failures, to a progression upwards—on stepping stones of his dead self to higher things. In Goethe's *Faust* the devil is cheated of his victim; in *The Marble*

Faun the moral is not, as it was in *The Scarlet Letter* and the earlier tales, that the wages of sin is death. In short, Hawthorne's final treatment of the problem of evil is that since it is an integral part of the nature of things, man must acknowledge it, for only by experiencing sin can he recognize it, and finally triumph over it. The knowledge and experience of sin thus become steps in the process of man's humanization. This view marks the difference between Goethe's and the earlier treatments of the Faust theme; and it suggests, despite the paucity of references to Goethe that is so striking in Hawthorne's books, that he took notice of Goethe's raising the theme above the level of the old chap books and morality plays, and that his final thoughts on the subject were colored by Goethe's view.

By and large, however, the influence of German literature on Hawthorne is relatively inconsequential. Most of Hawthorne's tales which suggest outside influences are traceable less to Germanic sources than to his peculiar temperamental inheritance.[122]

EDGAR ALLAN POE
(1809–1849)

Poe's Knowledge of German

While industriously and ingeniously discovering plagiarism in his contemporaries,[123] Poe emphatically denied that he himself borrowed from others. In the Preface to *Tales of the Grotesque and Arabesque* (1840) he publicly disavowed Germanic influence. After commenting on the grotesque and arabesque qualities of his stories and admitting that his "'phantasy-pieces' . . . *are* Germanic," he explains that "Germanism" is merely their "vein," that with "a single exception," none partakes of that "pseudo-horror . . . identified with . . . some of the secondary names of German literature."

If in many of my productions terror has been the thesis, I maintain that terror is not of Germany, but of the soul—that I have deduced this terror only from its legitimate sources, and urged it only to its legitimate results.[124]

In spite of this and similar disclaimers, neither Poe's contemporaries nor posterity have been willing to accept his protestation at face value, though great difference of opinion and much uncertainty upon that point still prevails. European critics in general have argued that Poe was under varying degrees of foreign influence; Americans are divided, not only among themselves but even in their own minds.[125]

In a consideration of this kind, beset by

the pitfalls of what the Germans call *Motivenjägerei*, the first inquiry concerns the facilities Poe had for knowing German literature both in the original and in translation. The question whether he read German has been discussed pro and con. Gruener, Cobb, and Campbell [126] hold that Poe knew enough German to read Hoffmann in the original; Woodberry,[127] Beale,[128] and Belden think he did not. Belden expressed the view of the latter group in this way:

> There is nothing to show that he read German, and there is much reason, in the lack of regular education in his hurried, hand-to-mouth career, to believe that he never undertook what in those days even more than now was an arduous task, the acquisition of that language. He could make effective use of a name now and then, or of an occasional phrase, but there is nothing to warrant the belief that he knew German well enough to detect the "manner" of a German book.[129]

This position is based on three arguments. Of these, the first, namely, that there is no record or authoritative statement that Poe studied or knew German, is irrefutable. The second claim, that he lacked, or failed to take advantage of, the opportunity to undertake the arduous task of learning German, is not warranted by what we know of Poe's linguistic abilities and of his literary interests. The third argument, that Poe's occasional use of German was only for effect, was meretricious, is a charge which, while not without some supporting evidence, is debatable. There can be little doubt that the sincerity of Poe's work suffers from his noxious habit of throwing a glamor of erudition over his writings by citing obscure authors and little-known treatises among which he had foraged with a special design—a method that betokens clever trickery even in its artfulness.[130] In itself, this practice is no more an argument against his knowledge of German than against his familiarity with French and Latin, both of which he knew well, even though his quotations in both are inexact at times.

In view of the testimony of teachers and schoolmates that Poe was uncommonly precocious, with a marked ability for language study, the acquisition of German need not have been an "arduous task."[131] What is more, Poe's year at the University came right at the time when the English-speaking world was becoming profoundly interested in German literature and thought, particularly of the Romantic school. Poe was already writing weird tales and seriously busying himself with poetry. The trend and spirit of German romanticism were sufficiently in accord with the temperament of the incipient author, ever alert for what he called "novel effects," to recommend themselves to his attention, either inside or outside his classes.[132] If he did not study German at Charlottesville, he must have given some attention to it almost immediately after his departure, for from the very beginning of his literary career there is evidence that he knew something of both the language and the literature of Germany. In a note to the poem "Al Aaraaf," first published in 1829, he quoted three lines from Goethe's "Meine Göttin."[133] In his first published tale, "MS. Found in a Bottle," referring to his hero's favorite studies, Poe wrote: "Beyond all things, the study of the German moralists gave him great delight."[134] Again, in "Morella" (1835), the heroine "placed before me a number of those mystical writings which are usually considered the mere dross of early German literature. These were her favorite and constant study— and . . . in the process of time became my own."[135] While such references, in and of themselves, mean little, they take on added significance from the fact that Poe's heroes, like Byron's, contain a good deal of himself.[136] There are also correct references to the German philosophers: Leibnitz is quoted once and referred to four more times, Kant is mentioned seven times, Schelling five times, Fichte thrice, and Hegel once.[137] Hegel is also quoted once and Schelling's idea of identity lies at the base of "Morella."[138] Poe's "philosophic Bon-Bon . . . a character of strange intensity and mysticism" is "deeply tinctured by the diablerie of his favorite German studies." "Clearly," concludes Killis Campbell, "Poe shared with the Transcendentalists an interest in German philosophy."[139]

Now, for the third argument, based on Poe's alleged superficiality of mind and display of erudition, notably in the foreign languages.[140] To begin with, there is scattered testimony proving Poe's general knowledge of considerable areas of German literature and thought. Altogether, his writings contain 128 easily identifiable quotations from and references to German authors. None of these, nor all of them combined, prove that Poe knew German literature at first hand, for he could have found many of them in English translation, though hardly all of them. They do illustrate his accuracy and discrimination in using names and quotations at the same time that they affirm his keen interest in a wide range of German thought and art.[141] "To garnish some trite context or give an air of superior learning to some critique," Poe most commonly used French, which he handled more fluently than the German; but when he does employ the latter, he shows a nice appreciation of its terms and demonstrates a correct knowledge of grammatical detail. He uses distinctive German words like *Schwärmerei* rather than some inexact English synonym.[142] He speaks of his own Philistine age as a "period not inaptly denominated by the Germans as 'the age of wigs,' *i.e.*, *Zopf-* or *Perückenzeit.*"[143] In Griswold's edition of the *Literati*, Poe's castigation of Thomas Dunn English ends in the epithet, "In character, a *windbeutel*,"[144] in which the German word speaks volumes. Again, he contrives to give a sentence a clever or humorous turn by using a German phrase.[145] While he does not often quote German expressions, when he does,

he gives them correctly and uses them tellingly.[146]

Finally there is more positive evidence of Poe's knowledge of German—evidence that would be absolutely convincing for almost any other author, and which, even considering Poe's love for mystification and dubious reputation for literary honesty, is all but conclusive.

The first case in point is found in the tale "The Premature Burial,"[147] in which Poe gives the details of a case of premature burial, taken, as he informs the reader, from a recent number of "'The Chirurgical Journals' of Leipzic[148]—a periodical of high authority and merit, which some American bookseller would do well to translate and republish." While it is not impossible that Poe had hit upon the case cited in some English or other European journal, or that someone had read and told him about it, the tone and the whole setting of the incident described suggest that he read the report himself, and that he consulted the "Chirurgical Journal" at other times for abnormal medical cases. There seems to be no special reason for Poe's wishing to display erudition in this instance, as he might in a learned review or literary essay.

The next case seems to furnish more direct, positive evidence. It is a passage from the German of Novalis prefaced to "The Mystery of Marie Rogêt,"[149] containing forty-five words, correctly quoted with the exception of what is obviously a typographical error. Poe adds a translation. There was at that time no complete translation of Novalis' work,[150] and only one book, as far as can be ascertained, included a translation of this particular passage. This book, Mrs. Sarah Austin's *Fragments from German Prose Writers* (London, 1841; reprinted by D. Appleton & Co., in New York, 1841), was noticed and reviewed at least five times in American magazines during 1841 and 1842,[151] and it is not unlikely that Poe knew the book.[152] The passage in question is No. 440 of Novalis' *Fragmente vermischten Inhalts* :[153]

Es gibt eine Reihe idealischer Begebenheiten, die der Wirklichkeit parallel läuft. Selten fallen sie zusammen. Menschen und Zufälle modifizieren gewöhnlich[154] die idealische Begebenheit, so dass sie unvollkommen erscheint und ihre Folgen gleichfalls unvollkommen sind. So bei der Reformation.[155] Statt des Protestantismus kam das Luthertum hervor.

The passage is translated by Mrs. Austin and by Poe as follows :[156]

MRS. AUSTIN

There are ideal *trains* of events which run parallel with the real ones. *Seldom* do they coincide. Men and *accidents* commonly modify *every* ideal event or train of events, so that it *appears* imperfect, and its consequences are equally imperfect. Thus it was with the Reformation,—instead of Protestantism, *arose* Lutheranism.

POE

There are ideal *series* of events which run parallel with the real ones. They *rarely* coincide. Men and *circumstances* generally modify *the* ideal train of events so that it *seems* imperfect, and its consequences are equally imperfect. Thus with the Reformation; instead of Protestantism *came* Lutheranism.

The two versions (major divergencies are indicated by italics) differ chiefly in the choice of words, which seem dictated more by taste than by the demands of exactitude. The translations are such as would be made by two persons independently of each other, both of whom understand German, but are not obliged to translate word for word or with the assistance of a dictionary.[157] This conclusion is supported by another German selection which Poe quotes in the original as a footnote in *Eureka*. This passage of seventy-six words from Alexander von Humboldt's *Kosmos* is much more difficult German than the paragraph from Novalis. Only two English translations

antedate Poe's: one by Prichard (London, 1845), the other by Sabine (London, 1847). The original, which Poe quotes letter perfect, without giving the source, runs as follows:

Betrachtet man die nicht perspektivischen eignen Bewegungen der Sterne, so scheinen viele Gruppenweise in ihrer Richtung entgegengesetzt; und die bisher gesammelten Thatsachen machen es auf's wenigste nich notwendig, anzunehmen, dass alle Theile unserer Sternenschicht oder gar der gesammelten Sterneninseln, welche den Weltraum füllen, sich um einen grossen, unbekannten leuchtenden oder dunkeln Zentralkörper bewegen. Das Streben nach den letzten und höchsten Grundursachen macht freilich die reflektierende Thätigkeit des Menschen, wie seine Phantasie, zu einer solchen Annahme geneigt.

Prichard's, Sabine's, and Poe's translations follow, in the order named :

If the non-perspective proper motions of the stars are considered, many of them appear groupwise opposed in their directions; and the data hitherto collected make it at least not necessary to suppose that all parts of our astral system, or the whole of the star-islands which fill the universe, are in motion about any great unknown, luminous, or non-luminous central mass. The longing to reach the least or brightest fundamental cause, indeed, renders the reflecting faculty of man as well as his fancy disposed to adopt such a proposition (Prichard, *Kosmos*, I, 154).

If we consider the proper motions of the stars, as contradistinguished from their apparent or perspective motions, their directions are various; it is not, therefore, a necessary conclusion, either that all parts of our astral system, or that all the systems which fill the universal space, revolve about one great undiscovered luminous or non-luminous central-body, however naturally we may be disposed to an inference which would gratify alike the imaginative faculty, and that intellectual capacity which ever seeks after the last and highest generalisation (Sabine, *Kosmos*, I, 135).

When we regard the real, proper, or non-perspective motions of the stars, we find *many groups of them moving in opposite directions;* and the data as yet in hand render it not necessary, at least, to conceive that the systems composing the Milky Way, or the clusters, generally, composing the Universe, are revolving about any particular centre unknown, whether luminous or non-luminous. It is but Man's longing for a fundamental First Cause, that impels both his intellect and fancy to the adoption of such an hypothesis (Poe's *Works*, XVI, 299).

A comparison of the three versions substantiates Gruener's judgment that Poe's is "surely as independent and original" as the others—a faithful rendition of the substance and form of the original, such as would be made by one thoroughly conversant with the original German, and hence feeling himself free to make changes not essential to the sense for the sake of a good literary translation. It might again be assumed that Poe secured someone to look up and translate for him the passage in the German text— something of a task, for the pretty bulky five-volume work of Humboldt's available in Poe's day had no index. The assumption is questionable when we take into account the frequency with which Poe would have had to rely upon such help. Among the 128 references to German authors and quotations from their writings, August Wilhelm Schlegel, whose *Lectures on Dramatic Art* Poe read, is oftenest alluded to. Schlegel is quoted twice and mentioned fifteen times.[158] Goethe is next with a dozen references[159] and four citations— two from "Meine Göttin" and two from "Das Veilchen."[160] It is likely that he knew also *Werther, Tasso,*[161] and, one would suppose, *Faust.* Schiller is quoted once and mentioned five times.[162] Bürger is referred to three times, and Herder, Körner, and Friedrich Schlegel each twice.[163] Musaeus, Wieland, Winckelmann, and Uhland are mentioned each once;[164] the dramatists Grillparzer and Öhlenschläger are mentioned in passing;[165] and a passage from Prince Pückler-Muskau's *Briefe eines Verstorbenen* is cribbed from Mrs. Austin's

translation, entitled *Letters by a German Prince.*[166] In his reviews of Longfellow's ballads, Poe discusses with discrimination a number of German ballads, and he ventures some generalizations concerning their nature. He finds that Longfellow's "German studies" have changed his "conventional habit of thinking,"[167] and that he is so "imbued with the peculiar spirit of German song that . . . he regards the inculcation of a *moral* as essential"[168]—a perfectly valid statement in respect to many German songs and "ballads." Poe quotes Tieck once[169] and refers to him five times.[170] He is also greatly interested in Fouqué, of whose *Undine* he wrote an appreciative review of ten pages in 1839.[171] He wonders, in one of the *Marginalia*, whether "anyone had remarked the striking similarity in tone between 'Undine' and the 'Libussa' of Musaeus"[172] —again a proper question to raise. In his review of Longfellow, he refers to Hoffmann's "Phantasy-Pieces of the Lorrainean Callôt,"[173] and himself projected in 1842 a new collection of his tales to be entitled "Phantasy-Pieces,"[174] obviously an inspiration from Hoffmann and Tieck's use of the terms *Phantasie* and *Phantasiestücke.*

Finally, Poe could hardly have hoped to achieve his position as a leading critic among a generation of writers who were all but' unanimous in reverencing German literature without making himself at home in that area; and when we add to this the fact that by temperament he was naturally more sympathetic toward German romanticism than any other literary school,[175] we have compelling reasons for believing with Professor Gruener, that Poe knew enough German "to read easy prose and, when necessary, to translate difficult prose with exactness and facility."[176]

Indebtedness to German Stories

Among the several groups or types into which Poe's stories fall, the hoaxes, extravaganzas, and satirical pieces show the fewest Germanic qualities, most of them being suggested by Poe's own observations on persons, events, and contemporary ideas and movements.[177] The second group, detective stories and ratiocinative tales, also contain little Germanic influence.[178] Yet the note which Poe prefixed to "The Mystery of Marie Rogêt" inevitably draws our attention to Novalis, notably to the passage from Novalis already cited regarding seemingly parallel circumstances and series of events. At the head of the story Poe wrote boldly:

What song the Syrens sang, or what name Achilles assumed when he hid himself among women, although puzzling questions, are not beyond *all* conjecture.—Sir Thomas Browne, *Urn Burial.*

To find answers to such questions (paralleling the way Poe goes about making his elaborate analyses and rationcinations) requires, he tells us, that he direct his attention to the seemingly trifling circumstances which seem to be coincidences but which are not coincidences for Poe. All events arrange themselves into a perfect train or series, and form the links of his logical processes;[179] it is by training his reasoning faculties upon these coincidences (as others regard them) that Poe solves the puzzles and mysteries of his tales of ratiocination: "Coincidences, in general, are great stumbling-blocks in the way of that class of thinkers who have been educated to know nothing of the theory of probabilities."[180] The fragment which Poe quotes from Novalis as a motto for "The Mystery of Marie Rogêt" has a like content. Furthermore, the *Fragmente* of Novalis, which Poe shows himself familiar with on two other occasions,[181] contain frequent repetitions of the same idea.[182] In view of Poe's interest in others of Novalis' works, it seems reasonable to conclude that he drew suggestions for his theory of coincidences, his "Calculus of Probabilities," from Novalis' *Fragmente.*

Romantic Stories

MESMERISM AND METEMPSYCHOSIS

It is in a third group of Poe's tales—stories portraying the conflict of powerful emotions, the growth of evil, revenge, disease, decadence, madness, hysterical or neurotic states of mind, *fixe Ideen*, mesmerism, hypnotism, metempsychosis, *Doppelgänger*—that we come to some of Poe's best tales, and to those in which "Germanism" is most palpable. Of these, perhaps the most startling are three in which Poe is concerned with mesmerism: "A Tale of the Ragged Mountains" (*Godey's Lady's Book*, April, 1844), "Mesmeric Revelation" (*Columbian Magazine*, August, 1844), and "Facts in the Case of M. Valdemar" (*American Whig Review*, December, 1845). They invite comparison with tales of the German romancers Tieck, Novalis, Kleist, and notably Hoffmann, who frequently occupied themselves with mesmerism in their stories.[183]

Alert for the novel and the fantastic, both Hoffmann and Poe were attracted by the doctrines of Mesmer and the theories of hypnotism. Disciples of the new theories tantalized themselves with promises of the discovery of the deepest secrets of nature. Hypnotism (magnetism, Hoffmann called it) plays a role in many of his tales, usually in terms of "das höhere geistige Prinzip," "eine freundliche feindliche Kraft," "innige geistige Verbindung," or "wunderbares psychisches Phänomen." In "Der Magnetiseur" and "Der unheimliche Gast"[184] Hoffmann based his plots upon the hypnotic relationship existing between his characters, the general features of the two stories, including plots, being very much alike, as Hoffmann himself admitted.[185]

The fact that both Poe and Hoffmann used the motifs of metempsychosis and of mesmerism in their tales is, by itself, insignificant; but when both united them in one story and both worked them out in almost identical terms, these similarities, extending sometimes to details, become meaningful; and when he consider the novelty of mesmerism at the time, it is safe to conclude that Poe did not accidentally hit upon the "same singular combination of singular motives."[186]

Hoffmann's "Magnetiseur" is much more complicated and less strictly unified than Poe's "Tale of the Ragged Mountains." There are three loosely connected parts. In the introduction a family group gathers before a cheerful fire. The Baron is induced to relate a tale that has to do with a dream and an experience of his youth, in which figures prominently an officer about whom hangs a fearful mysteriousness.

Seine Riesengrösse wurde noch auffälliger durch die Hagerkeit seines Körpers, der nur aus Muskeln zu bestehen schien; er möchte in jüngeren Jahren ein schöner Mann gewesen sein; denn noch jetzt warfen seine grossen schwarzen Augen einen brennenden Blick, den man kaum ertragen konnte; ein tiefer Fünfziger, hatte er die Kraft und die Gewandtheit eines Jünglings.[187]

The strangeness of his person, his temperamental attributes, a shady past, and the hypnotic power that he wields over others surround this Danish officer with an atmosphere of mystery and terror. The Baron comes at last to the climax of his story when he sees in a dream the Major enter his room at midnight and hears him say, "Armes Menschenkind, erkenne deinen Meister und Herrn! . . . Ich bin dein Gott der dein Innerstes durchschaut." The Baron proceeds: "Plötzlich sah ich ein glühendes Instrument in seiner Hand, mit dem er in mein Gehirn fuhr."[188] Terrified, the Baron awakes, and rushing to the window, where he hears a noise, he sees the Major disappearing through the garden gate into the open country beyond. The mystery of the situation is heightened by the fact that all doors and windows are locked. Other inmates of the house are aroused. They break into the Major's room and find him lying in his blood.

Thus ends the Baron's story. Following a general discussion of dreams, the Baron's son, Ottmar, relates a story told to him by his friend Alban, a convert to hypnotism or, as Hoffmann calls it, magnetism. The relationship of the characters is confusing. Ottmar relates the story as he heard it from Alban, whose story, in turn, deals with his friend Theobald, who is not otherwise related to the group in which the stories are recited. During Theobald's absence at a distant university, his fiancée comes under the influence of a stranger, an Italian officer, and becomes so enamored of him that she forgets her first lover. The story turns upon a theory of dreams. The girl is so beset by tormenting dreams of her Italian lover, who is called away on a campaign, that she becomes insane. Theobald, on returning home, finds her in this condition. He applies hypnotism. Slowly, his influence over the girl's dreams enables him to supersede the power the Italian holds over her, and finally she is completely restored (pp. 152–58).

Here begins the third, and central, part of the story. As Ottmar finishes his account, his sister Maria, who has shown signs of agitation during the preceding recital, falls into a faint. Ottmar's friend Alban, the "Magnetiseur," suddenly appears. He is attracted to Maria, and though he knows her to be the betrothed of Hypolit, he determines to cure her and at the same time bring her under the power of his will by magnetism. He succeeds, but on the wedding day she falls dead at the altar. Duels, catastrophe, and death follow for all members of the original group (pp. 158–75) except one, who lives to tell their tragic history.

At several points in the story the Baron expresses his distrust of Alban because he finds a singular resemblance between him and the Danish major, whom he had known in his youth. On the evening of Maria's wedding, the old Baron, meeting Alban in the corridor, mistakes him for the Major in the flesh (p. 174). The reader is left to infer that the Danish major of Part I of the story, though presumed dead long ago, is the Magnetiseur. Thus Hoffmann uses the theme of metempsychosis.

Poe's story uses the same motifs—hypnotism, metempsychosis, dreams, premonitions, and visions. As often in Poe's tales, there is no love episode. We learn of a singular relationship between Dr. Templeton, a physician, and Mr. Bedloe, an invalid.

Bedloe was singularly tall and thin. . . . His limbs were exceedingly long and emaciated. . . . His eyes were abnormally large. . . . In moments of exitement the orbs grew bright to a degree almost inconceivable; seeming to emit luminous rays, not of a reflected, but of an intrinsic lustre.

We recognize some of the same features that Hoffmann emphasizes. Like Hoffmann, too, Poe is undecided about the origin, the past, and the age of his character. Both authors are puzzled by his seeming old one moment, young the next. The men are alike also in retaining marks of their handsome youth, despite their present haggardness. Dr. Templeton, Bedloe's physician, is a "convert to the doctrines of Mesmer," and he used "altogether magnetic remedies" for his patient.[189] After detailing the relationship between patient and doctor, Poe proceeds to an account of Bedloe's visions and dreams on a solitary walk in the Ragged Mountains of Virginia. Growing tired, Bedloe comes to a secluded spot and feeling an "indescribable uneasiness" as a heavy mist and intolerable heat surround him, seats himself under a tree; he falls into a trance during which his senses become hyperacute. Looking up at the tree under which he is seated, he sees, to his surprise, that it is a palm.[190] Suddenly the fog lifts, and he perceives below him in the valley a bizarre scene—an "Eastern-looking city," swarming with Oriental people. He descends to find the city in "the wildest tumult and contention." It appears that the Indian inhabitants are fighting a "small party of men clad in garments half-Indian, half-European, and officered by a gentleman in a uniform partly British." Bedloe joins the smaller party; he and his allies are driven for refuge into a species of kiosk. Presently he observes an effeminate-looking person descend, by means of a rope knotted from the turbans of his attendants, from an upper window, leap into a boat, and make his escape. During a renewed attack on the kiosk, Bedloe rushes into the street to fight, but he is struck upon the temple by a poisoned arrow. "I reeled and fell. An instantaneous and dreadful sickness seized me. I struggled—I gasped—I died." When he comes to his original self (the change comes about as if by a galvanic shock), he finds himself again in the mountains. Slowly he proceeds on his way home, where he relates his experiences to Templeton and Poe. "And not even for an instant," he declares, "can I compel my understanding to regard it as a dream."[191] Dr. Templeton, Poe's *magnetiseur*, now produces a watercolor portrait, an exact likeness of Bedloe's features, and makes the following explanation:

You will perceive . . . the date of this picture . . . 1780. In this year was the portrait taken. It is the likeness of a dead friend—a Mr. Oldeb—to whom I became much attached in Calcutta, during the administration of Warren Hastings. I was then only twenty years old.
In your detail of the vision which presented itself to you amid the hills, you have described, with the minutest accuracy, the Indian city of Benares, upon the Holy River. The riots, the combats, the massacre, were the actual events of the insurrection of Cheyte Sing, which took place in 1780, when Hastings was put in imminent peril of his life. The man escaping by the string of turbans, was Cheyte Sing himself. The party in the kiosk were sepoys and British officers, headed by Hastings. Of this party I was one, and did all I could to prevent the rash and fatal sally of the officer who fell, in the crowded alleys, by the poisoned arrow of a Bengalee. That officer was my dearest friend. It was Oldeb. You will perceive by this manuscript, (here the

speaker produced a note-book in which several pages appeared to have been freshly written) that at the very period in which you fancied these things amid the hills, I was engaged in detailing them upon paper here at home (*Works*, V, 174–75).

The tale ends with the death of Bedloe, the result of Dr. Templeton's accidentally applying to his patient's temple a poisonous instead of a medicinal leech. Poe's (i.e., the narrator's) attention is arrested by the newspaper announcement of the death of Mr. *Bedlo*. He inquires of the editor regarding Mr. *Bedlo* and is told that *Bedlo* should have been printed *Bedloe*, with the final *e*— "merely a typographical error," explains the editor. "'Then,' said I mutteringly as I turned on my heel, 'then indeed has it come to pass that one truth is stranger than any fiction—for Bedloe, without the *e*, what is it but Oldeb reversed ? And this man tells me it is a typographical error²'" (*Works*, V. 176).

The doctrine of metempsychosis appears in the suggestion that Bedlo(e) is a reincarnation of Oldeb. However widely the stories differ in external particulars, the presence in both of metempsychosis, hypnotism, dreams, and the mysterious *magnetiseur* seems to involve something more than mere coincidence.[192]

In the opening sentence of "Mesmeric Revelation" Poe makes the bold declaration: "Whatever doubt may still envelop the *rationale* of mesmerism, its startling *facts* are now almost universally believed. Of these latter, those who doubt, are mere doubters by profession—an unprofitable and disreputable tribe."[193] After indicating that the knows several works on mesmerism, among them "the logical inquiry of Cousin and his European and American echoes," Poe goes on "to detail without comment the very remarkable substance of a colloquy between a sleep-walker and myself," the sleep-walker being a Mr. Vankirk, who had long suffered from phthisis, and whom Mr. P. as *magnetiseur*, had "been in the habit

of mesmerizing" and thus relieving. The conversation turns upon questions of the *magnetiseur* concerning the states of feeling of the patient, and resolves itself gradually into metaphysical gibberish, which is terminated suddenly by P's calling his patient to wakefulness. Less than a minute afterwards he expires, his corpse assuming the "cold rigidity of stone." The question involuntarily comes to P: "Had the sleep-walker, indeed, during the latter portion of the discourse, been addressing me from out of the region of the shadows ?"[194]

In the mesmeric state, says Poe, the external organs of sense are dull, while through "channels supposed unknown," matters beyond the scope of the physical organs" are clearly perceived. The same observations are made by Hoffmann.[195] But Poe was not content to stop there. If mesmerism enables us to learn profound truths from the "region of the shadows," why should it not be equal to preserving life itself ? This question he propounds in "The Facts in the Case of M. Valdemar."

In this story, M. Valdemar, with whom Mr. P. as *magnetiseur* professes to have long been *en rapport*, sends for the author just before his death, and gives him permission to perform upon him the experiment of prolonging life by mesmerism. At the moment that M. Valdemar seems to expire, P mesmerizes him and holds him in this state while he propounds questions to him. This condition endures for more than seven months. To all ordinary appearances, M. Valdemar is dead, but he still responds to P's passes; and upon P's question, whether he is still sleeping, the subject replies: "Yes; —no;—I *have been* sleeping—and now— now—I *am* dead."[196] However, examination shows that his tongue still moves, and that he still breathes. Eventually singular changes come over his features. Questioned about his wishes, M. Valdemar breaks forth: "For God's sake!—quick!—quick! —put me to sleep—or, quick!—waken me! —quick!—*I say to you that I am dead!*"[197]

The *magnetiseur* hastens to awaken him and succeeds.

"As I rapidly made the mesmeric passes, amid ejaculations of 'dead! dead!' absolutely *bursting* from the tongue and not from the lips of the sufferer, his whole frame at once — within the space of a single minute, or even less, shrunk—crumpled—absolutely *rotted* away beneath my hands. Upon the bed . . . there lay a nearly liquid mass of loathesome—of detestable putridity."[198]

The story illustrates how far Poe superseded Hoffmann in the realm of the horrible. Moreover, Hoffmann, though his tales end as tragically as Poe's, uses such incongruous touches as the humorously grotesque or the frankly supernatural that the reader is seldom deceived for long. Poe, on the contrary, is often serious and aims at convincing, to the point of shocking the reader if necessary. He puts his stories upon as reasonable (scientific or pseudo-scientific) a basis as the subject allows. Also, Poe's characters in these stories are neither weak, sentimental females of the Gothic type nor inexperienced, fantastic young swains; they are men who, though psychic or neurotic, are capable of reasoning and of proceeding effectively in their undertakings. Finally, while Hoffmann's hypnotists have the marks of extraordinary personages, bearing the outward stamp of wizards or magicians, Poe's differ little in outward circumstances from ordinary men. Dr. Templeton is described as a capable physician, and in "Mesmeric Revelation" and "The Facts of the Case of M. Valdemar" the *magnetiseur* is sufficiently commonplace not to warrant description at all. It is largely this greater seriousness, congruity, plainness, and directness that makes Poe's tales, though ghastlier than Hoffmann's, more convincing and more forceful.

THE *Doppelgänger* MOTIF

A theme not unlike metempsychosis that interested Poe at various times is the *Dop-* *pelgänger* motif. The idea of the double- or other-self is a very old one.[199] The German romanticists were especially fond of using it.[200] Fouqué used it in "Zauberring." Novalis made use of it in *Heinrich von Ofterdingen.* Hoffmann himself was frequently haunted by the idea of being pursued by his double.[201] The idea is basic in his story entitled "Doppelgänger," and he used it prominently also in "Der Elementargeist," "Der unheimliche Gast," and in "Der Sandmann," but it is in his "Elixiere des Teufels" that he comes closest to employing the idea as Poe used it in "William Wilson." The motif on which both narratives are constructed is that of the struggle for supremacy between good and evil in man. Both authors have availed themselves of the device of a double existence, mental and physical, to illustrate the tragic consequences of a separation of moral and physical identity.[202]

Hoffmann traces the growth of this "dunkle Macht" minutely from its first inception until, grown gigantic in its power, it plunges its victim into an abyss of crime. We follow the same development in Poe's tale. The difference in Poe's tale (and this adds force and gripping power in Poe's story) is that William is lost; the evil triumphs over the good. Hoffmann's Medardus thinks he has killed his double, that he is therefore lost; but in the sequel we learn that this last damning crime has not been committed. Medardus is reclaimed. While adapting Hoffmann's duelling scene, Poe, with a better estimate of its dramatic possibilities, makes the duel fatal to William's double, and therewith ends his story on a climactic, tragic note. What Medardus only fears becomes reality for William. William stabs his double, but sees him arise and hears him speak, no longer in a scraping whisper, but in the tone of his own voice:

"You have conquered, and I yield. Yet, henceforth art thou also dead—dead to the world, to Heaven and to Hope! In me didst thou exist—and in my death, see by this image, which is thine own, how utterly thou hast murdered thyself."[203]

Another motif that Poe appropriated but used to better advantage is the whispering voice of the *Doppelgänger*. Both Medardus and William are pursued by *hissed* and *whispered* utterances. With Hoffmann the exact correspondence of personal features and the whispering voice of Medardus' double have no special significance; they are the stock-in-trade of the double-motif. In making the two voices finally identical, by slow stages, Poe achieves an added and more forceful (because cumulative) final effect.[204]

By discarding much of Hoffmann's episodic matter, many nonessential complications, and all unnecessary characters, while concentrating upon the main line of action and the two focal characters, Poe heightens the effect. Hoffmann vacillates between the matter-of-fact and the supernatural, crossing and recrossing the border and leaving the reader in doubt until the very end, where everything is cleared up on natural terms.[205] Poe, instead, drives at once boldly into the realm of the supernatural and keeps the reader in an atmosphere frankly unearthly. "William Wilson" is constructed after Poe's own principles as laid down in the "Philosophy of Composition."[206] He started out to produce an awe-inspiring atmosphere of mystery, and in "looking about . . . for such combinations of event, or tone, as shall best serve . . . in the construction of the effect,"[207] he drew largely on Hoffmann's *Elixiere des Teufels:* first, for the criminal proclivities of his main character, second, for the *Doppelgänger* motif, third, for its typification of the good and evil forces in man, fourth, for the mysterious, solemn whispering and the final, exact correspondence of the double's voice, and fifth, for the murder of the double and the resulting extinction of the good principle in the murderer.

STORIES DEALING WITH *fixe Ideen*

A motif akin to the dual nature of man (typifying good and evil) is what Poe calls "the imp of the perverse." Poe and the German romantics knew it well—this desire to torture oneself, even to annihilate oneself. Corollary with it is the "desire to do wrong for the wrong's sake," in spite of it, nay, because of it.[208] Poe's "Imp of the Perverse" is one of a group of stories in which Poe develops this idea. After a six-page discussion of the spirit of perversity, Poe's character relates how he murdered a friend out of sheer perversity, going about it coolly, calculatingly, carefully destroying all possible clues that might lead to his detection. For a long time he reveled in the idea that he was absolutely safe. "But there arrived at length an epoch, from which the pleasurable feeling grew, by scarcely perceptible gradations, into a haunting and harassing thought . . . 'I am safe . . . if I be not fool enough to make open confession.'" Obsessed by the imp of perversity, he is finally driven to go before a judge and to inform against himself, consigning himself "to the hangman and to Hell," not because he is penitent, but because "the imp of the perverse" has driven him to destruction.[209] "The Black Cat" and "The Tell-Tale Heart" (both of 1843) develop the same theme with even greater intensity and effect and greater circumstantiality of detail. There is nothing in the work of the German *Romantiker* to equal these three tales of Poe.

But there is a motif very like it which they used often, and which Poe likewise employed. In general we may call it the *fixe Idee*—a kind of monomania, some singular thought which takes hold of a weakened, unbalanced, neurotic, or extraordinarily intense mind and turns into an obsession. Hoffmann, for instance, was harassed all his life by thoughts which drove him from self-contemplative brooding to thoughts of suicide. An ill-regulated imagination and an overdeveloped tendency toward the horrible and the distressing made him apprehensive of mysterious dangers; and the whole tribe of Demogorgons, apparitions, spectres, and goblins that filled his stories, though products of his imagination, were no less discomposing for him than if they had had real existence.[210] He wrote a number of stories dealing with such *fixe Ideen*, among them "Das steinerne Herz," "Meister Johannes Wacht," "Meister Martin, der Küfner, und seine Gesellen," and, more Poesque, the following: "Das Fräulein von Scuderi," "Der Sandmann," and "Die Jesuiterkirche in G——."

"Das Fräulein von Scuderi" is typical. The goldsmith, Cardillac, has a consuming passion for jewels and gold ornaments. As they take form under his deft fingers, they grow dearer and dearer to him, and he delays delivery as long as possible. Once they leave his hands, he finds no peace of mind until he has them again— anything, everything to get them again into his possession. To secure them, he kills, and kills again. He is perfectly conscious of the blood guilt which he is accumulating but is powerless to withstand the urge. As in the case of "The Imp of the Perverse," "The Tell-Tale Heart," and "The Black Cat," he finds no rest until the urge is satisfied. As in Poe's stories, there is no trace of penitence. So crime follows crime until he is driven to surrender and confession.[211]

In "Der Sandmann" a student named Nathanael becomes obsessed by the idea that one Guiseppe Coppelius, an alchemist, who has brought misfortune to his family, is haunting him. In his childish fancy Nathanael identifies Coppelius with the sandman of nursery lore, and visualizes him as a monster who stabs out children's eyes. As he grows older, he sees the evil spirit personified in this man who, after all, is little more than the creation of his overwrought fancy.[212] So fixed does the idea become that it robs him of his bride, throws

him into a frenzied fever, and leads him in the end to kill himself. His reason tells him that he is laboring under a delusion, but the imp of the perverse drives him on. The similarity in the mental states of Hoffmann's Cardillac and Nathanael and of Poe's characters dominated by perversity is apparent. Details in these stories, as well as in *Die Elixiere des Teufels*, parallel so closely Poe's "Tell-Tale Heart" that there may well be involved something more than mere coincidence. Particularly noteworthy is the identical use to which both writers put a mysterious knocking below the floorboards.[213] The idea of a man being hounded by his conscience or by some mysterious motive until he confesses his crime is, of course, not novel. "Murder will out," or "Die klare Sonne bringt's an den Tag," as the old folk saying has it, is not an unusual theme.[214] But Poe's use of the idea is on the same order as Hoffmann's; and since he appears to have borrowed, or adapted, other motifs from Hoffmann and otherwise shown himself akin to the German romancer, it is likely that he drew a suggestion for his "Tell-Tale Heart" from "Der Sandmann" and *Die Elixiere des Teufels*.

Among Poe's stories dealing specifically with women, "Berenice" (1835), "Morella" (1835), "Ligeia" (1838), and "Eleonora" (1842), all rest upon some form of *fixe Idee*. In "The Tell-Tale Heart" the film-covered eye of the victim motivates the entire story. In the woman-group of his tales Poe returned to the device of concentrating upon some personal feature: the eyes of Ligeia and of Eleonora, the melodious voice of Morella, the teeth of Berenice. "Berenice" is the most gruesome as we watch Agaeus driven by a ghoulish vampire desire to possess himself of the teeth of his beloved, deceased, and entombed Berenice. The words of Agaeus, "*Dicebant mihi sadales, si sepulchrum amicæ visitarem, curas meas aliquantulum fore levatas*," point toward a practice of the ancients—a practice which the romanticists were fond of treating—

namely, the love of dead bodies, the despoiling of corpses, and the annihilating power of love. If Poe turned to the German romantics, he found a number of instances upon which he could have drawn, for the Germans, like the English, had their graveyard literature.[216] The story in which the idea comes closest to that of Poe's is Hoffmann's "Der Vampyr," one of the group comprising "Die Serapionsbrüder" stories, which Poe drew upon on other occasions. In this story the curse of a hateful mother leads a young wife to a passion for corpses. Horrible is the scene in which the husband follows her to the cemetery and there sees her tearing with her teeth, like a hyena, a dead body which she has dug up.[217] While there is little resemblance between the action of Hoffmann's and Poe's stories, there is a striking similarity in motivation and characterization. As in Poe's story, there is a long struggle against the steady growth of the fearful, monomaniac desire. As in Poe's story, also (and unlike other examples cited above), the erotic impulse plays no part. Finally, there are the garments and other properties, bearing marks of the ghastly deed, which are used as evidence, as in "Berenice." In both stories, madness is the end.[218]

If in "Berenice" the perfect teeth of the lady become a prepossession in the lover's mind, in "Ligeia" it is her eyes that become the object of his monomania. The story bears remarkable analogies to the love episodes in Hoffmann's "Der Sandmann." Hoffmann's Clara is the prototype of Poe's Ligeia. Like Ligeia, Clara is passionately devoted; like her, too, her erudition is profound. Even more striking is the similarity of their persons. Like Poe's hero, Nathanael describes her perfections in detail, but always comes back to her eyes, which hold him most powerfully.[219] Poe dwells at length on "Those eyes! those shining, those divine orbs!"[220] But in an evil hour Nathanael forsakes Clara for the false image of a woman, a mere automaton.

So, too, Poe, in the trammels of opium, leads home a successor of the unforgotten Ligeia—the Lady Rowena. Ligeia is the embodiment of Beauty, not "classic" Beauty, yet Beauty in the highest earthly sense, "the symbol of that aethereal beauty the author himself adored."[221] Hoffmann's idea is the same.[222] Poe's love for Ligeia is not of the heart; it is of the mind. In the unremembered first meeting, in her all-comprehending knowledge, in the intellectual music of her voice, in the unsolved mystery of her eyes, we see Poe's embodiment in Ligeia of "Beauty as an idea." The Lady Rowena symbolizes the perverted taste, whose existence in Poe's mind is at length ended in that long mediation of his first pure love. The three or four ruddy drops[223] are potent distillations from the life-essence of the unperceived spirit, which thus replaces Rowena in his vision.[224] Poe himself commented on the idea developed in his story.[225] Concerning P. P. Cooke's criticism of "Ligeia,"[226] Poe wrote:

Touching 'Ligeia' you are right—all right—throughout. The *gradual* perception of the fact that Ligeia lives again in the person of Rowena is a far loftier and more thrilling idea than the one I have embodied. . . . And this idea was mine—had I never written before I should have adopted it—but there is 'Morella.' Do you remember that there the gradual conviction on the part of the parent is that the spirit of the first Morella tenants the person of the second? It was necessary, since 'Morella' was written, to modify 'Ligeia.' I was forced to be content with a sudden half-consciousness, on the part of the narrator, that Ligeia stood before him. One point I have not fully carried out—I should have intimated that the *will* did not perfect its intention—there should have been a relapse—a final one—and Ligeia (who had only succeeded in so much as to convey the idea of the truth to the narrator) should be at length entombed as Rowena—the bodily alterations having gradually faded away.[227]

Had Poe done this, i.e., had he intimated that the will did not perfect its intention (as Hoffmann did in his story), and had he in the end entombed Rowena as Ligeia, instead of leaving all questionable, he would have had exactly what happens in Hoffmann's story. Poe leaves the thing in the air; the reader does not know whether it is Ligeia who dies, or Rowena, or both. In the German story, Clara had warned Nathanael in words very like those used by Ligeia in her admonition that lack of will power would lead to ruination. As she predicts, Nathanael's weakness leads to his unhappy love, his madness, and finally his death.

"Morella" is, as Poe admits, very like "Ligeia," except that the idea is worked out to its natural conclusion. As in "Ligeia," the lover tells the story; and as in that story, he meets the lady by chance. Though he loves her, "the fires are not of Eros. . . . I never spoke of passion, nor thought of love." Their union is happy, but their happy relationship is based on Morella's prodigious learning. Together they bury themselves in metaphysical studies: "the wild pantheism of Fichte . . . and above all, the doctrines of *Identity* as urged by Schelling." But unlike Ligeia, Morella becomes the victim of a *slow*, consuming disease. Daily she sinks lower. As she dies, she gives birth to a child, which lives. The girl grows strangely in stature and intelligence. He beholds with terror the extraordinary mental development of the child. Daily she grows more like her mother, until the father shudders at the "too perfect identity." When she is ten years old, he takes her to be baptized. When the priest asks what name the child is to have, many names occur to him, but irresistibly, inevitably he utters the name "Morella."

What more than fiend convulsed the features of my child, and overspread them with hues of death, as startling as that scarcely audible sound, she turned her glassy eyes from the earth to heaven, and, falling prostrate on the black slabs of our ancestral vault, responded—'I am here.'— She died; and with my own hands I bore her to the tomb; and I laughed with a long and bitter laugh as I found no trace of the first in the charnal where I laid the second—Morella.[228]

In both stories Poe develops the idea that the second woman takes the form of the first, while the first becomes incarnate in the second. At the basis of Poe's stories lie two ideas. The first is summed up in the quotation from Joseph Glanvill placed at the head of "Ligeia":

And the will therein lieth, which dieth not. Who knoweth the mysteries of the will, with its vigor? For God is but a will pervading all things by nature of its intentness. Man doth not yield himself to the angels, nor unto death utterly, save only through the weakness of his feeble will.

The second is indicated by Poe's references to Schelling's Doctrine of Identity, but Poe goes no further than to allude to the German philosopher. Of Identity he has no more to say than this: "But the *principium individuationis*—the notion of that identity *which at death is or is not lost forever*, was to me at all times, a consideration of intense interest"; and, as he admits in the same breath, "not more from the perplexing and exciting nature of its consequences, than from the marked and agitated manner in which Morella mentioned them."[229] Nor is there anything in Poe's writings to indicate that he was familiar with the whole of Schelling's philosophy. Since there is evidence that he knew Novalis, and since he could have gleaned from Novalis all the ideas which he relates to Fichte and Schelling (for Novalis's *Fragmente* abound in quotations and paraphrases of them[230]) we may reasonably presume, in the absence of evidence of more than a general acquaintance with the German philosophers, that he derived most of his information on that score from Novalis. Indeed, we can find every one of Poe's ideas about the relation between the philosopher and the poet, about the relation between will and the power to do, and about the relations of the living and the dead tersely phrased in Novalis' *Fragmente*.[231]

Poe wrote two other tales that may be designated love stories: "The Assignation" (1835), which exploits the theme of the unhappy love of Prospero for the Marchesa de Mentoni, and "The Oval Portrait" (1842), which combines the love theme with that of the jealousy of art as a mistress. The resemblance of Hoffmann's "Doge und Dogaressa" and Poe's "The Assignation" has been noted repeatedly,[232] but the relationship is one that can easily be overemphasized. The love plot, which Poe may have adapted from Hoffmann, itself differs in many particulars from Hoffmann's. The setting of both is Venice, but the descriptions are not close enough to argue that one is derived from the other. Indeed, Byron's *Marino Faliero* and Delavigne's were already written and could have suggested Poe's tale. The difficulty here is that both Byron and Delavigne make the conspiracy of the old Doge and his tragic end the subject of their dramas. Hoffmann and Poe disregard this element entirely, while making the fate of the Dogaressa and her young lover of paramount importance. A fair statement of the case seems to be that Poe may have been attracted to the subject by Hoffmann's story. Definite influence is hard to establish.

The source of "The Oval Portrait" is more easily detected. Again, it is Hoffmann, as Cobb has pointed out.[233] Poe's story grows out of his contemplation of a picture, a device often used by Hoffmann, and with particular effectiveness in "Die Jesuiterkirche in G——," which appears to be the source of Poe's story. Both stories are told in the first person. The narrator in both cases finds a remarkable portrait, so striking that he is led to inquire further concerning it. Both learn—Hoffmann from a professor, Poe from a book—that the portrait is that of the wife of the artist who painted the picture; and what follows in both stories is an account of the life of the artist, illustrating the thesis that the price of success in painting a picture of his beloved is the life

of its object. The relationship between the artist and his model, between lover and beloved, is the same, but Poe's story is more closely constructed and more impressive in its climax. Hoffmann's artist fails in his attempt to paint the Madonna-like features of his wife until he kills her. Her death speeds his success. Poe's painter succeeds in his aim to paint her perfect portrait. Following the last stroke of the brush, "the painter stood entranced before the noble work . . . but . . . while he gazed, he grew tremulous and very pallid, and aghast, and crying with a loud voice, 'This is indeed *Life* itself!' turned suddenly to regard his beloved:—*She was dead!*"[234] His success results in her death. By a slight shift in handling the same material, and by reducing the length of the story from twenty-five to four pages, Poe made his story far more impressive. He omits Hoffmann's long discourses on the subject of art, which give his story a didactic tone. While using the same motifs, he established a closer causal relationship between the successful completion of the painting and the death of the model, and thus realized more nearly the dramatic potentialities of the action.

TALES OF HORROR

We come, now, to Poe's tales of terror, four of which—"Metzengerstein" (1832), "The Fall of the House of Usher" (1839), "The Masque of the Red Death" (1842), and "The Cask of Amontillado" (1846)— appear in subject matter and in tone to have parallels in German stories.

"Metzengerstein," when it first appeared in 1836, bore the subtitle "In Imitation of the German." This designation and, still more, the subject matter of the tale invite the *Motivenjäger* to seek a German source for the story, especially since it turns upon the theory of metempsychosis, this time the incarnation of the spirit of a man in that of a horse. German romantics often treated this, or similar, themes.[235] Germanic in general atmosphere as the story undoubted-y is, and offender on the score of "German-sm and gloom" though it was, there appears to be no specific German source for it. Poe's arch-revenge story, "The Cask of Amontillado," involuntarily suggests Kleist's "Hermannschlacht,"[236] in which Kleist probably outdid Poe; but the materials are so different that the influence of one on the other is out of the question. The grim horror of "The Masque of the Red Death" provokes comparison with such tales as Tieck's "Liebeszauber"[237] and Hoffmann's 'Der Sandmann,"[238] as well as "Klein Zaches, genannt Zinnober,"[239] but again, the similarities are superfical. A closer relationship seems to obtain between "The Fall of the House of Usher" and Hoffmann's "Das Majorat." The name of the hero of both stories is Roderick, and Hoffmann's castle is similar to Poe's house of Usher.[240]

But these features are the very ones which Scott had emphasized in his article on Hoffmann in the *Foreign Quarterly Review*.[241] He noted that the Baron's name is Roderick, and that his lady is "young, beautiful, nervous, and full of sensibility."[242] Scott's depiction of the exterior of Hoffmann's castle coincides in a number of important details with those accentuated in Poe's story.[243] Most important is Scott's description of the "chasm, which extended from the highest turret down to the dungeon of the castle." Poe observes that a 'barely perceptible fissure which, extending from the roof of the building in front, made its way down the wall in a zigzag direction, until it became lost in the sullen waters of the tarn."[244] Poe emphasized this detail and returned to it for its unifying effect at the end of the story.[245]

If Poe's "House of Usher" owes its setting to Hoffmann's "Majorat," its plot is more nearly an adaptation of Arnim's "Die Majoratsherren." Arnim's *Majoratsherr* is a fanciful young man who sees the real world only through the fantastic creations of his mind. A dark power hangs over his life and causes him, already lacking in courage and will power, to become entirely unhappy and renders him unable to take an active part in life. He spends his nights in mystical studies and phantasmagoric reveries. Like Poe's Roderick, he is a musican and poet, engrossed in odd, old books. Like Roderick, he plays on stringed instruments and sings romantic songs to the accompaniment of the mandolin. Like Roderick, his hearing is remarkably acute, for he can hear noises entirely inaudible to others. Like Roderick, he shuns the light, spending the day in sleep and the night in his dimly lighted study.[246] Like Roderick, he can resolve nothing; an emergency requiring resolute action leaves him helpless. He knows that a girl, who lives near his old *Majorat*, is the rightful heir to the possessions which he holds; and though he loves the girl, he lacks, like Poe's Roderick, the ability to right the wrong, however hard he tries. Finally, he sees Esther, the girl, choked to death but fails to go to her rescue. Only after she is dead, does he go to her, and then it is merely to die.[247] Like Roderick, he suggests the last stage of human decadence.

The heroes of both Poe's and Arnim's stories are the last of an old, once noble line, whose fate appears determined. Unable to cope with circumstances, they drift with them, and fall a prey to their own weakness. Their fate is closely linked with that of the ancestral castle. Usher lives in dread of the gray walls of the house, with which he believes his fate inevitably connected; like Arnim's *Majoratsherr*, he lives in fear of the dark, unfathomable evil that connects him with the *Majorat*.[248] In both stories the lady is temporarily entombed, and in both stories the hero knows she is not really dead.[249] Finally, they have the opportunity to save the girl, but they let the opportunity pass for lack of energetic action. Both in the end find their death with the lady.[250] How or where Poe read Arnim's tale cannot be determined, but it is hardly possible that Poe's story was written entirely independently of Arnim's.

A fourth group of Poe's short pieces—sketches, descriptive pieces, anecdotes, loosely constructed tales, and *jeux d'esprit* —warrant brief attention. Professor Wächtler, always on the lookout for psychological kinship between Poe and the *Romantiker— Gesinnungsverwandtschaft* he calls it—points out that Poe's attitude toward nature is the same as Hoffmann's. He cites, in support of his observation, parallel passages from Poe's "Island of the Fay" and Hoffmann's "Der goldene Topf."[251] While there are obvious similarities, they are not distinctive, extending as they do, little beyond the coincidence that both saw in nature a reflection of their own thoughts and feeling, fancy and imagination—a common trait of the romantic mind. To argue that Poe learned his *Naturanschauung* from Hoffmann is to force matters.

Poe's sketches in the metaphysical-mystical vein—"The Conversation of Eiros and Charmion" and "The Colloquy of Monos and Una"—remind the reader of Jean Paul's "Über den Tod nach dem Tod."[252] As in Poe's studies, the characters discuss the sensations of dying, the bodily changes, and the life after death. Two lovers meet in Aideen and compare their experiences, indulging in mystical conjectures and arguments regarding the significance of their experiences, and of life and death. The difference in the German sketch is that the conversation is carried on by people thoroughly alive— the whole is a play of fancy in which they indulge.[253]

Two other pieces, "The Spectacles" (1844) and "The Sphinx" (1846), seem to have drawn on Germanic sources. "The Sphinx" suggests Hoffmann's "Heimatochare,"[254] in which a fly is mistaken for a woman through an optical illusion; but Poe's story, in which a fly is mistaken for a monster, was probably inspired by Butler's "Elephant in the Moon."[255] The other story in which a defective eyesight figures is "The Spectacles." The point of the story is that a young man, who is nearsighted, thinks he sees a beauti-

ful young woman, who in reality is his great-great-grandmother. He woos and weds the lady, and does not discover, until he puts on his spectacles, that she is an ugly old woman of eighty-two. Hoffmann uses a similar motif several times. In "Klein Zaches, genannt Zinnober," in "Prinzessin Brambilla," and in "Meister Floh," a glass is used to similar purpose. In "Der Sandmann," Coppola, a glass-fitter, sells the student Nathanael a small glass, which, when he sees Olimpia through it, changes her image into that of the most beautiful woman for him. His exulting at having found so prodigious a beauty is very like Poe's. Similar, also, is his rage on finding that she is only an *Automat*. The difference in the two stories is that Hoffmann's tone is serious, while Poe is trying to be funny. The theme itself is a relatively common one.

In "Bon-Bon" (1835), one of Poe's earlier productions, we have a story after Hoffmann's fashion, with characters, situations, setting, and humor in the approved Hoffmannesque manner, except that Poe exaggerates everything in it just enough to make it a travesty on German metaphysics and German *diablerie*.[256] Indeed, when J. P. Kennedy wrote to Poe on February 9, 1836, concerning the eight tales which had appeared in the *Messenger*, characterizing them as *bizarreries* and gently lecturing Poe for indulging in the extravagant vein,[257] Poe replied:

Most of them were *intended* for half banter. . . . 'Lionizing'[258] and 'Loss of Breath' were satires properly speaking—at least so meant—the one on the rage of Lions, and the facility of becoming one— the other of the extravagancies of Blackwood.[259]

Poe here refers to the German tales which were flooding the market. As early as the twenties Irving had spoken of the wild tales of the German type as "the commonplace of the day." A decade later they had grown wilder and had invade-even the most conservative of British magazines.[260] This type of literature ran counter to Poe's conceptions of literary art. "While the public was revelling in the *Blackwood's* type of tale steeped in 'Germanism and gloom,' while the metaphysical cult, especially in New England, was discussing Swedenborgian mysticism, and the transcendentalists were loading the magazines full of the intricacies of German trancendentalism, he resolved to write tales that would out-Herod Herod."[261] To his "Loss of Breath" travesty in the *Messenger* he added the subtitle, "A Tale à la Blackwood." In this story he presses the popular manner to the extreme. Chamisso had written "Peter Schlemihl" and Hoffmann "Das Abenteuer der Sylvesternacht," in which the heroes lost their shadows; Fouqué's Undine had lived without a soul; Hauff's Dutch Michael had done very well without a heart; and Faust and Tom Walker had disposed of their souls; he would tell of the man who lost his breath. In the *Messenger* version, the worst extravagancies of which were not retained by Poe in the final reprint of the tale in the *Broadway Journal*,[262] we see him carrying his travesty to the last extremity. The hero is maimed, mangled, crushed, hanged, and buried alive; but being without breath, it is impossible for him to breathe his last. Consigned to the tomb, he industriously opens all the coffins, exposes the contents, finds in one of them his lost breath, and taking possession of it, is rescued, none the worse for his adventures. This is outdoing the Germans at their worst. Later he wrote the extravaganza, "How to Write a Blackwood Article" (1838) and added the story, "A Predicament," to illustrate the method. Travesty and burlesque can hardly go further.

Literary Principles—Poe's Debt to Schlegel

It remains, now, to consider Poe's critical theories, with reference especially to his pronouncements on the unity of effect or singleness of impression[263]—dicta which, as has been pointed out, Poe himself did not always follow.[264] That Coleridge, when Poe first discovered the *Biographia Literaria*, made a profound impression upon him is certain.[265] Poe's "Letter to B——" of 1831 demonstrates the fact that Coleridge more than any other critic supplied Poe with the groundwork of his literary theory about the time his critical personality was developing. Yet, as Professor Campbell has observed, pervasive and significant as Poe's debt to Coleridge was, it was "largely unsubstantial"[266]—vague and atmospheric rather than specific and verbal. His indebtedness to Schlegel, on the other hand, was specific, pointed, and consequently more influential and significant.

Poe does not directly name or quote Schlegel before September, 1835[267] (when he does both), while reviewing for the *Southern Literary Messenger*[268] R. Potter's translation of Euripides. The review incorporates two paragraphs quoted from Schlegel's *Lectures* and four pages of adaptation so bold and ascription so vague as to constitute plagiarism.[269] Of special importance here is Poe's first reference to that Ideality which Schlegel had found to be the distinctive characteristic of Greek dramatic poetry.[270] He proceeded at once to interpret Schlegel's *Idealität der Darstellung* (Black translates it "Ideality of the representation") as comprising both "ideality of conception" and "ideality of representation." Seven months later, while appraising the poems of Drake and Halleck, "the Faculty of Ideality" had become for Poe synonymous with "the sentiment of Poesy" itself.[271] In the meantime (reviewing Mrs. L. H. Sigourney's *Zinzendorff and Other Poems* for the *Southern Literary Messenger* of January, 1836), Poe had made another significant reference to Schlegel—significant because it embodies his first statement of his favorite doctrines of brevity and singleness of tone or effect:

In poems of magnitude the mind of the reader is not, at all times, enabled to include in one comprehensive survey the properties and proper adjustment of the whole. . . . But in poems of less extent . . . the pleasure is *unique*, in the proper acceptation of that term—the understanding is employed, without difficulty, in the contemplation of the picture *as a whole*—and thus its effect will depend, in a very great degree, upon the perfection of its finish, upon the nice adaptation of its constituent parts, and especially upon what is rightly termed by Schlegel, "the unity or totality of interest."[272]

A few lines further on he speaks of "totality of effect," a variant readily derived from Schlegel's "totality of interest." This article of January, 1836, contains Poe's first, still vague, formulation of the theory which, in 1842, he embodied in the famous passage beginning:

A skillful literary artist has constructed a tale. If wise, he has not fashioned his thought to accommodate his incidents; but having conceived, with deliberate care, a certain unique and single *effect* to be wrought out, he then invents such incidents—he then combines such events as may best suit him in establishing this preconceived effect.[273]

What is noteworthy is that in 1835, and perhaps earlier, Poe had read Schlegel's *Vorlesungen* (either in the Black translation of 1815 or in the 1833 Philadelphia reprint),[274] for in that year we find him turning Schlegel into grist for his mill. More than that, he does just what Coleridge had done before him:[275] he copies or paraphrases passages from Schlegel's *Lectures* and passes them off as critical formulations of his own.[276] Poe's coming upon Schlegel was no mere accident, for in following the early volumes of *Blackwood's*, he became familiar not only with Hoffmann and Hoffmannesque tales but with the Schlegel brothers, notably August Wilhelm, whose literary principles Lockhart worked hard to domesticate in England through the columns of the magazine.[277] But if Poe had never seen

a copy of *Blackwood's*, his acquaintance with Coleridge's writings, notably the *Biographia Literaria*, would still have introduced him to Schlegel. While it seems plausible, as Professor Stovall points out,[278] that Poe's reading of Coleridge antedates his firsthand acquaintance with Schlegel, it is certain that by 1835 he had turned to Schlegel himself, for he quotes and paraphrases passages directly from Schlegel's *Lectures*—passages not be found in Coleridge's writings. Thus, while he obviously derived his characterization of a poem as "opposed to a work of science by having for its *immediate* object pleasure, not truth . . ."[279] from Coleridge's *Biographia Literaria* (Ch. XIV), where the phraseology is almost identical, it is clear that Poe's theory of the totality of effect or unity of impression is not derived from Coleridge, who does not advance such a theory except to offer a few vague intimations of unity of tone as it is implicit in the doctrine of organic unity. Coleridge was only a cognate source with Schlegel for Poe's all-important doctrine of unity from which stems practically the whole of Poe's mature thought, whether literary theory, cosmogony, or philosophy.[280] Long before Poe formulated his famous pronouncements on unity, in his critiques and in *Eureka*, he had, during the first year of his connection with the *Messenger*, read in Schlegel (and inserted into the magazine) Schlegel's famous comment regarding Aristotle on the three unities. The connection is made obvious when the relevant passages in Schlegel and Poe are compared:

SCHLEGEL (BLACK'S TRANSLATION, P. 337):

It is amusing enough to see Aristotle driven perforce to lend his name to those three Unities, whereas the only one of which he speaks with any degree of fullness is the first, the Unity of Action. With respect to the Unity of Time he merely throws out a vague hint; while of the Unity of Place he says not a syllable.

Southern Literary Messenger I, XII (AUG., 1835), 698

Aristotle's name is supposed to be authority for the three unities. The only one of which he speaks decisively is the unity of action. With regard to the unity of time he merely throws out an indefinite hint. Of the unity of place not one word does he say.

These passages, taken in conjunction with Poe's acknowledgments in two reviews of about the same time, leave little doubt that by 1835 Schlegel more than Coleridge was Poe's mentor. More particularly, Poe derived his theory of the short story from Schlegel's explanation and criticism of the conventional interpretation of Aristotle on the unities by simply adapting certain ones of Schlegel's principles of dramatic literature to the short story. In discussing the "three unities" attributed to Aristotle, Schlegel wrote:

De La Motte, a French author, who wrote against the Unities in general, would subsitute for Unity of Action, the *Unity of Interest*. If the term be not confined to the interest in the destinies of some single personage, but is taken to mean the general direction which the mind takes at the sight of an event, this explanation, so understood seems most satisfactory and very near the truth (p. 243).

"*Unity of interest* being the aim of the dramatist, how does he proceed?" asks Schlegel. "The object proposed," he answers, "is to produce an impression[281] on an assembled audience, to rivet their attention, and to excite their sympathy and interest. In this respect the poet's occupation coincides with that of the orator. How does the latter attain his end? By perspicuity, rapidity, and energy.[282] Whatever exceeds the ordinary measure of patience must be diligently avoided. . . .[283] The dramatic poet, as well as the orator, must from the very commencement,[284] by strong impressions,[285] transport his hearers out of themselves, and, as it were, take bodily possession of their attention."[286] Poe expresses the

same idea when he insists, in his review of Hawthorne's tales, that a short story shall not be so long as to produce weariness in the reader;[287] and subsequently in "The Philosophy of Composition," he limited the length of a poetical composition still more severely.[288]

Poe, whose literary theories appear to have been formulated in a manner generally to suit his own peculiar literary abilities, was naturally led to deduce from the doctrine of effect its corollary concerning the length of a poem or story, namely, that it should be short—so short that it could be read at one sitting. It is for this reason, according to Poe, that the poem of about one hundred lines and the short story afford the greatest opportunity for achieving excellence.[289]

Finally, Poe borrowed from Schlegel illustrations for his arguments, as, for instance, in the case of the *Iliad*, which both critics assert secures a certain unity of action and totality of effect, not from a cause-and-effect relationship of the events, or the logical sequence of incidents, but rather from a great number of impressions, each separate and distinct from the one that precedes and the one that follows, yet all tending, in the end, to produce an impression or effect on the mind much like the bas-reliefs on a vase, which, while they are seemingly incongruous and isolated, yet give us a sense of unity, a totality of effect.[290]

Just as Poe derived from Schlegel his doctrine of effect, so he found Schlegel useful in formulating the theory of unity which underlies all his metaphysical thinking, especially as it was finally embodied in *Eureka*. In "The Philosophy of Antiquity"[291] he cites Schlegel, Tennemann, Tiedemann, and Lamprière as his sources, concluding that the point which all these writers have in common is the concept of unity as the elementary principle of existence.[292] Margaret Alterton has pointed out that his immediate source was principally Tennemann's *Manual of the History of Philosophy*, for his phraseology is almost identical with that of Tennemann.[293] Eventually Alexander von Humboldt (to whom Poe dedicated *Eureka*), as well as the cosmological theories of Newton, Leibnitz, Mädler, Argelander, Laplace, Herschel, Ferguson, Dick, Coleridge, Whewell, and the encyclopaedic works (old and new), contributed something to Poe's theories embodied in *Eureka*, but basically *Eureka* had its inception in Poe's mind chiefly in the concept of unity as derived from Schlegel and Tennemann.

Thus Poe adapted not only themes and motifs from the German *Romantiker*, but appropriated from the foremost of the German critics his most important critical principle. It was Schlegel who most profoundly influenced Poe's sense of literary form and technique, and it was from Schlegel that Poe adduced the first, and to this day, the most important critical theory that has been formulated for the modern short story, although, in the end, its effect was rather to cramp than to enlarge the sphere of development of that genre.

From the very beginning the American short story has drawn important and valuable materials from German literature. It is only fair to add that what it borrowed it often improved. To be sure, Hoffmann and Tieck especially had already made a beginning by going a step beyond the simple hair-raising tales of sensationalism and Gothicism by putting an idea, or allegory, into their narratives. More often, however, German writers of short prose fiction were content to tell their tale for its telling effect with little concern whether there was an idea behind it or enough weight to carry it over. Of technique, in the sense in which Poe conceived it, they knew little, except that somehow, some way, the story must be written so as to hold the

reader's attention. In their attempt to do this, they frequently piled ghost on ghost, horror on horror, and absurdity on absurdity (the development of the *Novelle* as a more legitimate artistic form came later). Irving, in general, was content to take a German story and transfer it to America, as in the case of "Rip Van Winkle" or "The Legend of Sleepy Hollow," whose chief difference from their models (and their chief virtue) lies in the fact that Irving was astute enough to give his tales an authentic setting, flesh-and-blood characters, and a delightful style. Hawthorne, though he cannot be said to have borrowed much directly from the Germans, nevertheless used themes and materials which are decidedly Germanic. In his handling of these materials, he advanced a step beyond Irving by using the Germanic grotesquery merely as a flavoring, a dress in which to clothe his allegory or moral or idea; and Poe went another step, by adding a clear-cut, workable technique to the short story. Thus we have represented in Irving, Hawthorne, and Poe, the first three stages which German blood-and-thunder material underwent in being transformed into American short stories. Irving used the material as he found it, merely adding a native locale or local color; Hawthorne gave it carrying power and weight by adding an idea; and Poe contributed to the material, and the idea a definite technique in terms of an effect to be created. Thus far the Germanic motifs and materials were beneficent for the development of the American short story. For several generations, the form, as imposed by Poe, persisted, until later nineteenth-century writers—among them Mark Twain, Bret Harte, and Sidney Porter—revolting against the strait-jacketing of Poe's set form, struck out on new paths, in the pursuit of which Germanic materials appear to have been of little significance. In its later developments the American short story grew more original by becoming more strictly American.

Nineteenth Century Poets, Novelists, and Critics

EARLY POETS

Drake and Halleck

During the closing years of the eighteenth century American dramatists exploited the more sensational features of Schiller and Kotzebue, and writers of prose fiction created a *Werther*-fever of their own, but American lyric and narrative poets before Bryant remained singularly oblivious of Germany,[1] except for a series of adaptations spawned by the story of Werther and Charlotte, several poems on the *Lenore*-motif, and scattered poetical effusions inspired by the sentimentally pious fare of a Gessner or a Klopstock. Despite his wide reading and a tour of Europe, Joseph Rodman Drake (1795–1820) made only a passing reference to Germany.[2] His friend, Fitz-Greene Halleck (1790–1867), came nearer to German literature, though not near enough for it to produce any marked effect on his poetry. Indeed, when in 1847, the first illustrated edition of his poems appeared, he was commended for having remained true to the natural, indigenous tradition instead of surrendering to "the dreamy and fanciful school of poetry to which German literature has given birth" in recent years.[3] Actually, however, he more than once glanced in the direction of the novel effects created by the German school, though he did not find all specimens equally praiseworthy. He disapproved heartily of *Faust* as "coarse, impious and impure, licentious and blasphemous," but explained "My dislike to [*sic*] German literature is confined to the 'Faust' of Goethe—the worst book in the strongest sense of the word *worst* that I have ever read through."[4] For Schiller he had a real fondness,[5] and even Goethe was not altogether objectionable, for among the four extant translations or adaptations which he made of German poets, two are from Goethe. While these transliterations betoken a mild interest in German literature spanning a period of nearly forty years, they have little intrinsic importance beyond the pittance they added toward the means by which a steadily growing number of American readers became cognizant of German poetry.

James Gates Percival

A contemporary who did much more in this vein was James Gates Percival (1795–1856), a scientist, lexicographer, and student of literature, who also versified in thirteen languages—among them, German. During his later years at Madison, Wisconsin, where he was state geologist, he wrote more verse in German than in English. He learned German about 1820, presumably to read the linguists Bopp and Grimm. Next, he turned to the German philosophers and became one of the first Americans to read Kant in the original. Soon his interest spread to Kotzebue, Lessing, Bürger, Voss, and finally to all German writers.[6]

William Cullen Bryant

By 1835, when William Cullen Bryant (1794–1878) first centered his attention on the language and literature of Germany, the poems which every school boy knows and his *Lectures on Poetry*, which embody his basic and abiding principles of literature, had already been written a decade or more, and the main lines of his literary development were already well drawn. His turn to Germany produced no radically new directions in either his literary theory or practice; but, as we shall observe, it did lead to a general broadening and enrichment of his literary personality.

Germany, which before 1835 had been for Bryant little more than a geographical or political fact,[7] became an object of interest for him during the first of his six trips to Europe, on five of which he included Germany in his itinerary. On his first European tour (1835) he entered Germany by way of the Tyrol.[8] The interest thus aroused led him to compose and publish, over a period of almost forty years, translations of nine German poems[9]—exactly equaling the number of his translations from the Spanish. Although Bryant was, especially during the earlier years of his journalistic career, all but preoccupied with other matters, he kept at his German.[10] Professor Tremaine McDowell thinks that

Bryant's first visit to Germany encouraged him to "dabble in blood,"[11] in such poems as "The Strange Lady," "The Hunter's Vision," and "A Presentiment."[12] One later poem that can properly be regarded as written under Germanic influence is "The Song of the Sower" (1859). It is much like Schiller's "Song of the Bell" in form, in the order of thought, and in the universalization of its theme, the fruitfulness of labor. While there are a few verbal and figurative similarities, a closer relationship is recognizable in the general theme, the tone, and the structure of the two poems.

For the rest, Bryant manifested an active interest in German literature and Germany generally.[13] He appeared on a number of public occasions to pay tribute to German achievements, and became known as an enthusiast for German culture.[14] In his commanding position as editor of the *New York Evening Post* and as a poet and critic of weight and influence, Bryant helped signally in acclimatizing German literary culture by presenting to his fellow-Americans a once strongly suspect literature as the veritable embodiment of respectability and gentility, a knowledge of which came to be the mark of a cultivated man.

HENRY WADSWORTH LONGFELLOW
(1807–1882)

Among the major American men of letters of his generation Longfellow is most deeply imbued with the spirit of German sentiment and song; and that is so because, more than any other, he was by temperament naturally susceptible to German literary influence, because he lived himself into the life of Germany during his periods of residence there, and because he consciously indulged his fondness for German literature after his return from abroad.[15]

First Trip to Europe, 1826–1829

The mounting enthusiasm in the vicinity of Boston for German literature had not yet penetrated very deeply the quiet, orthodox atmosphere of Bowdoin when Longfellow graduated in 1825; but the offer of the newly created professorship of modern languages at his alma mater, together with the suggestion that the eighteen-year-old professor-elect prepare himself for the post by studying abroad for a year, resulted in his seeking the advice of George Ticknor, who urged him to include Germany in his itinerary.[16]

In Paris, where he spent the first eight months, he found it difficult to fix his attention on studious pursuits. Dissatisfied with his progress in French, he yearned for the reputedly more romantic Spain. His half-year in Spain was spent mainly in Madrid, where he did not neglect to get letters from Irving to Rumigny, Böttiger, and Löwenstein in Dresden. His father, reading between the lines of his son's letters and recognizing a vacillating, romantic state of mind, recommended industry and economy at the same time urging that he proceed to Germany: "the German language will be more important to you as a literary man than any two other languages." But young Longfellow managed by stratagems and excuses (valid and otherwise) to indulge his romantic fancies for a full year in Italy (chiefly in Rome) before yielding to his father's entreaties that he push on to Germany. Even a letter from his Bowdoin classmate, Ned Preble, announcing his arrival at Göttingen and urging Longfellow to join him, had little effect, until news from his father that Bowdoin had changed the offer of a professorship to an instructorship, at a greatly reduced salary, roused him out of his lethargy and recalled to him the need for making the most of the little time that remained for the acquisition of German. After a brief visit to Venice and Trieste, he set out via Vienna and Prague for Dresden, meanwhile debating whether to follow Irving's advice to settle there or to push on to Göttingen. Irving's advice bore weight, all the more now that he was forming ideas for a Sketch Book in imitation of Irving's.[17] But at the end of a month in Dresden he was lonesome, homesick, and generally discontented. Dresden, he concluded, held "several inconveniences for a studious life"; moreover, Ned Preble beckoned from Göttingen. After paying calls to those who had befriended him, he left Dresden and arrived in Göttingen on February 23, 1829.[18]

Arrival in Göttingen brought the realization that his pleasant tour of Europe, already of three years' duration, must end soon; it could not go on—"a song sung

between acts." He determined to put an end to all vacillation and stop gathering nosegays and picturesque impressions. When he asked himself whether he was as well qualified to teach the foreign languages and literatures as Professor Ticknor was teaching them at Harvard, he shuddered. So he set to work to make up as much of the lost time of the past three years as possible in the few months that remained. If the Bowdoin matter should turn out badly and he missed the professorship, he would be thrown altogether on his own resources. In his diary he wrote: "I've kept close to my studies, almost to not going out of the house, and not allowing my eyes to wander from my book to look at the beautiful and modest Miss Young, my compatriot who lives across the street."[19] What he did not say was that he was spending most of his time acquiring what he had neglected in France, Spain, and Italy, and that practically all the books which he was drawing from the University library dealt with the literatures of these countries rather than with German literature.[20]

It is difficult to make an accurate appraisal of his linguistic achievements at Göttingen. Despite his resolutions, he did not attend as closely to his studies as Ticknor or Cogswell before him had done. He left Göttingen with little of the *Sprachgefühl* that he acquired seven years later at Heidelberg; still he came away, after a month in Dresden and three months in Göttingen, with some facility in the language, as is evident from the numerous, usually idiomatically correct German passages with which the pages of his journals and letters are studded.[21]

The Bowdoin Period, 1829–1835

The controversy over his professorial rank and salary at Bowdoin having been settled to Longfellow's satisfaction, he entered upon his duties there in August of 1829, but soon found his position anything but a sinecure.[22] German had a less prominent place in the curriculum than French and Spanish, but he managed to keep alive his interest in the language and its literature. In the meantime, he returned to his plan, first formed at Göttingen, to write "a kind of Sketch-Book of France, Spain and Italy." By March 9, 1833, he had enlarged the scope to include Germany, and in July of the same year appeared the first number of *Outre-Mer*, published in book form in 1835. Concerned though he is in this book primarily with romance materials, yet his experiences in Germany contributed more than a dash of German flavor.[23]

In spite of his success as a teacher, the satisfactions of an academic career, and a happy marriage, Longfellow was never really contented at Bowdoin.[24] He was hardly settled when he began looking for a better post. Carefully prosecuted relations with his friends at Harvard came to a fruitful conclusion in December, 1834, when President Quincy informed him of Professor Ticknor's impending retirement from the Smith Professorship of Modern Languages and of Longfellow's election to the position. He concluded with the suggestion that Longfellow prepare himself for the office by going to Europe for "a year or 18 months" at his own expense "for the purpose of a more perfect attainment of the German."

Second European Tour, 1835–1836

On April 10, 1835, Longfellow and his wife, accompanied by Miss Clara Crowninshield and Miss Mary C. Goddard, sailed from New York for London, where they enjoyed a month of sight-seeing and literary sociality.[25] Before setting out for Germany, Longfellow and his party proceeded via Hamburg, Copenhagen, and Gothenburg, to Stockholm, where they arrived at the end of June and spent most of the summer.[26] On arriving at Amsterdam (October 1), following a rough passage, his wife

was brought to the verge of death by the premature birth of her child, and the party was detained for nearly a month before proceeding via the Hague and Delft to Rotterdam, where Mary Longfellow again fell ill. While awaiting her expected recovery, he busied himself with Dutch, already begun at Amsterdam, and made occasional forays also into the Scandinavian literatures.[27] So he kept himself occupied until November 24, when his wife took a turn for the worse. Five days later she died. Distraught, he made the last arrangements for sending her body to America, and on December 2 he left, with Clara Crowninshield, for Heidelberg, where he hoped that immersion in books would occupy his mind to the exclusion of all other thoughts.

He proceeded rapidly up the Rhine and on December 11 arrived in Heidelberg,[28] where he took lodgings in the pleasant home of Frau Himmelhahn, who appears under that name as the aged Heidelberg gossip in the first edition of *Hyperion* (altered to "old Frau Himmelauen" in later editions).[29] Suffering the pangs of self-accusation and remorse for having insisted on leaving at once on the European journey against the advice of his parents, and well-nigh crushed by his loss, he sought forgetfulness in serious study. He had come well provided with letters to Heidelberg celebrities, and there was a round of visitations to professorial homes.[30] He lost no time resuming his study of the language, and before the end of 1835 could "hold his own eloquently in German discussions."[31]

In the area of modern German literature Longfellow contented himself for the time being with browsing more or less at random, as when, on December 18, he busied himself with a "little work containing Schleiermacher's Letters on Friedrich Schlegel's romance of *Lucinde*." But with the beginning of the new year, he began a more systematic study of German literature[32]— in pursuit of a plan to prepare a "Handbook" or "Syllabus" of the "Literature of the

Middle Ages" from the close of the fifth to the end of the fifteenth century.[33] Beyond this systematic study of earlier German literature, his diary reveals that he read a remarkable array of works.[34] Among them all, Goethe affected him most profoundly. With Clara he selected sixteen of the best of Goethe's lyrics for her album and himself read widely enough to catch the essential spirit of German lyric poetry.[35]

However important his discovery of the lyrical quality of German song was for the development of his own poetic craftsmanship, what is of more immediate significance is the effect upon him of his discovery of the deeper meaning of Goethe. He read *Faust* (with Clara), *Egmont*, *Werther*, *Wilhelm Meister*, Eckermann's *Gespräche*, *Dichtung und Wahrheit*, "Das Märchen", and *Die Geschwister*. The last, "trifling" though he considered its literary merits, yet contained "one or two touches of pathos, that brought tears into my eyes, and recalled the affection and devoted love of one that is gone."[36] He devoured *The Sorrows of Werther* and, though admitting that "such books are not favorites of mine" because they "leave in the soul . . . unrest and pain," he found the language and imagery "beautiful," and insisted that persons possessing "intellect" and "tenderness of heart" found the "peculiar tone of such books" altogether "ideal."[37] The sentiment of German romantic literature presented a mood that he could appropriate to his own heartache. He found his mood most perfectly reciprocated in Novalis, the young tragic poet who had wept alone over the grave of his beloved in the twilight and composed "Hymns to the Night" very much like some of the *Voices of the Night* that were beginning to shape themselves in the mind of the young American poet who also had loved and lost. He began to understand the language of the German romantic sentiment and to accept the mystical communion which Novalis established with the spirit of his departed beloved in the holy solitude of night.[38] The *Sturm-und-Drang* literature of sentiment perfectly accorded with his mood; and he read into *Werther*, *Meister*, *Faust I*, Fouqué's *Undine*, Jean Paul's *Titan*, and Novalis' *Heinrich von Ofterdingen* the story of his own life. The tragedy of Mary Longfellow's death was a humanizing experience that developed his emotional susceptibilities and prepared him for the keener intellectual perceptions and spiritual insights which he was soon to develop under the stimulus of Goethe's more strenuous doctrine of renunciation and persistence.[39]

As he read the German romantic poets, he saw a great diversity among them—even within individual ones of them. For example it seemed odd that Werther and Wilhelm Meister could both have been conceived by the same mind. The affinity that Longfellow's bleeding heart felt for the sorrowing Werther was neutralized by the New Englander's dislike of Werther's motives and actions. They seemed weak, pagan, terrible.[40] A work like *Wilhelm Meister* left an entirely different effect on his mind. It taught a doctrine of resolution, faith, work, and presented a pattern of conduct which Longfellow could appropriate to himself. Meister's life and Goethe's simple lyrics taught him much that he would not have understood a year earlier.[41] But he worked too steadily and soon felt exhausted. When Greene's young cousin, gay Samuel Ward, paused in his travels at Heidelberg, he awakened in Longfellow the *Wandertrieb*, which the approach of spring conspired to augment. He made several short excursions,[42] but by June 20 he recorded in his diary: "Torpor steals over me again. . . . My mind has lost its sensibility and does not feel the spur. I cannot study: and therefore think I had better go home." But because his friend Greene was still in Italy, he decided to travel through Austria, Switzerland, and across the Alps, instead of proceeding directly for America. Leaving Heidelberg on June 25, he began what proved a joyless trip, all set down later in *Hyperion* with sufficient circumstantiality to serve as a guidebook for any traveler who wishes to follow the same route.[43] Toward the end of July he joined the Appletons; two days later he wrote: "I now for the first time enjoy Switzerland," while Frances Appleton confided to her diary: "Have a nice walk with Mr. Longfellow to the old bridge. . . . Sketched. . . . A nice talk, delicious twilight." They sketched, they walked, they read poetry together: "Uhland and Count Auersberg [*sic*], till dinner." Longfellow accompanied them for a week of travel to Lake Lucerne, Zürich, and Schaffhausen.

My propitious star [he wrote] placed me in Mr. Appleton's travelling carriage with the two young ladies, who are all intellect and feeling. I cannot say what kind of country we passed through, for I hardly looked from the carriage window. . . . Our conversation was all that is gentle and fair; and we read the *Genevieve* of Coleridge, and the *Christabel*; and many other scraps of song; and the little German ballads of Uhland, simple and strange. And all this to me is a passion—a delight, strong and unchanging.

Fanny wrote more laconically: "Read German, Coleridge, etc., all the morning and saw no scenery." Later in the day, Longfellow's soul was still "filled with peace and gladness," but not many hours later came the enigmatic observation: " . . . and finally—Damnation."[44] This passage, read in conjunction with Book III, Chapter IX, of *Hyperion*, suggests that the young widower had overreached himself by the expression of some ardent sentiment and had been effectively checked by the young lady from Beacon Street. However, the journey went on, and so did the joint sketching, reading, and translating.[45] After nearly three weeks of such pleasant occupations, they stopped at Schaffhausen, where he received a peremptory letter from the faithful Clara (still in Heidelberg, and "out of patience waiting for an escort to Amer-

ica") that recalled him to his duty. Conscience-stricken, he tore himself away, and in three days reached Heidelberg, whence, a week later, they went via Paris to Le Havre and sailed on October 8, 1836.[46]

Cambridge, 1836–1842

Early in December, 1836, Longfellow took lodgings at Dr. Stearns' in Professors' Row in Kirkland Street, Cambridge, where C. C. Felton, the professor of Greek, also had his quarters, and prepared for his duties that were to begin with the opening of the second college term in January, 1837. However arduous his work became later, for the time being he had little to do but prepare a course of lectures.[47] He found time to see a good deal of Boston society and to act and dress the part of a dandy—enough to occasion some criticism in the sober Cambridge community; he seldom found it necessary to study at night.[48] Meanwhile he worked leisurely on a "course of lectures on German literature, to be delivered next summer": "I do not write them out, but make notes and translations. . . . In this course something of the Danish and Swedish (the new feathers in my cap) is to be mingled."[49]

On May 23, 1837, at the beginning of what was called the "first summer term," he gave the first of his series of "public Lectures." Seniors were required to attend, and members of the Law and Divinity schools were admitted. The discourses were liberally interspersed with translations (including his own), ranging from short pieces from Matthisson to a four-page selection of what Professor Hatfield calls "a rather astounding attempt at a translation of the original Hildebrandslied."[50]

Among the manuscript materials preserved in Craigie House are two bulky sets of lecture notes that can be identified with these early discourses. The notes on Goethe are the most extensive of the lot—as they should be. It is worth observing that in thus emphasizing Goethe, Longfellow was making an innovation at Harvard, for Goethe was still very much suspect, and Dr. Follen earlier had concentrated on Schiller and Körner, so that Longfellow was the first to introduce him effectively there.[51] His opinion of Goethe the man and poet was one of increasing sympathy. The unanimity of critical opinion against Goethe played its part in setting him against certain aspects of Goethe at the beginning; for, though he arrived at some of his judgments independently,[52] he neither exhibited much boldness or originality as a critic nor showed much interest in first principles and accordingly found it relatively easy to accept established opinion. Constitutionally conservative, he fell easily into the grooves of the genteel tradition as it was being formalized among his immediate friends at Harvard. He owed these men everything—including his position. And when he went with Felton to call on the Rev. Andrews Norton, he stepped warily when the discussion turned to the latest "infidel" philosophy of Germany which the "transcendental" Emerson was just now making bold to proclaim within the hallowed precincts of Harvard halls. When Norton thundered against the "Newness," Longfellow, who had neglected to inquire into these matters while in Germany, found it easier to nod a quiet assent than to offer contrary opinions on a subject about which he knew little. He must have felt that much of what was charged against the new school of thought was owing to traditional prejudice, but he was not one to speak out of turn. Similarly, when in the spring of 1839, Professor Felton brought over to Craigie House (whither Longfellow had transferred his quarters in August of 1837) his translation of Menzel's *History of German Literature*, seeking Longfellow's help and advice, Longfellow, whose lectures showed him forming a steadily more sympathetic and liberal attitude toward Goethe, suffered a relapse of critical opinion. Menzel's critical judgments of Goethe

seemed authoritative; and rather than trust to his own lights, Longfellow, then engaged on *Hyperion*, chose to present for public inspection the established opinions of Menzel rather than his own faltering conclusions. As things turned out, it was well that the book did not stir up a literary, or moral, controversy over Goethe, for the sentimental issue between himself and Frances Appleton (thinly veiled in the romance between Paul Fleming and Mary Ashburton) made trouble enough. But the fact remains that from a critical point of view, at least where Goethe is concerned, *Hyperion* is a botch. The real opinion of Longfellow is mixed up with that of Wolfgang Menzel and of current American judgment in degrees and proportions to leave the impression blurred. Paul Fleming, generally to be identified with Longfellow, usually represents the conservative moralist's point of view, which leads him to condemn Goethe's private life and the "immorality" of his works, while praising his craftsmanship. In the end, although many attitudes are presented, nothing is settled. The only conclusion possible is that Longfellow, at the age of thirty-two, did not know his own mind, or if he did, dared not avow it.

At the beginning of Chapter VIII of Book II, the Baron, generally Goethe's advocate, sets the stage for the argument by proclaiming "Goethe was a magnificent fellow."

Only think of his life; his youth of passion, alternately aspiring and desponding, stormy, impetuous, headlong;—his romantic manhood, in which passion assumes the form of strength; assiduous, careful, toiling, without haste, without rest [Goethe's 'Ohne Hast . . . ohne Rast'];—and his sublime old age,—the age of serene and classic repose, where he stands like Atlas, as Claudian painted him in the Battle of the Giants, holding the world aloft upon his head, the ocean-streams hard frozen in his hoary locks.[53]

Granted [replies Fleming]. What you glorify is what the world calls his indifferentism. It is precisely that in him, this cold detachment and self-culture in him, that I condemn.

And do you know [says the Baron] I rather like this indifferentism? Did you never have the misfortune to live in a community, where a difficulty in the parish seemed to announce the end of the world? or to know one of the benefactors of the human race, in the very storm and pressure period of his indiscreet enthusiasm? If you have, I think you will see something beautiful in the calm and dignified attitude which the old philosopher assumes.

An interesting example of how Longfellow transferred materials from his lectures to the book *Hyperion* is found in the concluding passage of his introductory lecture on Goethe:

And now tell me, young men, what do you think of it? From your own experience in the world—is it not best to take things coolly? . . . Have you never been in a troublesome community where a difficulty in the parish seemed to announce the end of all things? Have you never had the misfortune to know a fussy, indiscreet individual, whose bread-and-butter enthusiasm almost made you fall on your knees and implore peace? . . . How calmly the philosopher stands amid all this and says: that the best way to reform the world is to do one's own duty, and not the duty of others. Let each one labor in his sphere![54]

It would seem that while many of his friends still withheld their enthusiasm for Goethe's philosophy of life, Longfellow was viewing Goethe indulgently and with enough sympathy to defend him before his students. But obviously, these sentiments, uttered before adolescents in the semi-privacy of a classroom, was one thing; to publish them, where adults might read the opinions of Paul Fleming, whom everybody would identify as the Smith Professor at Harvard, was another matter. Prudence as the better part of valor won: the German Baron, who was beyond the reach of public attack, became the mouthpiece of these disturbing, if not dangerous, opinions; while the Harvard Professor preferred to have himself interpreted as repeating the

moral platitudes of contemporary gentility. One would like to believe that some of Paul Fleming's utterances are made tongue-in-cheek, but the instances where Longfellow braved the prevailing winds of doctrine are so few that the possibility is hardly admissible.

After Fleming expressed the wish that more of Goethe's defenders and defamers might practice Goethe's "philosophic coolness," instead of heaping ridiculous titles and epithets upon him,[55] the Baron observes "I confess he was no saint." Fleming, picking up the cue, does precisely what he has just condemned in the critics of Goethe, and breaks forth with some vehemence: "What I most object to . . . is his sensuality." The Baron has his answer ready (and there is something of Longfellow's own opinion in what he says): "Oh nonsense! Nothing can be purer than the Iphigenia. . . . Goethe is an artist, and looks upon all things as objects of art merely." Still Fleming demurs: "The artist shows his character in the choice of his subject. Goethe . . . gives us only sinful Magdalens and rampant Fauns. He does not so much idealize as realize." To this the Baron replies simply, "He only copies nature."

Here again the Baron has appropriated portions of the lecture notes of Professor Longfellow, who, discussing Goethe's style, spoke from the following notations:

Style: Looked upon all things as objects of art. Realized, not idealized. Reflection of earth lies nearer us than that of heaven. We take little thought of the moral impression. All we can require of the artist is not to choose immoral themes.

Naturalness. No effect, no struggle for effect.

"Immer hab' ich nur geschrieben
Wie ich's fühle, wie ich's meine."[56]

On the score of Goethe's philosophy of art, Professor Longfellow was ready to play the devil's advocate before his students; but in *Hyperion* he judiciously put such sentiments into the mouth of the irresponsible Baron. Fleming goes on to belabor Goethe, but is ready to agree that Menzel "goes too far" when he blames Goethe for being neither "politician" nor "missionary."[57] The running argument between Fleming and the Baron continues with further references to Goethe's life, his fame and influence, and finally ends when, passing a shop and seeing a full-length cast of Goethe in the display window, Fleming says: "But let us step in here. I wish to buy that cast." This is a poetization of Longfellow's buying in 1836 at Heidelberg the statuette of Goethe which stood, and still stands, on Longfellow's high study desk in Craigie House.

What has been detailed of Longfellow's patchwork process of bookmaking in the chapter on Goethe applies also to other chapters in *Hyperion*, notably those on Jean Paul, on the Lives of the Scholars, and on Literary Fame, all in Book I. The same method is used in the sketch of an artist's life in Rome and the picture of the Middle Ages (both in Book III) and in the chapter on Hoffmann of the last book.

During the second term of his second year at Harvard (1837–1838) Longfellow began his course on Dante,[58] and another on "Literature and Literary Life" was initiated on May 2, 1838. Precisely what the course included is not clear because the notes are no longer intact. Apparently he placed particular stress on German authors, the extant notes on Goethe, Jean Paul, Hoffmann, Tieck, Engel, and German popular tales being especially detailed and complete. The extent and proportion in which these were combined for the several courses during the years cannot now be determined,[59] but we can generalize regarding his lectures on German subjects to this extent: they show Longfellow "as a pioneer and prophet in the systematic presentation of German writers to the American public." His estimates, not usually profound, sometimes show an "uneven" or "disproportionate" emphasis,[60] but errors are rare, and

his judgments are fresh, derived from first-hand reading of primary sources. He steered clear of the "misty or rhapsodic phrases of the German critics," though in their delivery his lectures were perhaps a bit too much in the nature of "a dish of delicious and dainty devices," or, as young Hale put it, "too flowery."[61] On rare occasions the young professor permitted his erudition to get the better of his good sense of sound classroom technique by bringing in far-fetched allusions or questionable derivations; yet, on the whole, he succeeded in maintaining a sprightly style and avoiding the conventionally academic tone. In his first lecture on Goethe he stated his purpose and kept it steadily in mind in a manner that would delight the lesson-planners of today: it was to show "how Goethe, from a buoyant, cloud-capt youth, perfected himself, into a free, benignant, lofty-minded man." To illustrate, he translated the "Wanderer's Song in a Storm," and by way of recapitulation, he said:

In Goethe's development there are three periods:
(1) 1749–1776: Youthful passion, aspiring, desponding, infinite longings.
(2) 1776–1786: Fiery passion under control; passion assumes form of strength.
(3) 1786–1832: Classic repose: 'to stand like Atlas in the Battle of the Giants.' This last period is the important one.[62]

All in all, Longfellow's novel manner of introducing German writers to college students was a radical departure from the traditional pedagogic procedure.[63]

Obviously Goethe had a sympathetic and learned friend in this young professor, who worked seriously and lovingly at his task of indoctrinating successive classes of Harvard undergraduates, and who, if he had had more allies in equally strategic positions elsewhere, would have materially advanced the day when Goethe received an unprejudiced reception in America. Interested as

Longfellow was in many German writers, there was never, after he went to Cambridge, any doubt in his mind about Goethe's pre-eminence; and as his annual Goethe lectures became an institution, the feeling grew that not Schiller or Heine, not Luther or Kant, but Goethe was the German mind most deserving of attention.[64] While the regular repetition of his lectures on Goethe and the attendant steady mental occupation with his life and work alone might have led Longfellow eventually to jockeying himself into the position of regarding Goethe supreme, there were other, intrinsically more valid reasons for his championship of Goethe. However unlike he and Goethe were, Longfellow developed, especially during his own years of Storm and Stress (just before his second marriage) an ever growing and deeper appreciation of the applicability of Goethe's key doctrines to his own problems. As his aesthetic suscepti-bilities enlarged and his moral perceptions became liberalized (both partially under Goethean influence), Goethe the "Old Heathen" or "Old Humbug" assumed the stature, first, of a worldly-wise "German Horace,"[65] perhaps only "a rhymed Ben Franklin,"[66] but withal "a glorious speci-men of a man";[67] next, "the greatest name in German literature"[68] and finally, a "god,"[69] for whom he acknowledged having as late as 1871, "an ever-ascending regard."[70]

Longfellow never found his position at Harvard an easy one, and during the years before 1843, when his persistence finally broke down Frances Appleton's resistance, he endured frustration, unrest, indecision, and inner conflicts in proportions and de-grees symptomatic of Teutonic *Sturm und Drang*. His immersion in the romantic literature of Germany did much to nourish his perturbation. His love of Frances Appleton, nurtured amid the romantic surroundings of their first meeting in Ger-many, remained invested in the sentiment of German romance. Rebuffed, yet unwill-

ing to give up, he carried on a correspond-ence with Mary Appleton regarding their common interests in Heine, German popu-lar tales, *Faust*, and his literary plans (which seem to have included a design to write "a Faust-in-New-England sort of play"), and did not neglect to intimate his hope that Mary would intercede in his behalf with her sister. Choosing the German idiom as appropriate to the sentiment he hardly dared express, he wrote:

Ach, du schöne Seele! Es wird mir gar traurig zu Muthe, wenn ich daran denke, und sehe, wie der schöne Traum dahin zieht,—wie die Wolke sich theilt, und in Thränen zerfliesst, und um mich wird alles so leer, und in meiner Seele eine dunkle Nacht—eine dunkle sternlose Nacht!—Und dass [sic] hab' ich Dir auf Deutsch sagen müssen, weil eine fremde Sprache ist eine Art von Dämmerung und Mondlicht, worin man den Frauenzimmern allerlei sagen kann —und so herzlich treu! Eben so herzlich grüsse mir die liebe, liebe Fanny, die ich immer liebe, wie meine eigene Seele. Ach! dass [sic] bisschen Verstand, das einer ha-ben mag, kommt wenig oder gar nicht in Anschlag, wenn Leidenschaft wüthet. Wie wird mir das Herz so voll!—Das letzte Mal, das wir zusammen waren, gingen wir aus einander ohne einander verstanden zu haben: denn 'auf dieser Welt keiner leicht den andern versteht.' Und dass [sic] is gar zu traurig.[71]

The quotation near the end of this pas-sage is from the last sentence in Werther's letter, dated August 12, and the whole is cast into a decidedly Wertherish tone—a reflection of his reading. There can be no doubt that his lovesickness was real enough, but the record of that period of Long-fellow's life as revealed by Professor Thompson and as reflected in *Hyperion* makes it equally clear that his unhappiness was aggravated rather than assuaged by the literature of sentiment and romance in which he dwelt. Searching for a course of action that should alleviate his suffering, he only worked himself deeper into his gloomy thoughts. With Hawthorne he planned a book of tales and legends to be called *The*

Wonder Horn. Its relation to the Arnim-Brentano *Wunder-Horn*, which had thrilled him at Heidelberg, is not hard to discover, but nothing came of the plan. Numerous other literary projects all came to naught. Nothing could draw his attention for long from the unapproachable "Dark Ladie" in Beacon Street, and, what was almost as bad, his recurring moods of grief and loss and disturbing questionings regarding what the future course of his life should be—poet, teacher, scholar, or what? Sitting disconsolately in his Craigie House study and pondering the past and the future, life and death and the life hereafter, as he did with increasing frequency since Mary's death, he lapsed, on the evening of his thirty-first birthday, into that vague mood, compounded of nighttime and otherworldliness which he had found so moving in Novalis and Matthisson. Sorrow, which had taught him to look into his heart, also drove him into a dream-world refuge where the mystical experiences of the night conjured up "forms of the dear departed," a "Being Beauteous," who entered at the open door to take "the vacant chair" beside him and to "lay her gentle hand" in his. This is the mood that evoked the poem, "Evening Shadows," in which, following Novalis, he sought a kind of escape into the twilight of a world of phantoms that only prolonged his agony.

In the meantime his occupation with Goethe, notably *Faust, Wilhelm Meister,* and *Dichtung und Wahrheit,* taught him Goethe's sterner lesson of growth, through control of passion, to ultimate peace. But he found it easier to tell his students to emulate Goethe's perseverance in the struggle for self-conquest by doing what lies near than to follow that gospel himself. He struggled against morbidity and told himself repeatedly that one must "bear one's self doughtily in Life's battle and make the best of things" as they are. While reading *Wilhelm Meister* he wrote into his diary the maxims which had enabled Wilhelm to progress from an apprentice to a craftsman: "A man is never happy till his vague striving has marked out its proper limitation." "It is not of yourself that you must think, but of what surrounds you." "The safe plan is, always simply to do the task that lies nearest us."[72] In *Faust* (ll. 558–59) he found repeated the famous motto of Hippocrates, "Life is short, and art is long," that he had himself quoted in *Outre-Mer.*[73] So he concluded, "Art is long, life short, judgment difficult, opportunity transient—therefore, be doing."[74] Saturated with these ideas, he tried, on June 27, 1838, to set down this creed in "A Psalm of Life."[75] That this adaptation of Goethe's so-called *carpe diem* philosophy, combined with the *Tätigkeit* morality of *Faust* and *Meister,* was conscious appears in his first reading the poem at the close of one of his lectures on Goethe, evidently intending to emphasize the part of Goethe's message that impressed him most forcibly at the time. That it did so impress him is evident from his own observation: "I kept it ['A Psalm of Life'] for some time in manuscript, unwilling to show it to anyone, it being a voice from my inmost heart, at a time when I was rallying from depression."[76]

The parallels in a few instances are verbal. Goethe's "Die Kunst ist lang, und kurz ist unser Leben"[77] is very close to Longfellow's "Art is long, and Time is fleeting."[78] And his line, "Let the dead Past bury its dead" is close enough to Goethe's "Lass das Vergangene vergangen sein" (*Faust I,* l. 4518) to be recognized as an influence. Other parallelisms are not strictly verbal; yet one senses in the entire stanza in which the last-quoted line appears at once a reminiscence and a re-embodiment of the oft-repeated counsel of Goethe:

> Trust no Future, howe'er pleasant!
> Let the dead Past bury its dead!
> Act, — act in the living Present!
> Heart within, and God o'erhead![79]

But his battle was far from won, however often he told himself he must work in the present, must write himself clear of his troubles. There was no dearth of plans and projects,[80] none of which materialized except that his "Psalms" and "Ballads" were appearing in the newspapers and that his romance *Hyperion* (presenting the pageant of his bleeding heart) was given to the public in August of 1839. "I have written a Romance during the last year," he announced to his friend Greene, "into which I have put my feelings, my hopes and sufferings for the last three years. . . . The book is a reality; not a shadow or a ghostly semblance of a book."[81]

He had noticed in Goethe's life the same central idea upon which *Faust* and *Wilhelm Meister* turn. Following Goethe's example in the latter, he set himself to write an *Entwicklungsroman*, largely autobiographical in nature and showing "the passage of a morbid mind into a purer and healthier state."[82] *Hyperion* develops the same central theme already expressed in "A Psalm of Life." Both illustrate his tendency to identify his own problems with those expressed in his favorite German books. In his Harvard lectures he dwelt on the threefold pattern of growth as exhibited in Goethe's character and as developed alike in *Faust*, in *Wilhelm Meister*, and in *Dichtung und Wahrheit*.[83] Carefully pondering the message, he grasped and appropriated to his own problem Goethe's emphasis on the ennobling power gained through suffering. Already he felt better, and writing to Hillard, he spoke of his happy recovery from his "late serious accident in Beacon street"; yet characteristic of his still fluctuating moods, he closed the letter with a quotation from *Wilhelm Meister*:

Who ne'er his bread in sorrow ate
    Who ne'er the mournful midnight hours
Weeping upon his bed has sate,
    He knows you not, ye heavenly powers.[84]

The genetic relation between *Wilhelm Meister* and *Hyperion* is suggested by his using this quatrain as the motto for the first

edition of *Hyperion*. Complementary evidence appears in the Baron's characterization of Paul Fleming:

. . . you have a rakish look . . . you carry a cane, and your hair curls. Your gloves, also, are a shade too light for a strictly virtuous man. . . . Why the women already call you Wilhelm Meister.[85]

When Longfellow first reached Cambridge, he affected the dress and manner of Wilhelm Meister, so that in the staid and sober Cambridge society he "was not exempt from some social criticism"; and when he applied to Mrs. Craigie for rooms, she thought he had "somewhat too gay a look," and supposing him a student, at first refused to take him in.[86] In 1840, recalling the figure he had cut in Heidelberg society during the winter of 1835–1836, while participating in musical evenings and whist parties at the Hepp home, he sent a letter to the sprightly Julie Hepp, which he signed significantly "Wilhelm Meister":

Meine liebe Freundin!

Der Überbringer dieses ist der Herr Shaw aus Boston. Er wird den Winter in Heidelberg zubringen, und ich weiss ihm kein grösseres Vergnügen dort zu verschaffen als ihre Bekanntschaft. Er ist von einer sehr ansehnlichen Familie, hat viel Talent, und einen schönen Charakter. Ich bin überzeugt dass Er Ihnen gefallen wird.

Ich danke Ihnen recht sehr für Ihren lieben Brief des 26 Feb. Immer mit Freude denk' ich mich in Heidelberg zurück: und wahrscheinlich werden wir uns noch einmal dort treffen. Das wird aber nicht diesen Winter geschehen, also schicke ich Ihnen diesen jungen Freund um meinen Platz in ihrem Herzen und in den Whist Parthien zu behalten bis ich wiederkomme. Unterdessen rede ich mit Ihnen in den *Stimmen der Nacht* die ich Ihnen hinüber schicke, als ein Hauch von meiner Seele.

Ade! liebes Fräulein! Meine schönsten Empfehlungen an die Frau Mutter, Evchen und Eduard. Clara [Crowninshield] ist in Portland, dreissig Meilen von hier; immer wohl und immer geheimnisvoll, wie die Heldin eines französischen Romans.

Und so gute Nacht! Mit treuer Anhäng-
lichkeit, Ihr ganz ergebener

Wilhelm Meister[87]
Cambridge, den 28. Sept. 1840.

These circumstances help to explain why
Longfellow proceeded to depict in *Hyperion*
his bewilderment and loneliness following
the death of Mary and the turmoil of mind
occasioned by his unrequited love for
Frances Appleton in terms of the soul of a
youth, sustained by high aspirations, sur-
mounting all suffering and reaching a
victory far greater than Werther's "shoot-
ing-himself"—more like Wilhelm Meister's
triumph over vain strivings to attain the
victory. From this point of view, which (as
Longfellow said) "is *the* point,"[88] *Hyperion*
is but another sermon preached on the same
text of renunciation, practicality, and
action—already embodied in the "Psalms."

To supplement his travel experiences,[89]
Longfellow added the fruits of his intensive
reading at Heidelberg.[90] Especially noteworthy in this connection are the German
lyrics and the spirit of German song that
pervades the entire book. The Baron, "in
morning gown and purple-velvet slippers,"
is discovered lying on the sofa, strumming
the guitar and "humming his favorite song
from Goethe:

The water rushed, the water swelled,
A fisher sat thereby."[91]

And it is with equal naturalness that the
Polish Count serenades Emma of Ilmenau,
in a manner and under circumstances like
those in the scene of *Faust* where Mephistopheles sings before Margaret's door. In
this instance the song is "those beautiful
lines which Goethe wrote on the wall of the
summer-house at Ilmenau," which Longfellow renders

O'er all the hill tops is quiet now!
In all the woodlands hearest thou
    Hardly a sound!
The little birds are asleep in the trees;
Wait! wait! and soon, like these,
    Sleepest thou.[92]

For the rest, he incorporated into his
romance long sections of his college lectures
on Goethe and Jean Paul, Hoffmann and
others, usually casting them into the form
of argumentative conversations between
Fleming and the Baron. To enliven the
book he liberally introduced anecdotal
material drawn from the lives of German
literary men. The most obvious stylistic
influence on *Hyperion* is that of Jean Paul,[93]
rather in the nature of a momentary susceptibility to the stylistic features of Richter than an abiding influence. None of Longfellow's later works exhibits a like influence. What goes more directly to the heart
of the book—its burden of thought, or its
central idea—is more properly related to
Goethe. As Goethe had demonstrated in his
own life, as well as in *Faust, Wilhelm Meister*, and *Dichtung und Wahrheit*, so it was
Longfellow's intention to portray a restless
and agitated youth, filled with indefinite
longings and unrealizable yearnings in an
unknown Future, working his way out of
doubt, irresolution, and despair, by Goethe's
calm gospel of renunciation and the simple
philosophy of working in the Present.[94]

In so far as *Hyperion* was designed as a
means to write himself clear of his troubles
and to effect, possibly, a change of heart and
capitulation in Frances Appleton, the book
was, of course, a huge paradox—a circumstance of which he was probably only
vaguely conscious at the time. To win her,
who had "no talent for matrimony," by
telling her in a book of three hundred pages
that he desired nothing more than to forget
her—to shed no more tears over unrequited
love—that was surely a dubious procedure.
The entire book seemed to enforce the
climactic point of Suckling's poem (which
Longfellow had the tactless temerity to
quote in full), that since "nothing will make
her, The devil take her!"[96] A week
before the book appeared he confessed his
fear (as well he might) that the book would
be misunderstood; for after all his brave
resolutions, he had to admit: "I am as

much in love as ever. . . . The lady says she *will not*! I say she *shall*!" Everything else having failed, he resolved to stake all on one throw. So much of resolution he had, though of renunciation he had learned little. "Next week I shall fire off a rocket which I trust will make a commotion in that citadel. Perhaps the garrison will capitulate;—perhaps the rocket may burst and kill me."[97]

The rocket landed in the garrison on Beacon Hill without producing a capitulation, without any show of a white flag.[98] Four months later he met Frances Appleton on one of his walks in the vicinity of Beacon Hill. She passed without a sign. That night he wrote in his diary: "Met the stately dark ladie in the street. I *looked* and *passed*, as Dante prescribed. . . . It is ended."[99] So much for Goethe's resolution and renunciation, as resolving the affairs of a young man's heart.

Yet the sequel, as everyone knows, is that Longfellow's perseverance was rewarded three years later when she wrote that she was ready to let the "dead Past bury its dead," and Longfellow had cause to celebrate May 10, 1843, as a "Day forever blessed, that ushered in this *Vita N[u]ova* of happiness."[100] Two months later they were married, and as a token of her complete surrender of any lingering reproach she gave him her European sketch book, which they had made together in Switzerland eight years earlier, now beautifully bound in green Levant morocco and inscribed simply, "Mary Ashburton to Paul Fleming."[101]

The main tendency of *Hyperion* (insofar as it is possible to speak of a single tendency in so formless a book) is suggested by Goethe's *Entwicklungsroman*. Jean Paul influenced the style of the book, and a touch of Heine inspired some of the lighter irony in which the book abounds,[102] but what is of most significance is that *Hyperion* offered the first fair interpretation and panoramic view of the essential spirit of German

romantic literature to the American reader. Although Longfellow may have overestimated its intrinsic worth when he said in 1840, "It will take a good deal of persuasion to convince me that the book is not good,"[103] there can be no doubt about its historical importance in making Germany better known to Americans.[104]

Although the rocket's burst in the summer of 1839 almost killed him (as he prognosticated it might), life had to go on; and much of the year was spent reading widely, re-perusing Goethe's works, and helping Felton with his translation of Menzel's *History of German Literature*. The book appeared in 1840, and early in June Longfellow prepared a lengthy review of it, not as critical of Menzel's slashing attack on Goethe as one might expect from his foremost professional exponent in America.[105] Meanwhile he had gathered enough poems to make a little volume, which appeared as *Voices of the Night* in December, 1839, and into which went more of the stuff garnered in Germany. Although the book contains two of his "Psalms," their titles belie his true sentiments at the time: he was far from cured of the wavering between living bravely in the present and dwelling longingly in the sweetly sad realms of the past, of nighttime, and of visions. Moreover, the opening poem, the "Hymn to the Night," beginning with lines that Poe praised, is in perfect antithesis to the lessons of the "Psalms." He still hears "the sounds of sorrow and delight" in "the haunted chambers of the night," and finds "relief" from "the frenzy and despair" and "the apathy of grief" by drinking from "the cool cistern of the midnight air." The reference to "some old poet's rhymes" in the third stanza suggests literary influence,[106] and a search through the slender booklet reveals an abundance of it—from the German lyric writers, as one would suspect. Speaking of Arnim and Brentano's *Boy's Wonder-Horn*, which he had bought in Heidelberg, he had written in *Hyperion*:

I know the book almost by heart. Of all your German books, it is the one which produces upon my imagination the most wild and magic influence. I have a passion for ballads! . . . They are the gypsy-children of song, born under hedgerows, in the leafy lanes and by-paths of literature,— in the genial Summer-time.[107]

The type here mentioned is the German ballad of sentiment. His fondness for the other type, the ballad of action, of heroic love and feats of valor, was a later development. There is no trace of the latter in the *Voices* of 1839.

Voices of the Night includes, besides the "Psalms" with their Goethean lessons, a poem called "Flowers," which opens with an allusion to Carové's "Märchen ohne Ende." Similarly, "The Beleaguered City" relates the "old marvellous tale" of the *Nacht-Lager* which nightly "beleaguered the walls of Prague beside the Moldau's rushing stream." "There is a Reaper, whose name is Death," the opening line of "The Reaper and the Flowers," undoubtedly derives from the familiar *Volkslied*, "Es ist ein Schnitter, der heisset Tod," though (as Professor Hatfield has observed) the delicate treatment of the theme is far removed from the style of German folk poetry.[108] The volume also contains ten translations from the German, six of which had already appeared in *Hyperion*.[109]

Longfellow had considered introducing into *Hyperion* a long Scandinavian ballad "on the deeds of the first bold Viking who crossed to this western world, with storm spirits, and devil machinery under water,"[110] and on May 24, 1839, Felton first suggested a poem on the Round Tower at Newport.[111] "The Skeleton in Armor" and "The Wreck of the Hesperus" were written toward the end of 1840. They represent a new note in Longfellow's poetry—a turning away from the sentiments of German romance, which, as he was given to understand by the critics, involved rather too much reliance upon (or borrowing from) "foreign" materials, instead of the more

appropriate indigenous sources.[112] But Longfellow did not then, or later, entirely give up playing his more sentimental German tunes, least of all in *Ballads and Other Poems* of 1841. Among its more notable pieces were his versions of Uhland's "Das Glück von Edenhall" and of Pfizer's "Der Junggeselle," rendered with admirable fidelity while retaining the identical rhyme thrice-repeated in each stanza.[113]

Third European Trip, 1842

Despite a busy academic career, absorbing literary activity and a distinctly gratifying and steadily mounting reputation, evenings of convivial gaiety, and even attempts to fall in love with some one else, Longfellow found no effective balm for his heartache.[114] In April, 1842, he set out to seek a change of scene and to take the water cure of Marienberg at Boppard on the Rhine. There much of his unoccupied time was devoted to short foot-tours in the picturesque vicinity, often in the company of the vivacious Herr Landrat H. C. Heuerberger of St. Goar, the nearest considerable town up the river, where, as was natural, he soon met Heuberger's close friend and near neighbor, Ferdinand Freiligrath. Each admired the other's writings, and Longfellow immediately recognized in Freiligrath "a jovial, good fellow and a poet of genius," while Freiligrath, pleased that his American friend spoke "German well," found him "exceedingly charming and agreeable."[115]

During this third visit to Germany Longfellow perfected his understanding of the German temperament and gained a wide familiarity with the physical character of the Rhineland, as well as of other sections of Germany.[116] There appears to be more than a casual relationship between these stimulating experiences and his writing a few weeks before leaving Marienberg the poem "Mezzo Cammin" with its resolve "to build some tower of song with lofty parapet," for out of it grew *The Golden Legend*, at once the central portion of the trilogy which he deemed his loftiest undertaking and the most strictly Germanic of all his compositions.

During the rough ocean passage in late October, 1842, Longfellow overcame his dislike for occasional verse to the extent of writing a series of poems supporting the antislavery cause. Thus he finally composed what his friend Sumner had repeatedly urged but what he could not bring himself to write until Freiligrath's romantic poems about Negroes, wild animals, and exotic places showed him how he could combine antislavery sentiments with romantic word pictures. In the first letter to Freiligrath after his return to Cambridge, he acknowledged borrowing "one or two wild animals from your menagerie."[117]

Cambridge, 1842–1868

Life in Cambridge soon settled itself into its wonted if busy routine, except that his marriage in 1843 introduced a new peace and happiness and an enlargement of labors both literary and professional, and of domestic and social spheres.[118]

Poets and Poetry of Europe appeared in the summer of 1845, with a portrait of Schiller for the frontispiece. Among the German authors, Goethe had, in the first edition,[119] what might be considered a strictly proportionate share of the space. When a new edition appeared in 1871, Schiller's portrait was significantly replaced by Goethe's; and while no new translations from Schiller were added, Longfellow's own version of Goethe's two "Wanderer's Night-Songs" and extracts from Bayard Taylor's translation of *Faust II* were included—both changes symptomatic of the steadily growing importance of Goethe in Longfellow's estimation.

Evangeline (1847) has been a stumbling block at once to English readers who are congenitally opposed to hexameters and to German scholars[120] who would like to make

it an American imitation of *Hermann und Dorothea*. The argument runs usually as follows: first, Klopstock, Voss, and Goethe are forever associated with the modern revival of the classical hexameter, and Longfellow is the fourth in line, hence *Evangeline* is a "German" production; second, *Evangeline* and *Hermann und Dorothea* are both properly idyls; both deal with true love that does not run smooth when political affairs intervene; in both a parish priest appears who attempts to set things aright; in both idyllic scenes of domestic tranquility are drawn—therefore one derives from the other. True, Freiligrath, when he finished reading his friend's story, wrote to say that he regarded it "a masterpiece," and that he had placed the book on his shelves, "not near Voss' *Luise*, but near old Wolfgang's *Hermann und Dorothea*."[121] But, as Professor Hatfield has remarked, "there the resemblance ends. There is not one line which shows a direct imitation."[122]

For one thing, the circumstances that evoked the two poems are quite dissimilar. Goethe, aside from what he drew from Voss's *Luise*, got his story from *Das Liebthätige Gera gegen die Salzburgischen Emigranten* . . . (Leipzig, 1732).[123] Longfellow, as all the world knows, got his story from H. L. Conolly, who related it to Hawthorne in Longfellow's presence. His immediate source was native, and the adornments he added represent gleanings from a variety of American sources, notably books on Canada, Indian lore, Audubon, Sealsfield, and Banvard's panorama of the Mississippi.[124] But the most important differences arise from the two authors' different purposes. According to Scherer, Goethe represents in Dorothea that strength growing out of the sorrows of a woman who has been literally torn from her native soil, and who, in spite of adversity and lonely homelessness, develops an independence and resourcefulness, and in her heart, a tenderness for the needy and afflicted; and in Hermann the enduring and abiding strength of that culture which is fostered by the security of a regular, well-ordered existence and home life. Longfellow, on the other hand, presents only an impressive picture of love and constancy in the heart of a woman—a tale intended to inculcate the lessons of hope, endurance, and fidelity to an ideal.

In view of these broad disparities, it would seem that there is no necessary connection between the two poems. To be sure, Longfellow's library contained several copies (original and translated[125]) of *Hermann und Dorothea*, and we know that he read the poem in the original as early as June 10, 1838, finding it "a very simple, singular, and beautiful poem";[126] but following a brief reference to *Hermann und Dorothea* in 1840,[127] there are no further references in his diaries and letters until some thirty years later.[128] And there is nothing to suggest that he returned to it at the time he was working on *Evangeline*.[129] His adoption of the hexameter as his verse form could have come as readily from Voss (whose *Luise* he had known as early as 1839) or, what is most likely, from classical sources.[130]

During the years between publication of *Evangeline* (1847) and *The Golden Legend* (1851), Longfellow's life went on much as it had been. He kept supplementing his knowledge of the German authors, especially the more contemporary.[131] In the meantime he had his say on nationalism in American literature, voicing an opinion strikingly at variance with the one expressed in 1837 when, in reviewing Hawthorne's *Twice-Told Tales*, he had argued that in choosing native New England materials Hawthorne had selected "the right materials" for his stories. In *Kavanagh* (1849) he argued against the thesis that American literature, if it is not national, is nothing, by observing that while nationality is good, "universality" is better. "We shall draw from the Germans tenderness, from the Spaniards passion, from the French vivacity, to mingle more and more with our English good sense."[132] This doctrine of transplantation and acculturation is, of course, in perfect accord with his own endeavors as professor of modern foreign languages and literatures, with his practice of translating some of the best foreign specimens, and with his publication of the *Poets and Poetry of Europe*. His repeated periods of residence in Europe, notably Germany, and the literary and personal ties formed there, are in a large measure responsible for this change of front.

The Golden Legend, written during 1850–1851, has no close connection with Jacobus de Voragine's *Aurea Legenda*; it received its title because Longfellow considered the story, as he got it from Hartmann von Aue's *Der arme Heinrich*, "to surpass all other legends in beauty and significance." As early as November 27, 1839, he had considered whether he should work up something from Cotton Mather or write "a drama on the old poetic legend of *Der arme Heinrich*." "The tale," he added, "is exquisite. I have a heroine as sweet as Imogen, could I but paint her so."[133] Eventually it became the Second Part of his trilogy, *The Christus*, which was completed in 1871—thirty-two years after he first recorded his interest in the subject and fully thirty years after he conceived of it as part of his chief life work—"a long and elaborate poem by the holy name of Christ, the theme of which would be the various aspects of Christendom in the Apostolic, Middle, and Modern Ages."[134]

The drama as Longfellow wrote it enormously transcends the simple epic of the old Minnesinger.[135] *Der arme Heinrich* was available to Longfellow in Mailáth's *Altdeutsche Geschichte* (Stuttgart, 1809), which he discovered at Heidelberg in 1836,[136] and also in a complete prose version which his assistant Rölker made for him. Longfellow derived the central story directly from the Middle High German text, as well as from Rölker's manuscript, but he also drew heavily on Goethe's *Faust*.

Hartmann's simple epical poem presents, in its 1530 lines, an economically unified picture of religious faith in the Middle Ages. *The Golden Legend* finally achieves something of a unity of tone, but it is done by a variety of effects. Little of the simple atmosphere of pious faith remains. Prince Henry is no *armer Heinrich* as he is in Hartmann; he is a modern man whose simple faith has been destroyed by the modern enlightenment and its consequent inquisitiveness and skepticism.[137] But the closest parallel is not that between Faustus and Prince Henry. Longfellow's conception of Lucifer in the image of Mephistopheles represents his most direct debt.

The effort to unite in one poem the story of Heinrich von Hoheneck and that of Faust involved a fusion of the medieval and the modern man, the believer with the skeptic, that was only half successful. Poor Henry lacks the consistency of either Hartmann's Heinrich or Goethe's Faust; neither one nor the other, he is at best, a blurred image of both.[138] The verbal parallels are often very close,[139] but need no enumeration. Considering how often by 1850–1851 Longfellow had repeated his lectures and gone over the text of *Faust* with successive classes, we understand why there should be a great number of these reminiscences and parallels, voluntary and involuntary, in a poem whose leading characters are so much like those in *Faust*.[140]

Among the "Birds of Passage" poems published in the *Miles Standish* volume are several shorter pieces, of which "Victor Galbraith" is close enough to Mosen's "Andreas Hofer" to suggest a genetic connection. And the two very effective lines from the "Lapland Song," quoted at the end of each stanza of "My Lost Youth," were taken directly from Herder's *Volkslieder*.

Fourth Trip—Later Years, 1868–1882

Following the tragic death of his wife in 1861, Longfellow turned to translating Dante. A fourth and last sojourn in Europe, lasting fifteen months, was undertaken in 1868–1869. Traveling in a family group of ten, this expedition resembled more a *Völkerwanderung* than any of his three earlier journeys, which were more in the nature of a student's pilgrimage. Germany was traversed only cursorily.[141]

While German literature ceased to be a matter of insistent academic concern after 1854, Longfellow's reputation as an authority on German literature survived, he continued reading to enlarge his knowledge of classic authors and foraged widely among contemporary writers.[142] He produced also a few translations, one of which remains unsurpassed—the version of "Über allen Gipfeln," which he prepared in 1870 for the new edition of *Poets and Poetry of Europe* (1871).[143] Although none of his later poems depends as strongly upon German models as do the poems of his middle period, it was inevitable that certain German notes should make themselves heard.[144]

FROM FIRST to last, Longfellow's poems illustrate his absorption of the spirit of German poetry. He was, for his generation and in his locality, the representative of German letters. It was only natural that J. T. Fields should have been struck with the likeness of Longfellow's "private rooms to those of a German student or professor, —a Goethean aspect of simplicity and space everywhere."[145] As professor of modern languages and literatures in America's most influential university during the most formative decades of American cultural development, Longfellow stood in a unique position to introduce into American literature those better elements of European culture by which he hoped a too strict spirit of American nationalism would be transformed into a broader spirit of universality. To that end the atmosphere of "the castled Rhine" that pervades so much of his prose and verse—specimens of which still adorn every grade-school reader— provided a powerful leavening influence.

JAMES RUSSELL LOWELL
(1819–1891)

Acquaintance with German Literature

While Lowell's writings exhibit a wealth of German allusion, he was, among the middle generation of Brahmins, one of the most staunchly Anglophile; and the Germanic influences, except in the formulation of his critical principles, do not form as pervasive or as basic a part of his literary personality as in the case of Longfellow. The pronounced Germanic flavor which his allusions and references give to his writings was mainly a part of his academic nature. His highly allusive style illustrates his conviction, expressed in his essay on Carlyle, that "a great part of our pleasure in reading is unexpectedness." To achieve unexpected novelty, he ransacked all literatures for telling phrases and figures. What De Quincey called the "gluttony of books" is in a large measure responsible for the piquancy of Lowell's prose style, but his bookishness worked to the detriment of original ideas and the formulation of first principles in his critical and literary essays. For though he deprecated the book suffocation of Cotton Mather, Lowell himself had (as he said of Emerson) the keen eye for a "fine telling phrase that will carry true . . . like that of a backwoodsman for a rifle." Emerson, he observed, will "dredge you up a choice word from the mud of Cotton Mather himself"; yet Lowell was no less ready to ransack Mather or any other source of whatever age or clime if what he found could be made to add sparkle to his sentence. The result is what has been deplored in Lowell's character as a critic—that his literary essays are less statements and applications of fundamental critical principles than "clever" but essentially "random comment."[146]

Although he studied German during his undergraduate days at Harvard (1834–1838) and spent a year in Dresden (1855–1856) working hard on the German language and the forty volumes of Goethe's writings in preparation for his duties as Smith Professor of Languages and Literatures at Harvard, it was not until 1866 that he wrote his "Lessing," his single complete essay dealing with German literature. In his last public address, "The Study of Modern Languages," delivered before the Modern Language Association in 1889, Lowell expressed satisfaction at the fact that modern languages and literatures were being taught seriously and thoroughly in American colleges and universities. He had watched the development of foreign-language instruction at Harvard from the time when only French was taught, and that not regularly; when German was acquired, as he put it, only "by hook or by crook,"[147] through the decade of Follen's career there and the eras of Ticknor and of Longfellow, whom he was destined himself to succeed in 1855.

Lowell's letters and his commonplace book indicate a mild interest in German literature during his undergraduate days.[148] He proposed going to Germany to study law but seems to have accepted with good grace his father's veto of the plan. Upon reading Margaret Fuller's translation of Eckermann's *Conversations with Goethe*, he thought of "writing a series of communications for some periodicals in the form of Eckermann and Boswell,"[149] but never carried out the plan. At times he lost all patience with the "cant" of overenthusiastic Goetheans,[150] and not until he read *Wilhelm Meister* in 1840 did he find anything of Goethe's unqualifiedly delightful.[151] Even though he found many qualities of Goethe's admirable, Lowell remained inexorable in his condemnation of the great German's willingness, in order to satisfy his own intellectual curiosity, "to soil the maiden petals of a woman's soul": "to get the delicious sensation of reflex sorrow, he would wring a heart."[152] But if Goethe's morality troubled him, he could accept Schiller wholeheartedly, and his first book of poems, inspired by Maria White, bore a motto from Schiller's *Wallenstein*, "Ich habe gelebt und geliebt."

Preoccupied during the early forties with personal problems, journalism, and anti-slavery propaganda, Lowell made little more than passing references to things German;[153] but in 1848–1849 he became aware of the high quality of German literary criticism (theoretical and applied)[154] in which area he came to feel the Germans had made their greatest contribution. In 1851 the Lowells made the long-hoped-for-trip to Europe. Toward the end of their fifteen-month stay they paused briefly in Germany, but the visit bore no literary fruit, unless it revivified the phrase "Auf Wiedersehen," which Maria was fond of using during the early days of their love, and which her husband took for the title and burden of the memorial verses which he wrote shortly after her death in 1853. In 1855, in a series of lectures on the English poets, which won him the Smith Professorship at Harvard, Lowell made passing references to Fouqué, Jean Paul, Luther, Kepler, and Kant, and quoted Schiller.[155]

The year abroad (1855–1856) was in several ways a disappointment. Lowell had hoped to master German during the fall and winter, at the same time making himself proficient in the Spanish language, so that he might spend the spring in literary study in Spain. But German inflection and word order proved more troublesome than he had anticipated. He never appreciated linguistic study except as a means to an end; and his letters are full of complaints against *"der, die, das"* and against sentences in which "one sets sail an admiral with sealed orders, not knowing where the devil he is going till he is in mid-ocean."[156] The forty volumes of Goethe which he acquired and set himself to read also proved heavy going, although by late November he reporting reading 150 pages a day.[157] He soon resigned himself to devoting all the remaining months in Europe to acquiring the command of German that his position required. From time to time he expressed sober satisfaction at his progress, and occasionally his reading brought him a sense of intellectual enlargement,[158] but his letters seldom mention any great aesthetic delight experienced through his widening contact with German literature.[159]

The Harvard Professorship

During the first decade of his Harvard professorship Lowell seems to have made little use of his painfully acquired knowledge. For a time he taught a course in German literature,[160] of which there remain some manuscript notes for lectures on Middle High German literature, the *Nibelungenlied*, and Wolfram von Eschenbach[161]. It was not until 1868 and 1870 that the published essays on Shakespeare and on Dante indicated the full extent of his debt to German literary scholarship and criticism.[162] Later essays contain scattering references, but a surprisingly high proportion of all that Lowell had to say about German literature and criticism appears in the essays of the five years from 1866 to 1870. Even during these years the range of the allusions is not particularly wide. Perhaps a dozen new names are mentioned, but many of the references are inconsequential or satirical.[163] In the end, Goethe and Lessing emerge as the two who, in Lowell's estimation, stand head and shoulders above all other Germans.

Of the several Goethes whom Lowell considered, it was chiefly Goethe the man of wisdom and Goethe the critic that eventually meant most to him. *Faust* and others of his poetical productions served to embellish a sentence or garnish a text, but his "wise sayings" were treasured and quoted, sometimes repeatedly.[164] Lowell's essay on

Carlyle further emphasized Goethe's catholic wisdom as helping Carlyle break down the parochial standards and religious prepossessions of British criticism.[165] More important still for Lowell was Goethe's Shakespeare criticism. In his essay on "Shakespeare Once More" he emphasizes the powerful effect of Goethe's dictum "not to accept and take for granted, but to weigh and consider" in creating what is called the "productive" criticism of the Germans. He is not always in complete agreement with Goethe's individual judgments. Thus, while acknowledging the fecundity of Goethe's "distinction between ancient and modern drama" as resting on "the difference between *sollen* and *wollen*, between *must* and *would*," he points out instances in which this "conveniently portable" distinction has its "limitations."[166] and he questions the validity of Goethe's conclusion that Shakespeare was a greater poet than dramatist.[167] After acknowledging his debt to a number of German critics (among them Goethe, A. W. Schlegel, Gervinus, and Tieck), Lowell proceeds to apply the theory of "productive" criticism to *Hamlet*. In the process he must inevitably consider the oft-quoted criticism from *Wilhelm Meister*, with which, again, he finds himself in imperfect agreement.[168] Oftener than not, however, he accepts Goethe's pronouncements.[169]

It is significant that Lowell chose a critic as the subject of his one full-length essay on a German man of letters. His essay entitled "Lessing" afforded an opportunity for his most extended comments on German literary culture—on the genuine value as well as the ponderous pedantry of German scholarship, the recalcitrance of the language, the heaviness of German humor, the low state of German literature before Lessing, the quarrel between classical and romantic disciples, and the German Shakespeare criticism. Lessing himself Lowell rated a genius, though not a poetic genius; it was as man and critic, not as

poet or dramatist, that he valued him.[170]

Lowell's knowledge of German literary learning went beyond the great critics and the Shakespeare scholars[171] to include the students of Dante[172] and Chaucer[173] and the great linguists;[174] but his chief debt (as he freely acknowledged) was owing to the critical views of Lessing, Goethe, A. W. Schlegel, and the German aesthetic theorists, including Zeising and Vischer.[175] It is often difficult and sometimes impossible to determine whether a certain idea was derived directly from Lessing, Goethe, Schlegel, or Gervinus, whether it came by way of Coleridge, Lamb, Hazlitt, Carlyle, or Arnold, or possibly several of them jointly.[176] Yet the tone of his references and his frank avowals leave little room for doubting that in the realm of critical or aesthetic guidance he turned more frequently to German than to English critics even,[177] though for his numerous literary allusions, embellishments, and general stylistic garnishments, it was but natural that he should lay a heavier levy upon English than upon German writers.[178] Of Goethe, only *Faust I*, *Hermann und Dorothea*, and a few of the shorter lyrics touched that "something deeper than the mind" which Lowell felt it was the province of imaginative literature to stir and dilate. The dull, heavy unhappiness of his winter in "dreary Dresden" seems to have colored his subsequent approach to German letters. Want of style and heaviness of language destroyed his pleasure in much of the work of the lesser writers, while the too great freedom of some of the greater figures was objectionable on moral grounds. He could respect German literature, but he could not enjoy it. Despite the strong moral strains in Lowell's own poetry and criticism, he never, in theory, wavered from the position that the first duty of the muse is to be delightful; but he had as little stomach for the "questionable" morals of *Elective Affinities* as he had for the abstractions of *Faust II*. National tastes being what they are, it seemed to him that English, even French and Italian poetry, was more closely akin, more nearly consonant with, and better suited for the enrichment of the native tradition of American letters than the German could be.

OLIVER WENDELL HOLMES
(1809–1894)

The very Brahmin of the Brahmins and one of the hierarchs on whose image the Genteel modeled themselves, Holmes is different from the breed he helped to engender chiefly in one respect: he did not share fully with the succession of greater and lesser men, from Emerson to Stedman, their enthusiasm for German culture.[179] His life became wrapped up in the twin foci of Cambridge and Boston, and he developed a kind of provincialism that militated against the type of cosmopolitanism which the Transcendentalists espoused. "I have lived so long stationary," he confessed, "that I have become intensely local, and doubtless in many ways narrow."[180] Identification with a locality, he always maintained, is a surer passport to immortality than cosmopolitanism.[181] But, says the Autocrat to his fellow-boarders, "I was born and bred, as I've told you twenty times, among books and those who knew what was in books";[182] and accordingly, having handled books from infancy, he was not afraid of them.[183] When the subject of conversation round the breakfast table turns to Kant on Space and Time[184] or on the distinction between "understanding and reason,"[185] the Autocrat is not flustered. Indeed, at one point, he allows himself to discourse on distinctions between knowledge and truth in such a manner that, to check himself, he allows "the old gentleman who sat opposite" to sniff audibly and to observe that the Autocrat "talked like a transcendentalist." "For his part," he added, "common sense was good enough."[186]

Pre-eminently a Boston wit, Holmes was nonetheless a man of the world—an alert, worldly-wise, well-read, and if not receptive, at least sympathetic, observer. The *Autocrat* and its three successors are, like Thoreau's *Week*, a mine of allusions and quotations from diverse sources. But while references to Byron, Bulwer, Thomas Browne, Bacon, Swift, Shakespeare, and Latin authors, notably Horace, come "trippingly," the German writers supplied no strongly activating inspiration and are mentioned sparingly—usually *en passant*.[187] The conclusion must be that German literature and thought, except when used for superfical literary embellishment, served Holmes rarely. It was mainly in his thinking on scientific subjects that he looked abroad, but even in this area he got most of his training in Paris, and for the rest he relied mainly on English and American medical precedent; while in letters he was inspired chiefly by the principles of the Latin authors and the practice of the neo-classical school of English writers. The Germanic element stricken from his writings would substract little from the record as it stands.

JOHN GREENLEAF WHITTIER
(1807–1892)

German Legends, Tales, Scenery

As a youthful romanticist Whittier took hints from German legends of wizard, demon, and ghost. From time to time throughout his life he enjoyed vicarious or fanciful fireside journeys into the Rhineland. As a militant, religiously motivated reformer, he now and again turned to Luther for pattern and for warning. In his fight against slavery he became allied with a number of political refugees who espoused the abolitionist cause, and during his publicist career he repeatedly referred to German-American liberal publications and to the antislavery tradition of the Pennsylvania-Germans.[188] He felt an affinity with the German quietists and mystics and a friendly tolerance for those who were more ascetic and more concerned with the occult than he. Finally, he formed friendships with several American translators of German literature, notably Longfellow, C. T. Brooks, the Rev. Thomas Tracey, and Bayard Taylor, through whose translations and those of others he became familiar with the masterpieces of Goethe and Schiller and with the lyrics and tales of the German romantic writers.

The newspapers which Whittier edited and the magazines to which he contributed, especially for the years 1828–1838, when his mind was much occupied with the type of supernatural tradition dear to the German romantics, contain evidence of his early interest in the Faust story and other German legendary lore[189]—an interest that reappeared from time to time and extended far beyond the years usually set as bounding his period of fanciful romantic fondness for the lurid, the strange, the sensational, and the dreamy.[190]

Akin to Whittier's enjoyment of German romance was his pleasure in imagined German scenery. Germany was to him, as she was to other romantically-minded poets, a classic region of fable and romance; and allusions to the Rhineland especially came trooping to his imagination, during both the earlier period of his poetic career[191] and his later years.[192]

Abolitionism: Follen and Luther

Whittier's addiction to romantic supernaturalism in his early poetry was supplanted, in his more mature work, by Quaker humanitarianism, manifesting itself chiefly in the fight against slavery. In May, 1834, he attended an antislavery convention in Boston and heard a stirring address by Dr. Carl Follen,[193] whose reformist activities had already cost him his post in Jena and were soon to lose for him his professorship at Harvard. Until Follen's death in 1840 Whittier frequently worked with Follen on antislavery committees, and the relations between the two men were warmly affectionate, so that Follen's personal influence upon Whittier must be rated as cognate with that of Garrison in arousing his ardor for abolition.[194]

An even older presence in Whittier's mind was that of Martin Luther. Again and again, when the Abolitionists were reproached for stirring up discord, the Quaker poet reminded his antagonists how the leader of the Reformation had shaken the quiet of Christendom, irritated the rulers of the Church, rebuked the princes, and, planting his feet on the rock of principle, declared "I cannot otherwise."[195]

Germans as Poetical Subjects

The settlement in Pennsylvania of the German followers of William Penn was a subject of lifelong interest to Whittier. As early as 1835 he wrote a story about Penn's visit to Germany in 1677, in which he told how the stranger from England brought to the sweet enthusiast Lady Eleanora and her studious lover Ernest the message of the Inner Light.[196] In "The Pennsylvania Pilgrim" (1872) he wrote the exquisite idyl which stands a fitting memorial to the learning, piety, Christian charity, and gentleness of spirit of the German-American Quaker Pastorius, who drew up for the Germantown Friends the document which Whittier correctly described as "the first protest made by a religious body against Negro Slavery."[197]

Others of Whittier's poems suggestive of Germanic content include "Maud Muller," with a headnote explaining that its "somewhat infelicitous title" is derived from "the recollections of some descendants of a Hessian" named Muller, but that "the poem has no real foundation in fact." When a correspondent inquired whether the *u* in *Muller* should not be umlauted, Whittier replied, "Pronounce the name with either the Yankee or the German accent—it matters not which," and there is nothing to suggest that he thought a second time of his heroine's ancestry or national origin. Nor has the nationality of Barbara Frietchie's antecedents any significant relation to the ballad that bears her name. In "The Palatine" (1887) nothing is made of the fact that most of the unfortunate passengers on the wrecked and burned ship were German emigrants bound for Philadelphia.[198] In "Cobbler Keezar's Vision" (1861), however, the "tough old Teuton's" colorful recollections of his homeland and his scorn of his glum, psalm-singing Connecticut neighbors are essential elements in the texture of the ballad. The "Hymn of the Dunkers" (1877) is fraught with memories of the religious persecutions from which the German pietists fled, but these memories are subdued by the mystic calm with which the sisters in serene Kloster Kedar at Ephrata await the second coming of the Lord.[199] Another late poem which shows Whittier's continued responsiveness to German religious tradition is "The Two Elizabeths," read at the

unveiling of the bust of Elizabeth Fry at the Friend's School in Providence in 1885.[200] When, with the aid of Lucy Larcom, he edited *Child Life* (1872), a collection of poems, and a companion volume, *Child Life in Prose* (1874), he included a dozen selections from the German[201] as representative of the simple or pious sentiment he wished to perpetuate among children.

Without constituting a major or directive influence on Whittier, German motifs provided him with a significant supplementary source of subject matter and allusion. From first to last, he drew heavily upon the storied lore of ballad and legend for his narrative poetry and upon the lives of German mystics for his historical, as well as religious and humanitarian, poems. Lacking fluency in the language, he yet made several translations and adaptations of German poems. For the greater part, however, he relied upon such English translations as were available. Throughout his life he was aware of certain movements of German and German-American thought; from personal contacts and from reading he absorbed such elements as were congenial to his spiritual nature; but the currents of German thought that attracted an Emerson or a Parker left him cold, and his Quaker prepossessions kept him from entertaining sympathetically either the methods or the results of German critical theological investigations.

HENRY DAVID THOREAU
(1817–1862)

His Literary Personality

In a writer like Thoreau it becomes desperately hard to distinguish what the man read from what he was. For one thing, his deep-seated desire to be utterly himself and his horror of dependence make the attempt to find the sources of Thoreau a baffling process. Sharing the Transcendentalists' worship of self-trust and originality,

he yet absorbed from them much of their enthusiasm for books from many lands. They were constantly putting books into each other's hands. The first principle in Emerson's (and Thoreau's) theory of good books was that they must not be allowed to lie fallow or merely pass through the mind, but that their proper use lies in the reader's acting out the best of what he reads. Thoreau, even more resolutely than his mentor, Emerson, set out to make all his activities of one piece—to the point of steadfastly refusing to indulge in activities that could not be made to contribute directly to that purpose; but however many items he put down on his list of things without which he could get along, good books were not among his proscriptions. All his life he had ready access to books.[202]

But no man can be explained solely in terms of the books he read; and in Thoreau's case, instead of saving that he became what he read, it might better be said that his reading indicates what he was. His first published work, *A Week on the Concord and Merrimac Rivers* (1849), that "mine of quotations from good authors,"[203] is at once an "anthology carried on the frame of a story" and an authentic literary autobiography.[204] As such, it contributes, as do also the earlier volumes of his *Journal*, to our understanding of the books that were most vital to him, and occasionally we get a glimpse of how a Goethe or a Schlegel helped him to his characteristic ideas. For example, the passages on poetry and authorship in "Thursday" of the *Week* which culminate in the definition of a poem as "one undivided, unimpeded expression fallen ripe into literature"[205] is inspired by his reading of Goethe's *Autobiography*, *Wilhelm Meister*, and *Italian Travels*.[206] The immediate source is to be found in the *Journal* for November 15, 16, and December 8, 1837,[207] whence he transcribed whatever he wanted when he came to write the *Week*. But in this instance, as seemingly in others where Thoreau quoted or otherwise deferred to printed sources, the borrowed material did little more than embellish or round out the structure that Thoreau himself had reared. In this case, Goethe served as an example of the Man of Art as distinct from Thoreau's conception of the Man of Genius.[208] The main concept itself Thoreau had grasped long before—not from Goethe or Shakespeare or Emerson even, but from within the recesses of his own conscious-

ness, his inviolate personality. Goethe's literary career only served to supply a footnote, as it were, to document Thoreau's view of the simplicity, spontaneity, originality, and organic nature of art. For Thoreau's reading of Goethe did no more to make him a German than his reading of the *Bhagavad-Gita* made him a Hindu.

And yet Thoreau read much and was manifestly affected, for better or worse, by his reading.[209] The *Week* and *Walden* would hardly be recognizable without the portions deriving from Greek, Latin, Oriental, British, and other literatures. Without this literary background, the central body of thought that we recognize as being the heart of Thoreau would doubtless be intact, or nearly so; but the illustrations, or the "lustres" (to use an Emersonian expression) would be missing; and in at least a few cases we should miss certain Oriental concepts, Greek attitudes, and German ideas that must be regarded as more than mere marginalia or embellishments.

Very likely if, in 1856, Whitman had talked to Thoreau about the German transcendental philosophers as Thoreau talked to Whitman about the Orientals, and then asked whether Thoreau had read them, he would have replied, as Whitman did to Thoreau's inquiry about the Orientals, "No, tell me about them."[210] It is doubtful, as Professor B. V. Crawford has observed, that Thoreau, had he been asked, "would have acknowledged any important debt to the philosophical thought of Germany."[211] There is nothing to indicate that he read Kant or Schelling; and yet there can be little question that in one way or another (whether through Emerson, Coleridge, Carlyle, the reviews, or the transcendental climate around him), he learned something more than the dictionary definition of the word *transcendental*. During the years when he assisted Emerson in editing the *Dial*, he became familiar, as the copy and proof passed through his hands, with a considerable body of German transcendental ideas, pure and diluted; although it seems fairly obvious that he never divested himself of the misconceptions respecting Kantian epistemology that Carlyle (and through him, Emerson) put into circulation. This, however, was no great loss to Thoreau; for "metaphysics was his aversion," and "no work of metaphysics found room on his shelves unless by sufferance."[212] The twenty volumes of his *Writings* reveal few noteworthy German passages. On the first page of his journal he wrote, with apparent approval, "The Germans say, 'Es ist alles wahr wodurch du besser wirst,'" and during the first year of his journal-keeping he translated five passages from Goethe's *Tasso* and two from *Italienische Reise*,[213] but nothing in his later journals suggests that this kind of activity consumed much of his time. His library contained few German books.[214] His article on Carlyle makes it fairly clear that he was not fond of the involved German language, and there is good evidence for inferring that much of what he read during his later years of German authors was read in translation.[215]

Affinities with German Writers

Nonetheless, Thoreau was, first and last, affected in one way or another by various German writers. The technicalities of the romantic philosophers left him cold; he could not entertain either speculations on the special faculties of the mind or questions whether the "Not-Me" derives from the "Me" or the All from the Infinite Nothing.[216] Yet there are a number of striking coincidences of thought and mood, so that, as Paul Elmer More once observed, the whole body of German romanticism can be found reflected, explicitly and implicitly, in his journal and formal works.[217] For example, the metaphysical parallelism by which Schelling defined nature as visible spirit and spirit as invisible nature has its counterpart as much in Thoreau as in Emerson; but it would be a fruitless exercise

to try to ascertain whether Thoreau arrived at the same conclusion independently of Schelling, or derived it from Emerson, or through Emerson, or elsewhere. It is enough to point out that there is a remarkable similarity.[218]

Turning from these general affinities to more specific points of contact between Thoreau and German authors, we should note that Goethe meant more to him than any other German. Aside from seven translated passages which he wrote into his journal for 1837 (most of them subsequently transcribed into the *Week*) and the essay on Carlyle (where, of course, Goethe figures prominently), there are eight other noteworthy references to Goethe from which to construct Thoreau's opinion of Goethe.[219] Other German writers did not vitally interest Thoreau.[220]

German Criticism

In the essay on Carlyle, Thoreau speaks of "the German rule of referring an author to his own standard,"[221] meaning the sympathetic (or what Margaret Fuller called the "affirmative") type of literary criticism practiced by the German romantic critics and given wide currency among American Transcendentalists through Goethe's famous formulation of their creed and the Schlegel brothers' practice. Thoreau himself, in his critical essays, seems inclined to follow the Schlegel-Coleridge school of literary appreciation and critical evaluation, but he probably relied, in this department, more on Coleridge[222] than upon any firsthand familiarity with the German critics who followed in the wake of Herder. In one instance he spoke disparagingly of the excessive adulation heaped upon Shakespeare by the German romantic critics.[223] In his concept of the organic, however, it would seem that his relation to the Germans was mainly accidental. The idea of poetry as organic expression (as developed by Herder, Goethe, Schelling, and the Schlegels) had by the forties become a commonplace in transcendental New England. It had been given wide currency by Carlyle and Coleridge; it was repeatedly discussed in the *Dial*; and Emerson, as well as Margaret Fuller, never wearied of reenforcing the doctrine. Wherever Thoreau got the idea, he early conceived of poetry, not as imitation, but as expression—not as something made, mechanically shaped by rules imposed from without, but as something following the laws of organic growth. This led to his formulating distinct theories regarding intuition and form, genius and talent, which approximated rather closely those of Herder, Schelling, the older Goethe, and the Schlegels.[224]

Thoreau went beyond the Germans in one respect. His conception of the organic principle embraced far more than poetic expression, or even art in general. It furnished the key to his basic attitude toward the whole of life. He sought to "live as tenderly and daintily as one would pluck a flower," to make his life the outer expression of his inner organic principle of simple, sane, good living, which had its base no more in the natural and emotional man than in his mental and moral discipline.

My life hath been the poem I would have
    writ,
But I could not both live and live to utter it.

His practical Puritan idealism, by which he placed great store to foster growth of character through discipline, objected to the unrestained emotionalism of "Wertherish" literature, the unrealizable idealism that led to disillusionment, irony, and despair—all that which the older Goethe repudiated as *das Krankhafte*. He was fond of repeating after Samuel Daniel the lines,

Unless above himself he can
Erect himself, how poor a thing is man!

Thus it would seem that here, as in other instances, Thoreau succeeded in giving to

sentiments of whatever origin his own turn in a manner to make them his own.

A German writer who probably lent something to Thoreau's creed is Johann Georg Ritter von Zimmermann, whose *Betrachtungen über die Einsamkeit* (1784–1785) first became available in an English edition in 1791, and after 1793, in many American editions.[225] Thoreau listed the book in the inventory he made of his library in 1840,[226] and it may be presumed that he read it before he went to live in his hut at Walden Pond on July 4, 1845. We can be reasonably certain that the most direct motivation that led him to give solitary life a trial was the example of his friend and classmate Stearns Wheeler, who had lived in the woods near Flint's Pond.[227] Thoreau began to comment during 1841[228] on the desirability of finding a solitary retreat; and it does not seem far-fetched to conclude that his reading of Zimmermann's book at about this time should have suggested to him the idea, or, at all events, encouraged him in his resolution to put the theory of solitude into practice.[229] Impossible though it be to determine the degree or extent of influence, we may conclude that whatever Thoreau owes to Zimmermann he translated not merely into his writings but made a component part of his life—again illustrating, as in the case of his relation to Emerson, an instance of the disciple outdistancing the master.

German Scientists

Another group of German writers interested Thoreau—the savants, scientists, and travelers with scientific interests. He found their writings useful in his nature studies and used them accordingly, often quoting Konrad Gesner[230] and Alexander von Humboldt,[231] and occasionally Ida Laura (Reyer) Pfeiffer[232] and David Crantz.[233] His reading and use of Gesner and Humboldt provide good examples of what Channing had in mind when he said that Thoreau read with pen in hand making what he called "Fact-books—citations which concerned his studies."[234] The only other German with whom he occupied his mind to any considerable degree was J. A. Etzler, a native of Germany residing in Pennsylvania in 1833 when he published his *Paradise within the Reach of All Men, without Labor, by Powers of Nature and Machinery*, the second London edition (1842) of which Thoreau reviewed in the *Democratic Review* for November, 1843. The review, while significant as setting forth some of Thoreau's essential doctrines, is little to our purpose. The ideas presented in the book are not characteristically Germanic, and Thoreau's occupation with it sheds no light on our problem of German influence on him.

Everything considered, Thoreau was not much influenced by Germany. True, he understood well enough that when he avowed himself a Transcendentalist, as he freely did, the roots of the philosophy that he professed were understood to lie in Germany; but he did not have the curiosity about metaphysical roots that he had about Greek and Latin roots. There are affinities a-plenty between Thoreau's romantic ideas and those common among romantic writers of Germany, but who can say that Thoreau derived his sense of the organic from Schelling or Schlegel, or that his doctrines of work and renunciation are drawn any more from Goethe or Carlyle than from within himself? That Goethe's method of truthful and circumstantial description seemed an ideal which he strove to emulate, and that he was encouraged by Zimmermann to try solitude as a means to the end of humanistic control in his own life seem fair enough inferences; and there are other such particulars which he adapted to his purposes. But, taken altogether, foreign influences did not radically alter the man who resisted nothing more strenuously than influences from outside himself, and who must be put down in the end as having succeeded better than most of his contemporaries in remaining true to himself.

HERMAN MELVILLE
(1819–1891)

Literary Background

Ishmael's observation that a whale-ship had been his Yale College and his Harvard, too, has helped inspire the myth that as a young man Melville learned little about books. But overlooked is Ishmael's declaration that while he sailed through oceans, he also swam through libraries.[235] The publication of *Typee* (1846), a scant two years after his return from the South Seas, suggests that there was somewhere a preparation and literary foreground.[236] To be sure, he had still to write, partly to get them out of his system, his travel romances; but the germs of *Mardi*, *Moby-Dick*, and *Pierre* were already lodged in his brain. After the pap and pablum of his earlier "trash," as he styled his first books—"written to buy tobbacco with"[237]—he turned his back on light fiction and set off on his voyagings in the untracked seas among the Mardian islands: on voyagings that led from one metaphysical abyss to another. Already predisposed to speculation, he was plunged into the world of books and literati represented by the Duyckincks, who placed their libraries at his disposal.[238] Whatever he missed during his earlier years was made up by indefatigable reading after 1844, though it may be observed that this eager investigation of bookish lore brought him little peace of mind but only mounting rage at the necessity under which philosophy, including the Kantian criticism, put him to regard truth as dual, casting two shadows—one earthly, the other heavenly.

Interest in Religion and Philosophy

If anything was lacking before he wrote

Moby-Dick to turn his attention to German thought, the necessary stimulation came during his trip to Europe in the autumn of 1849. On the second day aboard the *Southampton*, Melville met "some very pleasant passengers," chief among whom were George J. Adler, lexicographer and Professor of German at New York University, and Dr. Franklin Taylor, a cousin of the translator of *Faust*—both of whom were versed in German philosophy. Adler immediately struck Melville as a capital fellow whose learning placed no barriers in the way of free intercourse, despite Melville's inexpert dialectical powers. On the day he met Adler, Melville "walked the deck with . . . [him], till a late hour, talking of 'Fixed Fate, Free-Will, foreknowledge absolute,' etc." Sizing up Adler as a "Coleridgean," he made this erudite linguist, "full of German metaphysics and discourses of Kant, Swedenborg, etc.," his "principal companion." There were evenings when, says Melville, "Adler and Taylor came into my room, and it was proposed to have whiskey punches. . . . We had an extraordinary time and did not break up till after two in the morning. We talked of metaphysics continually, and Hegel, Schlegel, Kant, etc., were discussed under the influence of the whiskey." These gaudeola, varied by whist, mock trials, and other jollifications, were oft-repeated throughout the voyage, during all of which the slightest excuse "Got—all of us—riding on the German horse again."[239]

We know little about the precise contents of Melville's library, or when and where the accessions were made; but knowing something of the philosophical problems that tantalized him and that form the crux of *Moby-Dick* and *Pierre*, we can understand why visitors to Arrowhead were struck by his "well-stocked library."[240] Apparently works of German authors included were not numerous;[241] yet somewhere along the way he picked up an acquaintance with at least the general significance of German transcendental philosophy and Biblical criticism. When, during 1856–1857, he visited the Holy Land, he found his mind "sadly and suggestively affected" by "the indifference of Nature and Man"[242] to all that should make Jerusalem sacred, and disenchanted by that "great curse of modern . . . skepticism." He charged men like Niebuhr and Strauss with having generated and encouraged it, and added, "Heartily wish Niebuhr and Strauss to the dogs.—The deuce take their penetration and acumen."[243]

This is but one instance among many of Melville's inability to choose between the Will to Believe and the Desire to Know[244]— a harassing indecision that sent him roaming through pagan and Christian philosophies, ancient and modern, to his own bewilderment.[245] The moderns, from Bacon to Schopenhauer, especially interested him because they were presumed to have had the last word.[246] Of the Germans, he appears to have known most about Kant.[247] How much of German philosophy he read in translation we have no way of knowing exactly, but it would seem odd, considering his rather systematic analysis of English thought from Bacon to Hume and his great interest in Schopenhauer, had he neglected Kant and Hegel altogether. It may be, of course, that he felt the conversations he had with men like Adler and Taylor sufficed for his purposes; but it seems more likely that by the time he wrote *Moby-Dick* (certainly by the time he considered the ambiguous moral problems of *Pierre*), he had either consulted Kant at first hand or had pondered long on what his informants had told him. Even earlier, Melville had mentioned Kant in *Redburn* and in *Mardi*,[248] in the latter book making Bardianna (whose whimsicalities and profundities Babbalanja is fond of quoting at length[249]) the mouthpiece of Kant.[250]

Mardi, the first of Melville's deeper books represents Taji-Melville following religious truth and political justice through all known and unknown parts of the world and finding both forever eluding him. His traveling companions elect to remain among the Serenians, in the land of Alma-Christ, which is governed by the laws of Christian love. They rest content in Christian faith. Taji finds their uncritical acceptance of faith, untested and unconfirmed by the absolute reason, incapable of satisfying his inquiring mind.

The problem at the beginning of Melville's quest concerns social justice, but it soon involves the nature of God, man's divinity, his immortality, moral nature, free will, evil. Questions regarding all these become explicit in *Mardi*, but none is solved. In the end it is explained, by those who find faith and "provisional" truth sufficient, that these final questions involve secrets which Oro-God guards. To divulge them would make man equal to God in knowledge, thus destroying the distinction between the human and the divine. Not content with this answer, which seems to Taji-Melville an evasion, he seizes the helm of his boat and, fixing his eye on eternity, steers for the outer ocean, to re-emerge in *Moby-Dick* as the questing, avenging spirit of Ahab determined to dispel the mysteries by reducing them to knowledge or to pull down heaven in the attempt. It was inevitable that sooner or later Melville's questions respecting God, immortality, and freedom would lead to the crucial one underlying all problems affecting the Ideas of the Reason, namely, the epistemological one which Kant had considered in his two Critiques. Melville saw that all answers must remain tentative until the validity of the Reason itself is established: all ontological problems, for example, remained riddles until the legitimacy of the reason to reduce its Ideas to knowledge is validated. Accordingly when Ahab rants and raves against the inscrutability of the universe, what tantalizes him is not merely that he lacks the ability either to prove or to disprove the validity of the Ideas of the Reason; what

particularly torments him is that, though he grinds away at the nut of the universe until it cracks his jaws, he finds himself baffled at the very outset by his inability to prove Reason itself capable of acquiring absolute knowledge on these high matters. It is not only that he finds himself confronted at every turn by the chasm that separates mind and matter but that the mind itself seems incapable of marking clearly the grounds, limits, and validity of human knowledge. Everywhere Ahab sees himself confronted by the grinning masks of subtle, elusive inscrutability.[251] The quenchless feud which he feels, and which Melville confesses "seemed mine,"[252] is against these masks, all incarnate in the white whale:

All visible objects . . . are but pasteboard masks. . . . If a man will strike, strike through the mask! How can the prisoner reach outside except by thrusting through the wall? To me, the white whale is that wall, shoved near to me. . . . I see in him outrageous strength, with an inscrutable malice sinewing it. That inscrutable thing is chiefly what I hate; and be the white whale agent, or be the white whale principal, I will wreak that hate upon him. Talk not to me of blasphemy, man; I'd strike the sun if it insulted me.[253]

The conclusion of the book, couched though it be in allegorical action instead of abstract proposition or syllogism, is, for every practical purpose, the same as that of Kant's first *Critique*. The marriage of mind and matter remains unconsummated, and human reason remains forever incapable of reducing its Ideas to scientific knowledge. It is hard to believe that Ahab had not pondered Kant's argument, and that the Kantian examination of the antinomies did not lend argument and illustration to the thought that Melville incorporated in the story of the whale hunt.

While Kant relegated the purely speculative reason to a position of exercising regulative functions only, at the same time denying it any constitutive powers, he had insisted that the results of his criticism were not altogether negative. Unable to supply us with knowledge of God, immortality, and freedom, nevertheless it is a gain if, in its purely regulative province, the Pure Reason can criticize and test our ideas affecting supersensible qualities if they come to us from some other source. There Kant might have stopped. But he was loath to rest his case on a purely theoretical or speculative basis, and was impelled, by a practical human desire as a moral and religious being, to re-examine the entire problem from the point of view of Practical Reason—on the basis of moral will. The result was the *Critique of Practical Reason*, in which he affirmed, in the realm of the *practice* of ideas, what, in the purely speculative or theoretical sphere, he had logically been compelled to deny. And it is worth noting that Melville's next step, in its broader aspects, parallel's Kant's second.

Although Ahab ended disastrously in his attempt to carry the turrets of heaven by escalade, Melville tried, in his next book, to have Pierre test the adequacy and validity of *moral* law. Having failed in the purely theoretical, he would test the practical sphere of rational activity. The difference between Melville and Kant here is that Melville still seeks for what he calls "the Ultimate of Human Speculative Knowledge,"[254] that is, he demands of moral truth the same finality which Kant had proved impossible in the first *Critique*, and simply posited in the second.[255] The result is that Pierre is befooled by Truth, Virtue, and Fate, and that he concludes "it is not for man to follow the trail of truth too far, since by so doing he entirely loses the directing compass of his mind." For like the Arctic explorer, when he finally reaches the pole, to whose barrenness the needle of his compass has led him, he finds that the needle "indifferently respects all points of the horizon alike."[256] The subtitle of the book is, appropriately, "The Ambiguities." The answers are all ambiguous.[257] Different as this conclusion is from that of Kant's

second *Critique*, there is still the singular parallelism of both men's examining the problem of knowledge on identical levels—the metaphysical and the moral—in a manner to suggest that Melville was not unaware of Kant's example.[258] The influence of Kant on Melville is not one of clear-cut concepts or precise propositions, but rather one of Melville's understanding and applying the main or broad conclusions of the Kantian criticism. His interpretation of Kant, as voiced by Babbalanja, Taji, Ahab, and Pierre, is that Kant had marked the boundaries of "the Empire of Human Knowledge."[259] Rightly or wrongly interpreted, Kant furnished Melville with the backbone upon which to build his anatomy of despair.[260]

Among German literary figures Melville had, with a few notable exceptions, little acquaintance. As has already been noted, he bought in 1849 a copy of Schiller's *Poems and Ballads;* in 1851, writing to Hawthorne, he mentioned Schiller's advocacy of an aristocracy of the mind, but added, "I don't know much of him."[261] In the case of Goethe, the situation was different, for Melville paid a good deal of attention to Goethe and was alternately attracted and repulsed by him. "As with all great genius," he concluded, "there is an immense deal of flummery in Goethe, and in proportion to my own contrast with him, a monstrous deal of it in me."[262] As regards the other German writers, convincing arguments have been presented by Professor Leon Howard (1) that Fouqué's Undine supplied more than a suggestion for Melville's conception of Yillah in *Mardi*, and (2) that Melville's flower symbolism (in *Mardi* as well as the rose imagery of his later poems) derives from that of Fouqué, Tieck, Novalis, and others of the German *Romantiker*.[263]

Melville was attracted to German thought in much the same way that Emerson was drawn to it—by the hope that it would help him in the problem of squaring his heart by his head. Like Emerson, too, he contented himself largely with information derived at second hand, and seldom got beyond the comprehension of general tendencies, except perhaps in individual tenets of Kant, in whom, be it observed, he only found his worst fears substantiated. For where Emerson felt German speculative efforts to constitute an affirmative Yea to human questionings, Melville interpreted their conclusions to be an Everlasting Nay.

"A pondering man," as he styled himself, unwilling to accept "the infinite cliffs and gulfs of human mystery and misery" that Dante first revealed to him,[264] he groped about in Kantian epistemology and Goethean "pantheism" and found that after vast pains of mining the pyramid, "with joy we espy the sarcophagus; but we lift the lid— and nobody is there!—appallingly vacant, as vast as the soul of man."[265]

MARGARET FULLER
(1810–1850)

Early Intellectual Interests

In evaluating the influence of German literature as distinct from theology and philosophy in the complex of forces that went to make up New England Transcendentalism, the career of Margaret Fuller, the Aspasia of the Transcendental high council, is highly significant. More than any other single influence, her activity as reviewer, translator, and conversationalist was the agency that brought German literature into the orbit of the Transcendentalists' interests. Just as the young theologians in the Divinity School were receptive to the pious emotion and high spirituality of Herder and Coleridge, so she was taken with the warm, enthusiastic accounts of German letters then being trumpted "by the wild bugle-call of Thomas Carlyle."[266]

Early in her prodigious program of German studies she perceived that metaphysics would be of inestimable value to her. She looked into Locke "as introductory to a course of English metaphysics, and then [Mme] de Staël on Locke's system," and progressed soon to Kant and the post-Kantians as necessary to one engaged in studying Lessing, Schiller, and Novalis and "meditating on the life of Goethe," but these first excursions into German transcendental speculation left her optimism a bit dashed. By 1836 she was ready to admit

the inadequacy of her metaphysical preparation, and the thought that she had considered "*writing* a life of Goethe" now "shocked her."[267] However, the propagation of the "spiritual philosophy" had gone so far in her day that, while it proved insufficient to plumb the deepest meanings of critical transcendentalism, it provided her with confidence in her own intellectual resources, even to the point that she could declare, with perfect sincerity, that she found in America "no intellect comparable to her own."[268] Much that she believed was not only intuitional in the sense in which Parker used the term, but was communicated to her in flashes of mystical insight, and her communication of that "truth" was in turn couched in metaphorical, dark, and obscure language. Yet at bottom there lies the great tradition of German idealism from Kant and Jacobi to Hegel.[269] On occasions she wrote of "faith" as contrasted with "understanding,"[270] thereby recalling the Carlylean re- or misstatement of Kant. Again, she would affirm, "Our lives should be considered as a tendency, an approximation only," and in so doing, call up an image of Kant's *Idee*, dimly apprehended.[271] She conceived of the unity of existence as "the natural life of the soul,"[272] as "the law and plan of God";[273] or (what is highly characteristic) she borrowed a term from the German to call it simply the life of "Poesie" or "Poesy." Though the archaism "poesy" was rarely used among the English romantics and was uncommon in modern English generally, it was a Germanism that Margaret became exceedingly fond of, and which she came to employ as a key element in her thought. In German (as antonym to *Prosa* and synonym for *Dichtung*) *Poesie* had been revived by recent romantic critics and poets, and was a favorite of Bettina, Novalis, Schelling, and Goethe. After 1836 Margaret used it freely to denote all forms of the aspiration toward the ideal, the fulfillment of the highest spiritual potentiality of man. It is, she would say, "the ground . . . of the true art of life; it being not merely truth, not merely good, but the beauty which integrates both."[274] In the end it became a term by which she could establish the identity of the aesthetic and the religious impulses (in their purest state): she called it directly "the spirit of religion. . . . In their essence and their end these (poetry and religion] are one."[275]

Thus the gradual elaboration of her concept of "poesy" as suggested by her German studies foreshadowed a marked growth of her interest in the arts as avenues to the spiritual life. Especially after removing in 1839 to Jamaica Plain her preoccupation with poetry, art, and music was pronounced. In the Boston community she had ready access to museums, galleries, and concert halls; she read Flaxman and Retzsch and made the acquaintance of Allston.[276] Though she undertook, at the urging of Dr. Channing, to make translations of the German philosophers, her enthusiasm for the study of the arts drew her attention away from metaphysics,[277] and she never completed any of these translations. The necessity, occasioned by her work on the *Dial*, for orienting herself in the basic principles of literary criticism, accentuated this tendency.[278] She never engaged in a concentrated study of philosophy as a pursuit in itself, and her cry in 1836, "O for a safe and natural way of intuition," represents a point of view she maintained for the rest of her life.[279]

In German literature she became speedily more expert, Emerson observing that she knew the subject "more cordially than any other person."[280] Between 1834 and 1838 she demonstrated her command of German by teaching it both in private and in Alcott's school.[281] She was convinced that her vocation was to be teaching,[282] however difficult that would be in an age when all posts in the higher schools were held by men.[283] By 1836 she wrote on the subject of teaching that it was her earnest desire "to interpret the German authors of whom I am so fond to such Americans as are ready to receive," their "kind of culture" being "precisely the counterpoise required by the utilitarian tendencies of our day and place."[284] She soon earned the name "Germanico."[285] As early as 1833 she recognized the need of a suitable organ for her purposes, and by March, 1835, she was actively planning, chiefly with Hedge, the "periodical" that eventually became the *Dial*, the fundamental aim of which was to draw New England into a closer relationship with the totality of western culture. Freely offering to "lend a hand" whenever it should be launched, she made clear that if the projector accepted her help, she would emphasize German literature.[286] "I fear I am merely 'Germanico,' and not 'transcendental.'"[287]

Goethe and Schiller

Her first tangible step toward popularizing German authors in America was an effort to bring Goethe out from under the cloud cast over him by Menzel's attack on his morality. To this end, she made a verse translation of *Tasso*. As soon as she completed it (March, 1834), she asked Hedge to submit it to Emerson, who read it but recorded no impression of it. All efforts to secure a publisher failed until the appearance of the second volume of her *Works*, edited posthumously by her brother, in 1859.[288] *Tasso* spoke directly to Margaret's heart, and she responded warmly to the human sympathy displayed by Goethe toward the problems of the artist. She did more. She identified her isolated existence with that of the frustrated, misunderstood poet.

Poor Tasso [she wrote to Emerson] in the play offered his love and service too officiously to all. . . . If I wanted only ideal figures to think about, there are those in literature I like better than any of your living ones. But I want far more. I want habitual intercourse, cheer, inspiration, tenderness. I want these for myself; I want to impart them.[289]

Emerson, who preserved the New England reticences, while regretfully confessing his "porcupine impossibility of contact" with other personalities, doubtless read this confession warily and counted it an embarrassing instance of her overwarm nature, which throughout the period of their friendship half-irritated him and impelled him to keep her at arm's length.[290]

Margaret's first publication was a translation of Eckermann's *Conversations with Goethe* (1839). She shortened the work slightly, omitting references to the *Farbenlehre* and certain other topics. Throwing light on the little-known later years of Goethe and displaying to full advantage the ripe wisdom, the humanity and profundity of his character, this work revealed an entirely new side of him; and many of the younger Transcendentalists must have felt as did Thomas W. Higginson: "It brought him nearer to me than any book, before or since, has ever done."[291]

Her publication in 1842 of a small portion of Bettina (Brentano) von Arnim's *Günderode* in English translation affords a glimpse into some special enthusiasms in the field of German literature about which she otherwise wrote very little. Margaret was fascinated by this German woman who had achieved success as an interpreter of the inner lives of the romantics.[292] She pored eagerly over Bettina's revelations about Goethe and the extended account of her love affair with the elderly poet, and found herself even more carried away by Bettina's second book, a fictionization of her correspondence with the melancholy young poetess Karoline von Günderode.[293] While somewhat shocked at the sensationalism and candor of the *Correspondence with a Child*,[294] she was delighted with the affecting and beautiful account of the friendship between two gifted girls as recorded in *Günderode*.[295] She saw in it a parallel to the intimacy and tender spiritual response that she herself was attempting to establish in her relations with the young girls who flocked about her in Boston.[296] Without pausing to consider whether the work would have any appeal to an American audience, she set about preparing a translation, the first installment of which she put on sale in Elizabeth P. Peabody's shop, though without identifying herself as translator. Thus the "somewhat angular Boston sibyl," as Henry James once characterized her,[297] not only attained a certain release from emotional tension which had been built up in her but made a covert appeal to have her kind of high-minded sensibility understood and recognized by unsympathetic Boston. She was revealing the strong undercurrents of genuinely romantic emotionality that linked her in spirit with such feminine rebels of her time as George Sand, Rahel, Mme de Staël, and Bettina. Needless to say, *Günderode* failed of its purpose.

The salutary effect of her criticism was that, through her continual attention to European writers and modes of thought, she was able to lead the writer and reader away from parochialism toward subjects and attitudes of universal validity. She defined the critic's function as an activity paralleling that of the creative writer, in which they strive together to realize the objective ideal standard that lies outside and beyond them both.[298] The critic, she says, must be accepted in the community of thinkers as one who keeps up a protestant spirit in the literary church. All literature is required to pass muster in the light of reason. This she considered a universal basis of criticism, and its best justification —a conception where both critic and writer are brought before the same bar and permitted to settle their differences on equal terms.[299] From this lofty critical eminence, she sought to review the literary productions of her time. From this point of view, American literature was for her but a small area of the totality of western culture. Her success on the *Tribune* under such an exacting master as Horace Greeley is a signal achievement in American letters, one that has given her the reputation of being "the best critic produced in America before 1850,"[300] only Poe disputing the position with her.

From the German romantic critics, Schlegel and Tieck, and from Goethe, she learned to apply the laws of historical development in the realm of literature even while, like them, she clung to the ideal principle as the ultimate goal.[301] She used both the ideal and objective criticism with success. The former principle, she held, is consonant with New England absolutism; the second is the naturalistic, organic, and at the same time artistic approach of Goethe and the historical school.[302] The former is in agreement with classical tradition in the drama, the latter with Shakespearean-historical tradition.[303]

Margaret's long struggle to understand Goethe involved the reading of all available works, memoirs, and letters. She recognized that in him there spoke a wise and experienced authority on the problems of life, who, observant and penetrating as he was, taught a doctrine of realism and renunciation very difficult either to refute or to accept. This dilemma, together with her fear of the impulses within her that seemed dangerously close to his own "paganism," made the study of Goethe a serious occupation for a full decade of her life. He alternately "solaced" and "disquited" her soul, yet provided for her the

greatest literary as well as spiritual experience.[304] By 1838 she had collected a large mass of notes on Goethe's life, which she tentatively promised to write for Ripley's *Specimens*, but which she never completed. There was no personality, either in books or among her acquaintances, who did more to emancipate her soul from the limitations of New England morality and the restrictions of femininity.

Critics before her were at a loss how to answer Menzel's charges, how to justify the ways of this man to the Puritan conscience.[305] She knew Goethe well enough to see that he lived by a morality and a religion of his own. She completely shifted the ground of argument: she defined morality, not as did the others, as conformity to absolute rules laid down by religious authority, but as conformity to the individual's own code as prescribed by his personality. From this point of view Goethe's life was, as she said, "active, wise, and honored,"[306] as consistent and beyond reproach as the Gods on Olympus. Her essays on Goethe in the *Dial* and her Preface to the *Conversations with Goethe*[307] are not principally criticisms of separate works but rather interpretations—remarkably modern in tone and depth of understanding—of the total personality of the man.[308] She was no "blind admirer" of the man, but her vision was not obscured by the search for values which he does not profess to have. In her essay on "Menzel's View of Goethe"[309] she continued her work of defining the limits and range of Goethe's mind, affirming again and again that we are not fitted to judge him unless we have studied him long and well. "He obliges us to live and grow, that we may walk by his side. . . . We doubt whether the revolution of the century be not required to interpret the quiet depths of his Saga." She predicted that the caviling at this or that fault in him will end "in making more men and women read these works and [go] 'on and on,' till they forget whether the author be a patriot or a moralist, in the deep humanity of the thought, the breathing nature of the scene."[310] She explained his career as determined by the environmental influence of his youth—as *the* one necessary to bring German literature to its fruition; though, again, she was careful to show the limits of his gifts, deploring the fact that he was not a poet-prophet, but "only a sage."[311]

Particularly appealing to her was the idea that the role of woman in society could be charted and illustrated by taking such Goethean types as Philine, Marianne, Natalie, Makarie, Ottilie, and Margarete as basic symbols for the range of feminine qualities and types. Goethe's ideal of woman, "das ewig Weibliche," was for her a key for interpreting woman's essential character and potentiality. In her feminist treatise *Woman in the Nineteenth Century* she made effective use of the Goethean gallery of female characters, drawing on her vast knowledge of those women who figured in the actual life of Goethe as well as on the creatures of his imagination. In the area of feminism, where Emerson failed her dismally, Goethe was able to supply her with the orientation and illumination which she so much desired, and which, more than anything else, became the mainspring of her genius and power. In short, the central doctrine that Margaret learned from Goethe (not Emerson) was self-reliance, self-culture.[312] It was this that liberated her from New England puritanism and taught her to resist the pressure of social convention under which her nature felt stifled. It encouraged her to take a bold stand on the "woman question," for it taught her that for all their well-meant chivalry, the men of her society were putting unfair restrictions on the lives of women. From Goethe, too, she learned to take a cosmopolitan view of literature—to look upon the advent of a *Weltliteratur* as the distinctive development of the future. Her discussion of American writers, her praise and blame of individual authors, are predicated on the conviction that the local and national must be harmonized with the ideal and universal.[313] Finally, she learned from Goethe much about the nature and history of art; only through him did she come to appreciate the great tradition of modern and classical sculpture, architecture, and painting.[314]

The Romantic School

Yet Goethe's liberalism, his precept of "extraordinary, generous seeking" alone never satisfied the demands of her idealistic nature. She belonged to a generation of romanticists, while Goethe stood apart from that movement, not at its center; he was too calm, too patient with the reality of life, too aloof.[315] Under his influence she could make heroic efforts to master her volatile feelings, to learn the lesson of resignation; but her glowing enthusiasm for Beethoven and her sympathy for the Romantic School show that this was not constantly in her power.[316] The reading of Novalis and Körner she found "a relief, after feeling the immense superiority of Goethe." She was enchanted while she read him, but found "when I shut the book, it seems as if I had lost my personal identity." At such times "the one-sidedness, imperfection, and glow of a mind like that of Novalis" seemed "refreshingly human" to her.[317] The part of her nature that was repulsed by Goethe's tepid equanimity turned, with true spiritual kinship, to the romantic sentiments of Jean Paul, Novalis, and Bettina and, above all, to the "Titanic utterances" of Beethoven.

Margaret's delight in the tenderness, fancy, and rich brilliance of Jean Paul made for direct sympathy with his message and point of view.[318] She found him the priest of natural religion, a "magnetic influence." Her Italianate soul[319] responded to Jean Paul's high coloring, his pure, sensitive heroes, his extravagant, rhapsodic passages of description, and his fondness for omens, puzzles, premonitions, and apparitions.

To become acquainted with Novalis was to indulge some of the same preferences. In 1832 she was studying Novalis and Goethe, and there were moments when she felt much more sympathy for the "wondrous youth" than for the old "master."[320] His religion of nature, his view of the external world as the image of the inward being, the mystical significance he attached to flowers, stones, and minerals—these found many echoes in her own thought. They gave stimulus and direction to the development of her esoteric mystical studies, which even to her closest friends remained an obscure, imperfectly realized phase of her thought.[321]

Her interest in Justinus Kerner also springs from her addiction to the occult. The lengthy account of his *Seherin von Prevorst*, inserted in *Summer on the Lakes* (pp. 125–64) presents the results of some pseudo-scientific investigations into spiritualistic and so-called "electrical" phenomena. A somnambulist from childhood, she could not let the occasion offered by Kerner's book pass without giving her observations to her readers.[322] All in all, she made no favorable impression on the public by displaying her preoccupation with these mysterious phenomena. It was precisely her penchant for mysticism,[323] nature-worship, and spiritualism that caused her New England neighbors—who possessed more of the witch-hunting spirit than they realized—to look upon her as a foreign creature, a Bacchante entirely out of place in the realities of American life.[324]

In her treatment of the ballad literature of Germany, Margaret performed a service to the literary culture of America. Her review of Simrock's *Rheinsagen* (1842)[325] showed an insight into the significance of folk poetry as a basis of a national literature. While most enthusiastic about *Rhein-Romantik*, she also emphasized the importance of the *Volkslied* as a social phenomenon,[326] and urged American writers to follow the German example of paying more

attention to their own heritage, including the fast-vanishing Indian lore.[327] She made a strong case for an indigenous American literature, rooted in the native past, and not merely imitative of the European.[328]

German Music

The romanticism of her nature is revealed most clearly in her passionate response to music. To hear the symphonies of Beethoven was, as she described it, the supreme spiritual and aesthetic experience of her life in New England.[329] In Beethoven she recognized a genius fired with the high idealism of the age, and in his music she heard the surging romantic affirmation of the universality and prophetic power that she demanded in the highest poetry. Knowing Beethoven, she could say that music was the highest of the arts.[330] She would have the soaring aspirations of her nature expressed not in imperfect words, but in appropriate music. The musical genius was the man completely dominated by "das Dämonische." Music transported her completely; it was a rapture, a fulfillment of her strongest "Sehnsucht."[331] It was for her the embodiment of that religion of nature wherein nothing is negation, and all is seen as the substance of the divine; in a sense, her form of Transcendentalism.[332] Her intense experience in music goes far beyond anything that we find in the other major Transcendentalists. Her dependence on it as a ministrant to the soul reveals her a person closely identified with romanticism in a pure and drastic form. Her utterances on the subject (often private poems not intended for publication[333]) lay bare the irrationalism and desperate romantic loneliness which are strong components of her mind. For a number of years she explored the possibility of finding the meaning and fulfillment of her life in art, above all in music. That this endeavor was difficult and indeed finally unsatisfactory is demonstrated by the fact that after 1844 she altered the direction of her interests and began to take an active part in practical issues, in prison reform, pauperism, education, and European political movements.[334]

MARGARET FULLER's influence was exerted in many ways. Not the least was her personal impact on leaders of the Transcendental movement—on Emerson, above all, but also on Clarke, Ripley, W. H. Channing, and their younger associates. Anyone interested in music or art or foreign literature knew what Margaret Fuller had said on these subject, for as Emerson remarked, "All the art, the thought, and the nobleness of New England, seemed . . . related to her and she to it."[335] It was her distinctive achievement to do for American criticism and literary culture what Parker did for American theology. The wide international viewpoint which she fostered became another strong characteristic of American Transcendentalism. German literature, which was in the ascendancy in that day, received the largest share of her attention because she recognized it as the fountainhead for the newer European movements.[336] In later years, after her removal to Italy and her sudden death in 1850, her efforts attained a wide effectiveness through the work of younger Transcendentalist disciples. By her example of faithful translation of the German classics, she encouraged Brooks and Dwight, to name the most prominent, to undertake similar projects; and by her discriminating critical labors, she hastened the assimilation of German authors into the receptive but nonetheless provincial community. In J. F. Clarke, who decades after her death was to become an authority in the field of primitive religions and mythology, we can see the shaping influence of her mind. Emerson's debt to her was at least as great as hers to him. W. H. Channing, another of her close friends, shared her sensitivity to the beauty of European art and literature. W. E. Channing the younger, C. P. Cranch, C. T.

Brooks, Bayard Taylor, and John Weiss can be considered as direct inheritors of her position in New England life, for they continued her pioneering work in translation and criticism from the point where she left it.[337]

American interest in German literature generally was in the ascendancy until well into the 50's though the attention focused on different groups of writers at different times. The high point of interest in theology was reached earliest—in the writings of Parker, Ripley, and Hedge. Then followed, with the stimulus of Margaret Fuller's essays, the study of Goethe and the German romantics. This phase culminated before 1865, by which time most of the larger pieces of translation from the German classics had been completed. After the Civil War came a wave of popularizing and imitation of relatively unimportant contemporary writers of fiction. The members of the Genteel Tradition—reared mainly by the Transcendentalists, to be sure, but developing a different social attitude altogether—now set up a new authoritarianism in taste. The deep, firsthand inspiration which the older generation had drawn from Germany had almost disappeared, leaving in its place a mere curiosity for the entertaining or the sentimental.

This superficial worshipfulness of all things German, of course, had already a long history before the so-called Genteel tradition became operative. The temptation on the part of the meagerly gifted to draw upon German materials in the vain hope thereby to give their effusions a certain afflatus as a substitute for what was inherently lacking goes back to the time when German literature first attracted attention. During the early years of the nineteenth century there was a rash of *Werther* adaptations and of Gothic productions faintly reminiscent of German horror. Later, and running parallel to the flow of books that came from the better Transcendentalist writers, there was a steady stream of second-

and third-rate books that claimed descent from the same spiritual source, and that had, indeed, a superficial overlay of Germanic inspiration. Examples that come to mind run from Mrs. L. H. Sigourney's *Zinzendorff* (1836) and Philip James Bailey's *Festus* (1839) to John Lothrop Motley's *The Chevalier de Satiniski* (1844) and Sylvester Judd's *Margaret* (1845). Representatives of a later generation are men like Richard Henry Stoddard and Thomas Bailey Aldrich, who, while they stood basically outside the Germanic tradition, did not entirely escape the contagion. Besides writing a biography of Alexander von Humboldt, Stoddard invested several of his poems in a German locale and apparently wrote his ballad "The Wine Cup" on the model of Uhland's "Glück von Edenhall"; while Aldrich's drama *Judith and Holofernes* appears to be a watered-down version of Hebbel's *Judith*. Meanwhile, on a more popular level, certain distinctive concepts originally derived from German books had become popular possessions, so that the Rev. Henry Ward Beecher, in sermons to his Plymouth Church in Brooklyn during the seventies, explained his emotional entanglements to his parishioners in terms of "elective affinities," and presumably was both understood and forgiven. Already in 1856, when Moncure D. Conway preached his farewell sermon in Washington he took his text "from Mignon's song in *Wilhelm Meister*" and quoted Mephistopheles, and assumed that his audience knew enough of Goethe to grasp his allusions. Years later, when he reported to his free-religionist congregation in Cincinnati his meeting with David Friedrich Strauss and

explained the latter's "purely anthropological view of immortality," he again presumed that his auditors comprehended him; but it does not follow that either he or his congregation had any longer the intense interest in the several schools of German Biblical criticism that had inspired the generation of Parker, Ripley, and Norton. These instances, and a hundred like them that could be cited, betoken an ever-widening popularity or speaking-acquaintance with concepts or tendencies stemming from Germany, but often lacking the intensity and absorption of interest of an earlier day. That is to say, there was, except among several groups of specialists, a certain dilution of that once clear stream of Germanic influence as it flowed through the thirties and forties, when it provided for many an exhilerating, sometimes intoxicating stimulant, until during the seventies and eighties it was taken, in many quarters, as a kind of postprandial concotion. In literary circles, a dash of German allusiveness served admirably for garnishment, ornamental embellishment, and a universally recognized sign of literary sophistication.

The Transcendentalists on the whole resisted this relative lowering of appreciation and taste; they stood out conspicuously as the only group (with the exception of professional teachers of German literature) whose interest in Goethe, for example, increased rather than diminished; but some of the youngest among them—men like C. T. Brooks and T. W. Higginson—no longer possessing the inspiration of the original Transcendentalists, followed in the easier ways of the Genteel traditionalists.

MINOR MOVEMENTS AND GROUPS

Transcendentalist Writers

GODWIN, WHEELER, HURLBUT

Directly out of the circles of the *Dial* and Brook Farm came a group of amateur

critics and translators who disappeared from view rather quickly, either because they turned to other interests or because their lives were cut off at an early age. George Bancroft's contributions were a few poems in Dwight's anthology of Schiller and Goethe, and George P. Bradford translated a small portion of the *Wahlverwandtschaften* for Frederic H. Hedge's *Prose Writers*; yet the latter is significant as the only sampling of Goethe's novel available to English readers before Boylan's version of 1854. Parke Godwin (1816–1904) was a Fourierite during his earlier years and editor of the *Harbinger*. With the assistance of Dwight and Dana, he translated Goethe's *Autobiography* in 1846, and with W. P. Prentiss the *Tales* of Zschokke. Later he contributed to *Putnam's* and other journals many critical articles on German literature, among the more notable one on Strauss in 1855 and another on Goethe in 1856. Charles Stearns Wheeler (1816–1843), tutor of Greek at Harvard from 1838 to 1842 and close associate of Thoreau, sent back from Heidelberg, whither he went in 1842, reports to the *Dial* on German books and authors, especially on philosophy. One was a lengthy transcript of Schelling's important *Introductory Lecture* delivered in Berlin in 1841. Finally, there was the young divinity student William Hurlbut, at Cambridge, who busied himself with translations from Heine during the forties. His article in the *Christian Examiner* for March, 1849, "The Religious Poetry of Modern Germany," was full of praise in the manner of Parker and Ripley for the "religious character" and the beautiful expression of "reverence and belief" to be found in Novalis, Schiller, Jacobi, and Herder.[338]

LOUISA MAY ALCOTT

Louisa May Alcott (1832–1888), who was as much a May as an Alcott, soon came to see some of her father's idealisms as eccentricities, and in her essay, "Transcendental Wild Oats," she touched on the comic side of Transcendentalism. However, as a girl she felt some of the enthusiasms of the day very keenly, particularly those affecting German romantic literature.[339] Never a close student, but always a great reader, she especially admired "Goethe, Emerson, Shakespeare, Carlyle, Margaret Fuller . . . Whittier, Herbert, Crashaw, Keats, Coleridge, Dante."[340] While she was trying out her pen, she was constantly in the company of her father's associates, especially Emerson and Parker. Not unnaturally, she expanded her reading in Goethe, and soon Schiller, Jean Paul, and Madame de Staël too became favorites.[341] In 1859, when she won her first literary triumph by selling a story to the *Atlantic* for fifty dollars, editor Lowell had some reason for wanting reassurance that her contribution was not a translation from the German.[342] Thereafter she sold readily enough what she called her "blood and thunder" stories and "rubbishy" tales,[343] but she soon tired of these and grew ambitious to write something touching her inmost thoughts. The result was her first novel, *Moods* (1864). It achieved a momentary success, but after a week people discovered that it belonged to the class of writings known as "transcendental."[344] Its fault was that it was too full of the thoughts inspired by her reading in books like *Werther* and *Elective Affinities*; and as soon as the dangerous word *affinities* was noised about by the reviewers and attached to the Warwick-Moor-Sylvia relationship, the popularity of the book fell off speedily. Having decided long before that the situation in Goethe's *Wahlverwandtschaften* was immoral, the New England public concluded that *Moods*, so obviously inspired by it, was also wicked. "I seem to have been playing with edge tools without knowing it," said Miss Alcott.[345]

She knew almost everybody even remotely connected with the Transcendental group from the time when she was a child through the period of the Concord School of Philosophy and the Radical Club. She often accompanied her father to the meetings; but since philosophy was early associated in her mind with poverty and suffering, she never felt its charms and contented herself with watching "the philosophers mount their hobbies and prance away into time and space," while she "gazed after them and tried to look wise."[346] Yet after the thorough immersion which she had in the Transcendental, Germanic climate of Concord, her books could not remain unaffected. They are full of German touches, ranging from allusions and quotations to German characters and whimsical references to German metaphysics.[347] More important as indicating Germanic inspiration is *A Modern Mephistopheles* (1877). Long desirous of writing another novel like *Moods*, into which she might pour more of her own thoughts than was possible in her popular stories, she wrote during the winter of 1876–1877 *A Modern Mephistopheles*, published the following April in the No Name Series. She wrote rapidly and *con amore*, fascinated by the excitement of the *incognito* afforded by the anonymity of the series. The book, she said, "had been simmering even since I read Faust last year," and she added, "Enjoyed doing it, being tired of providing moral pap for the young."[348] The book took its inspiration from *Faust* in the sense that it built on Goethe's conception of a Mephistopheles as a gentleman who moved in the best society.[349] All in all, though Louisa May Alcott never learned to handle the language competently and refused to concern herself actively with German metaphysics, the influence of German literary motifs on her work is more than superficial.

CHRISTOPHER PEARSE CRANCH

Christopher Pearse Cranch (1813–1892), one of the Transcendentalists associated with Margaret Fuller in cultivating the arts of poetry, painting, and music, was a Southerner by birth who entered Harvard in 1832 and thenceforth indulged his versatile talents.[350] Impressed by the preaching of Parker, Clarke, and W. H. Channing, he attended the Divinity School and accepted

various preaching engagements, but still remained undecided about his life work. At Bangor he met Hedge; while in Cambridge he practiced music whenever the occasion offered; and in 1836 he often enjoyed the company of a certain "musical German minister." His wanderings took him to Cincinnati in time to assist in the editing of the Transcendentalist journal, the *Western Messenger*, during the absence of Clarke.[351] During 1841–1844 he was often at Brook Farm, where he was always welcomed by the assembled company as one of their gayest and brightest wits. Even his caricatures of the Transcendental hierarchy, born of a sense of realistic objectivity and sketched with a sharp pencil, were objects of merriment.[352] He introduced them to the pleasures of hearing German *Lieder* such as Schubert's Serenade (*Ständchen*) and Erlking (*Erlkönig*). In 1841 he decided, as did others of the younger disciples of Margaret Fuller and Emerson, that his interests were too diversified to be cramped in the clerical mold. He was ready to substitute painting for sermon writing.[353]

The rest of his life was one of genial devotion to poetry, painting, and music.[354] He wrote children's stories and poems and translated from the Latin, French, and German. His first volume of poems (1844), dedicated to Emerson, contained several translations from the German. He became one of the group of artistic expatriates who spent long periods of time in the art centers of Europe. He continued to write poetry throughout his life, and once remarked he had "enough translations . . . of the German and Latin chiefly, to make a volume, but there is no demand for such ware."[355] Thus it happens that none but a remarkably small number of his translations are accessible today, though his friends enjoyed them and valued them highly.[356]

JOHN SULLIVAN DWIGHT

John Sullivan Dwight (1813–1893) dedicated a long life to the expounding of the Transcendental aesthetic and religious creed, and distinguished himself in a field which twenty years before had lain entirely uncultivated—the interpretation and criticism of music.[357] The study of German poetry and music were Dwight's two loves, which gradually supplanted his interest in a theological career. By 1837 he was preoccupied with his studies of literature, and in 1838 appeared his volume of translations, *The Select Minor Poems of Goethe and Schiller*, the second in Ripley's series of *Specimens*. It was precisely their shorter poems that were least known, and Dwight's book, which contained many of the best translations that have ever been made, led to a far more favorable reception of the authors than their dramas and novels alone had won for them. While he was assisted by a number of his Transcendentalist friends,[358] Dwight himself provided versions of admirable finish and tone and added some seventy pages of notes interpreting the poems against the background of their authors' thought. The volume has remained unsurpassed in its field during the century since its appearance, many of the versions still being accepted as standard.

His intermittent preaching was no great success. In November, 1841, he went to Brook Farm, where he taught harmony, voice, and piano, as well as Latin. Throughout this period he translated the texts of many German songs and hymns, especially from oratorio scores. Dwight led singing classes and choruses, instructed the members in the fundamentals of art, and he took pains to develop their talents. He lectured on musical subjects in Boston and New York and wrote much for the *Harbinger* and the *Democratic Review*, dwelling little on the technical aspects of music but attempting to convey in words the inner meanings of the musical message. Those who were unsympathetic with his approach (and there were many such) thought his utterances rhapsodical, flighty, abstruse. He had

a vibrant and loosely strung nature, extremely sensitive and responsive to art, perhaps too much at the mercy of the emotion that music generated in him.[359] For him, music contained the essence of the view of life that Emerson, Parker, and Ripley were grappling with in other media. The growing recognition of music as "the art of arts, the soul of them all," at the same time that "the law of social harmonies is being announced," seemed to him an all-important fact, and he was prepared to spend his life developing the analogy. Just as Ripley learned from Fichte that the propositions of metaphysics must be put to the test of practical experiment, so Dwight looked upon music not merely as a refuge of the soul, but as one of the avenues over which mankind is to pass into the realm of social harmony.[360] However visionary these reformist dreams may have been, Dwight's columns in the *Harbinger* were extremely successful in the sense that he made that paper one of the best musical journals the country had ever possessed.[361]

In 1850–1851 Dwight gave over his reviewing in favor of a new periodical venture. The Harvard Musical Association assisted him in raising a guarantee fund for a projected musical journal, which he was to edit and manage. The first number of *Dwight's Journal of Music* appeared on April 10, 1852, to continue an honored and influential career until 1881. What the reformers and social planners had been unable to effect at Brook Farm by immediate, practical experiment, Dwight hoped might be realized gradually through the refining, ennobling influence of the arts.[362] His *Journal of Music* was devoted to this end. In filling its pages, Dwight made no concessions to the relatively low state of popular knowledge and taste. He was "intensely German in his preferences," and he took the stand that the composers of the "classical" school from Mozart through Beethoven had carried the art to the apex of its development, though he did not neglect other national schools nor ignore contemporary figures and the advocates of program music.[363] In his last years, however, he found himself among the party of the old-fashioned—outmoded by the public taste that he had molded but that went beyond him in its enthusiasm for opera, program music, and theater music.

THOMAS WENTWORTH HIGGINSON

Thomas Wentworth Higginson (1823–1911) is a late Transcendentalist who, though not a writer of lasting importance, was an accomplished representative man of letters of the idealist tradition. His work as historian of the movement and biographer of Margaret Fuller and George Ripley is an invaluable contribution to our knowl·edge of the earlier phases of the Newness, and his long career is an excellent mirror of the changes in thought and feeling in Boston from the forties to the end of the century.[364]

Born and reared in the shadow of the Harvard buildings, Higginson grew up in intimate association with the Harvard teachers and students. He entered as a well-wishing friend the circle of young men at Brook Farm; this influence, he reported, made him a "half-way socialist for life." The writer who took strongest possession of him, after Emerson, was Jean Paul, whose memoirs Mrs. Eliza Buckminster Lee of Brookline made available in 1845. He eagerly read all new translations of Jean Paul as they appeared. Though his mastery of German was not complete, he was affected in his impressionable youth by romances, ballads, letters, and patriotic songs of the German romanticists then appearing in profusion from the American presses. He remained at Harvard through the year 1846–1847, his reading "tending more and more to Cousin, Jouffroy, Constant, Leroux . . . and the easier aspects of German philosophy," social reform finally superseding his interest in both philosophy and theology.[365]

As a mature writer Higginson came to look back on the forties as a period too strongly influenced by European romanticism, the great wave of enthusiasm in Jean Paul, for example, stemming largely from this absorption in the sentimental.[366] In his late years he appraised Germany as a great nation of science rather than of literature.[367] He was a *literatus* and genial gentleman representing the New England liberal tradition of his day. By and large, he was one of the group including Dwight and Brooks who took their cues from the earlier Transcendentalists, notably Margaret Fuller. But Higginson, while carrying forward the tradition of art and music which she initiated, tended to conventionalize it and to superimpose upon it a code which she would have been the first to denounce. Higginson never reached the depth of understanding of German literature that is found among its earlier students and translators.[368] As a late Transcendentalist, he joined forces with the disciples of gentility who patterned themselves after Longfellow, Holmes, Lowell, and Whitter. By gradually introducing an emphasis on propriety and decorum, the *literati* of his kind transformed the earlier insurgency into that branch of the Genteel Tradition in American art that is best exemplified, perhaps, by Charles Timothy Brooks.

The Genteel Writers

The Genteel Tradition in American literary culture embraces men of varying abilities, often totally different backgrounds, and sometimes sharply divergent personalities. Certainly they were less conscious of being a group at all than literary historians and critics today make them. Almost to a man, however, they were in accord in regarding German literature as the latest and finest flowering of literary culture. They believed that American letters stood to be enriched by the addition of a German leaven, and they did what lay within their powers to introduce that leaven. In this respect and in others, Charles T. Brooks, Bayard Taylor, G. H. Boker, Charles G. Leland, Edmund C. Stedman, and Richard H. Stoddard, each sought to emulate his elders, yet each missed the literary distinction of the older generation. These men were belated romanticists in a world already stirring with a new ferment—a world that was to repudiate them as the realistic movement gained power. Their roseate view of life, compounded of German idealism and romanticism, was ruthlessly swept away before the newer critical realism.

CHARLES TIMOTHY BROOKS

Though not a creative writer in his own right, Charles Timothy Brooks (1813–1883) was the most assiduous translator of German literature ever to appear on the American scene. On the whole his work was competent and skillful, and some of his productions have not been superseded to this day. Though a respected contemporary and friend of the Transcendentalists, he was never closely allied with the movement, except insofar as his literary interests coincided with theirs. Like them, he was attracted to Schiller, Jean Paul, and the romantic lyricists; but unlike the Transcendentalists, he tended to seek out the writings which displayed to best advantage the Germans' warmth of sentiment, didacticism, piety, and simplicity. He culled from the vast but then unknown reserves of recent German literature primarily those works that were distinguished by the qualities of gentleness, sweetness, moral purity, and optimism. A large segment of the American public demanded a belletristic fare of this kind, and Brooks's translations were popular successes. Occasionally he wrote articles on theological subjects, but his attitude was moderate, pacific, and spiritual in tone.[369]

Brooks absorbed the current of Transcendentalist doctrines in ethics and Bibli-

cal interpretation, and he owed to them, also, his early sympathy for such authors as Goethe, Rückert, Jean Paul, Freiligrath, and Schefer. In 1838 he published his first work of translation—the first American version of Schiller's *Wilhelm Tell*, and, excepting the versions done in England by S. Robinson (1825 and 1834), one of the earliest readable renderings of that work. From *Tell*, Brooks turned to the lyric, and in 1842 published *Songs and Ballads: Translations from Uhland, Körner, and Other German Lyric Poets*[370] as the fourteenth and final volume of Ripley's *Specimens*. The book was uneven in workmanship, containing not a few successful translations alongside some mediocre ones, just as there was an astonishingly wide range in quality between the better and the weaker specimens chosen for inclusion in the collection. In a similar way, his next volume, *Schiller's Homage of the Arts, with Miscellaneous Pieces from Rückert, Freiligrath, and Other German Poets* (1846), brings a varied selection of lyrics. It strikes somewhat more loudly than the first book the tone of social and political protest as expressed by Freiligrath, Herwegh, and Rückert. Brooks's next collection, *German Lyrics* (1853), devotes almost half its space to poems by Anastasius Grün (Count von Auersperg), but on the whole, the romantic tone still predominates. Uhland, Rückert, and Kerner, with their poetry of radiant sentiment and simple virtue, are clearly the poet's favorites among the more recent writers.

From the lyric, Brooks turned to Goethe and in 1856 published his version of *Faust I*. Coming as it did on the heels of a number of wretched attempts, this work enhanced the English reader's enjoyment and understanding of the work. Notwithstanding occasional mistranslations and "lapses into pedestrianism," Brooks's translation is a creditable piece of work, and one which had its influence on Bayard Taylor when, two decades later, he undertook the same task. Like Margaret Fuller and his teacher, Follen, Brooks was a warm admirer of Jean Paul. As early as 1843 he had praised this writer in an article in the *Christian Examiner*, and in 1847 he had published an excerpt from *Levana* in the *Christian Register*. Brooks remains to the present day the only translator of the *Titan* (1862), *Hesperus* (1864), and *The Invisible Lodge* (1883), three of the greatest of the author's long works. In sheer volume of output, Brooks's translations are monumental. His work with Jean Paul alone—an author notoriously hard to translate—amounted to over two thousand closely-packed pages.[371]

His representative position in the literary scene of his day makes his career a good measuring-stick of the tastes of his reading public. His translations represent that branch of German literature that was congenial to the temper of the genteel tradition, which Brooks did as much to call forth as to foster. Professor von Klenze's phrase for the interests of these "Victorians"—"meliorism unembarrassed by facts"—suggests the limits of their appreciation. They stopped this side of the vitriolic irony of Heine; they preferred the sentimental Auerbach to Keller; and they avoided or misunderstood the tragic depths of Hebbel and Grillparzer. The uncertainty of their literary standards is evident in the unevenness of their translations as well as in the absence of an assured sense of discrimination among the worst, the mediocre, and the best of German verse.

NATHANIEL PARKER WILLIS

Nathaniel Parker Willis (1806–1867) belonged to an older generation, but since his writings are similar to the product of the Genteel Tradition, he may be discussed with them. Finding journalism in America an uphill struggle, Willis seized the opportunity that came in 1831 to go to Europe as a traveling reporter and letter-writer. He was able to catch the American vogue for European sketches, or pencilings, as he called them, at its height, and his letters were widely printed in newspapers and magazines.[372] His best pictures of German scenes are to be found in *Pencillings by the Way* (1835), although the descriptions in *Invalid Rambles in Germany* (1845) are more detailed. Something of a dilettante, Willis looked on Europe superficially, more concerned with scenic details, imposing architecture, and picturesque folkways than with books, literary people, or ideas. He is the reporter who describes engagingly his first glimpse of the Rhine, presents the tourist's view of Cologne, or recounts the ordeal of customs inspection at the Prussian border.[373] A few of his stories have German settings: the locale of "The Icy Veil" is Leipzig at the time of the fair, "Love and Diplomacy" and "The Bandit of Austria" have a Viennese background, and the poem "To Ermengarde" has a German setting as well as German atmosphere. His occasional references to Goethe, Schiller, Jean Paul, or Tieck are of a kind to suggest that he did not penetrate into the inner spirit of their writings, and his notices of German composers sound artificial. He was at his best when he had something concrete to transcribe, but he had little of the essential Germany, beyond romantic coloring and picturesqueness, to pass on to his American readers.

BAYARD TAYLOR

Once one of the most famous American authors, Bayard Taylor (1825–1878) has paled in the eyes of twentieth-century critics, though his translation of *Faust* is still highly regarded. From the very beginning, with the publication of *Views Afoot* (1846), to his death in Berlin in 1878, his career is intimately bound up with the story of German-American cultural interchange. Standing at the very center of the group who formulated the Genteel Tradition in American letters, he was the perfect medium between German and American literary culture. The characterization,"Laureate of the Gilded Age," with all its implications of cultural pretense and limitation fits him perfectly.[374]

Before he left America for Europe, his imagination was aglow and dazzled by the stirring scenes and hallowed wonders in store for him. Leaving in July, 1844, he toured Scotland, England, and Belgium and arrived in Germany in September. He spent the winter in Frankfurt on the Main, and between May and July of 1845 he made a tour which included Leipzig, Dresden, Prague, Vienna, and Munich.[375] The manifold impressions of his rambles in the fascinating world of the European past were recorded in *Views Afoot, or Europe seen with Knapsack and Staff* (1846). From the outset he struck a clear, colorful style of writing, an extraordinary kind of verbal photography, and poured into his reminiscences all the youthful thrill of discovery and recognition which his impressionable nature felt at the sight of these wonders. *Views Afoot* was a successful book because it brought something vivid and original to the American reader. Devoted as it is in such large part to the romantic exploitation of German scenery, and coming in 1846 near the peak of the American interest in Germany, it forms an important contribution to the American conception of Germany. Like Longfellow's *Hyperion*, it takes for granted the romantic point of view, devotes little space to the discussion of current affairs, but paints in glowing, shimmering colors the pretty half-legendary picture of quaint customs and traditions, the reminiscences of medieval splendor, and the affecting stories of poets and musicians, that were part of the current myth.

On returning home, he kept up his contacts with Freiligrath by correspondence and hoped to publish a volume of translations of his poems. He continued to study German authors and to acquire a library of their works. However, the press of daily reporting prevented his writing of much poetry and pushed into the background the rich experiences of the previous years. When in 1847 he moved to New York, he was engaged for a time in translating articles from Brockhaus' *Conversationslexikon* for Griswold.

The record of the next decade is one of alternate travels, reporting, writing of travel accounts, and lecturing. In 1856 he was prevailed upon by German friends to pay them a visit in Gotha, from which point he made several excursions in Germany and Switzerland. He visited Rückert, Gerstäcker, Gutzkow, and Auerbach of the Dresden Circle, and Fritz Reuter, as well as some famous German scholars.[376]

Between sojourns in Europe, Taylor was busy on the American lyceum platform. Though he usually spoke on general topics, he lectured once on Alexander von Humboldt and occasionally on "The Life and Times of Schiller." From May, 1862, to the end of his life in December, 1878, he spent a full third of his time in Europe. He made Gotha his home, but from thence undertook elaborate trips of exploration into Iceland, Egypt, and "the least known corners and by-ways of Europe." His second book, *At Home and Abroad, First Series* (1859)[377] was in part a personal narrative of experiences in Germany; in substance and tone it was similar to *Views Afoot*.

At Home and Abroad, Second Series (1862) includes ten chapters on "A Home in the Thuringian Forest," the record of a stay there in July, 1861, with a faithful and charming re-creation of the daily lives of its people. Section IV of the book, "A Walk through Franconian Switzerland," is the narrative of a tour made in company with a German friend, a professor from Erlangen, who in 1816 had been a fellow-student of Ticknor and Everett at Göttingen. Because of his growing interest in Goethe and his project of writing a new biography, Taylor enjoyed exploring the localities associated with Goethe, and in preparation of his next book, *By-ways of Europe* (1868), he visited the home of the blacksmith ancestor of Goethe at Artern.[378] Forgotten as these travel sketches are today, they were immensely popular in Taylor's lifetime and were an important agent in shaping the American attitude toward Germany. Taylor wrote from the point of view of a tourist-reporter. He did not, like Parker, search out the social ills of Europe; nor was he, like the *emigrés* Cranch and Story, interested in the study of the musical and artistic life of the Continent. His judgments of German authors was bounded by a set of values that precluded an appreciation of such figures as Lenau, Grillparzer, Heine, or Keller. He understood best those men of the late romantic school who in Germany represented the same compromise of the bourgeois and the conventionalized romantic that was dominant at the moment in America.

There existed in his day no translation of both parts of Goethe's *Faust* in the original meters, and of really satisfactory versions of Part I none except Brooks's of 1856 and Miss Swanwick's of 1849. Burning with ambition to elevate his name into the first rank of American poets, Taylor seized the opportunity to try his prowess on the large task of translating *Faust*. "Indeed," he said, "an English 'Faust' seems to me the next best thing to writing a great original epic!"[379] He conceived the idea before 1850, but did not begin work until the autumn of 1863. After several years of interrupted work, he finished it early in 1871, afterwards spending a good many months more in the preparation of notes and comments, in which he hoped to "sum up all German criticism and comment . . . and especially to make the Second Part clear."[380]

Taylor's *Faust* remains the best-known and most often recommended English version, remarkable for its close fidelity to the original metres, rhyme, and sense, though lacking in richness, depth, and the intrinsic poetic beauty of Goethe's lines.

Since every translation of *Faust* becomes a single man's commentary upon the poem (in the sense that each reader or translator interprets and emphasizes its ideas in the light of his own philosophic and aesthetic position), the present-day reader often finds Taylor's version inadequate.[381] The work of scholars since Taylor's day has elucidated many passages which were misunderstood in 1870, so that the limitations of his translation are owing as much to Taylor's age as to Taylor himself.

In the midst of his work on *Faust*, Taylor was winning recognition as a student of German literature. In September, 1869, he accepted a nonresident professorship of German literature at Cornell University, and the following spring he delivered a course of lectures at Cornell on Lessing, Klopstock, Schiller, Goethe, and Humboldt. Later he expanded the list to twelve, to include the whole range of German literature. The full course was given on at least two other occasions at Ithaca and in several other cities.[382] His approach lacked the intense, personal, and almost fanatically dedicated spirit that had moved the earlier Transcendentalists. But insofar as he reached an immense audience, he outdid even Brooks in making *Faust* a part of our national culture.

During the last decade of Taylor's life he wrote a good deal of criticism, including some of German authors, which appeared in leading periodicals and was collected as *Critical Essays and Literary Notes* in 1880.[383] However, the main task of his last years was the projected great "double biography" of Schiller and Goethe.[384] But when he was appointed Minister to Germany in 1878, he had not yet written the first chapter. Although he was delighted at the prospect of living near the scenes of his newest book, ill health and the press of official duties prevented progress on the ambitious work, and it remained "written only on the tablets of his brain."[385]

In his later years Taylor ventured into

new poetic fields. Intensive study of *Faust* and other German poems prompted him to renounce his earlier "sensuous" style (which borrowed heavily from Shelley and Tennyson) in favor of a more "solid," more abstract and "philosophical, manner, traceable to Goethe more than to any other single writer."[386] Unfortunately these poems betray signs of imitativeness combined with lack of power and poetic content; the bare intellectual concepts do not come alive. Taylor was embarrassed by a lack of something real and heartfelt to say. It is for this reason that his version of *Faust*, though a remarkable performance in many ways, fails to give a true and full reflection of Goethe's meaning and poetry; why Taylor's criticism lacks originality and the marks of strong conviction in the principles and ideas discussed; why his lyrics, so brilliant on the first reading, seem hollow when reread;[387] and why, finally, his travel books, which promise to do no more than describe, remain his most individual and most successful work, although his *Faust* is a monument to his efforts of transplanting the culture of Germany in America. By virtue of his excellence as a journalist, he promoted in America a better understanding of German people, life, and literature.[388] For sheer quantity of information, skillfully and sympathetically presented, he was the most assiduous and devoted American student of German affairs in his time.

CHARLES GODFREY LELAND

No less a Germanophile than Bayard Taylor was his friend Charles Godfrey Leland (1824–1903). Exposed to German influences from earliest youth,[389] he was educated at Princeton, and then spent three years (1846–1848) at the universities of Heidelberg and Munich. Everything in Germany enchanted him.[390]

What a mighty fascination Germanism has over one who has been under its influence! It is the opium of the mind. . . . That strange feeling of God in all, of the Infinite, is everywhere in Germany. . . . Germanism, that mysterious wonderful spirit, impresses itself on everyone who lives unprejudiced in that country. . . . I shall never recover from Germany nor do I know a single person who has lived in Germany who does not prefer it to any other country.[391]

Although learning the language cost him "incredible labour,"[392] he mastered it so that it presented no barrier to his full, sympathetic entry into the spirit of the literature—until, in short, he felt himself qualified to translate the least translatable of German lyricists, Heinrich Heine. His predilection for Heine was owing largely to the fact that he had in himself something of Heine's combination of seriousness and humor, of tenderness and drollery.[393]

Leland's generation and later ones persisted in thinking of him primarily as the creator of Hans Breitmann, often to his annoyance identifying him with his hero. The earliest of the Breitmann ballads, "Hans Breitmann at the Barty," was "knocked off in a hurry" as a kind of relief from the tedium of journalism, but it was at once so popular that Breitmann soon developed into "a definite personality" as Leland added new episodes in the life of his comic rogue.[394] In the Preface to the English edition of 1871 Leland explained what he was about in creating the character:

Breitmann is one of the battered types of the men of '48—a person whose education more than his heart has in every way led him to entire scepticism or indifference, and one whose Lutheranism does not go beyond *Wein, Weib* und *Gesang*. Beneath his unlimited faith in pleasure lie natural shrewdness, an excellent early education, and certain principles of honesty and good-fellowship, which are all the more clearly defined from his moral looseness in details identified in the Anglo-Saxon mind with total depravity.

The dialect which Leland used in the ballads caused comment from the first. Even his friend Boker criticized Leland's inconsistencies in the Breitmann dialect; but Leland painstakingly justified his practice, explaining that though there is "actually no well-defined method or standard of German-English," he used "observation and care," as well as "suggestions of well-educated German friends," in recording the dialect in a "truthful form." Breitmann, he added, "in several ballads" is a "literal copy or combination of characteristics of men who really exist or existed, and who had in their lives embraced as many extremes as the Captain."[395] He soon went on to cast Teutonic legends into the same dialect.[396] One of his greatest hits was *De Maiden mid Nodings On*. It is a burlesque of the old tale of "Sir Rupert the Fearless, a Tale of the Rhine," which Leland carried in his memory for years, until, taking a cue from Goethe's "Wassermädchen," he saw the way to turn it to account. *De Maiden mid Nodings On* became at once a "delightfully grotesque morsel on every tongue."[397]

There is often in these dialect poems more than immediately meets the eye. "Breitmann's thoughts were ever soaring so to the infinite, so many tags of old verse and bits of old legends were ever running through his head, that only those familiar with German philosophy and literature appreciate the learning crammed into what, to the casual reader, seems mere 'comic verse.'"[398] In this way, Hans Breitmann did much to domesticate certain German concepts and folkways in America. Hans was not universally appreciated by the German-Americans,[399] but (as Leland observed) the Germans themselves recognized that the pen which poked fun at them was no poisoned stiletto. In Philadelphia, during his later years, Leland moved much in German-American circles and actively sought to promote cultural and social contacts between the German and English elements. He participated in German political and social meetings until he felt that the Germans considered him "almost so good ash Deutsh" and very "bopular" to boot.[400]

RICHARD HENRY STODDARD

In a man like Richard Henry Stoddard (1825–1903) is exhibited the potency of that bookish tradition which aroused in writers of moderate talents the desire to emulate such popular leaders as Taylor and Willis of the Genteel Tradition, whose veneration of German literary culture was integral with their credo. Stoddard had few advantages of education, but fondness for reading and ambition to make a literary career brought him into contact with Taylor, Boker, Aldrich, Winter, Willis, and Stedman. In 1858, while living with the Taylors, Stoddard wrote his life of Alexander von Humboldt, drawing heavily on Taylor's store of personal reminiscence to enliven the account.[401] Willis' European travel letters, likewise, served to attract and encourage Stoddard to the pursuit of letters. He once asserted that Goethe's *Essays on Art* helped him profoundly,[402] but very few of his poetical effusions show any direct or marked German influence.[403]

EDWARD EVERETT HALE

Edward Everett Hale (1822–1909) had the advantage of early contact with the German tongue.[404] Like the other Genteel writers, he toured through Europe and visited the famous scenes of southern Germany. His books contain numerous references to Germany and to German figures. Goethe and Schiller, in *Lights of Two Centuries* (1887), are singled out for special treatment, but the perfunctory tone of his remarks suggests that he was not deeply versed in either. In his booklet on Emerson, Hale's casual and general remarks about Emerson's indebtedness to German philosophy imply a familiarity with and mastery of the subject not borne out by the facts.[405] Indeed, this glibness, this tone of easy familiarity with world literature and philosophy, is put on as a badge of cosmopolitanism and of universality of taste by many who inherited the tradition of Longfellow, Lowell, and Holmes.

GEORGE HENRY BOKER

George Henry Boker (1823–1890), friend of Taylor and Leland, undertook private studies in German with the latter during their college years at Princeton.[406] His tour of Germany predisposed him to imbibe the generally romantic literary views of the Schlegelian school. Like the Germans, he held that great poetry embodies a philosophical idea, and he advocated the organic concept by which thought and design (*Gehalt* and *Form*) are viewed as flowing from a single source. In his poem *Königsmark* (1869) he drew on firsthand knowledge of Germany to picture corrupt eighteenth-century court life. "Countess Laura" is a poem that has superficial resemblances to Goethe's *Faust* and draws on other motifs of German romantic literature as well, but the influence goes no deeper than surface coloring and atmosphere. In his searches for poetic and dramatic themes, ranging through legends and romances from the Far East to the American Far West, he hit upon the intention of doing a dramatic poem to be entitled "Tannhauser,"[407] but nothing came of this enthusiastically adopted plan. On the whole, he was more responsive to the English, Spanish, and Italian traditions than to the German.

CHARLES DUDLEY WARNER

Charles Dudley Warner (1829–1902), famous editor of the Hartford *Courant*, struck out for a literary career upon graduating from Hamilton College in 1850. He made five journeys abroad that kept him altogether seven years away from home. Like Willis and Taylor, he became a writer of popular travel letters, his work appearing in *Harper's* and the *Atlantic*. His first journey (1868–1869) produced a volume of European impressions entitled *Saunterings*, in which chatty, familiar sketches of Germany make up a considerable portion.[408] Warner's forte in these essays was a kind of informal philosophic comment on men and manners, such as is well displayed in the chapter on Innsbruck in *A Roundabout Journey* (1883–1884). En route to Italy, his stay at the Golden Adler inn brought to mind the occasions when Goethe, Heine, Emperor Joseph II, and Andreas Hofer had stopped there; the author played over this rich history of the spot with an admirable imaginative reconstruction of literary and historical associations. In a sense, Warner's talent for compilation and his wealth of information brought, in his *Library of the World's Best Literature* (1896–1897), in 31 volumes, a fitting climax and monument to the endeavors of the Genteel Tradition to foster cosmopolitan literary culture in its time.

EDMUND CLARENCE STEDMAN

Edmund Clarence Stedman (1833–1905) was a member of the New York group of writers who shared with the "respectable" company of Taylor, Aldrich, Stoddard, and Gilder "the knighthood of the pen" and the prevailing views of gentility in American letters.[409] German literary names, titles, quotations, and allusions figure prominently in his works, notably his critical writings. Several of his books and essays on aesthetic theory are based directly upon the foundations of Lessing, Goethe, and Schopenhauer.[410]

As a literary critic of his own age, Stedman was inclined to interpret such writers as Poe, Longfellow, Whittier, Emerson, and Whitman against a European background.[411] He pointed out the ways in which Goethe, Richter, and Heine influenced Longfellow;[412] he indicated similarities between German romantic concepts of art and those of Poe and suggested that Poe was indebted to A. W. v. Schlegel for his theory of the "totality of effect" or "singleness of impression";[413] he compared Whitman's and Goethe's ideas on poetic prose;[414] and he drew parallels between Goethe and Emerson as leaders of their time.[415] He was an influential poet and critic, possessed of high, if not the highest seriousness, ideality, and range, without the admixture of sentimentalism or frivolity that spoiled so much of the work of his associates. His urbane pronouncements upon aesthetics and his cultivated judgments upon literature served the cause of American letters in his day. The ideas which he derived from Germanic sources were only supplementary to the main body of his fundamentally English theory and practice, but they served to counteract American provincialism and didacticism and to promote universality of aim and a devotion to the beauty and dignity of letters.

EUGENE FIELD

It is not clear whether Eugene Field (1850–1895) learned his German at college or taught himself. His tours of Germany in 1872 and 1889–1890 and his contacts with German-Americans, notably Carl Schurz, were doubtless of influence. By the time he accompanied Schurz on his campaign of 1874, Field had become sufficiently proficient in the English-German dialect to indulge his inordinate love of practical jokes at the expense of Schurz and his "thick-tongued" supporters.[416] Field's interest in Germany was primarily that of a connoisseur of German art objects or rare books,[417] or that of a seeker after oddities that could be turned to comic uses.[418] In his search for the humorous, he extolled the virtues of gosling stew as he had tasted it in Germany,[419] and in his curious mixture of German and English he sang the praises of German onion tarts,[420] while German *Kneipen*-life inspired him to compose four poems after the manner of the German drinking song.[421] He composed a poem on the German feather bed,[422] and he

scored a notable success with his "Der Niebelrungen und der Schlabbergasterfeldt," when he read it at a dinner in Chicago and again when it was given wide currency in the German-American press in German text.[423]

As would be expected, German legends appealed to him, and he turned several of them to comic or serious use, usually in his dialect.[424] He occupied himself very little with the heavier and more serious classics, concentrating instead on the *Lieder*, especially those of Heine and Uhland.[425] On the whole, the Germanic element in his work is superficial rather than deep. He illustrates the tendency of the disciples of gentility to preserve the refinements of the older school of Lowell and Longfellow without inheriting their intellectual force.

The Southern Writers

WILLIAM GILMORE SIMMS

The romantic culture of the South, even after the Civil War, continued to take its impress largely from the French in matters of taste, while in literary matters it followed with few exceptions, the tradition of English romanticism. William Gilmore Simms (1806–1870) was among the first, following Poe, to take some cognizance of German literary figures and motifs.[426] His *Wigwam and the Cabin* (1845) and the collection of stories published under the title *Carl Werner and Other Tales of Imagination* (1838) are indicative of the extent to which he dabbled in the grotesqueries of Germanic Gothicism, but the relationship is one chiefly of general kinship in tone rather than direct berrowing.

Closely associated with Simms, the Nestor of the group, were Henry Timrod (1826–1867) and Paul Hamilton Hayne (1830–1886), who combined their efforts in 1857 to found *Russell's Magazine*. During the three years that it flourished, this journal promised to compete for the position which the *Southern Literary Messenger* had attained under Poe's editorship, and which it still held, as the leader among Southern periodicals in devoting space to German literature. The war nullified all this; and the cultivation of German literature, which might have grown into something of consequence, is traceable today only as echoes in the writings of the Charleston group. In the case of Timrod, the most cleary recognizable German notes are several passages in his long poem, "A Vision of Poetry," that appear to be reminiscent of lines in *Faust*, and in Hayne the Germanic tones are even more evanescent.

JOHN ESTEN COOKE

John Esten Cooke (1830–1886), who aspired to do for Virginia what Irving, Cooper, and Hawthorne had done for their regions, was inspired mainly by Scott, but he also showed strong leanings toward German Gothicism and found the German romantics engaging—especially Jean Paul, to whom he devoted a chapter, "An Autumn Evening with Jean Paul," in *Leather Stocking and Silk* (1854). *Ellie* (1855) and *The Heir of Gaymount* (1870) contain German allusions, names, and characters, and, of course, in his *Virginia: A History of the People* (1833) he dwells at length on the German-American settlements; but most of his literary allusions appear to be derived from such sources as Carlyle, for example, provided.

SIDNEY LANIER

In the work of Sidney Lanier (1842–1881) the Germanic influence runs deeper. As a young man at Oglethorpe College he came under the spell of James Woodrow, who had taken a Ph. D. degree at Heidelberg and whom he credited with exerting the most "formative influence . . . in all my literary work."[427] Lanier formed an ambition to go to Heidelberg to prepare for a professorship

in an American university. It is not known how much of the German language and literature he learned from Woodrow, but he began to try his hand at translating some of Goethe's lyrics, and his earliest poems were observed to be in a Wertherish vein.[428] The Civil War destroyed his hopes of going to Germany, but the study of the language continued "his most important intellectual activity of this period."[429] By 1867, when *Tiger-Lilies* appeared, he had begun to formulate his characteristic theory of poetry. Most of his poems of the time are on melancholy themes associated with love and show a strong, sometimes strained tendency to the personification of natural phenomena and of abstractions. "Both tendencies need to be traced no further than to the influence of German poetry which he was so thirstily absorbing, to which tendency must also be ascribed Lanier's characteristic and often unfortunate tendency to use compound nouns and nominal adjectives."[430]

Tiger-Lilies has been called "a boyish record of one just initiated into the world of German thought."[431] So numerous are quotations from Carlyle, Richter, and Novalis that they interfere with the plot. The theme of the first part of the book is given a Germanic investiture of quotations and characters with German names. Gretchen and Ottilie reflect Lanier's reading of Goethe. Thalberg, the name given to Sterling House, is a translation of Montvale, the name of Sterling Lanier's Tennessee resort.[432] Gretchen speaks as Lanier imagines a newly-arrived German would speak English: "How ish all with your house? Und was für ein Man ish Mr. Cranston?" Rübetsahl is a free spirit, a haunter of the mountains, obviously inspired by Lanier's reading of the Rübezahl legends of Germany.[433] The Cranston-Rübetsahl relationship is comparable to the Mephistopheles-Faust relationship, and Ottilie says to Cranston, "O, Mephistopheles, play what pleases thy Satanic fancy."[434] Instead of laying the scene in Germany, which he had never seen but which he yearned for, Lanier in *Tiger-Lilies* brings Germany to America. Thus the novel becomes part of the literature of transplanted German romanticism.

Largely self-taught though Lanier was,[435] his German served to give him a wide and discriminating knowledge of German composers, among whom Schumann was his favorite.[436] Not equally familiar with all German achievements in art, literature, and science, he had rather an eclectic's knowledge of many fields; except for the arts of music and poetry, he was expert in none. In these two realms he studied intensively and thereby found the means to construct his unique fusion of music and poetry. In June, 1875, he published "The Symphony," a poem designed to demonstrate that love is music, that music is poetry, and that both are revelations of God.[437] The same idea

finds expression in *Tiger-Lilies* (1867), *The Science of English Verse* (1880), and *Music and Poetry* (1899). In elaborating this theory, Lanier drew on German romantic aesthetics as developed by Wackenroder, F. Schlegel, and Novalis. The German school regarded music as the most spiritual of the arts; poesy, in the words of Wackenroder, lay conquered at the feet of music. In his experiments with *"reine Poesie"* Tieck attempted to utilize tones and notes directly in poetry, and he sought in the novel *Franz Sternbalds Wanderungen* to resolve all life and poetry in music. Novalis, whom Lanier admired and frequently quoted, taught in *Heinrich von Ofterdingen* that it was the romantic destiny of language to become music, to be transformed into pure song. Catching hints also from Coleridge and Poe, Lanier embodied in his theory the sum of these romantic speculations on the possibilities of word music.[438]

WALT WHITMAN
(1819–1892)

The cosmic sweep of Whitman's "barbaric yawp,"[439] the comprehensiveness of such poems as "Salut au Monde," and the ease with which by the twirl of his tongue he "skirted sierras," "covered continents," and encompassed "worlds and volumes of worlds"[440] are at once disarming and suggestive that inquiries into his literary antecedents are petty. While admitting "I conned old times, I sat studying at the feet of the masters,"[441] he habitually denied having borrowed from them, and even in his later utterances took pains to say that he received the "precious legacies of the Old World" merely "to give them ensemble," to mold them into "modern American and democratic physiognomy."[442] Like Emerson, who resolved in 1835 "to utter no speech, poem or book that is not entirely and peculiarly my work," so Whitman recorded, among the notes made in prepa-

ration of *Leaves of Grass*, his intention to "make no quotations and no references to any other author."[443] Both resolutions were idle; and as inquiries are pushed forward, it becomes increasingly apparent not only that Whitman was one of the most widely (though not systematically) read of the major American authors of the last century,[444] but also that his reading colored his writings and in some instances supplied the main tenets of his doctrine.[445] If we investigate his claim that he was pre-eminently the "poet of science and democracy," we shall find him in the first area owing practically everything to his foraging among scientific books; and, as the poet of democracy (where he spoke more clearly from his own experience and conviction), we find him admitting that he found "in the formulas of Hegel" his "justification of New World Democracy,"[446] for "only Hegel is fit for America—is large enough and free enough."[447] Associated with his faith in democracy was his theory of a national new-world democratic literature, which he said he derived from Goethe, as Goethe had derived it from Herder.[448]

Early Contacts with German Culture

The question naturally arises: Where, when, and by what means did he acquire a sufficient knowledge of German thought and literature to form such basic judgments? He knew little or nothing of the German language.[449] His acquaintance with German literature appears to have received marked acceleration during 1846–1848 while he edited the Brooklyn *Daily Eagle*, from which time onward his German allusions come in great profusion.[450] In his capacity as editor he reviewed a number of German books that came to his desk.[451] In his published writings are upward of a hundred references to Goethe, approximately half as many to Hegel, and a like number to Kant; but of the three we cannot be sure that he read much beyond those works of Goethe's that were readily availabe in translation— notably the *Autobiography*—while of Kant and Hegel he obviously read nothing beyond what he could find in such books as Gostick's *German Literature* and Hedge's *Prose Writers of Germany*. For books and subjects requiring a knowledge of German —"the one language," he observed in 1888, "I am sorry I did not go into when I was young"[452]—he habitually resorted to his practice of "posting up" instead of reading closely or studying systematically. That some of this "posting up" was rewarding is abundantly apparent in the case of the *Nibelungenlied*, which, by whatever means the illumination came, supplied him with fertile suggestions and some of the essential elements of his distinctive theory of a national American literature and of the type of American bard that he envisaged.[453]

Literary Influences

Although Whitman said late in life that he was not a "constitutional reader," Emerson's opinion of him as a man who made a copious, if not thorough, survey of the world's books is quite correct.[454] In the process it was inevitable that he should learn something about German writers, though the evidence of what particular authors or books he knew best is not always conclusive. In the case of Goethe, for instance, he professed to know enough to justify his passing judgment upon him, even while confessing, in the next breath, "I know nothing about Goethe."[455] This is but one instance among the many contradictions in Whitman that involve little more than his love of paradox,[456] for it is evident (as will appear in the sequel) that he read at least portions of Goethe very attentively. Far from being borne out by the facts, his professed ignorance of Goethe is an aspect of the Whitman "pose" or "legend," which he himself did much to create and to perpetuate. In this instance we are concerned with that phase of Whitman the poseur which sought to deflect the reader's (or critic's) attention from the track of his foragings. In his published writings his "concern to conceal his indebtedness"[457] generally succeeds, but occasionally his phraseology is so close that the alert reader recognizes what amounts to a borrowing. One such instance occurs in his characterization of Goethe, who (he says) was, like Sophocles, one of those fortunate individuals endowed with "genius, health, beauty of person, riches, rank, renown and length of days, all combining and centering in one case."[458] The passage is recognizably like Hedge's observation in *Prose Writers*: "Sophocles alone, among the poets of all generations, may vie with him [Goethe] in this. . . . all things conspired for once to make a perfect lot: genius, organization, beauty of person, high culture, riches, rank, renown, length of days."[459] A nearer examination of this popular work on German writers reveals that it was one of three or four general sources from which Whitman derived more than he cared to acknowledge. A comparison of Whitman's introductory notes for a series of projected "Sunday evening lectures" on "Hegel and Metaphysics" with Cabot's remarks on Hegel in Hedge's *Prose Writers* illustrates the extent of his reliance on this book:

Hegel—born at Stuttgart in 1770—died at Berlin of cholera—educated at University of Tübingen—student of theology— matriculated in 1788, aged 18—then in retirement pursued extensive and severe courses of study. At 31 was a public lecturer at Jena, at the University—was an associate of Schelling—examined, in his lectures, the difference between Fichte and Schelling—edited a newspaper—then conducted an academy or gymnasium at latter place (as rector)—inaugurated and planned his great work of works. Was professor of philosophy at Heidelberg (1816–1818) and there published his Encyclopaedia, developing his whole philosophy.[460]* [*Writings*, IX, 167]

Whitman's relation to Friedrich Schlegel presents another interesting case. His notes do not indicate that he delved deeply into Schlegel's characteristic theories, but there is evidence of more than a schoolboy's interest in noting down dates and biographical facts. In 1847 he reviewed the Morrison translation of the *Philosophy of Life and Philosophy of Language* for the *Daily Eagle*; a decade later, while making notes on the

intention and meaning of *Leaves of Grass*, a passage in Gostick on F. Schlegel sufficiently rearoused his interest to make a sizable notation:

Friedrich Schlegel—1772–1829—one of two celebrated literary brothers—the other named Augustus. Had a strong predilection toward the wonderful and mysterious. 1803 entered Roman Catholic church. Wrote *Philosophy of History*, most valuable tenet of which is,—*"the inexpediency of destroying old institutions before new ideas are prepared to develop themselves in consistency with the order of society."* Lectures (History of Literature) 1811–1812 have chiefly extended his fame. *He makes literature the representative expression of all that is superior in a nation*, thus elevating it, especially poetry, far above the views of trivial and commonplace criticism, and regarding it as incorporating and being the highest product of human life and genius. He appreciates the great masters of all countries and sets them off from crowds of temporary persons. Prejudices.—But remember in reading these lectures Schlegel was full of prejudices of a zealous newly converted Roman Catholic.† [*Writings*, IX, 120–21]

The two passages which Whitman underscored—the first about the expediency of destroying old institutions before developing new ones in consistency with the order of society, and the other, about literature as the representative expression of all that is superior in a nation—are both paraphrasings of Gostick's account and represent what in Schlegel was significant for Whit-

---

* See Hedge, *Prose Writers*, page 446:
George Wilhelm Friedrich Hegel, the last of the four great German philosophers, was born August 27th, 1770, at Stuttgart, in the kingdom of Württemberg. . . . He was matriculated as a student of Theology in the University of Tübingen in the year 1788. After completing his University career, he pursued an extensive and severe course of study in comparative retirement, being meanwhile chiefly employed as a teacher in private families. In 1801 he became a public lecturer in the University of Jena, dedicating his first work to an examination of the difference between the systems of Fichte and Schelling. Here he continued to give courses of lectures, and to develope his own

system, until the taking of Jena by the French in 1806. For the next two years he edited a newspaper, then he was rector of a gymnasium in Nuremberg, where he perfected his most important work, in which he gave a new character to the whole system of logic. While professor of philosophy in Heidelberg (1816–18) he published his Encyclopaedia, in which his whole scheme of philosophy is contained. He was called to Berlin in the year 1818, and remained there until his death, on the fourteenth of November, 1831, when he fell a victim to the cholera.

† See Gostick, pages 278–79:
Friedrich Schlegel, the younger brother (1772–1829), wrote his work on the "poetry of

man. When they are considered in conjunction with what he derived from Herder about national literary expression, we see how vital they were for the formulation of Whitman's own literary doctrine.

Another important source of information for Whitman was Carlyle. The clue that leads to this conclusion is a notation made by Whitman in 1856 at the head of five pages of memoranda on Goethe's life, character, and writings: "Carlyle, in reviews and otherwise, seems to have been the introducer of Goethe and the principal German writers from 1827 onward 10 years."[461] Following the heading "Goethe," he added in parenthesis, "reading Carlyle's criticisms on Goethe." "His first literary productions [he continues] fell in his 23rd year. Sorrows of Werther in his 25th year." This is recognizable as a passage taken from Carlyle's essay of 1832 of "Goethe's Works": "His first literary productions fell in his twenty-third year; Werter, the most celebrated of these, in his twenty-fifth."[462] Thence he proceeded, point by point, to digest Carlyle's essay, except for occasional interpolations drawn from Carlyle's essay of 1828 entitled simply "Goethe."[463]

GOETHE

While it might be presumed that as a critic-journalist Whitman knew something about Goethe prior to November 19, 1846, when he published his review of Parke Godwin's translation of Dichtung und Wahrheit,[464] nothing of importance appears earlier. This review, in Mr. Holloway's estimation, is significant as throwing light upon the germination of the literary ideals which, during the next year, began to shape parts of Leaves of Grass.[465] The reviewer envisages a "prodigious gain that would accrue to the world" if more men, like Goethe, would write "LIFE instead of the million things evolved from Life—LEARNING," and he particularly commends

the simple easy truthful narrative of the existence and experience of a man of genius, —how his mind unfolded in his earliest years—the impression things made upon him—how and where and when the religious sentiment dawned on him—what he thought of God before he was inoculated with books' ideas—the development of his soul . . . with all the long train of occurrences, adventures, mental processes, exercises within, and trials without, which go to make up a man.[466]

---

the Greeks and Romans" in 1798. He was even more decided than his brother in opposition to the scientific character of some philosophical theories of his day. His mind had a strong predilection towards all that was wonderful and mysterious in literature as in religion, and the result of his studies was, that he entered the Roman Catholic church at Cologne in 1803, which produced some excitement in the literary world. . . . His lectures on the "Philosophy of History" were evidently written with religious and political purposes, to which he often sacrifices the fair and candid statement of facts. Perhaps the most valuable argument in these lectures is that which exposes the danger of "negative" reformation; or, in other words, the inexpediency of destroying old institutions before new ideas are prepared to develop themselves in consistency with the older society. . . . His lectures on the "Literature of all nations" (1811–1812) have chiefly extended his fame. . . . The great purpose of the author is to describe the development of literature, in its connec-

tions with the social and religious institutions of various nations and periods. He thus elevates literature, especially poetry, far above the views of trivial and commonplace criticism, and regards it in its highest and most important aspect, as the product of human life and genius in various stages of cultivation. The history of the world of books is thus represented as no dry and pedantic study, but as one intimately connected with the best interests of humanity. In the establishment of this "humanitarian" style of literature the services of Friedrich Schlegel were valuable. He endeavored to show the wide distinction between superior men of true genius and the crowd of frivolous writers who have in every period degraded the character of literature. His design was noble, though its execution was disfigured by prejudices, as the following summary will prove. [Here follows a summary of the Literature of All Nations, in which the reader is again warned against Schlegel's Roman Catholic prejudices, a warning Whitman faithfully recorded.]

These comments take on a special meaning when they are related to his stated purpose in *Leaves of Grass*: to portray a representative personality against the American background of democracy and science. Goethe's "intention of rendering a history of soul and body's growth" is echoed in his own plan for *Leaves of Grass* in the Preface of 1855: both are a record of "the development of the poet, the type-character, against the contemporary background."[467] At the time when Whitman first read Goethe's autobiography, he was looking, as Dr. Holloway has said, "for a biographical work—whether in prose or verse seemed to matter little—which should express the entire man very much as his own *Leaves of Grass* set out to do."[468] Here was a "road map" not only "of the life he was to live" but also "of the book he was to write."[469] Goethe's *Dichtung und Wahrheit* furnished not so much materials as inspiration for the work Whitman planned to write, but it was not the sole influence in directing the composition of *Leaves of Grass*. George Sand,[470] Carlyle,[471] and especially Emerson[472] had a share in it. However, priority of influence appears to belong to Goethe, whose autobiography had suggested a "ground plan" or "road map" as early as 1846, while Emerson appears not to have counted for much before 1850, when Whitman read *Representative Men*,[473] and when he may have heard the Concord sage lecture in Brooklyn. It was 1853 or 1854 before he was ready for the Emersonian message; only then had he "simmered" long enough for Emerson to bring Whitman's pot "to a boil."

While Whitman owed something to *Dichtung und Wahrheit*, he never became a close student of Goethe.[474] The only other work of Goethe's that left its residue on Whitman's mind was *Faust*, a book in which he said Goethe "drew deep water."[475] He repeatedly acknowledged reading it, but late in life he insisted that he had only "looked into it—not with care, not studi-

ously, yet intelligently, in my own way."[476] When his admirer, Doctor Bucke, pointed out parallels between *Faust* and *Leaves of Grass*, Whitman "appeared interested" but put him off saying, "It is striking, Maurice, though I don't know how well you would hold it against the scholars if they slapped back at you."[477] Soon thereafter Bucke again opened the subject in a letter, saying, "There are just two great modern books—Faust and Leaves of Grass"; and Traubel records Whitman's laughing "mildly" and then remarking airily that Bucke's bracketing him with Goethe represented "a modification of Doctor's partisanship." Then he added that Bucke "always goes far enough and on days when he feels particularly good he goes too far."[478] The complacency with which Whitman regularly accepted tributes, however fulsome, in other instances makes his protestations in cases where similarities between his poems and *Faust* were stressed singular enough to arouse the suspicion that comparisons on this head were not welcome to him,[479] and that, in this instance he took unnecessary pains to deny a connection which few people had thought important enough to mention.

But there are admitted similarities between the general aim of *Leaves of Grass* and *Faust*. Both are built on the theme of human effort, human striving. "The justification of evil, indispensable for keeping the equilibrium in the spiritual energy of mankind"[480] is a postulate as much of the Faustian creed as of Whitman's view of the world.[481] Inactivity and complacency spell stagnation in both books. But these are general ideas for which Whitman, who had read Milton, Emerson, and other expositors of the same theme,[482] was not necessarily indebted to Goethe, however suggestive or confirmatory Goethe's poem may have been on this score as, apparently, Hegel came to be later.[483]

ZSCHOKKE

Several circumstances suggest that Whitman derived something from Zschokke's *Autobiography*, and corroborative evidence appears in certain memoranda that Whitman made, presumably in 1848, from Zschokke's *Selbstschau*.[484] These notes include both comments and quotations— some exact, others modified in various ways by Whitman. It has been suggested that Whitman discovered in Zschokke "a kindred and congenial spirit," and that he "may have derived his conception of evil, politics, the individual, and religion from Zschokke before the reading of Emerson brought him to a 'boil.'"[485] A comparison of Zschokke's and Whitman's texts fails, on the ground of internal evidence, to substantiate these interesting suggestions. Parke Godwin's translation contained only Part I of Zschokke's *Selbstschau*, i.e., the biographical portion of the book. Part II, entitled "Welt-und Gott-Anschauung" and embodying the kind of sentiments that might have been useful to Whitman in the formulation of the creed that underlies *Leaves of Grass*, had not been translated and hence was not easily available to Whitman. Indeed, an attentive reading of Whitman's prose writings befoet 1848[486] serves to authenticate the fact thar many of the ideas characteristic of the 1855 edition of *Leaves of Grass*—democratic principles, political idealism, questionings of sense and outward things, individualism, and what he already called the "American identity"—were already firmly lodged in his mind. Their fruition, if they derived from anything outside Whitman himself, could as readily be related to his contacts with Emerson as well as to his random experience in the practical realm of living, rather than to Zschokke's autobiography, the most fruitful part of which for his purposes he probably never saw.

Nevertheless, Zschokke's book left its mark. Whitman's memoranda indicate that what impressed him most was Zschokke's simple, honest, straightforward account of himself. Already provided by Goethe's *Dichtung und Wahrheit* with one notable model of autobiography, he saw in Zschokke's book another. Paraphrasing Zschokke's purpose, Whitman observed, "the Life of Man is interesting and striking enough to stand by itself unwarped by the merit of the Author, or the celebrity of the Statesman."[487] In short, Zschokke's book helped confirm Goethe's example for his own plan of employing a simple, natural, autobiographical method for *Leaves of Grass*.[488] Nothing more seems to be involved.

HERDER

For the rest, Whitman's acquaintance with German literary personalities was neither extensive not profound; yet in a few particulars their influence was decisive. He applauded Herder's insistence on a national literature, and credited him with teaching the young Goethe that "really great poetry is always (like the Homeric or Biblical canticles) the result of a national spirit, and not the privilege of a polished or select few."[489] While this concept and the attendant idea of the poet's supreme position and function had become, under the auspices of the romantic dispensation, a commonplace, Whitman's direct attribution of the idea to Herder suggests that he knew what Herder had said on this score and was not merely echoing a widely current idea.[490] Passage after passage, in both Whitman's prose and poetry, parallels Herder's theory. As in Herder, Whitman's interest centers in poetry and on the influence of the "literatus."[491] "The topmost proof of a race is its own born poetry. . . . No imitations will do."[492] But we need not go on citing parallels from Whitman's pages, for we should have to reproduce large portions of *Democratic Vistas*, the several prefaces, "Poetry in America To-Day," "American National Literature," and several of the poems.[493]

HEINE

Heine is the other German literary figure

with whom Whitman occupied himself at some length. Whitman was drawn to Heine by a kinship of spirit, a like feeling for freedom and modernity, and by their common attack on outworn ideas. Heine was the one German poet whom he discussed at length and admired without qualification.[494]

MISCELLANEOUS INFLUENCES

Among his memoranda are mentioned a number of other German literary figures who engaged his attention at various times and in varying degrees. Among the older examples was the *Nibelungenlied*, which he kept coming back to, and regarding which he kept making notations. Luther similarly engaged his attention. If we consider the relative space he devoted in his "Notes and Fragments" an indication of his interest, we shall have to name first "the illustrious four"[495] among German philosophers—Kant, Fichte, Schelling, and Hegel —as most meaningful, for he devoted twenty pages to them.[496] Following them come Goethe with five pages; Richter, with two; F. Schlegel and Herder, one each; and Hans Sachs, Boehme, Leibnitz, Klopstock, Lessing, Schiller, Heine, Lenau, each, less than a page. Others include Freiligrath, Rückert, Uhland, and Hoffmann von Fallersleben (each mentioned twice), and Kinkel, Xavier, Tieck, Chamisso, and Schultze (each once).

Beyond some acquaintance with the literary theories of the Schlegels, of Herder, of Heine, and, of course, of the German romantic school generally (especially as affecting the criticism of Shakespeare[497]), Whitman was not deeply conversant with German criticism. In his essay on "Slang in America," he spoke appreciatively of the "honest delving" of German comparative philologists and the significance of their findings,[498] and he knew something of the archaeological discoveries of Schliemann. Among German historians, only Niebuhr is commemorated—in two brief paragraphs.[499]

He made some notes and preserved several newspaper clippings regarding Alexander von Humboldt,[500] and he got from such books as Gostick's *German Literature* some general conceptions of the influence of science on the thought of Schelling and Hegel. In the realm of German philosophical thought he attained, despite his reliance on secondary sources, a better orientation.

Philosophical Influences

WHITMAN'S PHILOSOPHIC PERSONALITY

Whitman's status as a philosopher is indicated by Horace Traubel's report of a conversation between Daniel G. Brinton, Whitman, and himself in 1888, when Brinton said to Whitman, "You give us no consistent philosophy." "I guess not," replied Whitman. "I should not desire to do so."[501] Hereupon Traubel suggested, "Plenty of philosophy but not *a* philosophy"; and Whitman added, "That's better —that's more the idea."[502] His meditations often sound like the stammerings of an adolescent bewildered by the multiplicity of impressions streaming in and upon him: "I cannot say to any person what I hear—I cannot say it to myself—it is so wonderful."[503] Humbled before "the puzzle of Being,"[504] he stands "baffled, balk'd," ready to admit, "I perceive I have not really understood anything."[505] This feeling of impotence provokes him to scorn philosophy: "Philosophies—they may prove well in lecture rooms."[506] "A morning-glory at my window satisfies me more than the metaphysics of books."[507] Yet he accepted without much discrimination all things and all philosophies: "I reject none, accept all."[508]

> I believe materialism is true and spiritualism is true, I reject no part . . . .
> I adopt every theory, myth, God, and demi-god.[509]

The wag points knowingly at the passage in the "Calmus" cycle of poems:

Here I shade and hide my thoughts, I
myself do not expose them
And yet they expose me more than all
my other poems.[510]

But when we lift the mystic curtain of
obscure terminology and tongue-in-cheek
paradox, we discover that the base of all his
thought is "the dear love of comrades,"[511]
essentially the Christian concept of brotherhood. This is the thought upon which the
poem, "The Base of All Metaphysics,"
turns:

Having studied the new and antique, the
Greek and Germanic systems,
Kant having studied and stated, Fichte
and Schelling and Hegel,
Stated the lore of Plato, and Socrates
greater than Plato,
And greater than Socrates sought and
stated, Christ divine having studied
long,
I see reminiscent to-day those Greek and
Germanic systems,
See the philosophies all, Christian
churches and tenets see
Yet underneath Socrates clearly see, and
underneath Christ the divine I see,
The dear love of man for his comrade, the
attraction of friend for friend,
Of the well-married husband and wife, of
children and parents,
Of city for city and land for land.[512]

"The base of all metaphysics" is not
"what the world calls logic,"[513] he told
Traubel. The rigorous method of the logician was not for him, though he honored
those who mastered it. He paid homage to
"wondrous Germans and other metaphysicians" for their contributions to the culture
of the America that is to be[514]—"to such as
German Kant and Hegel, where they,
though near us, leaping over the ages, sit
again, impassive, imperturbable, like the
Egyptian gods."[515]

What is to be made of these mutually
nullifying contradictions? Here, as elsewhere, Whitman's pose is the key. Having
set up, on the one hand, as the "great
accepter," unwilling to reject any phase or
part of the universe, however irreconcilable,[516] he yet felt the need, on the other
hand, for a philosophy broad enough to
bring harmony into this diversity. There
are indications that the cosmic inclusiveness
of his creed as enunciated in the earlier
editions of *Leaves of Grass* subsequently
occasioned moments of embarrassment,
notably during the period immediately
before his adoption of Hegelian absolutism
as a means at once to justify his assertions to
himself and to answer his critics.[517] A
number of circumstances converge to
indicate the nature of the dilemma in which
he found himself. In the first place, as his
vision expanded, he found himself checked
and amazed at every turn by newer and
greater contradictions, and often he could
think of nothing better to do than to throw
up his hands in a gesture compounded
of despair and bravado to assert his
"diversity" and "comprehensiveness," or
roundly to damn philosophy altogether. In
the second place, the oft-repeated criticism
of his gainsayers who charged him with
inconsistency wore on his equanimity; and
in the end his composure was ruffled by the
defection of several of his closest disciples,
like Brinton, who complained of the master's
contradictory principles.[518] Finally, his own
experience and growth resulted in a sober-
ing development that compounded his
difficulties as he progressed. As he gradually shifted from his earlier nationalistic,
pantheistic, not to say materialistic, and
egoistic tendencies to his later position
embracing more of internationalism, Christianity, idealism, and humanism,[519] Whitman felt increasingly the necessity for a
larger philosophy by which to justify his
changing views. There can be no doubt that
when he chanced upon Hegelian idealism
with its doctrine of the Absolute—in which,
by definition, all opposites find reconciliation—he clutched eagerly at its more
general phases as providing a system of
metaphysics large enough for America and
for himself.[520]

Conditioned as he had been by Emerson, as well as Hicksite Quakerism,[521] to accept the doctrine of spirit-mirrored-in-nature, he held that "Body and mind are one; an inexplicable paradox," as Whitman goes on to say in the notes for the projected series of lectures on the German idealists:

The varieties, contradictions and paradoxes of the world and of life, and even good and evil, so baffling to the superficial observer, and so often leading to despair, sullenness or infidelity, become a series of infinite radiations and waves of the one sea-like universe of divine action and progress, never stopping, never hasting. "The heavens and the earth" to use the summing up of Joseph Gostick whose brief I endorse: "The heavens and the earth and all things within their compass—all the events of history—the facts of the present and the development of the future (such is the doctrine of Hegel) all form a complication, a succession of steps in the one eternal process of creative thought."[522]

Here we arrive at once at the reason why Hegel appealed to Whitman and his chief source of information regarding Hegelian idealism, for the conclusion of the passage just quoted is closely adapted from the 1854 edition of Joseph Gostick's *German Literature* (p. 269):

The heavens and the earth, and all things within their compass, all the events of history, the facts of the present, and the developments of the future, may be (according to Hegel's doctrine) only so many steps in one eternal process of creative thought.

Whitman's pose complicates the problem of determining by what means he arrived at this Hegelian conclusion. To hear him tell it, he searched all philosophies, "the new and antique, the Greek and Germanic systems, Kant . . . Fichte, and Schelling and Hegel" before he found at last "the base and finale for all metaphysics" in Hegel.[523] That the search approximated anything as extensive and systematic as he suggests is unlikely. There can be no doubt that he searched, but all known facts indicate that the quest was a groping about

until he stumbled on Gostick's abstract. On the basis of all his published writings and those of his notes that are available, we must conclude, first, that the German idealists did not seriously engage his attention prior to his study of Gostick's book; second, that this could hardly have been many years before 1870;[524] and third, that his reading about the German metaphysicians was completed (perhaps it were more accurate to say, his conclusions regarding them had been formed) before the end of 1872, for in that year, when he published his small volume *As a Strong Bird on Pinions Free and Other Poems*, he appended an advertisement of *Leaves of Grass* in the form of an alleged quotation from John Burroughs which bears the unmistakable impress of Whitman's own hand:[525]

"The history of the book [*Leaves of Grass*], thus considered, not only resembles and tallies, in certain respects, the development of the great System of Idealistic Philosophy in Germany, by the 'illustrious four'—except that the development of *Leaves of Grass* has been carried out within the region of a single mind,—but it is to be demonstrated, by study and comparison, that the same theory of essential identity of the spiritual and material worlds, the shows of nature, the progress of civilization, the play of passions, the human intellect, and the relations between it and the concrete universe, which Kant prepared the way for, and Fichte, Schelling, and Hegel have given expression and statement in their system of transcendental Metaphysics—this author has, with equal entirety, expressed and stated in *Leaves of Grass*, from a poet's point of view . . . ."—*John Burroughs's Note.*[526]

Thus it appears that by the end of 1871 Whitman had got from Hegel and his German colleagues what was essential for his purposes, and that he wished *Leaves of Grass* in its several editions to be understood not merely as an exemplification of Hegelian philosophy but as paralleling, in its organic evolution, the development of the "great System of Idealistic Philosophy in

Germany," with the difference that what in Germany required the combined efforts of four men in America was done single-handedly. In his anxiety to give currency to the idea of *Leaves of Grass* as an organic outgrowth and a consistent illustration of the system of thought developed in successive stages by Kant, Fichte, Schelling, and Hegel, he repeated the idea three times in as many years in his advertisements. He also wrote it into his poem on "The Base of All Metaphysics," and he allowed W. D. O'Connor to say in a letter, dated February 22, 1883, to R. M. Bucke (a letter which Whitman took care to read and edit very carefully), "Walt Whitman had never read Emerson at all until after the publication of his first edition [of *Leaves of Grass*]. . . . But he *had* read Kant, Schelling, Fichte, and Hegel."[527] By 1883, Whitman's memory, like Mark Twain's in later years, had become facile and could recall some things that had not happened at all. He could *not* remember having read Emerson before 1855—Emerson whom in 1856 he called "dear Master"; but he could remember that he *had* read Kant, Fichte, Schelling, and Hegel before 1855—philosophers whom, as the sequel will show he hardly read at all, but only read about—and that, much later. In view of Whitman's repeated assertions that he not only considered carefully the systems of all four but that his writings represent an American poetic distillation of their "magnificent system,"[528] it behooves us to examine the matter in detail.

SOURCES OF GERMAN IDEALISM

Whitman's notes for the projected "Sunday evening lectures" aggregate twenty pages in the collected edition of his writings. After jotting down birth and death dates for the four German thinkers and adding two paragraphs of biographical facts concerning Hegel (taken directly from Hedge's *Prose Writers*), he launches into a discussion of the need for a precise metaphysical terminology not merely for the discovery of truth but the better to show the relations among philosophy, religion, ethics, and history. Hegel's strict logic observed this precaution scrupulously, and accordingly he "probably rendered greater service than any man we know, past or present."[529] Despite all this, transcendental philosophy failed to make any "notable increase or diminution" in ethics and religion. "Nor does the Hegelian system, strictly speaking, explain the universe, either in the aggregate or detail. . . . The Eternal mystery is still a mystery." But granting this limitation, there still remains "an entirely legitimate field for the human mind, in fact its chosen ground where all had before gone by default."[530]

Next, Whitman falls back on Hedge's *Prose Writers of Germany*:*

Penetrating beneath the shows and materials of the objective world we find . . . that in respect to human cognition of them, all and several are pervaded by *the only absolute substance* which is SPIRIT, endowed with the eternal impetus of development, and proceeding from itself the opposing powers and forces of the universe. A curious triplicate process seems the resultant action; first the Positive, then the Negative, then the product of Mediation between them; from which product the process is repeated and so goes on without

---

* Hedge, *Prose Writers*, p. 446:
There is one *Absolute Substance* pervading all things. That Substance is *Spirit*. This Spirit is endowed with the power of development; it produces from itself the opposing powers and forces of the universe. All that we have to do is to stand by and see the process going on. The process is at first the evolution of antagonistic forces; then a mediation between them. All proceeds by triplicate; there is the positive, then the negative, then the mediation between them which produces a higher unity. This again is but the starting point for a new series. And so the process goes on, from stage to stage, until the Absolute Spirit has passed through all the stadia of its evolutions, and is exhibited in its highest form in the Hegelian system of philosophy.

end. In his Introduction to the *Philosophy of History*, this is illustrated in the portion on "History as a manifestation of Spirit."[531]

Having said this, Whitman turns at last to a consideration of Hegel's predecessors. Biographical facts, derived in part from Hedge and more particularly from the encyclopedias,[532] are followed by a brief discussion of Kant's purpose and method, with emphasis upon his criticism—all obviously drawn from such popular sources as Hedge, Gostick, Madame de Staël, and the *Britannica*,[533] for of a firsthand acquaintance with any of Kant's works there is no suggestion.[534] In explanation of the problem which Kant attacked, Whitman reports, in Gostick's terms,* on the Locke-Leibnitz controversy as follows:

Long before, the speculations of Locke and the materialists had reached the formula that "there is nothing in the understanding which has not arrived there through the sense," Leibnitz had replied, "Yes, the understanding itself."[*Writings*, IX, 176]

From this point, again in Gostick's terms,† Whitman proceeds:

We must sum him [Kant] up briefly. Kant analyses, dissects, dissipates the vast suffocating miasma that had so long spread impediments to philosophy—discusses much—clears away, removes, sometimes like a surgeon's knife—yet in fact and after all decides little or nothing—is of indes-

cribable value—denies the possibility of absolute knowledge of the eternal world. . . . Kant's entire speculations are but a splendid amplification of this [Leibnitz's] reply. He endeavors to get at and state the philosophy of the understanding. The problem of the relation between understanding and the universe of material nature, he does not attempt to solve.

The pursuit or examination and elaboration of the inquiry, *Is a science of metaphysics possible and practicable?* involves the gist of Kant's entire labors. [*Writings*, IX, 176]

In the case of Fichte, to whom Whitman devotes the next two pages of his notes, he relied entirely on the *Britannica*. It is worth noting that while he understood "Subjectiveness" to have been Fichte's basic principle, this doctrine, by the time he made his condensation of the article in the *Britannica*, did not attract Whitman as it might have if he had come upon it at the time when he first composed "Song of Myself." Fichte's philosophy is acknowledged to be "simple, single, complete and logical as far as it goes," so that there "will always be a select class of minds, and superior ones, to whom Fichte's theory will be everything," but his subjective egoism is important for Whitman chiefly as representing one of the phases by which the critical philosophy came to fruition in Hegelian absolutism.[535]

Similarly, Schelling is important mainly because he attempted to answer "the

---

* See Gostick, page 269:

German philosophy, from the time of Leibnitz, to the present day, has been marked by its "Idealism." The writings of Locke, Condillac, and others led to the conclusion, "there is nothing in the understanding which had not arrived there through the senses." To this Leibnitz replied by saying, "Yes, there is the understanding itself."

† See Gostick, pages 266, 269:

Kant began his theories with the skepticism of Hume. Like Hume, he begins by denying the possibility of a real knowledge of the external world. He admits that we receive all the materials of our knowledge through the senses,

and that from these materials we induce general laws in accordance with the nature of the human understanding; but the question remains—Are these laws, or conclusions (which result from the constitution of the mind), in accordance with external truth or reality? Kant asserts that no proof can be given to this question.

. . . The whole of Kant's system was simply an exposition of all that was implicit in the remark of Leibnitz. Kant explained the laws of the understanding. But are these laws accordant with external truth or reality? Schelling and Hegel have endeavored to answer this question.

question left open by Kant with a doctrine of 'spontaneous intuition'"—by which the human mind and external nature are to demonstrate *"the essential identity of the subjective and the objective worlds,"* and thus to "restrain Fichte's all-devouring egoism."[536] Gostick, again, is the main source of information:

[Schelling] professes to largely answer the question left open by Kant with a doctrine of "spontaneous intuition"—in other words to solve the problem . . . with the theory that the human mind and external nature are essentially *one.* That which exists in concrete forms etc. in Nature exists morally and mentally in the human spirit. The difference between him and Fichte is that Schelling's philosophy is more largely objective.* [*Writings,*IX, 180]

No one of Hegel's three forerunners is entirely acceptable to Whitman; yet each in his way originated or carried forward "with epic succession, the modern system of critical and transcendental philosophy," until it reached its fullest expression in Hegel.[537] Together they are "the illustrious four."[538] "They fit into each other like a nest of boxes—and Hegel encloses them all."[539]

Of the major nineteenth-century American writers, Whitman expressed his appreciation of the German transcendental philosophers most enthusiastically. This circumstance is all the more striking because he, unlike the New England Transcendentalists (though he delved no deeper than they did into the "four great philosophers"), never fell into the error common among them of ascribing to these philosophers greater powers than they possessed or greater successes than they achieved. Without pretending to master their dialectics or to follow them in their more rigorous

methods, he recognized their limitations and the limitations of philosophy in general. He repeatedly remarked on the inability of the human mind to achieve absolute knowledge,[540] yet rated it an inestimable gain that the German transcendentalists had justified "the thought of universality."[541]

The longest consideration of the German idealists to be found in Whitman's published writings occurs in the section in *Specimen Days* (1882) entitled "Carlyle from American Points of View." Two observations are in order: first, it illustrates a method analogous to Emerson's transferring ideas and expressions from his notes and lectures to his essays; and second, it is entirely fitting that Whitman should have inserted his comments on German philosophy into the essay on Carlyle, who had supplied him with much information on the subject in the first place. In a comparison that Whitman makes between Carlyle and Hegel, he sets off Carlyle's "dark fortune-telling of humanity and politics" against the "far more profound horoscope-casting" of Hegel on the same themes.[542] Carlyle seems to Whitman to have done in the realm of literature what Kant did in speculative philosophy. Carlyle cleared away the "jungle and poison vines and underbrush," hacking valiantly at them, "smiting hip and thigh." Kant did the like in his sphere, and "it was all he profess'd to do; his labors have left the ground fully prepared ever since."[543] But the "main point of Carlyle's utterance was the idea of duty being done,"[544] and with this Whitman is off to a discussion of this "most profound theme that can occupy the mind of man," in the course of which his enthusiastic preoccupation with Hegel's "fuller statement of the matter" ("probably," says Whitman, "the last word that has been said upon it") soon

---

* See Gostick, page 269:
[Schelling] professes to solve it [the problem left open by Kant] by an appeal to "spontaneous intuition," which discovers that the human mind and external nature are essentially one, or, in other words, that the same intelligence which exists in a conscious state in man lives in an unconscious condition throughout the universe, pervading "all thinking beings, and all objects of all thought."

leaves Carlyle behind and forgotten. This inquiry involves the question: "What is the (radical, democratic) *Me*, the human identity of understanding, emotions, spirit, &c., on the one side, of and with the (conservative) *Not Me*, the whole of the material objective universe and laws, with what is behind them in time and space, on the other side?"[545] Although Kant explained the laws of the human understanding, he left this larger question an open one; "Schelling's answer" is valuable "as far as it goes"; only Hegel's more coherent metaphysical system provides a "substantial answer (as far as there can be an answer to the foregoing question)."[546] Hereupon Whitman proceeds to recount "a little freely," he admits, "Hegel's theories of metaphysics,[547] politics,[548] and theology,[549] in each instance drawing either upon his own notes or upon Gostick's account. Following this summary of Hegelian doctrine, "indispensable to America's future," he returns to Carlyle in order to call attention to the identity of purpose while contrasting the great divergence of method between the inspirational progressivism of Hegel and the drastic prescriptions and abysmic pessimism of Carlyle.[550] While the latter is "quite the legitimate European product to be expected," the formulas of Hegel are an "essential and crowning justification of New World democracy."[551]

Without being, in the strict sense, either scientist or philosopher, Whitman did possess, especially during his later life, a fairly consistent *Weltanschauung*; and that view of life was, in the main, in accord with the absolute idealism of Hegel. His universe like Hegel's, was fluid—in the eternal process of becoming, or progression, by orderly development, which is best described or explained metaphysically by the Hegelian triadic dialectic. The scientific conception of evolution, his faith in democracy and individualism, his transcendental doctrine of idealism, and his self-reliant trust in the godliness of man were all acquired long before he knew anything about Hegel, although the extension and final elaboration of these and related doctrines went forward under Hegelian auspices after he discovered the Hegelian framework about 1870. Most of the elements of Hegelianism which the successive and expanding forms of *Leaves of Grass* exhibit are properly regarded as basically Whitmanesque in inception, the Hegelian expression of them being in the nature of an overlay, a kind of rationalization of his own still more or less inchoate thinking, but indubitably his own. Hegel's influence on Whitman was in the nature of organizing and regularizing his thought, less in the nature of a great creative or originative force setting him off on a new tack; for by 1870 the direction of Whitman's mind was too clearly determined for Kant or Hegel or any other philosopher radically to deflect him from his course. But once he discovered and largely accepted the transcendental formulas of the "four great philosophers," his later poems, like his later prose, could not escape taking on admixtures from the German source.

The point is that his basic doctrines had involved him in so many contrarieties and contradictions that he all but despaired of his problem. It is worth noting that while, after 1870, he continues to stand perplexed before "the puzzle of puzzles," the mystery of Being, repeatedly calling attention to the inscrutability of life's deepest secrets,[552] he is now as anxious to find a consistent explanation and to have his philosophy appear harmonious as earlier he was content to shrug off the imputation of inconsistency.[553] Finding Hegel's doctrine "a reasoned apprehension of the absolute," he adopted it, according to his lights, as the only scheme of reference by which he could justify his thoughts to himself and himself to America. Hegel corroborated in the abstract what he had created in the concrete; and having offered himself to America as the poet of democracy and science, he appropriated Hegel in the same dual capacity—as a philosopher of democratic freedom and of "modern scientism."[554]

EVERYTHING considered, it is remarkable that a relationship so tenuous should have produced such startling results. It may be partly owing to the slight firsthand knowledge which Whitman had of "the great System of Idealistic Philosophy of Germany"[555] that he so readily found in it lessons for the future of America that he envisaged. Certainly it is a striking instance no less of the absorptive power of the American spirit than it is an example at once of the irony of history and the ambiguity of the Hegelian system that the "Prussian State- and Court-Philosopher" should find among his most notable disciples the American poet who called himself the poet of democracy and "the greatest *poetical* representative of German philosophy."[556] Finally, the impact of German thought is another instance to prove false the idea that the German influence subsided with the decline of Transcendental-Romanticism and the dawn of Realism in America. However, it is noteworthy that in his transitional position and in conformity with his predilections for science and his demand for a new literary spirit, Whitman turned his attention away from Kant and toward Hegel as more nearly consonant with the new science and the future democracy in the Western World.

LATER NINETEENTH-CENTURY WRITERS

John Burroughs (1837–1921)

John Burroughs was a literary naturalist who was familiar with not only the works of German scientists like Kepler, Helmholtz, Haeckel, and Weismann[557] but also a number of literary men, and he was genuinely fond of German music, especially Bach. Beethoven, and Wagner.[558] Since he was never in Germany,[559] his contacts with German culture were entirely through books and people. It is doubtful that he knew much of the language; his use of German words is rare. What he lacked of facility in German he made up through familiarity with writers in English and French who informed him about German science, philosophy, and literature, among them Coleridge, Carlyle, Hobhouse, Tyndall, Darwin, Huxley, Lodge, and later the French philosophers Bergson and Carrél. Emerson and Carlyle were two of his chief informants. For the rest, he depended on translations, of which there were a great many by his time. His references to German writers are numerous; they cover a wide range; and occasionally they are penetrating.

Of all Germans, Goethe is the subject of greatest interest to Burroughs. He is discussed, quoted, or paraphrased some sixty times. The greatest single source of his information was Eckermann's *Conversations with Goethe*, which he read in both Margaret Fuller's version of 1839 and the complete John Oxenford translation of 1850.[560] The materials derived from Eckermann are of various kinds, touching all sides of Goethe's character: Goethe's interpretation of happiness,[561] the necessity of personality and manliness in great literature,[562] his discussion of weather and the inhaling and exhaling of the earth,[563] his opinions of Dante,[564] his criticism of Byron,[565] points of similarity between Goethe and Kant,[566] the superiority of Eckermann over Goethe as an ornithologist,[567] Goethe's description of Scott as a "comprehensive nature,"[568] his discussion of the proper subjects for poetry,[569] his view of nature's beneficence,[570] his religious nature, which Burroughs considered inadequate for the modern world,[571] Goethe's foreshadowing of some of the ideas of modern scientists,[572] his wondrous insight and his cool, uncommitted moral nature,[573] and his "intense individual point of view."[574] Generally in agreement with Goethe's critical dicta—on Byron, Shelley, and Scott, for example—he disagrees with Goethe on the nature of the Beautiful as objective, holding instead that it is a subjective experience.[575] He cites Goethe upon the necessity of art to produce by semblance the illusion of a higher reality against the rising realists who, he feels, content themselves with "only common reality."[576] And he agrees with Goethe that "a loving interest . . . amounting to a one-sided enthusiasm, alone leads to reality in criticism."[577]

Discriminating as Burroughs doubtless sought to make his views of Goethe, all his observations taken together reveal little originality of judgment based on a close study of Goethe's writings in their entirety. There is about his remarks a tone of sincerity, but there is also about them the air of the man who relies chiefly on secondary sources and consequently does not trust himself to discuss minute details but courts safety by sticking close to established opinions, phrased often in striking, but none the less general terms.[578]

Interest in Henri Bergson led him to make a study of the translations and commentaries on Kant and Hegel that were available in English,[579] and in his book on Whitman he discussed the Hegelian influence on *Leaves of Grass*, professing to find Hegelian thought in Whitman "as vital as the red blood corpuscles in the blood."[580]

German literature enriched Burroughs' mind in many ways, but on the whole he read, following the practice of his friend Emerson, mainly for the lustres. Except in science, where he read for information, German writers provided him chiefly with points of comparison, allusions, embellishments—materials with which to garnish his style. Except for Goethe, no German literary figure added much to his stature; but no admirer of Burroughs would delete the German element that adds so much to the pungency of his style.

William Dean Howells (1837–1920)

William Dean Howells' acknowledged indebtedness, in *Criticism and Fiction* (1891) and elsewhere, to the English and Continental realists is so well known that the extraordinary catholicity of his literary taste, especially during his earlier years, is often forgotten. Even after the main lines of his realism were clearly drawn, the variety of his interests manifested itself—most notably in *My Literary Passions* (1895).[581] In his autobiographical *Years of My Youth* (1916) he described the excitement and intoxication that he felt as a youth of fourteen when, dedicating himself to literary pursuits with delirious obsession, he set himself to unlock the stores of foreign literatures by "studying four or five languages" and "reading, reading, reading."[582]

Early during his years as a compositor in his father's printshop he came under the spell of Heine through a German typesetter, and promptly proceeded to do battle with the German language.[583] Before he was eighteen, the witchery of Heine had led him to develop a fondness for all German literature, and his daily association and cultural contacts with the large German populations of Dayton and Columbus engendered a kind of frenzy for Germanism.[584] In retrospect, years later, this Teutonic phase of his self-culture seemed to him "fantastic," but there can be no doubt that at the time he was seriously affected, and that, however far he subsequently got away from these youthful enthusiasms, they left a substantial cultural residue in his mind.[585]

During his Ashtabula period, while foraging about for something to read, he came upon a copy of Schlegel's *Lectures on Dramatic Literature*. He chanced upon this book at an opportune moment, immediately after Spanish drama had engrossed his attention.

I cannot give a due notion of the comfort this book afforded me by the light it cast upon paths where I had dimly made my way before. . . . Of course, I pinned my faith to everything that Schlegel said. I obediently despised the classic unities and the French and Italian theatre which had perpetuated them, and I revered the romantic drama which had its glorious course among the Spanish and English poets, and which was crowned with the fame of Cervantes and Shakespeare whom I seemed to own, they owned me so completely.[586]

Even before he read Schlegel, he discovered Goethe, about whom he had more to say than about any other German except Heine. Taught that he should admire Goethe in all his parts, the youthful Howells was chagrined to discover that his "heart would not kindle at the cold altar of Goethe."[587] Even after he had formed his own literary theory, he found Goethe's novels crudely constructed, the dialogue stilted, and the tone too sentimental to suit his taste for realism.[588] Holding that "art, like law, is the perfection of reason," and that "whatever is unreasonable in the work of an artist is inartistic,"[589] Howells found distasteful Goethe's blending of the real and the unreal and his veiling of the reasonable behind the implausible. Finally, demanding a realistic portrayal of life that centered on normal, healthy people, he objected to the unmoral nature of Goethe's works.[590]

But Heine (he said) "dominated me longer than any author that I have known."[591] Aside from Heine's direct literary influence on individual poems, the earliest and in some respects most profound effect of Heine was to correct Howells' idea, learned from Goldsmith and Pope, that to be a writer he must adopt a literary attitude or pose—that he must "literarify" himself. This he thought, meant developing a certain type of style as far removed from reality as "acting which you know to be acting" is removed from life.

Heine at once showed me that this ideal . . . was false; that the life of literature was from the springs of the best common speech, and that the nearer it could be made to conform, in voice, look and gait, to graceful, easy, picturesque and humorous or impassioned talk, the better it was.

He did not impart these truths without imparting certain tricks with them, which I was careful to imitate as soon as I began to write in his manner, that is to say instantly. . . . But in all essentials he was himself, and my final lesson from him, or the final effect of all my lessons from him, was to find myself, and to be for good or evil whatsoever I really was.[592]

As he intimates, he did not learn this lesson at once, for in imitating Heine and copying his mannerisms, Howells was, of course, defeating his own purpose. A decade later Lowell, to whom Howells had sent some verses for the *Atlantic*, held them over until he could be reassured that they were original and not translations from Heine.[593] Later Lowell improved an opportunity to tell his young friend that he disliked the "pseudo-cynical" note which he detected as deriving from Heine, and advised him to "sweat the Heine out" of himself "as men sweat mercury out of their bones."[594]

The poem entitled "Pleasure-Pain," whose authenticity Lowell questioned, is among the most obviously Heinesque poems of Howells. The melancholy sigh, the longing, the disappointment, the passionate love coupled with the thought of death, that pervade Heine's poems are imitated in both manner and rhythm,[595] and the superscription from Heine, "Das Vergnügen ist nichts als ein höchst angenehmer Schmerz," further accentuates the relationship. Often the similarity extends only to mechanics and mood, both of which are followed rather faithfully in "While She Sang," identical in meter with Heine's "Lorelei." The same may be said for "Convention," a poem of eight lines; while the metrics of the "Elegy on John Butler Howells" bears a striking resemblance to that of Heine's "Belsazer." Occasionally, as in "A Poet," Howells seeks to combine the lyric note of longing with that of cynicism that is so characteristic of Heine; but the more striking parallelisms are usually in metrical arrangement, notably in the manner in which he seeks to imitate Heine's variations from two- to three-syllable feet and back again for lyric effect.

Except for his "saturation in Heine," from whom he unquestionably drew much support in developing his characteristic doctrines of writing "truthfully" or "realistically," the German writers left him relatively untouched.[596] The boundless enthusiasms of his youth, appropriately called "passions," however much they "emparadised" him at the time, were evanescent in their effect, as such infatuations often are. After all, Howells' technique was of the simplest kind—about as untheoretical as it could be. He set out simply to do for his place and time what "the divine" Jane Austen had done for hers. "The faithful treatment of material," once he realized that he must rid himself of imitation and mannerism, schools and cults, required little more than keeping his eyes straight ahead and setting down what he saw, and that simple procedure enabled him to make the boast that he could concentrate on his materials, or the selection of them, with a minimum of distraction by any theoretical or technical considerations of craftsmanship. In crediting Heine with showing him the way, he acknowledged Heine to be the one from whom he learned more than from any other literary source.

Henry James (1843–1916)

Germany was largely irrelevant for Henry James. As a lad of sixteen he spent a summer at Bonn, with tutors, busy with the German language and literary classics, in the faith that everything "so mystically and valuably Gothic" somehow was an agency "ministering to culture."[597] But he was not won over; and when, in 1872, his commission to write a series of European travel letters for the *Nation* again took him to Germany, he soon concluded that he was

done with Germany—that he could "never hope to become an unworthiest adoptive grandschild of the fatherland."[598] There are occasional references to Goethe and other Germans in his writings, [599] and for the sake of universality, he included among his social revolutionists in *The Princess Casamassima* (1886) a German named Schinkel along with Muniment of England and Poupin of France, and other German characters appear in others of his "international" stories; but fundamentally, he remained antipathetic toward Germany—an instinctive feeling that finally expressed itself in his embracing British citizenship as an act of protest against his native country's not coming promptly to the aid of the Allies in World War I.

Mark Twain (1835–1910)

Howells' observation that Mark Twain was "the most unliterary" literary man he had ever known engendered the myth that Mark Twain was a completely "self-made" writer "lacking in book learning,"[600]—that more than any other American writer, he dug into the native virgin soil and copied nature only. As the study of Mark Twain proceeds, it becomes steadily clearer that Mark Twain was unliterary only in the sense in which Howells was literary. He was fully cognizant of his shortcomings owing to the irregularity of his education. It required no Dr. Holmes to remind him that to be "self-made" was not synonymous with being "well-made."[601] But that he was ever driven by established opinion or "genteel" tradition into denying his own feelings and convictions about what he considered good or bad in art is refuted by numerous passages in *A Tramp Abroad*[602] and elsewhere. He once observed, "I ought to have recognized the sign—the old sure sign that has never failed me in matters of art. Whenever I enjoy anything in art it means that it is mighty poor."[603] But Mark Twain made a fine art of talking through his hat, and care must be exercised to recognize his drollery when we come upon it.[604] He was no more reticent about voicing his opinion of books or about quoting from them than he was about continuously repeating a word or phrase that suited him, all the resulting tautology notwithstanding.[605] But there is no profit in laboring the point. Mark Twain was unacademic but not unliterary.[606]

Among the 695 references to books and authors that I count in his published works, there are few allusions to Germans and fewer to writers in other foreign languages. There is nothing to indicate that in French or German, the languages which he knew best, he ever read a book in the foreign language if he could get it in translation.[607] Paine tells us that Mark Twain tried to learn German from an old German cobbler who lived in Hannibal, but his English was so meager that little was gained from him. It was not until he was fairly launched on his career as a writer that he began a more serious study of the foreign languages and literatures. Howells was of the opinion that Mark Twain knew German "pretty well, and Italian enough late in life to have fun with it."[608] Even after Samuel Clemens acquired fair facility in German during his several periods of residence in German-speaking countries, he continued "to have fun" with German, purposely exaggerating his difficulties with the language in order to capitalize on its absurdities, and ingeniously inventing unheard of linguistic atrocities for calculated comic effects. Many of his best passages in "The Awful German Language" and in the playlet which he composed in a jargon of German-English are felicitous hits only because the author, far from being the inept linguist that he represents himself, knows perfectly well what he is about.

RESIDENCE AT HEIDELBERG

During the first months of 1878 the entire Clemens family seriously undertook to learn German in preparation for a year which they intended to spend in Germany. A German nurse was engaged, and "the whole atmosphere of the household presently became lingually Teutonic."[609] Bayard Taylor, going on his appointment as Minister to Germany, accompanied them, and lessons were profitably continued aboard ship. The study was prosecuted even more vigorously immediately upon finding living quarters in the Schloss Hotel at Heidelberg, to the point, said Mark Twain, that all suffered nightmares. Little Susy wished that Rosa, the German nurse, were "made in English," and Clemens himself heartily damned the language time and again. But they all persevered, and by May 7, Mark Twain wrote to Bayard Taylor in that mixture of tongues for which he had a special gift:

Wir werden hier bleiben villeicht für drei Monate, zum Schloss-Hotel.—Dies hotel steht about fünf und siebenzig Fuss höher als das Schloss, und commandirt ein Aussicht welcher ohne Ahnlichkeit in der Welt hat. (Sie müssen excuse auskratchens, interlineations, u.s.w.)

Ich habe heute gecalled on der Herr Professor Ihne, qui est die Professor von Englischen Zunge im University, to get him to recommend ein Deutschen Lehrer für mich, welcher he did. Er sprach von mehrerer Amerikanischer authors, und meist günstiger und vergnügungsvoll von Ihrer; dass er knew you und Ihrer Lebe so wohl, durch Ihrer geschreibungen; und wann Ich habe gesagt Ich sollen Ihr schreiben heute Nacht gewesen if nothing happened, er bitte mich Opfer sein compliments, und hoffe Ihnen will ihm besuchen wenn du kommst an Heidelberg. Er war ein vortrefflicher und liebwürdiger and every way delightful alte gentleman.

Man sagt Ich muss ein Pass (in der English, *Passport,*) haben to decken accidents. Dafür gefelligt Ihnen furnish me one. Meine Beschreibung ist vollenden: Geborn 1835; 5 Fuss 8 1/2 inches hoch; weight doch aber about 145 pfund, sometimes ein wenig unter, sometimes ein wenig oben; dunkel braun Haar und rhotes Moustache, full Gesicht, mit sehr hohe Oren und leicht grau practvolles strahlenden Augen und ein Verdammtes gut moral character. Handlung-keit, Author von Bücher.

Ich have das Deutsche sprache gelernt und bin ein glücklicher Kind, you bet.[610]

On July 4, he addressed the American students at the University in the same kind of jargon.[611] Later from Munich, he wrote to Taylor that "the children talk German as glibly as they do English," but that his own facility in the language still left something to be desired. The oddities of the language continued to engage his attention, but he gave up actively studying German because it interfered with his writing. Triumphantly he reported that since he had "learned the German language and forgotten it again," he felt justified in resuming English once more.[612] He had attained a certain fluency, and he decided to forego accuracy, while he capitalized on his own mistakes, even to exaggerating them grossly and blaming all on the "awful" language itself. He reported with relish Twitchell's saying to him, on an occasion when he was speaking in English of some private matters which he did not want German bystanders to overhear, "Speak German, Mark,—some of those people may understand English."[613] Thus he practiced his atrocities on the language and stored up materials for his essay on "The Awful German Language," for the playlet *Meisterschaft*, and for the translation which he made of *Struwwelpeter* some years later.

The concern with German did not cease once the Clemenses returned home. The German nurse remained a fixture;[614] and as late as 1887, when the study of Browning was on the wane, the Browning Club was succeeded by (or blended with) a German Class which met at regular intervals at the Clemens home to study *"der, die, das"* and the *"gehabt haben's"* out of such texts as Meisterschaft and Ollendorff.[615] For their amusement and profit, Mark Twain concocted a play in three acts called *Meisterschaft*, a literary achievement of which he was proud. His struggles with German, his

studied corruptions of the language, an "innate gift of gab, and his western relish for sonorous idiom that underlay his love of declamation and profanity,"[616] all eminently prepared him for the writing of this farce. The play was given twice by the class "with enormous success," and it was published in modified form in the *Century* for January, 1888.[617]

BERLIN AND VIENNA

During the summer of 1891 and the following winter the Clemenses were again in Germany.[618] Mark Twain and his wife enjoyed the most flattering attentions from Berlin society, from Emperor William II on down, so much so that little Jean remarked, "Why, papa, if it keeps on like this, pretty soon there won't be anybody for you to get acquainted with but God"—a remark that he relished less and less the more he thought about it.[619] He was much in demand at the mighty *Kommers*, and it was for one of these occasions that he dug up a chapter of an essay in which he had made a beginning thirteen years earlier to "improve and simplify" the German language. Still intrigued by the mouth-filling compounds, he proudly produced a word of thirty-nine letters, which, as he observed, "merely concentrates the alphabet with a shovel."[620] The Berlin winter also yielded his essay on Berlin, "The German Chicago."[621] Most important, he came across the old nursery book of *Struwwelpeter* by Dr. Heinrich Hoffmann and straightway set to translating it for the edification of his children.[622]

The third period of residence in German-speaking countries came during 1897–1899, toward the end of the long lecture tour that resulting in *Following the Equator* (1897) and the settlement of Mark Twain's debts.[623] On November 21, 1897, the Concordia Club of Vienna honored him with a *Festkneipe*, for which all the great ones of Vienna assembled, and for whose delectation he spoke on "Die Schrecken der Deutschen Sprache."[624]

Thus by steps was produced "The Awful German Language," an essay which contains ample evidence to show that while in speaking German Mark Twain may have disdained to employ more than "a touch of good grammar for picturesqueness," he was far from uninstructed on the subject when it came to writing. For no one not thoroughly acquainted with the idiosyncrasies of the language could have butchered it as successfully as he did.[625]

In some respects the most important literary result of Mark Twain's Vienna period came as a consequence of his twice seeing Adolf von Wilbrandt's *Der Meister von Palmyra*, an impressive play in which Death, the principal character, is presented as all powerfull.[626] As one reads Mark Twain's commentary on the play, one feels that he found strong confirmation, not to say satisfaction, in the *Meister von Palmyra* for his own "sorry creed," as it took shape in his mind during the nineties. "The piece," he wrote, "is just one long, soulful, sardonic laugh at human life. Its title might properly be 'Is Life a Failure?' and leave the five acts to play with the answer. I am not at all sure that the author meant to laugh at life. I only notice that he has done it."[627] He then proceeds to elaborate on the lessons of the play in precisely the tone adopted in *What is Man?* and *The Mysterious Stranger*.

Germany provided Mark Twain not merely with the bewitchingly romantic atmosphere portrayed in *A Tramp Abroad* but also with a retreat from a life whose sorrows were bearing him down. He found the German language excruciatingly funny, but he also found in that language the play that gave him food for serious thought. Finally, it may be observed that, despite the fun he made of it, the language itself became a family possession of the type that entered into their daily lives. It developed overtones of meaning that only long familiarity could breed. An instance is the peculiar spell which the word *unberufen*

worked on all members of the family. It acquired a special meaning and became a kind of talismanic charm which the anxious watchers at the death-bed of Mrs. Clemens uttered—softly, half-superstitiously, half-religiously—as she made her last rally. On the simple marker which Mark Twain had placed at her grave he had inscribed, besides the name and record of birth and death, the words: "Gott sei dir gnädig, O meine Wonne!"

Bret Harte (1836–1902)

Previous to his appointment as consul to Crefeld in Prussia, Bret Harte had taken little notice of German literature.[628] When he sailed for Europe in 1878, he left his family in America, intending to have them join him after he was established. His early dislike of Germany appears in his first letters home: the climate, the officiousness, the militarism, and the scenery around Crefeld left much to be desired. Even the vaunted German opera displeased him: in *Tannhäuser* he found the singing, acting, orchestration notoriously bad, and he was disappointed in *Faust* and *Der Freischütz*. Aside from the ill health that troubled him during his first year in Germany, he had serious difficulties with the language, and the work incident to mastering the records of his office and organizing the consular service was very trying, for he had to rely largely on an interpreter.[629]

Soon after his arrival in Crefeld, the *Berliner Tageblatt* asked him to write a series of semi-monthly letters.[630] These letters of "impressions" turned out rather more "frank" and "outspoken" than the editor had bargained for, or the reading public liked; and by April, 1879 Harte gave up the plan.[631] Even before going to Germany, he had written a parody called "The Legends of the Rhine," in which he listed, recipe-like, the ingredients required for concocting a German legend. In Germany, when he set himself to turn to literary use some of the German lore that he found on every hand, this critical tone insinuated itself into his stories. In poems like "A Legend of Cologne," instead of surrendering to the atmosphere of romanticism as Irving and Longfellow had done, he adopted the quizzical tone of Mark Twain's Innocents. In "A Legend of Sammstadt" the hero drinks a glass of wine, inducing a dreamy state in which he relives the events related in an old German tale, but throughout the author remains critically aloof, and the whole is treated in the nature of a hoax. Altogether his nearest approach to an appreciative tone is struck in "Views from a German Spion," in which, after the manner of the Lady of Shalott, he views a street scene below his window by looking into a small mirror; but even in this sketch, his critical temper asserts itself in the inevitable comparisons which he draws between small-town life in Germany and America.[632]

After two years in Crefeld, Harte was transferred to Glasgow, and he never again saw Germany or his native land. The literature of Germany touched him but lightly. For the most part, the German influence on his writings is one of places and characters, or what might be termed local coloring.

Edward Rowland Sill (1841–1887)

In the case of Edward Rowland Sill, another one of the men interested in the *Overland Monthly* and, like Harte, long a resident of California, the purely literary influence was stronger than in Harte.[633] He early turned his attention to making German literature available through translation. In 1867 he proposed to Henry Holt a volume of Zschokke's tales, to be translated by himself and his friend Shearer, and the next year he prepared an English version of the novelized life of Mozart by Hermann Rau.[634] It is clear from his translation as well as from several of his critical essays, notably one on the art of translation

and another in which he compared French and German lyric poetry, that he had expert knowledge of both languages.[635] His literary ideal was Goethe, whose life and writings furnished him with anecdote and illustration for his own essays.[636] He was fond also of Kant and approvingly quoted Kant's ethical pronouncements.[637] Another work of serious import that interested him was F. W. von Humboldt's *Briefe an eine Freundin*.[638]

Most of Sill's essays, appearing in magazines as various as the *Overland*, the *Nation*, and the *Atlantic*, were unsigned, so that the establishment of his canon presents difficulties. The extent of Germanic influence on Sill will not be known until his writings are brought together; but it is apparent, on the basis of the available fragmentary collections of his prose and verse, that he repeatedly drew upon German authors for his own writings.

Ambrose Bierce (1842–1913?)

A self-educated adventurer in many realms and a bold pretender to universal learning, Ambrose Bierce declared on one occasion that a knowledge of foreign languages and literatures was of no use to a writer, only to claim at the next opportunity, expert linguistic attainments for himself in many languages.[639] It is generally believed that he attained in a considerable measure the scholarship to which, earlier, he pretended. His publication, in 1892, of a translation of Richard Voss's *Der Mönch von Berchtesgaden* is not conclusive evidence that he attained to competence in German, because it was in reality only an adaptation of Danziger's translation of the year before.[640] *The Devil's Dictionary*, appearing in installments from 1881 to 1906, affords some indications of Bierce's knowledge of German language and literature, as well as of philosophy, although much of it bears the earmarks of curious learning dug out of out-of-the-way places of a sort to suggest that he mastered all literary and philosophical books.[641] His spurious learning and his mock references to books only deepen the studied enigmatical nature of the man, whose unexplained disappearance about 1913 in Mexico came as a fitting climax to his odd career.

O. Henry (1862–1910)

Irregularly educated, O. Henry became a voracious reader, first, of all literatures in translation, and after 1882 (when he began to study German, French, and Spanish), in some cases in the original. Included among his earlier reading are some of the stories of Auerbach and the *Hammer and Anvil* of Spielhagen. After he went to live with the Halls in Austin, Texas, he paid some attention to the German language, but never progressed as far in that medium as he did in the Spanish. It may be that the large German population of San Antonio and Austin led him to resume studying German about 1894–1895, while editing the *Rolling Stone*, a humorous weekly, published in both cities and circulated in considerable numbers among the Germans of those localities. An illustration of a German musician brandishing a baton and some humorous verses below the picture cost him most of his German subscribers. Occasional references to Germany, German art and music and German architecture indicate that Germany appealed to his imagination, but there is little in his writings to suggest anything like a distinctly literary influence.

Recent Trends

By the time of O. Henry the prevailing emphasis on localism and veritism, that is to say, attention to the near at hand and to the factual, made romantic and transcendental Germany seem remote and inconsequential. In some realistic and naturalistic quarters everything German was foreign, exotic, false—at all events, inapplicable.

Veritism insisted upon the "truthful" depiction of the local American scene; and in the craftsmanship of people like Frank Norris and Hamlin Garland German sentiment and idealism alike ceased to have much significance.

However, with the advent of the local-color movement and its attention to regions, races, nationalities, and folkways, the German settler came in for his share of literary treatment. The occasional "Dutchman" who flitted across the pages of Cooper and Irving was invested with a new significance by the local colorist. The tendency is noticeable in John Esten Cooke, whose interest in Germany otherwise is nonexistent. His portraits of German settlements in Virginia and of individual German characters provide more than merely incidental touches. The same tendency is notable also in some of Edward Eggleston's novels of Indiana, especially in *The End of the World* (1872),[642] which embodies a highly successful rendition of the German-American dialect in the speech of Gottlieb Wehle.[643] The trend continued unabated, and finds exemplification in more recent times in the novels of Sinclair Lewis and Theodore Dreiser, the latter himself the son of German immigrants; and in an area like Pennsylvania, the Pennsylvania-German has been exploited for literary purposes not only by himself but by writers of non-German extraction.

While American literary interest in Germany underwent a general abatement with the rise of the realistic and naturalistic schools, Germanic influence never came to a sudden halt or a final period. Even the imagists, whose chief emphasis fell upon matters of technique (for which they found their models primarily in France and England), were not unacquainted with poetic trends among modern German poets. Amy Lowell and Ezra Pound are cases in point. Sara Teasdale's inspiration came not only from her early reading in Christina Rossetti, but quite as much from German lyricists.

especially Heine, with a translation of whose verses she busied herself while she was still a schoolgirl. John Gould Fletcher inherited through his mother, who was born of German immigrants and who never felt at home in America, his aspirations toward the aesthetic life of Europe, so that he became an expatriate, until his reading of Nietzsche and Spengler, together with events in Europe at the time of the first world war, led to his repatriation.

The impact on American writers of Schopenhauer's pessimism and von Hartmann's philosophy of the unconscious goes back as far at least as Edgar Saltus' *Philosophy of Disenchantment* (1885). It has been called "a pocket exposition of the doctrines of Schopenhauer and von Hartmann," jauntily concluding that "life is an affliction." A contemporary of his, who also represents the *malaise de la fin de siècle*, though from a very different angle, was Henry Adams, whose autobiographical *Education* spells out very precisely the crucial effect upon his turn from faith in unity to acceptance of chaos by the distressingly disintegrative complex of ideas stemming from Schopenhauer, Nietzsche, and Haeckel. *The Education of Henry Adams* (1907), obviously inspired by the *Erziehungsplan* of Goethe's *Autobiography* and *Wilhelm Meister*, explains in the chapter entitled "Teufelsdröckh (1901)" how his reading of Schopenhauer led him to proclaim that "the larger synthesis" of the Hegelian "principle of contradiction expressed by opposites" led inevitably to the conclusion that "in the last synthesis, order and anarchy were one, but that the unity was chaos." Thus prepared, he describes in the chapter called "The Abyss of Ignorance (1902)" how his "plunge" into the science of Wilhelm Ostwald, Ernst Mach, and Ernst Haeckel led at last to his initiation into "The Grammar of Science" by which he was forced to conclude (1) that "Chaos was the law of nature, and order was the dream of man," and (2) that "the mind could gain

nothing by flight or by fight" but must "merge in its supersensual multiverse, or succumb to it." This, in turn, led to the final phase of the education of Henry Adams by which he formulated the dynamic theory of history that fixed "1950 as the year when the world must go to smash."

The impacts of Haeckel on writers like Dreiser, of Nietzsche on Jack London and Frank Norris, and of Freud on Anderson, Hemingway, and the stream-of-consciousness writers are relatively recent but important phenomena that will long occupy the critic and historian of twentieth-century literature. In the drama, Eugene O'Neill admittedly learned much from individual Germans like Hauptmann, Kaiser, and Wedekind and from the entire tradition of *Expressionismus* in recent German literature. Men like T. S. Eliot have, of course, made the language and literature of Germany an integral part of their intellectual and aesthetic equipment. The writings of William Ellery Leonard breathe the very atmosphere of Germany, where he received much of his education. Even the naturalistic verse of Robinson Jeffers bears the mark of his years in Switzerland and Germany, so that while more immediate native concerns have largely displaced the powerful interest which classic German literature once evoked in American writers like Emerson and Longfellow, there is still an active and continuous stream of influence that shows signs of outliving even the catastrophe that German culture suffered during recent years.

The first comprehensive, though brief and necessarily very tentative, survey of what twentieth-century American authors owe to German critics and writers has been attempted by Professor J. Wesley Thomas in the concluding pages of his *Amerikanische Dichter und die deutsche Literatur* (Goslar, 1950).

In the meantime, especially since the end of World War II, we have witnessed a decided shift of emphasis and direction in

German-American cultural exchange. Germany, long the exporter to America, has become steadily more the importer from America[644]—a shift in cultural influence that promises to provide the counterpart in this century for that remarkable German cultural imperialism felt in the United States during the last century.

AMERICAN LITERARY CRITICISM

German literary criticism did not make itself felt in America until after 1820, partly because American critics were under English-Scottish tutelage,[645] and partly because German criticism itself was meager and derivative before the era of Lessing and Herder. The generation of Coleridge, Lamb, and Hazlitt, reading Schiller, Goethe, the Schlegels, Tieck, Gervinus, and Ulrici and probing into German idealistic philosophy, were the first to make extensive use of German criticism. Following a time lag of another decade or two, this body of German thought was transmitted to America, when W. H. Prescott, R. H. Dana, H. N. Hudson, Emerson, and Lowell fostered Schlegel-Coleridge-Carlylean criticism—a romantic approach to literature and art in general but especially to Shakespeare.[646]

THE CONCERN
WITH SHAKESPEARE CRITICISM

The effort of the Germans to incorporate Shakespeare into their literary tradition was the aspect of their criticism that received more notice in England than Lessing's examination of the broad principles of poetic creation, or the violent and provocative naturalism of the *Sturm und Drang* school, or the speculations on aesthetics of Kant, Schiller, Novalis, Wackenroder, and Schelling. German critical influence in nineteenth-century America can conveniently be studied in relation to Shakespeare, for virtually every literary principle advanced by German critics from Herder and Lessing to the Schlegels and Hegel was itself bound to be brought to bear on Shakespeare.[647] Shakespeare criticism came to be a common ground on which German and American critical opinion could meet most readily. Three broad, not always mutually exclusive, streams of critical opinion emanating from Germany had a deep and lasting effect: (1) the Schlegel-Coleridge view of Shakespeare as interpreted by such writers as Prescott, Dana, Whipple, Giles, Lowell, Emerson and Margaret Fuller; (2) German philosophical transcendentalism that inspired the transcendental critics, principally Margaret Fuller; and (3) the historical-scholarly school, inspired by Goethe and the Schlegels, introduced by the Ticknor-Everett-Bancroft generation, and adopted as the standard in method and point of view by our universities and graduate schools generally.

The extraordinary vogue of Shakespeare in Germany[648] between 1760 and 1780 encouraged the British to re-examine the bases upon which their own criticism had so long rested, and it inspired in them a renewed interest in their national past. Aided by the synthesizing efforts of the aesthetic philosophers, German criticism was at long last in a position to strengthen the critical revolt in England that had been germinating as far back as Addison, Steele, Lord Kames, Dr. Johnson, and the Wartons. The implications of the new criticism for the interpretation of Shakespeare may be reduced to the following principal points: (1) the effort of historical criticism to see Shakespeare in his own age and country; (2) the substitution of the principle of organic unity for the rules and authority of the French neoclassical school; (3) the attempt to read a philosophic content, a "larger unity," dramatic consistency, and central idea into the Shakespearean drama;[649] (4) the assertion of the artist's right to expression as opposed to the imitation of models; (5) the appearance of a note of appreciative sympathy, often mixed with sentimentality, in discussing Shakespeare; and (6) a strong feeling of national pride.

The Schlegel-Coleridge School

These romantic principles—especially the concept of organic unity, of the "myriad-minded" Shakespeare, and of Shakespeare's superiority to the "rules"—were at first attributed almost wholly to Coleridge.[650] An exception was an anonymous critic, writing in the *Analectic* for 1818,[651] who traced the new criticism to A. W. Schlegel and described the Coleridge-Hazlitt school as imitators of Schlegel, the "discoverer of Shakespeare." William Hickling Prescott (1796–1859), himself a disciple of Schlegel,[652] has the credit of introducing the Schlegel-Coleridge inspired views in a tentative way in essays appearing intermittently from 1823 to 1859.[653]

The *Lectures* (1834) of Richard Henry Dana (1787–1879) were more extensive and influential. Early convinced of the pre-eminence of Coleridge among critics, Dana followed the romantic interpretation of genius, condemned formal criticism by rules, and in 1834 delivered, in his eight lectures, the first organized American treatment of Shakespeare in the manner of Schlegel and Coleridge.[654] In the forties the succession went to a clergyman scholar, Henry Norman Hudson (1814–1886), who dedicated his *Lectures on Shakespeare* (2 vols., 1848) to Dana.

Hudson's *Lectures*, his *Shakespeare: His Life, Art, and Characters* (2 vols., 1872), and his twenty-volume "Harvard Edition" (1880–1881) established the German-inspired Coleridgean Shakespeare criticism on a broad footing in this country[655] and did much to domesticate it in academic circles. Hudson probably read no German,[656] but his *Lectures* of 1848 show that he made an early acquaintance with Coleridge and Lessing, Goethe, and A. W. Schlegel on Shakespeare (in translation).[657] In his 1872

volume on Shakespeare we find him quoting and citing in footnotes, in addition to the critics already named, Gervinus, Ulrici, and Karl Werder. Schlegel is most frequently quoted as an authority on the principle of organic unity, on the distinction between the classic and the romantic, and on the relation between the philosophical and moral in literature; in his moral interpretation of Shakespearean characters, Coleridge, Goethe, and Gervinus share equal honors as inspiring him. His borrowings are numerous, sometimes unacknowledged, and often *verbatim.*[658]

Edwin Percy Whipple (1819–1886) synthesized the efforts of his predecessors Dana and Hudson (whose work he knew and acknowledged), and he gave forceful, unified formulation to the theories which, in various states of disjointedness, they had fostered.[659] Beginning as a disciple of Coleridge, he came to accord Schlegel greater authority even than Coleridge except in one respect: Schlegel sometimes neglected the characters of plays when tracing out the pervading unity.[660] He expressed the common American attitude toward German scholarship when he found that, in their search for "ground ideas," the Germans sometimes arrived at little more than barren ethical, political, and social truisms.[661] In Whipple we find signs of the weakness which the slavish following of German criticism led to, and which ultimately produced a reaction. Refusing to resort to historical research on the grounds that the mystery of genius is impenetrable, American disciples fell back on a system of idolatry that left them little to do but to exclaim. On the constructive side, Whipple's contribution consisted in "pointing out how Shakespeare's productions fulfill the organic requirements of literature, how they exhibit Unity within Variety," and in "illustrating the ideal and representative quality of the poet's broadly diversified characterizations."[662]

Henry Giles (1809–1882), the disciple of

Coleridge, brought to a head most of the romantic attitudes and especially the tendency to read moral and philosophical ideas into the plays of Shakespeare. His *Human Life in Shakespeare* (1868) marks the climax of the Germanic character analysis linked with the search for "ground ideas" in Shakespeare. Aside from the attitudes of Lowell, Emerson, and Jones Very, the "sympathetic appreciation" derived from the German Romantic school became less ecstatic, critics of the opposition—Richard Grant White, Walt Whitman, George Wilkes, and the scholar-critics of the universities—insisting upon a more realistic and historical approach.

Meanwhile, James Russell Lowell, representing mainly the romantic point of view, had his say, as did also the Transcendentalists Margaret Fuller, R. W. Emerson, and Jones Very—critics whose work was not decisive, but is part of the story of how German Shakespeare criticism long domiated American literary theory even while it fostered an independent literary conciousness in the young nation.

Lowell was aware of the vast critical commonwealth of which he was a part. In his essay on "Shakespeare Once More" (whose title obviously echoes Goethe's "Shakespeare und kein Ende"), after distinguishing between the conventional "destructive" criticism and the Germans' "productive" approach, he lists Lessing, Goethe, Schlegel, and Gervinus as the line of succession in this tradition. A member of their school, he naturally showed similarities with all of them, just as they paralleled each other in many particulars, and frankly avowed himself in debt to them all.[663]

"Shakespeare Once More" is an example of Lowell's eclecticism and of his debt to German criticism and to Coleridge.[664] It lacks logical unity, except insofar as it discusses Shakespeare historically in relation to his time. Here Lowell probably followed a principle originally derived from Goethe.[665] Lowell indulges in romantic

ádoration and unqualified defense, joining Coleridge in his disagreement with Goethe when the latter maintained that "Shakespeare was a poet, but not a dramatist."[666] From Goethe and Schlegel came Lowell's formulation of the difference between the ancients and the moderns as the distinction between *must* and *would* (*sollen* und *wollen*) —that in general in the Greek drama Destiny is outside the control of the characters while in Shakespeare it lies within them. Again, Lowell agreed with the German school in regarding each of the plays as developing out of a central germinating idea and unifying principle. In applying the organic theory to *Hamlet*, Lowell (though he rejects Goethe's explanation of the tragedy) is as much in debt to Goethe's long discussion in *Wilhelm Meister* as to Coleridge, and in a lesser degree to Schlegel and Gervinus.[667] Goethe more than any other individual affected Lowell's personality as a critic, though he often found fault with Goethe, especially on the score of his not taking the critic's task and responsibility seriously enough.[668]

The theories and principles of Lowell's that derive most clearly from A. W. Schlegel, or the Coleridgean restatement of Schlegel, are the concept of organic unity, the division of the powers of the imagination, the critical terminology for dealing with the endless antitheses between fancy and imagination, talent and genius, understanding and reason, the real and the ideal, and so on, and the lofty conception of the function of the poet.[669] Finally, from both the German and the English romantic schools Lowell caught the contagion of Shakespeare-*Schwärmerei*, to which Coleridge gave expression when he said, "I have a smack of Hamlet myself."

Transcendental Criticism

The Germanic preoccupations of Prescott, Dana, Hudson, and Lowell were but a prelude to the more deeply tinged romantic

Germanicism of the American Transcendentalists, of whom Margaret Fuller, Emerson, and Jones Very may be taken as the types. The community of interests of their group, their co-operative, enthusiastic, and unselfish spirit, made it possible for them to absorb the German romantic conception of literature with thoroughgoing and radical completeness. They constituted the second prominent avenue by which German critical principles came to America.

Margaret Fuller's editorship of the *Dial*, her conversations, and voluminous critical writings combined to make her the leading critic of the movement. Her greatest achievements as critic were to break down the moral reservations of Puritan-conditioned American literary consciousness, as applied to Goethe, for example, and to affirm the legitimacy and respectability of what she termed "the gentle Affirmative School" of criticism.[670] What she had to say regarding first principles in criticism is significant. The Germans (Schlegel and Tieck) persuaded her to join the positive, constructive school which engages to "appreciate the good qualities." Yet, in "a time and place so degraded by venal indiscriminate praise as the present," she recognized also "the uses of severe criticism and of just censure" and was determined to "tell the whole truth, as well as nothing but the truth," so long (she added) as the "sternness be in the spirit of Love."[671] She called upon Goethe as her authority in applying the laws of historical development, and upon the German romantics to justify her faith in the ideal principle as the ultimate goal in literature.[672] Thus she sought to reconcile the ideal with the real—the appreciative with the historical, or the romantic vision with the historical present —both to be united in a millenial "golden age" when man will enjoy "the largest appreciation with every sign of life."[673] The ideal principle is consonant with traditional Puritan otherworldliness, the other with the naturalistic and organic school, and at the same time, with the historical school of Goethe and Schlegel. Her criticism of Goethe himself affords the best index of the remarkable success she achieved, by her fine insight and intuitive powers, in uniting all three. Not the least of her services in her time and place was her adoption of a broadly historical and cosmopolitan point of view, which helped to lead American literary consciousness out of its parochialism. From her serene eminence she surveyed the whole of American and British literature in its proper relation as but a small area in the totality of Western, not to speak of global, culture. Round her gathered the lesser writers of the Newness as well as the young artists, like Cranch, Dwight, and Brooks, whol earned from her the function of every art in the service of the ultimate, the Spirit.

While Emerson is not as much the critic as Margaret Fuller, his central and representative position among the Transcendentalists, together with his considerable amount of critical writing (including of course the essay on Shakespeare in *Representative Men*), justifies consideration of him in this connection. His attention to the German critical temper was aroused when he saw, as an undergraduate at Harvard, Everett and his associates, just returned from Göttingen, promoting the type of historical scholarship and criticism that the German universities fostered. Although he was never overfond of German historical research, he hoped to go to Germany to complete his education, but had to content himself, as far as the new criticism was concerned, with the new-found treasures of Coleridge and Carlyle. Following the advice of William who wrote in 1824 from Germany urging his younger brother to "read all the Herder you can get,"[674] he availed himself of the 1800 London translation by T. Churchill of Herder's *Outlines of a Philosophy of the History of Man*. Interested as he already was in science and in finding the key to a unified reading of the universe, the principle of organic development in history as presented by Herder in that book made a profound impression on him. Like Schlegel and Coleridge, Emerson began to distinguish between the organic and the mechanic. By the time he became associated with Margaret Fuller on the *Dial*, he was ready to assimilate the doctrine of the organic in art.[675] In July, 1841, he was recommending to a friend that, besides Wotton, Malone, Dr. Johnson, and Lamb, Schlegel's *Lectures on Dramatic Literature*, Goethe's critique of *Hamlet* in *Meister*, and his "Shakespeare and No End" were all "well worth reading."[676] As he studied the Germans on Shakespeare, he got much of the general critical views of Schlegel and Lessing, some of it direct, more of it through Coleridge.

The organic theory in art was readily, almost necessarily, brought to bear on the idealism with which he began and by which he sought, as he expressed it in *Nature*, to effect the marriage of mind and matter. Its formulation[677] came precisely, and significantly, at the moment when Emerson was concerned in "The Over-Soul" with the attempt to demonstrate that "the Universe is the externalization of the soul" and (shortly afterwards, in "The Poet") with the poet's need for expression: "The man is only half himself, the other half is his expression."[678] The expression being organic and deriving from "the nature of things," it must be one with Truth, Beauty, and Goodness. It cannot be otherwise, for "poetry was all written before time was."[679] Thus the unity and parity of the Emersonian Trinity of Truth, Beauty, and Goodness harmonizes with his conception of the innate need for expression;[680] the poet's symbols become legitimate forms of the ideal beauty, truth, and goodness, showing unity in variety. It is doubtful whether the Aristotelian concept of organic unity, as invested with new life by A. W. Schlegel, was equally portentous for any other American poet.[681] It rounded out and unified Emerson's philosophy of the function of art.

Emerson practiced various modes of criticism: He believed in judging books by absolute standards, but he often wrote sympathetically and romantically in the Schlegel-Coleridge-Lamb tradition. He voiced the reservations of the moral idealist, but admitted that Goethe and Coleridge "are the only critics who have expressed our convictions with adequate fidelity."[682] He also foreshadowed Whitman's realistic approach to Shakespeare and viewed him in relation to his age as dependent on his past, on tradition, and on books.[683]

Jones Very's view of literature and his interpretation of Shakespeare is so highly individual, based upon a mystical and religious concept of art, that it represents a kind of climax to the transcendental criticism in America. The German influence came to him indirectly through the agency of Coleridge. He found Shakespeare's greatness manifested in an *unconscious* revelation of the Divine, but considered his failure to express a *conscious* moral in the plays a serious limitation.[684] The type came to a period with him.

The Historical-Realist School

Upon the heels of the romantics and the Transcendentalists there followed Richard Grant White (1821–1885), who marks the advent of the historical-realistic criticism of Shakespeare. White took it to be his duty as editor to restore, as far as possible, the conditions of the past and to put the reader "in the same position for the apprehension of his author's meaning that he would have occupied if he had been a contemporary with him."[685] Though an early enthusiast for Coleridge and the German "sympathy" school, he later deplored the Coleridgean "hysterical ecstasy about Shakespeare," the "inflated nonsense" and the "pompous platitudes" of the philosophical critics.[686] He attacked the Schlegel-Coleridge school for failing to point out that Shakespeare depended upon his sources for the course of action in his dramas and for the motives of his characters.[687] He found the chief absurdity their attempt to discover how Shakespeare systematically set "forth a philosophy of life," a moral and "central informing thought in his dramas."[688] While he was never as far from the school of Schlegel and Coleridge as he thought himself to be, White's hard-headed common sense, thorough historical scholarship and persistent opposition to current "eulogistic gush" helped check the growth of the "philosophical" and prepared the way for the historical approach.

Walt Whitman ably seconded White's aim in insisting upon realistic interpretation. Attracted to Shakespeare all his life, often indebted to him, and oftener still concerned with assigning a place to him, Whitman charged Shakespeare with doing "everything possible . . . to make the common people common—very common indeed."[689] The poet of democracy and science, of the people and the future, Whitman isolated and rejected what he called the anachronistic features of Shakespeare's writings—his "feudalism."[690] Yet always seeking "lessons" for American democracy, he endeavored to absorb Shakespeare into the heart of American thought by Americanizing the ideas that the poet voiced. Even in the 1855 Preface he said, "America does not repel the past," and as he grew older, he came to feel more keenly that Shakespeare was one of the figures needed for the realization of the great New World democracy.[691]

Considering Whitman's view of the relations among past, present, and future, it was inevitable that he should be struck by Hegel's evolutionary philosophy of history, and that he should interpret Shakespeare in terms of it. Whitman's Hegelian reading of the universe is "clearly behind his steady efforts to discover Shakespeare's real 'lesson' for America. . . . The Past is a legitimate and necessary stepping stone to the Present; . . . hence, in their very opposition to Democracy, Shake-

speare's plays serve America."[692] Thus he could assign, in a roundabout way, a value to Shakespeare, even while he was dissatisfied with the episodes of Jack Cade and Joan of Arc, his history plays, and his style.[693] In this protest Whitman, along with Richard Grant White, marked a break in the romantic interpretation of Shakespeare in America. The social consciousness which made him cry out against the "lordly port" of Shakespeare and made him critical of the undemocratic, unrealistic "purpose" elegance of Shakespeare's style prepared the ground for later social, humanitarian, and realistic critics.

Over and above Whitman's Shakespeare criticism, but equally as important for his literary creed as the Hegelian concept of history, was an idea which he took over early from Herder (through Goethe). This was the theory "that really great poetry is always (like the Homeric and Biblical canticles) the result of a national spirit,"[694] and the corollary that a national spirit is the result of a really great poetry: "Immortal Judah lives, and Greece immortal lives, in a couple of poems."[695] Brooding upon this idea from the time of his apprenticeship to his last days in Camden, Whitman developed his thesis of a national new-world democratic literature, which earned for him the self-chosen title of "poet of democracy."

Whitman wished to be regarded not only as the poet of democracy but also as the poet of science. In respect to the latter, he held the scientific conception of nature as a reality independent of the Hegelian cosmic reason but determined by the processes of historical evolution.[696] Here again he is indebted to Herder, whose view of nature as beautiful and beneficent is more in accord with his thinking than the post-Darwinian conception. Familiar with the significance of Herder, in whom the dominant interests and assumptions of nineteenth-century science were already vital, and finding Herder's ideas consonant with those of Hegel and not contrary to later scientism,

Whitman found the scientific thought of Herder as applied to the philosophy of man, to nationality, to art, and to literature useful for his theorizing on science and democracy.[697]

To resume the discussion of Shakespearean criticism in America as affected by the Germans, we turn to George Wilkes (1817–1885), whom Whitman grudgingly acknowledged his successor in treating Shakespeare as the embodiment of "the spirit and letter of the feudal world."[698] Wilkes was a left-wing humanitarian and nationalist who presented what he called *Shakespeare from an American Point of View* (1876). He studied and collated the important commentaries from Dr. Johnson through Dowden, including the Germans Gervinus, Elze, Horn, Ulrici, Rötscher, Hebler, and Kreysig. His purpose was to "ascertain the character of Shakespeare's social and political sympathies from an American point of view,"[699] and to refute the advocates of the Baconian theory of authorship. Wilkes condemned what he considered Shakespeare's servility to the ruling classes and to the Church, his contempt for the working classes, his alleged hostility to the "march of democracy and liberal ideas."[700]

With the rise of the realistic and of the historical criticism in the universities, the Schlegel-Coleridge inspired Shakespearean school ceased to be a potent force in America. It had conferred the benefit of making nativism less blatant, inherited Puritanic moralism less rigorous, and critical procedures more philosophical, less opinionated, less provincial. Without the leavening, transmuting, and liberalizing effects of German romantic criticism, it would be hard to account for the relative critical maturity of the twentieth century.

WHILE German influences were hastening the ripening of an American criticism, scholars and students were becoming aware of German methods of literary-historical research. The so-called philosophical technique of historical investigation and interpretation, of textual criticism, and of scientific literary research as practiced in the German universities had won the attention and admiration of intellectual Americans. Soon after Madame de Staël and Carlyle described the method, Follen and Lieber exemplified it in our schools. Then followed the first generation of Americans who studied at Göttingen. Objective use of sources in furthering independent thought and research, systematic training in the use of libraries and laboratories, and meticulous documentation in the service of *Wissenschaft*, these features of the German methodology gradually won acceptance and overcame the commonly held view that German scholarship must be synonymous with pedantry. The importation of German professors and the education of more and more Americans in the German universities accentuated the trend. By the third quarter of the century the Germanization of the American university was well under way.[701] The Johns Hopkins University and the University of Chicago were no accidental creations; the ground had been preparing for fully half a century.

The new methods of study and of writing affected and partially engendered a new generation of scholar-critics in America. The influence is first detected in the new type of review-article that began to appear in the *North American Review* about 1820. Among the earliest is Edward Everett's fifty-five–page review of Goethe's *Dichting und Wahrheit*, written while Everett was still a student at Göttingen and published in January, 1817. This was followed by many essays on literary, historical, philosophical, religious, and generally cultural subjects, by Ticknor, Bancroft, Cogswell, and others, and by such German-American savants as Beck, Follen, and Lieber. They exhibited a new approach, in their point of view, their manner of applying philosophy to humanistic study, their regard for historical perspective, their careful examination and reliance upon primary sources, their methodical documentation, and their insistence upon the freedom of inquiry and the deduction of conclusions based on the evidence without regard to presupposition or tradition. Many who engaged in the new type of critical writing were academicians, among them Follen, Beck, Lieber, Stuart, Marsh, Francis, Hedge, Ticknor, Everett, Cogswell. Bancroft, and, later, Longfellow and Lowell. Their influence was exerted through the periodicals, in the classroom and lecture hall, and in books as various as Longfellow's early textbooks for language study and his *Hyperion* or Lowell's vast miscellany of critical essays.

Often this influence in scholarly method was related, as in the case of Lowell, to the historical type of criticism identified with Goethe and Schlegel, though others, of course, were also cognizant of the work of Sainte-Beuve, Taine, and other historical critics. Often, as in the case of Longfellow's early reviews or Margaret Fuller's criticism, it was connected with the romantic type of "affirmative" criticism. Again, as in the instance of the American Shakespeare critics, the method of German scholarship was identified with the "philosophical" type. However construed and employed, it prepared the way for the development of the literary scholarship currently in use. Our textual criticism, linguistic research, literary history, and our philosophically critical interpretation—all the academic disciplines most widely employed today bear the mark "Made in Germany."

Journalists and Editors

Editors and journalists were affected also. Everyone who had charge of a literary magazine or a periodical with a literary department had to take note of German literature. Some, like Joseph Dennie, set themselves to halt the advance of "Germanism" in the United States; but even

notable isolationists and nativists like Charles Fenno Hoffman took cognizance of it. Horace Greeley (1811–1872), during his long editorship, saw a considerable body of German literature pass across his desk. Thomas Holley Chivers (1809–1858), a contemporary of Poe and Margaret Fuller, moved in the literary circles where Germanism was the rage and was himself affected by all the prevailing forms of romanticism, though little of it came to him directly from German sources. Rufus Wilmot Griswold (1815–1857) occupied a like position, while as late a figure as Frank Stockton (1834–1902), though he cared little about trends in contemporary letters and less about the literary aims of his fellow-members of the Authors Club, was not untouched by German literature.

Recent Trends

While the inspiration of later critics like Howells and James came principally from English and French sources, they were conversant with German masterpieces and not unmindful of German critical theory. The same may be said of the versatile Henry Adams. William C. Brownell, G. E. Woodberry, S. P. Sherman, Paul Elmer More, and Irving Babbitt lived and wrote during a time when familiarity with German letters and criticism was part of the indispensable equipment of the critic. A journalist and editor of the type of Henry L. Mencken, himself of German parentage, came to be as much at home in German letters as in the literature of his own land. His essays form a *Schimpflexikon* that bristles with German terms and allusions, while his autobiographical books breathe the atmosphere of the Baltimore Germanland whence he stemmed and to which he retired in his later years. And critics of our own day who speak to a more than parochial audience from a more than journalistic point of view have made German (along with classical, French, and British) letters and literary criteria an integral part of their aesthetic possessions and prepossessions.

But the twentieth century is witnessing a remarkable shift of emphasis in German-American cultural interrelations. Germany, long preponderingly the exporter of books, is now (following her defeat in two world wars) the debtor nation. Since 1945 she has imported more books from abroad than she exported, and the proportion of German translations of foreign books to native productions has steadily increased. What is especially striking is that the once predominant interest on the part of Germans in England and English literary productions is (if bibliographical statistics provide a reliable index) rapidly shifting Americaward. Symptomatic as this tendency is of the increasingly influential role that America is playing in world affairs, it suggests that, while European influences in the United States are still potent, the reciprocal relationship is no less significant, and is daily growing stronger.

NOTES

Notes

INTRODUCTION

1. Chief among the attempted general treatments of the subject are Franz Löher's *Geschichte und Zustände der Deutschen in Amerika* (Cincinnati & Leipzig, 1847), Gustav Körner's *Das deutsche Element in den Vereinigten Staaten von Nordamerika, 1818–1848* (Cincinnati, 1880), Anton Eickhoff's *In der neuen Heimat* (N.Y., 1884), Herman J. Ruetenik's *Berühmte deutsche Vorkämpfer für Fortschritt und Friede in Nord-Amerika, 1628–1888* (Cleveland, 1888), Karl Knortz's *Das Deutschtum der Vereinigten Staaten* (Hamburg, 1898), Julius Goebel's *Das Deutschtum in den Vereinigten Staaten von Amerika* (Munich, 1904), Georg v. Bosse's *Das deutsche Element in den Vereinigten Staaten* (Stuttgart, 1908), *Drei Jahrhunderte deutschen Lebens in Amerika* (Berlin, 1909), and *German Achievements in America* (N.Y., 1916), Albert B. Faust's *The German Element in the United States, with Special Reference to its Political, Moral, Social, and Educational Influence* (2 vols., N.Y., 1909; rev. and enl. ed., N.Y., 1927; 1st ed. also in German, 2 vols., Leipzig, 1912), Oswald Lohan's *Das Deutschtum in den Vereinigten Staaten von Amerika* (Berlin, 1913), Frederick F. Schrader's *The Germans in the Making of America* (Boston, 1924), Colin Ross's *Unser Amerika. Der deutsche Anteil an den Vereinigten Staaten* (Leipzig, 1936), and Rachel David-DuBois and Emma Schweppe's *The Germans in American Life* (N.Y., 1936). *Das Buch der Deutschen in Amerika* (Phila., 1909), edited by Max Heinrici for the German-American National Alliance on the occasion of the 225th anniversary of the first German settlement in America, though in the nature of a jubilee publication, deserves inclusion in this list because it rises above the level common among books of its kind. One of the most satisfactory of recent books attempting to evaluate all the major immigrant contributions from the historian's point of view is Professor Carl Wittke's *We Who Built America: The Saga of the Immigrant* (N.Y., 1940).

2. See Charles A. Beard and Alfred Vagts, "Currents of Thought in Historiography," *Amer. Hist. Rev.*, XLII, iii (Apr., 1937), 465.

3. Preface, pp. vi–vii.

4. For other statistical data and comparative figures on immigration, see Faust, *op. cit.* (1927 ed.), I, 285; II, 13, 24, 27; and the U.S. Dept. of Labor, *Annual Report of the Commissioner-General of Immigration* (Washington, D.C., 1929), Table 83, pp. 186–87; see also pp. 182–83.

5. *Wis. Mag. of Hist.*, XIX, i (Sept., 1935), 101–2.

6. Inspired by the theory and example of historians like Turner and Paxson, American literary historians and critics called for a new deal. Professor Fred Lewis Pattee led the way in June, 1924, with his "call for a Literary Historian" in the *American Mercury*. Six months later Professor Norman Foerster proposed to the small nucleus of professors who then comprised the American Literature Group of the Modern Language Association of America the necessity for adopting a new point of view and distinctively literary criteria upon which to proceed in the reinterpretation of American literature. His proposals were published in the *Saturday Review of Literature*, April 3, 1926 (pp. 677–79), and reprinted the same year as a twelve-page pamphlet by the Houghton Mifflin Company, under the title, *New Viewpoints in American Literature*. The essay was reprinted in a volume entitled *The Reinterpretation of American Literature*, edited by Norman Foerster (N.Y., 1928), pp. 23–28, together with eight other essays by as many contributors, explaining and illustrating in some detail the plan proposed. In 1927 Professor Howard Mumford Jones published his *America and French Culture, 1750–1848* (Chapel Hill, 1927), the first significant example of what such a method of literary history could effect when applied to French cultural influence in America, although the methods and criteria employed by him differ markedly in some respects from the scheme proposed by Mr. Foerster. Since then other schemes of evaluation have been proposed

one of the most provocative of which is that outlined by Professor Oscar Cargill in his book *Intellectual America* (N.Y., 1941). His approach he calls the "Ideodynamic," in which Ideas are viewed as "on the March" and "in Conflict."

7. In the field of literary influence, for example, major bibliographical contributions include Bayard Q. Morgan's *Bibliography of German Literature in English Translation* (Madison, Wis., 1922; 2nd ed., Stanford, Calif., 1938); Edward Ziegler's *Translations of German Poetry in American Magazines, 1741–1810* (Phila., 1905); Frederick H. Wilkins' *Early Influence of German Literature in America 1762–1825* (N.Y., 1900); Scott H. Goodnight's *German Literature in American Magazines Prior to 1846* (Madison, Wis., 1907); Martin H. Haertel's *German Literature in American Magazines 1846–1880* (Madison, Wis., 1908); Lillie V. Hathaway's *German Literature of the Mid-Nineteenth Century in England and America as Reflected in the Journals, 1840–1914* (Boston, 1935); the joint work of W. M. Roloff, M. E. Mix, and Martha Nicolai, edited by B. Q. Morgan and A. R. Hohlfeld, *German Literature in British Magazines, 1750–1860* (Madison, Wis., 1949); and Oswald Seidensticker's *First Century of German Printing in America, 1728–1830* (Phila., 1893). This list can readily be supplemented by several hundreds of bibliographies on more restricted subjects.

8. Consider the significance of 7,858 items on a subject as severely limited as this bibliography is by its title. Dr. Meynen's work is especially thorough on the score of immigration and settlement and on the side of genealogy and local history (notably church, community, and county history), on arts and crafts, and on Pennsylvania-Dutch customs and folkways. He made no effort to cover German imprints published in America, or in Pennsylvania, or to prepare a check list of German newspapers and periodical literature, or even to indicate the extent of Pennsylvania-German dialect writings. In these several departments he contented himself with referring simply to such works as Seidensticker's compilation, Harold Bender's *Bibliography of Mennonitica Americana, 1727–1928* (Goshen, Ind., 1929), Daniel Miller's several studies of early German-American newspapers, John H. Flory's *Literary Activity of the German Baptist Brethren in the Eighteenth Century* (Harrisburg, 1900), Ammon M. Aurand's *A Pennsylvania German Library* (Harrisburg, 1930), and Harry H. Reichard's *Pennsylvania-German Dialect Writings and Their Writers* (Lancaster, 1918).

9. An excellent example of nice adjustment between this and the reciprocal point of view is explicit in Professor Morgan's bibliography of German literature in English translation. The book was designed to serve investigators who adopt either point of view, and it is being put to excellent use by students of English and American literature to study the modifying effect of German literature upon their literary culture no less than by Germans who, following the leads presented, may thus study German literature through the refracting judgment of American readers and the distorting medium of the English language. Factual and objective, Morgan's book is without thesis; it is concerned neither more nor less with the German than with the English and American aspects of the subject; it looks impartially both ways.

10. "The Influence of European Ideas in Nineteenth-Century America," *Amer. Lit.*, VII, ii (Nov., 1935), 244.

11. Similar difficulties beset the endeavors of the American student when he undertakes to trace the vogue and influence in Germany of American authors, let us say, of James Fenimore Cooper. Such studies are often strong on factual information regarding translations, editions, and sales statistics, but lacking on the interpretative side. They tell us little about the reasons why Cooper was read in Germany at a time when Hawthorne was not; nor do they dwell upon the effect which Cooper's stories of the new land exercised upon the *Europa-müden* of the nineteenth century. All too often students of comparative cultural relations have at their command a thorough understanding of the radiating culture and a correspondingly poor knowledge (not to say appreciation) of the receiving culture. It is this one-sidedness, this inability to see larger connections, and the consequent failure to add significant interpretations, that makes the books and monographs of many German students who attempt to deal with German-American relations so arid. They possess a profound knowledge of Kant and Fichte and Schelling, of German theology, or of German literature; but their ignorance of Emerson and Parker, of Concord and Boston, of American Unitarians and New England Transcendentalism is equally marked.

12. This criticism does not, of course, apply to many individual writers on the subject nor to all agencies and organizations set up to promote a better feeling between Germany and the United States. The Carl Schurz Memorial Foundation and, among the German-American historical associations, the Pennsylvania-German Society and the German-American Historical Society of Illinois can be cited as typical of those who have sought to keep partisanship out of their programs and their publications.

13. For example, the studies of Morgan, Wilkens, Davis, Goodnight, and Haertel of the vogue of German literature in America, together with the Hathaway and Morgan-Hohlfeld studies of German literature in British magazines, cover the ground with sufficient precision and completeness so that further efforts in the same direction cannot be undertaken with any assurance that the results will be commensurate with the labor required. Similarly, existing studies of the "German element" in communities, cities, and counties, histories of Gesang- and Turn-Vereine and other local German clubs, local church histories, and technographical surveys of Germans in countless localities already clutter up our book shelves and our bibliographies. However valuable their indefinite multiplication may be for investigators in other areas, the literary historian will lose little if he resigns these matters to the U.S. Census Bureau and to the historical and genealogical societies, local and national. There are dozens of other fields, thus far virtually uncultivated, that promise far greater and more rewarding yields.

14. This chaotic state of affairs is not peculiar to the department of German-American studies; it is even worse in French-American and Anglo-American areas. Indeed, until recently, the study of American literary culture itself was in a very poor state of organization, and it cannot be claimed that the ambitious bibliographical undertakings of the Federal Records Historical Survey, the Works Progress Administration, and the numerous historical studies carried on under federal and state auspices made much signal progress. Perhaps the most marked advance was made by the co-operative project, conducted under the supervision of Dr. Edward H. O'Niell, to compile a comprehensive Bibliography of American Literature. When this work stopped, it embraced complete bibliographies of 602 American authors, represented by a catalog of some 750,000 bibliographical cards (now deposited at the University of Pennsylvania). This bibliography is supplemented by a similar one begun earlier at New York University under the direction of Professor Oscar Cargill.

15. Complementary to this broad subject is the study of the several German church periodicals, of the type recently completed by Professor Victor Gimmestad, of Normal, Illinois—a history of the *Lutheran Quarterly Review*.

16. On the basis of the experience gained in compiling the *Bibliography*, the conclusion is unavoidable that the historians of American philosophy have been as lax about making such fundamental inquires as have the historians of American education. Except for certain trite observations whenever the names of German educational pioneers like Pestalozzi are mentioned, or the influence of the German university system upon Johns Hopkins is related, or the introduction of German at Virginia and Harvard as a subject of instruction is rehearsed, such histories of American education as we have offer little. An examination of thousands of pages of educational history does not produce convincing evidence that any appreciable advance has been made in this area in the half-century that has passed since the publication of B. A. Hinsdale's "Notes on the History of Foreign Influences upon Education in the United States," *Report of the Commissioner of Education for the Year 1897–1898* (Washington, 1889). I, 591–629, and George S. Viereck's "German Instruction in American Schools," *Report of the Commissioner of Education for 1900–1901* (Washington, 1902), I, 531–708, except for the publication in 1913 of Charles H. Handschin's *Teaching of Modern Languages in the United States* (U.S. Bureau of Education Bulletin, 1913, No. 3, Whole No. 510, Washington, 1913). Numerous documents repeat what Viereck, Hinsdale, and Handschin reported, and a few bring addenda for succeeding years; but none of them is basic in the manner of these earlier studies, and none is interpretative in a measure to make it of much value for the historian of American civilization.

17. There are basic studies of Pennsylvania-German authors and of their writings, several anthologies of Pennsylvania-German literature, and a few studies of German-American literary activity in other states or localities (such as the Metzenthin study for Texas); but Professor Faust's eighteen-page contribution to the *Cambridge History of American Literature*, published in 1921, remains the chief source of information on German-American literature in the German medium. My own brief treatment of the subject in "The Mingling of Tongues," *Literary History of the United States* (3 vols., N.Y., 1948), II, 676–93, III, 284–303, is nothing more than a sketchy summation.

18. See the interesting suggestions set forth in F. O. Matthiessen, *American Renaissance. Art and Expression in the Age of Emerson and Whitman* (London & N.Y., 1941). Professor Carl Bode (University of Maryland) is currently studying the American lyceum as a factor in the literary consciousness of the last century.

EARLY INTEREST IN GERMAN CULTURE

THE SEVENTEENTH CENTURY

1. See esp. Harold S. Jantz, "German Thought and Literature in New England, 1620–1820: A Preliminary Report," *JEGP*, XLI (Jan., 1942), 1–45.

2. This concern was not always with strictly philosophical or literary matters: it included commercial, ethnographical, scientific, geographical, theological, and many other human interests, fostered partly by the presence in America of sizable contingents of German immigrants and by the immigration companies and other agencies on both sides of the ocean, but also by more strictly "American" interests that may be called, for want of a better term, intellectual. The reciprocal relationship—German interest in America—has long been known to have been both early and extensive. See Paul Baginsky, *German Works Relating to America, 1493–1800* (N.Y., 1942). See further the *Bibliography of German Culture in America, to 1940*, by Pochmann and Schutz (Madison, Wis., 1953), hereafter cited as *Bibliography*.

3. See, for example, A. B. Faust, *The German Element in the United States* . . . (2 vols., N.Y., 1909; rev. ed., 2 vols, in 1, N.Y., 1927); Scott H. Goodnight, *German Literature in American Magazines prior to 1848* (Madison, Wis., 1907), pp. 12–15; Emma G. Jaeck, *Madame de Staël and the Spread of German Literature* (N.Y. & London, 1915), pp. 21–25, 251–99; Harold C. Goddard, *Studies in New England Transcendentalism* (N.Y., 1908), pp. 202–3; O. W. Long, *Literary Pioneers: Early American Explorers of European Culture* (Cambridge, Mass., 1935).

4. For Kuno Francke's several studies of this correspondence, consult the *Bibliography*. New England especially is represented as having been dedicated to a rigid theological, political, and social exclusiveness, tightly self-contained except for such contacts as she maintained with Puritan England. Unleavened by such Continental influences as New York, Pennsylvania, Georgia, and others of the Atlantic colonies felt, seventeenth-century New England is presumed to have been immune to intellectual infiltrations from Germany. Even for eighteenth-century New England, little attention has been given to Germanic influences beyond the exploratory study by John P. Hoskins (*Princeton Theol. Rev.*, V, i [Jan., 1907], 49–79; ii [Apr., 1907], 211–41), with reference especially to the impact of German pietism on American religious and social life, notably through the agency of the Moravians, the Wesleys, and Whitefield, in a manner that was not without its effects on

Jonathan Edwards and those large segments of the colonial populace that were affected by the Great Awakening. Then there follows a long barren stretch until we come upon John Quincy Adams, at the turn of the century, studying German during his ministership in Berlin and translating Wieland's *Oberon*, a document that remained more mythical than real until Professor A. B. Faust discovered the long-lost manuscript and edited it in 1940.

5. Virtually every account that deals with the introduction of German culture into America repeats the story of how Ticknor, spurred on by Charles Villers' *Coup-d'oeil sur les universités et le mode d'instruction publique de l'Allemagne protestante* (Kassel, 1808) and Madame de Staël's book, resolved to learn German preparatory to going to Germany, but found himself reduced to seeking instruction from a Dr. Brosius, an Alsatian teacher of mathematics in Jamaica Plain, until his friend Alex. Everett lent him a German grammar in French, and he had time to send for a German dictionary which he knew to be in New Hampshire. See *Life, Letters, and Journals of George Ticknor*, ed. by George. S. Hillard (2 vols., Boston & N.Y., 1877), I, 11–12.

6. What is left entirely unexplained is why these young men did not avail themselves of the several thousand volumes of German books on the Harvard library shelves. For details and some noteworthy discrepancies in these early accounts, see A. P. Peabody, *Harvard Reminiscences* (Boston, 1888), pp. 117–18; Mrs. Eliza Lee Cabot Follen, *Life of Charles Follen* (Boston, 1844), p. 105; and O. W. Long, *op. cit.*, p. 233, n. 116.

7. *PMLA*, V (1890), 5.

8. *Christian Rev.*, VI, xxiii (Sept., 1841), 454, 456. It may be observed that Moses Stuart knew better, for he was acquainted with William Bentley's circle, he repeatedly called on Bentley, and often borrowed German books from him.

For Bentley's position as a medium of German-American intellectual interchanges see Jantz, *loc. cit.*, pp. 31–45. Dr. Jantz's ingenious detective work at Worcester, in other New England depositories, and in special collections elsewhere, led to findings which he graciously placed at my disposal—many of them while they were still in manuscript form. While his systematic investigations, together with my own more modest and miscellaneous discoveries, are sufficient to modify our earlier view of New England insularity, Dr. Jantz's work is far from complete; hence there is every likelihood that the story as told in the pages immediately following will be much amended as his research progresses.

9. Buckminster was commissioned to inform Ticknor of his election on June 12, 1810. Following a protracted illness, Buckminster died in Ticknor's arms, in 1812. See *Journal of the Proceedings of the Anthology Society*, ed. by M. A. DeWolfe Howe (Boston, 1910), p. 231.

10. Convers Francis and Frederick Henry Hedge are others who claimed similar priority for their knowledge of German language and literature.

11. Charles H. Herford's *Studies in the Literary Relations of England and Germany in the Sixteenth Century* (Cambridge, 1886) and Gilbert Waterhouse's *Literary Relations of England and Germany in the Seventeenth Century* (N.Y., 1914) are suggestive of areas still unexplored. For Anglo-German literary relations of the eighteenth and nineteenth centuries the several bibliographical studies of Lawrence M. Price, Mary Bell Price, and Bayard Q. Morgan are most helpful. For other studies, and especially for significant investigations now in progress, consult the *Bibliography* (Index).

12. See Wilhelm Begemann, *Die Fruchtbringende Gesellschaft und Johan Valentin Andreae* (Berlin, 1911), and Felix E. Held, *Johann Valentin Andreae's Christianapolis: an Ideal State of the Seventeenth Century* (N.Y., 1916), esp. Ch. V.

13. Consult Mrs. Frances Rose-Troup's *John White . . .* (N.Y., 1930), pp. 43–47 *et seq.*, her *Massachusetts Bay Company and its Predecessors* (N.Y., 1930), and *Roger Conant and the Early Settlements of the North Shore of Massachusetts* (Roger Conant Family Assn., 1926); and Samuel E. Morison, *Builders of the Bay Colony* (Boston & N.Y., 1930), pp. 21–50.

14. See A. W. M'Clure, *The Life of John Cotton* (Boston, 1846), pp. 267–68, and Cotton Mather, *Magnalia Christi Americana* (2 vols., Hartford, 1855), I, 279.

15. See the book lists in Thomas G. Wright, *Literary Culture in New England, 1620–1730* (N.Y., 1920). Wright notes only four copies of Calvin's *Institutes* as against five copies of the writings of Pareus. See also Morison *op. cit.*, pp. 10, 57, 128, and his *Puritan Pronaos* (N.Y., 1936), p. 136.

16. After extensive investigations, Professor Jantz concludes that John Cotton's statement that he loved "to sweeten . . . [his] mouth with a piece of Calvin" as a kind of bedtime dessert (Mather, *Magnalia*, I, 274) stands as one of the *few* expressions by seventeenth-century Americans of a special preference for Calvin. They read Calvin, but not as exclusively (or even mainly) as we infer from the standard works on the subject. New England Puritans were not content with Calvin's *Institutes* alone or, for that matter, with the Bible alone. They searched all the available and reputable literature that held any promise of leading to the conclusions which they sought. They quoted Calvin less frequently than English theologians like Ames, Perkins, and Whitaker; when they went for authority to continental theologians, they consulted not merely Calvin but Luther and Pareus no less than others (Morison, *Builders of the Bay Colony*, pp. 57, 128).

17. Professor Morison remarks that although seventeenth-century New England theology was of the Calvinist family, it was not Calvinism; and there is a good deal of justice in his calling Jonathan Edwards "the first New England Calvinist" (*Puritan Pronaos*, p. 155), although Edwards himself might have denied such an allegation. It is to be observed that even in Edwards' day, by which time the so-called "hardening process" of Calvinism had set in, a man like John Barnard, though definitely identified with the conservative Mathers before 1710, in his autobiography (written during his eighty-fifth year) declared flatly that he read "all sorts of authors," but that he "never to this day read Calvin's works, and cannot call him master."—*Coll. Mass. Hist. Soc.*, 3rd ser., V (1836), 186.

18. See Luther's statement: "We are all Priests, as many of us as are Christians."—*Works of Martin Luther* (ed. by Henry E. Jacobs, 2 vols., Phila., 1915), II, 279; see further, *ibid.*, II, 68, 282, and compare V. L. Parrington, *The Colonial Mind* (N.Y., 1927), p. 9; Kuno Francke, *Social Forces in German Literature* (3rd ed., N.Y., 1899), pp. 150, 155, 156; M. S. Bates, *Religious Liberty: An Inquiry* (N.Y. & London, 1945), p. 419, as well as Luther's *Tischreden oder Colloquia* (hrsg. von Karl E. Förstermann, 4 Bde. in 2, Leipzig, 1846), IV, 156–75, 176–237, 456–72.

19. For a comparison of Luther and Calvin, consult James MacKinnon, *Luther and the Reformation* (London, 1925), and his *Calvin and the Reformation* (London, 1936); G. P. Gooch, and H. J. Laski, *English Democratic Ideas in the Seventeenth Century* (Cambridge, 1927), esp. p. 8; John N. Figgis, *Studies of Political Thought from Gerson to Grotius, 1414–1625* (Cambridge, 1916), p. 86. For Calvin's borrowings from Luther, see Preserved Smith, *The Age of the Reformation* (N.Y., 1920), pp. 163–64.

20. "Luther, it is true, taught that the State had the duty of protecting the true religion, but it was a negative duty. In Lutheranism the duty of the Church was to establish the Kingdom of God on earth; in Calvinism that was the

duty of the Church and State working intimately together."—William W. Sweet, *Religion in Colonial America* (N.Y., 1942), pp. 13–14. See also Gooch and Laski, *op. cit.*, pp. 2–3; Robert H. Murray, *The Political Consequences of the Reformation* (Boston, 1926), pp. 75, 90; R. H. Tawney, *Religion and the Rise of Capitalism* (N.Y., 1926), p. 88; and L. H. Waring, *The Political Theories of Martin Luther* (N.Y., 1910).

However, as far as early New England Puritans' dependence upon continental political theory goes, it appears that neither Luther nor Calvin was as decisive as Johannes Althusius, or Althaus (1557–1638). His Calvinistic view of the state as expressed in his *Politica methodica digesta* (1603) found its way to almost every seventeenth-century Puritan who interested himself in political theory and practice. His book achieved many editions and reprintings, for details regarding which see the introduction by Carl J. Friedrich in the modern edition of the book, reprinted from the third edition of 1614, Cambridge, Mass., 1932, as well as O. F. von Goerke, *The Development of Political Theory* (tr. by Bernard Freyd, N.Y., 1939), devoted almost exclusively to Althusius's political theory and its influence.

The great popularity of Althusius among New England colonists is due to several causes: (1) his widespread reputation as professor at Herborn, (2) his application of the Ramistic method to politics, which struck a responsive chord among the Puritans, who had a predilection for the Ramean logic, and (3) the consistency of his political theory with Puritan doctrine.

The copy of Althusius owned by the Mathers, preserved in the library of the American Antiquarian Society, shows annotations by Samuel Mather which particularly accentuate certain of the revolutionary-republican ideas that eventually led to democracy and independence. A thorough examination of the impact of Althusian thought upon colonial polity may well lead to a revision of the conventional view which finds the origins of American republican and revolutionary principles exclusively, first, in England, and, later, in France.

21. For American separatists, purifiers, and reformers, bent on liberalizing their church and state, Luther the "protestant" was inevitably more vital than Luther the "reactionary," regardless of what the final effect of his influence in his own country turned out to be. It is beside the point to argue that because Lutheranism in Germany promoted absolutism, Lutheran principles should have had an identical or similar development in America, where an entirely different set of conventions and environmental conditions obtained. Ideas of whatever kind, particularly ideas of reform, are adapted to or modified by existing conditions. In America, given certain contingencies favoring the growth of liberal tendencies in Church and State, certain ones of Luther's principles might achieve a degree or a kind of objectification impossible in older communities; while others of Luther's principles might be disregarded altogether.

22. Sweet, *op. cit.*, pp. 14–15; C. H. Smith, *The Mennonite Immigration to Pennsylvania in the Eighteenth Century* (Norristown, Pa., 1929), p. 37.

23. These eventually made their own distinctive contributions to eighteenth-century American religious, political, and social development. It may be observed at this point that the Lutherans of the recognized Lutheran Church in Germany (except for the Salzburger Lutherans who were persecuted by a Catholic archbishop) found little cause to migrate to America for religious reasons. This circumstance explains in large measure why German Lutherans did not emigrate in great numbers until later, when economic advantage rather than religious persecution made them seek new lands. It explains also why the Dunkers, Schwenkfelders, Inspirationists, and certain groups of German Reformed, as well as the Salzburgers, came early and in relatively large numbers. For a brief treatment of each, see W. W. Sweet, *op. cit.*, pp. 210–14, and for a longer discussion, Faust, *op. cit.*, I, 262, *et seq.* More special studies of individual groups can be located through the indexed *Bibliography*.

24. *Works*, II, 314.

25. *Works*, II, 233.

26. *Works*, II, 312.

27. The last four of these became vital issues in the Antinomian controversy provoked by Anne Hutchinson in 1636.

28. Parrington, *op. cit.*, p. 12. Luther set men free at once from the purely theological concept of moral law and from a purely supernatural moral system. Ethics became the real test of religion. If a man walks uprightly in love and mercy, that is a sign, and the only sign, that he is saved, and that he has a proper faith in God. With such a faith, the Christian's life will naturally and freely flower in moral virtue. To Calvin, such complete freedom seemed dangerous, and led, as American theocrats had bitter occasion to find in persons like Anne Hutchinson and John Wheelwright, to a confusion of imputation, justification, and sanctification, besides making a not-to-be-thought-of assault upon the social, economic, and political struc-

ture of the Puritan theocratic community. Thus while Luther confidently refused to abridge the Christian freedom of individual moral responsibility, Calvin and his followers timidly but fervently searched the letter of the Scriptures for prescriptions of human duties, and converted the free and natural ideal of Lutheranism into Puritan theocracy.

The basis of Luther's faith was his own experience, which he sought to confirm by the Scriptures; Calvin started with the Scriptures and searched them for God's prescriptions. And where Luther entrusted to the State the power of deciding what was in accord with the Gospel and stamping out divergencies, Calvin affirmed the medieval supremacy of the Church. Paradoxically, Luther's refusal to carry his religious democracy into politics ended in promoting political tyranny in his own country, while Calvin's emphasis on the power of God and submission to His will, when put to use in a new country, eventually resulted in strengthening the human power of the individual against all earthly authority. See further, John E. Randall, *The Making of the Modern Mind. A Survey of the Intellectual Background of the Present Age* (N.Y., 1926), pp. 151–53.

29. John Cotton, *A Modest and Cleare Answer to Mr. Balls Discourse on Set Formes of Prayer* (Boston, 1642), Ch. X, p. 44; Perry Miller, *The New England Mind* (N.Y., 1939), p. 468.

John Robinson was of a like mind when he observed that "Religion is not always sown and reaped in one age . . . . John Huss and Jerome of Prague finished their testimony a hundred years before Luther, and Wickliff well nigh as long before them, and yet neither the one nor the other with the like success as Luther."— Alex Young (ed.), *Chronicles of the Pilgrim Fathers of the Colony of Plymouth from 1602 to 1625* (Boston, 1841), p. 423.

"The character of New England Puritanism," concludes Professor Perry Miller, "was determined as much by questions which Luther and Calvin did not solve as by those which they did."—*The New England Mind*, p. 194. Thus John Cotton declared, "We may oppose Calvin's authority with reason. It's not the authority of *Calvin* that concludes for . . . but the reason . . . according to truth, that determines the question."—Quoted, *ibid.*, p. 93.

30. *Ibid.*, pp. 92–93.

31. See the letter written by John Davenport and signed by the New England clergy, as reproduced in Samuel Mather, *An Apology for the Liberties of the Churches in New England . . .* (Boston, 1738), pp. 151–66.

32. Quoted in Mather's *Magnalia*, I, 64; see also *Words of John Robinson's Farewell Address*

to the Pilgrims . . . (Boston, 1903), pp. 351–52; Ed. Winslow, *Hypocrasie Unmasked* . . . (Providence, 1916), p. 97; Alex. Young (ed.), *Chronicles of the Pilgrim Fathers* . . . (Boston, 1841), pp. 296–97; W. W. Fenn, "John Robinson's Farewell Address," *Harvard Theological Rev.*, XIII (1920), 323–39; and J. G. Powicke, *John Robinson* (London, 1920). Robinson's works are available in an edition prepared by Robert Ashton (3 vols., Boston, 1851).

John Cotton, no less than the good Robinson, lamented this disposition of reformed churches to "keep at a stay just where their reformers left them."—*A Modest and Cleare Answer*, Ch. X, pp. 44–47; M'Clure, *op. cit.*, pp. 214–15.

Orthodox Pilgrims were, of course, less Lutheran than Calvinist in their theology. See Williston Walker, *Creeds and Platforms of Congregationalism* (N.Y., 1893), pp. 60, 91; his *History of the Congregational Churches in the U.S.* (N.Y., 1894), p. 101; Morison, *Builders of the Bay Colony*, p. 57; and H. K. Rowe, *A History of Religion in the United States.* (N.Y., 1924), p. 22. They particularly disapproved of Smyth's acceptance of the Mennonite faith, and they reputedly left Amsterdam for fear of becoming involved in the disputes of the other religious communities established there. Yet their espousal of Calvinism seems to have been motivated as much by the hope that by cleaving to Calvin's clearly-stated and close-knit system they might escape the disintegrating forces of dispute, dissent, and schism as by any intrinsic love for the "points" of Calvin. For while they followed Robinson in his espousal of conservative Calvinism, including the doctrines of Election and Predestination, they heard him also, and attended to his counsel, when he warned them against being too rigid in their doctrine, because "The Lord hath *more truth* yet to break forth out of his holy word." See Walker, *History of the Congr. Churches*, pp. 101–2; H. M. Dexter, *Congregationalism* . . . (4th ed., rev., & enl., Boston, 1876), pp. 118–32; and Roland G. Usher, *The Pilgrims and Their History* (N.Y., 1918), p. 33.

Still more important, they championed the right of the individual to investigate the Scriptures, as that right had been proclaimed by Luther, and soon made the important discovery that this type of defense for their own secession from Pope and Archbishop involved permission also to differ from the minister or majority opinion regarding the meaning of Scripture. See Usher, *op. cit.*, pp. 43–44. They deviated also from the rigid path of Calvin's teachings in their form of church government, "employing in addition to Calvinist presbyterian customs, certain congregational characteristics," which appear to have been derived from Browne, Barrowe, Greenwood, Penry, and others (see W. Walker, *History of Congregational Churches*, pp. 118–27). Hence the search for origins of Separatist principles and practices leads not only to Calvin and Luther but also to doctrines and forms called Anabaptist, Brownist, Hussite, Lollard, and Congregationalist—relationships that deserve exhaustive investigation. It would seem, then, that it is as fallacious to assume that all New England Puritans were strict Calvinists as it would be to hold that all non-Calvinist Protestantism among them was inspired by Luther. See further Esther E. Burch, "The Sources of New England Democracy," *Amer. Lit.*, I, ii (May, 1929), 115–30.

33. But see O. C. Goodell's argument in *Hist. Coll. of the Essex Institute*, III (1861), 238–53, esp. 239, that antinomianism in Massachusetts derives mainly from Johannes Tauler. However, the Lutheran Agricola, rather than the Illuminated Doctor of Strasbourg is generally accepted as the founder of antinomianism.

34. For the issues involved, see Winthrop's *Journal* for Oct. 21, Nov. 17, 1636; Jan. 20, Mar. 7, May 17, Aug. 30, Nov. 1, 1637; Mar. 1 and 22, 1638.

The Antinomians were supported in their principles by William Coddington, John Clarke, and Henry Vane, and they also referred their accusers to the earlier teachings of John Cotton himself. Cotton, who had been Mrs. Hutchinson's spiritual adviser, was doubtless more responsible for her "heretical" opinions than he dared or cared to admit. If Mrs. Hutchinson was right in charging her former pastor with her opinions, one wonders whence he derived them, and whether his entertainment at Old Boston of such German refugees as Libingus, Saumer, and Tolner could have led to his defection from strict Puritan doctrine (see Mather's *Magnalia*, I, 279). At all events, Cotton found himself in a very uncomfortable position, and at the height of the controversy he meditated removing to New Haven. Instead, he compromised his views, and submitting to the manifold pressures seething about him, turned upon Mrs. Hutchinson, even to pronouncing sentence of banishment upon her.

35. James E. Ernst, *Roger Williams, New England Firebrand* (N.Y., 1932), pp. 422, 476, and *The Political Thought of Roger Williams* (Seattle, Wash., 1929), p. 19.

Quite probably all or most of the American Puritan divines who were trained at Cambridge read Luther during their university days.

36. Luther, "An Open Letter to the Christian Nobility," *Works*, II, 66, 69, 103, 108.

37. See his *Hireling Ministry None of Christ's*

(London, 1897), pp. 201, 290, 309, and Ernst, *Roger Williams, New England Fireband*, p. 487.

38. That is, he penetrated to the foundations of Christian liberty as implicit in the New Testament and took to heart the revolutionary ideas that underlie its teachings. See L. Fuerbringer, T. Engelder, and P. E. Kretzmann, *The Concordia Cyclopedia* (St. Louis, 1927), p. 424; for Williams' arguments, see *Publ. of the Narragansett Club*, I (1866), 299–300; III (1867), 214, 248, 349, 355, 366, 398; IV (1870), 187, 487; VI (1874), 401.

39. *Publ. of the Narragansett Club*, III (1867), 74–78; IV (1870), 222; VI (1874), 51, 263–68.

40. Ernst, *Roger Williams*, p. 483. While Luther held that "all the righteousness of the best men, their thoughts, good works, alms, prayers, and sufferings avail nothing before God," he held, with Williams, that good works would ordinarily follow faith, repentance, and election. See Luther's *Works*, I, 173–285.

41. Like Luther, Williams rejected the doctrine of unconditioned free will. See Luther's treatise on free will and his argument that man's future depends less on human free will than upon God's free grace; and compare Williams and Luther on this score with the difficult position into which Puritan theologians got themselves by their acceptance of Calvinistic predestination. On their efforts to square the doctrine of works with that of predestination, consult Professor Perry Miller's excellent discussion in *The New England Mind*, pp. 365–97, esp. pp. 366–70; also pp. 397–407, 444–50, 475–80.

42. For Gorton's troubled, peripatetic career in the colonies, see Adelos Gorton, *Life and Times of Samuel Gorton* (Phila., 1907).

43. Gorton, *op. cit.*, pp. 12, 146–48. During his later years Gorton became more moderate, leaving at his death some manuscripts now in the possession of the Rhode Island Historical Society, notably a commentary on the Lord's Prayer that suggests that Gorton was definitely, probably directly, under Luther's influence. The manuscripts await closer study than they have received. Indications of Lutheran content are to be gleaned from the extracts given in Lewis G. James, *Samuel Gorton: A Forgotten Founder of Our Liberties* (Warwick, R.I., 1896).

44. This conclusion is corroborated by Professor Jantz, whose survey of colonial libraries, or remnants of them, goes far beyond my own. Exact numbers and comparative figures on all libraries and library lists examined are promised by Dr. Jantz when he completes his comprehensive study (a few will be given below). Much of what follows regarding seventeenth-

and eighteenth-century libraries is based on Dr. Jantz's findings.

45. Samuel Fuller's booklist in 1638 included a Musculus; Captain Miles Standish's in 1656, *The State of Europe* and *The German History;* and Governor Bradford's in 1657, a copy of Luther *On the Galatians.* William Brewster's list of 1644, the first of any length and reasonable completeness, included a number of works by Germans, among them the theological works of Musculus, Oecolampadius, Lavaterus, Zanchius, Sohnius, Pareus, Piscator, Buxtorf, Wigandus, Chemnitz, Keckermann's *Systema Physicum,* and three English books on the German wars.— Jantz, *loc. cit.,* p. 5; T. G. Wright, *op. cit.,* pp. 254–65; *Records of the Colony of New Plymouth,* ed. by N. B. Surtleff (Boston, 1855), esp. Vols. I–IV, on the years 1633–1668; H. M. Dexter, "Elder Brewster's Library," *Proc. Mass. Hist. Soc.,* 2nd ser., V (1889–1890), 37–85.

46. Jantz, *loc. cit.,* p. 5; J. H. Suttle, "The Libraries of the Mathers," *Proc. Amer. Antiq. Soc.,* new ser., XX (Apr., 1910), 269–356. Buxtorf's *Thesaurus Grammaticus Linguae Sanctae Hebraeae* (1629) was one of the most generally used books among studious Puritans. The first literary use to which I find it put in America is in Richard Mather's Preface to the *Bay Psalm Book* (Cambridge, Mass., 1640).

47. John Harvard's gift includes two works of Luther and Melanchthon. See the Harvard Library *Bibliographical Contributions,* ed. by W. C. Lane, No. 27, pp. 5–14: "Books Given to the Library by John Harvard, Peter Bulkley, Sir Kenelm Digby, and Governor Bellingham." See also No. 55, pp. 26–28, as well as S. E. Morison, *The Founding of Harvard College* (Cambridge, Mass., 1935), p. 265; Alfred C. Potter, "Catalogue of John Harvard's Library," *Trans. Col. Soc. Mass.,* XXI (1919), 190–203; Henry J. Cadbury, "John Harvard's Library," *Trans. Col. Soc. Mass.,* XXXIV (1942), 353–77.

Subsequent bequests to Harvard almost invariably included German works. Of particular importance among seventeenth-century gifts are the Sebastian Münster *Cosmographia* from Peter Bulkley of Concord, scientific and mystical works from Sir Kenelm Digby, the friend of John Winthrop, Jr., and several scholarly and theological works from John Winthrop the Elder. See Robert C. Winthrop, *Life and Letters of John Winthrop* (2 vols., Boston, 1869), II, 438. That these gifts were not for naught appears from many contemporary references, among which may be cited Leonard Hoar's advice in 1661 to his nephew, then at Harvard, that he should study, in addition to the Bible, Petrus Ramus, and other fundamental sources, such universal reference works as Conrad Gesner's *Bibliotheca Universalis* (Zürich, 1545–1549), a catalog in the three learned tongues of all known writers and books, and Georg Draud's *Bibliotheca Classica* (Frankfurt-am-Main, 1611 and 1625), a catalog of books and authors not surpassed until Bayle's *Dictionary* appeared in 1697.

48. A list of his foreign correspondents published in Volume XL of the *Transactions of the Royal Society* (London, 1741), enumerates 81, of whom 15 are Germans, 3 are Englishmen who maintained close German connections, 5 Dutch, 3 Italian, 2 French, 1 Danish, and 1 Bohemian. Among the Germans, the best known are the chemist Johann Rudolph Glauber, the astronomer Johann Hevelius, the Hamburg physicians Paul M. Schlegelius and Johann Tanckmarus, and a well-known group of Germans residing in England: Samuel Hartlib, the friend of Milton's whom Winthrop held dear as "the great Intelligencer of Europe"; Heinrich Oldenburg, a founder of the Royal Society and its corresponding secretary for many years; and Prince Rupert of the Palatinate, who, after a tempestuous youth, had settled down in England, devoting himself to artistic and scientific pursuits. To this list Dr. Jantz has added the names of three other influential European men of learning: (1) Theodor Haak, a friend of Milton, translator of half of *Paradise Lost* into German blank verse, and generally accredited founder of the Royal Society; (2) "Mr. Morian," "Morlian," or "Morlean" (the name is variously transcribed in the Winthrop papers) to whom both Winthrop and his German correspondents invariably refer with respect and devotion; and (3) Augustinus Petraeus.

49. John Winthrop, *The History of New England* (ed. by James Savage, 2 vols., Boston, 1825–1826), II, 20. The library was steadily added to by his son Wait and his grandson John. Professor Morison thinks that Winthrop brought a thousand-volume collection of books with him when he emigrated in 1631. Of the 270 volumes which he considered, Mr. Morison classifies 135 as scientific works (including 52 devoted to chemistry), 61 religious, 36 as relating to history and belles-lettres, 24 on languages, law, and philosophy, and 12 on the occult sciences. See *Builders of the Bay Colony,* p. 272; *The Puritan Pronaos,* p. 130.

50. In 1812, Francis B. Winthrop gave to the New York Society Library 259 volumes. Another sizable portion of this colonial library, comprising "One hundred sixteen Volumes of Books and twenty three Pamphlets," was given by the same donor to the New York Hospital in 1812, whence it came, in 1892, into the possession of the New York Academy of Medicine

Library. Francis B. Winthrop also gave upwards of another hundred volumes of the Winthrop collection to the Massachusetts Historical Society. Since 1942, when Dr. Jantz published his "Preliminary Report," he has found two other sizable groups of Winthrop books—one at Yale University and the other at Trinity College—so that approximately a half of the thousand-volume Winthrop collection is now avaliable for analysis.

Regarding questions of provenience, see Herbert Greenberg, "The Authenticity of the Library of John Winthrop the Younger," *Amer. Lit.*, VIII, iv (Jan., 1937), 448–52. While a number of the Winthrop books represent accessions made by Winthrop's descendants—some of them, for instance, bear marks indicating that they were used as textbooks by late seventeenth- and eighteenth-century members of the family—Dr. Jantz is confident that his researches, when complete, will substantiate his belief that a much higher percentage of the extant books were acquired by Winthrop himself than Mr. Greenberg's figures (based on an examination of only the 259 volumes in the New York Society Library) indicate.

Professor Samuel Morison, tells us that half the books are in Latin, 71 in English, 23 in German, 17 in French, 12 in Dutch, 7 in Italian, 4 in Greek, and one in Spanish. A survey based on an examination of the books themselves, rather than on the *Catalogue of the Society Library* of 1850, whose short titles are often misleading or inaccurate, shows that there are at least 40, rather than 23, German books, exclusive of those now deposited in the New York Academy of Medicine, Yale University, and Trinity College. This number will doubtless be increased considerably when a classification is made of the 116 volumes and 23 pamphlets in the New York Academy of Medicine Library and of the smaller holdings of Yale and Trinity. Professor Morison's error may well be attributable to the circumstances that in several cases a number of separate publications are bound together in one volume, and that in seventeenth-century German books the upper part of the title page is often in Latin with the German title below, so that a work wholly in German may appear in a short-title catalog or a hastily made classification as a Latin work, when in reality it is a German book.

Of the four hundred–odd books examined by Dr. Jantz thus far, "all but a small portion" were acquired by John Winthrop, Jr., himself; later acquisitions, made by his descendants (since they include relatively few German titles) are of no particular significance for the matter in hand.

51. For Child, see G. L. Kittredge, "Dr. Robert Child the Remonstrant," *Trans. Col. Soc. Mass.*, XX (1919), 1–146, and Morison's excellent chapter on Child in *Builders of the Bay Colony*, pp. 244–68.

52. The concluding section of this work, on "Torwelsch," was abstracted in Alsted's *Encyclopaedia* (Nassau, 1630), one of the standard reference works used by seventeenth-century New Englanders. See T. G. Wright, *op. cit.*, pp. 30, 52, 59, 130.

53. Winthrop's copy shows interesting notes in the section on German language.—Jantz, *loc. cit.*, p. 11.

54. *Coll. Mass. Hist. Soc.*, 5th ser., I (1871), 160.

55. *Proc. Mass. Hist. Soc.*, XVI (June, 1878), 206–51, esp. pp. 210–11; also *Discovery*, VI (1925), 383–92.

56. See Jantz, *loc. cit:*, p. 11. Quite possibly others of Winthrop's papers and books disappeared or were destroyed earlier. For example, his father describes in his *Journal*, December 15, 1640, the havoc wrought by mice among his son's books while they were stored, temporarily, it is presumed, in a granary.

The history of the Winthrop library and the interest of Winthrop's descendants in German learning, while showing some interruptions, is more or less a continued story. The two sons of John Winthrop, Jr., especially Wait Still (1642–1717), carried on where his father had left off. He both preserved and added to the books he inherited; he wrote his name into many of his father's books and acquired additicnal German works. See the letter to his brother Fitz-John, asking him to procure the works of Glauber in an English translation.—"Winthrop Papers," *Coll. Mass. Hist. Soc.*, 5th ser., VIII (1882), 503, 511, 513, and Jantz, *loc. cit.*, p. 18. Wait's son John (1681–1747) became a scholar in his own right and was elected a Fellow of the Royal Society. He was honored in 1741 when the society dedicated to him a volume of its *Transactions* and again when the translation of the German-Latin work of John Andrew Cramer's *Elements of the Art of Assaying Metals* (London, 1741) was inscribed to him—both of them with references to his learned and distinguished ancestors (Jantz, *loc. cit.*, p. 18). Another John Winthrop (1714–1779), the grandson of Adam Winthrop (brother of John Winthrop, Jr.), carried forward the family tradition. In 1738 he was appointed Hollis professor of science at Harvard; and his son, James (1752–1821), became the close friend of William Bentley and, like him, an admirer of German learning as well as of the rising German literature—for all of which he acquired adequate representations for his library. Thus German learning and literature attained, around 1800, once again the position of importance for a Winthrop comparable to that which it had held during the middle of the seventeenth-century.

57. The significance of Samuel Lee as a popularizer in New England of the new discoveries and theories of science and as a directive force in the tentative explorations of Cotton Mather and his successors into such realms as are considered in *The Christian Philosopher* merits further investigation.

58. Jantz, *loc. cit.*, p. 23.

59. Educated in medicine at Leyden and Padua, and committed to liberal political and religious views, Child found his efforts to carry liberty as well as prosperity to the New Englanders rewarded by the imposition of fines (which Winthrop paid for him), confiscation of property, and imprisonment; yet he refused to be "weaned from New England for their discourtesye" and continued to offer his money for joint enterprises with Winthrop in the prosecution of scientific ventures in agriculture, chemistry, and metallurgy in the promotion of industrial projects, including a scheme to combine viniculture with silkworm culture, a fur trading company, blacklead mining, iron works, and salt wells.

60. Another popular volume among early colonial learned men, e.g., among the Mather books now in the Amer. Antiq. Soc. and among James Winthrop's books in Allegheny College. See also the book lists in Wright and in Morison.

61. According to Johann Conrad Creiling (*Die edelgeborne Jungfer Alchymia*, Tübingen, 1730), the writings of Eirenaeus Philalathes became as familiar to alchemists as their daily bread. He goes on to say that Philalathes was identified by some with "Dr. Zcheil, residing in America" (who is, of course, Dr. Child), and by others with "Georgius Sterkey, an apothecary in London." General opinion today agrees with G. L. Kittredge, who observed that Philalathes "was the creation of George Stirk's teeming brain and not too scrupulous conscience." See S. E. Morison, *Harvard College in the Seventeenth Century* (Cambridge, Mass., 1936), p. 78. It requires little more than a glance at the index of Professor Kittredge's *Witchcraft in Old and New England* (Cambridge, Mass., 1928) to discover the close relationships existing among German, English, and American witchcraft, necromancy, alchemy, and allied pseudosciences.

62. *Proc. Mass. Hist. Soc.*, XVI (June, 1878), 212–13. "Durie appealed to him and to John Norton particularly for New England support of his plan of Protestant union, in the further-ance of which he spent many years in Germany conferring with noted scholars. The replies of Davenport and Norton, quoted in part in Cotton Mather's *Magnalia* (I, 272–74, 297) were friendly in spirit and conciliatory in doctrine. Davenport shared many of Winthrop's scientific interests, corresponded with the London Germans, and received many books from them." —Jantz, *loc. cit.*, p. 12.

63. Master of Arts of Emmanuel College in 1603, he studied and practiced law in London for a decade, and then traveled on the Continent, stopping at Heidelberg, where he was well received at the court of the Elector Palatine and the Princess Elizabeth, daughter of James I. At Heidelberg, about 1618, David Pareus, the learned Reformed professor of theology, persuaded him to enter the ministry. His first living was the chaplaincy of the mercantile colony of the Eastland Company at Elbing, Prussia—the same Eastland Company of which the deputy-governor was Theophilus Eaton, later the organizer of the Massachusetts Bay Company, and the first governor of the New Haven Colony. He remained in Prussia long enough after the outbreak of the Thirty Years' War to see something of the Counter-Reformation, and then returned to England about 1624. After suffering the displeasure of his former friend, Laud, he emigrated to America in 1633, aged fifty-five, and soon settled at Aggawam.

64. For the popularity of Keckermann's books among students at Harvard, see Morison, *Harvard College in the Seventeenth Century*, pp. 157–58, and Arthur O. Norton, "Harvard Textbooks and Reference Books of the Seventeenth Century," *Publ. Col. Soc. Mass.*, XXVIII (Apr., 1933), 361–438, esp. pp. 379, 412–14.

65. For the widespread use of this book, as well as of others of Alsted's works, see Morison, *Harvard College in the Seventeenth Century*, pp. 147, 158–59, 162, 209, 217, 226, 273, and Norton, *loc. cit.*, pp. 383–84.

66. See *ibid.*, pp. 396–97, 421–22, 432–33; Louis F. Snow, *The College Curriculum in the United States* (N.Y., 1907), pp. 20–77 *passim;* and *New Englands First Fruits* (London, 1643), sec. 2.

67. For details, consult Morison, *Harvard College in the Seventeenth Century*, pp. 139–297, and Norton, *loc. cit.*, pp. 361–438. For textbooks in use in philosophy at Harvard during the seventeenth and eighteenth centuries, see Benjamin Rand, "Philosophical Instruction in Harvard University from 1636 to 1900," *Harvard Graduates' Mag.*, XXXVII (Sept., 1928), 29–47, and Snow, *op. cit.*, pp. 31–35, 46–48, 56–77, 78–116. For books in use at Yale during the eighteenth century, see *ibid.*, pp. 23–25,

37–39, 42–45, 51–54, 79, 90–92; at Princeton, pp. 38–39, 54–55, 72–73; at Columbia, pp. 56–72; at William and Mary, pp. 73–74; at the University of Virginia, pp. 75–76.

68. For example, as early as 1657 Elisha Cook (B.A., 1657) owned a copy of Buchler's *Thesaurus Poeticus*. John Hancock, a freshman in 1685, had another copy (Cologne, 1609, ed.). —Jantz, *loc. cit.*, p. 14; Morison, *Harvard College in the Seventeenth Century*, p. 178.

69. *Ibid.*, pp. 285–97; Morison, *The Founding of Harvard College* (Cambridge, Mass., 1935), pp. 263–70.

70. See Morison, *Harvard College in the Seventeenth Century*, p. 292. Apparently this weeding-out process continued regularly. In 1682 Cotton Mather, just then taking his second degree, purchased ninety-six volumes of duplicates for 43 pounds and 19 shillings, and his classmate, John Cotton, paid 30 pounds for "double books" in 1695. For details see C. S. Brigham, "Harvard College Library Duplicates, 1682," *Publ. Col. Soc, Mass.*, XVIII (1916), 407–17.

71. *Miscellanea Curiosa, sive Ephemerides Medico-Physicarum Germanicarum.*

72. Morison, *Harvard College in the Seventeenth Century*, p. 293; Alfred C. Potter, "Harvard College Library, 1723–1735," *Publ. Col. Soc. Mass.*, XXV (Feb., 1922), 1–13.

73. Compare the list given by Norton (*loc. cit.*, pp. 361–438) with that by R. F. Seyboldt, "Student Libraries at Harvard, 1763–1764," *Publ. Col. Soc. Mass.*, XXVIII (Apr., 1933), 449–61.

74. Among works of special interest are the *Ephemerides Brandenburgicae* (another scholarly periodical), Reuchlin's Hebrew grammar, Frischlin's Latin grammar, Serreius' Latin-French-German dictionary (Strassburg, 1603), Johan Clacius' (probably Clajus') German grammar (Leipzig, 1617), Luther's German New Testament (Wittenberg, 1595), the complete works of Jacob Boehme in German (1638), *De Signatura Rerum* (n.d.), and *Josephus Redivivus* (1631). Among significant newer works are those that came through Cotton Mather's German correspondents, August Hermann Francke, Bartholomaeus Ziegenbalg, and Anthony Wilhelm Boehm. The supplement of the catalog for 1724 lists additional titles.

75. Thomas Grocer's inventory in 1664 listed a "German Dyet" and "Praehes Emblems," the latter identified by Ford as Stephanus Praher's *Erste Thayl dess Podagraischen Fliegenwadels ...* Passau, 1614.—T. G. Wright, *op. cit.*, p. 54; Worthington C. Ford, *The Boston Book Market, 1679–1700* (Boston, 1917), p. 74.

76. Jantz, *loc. cit.*, p. 15.

77. T. G. Wright, *op. cit.*, pp. 121–23.

78. *John Dunton's Letters from New England* (Publ. of the Prince Soc., Vol. IV, Boston, 1867), pp. 314–19, esp. pp. 315–16.

79. Dieter Cunz, "John Lederer," *William and Mary Quar.*, XXII (1942), 175–85. Dr. Jantz has found among the Winthrop papers letters by and about him, as well as a thirteen-page manuscript in his handwriting.

80. *The Diary of William Bentley, D.D.* (4 vols., Salem, 1905–1914), II, 444.

81. *Ibid.*, II, 74, 200; IV, 435.

82. *New England Journal of Medicine*, Apr. 21, 1938.

83. Mather published *A Letter from the most ingenious Mr. Lodowick of Rhode Island, Febr. 1, 1691/2*, in which Lodowick is represented as professing to have been once a Quaker and as undertaking now to speak authoritatively concerning Quakers, at the same time endeavoring to deflate the claims of "the more learned sort of people called Quakers" to superior enlightenment by asserting that they had all their ideas at second hand from a German nobleman, who is left unidentified, but whose children he professes to have tutored. Regarding the identity of this nobleman, consult Thomas J. Holmes, *Cotton Mather: A Bibliography ...* (3 vols., Cambridge, Mass., 1940), II, 569.

84. *Diary of Samuel Sewall* (3 vols., Boston, 1878), I, 318, 391.

85. Judge Sewall, in his Letter Book, preserved a letter from Lodowick dated Leipzig, March 24, 1712, in which Lodowick gave him specific directions for the cure of an ailment diagnosed as "the Hypochondriack Evil" (see *Coll. Mass. Hist. Soc.*, 6th ser., II [1888], 25–29). As late as 1752 Thomas Prince, in the preface to a medical pamphlet mentioned "the learned Dr. James *Oliver* of *Cambridge*, one of the most esteemed *Physicians* in his Day, who had a singular Help in the Art of *Chemistry* by the ingenious Dr. *Lodowick* a *German*, who was also accounted an excellent *Physician*, and the most skilful *Chymist* that ever came into these Parts of America" (quoted by Samuel Abbot Green in *A Centennial Address ... June 7, 1881, before the Mass. Hist. Soc.* [Groton, 1881], p. 54).

Green also quotes (p. 37) a news item from the *Boston Weekly News Letter* of 1717 about another German physician in Boston, Sebastian Henry Swetzer, and his marvelous "cure" of a Negro. About the middle of the eighteenth century Dr. Johann Rhode was a prominent physician in New Haven (see Charles F. Bollman, "Zur Geschichte des Deutschtums in New Haven," *Deutsch-Amerikanische Geschichtsblätter*, XXVII–XXVIII [1927–1928], 216–24). There were also Germans in other professions around the turn of the century, e.g., Colonel

Wolfgang Romer, an army engineer in charge of New England fortifications between 1698 and 1705. See *Coll. Mass. Hist. Soc.*, 6th ser., III (1899), 336–37, 547–51.

86. Jantz, *loc. cit.*, pp. 16–17. The fullest account available on Lodowick is Dr. Jantz's "Christian Lodowick of Newport and Leipzig," *Rhode Island History*, III, iv (Oct., 1944), 105–17; IV, i (Jan., 1945), 13–26. Dr. Jantz, upon whose researches I have relied heavily for the facts adduced concerning the aforementioned German professional men in seventeenth-century America, is investigating, among other Germans in early New England, Captain John Luther, one of the first settlers of Rhode Island.

87. Rufus M. Jones, *Spiritual Reformers in the Sixteenth and Seventeenth Centuries* (London, 1914), esp. Ch. XII, "Jacob Boehme's Influence in England." See also his *Studies in Mystical Religion* (London, 1909), Chs. XII–XIX, as well as *Some Exponents of Mystical Religion* (London, 1910), pp. 199–200.

88. Harvard Library, *Bibliographical Contributions*, No. 27 (1888).

89. For example, the library of George Alcock, a medical student, included among eight German works Boehme's *De Signatura Rerum* (probably the J. Ellistone translation, London, 1651) as early as 1676.—S. E. Morison, "The Library of George Alcock, Medical Student," *Publ. Col. Soc. Mass.*, XXVIII (Feb., 1933), 350–57, esp. p. 356.

90. It is all too easy to overestimate the dogmatic exclusiveness of New England Puritanism and to assert that Puritans inexorably opposed all aspects of pietism and mysticism. For a corrective of this view, consult Professor Perry Miller's *New England Mind*, notably Ch. I and II, but also pp. 286–87, 372, 373, 396–97, 484–91.

91. While this influence never disappeared, it tended to fall behind the growing vogue of the Dutch and French scholars, until it was revived by the Harvard-Göttingen men about 1820.

THE EIGHTEENTH CENTURY

92. For brief treatments see A. B. Faust, *German Element . . .*, I, 47–52, and A. Steinmetz, "Kelpius, the Hermit of the Wissahickon," *Amer.-Ger. Rev.*, VII, vi (Aug., 1941), 7–11.

93. Julius H. Tuttle's list in "The Libraries of the Mathers," *Proc. Amer. Antiq. Soc.*, n.s., XX (Apr., 1910), 269–356, esp. pp. 313–56, when checked against the "remains" presented in 1814 to the American Antiquarian Society, is found to be very incomplete, at least sixty

titles of German authors now deposited in Worcester being omitted. Those of Mather's books that are now in the Massachusetts Historical Society Library are listed by Tuttle (*ibid.*, pp. 280–90). See also H. J. Cadbury, "Harvard College Library and the Libraries of the Mathers," *Proc. Amer. Antiq. Soc.*, L (Apr. 17, 1940), 20–48.

94. In addition to the common reference works and commentaries, it included such unique items as Trithemius' *Historia*, the *Epistolae Obscurorum Virorum*, Lemnius' *De Occultis Naturae Miraculis*, Carion's *Chronicon*, and two translations into English: *Causes of Pestilence* and Bucer's *Judgment on Divorce* (in the Milton translation). In 1676 Increase Mather acquired from Mrs. Bridget Usher Gesner's natural history, the works of Cornelius Agrippa, several of Buxtorf's works, and the *Laws of the Fraternities of the Rosie Crosse* by Michael Maierus.—Tuttle, *loc. cit.*, pp. 291–92.

95. *Increase Mather, the Foremost American Puritan* (Cambridge, Mass., 1925), and *Selections from Cotton Mather, with Introduction and Notes* (N.Y., 1926); consult also the bibliographies in Perry Miller and T. H. Johnson (eds.), *The Puritans*, pp. 821–31, esp. pp. 829–31.

96. It is not to be presumed, of course, that a reference by Cotton Mather ("book-suffocated" as he was) to a German author or book is presumptive evidence that he knew the author at first hand or that he had the book before him. Often Cotton Mather quoted at second- and third-hand. Professor Murdock reminds us that if one reads Mather's *Christian Philosopher* with Ray's *Wisdom of God Manifested in the Creation* and his *Physico-Theological Discourses*, Wm. Derham's *Physico-Theology*, Dr. Cheyne's *Philosophical Principles of Religion*, and Grew's *Cosmologia Sacra* open before him, he will discover that much of what Mather says— particularly by way of quotation or reference to authorities—derives from these books, "or from others like them."—*Selections from Cotton Mather*, Intro., p. 1.

97. Here may be mentioned the most oft-used German works in the Mather collection, the *Acta Eruditorum* and the *Miscellanea Curiosa* ("the German Ephemerides," in Cotton's phrase)—both many times acknowledged as the sources of Mather erudition, and equally often unacknowledged.

98. While writing his *Christian Philosopher*, Mather found Alsted as indispensable as Drew's and Derham's physico-theological books. The *Theologia Naturalis* turns out to be the source of many of Mather's longer quotations. See, for example, "Essay XXVI: Of the Vegetables."

99. *Miscellanea Curiosa sive Ephemeridium*

Medico-Physicarum Germanicarum, etc., acquired by Mather during his university days, formed perhaps the one reference work of his that he found most useful. In this case, as in the case of Alsted's compends, Mather's methods illustrate the not uncommon practice of students to revert to the books which early study and long use have made familiar. For a good illustration of the use to which he put his "German Ephemerides," see "Essay XXXII: Of Man" in *The Christian Philosopher*. This book is but one among many that demonstrate the method by which the learned Mathers arrived at their reputation of being "walking libraries." Cotton's *Magnalia*, with its various contents—historical, political, theological, cosmological, astrological, etc.—is another illustration of how, in the numerous departments of learning that engaged his attention, he went to corresponding German sources. What I have been able to learn about the six massive manuscript folios of his *Biblia Americana* suggests that in this department of learning he was equally dependent upon the findings of German theologians, most likely drawn at second-hand from his "German Ephemerides."

100. Reprinted, largely from the originals in the American Antiquarian Society, by Kuno Francke, "Cotton Mather and August Hermann Francke," *Harvard Studies and Notes in Philology and Literature*, V (1896), 55–67; "Further Documents Concerning Cotton Mather and A. H. Francke's Correspondence," *Americana Germanica*, I (1897), 39–45; and "The Beginnings of Cotton Mather's Correspondence with A. H. Francke," *Philol. Quar.*, V (July, 1926), 193–95.

101. Francke inspired him to write a thirteen-page treatise, *Nuncia Bona a Terra Longinqua. A Brief Account of Some Good & Great Things A Doing For the Kingdom of God in the Midst of Europe* (Boston, 1715, reprinted in *Americana Germanica*, I, iv [1799], 54–66), a spirited recapitulation of the account given him of Francke's numerous pietistic, charitable, missionary, and educational activities, interspersed with Mather's own reflections and moral exhortations. Francke is the "pure, undefiled" minister of God on Earth, whose "Notable Improvements" are so truly "Miraculous" as to make him "the Wonder of Europe."—*Nuncia Bona*, pp. 2, 11–12.

102. Boehm had studied at Halle in 1693 and had been a "table inspector" at Francke's Orphan House. In 1701 he went to England as tutor, and in 1705 he was appointed Court Preacher to Prince George of Denmark, a position he held until his death in 1722. He was a forerunner of the German ministers who came, under the four Georges, to hold increasingly influential positions in the English court; for under the Hanoverians, who were Lutherans, their churches received the benefit of whatever royal prestige and favor could bestow. Boehm, for example, was already sufficiently in Queen Anne's confidence for her to accede to his request that she provide for the successive waves of Palatines who came to London en route to the new world and who totalled, by 1709, some 13,000. See Faust, *op. cit.*, I, 73–81; W. A. Knittle, *The Early Eighteenth Century Palatine Emigration . . .* (Phila., 1937); Jöcher's *Allgemeines Gelehrten-Lexikon*, I, 1170; H. E. Jacobs, *History of the Evangelical Lutheran Church in the United States*, (N.Y., 1893), pp. 143–44.

103. These works, as we shall observe, were not without their effect on the Wesleys and on Whitefield. In 1751, the close-calculating Franklin considered Arndt's *True Christianity* sufficiently popular to warrant his publishing an edition de luxe.—John P. Hoskins, "German Influence on Religious Life and Thought During the Colonial Period," *Princeton Theol. Rev.*, V, ii (Apr., 1907), 211–13.

104. What is more, Mather, on April 27, 1716, presented "unto our poor College . . . certain Books that are of great improvement and influence in ye famous Frederician University and of a tendency to correct ye wretched methods of education there; and ye works of Arndt (de vero Christianismo) and Franckius and Langius [Joachim Lange]."—*Diary*, Apr. 27, 1716.

On June 6, 1716, Mather rejoiced at learning that his *Magnalia* had fallen into Boehm's hands. He wrote immediately to Boehm, professing to believe "ye American puritanism to be so much of a piece with ye Frederician pietism, that if it were possible for ye book to be transferred unto our Friends in ye Lower Saxony, it could be . . . a little serviceable to their religious institutions." Mather, be it observed in passing, was fond enough of his own "little engines of piety" to send several of his shorter treatises to Boehm, enjoining him to distribute them as fast and as far as he could, even to "ye Malabarian Missionaries."

105. Along with Luther's *Colloquies*. The first page of this list is reproduced in facsimile in Ora E. Winslow, *Jonathan Edwards* (N.Y., 1940), p. 120; see also Thomas H. Johnson, "Jonathan Edwards' Background of Reading," *Publ. Col. Soc. Mass.*, XXVIII (Dec., 1931), 193–222.

106. Further indications of the Mathers' strong interest in German pietism appear in their efforts to gain all available information on the Hallesche Stiftungen, especially of the methods by which Francke inculcated piety

among his charges in the Orphanage. See Cotton's numerous references in the *Diary* for the years 1709–1724. Cotton was especially lavish in sending "packetts" of books and "treatises," and several times "small presents of gold." Moreover, the touching story of Christlieb Leberecht von Extor, widely circulated in Germany, England, and America, moved both father and son to write on the subject: Increase, *An Earnest Exhortation to the Children of New England* (Boston, 1711), and Cotton, *Man Eating the Food of Angels* (Boston, 1710). It would seem that Cotton Mather wrote sincerely when he declared in 1715, "The World begins to feel the Warmth from the *Fire of God* which thus flames in the Heart of *Germany*, beginning to extend into many Regions; the whole World will e're long be sensible of it!"—*Nuncia Bona a Terra Longinqua*, p. 9.

107. Letter to Boehm, June 6, 1717 (see *Harvard Studies . . .*, V [1896], 63); *Nuncia Bona a Terra Longinqua*, pp. 2, 9, 11; Mather's *Diary*, Oct. 9, 16, 1716.

108. The German titles were omitted because German type was lacking in Boston.

109. Kuno Francke, *Harvard Studies . . .*, p. 66.

110. For example, his copy of Paul Freherus' *Theatrum Virorum Eruditione Clarorum* (Nürnberg, 1688) contains many notes in his handwriting indicating that he used the work for illustrations of almost every kind.

111. When, after an extensive visit among the Salzburgers in Georgia and a tour of Carolina, Pennsylvania, New York, and Rhode Island, Urlsperger's young friend, Baron P. G. F. von Reck, came to Boston in the winter of 1733–1734, Governor Belcher entertained him in his home and provided him with letters of warm commendation. Subsequently he corresponded with Urlsperger himself concerning pietism in general and the Georgia Salzburgers in particular. See the Belcher Papers, Part II, in *Coll. Mass. Hist. Soc.*, 6th ser., VIII, 88–89, 122, 395, 466, 474.

112. *Diary*, IV, 318 (Feb. 26, 1815).

113. His chief German correspondent was the Rev. Samuel Urlsperger, Sr., pastor of the Church of St. Anna in Augsburg.

114. A very large portion of this collection is preserved in the Boston Public Library which printed a catalog of it in 1870, with a preface by Justin Winsor.

115. For texts in use at Yale, see L. F. Snow, *op. cit.*, pp. 23–25, 37–39, 42–45, 51–54, 79, 90–92; Franklin B. Dexter, "The First Public Library in New Haven," *Papers of the New Haven Hist. Soc.*, VI (1900), 312–13.

116. T. H. Johnson, *loc. cit.*, pp. 197, 220.

Students at Yale recited out of Wollebius' theological works from 1720, when Edwards used the book as a text (see Alex. Cowie, "Educational Problems at Yale College in the Eighteenth Century," *Tercentenary Commission of the State of Conn. Hist. Publ.*, LV [New Haven, 1936], 16), until at least 1779, when Wollebius was still a standard text for the senior class. See Theo. D. Woolsey, *An Historical Discourse . . . Aug. 11, 1850* (New Haven, 1850), p. 119.

117. T. H. Johnson, *loc. cit.*, pp. 183–222. Francke's *Letter Concerning . . . Preaching* enjoyed a considerable popularity and was printed in Boston twice in 1740, in John Jennings' *Two Discourses*. Another of Francke's works, *Nicodemus: or, A Treatise against the Fear of Man* (probably in Boehm's translation), appeared in Boston in 1744; and John Wesley's abridgment of it remained popular throughout the century. See Richard Green, *The Works of John and Charles Wesley. A Bibliography* (London, 1896), p. 14.

118. See Wesley's *Journal*, ed. by N. Curnoch (8 vols., N.Y., 1909–1916), Jan. 23–25, 1736, *et seq.*; H. E. Jacob, *op. cit.*, pp. 169–79; C. T. Winchester, *John Wesley* (N.Y., 1906), pp. 40–52, 61–63; Luke Tyerman, *The Life and Times of the Rev. John Wesley* (3 vols., N.Y., 1872), I, 174–211; P. A. Strobel, *The Salzburgers and Their Descendants* (Baltimore, 1855), pp. 78, 81–82; and James T. Hatfield, "John Wesley's Translation of German Hymns," *PMLA*, XI, ii (1896), 174–81.

119. See Wesley's testimony, *Journal*, June 14—Sept. 16, 1738; Nov. 1–10, 1739; and June 1—Aug. 8, 1741.

120. All three emphasized the subjective side of religion, seeking to restore to the soul its oneness with the Divine and insisting that true religion is a matter of experience as well as of belief. In one sense, this emotional religion was a revival of sixteenth-century Reformation doctrine, whose essence had been an appeal to the individual conscience. In another sense, it was a reaction against the empty formalism and sterile dogmatism which had settled upon the Church after it had become a political as well as an ecclesiastical institution. In some respects it paralleled the efforts of the English Independents; in others it sought to counteract them. It particularly aimed at the destruction of the half-hearted, rational, deistic method. Paradoxical as it appears, it was also, in its practical aspects, in revolt against the doctrine of salvation by faith alone and against the laxity in religious practice that had followed a too literal application of the Lutheran principle. German pietists and quietists, Salzburgers, Moravians,

and Methodists alike endeavored to restore good works to their proper place in religious life. In this respect they represented a reaction against Luther. Schools for orphans, the care of the poor, the sick, the aged, preaching in prisons, and other charitable and pious endeavors bear witness to their philanthropic and missionary zeal. Francke's "Pädagogium" at Halle and his far-flung missionary work, Wesley's school at Kirkswood and his orphanage at Newcastle, Whitefield's orphan-house at Savannah, Edwards' missionary work at Stockbridge, and David Brainard's activities in New Jersey are all manifestations of this humanitarian impulse.

121. A noteworthy manifestation, aside from philanthropic and humanitarian reform programs, is the rise of pietistic middle-class literature as represented by Gellert, Gessner, Bodmer, Klopstock, and Wieland in Germany and the works of Lillo and Richardson, the Wesleyan hymnody, and the cheap Methodist press in England. In America, while such quietistic enterprises as those of Kelpius and of Zinzendorf in Pennsylvania and of Bolzius and Grunau in South Carolina were primarily religious in inspiration, they aimed also at the establishment of an ideal Apostolic social organization, based sometimes upon community of goods and always upon a greater degree of social equality and political justice than they believed realizable in Europe.

122. For the hardening process that had gained ground in the New England of Edwards' youth, see the central thesis of Professor Perry Miller's *Jonathan Edwards*, (N.Y., 1949). In the Middle colonies the great diversity of race, doctrinal opinion, and ecclesiastical connection promoted what "right-thinking" New Englanders looked upon as an anarchical state of religion. Those churches—English, German, and Dutch—which depended for support on transatlantic hierarchies all suffered from lack of support and especially from a shortage of pastors. The Quakers had entered the second phase of their development and had ceased active proselyting. The Presbyterian Church, with headquarters in Philadelphia, though well-organized, was small; and if the efforts of William Tennent and his four preaching sons to revitalize it are any indication of its status, it was subject to schisms and embroilments—in no position to take a commanding lead among colonial denominations. The Dutch Reformed Church in New York and New Jersey was dwindling before the onslaught of trade and commercialism, changes in language, and a lack of ministers. The numerous German sects, hedged about by barriers of language and racial feel-

ing, were torn by internal strife and were suffering from a woeful dearth of ministers until the threat of Zinzendorf to unite all under the Moravian banner finally brought some response to the repeated calls for help. The Lutheran Church in Halle bestirred itself and sent Heinrich Melchior Mühlenberg in 1741, and five years later the German Reformed Church sent Michael Schlatter—men who became the leaders and unifiers of their respective churches. The independent German sects, while numerous, were scattered from New York to Georgia. Finding all restraints removed in America, they followed their own inclinations to extreme pietism (even forms of monasticism) and hence failed to attain solidarity or to wield any considerable influence beyond their immediate spheres. The intricate and, in some cases, tragic embroilments among Lutherans, the German Reformed bodies, and the lesser groups of German sectarians are summarily related by Faust (*op. cit.*, I, 48–52, 111–48, esp. pp. 113–15) and more circumstantially by Dr. Heinz Kloss, *Um die Einigung des Deutschamerikanertums* (Berlin, 1937), esp. pp. 89–116.

123. In the meantime, Edwards' early efforts were followed almost immediately by scattered revivals at Newark, N.J., under Jonathan Dickinson; at New Brunswick, in the church of Gilbert Tennent; and at Londonderry, Pa., by Samuel Blair. All these early revivals were local, and there was little sign that they would become extensive until the Wesleyans, imbued with German pietism, made the revival general.

124. John was going as chaplain to the colony at Savannah and missionary to the Indians, and Charles as secretary to Governor Oglethorpe. Aboard ship was David Nitschman, a Moravian bishop (whom the Wesleys had met at the house of James Hutton in London), with twenty-six Brethren. On the third day out John Wesley undertook the study of German. Before the voyage was over, he had translated a number of German hymns, five of which he included in his *Collection of Psalms and Hymns* (Charleston, S.C., 1737). On arriving at Savannah, he was able to minister to the German congregation there in their native tongue.

125. Johann Arndt (1555–1621), "a lover of the sincere Christianity of the heart" (so the legend on his tombstone runs), had sought to keep alive during the difficult years preceding the Thirty Years' War a religion founded on Scripture and developed in the individual through prayer, the practice of godliness, the emulation of Christ, and the cordial love of God and one's neighbor. In his book he insisted upon the mystical union of the soul with God, at the sametime urging the necessity of good works

as a means to Christian growth. His book stood almost alone in its day in protesting against the one-sided doctrinaire separation of faith and living, of justification and sanctification, of religious knowing on the one hand and religious feeling and willing on the other. Spener delivered a series of sermons with Arndt's book as his text, and declared its value next to the Bible and Luther's works. It was a favorite with Francke and with A. W. Boehm, who, seeking to enkindle religious enthusiasm and missionary zeal in England of the kind he had known at Halle, chose to translate it. Reprinted almost annually from its first publication, Arndt's *True Christianity* stands first among books of a devotional character to preserve the gentle, introspective, practical type of Christianity among the German people. For its impact on Whitefield, see Luke Tyerman, *George Whitefield* (2 vols., N.Y., 1877), I, 107, 112; also John Wesley's *Journal*, Mar. 24, Apr. 31, 1736, and Aug. 10, 1738.

126. Tyerman, *Whitefield*, I, 16–17, 89, 109, 143.

127. *Ibid.*, I, 142, 308, 358, 392, 443; II, 20, 44, 383; Whitefield, *Continuation of the Account of the Orphan-House* (Edinburgh, 1742), pp. 17, 19, 26.

128. Tyerman, *Wesley*, I, 174–78, 180, 188, 190–96. In June, 1738, three weeks after his conversion, Wesley set out to pay a visit to Zinzendorf at Marienborn, to inspect the Franckian institutions at Halle, and to see Herrnhut, where he remained until August 12, participating freely in all the Moravian exercises, conferring with Christian David (the colorful "Bush-Preacher"), Michael Linner, David Nitschmann, Martin Döber, Augustine Neusser, David Schneider, and Arvid Gradin. Upon returning to London, he testified, "I would gladly have spent my life there. Oh when shall this Christianity cover the earth?" He rejoiced that the Moravian Society in Fetter Lane had grown during his absence from ten to thirty-two members. Its organization was destined to exert a powerful shaping influence on the future organization of Methodism.— *Ibid.*, I, 196–207; *Journal*, Aug. 1–12, 1738.

On Whitefield's return to London, he attended a love-feast in Fetter Lane (Dec. 6, 1738) and was a good deal surprised to find the new turn which Moravian piety had taken under Böhler's leadership. What surprised him even more was Wesley's preaching salvation by faith in Jesus Christ without regard to works. By January 8, 1839, Whitefield, too, was committed to the doctrine, and according to his own testimony, he confuted "a virulent Opposer of the Doctrine of the New Birth and Justification

in the Sight of God by Faith only." Up to the time of his next embarkation for America, Whitefield, like Wesley, improved every opportunity to participate in the services of the Moravian Society and to become really, if not nominally, one of the Brethren.—Tyerman, *Whitefield*, I, 148–50, 155, 162, 172, 214, 216; Whitefield's and Wesley's journals for the period; and Hoskins, *loc. cit.*, p. 221.

Subsequently the Wesleys and Whitefield split with the Moravian Society. Among the more important reasons for Wesley's departure was the Moravians' tendency toward quietism. Their insistence that there are no degrees of faith, and that the way to obtain it is not to use the means of grace but "to wait for Christ and be still" seemed to Wesley an open invitation to Antinomian heresies. Wesley, whose strength lay in organization, felt compelled to form societies of his own. In 1740 he organized the first Methodist Society, modeled in all essentials of organization on the Moravian Society in Fetter Lane, differing mainly in the doctrinal points indicated. Henceforth his work lay apart from that of the Moravians, but he never felt any bitterness toward them, and he always freely acknowledged his indebtedness to Moravian doctrine and practice.—Tyerman, *Wesley*, I, 307–9, 311, 336; *Journal*, June 4, 1742.

129. Even the Presbyterian Church caught the evangelical tone and felt the impact of pietism through the relationship between Gilbert Tennent, pastor in New Brunswick since 1727, and Theodor Jacobus Frelinghuysen, the Dutch Reformed pastor at Raritan. The latter had come under the influence of the pietism, which had spread from Germany to Holland, before he came to America in 1721. The chief point of his powerful preaching was his discriminating view of the nature of personal conversion, and he earnestly advocated the pietistic doctrines of regeneration, repentance, faith, and holiness, demanding a clear and consistent account of the convert's religious experience. In these matters he said he took Frelinghuysen for his model to become, in Leonard Woolsey's estimation, "as truly the son of Freylinghuysen as Timothy was of Paul."—*Hist. of Amer. Christianity* (N.Y., 1900), pp. 81, 141–42, 162–63).

The individualistic and emotional character of evangelical Christianity proved particularly advantageous to the growth of the Baptist churches. Many of the revival enthusiasts, when they separated from the orthodox organization, turned Baptist. In the South, the work of winning converts to the Baptist Church was especially successful. When it is considered that today Baptists and Methodists, similar in their emotional appeal and the revival methods of evangelization (whatever else their differences), outnumber all other Protestant denominations, the tremendous influence flowing from the Great Awakening, and through it, from German pietism, becomes apparent.

130. For the rise of hymn-singing under the guidance of Melanchthon and Luther and the importance of Germany as a hymn-producing country, see Clifford L. Hornaday, "Some German Contributions to American Hymnody," *Monatshefte für deutschen Unterricht*, XXXII, ii (Mar., 1940), 120–27. Although Isaac Watts already had come in contact with German pietism through his friend A. W. Boehm, the first really important step toward a new hymnody was taken by John Wesley. Henry E. Jacobs offers plausible evidence that the inspiration for Charles Wesley's "Jesus Lover of My Soul" was derived from the sight of the Moravians, during the violent sea storm, singing their hymns and relying upon God in things temporal as well as spiritual.

131. For details regarding the authorship of these hymns, see Hatfield, *loc. cit.*, pp. 171–99, esp. pp. 174–81; Hornaday, *loc. cit.*, pp. 120–27; and Henry Bett, *The Hymns of Methodism in Their Literary Relations* (London, 1920), pp. 8–18.

132. Charles Wesley's reliance upon German pietistic hymns has been recognized by hymnologists like W. Garrett Horder (*The Hymn Lover*, N.Y., 1896, p. 113) and Henry Ward Beecher, who wrote in the Preface to his hymnal: "His [Charles Wesley's] hymns are only Moravian hymns resung." One of Charles Wesley's most popular hymns, placed first in most Methodist hymnals, "O for a thousand tongues to sing / My great Redeemer's Praise," evidently relies heavily on Johann Mentzer's "O dass ich tausend Zungen hätte," written about 1714. It was in Freylinghausen's collection, which was used by the Wesleys during the period of their ministry in Georgia. See further, Tyerman, *Whitefield*, II, 148, 295, and Hoskins, *loc. cit.*, p. 235.

133. A related force was the introduction, first into England and soon after into America, of German pietistic literature. The middle of the eighteenth century saw the rise in both Germany and England of a sentimental, moral, didactic tendency in literature that appealed especially to the middle and lower classes, and that was closely associated with this new moral (sometimes sentimental) emotionalism. In this category the first notable German book to achieve popularity in England was Gellert's *History of the Swedish Countess G—* (London, 1752), followed in 1761 by Gessner's *Death of*

Abel, translated by Mary Collyer. Two years later came her translation of Klopstock's *Messias* and his sacred drama *The Death of Adam*. In 1764 appeared Wieland's *Trials of Adam*, another Biblical play; in 1767, Bodmer's *Noah*, a Biblical epic; in 1772, Haller's didactic romance *Usong;* and in 1780 his *Letters to His Daughter on the Truths of the Christian Religion*. In America these works were equally popular and several of them enjoyed an even greater vogue than in England. For example, twenty-three editions of Gessner's *Death of Abel* were printed in places ranging from Concord, N.H., and Newport, R.I., to Philadelphia and Baltimore before the public became surfeited with this sentimentally pious fare, and before the more hearty productions of Lessing, Goethe, and Schiller got a hearing. Even then, the classical German authors made slow headway against a firmly entrenched opposition to what American readers (nurtured first on puritanical and later on pietistic literature) had been taught to consider impious or profane. The religious leaders of evangelical religion had thoroughly indoctrinated their middle-class followers to read only moral prose and sacred poetry and to eschew all worldly and "fleshly" literature as soul-withering.

134. Although the Moravian school at Nazareth, Pa., was early destroyed in the Indian wars, and Whitefield's "Pietas Georgiensis" was swept away by the Revolution, their example was not lost, and the nineteenth century went on to imitate these earlier examples and set in motion a program of humanitarianism such as the early evangelists could hardly have envisaged.

135. Jacobs, *op. cit.*, 446–47.

136. Accurate figures are hard to secure, but the following, taken from the Census report of 1900, from Faust, *op. cit.*, II, 409–29, and from H. K. Carroll's *Religious Forces of the United States* (N.Y., 1893), as well as from statistics gathered by Carroll in his "Statistics of the Churches of the U.S.," in *The Christian Advocate* for Jan. 5, 1905 (pp. 17–20), appear to represent a fairly accurate view of the relative number of communicants in the more prominent sectarian bodies in the United States. No effort is made to list all denominations.

Catholic (incl. German Catholics)	10,233,824
Methodist (incl. German Methodists)	6,251,738
Baptist (incl. German Baptists or Dunkards)	5,150,185
Lutheran (incl. 187,432 of the German Ev. Synod)	1,789,766

Presbyterian	1,687,697
Protestant Episcopal	807,924
Congregational	667,951
Reformed (incl. 263,954 German Reformed)	401,001
Mormon	343,250
United Brethren in Christ (Moravian)	273,200
Evangelical Association	164,709
Jewish	143,000
Friends	117,065
Dunkards	114,065
Unitarians	71,000
Mennonites	60,953
German Ev. Protestant (Freethinkers)	36,156
Unitas Fratrum (Moravians, not to be confused with the United Brethren in Christ)	16,327
Schwenkfelders	600

These figures vary considerably from those for 1942 as given in Willard L. Sperry, *Religion in America* (Cambridge, Mass., 1945), App. C., pp. 285–87. The nine churches having the largest membership in 1942, according to Sperry, are the following:

Catholic	22,945,247
Baptist	11,253,559
Methodist	8,303,203
Lutheran	4,814,855
Jewish	4,641,184
Presbyterian	2,796,051
Protestant Episcopal	2,074,178
Disciples of Christ	1,655,680
Congregational	1,052,701

In addition to showing the interchange of Baptists and Methodists for the second and third places and the phenomenal growth of the Jewish church and the Disciples of Christ, the table is interesting as showing that the Lutheran church (represented in 1942 by twenty denominations) has maintained its position as the fourth largest church body in the United States.

137. For efforts in this direction, see Faust, *op. cit.*, II, 409–29, and the *Bibliography* for studies of individual German churches in the United States.

138. For exceptions, see Faust, *op. cit.*, I, 247–62 and the index to the *Bibliography* under the names of the New England states.

139. Faust, *op. cit.*, I, 126. At least one other, similarly abortive, attempt to do the same thing had been made forty years earlier by Kelpius, one of the mystics of the Wissahickon (*ibid.*, I, 50, and Heinz Kloss, *op. cit.*, pp. 95–98

et seq.). Proceedings and minutes of several of these interdenominational meetings are described by Gerhard Friedrich, "The A. H. Cassel Collection at Juniata College [Huntington, Pa.]," *Amer.-Ger. Rev.*, VII, vi (Aug., 1941), 18–21, esp. p. 19.

140. The chief anti-Herrnhut attack came from Gilbert Tennent (himself not untouched by pietism) when he published in Boston in 1743 his *Necessity of Holding Fast the Truth*. A commendatory preface was signed by five prominent ministers, including Benjamin Colman. Another opponent was Henry Rimius, whose publications during the 1750's had a considerable circulation in America—notably his *Narrative of the Moravians* (London, 1754).

141. Byrd prepared an elaborate 228-page *Natural History of Virginia, or Newly Discovered Eden*, descriptive of his large Roanoke tract in glowing terms, and had it translated and printed in Bern, Switzerland, with the object of enticing settlers. The book has recently been retranslated into English by R. C. Beatty and W. J. Mulloy (Richmond, 1940). Several groups of German and Swiss immigrants started for his lands only to be sidetracked. Once he almost sold 33,400 of his 180,000 acres to a Swiss immigration and settlement society; but in the end he had to content himself with the Scotch-Irish, whose swarming into Virginia, "like the Goths and Vandals of old," he did not like.—*Ibid.*, pp. xix–xxvi.

142. *Works* (Sparks ed., 10 vols., Boston, 1840), VII, 71–73.

143. *Provincial Society* (N.Y., 1927), p. 7.

144. Faust, *op. cit.*, I, 30–47; see also the *Bibliography* (index).

145. Printed by Christopher Saur (Phila., 1750). Dock's work was translated and edited by Martin Brumbaugh (Phila., 1908). This work includes a life of Dock and illustrations showing some of his schoolroom furniture.

146. C. H. Handschin, *The Teaching of Modern Languages in the United States* (U.S. Bureau of Ed. Bulletin, 1913, No. 3, whole no. 510), pp. 51–53.

Some of these German schools early attained an influence beyond their immediate localities. Zinzendorf's school at Bethlehem and his seminary for girls attracted scholars from some of the most noted families. The two daughters of General Greene and Alma Allen, a niece of Ethan Allen, were educated there; and Mrs. Thomas Lee of Virginia, President Washington's niece, on the recommendation of the President, sought admission for her daughters there.—Rachel DuBois and Emma Schweppe, *The Germans in American Life* (N.Y., 1936), pp. 48–49.

147. M. D. Learned, "The Teaching of German in Pennsylvania," *Americana Germanica*, II, ii (1898–1899), 73.

148. See Felix Reichman, *The Muhlenberg Family* . . . (Phila., 1943); Frederic S. Klein, "The Spiritual and Educational Background of Franklin College," *Amer.-Ger. Rev.*, IV, iv (June, 1938), 39–43.

149. Educated in medicine, botany, and mineralogy at Erlangen, Berlin, Prague, and Vienna, Schoepf came to America in 1777 as chief surgeon to the Ansbach troops. In 1783 he asked leave to remain to make a naturalist's tour of the colonies. Leaving New York on July 22, 1783, he passed through New Jersey to Philadelphia, and after a circuitous tour of Pennsylvania, proceeded from Pittsburgh toward the Potomac by way of Warm Springs, in Berkeley County, Va., to Baltimore, Alexandria, Georgetown, and Annapolis, arriving again in Philadelphia on October 31, 1783. Here he was much interested in the controversy then raging over play-acting and also in the several learned and artistic efforts then emerging. But he was soon off again on more travels. While the fall and winter months were not ideal for botanical and geological studies, he had excellent opportunities for observing social and political conditions. He saw the Pennsylvania assembly at work; he was in Baltimore at the time the Glebes question was uppermost. Proceeding *via* Lancaster, York, and Frederick, he went to Richmond. Here he spent many December evenings in Formicola's tavern, where "Generals, Colonels, Captains, Senators, Assemblymen, Judges, Doctors, Clerks, and swarms of Gentlemen of every weight and calibre sat about the fire, drinking, smoking, singing and telling anecdotes." Heheard Patrick Henry speak, observed the factionalism between eastern and western Virginia, and participated in a spirited discussion with some agreeable gentlemen of Smithfield on the "Nation of Virginia." By January he was in Charleston in time to attend the sessions of the Assembly in 1784 and to hear the debates over the Society of Cincinnati. Early in March he sailed for Florida and thence to the Bahamas, returning to New York and finally to Germany in the latter part of the same year. For the rest of his life he was diligent in pushing his scientific investigations at the same time that he held many positions of public trust.—Alfred J. Morrison, "Doctor J. D. Schoepf," *German-American Annals*, XII, v–vi (Sept.–Dec., 1910), 256.

150. *Reise durch einigen der mittlern und südlichen vereinigten nordamerikanischen Staaten . . . 1783 und 1784* (2 Bde., Erlangen, 1788), II, 336;

see also I, 128. Other significant works dealing with the new world include (1) *Über Klima, Witterung, Lebensart und Krankheiten in Nordamerika* (in Meusel's *Historische Literatur*, 1781, and in modified form in his *Reise*, Vol. II); (2) *Von dem gegenwärtigen Zustand in Nordamerika, aus dem Lande selbst, im Jahre 1783* (in Schloezer's *Staats-Anzeigen*, Vol. VII [1785], in 4 installments); (3) *Vom amerikanischen Frosche* (in *Naturforscher*, No. 20, 1874); (4) *Der gemeine Hecht in Amerika* and *Der nordamerikanische Haase* (*ibid.*); (5) *Beschreibung einiger nordamerikanischen Fische, vorzüglich aus dem newyorkischen Wassern* (in *Schrift der Berliner Gesellschaft naturforschender Freunde*, II [1788], 138–90, and said to be "the first ichthyological paper ever written in America or concerning American species"); (6) *Materia medica americana, potissimum regni vegetabilis* (Erlangen, 1787), said to be "the first treatise in this department, and the authority well into the nineteenth century (see G. B. Goode, *Beginnings of Natural History in America*, Smithsonian Institution Report, 1897, II, pp. 396f.); (7) *Beiträge zur mineralogischen Kenntnis des östlichen Theils von Nordamerika* (Erlangen, 1787), commonly regarded as "the first work on American geology" (see G. P. Merrill, *Contributions to the History of American Geology*, Smithsonian Institution Report, 1904, p. 208); (8) *Historia Testudium* (Erlangen, 1793–1801), rated as "one of the earliest monographs of the Testudinata" by Goode, (*op. cit.*, II, 397); (9) a description of the birds of North America which came under his observation, the manuscript of which was lost at sea between Virginia and South Carolina. —Alfred J. Morrison, *loc. cit.*, pp. 256–57.

His *Travels*, exhibiting the author's keen and ubiquitous curiosity and a manner often as engagingly observant of men, manners, and customs as it was scientifically precise regarding the fauna, flora, and other natural phenomena of America, remains his chief monument. As a one-time member of the Ansbach troops, Schoepf never became enthusiastic about American independence and liberty; yet he wrote unpatronizingly and objectively, devoting his trained attention not only to botanical, zoological, and geological facts but also to the economic phases of plant life in the South as they were affected by plantation and marketing methods then in vogue, rice and indigo production in South Carolina, water courses, mountain ranges, mineralogical deposits, and the commercial and trade relations of all the colonies, incidentally tying in much ethnographical, linguistic, and general cultural information.

151. Spelled variously Priber, Pryber, and Preber. Once, in a statement of the public debt

of South Carolina for 1738–1739, when the expense of a party sent among the Cherokees to arrest him is recorded, he is called Dr. Priber. All contemporary accounts agree (however widely they differ on other points) that he was a man of parts, "conversant with most of the arts and sciences" and "adorned with every qualification that constitutes a gentleman." See V. W. Crane, "A Lost Utopia of the First American Frontier," *Sewanee Rev.*, XXVII, i (Jan., 1919), 48–61.

152. Described by General James Oglethorpe as "a very extraordinary Kind of a Creature," speaking "almost all languages fluently, particularly English, Dutch, French, Latin and Indian," Priber lived among the Indians, adopting their customs even to trimming his hair in Indian fashion and painting himself "as they did, going generally almost naked except a shirt & a Flap."

153. Equally bad was "a Book . . . of his own Writing ready for the Press, which . . . lays down the Rules of Government which the town is to be governed by; to which he gives the Title of Paradise; He enumerates many whimsical Privileges and natural Rights, as he calls them, which his Citizens are entitled to, particularly dissolving Marriages and allowing community of Women, and all kinds of Licentiousness; the Book is drawn up very methodically, and full of learned Quotations; it is extreamly wicked, yet has several Flights full of invention; and it is a Pity so much Wit is applied to so bad Purposes." This manuscript and that of a dictionary of the Cherokee language seem irretrievably lost. See V. W. Crane, *loc. cit.*, pp. 57–61.

154. *The History of South Carolina* (4 vols., N.Y., 1934), I, 351.

155. Louis Viereck accords this honor to Saur. See "German Instruction in American Schools," *Report of the Commissioner of Education for the Year 1900–1901* (Washington, D.C., 1902), I, 542.

156. Attention to this visit was first called by B. A. Hinsdale, "Notes on the History of Foreign Influence upon Education in the United States," *Report of the Commissioner of Education, 1897–1898* (Washington, D.C., 1899), I, 604–7. See also J. G. Rosengarten, "American History from German Archives with Reference to German Soldiers in the Revolution and Franklin's Visit to Germany," *Proc. & Add., Pa. German Soc.*, XIII (1902), 50–68. An interesting conversation with Franklin is recorded by Dr. Gottfried Achenwall of Göttingen in *Einige Anmerkungen über Nordamerika . . . aus mündlichen Nachrichten des Hrn. Dr. Franklins* (Hanover, 1768).

157. The same periodical reported, on Sep-

tember 27, 1766, that Pringle and Franklin visited Mr. Hartmann in Hanover, in order to see his apparatus for electrical experiments (see B. A. Hinsdale, *loc. cit.*, p. 605). In 1796 Joseph Willard, President of Harvard, was elected to membership to succeed Franklin.—Willard's *Memories of Youth and Mankind* (2 vols., Cambridge, Mass., 1855), I, 147.

158. *Selbstbiographie* (2 vols., Göttingen, 1798), I, 490–91.

159. Episcopal, Presbyterian, Lutheran, German Calvinist, Baptist, and Roman Catholic.— Geo. B. Wood, "The History of the University of Pennsylvania . . . to 1827," *Memoirs of the Pa. Hist. Soc.*, III, i (1834), 219.

160. Kunze (1744–1807) had established a German school in imitation of the Klosterburg seminary as early as 1773, with himself and a Mr. Lips, an experienced teacher from Halle, as the faculty. He appears to have encountered little trouble finding the necessary 24 subscribers, each contributing ten pounds. The sons of subscribers received free tuition; others paid. Three classes were formed, and thus was introduced, under the title of "German Seminary," the first school devoted to German instruction. This seminary must be recognized as another direct influence of Francke's Pedagogical Institute at Halle.—Carl F. Haussmann, *Kunze's Seminarium . . .* Americana Germanica Monograph ser., No. 27 (Philadelphia, 1917).

Kunze, as an influential member of the German Society (founded in 1764 for the protection of German immigrants) urged that body to found a German library and to provide the means for the instruction of poor children in both English and German. Those who excelled were to proceed to the University.

161. Viereck and Hinsdale are our authorities for the assertion that this event inspired Benjamin Smith Barton, a native of Lancaster (a student in the University of Pennsylvania at the time) to go to Göttingen, where he took the degree of doctor of medicine in 1789. He is said to be the first Anglo-American student to receive a degree from a German university. Barton became a prominent physician in Philadelphia, wrote a number of scientific papers and books, and in 1813 succeeded Benjamin Rush as professor of medicine at the University of Pennsylvania.

Another Anglo-American who early studied at a German university was a young man named White, who studied mathematics at Göttingen during the winter semester of 1782–1783; but nothing more is known about him, and it seems unlikely that he received a degree. See Daniel B. Shumway, "The American Students of the University of Göttingen," *German-American*

Annals, XII, v–vi (Sept.–Dec., 1910), 172–254, esp. pp. 172–73.

162. To be sure, the principles of political liberalism from Luther through Althusius to Pufendorf were not forgotten by the more learned type of man like Samuel Mather, who took an active part in the pre-Revolutionary agitation, or like Thomas Jefferson, who freely acknowledged his debt to Pufendorf both during and after the war. A study like Alice M. Baldwin's *New England Clergy and the American Revolution* (Durham, N.C., 1928) accentuates the fact that the Congregational clergy played a very prominent role in preparing the field for the harvest which men like Paine and Jefferson were to reap, and that in the process they drew upon many authorities, including German exponents of natural rights and other revolutionary principles. However, once the agitation reached the stage of harangue and pamphlet the turbulence of the times left little opportunity for consulting any but the more immediate authorities. Propaganda was conducted by men of the readier sort like Paine, for whom revolutionary doctrine as it had been promulgated in France and as it had developed slowly in England since the days of Locke was authority enough. Kant, Fichte, Schelling, and Hegel had not yet advanced their philosophies; and if they had, they could hardly have served the rough and ready purposes of the eighteenth-century revolutionists. They were to have their day in the next century when Americans put them to use in quite another way.

163. The extraordinary vogue and influence which Pufendorf attained in eighteenth-century America was doubtless owing partly to the fact that four of his principal works had become available in English translation by 1700. See B. Q. Morgan, *op. cit.*, p. 383. For indications of the widespread use of Pufendorf in American colleges during the eighteenth century see Anna Haddow, *Political Science in American Colleges and Universities 1639–1900* (N.Y., 1939) pp. 11–14, 26–28.

164. T. H. Johnson, *loc. cit.*, p. 211, and F. H. Foster, *A Genetic History of New England Theology* (Chicago, 1907), p. 48.

165. Herbert and Carol Schneider, *Samuel Johnson* . . . (4 vols., N.Y., 1929), I, 495–526: "Catalog of Books Read by Samuel Johnson from 1719 to 1756." This list includes numerous references to his reading of German works from the Nürnberg *Miscellanea Curiosa* about 1719 to Rimius' *Narrative of the Moravians* in 1754.

166. The title appears frequently in colonial inventories and book lists, and several copies survive. One, in the American Antiquarian Society, once belonged to William Bentley,

prominent in the promotion of German-American relations about 1780–1820.

167. Both editions contained—besides the formal grammar—reading selections, such as German proverbs, excerpts from newspapers, "deutsche moralische Stücke," and five of Gellert's fables in verse.

168. Also listed are travel books, memoirs, and letters, including Baron Bielefield's *Letters*, Frederick the Great's *Memoirs of the House of Brandenburg*, the Herrnhuter David Crantz's *History of Greenland*, Engelbrecht Kaempfer's *History of Japan and Siam*, Johann Georg Keysler's (also Keyssler) *Travels through Germany*, Stralenburg's *Description of Russia*, and an *Account of Switzerland*.

169. One of the earliest books of this class was Charles Burney's *The Recent State of Music in Germany, the Netherlands, and the United Provinces; or, the Journal of a Tour through those Countries, Undertaken to Collect Materials for a General History of Music* (London, 1773). Far from being only a collection of musical data, the section of this book that is devoted to Germany contains also much information about the state of literature in Germany before the period of *Sturm und Drang*, and accounts of Burney's meetings with German writers and musicians.

One of the most popular books of the type in both England and America was Baron Johann Kaspar Riesbeck's *Briefe eines reisenden Franzosen über Deutschland* (1780), translated into English in 1787, and often reprinted. From it many Americans, among them W. Irving and C. B. Brown, derived their first idea of some of the more eminent German figures in literature, the arts, and scholarship; while people like William Bentley, who were already initiated, supplemented their store of information from this source.

Finally, William Coxe's *Travels in Switzerland* (1789) was timed just right to promote the vogue of Gessner, Haller, Lavater, and other Swiss writers; and Count Frederick Stolberg's *Travels in Germany* (1796–1797) helped to accentuate the movement already fairly begun.—Jantz, *loc. cit.*, p. 28.

170. Fred. H. Wilkens, "Early Influence of German Literature in America," *Americana Germanica*, III, ii (1901), 8–10; Goodnight., *op. cit.* p. 23, and Goodnight's List A.

171. F. H. Wilkens, *loc. cit.*, pp. 48–49, 66–68, 84.

172. Goodnight, *op. cit.*, pp. 26–27.

173. *Ibid.*, p. 30, and Wilkens, *loc. cit.*, p. 104. Zimmermann's *Strictures on National Pride* (*Vom Nationalstolze*) was printed in Philadelphia as early as 1778.

174. For details, titles, dates, and the vogue of these vapid fictional effusions, see Wilkens, *loc. cit.*, pp. 39–42, and Morgan's bibliography.

175. For particulars, see Wilkens, *loc. cit.*, pp. 36–42, and Haney, *loc. cit.*, pp. 144–45.

176. Wilkens, *loc. cit.*, pp. 37–38; Goodnight, *op. cit.*, pp. 29–30; Morgan's bibliography.

177. Several of the titles in the following partial list from Dabney's *Additional Catalog* (Salem, 1794) reveal the type of subliterary books that had come into vogue: *Baron of Manstow; Castle of Wolfenbach; Christiana, Princess of Swabia; Memoirs of Count Cronstadt; The Female Werther; The German Gil Blas, or the Adventures of Peter Claus; History of Count Gleichen; Letters of Albert to Charlotte; Popular Tales of the Germans; Radizal, a Novel; Rosenberg, a Legendary Tale.*—Jantz, *loc. cit.*, pp. 29–30.

Other books that fed the same taste and that achieved a good deal of notoriety were John Robison's anti-Illuminati tract, entitled *Proofs of a Conspiracy* (1795); Christine Benedikte Naubert's *Hermann und Unna,* translated as *Hermann and Unna: A Series of Adventures of the Fifteenth Century in which the Proceedings of the Secret Tribunal, under the Emperors Winceslaus and Sigismund, Are Delineated* (Dublin and London, 1794; London, 1796); Schiller's *Geisterseher,* translated by David Boileau, appearing in London in 1795, twice in America (N.Y. and Charleston) in 1796, and in a new translation by William Render (N.Y.) in 1800, and again in 1801; Cajetan Tschink's *Geisterseher,* translated by Peter Will as *The Victim of Magical Delusion* (London, 1795; republished in N.Y., 1796–1797); Karl Friedrich Kahlert's *Der Geisterbanner,* tr. by Peter Teuthold as *The Necromancer; or a Tale of the Black Forest* (London, 1794); Karlos Grosse's *Der Dolch,* translated as *The Dagger* (London, 1795); Grosse's *Der Genius,* translated by James Trapp as *The Genius; or the Mysterious Adventure of Don Carlos de Grandez* (London, 1796), and also by Peter Will as *Horrid Mysteries* (London, 1796). See Harry Warfel, "Charles Brockden Brown's German Sources," *Mod. Lang. Quar.,* I, iii (Sept., 1940), 357–65. The list can be readily extended by searching Morgan's bibliography and by consulting such special studies as Christine Touaillon, *Der deutsche Frauenroman des 18. Jahrhunderts* (Wien and Leipzig, 1919); Marianne Thalmann, *Der Trivialroman des 18. Jahrhunderts und der romantische Roman. Ein Beitrag zur Entwicklungsgeschichte der Geheimbundmystik* (Berlin, 1923); and Agnes G. Murphy, *Banditry, Chivalry, and Terror in German Fiction, 1790–1831* (Chicago, 1935), as well as such

works as Edith Birkhead's *The Tale of Terror* (London, 1921).

178. See Wilkens, *loc. cit.*, pp. 10–36, and below.

179 See B. Q. Morgan's judgments, *op. cit.*, Nos. 83, 5093, 5280, etc.

180. Among his more important translations are the following: Cajetan Tschink's *Victim of Magical Delusion* (3 vols., London, 1795); Lavater's *Secret Journal of a Self-Observer* (London, 1795); Karl Grosse's *Horrid Mysteries* (4 vols., London, 1796); Kotzebue's *Sufferings of the Family of Ortenberg: a Novel* (3 vols., 1799; 2 vols., Dublin, 1799; 2 vols. in 1, Phila., 1800); Kotzebue's *Constant Lover; or, William and Jeanette: a Tale* (2 vols., London, 1799; Boston, 1799, and again in 1801); Adolf Knigge's *Practical Philosophy of Social Life* (2 vols., London, 1799; N.Y., 1805); Lafontaine's *Romulus* (2 vols., London, 1799; Baltimore, 1814); Johann A. Leisewitz' *Julius of Tarentum: a Tragedy* (London, 1800); Lavater's *Pastor's Legacy: Devotional Fragments from Lavater; or On the Nature, Excellency, and Necessity of Faith* (London, 1805); Ernst Arndt's *Spirit of the Times* (London, 1808); E. T. A. Hoffmann's *The Entail (Das Majorat;* Heidelberg, 1829); Aloys Schreiber's *Complete Guide on a Voyage on the Rhine . . . on the Moselle . . .* (Heidelberg, 1835); and Schreiber's *Traditions of the Countries of the Rhine* (Heidelberg, 1836).

181. *Old New York: or Reminiscences of the Past Sixty Years* (N.Y., 1858), p. 46; see also his reminiscences in the *International Magazine,* V, ii (Feb. 1, 1852), 253–66, esp. p. 261. According to Francis, Will returned during 1799 to London and published there, before the year was out, his translation of Knigge's *Practical Philosophy.* The facts seem to be that Will remained in London throughout 1799 and 1800, busy with his duties as "Minister of the German Reformed Church in the Savoy," as translator of the volumes listed above, and as the active collaborator with Constantin Geisweiler in editing a periodical called *The German Museum.* No doubt its demise in 1801 was one of the circumstances that led him to go to America later in the same year or early in 1802. At all events, during 1802–1803, the Rev. Samuel Miller spoke of him as "lately of London, at present minister of the German Calvinist Church in the city of New York." See Miller's *Brief Retrospect of the Eighteenth Century* (2 vols., N.Y., 1803), II, 271, note x. Will is also listed in the "Chronological List of Ministers" under the date of 1802 in Ed. T. Corwin, *A Manual of the Reformed Church in America* (3rd. ed., N.Y., 1879), p. 659. A few other biographical facts are supplied in H. E. Scriba, *Biographisch-litera-*

risches Lexicon der Schriftsteller des Grossherzog-thums Hessen . . . (Darmstadt, 1843), but the identification of Peter Will and virtually all that is known about his many activities is owing to the brilliant detective work of Professor Jantz. See his "Samuel Miller's Survey of German Literature, 1803," *Germanic Rev.*, XVI, iv (Dec., 1941), 268–70.

182. See, for example, Francis Dana Channing's "Brief Review of the Progress of Literature in Germany" (admittedly an abridgment of Will's "Historical Account" that had run in *The German Museum* throughout 1800–1801) in the *Literary Miscellany*, I, i (July, 1804), 26–32; ii (Oct., 1804), 122–30; iii (Jan., 1805), 225–32.

183. Even among the Pennsylvania Germans the worst epithet that one could apply to another was "du verdammter Hess."—Dubois and Schweppe, *op. cit.*, p. 38. However, once the stress of war had subsided, even Hessians came to be viewed tolerantly. Practically all of the Hessian soldiers who had been captured and many others who had been left in the colonies at the close of the war settled in the midst of the American populace, intermarried, and found a place among the American people without any marked friction.

184. Goodnight, *op. cit.*, pp. 18–19.

185. Piqued at Frederick's turning down Franklin's request for aid in the colonial struggle for independence on the ground that he had been born a king and that he would not employ his power to spoil the trade, Franklin wrote two satires on the German monarch, but these were aimed more at England than Germany, and obviously did not irreparably damage Frederick's reputation in America.

186. H. W. Fischer, "Frederick the Great, America's Friend," *Amer.-Ger. Rev.*, I (1898), 7.

187. Steuben's signal service as Washington's inspector-general and drill master is well known. Consult the *Bibliography* for the numerous books and articles appraising his part in the Revolution. It is interesting to note that already before the war, Americans had formed a very high opinion of the military tactics of Frederick and his officers. As early as 1768, Samuel Corwin mentions the "King of Prussia's Rules of Infantry" as authoritative. Steuben's own *Regulations for the Order and Discipline of the Troops of the United States* (1794, 1802) became, and long remained, the official manual of the U.S. armies.

188. New York especially attracted, during the seventeenth and even more during the eighteenth century, merchants of wealth and social distinction from the old commercial cities of Germany—among them the heads of the Van der Beeck, Santford, Ebbing, Leisler,

Schrick, and Meyer families. The prosperous merchant Augustin Hermann, the ship surgeon and colonial physician Hans Kierstede of Magdeburg, and the importer Joachim Peter Kuyter of Dithmarschen are others whose activities merit minute investigation. Their work as international intermediaries was carried on at the turn of the century by individuals like Matthias Müller, Jeremiah Kähler, and the Crowninshields. See Lohr, *The First Germans in North America and the German Settlement in New Netherlands* (N.Y., 1912), p. 13. Emil Meynen's *Bibliography of German Settlements in Colonial America* . . . provides numerous suggestions for the researcher in this field. Professor Jantz has called my attention to John Olaf Evjen's *Scandinavian Immigrants in New York, 1630–1674* (Minneapolis, 1916) as supplying a number of leads. The entire area of investigation, especially as it involves early travelers, traders, and merchants, remains almost unexplored except for the fruitful work of Mr. Jantz.

189. *Oberon: A Poetical Romance in Twelve Books*, tr. from the German of Wieland by John Quincy Adams; ed. with Intro. and Notes by A. B. Faust (N.Y., 1940). I have endeavored to appraise its significance in a review in *Mod. Lang. Notes*, LVI, iii (Mar., 1941), 225–27.

190. While John Adams' library contained many German literary titles, among them the works of Lessing, Wieland, Herder, Kotzebue, Goethe, and Schiller, he owned few books of German philosophy. However, his son, John Quincy Adams (1767–1848) acquired a number of philosophical works, among them the Riga edition of Kant's *Kritik der reinen Vernunft*. What particular role the Adams letters and books played in the adventures of younger Americans in the realm of German literature and thought remains to be investigated.

191. *The Autobiography, Reminiscences, and Letters of John Trumbull* (New Haven, 1841) contains several lithographic reproductions of these sketches. For the journals of the German tours, see pp. 120–40, 179–82, 219–22.

192. William Bentley, *Diary* (4 vols., Salem, 1905–1914), I, 47; Jantz, *loc. cit.*, pp. 30–31.

193. Both Bentley and Ebeling have been subjects of investigation, but neither of them was examined for his importance in furthering German-American cultural contacts until Dr. Jantz undertook the study and prepared for the Anglo-German Group of the Modern Language Association, in December, 1939, a brief report (extended and published in *JEGP* for January, 1942) summarizing the results of his preliminary investigation of the Ebeling-Bentley materials deposited in the American Antiquarian Society and the Massachusetts Historical

Society, supplemented by the printed diary of Bentley and the published correspondence of Ebeling. The bulk of Ebeling's letters has been published in *Proc. Amer. Antiq. Soc.* for 1925; lesser portions appear in *Proc. Mass. Hist. Soc.* for 1826 and the *Coll. Mass. Hist.* for 1891.

194. In addition to general and statistical information on physical America, events in American history, and translations of various political, descriptive, and statistical pamphlets relating to America, he reproduced such choice items as Washington's diary of 1753, the Articles of Confederation, and the parts of Thomas Paine's *Common Sense* that had previously been suppressed in Germany.

195. The last volume was dedicated to William Bentley, Samuel Miller, Samuel Latham Mitchell, and Henry St. George Tucker. The contents of the seven volumes completed are: I. New Hampshire, Massachusetts, 1783 (2nd ed., increased from 1135 to 1519 pages, 1800); II. Rhode Island, Connecticut, Vermont, New York, 1794; III. New York, New Jersey, 1796; IV. Pennsylvania, 1797; V. Delaware, Maryland, 1799; VI. Pennsylvania (enlarged), 1803; VII. Virginia, 1816. Ebeling's manuscripts and partially completed accounts of other states and of the new western territories came to Harvard along with his collection of books and maps in 1818, but are no longer to be found. No more of Ebeling's manuscripts were published, though Edward Everett had, at the time of the purchase, pledged Harvard College to the obligation of continuing the publication of Ebeling's geography.—Jantz, *loc. cit.*, p. 32.

Among Ebeling's other works was his publication, during 1795–1797, of the *Amerikanisches Magazin*, by which he sought to carry on the work, already initiated in the *Amerikanische Bibliothek* two decades earlier, of instructing his countrymen about America. The periodical printed what is probably the first account made available to German readers of American literature, together with sketches of prominent German-Americans like General von Steuben and articles by others, such as H. E. Mühlenberg, as well as reviews, translations, and summaries of American books, scientific and literary. He also published ten volumes of *Neue Sammlung von Reisebeschreibungen* (Hamburg, 1780–1790).

196. Besides those already mentioned, Ebeling maintained contacts with Jeremy Belknap, Joel Barlow, Secretary of State Timothy Pickering, Thomas Jefferson, Noah Webster, Mathew Carey, John Ormond, Dr. Benjamin Smith Barton, David Ramsey, Jedidiah Morse ("The American Geographer" of Charlestown, Mass.), Jacob Crowninshield (the merchant-prince of Salem, who declined Jefferson's appointment as Secretary of the Navy), Isaiah Thomas (founder of the American Antiquarian Society), President Timothy Dwight of Yale, General John Fiske, Joseph Story, Samuel Miller, Dr. Samuel Latham Mitchell, Judge Henry St. George Tucker, Bishop James Madison (President of William and Mary College), Charles Gheguiere of Baltimore, Dr. H. E. Mühlenberg (the theologian and botanist), President Joseph Willard and Professor Joseph McKean of Harvard, and the Rev. John Eliot (corresponding secretary of the Massachusetts Historical Society, 1799–1810), and his successor, Abiel Holmes, and most important of all, the Rev. William Bentley of Salem.

197. The earlier numbers of the *North American Review* contain numerous references to Ebeling, and No. 22, dated December, 1818, recounts gleefully the story of how a Yankee had carried off the prized library before King Frederick III. of Prussia. It may well be that Goethe heard of this transaction, and that this circumstance, coupled with the pleasant relations which the young Harvard men established with him through their visitations, led him to present a twenty-volume set of his works to the Harvard library.

198. See *Proc. Amer. Antiq. Soc.*, n.s., XXXV (Oct., 1925), 286, 408, 417–19; Bentley's *Diary*, IV, 91. Ebeling dedicated the first volume of his geographical history of America to Sieveking.

199. *Proc. Amer. Antiq. Soc.*, n.s., XXXV (Oct., 1925), 291, 428.

200. While Bentley occasionally complained of "a great sense of duty in providing Books in return for his [Ebeling's] donation," he attended conscientiously to Ebeling's wants. See Bentley's *Diary*, II, 194, and *Proc. Amer. Antiq. Soc.*, n.s., XXXV (Oct., 1925), 377–78. The exchange of books between Ebeling and Bentley must have been well in excess of a thousand volumes, on either side.

201. This practice he kept up from June 6, 1795, when he sent Bentley a "box of books and maps," at the same time that he promised to "gather and send more German books on American history," and offered "to sell copies of Belknap's books in Germany," to May 22, 1815, when he dispatched three boxes of books to Bentley, containing 44 titles (146 volumes) of German theological, philosophical, historical, scientific, and literary works. On January 3, 1817, followed 22 additional volumes, and on May 12, he sent 12 more.—*Proc. Amer. Antiq. Soc.*, n.s., XXXV (Oct., 1925), 288, 419–22, 434, 435, 441–42.

On intimate terms with many of the greater German literary figures of his time, notably with those of Hamburg, Ebeling was in a favored position to report to his American friends on Lessing, Voss, Matthias Claudius, the Stolbergs, the Reimaruses (father and son), and Klopstock. Among university men, he knew best those of Göttingen—Blumenbach, Heeren, Benecke, Schlözer, and Eichhorn among others —and he did much to call to the attention of Americans the Göttingen scholars among whom he was best known. He actively concerned himself about the welfare of American students at Göttingen, and Ticknor, Everett, Cogswell, and Thorndike acknowledged their debt to him and paid him visits at Hamburg. Besides supplying the university library with important new books on America, he wrote a number of reviews for such works as the *Göttingische gelehrte Anzeigen*. In 1797 he began to send to his American correspondents, notably Bentley, the chief German periodicals, such as the literary gazette of Gotha. On March 28, 1799, he sent the *Jenaische allgemeine Literatur Zeitung* for 1791–1797, and by 1805 he was sending not only current numbers but back volumes of the *Göttingische gelehrte Anzeigen*, *Berlinische Monatsschrift*, *Neue allgemeine Bibliothek*, and hundreds of individual numbers or volumes of lesser German periodicals.

Not much interested in metaphysics, and not at all in the new Kantian speculative philosophy, Ebeling nevertheless several times reported on Kant and his followers, usually depreciatingly as being obscure, "scholastical," or paradoxical. He never relinquished his dislike of the *Jenaische allgemeine Literatur Zeitung* for its championship of the transcendental philosophy. When, on August 1, 1810, he sent additional numbers of the periodical to Bentley, he added, "[It] has a few fellow authors of the first rank as Voss, late Mr Muller, Wolf, Goethe, but is the seat of faction in Poetry [and in] Philosophy adheres blindly to the Natural philosophy of Schelling and Fichte, which is entirely metaphysical fancied stuff." This objection to the alleged skeptical cast of Fichte's and Schelling's philosophies is the same so often voiced later by American watchdogs of orthodoxy, and quite possibly some part of American suspicion may be related to this earliest representation under which German critical transcendentalism was introduced into America.

202. Bentley's *Diary*, I, ix, xx, xviii, 43; J. T. Buckingham, *Specimens of Newspaper Literature* (2 vols., Boston, 1850), I, 336, 342–44.

Basing his estimates on the prices paid at the auction of Buckminster's books in 1812, Dr. Eliot valued Bentley's library at $6,000.— *Diary*, IV, 112. Unfortunately, near the time of his death, Bentley became piqued at the failure of Harvard to acknowledge his scholarship, revoked an earlier will by which Harvard would have become the sole recipient of his books, manuscripts, maps, and periodicals, and gave his classical and theological library instead to Allegheny College, Meadville, Pa., where it was soon dissipated. His German, Persian, Arabic, and Chinese books and 56 manuscripts of varying length went to the American Antiquarian Society. Subsequently Harvard acquired fragments of Bentley's collection, which she might have had intact had she acted a few months earlier in her belated bestowal of the degree of Doctor of Divinity upon her learned son.

203. His most ambitious historical undertakings, including an exhaustive history of Salem, on which he worked for years, remained unpublished at his death. The exception is the first installment of his history of Salem, which was published in the *Coll. of the Mass. Hist. Soc.*, VI (1799), 221–88.

204. Sometime before 1785, when he started his catalog and book accounts, he acquired a small stock of German books, moral weeklies, devotional works, and miscellaneous items from a German family named Helms, of whom little is known except that when they moved to Salem, they brought a considerable library with them.—Jantz, *loc. cit.*, pp. 30, 35–36.

205. Bentley picked up German lore and German books whenever he had the opportunity. Even Salem was not entirely destitute of people who could supply his wants. In 1792, for example, he acquired Rabener's *Satyren* (4 vols., Vienna, 1765) from a Mrs. Heymel, evidently a German resident of Salem. Another well-known German in Salem at this time was George Heussler, a landscape gardener, seed merchant, and exporter, whose friendship Bentley cultivated. His friend General John Fiske, when he returned from his travels in Germany, brought him a seven-volume work on German commerce and law. In 1794 William Priestley, son of the famous Joseph Priestley, with whom Bentley corresponded, twice visited him in Salem and gave him a handsome edition of Gessner's *Werke*. In the same year Bentley took eight lessons at nine shillings each in German pronunciation from Frederic Jordy, a Rhinelander, who had come to Salem in 1792, and who taught both French and German. In the same year, too, Bentley began negotiations that led to the Ebeling-Bentley correspondence. In June, 1794, Ebeling had sent Jeremy Belknap the first volume of his geographical history of America, which Bentley borrowed. Then, in quick succession, Captain Allen brought him a copy from Germany, and the famous mer-

chant Elias Heskett Derby gave him another. By June 28, 1795, Ebeling himself forwarded a copy of the second volume of the work, and thereafter the correspondence was fairly launched.

Among Bentley's many friends was the Crowninshield family, notably Jacob, one of the younger and ablest of the Crowninshields, who received most of his education informally from Bentley, and who later brought him numerous objects from foreign lands for his museum of natural history, as well as books for his library. For Jacob and his brother Benjamin, Bentley traced their German ancestry back to Dr. Johann Kaspar Richter von Kronenscheldt, a German physician who settled in Salem a century earlier; and they reciprocated, Jacob as we have seen, and Benjamin, while Secretary of the Navy, by sending Bentley copies of important state papers from Washington for transmission to Ebeling. Bentley also prepared several of the younger Crowninshields for college, and in the case of one, at least, included in his instruction a thorough introduction to the history and literature of Germany.—Jantz, *loc. cit.*, pp. 36–37; *Diary*, II, 74, 200; III, 13; IV, 435.

206. *Diary*, I, 66, 333, 340.

207. These newspapers, which came in 1818 to the Harvard College Library, by the purchase of Israel Thorndike, form one of the most valuable adjuncts of the Harvard collection of periodicals.

208. *Dawson's Historical Mag.*, 3rd ser., II (Oct., 1873), 249. John Adams' equally high opinion is quoted in Bentley's *Diary*, I, xviii. See also J. T. Buckingham, *op. cit.*, II, 341–50.

209. Printed in 1803 by another of Bentley's friends, Isaiah Thomas of Worcester. Thomas also printed a *Faust* book in 1795. As his own work on the *History of Printing* progressed, Thomas became more and more interested in German literature; and his careful investigation, then and later, of Pennsylvania-German printers and imprints formed an important contribution to German-American studies. Ebeling, for his part, appraised Thomas' *History* as "very valuable and learned," and forthwith began an exchange of letters, information, and gifts with him.—*Proc. Amer. Antiq. Soc.*, n.s., XXXV (Oct., 1925), 426, 430.

210. These details, derived from the MS materials in the American Antiquarian Society, are communicated to me by Professor Jantz. See also Jantz, *loc. cit.*, p. 39.

211. For a history of this ferment, see Vernon Stauffer, *New England and the Bavarian Illuminati* (N.Y., 1918).

212. *Proc. Amer. Antiq. Soc.*, n.s., XXXV

(Oct., 1925), 311. The entire letter is reproduced, *ibid.*, pp. 307–34.

213. Professor Jantz, after examining Bentley's catalogs and book accounts, as well as the remnants of his library, concludes that Bentley had by 1805 some 250 volumes in German, and by 1819 over 1,000.

214. Long profoundly interested in advancing music, vocal and instrumental, in and out of church, he organized several "Singing Schools." He became one of the most ardent advocates in New England for the introduction of German music, and co-operated with the German Hans Gram, the Dutchman P. A. von Hagen, and later with Gottlieb Graupner in furthering the cause. Out of the singing schools grew the Salem Handel and Haydn society, the earliest beginnings of which go back to about 1809, although it did not become really flourishing before 1817.

An interesting circumstance is that von Hagen changed his name from *van* to *von* when he came to America, in order to enhance his prestige as a musician—a change which all the more underscores German musical leadership in America even during the opening years of the nineteenth century.

215. Bentley's nephew, William Bentley Fowle, carried on his uncle's interests, particularly in education, and formed a direct link to connect Horace Mann with this earlier tradition.

216. Buckminster is reputed to have returned with some 3,000 volumes, of which it may be presumed a considerable portion was German. When Bentley inspected his library in 1809, he called it "elegant."—*Diary*, III, 458; Jantz, *loc. cit.*, p. 42.

217. *Sermons of the Late Rev. J. S. Buckminster* (Boston, 1814), "Memoir," p. xxx. Buckminster's sister Eliza later achieved distinction as a translator and biographer of Jean Paul.

218. See *Anthology Society. Journal of the Proceedings of the Society which Conducts the Monthly Anthology & Boston Review, Oct. 3, 1804, to July 2, 1811*, with an introduction by M. A. DeWolfe Howe, Boston, 1910.

219. It is clear that during the eighteenth century a knowledge of German, while still rare, was far from nonexistent in America. John Quincy Adams, William Bentley, William Jenks, Benjamin Barton Smith, the Vaughan brothers, and James Winthrop—all in the *Dictionary of American Biography*—attained a mastery of the language before 1800. Many more prominent men had a fair knowledge of German—among them John Adams, Joel Barlow, Jacob Crowninshield, John Eliot, John Trumbull, Samuel Williams, and, slightly later, J. S.

Buckminster, Andrews Norton, Samuel C. Thatcher, Sidney Willard, Alexander Everett, George Ticknor, and the Harvard-Göttingen group.

220. Harry R. Warfel, *Noah Webster* (N.Y., 1936), pp. 348, 350, 358, 360.

221. *Proc. Amer. Antiq. Soc.*, n.s., XXXV (Oct., 1925), 424, 426–28, 439, 443–44, 446–50; Peabody, Andrew, *Harvard Reminiscences* (Boston, 1888), pp. 92–93; Jantz, *loc. cit.*, pp. 43–45.

THOUGHT CURRENTS OF THE NINETEENTH CENTURY

THE GROWTH OF INTEREST IN GERMANY

1. Before the Revolutionary War there had been only nine institutions of collegiate rank. By 1800 there were nineteen—still a relatively small number when compared with 181 in existence at the outbreak of the Civil War, but already there were signs of a desire to break through traditional conformity and uniformity of doctrine. See G. P. Schmidt, "Intellectual Cross-Currents in American Colleges," *Amer. Hist. Rev.*, XLII, ii (Oct., 1936), 46; G. S. Hall, "On the History of American College Textbooks and Teaching . . .," *Proc. Amer. Antiq. Soc.*, n.s., IX (1894), 138.

2. I, vii, Preface. Miller was active in many directions. About 1799 and later he was intimate with Charles Brockden Brown, then associated with the *Monthly Magazine and American Review*. Something of Miller's associations with Brown's coterie can be reconstructed from unpublished correspondence with his old friend, the Rev. John Eliot of Boston. The Miller Papers are in the New York Historical Society, and the Eliot letters are in the Massachusetts Historical Society, where Professor Jantz (to whom I am indebted for this information) has examined them. See Jantz, "Samuel Miller's Survey of German Literature, 1803," *Germanic Rev.*, XVI, iv (Dec., 1941), 267–77, esp. p. 270. Miller was of special service to Ebeling in supplying him with information for his seven-volume history of the United States, and Ebeling reciprocated by sending materials for Miller's projected history of New York. Miller's later activities as a prolific author on a broad range of subjects besides history and biography, his professorship of church history in the Princeton Theological Seminary (of which he was the founder), his corresponding membership of numerous historical societies, his founding and presidency of the New York Bible Society, his trusteeship of Columbia College and of the College of New Jersey, and his authorship of *The Life of Jonathan Edwards* (1837) are suggestive of the position he occupied in the intellectual life of the nation before 1850.

3. See his prefatory statement (I, xii, and II, 22–23, 26, and note). Miller's strictures are based chiefly on an article in the London

Monthly Review for January, 1799, by William Taylor, which reviews A. F. M. Willich's *Elements of Critical Philosophy* . . . (London, 1798), itself based largely upon Johann C. Adelung's summary *Geschichte der Philosophie* . . . (Leipzig, 1787–1788) and F. A. Nitsch's superficial *General View of Professor Kant's Principles* . . . (London, 1796).

Another account of Kant, as early as Miller's though far less extended, was the notice of the "Critical Philosophy" by an anonymous "Illustrious Frenchman" which appeared in the third volume of the Supplement to the American reprint of the *Encyclopaedia Britannica* (Phila., 1803). But the unsympathetic nature of the article, together with the severely critical comments of the Scottish editor, Dr. George Gleig, vitiated whatever value such an essay in a cyclopedia might have had by way of informing the American reader on German thought.

4. II, ii, 23, 26.

5. II, 24–26, 27–28. Lossius, Tetans, Feder, Kruger, Mendelsshom (*sic*), Fuhte (a typographical error for Fichte), Born, Beck, Mellin, Eberhard, Tiedemann, and Maas are listed as other zealous participants, pro and con, in the controversy provoked by the Kantian system (II, 452). Among other German philosophers, Leibnitz is accorded the most space and praise, though Wolff is also prominently mentioned (II, 14–17, 19).

6. Only those who receive more than cursory attention are counted in these figures.

7. This is not to imply that Miller brought to his task any profound firsthand knowledge of German literature (though he had some), but rather that he used numerous sources of information. Indeed, one of the particular features of the *Retrospect* for that day is that it contained numerous citations and references, in footnotes and appendices, to sources (many of them German sources), thus supplying American readers with what amounted virtually to a bibliography of references pertaining to German scholarship, literature, philosophy, and science. The degree to which this bibliographical information was used by readers can be surmised from the indication that we have of how carefully men like William Bentley of Salem and Joseph Buckminster of Boston worked through their copies of the two-volume work

for these hints that might lead to the opening up of new areas and an extension of knowledge in others already more or less familiar to them. Miller's broad survey was all the more effective because German achievements were set against the background of all other European as well as American accomplishments, thus providing the reader with a perspective which made comparisons inevitable and prompted the conclusion that Germany had undergone a "literary" awakening which merited more than passing attention.

Besides the shortcomings already mentioned, Miller's book exhibits others of the faults common to critical writing of the day—a certain critical superficiality, an erudite, rhetorical style, a certain smugness in passing off-hand moral judgments, and a degree of derivativeness. But as Dr. Jantz has observed, Miller shows also in a marked degree the "strong, active, youthful characteristics of a progressiveness, earnest curiosity, and eagerness to acquire all that is newest and best in the world." It is to be remarked that Miller was barely thirty when he began the book and only thirty-three when the two volumes were published in 1803.

8. Including the cultivation of the language by Luther for literary purposes, its progressive replacement of Latin for meritorious work, and the development of taste in belles-lettres in place of the tedious, pedantic compilations of earlier periods. He mentions as pioneers in this work Thomasius, Leibnitz, Wolff, Dunkelberg, Mosheim, Gottsched, Adelung, Schlegel, and others, especially emphasizing the effects which Gottsched's labors and philological controversies with Bodmer and Breitinger had in this respect, and not neglecting the contributions of such writers as Haller, Gessner, Gellert, Wieland, Lessing, Herder, Goethe, and Schiller. Three epochs are delineated by which German has become "one of the most copious, energetic, and fashionable languages in Europe" (II, 111–12, 317–19).

9. II, 56–57, 60, 64–70, 324–25. Reinke the Michaelises, Eichhorn, Reimarus, Ludolf, Hezel, Schroeder, Wohl, Hirt, Tychsen, Paulus, and Haase are enumerated, and the appointment in 1779 of the Rev. Dr. Kunze to the professorship of oriental languages at the University of Pennsylvania and in 1784 to a similar post at Columbia University is mentioned as evidence that their work is bearing fruit in America. Several of these orientalists, together with the classical scholars, will be recognized as the group that soon became more than names to the Harvard-Göttingen group and to all young Americans with scholarly ambitions, as well as to the older defenders of the faith of

whatever persuasion from Calvinist to Unitarian.

10. In concluding, Miller tempers this long catalog of praiseworthy accomplishment with a reservation or two; for while Germany "has in several respects pushed her literary progress to a degree hitherto attained by no other nation," thus affording "a striking example of the influence of literature on the national character . . . it may be questioned whether the friend of sound and useful learning can contemplate her literary aspect with unmingled pleasure." For "there is such a thing as an injurious multiplication of books, even when they are all individually harmless; but where a considerable portion of them bear a corrupt character, every increase of their number will give the friend of human happiness a mixture of pain. There is no country on earth (unless, perhaps, we must except France) in which literary enterprise is made the medium for conveying so much moral and theological poison as in Germany" (II, 329–30).

11. Among the most important of these, Miller discusses the significance of Meiner's *Physical History of Man* and Herder's *Outline of a Philosophy of the History of Man*, adding that while he does not know the former, he has read the latter. He devotes a good deal of space to Lavater's *Physiognomy*. Under "History," Brucker's *History of Philosophy* and Winckelmann's *History of the Art of Antiquity* are recommended—both books soon to become well known in America and England through translation (I, 118, 146, 431–34).

In the section on "Romances and Novels," he emphasizes the fecundity of the Germans in producing works in the Gothic strain and singles out Schiller's *Geisterseher* and Peter Will's translation of Tschink's *Geisterseher* (*The Victim of Magical Delusion*, 1795) as of particular import and popularity, however questionable in moral effect. The *Agathon* of Wieland is presented as a classic example of the German novel, and Lessing's critique of it is mentioned; Goethe is rated as second to Wieland in this genre (II, 167, 170–71).

Aside from the more extensive discussion of German poets and poems in the chapter on "Poetry", Haller, Klopstock, Wieland, Voss, Gellert, and Goethe receive separate treatment elsewhere (II, 182–83, 187–88, 189, 195, 198, 479, 481). "The *Faust*, of the celebrated Goethe," says Miller, "occupies a high place in the list of modern satirical writing"—a judgment not to be regarded as odd as it appears to us of a later period who are apt to forget that in 1803 only the published *Fragment* was generally available.

Among descriptive poets Miller singles out for praise particular poems by Kleist, Gessner, Klopstock, Weisse, and Wieland; and among dramatists Goethe and Schiller are similarly treated, while Kotzebue is said to be "so generally known," especially in America, that a discussion of his works is "altogether unnecessary" (II, 202, 204, 206, 220–21, 481).

12. Not as well read in German reference works as Bentley, for instance, Miller nevertheless used to good advantage such works as Adelung's *Grammar of the German Language* and his *Complete Dictionary of the High German Language*, Alsted's *Encyclopedia*, Bielefeld's *Elements of Universal Education*, and Varentrapp and Wenner's *Allgemeine Encyclopedie der Künste und Wissenschaften*. The numerous references to Professor Kunze (II, 8, 13–14, 56, 68, etc.) suggest that he may have derived assistance from Kunze, Professor of Oriental Languages at King's College.

13. The "firsts" to which Miller's *Retrospect* may lay claim are numerous and notable. It incorporates, says Professor Jantz, the first American discussion of the development of the German language to a leading position in Europe; the first extensive treatment of German philosophy, including the first discussion of Kant; the first discussion of certain important works of Haller, Kleist, Lessing, Wieland, Herder, Goethe, Voss, and others (not to mention the numerous scholars of equal fame at that time); the first general discussion of the whole of German intellectual life and literary activity; and finally, the first appraisal of early American-German intellectual contacts.

14. In the meantime he had been appointed, in 1811, to the first lectureship in Biblical criticism at Harvard, in preparation for which he perfected himself in German as a necessary preliminary. He died quite suddenly in 1812, leaving but a few fragments of his research.

15. Considering the intimate friendship that existed between Buckminster and Emerson's father, young Emerson's fondness for Buckminster is not surprising. His father had been, with Buckminster, a founder of the Anthology Club, and from 1804 until his death, he had conducted the *Monthly Anthology*. Young Emerson found in the family library a file of the *Monthly Anthology* and a copy of Buckminster's sermons. We know he prized the latter highly.

16. Bentley's case, since he was a New Yorker, is not parallel, while John Quincy Adams, of course, had no particular interest in theology.

17. See Ticknor's *Life, Letters, and Journals* (2 vols., Boston, 1877), I, 8–12.

18. II, iii (Sept., 1798), 151–53.

19. What is most remarkable about this early essay is its tolerant tone. The author likens Kant's findings to the discovery of Copernicus, who illustrated that "the phenomena of the heavenly bodies did not entitle [us] to attribute to them the various cyclar and epicyclar motions of the Ptolomaic [*sic*] system, that . . . we can be assured of nothing more than the existence of those bodies, and that the different changes in their appearance might as well be explained by supposing a change in our situation as . . . in theirs."

20. *Port Folio*, I (Jan. 10, 1801), 9; also in *Letters of Silesia* (London, 1804), pp. 22–23.

21. The same number of the *Register* contains this remark (doubtless Bentley's): "An able writer in the Chronicle assures us, that the author of the invective to be found in a Boston Newspaper, against German literature, of which he knows nothing, and against German philosophy, which he grossly misrepresents, is the same, that was the tool of a party two years ago, to sound the alarm of an Illuminati." The Boston newspaper referred to has not been identified.

22. In 1804 the *Connecticut Evangelical Magazine* (V, iii, 93–105) printed a twelve-page essay on the "State of Religion on the Continent of Europe," with special reference to Germany and the bearing of German philosophy on theology, and the next year the *Monthly Anthology and Boston Review* (II, xi, 498) noticed the publication of Leibnitz' *Letters* at Hanover; in December, 1806, the Boston *Emerald, or Miscellany of Literature* (I, xxxii, 382) considered a ten-line note on Kant sufficient because he was reported "sinking into oblivion." Meanwhile more and more journals were devoting space to the pietistic works of Lavater, Klopstock, Wieland, Gessner, and to the *Sturm-und-Drang* effusions of Schiller and Goethe, as well as to the sentimentalities of Kotzebue. Considerable journalistic interest centered upon the publication in 1806 at Worcester, by I. Thomas, of Zollikofer's *Twenty-Two Sermons on the Divinity of Man* and, the next year, of his *Exercises of Piety*. In 1808 both the *Monthly Anthology and Boston Review* (V, 397) and the Boston *Panoplist* (IV, 286) reported as an important forthcoming publication a new edition of Zimmermann's *Solitude* (published in New London, Conn., by Thomas and Whipple, in 1808), a pseudo-philosophical work that had attracted attention in America as early as 1791, when J. B. Mercier's translation appeared in London, and that retained its appeal for a half-century (British, French, and American editions; see B. Q. Morgan, *op. cit.*,

pp. 542–44) until the time of Thoreau, who appears to have found inspiration in Zimmermann's meditations of solitude for his experiment at Walden. By 1809 American interest in Germany had assumed proportions sufficient for the *Monthly Anthology and Boston Review* (VI, 358) to hail as a significant event the publication by I. Thomas of Lancaster, Pa., of Hamilton and Ehrenfried's *German-English and English-German Dictionary*, the first noteworthy publication of its kind in America for the use of the general reader. During the next few years other journals joined the *Monthly Anthology* in bringing increasingly informative intelligences regarding the publication of books in Germany, statistics regarding the Leipzig Book Fair, and long reviews (often aggregating fifty to a hundred pages) of the more significant among recent German works (consult Goodnight, *op. cit.*, pp. 122 f. for details), while editorial concern with German plays, especially those of Kotzebue, Zschokke, and Schiller, as represented on the Boston, Philadelphia, and New York stages became common (see *ibid.*, p. 122).

23. This acceleration is demonstrated in the lists prepared by S. H. Goodnight.

24. III, 214–16. The next year there followed a forty-five–page review of Goethe's autobiography (IV, 217–62).

25. IV, 166–76.

26. *Works of John Adams* (10 vols., Boston, 1850–1856), X, 57.

27. Except for a brief note by Roy A. Tower in the *Philological Quarterly*, VII, i (Jan., 1928), 89–90.

28. *Discourse on the Necessity and the Means of Making Our National Literature Independent of That of Great Britain* (Phila., 1843), pp. 24–25. Du Ponceau neglects to mention a fifth journal, the *Columbus* of Hamburg.

29. The materials (says the editor) are not derived from English or French sources but directly from America, the land to the promotion of whose interests the "Institute" is dedicated. Dependable informants support both editors—one of whom, "Hermann," lives in New York, the other, "Göschen," in Leipzig. This arrangement of close interdependence and rapport insures at once nonpartisan reporting and a steady supply of news for the transmission of which German, American, Dutch, and British ships are used. Even mishaps at sea, while they may interrupt the steady flow of news, cannot prevent the regular appearance of the paper, for there is constantly at hand an abundance of important matter that does not depend upon immediate timeliness.

30. For other details and arrangements, as well as rates, see Henry A. Pochmann, "Early German-American Journalistic Exchanges," *Huntington Lib. Quar.*, XI, ii (Feb., 1948), 161–79, esp. pp. 168–70.

31. The reasons given are that American newspapers are now arriving in such abundance as to make abstracting them an impossible task, and that the fast courier-ships between America and England enable the British to get the news much earlier than it can be received in Leipzig, so that English bulletins and newspapers reach Germany before the ships bearing the news arrive in German ports.

32. Five numbers, January 31 to May 23, 1820, vary from eight to sixteen pages per issue. The sixth and last number of thirty-two pages, edited by "An American" instead of "Hermann," appeared in January, 1821.

33. Most of the first number is devoted to the persecutions of Jews in Germany, said to be no worse than among "the *free* and *enlightened* people of Republican America." The topic is pursued at lesser length in Nos. 3 and 4. Number 2 presents extracts of poetry in translation, book notices, general literary intelligence, and notes on astronomical, political, and scientific matters in Germany. Number 3, aside from the literary notices common to all installments, relates the history of the German Society of the City of New York. The most notable feature of No. 4 is a letter from an unidentified American traveling in Germany, at once highly complimentary of Germany and the Germans, whom he finds entirely unlike the "dull, heavy, plodding thinking machines" as they are often drawn, and expressing gratification at their lively interest in America. Number 5 contains an essay on German archeological investigations in Babylon, another on political theories in Germany, comments on the work of *Amerika dargestellt durch sich selbst* in establishing favorable German-American relations, and notices of the affairs and publications of the American Philosophical Society, the New York Historical Society, and the Literary and Philosophical Society of New York, a biographical sketch of Bach, figures on German population and emigration, and miscellaneous correspondence. Number 6, in addition to the usual literary and scientific intelligences, contains (1) a review of Adam Storck's translation of Scott's *Lay of the Last Minstrel* (Bremen, 1820) and *The Lady of the Lake* (Essen, 1819); (2) a critical review of Thomas Hodgskin's *Travels in the North of Germany* (2 vols., Edinburgh, 1820), which is said to display "a lamentable ignorance of things known to the merest tyro of German scholarship" and an utter inability to "comprehend anything of the peculiar spirit . . . of the great German authors." "The

excellent judge complains," says Hermann, "that in Kant he finds *abundance of words, but no thoughts*; and he talks of people being 'acquainted with Goethe from the Edinburgh Review.'" There are (3) reprintings of German reviews of American publications; (4) a notice of German scientific books given to the Literary and Philosophical Society of New York and to the Teutonic Lyceum of New York by donors in Germany; and (5) extracts from a "distinguished Literary Gentleman, residing in Massachusetts," who reports on the enthusiasm among his friends in the vicinity for studying German. Among the literary notices is one announcing that the "celebrated Pestalozzi" is preparing his works for a new edition, to be put into English, and that "several Englishmen are now in his institution," among them Lord Greaver, who "has taken lodgings in Castle Yverdun, and studies the interesting subject with great zeal, in order to . . . introduce it into England." Another announces the publication at Weimar of a five-volume edition of Franklin's works, correspondence, and life. The University of Göttingen is reported to have sixty-five professors and 1,118 students, of which number 544 are foreigners. Finally, there is a postscript announcing receipt of "new assurances of the perfect approbation with which *The German Correspondent* is regarded in Germany" and promising numerous interesting innovations. With this encouraging note *The German Correspondent* came to a sudden end, a year after its foundation, immediately after it had quadrupled its size and, as far as can be discovered at this distance, when everything seemed most favorable for its continued success.

34. The only complete file that I have found of *Amerikanische Ansichten von dem Gottesdienst und andere Eigenheiten der Mosheimschen Gesellschaft in Philadelphia zugeeignet und monatlich herausgegeben von Pastor* [J. K.] *Plitt* (10 nos., Jan.–Oct., 1820, Phila., Michael Billmeyer, 1820) is that in the Krauth Memorial Library of the Lutheran Theological Seminary in Germantown, Pa.

35. Among noteworthy items publicized were reports of the transactions of the several standing committees of the society, reports on the activities of the American Philosophical Society, reviews of books like M. v. Fürstenwärter's *Der Deutsche in Nord-Amerika* (Stuttgart & Tübingen, 1818), literary intelligences from Germany, data on the variety of German sects found in the United States, and essays on the effects of the American language upon German as used in America. Respecting German in America, the editor promised to maintain a high standard of pure German, literary and uniform, showing a minimum of such dialectal differences as were developing from Pennsylvania to Georgia. In No. 2 he ridicules wittily what he calls "Verdeutschungssucht," or the inordinate opposition among Germans in America to all Americanism. The language problem, particularly as it affected German churches in America, frequently forms the subject of the editor's sensible comment (see I, iv, 27, 29; ix, 71; and x, 71, 73). Some of the articles are intended primarily for the information of Germans in Europe, but most of the magazine is devoted to the instruction of Germans in America. One of the most noteworthy contributions is an essay on Anglo-American enthusiasts for the German language and German culture—listing twelve professional men and civic leaders of Philadelphia, headed by Du Ponceau, who is said to have pursued his German studies for the last fifteen years, and whose library, "one of the richest in the U.S., lacks no significant German work." Other noteworthy items include reports on educational methods in the Franckische Akademie, on Germans in Brazil, on the DeWette-Sand correspondence, and on *Proselytenmacherei* (the mania for proselytizing). For other details, see Pochmann, *loc. cit.*, pp. 174–77.

36. Fourteen vols., Hamburg, Hoffmann, Jan., 1825–Mar., 1832.

37. *Atlantis. Journal des Neuesten und Wissenswürdigsten aus dem Gebiete der Politik, Geschichte, Geographie, Statistik, Kulturgeschichte, und Literatur der nord- und südamerikanischen Reiche mit Einschluss des westindischen Archipelagus.* Hrsg. von Eduard Florens Rivinus in Phila. 6 nos. in 2 vols., Leipzig, J. C. Hinrichs, 1826–1827.

38. For Rivinus, see *Deutsch-Amerikanisches Magazin,* I, iii (Apr., 1887), 327–33.

39. Designed primarily for European consumption, it contained regular intelligence under the following classifications: "(1) Zeitgeschichte der amerikanischen Staaten und Colonien; (2) Beiträge zur Erdbeschreibung; (3) Völkerkunde; (4) Religionszustände; (5) Statistik; (6) Biographische Beiträge; (7) Merkantilische Notizen; (8) Amerikas Naturgeschichte, Industrie, Landbau und Geologie; (9) Poesien und Erzählungen; (10) Amerikanische Charakterzüge; (11) Aufsätze aus brieflichen Mittheilungen und denen in Amerika erschienenen Blättern."

40. Since both the *Atlantis* and *Columbus* were designed mainly for European readers, their immediate influence in America was smaller and their general significance for our purpose less, despite their wide circulation in

Europe, than that of the earlier periodicals edited by Göschen, "Hermann," and Pastor Plitt, who directed their journals to readers on either side of the Atlantic.

41. Professor Orie W. Long's *Literary Pioneers: Early American Explorers of European Culture* (Cambridge, Mass., 1935; hereafter cited as Long) recounts with great circumstantiality of detail the careers of George Ticknor, Edward Everett, Joseph G. Cogswell, George Bancroft, H. W. Longfellow, and John L. Motley. Mr. Long has treated Frederic H. Hedge in a fifty-three-page brochure entitled *Frederic Henry Hedge: A Cosmopolitan Scholar* (Portland, Me., 1940). James T. Hatfield's *New Light on Longfellow* (Boston, 1933) is equally detailed regarding Longfellow's position as an intermediary of German culture.

42. Ticknor spent the winter of 1814–1815 visiting John Randolph in Philadelphia, President Madison in Washington, Chief Justice Marshall in Richmond, and Jefferson at Monticello, acquiring information and advice regarding his proposed tour. Friendship with Jefferson turned out to be especially fruitful. Ticknor became Jefferson's literary agent in Germany, France, England, and Italy, executing many commissions for the purchase of books. For example, in the summer of 1815 Ticknor shipped some of the best German editions of the classics to Jefferson, among them Homer and Virgil by Christian G. Heyne, Aeschylus by Christian G. Schütz, Juvenal by Georg A. Ruperti, and Tacitus by J. J. Oberlin. For his part, Jefferson drew inspiration and advice from Ticknor when he came to establish the University of Virginia, and he repeatedly tried to persuade Ticknor to join the faculty at Charlottesville. For Jefferson's appreciation of Ticknor (and of the scientific method of textual criticism developing in Germany) see his letters to Ticknor printed in O. W. Long, *Thomas Jefferson and George Ticknor* (Williamstown, Mass., 1930), and Long, pp. 3–62.

43. Although he spoke of closing "the last wearisome semester" of his labors at Göttingen on March 26, 1817, his letters show that this weariness stemmed from a too steady attention to his ambitious lecture and study program rather than from any tedium attaching to the subjects studied. His communications on the intellectual life of Germany are both detailed and penetrating. Before he had been four months at Göttingen, he was elected, along with Edward Everett (who had sailed with him on April 16, 1815, four days after his inauguration as Eliot Professor of Greek Literature at Harvard), a member of the exclusive "Literary Club," consisting of a small number of carefully selected professors and students. (For details on Ticknor's Göttingen sojourn, see Long, esp. pp. 14–33). He improved every opportunity during vacation periods to make excursions into the highways and byways of Germany. In 1815 he and Everett visited Hanover, where they met the original of Goethe's Lotte. The next year (September–December) they toured Saxony and Prussia, visiting Leipzig, Dresden, Wittenberg, and Halle, returning *via* Weimar and Jena. On October 25 they called on Goethe at Weimar, thus becoming the first, save one, of the American visitors who henceforth beat a path to Goethe's house (Goethe had received Aaron Burr in January, 1810; see E. G. Gudde, "Aaron Burr at Weimar," *South Atl. Quar.*, XL, iv [Oct., 1941], 360–67). Their visit was no less important for Goethe than it was for his American admirers. He began now actively to familiarize himself with America, and the result was an ever-widening sphere of contacts with America and Americans. See H. S. White, "Goethe in America," *Goethe Jahrbuch*, V (1884), 219–56; *Goethe's Gespräche* (Leipzig, 1889), III, 269–71; also *Goethe Jahrbuch*, XXV (1904), 3–37; and Long, pp. 26–29.

44. Going thither, he paused at Kassel to meet Voelkel, the classical scholar, and visited Marburg and Giessen. At Wetzlar he was interested in the scenes associated with *Werther*; at Frankfurt he met Friedrich Schlegel; at Heidelberg he was entertained by Johann Voss, who told him a great deal about Klopstock, Hölty, and the Stolbergs. Among the most interesting and intimate associations that Ticknor formed during his five months in Paris were those with A. W. Schlegel and A. von Humboldt.—Long, pp. 31–32.

45. Letter to George Bancroft, Dec. 30, 1825, in the Massachusetts Historical Society.

46. Before this time the Harvard Corporation had voted "permission" for one Meno Poehls of Hamburg "to give private lessons in German to such students . . . as may choose to attend him." The Harvard catalog of 1820 lists one Frederick S. Gustorf as "Private Teacher of German."

47. See *Life, Letters, and Journals of George Ticknor*, I, 87–89, 98; Long, pp. 26–27.

48. He wanted to see America adopt much, though not all, of what he observed, for in Germany, as elsewhere, the found "men of great learning and men of little learning, and men of no learning at all." For details, see Long, pp. 18–19, 24, 27, 230 n. 272.

49. *Ibid.*, 19–20, 30–31, 33, 52; Long, *Thomas Jefferson and George Ticknor*, pp. 26–28.

50. Long, *Jefferson and Ticknor*, pp. 49–50.

51. See Ticknor's *Remarks on Changes Lately*

Proposed or Accepted in Harvard University (Boston, 1825).

52. The liberal tradition in his own department was carried forward by Longfellow, who succeeded him from 1836 to 1854, and subsequently by Lowell, from 1854 to 1872.

53. For particulars, see Long, pp. 55–61.

54. Graduated from Harvard with highest honors at seventeen, he pursued graduate literary and theological studies for several years and succeeded, in 1814, to Buckminster's pulpit in the Brattle Street Church. Well prepared, according to contemporary American standards, in the classical and several modern languages (including a reading knowledge of German, acquired under the stimulation and direction of Moses Stuart of Andover), he was appointed Eliot Professor of Greek Literature at Harvard in 1815, but granted permission to travel for two years before assuming his duties.

55. Proc. Mass. Hist. Soc., VIII (Jan., 1865), 137–41.

56. During the spring and summer of 1816 his letters to his brother are full of plans to translate Klopstock's Messias and have it ready for publication on his return to America, but the project came to naught.—Long, pp. 66–67.

57. Letter, Oct. 2, 1815, in the Massachusetts Historical Society, quoted in Long, p. 238, n. 19.

58. Goethe Jahrbuch, XXV (1904), 5–6.

59. On October 25, 1817, in a tone that suggests gratification at the results of his efforts, he wrote to his brother, "I have received a letter from the College ordering 20 German Grammars, 20 German Dictionaries, 5 Schneider's German Greek Lexicon, 20 Schleussner's etc. So that German seems to look up."—Long, p. 238, n. 32.

60. Ibid., pp. 79–80, 90; North Amer. Rev., VII (July, 1818), 288; VIII (Dec., 1818), 208.

61. See his letter to Stephen Higginson, Sept. 17, 1817, printed in Harvard Graduates' Mag., VI (Sept., 1897), 14.

His comments on Göttingen varied from time to time. For example, a year after taking the doctorate, he wrote from Rome to Bancroft, then at Göttingen, "With respect to a degree, if they are willing to give it to you without examination, as they did mine, and you have nothing better to do with 60 or 70 Thalers, you can take it" (Long, p. 269, n. 36). Generally, however, he referred to Göttingen more appreciatively in some such terms as "the famous fountain of European wisdom" (Harvard Graduates' Mag., VI, Sept., 1897, 14); and years later he said, "I left Germany in the fall of 1817, strongly attached to that country, and

after deriving in my opinion very great advantages from my intercourse with learned men in various parts of it and especially from the course of studies which I pursued at Göttingen."—Long, pp. 71, 239, n. 37.

For the rest of his European sojourn, he spent the winter of 1817–1818 in Paris, continuing his studies of Greek and Italian and cultivating Alex. von Humboldt, Benj. Constant, Madame de Staël, and Lafayette. In London he called on Dr. Nöhden, "whom I had seen once in Göttingen, and whose German Grammar I had diligently studied. He also called on Wm. von Humboldt, who "was quite pleased to find I had read his own German translation of the Agamemnon of Aeschylus" (Journal, May, 1818; Long, p. 239, n. 40). In both London and Edinburgh later he had access to the same distinguished circles of literary people in which Ticknor moved so agreeably later in the same year. After a winter in Rome and a tour of Greece, he returned on October 7, 1819, to Boston to assume his duties as Professor of Greek at Harvard.

62. Letters of Ralph Waldo Emerson (ed. by R. L. Rusk, 6 vols., N.Y., 1939), I, 76; see also pp. 78, 84. In the meantime he heard Everett's "Introductory Lecture" and as many others as were open to him, and recorded his unqualified admiration of Everett's inspiration, eloquence, and tremendous stock of factual knowledge. Forty years later, writing his "Historic Notes of Life and Letters in New England," Emerson likened Everett's influence on the young people of his day to that of Pericles in Athens:

"Germany had created criticism in vain for us until 1820, when Edward Everett returned from his five years in Europe, and brought to Cambridge his rich results, which no one was so fitted by natural grace and the splendor of his rhetoric to introduce and recommend. He made us for the first time acquainted with Wolff's theory of the Homeric writings, with the criticism of Heyne. The novelty of the learning lost nothing in the skill and genius of his relation, and the rudest undergraduate found a new morning opened to him in the lecture-room of Harvard Hall."—Works (Centenary ed., 12 vols., Boston, 1903–1905), X, 330.

Emerson continues in this vein for the length of five pages. In his Journal for 1851 (VIII, 225–26) he wrote: "Edward Everett had in my youth an immense advantage in being the first American scholar who sat in the German universities and brought us home in his head the whole cultured method and results,—to us who did not so much as know the names of Heyne, Wolf[f], Hug[o], and Ruhnken. He dealt out his treasures, too, with such admirable prudence, so temperate and abstemious that our wonder and delight was still new."

Samuel E. Eliot, on the other hand, thought Everett's lectures "rather calculated to set forth the amount of the professor's studies than to do any particular benefit to the students."—Bancroft MSS, Mass. Hist. Soc., quoted in Long, p. 73.

But admirers of Emerson's sort seem to have been in the vast majority. See, for example, the testimonials in Andrew P. Peabody's *Harvard Reminiscences*, p. 93, and the tributes collected in the *Proc. Mass. Hist. Soc.*, VIII (Jan., 1865), 161–70.

63. For his classes he prepared and, in 1822, published a translation of Philipp Karl Buttmann's *Greek Grammar*, and the next year a Greek reader based on that by Friedrich Jacob. Both were reviewed by Bancroft in the *North Amer. Rev.* (Jan. & Apr., 1824).

64. In his lectures Everett was often lavish in his praise of German thought, scholarship, and literature. He particularly singled out Goethe, Schelling, Oken, and Hegel as having been helpful to him and as worthy of consideration. Of especial importance is his address on "American Literature," delivered on August 26, 1824, before the Phi Beta Kappa Society of Harvard. In it he exhibited a keen grasp of the situation of his day, espoused the cause of higher education after the German example, and expressed his conviction of the scholar's responsibility to lead—a belief which seems to have been inspired by his study of Fichte's ideal of the scholar and his national mission. It, in turn, helped inspire Emerson's classic statement, thirteen years later, when he stood in Everett's place before the same society and addressed them on the subject of "The American Scholar."

65. Conveniently located by consulting Goodnight, *op. cit.*, pp. 138, 146, 149.

66. *North Amer. Rev.*, X (Jan., 1820), 115–37.

67. July 6, 1825, Jefferson MSS, Lib. of Congr., quoted in Long, pp. 73–74.

68. July 21, 1825, Jefferson MSS, Lib. of Congr., quoted *ibid.*, p. 74.

69. Not only in academic matters but in his personal desires, as when he asked for permission to reside in Boston while teaching in Cambridge, or when he asked to be sent on an expedition to revolutionary Greece (Long, p. 75). As early as April 13, 1821, he wrote to Judge Joseph Story, one of the Harvard Overseers: "You have occasionally, though undesignedly, placed a thorn in my side, by remarks which you have dropped, that you thought I would have been a good lawyer;—the rather as I find I am a poor professor. From the first week of

my return hither, I saw that our university—as good I doubt not as the state of society admits —would furnish me with little scope for the communication of the higher parts of ancient literature, and that a good grammatical driller, which I cannot consent to be, is wanted. But I find that the whole pursuit, and the duties it brings with it, are not respectable enough in the estimation they bring with them, and lead one too much into contact with some little men and many little things" (original in Mass. Hist. Soc., quoted in Long, pp. 74–75).

70. Emerson's *Journals*, VI, 257 (Sept., 1842; see also *Works*, X, 330–38.

71. See, for example, the letter written on Nov. 9, 1835, while he was Governor of Mass., to Prof. Blumenbach of Göttingen, admitting that while he had lost some of his facility in speaking and writing "for want of practice," he continued to read German "with pleasure and ease," as, he went on to say, he retained "an affectionate remembrance" of his "German friends."—MS letter in library of Univ. of Göttingen, quoted in Long, p. 75.

72. Edward E. Hale, *Memories of a Hundred Years* (2 vols., N.Y., 1902), II, 14–15.

73. Emerson, who attended the inaugural exercises, wrote on May 1, 1846: "The satisfaction of men in his appointment is complete. Boston is contented because he is so creditable, safe, prudent, and the scholars because he is a scholar, and understands the business."—*Journals*, VI, 168.

74. MS diary, May 1, 1846, preserved at Craigie House, and quoted in Long, p. 76.

75. For details, see Paul R. Frothingham, *Edward Everett, Orator and Statesman* (Boston & N.Y., 1925), pp. 265–301.

76. Anna E. Ticknor, *Life of J. G. Cogswell as Sketched in His Letters* (Cambridge, Mass., 1874), p. 51. One gathers, however, that he never fully succeeded in subjecting himself to the discipline required, for a chance remark of Dissen's that after spending eighteen years, sixteen hours daily, exclusively on Greek and still being unable to read a page of Greek tragedy without the aid of a dictionary, led him to strike Greek from his list of studies.—*Harvard Graduates' Mag.*, VI (Sept., 1897), 12; see also pp. 9–10.

77. Long, pp. 78, 240, n. 5.

78. Anna E. Ticknor, *op. cit.*, p. 57

79. *Ibid.*, pp. 60–61.

80. Long, p. 241, n. 12.

81. *Harvard Graduates' Mag.*, VI (Sept., 1897), 12–13; Long, pp. 83, 241, n. 15

82. *Ibid.*, p. 83.

83. Anna E. Ticknor, *op. cit.*, p. 73.

84. Although Cogswell had resolved by now

to prove to his friends that he was not a "wayward, froward child," he was still unable to settle on a vocation. "When I return to America," he wrote on May 4, 1819, "I mean to listen to the calls of reason and duty and if these take me to the Poles or sit me quickly down in New England, I shall cheerfully obey their dictates and go on my way rejoicing." But he was sufficiently mindful of the future to take the Göttingen doctorate in August, 1819.—Long, pp. 85–87.

85. Cogswell's account of his country and countrymen inspired Goethe to read more widely concerning the new world and to say, "If I were twenty years younger, I should sail for North America." He avowed more affection for Cogswell than for any other American of his acquaintance and spoke of him as "ein lieber Mann."

86. Long, pp. 90, 242, n. 34.

87. See Alfred A. Potter and C. K. Bolton, *The Librarians of Harvard College*, 1667–1877 (Cambridge, Mass., 1897), pp. 36–37; also Cogswell's article "On the Means of Education, and the State of Learning in the United States," *Blackwood's Edin. Mag.*, IV (Feb., 1819), 546–53, which contains (pp. 552–53) his criticism of American libraries.

88. Cogswell had met Bancroft earlier at Göttingen. Bancroft had entertained the idea of founding "a high school of the German character" as early as January, 1819, when he communicated his design to Dr. Kirkland, who encouraged him in his plans. He had inspected a number of schools in Berlin and the celebrated Schulpforta, consulted Schleiermacher, and had drawn up a plan of organization for what he considered an institution ideally adapted to Massachusetts.

89. Long, pp. 141–44. For the principles of organization and particulars of indebtedness to European models, consult Cogswell and Bancroft's *Prospectus of a School to be Established at Round Hill, Northampton, Mass.* (Cambridge, June 20, 1823); *Some Account of the School for the Liberal Education of Boys Established on Round Hill . . .* (n.p., 1826); and *Outline of a System of Education at the Round Hill School* (Boston, 1831).

90 Anna E. Ticknor, *op. cit.*, p. 160.

91. While casting about for something to do, he engaged himself for two years to superintend an Episcopal school for boys in Raleigh, N.C., where he was surprised to find that he could employ successfully a system of "German ideals . . . more severe" even than any he had thought of applying to his New England scholars at Northampton.—*Ibid.*, p. 197. In 1836, he returned North to tutor the three sons of

Samuel Ward, but in October he joined Francis C. Gray on a tour of Europe.

92. See, e.g., his essay on "University Education," *N.Y. Rev.*, VII (July, 1840), 109–36. Consult also Goodnight, *op. cit.*, for the years indicated.

93. H. M. Lydenberg, "A Forgotten Trail Blazer," *Essays Offered to Herbert Putnam* (New Haven, 1929), p. 302; see also pp. 303–14, as well as Lydenberg's *History of the New York Public Library* (N.Y., 1926), pp. 1–56, and Fred Saunders, *Historical Sketch of the Astor Library* (N.Y., 1895).

94. Letters of introduction from Everett to Benecke, Gauss, Blumenbach, Eichhorn, and Dissen prepared for their ready access to the innermost circles, if such a preparation was at all necessary for this latest contingent of "neue Amerikaner." By September 5, writing to Andrews Norton, then librarian at Harvard, Bancroft rated himself fortunate to be in "the land of learning, of literature, of science . . . the pure fountain of wisdom" and "to drink of her unpolluted waters and be refreshed" (Long, p. 109; Mark A. DeWolfe, Howe, *The Life and Letters of George Bancroft*, 2 vols., N.Y., 1908, I, 30–44; hereafter cited as Howe). Feeling the inadequacy of his German, which he learned from Professor Sidney Willard (himself self-taught), Bancroft set at once to perfect himself in the language, and apparently succeeded in record time, for by June of the following year he reported, with justifiable pride, to his friends in America that he had gone to "a village in the vicinity and delivered a sermon in the German language" (Long, p. 111).

95. Long, p. 112; Howe, I, 48–58, 63–64.

96. Long, pp. 114–15.

97. "This degrading love of money is carried beyond all bounds." So far is learning reduced to the rules of trade that an inquiry of a Göttingen professor after information not immediately related to the matter in hand invariably meets with the reply, "It would cost me time to tell you, but you can hear what I have to say on the matter, in a course I am going to deliver next term," that is, by paying the fees and presenting a properly endorsed receipt.—Long, p. 120.

98. "They have no idea of the sublimity or sanctity of their science. 'Tis traduced to a mere learning. I never hear anything like moral or religious feeling manifested in their theological lectures. They neither begin with God nor go on with him, and there is a good deal more religion in a few lines of Xenophon, than in a whole course of Eichhorn. Nay, the only classes, in which I have heard jests so vulgar and indecent, that they would have disgraced

a jailyard or a fishmarket, have been the theological ones. The bible is treated with very little respect, and the narratives are laughed at as an old wife's tale, fit to be believed in the nursery."—Long, p. 120.

99. E.g., Long, pp. 121–24, 127–30, 131, 134–36, and Howe, I, 84–87, 89–92.

100. Letter of Aug. 19, 1820, quoted in Long, pp. 127–30; see also Howe, I, 77–78.

101. July 18, 1821, printed in Howe, I, 111.

102. Howe, I, 155–57.

103. Emerson, too, while he considered Bancroft "a perfect Greek scholar," who had made good use of his time in Germany, admitted that he needed "a good deal of cutting & pruning." —*Letters*, I, 127 (Jan. 23, 1823). See also Higginson's opinion as given in *Harvard Graduates' Mag.*, VI (Sept., 1897), 17.

As a young man Bancroft had a faculty for going against the current and for attracting the attention and often the ill-will of the conservative-minded, who thought him eccentric or foolish. In Germany, he felt, he was "all too American" to get on smoothly; but when he returned to his own country, he seems not to have realized that it was chiefly his foreign manners and views, social and professional, that provoked irritation in Cambridge. Even before he entered upon his duties at Harvard, he told Norton, "I do not expect to be popular, because I intend to require more than has been usual." In external matters he imitated the German professors, and was exacting in his assignments, while the boys retaliated by congregating under his study windows in the college yard and singing a ditty beginning, "Thus we do it in Germany." If his Germanized manners offended in America, his ultra-Americanism was one of the contributing factors that made him unhappy in Germany. For example, on July 4, 1820, his pent-up dissatisfaction with the Germans, their customs, and their institutions, overflowed in a grandiloquently jingoistic Fourth-of-July oration, delivered to an audience of one—Robert Bridges Patton of Middlebury College, the only other American in Göttingen at the moment. This was followed, after a poem by Patton, with a round dozen toasts to George Washington, the President of the United States, the American flag, the heroes of '76, American liberty, American institutions, etc., etc. See Long, pp. 124–27.

104. Compare his letters printed in Long, pp. 121–23, with the stock criticisms as they appear in Goodnight, pp. 33–107.

105. Mindful of the practical value of the Göttingen doctorate, he presented himself for examination before eight members of the faculty, defended successfully nine theses, according to requirements, and on September 9, 1820, became "Dr., *Herr* Doctor," as he put it. —Long, p. 130; Howe, I, 78–84.

106. The longer he remained, the more Berlin pleased him. His frank condemnation of certain aspects of Göttingen and his equally frank glorification of the Royal Friedrich Wilhelm University in Berlin supply one of the causes that turned the trek of American students, during the 30's, increasingly toward Berlin. See the lists of students at the several German universities before 1850, as presented in A. B. Hinsdale, "Notes on the History of Foreign Influences upon Education in the United States," Ch. XIII, in the *Report of the Commissioner of Education for the Year 1897–1898* (Washington, D.C., 1899). It is noteworthy that Halle, which had so delighted Ticknor, particularly disgusted Bancroft. He would not go there, he wrote to Norton, "for all the Hebrew Gesenius has in his scull or his library . . . If Göttingen is a little hell, Halle is the place the devil would blush to show his face in."—Long, p. 248.

107. On his first visit to Hegel, he put him down as "very sluggish for one of Schlegel's school," and at the end of the course observed that the time spent listening to Hegel's "display of unintelligible words" was so much time "lost" (Long, pp. 132, 248, n. 5; Howe, I, 92). Concerning Wolf, he sent President Kirkland the following, not entirely consistent report: "He is a genius of the first order; one of the few great men it has been my lot to meet in Germany . . . the most learned man on the continent . . . But Wolf has neither dignity of character, nor purity of morals . . . is stubbornly vain, childish, licentious."—Long, p. 132; Howe, I, 47, 92–93, 96. Schleiermacher made altogether the most favorable impression: "Schleiermacher delighted me extremely . . . [His] mode of preaching is very dignified and severe. Language flows from his lips fluently . . . the best extempore speaker I have ever heard . . . . He is a preacher for the understanding, not for the heart."—Long, p. 132; Howe, I, 97. See also the praise he bestowed on Schleiermacher in his letter to Kirkland, Nov. 5, 1820, printed in Long, p. 132.

108. Fired by Schleiermacher's lectures on education, he began to contemplate principles and plans for Germanizing American secondary education. Although Humboldt pointed out to him several good reasons why such plans would be hard to realize in America, when Bancroft's term at Berlin came to a close in February, 1821, he spent four days at Schulpforta, ostensibly to look after young Hedge (who was caus-

ing trouble by his "impertinence and undescribable Faulheit"), but really, one would gather from his enthusiastic comments at the time, to study the history, organization, equipment, discipline, modes of instruction, and general life of the famous school there. He was acquiring data for the formation of a school on the German model in America. As early as January, 1819, he had written Kirkland regarding such a possibility, and Kirkland had encouraged him. Now that Schleiermacher had revived his interest in the project, his letters became replete with details concerning German schools, Fichte's ideals, Schleiermacher's principles, and Pestalozzi's and Fellenberg's methods. See Long, pp. 133, 142–44.

109. Long, p. 138. For a more circumstantial account of Bancroft's experiences at the German universities, see the excellent study by Russel B. Nye, which has appeared since this section was written.—*George Bancroft, Brahmin Rebel* (N.Y., 1944).

110. Long, pp. 141–42.

111. More the scholar than the administrator, Bancroft devoted all his time to teaching, teaching German, the classics, and history; but when G. H. Bode joined the staff in 1825, Bode took over the German classes. Although eminently fitted and trained for scholarly research, Bancroft was not a highly successful teacher. His lack of sympathetic understanding of young students and his eccentric, romantic, and emotional temperament made him unpopular with the boys.

112. A Greek grammar, abr. and tr. from that of Philipp C. Buttmann (1824); a Latin reader, tr. from the 5th ed. of Christian F. W. Jacobs (1825); *Cornelius Nepos*, from the 3rd ed. by J. H. Bremi (1826); and a Latin grammar, tr. from the German of C. G. Zumpf (1829).

113. Chief among these were a review of Schiller's *Minor Poems* in the *North Amer. Rev.*, Oct., 1823, and two essays—"The Life and Genius of Goethe," *loc. cit.*, Oct., 1824, and "The Writings of Herder," *loc. cit.*, Jan., 1825. Beginning in 1827, he published a series of articles on "German Literature" in the *Amer. Quar. Rev.*, based on recent German publications and outlining the development of German literary culture. When John S. Dwight published, as No. 3 of Ripley's "Specimens of Foreign Standard Literature," his *Select Minor Poems from . . . Goethe and Schiller* (Boston, 1839), Bancroft wrote his last long review in this category for the *Christian Examiner*, July, 1839. In it he incorporated a scathing attack on Goethe's personality and character, thus revealing a tendency in his own development toward conservatism between 1824 and 1839.

114. When, in accordance with its custom of renewing degrees on fiftieth anniversaries, the University of Göttingen sent a special deputy to Berlin to present the new diploma, Bancroft, later recalling the event, said, "I answered him in German, giving an account of Göttingen in my day," at the same time relating something of his student days at Berlin and of his associations with Hegel, Wolf, Humboldt, and Schleiermacher (Long, p. 157). Numerous other honors came to him from Germany. He became one of the original members of the Goethe Club in New York City. To the end, as earlier in his life, he maintained a certain Germanic air about him, and there was a story current during his last years in Washington to the effect that when a stranger, who had repeatedly observed an old man of peculiarly military bearing riding past the Soldiers' Home, asked a guard who the old gentleman was, received for his reply, "Why, that's an old German named Bancroft."

115. See Michael Kraus, "George Bancroft 1834–1934," *New Eng. Quart.*, VII, iv (Dec., 1934), 662–86, esp. pp. 667–68, 683.

116. M. A. DeWolfe Howe, in *Harvard Graduates' Mag.*, XVI (June, 1908), 652.

117. J. S. Bassett (ed.), "Correspondence of George Bancroft and Jared Sparks, 1823–1832," *Smith College Studies in History*, II (Jan., 1917), 73.

118. Wm. Charvat and Michael Kraus (eds.), *William Hickling Prescott* (Amer. Writers Series, N.Y., 1943), pp. xxvi–xxvii, xxix; George Ticknor, *Life of Prescott* (Boston, 1864), pp. 68–69.

119. In 1832 he credited the Germans with "throwing the light of learning on what before was dark and inexplicable," no other nation having done "so much to lay the foundations of that reconciling spirit of criticism, which, instead of condemning a difference of taste in different nations as a departure from it, seeks to explain such discrepancies by the particular circumstances of the nation."—*Biog. and Crit. Misc.* (Boston, 1850), p. 254.

120. He concluded that Humboldt, as "the first, almost the last writer on these topics," made his "theories conform to the facts, instead of binding his facts to theories," and hence merits "the name of a philosopher."—Ticknor, *Life*, p. 195. When his *Conquest of Mexico* (1843) won for him the admiration and fellowship of Humboldt and, in 1845, membership in the Royal Society of Berlin, he was elated.—G. P. Gooch, *History and Historians in the Nineteenth Century* (N.Y., 1935), p. 414; Ticknor, *Life*, p. 203.

121. Finding the English edition of Ranke's *Spanish Empire* ill printed, Prescott had four

copies of the part touching Philipp II struck off in a large type, so that whenever his eye would permit the indulgence, he might recur to it "as a manual and guide."—Ticknor, *Life*, p. 290; see also pp. 171, 287.

122. Parker also found *The Conquest of Mexico* lacking in philosophical background, and charged that Prescott seemed to know "nothing of the philosophy of history, and little, even of political economy."—Parker, *Works* (14 vols., London, 1863–1871), X, 116, 153. But Parker, be it remembered, had immersed himself in German Biblical research, had gone over completely to the German school, and was not the man to be pleased by methods short of the severity of the strictest critical ones.

123. Chas. H. Farnham, *Life of Francis Parkman* (Boston, 1901), pp. 183–84; Wilbur Schramm (ed.), *Francis Parkman* (Amer. Writers Series, N.Y., 1938), pp. lii, liv, lv, lvii; Wm. T. Hutchinson, *The Marcus Jernegan Essays in American Historiography* (Chicago, 1937), p. 50.

124. After spending the years 1825–1827 at the Round Hill School and acquiring the rudiments of German, French, Greek, and Latin, Motley went to Harvard, where he graduated in 1831. At the college exhibition during his senior year the seventeen-year-old lad delivered an address on "The Genius and Character of Goethe," which Cogswell thought good enough to send to Goethe's daughter-in-law, Ottilie, who wrote to say, "I wish to see the first book that young man will write."

125. He attended Hugo's lectures on civil law and in the next semester added "Heeren's lectures on History" and "Saalfeld's Political lectures." After two semesters at Göttingen, where he partook more freely than his predecessors of German student life, and where he formed lifelong friendships with Graf Alex. Keyserling and Otto Bismarck, he proceeded to Berlin; but being more interested in belles lettres than historical subjects, and finding at Berlin no great "menagerie" of literary lions (he appears to have overlooked Ranke), he set forth in the spring of 1834 on his travels, which included a number of the principal German cities. Disappointed at having arrived in Europe too late to see Goethe, he nevertheless visited Weimar and was graciously entertained by Ottilie. At Dresden he met Tieck, and proceeded thence *via* Vienna, through the Tyrol and southern Germany, to Paris. After tours of Italy and England, he returned to America in the autumn of 1835.—Long, pp. 202–4, 208–12.

126. For details of the Motley–Bismarck relationship, see Long, pp. 221–24.

127. C. P. Higby, and B. T. Schantz, (eds.), *John Lothrop Motley* (Amer. Writers Series, N.Y., 1939), pp. lxxv–lxxvii.

128. Fortunately he had become acquainted at Göttingen and Berlin with the painstaking process of minute research, and he knew something of how German libraries were arranged, so that when he applied for help to Dr. Klemm, the chief librarian at Dresden, and to Herr von Weber, the head of the Royal Archives of Saxony, he was prepared to proceed with a minimum of lost motion. In Germany, as later in Holland, the custodians of printed and manuscript sources co-operated fully in supplying him with the desired materials.

129. His later work does not exhibit any marked changes in method or manner, except that he came to rely more and more on manuscript materials, and that with practice he gained facility in writing and a more assured style. His apprehension of the dramatic power of great painting led him to develop a style embodying dramatic and pictorial painting in his presentation of men and events in a manner essentially alien to the severely objective and critically restrained German method of historical writing. In whatever degree he fell short of equaling the German historiographical scientists, his books became models which later American historians sought to equal or surpass in critical accuracy and scientific objectivity.

130. He was the second American to win the Ph.D. degree from the University of Göttingen. He matriculated in the theological faculty but devoted himself mainly to the ancient languages, and subsequently became a noted Greek scholar and professor of that subject at Middlebury, later at Princeton, and finally at the University of the City of New York.

131. On his return he was for several years the editor of the *Baltimore American*. He became a prolific writer, produced translations of *Don Carlos* in 1836 and the correspondence between Goethe and Schiller in 1845, and a life of Goethe in 1872.

132. For a complete list of Americans studying at Göttingen, see Daniel B. Shumway, "The American Students of the University of Göttingen," *Ger.-Amer. Annals*, n.s., VIII, v–vi (Sept.–Dec., 1910), 171–254. Shumway's list extends to 1910. The statistical data which he presents (too detailed for summation here) are indicative of how thoroughly the Göttingen influence insinuated itself into the intellectual life of the United States.

133. From 1828 to 1831 Dwight and his brother Sereno operated a Gymnasium at New Haven on the order of the Round Hill School.

134. C. F. Thwing, *The American and the German University* (N.Y., 1928), pp. 12–39, 42–43.

135. The figures are those of Louis Viereck in his "German Instruction in American Schools," *Report of the Commissioner of Education for the Year 1900–1901*, Washington, D.C., 1902. For other significant figures and conclusions, see D. B. Shumway, *loc. cit.*, pp. 171–96, and A. B. Faust, *op. cit.*, II, 231.

136. They themselves were preceded by three or four others, who, however, failed to achieve the fame of Ticknor and Everett, and they consequently count for less in the cultural history of the United States as it is preserved in the written record. See D. B. Shumway, *loc. cit.*, pp. 172–73.

137. He became acquainted with Pestalozzi and Fellenberg, and upon his return published a report in two volumes entitled *A Year in Europe*, which included extended accounts of his visits to Yverdun and Hofwyl, as well as other institutions. In the opinion of Henry Barnard, "No volume in the first half of the 19th century had so wide an influence on the development of our educational, reformatory, and preventive measures, directly or indirectly, as this."

138. This projected institution, proposed chiefly by the Chevalier de Beaurepaire, was to be a kind of French academy of Arts and Sciences at Richmond, with branch academies in Baltimore, Philadelphia, and New York, with widespread international affiliations with the royal societies of London, Paris, Brussels, and other learned bodies, together with an elaborate hierarchy of officers, professors, resident and nonresident associates selected from both hemispheres. Fantastic as the scheme now appears, it had a good deal of support, and some money was collected (especially in France) toward its establishment, when the French Revolution stopped the proceedings. Jefferson, who was loath to give up the project, for a while cherished a scheme of "removing bodily to Va. the entire faculty of the Swiss Collège of Geneva." His preoccupation with these plans for a "French" institution doubtless explain why, when in 1788, he made a coach trip up the Rhine as far as Mannheim, he made no note in the written accounts of the trip of German educational or literary accomplishments but concentrated on certain sociological, agricultural, and topographical features of Germany. See Marie Goebel Kimball, "Thomas Jefferson's Rhine Journey," *Amer.-Ger. Rev.*, XIII, i (Oct., 1946), 4–7; ii (Dec., 1946), 11–14.

139. Ticknor had labored, since the summer of 1821, for "more freedom in the choice of subjects" with only partial success at Harvard. Mindful that his institution would be less encumbered by what he called the "ecclesiastical leaven" than Harvard, Jefferson announced, on July 16, 1823, "We shall . . . allow them [the students] uncontrolled choice in the lectures they choose to attend, and require elementary qualifications only, and sufficient age" (Long, *Thomas Jefferson and George Ticknor*, pp. 33–34; Jefferson's *Works*, Library ed., XV, 454–57). At Harvard Ticknor and his colleagues were soon checkmated in their efforts; by 1827 their reforms were abandoned in all but Ticknor's own department. Until after the administration of Everett (1846–1849) little progress was made. Free election was reinstituted between 1872 and 1885 by President Charles W. Eliot, but by that time Michigan, Cornell, and Hopkins had entered the field and made advances in this direction quite apart from earlier efforts at Harvard. Hence it seems that to Jefferson rather than Eliot belongs the honor of being the first successfully to introduce the elective system.

140. When, on March 17, 1825, the University of Virginia formally opened its doors, German was offered, under Blaettermann's tutelage, along with French, Italian, Spanish, and Anglo-Saxon, as a language that "now stands in line with that of the most learned nations in richness of conditions and advance in the sciences." See Jefferson's plans for the University as proposed to the Virginia Legislature. Of the first class of 116 students at Virginia, 64 studied German. By 1854 the number was 200, and in 1869 a knowledge of German and French was made obligatory for the degree of Master of Arts.

141. *And Gladly Teach* (Boston & N.Y., 1935), pp. 88–89.

NEW ENGLAND TRANSCENDENTALISM

142. This threefold derivation is emphasized by W. H. Channing: "In part, it was a reaction against Puritan Orthodoxy; in part, an effect of renewed study of the ancients, of Oriental Pantheists, of Plato and the Alexandrians, of Plutarch's morals, Seneca and Epictetus; in part a natural product of the culture of the place and time. On the somewhat stunted stock of Unitarianism . . . had been grafted German idealism, as taught . . . by Kant and Jacobi, Fichte and Novalis, Schelling and Hegel, Schleiermacher and De Wette, by Madame de Staël, Cousin, Coleridge, Carlyle; and the result was a vague yet exalting conception of the godlike nature of the human spirit."—*Memoirs of Margaret Fuller Ossoli* (2 vols., Boston, 1881), II, 12.

143. O. B. Frothingham, *Transcendentalism in New England* (N.Y., 1886), pp. vi–viii, 136.

This dual nature was observed as early as 1842 when Noah Porter remarked: "The word Transcendentalism . . . has two applications, one of which is popular and indefinite, the other philosophical and precise. In the former sense it describes men, rather than opinions, since it is freely extended to those who hold opinions, not only diverse from each other but directly opposed."—*American Biblical Repository*, 2nd ser., III (July, 1842), 195.

From the beginning, no one, not even the members, quite agreed on what Transcendentalism was. There was more agreement on who were and who were not Transcendentalists, though even here there were differences of opinion. To the earlier generation belonged Dr. William Ellery Channing (1780–1842), Convers Francis (1795–1865), Amos Bronson Alcott (1799–1888), Wm. Henry Furness (1802–1896), George Ripley (1802–1880), Orestes A. Brownson (1803–1876), R. W. Emerson (1803–1883), Elizabeth P. Peabody (1804–1884), F. H. Hedge (1805–1890), Wm. H. Channing (1810–1884), James F. Clarke (1810–1883), Sarah Margaret Fuller (1810–1850), Theodore Parker (1810–1860), C. P. Cranch (1813–1893), J. S. Dwight (1813–1864), and H. D. Thoreau (1817–1862). Whether Nathaniel Hawthorne (1804–1864) should be listed with them poses several nice questions. Hedge named Caleb Stetson, Mrs. Sarah Ripley, Jones Very, and Robert Bartlett as other members of the Transcendental Club, and among occasional visitors he mentioned George Bradford, Samuel Osgood, Ephraim Peabody, and George Putnam. Among the later Transcendentalists were Cyrus A. Bartol (1813–1900), John Weiss (1818–1879), Samuel Longfellow (1819–1892), J. E. Cabot (1821–1903), O. B. Frothingham (1822–1895), Samuel Johnson (1822–1882), T. W. Higginson (1823–1911), David A. Wasson (1823–1887), Moncure D. Conway (1832–1907), and George Willis Cooke (1848–1923).

144. Lowell called it "the protestant spirit of Puritanism seeking a new outlet and an escape from forms and creeds."—*Works* (Ed. de luxe), II, 137.

145. Frothingham, *op. cit.*, 302. This admission, by one on the inside, explains why those on the outside considered Transcendentalism incomprehensible. The uninitiated called it nonsense and moonshine. Members of the group themselves were conscious of their reputation for shadowy vagueness. Said Thoreau: "I should have told them at once that I was a transcendentalist. That would have been the shortest way of telling them that they would not understand my explanations."—*Journal*, V, 4 (Mar. 5, 1853). Emerson himself sometimes poked sly fun at the whims and oddities of his confreres, while good Transcendentalists like Clarke and Cranch enjoyed making humorous drawings of the brethren. See F. D. Miller, *C. P. Cranch and his Caricatures of New England Transcendentalism* (Boston, 1951). Emerson's efforts to explain Transcendentalism were unavailing; the public either oversimplified his meaning or roundly pooh-poohed it. As early as 1836 one of his Concord neighbors explained, with a wave of the hand, that Transcendentalism meant simply "a little beyond" (Emerson's *Journals*, Cent. ed., IV, 114). Even Dickens was given to understand "that whatever was unintelligible would be certainly transcendental" (*American Notes*, in *Works*, Household ed., I, 51–52). A teacher, taking his pupils on a Mississippi riverboat excursion, explained, "See the holes made in the bank yonder by the swallows. Take away the bank, and leave the apertures, and this is Transcendentalism."—Clarence Gohdes, *Periodicals of Transcendentalism* (Durham, N.C., 1931), p. 8.

The theologians were more serious. "To me," said the Rev. John Pierce, "it is like the tale of an idiot, full of sound and fury, signifying nothing" (*Proc. Mass. Hist. Soc.*, 2nd., V, 227, Jan., 1890). A Baltimore clergyman described it as "a new philosophy . . . maintaining that nothing is everything in general, and everything is nothing in particular."—M. D. Conway, *Emerson at Home and Abroad* (Boston, 1862), 187–88. For most people, Transcendentalism was anything that lay beyond the realm of common sense, whether in thought, word, or deed.

146. Frothingham, *op. cit.*, p. 355; see also pp. 153–58.

147. *Works* (Cent. ed., 15 vols., Boston, 1907–1913), VI, 37.

148. The Transcendental hierarchy was recruited chiefly from the Unitarian clergy. First and foremost as the greatest preacher of his generation stood W. E. Channing, a kind of godfather of the Transcendentalists, though not strictly one of them. Others who were, or had been Unitarian clergymen include Emerson, Ripley, Dwight, Cranch, Parker, and W. H. Channing. Alcott, though without a pulpit, was a preacher all his life; while Brownson was a preacher of all orders in succession. Among the younger men, Samuel Longfellow, Johnson, Higginson, and Bartol were Unitarian ministers.

149. It was generally agreed that Transcendentalism, this latest form of infidelity, was the result of erstwhile Unitarians, like Emerson and Parker, going in pursuit of foreign gods— German theologians and German metaphysi-

cians. For a lucid presentation of the issues involved, see Clarence H. Faust, "The Background of the Unitarian Opposition to Transcendentalism," *Mod. Philol.*, XXXV, iii (Feb., 1938), 297–324. "This movement," contended W. D. Wilson, "grew out of the Unitarian movement. It did not, however, grow out of Unitarian theology. It is not a carrying out of Unitarianism, for the two systems have different starting points, and tend to different directions. . . . The association is, philosophically speaking, purely accidental."—*Dial*, I (Apr., 1841), 421. Professor Henry D. Gray, too, concludes: "However much more it may have been, Transcendentalism was a development in the history of the Unitarian church."—*Emerson: A Statement of New England Transcendentalism* (Stanford University, 1914), p. 11.

150. XII (Jan., 1840), 71. That German metaphysics and theology were mainly responsible for the "atheistical tendencies" among the Transcendentalists was assumed by almost everybody. See C. H. Faust, *loc. cit.*, 304–5, 307, 316–24; *Christ. Exam.*, XXIII (Nov., 1837), 181–82; XXV (1836), 266 ff., XXXI (1841), 98 ff; XXXII (1842), 251 ff.; and Parker's "Experiences as a Minister," *Works*, XIII, 324–25.

151. Frothingham, *op. cit.*, p. 153; Emerson, *Works*, I, 340–42, 347–48.

152. Horace Mann was agitating for educational reforms, and Elizabeth P. Peabody, among others, was beginning to evolve a system of kindergarten education. The temperance movement was attracting attention, and Pierpont quit the pulpit because people were not ready to become total abstainers. The first national temperance convention was held in 1813, and in 1838 a prohibitory law was passed in Massachusetts. Conventions of all kinds were held, and newspapers espousing all sorts of ideas and reforms appeared, among them the *Non-Resistant*, begun in Boston in 1839 and edited by Garrison, Edmund Quincy, and Maria W. Chapman. In 1840 the Anti-Slavery Society split because women demanded to speak on its platform. Soon after a women's convention was called. Emerson resigned his ministerial charge because of religious scruples; Ripley and Parker preached naturalism; Abner Kneeland was preaching materialism. In 1838 George Combe came to this country and aroused unbounded expectations among the phrenologists. About the same time spiritualism began to claim attention; mesmerism, clairvoyance, and kindred subjects electrified the people. Homeopathy, hydropathy, the Graham diet, and the Thomsonian cure came in for their share in the effort to redeem human life. Some

forswore the use of cotton because it was produced by slave labor; others refused to wear woolen goods lest they rob the sheep of their natural defenses. Many became practicing vegetarians; some denied themselves not only meat but also tea and coffee. In the midst of all these reformations and dreams appeared William Miller to prophesy the end of all things and to do a brisk business selling ascension robes.

Nearly all the disciples of the Newness were affected by this ferment. Thoreau declared his independence of all visible churches, announcing that he had never joined one and would henceforth withhold his money. Next, he led a one-man secession movement and, protesting taxes and an unjust war with Mexico, found himself lodged in jail. Shortly after this clash with the state, he went to Walden Pond to live in seclusion. On the social front, Brownson advocated ideas and a program that were too extreme even for the disciples of the New Views, so that after the first meetings, he became "unbearable" and "was not afterwards invited." Margaret Fuller conducted her remarkable conversations in Boston and elsewhere. Francis, Hedge, Ripley, and Clarke were reading the German theologians and publicly defending them. Alcott left his Temple School, went to Concord, and there lived by manual labor, and nibbled his celery and asparagus at the wrong end. Only the "heaven-aspiring" vegetables were proper food: potatoes because they grew underground and carrots because they grew downward were proscribed. Emerson helped him procure the means for going to England, there to establish a school which should realize the idea conceived in Boston, only to have Alcott return with Charles Lane and establish Fruitlands at Harvard, Mass.—another one of the numerous attempts looking forward to the new order. Robert Owen's enterprise at New Harmony was followed by others; the writings of Fourier were interpreted by Albert Brisbane and given currency in Greeley's *Tribune*, which absorbed new ideas like a sponge. The Brook Farm community was established in 1841, Hopedale the same year, and Northampton in 1842.

Among the more notable combinations were the conventions of the "Friends of Universal Reform" held in the Chardon Street Chapel, Boston. Their purpose was to revitalize the old church forms and doctrines. Three meetings, each of several days' duration, were held during 1840–1841, to discuss the institution of the Sabbath, the church, and the ministry. Edmund Quincy was moderator; Brownson was one of the chief speakers; Alcott found himself at home on the platform; Emerson attended and served on committees but did not speak; but he did print, in the *Dial*, what he considered the best speech delivered, by Nathaniel H. Whiting, a mechanic. Later he reported, with a good deal of detachment:

"A great variety of dialect and costume was noted; a great deal of confusion, eccentricity, and freak appeared, as well as zeal and enthusiasm. If the assembly was disorderly, it was picturesque. Madmen, madwomen, men with beards, Dunkers, Abolitionists, Calvinists, Unitarians and philosophers,—all came successively to the top, and seized their moment, if not their *hour*, wherein to chide or pray or preach or protest."—*Works*, X, 374; see also the opening paragraphs of Lowell's essay on Thoreau.

153. The Brook-Farm Institute of Agriculture and Education of 1841–1846 and the *Dial* of 1840–1844 were admittedly among its more tangible and representative manifestations, but neither was, in the philosophical sense of the word, Transcendental. While Brook Farm had its inspiration in the New Views, not one of the four generally regarded as the leading Transcendentalists—Emerson, Margaret Fuller, Parker, and Alcott—went to live at Brook Farm or invested their money in it. The *Dial* indicated, through the balanced nicety of its good will toward the community, sympathy for the aims of its founders but inability to subscribe to the theories underlying the experiment or the practices actually put in operation there. The collectivism upon which Brook Farm was founded did not chime harmoniously with the extremely individualistic base upon which the Transcendentalist built his faith. Emerson, when Ripley pressed him to join the Association, said, "At the name of a society my repulsions play, all my quills rise and sharpen" (*Letters*, II, 368–71, Dec. 14, 1840; *Journals*, V, 473–74). "He never spoke of Brook Farm," says Lindsay Swift (*Brook Farm*, p. 52), "without conveying to the finest sense the assurance that someone was laughing behind the shrubbery." Similarly, the other characteristic venture of the Transcendentalists, the *Dial*, did not satisfy all Transcendentalists, in either policy or accomplishment—no, not even the editors, assistant editors, and contributors.

154. *Emerson . . .*, pp. 14–15.

155. *Studies in New England Transcendentalism* (N.Y., 1908), pp. 107–8.

156. T. W. Higginson, *Writings* (7 vols., Boston, 1900), II, 12.

157. Gohdes, *op. cit.*, p. 12.

158. My italics. The qualification implied in the italicized phrase throws the meaning of the term *Transcendentalism* open to a wide variety of interpretations.

159. G. W. Cooke, *An Historical and Biographical Introduction to Accompany the Dial as Reprinted in Numbers for the Rowfant Club* (2 vols., Cleveland, 1902), I, 1.

160. There was nothing in Hobbes's materialism, Locke's sensationalism, or Hume's skepticism to encourage an enthusiastic and live religion. Based on the cold light of reason and nature, it could not logically admit either enthusiasm or ecstasy. The result was a frigid, empty theism—what Emerson spoke of as "the pale negations of Boston Unitarianism." Parker, too, was aware of this spiritual sterility: "I felt that the 'liberal' ministers did not do justice to simple religious feeling; to me their preaching seemed to relate too much to outward things, not enough to the inward pious life; their prayers felt cold." Writing of Massachusetts, Emerson said, "From 1790 to 1820, there was not a book, a speech, a conversation, or a thought in the State."

161. "From 1830 to 1840," testified Mrs. Caroline Dall, "was a period of mental activity. It produced some confusion when Leibnitz, Spinoza, Kant, Goethe, Herder, Schleiermacher, and Jean Paul came sailing at once into Boston harbor and discharged their freight. The wharves were littered with the spoils of a century. Idealism, which had originated with Anne Hutchinson, was now imported in foreign packages from France and Germany."—*Transcendentalism in New England* (Boston, 1897), pp. 12–13.

162. Transcendentalism was essentially a young people's movement. In 1836, the leading adherents averaged thirty years of age. Their teachings were most eagerly caught up by the young. See Lowell's essay on Emerson as well as Emerson's observation, "The old people suspect and dislike me, the young love me."—*Journals*, V, 270–71.

163. Elizabeth P. Peabody, *Reminiscences of the Rev. William Ellery Channing* (Boston, 1880), p. 56.

164. W. H. Channing, *The Life of William Ellery Channing* (Boston, 1899), p. 276; also *Works* (new and complete ed., Boston, 1903), pp. 272–73.

165. W. H. Channing, *Life*, pp. 39, 54–57, 87–88; Peabody, *Reminiscences*, pp. 367–68. He retained, even in his late years, a vivid recollection of how, during his undergraduate days at Harvard, after reading Hutcheson, there came to him an intense intuitive experience which marked a "new spiritual birth." Realizations of the dignity of human nature, of the beauty of disinterested love, of man's position

in an order of eternal progression penetrated his soul and dominated his thinking. His reading of Ferguson on Civil Liberty led him to apply to society what Hutcheson had taught regarding the tendency of the human soul toward moral perfection, an application that led to Channing's conception of social progress.— *Life*, 32–33; Goddard, *op. cit.*, p. 46.

166. *Life*, p. 34; *Reminiscences*, pp. 367–68. Later students seem to find not necessarily that Kant depended upon Price but that there does exist a striking parallelism in general tendency of moral thought. For able but contrasting views, see James Martineau's *Types of Ethical Theory* (2 vols., Oxford, 1885), II, 439–47, and Leslie Stephen's *History of English Thought in the Eighteenth Century* (2 vols., London, 1876), II, 12–15. Both find in Price anticipations of Kant: Stephen, of Kant's Categorical Imperative, and Martineau, of his distinction between the pure and practical reason.

167. *Reminiscences*, pp. 9, 70, 72, 75–77, 80–81, 127, 134, 143, 158, 188, 364, 441; *Life*, pp. 275–76, 341; *Works*, pp. 161–62.

168. This bore fruit, in 1830, in the form of Miss Peabody's publication of her translation of *Self-Education; or, the Means and Art of Moral Progress* (reprinted 1832 and again in 1833). When De Gerando wrote to Miss Peabody requesting information on religious views in America, Channing himself responded on June 29, 1831. In view of these circumstances it seems not unlikely that De Gerando's *Histoire comparée des systèmes de philosophie* (Paris, 1804), which the *North American Review* reviewed enthusiastically in 1824 (XVIII, 234–66), should have been known to him. This is the work on which Emerson fell with so much relish in 1830. The contribution of De Gerando's to the rise of new ideas in New England has been discussed by Howard M. Jones in *America and French Culture, 1750–1848* (Chapel Hill, 1927), pp. 463–64.

169. *Reminiscences*, p, 351. Cousin's *Introduction* was translated by Henning Gottfried Linberg (Boston, 1832).

170. Tr. by Caleb S. Henry (Hartford, 1834) as *Elements of Psychology: Included in a Critical Examination of Locke's Essay on the Human Understanding*.

171. His nephew-biographer tells us: "In Kant's doctrine of the Reason he found confirmation of the views which, in early years received from Price, had quickened him to ever deeper reverence of the essential powers of man. To Schelling's sublime intimations of the Divine Life everywhere manifested through nature and humanity, his heart, devoutly conscious of the universal agency of God, gladly responded. But above all did the heroic stoicism of Fichte charm him by its full assertion of the grandeur of the human will."—*Life*, p. 275.

172. *Reminiscences*, p. 350.

173. *Reminiscences*, pp. 213, 250; see also Geo. W. Spindler, *Karl Follen: A Biographical Sketch* (Chicago, 1917), pp. 107–8.

174. Follen's diary, kept from November 5, 1827, to February 26, 1828, although only fragmentarily reproduced in the biography his widow prepared indicates that he spent on the average at least one day a week with Channing in private conversation. Among the subjects discussed, the following are representative: the personality of God, the nature of Christ, immortality, free agency, moral and religious education, Christianity as a particular form of religion, religious instruction of children, the value of imaginative literature and of fiction in general, Schiller's idea of co-operation of kindred minds for the discovery of truth, German art and literature, the moral teaching of Fichte, the theological contributions of De Wette and Schleiermacher, and the philosophies of Kant, Fries, and Schelling (*Works*, I, 180–246 *passim;* Spindler, *op. cit.*, pp. 106–7, 167–68). Follen's diary records evenings when he read to Channing from such works as Foster's *Rise and Progress of Religion*, Tennemann's *History of Philosophy*, and De Gerando's discussion of Kantian idealism. To Miss Peabody, Channing avowed his opinion of Follen as his superior in learning and Christian character (*Reminiscences*, p. 301). Doubtless Follen was the determining factor in changing Channing's view of German literature. In 1823, laboring under the impression that German thought was subversive to true Christianity, he cautioned William Emerson against studying in Germany (Frothingham, *Life of George Ripley*, pp. 20 ff.); five years later, prompted by Follen, he himself undertook to learn German in order to gain a firsthand knowledge of German thought (Spindler, *op. cit.*, p. 158). The evidence that he succeeded in learning German is inconclusive. Generally, it seems, he contented himself with French and British restatements of German philosophy or Follen's more authoritative explanations.

175. *William Ellery Channing* (Boston & N.Y., 1903), p. 383.

AVENUES OF TRANSMISSION

176. René Wellek, *Immanuel Kant in England* (Princeton, 1931), p. 5.

177. Other deterrents included British theological orthodoxy and prejudice. Consider, for example, the translation of Tennemann's

Grundriss by the Rev. Arthur Johnson, who, in order to appease his own religious conscience, permitted himself some rather unusual liberties as a translator. He not only substituted terms and otherwise modified Tennemann's text but confessed that he "judged it better to omit altogether a few passages which appeared to militate against Revealed Religion rather than alter or soften them." He solemnly warned the reader against Kant, and as for Fichte and Schelling, "the most fanatical dreams of the wildest religious enthusiasts were never more repugnant to common sense than . . . the Absolute Identity of Schelling or the *Ego* and *Non-Ego* of Fichte" (first ed., 1832, Preface, p. xi). For similar wholesale condemnations in the more academic English philosophical books, see J. D. Morrell, *Historical and Critical View of the Speculative Philosophy of Europe in the Nineteenth Century* (4 vols., London, 1846), II, 156–58, 159; Robert Blakey, *History of the Philosophy of Mind* (4 vols., London, 1850), IV, 158; and George H. Lewes, *Biographical History of Philosophy* (Library ed., London, 1857), p. 725.

178. *A General View of Professor Kant's Principles Concerning Man, the World, and the Deity, Submitted to the Consideration of the Learned.* By F. A. Nitsch, Late Lecturer on the Latin Language and Mathematics in the Royal Frederician College at Königsberg, and Pupil of Professor Kant (London, 1796), 234 pp.

179. *Elements of Critical Philosophy: Containing a Concise Account of its Origin and Tendency; a View of All the Works Published by its Founder, Professor Immanuel Kant, and a Glossary of Terms and Phrases* . . . (London, 1798), 183 pp. This book is little more than a chronological listing, with tables of contents or chapter headings, of thirty of Kant's principal works, including the two *Critiques*, and of fourteen of his minor works, together with a translation of Joh. Schultze's *Synopsis of the Critical Philosophy.*

180. This is really a translation of Ignatz Sigismund Beck's *Erläuternder Auszug aus den kritischen Schriften des Herrn Professor Kant auf Anrathen desselben* (Riga, 1793), published in London, but actually printed in Altenburg, 1798, under the title of *Principles of Critical Philosophy, Selected from the Works of Emmanuel Kant by I. S. Beck. Translated by an Auditor of the Latter.*

181. Ascribed by George M. Duncan to A. F. M. Willich, in "English Translations of Kant's Writings," *Kantstudien*, II (1898), 253–58.

182. For the chief bibliographical facts regarding early English renditions of Kant, see Morgan, *op. cit.*, Nos. 4787–89, 4801, 4810–11, 4819–20, 4838, 4850a, 4851.

183. See Wellek, *op. cit.*, pp. 28–38; also John H. Muirhead, *Coleridge as Philosopher* (London & N.Y., 1930), pp. 422–36. Thos. Brown's review, in 1803, of Charles Villers' *Philosophie de Kant ou Principles Fondamentaux de la Philosophie Transcendentale* (2 vols., Metz, 1801) is of some significance (1) because of Brown's importance, for he later became Dugald Stewart's successor at the University of Edinburgh, (2) because Villers' book was the chief source of popular information on Kant in French until it was superseded by Madame de Staël's, and (3) because the review appeared in a very conspicuous place, the first number of the *Edinburgh Review* (Jan., 1803), pp. 253–80. The essay was known to both Wm. Drummond and Dugald Stewart. See Stewart's *Complete Works* (ed. by Wm. Hamilton, 11 vols., Edinburgh, 1854–1860), V, 117.

184. A brief treatment of the Kantian time-space problem in his *Philosophical Essays* (1810) may be disregarded. See *Collected Works*, pp. 420–22.

185. Wellek, *op. cit.*, pp. 40–41, 273.

186. In 1817 Wirgman sent Stewart an article on metaphysics which contained a good account of Kant's main points. This Stewart acknowledged, but added that there was "little probability" that he would change his views at the same time that he offered to subscribe for Wirgman's projected (but never completed) translation of Kant's first *Critique*. Wirgman's efforts to introduce Kant into England were continued throughout his lifetime, from 1795 to 1838. Notwithstanding Coleridge's snap judgment of him as knowing "nothing about Kant—a mere Formalist—a Buchstabler," Wirgman was far from being the worst expounder of Kantism in England. For his relations with Coleridge, H. C. Robinson, Madame de Staël, and De Morgan, see Wellek, *op. cit.*, pp. 40, 211–42, and Fr. Ueberweg, *Hist. of Philosophy from Thales to the Present Time*, tr. by Geo. S. Morris (2 vols., N.Y., 1874), II, 434.

187. *Collected Works*, V, 117–18.

188. Chiefly (1) G. G. Johann Buhle, *Histoire de la Philosophie moderne* (9 vols., Paris, 1817), a translation of the original German edition (8 vols. in 9, Göttingen, 1796–1804); (2) Willich, (3) Nitsch, (4) Madame de Staël, and (5) J. M. De Gerando, *Histoire comparée des systèmes de philosophie* (2 vols., Paris, 1804).

189. The misapprehension involved here is doubtless owing to Stewart's reliance on Nitsch, whose refinements upon reason, understanding, and sensibility, present these faculties under very novel colors. See Nitsch, *op. cit.*, p. 40.

190. Without discerning the principles on

which Kant deduced the categories, but identifying them with Cudworth's conglomeration of innate ideas, he quotes verbatim, in a footnote in the Appendix, the Kantian categories from Willich. Depreciatingly he adds: "These tables speak for themselves without further comment." And with this flourish Stewart is off to matters of greater moment—matters which he came little nearer comprehending—namely, Kant's practical reason, free will, morality in general, and religion. Kant is generously excused of the intent "to establish a system of skepticism"; his inquiries simply got out of hand. Hence the "*Practical Reason* is a wing which Kant prudently added to his edifice, from a sense of the inadequacy of the original design, to answer the intended purpose." Unfortunately "the whole of Kant's moral superstructure will be found to rest ultimately on no better basis than the metaphysical conundrum, that the human mind (considered as a *noumenon* and not as a *phenomenon*) neither exists in space nor in time."

191. Stewart, *General View*, pp. 245–46; compare De Gerando, *Histoire comparée*, II, 244 ff.

192. He quotes Madame de Staël's account of Fichte's announcement that "in his next lecture he 'was going to create God,' . . . meaning that he intended to show how the idea of God arose and unfolded itself in the mind of man."—*De l'Allemagne* (London, 1813), III, 107. Most of the two pages are devoted to De Gerando's exposition of Fichte's equation, ego = ego, and its implications, of the "unparalleled absurdity" of which Stewart says simply, "I cannot make anything." Compare Stewart, *op. cit.*, pp. 249–50, and De Gerando, *op. cit.*, II, 314. Then he proceeds to Schelling, who gets a bare page of commentary, quoted, first, from M. G. Scheringhauser's article in the London *Monthly Magazine* for October, 1804, to the effect that Schelling's mystical transcendentalism has led a number of his Protestant disciples to embrace Catholicism, "not as a true religion, but as the most poetical" (XVII, 207; cf. *General View*, p. 251), and second, from De Gerando, who regards the "system of Schelling but an extension of that of Fichte, connecting with it a sort of Spinozism grafted on Idealism." Following a mere mention of Jacobi, Meiners, Herder, and Reinhold, whose works lay unread in Stewart's study, the venerable Professor of Moral Philosophy of Edinburgh passed on to a sixty-four-page eulogy of his beloved Scottish philosophy of common sense, firmly convinced that the latter had nothing to fear from the thoroughly discredited critical philosophy of Germany.

193. *Journals* (10 vols., Boston, 1909–1914),

I, 289–90. A few years later James Marsh of Vermont appraised Stewart more critically and correctly as one of the chief deterring influences in America to a reception of Kantian idealism. See Jos. Torrey, *Remains of James Marsh . . . with a Memoir* (Boston, 1843), p. 137 (Mar. 23, 1829).

194. See his review of Cousin's *Cours de Philosophie* in the *Edinburgh Rev.*, L, xlix (Oct., 1829), 194–221, reprinted in *Discussions on Philosophy and Literature, Education, and University Reform* (London, 1852), esp. pp. 24–25. Sir James Mackintosh's earlier study of German in 1804–1805 with the view to read Kant had born little fruit. See *Memoirs of Sir James Mackintosh* (Boston, 1853), I, 260; Wellek, *op. cit.*, pp. 49–50.

195. See Hamilton's review of Johnson's translation of Tennemann's *Grundriss* (London, 1832) in the *Edinburgh Rev.*, LVI, cxi (Oct., 1832), 160–77; repr. in *Discussions*, pp. 98–116.

196. *Discussions* (Edinburgh & London, 1866), p. 11. The italics are Hamilton's.

197. *Ibid.*, p. 12. The force of the word *constitutive*, if Emerson, for instance, read it in this context, was doubtless lost to him. As we shall have occasion to observe later, Emerson seems never to have distinguished clearly between the constitutive and the purely regulative aspects of the reason.

198. Himself far from a professing Kantian, yet confessing "sincerest admiration" for Cousin's "character and accomplishments," while dissenting from "the most prominent principle of his philosophy" (*ibid.* p. 7) and objecting to Cousin's easy popularization of critical transcendentalism, Hamilton was, nevertheless, the best commentator on German thought in Britain up to his time and the first "authority" on German philosophy available to Emerson in America before he turned to a more earnest study of Coleridge.

Hamilton outlines four fundamental positions with respect to the Absolute (Unconditioned): "(1) The Unconditioned as uncognisable and inconceivable; its notion being only negative of the Conditioned, which last can alone be positively known or conceived. (2) It is not the object of knowledge; but its notion, as a regulative principle of the mind itself, is more than a mere negation of the Conditioned. (3) It is cognisable, but not conceivable; it can be known by a sinking back into identity with the Infinito-Absolute, but it is incomprehensible by consciousness and reflection, which are only of the relative and the different. (4) It is cognisable and conceivable by consciousness and reflection, under relation, difference, and plurality."—*Discussions*, p. 12. The first of these positions Hamilton himself subscribes to; the second is the position held by Kant; the third, by Schelling; the last by Cousin. The last three are arranged, according to Hamilton, in the ascending order and degree of error which the philosophy of the Absolute presents.

Hamilton regards as "conclusive Kant's analysis of Time and Space into formal necessities of thought (without however admitting that they have no external or objective reality)," but he cannot "help viewing Kant's deduction of the 'categories of Understanding,' and of the 'Ideas of speculative Reason,' as the work of great but perverse ingenuity" (*Discussions*, p. 16). Kant distinguishes Reason from Understanding "simply on the ground that the former is conversant about, or rather tends toward, the Unconditioned." Actually "both faculties perform the same function, both seek the one in the many; the Idea (*Idee*) is only the Concept (*Begriff*) sublimated into the inconceivable," and "Reason is only the Understanding which has 'overleaped itself.'" While Kant has shown that the Idea of the Unconditioned can have no objective reality—that it conveys no knowledge—and that it involves the most insoluble contradictions, he ought to have shown, also, that the unconditioned has no objective application, because it has, in fact, "no subjective affirmation". Thus, in Hamilton's estimation, Kant "stands intermediate between those who view the notion of the Absolute as the instinctive affirmation of an eccentric intuition, and those who regard it as a factitious negative of an eccentric generalisation." If, says Hamilton, analysis were reduced to its ultimate simplicity, thought would have to be discriminated simply into *positive* and *negative*, "according as it is conversant about the Conditioned and the Unconditioned," and Kant's twelve categories would thus be included under the former, and his three Ideas of Reason under the latter; whence it would follow that the contrast between Understanding and Reason would disappear altogether." —*Discussions*, pp. 16–17.

Since the speculative Reason, "on Kant's own admission, is an organ of mere delusion . . . his doctrine leads to absolute skepticism"; for "if our intellectual nature is perfidious in one revelation, it cannot be presumed truthful in any; nor is it possible for Kant to establish the existence of God, Free-Will, and Immortality, on the supposed veracity of reason, in a practical revelation, after having himself established its mendacity in a speculative." Thus, while Kant annihilated the older metaphysics (for which Hamilton praises him), he retained "within the bosom of his own philosophy" the germ of "a more visionary doctrine of the Absolute (Infinito-Absolute) than any of those refuted." Having slain the body, he failed to exorcise the spectre of the Absolute, which continues to haunt its followers—Bouterwek, Bardili, Reinhold, Fichte, Schelling, Hegel, and sundry others—all endeavoring, according to their several abilities, "to fix the Absolute as a positive knowledge."—*Discussions*, p. 18. This is followed by an exposition, first, of Schelling, and then of Cousin, in whom the shortcomings of the third and fourth positions enumerated above are discussed.

199. See his attack on Hegel in 1852, *Discussions* (London, 1852), pp. 21, n., 21–24; also Muirhead, *op. cit.*, pp. 427–28.

200. The misunderstanding of Hegel by Englishmen was heightened by the inherent difficulties of his language. Lewes indicated a major difficulty when he observed that Hegel differs from Kant, Fichte, and Schelling in that, while they carry forward a certain tradition of terminology and methodology, in Hegel a new nomenclature has to be mastered. Hegel had, it seemed, succeeded all too well in his avowed intention "to teach philosophy to speak German." For twenty or more years British academic philosophers went their ways unconcerned about Hegel.

201. See *Philosophical Remains*, III, 545–68; Muirhead, *op. cit.*, pp. 436–38.

202. *Modern Philosophy* . . . (London, 1862), pp. 619–38.

203. Heretofore only two of Hegel's works had been available in English: (1) H. Slowman and J. Wallon's fragmentary translation of the *Logic* in 1856, and (2) Sibree's translation of *Lectures on the Philosophy of History* (London, 1857).

204. Muirhead, *op. cit.*, pp. 444–45; *The Secret of Hegel* (2nd ed., Edinburgh, 1898), Preface.

205. De Quincey's translation of Kant's essay on "The Idea of a Universal History on a Cosmopolitan Plan" had appeared in the *London Magazine* for October, 1824 (X, 385–93). Before that date, the *Morning Chronicle* had printed a series of letters on German philosophy, notably one by Henry James Richter, for March 12, 1814. The same writer published, in 1817, a philosophical satire entitled *Day Light, a Recent Discovery on the Art of Painting; with Hints on the Philosophy of the Fine Arts and on the Human Mind at First Discovered by Emmanuel Kant* (London, 1817), in which Kant appears as a star witness for the doctrine of ideality of art and the creativeness of the human mind. For a brief account of Richter, who

was a friend of William Blake, and whose propagandist activities for Kant extended from 1797 to 1855, see Wellek, *op. cit.*, pp. 205–11. Two years later came the first actual translation (properly so called) of Kant's works in John Richardson's *Prolegomena to Every Future Metaphysics Which Can Appear as a Science* and Kant's posthumous work on *Logic*, the latter with a biographical appendix. These two were republished, together with a third work, entitled "An Enquiry, Critical and Metaphysical, into the Grounds of Proof for the Existence of God, and into Theodicy, a Sequel to the Logic and Prolegomena . . . printed in 1819, now first published in 1836"—all under the title of *Metaphysical Works of the Celebrated Immanuel Kant* (London, 1836; see Muirhead, *op. cit.*, p. 431; Wellek, *op. cit.*, pp. 18–19). In 1823 appeared Wirgman's *Science of Philosophy, i.e., An Entirely New Complete and Permanent Science of Philosophy Founded on Kant's Critic of Pure Reason*, published by the press of *Encyclopedia Londonensis*, and comprising 200 folio pages full of blusterous polemics directed chiefly against Stewart and long quotations from Nitsch, Willich, Richter, Reinhold, Lambert, Villers, Madame de Staël, and Christian and William Snell—all bountifully embellished with plates and diagrams in brilliant colors.

The production of complete and authoritative translations of Kant's writings proceeded slowly. Francis Hayward's translation of Kant's *Critique of Pure Reason* was published in London in 1838 by Pickering (2nd ed., London, 1848), followed by that of J. M. D. Meiklejohn (London, Bohn, 1845; repr., 1855); while Max Müller's long standard rendition did not appear until 1881, to be followed by Norman Kemp Smith's in 1929. A part (about one half) of the *Critique of Practical Reason* became available to English readers in J. W. Semple's volume, *Kant's Metaphysic of Ethics* (Edinburgh, 1836), and two years later the same translator presented *Die Religion innerhalb der Grenzen der blossen Vernunft* as *Kant's Theory of Religion* (London, 1838). Thomas K. Abbott's *Critique of the Practical Reason* did not appear until 1873. In 1836 the French life of Kant by the Swiss Phillip Albrecht Stapfer was translated by Charles Hodge. For a fuller list of Kant translations see George M. Duncan, *loc. cit.*, pp. 253–58; B. Q. Morgan, *A Critical Bibliography of German Literature in English Translation* (2nd ed., Stanford Univ., 1938), pp. 257–61 (for Fichte, see pp. 113–14; for Schelling, p. 407; for Hegel, pp. 216–17). For the progress of German philosophy in making itself felt in British thought since 1830, see Wellek, *op. cit.*, pp. 245–62; Muirhead, *op. cit.*, p. 447; J. E. Creighton,

"The Philosophy of Kant in America," *Kantstudien*, II (1898), 237–62; J. H. Muirhead, "How Hegel Came to England," *Mind*, XXXVI (1927), 423–27, and "How Hegel Came to America," *Philosophical Rev.*, XXXVIII (1928), 226–40.

206. *Works* (Shedd ed.), III, 257; see also IV, 400; Wellek, *op. cit.*, pp. 69–73, and *Unpublished Letters of Samuel Taylor Coleridge* (ed. by Earl L. Griggs, Amer. ed., 2 vols., New Haven, 1933), II, 264.

207. Among the latest and most informative contributions is Joseph W. Beach, "Coleridge's Borrowings from the German," *ELH*, IX, i (Mar., 1942), 36–58.

208. Especially by Professors Wellek, Muirhead, and Alice D. Snyder. See her *Coleridge on Logic and Learning* (New Haven, 1929).

209. These include Mendelssohn's *Morgenstunden*, erster Theil, 1790, and *Jerusalem* (1781); Maass's *Versuch über die Einbildungskraft* (1797); Wolff's *Rational Thoughts on the Powers of Understanding* (Engl. tr., 1777); Kant's *Vermischte Schriften* (3 vols., Halle, 1799), *Die Religion innerhalb der Grenzen der blossen Vernunft* (1793), and *Metaphysik der Sitten* (1797); Fichte's *Bestimmung der Menschen* (1800), and *Versuch einer Kritik aller Offenbarung* (1792); Schelling's *Ideen zu einer Philosophie der Natur* (1803), and *System des transcendentalen Idealismus* (1800); Hegel's *Wissenschaft der Logik* (1812–1816); and Tennemann's *Geschichte der Philosophie* (12 vols., 1794).

210. Most of these are reproduced in Alice D. Snyder, *op. cit.*; see also Julian Ira Lindsay, "Coleridge Marginalia in Jacobi's *Werke*," *Mod. Lang. Notes*, L, iv (Apr., 1935), 216–26. In addition, Muirhead drew upon the two volumes of Coleridge's *Marginalia* which contain numerous notes by Coleridge on Kant's *Kritik der reinen Vernunft* and his *Allgemeine Naturgeschichte und Theorie des Himmels*, on Jacobi's *Ueber die Lehre des Spinoza in Briefen an den Herrn Moses Mendelssohn*, and on William Law's translation of Boehme.

211. Here are to be enumerated chiefly the two-volume *Logic*, the three-volume, vellum-bound *Opus Maximum*, two volumes of *Marginalia*, and an *Autograph Notebook*.

212. Muirhead, *Coleridge as Philosopher*, p. 15. Professor Wellek, in his finely analytical study of *Kant in England*, is not quite as positive on the score of Coleridge's originality and consistency. Wellek seems to demonstrate, first, that Coleridge's several philosophical works (including the MS "Logic") are everywhere permeated with Kantian thought and phraseology; and second, that while his impor-

tant criticism of Kant is borrowed from Schelling, it did not lead, as in Schelling, the way to Hegel's synthesis, but only to "a deeper and more pernicious dualism" (p. 101). Since in the latter conclusion much depends on the interpretation of the word *dualism*, the point remains debatable. Coleridge emphatically denied the charge, and Muirhead's argument runs contrary to Wellek's. Indeed, the latter himself moderates his charge by observing that among the English romantics "only in Coleridge [do] we leave thought which is an integral part of poetry for thought which can be expressed in logical form and can claim comparison with the systems of the great German philosophers of the time" (p. 139). See also Elisabeth Winckelmann, *Coleridge und die Kantische Philosophie* (*Palaestra*, No. 184, Leipzig, 1933).

213. These contributions, Professor Muirhead finds, grew out of Coleridge's fundamental dissatisfaction with the effort of contemporary philosophy to reduce everything by "triumphant analysis" to its component elements, thus reducing poetry, religion, and morals to the realm of "unanalysable feeling." See Muirhead, *op. cit.*, pp. 29, 30–33; S. F. Gingerich, "From Necessity to Transcendentalism in Coleridge," *PMLA*, XXXV, i (Mar., 1920), 1–59; and Claud Howard, *Coleridge's Idealism* . . . (Boston, 1924). Possessed of a temperament in some respects distinctly favorable for philosophical pursuits and with a vastly larger amount of sustained effort than he has been credited with, Coleridge labored to establish a philosophical position, the central point of which Muirhead defines as "that of the true meaning and place of Individuality in the world both of nature and of man" (*op. cit.*, p. 263).

This is not to maintain that Coleridge possessed a naturally great philosophic personality. He lacked a sense for the subtle shades of terminological differences in different thinkers; he did not always exercise a nice discrimination, and he seems not always to have been fully aware of the wide implications of individual theoretical propositions. These shortcomings, serious as they were for a philosopher as eclectic in method as Coleridge was, led him to construct, of his own ideas and those he borrowed or adapted, a building which, as Professor Wellek suggests, is not truly a unit, but rather a Kantian structure with liberal trimmings from Schelling, standing upon a Platonic foundation, and surmounted by an Anglican roof— in short, a typically Coleridgean building. But a building it is, whatever we may think of its consistency of style.

Muirhead's method of reviewing Coleridge's doctrine in the light of all the old and much new evidence emphasizes the necessity for dismissing the off-hand or biased judgments regarding Coleridge's "fragmentariness and slothfulness" as a thinker on the one hand and his "abstruseness and unintelligibility" on the other—for discounting the quips about his "logical swimming bladders" and "transcendental life preservers" made by Carlyle, who, of all men that claimed the right to judge, had the least right to call Coleridge a shyster in philosophy or to accuse him of misinterpreting the Germans. While the several works of Coleridge, taken separately, appear fragmentary, they are less so when viewed together. Completeness in itself, if made the sole test of greatness in philosophy, would do serious damage to the reputation of philosophers commonly lodged among the "greatest." Moreover, disciples of Coleridge like T. H. Green and J. H. Stirling, in substantial agreement upon what constitutes the essentials of his philosophy, discovered no fundamental inconsistencies and did not complain of abstruseness; and they found no cause to accuse him of misunderstanding and misinterpreting Kant and the German transcendentalists generally, although his American disciples, notably Marsh, had trouble following him on *all* points. As will appear in the sequel, Emerson, too, was at some points rather wide the mark in his understanding of both Coleridge and Kant.

214 *Letters* (ed. by E. H. Coleridge, 2 vols., Boston & N.Y., 1895), I, 348; also p. 341, note.

215. Letter to Poole, Mar. 23, 1801, *Letters*, I, 352.

216. *Biog. Lit.*, Ch. IX, in *Works* (Shedd ed.), III, 256–58. In subsequent references the Shedd edition is used unless otherwise indicated.

217. *Ibid.*, III, 258.

218. Compare *ibid.*, pp. 258–59, and Schelling's "Einleitung" in *Ideen zu einer Philosophie der Natur* in *Sämmtliche Werke*, II, 11–56. See Ch. XII of *Biog. Lit.* for Coleridge's acknowledgment of indebtedness to Schelling.

219. *Biog. Lit.*, Ch. IX, pp. 260–61. In a letter, dated Dec. 15, 1817, Coleridge says: "Fichte in his moral system is but a caricature of Kant, or rather, he is a Zeno, with a cowl, rope, and sackcloth of a Carthusian monk. His metaphysics have gone by; but he hath the merit of having prepared the ground for, and laid the first stone of, the dynamic philosophy by the substitution of Act for Thing" (*Letters*, II, 682). In the same letter he criticizes Kant's "stoic principle" as "false, unnatural, and even immoral," while Kant's "remarks on prayer in his 'Religion innerhalb der reinen Vernunft,'" are as "crass, nay vulgar and as superficial even in

psychology as they are low in taste." But, he adds, "with these exceptions, I reverence Immanuel Kant with my whole heart and soul, and I believe him to be the only philosopher for *all men* who have the power of thinking."

220. See, for a detailed examination of Coleridge's indebtedness, Henry H. Coleridge's introduction to the 1847 edition of the *Biographia Literaria*, conveniently available in the Shedd edition of Coleridge's *Works*, III, xi–cxl; see also III, 691–751.

221. *Biog. Lit.*, p. 262.

222. *Table Talk*, June 28, 1834, *Works*, VI, 521; cf. Muirhead, *op. cit.*, p. 56.

223. Already *The Friend* [says Wellek, *op. cit.*, pp. 102, 108] shows everywhere how Kant's teaching has become central for Coleridge's thought . . . determining the essentials of [his] theoretical doctrines and coloring even the minutest tags of his terminology . . . . Everything is there: the threefold division of the mind, space and time as forms, the categories, the Ideas of Reason . . . etc." However, in his interpretation of Reason, as expounded in *The Friend*, Wellek holds that Coleridge veered too much toward "the old meaning of intellectual intuition."

224. Although the *Biographia Literaria* is the least philosophical of his later works and the least Kantian, the dominant influence being that of Schelling, still the Kantian terminology is everywhere apparent, and the Kantian moral foundations of religion are used to refute the depersonalized God of Fichte on the one hand, and, on the other, Kant's tripartition of the mind is cited in support of the Schellingian trichotomy of subject-object-absolute identity as opposed to the older dogmatic principle of dichotomy. See Wellek, *op. cit.*, pp. 114–16, 120–21, 284, notes 243–55.

225. Although Coleridge continued to putter with the *Logic* until 1827, we know that in 1822 it was substantially in the shape in which it is today (see Snyder, *op. cit.*, pp. 51–74, esp. pp. 62–72). Because its composition falls between the *Biographia Literaria* and the *Aids*, the evidence which it affords of Coleridge's knowledge of Kant is significant. Muirhead and Wellek are in complete accord on the score of Coleridge's correct interpretation of Kant in the *Logic*. Says Wellek: "As an exposition of Kant, the *Logic* ranks high indeed . . . . The distinction between Reason and Understanding appears in a correctly Kantian sense: Reason as the source of principles, Understanding as the faculty of rules; or Reason as the power of Ideas contradistinguished from Understanding as the faculty of conceptions . . ." (*op. cit.*, pp. 121–22).

226. Coleridge suggested in *The Friend* (*Works*, II, 144–45, 526) and elswhere (*Works*, I, 153, 167–68, 228, 251, and V, 40) that Harrington, Hooker, Bacon, Shakespeare, Hobbes, Milton, Jacobi, Hemsterhuis, Jeremy Taylor, Archbishop Leighton, and John Smith the Cambridge Platonist, all anticipated Kant in distinguishing between understanding and reason. He need not have stopped there but might have gone back, as Dr. Wellek suggests, to Plato and Aristotle, or at least as far as Thomas Aquinas, "who sharply distinguished between ratio and intellectus, though intellectus is for him a higher faculty, while reason is the discursive reason which Kant and Coleridge call understanding" (*op. cit.*, p. 103). Indeed, Plato, in the *Republic*, had come close to the Kantian distinction in what he called *Nous* and *Dianoia*, customarily translated as Reason and Understanding, respectively. "By the latter we apprehend the truths of mathematical and physical science; by the former the legitimate and absolute realities on which these depend."—A. W. Benn, *The History of English Rationalism in the Nineteenth Century* (2 vols., London, 1906), I, 255. Aristotle modified and in his manner simplified this Platonic distinction by stripping off all the transcendent implications which Plato had imputed to the Reason, so that from the time of St. Augustine to Sir William Hamilton, Reason, in the sense of *Nous*, was regarded generally as the faculty of intuitive truths as distinct from discursive reasoning. This gave rise to all kinds of confusion in terminology and thinking, of all of which Coleridge was well aware. Even his beloved Bacon was guilty. "Bacon himself," says Coleridge (*Aids*, p. 241), "does in sundry places use the term *reason* where he means the understanding, and sometimes, though less frequently, understanding for reason. In consequence of thus confusing the two terms, or rather of wasting both words for the expression of one and the same faculty, he left himself no appropriate term for the other and higher gift of reason, and was thus under the necessity of adopting fantastical and mystical phrases, for example, the dry light (lumen siccum), the lucific vision, and the like, meaning thereby nothing more than reason in contradistinction from the understanding." Leighton, too, has not escaped this error: "In the preceding Aphorism, by reason Leighton means the human understanding, the explanation annexed to it being (by a noticeable coincidence) word for word, the very definition which the founder of the Critical Philosophy gives of the understanding—namely, 'the faculty judging according to sense.'" See also *Works*, I, 233–34, 236, 264–65.

In short, while Coleridge looked upon his countrymen as having anticipated the transcendentalists of Germany in some of their important conclusions or results, he was cognizant of the wide differences of terminology and method employed by one and the other. From first to last, he sought to effect a satisfactory correlation between what he considered the truth of his beloved Platonists, on which his youth had fed, and the precise methodology, on which he sought to discipline his mature thought. For the more important references bearing on this attempt, see *Works*, I, 128, n., 166, 198–99, 200, 209–12, 234–36, 241–43, 246, 272, 284–86, 292, 321, 367, 450, n., 594; II, 96, 103, 106, 139–40, 143–45, 164, 176, 179, 286, 389, 402–5; III, 218, 258, 296; IV, 398; V, 15–16, 29, 38–40, 81–82, 112, 115–16, 181, 202–3, 206, 209, 267–68, 378, 551, 557–58; VI, 265, 369–70, 502; *Anima Poetae*, ed. by E. H. Coleridge (Boston & N.Y., 1895), 2, 78–79, 89, 127–28, 130–31, 170; and *Biog. Lit.* (ed. by J. Shawcross, 2 vols., Oxford, 1907), I, xvii, xxvii–xxviii, xxx; and Claud Howard, *Coleridge's Idealism: A Study of Its Relationship to Kant and to the Cambridge Platonists* (Boston, 1924).

227. *Works*, I, 241.

228. *Critique of Pure Reason* (Müller tr.), pp. 57, 67, 80–81, 97–98, 103–5, 114–16, 242–45, 247, 274, 517; also Bk. I, Ch. II, sec. iii.

229. *Works*, I, 241–67.

230. Similarly, Coleridge's next sentence regarding the Reason as "the power of universal and necessary convictions, the course and substance of truths above sense, and having their evidence in themselves," if taken without reference to what follows, seems oversimplified. The long "Comment" that follows amplifies this first generalization, brings it in accord with the meaning of Kant, and renders the Kantian distinction between pure and practical reason quite correctly. Coleridge lent his best abilities to drawing these distinctions; he rests his hopes of "carrying the Reader along with him through all that is to follow . . . on his success in establishing the validity and importance of the distinctions"; and it is impossible to feel that he is insincere, or that he would rest his case on falsely drawn distinctions. See C. R. Sanders, "Coleridge, F. D. Maurice, and the Distinction between the Reason and the Understanding," *PMLA*, LI, ii, (June, 1936), 459–74.

231. Whatever Coleridge's understanding was earlier, by 1822, when the *Logic* was substantially in the shape in which it is today, he had arrived, by the aid of Kant, at a clear apprehension of the relation of sense to understanding, and of understanding to reason, and he differentiated clearly between regulative and

constitutive, between pure and practical reason. See Muirhead, *op. cit.*, pp. 66–67; Wellek, *op. cit.*, pp. 121–22, 124–32, 285, notes, 294–361.

232. Wellek, *op. cit.*, p. 132; see also p. 285, and E. Winckelmann, *Coleridge und die Kantische Philosophie*, pp. 132–42.

233. "Coleridge's Marginalia in Jacobi's *Werke*," *Mod. Lang. Notes*, L, iv (Apr., 1935), pp. 216–26.

234. His study showed him that Schelling was much too much the "Grand Seignior of the *allein-selig* [*sic*] *Philosophie* to be altogether trustworthy," while Jacobi was but a "rhapsodist, excellent in sentences all in *small capitals*," whose "scheme ' resolves itself into "golden mists" (*Letters*, II, 683). The reasons which led him, on purely rational grounds, to repudiate Schelling operated equally to discredit Jacobi—Schelling on the ground that his philosophy is "in the first sense . . . *überfliegend*, and in the literal sense scandalous," i.e., "essentially pantheistic," and Jacobi on the score of the "indefiniteness of his suprarational theism" (*Works*, III, 709; see also III, 268, 710). On the question—the only one of significance in this connection—of how closely Coleridge's "Reason" approaches the "Gefühl" of Jacobi, Coleridge says specifically in *The Friend*:

"I should have no objection to define reason with Jacobi . . . as an organ bearing the same relation to spiritual objects, the universal, the eternal, and the necessary, as the eye bears to material and contingent *phenomena*. But then it must be added that it is an organ identical with its appropriate objects. Thus God, the soul, eternal truth &c., are the objects of reason; but they are themselves reason."—*Works*, II, 143–45.

This qualification of Coleridge's is all-important and indicates the point at which Coleridge insisted on going beyond Jacobi's "reason as the inward eye." Coleridge points out that the "object" of reason is not anything that bears comparison with the confused, comparatively structureless objects of sense perception . . . but something that possesses internal organization and structure and is, in a word, logos or reason—a view which Jacobi was bound, by every law of consistency, to repudiate. For Jacobi, be it remembered, "a known God would be no God." The Understanding leads inevitably to fatalism and atheism; only through what Jacobi calls variously intuition, divination, feeling, and faith can God, immortality, truth, beauty, and goodness be apprehended. For Coleridge, on the contrary, the problem of philosophy is to *know*, not merely phenomena but also spiritual objects—to find the unity of knowledge. The grand problem and its distinctive character, says he, is "to find a ground that is unconditioned and absolute, and thereby to reduce the aggregate of human knowledge to a system" (*Works*, II, 420). One point on which he never wavered, either in his published or his unpublished writings, is to assert that the "work of the reason, as the highest of which the mind is capable and as an expression of its own inner unity, is in essential continuity with that of the sense and understanding." See *Works*, I, 210, 456; also Muirhead, *Coleridge Studies by Several Hands* (London, 1934), p. 192.

235. *Works*, II, 144, n.

236. *The Friend*, written with the "one main purpose" of drawing the Kantian distinctions "as both an indispensable condition and a vital part of all sound speculation," supplies abundant evidence in the Fifth Essay of the First Landing Place that for Coleridge the reason is more than merely the vision of spiritual realities, and that understanding does more than generalize and arrange the phenomena of perception. By 1822, when the greater part of the *Logic* was already composed, he was definitely and completely under the guidance of Kant. It would be extraordinarily strange if, in 1825, when the *Aids* was published, he should have repudiated what he had been years toiling out, or gone back to the old faith and intuition of Jacobi, which he had discarded a decade earlier, or been content with the mysticism of Schelling after having deliberately repudiated him, at the same time that he had committed himself to the epistemology of Kant. On this score, see Snyder, *op. cit.*, pp. 135–36.

237. *Works*, I, 367; see also I, 209–10, 211–12, 242, 484.

238. See Coleridge's criticism of John Smith, the Platonist, whom he otherwise repeatedly praised (*Works*, V, 268), as well as Professor Howard's argument (*op. cit.*, p. 78) of Coleridge's greater reliance upon Kant than upon his prior study of the Platonists.

Although Coleridge's "truths of reason" appear to be revelatory in a degree, they were to Coleridge something more than sheer revelation, and depended for their validity upon the design of nature on the one hand and upon the divine harmony of moral truth on the other. In his attempt to establish ethical laws as absolute, he sided with Kant, who, contrary to the Platonists' intuitive grasp of moral law, held that the only means for knowing them was by an analysis of the concept of duty. On the other hand he agreed more nearly with the Platonists in their view of morals and religion as inseparable rather than with Kant's view of religion as subsidiary to morals. But his agree-

ment was one with a difference. So far from being mere intuitive commands, moral laws were for him the demands of the categorical imperative that was at once a categorical and a divine command. See his definition of the categorical imperative, *Works*, I, 131; V, 557–58; VI, 369–70). It is chiefly the spiritual *tone* in which he invests the Kantian principles that make them seem nearer the Platonists than Kant. *Cf.* Howard, *op. cit.*, pp. 71, 75–78, 80.

239. *Works*, II, 103.

240. *Letters*, II, 681–82.

241. *Works*, III, 258.

242. *Works*, I, 211–12; see also 30–33, 209–10.

243. *Works*, IV, 400; see also I, 209–10, 484, and *Unpublished Letters of Coleridge*, II 264.

244. These doctrines are discussed by Howard, *op. cit.*, pp. 88–97, and in greater detail by Muirhead, *op. cit.*, pp. 217–55, esp. pp. 222–51, in a way to demonstrate how in every case the Kantian criticism radically altered his Platonic heritage.

245. Howard, *op. cit.*, p. 46.

246. See his comments on atheism and pantheism, *Works*, V, 462.

247. Muirhead, *op. cit.*, pp. 121–36, 263; *Works*, I, 373, 374; II, 417–48. A comparison of the passage from MS. C, quoted by Muirhead (*op. cit.*, p. 121), with passages from Emerson (cited in H. H. Clark's essay on "Emerson and Science," *Philol. Quar.*, X, iii [July, 1931], 225–60) reveals startling coincidences between Coleridge's and Emerson's views of science and of nature.

248. His later views of Nature and of Man as a progressive system of embodied and individualizing activity that form the basis of his "principle of Individuation" were first published in his *Theory of Life* in 1848, but the idea had been abundantly available to American Transcendentalists since 1831, when the first American edition of *The Friend* appeared. See *Works*, II, 417–22, 442–48, 448–57; also I, 357–62, esp. pp. 357–59, 375; and Seth B. Watson, *Coleridge's Theory of Life* (Phila., 1848), pp. 7–16. This principle is not to be forgotten in any consideration of how Emerson, for example, came by his ideas (expressed in *Nature, Self-Reliance*, and elsewhere) of Individualism as the proper principle of Man, of individuation as the ruling process of Nature, of the One and the Many, and of his general position with regard to idealism, whether of Platonic, Kantian, Berkeleyan, Coleridgean, or some other derivation. Coleridge's influence in inciting others to think is quite as important as his supplying them with the materials for thought. See the testimony of Theodore Parker in his "Experiences as a Minister," *Works* (Cent. ed.,

15 vols., Boston 1907–1913), XIII, 309–10.

249. See Melvin M. Rader, "Presiding Ideas in Wordsworth's Poetry," *Univ. of Wash. Publ. in Lang. and Lit.*, VIII, ii (Nov., 1931), 189–93. Newton P. Stallknecht (in "Wordsworth and Philosophy," *PMLA*, XLIV, iv [Dec., 1929], 1137–43) makes an attempt to link passages in Wordsworth's *Excursion* with Kant.

250. "Ode on the Intimations of Immortality," ll. 145–49.

251. *Excursion*, Bk. IV, ll. 66–102, lines which drift into neo-Platonic ecstasy; "Tintern Abbey," ll. 95–102; *Excursion*, Bk. IX, ll. 101–19; and Preface to the *Excursion*, ll. 63–71.

252. See John Veitch, *Memoir of Sir William Hamilton* (Edinburgh & London, 1869), pp. 88–89.

253 He knew little about Fichte and Schelling, although he heard the latter's lectures at Jena. For Robinson's knowledge of Kant, see Wellek, *Kant in England*, pp. 140–59. His sojourn in Germany is described in his *Diary, Reminiscences, and Correspondence* (ed. by T. Sadler, 2nd ed., 3 vols., London, 1869) for the years 1800–1805. See also *Crabb Robinson in Germany* (ed. by Edith J. Morley, London, 1929).

254. Of some importance for Americans were his relations with Madame de Staël in Weimar during the first months of 1804, when, according to Robinson, "she was pleased to compliment me by declaring that I was the only person who had been able to give her any clear notion of German philosophy." At about the same time he confided to Thomas Robinson: "She . . . is absolutely incapable of thinking a philosophical thought . . . . Of course, she cannot underst [an]d properly speaking a syllable of the new Phil[osoph]y."—*Crabb Robinson in Germany*, pp. 134, 139. If Robinson's judgment is correct, his observation provides a clue to the reason why her book *De l'Allemagne* is so weak and inconclusive on the subject of German critical transcendentalism.

255. The first essay appeared in the issue of November 13, 1813; reprinted in *New Writings of William Hazlitt* (2nd ser., coll. by P. P. Howe, London & N.Y., 1927), pp. 27–34.

256. This essay, entitled "Madame de Staël's Account of German Philosophy," appeared under the dates of February 3 and 17, March 3, and April 8, 1814; reprinted in *Collected Works* (ed. by A. R. Waller and Arnold Glover, 12 vols., London & N.Y., 1902–1904), XI, 162–86. In a later article, "Mr. Locke a Great Plagiarist," in the *Examiner* for February 25, 1681 (reprinted in *Works*, XI, 284–90), Hazlitt taxes Dugald Stewart with undue neglect of Kant;

but in his review of Coleridge's *Biographia Literaria* in the *Edinburgh Review* (XXVIII, lvi [Aug., 1817], 488–515), after referring to Kant as "the great German oracle," Hazlitt goes on to speak of Kant's philosophy as "the most wilful and monstrous absurdity that was ever invented." See also Wellek, *op. cit.*, pp. 154–71.

257. One of the few Englishmen of his day able to read German readily, he early assumed an attitude of superiority toward all other commentators on the Germans—Willich and Nitsch being "very eminent blockheads," Drummond and Wirgman are not worth his time, while Thomas Brown, Dugald Stewart, and Madame de Staël content themselves with "drawing their information from [such] imbecile French books" as the "entirely childish" essay by Villers or the books of De Gerando. Coleridge alone knows Kant, but, of course, he lacks all "talent of communicating any sort of knowledge."

258. *Writings* (Masson ed., X, 64–80). The phrases quoted are from X, 66, 68–69, 77.

259. XXI, cxxii, 135–58; reprinted in *Writings*, IV, 323–79.

260. XXVIII, clxix, 244–68; *Writings*, VIII, 84–126.

261. XXVIII, clxix, 248, 254, 255. The same vein is continued in an essay, "German Studies and Kant in Particular" for *Tait's Edinburgh Magazine* (n.s., III, 355–60; *Writings*, II, 81–109), wherein he asserts that he had discovered as early as 1805, that Kant's philosophy "destroys by wholesale and . . . substitutes nothing." Then he proceeds, with characteristic inconsistency, to give a rather accurate account of Kant's purposes and to sing Kant's praises for having established "an order of ideas . . . which all deep philosophy has demanded, even when it could not make good its claim." "This," he concluded, "has been fulfilled [by Kant] without mysticism or Platonic reveries" (*Writings*, II, 99).

262. *London Mag.*, IX (Apr., 1824), 381–88; *Writings*, XIV, 46–60.

263. *London Mag.*, IX (May, 1824), 489–92; *Writings*, XIV, 61–68.

264. *London Mag.*, X (Oct., 1824), 285–93; *Writings*, IX, 428–44.

265. *Tait's Edin. Mag.*, IV (Nov., 1833), 165–79; *Writings*, XIV, 69–93. This translation he followed thirteen years later with a detailed explanation, printed under the title, "System of Heavens," *Tait's Edin. Mag.*, n.s., XIII (July, 1846), 566–79 (*Writings*, VIII, 7–41). For other references to Kant and German philosophy, see *Writings*, V, 336–37; X, 122, 160–61; XI, 11–12, n.; XII, 259, 262–63. In the last

two references, Kant's ideas of God are given correctly, and so far from being a shuffling, lying sycophant, he is now (1858) spoken of as "the most sincere, honorable, and truthful of human beings."

266. Four other contributions to be listed were his essays on "Herder," *London Mag.*, VII (Apr., 1823), 372–80 (*Writings*, IV, 380–94); "Goethe," *Encyclopaedia Britannica*, 7th ed.; "Schiller," *ibid.*; and his translation of Tieck's "Love Charm," *Knight's Quar. Mag.*, of 1835 (*Writings*, XII, 434–63).

The most recent evaluation of De Quincey's philosophical stature is an article by Professor René Wellek entitled "De Quincey's Status in the History of Ideas," *Philol. Quar.*, XXIII, iii (July, 1944), 248–72, in which he dissents radically from the high estimation of De Quincey by Sigmund K. Proctor, in *Thomas De Quincey's Theory of Literature* (Ann Arbor, Mich., 1943).

267. See his "Signs of the Times," *Crit. and Misc. Essays* (Vols. XXVI–XXIX of *Works*, Centenary ed., ed. by H. D. Traill, 30 vols., N.Y., 1896–1901), II, 64. All references, unless otherwise indicated, are to the Centenary edition.

268. In addition to the comprehensive study of Charles F. Harrold, *Carlyle and German Thought: 1819–1834* (Yale Studies in English, No. LXXXII, New Haven, 1934), among the more important recent investigations of Carlyle's German affinities are to be noted the following: C. E. Vaughan, "Carlyle and His German Masters," *Essays and Studies by Members of the English Association* (Oxford, 1910), pp. 168–96; A. Hildebrand, *Carlyle and Schiller* (Berlin, 1913); W. Morgan, "Carlyle and German Thought," *Queen's Quar.*, XXIII (1915–1916), 438–52; Theo. Geissendoerfer, "Carlyle and J. P. F. Richter," *JEGP*, XXV (1926), 540–53; B. H. Lehmann, *Carlyle's Theory of the Hero* . . . (Durham, N.C., 1928); C. F. Harrold, "Carlyle's Interpretation of Kant," *Philol. Quar.*, VII (1928), 345–57; René Wellek, "Carlyle and German Romanticism," *Xenia Pragensia* (Prague, 1929), pp. 375–403; Marg. Storrs, *The Relation of Carlyle to Kant and Fichte* (Bryn Mawr, Pa., 1929); C. F. Harrold, "Carlyle and Novalis," *Studies in Philology*, XXVII (1930), 47–63; Suzanne Howe, *Wilhelm Meister and his English Kinsmen* (N.Y., 1930); René Wellek, *Kant in England*, pp. 183–202; Hill Shine, "Carlyle and the German Philosophy Problem during the Year 1826–1827," *PMLA*, L (1935), 807–27; René Wellek, "Carlyle and the Philosophy of History," *Philol. Quar.*, XXIII, i (Jan., 1944), 55–76.

269. "Varnhagen von Ense's Memoirs," *Crit. and Misc. Essays*, IV, 108.

270. H. L. Stewart, "Carlyle's Conception of Religion," *Amer. Jour. of Theol.*, XXI (1917), 46.

271. Harrold, *Carlyle and German Thought*, pp. 7–8.

272. Harrold suggests quite correctly that Carlyle seems to have been interested less in the whole thought of an author than in individual ideas or passages. He was particularly fond of aphoristic literature, such as Novalis' *Fragmente*, Goethe's *West-Östlicher Divan*, *Maximen und Reflexionen*, Richter's *Wahrheit aus Jean Pauls Leben* and *Des Feldpredigers Schmelzle Reise*. Apparently he made little effort to read all the writings of a given author or to form consistent and systematic estimates of the total significance of any of them. Even Richter, Novalis, and Goethe, to each of whom he devoted long discussions, he did not completely evaluate either for himself or for his reader. His strong moral bias caused him to steer a rather narrow course between the romantic aesthete and the theoretical transcendentalist. Not enough artist, he was too much moralist to appreciate fully Goethe the novelist; not enough philosopher, he was too much the artist, to fathom Kant the epistemologist. His knowledge of Germany, of German literature, and of German philosophy presents the peculiar paradox of wide and detailed learning with sudden and complete gaps. "He mentions many German authors and books, but many of them were known to him by name and title only, so that the number of mentionings is not always indicative of his knowledge. Even after the translation of *Wilhelm Meister* (1824), he knew few German authors; and for the composition of *German Romance* he sought the advice of Henry Crabb Robinson. While he doubtless knew Schiller and Goethe well, his authoritative tone in pronouncing judgments on Kant serves only poorly to conceal his remarkable ignorance of even the basic ideas of Kant."—Harrold, *op. cit.*, pp. 9–10.

273. "Goethe especially," said Carlyle, "was my evangelist"; and we may believe with Edwin D. Mead that Carlyle, if he was anybody's disciple, was Goethe's. See Mead's "Emerson and Carlyle" in *The Influence of Emerson* (Boston, 1903), p. 223.

274. Naturally he knew *Wilhelm Meister*, and only slightly less intimately *Dichtung und Wahrheit*, the epigrammatic verses, the Proömion, Symbolum and Zahme Xenien. *Faust*, although it was the work through which Goethe was introduced to him, he read only once before 1828, and then only Faust's curse and the song of the Earth Spirit seem to have impressed him strongly. However, Goethe's gift of *Helena*

sent him back to *Faust*, which he came eventually to read with renewed pleasure, although he placed Part II above Part I. See Harrold, *op. cit.*, pp. 10, 250; W. F. Hauhart, *The Reception of Goethe's Faust in England* . . . (N.Y., 1909), Ch. III; and W. A. Speck, "New Letters of Carlyle to Eckermann," *Yale Review*, n.s., XV, iv (July, 1926), 736–57.

275. Harrold, *op. cit.*, p. 11.

276. *Early Letters of Thomas Carlyle, 1814–1826* (ed. by C. E. Norton, London, 1886), p. 159.

277. A notable exception occurs in his *Life of Schiller* (Centenary ed., p. 112), where he professes to have "only a very limited acquaintance with the subject"—a statement the truth of which the attentive reader has doubtless already gathered from Carlyle's remarkable statement on the page preceding, namely, that Kant's metaphysics and logic are "scarcely to be traced in any of Schiller's subsequent writings [i.e., subsequent to *ca.* 1793]."—*Ibid.*, p. 111; see also pp. 108, 114. Further light is shed on his "limited acquaintance" with the German philosophers by his letter to Francis Espinasse, August 28, 1841:

"It is many years since I ceased reading German or any other metaphysics, and gradually came to discern that I had happily got done with all that matter altogether . . . .

"Those two little books of Fichte [*Über das Wesen des Gelehrten*] and Schelling [*Über die Methode des akademischen Studiums*] are bright in my memory beyond all others that I have read on the subject. Perhaps there is not elsewhere, for a British student, as much interest and novelty extant, in equal comprehension, in the whole literature of German philosophy. One other book I also favorably remember: The Life of Fichte, by his Son. . . .

"I may say further that after all the Fichteisms, Schellingisms, and Hegelisms, I still understand *Kant* to be the great authority, the prime author of the new spiritual world, of whom all others are but superficial, transient modifications . : . . What better can you do than vigorously set to the *Kritik der reinen Vernunft* . . . and resolutely study it and re-study it . . . . You will find it actually capable of being understood, rigorously sequent . . . really one of the best metaphysical studies that I know of. Once master Kant, you have attained what I reckon most precious: namely, deliverance from the fatal incubus of Scotch and French philosophy, with its mechanisms and Atheisms . . . ."—Francis Espinasse, *Literary Recollections and Sketches* (London, 1893), 58–59.

278. *Love Letters of Thomas Carlyle to Jane Welsh* (ed. by Alex. Carlyle, London, 1909), II, 324. But see *Two Note Books of Thomas Carlyle* . . . (ed. by C. E. Norton, N.Y., 1898), pp. 112–13, where he claims familiarity with only "100 pages."

On the question of how and where Carlyle gathered his conceptions of Kantian philosophy see the penetrating article by Professor Hill Shine, *loc. cit.*, pp. 807–27; also his *Carlyle's Fusion of Poetry, History, and Religion* (Chapel Hill, N.C., 1938).

279. See also Harrold, *op. cit.*, p. 12, and Shine, *PMLA*, L, ii (Sept., 1935), 810.

280. *Wotton Reinfred* in *The Last Words of T. Carlyle* (N.Y., 1892), pp. 83–85, 86–87, 136–39. Nor is there anything to indicate that Carlyle had, by this time, grasped the ethical (or practical) philosophy of Kant (see *ibid.*, pp. 95, 136–39). For Carlyle's divergences from Kantian ethics, see Harrold, *op. cit.*, 135–47. There is no evidence to show that Carlyle had, by this time, read either the second *Critique* or the *Grundlegung zur Metaphysik der Sitten*, or, for that matter, that he ever read them. What he knew of Kant's practical philosophy he appears to have derived entirely at second hand. Indeed, Carlyle's "imperative" is more like Calvin's than Kant's.

281. *Crit. and Misc. Essays*, I, 76.

282. See Shine, *loc. cit.*, pp. 807–27, and Harrold, *op. cit.*, p. 252, n. 30. Into his notebook Carlyle wrote a number of notations which Professor Shine finds are derived from his reading of Phillip Albrecht Stapfer's "Problème de l'esprit humain" in *Revue Encyclopédique* for July, 1827 (XXXIII, 414–31). The last of these notes reads: "Kant reminded me of father Boscovich; but alas: I have only read 100 pages of his works. How difficult it is to live! How many things to do, how little time to do them! T.C."—*Two Note Books* . . . pp. 112–13.

283. *Crit. and Misc. Essays*, I, 69–70.

284. *Ibid.*, p. 81. The terminology here suggests not only Jacobi's intuition and faith but also Dugald Stewart's peculiar misconstruction of Kant. For Stewart's profound influence on Carlyle's misconceptions of Kant, see Harrold, *op. cit.*, pp. 33–40, 121–22. Although Carlyle said of Madame de Staël that "this gifted lady's *Allemagne*, in doing so much to excite curiosity, has done little to satisfy . . . it" (*Crit. and Misc. Essays*, I, 35; *Early Letters*, p. 170), several of her misconstructions of German transcendental philosophy are repeated in his essays. See Harrold, *op. cit.*, pp. 58, 259–60. Her book provided him with a tentative prospectus of German writers. Like Madame de Staël, he was actuated primarily by religious motives,

and, following her, he interpreted the new movement in Germany less in terms of metaphysics than in terms of a unification of faith and knowledge, religion and science.

Another medium of Kantian ideas was Carl L. Reinhold's *Briefe über die Kantische Philosophie* (Leipzig, 1885–1887), which considered chiefly Kant's practical philosophy. See *Two Note Books*, p. 102, and Harrold, *op. cit.*, pp. 58–59.

285. See Harrold, *op. cit.*, pp. 141–42.

286. *Crit. and Misc. Essays*, I, 82. The province of the Understanding is to "all strictly speaking, *real* practical and material knowledge, Mathematics, Physics, Political Economy, the adaptation of means to ends in the whole business of life." "Appointed to obey Reason," if the Understanding is permitted to rule Reason, it spells the "ruin of the whole spiritual man" (*ibid.*, I, 82), for the Understanding leads to Atheism in religion, Utilitarianism and Egoism in morals, and to empty formalism in aesthetics. These misconceptions, as we shall see, Emerson took over bodily from Carlyle.

287. *Ibid.*, I, 83. In view of this conclusion, which resolves itself essentially into that of the Common-Sense school (giving unto science the things that belong to science and unto religion those belonging to religion), it is hard to understand Carlyle's rejection of Dugald Stewart's criticism of Kant (*ibid.*, I, 29, n.), except that Carlyle's views were often inconsistent and inconstant, indefinite and inconclusive. Professor Harrold has pointed out the "miscellaneous character of Carlyle's thought" and indicated the ease with which Carlyle could corral on a single page, and under a single term, not only Fichte, Tieck, Kant, and "Kantism and German metaphysics generally" but also Bishop Berkeley, Father Boscovich, Sir William Jones, and Dugald Stewart. See "Novalis," *Crit. and Misc. Essays*, II, 23. Similarities between the ideas of Carlyle and those of Kant lie oftener in the word than in the fundamental idea itself.

288. In defense of German idealism, Carlyle maintains that it is no argument against the Idealist "to say that since he denies absolute existence of Matter, he ought in conscience to deny its relative existence."—*Ibid.*, II, 22–24.

289. *Ibid.*, II, 26–27.

290. "If the logical mechanism of the mind is arbitrary, so to speak, it will follow that all inductive conclusions, all conclusions of the Understanding, have only a relative truth, are true only for *us*, and *if* some other thing be true." Reason, on the other hand, "the higher faculty in man than Understanding [is] the pure ultimate light of our nature, wherein . . . lies the foundation of all Poetry, Virtue, Religion,

things which are properly beyond the province of the Understanding, of which the Understanding *can* take no cognisance, except a false one." —*Ibid.*, II, 27. These misconceptions, too, Emerson absorbed.

291. *Ibid.*, II, 27. See also III, 318.

292. For details, see Harrold, "Carlyle's Interpretation of Kant," *Philol. Quar.*, VII, iv (Oct., 1928), 345–57, esp. pp. 349–56.

293. It is emphasized not only in the section on "Natural Supernaturalism" and elsewhere in *Sartor* but also in "Goethe's Helena," *Crit. and Misc. Essays*, I, 166, and "Taylor's Historical Survey of German Poetry," *ibid.*, II, 355–56.

Apart from the general quickening effect of Kantian idealism as Carlyle conceived it, and as he re-echoed it in his rhapsodical statement of the Philosophy of Clothes, the rest of *Sartor* (notably in its identification of the microcosm with the macrocosm, of man with God, and of Nature with "the living Garment of God"), seems to derive less from Kant than from Goethe and Fichte, especially the latter. See *Crit. and Misc. Essays*, III, 76; IV, 109.

294. Letter, Aug. 28, 1831, in Epinasse, *op. cit.*, p. 59; also pp. 56–60, and D. A. Wilson, *Carlyle at His Zenith*, 1848–1853 (London & N.Y., 1927), pp. 63–64, 374; "Shooting Niagara: and After?" in *Crit. and Misc. Essays*, V, 29; and *William Allingham: A Diary*, ed. by H. Allingham and D. Bradford (London, 1908), p. 264.

295. Epinasse, *op. cit.*, pp. 220–21.

296. P. 145.

297. For Carlyle's later views see D. A. Wilson, *op. cit.*, pp. 203, 204, 273, and Harrold's review of Marg. Storrs's *Relation of Carlyle to Kant and Fichte* in *Mod. Phil.*, XXVII, ii (Nov., 1930), 243.

298. To be considered in this connection is Nietzsche's comment on "the absurd muddleheaded Carlyle, who sought to conceal under passionate grimaces what he knew about himself: namely, what was lacking in Carlyle—real power of intellect, real depth of intellectual perception, in short philosophy" (*Beyond Good and Evil*, par. 252).

299. Although Carlyle quoted Jacobi only once (*Crit. and Misc. Essays*, II, 27) and mentioned him rarely, they had much in common, and doubtless Jacobi lent many an argument to the confusion that Carlyle wrought in his own mind in trying to equate Kantian epistemology with Kantian conclusions. Dualists alike, and unable to reconcile the claims of the head with those of the heart, Jacobi's pietism and Carlyle's Calvinism conspired in both, alike, to rule out the purely rational faculty as affording any real knowledge of spiritual matters. The highest

faculty of man was for both a divining instinct which has access to realms of "truth" beyond all purely intellectual efforts. The celerity with which Jacobi changed his term *Glaube* (belief or faith) to *Vernunft* (reason) contributed to Carlyle's undoing as a metaphysician and led him eventually to follow Jacobi's uncritical example of adopting the Kantian terminology without the Kantian meaning—of using Kantian reason, for example, to designate the very un-Kantian idea of Faith. This Jacobian "reason" in the end becomes "spiritual discernment," and as such has nothing in common with the purely regulative nature of Kant's pure reason. It is essentially "a sea of light," "a spiritual eye for spiritual objects," or as Carlyle puts it simply, "all true Christian Faith and Devotion" (*ibid.*, II, 27). In thus interpreting Kant *à la* Jacobi, Carlyle compounded the confusion among many American readers whose grasp of Kant on Coleridgean terms was none too adequate. For details of Jacobi's influence on Carlyle, see Wellek, "Carlyle and German Romanticism," *Xenia Pragensia*, pp. 401–3; Harrold, *op. cit.*, pp. 17–18, 124–27, 131–44; and A. W. Crawford, *The Philosophy of J. H. Jacobi* (N.Y., 1905), pp. 18–19, 27–29, 38–40.

300. The references and arguments are given in detail in the studies by Harrold and Storrs, and therefore are not repeated here.

301. Harrold concludes that "whenever Carlyle momentarily speaks like a philosopher, it is as a follower of Fichte. Of all German metaphysicians, Carlyle understood him most naturally and interpreted him with the least sacrifice of the original meaning."

302. To Schelling's *System of Identity* (he admitted) he could "attach next to no meaning."—*Two Note Books*, p. 113.

303. Notably as Novalis seemed to confirm Fichte's refutation of the substantiality of matter and in his conception of history.

304. Especially in regard to Symbolism.

305. Of Schiller's Jena lectures he said: " . . .there perhaps has never been in Europe another course of history sketched out on principles so magnificent and philosophical." The very first lecture contains these several points which Carlyle incorporated in his own theory and practice: namely, that great blanks in history can never be filled; that, even at its best, history is only a collection of fragments; that only the Infinite Spirit can see the whole history of man; that teleology, with its emphasis on the inner and active purpose of history, is essential in making history intelligible; that only the philosophical historian, never the mere fact-gatherer, can recreate and revitalize the past; and that any given period or phase of history is but a part of the greater cosmic process in which moral ideas are seeking realization.

306. Less sweeping, yet significant as influencing Carlyle's thinking in more or less isolated instances (as Harrold has demonstrated) are the works of Lessing, Schleiermacher, Mendelssohn, Werner, Hoffmann, Fouqué, and Tieck.

307. This selective method found rich pickings in the aphoristic writings of Novalis, Goethe, and Jean Paul; but he applied it also to more rigorously and organically constructed discourses, often lifting what pleased him without regard to the context or the implications in the original text. In Fichte, he seized upon the concept of the "Divine Idea at the Bottom of Appearance" but ignored the relation between the finite and infinite egos. In Novalis, he admired the idea that religion is the essence of society, but was silent on Novalis' audacious query about the close relations among religion, lust, and cruelty. Noncommittal on the total significance of an author, he was content for the most part with squaring any given new idea with his own preoccupations and adopting or rejecting it accordingly, without bothering to relate the old and new alike to any basic and coherent body of principles. He was not above modifying an author's thought and combining it with the thoughts of others or his own, thus getting something quite different from what the original author intended. In this way he·modified what he conceived to be Kant's reason by combining it with accretions from Fichte, Jacobi, and Novalis, and got a "blend of intellectual intuition, mystical communion, and moral revelation," by means of which he asserted the possibility of man's knowing and communing with the divine, immanent reality.

308. After 1834, he "ceased reading German and any other metaphysics and came to discern that . . . [he] had happily got done with that matter altogether."—Espinasse, *op. cit.*, p. 58.

309. Little concerned with philosophic consistency, he preached a doctrine of regeneration to a materialistic and hedonistic age, in the process of which he popularized the ethical ideas of Goethe, the religious implications of Kant (as he saw them), of Fichte, and of Novalis, and the moral inspiration of Jean Paul. He clung to his preoccupations, refusing to let go of such fundamental conceptions learned from the "German writers" as the conviction that the subjectivity of time and space guarantees the supremacy of mind and spirit over matter and body. His ideas on reason and understanding, the organic principle of the universe, the symbolism of Nature remained integral parts of his creed. But his God became less

the God of German transcendentalism and more and more the God of the old Christian faith—less the Divine Idea and more the Maker. But he remained steadfast in his convictions regarding moral right as the only reality, the duty of obedience and self-annihilation, the religious nature of work, the organic order of things, and the importance of heroes. His disparaging remarks about all "that multifarious business of German philosophy" to the contrary, he remained profoundly indebted to Goethe, Schiller, Kant, Fichte, and other German writers.

310. Emerson's *Journals*, II, 515 (Oct. 1, 1832).

311. On the score of Carlyle's early vogue in America, see Wm. S. Vance, "Carlyle in America before *Sartor Resartus*," *Amer. Lit.*, VII, iv (Jan., 1936), 363–75, and George Kummer, "Anonymity and Carlyle's Early Reputation in America," *ibid.*, VIII, iii (Nov., 1936), 297–99.

312. See Emma G. Jaeck, *Madame de Staël and the Spread of German Literature* (N.Y., 1915).

313. George Ticknor, for example, recalled later: "The first intimation I ever had on the subject was from Madame de Staël's work on Germany, then just published."—*Life, Letters, and Journals*, I, 11–12. Her praise of the German universities led him to complete his education in Germany. Edward Everett credits her with having inspired him to acquire a better knowledge of German literature.—Long, pp. 18, 68. Moses Stuart, Alex. H. Everett, James Marsh, George Bancroft, Joseph G. Cogswell, Charles Timothy Brooks, George H. Calvert, George Ripley, John S. Dwight, James F. Clarke, Theodore Parker, Margaret Fuller, R. W. Emerson, and Henry W. Longfellow, all were incited by her book either to undertake the study of the German language and literature or to pursue more vigorously such studies as they had already initiated. See *Remains of James Marsh . . . with a Memoir*, p. 34; Emerson's *Journals*, II, 128, Nov., 1826.

314. On the score of the misconceptions and misconstructions which she spread concerning German literature and literary figures, see Harrold, *op. cit.*, pp. 40, 50, 55–59, 140, 259–60; Jaeck, *op. cit.*, p. 92; and Jean Paul's review of her book (tr. by Carlyle) in *Fraser's Mag.*, I, i (Feb. 1830), 21–37, iv (May, 1830), 407–13, reprinted in *Crit. and Misc. Essays*, I, 476–502.

315. *Love Letters of Thomas Carlyle and Jane Welsh*, I, 3.

316. *Early Letters . . .*, ed. by C. E. Norton, p. 170.

317. Indicative of these preoccupations in connection with German thought are the facts (1) that Jacobi receives an unduly prominent place in her book, (2) that Kant is slurred over in the fashion indicated below, and (3) that twelve chapters are devoted exclusively to religious sects, not to mention many digressions and interpolations on religious subjects introduced in other chapters.

318. *Germany*, with notes and appendices by O. W. Wight (2 vols. in 1, Boston & N.Y., 1859; repr., 1887), II, 161.

319. When O. W. Wight edited her book, he felt constrained to add more than a hundred pages of notes designed to provide the necessary substance that Madame de Staël had omitted. His chief sources are Sir William Hamilton's *Discussions of Philosophy*, Schwegler's *History of Philosophy* (Seelye translation), Tennemann's *Manual of Philosophy*, Carlyle's *Essays*, Cousin's *Lectures on the True, the Beautiful, and the Good*, Max Müller's *German Classics*, and J. H. Allen's article on "Recent German Theology,' *Christ. Exam.*, LXII (Nov., 1857), 431–40.

320. After the long sections on German ethics are stripped of their dross, this much remains: "Kant, Fichte, and Jacobi have combated with success" the system of ethics founded on personal interest (p. 232), for their "idealistic philosophy has a tendency, from its very nature, to refute ethics founded on individual or national interest" (p. 251). Kant and Fichte aimed at giving the "law of duty a scientific theory, and an inflexible application" (p. 262); "those at the head of whom Jacobi is placed, take religious sentiment and natural conscience for their guide . . . ; a third group, making revelation the basis of their belief, endeavor to unite sentiment and duty, and seek to bind them together by a philosophical interpretation." And without so much as hinting at the processes by which these objectives are sought, she is off to fresh fields and pastures new, though she does add that all three of these systems combat the morality of self-interest, which "has now scarcely any partisans in Germany; evil actions may be done there, but at least the glory of what is right is left untouched" (p. 263). Her treatment of Jacobi affords an illustration of her inability to judge the relative importance of individual figures. Jacobi is allotted fourteen pages (pp. 184–87, 257–66), Fichte is dismissed with seven, Schelling gets five, and Hegel is not so much as mentioned.

321. Carlyle was not far wrong when he observed that her book made all the world aware "that the Germans are something; something independent and apart from others; nay, something deep, imposing, and, if not admirable, wonderful." He was right, also, in adding,

"But what that something is, indeed, is still undecided; for this gifted lady's *Allemagne*, in doing so much to excite curiosity, has still done little to satisfy it or even to direct it."—"State of German Lit.," *Edin. Rev.*, XLVI, xcii (Oct., 1827), 311; *Crit. and Misc. Essays*, I, 35; also Jean Paul F. Richter's review of *De l'Allemagne* translated by Carlyle for *Fraser's Mag.*, 1830, and reprinted in *Crit. and Misc. Essays*, I, 476–502. "Madame de Staël," says Jean Paul, "had this advantage, that she writes specifically for Frenchmen; who, knowing about German art and German language simply nothing, still gain somewhat, when they learn never so little" (*ibid.*, I, 477). Throughout the essay he is severely critical of her extraordinary "naivete," her "superficialities," "whimsicalities," and "misapprehensions." See esp. I, 494–502.

322. *Introduction to the History of Philosophy* (Boston, 1832). The substance of this book originally formed the first thirteen of a series of lectures delivered by Cousin in Paris in 1828 and published in Paris the next year.

323. Hartford, 1834. Originally Lectures XVI–XXV of a course delivered in Paris in 1829 and published the same year.

324. *Elements of Psychology*, pp. xv–xvi.

325. *Ibid.*, pp. xvii–xxxiv.

326. *Ibid.*, p. xvii.

327. *Ibid.*, p. xviii.

328. The three elements find their unity in reason, which itself is divisible into the three inseparable, equally essential, and primitive elements of the finite, the infinite, and the necessary relations between the two. Together they constitute "at once a triplicity and a unity." Reason, which manifests itself in these three ideas, is not individual or personal; it is absolute and divine; and the ideas in human intelligence are a manifestation of the absolute intelligence and a true revelation of the divine in the human. Similarly, creation is nothing else than the necessary development of the infinite in the finite, of unity in variety; and the universe is but the reflection of God's being, a development of his existence. God is the cause; the universe is the effect.—*Ibid.*, pp. xvii–xx; also *Introduction*, Lectures IV and V.

329. By the spontaneity of reason is meant "that development of reason anterior to reflection, that power of reason to seize upon truth at first sight, to comprehend it, and admit it, without asking or giving an account of its doing so."—*Introduction*, Lectures V and VI; see also *Elements*, Intro., p. xxi.

Reflection, on the other hand, applies itself to the elements given in spontaneity, analyzes and discriminates the facts contained in the primitive synthesis, recognizes these characteristics, and receives these fundamental elements of thought as ideas, laws, principles, or categories (*Introduction*, Lectures V and VI). For an ingenious argument in support of the unity-in-triplicity of the human consciousness, of the subjectivity of Sensibility and Will, and of the objectivity of Reason, see Orestes A. Brownson's exposition of Cousin in the *Boston Quar. Rev.*, II (Jan., 1839), 47–49, and II (Oct., 1839), 169–76, 178–79.

330. *Introduction*, Lect. IV, p. 109.

331. For the detailed argument, see *Elements*, Intro., p. xxiii.

332. *Introduction*, Lecture VI, p. 170. "Nature and God may be objects of our faith, but not objects of knowledge. Thus Kant comes out to absolute skepticism, in regard to ontology,— a skepticism against which he finds no refuge, except in the sublime inconsistency of giving to the laws of the practical reason more objective reality than to those of speculative reason; —an inconsistency which Fichte demonstrated and demolished."—*Elements*, Intro., p. xxiv.—

333. *Introduction*, Lecture VI, p. 170.

334. *Ibid.*, p. 167. "If Kant, within his own profound analysis, had seen the source of all analysis . . . he would have seen, that nothing is less individually personal than reason, and particularly, as it appears in the phenomenon of pure affirmation . . . and that the truths which are thus given us are absolute truths. . . . Truth itself is absolute; and in like manner, what we call reason, is truly distinct from ourselves. . . . The demonstration of the independence of the truths perceived by reason is the characteristic mark of the spontaneity of reason . . . . When we speak of God, we have a right to speak of him according to our dictates, according to the dictates of that reason which represents him."—*Ibid.*, pp. 171–72.

335. *Ibid.*, pp. 173–74. While Cousin credits Kant with having enumerated and analyzed correctly the elements of human intelligence, Kant failed in their reduction. In regard to the absolute and infinite, Kant made it merely a regulative principle of thought, and denied explicitly the possibility of any knowledge beyond the science of the subjective. Moreover, he denied that the subjective, considered as intelligence, affords any ground for the assertion of a corresponding reality. But God *is* a necessary conception, an object of invincible faith. Kant's only legitimate ground for this faith is the moral interest of the practical reason, which, contends Cousin, cannot be taken as a scientific basis. "Considered as such, it is equally subjective as the regulative principles of the speculative intelligence, and equally liable to the objections which he urges against

the latter, when applied to the limits of consciousness . . . . Thus that which was already subjective in the timid and inconsequent Idealism of the Scottish school, became more decisively subjective in the Idealism of Kant; and neither of them establish the infinite as an object of knowledge."—*Ibid.*, p. xxvii.

This objective Cousin claims to reach. He joins with Schelling against Kant in denying the personal and subjective nature of intelligence, and in asserting for philosophy a positive science of the infinite, *immediately* known by the intelligence as impersonal and divine. At this point his editor, Henry, adds: "But while Schelling, if we do not mistake him, denies this knowledge to the consciousness, and refers it to a capacity for knowledge about consciousness, which is the absolute identity of being and knowing, of the finite and the infinite —Cousin maintains that consciousness is necessarily implied in intelligence, and that the knowledge of the infinite is given in the spontaneous consciousness as above explained."— *Ibid.*, pp. xxvii–xxviii.

336. *Journals*, IV, 404 (Mar. 5, 1838).

337. *The Flowering of New England, 1815–1865* (New York, 1936), p. 191.

338. Cousin's facile distinction between spontaneous and reflective reason solved not only Kant's dilemma but explained also the identity and diversity of humanity—and the history of the world and of philosophy. As spontaneity is the element of agreement, and reflection of difference, so men agree in spontaneity and differ in reflection. In this instinctive and spontaneous form, reason is everywhere the same and equal to itself, in all generations, in all places, and in all individuals. Reflection, on the contrary, as the element of difference, is the source of all diversity in mankind, their differences and errors of opinion and character. Thus Faith in God is a necessary faith, a spontaneous truth, for the whole human race; Atheism, in strictness, has no existence. It is nothing more than an individual madly opposing his will to the spontaneous reason, and rests on nothing better than the errors of reflection, which, in turn, rest upon variables. See *Introduction*, p. 176; *Elements*, Intro., p. xxvi.

What reflection is to the individual, history is to the race. Hence the distinguishing character of different epochs in the history of mankind as well as in the history of philosophy, is found in the predominance of some one element of the intelligence. See *Elements*, Intro., p. xxvi, and *Introduction*, Lecture VI, pp. 176f.

Fortunately errors of reflection can be corrected and eliminated by referring them back to

some fundamental axiom of faith, the verity of which is asserted by the spontaneous reason and the primal fact of affirmation. Hence Cousin becomes a strong advocate of the doctrine of perfectibility and of an historical optimism in which history is viewed as the plan of providence (*Introduction*, Lecture VII, pp. 188–226). These ideas are further expounded in Lecture VIII, pp. 227–49, and lead (in Lecture IX, pp. 250–91) to a discussion of nations and (in Lecture X, pp. 293–327) of heroes and the epochs most favorable to their rise. He finds that the "two most eminent manifestations of the energy of the human mind are action and thought," and that these are displayed "in highest degree on the field of battle and in the closet" (*ibid.*, p. 323). The next lecture (pp. 329–62) reviews the several theories of history, including that of Herder and its merits and defects, as Cousin sees them. The remaining lectures (XII, pp. 363–404; XIII, pp. 415–43) are devoted to the history of philosophy, with special reference to Tiedemann as the product of the Lockean tradition and Tennemann as the product of Kantism. Their opposite points of view are emphasized, their merits and defects weighed, and the present state of philosophy estimated. Philosophy is in a bad way everywhere but in France; for German philosophy is in a state of "decomposition" (p. 410), southern Europe is still too much in the toils of theology, English philosophy has been dead for more than a century, and only in France has philosophy a fair chance, and that only through the agency of eclecticism (pp. 422–23). This paean of self-adulation and propaganda (to the length of two lectures) ends in Cousin's repetition of his "profession of faith": "I believe that in Christianity all truths are contained; but these eternal truths may and ought to be approached, disengaged, and illustrated by φhilosophy. Truth has but one foundation; but truth assumes two forms, namely, mystery and scientific exposition; I revere the one, I am the organ and interpreter of the other" (p. 442).

And that every reader was left to make the most of. Some of his readers—Brownson, for example—for some time affirmed eclecticism to be God's own word, only to find eventually another and truer God. Others—Emerson, for example—apparently never made much of it; while J. Elliot Cabot, in what was virtually his first word to appear in print, resolutely attacked Cousin's "charlatanism" as a philosopher. See Cabot's "Introductory Remarks" to his translation of Kant's *Critique of Judgment* printed in Hedge's *Prose Writers of Germany*, 3rd ed., p. 62.

339. Henry's translation reached its fourth

edition in 1856, the second edition (N.Y., 1838) having been prepared for use in colleges. Altogether nine of Cousin's works were translated in America, wholly or in part, during the high tide of Transcendentalism, five of them before 1842. Among his works enjoying the greatest vogue were J. C. Daniel's version of *The Philosophy of the Beautiful*, in 1848; O. W. Wight's rendition of Cousin's *Course of the History of Modern Philosophy* (2 vols., N.Y., 1852; repr., 1854, 1866, 1869, 1877, 1889); *Lectures of the True, the Beautiful, and the Good*, by the same translator (N.Y., 1854; enl. ed., 1861; repr., 1866, 1879); and, of course, George Ripley's *Philosophical Miscellanies* . . . (2 vols., Boston, 1838).

One other service of Cousin's popularizing German thought in America is represented by his translation of Wilhelm Gottlieb Tennemann's *Grundriss* (*Manuel de l'histoire de la philosophie*, 2 vols., Brussels, 1837), although this book had enjoyed some popularity even earlier in the English version, of 1832, made by the Rev. Arthur Johnson (*Manual of the History of Philosophy*, Oxford, 1832; rev., enl., and cont'd. by J. R. Morell, for the Bohn Library, London, 1852).

Meanwhile seven of Jouffroy's works were translated, the most important of which, after Ripley's selections in the *Philosophical Miscellanies* of 1838, was Robert N. Tappan's translation, in 1862, of Jouffroy's *Moral Philosophy*. In comparison with Cousin and Jouffroy, Constant was neglected except for what appeared by him and about him in the periodicals of the time and in Ripley's anthology. See Walter L. Leighton, *French Philosophers and New England Transcendentalism* (Charlottesville, Va., 1908), pp. 31, 40; and Howard M. Jones, *America and French Culture, 1750–1848* (Chapel Hill, 1927), p. 461.

340. These volumes of 383 and 376 pages, published in Boston in 1838, formed Volumes I and II of Ripley's fourteen volumes of *Specimens of Foreign Standard Literature*.

341. XXIX (July, 1829), 67–123.

342. X (Dec., 1831), 291–311.

343. Cf. H. M. Jones, *op. cit.*, p. 465.

344. I (Jan., 1832), 22–23.

345. XXXV (July, 1832), 19–36.

346. See also *Amer. Quar. Observer*, I (July, 1833), 177; III (Dec., 1834), 354–56.

347. VII (Mar., 1835), 89–127.

348. *Christ. Exam.*, XXI (Sept., 1836), 36–64.

349. *Boston Quar. Rev.*, I (1838), 86. Italics are mine. A year later, Brownson reiterated: "We say again that M. Cousin is not a Transcendentalist, as the term appears to be understood in this community. It is not easy to de-

termine what people mean by the term . . . ; but we suppose they mean to designate by it, when they use it as a term of reproach, a man who in philosophizing, disregards experience and builds on principles obtained not by experience, but by reasoning *a priori*. In this sense Cousin is not a Transcendentalist; nor, indeed, was Kant."—*Ibid.*, II (Jan., 1839), 27, 20.

350. See III (Dec., 1838), 590–613, and IV (Mar., 1839), 21–36.

351. "Transcendentalism," *Princeton Rev.*, XI (Jan., 1839), 37–101, esp. p. 99. Emerson's address, they go on to say, "is before us. We have read it, and we want words with which to express our sense of the nonsense and impiety which pervade it. It is a rhapsody, obviously in imitation of Thomas Carlyle. . . . The principles upon which Mr. Emerson proceeds, so far as he states them, are the same with those of M. Cousin. . . . In a word, Mr. Emerson is an infidel and an atheist, who nevertheless makes use, in the esoteric sense of the new philosophy, of the terms and phrases consecrated to a religious use."—*Ibid.*, pp. 95, 97–98.

Doubtless the publication, in 1838, of Ripley's *Philosophical Miscellanies* had added to the provocation that Alexander and Dod felt.

352. See *Journals*, IV, 400 (Mar. 4, 1838), and IV, 404–5 (Mar. 5, 1838).

353. II (Jan., 1839), 27–35; (Apr., 1839), 169–87; (Oct., 1839), 435–48; also I (Oct., 1838), 433–44, for his review of Ripley's *Philosophical Miscellanies*.

354. *Ibid.*, II (Jan., 1839), 43, 49.

355. *Ibid.*, II (Jan., 1839), 178–79; III (Apr., 1840), 201.

356. H. M. Jones, *op. cit.*, p. 467; I. W. Riley, *American Thought* . . ., pp. 395–97; R. L. Rusk, *Literature of the Middle Western Frontier* (2 vols., N.Y., 1925), I, 51.

357. Forming volumes V and VI of Ripley's *Specimens of Foreign Standard Literature*.

In order to correct "such gross misconceptions" as still prevail, "notwithstanding the full expositions which have been laid before the public, the editor, W. H. Channing, makes known "the true position" which the writers of the eclectic school occupy (*Introduction*, 1848 ed., I, xi). The French school is credited with having performed three great services: (1) while they acknowledged the value of Reid's method and his "first truths," they went beyond him to clear away the inanities of common-sense based on observations that were "hasty, partial, and confused" (*Ibid.*, p. xii); (2) they recognized the great work done by Kant in substituting "spiritualism in place of sensualism forever," but failed to be satisfied with Kant's "system of skepticism," which asserted "that we have no means of proving the existence of objective realities" (pp. xiii–xiv); and (3) they adopted the best of both the Scottish school, which had been devoted to psychology, and of the German, which was given to ontology and logic, and "blended them with a method of their own" (p. xiv). Maine de Biran and Royer-Collard are said to be the originators of the school. Cousin has given it its widest celebrity, and Jouffory is well fitted to advance the movement "from his habit of patient observation, his liberal spirit, and perfect simplicity and method of style" (p. xv). Taking a hint from the German concern with ontology, but reversing the process of the Germans, who "begin with the absolute and descend to man, the French begin with man and ascend to the absolute" (p. xvi). Channing's introduction did little toward teaching his countrymen the Kantian epistemology; while Jouffroy's text itself did little more than represent Kant as an exponent of the "Skeptical School" of ethics; but no concerted effort was made to explain, defend, or refute him.

358. W. D. Wilson, in I (July, 1840), 99–117. Led by George Ripley, who organized a class to study Cousin, several Brook Farmers (notably Mrs. Kirby) found eclecticism "inspiring and delightful." See Caroline Dall, *Transcendentalism in New England* (Boston, 1897), p. 28.

359. III (July, 1840), 265–323; see also *Princeton Rev.*, XI (Jan., 1839), 37–101, and XII (Jan., 1840), 31–71.

360. XXVIII (May, 1840), 137–47.

361. LIII (July, 1841), 1–40.

362. XLI (Febr., 1840), 382–414.

363. I (Mar., 1841), 276–87. Cousin is introduced as the "best equipped living writer to interpret the 'critical philosophy' of Kant" (p. 276). While a good deal is promised, little is presented; for the first essay contributes little more information regarding Kant than that "*the law of duty* . . . is the center of Kant's morality, and his morality is the center of his philosophy" (p. 285). Neither Cousin nor Kant is mentioned in succeeding numbers of the short-lived *Eclectic*.

364. Samuel Johnson, one of the later generation of Transcendentalists, recalled in 1880, as among his "happiest recollections" of his undergraduate years at Harvard (where he graduated in 1842) his reading with Dr. James Walker "portions of Locke, in Cousin's Lectures on Psychology, translated by Dr. Henry, and Jouffroy's Ethics translated by Mr. Channing." —Johnson's *Lectures, Essays, and Sermons* . . . (Boston, 1883), p. 5.

365. LIV (Apr., 1842), 356–97.

366. *Democratic Rev.*, XII (May, 1843), 457–74.

367. Girard, "Du Transcendentalisme considéré essentiellement dans sa définition et ses origines françaises," *Univ. of Calif. Publ. in Mod. Philol.*, IV, iii (Oct. 18, 1916), 351–498; Michaud "Le Transcendentalisme d'après l'histoire," *Mod. Philol.*, XVI, viii (Dec., 1918), 393–411. For corrections of their errors of omission and commission, ill-founded assumptions and preoccupations, nationalistic bias, and misinformation on American factors, see the review by Professor George Sherburn in *Modern Philology*, XV (Sept., 1917), 317–20, and Ronald V. Wells, *Three Christian Transcendentalists: James Marsh, Caleb Sprague Henry, Frederic Henry Hedge* (N.Y., 1943), pp. 10–13.

368. For example, he finds in the sixteen numbers of the *Dial* only fifteen references to Cousin, Jouffroy, and Fourier, while Plato alone gets thirty references and Fichte twenty (p. 92).

Much has been made of the fact that Ripley selected for the first of his *Specimens of Foreign Standard Literature* the philosophy of France rather than that of Germany; but it must be borne in mind that Ripley, as he planned the *Specimens*, proposed to publish translations from only four French authors as opposed to fourteen Germans, and that of the fourteen volumes which appeared, only four deal with French as against ten with German writers. The volumes, in the order of their publication, are as follows:

I–II. *Philosophical Miscellanies, Translated from the French of Cousin, Jouffroy, and Benjamin Constant* . . . by George Ripley, 2 vols., Boston, 1838.

III. *Select Minor Poems, Translated from the German of Goethe and Schiller*, ed. [and tr. in part] by John Sullivan Dwight, 1839.

IV. *Conversations with Goethe in the Last Years of his Life. Translated from the German of* [J. P.] *Eckermann*, by Margaret Fuller, 1839.

V–VI. *Introduction to Ethics, Including a Critical Survey of Moral Systems, Translated from the French of* [*Th. S.*] *Jouffroy*, by Wm. H. Channing, 2 vols., 1840.

VII–IX. *German Literature, Translated from the German of Wolfgang Menzel*, by C. C. Felton, 3 vols., 1840.

X–XI. *Theodore; or The Mystic's Conversion. History of the Culture of a Protestant Clergyman, from the German of* [*W. L.*] *De Wette*, by James F. Clarke, 2 vols., 1841.

XII–XIII. *Human Life, or Practical Ethics, from the German of [W. L.] De Wette*, by Samuel Osgood, 2 vols., 1842.

XIV. *Songs and Ballads. Translated from Uhland, Körner, Bürger, and other German Lyric Poets* . . . by Charles T. Brooks, 1842.

369. Cf. W. F. Leighton, *op. cit.*, pp. 92–99; H. M. Jones, *op. cit.*, p. 462; I. W. Riley, *op. cit.*, p. 389.

370. The American translation of his *Introduction* led to a friendship and correspondence with Linberg, followed two years later by a similar connection with Henry, Professor of Philosophy at the University of the City of New York. He thanked Brownson for advocating eclecticism, and George Ripley for putting first in the *Specimens* his writings and those of his colleagues, Jouffroy and Constant. As early as 1834 he had expressed gratification at the use made of his educational treatises in Massachusetts and New Jersey, and the founding of Girard College by a Franco-American was another source of satisfaction. See H. M. Jones, *op. cit.*, p. 471.

371. Murdock's explanation, moreover, does not tally with that given by Emerson in his essay on "The Transcendentalist" (*Works*, Cent. ed., I, 327–66); with Theo. Parker's disquisition on "Transcendentalism" (*Works*, Cent. ed., VI, 1–38); with W. D. Wilson's account in "The Unitarian Movement in New England," *Dial*, I (Apr., 1841), 409–43; or with other contemporary testimonials of prominent exponents as well as opponents of the movement, as will appear in the pages immediately following.

372. For the differences between the Transcendentalists' "intuition" and the Kantian use of the term, see Norman K. Smith, *A Commentary on Kant's "Critique of Pure Reason"* (2nd ed., rev. & enl., London, 1923), pp. 81–82. Compare the use to which it is put in Barnas Sears's review of J. F. Clarke's translation of De Wette's *Theodore* in the *Christ. Rev.*, VI (Dec., 1841), 541.

373. Cousin, *Introduction to the History of Philosophy* (tr. by H. G. Linberg, Boston, 1832), pp. 163, 166, 167, 179.

374. James Murdock, *op. cit.*, p. 179.

375. Geo. W. Cooke, *op. cit.*, II, 73. Brownson was one of those sincere but unfortunate persons who is carried away by the last book he reads. Van Wyck Brooks says of him: "Every thinker he read, Lamennais, Jouffroy, Comte, Saint-Simon, Owen, overthrew all his previous views, and he rushed from one position to another, with a headlong, headstrong vehe-

mence, telling the world each time how right he was."—*The Flowering of New England*, p. 247.

376. Published originally in Paris, 1804; 2nd ed., rev., corr., and enl., 4 vols., Paris, 1822–1823; reviewed in *North Amer. Rev.*, XVIII (Apr., 1824), 234–66.

377. *Journals*, II, 329–30 (Oct. 27, 1830); see also pp. 330–45.

378. See *ibid.*, p. 451 (Jan. 20, 1832), where Cousin is quoted for the first time: " 'O Reason, Reason, art not thou he whom I seek?' Fenelon *apud* Cousin." Cousin is again mentioned on November 13, 1832 (*ibid.*, p. 529), but there is no indication that Emerson read Henry's translation of the *Cours de l'histoire de la philosophie moderne* in 1832, when it first appeared.

379. Translated by Cousin under the title *Manuel de l'histoire de la philosophie*, Paris, 1829.

380. *Journals*, III, 156 (June, 1833); see also III, 170 (July 15, 1833).

381. *Ibid.*, II, 268 (Oct. 8, 1829).

382. *Ibid.*, pp. 277, 278 (Dec. 10, 13, 1829).

383. *Ibid.*, p. 280.

384. *Ibid.*, pp. 329–30.

385. *Ibid.*, p. 515.

386. *Ibid.*, p. 278.

387. *Ibid.*, p. 515.

388. *Ibid.*, IV, 400 (Mar. 4, 1838); see also IV, 404–5.

389. The only praise Cousin ever elicited from Emerson was in connection with his appreciation of Cousin's "magnificent *Republic.*"—*Ibid.*, VII, 56 (1845).

390. A noteworthy exception is Ripley, who set out boldly in his several letters addressed to Norton to bring Schleiermacher and De Wette into the argument.

391. On this score, see the Rev. Daniel Dana's article, "On the Modesty Becoming a Christian Minister," *Amer. Quar. Register*, XI (Aug., 1838), 55–63, esp. pp. 59–60. See also Bancroft's repeated protestations written from Germany in 1819 to President Kirkland, Andrews Norton, and others that he remained unaffected by German atheism and German theology, except insofar as the latter was "merely critical."—M. A. DeWolfe, *Life and Letters of George Bancroft*, I, 56, 64 *et seq.*

392. Cambridge, 1839, pp. 9, 10, 11, 29, 36–64.

393. The *Discourse* itself, of course, deals in no personalities and mentions no names, but the two "Notes," of eleven and fourteen pages, appended in the printed version of the address (pp. 39–64) make it abundantly clear what was in Norton's mind. Here De Wette, Schleiermacher, and Strauss are roundly castigated. Incidentally, Norton's notes, which include

copious extracts and translations from German theologians and Biblical commentators, show him to have been well read in this area and every bit a match for Ripley in his ability to handle German.

394. *Letters on the Latest Form of Infidelity* (Boston, 1840), 129, 130–31.

395. Both are conveniently turned to, *ibid.*, pp. 161–246 and 247–401, respectively.

396. Except once as the editor of Descartes' *Les Principes de la Philosophie.* However, Coleridge's opinion of Spinoza (as given in the *Biog. Lit.*, Amer. ed., 1817, pp. 93–94) and his distinction between Reason and Understanding. as well as his definition of intuition as a generalizing faculty of the understanding are quoted from the *Aids to Reflection*, Marsh ed., Appendix, pp. 313, 329.

397. XI (Jan., 1839), 37–101.

398. Coleridge and Cousin are merely the means through which our *philosophemeta* are received "by a double transportation" (*ibid.*, p. 42). After indicating the general significance of Kant as a metaphysician, the authors discuss Kant's "synthetical judgments *a priori*" (pp. 44–46), name and explain briefly the categories of the Understanding (p.47), distinguish between Pure and Practical Reason, and enumerate the postulates of the latter (pp. 47–50). Fichte is disposed of in short order, but Schelling's theory of the identity of Ego and Non-Ego, his *Naturphilosophie*, and his pantheism are discussed (pp. 54–58), while Hegel's doctrine that "God exists only as knowledge, as an Idea," is given as the cause of Hegel's "nihilism" (pp. 56–61). Cousin is classed "with the German school, because the chief part of his philosophy is evidently derived from that source" (p. 64), but his is only a "mock-German metaphysics" (p. 87). His spontaneous reason and its far-flung theological implications are then discussed; but his system, "as far he has developed it, is to the last degree superficial and conceited. . . . it does in truth but skim the surface of things, and then fly off in . . . unmeaning abstractions" (p. 91); "the witch jargon he employs only confuses" (p. 92). The essay is liberally documented with footnotes, indicating that the writers had Kant, Jacobi, Fichte, Schelling, Hegel, Coleridge's *Friend, Aids,* and *Biographia Literaria,* and Linberg's and Henry's translations before them as they wrote.

399. *Princeton Rev.*, XII (Jan., 1840), 31–71.

400. When, in the same year, Norton edited and republished this essay, along with that by Alexander and Dod on "Transcendentalism," he appropriately renamed it "The School of Hegel." This reprint (Cambridge, 1840) did

much to give currency to the controversy. In addition to the German writers listed, he appears to have been familiar also with the works of Tholuck, Ruge, Bayrhoffer, Leo, Becker, Menzel, Vischer, Weise, and Hengstenberg.

401. The profuse footnotes indicate that, like Alexander and Dod, Hodge was thoroughly schooled in the German language and in German theology. See also the Rev. Henry Ware's article on Transcendentalism in the *Christian Examiner* for July, 1840 (XVIII, 378–89), which takes cognizance only of the Germans—Kant, Fichte, Schelling, and notably Hegel—"whose philosophy seems to be a concentration of all the vices" of all the German philosophers. In Hegel Ware finds the fountainhead of all the iniquities of American Transcendentalism. Francis Bowen, writing a year later, in the same journal, reaches a similar conclusion. See XX (May, 1841), 189–223.

402. P. 65.

403. *Christ. Exam.*, XXVIII (Nov., 1839), 221–35.

404. On this head, consult C. H. Faust, "The Background of the Unitarian Opposition to Transcendentalism," *Mod. Philol.*, XXXV, iii (Feb., 1938), 297–324, esp. pp. 304–5, 316–22.

405. The reputation of the French as popularizers was well understood, and Cousin and Jouffroy were recommended as best suited to the tired businessman for his family hours. See William Girard, *loc. cit.*, p. 454; George Sherburn's review of Girard in *Mod. Philol.*, XV, v (Sept., 1917), 319; and Samuel Osgood's review of Ripley's *Specimens* in *Christ. Exam.*, XXVIII (May, 1840), 137–47: "The French, indeed, are masters of the intellectual mint, they understand how to give thought such shape that it will pass current. Commend me to the Germans for skill, ardor, and patience in digging out the precious metal from its depths, and to the English for readiness and talent to use it in actual business; but it must first pass through the French mint and take the form and beauty that fit it for practical purposes" (pp. 137–38). "This," suggests Professor Sherburn, "seems to present the usual view and to explain perhaps why Ripley's early *Specimens* were from the French rather than German philosophers."

406. See his reviews of Herder's *Spirit of Hebrew Poetry*, tr. by James Marsh (2 vols., Burlington, Vt., 1833), in *Christ. Exam.*, XVIII (May, 1835), 167–221; of Herder's *Werke* (18 vols., Stuttgart, 1827–1835), *ibid.*, XIX (Nov., 1835), 172–204; and an essay on "Schleiermacher as a Theologian," *ibid.*, XX (Mar., 1836), 1–46.

407. For Herder's poetry, see E. Z. Davis *Translations of German Poetry in Amer. Mags.,*

1741–1810 (Phila., 1905), and M. D. Learned, "Herder in America," *Ger.-Amer. Annals*, VI, ix (Sept. 1904), 536–628.

    408. V, 258, 373–75.

    409. VIII, 233–37, 417–29; IX, 1–11, 81–88, 171–76, 241–54.

    410. I, 103.

    411. XX, 138–48.

    412. III (1826), 307.

    413. IV, 123–26.

    414. Two vols., Burlington, Vt., 1833.

    415. XVIII (May, 1835), 167–221. Ostensibly a review of Marsh's translation of *Vom Geist der ebräischen Poesie*, but really an extended biographical sketch drawn from *Erinnerungen aus dem Leben von Herder*, by Marie Caroline Herder (Stuttgart, 1830), *Herders Leben* by Carl L. Ring (Karlsruhe, 1832), and *Herders sämmtliche Werke* (ed. by Johann G. Müller, 18 vols., Stuttgart, 1827–1830). Thankful that German literature in good translations is fast becoming known in America, Ripley regrets that he "cannot make so favorable a report of the prospects of German theology," Americans being still ignorant of the "masterly intellects" of Germany in theological matters (p. 167). Mindful that German theology will not "settle any theological controversies now pending," he yet earnestly recommends "a sober examination of . . . the massive theological learning of Germany" to all religious-minded Americans (p. 168). Marsh's translation is praised as supplying the right kind of information. Unfortunately his rendition has killed much of the vivacity of Herder's original text (pp. 169–70). Three pages are devoted to discrepancies between the German and English versions (pp. 170–74). The remainder, and by far the longer portion, of the essay is devoted to Herder's life (pp. 170–211) and character (pp. 211–21).

    Ripley's essay was logically completed a year later by his article in the same journal (XIX, 172–204) on "Herder's Theological Opinions and Services," which is more properly a review of his *Werke*. See also XX (1836), 1–46.

    416. The *North American Review* for April, 1836 (XLII, 299–334), discussed at some length Herder's poetry in a longer discourse on German popular poetry (*ibid.*, pp. 265–339). In 1839 the *Baltimore Quarterly Review* (II, 77) brought out a translation of Herder's legendary ballad, "Die Geschwister," and the *Southern Literary Messenger* printed a version of "Das Grab" (V, 149). In his "Letter to a Theological Student," in the *Dial* for 1840 (I, 187), Ripley recommended Herder's *Letters* to all and sundry.

    417. For other works of Herder's available in translation, see Morgan, and for later periodical concern with Herder, see the bibliographies by Goodnight and Haertel. Three essays are particularly noteworthy: (1) Samuel Osgood's "Modern Ecclesiastical History," *Christ. Exam.*, XLVIII (May, 1850), 423–26; (2) H. J. Werner's review of *Von und an Herder*, *ibid.*, LXXII (July, 1862), 137–41; and (3) Karl Hildebrandt's essay of 124 pages in the *North American Review* for July and October, 1872, and April, 1873.

    418. Not to be overlooked, however, is the fact that De Wette had two personal disciples in America as early as 1824: first, his stepson, Dr. Carl Beck, who taught Latin at Harvard from 1832 to 1850, and second, Dr. Carl Follen, teacher of German at Harvard from 1825 to 1835. De Wette and Follen had jointly edited the literary journal at the University of Basel in 1821. See W. E. Channing, *Death of Follen* (Boston, 1840), p. 28.

    419. Translated by J. F. Clarke (2 vols., Boston, 1841; repr., 1856). It had already run serially in the *Western Messenger* (Louisville), of which Clarke was editor, during 1836–1837.

    420. Translated by Samuel Osgood (2 vols., Boston, 1842; repr., 1856); reviewed by C. F. Brooks in the *Christian Examiner*, XXXIII (Nov., 1842), 252–57.

    421. VI, 537–57.

    422. XXXI, 348–73.

    423. Sears knows "no theologian and biblical critic in whose works there is so much to admire, and at the same time so much to censure, as in those of De Wette" (p. 537). It might be observed here that Sears, the editor of the *Christian Review*, only recently returned from a visit to Germany, was usually more uncompromisingly critical where German theology is concerned. See, for example, his article on "German Literature" in the *Christian Review*, VI (June, 1841), 269–84—to the charges of which Moses Stuart felt constrained to reply in the next number (pp. 446–71). Sears goes on to criticize De Wette for adopting in his *Theodor* the philosophy of Fries and for supposing he found therein proof that "the mind itself is a source of intuitive truth," as "an all-sufficient guide in the criticism of divine revelation." He has nothing but censure for Fries's system which "appears to hold a middle-place between Kant and Schelling, and to unite the two" (pp. 540–41). He criticizes De Wette for setting aside the conclusions of the understanding by the authority of our moral feelings or intuitions without specifying the tests to which the latter are subjected (p. 543). With the position held by De Wette in regard to the canonical authority of the Scriptures (pp. 544–51) and his view of

faith (pp. 551–56) Sears is in substantial agreement.

Cyrus A. Bartol, one of the younger Transcendentalists, agrees with De Wette's views of justification by faith, which, he adds, are "not new to theologians among ourselves" (p. 349), but he differs radically on the relation found in De Wette "of Naturalism and Spiritualism in the true interpretation of the Christian Birth" (p. 350), and on the question, "Is Christianity a development of the natural powers of the human mind, or a spiritual interposition of God?" (p. 350). This leads to a critique of De Wette's treatment of miracles (pp. 351–58), the character of Christ (pp. 358–62), the faults of a too-exclusive supernaturalism (pp. 363–70), and the faults to a too exclusive rationalism as totally unfit for the mass of mankind (pp. 371–73).

Among other noteworthy articles are two by Samuel Osgood in the *Christ. Exam*: (1) "De Wette's Views of Religion and Theology," XXIV (May, 1838), 137–71, and XXV (Sept., 1838), 1–25, and (2) "De Wette and Schleiermacher's Ethics," XXIX (Nov., 1840), 153–74, and XXX (May, 1841), 145–73; also Osgood's rev. of De Wette's *Manual on the New Testament, ibid.*, XXXIV (Mar., 1844), 284–86; and an article on *Dr. Martin Luthers Briefe. By De Wette*, repr. from the *Edinburgh Rev.*, in *Littell's Living Age* (Boston), VI (1845), 325–39.

424. Two vols., Boston, 1843; 2nd ed., 1850; 3rd ed., 1858. On the vogue of Parker's translation, see Wm. F. Warren's "Theodore Parker: The Good and Evil in His Opinions and Influence," in *Parkerism* (N.Y., 1860).

425. Tr. from the 5th, improved and enl. German ed., Boston, 1858; rev. by G. R. Noyes in *Christ. Exam.*, LXV (July, 1858), 140–46.

426. However, the victory was not won without a struggle. For example, the *Christian Examiner* alone, during the twenty years which elapsed between 1838, when it first noticed De Wette, and 1859, when it reviewed the third edition of Parker's *Canonical Scriptures* devoted ten articles, comprising 180 pages, to the subject, and other religious periodicals showed a similar interest.

427. Notably his *Critical Essay on the Gospel of St. Luke* . . . tr. by C. Thirlwall (London, 1821); Schleiermacher's *Introduction to the Dialogues of Plato*, tr. by Wm. Dobson (Cambridge, Engl., 1836); and *Brief Outline of the Study of Theology* . . . tr. by Wm. Ferrier (Edinburgh, 1850).

428. O. B. Frothingham, *George Ripley* (Boston, 1883), p. 229.

429. Ripley translated the fifth of Schleiermacher's *Reden über die Religion*, today conveniently turned to in *The German Classics*, ed.

by Kuno Francke and W. G. Howard (20 vols., N.Y., 1913–1915), V, 19–30.

430. While editorial concern was neither spirited nor sustained, it continued intermittently from 1938, when Parker first introduced Schleiermacher through the columns of the *Christian Examiner*, until November 22, 1868, when a Schleiermacher Centennial was held by the united Unitarian congregations of New York City. See Samuel Osgood's article on the centennial, *Christ. Exam.*, LXXXVI (Mar., 1869), 171–91. In the meantime, the *Examiner* had, on three other occasions, devoted space to Schleiermacher's theology: in May, 1850, when Samuel Osgood had discussed him (XLVIII, 427–32) in relation to "Modern Ecclesiastical History"; in H. Davis' "Schleiermacher," LIII (July, 1852), 66–93; and in Miss L. P. Hale's "Life of Schleiermacher," LXXII (Jan., 1862), 109–23. All in all, the *Examiner* published five articles, totaling 117 pages, on Schleiermacher —an indication that he is of more than passing interest in any study of American theology that concerns itself with origins and influences.

431. For example, as early as 1834, Hedge read to Emerson what the latter termed "fine things out of Schleiermacher" (*Journals*, III, 393, Dec. 14, 1834); and in September, 1838, Emerson linked the writings of Schleiermacher with those of Goethe as desirable to read (*ibid.*, V, 37). See also the discussions below of Ripley, Parker, and Clarke.

432. *Princeton Rev.*, IX, 198–215. In Strauss's book, says the reviewer, "infidel theology appears to have reached its consummation" (p. 108). The *Southern Rose* (Charleston) took notice of it in 1839 (VII, 285) by reprinting a critical estimate of it from the London *Foreign Quarterly Review*.

433. XXVIII (July, 1840), 273–316.

434. Tr. by E. Littre (2 vols., Paris, 1838–1840).

435. Tr. by George Eliot from the 4th German ed., London, 1846. For other British eds., see Morgan.

436. Following an honestly executed and detailed summary, chapter by chapter, of *Das Leben Jesu* (pp. 280–306), Parker devoted ten pages (pp. 307–16) to pointing out the "false principles, extreme conclusions, and extravagances" in Strauss's book, but concluded in a manner which, although he himself was incapable of accepting the conclusions of Strauss, nevertheless indicates how effectively liberalism had proceeded by 1840 to break down the entrenched dogmatism of fifteen or twenty years before. In 1820 or even 1825 none but the veriest heretic would have admitted, as Parker did, on the mere testimony of Dr. Ullmann, that

Strauss is no atheist but "a religious man." Nor is it likely that at that time all Boston harbored a theologian who would have dared write and subscribe his name, as Parker did, to the passage in which he speaks of Strauss as "an individual raised by God" to discover "a great truth, which marks an epoch, and by its seminal character marks the coming ages . . . . Before mankind could pass over the great chasm between the frozen realm of stiff super-naturalism, and lifeless rationalism, on the one side, and the fair domain of *free religious thought*, where the only *essential* creed is the Christian motto, 'Be perfect, as your Father in Heaven is perfect,' and the only *essential* form of Religion is love to your neighbor as to yourself, and to God with the whole heart, mind, and soul, on the other—some one must plunge in, devoting himself unconsciously, or even against his will, for the welfare of the race. This hard lot Strauss has chosen for himself, and done what many we fear wished, but none dared to do. His book, therefore, must needs be negative, destructive, and unsatisfactory. It pleases no one. It is colder than ice . . . the most melancholy book we ever read . . . . But it only marks a period of transition"—a necessary phase presaging great advances to be made on the basis of it. For Strauss is not representative of the German theologians or the German people; they will transcend him (pp. 314–15).

437. See, e.g., the article by G. E. Ellis on Strauss in the *Christ. Exam.* for Nov., 1846, in which he assumes that every reader of the *Examiner* is familiar with the doctrines of Strauss—so much so, in fact, that many people in America have ceased to think of them as originating in Germany but regard them rather as of American origin (XL, 314–54, esp. 313–14). Indicative of the interest in Strauss is the fact that between January, 1839, and November, 1847, the *Christian Examiner* devoted five articles, totaling 123 pages, to *Das Leben Jesu*. Aside from those by Parker and Ellis (already mentioned), these are by Henry Ware, Jr., (Jan., 1839), Stephen G. Bulfinch (Sept., 1845), and Geo. R. Noyes (Nov., 1847). Two articles on Strauss appeared later, one by O. B. Frothingham (Mar., 1865), who, in reviewing the new French translation by A. Nefftzer and C. Dollfus (2 vols., Paris, 1864), finds it an "interesting and valuable book," though it "lacks the warmth the glow, the human interest, that carries us along in the brilliant romance which Renan calls the life of Jesus" (p. 287), published orig-inally in 1863 and first translated into English by C. E. Wilbour (N.Y., 1864).

438. For example, the influence of Strauss on the theology of Parker, especially in what

he called his "Absolute Religion," is not hard to discern in such works of his as "Some Account of My Ministry" and "Experiences as a Min-ister." A thorough examination of the precise extent to which Parker followed the German critics is in order.

439. Of course, there were notable excep-tions. For instance, Andrews Norton, though himself a student of German, would not allow his son to study the language at Harvard for fear that it would corrupt his Unitarianism.

440. We have already observed how handily men like Ripley, Norton, Sears, W. H. Chan-ning, Bartol, and Parker could refer to German theological scholarship. The list, as will appear, can be widely extended. A case in point is Stephen G. Bulfinch, who, in the course of his review, speaks with some degree of discrimi-nation of Niebuhr, Eichhorn, Bauer, Gabler, Paulus, Heyne, Neander, De Wette, Ullmann, Tholuck, Herder, Schleiermacher, Kant, Schel-ling, Jacobi, Eschenmayer, Menzel, and Weisse. See also J. H. Allen's "Recent German Theol-ogy," *Christ. Exam.*, LXIII (Nov., 1857), 431–40, in the course of which he refers to fifty theologians. While Emerson left the church with a yawn in 1832, he continued for some years to read rather widely in the theological literature of the time. He does not mention Strauss's *Life of Jesus* before Jan. 15, 1848 (*Journals*, VII, 396), but his words imply a prior familiarity with the book, as well as with Tholuck's reply, and a full understanding of the issues involved.

441. After graduating second in the class of 1797 at Yale, Murdock (1776–1856) held a pastorate in Princeton, Mass., 1802–1815; became professor of learned languages at the University of Vermont, 1815–1818; declined a professorship of languages at Dartmouth in 1818; became the Brown Professor of Sacred Rhetoric and Ecclesastical History in the seminary at Andover, 1819–1828, where he was dismissed because of his unwillingness to see ecclesiastical history crowded out of the curric-ulum in favor of sacred rhetoric. He settled in New Haven in 1829, and devoted the rest of his life to Christian scholarship.

442. For a statement of his aims, see the Preface. As to his sources, he says: "The principal authorities consulted in the twelve first chapters of the work are *W. G. Tenne-mann's* Grundriss der Geschichte der Philo-sophie, ed. 1829: *T. A. Rixner's* Handbuch der Gesch. der Philos. ed. 1822: *W. T. Krug's* Encyclopadie. ed. 1824. In the remaining chapters the authorities are generally stated in the work. While writing the four chapters on the Kantean Philosophy, the author had not

the Critik der reinen Vernunft before him, but relied upon very copious *extracts* which he made from that work about eight years ago. Since obtaining the Critik, he has not had the leisure for a thorough verification; but he hopes his statements will be found to be substantially correct."

443. Chapter V treats the following topics: (1) Kant as the critic of sensation, (2) his conceptions of time and space, (3) Kant's fundamental problems, (4) the distinction between knowledge *a priori* and *a posteriori*, (5) analytical and synthetical judgments, and (6) Kant's definitions of Sensation, Understanding, and Reason (pp. 44–54). The next chapter analyzes the sphere and 'the materials of the Understanding and presents in some detail the categories (pp. 65–67). In Chapter VIII (pp. 68–78), which is devoted to Kantian Reason, speculative or theoretical Reason as imparting rational knowledge is distinguished from practical or moral reason as enjoining upon us rational conduct. This is followed by an exposition of the transcendental ideas of pure Reason and a discussion of the difference between transcendental and natural theology. The eighth chapter (pp. 79–92) deals with the results to which the critical philosophy leads, with emphasis upon the disciplines of pure Reason in its dogmatic, its polemic, and its hypothetical uses, and upon the canon of pure Reason as it centers upon the problems of the freedom of will, the immortality of the soul, and the existence of God, as well as questions involving the effects of this philosophy upon opinion, knowledge, and faith. This chapter ends with Murdock's restatement of his purpose, which, be it added, he accomplished rather more successfully in fifty pages than one would expect—namely, to present Kant "fairly and intelligibly" so that the reader "might form some correct estimate of the merits and demerits of this coryphaeus of modern German philosophers" (p. 92). Earlier in the volume (p. 47) he says that he is not acquainted at first hand with Kant's "Critic of Practical Judgment, his Critic of the Judging Faculty, his Prolegomena of Every Future System of Metaphysics . . . a Foundation for the Metaphysics of Morals, &c. &c."

444. Tr. by Francis Hayward, London, 1838; 2nd ed., 1848; tr. by J. M. D. Meikeljohn, London, 1855.

445. Elisa Lee Follen, *Life of Charles Follen*, I, 145, 149, 617.

446. *Life and Letters of George Ticknor*, I, 11–12. In his *Inaugural Address* of 1831, Dr. Follen put back fifty years the date when no German grammar or dictionary was to be found in Boston. "Now," he added, "there are a number of persons who speak, and a large number who read and enter into the sense and spirit of German."—*Works*, I, 132.

447. *Ibid.*, I, 140.

448. *A Literary History of America* (New York, 1900), p. 295. See also the later testimony of Henry Adams in *The Education of Henry Adams* (Boston & N.Y., 1918), Chs. IV and V.

EARLY EXPONENTS IN NEW ENGLAND

449. F. L. Jahn, *A Treatise on Gymnastics*, tr. by Carl Beck (Northampton, Mass., 1828). Lieber reviewed the book in the *American Quarterly Review*, III (Mar., 1828), 126–50.

450. For further educational services, see George W. Spindler, *Karl Follen: A Biographical Study* (Chicago, 1917), pp. 2–3.

451. Some information concerning Beck's activity in public affairs can be gathered from Wm. Newell's *Christian Citizen: A Discourse Occasioned by the Death of Charles Beck. Delivered March 25, 1866, before the First Parish Church in Cambridge* (Cambridge, 1866); Andrew P. Peabody's *Harvard Reminiscences* (Boston, 1888); and John L. Chamberlain's *Harvard University* (Boston, 1900). A new study of Beck is in order, however.

452. The more important of these are his *German Reader for Beginners* (1826) and his *Practical Grammar of the German Language* (1828), which were used consistently at Harvard and elsewhere as the *sine qua non* of instruction in German well into the sixties. From these simple books many of the leaders of American thought and affairs derived their first knowledge of German arts and sciences. It is doubtful that any single one of the many German readers and grammers that have since appeared can boast similarly significant results. The *Grammar* reached its twenty-first recorded printing in 1859. Among significant data for these two volumes are the following:

German Grammar for Beginners: Deutsches Lesebuch für Anfänger, Cambridge, 1826. vii + 255 pp.; 2nd ed., 1831. xix + 256 pp.; 3rd ed., 1836. 232 pp.; repr., 1839. 220 pp.; 10th ed., 1845. 222 pp.; new ed., with additions by G. A. Schmitt, Boston & Cambridge, 1858. xv + 326 pp.; repr., 1867.

A Practical Grammar of the German Language, Boston, 1828. xix + 282 pp. The Preface carefully explains the author's utilization of and improvement upon Georg Heinrich Noehden's *Elements of German Grammar* (London, 1800; 5th ed., 1827) and John Rowbotham's *Practical German Grammer* (London, 1824) and his employment of Du Ponceau's philological theories as published in *Transactions of the American*

Philosophical Society (I, xvii [1818], 228–64), together with principles derived from Adelung's and the Grimm brothers' grammars and the German prosody of Voss and Schlegel. The second edition appeared in Cambridge in 1831; 3rd ed., Boston, 1834; repr. 1835, 1837; 6th ed., Boston, 1838; repr., 1839; stereotyped ed., Boston, 1839; repr., 1841, 1844; 10th ed., 1845; 11th ed., 1845; 14th ed., 1849; 21st ed., 1859. Follen's was the first German grammar to come into general use in American schools. Although John James Bachmair's *Complete German Grammar*, originally printed in London, had been republished in Philadelphia, by H. Miller, as early as 1772 and reprinted in Philadelphia in 1788, it never was widely used in college classes.

Another of Follen's books designed for use in teaching was his *Luther's German Version of the Gospel of John, with an Interlinear Translation, for the Use of Students* (Boston, 1835, 160 pp.). It seems probable, also, in view of Follen's having promised something of the sort, that he was responsible for the preparation of *German Dramas, from Schiller and Goethe, for the Use of Persons Learning the German Language* (Boston & Cambridge, 1831); repr. by Charles Folsom, the University printer, in 1833. The "Advertisement" states that the text is adapted to follow Follen's *Lesebuch* and is designed for students at Harvard. The book contains *Maria Stuart* (pp. 1–185) and *Tasso* and *Egmont* (pp. 186–422).

453. Many of his sermons are printed in Volume II of Follen's *Works*.

454. L. L. Mackall, writing in the *Harvard Graduates' Magazine* (XI, 492) for March, 1903, reported finding in a Boston bookstore two paper-covered German books printed in 1829, on the outside of each of which was pasted a printed list of rules and bylaws, and on one of them, following the heading, "German Society, 1828," the following names: C. Follen, S. A. Eliot, G. Ticknor, S. H. Perkins, Wm. T. Andrews, F. C. Gray, J. Pickering, N. L. Bowditch, C. Wigglesworth, F. Lieber, Mr. Miesegalo, T. Searle, J. M. Robinson. Follen's leading role in his effort to foster and spread a knowledge of German culture is hardly to be doubted.

455. In her *Reminiscences*, Elizabeth Palmer Peabody related how, during the autumn of 1827, a series of informal meetings was begun—some meetings at Dr. Channing's and some at the home of Jonathan Phillips—for discussing the general subject of the education of children. Among those in attendance were the Channings, Phillips, Dr. Follen, the Peabody sisters, and occasionally G. F. Thayer and William Russell, editor of the *Journal of Education*. "The con-versation soon ranged over every department of education, inquiring into the comparative study of languages, ancient and modern, and into science, history, fiction, and poetry as a means to education."—*Reminiscences*, pp. 213, 250. See also G. W. Spindler, *Karl Follen: A Biographical Study* (Chicago, 1917), pp. 107–8; and *Sprague's Annals*, VIII, 644. Miss Peabody adds that among minds as harmoniously disciplined yet as utterly different as Channing's, Follen's, and Phillips', these discussions became very rich, and that Follen earnestly espoused Froebel's principles by maintaining that the child should be handled not with reference to the future, but to his present perfection.—*Reminiscences*, p. 256. She goes on to recount details of Follen's principles, as enunciated by Pestalozzi and Froebel, so that when she heard later about the New Education (in which she herself came to take a leading part) she found nothing essentially different from what Follen had advocated half a century earlier.—*Ibid.*, p. 257.

Follen was probably the first to introduce Froebel's ideas in the United States, although Froebel's writings and ideas did not gain wide-spread currency before the mid-nineteenth century, when the kindergarten movement got under way. However, Pestalozzi's works were issued from American presses much earlier: (1) Pestalozzi's *Leonard and Gertrude. A Popular Story, Written Originally in Germany, Translated into French and now Attempted in English, with the Hope of its being Useful to all Classes of Society* (Phila., 1801, 276 pp.); (2) Solyman Brown's *Comprehensive Views of the Systems of Pestalozzi and Lancaster . . .* (N.Y., 1825. 34 pp.); (3) *Letters of Pestalozzi on the Education of Infancy. Addressed to Mothers* (Boston, 1830. viii + 517 pp.); (4) numerous British publications; and (5) items enumerated in the section on Alcott.

456. *Works*, I, 160, 163–64, 167, 172–79, 180–246.

457. Follen declared upon landing in America his intention of becoming an American citizen and set about promptly to master the language. Before the end of the year he was giving public lectures in Boston on civil law in the English language. Particularly significant for information on Follen's career as a public figure is Kuno Francke's essay in the *Papers of the Amer. Hist. Assn.*, V (1891), 65–81; Dieter Cunz's essay in the *Amer.-Ger. Rev.*, VII, i (Oct., 1940), 25–27, 32; and Spindler's full-length biography.

458. For example, one evening he discussed German art and literature for such an assembled group, and during several evenings he entertained another informal audience by reading

and explaining Gower's translation of *Faust* so effectively that they agreed that no one but Shakespeare had written with a power equal to Goethe's. On other occasions he gave descriptions of German student life, or discussed the works of such men as Herder, Jean Paul, Schiller, Kant, and Fries.

459. James Marsh of Vermont was one of the first who sought to plant the seeds of German theological and philosophical learning in America. Elected to the presidency of the University of Vermont in 1826, he set about immediately to reorganize the university on Coleridgean and Kantian terms. See his *Exposition of the System of Instruction Pursued in the University of Vermont* (Burlington, Vt., 1829; 2nd ed., 1831). In 1829 he edited the first American edition of Coleridge's *Aids to Reflection*, prefaced by a long "Preliminary Essay," sufficiently acute in its explanation of Kant and Coleridge to be called "the first publication of American transcendentalism." In 1833 followed his translation of Herder's *Spirit of Hebrew Poetry*. Meanwhile he had sought Follen's assistance in his efforts to fathom German philosophy. Follen replied in a long letter (*Remains*, pp. 151–53), in which he recommended the Anthropology of Kant, the psychologies of Carus and Fries, Tennemann's history of philosophy, and Schultze's and Tasche's works on logic, the last of which was compiled from notes taken on Kant's lectures. Further, he offered to send books from his own library and invited "a frequent exchange of thought" with Marsh "upon subjects of such deep interest to both of us."—*Ibid.*, pp. 152–53. Follen was both stimulating and helpful to Marsh in his work of translating Bellermann and Hegewisch and in projecting his works on psychology and logic. Both of these undertakings remained incomplete at Marsh's untimely death in 1842. Of the former a few chapters are reprinted in the *Remains* (pp. 239–367). Only notes remain of the system of logic, which was begun at Follen's suggestion, and which was to follow in its general divisions and arrangement the work of Fries. Of several translations of German philosophical works undertaken, none was completed.—*Ibid.*, pp. v–vi. The relations indicated here between Follen and Marsh (and with Henry, with whom Follen projected the establishment of a "philosophical journal") suggest that Follen's influence as an authority on German thought made itself felt in various directions. His connection with the Vermont Transcendentalists, as we shall have occasion to observe later, is of primary importance.

460. In 1842, when Follen died, W.E. Channing's parishioners denied Channing the use of his own church for the funeral services of the abolitionist Follen, one of Channing's most intimate friends.—Mrs. John T. Sargent (ed.), *Sketches and Reminiscences of the Radical Club of Chestnut Street, Boston* (Boston, 1880), pp. 372–73.

461. Of his numerous discourses on German literary subjects, only his lectures on Schiller remain. These were published in 1833 and are reprinted in the *Works*.

462. For details on his close and important associations with Unitarians of the time, see esp. Spindler, *op. cit.*, pp. 146–72 and below, under Marsh and under Hedge.

463. His formal connection with the Divinity School was terminated in the autumn of 1830, when Dr. John Gorham Palfrey became professor of ethics. Thereafter Follen devoted his full teaching time to his professorship of German, although his interest in ethics and philosophy generally continued as an absorbing extracurricular activity, and he lost no opportunity to advance the popular knowledge of German philosophy among Americans. See Spindler, *op. cit.*, pp. 123–26.

464. *Works*, I, 290.

465. *Ibid.*, V, 134.

466. Although there were, as we have seen, several individuals who had made a consideration of Kantian philosophy their concern, the popular mind, before 1830, knew little about the critical philosophy beyond what people like President Timothy Dwight and the Rev. Samuel Miller had said about it. "Pope" Dwight, in his "Century Discourses" (1801) at Yale had referred to Kant as a subverter of morals; and Samuel Miller, in his *Retrospect of the Eighteenth Century* (1803) repeated the charge that the Kantian philosophy served only "to delude, to bewilder, and to shed a baneful influence on the true interests of man" (II, 27). I. W. Riley, in his *American Thought* (2nd ed., N.Y., 1915, pp. 229–38) places the date for the first sympathetic interpretation of Kant in America in the fifth decade of the last century, and cites as evidence the works of two Reformed Pennsylvania-Germans: Frederick A. Rauch's *Psychology* of 1840 and S. S. Schmucker's *Mental Philosophy* of 1842. Follen's lectures, however, antedate these works by a full decade, as do also the efforts of Marsh and Hedge.

467. Introduction to his *Inaugural Discourse*, repr. in *Works*, V, 125–52.

468. See the first lecture on "Moral Philosophy." The fourth deals more specifically with Kant's moral philosophy.

469. In the first of his lectures, Follen outlined his plan, namely, to present "an intellec-

tual account . . . with historical accuracy" of the systems of Plato, Aristotle, Zeno, Epicurus, Spinoza, and Kant and to "give a critical exposition of their peculiar excellences and defects" (*Works*, III, 14–15). After this survey of the leading ethical systems before Kant, Follen introduces Kant himself in the fourth lecture with a preliminary outline of his general "system of intellectual philosophy" (*ibid.*, p. 79). In his references to Kant's Space, Time, and the Categories as "innate ideas" or "inherent forms," Follen doubtless does violence to the Aesthetic of Kant's first critique, but it does not follow that because the limitations of time in a lecture and the greater limitations of comprehension among his auditors (whose orientation in the critical terminology was nil) forced him to adopt a familiar and popular terminology, that he therefore misunderstood Kant on these points. It is abundantly evident from subsequent portions of this and other lectures that he had studied the two Critiques closely. It is to be observed, too, that however critical of Kant Follen was in the moral lectures of 1830–1831 (even imputing to Kant's philosophy the possibility of being put to atheistical uses), in the *Inaugural Discourse* (*ibid.*, V, 125–52), on September 3, 1831, he attributed to German philosophy, as "the science of sciences," the great flowering of German literature and the phenomenal progress made by German scientists (*ibid.*, p. 133). He felt duty-bound to deny the accusation that German philosophy tends toward "materialism and skepticism" and a "denial of those spiritual realities which form the foundation of the Christian faith" (*ibid.*, p. 135). Of his projected *Psychology* too little was written to give any accurate idea of his system. What survives is printed in *Works*, III, 325–63.

470. *Works*, III, 83. After presenting, in the first lecture, an outline of the second Critique that covers two and one-half pages in the published works, Follen proceeds to list what he conceives to be the "most important objections," leaving for the next lecture his criticism of the Kantian categories and the conclusion of his remarks on the Kantian system (*ibid.*, pp. 86–92). Disagreeing with the "subjectivism" involved in the Kantian definitions of Time and Space as mere categories of mental forms (*ibid.*, pp. 86–87) and demanding a more direct approach such as Fries had made, Follen attacks what he calls the fallacious tendency in Kant to view man in "a double aspect, each excluding the other": (1) "as a pure self-determined intelligence," and (2) "as an object of sense" (*ibid.*, pp. 87–88). This dual view of man leads Kant to make a divorce between the rational and the

sensible world that forced him to adopt, or at all events to play into the hands of the proponents of, an absolute idealism (meaning Fichte and Schelling, for of Hegel he appears to have known little), "which could easily be used as an instrument against itself, and thus again be converted into absolute skepticism, which Kant had set out to refute" (*ibid.*, p. 90).

471. *Ibid.*, p. 90.

472. *Ibid.*, pp. 81–92.

473. In the sixth lecture, Follen goes on to criticize the Kantian categories of the Understanding (*ibid.*, pp. 111–13), and then to add a more explicit statement of his more individual objections to Kant's general theory of cognition (pp. 114–18). These objections appear in several connections during the course of the following lectures. See, for example, *ibid.*, pp. 117–18. In the remaining ten lectures he refers repeatedly to Kant, who, despite sharp differences, is still Follen's acknowledged master, and the fourteenth lecture concludes with an eloquent expression of the hope that the free German system of philosophy and the enlightened German university system may be combined with and "perfected by the genius of American freedom" in religion, philosophy, and politics. —*Ibid.*, pp. 294–95.

474. The question of Follen's indebtedness to Schiller is interesting, and, in the case of his ethical convictions, important. Follen's published utterances, both in his lectures on Schiller and in the introduction which he wrote for the first American reprint of Carlyle's *Life of Schiller* (1833), repeatedly profess his admiration for Schiller's worship of freedom. Repeating Goethe's well-known dictum that "Schiller preached the doctrine of freedom," Follen explained that while the word *freedom* is to be understood in the Kantian sense as synonymous with the moral nature of man, it means in Schiller also the enthusiasm for freedom which is the living spring of true humanity, and that, as such, it finds one of its most notable expressions in poetry. "Schiller's poetry is distinguished," he says, "by its moral character. But its morality is not that of a philosopher who insists on an entire separation of the moral principle from all natural desires, nor that of the theologian who maintains that holiness consists in denying and crucifying the natural affections. It is a morality that flows from the heart freely and bountifully, receiving and merging in its wide and deep channel all natural desires and affections. It is the morality of nature, the beauty of holiness, the quickening spirit of love and happiness."

The importance of Schiller's morality to Follen personally appears in the second of his lectures on Schiller, which contains a résumé of the *Robbers*. In concentrating on Carl Moor's bold attack on tyranny, says Follen, the critics usually overlook completely "the sublime moral" of the play, namely, "the tragic results that accrue to him who of his own free will cannot yield obedience to the moral law." In Moor's headlong career, Follen saw, in epitome, what his own youthful career in Germany might have led to if he had not won the victory over self.

475. *Works*, III, 225 ff.

476. In this respect Follen is in close agreement with most of the New England Transcendentalists, who objected to Kant's close identification of religion with morality. Quite possibly Follen predisposed them to take this position of dissent from the Kantian position as well as from the same ultimate conclusion to which their own Unitarian principles would logically have led them. See the differentiation between religion and ethics that Emerson made in the section on "Idealism" in Nature.

477. Follen defines morality as the direction of the mind towards the happiness that results from a striving after the greatest efficiency, after perfection; while religion is the direction of the mind toward the happiness which results from the desire and belief that the world is so constituted and governed as to make possible this greatest perfection. The attainment of this perfection, however, depends not solely upon man himself, upon his faculties and moral effort, but also, partly, upon Providence, upon the power which has created the universe in such a way that man is aided in his striving after it. Furthermore, man's desire and belief that the world is so organized and regulated as to conform to his wants and needs is, in Follen's view, the foundation of religion; from this desire and belief proceeds man's restless striving after an ever-enlarging sphere of existence and action. See esp. Follen's first lecture, *Works*, III, 3–19, and Spindler, *op. cit.*, p. 174. "The moral man," as Follen explains it, "is like the husbandman who expects the harvest as a result of his own painstaking efforts in preparing the soil and sowing the seed; but the religious man recognizes that the seed sown will not yield the desired harvest unless sunshine and rain are sent by the Almighty's hand."

478. Here enters an intriguing question, namely, to what extent this may represent an influence upon Follen's thought from Constant, whose religious views closely parallel those expressed by Follen. He was familiar with this phase of Constant's theology. See, for example, *Works*, III, 229 ff., and V, 266, and the essay, "Constant on Religion," *Amer. Quar. Rev.*, XI (Mar., 1832), 103–21.

479. Spindler, *op. cit.*, pp. 174–75.

480. Compare Schleiermacher's *Reden über die Religion* and his *Glaubenslehre* with Follen's tract on "Religion and the Church," *Works*, V, 254–313.

481. *Works*, V, 254.

482. The sentiments expressed in this letter, reprinted as No. XIII of "Follenbriefe" by Hermann Haupt in *Jahrbuch der Deutsch-Amerikanischen Historischen Gesellschaft von Illinois*, XIV (1914), 26–28, parallel closely many of the principles enunciated by Schleiermacher, namely: the repudiation of irrational devotion to creeds; the differentiation between dogma and religion; the union of all sects in one church; the conception of religion as consisting at once of feeling, piety, and reverent contemplation of God; the sublime work of nature and art as the expression of an immanent Deity—as a symbol through which the mind and heart are directed toward the one eternal God; and the Christian church as an association of pious men for mutual aid and cultivation of a closer relation to God. Along with Schleiermacher, Follen emphasizes the social nature of religion. The church is not merely an instrument for moral education; it is an association of people seeking after religious truth through the mutual exchange of views. The greater the variety of these views, the better; for each individual is in this way more apt to find that which will satisfy his particular needs.

483. Concerning the influence of Follen upon his students, a number of men testify. See W. H. Channing, "Life and Writings of Dr. Follen," *Christ. Exam.*, XXXIII (Sept., 1842), 33–56, esp. p. 52: Andrew P. Peabody, *Harvard Reminiscences*, pp. 117–23; Follen's *Works*, I, 260–62; Josiah Quincy, *History of Harvard University*, II, 383; Sprague's *Annals*, VIII, 547; Ed Livingston's letter, quoted in *Works*, I, 308 the class oration (1832), quoted in *Works*, I 312; and the editorial by J. F. Clarke in the *Western Messenger* for October, 1836.

484. See Thomas S. Baker, "America as the Political Utopia of Young Germany," *American Germanica*, I, ii (1897), 62–102.

485. *Democratic Rev.*, V, xv (Mar., 1839) 288–308; repr. in *Works*, V, 314–73.

486. *Works*, III, 7–9.

487. *Ibid.*, p. 253. This is, of course, strongly suggestive of Kant's "Metaphysische Anfangsgründe der Rechtslehre" (*Kants Werke*, ed. by E. Cassirer), VII, 43.

488. *Works*, III, 270.

489. *Ibid.*, pp. 274, 278, 282–87, 289–90.

490. *Ibid.*, V, 197, 204, 207–16.

491. Specific influences of Follen's view upon those of his associates are hard to sub

stantiate, but the direct relationship existing among them and their common interests in the transcendental, romantic, and humanitarian ferment makes the presumption strong. Additional justification for relating the New England Transcendentalists and reformers like Garrison and Sumner to German political idealism, as represented by Kant, Fichte, and Hegel, and for regarding Follen as the link or intermediary appears in the pecular ethical basis which both parties gave to politics. For a detailed discussion of the relations between Follen's theory and practice and those of Channing, Garrison, Sumner, Parker, and Emerson, see the unpublished dissertation of Charles B. Robson, "The Influence of German Thought on Political Theory in the United States" (Univ. of North Carolina Library, 1930), esp. pp. 100, 103–22.

492. C. B. Robson, *op. cit.*, pp. 124–25.

493. Compare Kant's *Critique of Practical Reason* (Abbott trans.), sec. iii, with Emerson's *Journals*, III, 235, and J. E. Cabot, *Memoir*, I, 246–47.

494. See Emerson's *Works*, III, 212, as well as the suggestive discussion of Emerson's indebtedness to Kantian ethics, beginning page 299 in John S. Harrison's *Teachers of Emerson* (N.Y., 1910).

495. Robson, *op. cit.*, pp. 125–26. See also Hegel's *Philosophy of Right*, tr. by S. W. Dyde (London, 1896), pp. 127–29, and Bernard Bosanquet, *The Philosophical Theory of the State* (London, 1899), Chs. IX and X.

496. *Works of W. E. Channing*, (10th ed., 6 vols., Boston, 1849), V, 256.

497. Robson, *op. cit.*, p. 128.

498. Although Emerson was not then taking part in the regular exercises of the Divinity students, Follen could hardly have failed to attract his attention, omnipresent as he was at the time. However, Emerson's diary is completely innocent of any references to Follen during these years.

499. There were other factors that should have conspired to make Emerson notice Follen, who was in Cambridge the example, *par excellence*, of the German university-trained scholar. We know that he carefully appraised others who had enjoyed the advantages of a German education. For example, Bancroft, who had gone to Germany in 1818 and fallen completely under the spell of Schleiermacher's educational and religious views, was, upon his return, all but idolized by Emerson as an incipient Hercules in American learning.—J. E. Cabot, *Memoir*, I, 93–94, 98, 105. See also Emerson's adulation of Everett upon his return from Germany (*Letters of R. W. Emerson*, ed. by R. L. Rusk, I, 76. 78, 84; Emerson's *Works*, X,

330–31; *Journals*, VIII, 225–26). It will also be recalled that after graduating in 1821, Emerson had for two years assisted his brother William as a teacher, an enterprise which was discontinued when William went to Göttingen to study divinity—another circumstance that might have directed his attention toward Follen.

500. Cabot, *Memoir*, I, 145; see also *Letters*, I, 260 (Jan. 28, 1820).

501. Cabot, *Memoir*, I, 159.

502. Emerson, in a letter to William Emerson, quoted in Cabot, *Memoir*, I, 218.

503. *Letters*, I, 154 (Nov. 20, 1824); see also *ibid.*, pp. 143, 149.

504. Cabot, *Memoir*, I, 109.

505. *Ibid.*, I, 139.

506. *Journals*, I, 82 (June 10, 1821).

507. *Ibid.*, pp. 289–90 (Nov., 1822).

508. *Ibid.*, p. 288 (Apr., 1822). See also Mary S. Withington, "Early Letters of Emerson," *Century Magazine*, XXVI (July, 1883), 454.

509. Cabot, *Memoir*, I, 139; *Carlyle-Emerson Correspondence*, I, 29–30, 39–40.

510. For details of this long struggle, see the section below on Emerson.

511. III (Mar., 1831), 127–51.

512. *Journals*, II, 542.

513. *Carlyle-Emerson Correspondence*, I, 34, 53–63 *et seq.*

514. *Ibid.*, I, 55.

515. O. B. Frothingham, *George Ripley* (Boston, 1883), pp. 96–97.

516. XI (Jan., 1832), 373–80; see esp. pp. 374–77, containing a high tribute to Kant.

517. H. C. Goddard, *op. cit.*, p. 85; Henry S. Commager, *Theodore Parker* (Boston, 1936), pp. 31–32; John Weiss, *Life and Correspondence Theodore Parker* (2 vols., Boston, 1863), I, 49.

518. Commager, *op. cit.*, pp. 30–32, 34, 38–39 *et seq.*; O. B. Frothingham, *Theodore Parker: A Biography* (Boston, 1874), pp. 34–39; J. F. Clarke, *Memorial and Biographical Sketches* (Boston, 1878), p. 120.

519. Spindler, *op. cit.*, p. 143; John W. Chadwick, *Theodore Parker* (Boston, 1900), p. 84; and Edwin D. Mead, *The Influence of Emerson* (Boston, 1903), p. 110.

520. Commager, *op. cit.*, p. 55.

521. Odell Shepard, *Pedlar's Progress. The Life of Bronson Alcott* (Boston, 1937), pp. 112–37.

522. F. B. Sanborn and W. T. Harris, *A. Bronson Alcott: His Life and Philosophy* (2 vols., Boston, 1893), I, 118, 289.

523. Clarke entered Harvard in 1825, graduated with the class of 1829, then entered the Divinity School, and thus remained for another year in direct touch with Follen. Six years later,

shortly after Follen left Harvard, Clarke commented editorially upon his former teacher in the *Western Messenger* (Oct., 1836): "We are glad to see in the July number of the London and Westminster Review a high tribute to that distinguished scholar, philosopher, philanthropist, and Divine, Dr. Charles Follen. Our regard for that gentleman is so great that we rejoice in every tribute paid to his worth. His life has been one of conscientious sacrifice to principle. We knew him chiefly as an instructor in the course of his professional duties. Our whole class loved him—a feeling towards an instructor very unusual among captious and restless collegians . . . . We never hear his name pronounced without giving him a blessing. . . . We sincerely hope that he may find some sphere of action in which his large talents and his great learning in law, philosophy, belles-lettres, and theology may be more widely felt in our country. He has indeed already done much for German literature among us and has acquired a high reputation as a lecturer in civil law."

524. R. W. Emerson, W. H. Channing, and J. F. Clarke, *Memoirs of Margaret Fuller Ossoli* (2 vols., Boston, 1874), I, 114. Carlyle's articles had been appearing for five years without eliciting from her such a resolution as this one, dated January, 1833: "I have now a pursuit of immediate importance: to the German language and literature will I give my undivided attention"; we may therefore assume that it was Follen more than Carlyle who supplied the initial urge, although the influence of Carlyle was to become cumulatively stronger in later years. Earlier even than Carlyle, there had been Madame de Staël's book, which had not, however, actually provoked her to study German. Concerning the major influences which turned her toward German art and thought, we cannot be far wrong when we sum up the matter thus: Madame de Staël prepared the soil, Dr. Follen sowed the seed, and Carlyle supplied the sunshine and showers for the future harvest. Cf. Spindler, *op. cit.*, p. 144.

525. T. W. Higginson, *Margaret Fuller Ossoli* (Boston, 1898), p. 41.

526. Emerson, Channing, and Clarke, *Memoirs . . .*, I, 117.

527. The titles which Frothingham gave to the hierarchy among them is suggestive. There was Emerson the Seer, Alcott the Mystic, Margaret Fuller the Critic, Parker the Preacher, Ripley the Man of Letters, and a number of minor "Prophets." But among them all there was no "Philosopher."

528. O. B. Frothingham, *Transcendentalism in New England*, p. 286. Here, as in so many cases, the shrewd intuitive powers of Margaret

(her "genius") led her to make a guess which was not far off center. Spinoza might, indeed, have served well; but Schelling and Kant, as she later learned, were the intermediary minds with which she ought to be acquainted in order to know Jacobi.

529. *Ibid.*, p. 296.

530. John W. Chadwick, *Theodore Parker*, p. 92; H. S. Commager, *Theodore Parker*, pp. 70–71.

531. J. H. Muirhead, "How Hegel Came to America," *Philosophical Rev.* XXXVIII (1928), 228.

532. Commager, *op. cit.*, p. 32.

533. Resolved to adapt himself completely to his "new mother country," he soon knew most of the famous men of the day. In 1826 he became editor of the *Readinger Adler*, the "Berks County Bible," through which his ideas gained wide currency.

534. He formed a lofty vision of "the American Destiny," visualizing a nation of 150 million people, with cities containing millions, a nation of commanding industrial strength and unequalled sea power. He foretold a "future confederation of the American peoples," and as early as 1830 advocated the construction of the Panama Canal. For an account of his far-flung commercial activities in America, see Hanns G. Altner, "Friedrich List (1789–1846), *Amer.-Ger. Rev.*, V, i (Sept., 1938), 12–13. Retained by the Pennsylvania Society for the Promotion of Manufactures and Mechanic Arts as speaker, editor, and pamphleteer, he wrote a number of important letters and reports. The famous pamphlet entitled *Examination of the Boston Report* (1828), generally attributed to Mathew Carey, was in reality written by List. He did not, of course, effect a revolution single-handedly. His principles are closely allied to those of Alexander Hamilton, whose *Report on Domestic Manufactures* (1791) he studied closely, as well as the writings of Clay, Ingersoll, and the Careys; but it is not too much to say, according to M. E. Hirst (*Life of Friedrich List . . .* London, 1909, p. xx), that "most of the ideas that underlie modern tariffs, both in the old world and in the new, were originated or formulated by List."

Having been influential in carrying Pennsylvania for Jackson, List was rewarded in 1830 with a diplomatic post in Germany, where he spent the rest of his life organizing an economically united Germany, which afterwards found its political realization through Bismarck. In 1842 he published his famous *Nationale System der politischen Oekonomie*, which became the textbook of German political economists and was translated and printed in

Hungary (in 1843 and again in 1916), France (1851, 1857), Great Britain (1854, 1885, 1904–1905, 1909, 1922), the United States (1856, 1904, 1909), Australia (1860), Sweden (1888), Russia (1891), and Italy, China, and Japan (1936).

Like many another prophet, he won few rewards at home during his lifetime. Although he continued to write voluminously and remained active on many fronts, his internationalism failed to win a responsive ear in Germany. German economists believed him when he foretold the exploitation of the Danube basin, the British land highway to India, the Trans-Siberian railroad, and the Suez and Panama canals; they were less attentive to his prophecies of an "Alliance of Nations," a "World Court," and a "Pan-American Conference." However much he emphasized an enlightened internationalism, what he had to say about "Weltwirtschaft," "Weltpolitik," and "Weltmacht" more nearly accorded with their ideas and provided the slogans and springboards for the *Grossraumwirtschaft* of Nazi Germany a century later.

535. Wherever and whenever in the United States discussion and legislation referred to a balanced agricultural and industrial program, List's principles emerged. They received particular emphasis in the work of Simon N. Patton (1852–1922), Professor of Economics at the University of Pennsylvania, and during McKinley's administration they were reputed to have been the basic inspiration alike of the American tariff and foreign policy. They are most readily traced in the theories advanced by many of the three score or more young American economists who studied in the German universities, then most rampantly Listian. Economists like Johannes Conrad at Halle thought of themselves as public servants dedicated to the creation of a greater Germany and a better world, and American students caught the contagion. Richard T. Ely, who returned in 1881, not only glorified his professors Conrad, Knies, and Wagner as "humanitarians" creating "a better world" but preached the doctrine that America must follow the German example. See Ely's statement in "The Founding and Early History of the American Economic Association," *Amer. Econ. Rev., Suppl.*, XXVI, i (Mar., 1936), 141–50, esp. pp. 143, 145. American classical economists, typified by Sumner, Godkin, Wells, and Newcomb (relying mainly upon Smith and Ricardo), were not easily dislodged from their strategic positions, but the insurgents were aggressive, and the organization in 1855 of the American Economic Association by men like Simon N. Patton, Henry C. Adams, R. A.

Seligman, Alex. Johnson, Ed. J. Jones, John Bates Clark, and R. T. Ely, served notice, as Ely observed, that having "tasted the new and living economics which was taught in German universities," they "felt called upon to fight those who we believed stood in the way of intellectual expansion and social growth." Associated with them were men like Andrew D. White, late minister to Germany and first president of Cornell, Washington Gladden, and young Woodrow Wilson, who were soon to make their influence felt. They drew up a statement of principles in conformity with the German ethical superstructure as formulated by List and his university disciples, namely that what *is* must be made to conform with what *ought to be*—that economics must be consonant with ethics. See Ely, *The Ground Under Our Feet* (N.Y., 1938), pp. 132, 144; also his *Social Aspects of Christianity and Other Essays* (N.Y., 1889), pp. 113–32, esp. p. 122.

536. R. H. Gabriel, *The Course of American Democratic Thought* (N.Y., 1940), p. 297.

537. Born in Berlin in 1800, Lieber fought against Napoleon in 1815, became closely associated with Turnvater Jahn in his efforts to resurrect the fallen German nation, incurred the displeasure of the government, and was arrested and imprisoned for several months. Upon his release, finding the Prussian universities closed to him, he went to Jena and took the doctorate there in 1820. After an unhappy experience in his efforts to help Greece regain her independence, he went in 1822 to Rome, where he applied for assistance to the German historian Niebuhr, then ambassador to Rome. Niebuhr engaged him as tutor, to his son. In 1823 Lieber returned to Berlin, was rearrested, and on being released, set out for London in 1825, where he picked up a scant livelihood as reporter and correspondent for German newspapers. It was now that Follen, failing in his efforts to get Turnvater Jahn himself to conduct his successful Gymnasium in Boston, accepted Jahn's recommendation of Lieber for the post. Both Jahn and Niebuhr urged Lieber to go to America, the latter advising him to remain a German citizen and not to engage in political controversy or write political dissertations. Lieber promptly disobeyed both admonitions. He became an American citizen in the shortest time the law allowed, and won enduring fame by his great political writings. Symptomatic of Lieber's attitude toward America is a letter, written April 23, 1847: "I love my country . . . but when they talk of Germanizing America, I spurn the idea . . . . What, Germanize America and draw out of our country the Anglican institutions as the bones

of a turkey, and leave a lump, fit only to be dispatched ? No, no—modern liberty, people may say what they like, is . . . essentially Anglican liberty; develop, modify, change, trim, improve, but keep the backbone."— Chester S. Phinney, *Francis Lieber's Influence on American Thought and Some of His Unpublished Letters*, Diss., Univ. of Pa. (Phila., 1918), p. 33.

538. President Gilman of the Johns Hopkins University said that "of the Americans devoted to public affairs, from 1840 to 1870, it may be said that Lieber knew every one worth knowing."—*Ibid.*, p. 54.

539. In 1838, young Thoreau, just graduated from Harvard, found the *Americana* the only encyclopaedia to which he could turn for such information as he needed for his school-teaching career.—Thoreau's *Writings* (Walden ed., 20 vols., Boston, 1906), VI, 19.

540. Here are to be listed (1) *Manual of Political Ethics*, 2 vols., 1838; (2) *Legal and Political Hermeneutics*, 1839; (3) *Civil Liberty and Self-Government*, 2 vols., 1853; and (4) *Instruction for the Government of the Armies of the United States in the Field*, 1863. Besides these Lieber produced a number of shorter works on timely subjects.

541. Calhoun and others before him had denounced French romantic theories of government; Webster had expounded the conception of the organic nature of the federal compact; and Story had derived a legal conception of the organic nature of the union in terms of the Constitution. But Lieber first provided a philosophy for this conception, and he went beyond all three in elaborating a theory of the state in terms of an historical evolution that derives its form and spirit from social developments and needs.

542. The degree of Lieber's dependence on Kant for the idea of the essential and inalienable moral character of the individual as a basis of political theory and law can be gauged by comparing two passages: one, from Kant's *Metaphysische Anfangsgründe der Rechtslehre* (*Werke*, 8 vols., Leipzig, 1867–1868, VII, 39), the other, from Lieber's *Political Ethics*, I, 202.

Another influence of importance is that of his teacher and benefactor Niebuhr. See *Miscellaneous Writings of Francis Lieber: Reminiscences, Addresses, and Essays*, ed. by D. C. Gilman (2 vols., Phila., 1881), I, 54, 56, 73, 90. Lieber's interest in historical study, his conception of the complexity and continuity of social relations, and his feeling for the necessity of bringing practical and historical knowledge to bear upon the problems of political science are owing mainly to Niebuhr (see *Manual of*

Political Ethics, I, 336). To him, but also to Savigny, Grimm, and others of the German political scientists, may be related his love for philosophical investigation, his use of the analytical method of history, and the relation of words as a means to explain political and legal concepts.

543. For more detailed studies of Lieber's political views, see Ernest Bruncken, "Francis Lieber: A Study of a Man and an Ideal," *Jahrbuch der Deutsch-Amerikanischen Historischen Gesellschaft von Illinois*, XV (1915), 7–61; V. L. Parrington, *The Romantic Revival in America* (*1800–1860*), pp. 93–98; Merle Curti, "Francis Lieber and Nationalism," *Huntington Libr. Quar.*, IV, III (Apr., 1941), 263–92; and Bernard E. Brown, *American Conservatives: The Political Thought of Francis Lieber and John W. Burgess* (N.Y., 1951).

544. Follen also had been brought up under the rigorous discipline of German scholarship; but he did not emphasize the importance of scientific scholarly procedure to the same extent that Lieber did. Moreover, Follen's influence in this direction was more narrowly confined, first, because his publications, illustrating such methods, did not circulate as widely as Lieber's; second, because he did not enjoy the same wide and varied personal contacts; and third, because Follen died prematurely in 1842, while Lieber lived, active to the last, until 1872.

545. See Lieber's statement explaining and justifying his painstaking method of quoting exactly and of giving full titles, chapter and verse, and relevant bibliographical data in all his references, in Thos. S. Perry, *Life and Letters of Francis Lieber* (Boston, 1882), pp. 134–35.

546. Beck, Follen, and Lieber were only among the first in the nineteenth century of a long succession of Germans and, subsequently, of native-born Americans who furthered the advance of Germanic scholarly methodology in the United States. After the generation of Everett, Ticknor, Cogswell, and Bancroft, came a group like Theodore Dwight Woolsey (1801–1899), who studied in Germany under Hermann, Curtius, and Welcker and spread Boeckh's ideal of *Altertumswissenschaft* in American academic circles. In lexicography, men like George Martin Lane (1823–1897), who began his studies under Beck at Harvard and continued under Hermann, Welcker, Heyse, and Curtius at Göttingen, Berlin, Bonn, and Heidelberg, led the way; while James B. Greenough (1833–1901) was strongly influenced in his work by the German originators of the comparative linguistic method; and the conquest of German methods in the more general field of philological investigation was assured with the return from

the German universities of men like William W. Goodwin (1831–1912), Basil L. Gildersleeve (1831–1924), William D. Whitney (1827–1894), and Francis J. Child (1825–1896). The history of how German methods came to prevail in American scholarship and research is beyond the scope of this book. A brief account is to be found in the *Cambridge History of American Literature*, IV, 444–91.

547. Emerson was notoriously impatient of details and minutiae, and he was inclined to regard mere consistency as foolish consistency —as the hobgoblin of little minds and of old women. While rigor of scholarly method and depth in philosophy are not necessarily identical, slovenliness in the one is often attended by shallowness in the other. But this lesson, as applied to philosophy, came too late, if it came at all, to Emerson. Of philosophic originality Emerson's mind possessed enough; of mental discipline, of system and method in his thinking, he had little. Too impatient to follow Kant through the successive stages and details of his minute analysis of Sensation, Understanding, and Reason, but proceeding directly to apply the Kantian epistemology to his philosophic problems in his first published work, without first mastering his epistemology, he found himself involved in all manner of difficulties and forced to admit, near the end of his essay on *Nature*, that the means were not adequate for his purpose: that transcendental idealism at best was but an introductory hypothesis—suggestive and therefore useful, but still only a theory—by which to account for nature and spirit by other weights and measures than those of carpentry and chemistry. And what is true for Emerson is true, in varying degrees, of others of the New England Transcendentalists.

548. Productive of many practical reforms, good literature, and a revitalized religion—high-minded and earnest to the core—New England Transcendentalism, considered as a philosophy, was little more than a bubble that burst—as nothing when compared with the movement in Germany whence it claimed descent. A later revival, in the St. Louis Movement, made fewer converts and left a lesser literature, but it produced a more coherent philosophy (symbolized by the twenty-two solid volumes of the *Journal of Speculative Philosophy* as against four volumes of the ethereal *Dial*) and exerted a more abiding intellectual influence, whence the academic and professional philosophers carried it forward. For details, see the last chapter of my booklet on *New England Transcendentalism and St. Louis Hegelianism* (Phila., 1949).

549. The year after Lieber's *Civil Liberty and*

Self-Government appeared, Emerson quoted Lieber's theories as confirming his own (*Journals*, VIII, 459, 1854), and after Lieber went to Columbia, he spoke of him as the foremost political scientist in America.—*Journals*, IX, 212 (June, 1859); X, 55 (1864).

550. Phinney, *op. cit.*, p. 40. Regarding the wide influence of these *Instructions*, see Elihu Root, "Francis Lieber. Address read before the American Society of International. Law, Washington, D.C., April 24, 1913," *Jour. of International Law* (July, 1913), p. 457. When Bluntschli wrote his famous *Modernes Völkerrecht*, he gave credit to Lieber for having made "the first codification of International Articles of War" and acknowledged basing his own work on that of Lieber (*ibid.*, p. 458). Ernest Nys declared that Lieber's ideas "penetrated not only the scientific world through the works of Bluntschli but by the work of the Conference of Brussels, in 1874, and The Hague, in 1899 and 1907, they have penetrated international politics." See Phinney, *op. cit.*, pp. 42–46, where Bluntschli's and Lieber's paragraphs are juxtaposed in parallel columns. For similarly close parallels between Lieber and the articles of the Hague Conference of 1899, see Elihu Root, *loc. cit.*, pp. 466–69. Regarding Lieber's influence on the Brussels Conference and the first Hague Conference, see F. W. Holls, *The Peace Conference at the Hague* (N.Y., 1900), p. 150, and the *Miscellaneous Writings* of *Francis Lieber*, I, 14.

551. Bluntschli spoke of Lieber in New York, Edouard Laboulaye of Paris, and himself in Heidelberg as forming, from 1860 to 1870, "a scientific clover-leaf representing the international character of French, German, and Anglo-American culture."—Lewis R. Harley, *Francis Lieber: His Life and Political Philosophy* (N.Y., 1899), p. 178.

552. In 1845, Judge Story made a determined effort to bring Lieber to Harvard. Finding no funds available for the purpose, he initiated a financial campaign designed to endow a professorship for him, but Story's death in 1847 brought the move to naught.

553. For evaluations of Lieber's contributions, see the comments in Phinney (*op. cit.*, pp. 53–55) of such men as Daniel C. Gilman, Theo. D. Woolsey, W. H. Prescott, Rufus Choate, Henry Clay, Chancellor Kent, Judge Story, George Bancroft, Sheldon Ames, Simon Greenleaf, Ernest Nys, Ernest Creasy of London, the Italian jurist Garelli, Judge M. Russell Thayer, and Elihu Root; and see *DAB*, IX, 237; M. R. Thayer, *The Life, Character, and Writings of Francis Lieber* (Phila., 1873), pp. 23–29; Lieber's *Miscellaneous Writings* (2 vols.,

Phila., 1873), I, 80; Elihu Root, *loc. cit.*, pp. 457–66; L. R. Harley, *op. cit.*, p. 67; Herbert B. Adams, *The Study of History in American Colleges and Universities* (Bur. of Ed. Cir. of Inform., 1887, No. 2, Washington, D.C., 1887), p. 69; and *Amer. Pol. Sci. Rev.*, XVI (1923), 290.

554. Edward L. Pierce, *Memoir and Letters of Charles Sumner* (4 vols., Boston, 1877–1894), I, 158–60.

555. *Ibid.*, I, 45.

556. George H. Haynes, *Charles Sumner* (Phila., 1909), p. 46, n. 1.

557. Pierce, *Memoir*, III, 74.

558. Sumner carried letters of introduction to Thibaut and Mittermeier from Lieber, just as Longfellow did in 1836.—Pierce, *Memoir*, I, 186, 197. Although Sumner studied German diligently, he regretted having to leave Germany before he had fully mastered the language. Upon his return home, he wrote to Lieber: "Germany I left too soon; but I loved it well. Were I a man of fortune . . . I should first direct my steps to Germany." Subsequently he appears to have improved his command of German, for letters written during 1857 and 1858 breathe a spirit of appreciation of literary Germany that could hardly have been inspired through the medium of translation solely. There is evidence that he had read Lessing's *Nathan*, Goethe's *Werther*, some of Schiller (possibly all), Körner, Uhland, Richter, and much of Luther.—*Ibid.*, ii; Pierce, *Memoir*, I, 144, 214; II, 135, 145, 164, 179, 214; III, 570.

559. *Ibid.*, I, 189.

560. *Ibid.*, p. 189; II, 121.

561. *Ibid.*, I, 160; III, 67.

562. *Ibid.*, III, 601–2.

563. "German Idealism and American Theories of the Democratic Community," *Jour. of Politics*, V, ii (Aug., 1943), 213–36.

564. "Influence of German Thought on Political Theory in the United States on the Nineteenth Century," Diss., Univ. of North Carolina, 1930.

565. *Political Science in American Colleges and Universities, 1636–1900*, N.Y. and London, 1939. The subject is also dealt with by Charles A. Beard, "The Study and Teaching of Politics," *Columbia Univ. Quar.*, XX (June, 1910), 268–74; Manley O. Hudson, "The Teaching of International Law," *Proc. of Third Conf. of International Law, April 25–26, 1928* (Washington, D.C., 1928), pp. 68–76, 178–89; Joseph McGoldrick, "Political Science in the College," in *Redirecting Education* (ed. by R. G. Tugwell and L. H. Keyserling, N.Y., 1934), I, 225–58; Frederick Pollock, *History of the Science of Politics* (N.Y., 1833); David Y. Thomas, "Political Science in Southern Universities, "*Sewanee*

Rev., XVI (Oct., 1908), 466–71; Milton W. Thompson, "The Present Status of University Instruction in Political Science," *Historical Outlook*, XXIV (Mar., 1933), 141–46; W. W. Willoughby, "Political Science as a University Study," *Sewanee Rev.*, XIV (July, 1906), 257–66.

For economics, see James F. Colby, "Economics in Early American Colleges," *Nation*, LXIII (Dec., 1896), 494; Charles F. Dunbar, "Economic Science in America, 1776–1876," *North Amer. Rev.*, CXXII (Jan., 1876), 124–54; Lewis A. Haney, *A History of Economic Thought*, (N.Y., 1911); Edwin R. A. Seligman, "The Early Teaching of Economics in the United States," in *Economic Essays Contributed in Honor of John Bates Clark* (N.Y., 1927), pp. 283–320; E. R. A. Seligman, "Economics in the United States: An Historical Sketch," in *Essays in Economics* (N.Y., 1924), Ch. IV, pp. 122–60; and Elbert V. Willis, "Political Economy in the Early College Curriculum," *South Atl. Quar.*, XXIV (Apr., 1925), 131–53.

566. The subject is treated in varying degrees of thoroughness by George B. Adams, "Methods of Work in Historical Seminaries," *Amer. Hist. Rev.*, X (Apr., 1905), 521–33; Herbert B. Adams, *The Study of History in American Colleges and Universities*, Bur. of Ed. Circular of Information, No. 3, 1887 (Washington, D.C., 1887); C. A. Beard and Alfred Vagts, "Currents of Thought in Historiography," *Amer. Hist. Rev.*, XLII, iii (Apr., 1937), 460–83; Michael Kraus, *A History of American History* (N.Y., 1937); Allan Nevins, *The Gateway to History* (Boston, 1938); James T. Shotwell, *An Introduction to the History of History* (N.Y., 1922); James W. Thompson, *History of Historical Writing* (2 vols., N.Y., 1942). See also Harry Elmer Barnes (ed.), *The History and Prospects of the Social Sciences* (N.Y., 1925); L. L. Bernard and J. S. Bernard, "A Century of Progress in the Social Sciences," *Social Forces*, XI (May, 1933), 485–505; L. L. Bernard, "The Social Sciences as Disciplines: United States," in *Ency. of the Soc. Sci.*, I, 324–49; James Bryce, "Relations of Political Science to History and to Practice," *Amer. Pol. Sci. Rev.*, III (Feb., 1909), 1–19; Gladys Bryson, "The Comparable Interests of the Old Moral Philosophy and the Modern Social Sciences," *Social Forces*, XI (Oct., 1932), 19–27; John W. Burgess, "Political Science and History," *Annual Report of the Amer. Hist. Assn. for the Year 1896* (Washington, D.C., 1897), I, 203–11; James W. Garner, *Political Science and Government* (N.Y., 1932), Chaps. I–III, pp. 1–45; Wm. B. Munro, "Political Science," in *Teaching of the Social Sciences* (ed. by Edgar Dawson, N.Y., 1927), Chap. VII, pp.

158–85; Howard Odum (ed.), *American Masters of Social Science* (N.Y., 1927); John C. Schwab, "The Yale College Curriculum, 1701–1901," *Educational Rev.*, XXII (June, 1901), 1–17.

567. After graduating from Yale in 1799, Stuart taught a while and then turned to the law. Admitted to the bar in 1801, he never practiced, but his legal studies had some effect on the tenor of his thoughts as well as on his work as a professor of theology. During a two-year appointment as a tutor at Yale, he prosecuted theological studies. In 1804 he was licensed to preach, and subsequently he served four years in a regular pastorate at New Haven.

568. "Before I obtained Seiler," he said, "I did not know enough to believe that I yet knew nothing in sacred criticism."—*Christ. Rev.*, VI (Sept., 1841), 449.

569. See O. W. Long, *Literary Pioneers*, pp. 63–64, 237, n. 6.

570. Eliza Lee Follen, *op. cit.*, p. 188.

571. Something of the remarkable influence of the latter will be gathered from the following bibliographical facts: Second ed., assisted by Edward Robinson, Andover, 1823; same, 1824; 3rd ed., Andover, 1828; same, 1829; Phila., 1830; 4th ed., Andover, 1831; Oxford, 1831; same, 1832; 5th ed., Andover, 1835; Oxford, 1838; 6th ed., Andover & London, 1840. Although the book antedated the *Hebrew Grammar* (1830) by Dr. Samuel Lee of Cambridge by almost a decade, yet Stuart's work was commended by Dr. Nicol, Regius Professor of Hebrew at Oxford, as the best Hebrew grammar extant. The fourth American edition was accordingly reprinted at Oxford in 1831 and used as a textbook by Dr. Nicol's successor, Dr. E. B. Pusey.

572. Emma G. Jaeck, *op. cit.*, pp. 264–75.

573. Daniel D. Williams, *The Andover Liberals* (N.Y., 1941), p. 17.

574. Emma G. Jaeck, *op. cit.*, p. 275.

575. For a discussion of the issues between Stuart and Channing, see C. H. Faust, "The Background of the Unitarian Opposition to Transcendentalism," *Mod. Philol.*, XXV, iii (Feb., 1938), 297–324, esp. pp. 302–5, 317–18.

576. The first edition was exhausted in a week; two more printings were called for in America and three in England. See *Allibone's Dict.* (Phila, 1899), II, 2293.

577. Andover, 1822; ed. by E. Henderson, London, 1827; 3rd ed., Andover, 1838; 4th ed., Andover and N.Y., 1842.

578. Andover, 1825.

579. Andover, 1829; 2nd ed., Andover, N.Y., and Oxford, 1832; 3rd ed., Oxford, 1834; 3rd American ed., Andover and N.Y., 1838.

580. Andover, 1829.

581. Andover, 1834; Edinburgh, 1836; same, 1837; London, 1838; 2nd ed., Andover, 1841; reprinted, 1850, 1857.

582. Second ed., N.Y., 1851.

583. Ed. by E. Henderson, London, 1828; 2nd ed., Andover, 1833; ed. by E. Henderson, London, 1833–1834; 4th London ed., 1837; repr., 1846, 1851, 1856, 1864; 3rd American ed., by Rev. R. D. C. Robbins, Andover, 1854; 4th American ed., by Robbins, Andover, 1860.

584. See Emma G. Jaeck, *op. cit.*, p. 277; Wm. F. Albright, "Moses Stuart," *DAB*, XVIII, 175; *Allibone's Dictionary*, II, 2293–95.

585. Andover, 1831; ed. by J. P. Smith and E. Henderson, London, 1833; 2nd American, ed., Andover, 1835; repr. as 3rd ed., London, 1836; same, 1838; 4th, 5th, and 6th London eds., 1851, 1853, 1857; 3rd and 4th American eds., by R. D. C. Robbins, Andover, 1854, 1859.

586. Two vols., Andover, 1845; London, 1845; same, 1847, 1850, 1854, 1865; Andover, 1851.

587. Andover, 1850.

588. N.Y., 1851; ed. by Robbins, Andover, 1862.

589. N.Y., 1852.

590. Among other significant publications of Stuart's tending in the same direction are to be listed the following translations and original compositions: (1) *Letter to the Rev. Samuel Miller on the Eternal Generation of the Son of God* (Andover, 1822); (2) *Two Dissertations on the Atonement* (Andover, 1824); (3) *Examination of the Strictures upon the American Education Society, in a Late Number of the Biblical Repertory* (Andover, 1829); (4) *Exegetical Essays upon Several Words Relating to Future Punishment* (Andover, 1830; Edinburgh, 1848); (5) *A Letter to W. E. Channing, D.D., on the Subject of Religious Liberty* (Boston, 1830; 4th ed., 1831); (6) *Is the Mode of Christian Baptism Prescribed in the New Testament?* (Andover, 1833; 2nd ed., Nashville, 1856); (7) *Cicero on the Immortality of the Soul, with Notes and an Appendix* (Andover, 1833); (8) Friedrich Schleiermacher, *On the Discrepancies between the Sabellian and Athanasian Methods of Representing the Doctrine of a Trinity in the Godhead* (tr. with Notes and Illustrations, Andover, 1835); (9) *Philological View of Modern Doctrines of Geology* (Andover, 1836); (10) *Hints on the Interpretation of Prophecy* (Andover, 1842); (11) *Critical History and Defence of the Old Testament Canon* (Andover, 1845; repr., 1846, 1865; ed. by Sam. Davidson, London, 1849; ed. by Rev. P. Lorrimer, Edinburgh, 1849; same, London, 1849); (12) *Miscellanies . . .* (Andover, 1846); (13) *Letter to the Editor of the North American Review on Hebrew Grammar* (Andover, 1847); (14) *Conscience and*

Constitution; with Remarks on the Speech of Webster on Slavery (Boston, 1850). See further *Allibone's Dictionary*, II, 2293–95.

591. VI, xxiii (Sept., 1841), 446–71.

592. VI, xxii (June, 1841), 268–84.

593. See Sanborn's letter, quoted in S. H. Goodnight, *op. cit.*, p. 54.

594. Stuart, of course, did not bring about this change single-handedly. As has already become abundantly evident, he had his helpers among German-born and American-born students, most particularly among the Transcendentalists. But as much as any other individual, he was responsible. A decade after his death the acknowledgment was publicly made. See *Evangelical Rev.* (July, 1862), p. 151; also *ibid.* (July, 1863), p. 466.

595. F. H. Foster, *A Genetic History of New England Theology* N.Y., 1907), p. 289; Daniel D. Williams, *op. cit.*, p. 17.

596. J. L. Blake (*Biographical Dictionary*, 13th ed., N.Y., 1856, p. 1194) found also among Stuart's students more than a hundred foreign missionaries and about thirty who became translators of the Bible. See also *Allibone's Dictionary*, II, 2295.

597. At Dartmouth his interest had centered upon the ancient languages and literatures, especially the Greek. The "old English writers," i.e., the Cambridge Platonists, served for his "lighter reading."

598. See his letter to Coleridge, March 23, 1829, in Joseph Torrey (ed.), *The Remains of the Rev. James Marsh . . . with a Memoir of His Life* (Boston, 1843), pp. 135–38.

599. *Ibid.*, pp. 29–30, 36–38, 40.

600. *Ibid.*, p. 43.

601. Reprinted in America in 1817. He had first read the *Biographia* in 1819.—*Ibid.*, p. 135.

602. *Remains*, pp. 43, 116.

603. The evidence appears in an essay which he wrote for the *North American Review*, XV, i (July, 1822), 94–131. See Marjorie Nicolson's essay on "James Marsh and the Vermont Transcendentalists," *Philos. Rev.*, XXXIV, i (Jan., 1925), 34.

604. *Remains*, pp. 51, 56, 76, 110.

605. Reprinted, *ibid.*, pp. 556–84.

606. A study of this influence, called for by Professor Nicolson a quarter centrury ago, still remains to be made, although Professor John Dewey's essay, originally delivered as a lecture at the University of Vermont on November 26, 1929, in commemoration of the centenary of Marsh's "Introduction" to Coleridge's *Aids to Reflection*, and published in the *Journal of the History of Ideas* (II, ii [Apr., 1941], 131–50) contains, on pages 144–45, some pertinent remarks on Marsh's educational theory and,

on pages 145–50, an illuminating discussion of his social and political philosophy. To the purpose, also, is a series of articles on education that Marsh contributed to the *Vermont Chronicle* during 1829 over the signature of "Philopolis."

607. The faculty published a pamphlet setting forth the new course of study: *Exposition of the System of Instruction and Discipline Pursued in the University of Vermont* (Burlington, 1829; 2nd ed., enl., 1831). This announcement was widely publicized among other New England colleges, where it was variously received—sometimes with fervor, sometimes with disdain, but always with interest. Coming at the moment when Marsh's edition of Coleridge's *Aids* was engaging widespread attention, few attentive readers failed to grasp the obvious connection.

608. See *A Historical Discourse by Rev. John Wheeler, D.D. . . .* (Burlington, 1854), p. 38. Also abstracted in Duyckinck's *Cyclopaedia of American Literature*, I, 834.

609. Besides defending the grammatical and linguistic interprepation of the Scriptures and horrifying the orthodox by supporting Stuart's findings and championing the value of German theological criticism, he espoused the doctrines of Original Sin, Atonement, and Redemption in substantially Coleridgean terms. See *Remains*, p. 137.

610. See the "Advertisement," in which Coleridge says that in its inception, *Aids to Reflection*, too, was to have been primarily a book of "Selections from the Writings of Archbishop Leighton."—*Aids*, ed. by Marsh (Burlington, 1829), p. lv.

611. Marjorie Nicolson, *loc. cit.*, p. 38.

612. *Prose Writers of America* (Phila., 1849), p. 440; see also *Remains*, p. 92.

613. *Aids*, p. xiv. Compare Coleridge's "Reflections Respecting Morality," *Aids*, p. 35. In the course of the "Preliminary Essay," Marsh repeatedly emphasizes the idea that a thinking man "has and can have but one system in which his philosophy becomes religious and his religion philosophical." This assertion of the inherent rationality of Christian truth, at once the animating principle of Coleridge and of Marsh, naturally conditioned the latter to become the disciple of the former when he found the doctrine so explicitly stated in the *Aids*. Moreover, the combination by Coleridge of the doctrines of seventeenth-century English divines, themselves under the spell of Plato, with the German transcendental philosophy as a framework upon which to reconstruct a spiritual religion (which had been obscured and depressed under the influence of Locke and the

Scottish school) appealed to Marsh. It was in the search for a spiritual and personal religion that he turned to Coleridge and through Coleridge to Kant.

614. Yet in the "Preliminary Essay" proper Marsh nowhere draws the distinction itself, although there are numerous references to the extreme importance and significance of it for all departments of human thought and action. See, for example, pp. xv, xviii, xx, xxiii, xxv, xxviii, xxxix–xl, xlii–xliii, xlvi, xlviii. Indeed, he studiously avoids drawing the distinction, adding, "My object is merely to illustrate its necessity, and the palpable obscurity, vagueness, and deficiency, in this respect, of the mode of philosophizing, which is held in so high honour among us. The distinction will be found illustrated with some of its important bearings in the work, and in the Notes and Appendix; and cannot be too carefully studied . . . . Indeed, could I succeed in fixing the attention of the reader upon this distinction, in such a way as to secure his candid and reflecting perusal of the work, I should consider any personal effort and sacrifice abundantly recompensed" (p. xliii, and note 23, p. 262).

615. It has been charged that Marsh sometimes uses the word *reason* to designate the logical faculty, and again, as the equivalent of intuition; that sometimes his distinction between reason and understanding is no more than the distinction between truths that are self-evident and truths that are derivative.

616. Such is the general argument on pages xiv–xxxviii, whence he concludes: "It must have been observed by the reader of the foregoing pages, that I have used several words, especially *understanding* and *reason*, in a sense somewhat diverse from their present acceptation . . . . The ambiguity spoken of, and the consequent perplexity in regard to the use and authority of reason, have arisen from the habit of using, since the time of Locke, the terms understanding and reason indiscriminately."

617. *Aids*, p. xli.

618. *Aids*, pp. lviii, and 1 and 21 of the text; and notes 3 and 4, pp. 252–54.

619. *Aids*, note 22, pp. 260–61; see also p. xlviii.

620. See also Marsh's letter to Coleridge, dated March 23, 1829, printed in *Remains*, p. 137. The extreme need for a distinct terminology became most apparent to him when he set to writing his own "Psychology" (*ibid.*, p. 246). All his life, the lack of precise terminological tools frustrated his efforts and in the end spelt his defeat in the philosophical works which he planned but failed to complete. In 1837, after he had written at some length on the relation

of being and immortality to the Understanding and Reason, he felt constrained to admit: "I am aware that what I have said is not all very perspicuous, and that I have, especially in the last long paragraph, made transitions which it may be difficult to follow. Still, I know not that I should better it, without writing a system, so as to place all the parts in their proper relation to the whole, and thus show where the understanding belongs."—*Ibid.*, p. 397.

621. Coleridge's trustworthiness is discussed in the section, above, on Coleridge's position as an intermediary between German and American thinkers.

622. Here are included chiefly Bacon, More, and Leighton. See the Preliminary Essay, pp. xxviii–xxxix, xlvi; among the Notes, note 43 (p. 280), note 50 (pp. 288–90), note 59 (p. 305), notes on pages 316–21, note 65 (p. 323); and in the Appendix, pp. 375, 395–97.

623. See the passages in Chapter IX of *Biographia Literaria*, immediately preceding his blanket acknowledgment of indebtedness to Kant, whose every point Coleridge professed to understand in 1817, when that book was published.

624. See *Aids*, pp. 136–37. The inference in such passages as those on pages 137 and 145 is that Leighton and Kant were co-discoverers of the correct definitions. Kant is mentioned specifically only three times in the *Aids* (on pp. 137, 145, and 396).

To demonstrate coincident definitions in Leighton and Kant, Coleridge adduced a passage from Leighton: "Faith elevates the soul not only above sense and sensible things, but also above reason itself. As reason corrects the errors which sense might occasion, so supernatural faith corrects the errors of natural reason judging according to sense." At this point Coleridge added that if we substitute "reason" for the word "faith" in the passage quoted, and replace "natural reason" with "understanding," we shall find Leighton's definition to be, "word for word the very definition which the founder of critical philosophy gives to understanding, namely, 'the faculty judging according to sense'."—*Works*, Shedd ed., 1853, I, 241; see the whole of Aphorism VIII, *ibid.*, pp. 236–53; compare *Aids*, Marsh ed., 139, and the whole of Aphorism VIII, *ibid.*, pp. 135–45.

But such subtractions, additions, and substitutions, while they convert Leighton's passage into Kantian terminology, also convert his meaning into something other than Leighton intended. Passages such as these illustrate Coleridge's enthusiasm for the distinction between Reason and Understanding outrunning his discretion. Seldom was a prophet more inspired by a philosophical principle than was Coleridge by this one, and, we may add, seldom has one principle transmitted more enthusiasm than this one did to the men of the first half of the nineteenth century. So great was its significance for Coleridge that he took it, as he said, as "a magnificent theme, the different parts of which are to be demonstrated, developed, explained, illustrated, and exemplified" in all his philosophical works. See Claud Howard, *Coleridge's Idealism*, pp. 39, 47. When Coleridge is interested in giving weight and emphasis to this great seminal principle, he is so imbued with its importance that he sees reflections of it in writers whose view of the distinction was quite different from his own (and Kant's), however nearly they may have arrived at conclusions consonant with his own. It should be observed that when Coleridge is making notes for his own use, instead of publicizing the doctrine, he acknowledges more frankly, "How often have I found reason to regret, that Leighton had not clearly made out to himself the diversity of reason and understanding?" See *Works of Robert Leighton*, Aikman ed. (Edinburgh, 1835), pp. 352–53. See also his explanation of "the grounds of all Jeremy Taylor's important errors" in *Works*, Shedd ed., 1853, V, 181, 205, 209, as well as his criticism of the errors arising in Bacon and Harrington—all because they did not consistently distinguish between Understanding and Reason (*ibid.*, I, 236, 240–41, 264–65, and esp. 306–7).

It may well be, of course, that Marsh, in his efforts to popularize Coleridge's philosophy, consciously soft-pedalled the influence upon him of German philosophy (which he knew to be widely suspect in America) at the same time that he related Coleridge's ideas more immediately to the revered English Platonists.

625. John Dewey (*German Philosophy and Politics*, N.Y., 1915) reminds us, however, that German transcendentalism, purely critical and speculative though it was in the beginning, itself rapidly developed the most far-reaching practical applications—in religion, in politics, in art. William James maintained that Kant had been anticipated by the English theologians and the Cambridge Platonists, and A. O. Lovejoy has argued that the "Kantian doctrine was destitute of any radical originality; that none of the more general and fundamental contentions of the *Kritik der reinen Vernunft* were particularly novel or revolutionary at the time of their original promulgation [although there had been no such analyses and demonstrations as Kant supplied]; and that the principal developments of post-Kantian philosophy, even in the ostensibly Kantian schools, were not de-

pendent upon the interposition of the ingenious complexities of the critical system, but were present in germ, sometimes in fairly full-blown form, in the writings of Kant's predecessors and contemporaries," chiefly the English Platonists. See Lovejoy's "Kant and the English Platonists," in *Essays Philosophical and Psychological in Honor of William James* (N.Y., 1908), pp. 266–301. More immediately useful for our purposes is the careful inquiry into Coleridge's sources by Claud Howard in *Coleridge's Idealism: A Study of Its Relationships to Kant and to the Cambridge Platonists* (Boston, 1924). He seeks, first, to relate to Kant the anticipations which he finds in the writings of Cudworth, More, Hooker, Taylor, Leighton, Smith, Whitcote, and Culverwel; next, he seeks to describe Coleridge's attempted correlation of Kant's critical philosophy with the English anticipations of it; and finally, he undertakes to show the essential nature of the fused product that resulted in the mind of Coleridge. See esp. pp. 32–69, 87–97, 98–101.

626. See Coleridge's *Works*, Shedd ed., I, 94. It is not to be inferred, of course, that Marsh was ignorant of Coleridge's stricter reliance upon Kant than upon the seventeenth-century divines, for in preparing his edition of the *Aids*, he reread *The Friend* and the *Biographia Literaria* too attentively to have missed the import of Coleridge's flat statements of indebtedness. Moreover, a letter from Marsh to Coleridge, dated March 23, 1829, leaves no doubt on this point.

627. See Marjorie Nicolson, *loc. cit.*, p. 49.

628. See, for example, Marsh's "Letter to a Friend," entitled "On the Relation of Man's Personal Existence and Immortality to the Understanding and the Reason," dated Dec. 4, 1837, and printed in *Remains*, pp. 391–97. That his interest in Kant ever transcended this practical point of view is doubtful. His works on psychology and on logic, which he projected but never executed, might ultimately have led him to make a more detailed inquiry into Kant's purely speculative argument; but at his death in 1842 he had done little more than sketch some preliminary notes for these works. On the strength of these, little conclusive evidence appears.

629. See, for example, Coleridge's consistent use of the Kantian phraseology in such passages as those on pp. 137 and 142–45, as well as in the Glossary of terms from Appendix E of the *Stateman's Manual*, all of which Marsh felt constrained to reproduce for his edition of the *Aids*, pp. 395–99.

630. The extraordinary trouble to which Marsh went to explain Coleridge on Under-

standing and Reason appears in the pains he took to collect all the passages from Coleridge's published works which bear on the subject and in the cross references which he supplied. The more important notes and cross references intended to serve as guideposts for the reader are found on pp. xiii, xv, xix, xlvi, xlvii, 274, 279, 306, 328, 329. Aside from the long "Preliminary Essay," the other passages in the *Aids* to which Marsh called attention as being of value to the reader in an effort to get the correct distinction include this imposing array of references—(1) from the text: pp. 87–92, 102–5, 132–34, 135–45, 151–56, 160–63, 183–84, 193–94, 205–6, 211–13, 238–46; (2) from among the Notes: note 22 (pp. 260–61), n. 23 (pp. 261–62), n. 29 (p. 274), n. 43 (pp. 279–81), n. 50 (pp. 284–91), n. 51 (193–94), n. 55 (197), n. 59 (304–21, esp. 309–10), n. 64 (pp. 322–23), n. 66 (pp. 323–26), n. 67 (pp. 326–28), n. 78 (pp. 336–37); and (3) from the Appendix: pp. 343–99, esp. pp. 371–72, 374–75, 395–99. Most important, in Marsh's opinion, is the application of these distinctions for matters of faith. Accordingly, on page 279, he refers the reader specifically to passages on "pp. 108–20, 132–34, 192–94, 204–6, and the appendix to the first Lay Sermon republished at the end of the Volume."

631. *Critique of Pure Reason*, Müller trans., p. 242.

632. *Jour. of the Hist. of Ideas*, II, ii (Apr., 1941), 137.

633. Fries's influence is discussed below.

634. One aspect of Marsh's Aristotelianism (or his inability consistently to steer clear of what his reading in scientific books had impressed upon his mind) is seen in his treatment of space and time. Like Kant, he speaks of mathematics "as a science of space and time," of "necessary and therefore *a priori* forms of perceptual experience," but he also has in mind "the absolute space and time of Newtonian physics and not just mental forms." At all events, he does not always differentiate between the older and the Kantian concepts of space and time, and ordinarily infers that the powers of the mind, or of the self, are called forth only by objects correlative to them. See John Dewey's more detailed analysis, *loc. cit.*, pp. 138–40. It should be observed, however, that Marsh's inconclusive treatment of space and time appears mainly in his edition of the *Aids*, and that Dewey's criticism does not apply with equal force to Marsh's later writings.

Marsh's failure to isolate what he regards as an ascending and connected series of Sense-Understanding-Reason from the rational universe is what may be attributed to the Aristotelianism in his thinking. While there is no evidence to show that he read Schelling, in whose system he would have come upon the view of the subject as being in opposition to its object, there is evidence that he read something of Fichte's and knew the general doctrine of Fichte's subjective idealism (see his essay in *North Amer. Rev.*, XV [July, 1822], 123]. Yet there is in Marsh, instead of any tendency to put the subject in opposition to the object, the Hegelian tendency to regard the subject as coming most completely to himself in the rational will—"as the culmination, the consummation, of the energies constituting the sensible and physical world." See John Dewey, *loc. cit.*, p. 139. This tendency is not referable to Hegel. It goes back to Marsh's wide reading in the scientific writings of the day (and ultimately through the Baconian tradition to Aristotle), where he found evidence for the idea that nature presents an ascending scale of energies in which the lower are both the condition and the premonitions of the higher until the self-conscious mind itself at the apex is reached. Why this particular interpretation appealed to him and how it enabled him to use what he considered the Kantian tripartition of the mind for his purposes in reconciling religion and philosophy we shall have occasion to consider later.

635. See, in the Müller tr., pp. 41, 56–57, 242–45, 247, 274, 459, 517.

636. Discussed above, in the section on Coleridge.

637. It should be said, in fairness to Marsh, that while he made no amplification, in his edition of the *Aids*, of this limited view of Understanding, his "Letter to a Friend on the Relation of Man's Personal Existence and Immortality to the Understanding and the Reason" indicates that by December 4, 1837, when it was composed, he had revised his phraseology to bring his interpretation more nearly in accord with that of Kant. While he repeats Coleridge's phrase, "the faculty judging according to sense," he goes on to warn the reader "not to conceive it as being produced out of our sensuous nature."—*Remains*, pp. 392, 394–95.

638. To the inevitability of errors of this sort Kant himself had called attention in the *Critique of Pure Reason*, Müller tr., pp. 240–41.

639. *Ibid.*, pp. 11–12. The passage in which these statements are made is one of several which Coleridge arranged in parallel columns, the juxtaposition being designed to help elucidate the distinction between Understanding and Reason. But see, also, the last two paragraphs of the eighth "Aphorism on Spiritual Religion" (*Aids*, p. 145), where Coleridge implies that the difference between Reason and

Understanding is mainly one by which the former proceeds *a priori* and the latter *a posteriori*.

Coleridge was too much the poet to follow Kant's method of simple iteration to enforce a meaning. Instead, his fear of writing monotonously led him to present his definitions under as many varying lights and points of view as possible. This trait, Frederic Henry Hedge, one of the earliest and best American commentators on Coleridge and Kant, emphasized as being the chief difficulty which readers experience in attempting to follow Coleridge's thought. See *Christ. Exam.*, XIV, i (Mar., 1833), 116–18.

640. See, for example, p. 145 and n. 59 (pp. 304–5, 308–10) ; also pp. 371–72 of the *Aids*, where Coleridge clearly distinguishes, according to the Kantian criteria, between Reason and Understanding, between *a posteriori* and *a priori* knowledge, and between the pure and the practical Reason (see also pp. 137–39, 142–45, 205–7, 303–4, and 308–10, and compare with Kant's *Critique of Pure Reason*, pp. 171, 242–45, 537, and, as he refers to the Understanding, *ibid.*, pp. 41–42, 56–57, and 103–4). Here Marsh adds gratuitously nine and one-half pages of explanatory matter of his own, together with illustrations drawn from Coleridge's *Friend* and Henry More's *Antidote Against Atheism*, in the course of which he succeeds in hindering rather than helping the reader to grasp what Coleridge has just labored to explain. He speaks in one instance of "the relation of reason, as the power of spiritual intuition in man, to the Supreme Reason" in a manner to suggest that if he had, indeed, understood Coleridge a moment before, he had already forgotten that the Coleridgean distinction proscribed the indiscriminate use of terms like *intuition* and *reason*, the former being reserved to the intuition of sensibility (Kant's *Anschauung* of *Sinnlichkeit*), while the latter is described as "the faculty of producing unity among the rules of the understanding according to principles" (see *Critique of Pure Reason*, pp. 15, 242–43).

To be sure, Coleridge himself had not added anything to the clarity of the passage under consideration by introducing the figure of the "inward eye" or by using the words *Spirit* and *Soul* (*Aids*, pp. 308, 137, 142, 309); but these terms do not materially modify or destroy the essential meaning that he aims at in this note. However, Marsh's fondness for More, Cudworth, and others of the seventeenth-century Platonists led him sometimes to reinterpret Coleridge's interpretation more liberally than even Coleridge's liberal precedent justified.

641. See Coleridge's statement in the Preface and Marsh's repetition of it in his essay regarding the didactic and dogmatic rather than the speculative nature of the *Aids*, the aim being practical rather than theoretical.

642. See *Critique of Pure Reason*, Müller tr., pp. 238–42, 243–45, 508–10, 514–17.

643. *Ibid.*, p. 379.

644. *Ibid.*, pp. 563–64.

645. *Ibid.*, pp. 514, 558–64.

646. *Ibid.*, p. 655.

647. *Ibid.*, p. 654; see also p. 274.

648. That Coleridge attached relatively more significance to the practical than to the pure Reason appears from such a passage as the following: "But if not the abstract or speculative Reason, yet a reason there must be in order to [form] a rational Belief—then it must be the *Practical* Reason of Man, comprehending the Will, the Conscience, the Moral Being with its inseparable Interests and Affections—that Reason, namely, which is the Organ of *Wisdom* and (as far as Man is concerned) the Source of living and actual Truths."—"Aphorisms on Spiritual Religion," *Aids*, p. 375. And see Essay XI, second section of *The Friend* (Shedd ed., pp. 458–72), where Coleridge attempts to "fill up . . . the chasm" by means of "the moral being."

649. *Aids*, pp. 205–7.

650. *Ibid.*, pp. 115, 137.

651. *Critique of Pure Reason*, p. 562.

652. *Ibid.*, pp. 496–99, 518–20, 562.

653. Note 75, *Aids*, p. 334.

654. On this score he found in Coleridge only one brief note, and that (in the *Statesman's Manual*) seemed to leave the question upon which Kant had insisted open for debate. For Coleridge had only this to say: "Whether ideas are *regulative* only, according to Aristotle and Kant; or likewise *constitutive*, and one with power and Life of Nature, according to Plato and Plotinus . . . is the highest *problem* of philosophy, and not part of its nomenclature" (quoted by Marsh in *Aids*, p. 396). What Marsh could not know, unless he consulted Kant himself on this head, was the extreme importance, in the system of critical transcendentalism, that Kant attached to this distinction. See *Critique of Pure Reason*, pp. 517–18, 539. Contrast with Kant's cautious statements, Coleridge's note, Appendix A, *Aids*, p. 367.

655. *Remains*, pp. 135–36.

656. *Aids*, pp. xx, xxii.

657. *Ibid.*, pp. xxix–xxx.

658. *Ibid.*, pp. xv, xxiv–xxv.

659. When we search for reasons why Marsh failed to interpret clearly and precisely Kant's distinctions, we find two conditioning forces within Marsh that predisposed him to read into the Kantian epistemology certain preposses-

sions of his own. One of these stems from Aristotle, the other from Christianity. The former predisposed him to see the space and time relationships of Sense and the categories of the Understanding as more than merely passive forms, remaining inactive until called into action by the actual relationships which subsist among objects. In the Kantian epistemology there is no necessarily progressive development by which the Senses feed into the Understanding and both into the Reason. Marsh was able to break through this insularity among the faculties by adopting, instead of the Kantian separatedness, the Aristotelian connectedness of the mind's faculties, the senses supplying the materials of the Understanding, and the Understanding in turn actualizing these potentialities and supplying the Reason with the materials upon which to exercise itself. This scheme frees man, on purely natural grounds, for the possibilities of development and progress. On this score, see John Dewey's careful interpretation of Marsh, *loc. cit.*, pp. 139–42.

But if this is an Aristotelian interpretation of Kant, it should be observed that Marsh also separates himself in at least one important respect from Greek thought by introducing elements that are foreign to it, namely (1) the concept of mind as identical with the self, an identification that is alien to classic thinking, and (2) the concept of reason as will, i.e., of a "power to institute and seek to realize ends that are universal and necessary"—that are supplied by nature, but that flow from its own nature as a personal rational self. As Marsh himself points out, both ideas stem from, and are consonant with, Christianity. Where Aristotle, for example, held that "reason could be actualized by contemplative knowledge apart from any effort to change the world of nature and social institutions into its own likeness and embodiment," Marsh, following the spirit of Christian teaching, denies any such possibility, holding instead that "Reason can realize itself and be truly aware or conscious of its own intrinsic nature only as it operates to make over the world, whether physical or social, into an embodiment of its own principles." He condemns nothing so vehemently as the purely speculative tendency which would separate knowledge and the intellect from action and will. "By its own nature, reason terminates in action, and that action is the transformation of the spiritual potentialities found in the natural world, physical and institutional, into spiritual realities."—See Dewey, *loc. cit.*, p. 141; also pp. 142–50, and Marsh's "Discourses," printed in the latter half of *Remains*, "On Conscience," "On Hypocrisy," "On the Nature, Ground and Origin of Sin,"

"On Man's Need of Christ," and his "Tract on Evangelism." The basis of what immediately precedes in this note derives less from the *Aids* than from his later, more mature, though incomplete, writings in which Marsh sought to construct a comprehensive philosophy of his own.

660. *Remains*, p. 137.

661. *Ibid.*, p. 112.

662. *Ibid.*, p. 152.

663. *Ibid.*, pp. 291–97, 368–90.

664. *Ibid.*, pp. 187–210.

665. Marsh treats, in this instance, of space and time in equivocal terms, as representing quantities or qualities both "in the sphere of the outer senses" and "in our outward consciousness."—*Ibid.*, p. 191. A footnote refers the reader equally to Kant's *Kritik der reinen Vernunft*, erster Theil, and to Newton's *Principia*. However imperfectly Marsh had grasped these pure forms of Kant while he was preparing the *Aids*, successive passages in this Outline demonstrate that he was by now familiar with the Kantian concepts of space and time, but that he could still lapse into his earlier view of them. See *ibid.*, pp. 195–97, 302–4, 309–16, and compare with passages on pages 191–93.

666. *Ibid.*, p. 197. There are references also to Kant's *Naturwissenschaft* (*ibid.*, pp. 191, 197), his *Gedanken von der wahren Schätzung der lebendigen Kraefte* and his *Himmels System*, both in Volume I of *Vermischte Schriften* although no edition is specified (pp. 197, 203). The same notes refer also to Fries's *Mathematische Naturphilosophie* and his *System der Logik*, as well as to Oersted's *Identité des forces chimiques et electriques* (pp. 194, 197).

667. *Remains*, pp. 211–38.

668. *Ibid.*, p. vii. His reliance on Fries and Carus reflects Follen's influence.

669. *Ibid.*, pp. 239–367.

670. *Remains*, p. 118. See also his statement in "Psychology" (*Remains*, pp. 244–47) of the linguistic difficulties that beset the epistemologist.

671. *Remains*, p. 118.

672. In view of Coleridge's poor health at the time and his carelessness as a correspondent, not too much importance is to be attached to Coleridge's seeming neglect of his American disciple. To Americans who subsequently visited him at Highgate, he always expressed gratification at Marsh's service in spreading his doctrines in the New World; while his most intimate associates, among them Henry Nelson Coleridge, James Gilman, and J. H. Green, wrote highly appreciative letters to Marsh. When Coleridge's nephew prepared the 1839

edition of the *Aids*, instead of writing a new introduction, he simply reprinted Marsh's essay, with the explanation that he saw no need for doing again what had already been done well.

673. Convinced that psychology, based on internal evidence, must form the foundation of all philosophizing, Fries concluded that psychology must rest, first of all, upon empirical knowledge, for we become conscious of *a priori* cognitions only through *a posteriori* experience. Accordingly he set himself to establish Kant's criticism of reason on such a psychological basis. Like Kant, Fries stresses the necessity of criticizing the faculty of cognition, but he finds three fundamental faults with Kant. First, he dissents from what he calls Kant's "phenomenalism," or his subjective view of nature, by which space and time are merely mental forms or avenues of apperception, and insists upon a closer indentification of subject and object—a doctrine which, as we have observed, Marsh was prepared to accept as consonant with what he had read in books of science. Second, Fries objects to what he calls a vicious arrangement of Kant's doctrine by which the value of the categories depends upon transcendental proofs and ideas upon moral proofs, instead of rising, without any proof, to the immediate "knowledge of reason." Third, he objects to what he believes to be Kant's confounding psychological ideas with philosophy, and not properly distinguishing the aids which psychology furnishes to metaphysics from metaphysics itself. Fries maintains that he has corrected the errors of Kant, and that he has placed the *doctrine of belief* (which he considers the "focus of all philosophical conviction") on a sound basis. This he claims to have effected by means of researches carried on in the spirit of Kant himself. Starting with Kant by making the limits of science his starting point, he goes beyond Kant and arrives at once at the *pure faith of reason* in that which is eternal, a faith that is strengthened by presentiment (*Ahnung*). Knowledge, or science, is concerned only with sensuous phenomena; the true essence of things is the object of belief, which is the offspring of the limitation itself of knowledge. Here, again, in placing feeling and presentiment above science, Fries approaches the doctrine of Jacobi, though by different methods.—See Ueberweg, *op. cit.*, II, 195, 201–3, and Tennemann's *Manual of the History of Philosophy*, tr. by Arthur Johnson (London, 1852), pp. 467–69.

674. On the importance attached to precisely these elements of Fichte and Schelling as being the "most important victories" by which Kant's "revolution in philosophy" was consummated, see Chapter IX of the *Biographia Litera-*

ria. That Marsh appears to have followed Coleridge in attaching unusual significance to Fichte and Schelling, particularly the latter, appears from his inclusion, in connection with note 29, p. 275, of his edition of the *Aids*, a lengthy quotation from *The Friend* (III, 166–68) on Nature, the Dynamic, Phaenomenology, and Natural Philosophy—all bearing unmistakable Schellingian marks.

675. And, we might add, admixtures also of Herder, of Schleiermacher, of Schiller, and of Goethe.

676. XIV, i, 180–29. The essay is of importance (1) because it was the first review article written by an American that interpreted German thought correctly, (2) because in it was used for the first time in America the term *transcendental philosophy* in the sense in which it was soon to be understood by the New England Transcendentalists, and (3) because it served as one of the early important sources for Emerson's knowledge of Kant, Fichte, and Schelling.

677. Writing five years after the death of Marsh and almost twenty years after the appearance of Marsh's edition of the *Aids*, Porter put down this considered opinion:

"*The American disciples* of Coleridge have been numerous . . . and they have certainly been sufficiently diversified. Indeed his influence in this country has been wider . . . than in England. . . . There are many hundreds now living on whose minds his writings dawned like a new light, and on whose ears his words fell like a trumpet note, to stir all their better nature, and to strengthen and confirm their broken purposes. . . . Coleridge had the advantage of being introduced to our theological arena by one of the most distinguished of our scholars. . . . President Marsh will not soon be forgotten. . . . His essay preliminary to the *Aids to Reflection* and his criticism of Stuart's *Commentary on the Hebrews* are among the first specimens of writing of their kind. . . . The influence of Coleridge on the philosophy and theology of New England has been, in some respects, what President Marsh desired it should be. It has opened new fields of inquiry and put us in possession of other modes of viewing religious truths. It has brought within our notice writers who used to be unknown to our libraries. It has rendered our theology tolerant . . . at the same time it has made it free. . . . Above all, it has contended for a wakeful, thorough, and scientific theology, in which, let alarmists and incapables say what they will, rests the hope of the church."—IV, 161–63.

678. Burlington, 1830. See *Remains*, p. 103. Of this work only the first volume was pub-

lished. It included Howe's *Blessedness of the Righteous* and Bates's *Four Last Things*.

679. First American edition from the second London edition, Burlington, 1831.

680. Burlington, 1833.

681. Burlington, 1837.

682. As an indication of the effectiveness of some of his disciples might be mentioned the work of William Greenough Thayer Shedd, who was graduated from the University of Vermont in 1839, served as minister of various congregations in Vermont and New York and as professor at the University of Vermont, 1845–1852; in the Theological Seminary at Auburn, N.Y., 1852–1853; Andover, 1853–1862; Union Theological Seminary, 1863; and in 1854 brought out the long-standard seven-volume Shedd edition of Coleridge's works.

683. The connections between the Vermont and Concord groups is a matter that needs more attention than can be devoted to it here. It must suffice to point out that Marsh was often in Boston, was well acquainted with Channing, Ticknor, and Bancroft, as well as with many of the "Transcendentalists," and doubtless agreed heartily with many of their aims and aspirations. In the Brook Farm experiment, however, he had little faith. "The schemes cherished in New York," he wrote in 1841, "are very nearly of the same character, I suppose, as those which Mr. Ripley and others are going to commence near Boston on the first of April (an ominous day!) and it may be prudent for the New Yorkers to wait the result of their experiment. . . . The grand error I take to be in the hope which he [Ripley] indulges of finding men in this world sufficiently under the law of pure reason, or even sufficiently raised by divine grace above the selfishness of human nature, to live together on such terms as they propose. . . . These reformers . . . hope to redeem the world by a sort of dilettanti process, to purge off its grossness, to make a political paradise in which hard work shall become easy, dirty things clean, and a churl a churl no longer."—George B. Cheever, "Characteristics of the Christian Philosopher," *The Dartmouth* (1844), p. 67. The entire letter is quoted in Appendix D of Ronald V. Wells's *Three Christian Transcendentalists* . . . (N.Y., 1943), pp. 163–68.

684. After graduating from Harvard in 1815 and remaining three years in the Divinity School, he was ordained on June 23, 1819, as the minister of the church at Watertown, Mass., where he remained for twenty-three years. In 1842 he succeeded the Rev. Henry Ware, Jr., as Parkman Professor of Pulpit Eloquence and Pastoral Care at Harvard, and held that office until his death in 1863.

685. By 1835 he had read Herder's *Spirit of Hebrew Poetry*, Berger's *Einleitung in das neue Testament*, De Wette, Ilgen, Eckermann, Bauer, Corrodi, and other Germans. The *Catalogue of a Portion of the Libraries of the Rev. Convers Francis and His Sister* (Boston, 1887) includes titles (many of them in translation) of such writers as Neander, Tennemann, Fichte, De Wette, Niebuhr, Ramdohr, Humboldt, Ranke, Lessing, Tauler, Luther, Melanchthon, Hutton, and Dürer. The more recent German theological writers of the Tübingen School are conspicuously absent. See *Proc. Mass. Hist. Soc.* (1863), p. 6; *ibid.* (1866), p. 242; Odell Shepard, *Pedlar's Progress* . . . (Boston, 1937), p. 260; Clarence Gohdes, *op. cit.*, p. 78, n.; and O. B. Frothingham, *Boston Unitarianism, 1820–1850* (N.Y., 1890), p. 186.

686. H. S. Commager, *Theodore Parker* (Boston, 1936), pp. 24–25; H. C. Goddard, *op. cit.*, pp. 85–86; O. B. Frothingham, *Transcendentalism in New England*, pp. 353–54.

687. See John Weiss, *Discourse Occasioned by the Death of Convers Francis* (Cambridge, Mass., 1863), p. 28; H. S. Commager, *op. cit.*, p. 71. Francis' article on Reinhard's *Life and Writings* for the *Christian Examiner* (XIII, ii [Jan., 1833], 364–86) included a serious discussion of the claims of German theology and left little doubt about his position. His contributions to the strongly pro-Transcendentalist organ, the *Western Messenger* (see II [1837], 340) re-enforced it.

688. Frothingham, *Transcendentalism in New England*, pp. 345–54; Frothingham, *Boston Unitarianism*, pp. 186–87; Gohdes, *op. cit.*, pp. 40, 223.

689. The son of Levi Hedge, Professor of Logic, Ethics, and Metaphysics at Harvard from 1810 to 1832, he received his early education from his father and a tutor, young George Bancroft, so that he was ready for college at the age of twelve. Being too young to enter Harvard, but having shown a marked aptitude for acquiring foreign languages, he was sent in 1818 to Germany, in charge of Bancroft, himself only eighteen at the time. The latter had just graduated from Harvard College and intended to complete his education at Göttingen. In Germany, young Hedge studied for four years in various Gymnasia, chiefly at Schulpforta under the celebrated teacher David Ilgen. Although he later expressed the belief that as a foreigner in Germany he had been too much indulged and left too much to his own devices, so that he might have made better progress if he had stayed at home, he seems, nevertheless, to have made substantial acquisitions. In 1822, he returned to enter Harvard with advanced

standing. Immediately after his graduation in 1825, President Kirkland offered him an instructorship in German, which the young man declined in favor of three years in the Divinity School, where he began his friendship with Emerson, another divinity student. On May 20, 1829, he was ordained at West Cambridge (now Arlington), Mass., Emerson having been ordained two weeks earlier. Hedge served as Unitarian minister at West Cambridge, 1829–1835; Bangor, Me., 1835–1850; Providence, R.I., 1850–1856; Brookline, Mass., 1856–1872. He was editor of the *Christian Examiner*, 1857–1861; President of the American Unitarian Association, 1859–1862; Professor of Ecclesiastical History in the Harvard Divinity School, 1857–1876; especially appointed instructor in ecclesiastical history for the year 1877–1878; and Professor of German Literature in Harvard College from 1872 until his retirement in 1882. He continued to live in Cambridge until his death in 1890.

690. The Harvard-Göttingen men, except for some minor excursions into philosophy and some attention to theology, had concentrated their efforts on philological matters, so that the knowledge which they brought back with them regarding German critical transcendentalism was relatively slight. On the other hand, Hedge, when he stood in 1870 before a group of Germans assembled in Faneuil Hall, Boston, could truthfully say, "I am a German by intellectual descent. . . . Germany is the fatherland of my mind. It was there I first drew the breath of intellectual life [and] . . . imbibed my first ideas of poetry and philosophy."—*Index*, I, xxxv (Aug. 27, 1870), pp. 2–3.

691. George Ripley and George Bradford, "Philosophical Thought in Boston," in Winsor's *Memorial History of Boston*, IV, 307; *Nation*, LI, mcccxiii (Aug. 28, 1890), 165. T. W. Higginson, *Margaret Fuller Ossoli* (Boston, 1884), p. 44; John W. Chadwick, *Theodore Parker*, p. 82; *Emerson's Journals*, IV, 235; V, 206.

692. On December 22, 1833, writing to his brother William, Emerson said: "Henry Hedge is an unfolding man who has just written the best pieces that have appeared in the Examiner and one especially was a living leaping Logos, & he may help me."—*Letters*, I, 402; see also *ibid.*, I, 29–30; *Carlyle-Emerson Correspondence*, I, 25; II, 165, 170–71; and J. E. Cabot, *Memoir* . . . , I, 216. The articles referred to are on Coleridge (*Christian Exam.*, XIV [Mar., 1833], 108–29) and on Swedenborg (*ibid.*, XV [Nov., 1833], 193–218). See further, O. W. Long, *Frederick Henry Hedge. A Cosmopolitan Scholar* [Portland, Me., 1940), pp. 18–24, 31–48.

693. See Hedge's circumstantial letter of February 1, 1877, to Mrs. Caroline Dall, in answer to her inquiry regarding his early association with the Transcendentalists, in Caroline Healey Dall, *Transcendentalism in New England: A Lecture Delivered before the Society of Philosophical Enquiry, Washington, D.C., May 7, 1895* (Boston, 1897), pp. 14–17.

694. *Christian Exam.*, XIV, i (Mar., 1833), 109–11.

695. *Ibid.*, p. 119.

696. *Ibid.*, pp. 120–21.

697. *Ibid.*, p. 123. In calling attention to the primarily *critical* aspect of Kant's work, he was the first to correct the false emphasis upon the practical aspect of Kant's thought to which Coleridge and Carlyle led Americans to attach a disproportionate importance. Fourteen years later, in his *Prose Writers of Germany*, Hedge again carefully distinguished between Kant as the founder of the *critical method* and his followers as promulgators of the *transcendental philosophy*.

698. *Ibid.*, pp. 120–21. While "interior consciousness" is called by Hedge "a free intuition" that "can only be attained by a vigorous effort of the will," he is careful to point out that it is "distinguished from the common consciousness by its being an active and not a passive state" (*ibid.*, p. 119). It has nothing to do with intuitive divination.

699. "When this step is accomplished, the system is complete, the hypothetical framework may then fall, and the structure will support itself." This, adds Hedge, is "the *ideal* of the method proposed; we are by no means prepared to say that this ideal has been achieved, or that it can be achieved."—*Ibid.*, p. 121.

700. "In him intellectual philosophy is more ripe, more substantial, more promising, and if we may apply the term to such speculation, more practical than any of the others" (p. 125). Hedge's translation of Schelling's first Berlin lecture, in the *Dial* for January, 1843 (III, iii, 398–404), is another indication of his preference for Schelling.

701. In concluding his essay, Hedge mentions Hegel, Oken, Fries, Reinhold, Krug, and Plattner, but of them (he adds) "our information would not enable us to say much, and our limits forbid us to say any thing" (p. 125).

702. "In theology this method has been most conspicuous. We are indebted to it for that dauntless spirit of inquiry which has investigated, and for that amazing erudition which has illustrated, every corner of biblical lore. Twice it has saved the religion of Germany,— once from the extreme fanatic extravagance, and again, from the verge of speculative infidel-

ity. But, though most conspicuous in theology, this influence has been visible in every department of intellectual exertion to which the Germans have applied themselves for the last thirty years. It has characterized every science and each art, and all bear witness to its quickening power. A philosophy which has given such an impulse to mental culture and scientific research, which has done so much to establish and to extend the spiritual in man, and the ideal in nature, needs no apology; it commends itself by its fruits, it lives in its fruits, and must ever live" (pp. 126–27).

703. He regarded Schopenhauer as a much truer continuator of Kant than Hegel, whom he regarded always something of a charlatan. See "Frederick Henry Hedge," *Nation*, LI, mcccxii (Aug. 28, 1890), 166. W. T. Harris credited Hedge with being the first to make the American public acquainted with Schopenhauer, through his essays in the *Christian Examiner*. See *Journal of Speculative Philosophy*, XI, i (Jan., 1877), 107.

704. Averse to identifying himself positively with any party, and opposed to purely speculative philosophy, he was never a systematic philosopher. His importance as an intellectual force upon the minds of his associates was consequently all the greater, for they agreed with him in depreciating all pure speculation and dialectics as so much jargon. If his had been a profoundly technical system, his effectiveness among them could hardly have been as potent as it was. Instead, he brought them an atmosphere, a philosophical attitude, a *Weltanschauung*, expressed more in terms of tendencies and significances than technical details, with only as much of abstruse foundations as their understanding seemed to demand, and no more. See J. H. Allen, "Memory of Dr. Hedge," *Unitarian Rev.*, XXXIV (Sept., 1890), 269.

As editor of the *Christian Examiner*, he espoused no cause and was frankly intolerant of all attempts to organize Unitarian societies into large associations. As a professor in the Divinity School, he objected to the audacities of the western Unitarians, but himself complacently doubted personal immortality while cheerfully relegating the entire realm of nature to the devil. He was cautious about accepting the theory of evolution, but was often bold, even rash, in his own speculations. The Unitarians of the old school never liked his insistence that in the old Arian controversy Athanasius was more nearly right than Arius. His sermon in 1864, before the graduating class of the Divinity School, on "Anti-Supernaturalism in the Pulpit" was hailed with a tumult of acclaim by the conservatives, but it requires little

effort to find in his own writings striking examples of the tendency which, on that occasion, he so much deplored. Like Emerson, he felt no need to be always consistent; and when, on one occasion, he was told that the facts were against him, he replied, "So much the worse for the facts."—Cyrus A. Bartol, *Radical Problems*, p. 70. While this general independence of mind occasioned an awkward sort of unpredictability regarding what he might do or say in any given situation, and while it led sometimes to startling and even annoying results, it led, also, to his exerting an influence on several factions. It may also explain why he was not a really vigorous leader in any one of them.

705. In metaphysics fundamentally a follower of Kant, he modelled his religion more closely after that of Schleiermacher, the influence of whose doctrines is most readily discernible, from introduction to conclusion, in his *Reason in Religion* (1865).

706. In the Dudleian lecture delivered at Harvard in 1851 on the subject of "Natural Religion" (partially printed in the *Christ. Exam.* for Jan., 1852), he took the position that all religious truth is properly revealed, that it belongs to a higher power than understanding, and that it derives its original life from revelation. But what constitutes the most striking part of the discourse is his criticism of the common argument of the existence of God from instances of design in the universe. It is worthless as "proof," for in all such reasoning we carry with us the idea of God already existing in our mind and in no way dependent on the instances of design. This argument establishes nothing more than "the wonderful mechanician, the unfathomable artist." "What religion wants and declares is a Father in Heaven, a moral governor and judge of the rational world. Of this God the natural proofs are our own consciousness, our moral instincts, and the universal account of mankind" (LII, 131–33).

707. Yet the frequency with which the book was reprinted indicates something of its importance for later generations. Published originally by Carey and Hart in Philadelphia, in 1847, it was reprinted in 1848; it went into a second edition in 1849, and a third, published by C. S. Francis of New York, in 1855. A new edition, revised and enlarged, was supplied by Potter and Coates, Philadelphia, 1870. In view of these data and the fact that the 567 finely printed, double-columned pages contained eleven pages of translations from Kant's *Critique of Judgment* and *Concerning Eternal Peace*, twenty from Fichte's *Destination of Man*, twelve from Schelling's lecture *On the Relation of the Plastic Arts to Nature*, ten from Hegel's *Philosophy of*

History, and seventeen from F. Schlegel's *Philosophy of History* (not counting biographical and critical sketches), to say nothing of extracts from the aesthetical writings of Lessing, Mendelssohn, Wieland, Herder, Schiller, and A. W. Schlegel and the more popular or less technically philosophical writings of Boehme, Möser, Lavater, Jacobi, and Novalis—in view of these facts, it seems unwarrantable to dismiss this book as of no philosophical significance because it contained "nothing philosophic except Fichte's Destiny of Man." See René Wellek, "The Minor Transcendentalists and German Philosophy," *New Eng. Quar.*, XV, iv (Dec., 1942), 658. As first arousing Brokmeyer's interest in Hegel, it played a prominent part in generating the St. Louis School of Philosophy.

708. The selections from Kant's *Critique of Judgment* and *Concerning Eternal Peace* are by J. E. Cabot, only the six-page translation of the "Supposed Beginning of the History of Man" being by Hedge himself, while all but two of the twelve pages devoted to Hegel are the work of an anonymous "friend" (the Rev. Henry B. Smith). For the selections from the more distinctively literary figures, Hedge drew heavily upon Carlyle's *German Romance*. The translations from Schiller, however, are by John Weiss; the *Titan* of Jean Paul, by C. T. Brooks; Goethe's *Wahlverwandtschaften*, by George Bradford; Schleiermacher's *Church and Priesthood*, by George Ripley; and Schelling's *Relation of the Plastic Arts to Nature*, by J. E. Cabot.

709. Several of the latter Emerson thought good enough to publish in the *Dial* (I, iii [Jan., 1841], 290–91). One, entitled "Questionings, or The Idealists," written about 1834, is also preserved in Emerson's *Parnassus* (1875).

710. *Jour. of Speculative Philos.*, XV, i (Jan., 1881), 77; F. B. Sanborn (ed.), *The Genius and Character of Emerson* . . . (Boston, 1884), p. xv.

711. Luther's "Ein' feste Burg ist unser Gott" received its classic expression in English from him. For his other translations, see O. W. Long, *Hedge*, pp. 23, 28–31.

712. This work, based on his Harvard lectures, has been rated as more finished than James K. Hosmer's *Short History of German Literature* (1879) or Bayard Taylor's academic lectures collected as *Studies in German Literature* (1879). It was "the most complete treatment of German literature up to that time."— Long, *op. cit.*, p. 44.

713. His religious opinions are elaborated chiefly in *Recent Inquiries in Theology* (1860), *Reason in Religion* (1866), *The Primeval World in Hebrew Tradition* (1870), *Ways of the Spirit and Other Essays* (1877), *Personality and Theism* (1887), and *Martin Luther and Other Essays*

(1888). His philosophical opinions are best studied in *Atheism in Philosophy and Other Essays* (1884). This volume reproduces his essay on Kant, another on Leibnitz (originally printed in the *Atlantic Monthly* for June, 1858), and an extended version of his essay on Schopenhauer, originally published in the *Christian Examiner* for January, 1864. His translation of Leibnitz' *Monadology* appeared in the *Journal of Speculative Philosophy* for July, 1867 (I, iii, 129–36). An interesting sidelight regarding Hedge is provided by Harris' printing in the same journal for January, 1877 (XI, i, 107–8), twenty-eight questions bearing on Kant, Schopenhauer, and Hartmann which he selected from a list of questions prepared by Hedge as University Examiner at Harvard. See *DAB* for other titles.

714. Henry D. Gray, *op. cit.*, p. 17.

715. Sermon on "The Philosophy of Man's Spiritual Nature in Regard to the Foundations of Faith," published in the *Christian Examiner* in 1834, reprinted the same year as tract No. 87 of the American Unitarian Association, and finally republished in his volume of sermons, *Reason, Faith and Duty* (1876).

716. Yet in his capacity as Alford Professor of Moral Philosophy at Harvard he conscientiously read the German philosophers from Kant through Hegel, as well as Cousin and Jouffroy. He never entered fully into the spirit of transcendental philosophy, nor found in it the spiritual element he sought, but contented himself by combining common-sense rationalism with a simple piety and a lofty ethical tone. For him, as for Channing, philosophy served mainly as a basis for religion. Schleiermacher and De Wette were, therefore, more to his liking than Kant and Hegel. Though a theological liberal, he was temperamentally conservative and cautious; he kept clear of reform agitations, considered Theodore Parker a "phenomenon," and made it his practice, as he said, never to preach about anything until after people in the omnibus had stopped talking about it.

717. O. B. Frothingham, *Transcendentalism in New England*, pp. 120–22.

718. For convenience of reference, the names are arranged alphabetically, and dates are added. Further details regarding their position are given below. Consult the index. Of the men named, the Congregationalists Hodge and Porter and the Baptist Sears studied in German universities, and several others traveled in Germany.

719. Despite Ware's fulminations against the German theologians on other occasions, he wrote, on February 22, 1829, to Wm. Barry, then studying in Germany: "Your opportunities for

study are truly enviable . . . . It might almost make one sigh to think of your listening to Blumenbach and Heeren, (of whom we hear so much, but are condemned to know nothing personally,) and perfecting yourself in a language which is to be the key to many stores of delightful literature and sound learning, to which we have no access."—John Ware, *Memoir of . . . Henry Ware, Jr.* (2 vols. in 1, new ed., Boston, 1854), p. 22.

720. A member of the class of 1804, he pursued graduate studies for four years longer, became a tutor in 1811, librarian and lecturer in 1813, and professor in 1819. After his resignation in 1830, he remained in Cambridge, informally yet closely identified with the Divinity School until his death in 1853.

721. To be listed are (1) *A Statement of Reasons for Not Believing the Doctrines of Trinitarians* (Boston, 1833); (2) the several pamphlets which he contributed to the controversy over the "latest form of infidelity"; (3) *The Evidences of the Genuineness of the Gospels* (3 vols., Boston, 1837–1844; 2nd ed., 3 vols., 1846–1848; 3rd ed., abridged, ed. by C. E. Norton, 1 vol. 1867); (4) a collection of essays and discourses entitled *Tracts on Christianity* (Boston, 1852); (5) *The Internal Evidences of the Gospels . . . with Particular Reference to Strauss' "Life of Jesus"* (2 pts. in 1 vol., ed. by C. E. Norton, 1856, preface, 1855); and (6) *A Translation of the Gospels with Notes* (ed. by C. E. Norton, 2 vols., Boston, 1856).

722. Preface to 2nd ed. (Boston, 1846–1848), I, v. Except where otherwise indicated, all references to the *Evidences* are to the third edition, abridged, readily available for reference today. This abridged edition presents (pp. vii-viii) a "List of the Principal Omissions in the Present Edition," the most important for our purpose being Note A (pp. iii–xxxiv in the 1st ed.). It contains an elaborate analysis of Griesbach (pp. iv–x, xviii–xxi, xxiii–xxiv, xxix–xxxiv), as well as discussions of Eichhorn (pp. xi, xxiv–xxv), Scholz (pp. xi, xxxi), Semler (p. xii), Bertholdt (pp. xix–xx), and Hug (pp. xxiv–xxv). All these passages (says Norton, in the 2nd ed., I, v) were omitted in later editions because they consist "principally of statements and arguments, which, having been once made, it is not worth while to repeat, because they concern errors of the day, that have not their origin in any essential or permanent aspect of the subject to which they relate." They are of interest to us only as indicating the extent of Norton's familiarity with the German writers named.

723. They include Baur (pp. 180–82); Eichhorn (pp. 2, 5–10, 24–27, 36–37, 52–55, 60–67, 388–89, 488–91, 499, 501–2, 507, 545, 548, 560, 566–67); Gieseler (p. 546); Griesbach (pp. 45, 129, 421, 425, 444); Hahn (pp. 178, 341); Hegel (pp. 180–81); Less (p. 3); Michaelis (pp. 60, 490); Mosheim (p. 281); Neander (p. 546); Olshausen (p. 546); Postel (pp. 370–74); Scholz (pp. 19–23); Semler (pp. 30, 546); Strauss (pp. 149, 379); Stroth (p. 115); Tennemann (p. 182); Wetstein (pp. 450, 456); Wegscheider (p. 178).

724. While it does not follow that Norton had before him the books of all the Germans whom he cited or quoted (for he doubtless relied on secondary sources in some instances), there can be no doubt that he had the originals of the majority named on his desk as he wrote, for many of them were not available at the time in either translation or digest. Moreover, in the first part of the *Internal Evidences*, which he devoted to an examination and criticism of the myth theory of Strauss, and where he had an English translation of *Das Leben Jesu*, he often printed passages both in the original and in a translation of his own because he found the existing English version inaccurate or misleading (see pp. 150, 153–54, 546, n.). Part I, devoted to taking "particular notice of the late attacks of the infidel theologians of Germany on the credibility of the Gospels" (p. 5), presents the negative part of his argument, directed chiefly against Strauss "as a representative of the class" (p. 7). Others, including Müller (pp. 22–23), Hegel (pp. 54–55, 155), Paulus (p. 101), and Schelling (p. 155), receive their share of Norton's censure for having promulgated a "false philosophy" that has not only "unsettled all just notions of the political relations of men, but, through its irreligion and demoralizing character, done very much to destroy . . . all right conceptions of our duties" (p. 177).

The notes which accompany the second volume of his *Translation of the Gospels* cite besides classical, English, and French exegetes, the German reference works of Wetstein (pp. 60, 74, 77, 80, 153, 250, 315, 385), Schoettgen (pp. 71–86), Schleissner (p. 88), Winer (pp. 89, 223, 469), Gesenius (p. 89), Hengstenberg (p. 319), and Buxtorf (p. 469).

725. I, i (Jan., 1839), 87.

726. *Ibid.*, pp. 87, 104–12.

727. As one example among many, see the tolerant view expressed by Charles A. Aiken of Andover in his essay on "The Comparative Value of English and German Biblical Science" in *Bibliotheca Sacra*, XI, xli (Jan., 1854), 67–86.

THE TRANSCENDENTALIST WRITERS

RALPH WALDO EMERSON

1. See his statements: (1) "I cannot myself use that systematic form which is reckoned essential in treating the science of the mind" (*Works*, Centenary ed., XII, 11); (2) "I confess to a little distrust of that completeness of system which metaphysicians are apt to affect. 'Tis the gnat grasping the world" *ibid.*, XII, 120); (3) "The moment it [philosophy] would appear as propositions and have a separate value, it is worthless" (II, 329); (4) "I simply experiment, an endless seeker with no Past at my back" (II, 318); (5) "I know better than to claim any completeness for my picture. I am a fragment, and this is a fragment of me" (III, 83); (6) Emerson's letter to the Rev. Henry Ware, Jr., Oct. 8, 1838: "I have always been, from my very incapacity of methodical thinking, 'a chartered libertine,' free to worship and free to rail . . . . I could not possibly give an account of myself, if challenged. I could not possibly give you one of the 'arguments' you cruelly hint at, on which any doctrine of mine stands. For I do not know what arguments mean in reference to any expression of a thought. I delight in telling what I think, but if you ask me how I dare say so, or why it is so, I am the most helpless of mortal men." This reply to Ware was obviously designed chiefly to disarm the opposition and to forestall the possibility of a sharp theological debate (for which Emerson had no relish, and in which he would inevitably have been worsted by better theoretical theologians than he ever hoped to be); yet it seems clear that Emerson did indeed lack the discipline of a strict metaphysician.

2. Charles J. Woodbury, *Talks with Ralph Waldo Emerson* (N.Y., 1890), p. 60.

3. Emerson's confessions, or boasts, of inconsistency and formlessness gave rise to a judgment which became traditional, namely, that he was unable to think consecutively. See, for example, Lowell's essay on "Emerson the Lecturer"; the biographies by O. W. Holmes (Boston, 1885), p. 390; Geo. E. Woodberry (N.Y., 1907), p. 176; Richard Garnett (London, 1888), p. 93; and the more recent views expressed by Van Wyck Brooks (*America's Coming of Age*, N.Y., 1915, pp. 70–75), Henry S. Canby (*Classic Americans*, N.Y., 1931, pp. 150–51), V. F. Calverton *The Liberation of American Literature*, N.Y., 1932, pp. 254, 255, 261, 270), and Ludwig Lewisohn (*Expression in America*, N.Y., 1932, pp. 117–19). On the other hand, for statements of Emerson's fundamental consistency, see Horace Mann (quoted in Moncure D.

Conway's *Emerson at Home and Abroad*, Boston, 1882, p. 149), Edwin D. Mead (in F. B. Sanborn's *Genius and Character of Emerson*, Boston, 1885, p. 236), S. Law Wilson (*The Theory of Modern Literature*, Edinburgh, 1899, p. 105), John Dewey (*Internat'l. Jour. of Ethics*, XIII [1903], 405), Hugo Münsterberg (*Harvard Psychology Studies*, II, 17), P. E. More (*Shelburne Essays*, First Series, Boston, 1904, pp. 73–74), and O. W. Firkins (*Ralph Waldo Emerson*, Boston, 1914, p. 299).

See, further, Emerson's statement immediately following his denial of the ability to use "that systematic form which is reckoned essential in treating the science of the mind": "But if one can say so without arrogance, I might suggest that he who contents himself with dotting a fragmentary curve, recording only what facts he has observed, without attempting to arrange them within one outline, follows a system also,—a system as grand as any other, though he does not interfere with its vast curves by prematurely forcing them into a circle or ellipse, but only draws that arc which he clearly sees, or perhaps at a later observation a remote curve of the same orbit, and waits for a new opportunity, well assured that these observed curves will consist with each other . . . . Metaphysics is dangerous as a single pursuit . . . . The inward analysis must be corrected by roughest experience. Metaphysics must be perpetually reinforced by life . . . . I think metaphysics a grammar to which, once read, we seldom return . . . and I want only a teaspoonful in a year . . . . My metaphysics are to the end of use."—*Works*, XII, 11–13.

4. J. E. Cabot, *Memoir*, I, 329.

5. *Journals*, VI, 26 (Aug. 22, 1841); see also *Works*, I, 410–11.

6. Sweeping as Emerson's profession of indebtedness to Platonism appears to be (notably in the essay on Plato), a perusal of others of Emerson's statements illustrates the fact that there are others to whom he made much the same acknowledgment. As a lecturer he often allowed himself the luxury of overstatement for the sake of emphasis. His various utterances on Goethe, for example, or on Shakespeare are hardly less laudatory; while the essay on Swedenborg, or that on Montaigne, if taken by itself, might lead the reader to the conclusion that the chief influence on Emerson was exerted either by the mystical Swedenborg or by the skeptical Montaigne—an inference that would be very wide the mark.

7. For indications of how easily these influences lend themselves to overstatement, see

Isaac T. Hecker, "Two Prophets of This Age," *Catholic World*, XLVII (1888), 684, and Geo. W. Cooke, *An Historical and Biographical Introduction to Accompany the Dial*, I, 1–12.

8. *Journals*, IV, 256 (July 19, 1837); see also VII, 69–70 (1845).

9. *Works*, III, 233.

10. Cabot, *Memoir*, I, 289, 290–91.

11. *Journals*, IV, 286.

12. *Ibid*, VII, 329 (Sept., 1847).

13. That he considered the tradition of books noble requires no further substantiation than a perusal of the essay on "Books." Holmes's collation (based on the published writings of Emerson) of 3,393 named references, relating to 868 different authors, is indicative of the regard in which Emerson held books (Holmes's *Writings*, Riverside ed., 14 vols., Boston & N.Y., 1906, XI, 295). If to these are added those found in the *Journals* and in writings of Emerson that have appeared since Holmes made his count, the first number would easily be quadrupled, and the latter doubled. This revised count (as made in this study) shows that some names (Napoleon, for instance) should be moved down, while others (Luther, Milton, Goethe, Carlyle, and Coleridge, for example) should be moved up in the scale.

14. *Journals*, VIII, 528 (Feb. 25, 1855); see also II, 249 (1830); IV, 8 (Jan. 24, 1836); and O. B. Frothingham, *George Ripley* (Boston, 1882), pp. 266–68.

15. *Journals*, VIII, 528 (Feb. 28, 1855). "Only the inventor . . . knows how to borrow," he wrote in his *Journal*, III, 143 (Dec. 24, 1834). A good key to the Emersonian workshop is furnished by the essay on "Quotation and Originality," where he says, among other things: "Original power is usually accompanied by assimilative power, and we value in Coleridge his excellent knowledge and quotation perhaps as much, possibly more, than his original suggestions . . . . Next to the originator of a good sentence is the first quoter of it . . . . Genius borrows nobly . . . . The nobler the truth or sentiment, the less imports the question of authorship. It never troubles the simple seeker from whom he derived such and such a sentiment." And to illustrate his point, he quoted someone without attribution, on quotation: "It is," he added, "no more according to Plato than according to me."—*Works*, VIII, 190–93; see also *Journals*, X, 218–22.

16. *Journals*, II, 441. "Whoever expresses to us a just thought," said Emerson, "makes ridiculous the pains of the critic who should tell him where such a word has been said before" (*Works*, VIII, 192). Critics and scholars alike were sometimes cavalierly handled by Emerson. The scholar, he said, has often to run to his books for the answer to the simplest question (*Journals*, III, 557), and the critic too often bores into books merely that he may bore (V, 562). Yet questions regarding sources and origins troubled him: the idea of being dependent at all was a disquieting thought. Twenty years after he published *Nature*, he set down in his journal what seems to have given him some satisfaction: "My son is coming to get his Latin lessons without me. And I am coming to do without me. My son is coming to do without Plato, or Goethe, or Alcott."—*Journals*, IX, 37 (1856).

17. *Ibid.*, II, 447 (Jan. 9, 1832); see also III, 418–19 (Dec. 28, 1834), X, 382 (1872), and esp. Cabot, *Memoir*, I, 290–91, for Emerson's indifference to the relative antiquity or modernity of a truth.

18. *Journals*, IV, 23–24 (Mar. 14, 1936). Charges of plagiarism he was inclined to minimize or ignore altogether, saying, "The very plagiarism to which scholars incline (and it is often hard to acknowledge a debt) arises out of the community of Mind."—*Ibid.*, IV, 131 (Oct. 29, 1836). See also III, 363, and IV, 171.

19. "He borrowed from everybody and every book," wrote his friend Holmes, "not in any stealthy or shamefaced way, but proudly, royally, as a king borrows from one of his attendants the coin that bears his own image and superscription."—Holmes, *Emerson*, p. 221. This observation harmonizes with Emerson's own statement: "Rather let me be 'a pagan suckled in a creed outworn' than cowardly deny and conceal one particle of my debt to Greek art, or poetry, or virtue. Certainly I would my debt were more, but it is my fault, not theirs, if 't is little."—*Journals*, III, 418–19 (Dec. 28, 1834); see also III, 381, and IV, 189–90.

20. "This book," he wrote in January, 1834, "is my Savings Bank. I grow richer because I have somewhere to deposit my earnings; and fractions are worth more to me because corresponding fractions are waiting here that shall be made integers by their addition."—*Journals*, III, 246.

21. Let him who doubts this compare carefully Carlyle's "Novalis" with Emerson's *Nature*.

22. *Journals*, II, 515 (Oct. 1, 1832).

23. A sane treatment of the subject "Emerson and Quakerism" is by Prof. F. B. Tolles, *Amer. Lit.*, X, ii (May, 1938), 142–65.

24. The authority for the statement rests chiefly upon the evidence of the Rev. David Greene Haskins (*Ralph Waldo Emerson: His Maternal Ancestors, with Some Reminiscences of Him*, Boston, 1886, p. 48), to whom, because

Haskins insisted upon Emerson's defining his religious position, Emerson reputedly made the remark. What easier way out of such prying questions and unwelcome demands (behind which Emerson's experience taught him lurked further demands for "arguments" and "reasons" for his beliefs) than to say simply, "I am more of a Quaker than anything else. I believe in the 'still, small voice,' and that voice is the Christ within us." One remembers that he had put off Henry Ware's questions in the same way.

25. That Emerson read Fox and that he maintained cordial relations with a number of Quakers at various times the diaries and letters of Emerson show; but he steered clear of subscribing to Quakerism or of identifying himself with the sect. Quakerism, like Catholicism, both attracted and repulsed him. In "The Problem," Emerson professed to be allured by the vest of the cowled churchman, but he could not have endured it on himself. Just as his innate Protestantism prevented his acceptance of Catholicism, so his inbred Puritanism and ingrained Unitarianism found something Quakerish in Quakerism that he could not accept. Zealotry and fanaticism were popularly identified in New England tradition with the disciples of John Fox, and it will be recalled that during the period of his struggle to come to terms with himself and his congregation regarding certain rites and ceremonies, Emerson carefully searched himself to make sure he was not "sticking at gnats" and otherwise acting "Quakerish." When he finally came actively in contact with a family of Quakers at New Bedford, he commented at length on some of their customs, but concluded, as if it were a matter of surprise to him, "But many of them are excellent people."—*Letters*, ed. by R. L. Rusk (6 vols., N.Y., 1939), I, 400. See also his letter to Benjamin Peter Hunt, Jan. 23, 1835, in which Emerson asks, "Did you ever meet a *wise Quaker?* They are few." Although he gives these few credit for being "a sublime class of speculators," their religion is one which it is impossible to deny or confirm. He implies that he would prefer more certitude, such as can be found in "those laws of terrible beauty which took the soul of Newton and Laplace and Humboldt."—*Letters*, I, 433. The implications in these comments are fairly obvious and should be borne in mind, for it is easy to mistake mere coincidences for influences.

26. *Journals*, V, 484.

27. H. D. Gray, *Emerson. A Statement of New England Transcendentalism as Expressed in the Philosophy of Its Chief Exponent* (Stanford Univ., 1917), p. 32.

28. *Journals*, X, 300.

29. See Merrell R. Davis, "Emerson's 'Reason' and the Scottish Philosophers," *New England Quar.*, XVII, iii (June, 1944), 209–28.

30. For instance, his brilliant essay on the "Over-Soul"—suggesting, as it does wonderful reaches or insights into the truth to those who have had inspirational experiences or illuminations like Emerson's own, but suggesting little to all those who have not had them—becomes essentially a restatement of the mystic's creed. It identifies Emerson's search for reality with the unexplained and undemonstrable assumption of all mysticism, namely, that the soul perceives truth because it is part of the all-knowing Reality. "How," asked Emerson, in his faltering philosophical way, "can we speak of the action of the mind under any divisions, as of its knowledge, of its ethics, of its works, and so forth, since it melts will into perception, knowledge into act? Each becomes the other. Itself alone is. Its vision is not like the vision of the eye, but is union with the things known" (*Works*, II, 325), whence follows, in Wordsworth's words, "that serene and blessed mood" by which we are laid asleep

In body, and become a living soul:
While with an eye made quiet by the power
Of harmony, and the deep power of joy,
We see into the life of things.

See also the following passages from the "Over-Soul" (*Works*, II, 269–74, 279): "Within man is the soul of the whole; the wise silence; the universal beauty, to which every part and particle is equally related; the eternal *ONE*. And this deep power in which we exist and whose beatitude is all accessible to us, is not only self-sufficing and perfect in every hour, but the act of seeing and the thing seen, the seer and the spectacle, the subject and the object, are one. We see the world piece by piece, as the sun, the moon, the animal, the tree; but the whole, of which these are the shining parts, is the soul. Only by the vision of that Wisdom . . . by yielding to the spirit of prophecy which is innate in every man, we can know what it saith . . . . All goes to show that the soul of man is not an organ, but animates and exercises all organs; is not a function, like the power of memory, of calculation, of comparison, but uses these as hands and feet; is not a faculty, but a light; is not the intellect or the will, but the master of the intellect and the will; is the background of our being, in which they lie;—an immensity possessed and that cannot be possessed . . . . When it breathes through his intellect, it is genius; when it breathes through his will, it is virtue; when it flows through his affection, it is love. And the blindness of the intellect begins when it would be something of it-self . . . . The soul circumscribes all things . . . it contradicts all experience . . . it abolishes time and space . . . . Before the revelations of the soul, Time and Space and Nature shrink away . . . . The soul looketh steadily forwards, creating a world before her, leaving worlds be-hind her. She has no dates, nor rites, nor per-sons, nor specialties nor men. The soul knows only the soul; and the web of events is the flow-ing robe in which she is clothed . . . . The soul is the perceiver and revealer of truth . . . . We know truth when we see it, from opinion, as we know when we are awake that we are awake."

31. "Emerson and Science," *Philol. Quar.*, X, iii (July, 1931), 225–60.

32. It is significant that among his very first efforts at composition are two prize essays, one on Socrates and the other a survey of ethical philosophy, and that among his very latest pub-lished works (and he worked at it for more years than he did on any other of his writings) is his *Natural History of Intellect*. There are, moreover, numerous direct statements in which he sides with the scientist and the philosopher. Some of these will appear in the sequel. Here only one is cited. As early as December 30, 1826, writing to his brothers Charles and Ed-ward, he said what takes on added significance because he mentions Kant specifically: "It cannot be a matter of new speculation to you, —the effect of science on the bulk of mankind. That the effect of successful abstruse inquiries is minute, and for long periods, inappropriate is the burthen of many a sigh. But that in the end Jack and Gill [*sic*] are the better for the painful speculations of Leibnitz and Kant is equally undeniable."—*Letters*, I, 181.

33. "Plato," *Works*, IV, 47–48.

34. "Nature," *Works*, I, 66.

35. Already during his college days he was convinced that "of all sciences the science of the Mind is necessarily the most worthy and elevating." "But," he added, "it cannot pre-cede the others."—*Journals*, I, 59 (1820).

36. *Works*, I, 47–48.

37. "The uniform effect of culture on the human mind [is] not to shake our faith in the reality of particular phenomena, as of heat, water, azote; but to lead us to regard nature as phenomenon, not a substance; to attribute nec-essary existence to spirit; to esteem nature as an accident and an effect."—*Works*, I, 48–49.

38. Cabot (*Memoir*, II, 78) quotes a letter from Emerson to Margaret Fuller, in which Emerson recalls the joy with which "in my boyhood I caught the first hint of the Berke-leyan philosophy, and which I certainly never lost sight of afterwards."

39. *Works*, VIII, 223.

40. *Ibid.*, p. 66.

41. For the years prior to the publication of *Nature*, the following *Journal* references, by years, indicate the insistence with which the problem of dualism engaged his mind: I (1820), 59–60, 63–64; (1822), 98–99, 112, 127, 133, 134, 147–48, 155–56, 164, 167–69, 183–84, 186–87, 188–90, 199; (1823), 209, 216, 221–22, 225–26, 228–29, 238–39, 250–52, 258, 290–91, 301, 312, 313, 324; (1824), 345, 348–49, 361, 378–79; II (1826), 104–5; (1827), 145, 159–60, 167–68, 173, 217, 223–24; (1828), 230–31, 237; (1829), 269, 273; (1830), 288, 290–91, 304, 310, 317, 320–21, 323, 324, 334, 338, 341, 342, 343–44, 347–50; (1831), 357–58, 361, 362, 368, 404, 409, 414, 422, 425, 435, 438; (1832), 445, 478, 490–91; III (1833), 13, 15, 163, 192–93, 196, 199–201, 207, 210, 212, 213, 223, 224, 226, 227, 228, 235–37; (1834), 253–54, 267–68, 272–73, 274, 275, 283' 284, 288, 290–97, 305–6, 307, 308–9, 310–11, 314, 323, 324, 326–27, 330, 341–42, 343, 349, 352, 353, 362, 377, 381, 388–90, 392, 393, 397–98, 415, 416, 422–23; (1835), 452, 455, 467, 468, 488, 489–90, 492, 495, 500, 512–14, 517, 525–28, 529, 539; IV (1836), 12–14, 59–61, 65, 67–68, 71, 76, 78, 92–94, 115–19, 121, 126–29.

42. *Journals*, I, 209–11. See also II, 137–38 (Dec. 12, 1826). The origin of this conviction can be traced back in the *Journals* to July 13, 1822 (I, 162–63); see also I, 186–87 (Nov. 1, 1822). Even earlier, in his second Bowdoin prize essay, on "The Present State of Ethical Philosophy" (1821), he had declared: "Morality is constituted the rule by which the world must stand."—E. E. Hale, *Ralph Waldo Emerson, Together with Two Early Essays by Emerson* (Boston, 1904), p. 133; see also pp. 132, 134, 135.

43. *Journals*, I, 78 (Mar. 14, 1821); see also I, 82.

44. See the references cited above. The more he contemplated the problem, the more he be-came convinced of its inscrutability, even to saying, "The Platonist . . . did not widely err who proclaimed the existence of two warring principles, the incorruptible mind, and the mass of malignant matter."—*Journals*, I, 148 (June 10, 1822).

45. *Journals*, I, 155 (June, 1822).

46. *Ibid.*, II, 178 (Mar. 11, 1827).

47. *Ibid.*, p. 289 (Feb. 3, 1830); see also the earlier interchange of letters between himself and Aunt Mary, some of which are printed in Rusk's *Life* and *Letters*.

48. *Journals*, I, 290–91 (Oct., 1823), 361 (Apr. 18, 1824), 29 (1824); II, 124 (Oct., 1826), 298 (June 2, 1830), 456 (Jan. 26, 1832).

49. *Ibid.*, II, 132 (1826), 191–94 (1827).

50. *Ibid.*, pp. 155–56 (1827), 161 (1827), 183 (Apr. 6, 1827), 185–91 (1827).

51. The number in parentheses following the name indicates the number of references to be found in Emerson's *Journals, Letters,* and *Works* to writers with whom he occupied himself most intently chiefly during the twenties and thirties. The numbers are only approximately indicative of Emerson's interests, since no distinction in the count is made, in the case of Plato, for example, between a passing reference to him and a quotation from him, or between a passage of a page or two and a full-length essay like "Plato" in *Representative Men.* In view of the very incomplete indexes to the ten volumes of printed *Journals* and the twelve-volume Centenary edition of his *Works,* it is unfortunate that space does not permit giving full volume and page references instead of these summary figures. I have on file the complete references and shall be glad, insofar as I may be able, to supply them to interested students of Emerson. These references are also recorded on the first manuscript draft of this book, deposited in the University of Wisconsin Library. Since these counts were made, Kenneth W. Cameron's genetic studies have appeared. His *Ralph Waldo Emerson's Reading* (Raleigh, 1941) is especially suggestive in this connection.

52. For Emerson's relation to Swedenborg see the several studies by Clarence P. Hotson, conveniently located by referring to Lewis Leary, *Articles on American Literature Appearing in Current Periodicals, 1920–1945* (Durham, N.C., 1947), pp. 52–53.

53. Not specifically named. During the twenties Emerson's knowledge of German theological research was derived almost wholly from secondary sources.

54. See *Journals,* I, 188 (Nov. 16, 1822), 209–11 (Jan. 11, 1823); II, 137 (Dec. 16, 1826).

55. *Ibid.*, I, 78 (1821).

56. *Ibid.*, p. 379 (May 2, 1824). There were times when he could say, "Plato, thou reasonest well, but Christ and his Apostles infinitely better,—not through thy fault, but through their inspiration," only to conclude, a little later: "We know that all speculation . . . . pushed to an extreme is inconclusive and idle, for the nature of matter, as of mind, is buried in inscrutable night, and that we are fools to fear Matter when we do not know that there is any such thing."—*Ibid.*, pp. 382–83 (1824); II, 105 (June 15, 1826).

57. See, for example, *ibid.*, II, 158–59 (Jan., 1827).

58. *Ibid.*, p. 165 (Jan. 30 [?], 1827).

59. *Ibid.*, I, 360.

60. *Ibid.*, p. 361 (Apr. 18, 1824). Far from being sure of his ground, he was nevertheless resolved to follow the overpowering inner urge to assume the ministry. Very probably the decision of his brother William (gone to study theology in Germany) to forsake divinity and thus reject the family calling, even against the advice of Goethe (who had counseled him to master his scruples rather than disappoint the hopes of his family)—very probably this circumstance strengthened his determination to study divinity. Certainly his family, his mother most of all, would be disappointed if not one of her sons followed the traditional calling.

Although there is no reference to the effect in the early journals, we cannot be far wrong in surmising that the practical and worldly advice of the old Goethe to William Emerson struck his younger, intensely idealistically-minded brother Waldo forcibly and unfavorably. This first disappointment in Goethe as a moralist was recalled later when he undertook to read Goethe's works; it predisposed him to accord Goethe only his "qualified admiration." —See *Letters,* I, 160–62, where are printed portions of William's account of his visit to Goethe in 1824.

61. *Journals,* II, 158–59 (Jan., 1827). Obviously neither Scottish common sense nor Platonic idealism was adequate for his purposes.

62. *Ibid.*, p. 162.

63. *Ibid.*, p. 166.

64. *Ibid.*, p. 167 (Feb. 16, 1827).

65. *Ibid.*, p. 173 (Feb., 1827); see also pp. 201–2 (May 5, 1827), 217 (Oct., 1827), 223–24 (Dec. 17, 1827), and so forth.

66. It is doubtful, for example, whether Emerson, after he had caught the light from Coleridge and Kant, would have been able to "love and honour" Prince Napoleon Achille Murat, "the intrepid doubter" and "consistent Atheist," as frankly and sincerely as he did in 1827, or allowed his arguments to go unchallenged.

67. *Journals,* I, 83; II, 129, 164; *Letters,* I, 104.

68. *Letters,* I, 149 (Sept. 12, 1824).

69. *Ibid.*, pp. 154–55 (Nov. 20, 1824).

70. *Ibid.*, pp. 149–50 (Sept. 12, 1824).

71. *Ibid.*, p. 152.

72. *Ibid.*, pp. 76, 78, 84; VI, 254–57; *Works,* X, 330–35.

73. *Letters,* I, 84, 114, 127, 134, 135.

74. *Ibid.*, p. 306 (Mar., 1819).

75. That is, all but the "Ode on Intimations of Immortality." See *Journals,* II, 105–10 (June 30, 1826). The very interesting manner in which Emerson proceeded from a critical, sometimes almost abusive, attitude to a sincere appreciation of Wordsworth can be studied by referring

to the indexes of the *Journals, Letters*, and *Works*; see also Townsend Scudder, *The Lonely Wayfaring Man* (London and N.Y., 1936), pp. 29–30; C. J. Woodbury, *Talks with Ralph Waldo Emerson* (London, 1890), pp. 44–46; and Cameron, *op. cit.*, pp. 50 (1828), 39 (1858), 40 (1869), 42 (1872).

76. Although Emerson had withdrawn *Biographia Literaria* from the Harvard Library as early as November 16, 1826 (Cameron, *op. cit,*. p. 46), the *Aids to Reflection* is first mentioned in the *Journals* on October 9, 1829. See also *Letters*, I, 291 (Jan. 4, 1830), where Emerson speaks of reading "Coleridge's Friend—with great interest; Coleridge's 'Aids to Reflection' with yet deeper; Degerando, Hist. Comparée des Systèmes de Philosophie, I am beginning on the best recommendation."

77. *Journals*, II, 278–79 (Dec. 13, 1829).

78. The question which may be raised at this point regarding whether Plato taught a dualistic or monistic philosophy is beside the point; for Emerson, following Thomas Taylor's translation and more particularly the interpretation as given by Plotinus and Proclus, interpreted Plato through their eyes and regarded his philosophy as plainly dualistic. On this point Emerson's direct statements, made at the time under consideration, leave no doubt, however he came to interpret Plato in later years. To be sure, Jowett's translation (1871) came to his shelves, but too late to wield any considerable influence.

79. Emerson's turn from Platonic to German idealism is here referred to as a repudiation of Platonism, even in the face of the impassioned gratulation accorded to Plato in the essay on Plato in *Representative Men* (written *ca.* 1846), where Plato is made synonymous with philosophy, and philosophy with Plato (*Works*, IV, 40). But this discourse is the product of Emerson the lecturer, in which capacity he often allowed himself the luxury of superlatives for the sake of emphasis. Moreover, *Representative Men* was produced at a time when Emerson had, indeed, turned back from Kant to Plato (see below). Consider also the essay on Swedenborg, where the Swedish philosopher looms as "a colossal soul," second almost to none; whereas in the privacy of his journals, Emerson speaks of Swedenborgianism as "one of the many forms of Manicheism," denying "the omnipotence of God or pure spirit" and as introducing "unnecessary machinery" (*Journals*, V, 80, 110). So, too, for Plato. However hard Emerson tried to elevate Plato beyond the reach of man, he had in the end to record, in the privacy of his diary, that Plato was but the "great Average Man" (*ibid.*, p. 369). Plato is similarly designated in *Representative Men*, but the phrase as used there

carries a sense of approbation which it does not possess in the context of the *Journals*, where it carries a connotation of criticism. Believing as Emerson did in the cumulative progress of the mind of man, he observed that it would be unnatural, indeed, if Plato, living ages before Kant, had made discoveries that remained unknown to his successor. On April 16, 1835, in the very midst of his most intensive study of the Kantian distinctions and their application, he paused to record this question and answer: "Plato had a secret doctrine,—had he? What secret can he conceal from the eye of Montaigne, of Bacon, of Kant?" (*Ibid.*, III, 468). By his own theory, never held more firmly than at this time, that he who lives last stands the best chance to know most, it followed that Kant, who "climbed from round to round the steps of the mysterious ladder which is the scale of metaphysical powers," might well have outstripped Plato, as well as Montaigne and Bacon, in the race for knowledge and wisdom.—*Ibid.*, X, 461 (1876).

80. Cabot, *Memoir*, I, 131.

81. *Ibid.*, pp. 140–42.

82. *Ibid.*, pp. 147–48.

83. Feb. 8, 1832; see *Journals*, II, 356.

84. *Ibid.*, pp. 356–57 (Feb. 13, 1831).

85. *Ibid.*, pp. 357–58 (Feb. 23, 1831).

86. The journals and letters contain only one earlier reference to Reason and Understanding. This occurs on September 7, 1822 (*Journals*, I, 167–68), but the two terms are there used indiscriminately and not at all in the Coleridge–Kantian sense that he began to grasp about 1831. Though he was, in 1822, as poignantly aware of the irreconcilable elements of the Platonic dualism on which he had been nurtured as he was in 1831, when he was making some progress toward effecting a reconciliation, his uncertain allegiance before 1829 to Platonic idealism on the one hand and to Scottish common sense on the other, blinded him to the importance of the distinction until Coleridge opened his eyes.

87. *Cambr. Hist. Engl. Lit.*, XVIII, 7.

88. Besides using Madame de Staël's *Germany*, Stewart's *Dissertations*, and De Gerando's *Histoire Comparée*, Emerson frequently found it more convenient, rather than go to original sources, to read such compilations as the following: *The Library of Useful Knowledge* (see *Journals* for 1832–34), the *American Encyclopaedia* (see *ibid.*, II, 460–61; III, 252, 517; IV, 101), Cousin's translation of Tennemann's *Grundriss der Geschichte der Philosophie* (*ibid.*, II, 451; III, 240), Linberg's translation of Cousin's *Introduction to the History of Philosophy*, Barchou de Penhoen's *Histoire de la philosophie allemande depuis Leibnitz jusqu'à Hegel* (*ibid.*,

VI, 142–45), Müller's *Universal History*, (*ibid.*, III, 572; IV, 94, 378, 381), Mary Somerville's *Mechanism of the Heavens*, and elementary surveys of chemistry, geology, and botany, as well as popularly written accounts of scientific expeditions and voyages. In 1868 he said, "Ah, what a blessing to live in a house which has on the ground-floor one room or one cabinet in which a Worcester's Unabridged; a Liddell and Scott; an Andrews and Stoddard; Lemprière's Classical; a '*Gradus Ad Parnassum*'; a Haydn's *Dictionary of Dates*; a Biographie Générale; a Spier's French, and Flügel's German Dictionary, even if Grimm is not yet complete . . . are always at hand."—*Journals*, X, 261.

Bred of the same motive that sent him to encyclopaedias was his preference for translations to the necessity of acquiring foreign languages: "The cheap press and the universal reading, which have come in together, have caused a great many translations to be made from the Greek, the German, the Italian, and the French. Bohn's Library now furnishes me with a new and portable Plato, as it had already done with new Goethes: and John Carlyle translates Dante. To me the command is loud to use the time by reading these books, and I should as soon think of foregoing the railroad and the telegraph as to neglect these books." —*Journals*, VIII, 34–35.

89. Probably *A General View of the Progress of Metaphysical, Ethical, and Political Philosophy, since the Revival of Letters* (Boston, 1822). "It saves," said Emerson, "a world of reading by laying open the history and moral and intellectual philosophy since the Revival of Letters . . . . It is a beautiful abridgment of the thousand volumes of Locke, Leibnitz, Voltaire, Kant and the rest."—*Journals*, I, 289–90; see a similar statement in *Letters*, I, 225.

90. He continued naively to concern himself with Madame de Staël's superficial volume even after he had, on his own account, gone on to better commentators and to a firsthand acquaintance with German art and thought. Here, as elsewhere, he displayed something of the child's fondness for the thing which it has known longest and knows best.

91. First mentioned in the *Journals*, II, 279 (1829). See also II, 283, 327–28.

92. *Journals*, II, 330–45; see also *Letters*, I, 290, 306.

93. Chiefly early Greek philosophy.

94. Through De Gerando, he turned to Anquetil-Duperron, and thus learned something about Zoroaster and Confucius. See *Journals*, II, 333–35.

95. The influence of Cousin on Emerson was very transitory. He soon put aside Cousin's "pompous eclecticism" as less worthy of consideration than Coleridgean transcendentalism. See *Letters*, I, 123. Similarly Jouffroy, although Emerson had heard him lecture at the Sorbonne in 1833, left him cold. See *Journals*, III, 156, 170.

96. *Journals*, II, 330. See also Cameron, *op. cit.*, pp. 17 (Feb. 1, 1830), 18 (Apr. 6, 1831). Arthur Christy (*The Orient in American Transcendentalism* [N.Y., 1932], p. 278) has searched the records and found that Emerson drew Volumes I and II of De Gerando's *Histoire* (Paris, 1804, 4 vols., 2097 pp.) from the Boston Athenaeum on January 11, 1830, and Volume IV on February 1 of the same year. On April 6, 1831, he again drew De Gerando's work from the library, but there is no indication of the volume or volumes withdrawn.

97. *Journals*, II, 330–32 (Oct. 27, 1830); see also *Works*, IV, 117, V, 240, and *Journals*, IV, 118–19 (Nov. 4, 1838).

98. See *Journals*, II, 317 (Nov. 3, 1830).

99. *Journals*, II, 362 (Mar. 4, 1831).

100. See *Journals*, II, 330 (Oct. 27, 1830).

101. Herein lay the germ of his discontent with what he considered outmoded and outgrown forms and observances in the church. See Cabot, *Memoir*, I, 160.

102. Among characteristic diary entries recording examples that support this belief are the following: *Journals*, II, 368, 377–78, 387, 404, 415, 422, 435; III, 445.

103. Bacon is mentioned altogether eighty-eight times in the *Journals*, *Letters*, and *Works*.

In the following list the number in parenthesis represents the number of references counted. The method of counting is the same as that used in the list above.

104. As in the case of the names enumerated earlier, exact volume and page references are on file and available to interested students.

105. Emerson was familiar with the general significance of Darwin's *Origin of Species* as early as February 5, 1860, when he professed, in a letter to his wife, written from Lafayette, Ind., his chagrin at his inability to obtain a copy of "Darwin on Species . . . which I had depended on as a road book . . . . It has not arrived in these dark lands" (*Letters*, V, 195). On the same western journey, in Cincinnati, Emerson delighted Moncure D. Conway by "talking over with me the great discovery of Darwin."—Conway, *Autobiography, Memories and Experiences* (2 vols., Boston, 1904), I, 282. By May, 1860, he was discussing species with Agassiz and Thoreau. See *Journals*, IX, 270; also *Letters*, VI, 63 (Mar. 16, 1869). As a diligent amateur reader of scientific treatises, Emerson was, of course, familiar with pre-Darwinian

speculations on evolution, and his journals contain a number of anticipatory statements of the general idea of Darwinian development. See *Journals*, IV, 303–4 (Oct., 2, 1837) *et seq.*; see also *Journals*, IX, 270 (1860); X, 344 (1870), 423 (1873); *Letters*, V, 195 (1860), VI, 63 (1869), VI, 195 (1871); and *Works*, VIII, 7 ff.; and Joseph W. Beach, "Emerson and Evolution," *Univ. of Toronoto Quar.*, III, iv (July, 1934), 474–97.

106. Among other influential authors whom Emerson consulted in the succeeding years—including scientists, travelers, men of letters, philosophers, historians, economists, sociologists—are to be listed the following (arranged roughly in the order of the first appearance of their names in Emerson's journal and letters): Robert Owen (10), Dr. Spurzheim, the phrenologist (13), Leonhard Euler (13), Erasmus (2), F. A. Wolff (6), Winckelmann (14), Diderot (8), Oegger (3), Johannes von Müller's *Universal History* (7), Jacob Boehme (19), De Condelle (3), Joseph Black (2), Thomas Paine (2), Cobbett (3), Niebuhr (17), Heeren (16), Everard Home (2), Robert Leighton (1), John Ross's *Voyages* (1), Bartram's *Travels* (1), O'Connell's *South Sea Islands* (5), Richard Bentley (6), Champollion (1), Capt. James Cook's *Voyages* (3), McClelland's *Geology* (1), Leyden (1), Spinoza (8), Bell's *Bridgewater Treatise on the Hand* (4), R. Bacon (6), Proclus (19), James Bruce's *Travels* (1), Belzoni's *Pyramids* (5), Caillaud's *Travels* (2), von Ranke (1), Fourier (22), Lorenz Oken (10), Strauss (4), Lieber (3), Herbert Spencer (3), Wm. Hamilton (4), Edward Forbes (7), Wm. Buckland (4), Robert Brown (2), Wm. Spence (1), Emmanuel V. Scherb (5), J. B. Stallo (3), Liebig (2), Mülder (3), Oersted (1), Berthollet (2), Renan (3), Schopenhauer (2), J. H. Stirling (16), Comte (1), H. James (9), Wm. James (2), James McCosh (1), Tyndall (3), Hendrik Steffens (1), and Haüy (2).

107. See the editors' remarks in *Journals*, II, 365; also III, 17–18 (Jan. 15, 1835).

108. As early as 1827 he had deplored, as one of the "Peculiarities of the Present Age," men's cultivation of "the knowledge of anecdotes . . . instead of systematic pursuit of science" (*Journals*, I, 164). In 1834, he recognized his "own time" as "the era of science," and believed that "the benefits thence derived to the arts and to civilization are signal and immense." See Cabot, *Memoir*, II, 712, Appendix F, containing an abstract of the lecture on the "Naturalist," May 7, 1834; also "Progress of Culture," *Works*, VIII, 221. It is significant that on February 1, 1832, in advising his wife's young cousin, Elizabeth Tucker, on a course of reading, he should have included, in a list of twenty-seven titles,

three novels, five historical works, five religious books, six volumes of poetry, and eight scientific books. Two years later, writing to his brother William, he said: "Did you ask me what I am doing? I have written three lectures on Natural History and of course reading as much geology, chemistry and physics as I could find."—*Letters*, I, 404.

109. At the age of seventeen, Emerson observed: "With regard . . . to the study of Natural Philosophy, I do not think any one study so contributes to expand the mind as our first correct notions of this science."—*Journals*, I, 60. In his seventieth year, he confessed: "If absolute leisure were offered me, I should run to the college or scientific school which offered the best lectures on Geology, Chemistry, Minerals, Botany."—*Journals*, X, 393 (Aug. 31, 1872).

110. *Indoor Studies* (Boston, 1904), p. 80.

111. M. D. Conway, *Emerson at Home and Abroad*, p. 335; see also Conway, "Transcendentalists of Concord," *Fraser's Mag.*, LXX, cccxvi (Aug., 1864), 257.

112. It is a mistake to assume that Thoreau was solely responsible for Emerson the naturalist. Although Thoreau helped make a better botanist of his friend than he had been before his contacts with the captain of huckleberrying parties, Emerson the poet-naturalist was already well formed in 1833, when Thoreau was just setting off for college. Returned from Europe, where his visits to the Parisian museums and his attendance upon the lectures of the leading scientists of France had helped inspire him to write a book on "the Nature of Things," Emerson divided his time between writing lectures for a livelihood and attuning his soul to nature. His efforts to peep and botanize are recorded in his observations made at Newton, Mount Auburn, and Roxbury, before his residence in Concord. "Natural History," he told himself on April 27, 1834, "gives *body* to our knowledge. No man can spare a fact he knows. The knowledge of nature is most *permanent*; clouds and grass are older antiquities than pyramids or Athens; then they are *most* perfect."—*Journals*, III, 284.

To Lydia Jackson, who urged Plymouth over Concord as a home, he wrote during his courtship, "I must win you to love it [Concord, where he felt he could indulge his love for nature more freely than at Plymouth] . . . . I am a poet in the sense of a perceiver and a dear lover of the harmonies that are in the soul and in matter, and specially of the correspondence between these and those. A sunset, a forest, a snowstorm, a certain river-view, are more to me than friends, and do ordinarily divide my day with my books . . . . Now Concord is only one of a hundred towns in which I could find these necessary objects, but Plymouth, I fear, is not one. Plymouth is streets."—Cabot, *Memoir*, I, 236–37.

Yes, indeed, if he would write a *De Rerum Natura*, he must live close to nature and learn her secrets.

113. The more significant passages in the *Journals*, beginning with 1833, are the following: III, 17–18, 118, 129, 170, 173, 175, 180, 187, 190–92, 192–93, 194–96, 225–26, 226–28, 246 (1833), 247, 270–71, 290–91, 292–96, 296–97, 298, 299–300, 304–5, 305–7, 343, 393 (1834), 482, 513–14, 518–19, 559 (1835); IV, 12–14, 17, 21–22, 27, 32–33, 59–60, 90–95, 115, 122, 129–31, 131, 146, 149, 169 (1836), 187, 201–2, 294, 303–4, 311–12, 353, 377–78 (1837); V, 12, 92–94 (1838), 463–64, 473 (1840), 506–7; VI, 143 (1841), 246 (1842), 428, 462 (1843), 490, 529, 532 (1844); VII, 51–52, 58, 69–70, 104 (1845), 190, 312 (1846), 415, 420–22, 558 (1848); VIII, 9, 19, 32, 49–51, 57–58 (1849), 91, 105, 139 (1850), 177, 208, 214, 249, 252 (1851), 406, 412–13, 419–20 (1853), 465 (1854), 505, 525, 536, 546, 565 (1855); IX, 30–33, 43–44, 59–60 (1856), 106–8, 112–13, 123–25, 129, 134, 138 (1857), 155 (1858), 278 (1861), 440 (1862), 520–21 (1863); X, 60–61, 65–66 (1864), 103, 123, 134, 136–37, 139–40, 164, 169 (1866), 204–5, 211, 219 (1867), 238, 264–65 (1868), 283, 284–87, 298–302 (1869), 363–64, 366–67 (1871), 393, 422–23 (1873), 455 (1861–1872), 462 (1876); see also *Letters*, I, 389–91 (1833), 401–5 (1834); II, 41 (1836), 138–41, 164–65 (1838); IV, 46–51, 70, 87 (1848); VI, 63 (1869), as well as "Life and Letters in New England," *Works*, X, 328–39. For some indication of Emerson's concern with science before 1833, see such typical passages in the *Journals* as I, 324–27 (1827); II, 362 (1831) and 488 (1832).

114. See, for example, the emphasis placed upon the transcendentalist's concern with nature and science by Carlyle in his essay on Novalis.

115. *Works*, I, 329, 330, 332–33. See also *Journals*, IV, 12 (Feb. 12, 1836): "The idealist regards matter scientifically; the sensualist exclusively. The physical sciences are only well studied when they are explored for ideas . . . I have no hatred of the round earth and its gray mountains. I see well enough the sand-hill opposite my window. I see with as much pleasure as another a field of corn or a rich pasture, whilst I dispute their absolute being. Their phenomenal being I no more dispute than I do my own. I do not dispute, but point out the just view of viewing them." See further, *ibid.*, IV, 13–14, and *Works*, I, 47–49, 59, 62–63.

116. *Works*, I, 340. For other significant references to Kant, see *Journals*, II, 526 (Oct. 28, 1832), 529 (Nov. 12, 1832); III, 199 (Sept. 8, 1833), 468 (Apr. 16, 1835); IV, 256 (July 19, 1837), 456 (May 24, 1838), 473 (June 12, 1838); V, 306 (Oct. 28, 1839); VI, 143 (1841), 482 (Dec. 31, 1843); VII, 152 (1846); VIII, 210 (1851), 255 (1851), 530 (Feb. 24, 1855), 543 (1855); IX, 294 (1860), 349 (1861), 520 (1863); X, 52–53 (1864), 211 (1867), 224 (1867), 455 (1862–1863), 461 (1862–1863); *Works*, I, 339; II, 287, 343; VII, 27; VIII, 131; X, 92, 328, 455, 461; *Letters*, I, 181 (Dec. 30, 1826), 273 (July ? 15 ? 1829), 412–13 (May 31, 1834); II, 135 (May 24, 1838); III, 243 (Feb. 26, 1844); IV, 104 (Mar. 3, 1870). Among references to Kant not printed in the published *Journals*, see MS Journals, "AC. 1859," p. 218, and "LN. 1866," p. 279. See also C. J. Woodbury, *op. cit.*, p. 109.

117. *Works*, X, 338. Thus Goethe became "the interpreter between the real and the apparent world."—*Letters*, II, 202–3 (June 7, 1839).

118. See the extended quotations in *Journals*, II, 348–51, and the following more important references to Goethe during the period from 1830 to 1840: II, 330, 348–51 (1830), 502, 511, 524, 529–30, 541 (1832); III, 66, 71, 113, 147, 182, 241 (1833), 247, 251–53, 263, 273, 279, 284, 293–95, 299, 302, 309–10, 313–15, 363, 371–72, 385, 428 (1834), 453, 462, 464, 474, 477, 503 (1835); IV, 16–18, 27, 28, 31, 34, 37, 72, 79, 81, 90, 94, 99, 115–17, 157, 174 (1836), 187, 194, 199, 201–2, 213, 217–22, 224, 225, 324, 383 (1837), 452, 468; V, 17, 45, 57, 59–60, 109, 112–13, 133, 145, 153, 154 (1838), 222 (1839), 294–95, 502 (1840). For subsequent references, see V, 506 (1841); VI, 249 (1842), 466 (1843), 514, 544–45 (1844); VII, 77 (1845), 176 (1846), 280–83, 291–92, 303, 329 (1847); VIII, 16, 35, 39–70, 77 (1849), 90–92 (1850), 169, 245, 249 (1851), 489, 501 (1854); IX, 20, 24, 37 (1856), 212–13 (1859), 314 (1861), 471 (1862); X, 177 (1866), 300 (1869), 423 (1873). See also the early letters in the *Carlyle-Emerson Correspondence*, esp. I, 29 ff., 311; *Letters*, I, 161–62, n. 11 (1825), 254 (1828), 305 (1830), 354, 358 (1832), 373 (1833), 425–26 (1834); II, 32–33 (1836), 57, 68, 70–71, 72, 76–77, 88, 100 (1837), 135, 136, 164 (1838), 192, 197, 202–3, 208, 220, 222, 228, 236 (1839), 305, 315, 368 (1840), 425–26, 436, 445, 451 (1841); III, 43, 73, 83, 108–9 (1842), 220, n. 408 (1843), 279, 285–86, 304, 306 (1845), 336, 359 (1846); IV, 46 (1848), 257 (1851), 488–89 (1855); V, 205, 230 (1860); VI, 190 (1871); *Works*, III, 55; IV, 261–91 (esp. 273–75), 295–96, 366–78; V, 4; VII, 323; IX, 377; X, 328, 338, 342; XII, 284–85; Cameron, *op. cit.*, pp. 47 (Dec. 5, 1828), 19 (Aug. 13, Aug. 16, and Aug. 20, 1832), 22 (Feb. 28, 1835), 49 (Mar. 14, 1849), 26 (Jan. 7,

1851), 33 (Feb. 21, 1861), 41 (Apr. 25, 1870); O. W. Holmes, *Emerson*, pp. 60–61; and F. B. Wahr, *Emerson and Goethe* (Ann Arbor, Mich., 1915), esp. pp. 67–76.

119. To Convers Francis Emerson confessed on April 24, 1837: "I think he must be a very strong or a very weak man who can read his [Goethe's] books with impunity, without feeling their influence in all his speculation. Then there is something gigantic about the man, measure him how you will; his field of thought is immense; his acquisitions right German in their variety and thoroughness, and his point of view always commanding. But I will not start such a lion in the corner of a note, but keep this game for the time when I see you."—*Letters*, II, 72.

120. Emerson borrowed from the Harvard College Library Volume III of Goethe's *Werke* (probably in the Stuttgart-Tübingen edition) on December 5, 1828 (*Letters*, I, 305, n. 59). By June 27, 1830, he had read Francis L. Gower's translation of *Faust* (London, 1823). See *Letters*, I, 305. An item in *Journals*, IV, 17, indicates that by February 28, 1836, he had acquired the forty-volume Stuttgart-Tübingen, 1827–1830, edition of Goethe. Other entries in the *Journals* suggest that this forty-volume set may have been acquired as early as 1834. On August 8, 1836, he bought, in Boston, the fifteen volumes of Goethe's *Nachgelassene Werke* (Stuttgart and Tübingen, 1832–1833). In 1840 he boasted to Carlyle of having fifty-five volumes of Goethe and of having "contrived to read almost every volume." "But," he added, "I have read nothing else [presumably in the German language] . . . I have not looked even into Goethe for a long time."—*Carlyle-Emerson Correspondence*, I, 311.

121. *Journals*, III, 284 (Apr. 27, 1834), 293–95 (May 3, 1834); IV, 115–17 (Oct. 13, 1836).

122. *Works*, IV, 273–75.

123. *Journals*, V, 154; *Letters*, II, 164 (Sept. 28, 1838).

124. Yet he wrote to Hermann Grimm as late as 1871, "For Goethe I have always an ascending regard."—Wahr, *op. cit.*, p. 77.

125. *Works*, IV, 275. See also IV, 107–9, 261–90; VIII, 7–11; X, 337–38 (where reference is made to the ideal natural philosophy of Schelling and Oken and the metaphysics of Hegel as of a piece with Goethe's theory); and Cabot, *Memoir*, II, 725.

Goethe exerted a definite influence on Emerson's "The Humanity of Science" of 1836—the second in a series of twelve lectures entitled "The Philosophy of History." In it he relates his central thought directly to Goethe, who is credited with having reduced "the plant to a leaf, the animal to a vertebra."—*Ibid.*, II, 725.

He derived this idea from Goethe at least as early as April 27, 1834. See *Journals*, III, 284; also 292–95; IV, 114–17, esp. p. 116.

126. *Journals*, IV, 21–22 (Mar. 11, 1836); also 27 (Mar. 17, 1836), 28–30 (Mar. 21, 1836).

127. *Werke* (55 vols., Stuttgart & Tübingen, 1827–1833), XXII, 245.

128. *Journals*, IV, 28 (Mar. 21, 1836). In succeeding sections, Emerson aped the words and ideas of the passages quoted from Goethe.

129. See Cabot, *Memoir*, I, 154 ff.; also H. H. Clark, *loc. cit.*, p. 236.

130. *Journals*, II, 490–91 (May 26, 1832).

131. *Ibid.*, II, 492 (June 2, 1832).

132. Cabot, *Memoir*, I, 155–56.

133. *Ibid.*, p. 158.

134. *Works*, XI, 1–25; *Letters*, I, 355–57 (Sept. 11, 1832).

135. Although the form and theatricals of *Wilhelm Meister* repel him, he goes on to quote approvingly Schiller to the effect that in this book Goethe "leads a child of nature up from the period of 'Apprenticeship' to that of 'Self production' and leaves him assured on the way to infinite perfection."—*Letters*, I, 354.

136. Cabot, *Memoir*, I, 158.

137. *Ibid.*, p. 173; see also pp. 174, 175.

138. Emerson's first reading of Carlyle appears to date back to October 31, 1827, when he urged his brother William to read "in the last Edin. Rev. XCI p. 185 . . . an account of Richter wh. exactly describes Aunt Mary's style."—*Letters*, I, 218. Five years were to elapse before he learned the author's name. For Carlyle's early vogue in America see Wm. S. Vance, "Carlyle in America before *Sartor Resartus*," *Amer. Lit.*, VII, iv (Jan., 1936), 363–75, and George Kummer, "Anonymity and Carlyle's Reputation in America," *Amer. Lit.*, VIII, iii (Nov., 1936), 297–99.

139. *Journals*, III, 515.

140. *Ibid.*, p. 524.

141. *Ibid.*, pp. 329–30, 350 (1830), 424, 443 (1831), 519, 542 (1832); III, 115, 117, 159, 181–82, 185 (1833) *et seq.*

142. For details, see *Journals*, III, 25–154, and *Letters*, I, 362–86.

143. Paris, for all its spectacular and dazzling sights, held little for him beyond the collections in the museum of natural history. He was restless to be on his way to England and Scotland. For details on his residence in Paris see *Journals*, III, 155–71, and *Letters*, I, 386–91.

144. He had fraternized briefly with Cranch in Rome. See *Journals*, III, 87–88, 90, 97.

145. Had the European tour been made a year earlier, the very name of Carlyle would have been unknown to him. Coleridge was then in the foreground. But in the meantime the

fervor of Carlyle's moral suasion (coming at precisely the time when Emerson stood most in need of moral support) had found a ready reception in Emerson's heart, while the metaphysical abstractions of Coleridge momentarily faded into the background. Eventually, Coleridge won the ascendency (as we shall observe later); but during 1833 Carlyle was more immediately attractive.

146. Everett's lectures that Emerson heard dealt more with German criticism and historical research than with theology or philosophy. See *Works*, X, 330–35, 574.

147. In 1867 Emerson recalled that "Dr. [Nath.] Frothingham, an excellent classical and German scholar, had already made us acquainted, if prudently, with the genius of Eichhorn's theologic criticism. And Professor [Andrews] Norton a little later gave form and method to the like studies in the then infant Divinity School."—*Works*, X, 335.

148. Possibly as early as 1821–1822. See E. E. Hale, *Ralph Waldo Emerson . . .*, p. 100.

149. Cabot, *Memoir*, I, 138; *Journals*, II, 77–78, 83, 117, 143 (1826), 164 (1827), 273 (1829), 289 (1830) *et seq.* See also I, 288 (1822), 335 (1823); II, 33 (1824), 124 (1826).

150. *Journals*, II, 143 (1826), 233 (1828?); IV, 94 (Sept. 23, 1836). Yet, when his address before the Divinity School aroused the spirited Norton-Ripley controversy in 1839, which centered more upon German "infidelity" than upon the Emersonian version of it, Emerson was doubtless a little surprised to find his name linked so prominently with those of Herder, Schleiermacher, and De Wette, on the one hand, and with Cousin and Jouffroy, on the other, as being alike shoots off the parent stem of German philosophy represented by Kant, Fichte, Schelling, and Hegel. The actual connection between Emerson and German theologians like De Wette, Tholuck, and Strauss was, prior to 1838, certainly tenuous. After this date, he could hardly have remained ignorant of them —if for no other reason than that his adversaries forcibly brought them to his attention by their elevating him into the same hierarchy of infidelity and iniquity and insisting upon his descent from them. Although a few among the leadership were well enough informed, the general ignorance among the orthodox clergy of any discriminating knowledge of German theology was profound. The result was that all Germans alike were under suspicion—Herder as much as Strauss, and Schleiermacher only a little less than Hegel.

151. *Journals*, III, 393 (Dec. 14, 1834). An interesting exchange of letters between J. F. Clarke, by now editor of the *Western Messenger*

in Louisville, Ky., and Emerson, while it presents no conclusive evidence, nevertheless prompts conjectures regarding the extent of Emerson's knowledge of Schleiermacher prior to the Norton-Ripley controversy.

Emerson had written to Clarke urging him to publish his two essays on Goethe and Carlyle, written some time earlier and only recently transmitted to him in manuscript form through Eliz. P. Peabody. See Holmes, *Emerson*, pp. 60–61. Clarke replied that the essays had been written in reply to "Mr. Norton's affront on my favorites," but having grown in "self-confidence and self-respect," he preferred to "put back the shaft into the quiver" rather than "launch an arrow at a respectable senior"; for his desire was to "abuse Nortonism instead of Mr. Norton" (*Letters*, I, 425, Jan. 18, 1835). Meanwhile Clarke advanced a counter proposal:

"There is something I wish you to do and that is to write an article about Schleiermacher the German Platonic, Calvinistic, Spinozaic, but wholly original theologian. De Wette says he is the greatest theologian since Calvin and Melanchthon. Neander thinks he makes an epoch. At his death all Berlin was in tears as when the Queen of Prussia died. He was a faithful pastor ministering to the spiritual wants of high and low, rich and poor, one with another. Depth, Clearness, Freedom in thought united with Loftiness, Warmth and Earnestness of Sentiment composed his peculiar character. He spurned equally the shallowness of rationalism and the cant of pietism—he had a soul above it all. His 'lectures to the Educated' which first appeared in the last century made a great and salutary influence in the pool of theology. He sets forth in that the infinite intellectual dignity and moral of the religious principle. His religion was one of power, love and sound mind if any one's. Now if you have read him, pray write something about him in the Examiner—if not read him, and then you will write."—*Letters*, I, 425–26 (Jan. 18, 1835).

Another interesting aspect of this letter is that it first called Emerson's attention to Margaret Fuller: "There is one in your neighborhood (Groton)," writes Clarke," who has drank [*sic*] very deep of the spirit of German literature. I know not whether you are acquainted, though I think you must be somewhat at least with Miss Margaret Fuller. She has translated the Tasso beautifully into English blank verse. Do you see Henry Hedge often? I had a letter from him not long since in which he speaks of going to Bangor."—*Letters*, I, 425.

152. *Journals*, IV, 235 (Dec. 14, 1834).

153. *Journals*, II, 526 (Oct. 28, 1832). Emerson first mentioned Kant's name in a letter

dated December 30, 1826; but it was not until 1832 that his concern with Kant became intense. This interest is partly a reflection of his withdrawal from the Boston Athenaeum, between March 21 and April 3, 1832, of F. A. Nitsch's *General and Introductory View of Professor Kant's Principles Concerning Man, the World, and the Deity* (London, 1796). See Cameron, *op. cit.*, p. 19.

154. *Journals*, II, 422 (Oct. 24, 1831).
155. *Ibid.*, p. 502 (Aug. 11, 1832).
156. *Ibid.*, III, 260 (Aug. 12, 1834).
157. *Ibid.*, p. 393 (Dec. 14, 1834).
158. *Letters*, III, 77 (1842).
159. *Ibid.*, pp. 54, 70–71 (1842).
160. *Journals*, VII, 152 (1846).
161. *Ibid.*, p. 296 (1846).
162. *Ibid.*, VIII, 418 (1853). However, Jacobi is mentioned prominently in "The Transcendentalist" (*Works*, I, 336), which was first delivered as a lecture in January, 1842. Emerson's first real contact with Jacobi, after Madame de Staël's enthusiastic but superficial account of him, doubtless came through Marsh's edition of Coleridge's *Aids* as well as the *Friend*, when he turned to these works late in 1829. On March 24, 1873, he borrowed Volume II of the eight-volume edition of Jacobi's *Werke* (Leipzig, 1812–1825) from the Athenaeum and before returning it a month later (see Cameron, *op. cit.*, pp. 23, 81), copied from it the quotation later incorporated in the essay, "The Transcendentalist." There is nothing to suggest that he again looked into any of Jacobi's works, though he had readily available, of course, such commentators as De Gerando and Tennemann.

163. *Journals*, II, 330 (1830). It is not to be inferred that Emerson read all the German authors listed below, either in the original or in translation. Precisely when and how he acquired competence in the language still involves questions to which only relative answers can be given. What is certain is that this knowledge was acquired between 1828, when he waved aside Hedge's suggestion that he learn the language by saying that since he had managed for so long without it, he could not consider it very important (Cabot, *Memoir*, I, 138), and 1840, when, replying to Carlyle's pointed question whether he read German or not, he said that he had fifty-five volumes of Goethe and had contrived to read nearly all of them (*Carlyle-Emerson Corresp.*, I, 311). Since he added that he had not looked even into Goethe for a long time, it may be presumed that he had learned German some years before—possibly shortly after his visit to Carlyle in 1833. Emerson's observation *à propos* of Margaret Fuller's "five or six lessons in German pronunciation," which she administered

during April and May of 1837, to the effect that it was done "never by my offer and rather against my will each time" (*Journals*, IV, 225), has no necessary bearing on his *reading* knowledge of German at the time. All indications point to the conclusion that he was self-taught in German.

However and wherever he acquired his German, those who persist in raising an eyebrow at Emerson's professed knowledge of Goethe's fifty-five volumes have recently had their answer in the essay by Professor Y. D. Yohannan in *American Literature*, XIV, iv (Jan., 1943), 407–20, on Emerson's translations from the Persian on the basis of the German translations by Baron Joseph von Hammer-Purgstall. It is now established that in his effort to render accurately some seven hundred lines from Hammer-Purgstall's *Diwan von Mohammed Schemsiddin Hafis* (Stuttgart and Tübingen, 1812–1813) and his *Geschichte der schönen Redekünste Persiens mit einer Blüthenlese aus zweihundert persischen Dichtern* (Wien, 1818), Emerson proceeded with such remarkable fidelity to the German before him (he knew no Persian) that Professor Yohannan found it necessary to call attention to only three "significant examples" of mistranslation, one of which is obviously consciously perpetrated (*ibid.*, pp. 409–10).

To be sure, Emerson liked translations, compendia, and short cuts. If he wanted to go to Boston, he preferred crossing the bridge to swimming the Charles River. But he was also wise enough to know that if there were a treasure at the bottom of the river, he had to dive for it. Before he took the plunge, however, he wanted reasonable assurance that there was a treasure, and that he had located the right spot. He detested random, ineffectual effort. Just as he hesitated to follow William to Germany unless he could count his gains, so he refrained from diving into the depths of German until Carlyle, Coleridge, and all the world assured him that it would be worth the effort. Not given to doing things by halves or of misrepresenting his attainments, his profession to Carlyle that he made himself master of Goethe's voluminous writings is neither an idler's nor a liar's boast.

164. *Journals*, II, 330, 350–51 (1830); V, 154 (1837); IX, 349 (1861); X, 196 (1867).

165. *Ibid.*, II, 377–78, 423 (1831), 525–27, 541 (1832); III, 262, 347, 363 (1834); IV, 94 (1836), 357, 383 (1837); VI, 512 (1844); VII, 48 (1845); VIII, 554 (1855); see also *Works*, III, 89; VI, 254; VIII, 185, 329; *Letters*, I, 354, 358 (1832), 413 (1834); II, 57 (1837), 235 (1839), 265, 269, 354, n. 421 (1840); IV, 190 (1850); Cameron, *op. cit.*, pp. 18, 27, 41.

166. References are given above.

167. *Journals*, II, 330, 348–49, 351 (1830); III, 237 (1833), 313–15, 428 (1834); IV, 383 (1837); VII, 151 (1846); *Works*, IV, 280; and Cameron, *op. cit.*, pp. 23, 26, 42.

168. *Journals*, II, 401, 443 (1831); II, 541 (1832); III, 272 (1834); IV, 94 (1836); V, 154 (1838); VI, 138 (1841), 488 (1844); *Works*, III, 46; X, 169; and *Letters*, II, 424–26 (1841); III, 98, 100 (1842), 116 (1843).

169. *Journals*, III, 524, 570, 574 (1835); IV, 421; V, 154 (1838); VI, 142 (1841), 377–78 (1843), 517–18 (1844); VII, 152 (1846), 515 (1848); VIII, 549–51 (1855); *Works*, III, 34, 187; IV, 117, 143; VIII, 277; *Letters*, III, 23, 96 (1842); and MS Journal, "VA. 1862–63," p. 290.

170. *Journals*, III, 451 (1835); IV, 378, 383 (1837); V, 154 (1838); VI, 138, 145 (1841); VIII, 91–92 (1850), 323 (1852); X, 185 (1867); *Letters*, III, 116 (1843); *Works*, VI, 181, 286, 412–13; VII, 202.

171. *Journals*, IV (1836), 383 (1837); *Works*, XII, 325; and Cameron, *op. cit.*, pp. 21, 22, 23, 26, 29, 30, 40.

172. *Journals*, IV, 84, 174 (1836); 378, 383 (1837); 389; V, 154 (1838); VIII, 289 (1852), 524, 552–53, 587 (1855); X, 54–55 (1864); *Letters*, IV, 510 (1855); V, 99 (1858); *Works*, VIII, 43, 282; XI, 299; XII, 95; Cameron, *op. cit.*, pp. 29 (Apr. 1, Apr. 11, 1855), 49 (May 18, 1855).

173. *Journals*, IV, 94, 174 (1836), 17, 26–27; V, 17, 37, 68, 154 (1838); VIII, 106 (1850); *Letters*, II, 154, 158, 174–75 (1838); III, 116 (1843); IV, 185 (1850); *Works*, II, 19–21; VII, 99. Among German historians, Heeren undoubtedly exerted the greatest influence on Emerson's lectures and essays. See *Journals*, V, 68 (1838), and IV, 17 (1838).

174. *Letters*, II, 373 (Dec. 21, 1840).

175. *Journals*, III, 260 (1834); IV, 94, 174 (1836), 473; V, 154 (1838); VI, 62 (1841), 249 (1842); VII, 151 (1846); VIII, 530 (1855); X, 34 (1864), 318 (1870); *Letters*, IV, 24 (1848); *Works*, I, 336; see also *Journals*, III, 250 (Jan. 21, 1834), 259 (Feb. 12, 1834); Cameron, *op. cit.*, p. 34 (Feb. 12, 1863); C. J. Woodbury, *Talks with Emerson*, p. 54; and *Emerson's* MS Journal, "VA. 1862–63," p. 287.

176. *Journals*, II, 422, 443 (1831); III, 466, 503 (1835); IV, 473 (1838); VI, 138 (1841); VII, 143 (1845), 151–52 (1846); VIII, 69, 76–77 (1849), 126, 128 (1850), 506 (1854), 530 (1855); IX, 295 (1861); X, 34, 52–53 (1864), 455 (1862–1872); *Letters*, III, 76–77, 84 (see also *Dial*, III, 280, for Oct., 1842), 98, 100 (1842), 293, 298–99, 303–4 (1845), 343, 345, 346, 363 (1846); VI, 245–46 (1873); *Works*, I, 338; III, 32; V, 242;

VI, 12; VIII, 131; XII, 70, 430; MS Journals, "TU. 1849," p. 22; "ZO. 1856," pp. 98, 154; "GL. 1861, 1862 1863," p. 248; "VA. 1862–63," p. 290.

177. *Journals* II, 502, 542 (1832); VII, 151–52 (1846); VIII, 69, 76 (1849), 530 (1855); IX, 22, 36 (1856); X, 34, 52–53 (1864); 143–44, 177 (1866), 248, 263 (1868), 318, 321, 337 (1870), 423 (1873), 455, 460, 462 (1862–1872); *Works*, II, 343; V, 242; VIII, 131; X, 328, 338; *Letters*, III, 98–99 (1842); IV, 530–31 (1855); V, 421–22 (1865), 521 (1867); VI, 18, 20 (1868), 104 (1870); Cameron, *op. cit.*, p. 37 (Nov. 4, 1865); MS Journals, "TU. 1849," p. 22; "ZO. 1856," p. 182; "AC. 1856," p. 218; "VA. 1862–63," p. 286; and "LN. 1866," p. 248.

178. *Works*, I, 335 (Jan., 1842); *Journals*, VIII, 418 (1853); IX, 254 (1859); also *Works*, I, 336; VI, 191.

179. *Journals*, III, 393 (1834); V, 37, 164 (1838); VI (1841); VII, 32 (1845), 151 (1846); X, 380 (1872), 445 (1875); *Letters*, I, 425–26 (1834); Cameron, *op. cit.*, p. 48 (Sept. 2, 1846, Nov. 8, 1848).

180. See Cameron, *op. cit.*, pp. 22 (May 28, 1835) 26 (Nov. 4, 1845).

181. *Journals*, III, 348, 428 (1834), 505, 531, 575 (1835); IV, 26 (1836), 374 (1837), 408 (1838); V, 154 (1839); *Letters*, I, 450 (1835); II, 347, n. 398; III, 246 (1844); *Works*, X, 337.

182. *Journals*, III, 348, 356 (1834); *Works*, I, 56; V, 252.

183. *Journals*, III, 428 (1834); IV, 378, 383 (1837); *Works*, X, 337; XII, 328.

184. Cameron, *op. cit.*, p. 23 (Apr. 5, 1836).

185. *Ibid.*, p. 23 (Apr. 21, 1836).

186. *Journals*, III, 473 (1835); IV, 94 (1836); VI, 249, 253, 283 (1842); VIII, 574 (1855); IX, 229 (1859), 371 (1862), 496–97, 580 (1863); *Works*, II, 179; X, 20; XI, 350–51; *Letters*, I, 218 (1827), 383 (1833), 438 (1835); II, 269, 287 (1840) III, 92 (1844); 346 (1846); 411 (1847); Cameron, *op. cit.*, p. 30 (Mar. 28, 1857).

187. *Journals*, IV, 94, 174 (1836); VI, 138 (1841); *Letters*, III, 98 (1842), 116 (1843).

188. *Journals*, II, 502 (1832); 524 (1836); *Works*, VI, 6.

189. *Journals*, IV, 9, 174 (1836), 362 (1837); Cameron, *op. cit.*, p. 22 (Feb. 2, 1836).

190. *Journals*, III, 505–6, 512–15, 527 (1835).

191. *Ibid.*, III, 572, 575 (1835); IV, 94 (1836), 378, 381 (1837); *Letters*, III, 23, 96 (1842).

192. *Journals*, IV, 205, 383 (1837); *Letters*, II, 68, 70–71 (1837).

193. *Journals*, IV, 383 (1837); *Letters*, II, 68, 70, 71, 76–77 (1837).

194. *Journals*, IV, 199–210, 217–18 (1837); *Letters*, II, 57, 64–65, 67–68, 72, 77, 87 (1827), 197, 201–3 (1839); IV, 266 (1850), 503 (1855).

195. *Journals*, V, 502 (1840); *Letters*, II, 388 (1841); III, 29 (1842); IV, 266 (1850).

196. *Journals*, V, 154 (1838), 237 (1839), 502 (1841); VI, 229 (1842); VIII, 178 (1851); IX, 61 (1856); 212–13 (1859); X, 310 (1870); *Works*, III, 55; VI, 163; *Letters*, II, 29 (1836), 136 (1838), 374 (1847); IV, 222, 226 (1850).

197. *Journals*, VIII, 474–75 (1854); MS Journal, "VA. 1862–63," p. 287.

198. *Journals*, I, 222, 298 (1823); II, 34 (1824), 414 (1831); III, 350 (1834); V, 143 (1841); VIII, 16 (1849), 490 (1854); IX, 294 (1861); *Works*, IV, 105; VII, 158; X, 133; *Letters*, I, 181 (1826), 376, 383 (1833); II, 365 (1840); Cameron, *op. cit.*, p. 46 (Feb. 17, 1825).

199. *Journals*, III, 428 (1834); IV, 378, 383 (1837); VIII, 289 (1852); *Letters*, VI, 50 (1868); *Works*, X, 330.

200. References are given above.

201. *Journals*, II, 143 (1825–1826), 233 (1828); IV, 94, 174 (1836), 383 (1837); V, 133, 154 (1838); *Letters*, I, 153, n. 62 (1824), 161, n. 12; II, 70–71 (1837); Cameron, *op. cit.*, pp. 47 (Feb. 1, 1829), 18 (Aug. 1, 1831).

202. *Journals*, I, 83 (1821); III, 279, 356 (1834); IV, 94, 137, 146 (1836); V, 154 (1838); VI, 400 (1843); VII, 100 (1845), 370 (1847); VIII, 16 (1849); IX, 30–31 (1856); 521 (1863); X, 298–99 (1869), 350 (1870); *Letters*, I, 433 (1835); III, 77 (1842); *Works*, III, 172, 323; VII, 323, 488; IX, 457; X, 131; XI, 51, 455–59.

203. *Journals*, II, 446–47, 456, 542 (1832).

204. *Letters*, I, 425 (1834); III, 100 (1842), 374 (1847).

205. *Ibid.*, III, 96 (1842).

206. *Journals*, II, 416 (1831), 473, 475, 542 (1832); III, 348, 350 (1834); IV, 174 (1836), 337 (1837); *Letters*, III, 96 (1842), 230 (1843); *Works*, I, 113, 281; Cameron, *op. cit.*, pp. 19 (1832), 23 (1836).

207. *Journals*, IX, 398, 450, 459, 495 (1862), 505 (1863); X, 310, 315–16, 344 (1870), 423 (1873), 445 (1875); *Works*, X, 105, 110, 112; *Letters*, II, 192 (1839); VI, 190 (1871); Cameron, *op. cit.*, pp. 32 (Sept. 5, 1860), 34 (Mar. 10, Apr. 6, Apr. 13, 1863), 35 (Feb. 10, 1864), 36 (July 9, 1864), 41 (Jan. 29, Feb. 17, Mar. 7, July 7, 1870), 51 (July 13, 1870), 42 (Dec. 28, 1871).

208. *Works*, XII, 399.

209. *Letters*, III, 103 (Dec. 12, 1842).

210. *Journals*, VI, 357 (1843); *Letters*, III, 176, 194 (1843); 363 (1846); *Works*, XII, 399.

211. *Letters*, V, 80 (June 28, 1857).

212. *Journals*, VII, 236 (1846); VIII, 81 (1849); IX, 580 (1863); *Works*, VIII, 237–65, 421–22.

213. *Journals*, VII, 396 (1848); *Letters*, IV, 531, n. 132; V, 28 (1856); Cameron, *op. cit.*, 40 (Mar. 29, 1869).

214. *Journals*, VII, 152 (1846).

215. *Letters*, III, 77 (1842); *Journals*, VII, 151 (1846); VIII, 76 (1849), 128 (1850); *Works*, X, 338; MS Journals, "AZ. 1850," pp. 49, 52, 53, 54, 166.

216. *Letters*, III, 54, 70–71 (1842), 129 (1843); *Journals*, VII, 296 (1848).

217. *Letters*, IV, 390 (1853).

218. *Ibid.*, III, 243 (1844); *Journals*, VIII, 459 (1854); IX, 212 (1859); Cameron, *op. cit.*, pp. 28 (1854), 36 (1864).

219. *Letters*, IV, 130 (1849); IV, 276 (1852); V. 14 (1856); *Journals*, VIII, 69 (1849), 246 (1851).

220. *Journals*, VIII, 77 (1849); X, 423 (1873); *Letters*, IV, 470 (1854).

221. *Journals*, VIII, 487 (1854); X, 423 (1873).

222. *Ibid.*, IX, 30 (1856); *Works*, VIII, 222; X, 183.

223. *Journals*, IX, 30–31 (1856).

224. *Letters*, IV, 390 (Oct. 12, 1853).

225. *Journals*, VII, 236 (1846); VIII, 157 (1850); Cameron, *op. cit.*, p. 18 (Dec. 23, 1831).

226. Cameron, *op. cit.*, pp. 33 (Sept. 10, 1861, Feb. 26, 1962), 39 (Oct. 11, 1867, Apr. 4, 1868), 43 (June 13, 1872).

227. *Journals*, VIII, 425–26 (1853); Cameron, *op. cit.*, pp. 28 (1853), 39 (1854).

228. *Journals*, IX, 233 (1859); IX, 307 (1861); X, 142 (1866), 411–12 (1873); *Works*, VIII, 183–84; *Letters*, V, 111 (1858), 157 (1859), 221–22 (1860), 238, 249 (1861), 514, 543, n. 259 (1867); VI, 12 (1868), 142, 179, 187–90 (1871), 204 (1872); Cameron, *op. cit.*, pp. 37 (Aug. 19, 1865), 38 (Aug. 25, 1866); and *Correspondence between Ralph Waldo Emerson and Hermann Grimm*, ed. by F. W. Holls (Boston, 1903).

229. *Letters*, VI, 274–75, 282, 287 (1875); Cameron, *op. cit.*, p. 26 (Oct. 15, 1864).

230. *Journals*, X, 33–34 (1864); *Works*, VIII, 138.

231. *Journals*, VIII, 351 (1852).

232. Professor Cameron's list of Emerson's withdrawals from libraries indicates that among other significant German authors and titles that engaged Emerson's attention are the following: August von Boeckh's *Public Economy of Athens* (see Cameron, *op. cit.*, p. 48 [Mar. 30, 1847]); Friedrich Buechner's *Kraft und Stoff*, tr. by J. F. Collingwood (*ibid.*, p. 37 [Aug. 19, 1865]); Ludwig Preller's classical studies (*ibid.*, p. 49 [Mar. 25, 1868]); Friedrich Raumer's English studies (*ibid.*, p. 29 [July 26, 1854]); K. Ritter's *Comparative Geography of Palestine* (*ibid.*, p. 38 [May 13, 1867]); Albert Schwegler's *History of Philosophy*, tr. by James H. Stirling (*ibid.*, p. 40 [Aug. 30, 1869]); Adolf Stahr's *Weimar und Jena ibid.*, p. 40 [Nov. 21.

1868]); Gustav Waagen's *Treasures of Art in Great Britain* tr. by H. E. Lloyd (*ibid.* p. 25 [June 28 1842]); and Karl Witte's *Dante Forschungen* (*ibid.*, p. 43 [Nov. 12, 1872]).

233. Cabot, *Memoir*, I, 139.

234. *Journals*, IV, 286. Coleridge's name is added, almost as if it had been an afterthought. Had the note been written prior to 1833, instead of in 1837, the name of Coleridge would doubtless have come first, and Wordsworth's would probably have been omitted altogether, for as short a time as eight months before his visit to Ambleside, he "never read Wordsworth without chagrin."—*Journal*, II, 534. In March, 1819, Wordsworth's poetry had seemed to him "the poetry of pigmies" (*Letters*, I, 306), and as late as Oct. 22, 1835, he complained of the platitudes in Wordsworth (*Journals*, III, 561). Even on the occasion of his visit to the old poet, who had insisted on reciting schoolboy-wise some of his verses to the young American, Emerson (at least so he professed later) had hardly been able to contain himself sufficiently to avoid laughing in his face. See *Journals*, III, 182, and *English Traits* (*Works*, V, 22–23). However, see T. Scudder, *op. cit.*, 29–30, where the account of this episode, re-examined in the light of unpublished fragments of the journals, is modified somewhat. Only after Coleridge's critical writings stimulated him to a more sympathetic reading of Wordsworth's poetry did he overcome his antipathy. For Emerson's later judgments of Wordsworth, see *Journals*, III, 457 (1835); IV, 286 (1857); X, 68–69 (1864).

235. Emerson had drawn the *Biographia Literaria* from the Harvard College Library as early as Nov. 16, 1826; see *Letters*, I, xxxvi, 286, n. 99. The more important references to Coleridge include the following: *Journals*, II, 268, 277–78, 280 (1829), 320 (1830), 377, 405, 430, 444 (1831); III, 174, 181, 185 (1833), 262, 295, 328, 348, 367, 371, 405, 428 (1834), 439, 463–64, 466, 489, 494, 503, 508, 536, 539–40, 567 (1835); IV, 63, 93, 152–53 (1836), 279, 286, 356 (1837); V, 109, 112, 119, 133, 140–41, 143 (1838), 528 (1841); VI, 138 (1841), 266 (1842); VII, 329 (1847); VIII, 558, 579 (1855); X, 350 (1871); *Letters*, I, 291 (1830), 393, 397, 402, n. 133 (1833), 412 (1834), 432–33, 440, 448 (1835); II, 30 (1836), 78, n. 92 (1837), 126, 173 (1838), 226 (1839), 425–26 (1841); III, 64 (1842); IV, 26 (1848), 265–66 (1851); VI, 19 (1868); *Works*, V, 10–14; X, 343; Cabot, *Memoir*, II, 723–24; index to *Works*.

236. For the more important references to Carlyle, see *Journals*, II, 515, 524, 525–30, 541–42 (1832); III, 28, 159, 180–82, 185–86, 188, 190, 198, 241 (1833), 272, 274, 294, 299, 313–15, 321, 338, 348, 424 (1834), 457, 472, 486,

557, 573 (1835); IV, 85 (1836), 180–81, 195–96, 198, 212–13, 217–18, 238, 258–59, 272–74, 286, 287, 288, 346, 363, 383 (1837), 389, 398–99, 405–6, 410, 411, 446; V, 4, 17, 90, 153 (1838), 213, 352 (1839), 377, 440–41, 487 (1840), 520, 557, 571 (1841); VI, 222, 251–52 (1842), 387, 389, 394–95, 400, 403, 410 (1843); VII, 152, 196–97, 216, 224–25 (1846), 285, 344–48, 367 (1847), 384, 392, 402–4, 437, 439–40, 441–43, 445, 561 (1848); VIII, 91, 123 (1850), 169, 250, 261–62 (1851), 463 (1854), 579 (1855); IX, 195–96, 204, 212–13 (1859), 423–24, 465 (1862), 529 (1863); X, 63 (1864), 104, 116, 122 (1865), 217 (1867), 315 (1870), 349, 357 (1871), 397 (1872), 415 (1873), 445 (1875), 476 (1875–1881); Cabot, *Memoir*, II, 724; *Carlyle-Emerson Corresp.*; and the indexes to *Works* and *Letters*.

237. *Works*, V, 14.

238. Scudder, *op. cit.*, p. 14.

239. Frank T. Thompson, "Emerson's Indebtedness to Coleridge," *Studies in Philology*, XXIII, i (Jan., 1926), 55–76; N. Foerster, *American Criticism* (Boston and N.Y., 1928), pp. 62–63.

240. *Carlyle-Emerson Correspondence*, II, 217 (July 17, 1850).

241. *Journals*, VII, 442 (Apr. 25, 1848).

242. Scudder, *op. cit.*, pp. 60, 209.

243. *Carlyle-Emerson Correspondence*, II, 217.

244. *Journals*, III, 180.

245. *Ibid.*, pp. 185–86 (Sept. 1, 1833).

246. *Ibid.*, p. 190 (Sept. 2, 1833).

247. One of Emerson's erstwhile scholars at Chelmsford.

248. *Journals*, III, 185–86.

249. *Journals*, III, 186 (Sept. 1, 1833). The same ideas are expressed on August 30, 1833, in a letter to Alex. Ireland. Emerson adds: "Carlyle does not pretend to have solved the great problems but rather to be an observer of their solution as it goes forward in the world. I asked him at what religious development the concluding passage in his piece in the Edin. Review upon German Literature (say 5 years ago) and some passages in the piece called Characteristics, pointed? He replied, that he was not competent to state it even to himself—he waited rather to see.—My own feeling was that I had met with men of far less power yet greater insight into religious truth."

Either Emerson had read Carlyle's essays very attentively some years earlier, when he first came upon them, or he had refreshed his memory since then. His reference to Carlyle's essay in the *Edinburgh Review* is undoubtedly to that on the "State of German Literature" (1827), reprinted in *Critical and Miscellaneous Essays*, I, 20–65, and the passage referred to is Carlyle's attempted explanation of Kantian transcendentalism and its significance in shaping German religious thought. See *ibid.*, pp. 56–65.

250. *Journals*, III, 188 (Sept. 2, 1833).

251. *Ibid.*, p. 199 (Sept. 8, 1833).

252. *Ibid.*, p. 205 (Sept. 16, 1833).

253. *Ibid.*, p. 200 (Sept. 8, 1833).

254. *Ibid.*, p. 201 (Sept. 8, 1833).

255. *Ibid.*, p. 196 (Sept. 8, 1833).

256. *Ibid.*, p. 196.

257. *Ibid.*, p. 246 (Jan., 1834).

258. *Ibid.*, pp. 207–8 (Sept. 17, 1833).

259. *Ibid.*, pp. 209–10 (Sept. 17, 1833). It is unnecessary to connect this view of ethics with the practical idealism of Kant in the second *Critique*. In an essay entitled "Civilization," delivered in Washington in January, 1861, and printed in *Society and Solitude* (1870), Emerson quoted Kant's Categorical Imperative; but there is little to suggest that he knew much about Kant's second *Critique* in 1833. It is enough to say that, as in his innate tendency to idealize, without benefit of either Plato or Kant, so he arrived independently at this view of a rigorous Kantian ethics. Later he derived satisfaction in finding that Kant had taken a similar view, but he did not derive the doctrine itself from Kant. In the realm of ethics he was his own sufficient source.

260. *Journals*, I, 361 (Apr. 18, 1834). Even now he said: "The men of strong understanding . . . cut me short—they drive me in a corner—I must not suggest. I must define . . . . I avoid and defy them."—Rusk, *Emerson* (N.Y., 1949), pp. 235–36.

261. *Works*, IX, 315; also IV, 83–84. Aboard ship, on September 8, 1833, he wrote: "I believe that the error of religionists lies in this, that they do not know the extent or the harmony of the depth of their moral nature; that they are clinging to little, positive, verbal, formal versions of the moral law, and very imperfect versions too, while the infinite laws, the laws of Law, the great circling truths whose only adequate symbol is the material laws, the astronomy, etc., are all unobserved.—*Journals*, II, 199. Four years later he observed: "When the conversation soars to principles, Unitarianism is boyish."—*Ibid.*, IV, 345 (Oct. 28, 1837).

262. *Ibid.*, III, 18.

263. *Ibid.*, p. 196 (Sept. 6, 1833).

264. *Ibid.*, pp. 192–93; Cabot, *Memoir*, I, 248, 259.

265. This design was never executed except insofar as the brief sections on "Idealism" and "Spirit," incorporated in *Nature*, may be considered as carrying out this plan.

266. *Letters*, II, 26.

267. *Ibid.*, p. 32. The italics are added.

268. It will be observed that the Paris to which Oliver Wendell Holmes's "Good Americans" go "when they die" offered little to hold Emerson's interest in 1833. The Jardin des Plantes was another matter. So were the lectures at the Sorbonne, where he heard Gay-Lussac, Thenard, Jouffroy, and other "first" scientists of France. The significance to him of the great Parisian museums of natural history can be gauged by the references he made to them in his journals and in his recurrence to them in his lectures. The well-worn program of the Sorbonne lectures he preserved among his slender store of mementos to the end of his days. See *Journals*, III, 156, 161–64, 170; Cabot, *Memoir*, II, 640, 710; *Works*, XII, 3, 22; Bliss Perry, *Emerson Today*, p. 42; *Letters*, I, 387, n. 90.

Standing before the glass cases and exhibition cabinets in Paris, Emerson the naturalist was born. He resolved to write another *De Rerum Natura*. In the *Gift* for 1844, he wrote: "The universe is a wilder puzzle than ever, as you look along this stark series of once animated forms—the hazy butterflies, the carved shells, the bird, beast, worm, snake, and fish, and the upheaving principle of life everywhere incipient, in the very rock aping organized forms. Whilst I stood there, I yielded to the singular conviction, that in all these rich groups of natural productions which surrounded me, and in all the vast system which they represented, not a form so grotesque, so savage, so beautiful, but is an expression of some property in man the observer. I felt . . . an occult relation between the crawling scorpion, the flowering zoophyte, and man. I was moved to strange sympathies. I said, 'I will listen to this invitation; I also am a naturalist.'"—Perry, *op. cit.*, p. 44.

Commenting on the "occult relation between the very scorpions and man" in his diary on July 13, 1833, he said: "I feel the centipede in me,—cayman, carp, eagle, and fox. I am moved by strange sympathies; I say continually 'I will be a naturalist.'"—*Journals*, III, 163.

Returned to Boston, he delivered, beginning on November 4, 1833, his first lectures as a layman. The titles are self-explanatory: "Natural History," "On the Relation of Man to the Globe," "Water," and "The Naturalist" (see the abstracts of these lectures in Cabot's *Memoir*, II, 710–12). "It is in my judgment," so he opened the first of these discourses, "the greatest office of natural science (and one which as yet is only beginning to be discharged) to explain man to himself"; and he concluded: "The laws of moral nature answer to those of matter as face to face in a glass."—Quoted by

Perry from an unpublished MS, *op. cit.*, p. 45.

This last idea became a firm conviction, and he used the same words tellingly in his first published book three years later (*Works*, I, 32–33). The only difficulty that remained was to explain *why* the face in the glass answers to that of the beholder, *why* the laws of nature are but different versions of the laws of ethics. This problem led him into deep water—over his head. The next year he wrote:

"I am wading—sometimes overhead—in the most ambitious Course of Lectures—a little precipitately undertaken—once a week on a new subject, and each subject the Universe seen from one side; so that the Lecturer's task seems to be nothing less than Puck's 'I will put a girdle round about the world in forty minutes' —say sixty rather."—*Records of a Lifelong Friendship, 1807–1882. R. W. Emerson and W. H. Furness*, ed. by Wm. Howard Furness (Boston, 1910), p. 5.

The same year he resolved "to write the natural history of reason," and though he found himself unequal to the task, he "returned to the project again and again" until finally, in 1870, when he printed his Harvard lectures, unsatisfactory though they had turned out to be to himself, he gave them the old title, *The Natural History of Intellect.*—Cabot, *Memoir*, II, 633, 644.

Truly, Emerson the philosopher died hard. Though he forsook the pulpit, he remained all his life a preacher. Condemning eloquence, he yet hankered after a professorship of rhetoric at Harvard. Though he professed to believe that no wise man would look twice into a metaphysical book, he made this confession to Margaret Fuller: "Does not James Walker [of Harvard] want relief, and let me be his lieutenant for one semester to his class in Locke?"—Cabot, *Memoir*, II, 557–58; *Letters*, IV, 63 (Apr. 25, 1848). Among the last thoughts inscribed in his journals is this one: "Philosophy is called the homesickness of the soul" (*Journals*, X, 469). Compare *Novalis Schriften* (4th ed., 2 vols., Berlin, 1826), II, 116. Emerson's source was probably Carlyle's essay on Novalis (*Crit. and Misc. Essays*, I, 29), where the passage is rendered: "Philosophy is properly Homesickness; the wish to be everywhere at home. Novalis has it more properly thus: Philosophy is homesickness, a yearning to be at home in the All." Whatever the source, Emerson was, in more ways than one, sick for and sick of philosophy; and he died without finding a cure.

269. *Works*, I, 4.

270. *Works*, I, 339–40.

271. *Journals*, I, 210 (Jan. 11, 1823).

272. *Ibid.*, II, 357–58.

273. *Ibid.*, III, 346, 347–49 (1834), 565 (1835); IV, 27, 41 (1836); V, 545 (1841).

274. May 9, 1836. See *ibid.*, IV, 39–50, 63, 139–41 (1836), 409 (1838); V, 545, 546–47 (1841); VI, 394 (1843).

275. *Ibid.*, III, 361 (Nov. 15, 1834). On Emerson's feeling toward Concord, see M. D. Conway, *Emerson at Home and Abroad*, pp. 185–206; Ed. W. Emerson, *Emerson in Concord: A Memoir* . . . (Boston, 1889); and Randall Stewart, "The Concord Group," *Sewanee Rev.*, XLIV (Oct., 1936), 434–46.

276. A phrase derived from Bacon and De Gerando. See *Journals*, II, 330 (Oct. 27, 1830); III, 489 (June 10, 1835).

277. *Ibid.*, III, 235 (Dec., 1833).

278. Cabot, *Memoir*, I, 246. The passage is found in *Journals*, IV, 235–37, and represents a rather clearheaded perception of the Kantian distinction. It belongs rather to the end than the beginning of the period during which Emerson contemplated the Understanding-Reason problem and its relation to his problem. See the testimony of Edward Waldo Emerson, who, in editing the Centenary edition of his father's writings, dated the passage 1835.—*Works*, XII, 421–22. See also *Carlyle-Emerson Corresp.*, I, 50 (Mar. 12, 1835), and my essay, "The Emerson Canon," *Univ. of Toronto Quar.*, XII, iv (July, 1943), 476–84.

279. Understanding and Reason are not, in these two instances, consistently emphasized with capital letters, by which he later habitually distinguished them; indeed, there is, in the interpretation given them, no indication of anything more than a loose parallelism between mind and matter—certainly no glimmering of an understanding of the transcendental forms of Kant.

280. *Journals*, III, 235–37 (misdated 1833; more likely, June, 1835; see Cabot, *Memoir*, I, 246, and *Journals*, III, 489 [June 10, 1835], where Emerson says pointedly: "I endeavor to announce the laws of the First Philosophy"). Other references include the following: *Journals*, III, 210–11, 330, 376–77, 389–90, 392–94 (1834), 433, 435, 455, 456, 467–68, 488, 489–90, 492, 499–500, 519, 525–26, 529, 539–40, 567 (1835); IV, 11–14, 21–23, 25–27, 28–29, 32, 33, 37, 59–61, 65, 71, 73–74, 76, 78 (1836); also *Letters*, I, 412–13 (1834); II, 29–30 (1836).

During the remaining months of 1836, after *Nature* was published, the Understanding-Reason problem occupied Emerson (so far as the *Journals* indicate) ten more times: *Journals*, IV, 92–94, 102–3, 115–17, 118–19, 121, 122, 124, 126–29, 131, 164 (1836). Thereafter, the matter is referred to specifically in the *Journals* as follows: IV, 241, 355, 380–81 (1837); V, 13,

57, 92–93 (1838), 310 (1839). With this last reference (Nov. 3, 1839), Emerson is done with the Reason and Understanding. Only once more, between 1839 and about 1855, when his thinking entered another phase, does he revert to the subject—on August 17, 1843 (*Journals*, VII, 431). By 1840, the poet had extracted all the distinction held for his purposes, and he was ready to relinquish the terms to the philosophers.

281. *Journals*, III, 405.

282. See Emerson's restatement of the Coleridgean emphasis on the relation of language to thought, *Journals*, III, 439 (Jan. 13, 1835), 491 (June 20, 1835), and IV, 146 (Nov. 10, 1836); see also the "Author's Preface," *Aids to Reflection*, Shedd ed., p. 114; Marsh ed., pp. lviii–lix. For other significant references in the *Journals* that shed light on the question of Coleridge's relation to Emerson at this particular stage of Emerson's philosophical development, see III, 371, 379, 383, 405 (1834), 503, 540, 567 (1835).

283. *Journals*, III, 439 (Jan. 13, 1835). It is worth noting, also, that Emerson was consulting Hedge on philosophical problems during the winter of 1834–1835.

284. See *Journals*, III, 295–96 (May 6, 1834); *Letters*, I, 412 (May 31, 1834).

285. *Friend*, Shedd ed., pp. 420, 422; *Works*, I, 33.

286. *Journals*, III, 25–26 (Mar. 17, 1836).

287. Even after he had worked out his problem—at least to his own satisfaction—he cried, "Why must always the philosopher mince his words and fatigue us with explanation?"—*Journals*, III, 467 (Apr. 16, 1835). See also his objection to metaphysics, voiced when he was 67, *ibid.*, X, 336–37 (Oct. 6, 1870).

288. For this part of his definition he could hardly have found authority in Kant. It reflects (1) Carlyle's interpretation, rather misinterpretation, as given in his essays on "Novalis" and the "State of German Literature," and (2) the Scottish identification of the intuitive moral will with reason, as he had been taught at Harvard College.

289. In thus giving the functions of the Understanding, Emerson was doing little more than paraphrasing Marsh's Preliminary Essay to his edition of the *Aids*, which lay before him. See p. 96, Shedd ed., and p. xi, Marsh ed.

290. Another reflection of Carlyle's misconstructions.

291. Compare *Journals*, IV, 74 (June 22, 1836), where the same idea is repeated.

292. Schiller's *Don Carlos*, IV, xxi, 90–91. Probably quoted from Carlyle's *Life of Schiller*, Centenary ed., *Works*, XXV, 67.

293. See *Journals*, III, 299 (May 21, 1834).

294. *Letters*, I, 412–13 (May 31, 1834); imperfectly and partially quoted in Cabot, *Memoir*, I, 218.

295. The passage indicates that Emerson, following Coleridge and Marsh, repeated the fallacious argument that Bacon, Milton, and the British idealists had all anticipated Kant in drawing the distinction between Understanding and Reason. See *Table Talk*, Shedd ed., p. 336; the last paragraph in Appendix E of *The Statesman's Manual: A Lay Sermon; Aids to Reflection*, Shedd ed., pp. 210–12, 215, 222–23, 233–36, 263–65, 460; *Aids*, Marsh ed., pp. 111, 115, 118–20, 131–35, 144–45, 155–57, 375–76.

296. *Journals*, III, 310.

297. *Ibid.*, p. 300.

298. *Ibid.*, p. 377.

299. *See* Chs. V–XI of *Germany*, Wight ed., II, 146–230.

300. See *Aids*, Shedd ed., *Works*, I, 234–36, 2252–53; Marsh ed., pp. 131–35, 144–45.

301. *Aids*, Shedd ed., pp. 257–59, 368–72; Marsh ed., pp. 149–51.

302. Only when the Understanding "usurps the name of Reason," says Coleridge, does it join "the banners of Anti-Christ, at once the pander and prostitute of sensuality, and whether in the cabinet, laboratory, the dissecting room, or the brothel, alike busy in the schemes of vice and irreligion."—*A Lay Sermon*, App. B (*Works*, Shedd ed., I, 464; Marsh ed., p. 378). Note Coleridge's failure in this passage to distinguish between Pure and Practical Reason.

303. *Crit. and Misc. Essays*, II, 27. For similar constructions by Carlyle of the Kantian distinction, see his essay on the "State of German Literature," *ibid.*, II, 74–83, esp. p. 82.

304. Emerson's firsthand knowledge of Jacobi in 1834 was nil. The first reference to Jacobi in his diaries is dated September 8, 1835, and is in no sense indicative that Emerson had Jacobi before him even then.

305. Unless the editors of the *Journals* are in error, this book, bearing the publisher's date of 1835, was in Emerson's hands on December 2, 1834. See *Journals*, III, 379. On that day he quoted from "*Table-Talk*, 362, folio edition." See also *Journals*, III, 383 (Dec. 6, 1834), and *Letters*, I, 448 (July 27, 1835), where Emerson records the opinion that "Coleridge's Table Talk is, I think, as good as Spence's or Selden's or Luther's; better."

306. *Journals*, III, 295 (May 3, 1834).

307. See Carlyle's apology on this score in *Crit. and Misc. Essays*, I, 83.

308. See *Journals*, III, 573 (Dec. 7, 1835).

309. A copy of Cousin's *Cours de Philosophie* (Paris, 1828), bearing Emerson's signature is still in Emerson's house in Concord.

310. *Letters*, I, 322–23 (May 24, 1831).

311. See *Journals*, III, 451 (Jan. 20, 1832), and *Letters*, I, 346 (Mar. 5, 1832). Doubtless he had read, two or three years before, Sir Wm. Hamilton's long review of Cousin's *Cours de Philosophie* in the *Edinburgh Rev.*, L, cxix (Oct., 1829), 194–221. See *Letters*, I, 322, n. 26 (May 24, 1831).

312. *Journals*, II, 451.

313. *Ibid.*, pp. 529, 542; *Letters*, I, 346.

314. *Journals*, III, 389–90 (Dec. 9. 1834). But the democrat in him impelled him to make this qualification; "Democracy, freedom, has its roots in the sacred truth that every man hath in him the divine Reason, or that, though few men since the creation of the world live according to the dictates of Reason, yet all men are created capable of so doing. That is the equality and the only equality of all men. To this truth we look when we say, Reverence thyself; Be true to thyself. Because every man has within him somewhat really divine, therefore is slavery the unpardonable outrage it is." And this principle, after doing service in *Nature*, the *American Scholar* and Divinity School addresses, *Self-Reliance*, and elsewhere, was kept against the day in 1848 when he wrote the lecture on "Aristocracy."—*Works*, X, 29–66, 519–20.

315. *Letters*, II, 123 (Mar. 27, 1838). Into his diary he had written three weeks earlier: "I told Alcott that in the city, Cousin and Jouffroy, and the opinion of this and that Doctor, showed very large; a fame of the book-stores seemed commanding; but as soon as we got ten miles out of town, in the bushes, we whistled at such matters, cared little for societies, Systèmes, or book-stores. God and the world return again to mind, sole problem, and we value an observation upon a brass knob, a genuine observation on a button, more than whole encyclopedias. It is even so; as I read this new book of Ripley's it looks to me—neat, elegant, accurate, as it is—a mere superficiality: in my Jack Cade way of counting by number and weight, counting the things, I find nothing worth in the accomplished Cousin and the mild Jouffroy; the most unexceptionable clearness, precision and good sense,—never a slip, never an ignorance,—but unluckily, never an inspiration. One page of Milton's poorest prose tract is worth the whole."—*Journals*, IV, 400 (Mar. 4, 1838).

Still not out of breath the next day, he added: "Of the French Eclecticism, and what Cousin thinks so conclusive . . . I would say there is an optical illusion in it.

"Take Cousin's Philosophy . . . this book . . . ought to be wisdom's wisdom, and we can hug the volume to our hearts and make a bonfire of all the libraries. But here are people who have read it and still survive, nor is it at once perceptible in their future reasonings that they have talked with God, face to face. Indeed I have read it myself, as I have read any other book. I found a few memorable thoughts, for Philosophy does not absolutely hinder people from having thoughts, but by no means as many memorable thoughts as I could have got out of many another book, say, for example, Montaigne's essays."—*Journals*, IV, 404–5. See also *Letters*, III, 20 (Mar. 1, 1842), where, specifically referring to Ripley's championship of Cousin, he says, "I was driven at once to say . . . 'There is no hope for an Eclectic'; I must unfold my own thought."

Ripley appears to have been the only one among the leading Transcendentalists who was carried off his feet, momentarily at least, by Cousin. Theodore Parker, for example, soon recognized Cousin's eclecticism as a "brilliant Mosaic . . . but not satisfactory."—Parker, *Works*, Cent. ed., XIII, 301.

316. Oddly enough Emerson mentions Hamilton only twice before 1848, when he heard him lecture. But considering Hamilton's seven essays bearing on German thought in the *Edinburgh Review* between 1829 and 1836 (conveniently turned to in his *Discussions of Philosophy* . . . Edinburgh, 1852) and Emerson's known familiarity with that periodical during these years, it is all but certain that he was familiar with the Scot's strictures on and misinterpretation of what he called the "Infinito-Absolute" philosophy of Cousin and Kant, between whom he did not differentiate very clearly. See *Letters*, I, 320–23, n. 26 (Mar. 30, 1830), where, referring to the essay on Cousin in the *Edinburgh Review* for October, 1829, he asked William, "Do you read the Edinburgh? The new article on Cousin's Philosophy is said to be great—a key to the whole German system. I can't understand it at all." At this admission we need not wonder, for Hamilton misconstrued not only the Kantian distinction between Understanding and Reason but also confused the Pure with the Practical Reason and thus failed to explain the several purposes of Kant in the two critiques.

317. See *Journals*, III, 292, 298, 414 (1834), 435, 455–56, 467, 488, 492, 500, 539 (1835), IV, 73–75 (1836).

318. *Journals*, III, 398 (Dec. 20, 1834).

319. *Ibid.*, p. 457 (Apr. 16, 1835).

320. *Ibid.*, IV, 74 (June 22, 1836); see also III, 308 (June 18, 1834), where Understanding "in its right place," is called "the servant of the Reason." In such an essay as Carlyle's "Novalis" (1829), which Emerson perused and re-perused, both the Reason-*contra*-Understanding

and the Reason-*supra*-Understanding relationships are repeatedly emphasized. See, for example, *Crit. and Misc. Essays*, II, 24–28. Here Emerson found employed phrases that later came to be his own: "Light of Reason," "majesty of Reason," "the vassal Understanding," "Nature, the mysterious Garment of the Unseen," and the doctrine of circles, or Sphericity. For other examples, see "Characteristics," *ibid.*, III, 40–45, and "State of German Literature," *ibid.*, I, 74–84.

321. *Table Talk*, Shedd ed., 313 (May 14, 1830).

322. *Crit. and Misc. Essays*, I, 81.

323. Phases like this one, where the "practical" and aspects of the "pure" reason are obviously confused or left undifferentiated, were to cause Emerson much trouble.

324. *Crit. and Misc. Essays*, II, 27.

325. *Ibid.*, II, 26–28; see also I, 82.

326. See Hill, Shine, "Carlyle and the German Philosophy Problem during the Year 1826–1827," *PMLA.*, L, iii (Sept., 1935), 810. Compare *Crit. and Misc. Essays*, II, 26.

327. *Two Note Books*, pp. 221–22.

328. Wm. Allingham, *A Diary* (London, 1907), p. 273.

329. Hill Shine, *loc. cit.*, p. 810.

330. On secondary sources from which Carlyle could have derived his misinformation, see *ibid.*, pp. 813–27.

331. See *Journals*, III, 292, 298, 414 (1834), 435, 455–56, 467, 488, 492, 500, 539 (1835).

332. Especially with regard to the essential differences between constitutive and regulative forms of thought. See *Table Talk*, Shedd ed., pp. 336 (July 2, 1820), 502 (Feb. 22, 1834); the last paragraph of Appendix E of the *Statesman's Manual*; and *Aids*, Shedd ed. 215–23, 233–36, 248–53, 460, 464 (Marsh ed., 115–20, 132–35, 144–45, 375–76, 386).

333. *Journals*, IV, 74 (June 22, 1836).

334. *Letters*, I, 432.

335. *Journals*, III, 540.

336. A reference to Turner's *History of the Anglo-Saxons*, which Emerson was reading at the time.

337. *Journals*, III, 567.

338. As in "Novalis," *Crit. and Misc. Essays*, II, 25–27.

339. *Journals*, III, 573 (Dec. 7, 1835). The italics in this passage are added.

In the course of his lectures on "English Literature," delivered during the winter of 1835–1836, Emerson credited Coleridge with having "taken the widest survey of the moral, intellectual, and social world" (Cabot, *Memoir*, II, 723); and in *English Traits*, twenty years later, he spoke of Coleridge as the one "who wrote and

spoke the only high criticism in his time," while Carlyle "was driven into the preaching of Fate" (*Works*, V, 248, 249). In his English notebook Emerson observed concerning Carlyle: "It is droll to hear this talker talking against talkers, and this writer writing against writing . . . . He is a bacchanal in the strong waters of vituperation" (*Works*, V, 387; see also *ibid.*, V, 318–23; Conway, *Emerson at Home and Abroad;* and Scudder, *The Lonely Wayfaring Man*).

Carlyle, on his side, having already "happily got done with all that matter [philosophy] altogether," twitted his American friend unmercifully about the plans for the projected "book or journal" to be known as "The Transcendentalist" (to be edited by Hedge) and about the plans for establishing in Boston "the First Philosophy."

340. See the section on Carlyle above; also Shine, *loc. cit.*, p. 810

341. *Carlyle-Emerson Corresp.*, I, 67 (May 13, 1835).

342. *Journals*, VI, 222–23 (July 12, 1842).

343. *Journals*, VIII, 261 (Oct. 27, 1851). "In Carlyle, as in Byron," Emerson wrote on June 4, 1847, "one is more struck with the rhetoric than with the matter. He has a manly superiority rather than intellectually . . ." (*Journals*, VII, 285).

344. For details, see Scudder's *Lonely Wayfaring Man*.

345. *Journals*, III, 489.

346. *Journals*, II, 235–36 (June, 1835? Misdated in the published *Journals* as 1833).

347. *Table Talk*, Shedd ed., p. 265 (Jan. 6, 1833).

348. *Journals*, III, 236–37 (June, 1835?)

349. *Crit. and Misc. Essays*, II, 26, 50; see also I, 58–61, 70–86.

350. *Journals*, III, 237.

351. *Crit. and Misc. Essays*, II, 27.

352. Consider, for example, Goethe's distinction between *Gefühlsmensch* and *Verstandesmensch*.

353. See Schiller's numerous parallels drawn in his *Über naive und sentimentalische Dichtung*.

354. *Journals*, IV, 11–14 (Feb. 24, 1835); see also IV, 78 (July 30, 1836).

355. *Ibid.*, IV, 76 (June 24, 1836).

356. *Ibid.*, III, 330–31 (Aug. 17, 1834).

357. *Ibid.*, IV, 37–38 (Apr. 19, 1835).

358. *Ibid.*, III, 389 (Dec. 9, 1834).

359. *Ibid.*, p. 519 (July 31, 1835).

360. *Ibid.*, IV, 119 (Oct. 15, 1836).

360. *Ibid.*, IV, 119 (Oct. 15, 1836).

361. *Ibid.*, III, 455 (Mar. 19, 1835).

362. *Ibid.*, IV, 14 (Feb. 24, 1836).

363. *Ibid.*, III, 310 (June 20, 1834).

364. *Ibid.*, pp. 310–11.

365. *Ibid.*, pp. 330–31 (Aug. 17, 1834).

366. *Ibid.*, p. 343 (Sept. 15, 1834); also p. 434 (Jan. 8, 1835), and IV, 52–53 (Mar. 22, 1835).

367. *Ibid.*, III, 376 (Dec. 2, 1834).

368. *Ibid.*, p. 377.

369. *Ibid.*, p. 393 (Dec. 14, 1834); also V, 310–11 (Nov. 3, 1839).

370. *Ibid.*, III, 393.

371. *Ibid.*, p. 398 (Dec. 20, 1834).

372. *Ibid.*

373. *Ibid.*, p. 427 (Dec. 29, 1834).

374. *Ibid.*, p. 467 (Apr. 14, 1835); IV, 11 (Feb. 24, 1836).

375. *Ibid.*, III, 488 (June 4, 1835); also IV, 380–81 (Dec. 18, 1837).

376. *Ibid.*, III, 474 (May 9, 1835); also VI, 86 (Oct. 9, 1841), 370–71 (Mar. 23, 1843), and "Genius" in the index to the *Journals*.

377. *Ibid.*, III, 489 (June 4, 1835).

378. *Ibid.*, p. 492 (June 21, 1835).

379. *Ibid.*, p. 525 (Aug. 1, 1835); also *Works*, VIII, 28.

380. *Journals*, III, 529 (Aug. 3, 1835): "I suspect that wit, humor, and jests admit a more accurate classification by the light of the distinction of the Reason and the Understanding."

381. *Ibid.*, IV, 13 (Feb. 24, 1836).

382. *Ibid.*, p. 14.

383. *Ibid.*, p. 71 (June 17, 1836); also pp. 115–16 (Oct. 13, 1836), 122 (Oct. 20, 1836), 248 (May 26, 1837).

384. *Ibid.*, p. 72 (June 17, 1836).

385. *Ibid.*, p. 113 (Sept. 30, 1836).

386. *Ibid.*, p. 121 (Oct. 19, 1836); also p. 126 (Oct. 25, 1836).

387. *Ibid.*, p. 124 (Oct. 24, 1836).

388. *Ibid.*, III, 295 (May 3, 1834).

389. Notably in the last seven Essays of the Second Section (*Friend*, Shedd ed., pp. 417–72), where he endeavors to reconcile Platonic thought with Baconian methods and emphasizes the extreme importance of the transcendental methodology.

390. *Journals*, III, 295–96 (May 3–6, 1834).

391. By the end of 1834 the importance of Coleridge for Emerson may be gauged by his asking, "Why, O diffusers of Useful Knowledge, do you not offer to deliver a course of lectures on Aristotle and Plato, or on Plato alone, or on him and Bacon and Coleridge?"—*Journals*, III, 386 (Dec. 8, 1834). Two weeks later Coleridge is credited with having "thrown many new truths into circulation" (*Journals*, III, 405). Increasingly we come upon entries beginning with "Coleridge said," until in August of the following year, he is apostrophized as an "acute psychologist" (*Journals*, III, 540), and four months later Carlyle's speculative powers are put down as "limited" (*Journals*, III, 573).

392. *Aids*, Shedd ed., pp. 210–12, 215, 234; see also pp. 31–32.

393. *Ibid.*, pp. 241, 460.

394. *The Friend*, Shedd ed., p. 420.

395. *Works*, I, 3–4.

396. See, for example, *Aids*, Shedd ed., I, 393–95, and *Biog. Lit.*, Shedd ed., pp. 706–9; also "Novalis," *Crit. and Misc. Essays*, II, 25.

397. Steady reader that Emerson was of the British reviews, he might have encountered the Kantian phraseology several times, notably in Sir William Hamilton's essay in the *Edinburgh Review* for January, 1836. See XLII, 448.

398. See Carlyle's "Novalis," *Crit. and Misc. Essays*, II, 21–25, and *Journals*, III, 321.

399. In Chapter I, on Commodity, of course, Emerson applies only Sensation and Understanding, since Commodity does not supply materials for the Reason to work upon. Conversely, in the chapter on Discipline, Emerson omits Sensation, since Nature's use as Discipline is operative only in the realms of Understanding and Reason. In the chapters on Beauty and on Language, however, the Kantian tripartition is applicable, and is applied by Emerson in 1–2–3 order in each case.

400. *Works*, I, 15–19.

401. *Ibid.*, pp. 19–21.

402. That is, Reason understood here as the "higher," or Practical, Reason.—*Ibid.*, pp. 22–24.

403. To be sure, all this is presented without the Kantian "transcendental unit of apperception," without the forms of *Empfindung*, the categories of *Verstand*, or the Ideas of *Vernunft*, without explanation of the terms *a priori* and *a posteriori*. It is presented without analytic or dialectic, without postulates or antinomies, without the distinctions between pure and practical reason, and without a formal definition of the *Ding-an-Sich*, which the former strives vainly to apprehend, or the categorical imperative, which the latter seeks to formulate. Yet it is perfectly satisfactory as far as it goes. The guide here is obviously Coleridge.

404. In the edition of the *Aids* that lay before Emerson, Marsh had reprinted in Appendix C, Coleridge's *Hints toward the Formation of a More Comprehensive Theory of Life*, in which this schema is fully developed; see also *Biographia Literaria*, Shedd ed., 706.

405. Individual passages, such as those on Linnaeus and Buffon, can be related first to the journals and thence to his reading in Coleridge and in scientific books. In the third section of the chapter on Language are incorporated sentences, the exact phrasing of which dates back as far at least as November, 1833: for example, the statement that "the laws of nature answer

to those of matter as face to face in a glass."
On the other hand, the source of the passage
which calls material objects "kinds of *scoriae*
of the substantial thoughts of the Creator" occurs in the *Journals*, III, 513 (July 24, 1835),
where they are quoted directly from Oegger's
True Messiah, to the manuscript of which he
had access before Margaret Fuller set to work
translating it. These circumstances suggest derivations from sources other than Coleridge and
the critical transcendentalists of Germany—
sources which need further investigation.

All this lends support to the idea that the
further Emerson got into his undertaking, that
is, the nearer he approached the chapters on
Idealism and Spirit, the more difficulties he encountered. Obviously parts of Chapter IV were
phrased as late as July, 1835; and as we shall
have occasion to observe later, some of the sections on Discipline (representing the fourth and
highest use of Nature) waited until mid-July of
1836 to receive their final form. See *Journals*,
IV, 67–68.

406. *Works*, I, 26; cf. sec. 2 of Ch. III, on
Beauty.

407. *Ibid.*, p. 36.

408. *Ibid.*, p. 47.

409. *Ibid.*, p. 36.

410. On this score, compare also "The Sover-
eignty of Ethics" (*ibid.*, X, 184–85), first printed in 1878 but composed of notes and lectures
dating from 1859 and 1869.

411. *Ibid.*, I, 43.

412. *Ibid.*, p. 41.

413. *Ibid.*, p. 44.

414. *Ibid.*, pp. 41–42.

415. *Ibid.*, p. 43.

416. *Ibid.*, p. 44.

417. *Ibid.*, p. 41; see also pp. 40, 44.

418. The relation of Carlyle's essay to Emerson's *Nature* is close. See especially "Novalis"
(*Crit. and Misc. Essays*, I, 24, 26, 27–28, 29, 32,
35, 40–41) and "State of German Literature"
(*ibid.*, pp. 58 ff). Indeed, except for the illustrations drawn from natural science and the home-
spun phrases and figures, Emerson's *Nature*
contains few ideas that have not their counterpart in Carlyle's words on Novalis or in the
quotations from Novalis that are adduced for
illustrative purposes.

419. *Works*, I, 47. In this section we come
upon another instance of Emerson's peculiar
errors in attributing ideas or quotations to their
proper sources. Turgot is credited (*ibid.*, p. 56)
with the statement: "He that has never doubted the existence of matter may be assured he
has no aptitude for metaphysical inquiries."
Now, it happens that Turgot was not one regarding whom Emerson had any direct knowl-

edge. Indeed, a search of Turgot's writings does
not reveal the source of the statement there.
Most probably Emerson confused Turgot with
Dugald Stewart, in whose *Dissertation* he could
have come upon the idea as early as 1822. See
Journals, I, 289–90. The same idea is repeated
in Carlyle's essay on Novalis in the *Foreign
Rev.*, IV (1829), 97–104; cf. *Journals*, II, 229–
30, and *Crit. and Misc. Essays*, II, 23. Emerson's
misattribution seems all the more strange because he was rereading Stewart in September,
1830. See *Journals*, II, 308, 310, 321.

420. *Works*, I, 51.

421. *Ibid.*

422. *Ibid.*, pp. 47–49.

423. *Ibid.*, pp. 49–50.

424. This represents no more than many romantic post-Kantians did. It is not very different from the uses to which Kant was put by
Novalis and Schleiermacher or by Wordsworth
and Coleridge. Insofar as this is true, Emerson
is as nearly related to German and English romanticism as to the founder of German critical
transcendentalism. So much it seems safe to
say; to insist upon a nearer relation to Kant, at
the time when *Nature* was being written, would
seem to be unwarrantable.

425. *Works*, I, 56–57.

426. *Ibid.*, p. 59.

427. *Ibid.*, pp. 50–59.

428. *Ibid.*, p. 62.

429. *Ibid.*, p. 63.

430. For, says Emerson, if idealism does
nothing more than "deny the existence of matter, it does not satisfy the demands of the spirit.
It leaves God out of me." He cannot rest his
case thus and pass up the other two questions.
For "when, following the invisible steps of
thought, we come to inquire, Whence is matter?
and Whereto? many truths arise to us out of
the recesses of consciousness. We learn that
the highest is present to the soul of man; that
the dread universal essence, which is not wisdom, or love, or beauty, or power, but all in one,
and each entirely, is that for which all things
exist, and that by which they are; that spirit
creates; that behind nature, throughout nature,
spirit is present; one and not compound it does
not act upon us from without, that is, in space
and time, but spiritually, or through ourselves:
therefore, that spirit, that is, the Supreme
Being, does not build up nature around us, but
puts it forth through us, as the life of the tree
puts forth new branches and leaves through the
pores of the old . . . . Man has access to the
entire mind of the Creator, is himself the creator
in the finite . . . . The world proceeds from the
same spirit as the body of man. It is a remoter
and inferior incarnation of God, a projection of

God in the unconscious . . . ."—*Works*, I, 63–65.

There is nothing to suggest that Emerson identified the process by which he followed "the invisible steps of thought" to his essentially intuitive divinations arising out of the "recesses of consciousness" with the labored steps by which Kant's practical Reason arrived at its "affirmations," though it goes without saying that he was less interested in the process than in the results.

431. *Works*, I, 10.

432. *Ibid.*, III, 235–36.

433. *Ibid.*, II, 268.

434. The following passage from *Journals*, III, 235–36, is misdated 1833 by the editors, as has been explained above. It was undoubtedly written in 1835.

435. *Journals*, III, 235. The remainder of this passage, as quoted, is as given by Cabot (*Memoir*, I, 246–47), and his version differs markedly from that printed in the *Journals*.

436. *Works*, I, 63. Assured and even dogmatic as Emerson's expression is in *Nature* (except for this one reservation), his journals show him repeatedly humbling himself before his problem.

437. *Works*, I, 67; see also pp. 10, 34–44. This passage, say the editors of the *Journals* (I, 412, n.), was inspired by Emerson's visit to the Jardin des Plantes.

The chapter heading "Prospects" itself suggests that the theory advanced in *Nature* is not to be thought of as final. In sending the booklet to Carlyle, Emerson spoke of it as the first chapter of something greater, as "an entering wedge to something more worthy and significant." Carlyle, who considered the gaps and breaks in the philosophy outlined immaterial, if he noticed them at all, replied that he would "call it rather a Foundation and Ground Plan on which you may build whatsoever of great and true has been given you to build."—*Carlyle-Emerson Corresp.*, I, 112; *Works*, I, 410–2.

438. *Works*, I, 36.

439. *Ibid.*, p. 40.

440. *Ibid.*, p. 61.

441. Consult Joseph W. Beach, "Emerson and Evolution," *Univ. of Toronto Quar.*, III, iv (July, 1934), 474–97, and Harry H. Clark, *loc. cit.*, pp. 225–60.

442. *Works*, I, 10. This conviction dates back as far at least as 1833. See Cabot (*Memoir*, II, 710), who misdates the lecture 1832. It was first delivered in 1833. See Bliss Perry's *Emerson Today*, p. 45.

443. *Works*, I, 61.

444. *Ibid.*, pp. 403–4, notes.

445. It should be observed, however, that before the year was out he had advanced one step (though a short one) beyond the merely "occult" relation between man and vegetable —the impact, it seems, of acquaintance with Lamarck. See the synopsis of Emerson's lecture on "The Philosophy of History," delivered Dec. 8, 1836, as printed in Cabot's *Memoir*, II, 725; see also p. 734.

Emerson's development from this position toward that of Darwin (which he never fully reached) was very slow and gradual. We shall consider later his subsequent concern with the advance of science and scientific theory. It forms another important chapter in the history of Emerson's philosophic development and impinges upon the questions regarding Germanic influence upon Emerson. For the moment it is enough to remark that *The Origin of Species* (1859) went unnoticed in his journals for a number of years because he had already extracted from Stallo's *Principles of Nature* (1848) as much as he wanted at the time of Darwinian evolutionary theory. As late as 1873 he observed: "Darwin's Origin of Species was published in 1859, but Stallo, in 1849 [*sic*] writes, 'animals are but foetal forms of man.'"—*Journals*, X, 423.

446. At the beginning of this period man is conceived as "the point wherein matter and spirit meet and marry. The Idealist says, God paints the world around your soul. The spiritualist saith, Yes, but lo! God is within you. The Self of self creates the world through you, and organizations like you. The Universal Central Soul comes to the surface in your body."—*Journals*, IV, 78 (July 30, 1836). Here the idealist and the spiritualist, the doctrine of transcendence and that of emanation, exist side by side.

The next year he is wrestling with his problem still in the same fashion: "Who shall define to me the individual? I behold with awe and delight many illustrations of the One Universal Mind. I see my being imbedded in it; as a plant in the earth so I grow in God. I am only a form of him. He is the soul of me. I can even with a mountainous aspiring say, *I am God*, by transferring my *me* out of the flimsy and unclean precinct of my body . . . . How came the Individual, thus armed and impassioned, to parricide thus murderously inclined, ever to traverse and kill the Divine Life? Ah, wicked Manichee! Into that dim problem I cannot enter. *A believer in Unity, a seer of Unity, I yet behold two . . . . Cannot I conceive the Universe without a contradiction?*" (italics mine). *Journals*, IV, 247–49 (May 26, 1837).

447. What troubled Emerson as much at this point as his failure in *Nature* to establish a sys-

tem of Identity on solid metaphysical grounds was the position of man in which the philosophy expressed in *Nature* left him—a philosophy by which the individual is part and parcel of God, God is pure spirit, and the world, so far as man is concerned, is an illusion used by God to educate individuals who are, after all, not individuals at all. In this case, the individual seemed lost in God; while, in the evolutionary theory, he seemed in danger of being swallowed up in an overpowering, impersonal, natural reality.

448. The name at least of Plotinus was known to Emerson as early as 1830; but in 1837 he became the object of close attention. Proclus begins to be mentioned prominently in 1838. Thereafter the entire galaxy of neo-Platonists is consulted for light. For a detailed, but overenthusiastic, treatment of the neo-Platonic influence on Emerson, see J. S. Harrison, *The Teachers of Emerson* (N.Y., 1910). Professor F. I. Carpenter's *Emerson and Asia* (Cambridge, Mass., 1930), as the title suggests, adds information, which is essential to any effort to evaluate the elements of Emerson's thought that derive from Greek sources.

It may be observed that Emerson was inclined to be profoundly affected by the last book which he had read, especially when that book struck a sympathetic chord. This is not to suggest that he accepted docilely whatever he found, or that he slavishly echoed whatever he could use. It is simply to record a fact which is apparent again and again in the history of Emerson's concern with books.

449. *Journals*, IV, 380–81 (Dec. 18, 1837). The extent of Emerson's deflection from the course which Coleridge had charted for him a few years before in the realm of critical transcendentalism may be gauged by his designation of the *Trismegisti* as "that lofty and sequestered class who have been its [the pure intellect's] prophets and oracles, the high-priesthood of pure reason."—*Works*, II, 345; see also II, 427, notes, where Plato, Plotinus, Porphyry, Synesius, Proclus and the other Neo-Platonists influenced by Oriental thought —these "great spiritual lords who have walked in the world"—are again named "the high-priesthood of the pure reason." Obviously the word *reason* has taken on new (un-Kantian) connotations.

450. *Journals*, IV, 381 (Dec. 18, 1837). This is followed by the passage, eventually used as the second paragraph in the essay on "Intellect " which, together with what was drawn from various lectures dating to 1836–1839, serves as the best *gradus* to a view of Emerson's thought of these years. See *Works*, II, 325–26, 437–38, notes.

451. The contrast here between the adult and the child suggests kinship with similar ideas in Wordsworth's "Ode," Schiller's *Über naive und sentimentalische Dichtung*, Herder, Hamann and beyond them, Plato. It is doubtful that Emerson read Schiller's work *On Naive and Sentimental Poetry*, but he was familiar with Carlyle's *Life of Schiller*, which contains passages of striking similarity to that quoted. See Carlyle's *Works*, Centenary ed., XXV, esp. 98, 198, 199.

452. *Journals*, IV, 383 (Dec. 18, 1837).

453. *Works*, II, 327.

454. See *Works*, II, 426–27, notes, and Cabot, *Memoir*, II, 737–40.

455. That he did struggle with this idea the essays mentioned amply demonstrate. See for example, "The Over-Soul," *Works*, I, 268–69, 271–72, 276, 279, and esp. 280–82, 292, 294–97, and "The Method of Nature," *Works*, II, 194, 197, 199–200, 210, 221, 223.

Indeed, both series of the *Essays* (1841 and 1844) are worth studying with the design to trace the neo-Platonic elements in them. Especially to the point, besides the references already specified, are "Compensation" and "Spiritual Laws" of the First Series and those on "Nature" and "Nominalist and Realist" of the Second. "Circles" (written mainly during 1840), permeated as it is with neo-Platonic ideas, exhibits already another tendency—that of a return to science and an attempt to proceed to the principle of evolution; it demonstrates most clearly a growing dissatisfaction with the inconclusiveness of intuitional mysteries and marks the beginning of a return to science and philosophy—the last phase of Emerson's philosophic development.

456. That is, during 1837–1840 Emerson turned more and more from metaphysical speculation to history and biography—from theory to practice. It is noticeable, also, that about 1838, as his interest in metaphysics decreases, his references to Coleridge fall off, while those to Carlyle continue unabated—partly, of course, because of the close personal relations with Carlyle, following Coleridge's death in 1834. While he was aware that metaphysically Carlyle was dead, Emerson nevertheless turned to him for inspiration and affirmation regarding practical matters—for ethical but no longer for metaphysical principles. A comparison of Carlyle's *Heroes* and Emerson's *Representative Men*, in spite of the large differences, serves to illustrate their relationship.

457. Emerson's philosophic career up to this point is, in some respects, similar to O. A. Brownson's going from creed to creed, each time knowing that he was right and the last

time (or two) knowing that he "could not be wrong." The difference is one of degree, not of kind.

The last change that Emerson had undergone is best gauged by comparing the *Nature* of 1836 with the second essay on Nature that he wrote during the early forties. The question with which Nature confronts him is the same; but in assaulting the problem, he does not now, as he had in 1833–36, array in due order the epistemological forces of the transcendental method. Now, as then, he concludes that he cannot solve Nature's riddle; but now he humbly considers that it was not intended that he should, and lets it go at that.

458. For a consideration of Emerson's earlier concern with evolution, it is important to take into account what he derived of the Hunterian theory from Coleridge's *Friend* and *Aids* and from Dr. Abernethy's *Lectures;* his first contacts, in 1830, with Lee's *Life of Cuvier;* in 1835, with Oegger's *True Messiah, or the Old and New Testament Examined According to the Principles of the Language of Nature;* with Lyell's *Principles of Geology,* and, perhaps through Lyell, with Geoffroy Saint-Hilaire; in 1836, with Lamarck; in 1838, with Charles Bell's *Treatise of the Hand . . . Evincing Design;* and in 1844, with Robert Chambers' epochal *Vestiges of Creation.*

459. To Professor J. W. Beach belongs the credit of being the first to point out the possible significance of this book. A more exhaustive study reveals even greater influence than Mr. Beach intimated might be discovered from this quarter.

460. Johann Bernhard Stallo (1823–1900) was a now-forgotten German-American journalist, lawyer, politician, diplomat, statesman, and professor of science and mathematics at St. Xavier, Cincinnati, and St. John's, Fordham, N.Y.

461. To be sure, Emerson had, in 1841, read with considerable interest Barchou de Penhoen's *Histoire de la philosophie allemande depuis Leibnitz jusqu'à Hegel* (2 vols., Paris, 1836), and paused long enough to copy extracts concerning Boehme, Kepler, Leibnitz, Newton, and Kant (see *Journals,* VI, 142–46); but the succeeding sections of the journals exhibit no evidence that this was followed up, as it would have been in the early thirties, or as it was to be during the fifties and sixties (whenever he came upon such a book) by further reading and a tracing out of leads supplied or suggested by it. The causes for this doubtless lie in the facts (1) that Emerson was not, in 1841, primarily interested in either metaphysics or science, and (2) that he had not progressed, through the trials and errors of the years, to the point where he would once again be eager and consider himself capable (as he had believed himself earlier) of proceeding to a new synthesis.

462. Emerson's published journals do not indicate the precise date in the year of 1849 when he turned to Stallo's book. Possibly it was called to his attention as early as March, 1848, when James E. Cabot's laudatory review appeared in Parker's *Massachusetts Quarterly Review,* I, ii (Mar., 1848), 263–65. The plans for this new journal were perfected in Emerson's home in May of 1847 (see *Journals,* VII, 268–69), and Emerson wrote the editors' manifesto for the new magazine.

463. See *Journals,* VIII, 76 (Dec. 14, 1849), and esp. *Works,* VIII, 7, and 359–62, for interesting leads to the study of Emerson's progress from an earlier attention to the theory of "arrested and progressive development . . . the electric word pronounced by John Hunter a hundred years ago" to his more mature reflections on Darwin's theory.

It is not clear precisely by what means, other than Stallo's book, Emerson came by his knowledge of Oken. He mentions Oken as early as August 4, 1842, in a letter to John H. Heath (then in Berlin) as "a continuator of Schelling's thought," and gives him the title of "hero" for the "grandeur of his attempt to unite natural and moral philosophy."—*Letters,* III, 76–77. See also *Journals,* VII, 151 (1846). These references antedate Emerson's reading of Stallo, who devotes a good deal of space to Oken's philosophy of nature (see esp. pp. 258, 313). Whether Emerson read Oken, or about him, before 1849 or not, it is clear that Stallo forcibly called (or recalled) Emerson's attention to him, for most of the quotations from Oken which he copied into his commonplace book in 1850 are derived at second hand from Stallo.

As an evolutionist, Oken is known for his theory of the origin of life in the *Ur-Schleim.* Professor Beach has suggested that Emerson's "fluid in an elastic sack," the "infusoria," or microscopically minute bladders with fluid content, may be the stuff which makes up the primary sea-slime of Oken's theory.

It is worth noting that while Emerson regarded the theory of spontaneous generation (or "equivocal generation") as a scientific humbug in 1831, his reading in Chambers, Goethe, and Stallo, and others considerably altered his views by 1849. See, for example, what he made of this theory in 1854, when he wrote the introduction for "Poetry and Imagination," esp. *Works,* VIII, 7–8, and 358–60, notes.

As the analysis of Emerson's knowledge of science proceeds, it is becoming more and more obvious that the claims of earlier students of Emerson to the effect that he anticipated Darwin by five years (even twenty-five years, in the case of *Nature*) are overstated. The fact seems to be rather that some years were to pass after the appearance of Darwin's epoch-making book on species before the *full* significance of the new marshalling of scientific data and of the theories derived thence dawned on Emerson. His conception of evolution prior to his reading of Darwin underwent a gradual development from (1) the vague theories of development as he found them in his reading of the ancient philosophers, to (2) the Hunterian and Coleridgean theory of the scale of being with which he became familiar in 1829, to (3) Cuvier's fourfold classification of the animal kingdom, as he read about it in Lee's *Life* in 1830, to (4) Chambers' anticipation of Darwinian evolution, in 1844–1845 (*Journals*, VI, 550; VII, 51–53), not to mention supplementary information derived from numerous other scientific and pseudo-scientific sources, among which the neo-Platonic tradition must be reckoned as one and the Schellingian *Natur-Philosophie* another. The transition from the Hunterian chain-of-being theory to that of Darwinian evolution involved no such antagonisms for Emerson's mind as did the "bestial theory" to Coleridge's religious prepossessions, or his demands for philosophic consistency, either. For the transcendental cast of Emerson's mind was one in which intellectual contrarieties sometimes succeeded in living happily together in a sort of benign solution. Moreover, Emerson was exposed to scientific influences which Coleridge did not live to encounter. For examples of how easily Emerson was prepared to pass from the graduated-scale-of-being theory to that of transmutation of species, shortly after reading *Vestiges of Creation* during 1844–1845, see *Journals*, VII, 51–52, 58, 69–70, 104 (1845), and "Nature" (written in 1840–1841), *Works*, III, 167–96.

Emerson's transition from the scale-of-being to a more strictly evolutionary phase of his thinking was made very gradually. A detailed analysis of this transition would assuredly prove interesting. Such a study would have to distinguish carefully between the theory embodied in the quotation printed by Cabot (*Memoir*, I, 223–24) from Emerson's lecture in December, 1833, "On the Relation of Man to the Globe," and what is sometimes confused with it, i.e., the doctrine of evolution as transmutation of species, as Emerson conceived it increasingly after 1845 and certainly after 1849, when he read Stallo, who carefully drew the distinction between the old and the new. See Stallo's *First Principles*, 407–11.

Virtually unexplored but important is the question of precisely how much Goethe's scientific ideas influenced Emerson. During the thirties he worked carefully through Goethe's three more important scientific treatises and extracted for his journals the essential ideas from them. By September, 1843, he rated the second part of *Faust* "the grandest enterprise of literature . . . since the *Paradise Lost*" (*Journals*, VI, 466). An attentive reading of his essay on Goethe in *Representative Men* (1850), particularly of the passage devoted to *Faust II* (*Works*, IV, 271 ff), will indicate that little of the full significance of that work was lost to him.

It is to be borne in mind, also, that much may have come to Emerson from sources the evidences of which time has obliterated, such as the conversations he had with scientists. From Thoreau he undoubtedly learned much of botany, though he came in the end to be repelled by Thoreau's argumentativeness. There are indications in Holmes's biography of Emerson that the professor of anatomy at Harvard sometimes discussed scientific matters with the seer of Concord; and Agassiz tells us that he preferred Emerson's conversation on scientific subjects to that of any other man. See *Journals*, IX, 520–31; X, 60–61; 75 (1864); also VI, 395; VIII, 69; X, 208; *Works*, X, 466; Firkins, *Emerson*, p. 94; Cabot, *Memoir*, I, 270, 272, 282; *Carlyle-Emerson Corresp.*, II, 204; R. M. Gay, *Emerson* (N.Y., 1928), pp. 135, 161; Mark Van Doren, *Thoreau* (Boston, 1916), p. 123, and notably the letters of 1848 (as edited by R. L. Rusk) which record the pleasure Emerson found in the company of British scientists during his second visit to Europe.

464. On Saint-Hilaire, consult the essays by Professors Clark and Beach.

465. Emerson had grasped related ideas (such as that on "sphericity") as early at least as 1840, when "Circles" was written; he had, moreover, encountered the ancient doctrine of a "flowering" in Heraclitus, to whom De Gerando had sent him in 1830, and from whom he seems to have borrowed, in 1841, the idea for "Woodnotes II":

> Onward and on, the eternal Pan
> Halteth never in one shape,
> But forever doth escape,
> Like wave or flame, into new forms
> Of gem, and air, of plants and worms.

After reading Chambers' *Vestiges of Creation*, he wrote in 1845 (*Journals*, VII, 58) what seems to be an advance upon the idea expressed in "Woodnotes II":

As creeps from leaf to leaf the worm,
So creeps its life from form to form,
And the poor emmet on the ground
On the march of centuries is bound.

Indeed, many years before, he had found in Madame de Staël's characterization of German philosophy not only the doctrines of the analogy between mind and matter, of the microcosm (earlier noted in Aristotle, *Journals*, II, 347), of unity in variety and variety in unity, but also the idea, attributed to Goethe, that man's mind *"is always advancing, but in a spiral line."* See de Staël's *Germany* (Wight ed., 1859), II, 218–19, 225. However, these and all other early instances miss the precise mark in one way or another, so that the almost exact parallelism of idea and expression, together with the identity of dates between Emerson's reading about the idea in Stallo and his rephrasing of the motto for the 1849 edition of *Nature*, suggests that we have here more than a mere coincidence.

466. Consult indexes to *Letters* and *Journals*.

467. See *Journals*, X, 248 (June 16, 1868), and *Works*, XII, 13.

468. Fichte's more technical works were not available in English translation during Emerson's productive life; but beginning in 1844, when Wm. Smith translated and Chapman published, in London, *The Characteristics of the Present Age*, the more popular works became accessible to the British and American reader. On this score, see B. Q. Morgan, *op. cit.*, pp. 113–14.

469. *Journals*, III, 260 (Feb. 12, 1834).

470. *Journals*, X, 318 (1870).

471. *Crit. and Misc. Essays*, I, 60.

472. Wight's ed., N.Y., 1859, II, 193–94.

473. In 1847 Fichte merely reinforced the practical message that Emerson had taught years before. Similarly Strauss (who came prominently to his attention about this time) only advanced a criticism of the Christian tradition which Emerson had not only theorized upon in his own way but actually put into practice years before by renouncing that traditionalism.

474. See Fichte's Preface, as reproduced in Hedge's *Prose Writers* (3rd ed., N.Y. and London, 1855), pp. 384–85.

475. *Journals*, IV, 248–49. Compare Hedge, *op. cit.*, pp. 391 ff.

It is significant that after 1850, when Emerson returned to a reconsideration of German idealism, he never included Fichte in his lists of German thinkers whom he accorded first praise. Kant, Schelling, and Hegel are always named; Schleiermacher and Schopenhauer, sometimes;

Fichte, never. It is questionable, also, whether Emerson was prepared, even in 1847, to advance to Fichte's "rigid determinism" and "strict necessity" in nature, as promulgated in *The Destination of Man*. Emerson never quite subscribed to a naturalistic view of nature. In spite of his belief in the "reign of law," he never relinquished the notion of either an "occult" or a "moral" relation between Nature and Spirit —not even during the period when he came most under the influence of the evolutionary theorists.

476. Hedge, *op. cit.*, p. 400; see also pp. 401–2. Emerson the Believer might readily acquiesce in such a fatalistic or passive conclusion, but Emerson the Inquirer could hardly have agreed with it, or rested the case with Fichte when the latter concluded: "All my questions are solved." —*Ibid.*, p. 402.

477. How differently Emerson might have reacted toward Fichte if he had ever turned to his more technical works we need not inquire, however nearly they agreed on such points as the immutability of moral law, on freedom, on the individual, on optimism and the belief in the progress of culture, on nature's ability to contradict herself, on the practical reason as the "root of all reason," and on the "sublimity of Action through Will." Practically, Emerson had advanced to Fichte's position long before he discovered the "grand unalterableness of Fichte's morality." If Emerson had been reminded of the similarities between his own philosophy of practice, or "use," and Fichte's ethics, he might have observed that nothing more was involved than another instance illustrating his principle that "there is one mind, and every man is a porch leading into it."—*Journals*, IV, 171 (Dec. 10, 1836).

478. See for example, IX of *Biographia Literaria*. Schelling is mentioned in Emerson's *Journals* (II, 422) as early as October 24, 1831.

479. *Journals*, IV, 473 (June 12, 1838); also *Works*, I, 161.

480. The italics are added. Obviously this claim is not to be taken literally.

481. *Journals*, VII, 151–52 (Mar. 24, 1846). Emerson's reading of Boehme, begun in 1835, proceeded haphazardly until May 8, 1844, when he observed: "I have never had good luck with Behmen before today. And now I see that his excellence is in his comprehensiveness, not, like Plato, in his precision. His propositions are vague, inadequate, straining. It is his aim that is great. He will know, not one thing, but all things. . . . . Jacob Behmen is a great man, but he accepts the accommodations of the Hebrew Dynasty. Of course he cannot take rank with the masters of the world. His value, like that of

Proclus, is chiefly for rhetoric."—*Journals*, VI, 517.

482. See the numbers for January and April, 1843. Already in August, 1842, Emerson had admitted to John F. Heath, then in Berlin, where Schelling was lecturing, that "to hear Schelling might well tempt the firmest rooted philosopher from his home." "I confess," he went on, "to more curiosity in respect to his opinion than to those of any living philosopher," and he concluded his letter with the wish that Heath would return home soon bringing all of Schelling's best thoughts with him.—*Letters*, III, 76–77.

483. *Ibid.*, p. 77; see also pp. 70–71, 98–99, 100, 243.

484. *Ibid.*, pp. 98–99 (Nov. 21, 1842).

485. *Ibid.*, p. 243 (Feb. 26, 1844).

486. *Ibid.*, p. 290 (June 26, 1844).

487. *Ibid.*, p. 296 (June 12, 1845).

488. *Ibid.*, pp. 298–99 (Sept. 1, 1845).

489. *Ibid.*, pp. 303–4 (Sept. 28, 1845).

490. *Ibid.*, p. 343 (Aug. 19, 1846).

491. *Ibid.*, pp. 345–46.

492. *Journals*, VII, 152 (Mar. 24, 1846).

493. *Ibid.*, VIII, 69 (Nov. 17, 1849).

494. *Ibid.*, p. 16 (1849).

495. *Ibid.*, p. 249 (1851).

496. *Ibid.*, pp. 529–30 (Feb. 24, 1855).

497. *Ibid.*, p. 124 (Sept. 1, 1850).

498. *Ibid.*, p. 225 (1851).

499. This snap judgment regarding a Hindu element in Hegel appears substantially the same as that of W. T. Harris, a profounder student of Hegel than Emerson. See Harris, *Hegel's Logic* (Chicago, 1890), Preface, pp. xiii–xv; also Kurt F. Leidecker, "Harris and Indian Philosophy," *Monist*, XLVI, i (Jan., 1936), 112–53.

500. *Journals*, VIII, 69 (Nov. 17, 1849). Obviously this quotation is derived at second hand from Stallo. See the chapter on Schelling, *op. cit.*, pp. 214–29, esp. pp. 221, 222–24.

501. *Journals*, VIII, 77 (Dec. 14, 1849); also X, 423 (1873). The printed journals contain only three of Emerson's extracts from Stallo (by no means the most significant). The MS journals contain ten others.

502. *Ibid.*, VIII, 246 (July, 1851).

503. *Ibid.*, p. 533 (Aug., 1855).

504. *Journals*, IX, 419–20 (May, 1864), *et seq.*

505. *Ibid.*, pp. 30–31 (Apr. 5, 1856); see also X, 455 (1876): "The analysis of intellect and Nature which the grand masters, Heraclitus, Parmenides, Plato, Spinoza, Hume, Kant, Schelling, Hegel have attempted are of primary value to science . . . ."

506. "Poetry and Imagination" (written *ca.* 1854), *Works*, VIII, 8.

507. *Journals*, VIII, 46–47.

508. *Ibid.*, p. 77 (Dec. 14, 1849). Stallo (*op. cit.*, p. 17) has: "The figurations of nature must be more than a *symbol*,—they must be the gesticular expression of nature's inner life . . . ."

509. Omitted from the published *Journals*. Here reproduced from the MS Journal marked "AZ. 1850," p. 52. Emerson records the source correctly as Stallo, *op. cit.*, p.35.

510. MS Journal, "AZ. 1850," p. 52; quoted from Stallo, p. 58.

511. *Journals*, VIII, 77; MS Journal, "AZ. 1850," p. 53; source is Stallo, p. 16.

512. MS Journal, "AZ. 1850," p. 43; Stallo, p. 93.

513. MS Journal, "AZ. 1850," p. 53. I have been unable to find the exact source in Stallo, but passages on pages 108, 256, and 304 may have supplied the necessary suggestions.

514. MS Journal, "AZ. 1850," p. 53; quoted from Stallo, p. 304; see also p. 121, where Stallo's statement reads: "Oken sometimes defines animals as foetal men."

515. MS Journal, "AZ. 1850," p. 53; Stallo, p. 291.

516. MS Journal, "AZ. 1850," p. 53; Stallo, p. 192. For further references to Stallo, see *Journals*, X, 423 (1873), and the following notations under the heading of "Stallo: Oken": "The whole bird is a respiratory organ" (MS Journal, "AZ. 1850," p. 54; Stallo, p. 322). "The bird is an animal of song in full organization: in it nature attains to complete hearing and speaking" (MS Journal, "AZ. 1850," p. 54; Stallo, p. 322). "Hegel, or Oken, or whosoever shall enunciate the law which necessitates gravitation as a phenomenon of a larger law, embracing mind and matter, diminishes Newton" (MS Journal, "AZ. 1850," p. 166).

517. *Journals*, VIII, 77–78. This idea of eras or cyclic development becomes henceforth a common one in Emerson's journals. See, for example, IX, 295 (1861); for additional data consult the indexes of the *Journals* and the *Works* under the heads of Absolute, Identity, Polarity, Bi-polarity, Organic, Transition, Rotation, Bias, and Idealism.

In what Emerson says about cyclic development, the influence of Herder should be considered. Emerson's interest in Herder dates back at least to 1824 (see *Letters*, I, 153, 161), by which time he asked William (then in Germany) to send him "an English translation of Herder's phil. of history." Such ideas as the Greek deification of nature and the theory of cyclic, genetic development in man's view of nature are prominent in Herder's historical and critical works; see esp. *Ideen zur Philosophie der Geschichte der Menschheit*, Bk. XIII. This book became available in English in 1800.

518. *Journals*, VIII, 487 (1854), X, 462–63 (1862–1872), and *Works*, VIII, 4–11, 66; XII, 17, 19–20.

519. The relative influence of these several men can be studied through key references to be located in the *Journals, Letters,* and *Works* by consulting the indexes.

520. *Journals*, X, 205 (1867).

521. *Ibid.*, pp. 205–6 (1867).

522. For Emerson's sources of the doctrines of Identity and the Absolute, see Stallo, pp. 335–44, 400–7.

523. *Journals*, VIII, 69 (1850); see also MS Journal, "AZ. 1850," 53 (reproduced above), and MS Journal, "GL. 1861, 1862, 1863," p. 248, as well as *Journals*, VIII, 126 (1850), and X, 206 (1867), where he asserts that "the laws below are sisters of the laws above." Compare the introduction to "Poetry and Imagination," written *ca.* 1854 (*Works*, VIII, esp. 4–11), with Part I of Stallo's book, notably the chapter on Schelling, for a very interesting parallel illustrating how closely Emerson followed Stallo on both Schelling and Hegel. See Stallo, pp. 214–19, and 221, 222. The source of Emerson's statement appears to be Stallo, p. 222, except that Emerson substituted *union* for *identity* in Stallo's statement that "the Absolute . . . is the identity of the Ideal and the Real . . . ."

Just as Emerson found in his reading of Stallo an anticipation by ten years of Darwinian evolution, so Henry Adams in 1903, when he tried to read the new "Grammar of Science" as typified by Karl Pearson, found in it "little more than an enlargement of Stallo's book already twenty years old." However, there is a vast difference between the effect Stallo had on the two seekers. Emerson reed Stallo in a way to confirm his faith in the Absolute as "the identity of the Ideal and the Real." The younger man read in Stallo's "Concepts of Modern Science" (as he calls Stallo's *Concepts and Theories of Modern Physics* of 1882) a confirmation for his view of "Twentieth-Century Multiplicity." See *The Education of Henry Adams* (Boston, 1927), 377, 449, 452.

524. Omitted in the *Journals*; here quoted from MS Journal, "TU. 1849," p. 22. Compare *Journals*, VIII, 126, 506; IX, 295; and XI, 317–18.

525. This statement, like the second of Schelling's above, is several times exactly repeated by Emerson at this time and later. See MS Journal, "ZO. 1856," p. 154 (not in *Journals*), and MS Journal "LN. 1866," p. 19 (*Journals*, X, 144). See also *Journals*, XI, 317–18 (1870), and *Works*, VIII, 1–11.

526. *Journals*, X, 423 (1873); MS Journal, "ST. 1870–1875," p. 218.

527. See *Journals*, VII, 69–70 (1845). A more specific source for the phrase than Chambers, who uses the words but not in the sequence and contiguity in which Emerson does, it seems to me, is Hoefer's *Nouvelle Biographie Générale*. See the passage in *Journals*, X, 265 (1856), which he derived thence.

528. Much has been made of a passage in the introduction to "Poetry and Imagination" (*Works*, VIII, 7) as indicating that Emerson arrived at the theory of evolution about 1853–1854, when most of this essay was written. The passage in question is this: "The electric word pronounced by John Hunter a hundred years ago, *arrested and progressive development*, indicating the way upward from the invisible protoplasm to the highest organisms, gave the poetic key to Natural Science, to which the theories of Geoffroy Saint-Hilaire, Oken, of Goethe, of Agassiz and Owen and Darwin in zoology and botany, are the fruits,—a hint whose power is not yet exhausted, showing unity and perfect order in physics." Unfortunately for the validity of this claim, an examination of the lecture as given in 1854 does not reveal the passage. Evidently it was written and inserted, probably between 1865 (when he jotted down in his journal the passage from which the published version was later elaborated) and 1876 (when it was first printed). See *Journals*, X, 265, and *Works*, VIII, 357–58, notes.

529. In his later years Emerson preferred to use the words *transit* and *transition* rather than *evolution*. For examples, see *Journals*, VIII, 501 (1854), 529–30 (1855), X, 457–58, 462–63 (1862–1872). Similarly, he preferred the word *bias* to *individualism* or *originality*, as used during his earlier periods. See *Journals*, VIII, 226 (1851), 543 (1855), IX, 539 (1863), X, 22–23 (1864), 146–47 (1866).

530. See *Works*, XII, 17: "Matter is dead Mind." On this score, see Stallo, pp. 108–9, and esp. pp. 16–21.

531. *Works*, VIII, 4, 5, 7–8; see also *Journals*, X, 457: "Transition [meaning evolution] is the organic density of the mind . . . . 'Tis the great law of Nature, that the more transit, the more continuity. . . . What we call the Universe to-day is only a symptom or omen of that to which we are passing. Every atom is on its way onward. The universe circulates in thought."

532. *Works*, pp. 7, 8. The doctrine of polarity Emerson found conveniently stated in Stallo's discussion of Schelling, *op. cit.*, pp. 223–24.

533. Emerson himself suggested as much in his *Journals*, X, 459–60: "Natural Sciences have made great strides by means of Hegel's dogma which puts Nature and thought, matter

and spirit, in right relation, one the expression or externalization of the other." See also pp. 455, 462–63.

534. *Journals*, V, 206 (May 26, 1839); see also IV, 248–49, 250, 278–79 (1837).

535. "Circles," *Works*, II, 309–10; see also *Journals*, V, 223 (June 18, 1839).

536. Each of these propositions is thrice set down exactly in Emerson's daybooks, and repeated in *English Traits* (*Works*, V, 242); while the general ideas are reverted to many more times.

537. This sentence, quoted from Schelling, Emerson first wrote on his blotter on October 24, 1831 (*Journals*, II, 422). He repeated it in in 1850 and 1870 (*Journals*, VIII, 126, and X, 317–18.

538. Quoted from MS Journal, "AZ. 1850," p. 279, which shows several variations from the printed *Journals*, VIII, 126 (1850).

539. *Journals*, X, 318 (1870).

540. MS Journal, "ZO. 1856," p. 98.

541. MS Journal, "ZO. 1856," 154.

542. MS Journal, "DL. 1860–1866," p. 248.

543. *Journals*, IX, 30 (1856).

544. An example of how Emerson associated Hegel's doctrine of thought as Absolute with Schelling's philosophy of Identity as consuming all diversity occurs in the section of *English Traits* entitled "Literature." Here he links together, as two great interdependent germinal generalizations, or "constants" in the "vast kingdoms of thought," (1) "Hegel's study of civil history, as the conflict of ideas and the victory of the deeper thought" and (2) "the identity-philosophy of Schelling, couched in the statement that 'all difference is quantitative.'" —*Works*, V, 242; see also X, 338, and *Journals*, X, 137 (1866), and 205 (1867), where he professes, on the basis of Schelling and Hegel, to "see the law of all nature in Identity and Centrality." Identity is conceived as "One law [that] consumes all diversity."

Emerson apparently made less of Hegel's doctrine of opposites than did Whitman, but the passage just quoted (if there were not a dozen besides) is sufficient refutation of the idea that Emerson shut his mind entirely to the antithetical forms of the Hegelian thought processes. After his careful reading of Stallo's book he could hardly have remained unaware of the Hegelian doctrine of opposites.

545. This work of reference Emerson mentions frequently between 1862 and 1870. See esp. *Journals*, X, 322 (1870): "I find *Nouvelle Biographie Générale* a perpetual benefactor,— almost sure on every consultation to answer promptly and well. Long live M. Docteur Hoefer!"

It is to be noted that Emerson, especially during his later years, often preferred to read about scientists and metaphysicians than to read their writings. We have already observed the high repute in which he held encyclopedias and handbooks. In 1871, he again confessed his dislike for the reading of technical works: "Physicists in general repel me. I have no wish to read them, and thus do not know their names. But the anecdotes of these men of ideas awake curiosity and delight."—*Journals*, X, 364; consult also X, 365–73. Anent his reading of foreign works, he admitted: "The respectable and sometimes excellent translations of Bohn's Library have done for literature what railroads have done for internal intercourse. I do not hesitate to read all the books I have named, and all good books, in translations. What is really best in any book is translatable . . . . I rarely read any Latin, Greek, German, Italian, sometimes not even a French book, in the original, which I can procure in a good version. I should as soon think of swimming across Charles River when I wish to go to Boston, as of reading all my books in originals when I have them rendered for me in my mother tongue." *Works*, VII, 203–4.

Thus he turned, now more than ever, to biographical dictionaries, commentators, expositors of science and philosophy, and various other digests and compendia. Instead of returning to a firsthand reading of Schelling, for example, he relied on Stallo's *First Principles* and von Ense's *Tagebücher*, a complete set of which he seems to have possessed, and through which he appears to have worked. See *Journals*, X, 310, 445. Indeed, Emerson had no scruples about preferring as authorities the daily newspapers to the staid *Edinburgh* or the reputable *North American*, and repeatedly preserved the phrases and sentences of some nameless hack or journalist provided his words struck a responsive chord. See *Journals*, X, 33–34 (1864).

546. MS Journal, "ZO. 1856," 154. The quotation is repeated in MS Journal, "LN. 1866," p. 19 (printed in *Journals*, X, 144, 1866). See also Stallo, pp. 492–93, as well as pp. 500–1, 509–10, 515, 519–20.

547. MS Journal, "ZO. 1856," p. 182.

548. MS Journal, "VA. 1862–63," p. 286. The fact that Hegel was anticipated by Heraclitus in the idea of things being in a state of becoming was not, in Emerson's opinion, derogatory to Hegel. On the Heraclitus-Hegel relationship, see *Journals*, X, 321 (1870), where he implies that although both anticipated his own reaching this thought, it is nonetheless his own.

Emerson's reference to Hoefer's *Nouvelle Biographie Générale* is easily identified as referring to Volume XXIII, pp. 743-44, although Emerson had read the same statement regarding the Heraclitus-Hegel relationship in Stallo (pp. 49–50, note) in 1849. See the entire passage on Hegel in Hoefer (*op. cit.*, XXIII, 729–53), which Emerson considered carefully about 1862–1863.

549. *Journals*, X, 240 (May 22, 1868); see also *Letters*, VI, 18–19 (June, 1868).

550. *Journals*, X, 101 (1865).

551. *Ibid.*, p. 343 (1870).

552. *Ibid.*, pp. 310, 322, (1870); p. 445 (1875).

553. See, for example, *ibid.*, pp. 116 (1865), and 143–44 (1866).

554. *Ibid.*, p. 130 (Jan. 5, 1866).

555. See "Eloquence," *Works*, VIII, 131, where he speaks of the "metaphysical *zymosis* [of Germany] culminating in Kant, Schelling, Schleiermacher, Hegel, and so ending." It is significant that Fichte is omitted from all of Emerson's later tributes to German philosophers.

556. *Letters*, VI, 291 (Mar. 2, 1876).

557. See *Journals*, X, 21, 25–26, 33 ff. (1864). Something, too, may have come from Alcott, who, like himself, was extending his lecture tours to include St. Louis and other centers of Hegelianism in the West, and with whom he compared notes on American *versus* European thought, and especially on Western *versus* New England thought. See *ibid.*, pp. 53, 56 ff.

558. *Letters*, IV, 530–31 (Sept. 26, 1855).

559. *Ibid.*, V, 421–22 (July 18, 1865).

560. *Ibid.*, p. 514 (Apr. 4, 1867).

561. See *ibid.*, p. 456, n. 54, and V, 514, n. 140.

562. In the list of members as given by William Schuyler (see his article, "German Philosophy in St. Louis," *Bull. of the Washington Univ. Assn.*, No. 2, Apr. 23, 1904 [St. Louis, 1904] pp. 72–73), eighteen individuals are listed as "directors," thirty-five as "associates," and forty-nine "auxiliaries." All of the last group lived at a distance from St. Louis. It included men like A. B. Alcott, F. B. Sanborn, J. E. Cabot, D. A. Wasson, F. H. Hedge, John Weiss, and Emerson in New England; J. B. Stallo and August Willich of Cincinnati; J. H. Stirling of Scotland and T. Collins Simon of England; A. Vera of Italy; Jos. de Fonfride of France; and Karl Rosenkranz, Franz Hoffmann, Friedrich Kapp, Ludwig Feuerbach, Moritz Carrière, Jakob Bernays, and J. H. Fichte of Germany.

563. *Letters*, V, 521 (June 28, 1867).

564. *Ibid.*, VI, 15, 18–19, 201, 280, 284, 285–86.

565. *Ibid.*, pp. 103–4 (Mar. 3, 1870).

566. The Harvard catalog for 1869–1870 records an enrollment of only seven students for this course of lectures given by as many men. Emerson's own lectures in the course began in April.

567. *Letters*, VI, 104. Thomas Davidson's article on "Parmenides" appeared in the first number of Volume IV, which apparently Emerson had just received from St. Louis.

568. Although the *Journal* was a quarterly, Volume I contained only three numbers, so that the serial number does not proceed regularly by multiples of 4 per volume. Whole Number 12, therefore, is bound as Number 1 of Volume IV.

569. Yet the fact that he had the first three volumes of the *Journal* put in permanent bindings indicates that he valued their contents. His resolution formed on March 3, 1870, "to read them much in the next month" (presumably by way of preparation for his Harvard lectures on the natural history of intellect, to be delivered during April and May) seems significant. If he kept the resolution to read, then or later, the first twelve numbers, he became acquainted with a considerable body of information on German systems of thought, for they included, among other provocative essays (1) Harris' smashing twenty-page attack upon the entire Spencerian dispensation, (2) Kroeger's translation of Fichte's *Science of Knowledge*, (3) several expository articles on Kant's system of transcendentalism (including Kroeger's excellent essay in Vol. III), (4) Thomas Davidson's translation of Schelling's "Introduction to the Philosophy of Nature," (5) Bénard's analysis of Hegel's Aesthetics, (6) Harris' essay on "Hegel's First Principle," and (7) Harris' translations from the *Phenomenology* and the *Logic*, together with articles on Leibnitz, Winckelmann, Swedenborg, Cousin, Berkeley, Schopenhauer, and Goethe.

570. The Kant celebration is reported in the *Journal of Spec. Phil.*, XV, iii (July, 1881) 303–21, and discussed at some length in my book on *New England Transcendentalism and St. Louis Hegelianism* (Phila., 1948), p. 87 ff.

571. *Journals*, X, 137 (1866); see also X, 139.

572. MS Journal, "LN. 1866," p. 19.

573. See *Natural History of Intellect* in *Works*, XII, 13.

574. MS Journal, "NY. 1868–1870," p. 58; slightly altered in Journals, X, 248.

575. MS Journal, "NY. 1868–1870," p. 251; slightly altered in *Journals*, X, 321.

576. MS Journal, "AC. 1859," p. 218; not in printed *Journals*.

577. *Journals*, X, 455 (1876).

578. *Journals*, X, 53 (1864).

579. *Works*, XI, 458.

580. MS Journal, "ST. 1870–1875," p. 25.

581. MS Journal, "SO. 1856," p. 64 (printed with minor variations in *Journals*, IX, 22). See also X, 43 (1864). For other tributes to the Germans, see *Works*, IV, 281; V, 55, 244, 254; XI, 458; XII, 312

OTHER EARLY TRANSCENDENTALISTS

582. See his letter of May 15, 1820, in O. B. Frothingham's *George Ripley* (Boston, 1882), pp. 9–10, 17; cf. Emerson's *Letters*, I, 152.

583. His biographer lists the following: "... much of Kant, Schleiermacher, Herder, De Wette, Cousin, Jouffroy; something of Hegel; Schopenhauer's 'Die Welt als Wille und Vorstellung' (1819); the latest known volumes of Biblical criticism; Paulus, Bauer, Tholuck, Lücke, Bertholdt's 'Einleitung,' Winer's 'Handbuch der theologischen Literatur,'" and a host of histories of philosophy, literary writings, and moral tracts. Others listed include Bretschneider, Ammon, Reinhard, Ritter; Constant, Vico, Fichte, Cabanis, Eichhorn; a "few books now forgotten, about the origin of Christianity; a little of Goethe and Schiller, Luther's Werke, Baumgarten-Crusius; Heydenreich's 'Betrachtungen,' and 'Natur und Gott, nach Spinoza,' Wieland's 'Über Wunder,' Gfrörer's 'Giordano Bruno,' and miscellaneous works in morals and philosophy."—Frothingham, *op. cit.*, p. 46. Ripley's library, called "the finest of its kind in Boston," was large enough to be pledged as security for $400 in 1840, when Ripley was raising the money to organize the Brook Farm community. The failure of the Farm later was hardly a deeper loss for Ripley than the consequent loss of his library, though he drew some consolation from the fact that his beloved books went to Theodore Parker. See H. S. Commager, *Theodore Parker* (Boston, 1936), p. 51.

584. *Christ. Exam.*, IX (Sept., 1830), 70–107. Like Coleridge, he depended to a great extent on the Cambridge Platonists, but his attitude toward Coleridge is distinguished from that of his fellow-Transcendentalists by his being less ready than they to endorse Coleridge's principles—mainly because he finds Coleridge too "obscure" on many points (*ibid.*, pp. 71, 73). Instead, he professes to "look with deepest interest mingled with cheerful hope, on the progress of the eclectic school in France, of which Cousin, Roger Collard, Jeoffroy [*sic*] and Degerando are distinguished representatives" (p. 104). At the same time he recognizes the fact that the new religious and philosophical impulse that is converting his "age of superficial, sensuous philosophy" bears the mark,

"made in Germany," whence has "emanated more of the intellectual light on the deepest subjects of philosophic inquiry, than most writers of our language have yet been ready to acknowledge." Under this impulse "the best minds of France are awakening to more serious and elevated views of human nature," and he fervently hopes that Americans may follow the French example (p. 104).

585. Ripley initiated his fourteen-volume series of "Specimens of Foreign Standard Literature" with his own *Philosophical Miscellanies, Translated from the French of Cousin, Jouffroy and Benjamin Constant* (2 vols., Boston 1838). Although the remaining twelve volumes in this distinguished series include only two more volumes from the French, the other ten being specimens of German literature and philosophy, Ripley's interest in French eclecticism was greater and somewhat longer sustained than was Emerson's, who early found "an optical illusion" in it. See Emerson's *Journals*, IV, 404 (Mar. 5, 1838). No attempt is made here to evaluate the final importance of French influence upon Ripley. However, the conclusion reached by W. L. Leighton, in his *French Philosophers and New England Transcendentalism* (Charlottesville, Va., 1908), p. 93, is applicable to Ripley as well as to the movement as a whole: "the influence of French philosophy is, in proportion even to German influence alone, slight."

586. *Christ. Exam.*, X, 273–96.

587. *Ibid.*, XI, 347–73.

588. *Ibid.*, pp. 373–80. He indicts the American college and university system for neglecting literature, history, and philosophy, and recommends the cultivation and study of all branches of German scholarly and belletristic writing as being at once the most "profound" and the "most original." He attacks as false the contention that the mastery of German is difficult, and as pusillanimous the prejudiced orthodox who consider the Germans as given "to mysticism, rhapsody, wild and tasteless inventions in poetry, and dark and impenetrable reasonings in metaphysics." His championship of Kant as having contributed "more light" than any other "since the brightest days of Grecian philosophy" is particularly vigorous. Having considered the Coleridgean restatements of Kant as well as the tenets of the German philosopher himself, Ripley finds (contrary to general contemporary opinion) the minds of Kant and Coleridge not at all alike, however well they may agree on some important propositions. In concluding, he denies the charge that German philosophy is irreligious, by pointing to Tholuck as a staunch defender

of Calvinism, who will counterbalance the pantheistic tendencies of Schelling and Hegel.

589. The *Cyclopedia of Literature and the Fine Arts Comprising Complete and Accurate Definitions of All Terms Employed in Belles-Lettres, Philosophy, Theology, Law, Mythology, Painting, Music, Sculpture, Architecture, and All Kindred Arts*, comp. and arr. by George Ripley and Bayard Taylor (N.Y., 1854) dispels any doubt that may be entertained on that score. Ripley, who prepared the sections relating to philosophy and theology, in the sections on Kant (pp. 337–38), on Transcendentalism (p. 605), on Reason (p. 510), and on Rationalism (pp. 510–11), meticulously defined and explained the Kantian tripartition of the mind's faculties, indicated the place and significance of space and time for the Kantian sensation, of the categories for the understanding, and of the ideas for the reason, at the same time giving examples and distinguishing between the regulative and constitutive forms of the reason, while marking the distinctions between theoretical and practical reason (pp. 337–38) and between the transcendental and the transcendent (p. 605). These distinctions and their significance are further discussed in the section on "Reason" by relating them to and contrasting them with the systems of Locke, Hume, and Stewart (pp. 510–11); while the import of the Kantian criticism for Biblical criticism is discussed in the section on "Rationalism" in reference to seventeenth- and eighteenth-century deism and the Germans Baumgarten, Michaelis, Semler, Eichhorn, Paulus, Bretschneider, and Strauss (p. 510).

590. However, he viewed God as a personal Divinity, and at one of the meetings of the Transcendental Club, in February, 1838, is recorded as having taken exception to the impersonal conception of God as put forth by Emerson.—Frothingham, *op. cit.*, pp. 49–50, 56.

591. For example, his discussion of Mackintosh's book on ethical philosophy is an incisive and fair commentary not visibly affected by his own predilection for Kant and Coleridge. See *Christ. Exam.*, XIII (Jan., 1833), 311–32.

592. *Christ. Exam.*, XVIII (May, 1835), esp. pp. 167–69.

593. *Ibid.*, pp. 171–72; also p. 197.

594. He approved of Herder's campaign to deflate Kantism as "the ultimate and exclusive philosophy of human nature" and acclaimed his success in making the system "lower its pretensions."—*Ibid.*, pp. 188–89, 209. For a good statement of Ripley's dislike for what he called "the anatomical spirit" of German speculations see his article on Fichte in the *Harbinger* for April 18, 1846 (II, 297), where German philosophy is represented as having failed to solve "the mighty problems of Divine Providence and Human Destiny," thus demonstrating the fruitlessness of a method too exclusively speculative, although Fichte himself is praised for having recalled man to search "the depths of his own soul" for the "instinctive sense of justice, duty, universal harmony and unity."

595. This interest is traceable directly to Herder and Schleiermacher. His opinion of the latter he stated to Parker as late as 1852: "I regard Schleiermacher as the greatest thinker who ever undertook to fathom the philosophy of religion."—Frothingham, *Ripley*, p. 229.

596. *Christ. Exam.*, XIX, 172–204, esp. pp. 172–76.

597. *Ibid.*, XX, 1–46, esp. p. 4.

598. *Ibid.*, XXI (Nov., 1836), 226–54.

599. *Ibid.*, XXI, 285–98.

600. Meanwhile he was opening up yet another avenue by which European ideas were to gain currency in America, for in 1838 he published the first of his series of translations, the *Specimens of Foreign Standard Literature*. In the fourteen volumes published between 1838 and 1842, the French Cousin, Constant, and Jouffroy and the Germans Goethe, Schiller, Uhland, Körner, Bürger, Menzel, and De Wette were brought before the public in competent translations by such writers as J. S. Dwight, Margaret Fuller, C. C. Felton, S. Osgood, J. F. Clarke, and Ripley himself.

601. For details, including excellent bibliographical notes, see C. H. Faust's essay on "The Backgrounds of the Unitarian Opposition to Transcendentalism," *Modern Philol.*, XXXV (Feb., 1938), 297–324.

602. *Ibid.*, pp. 300–305. Some of the orthodox were confident in their prophecies that these scorners of revelation and exalters of reason would soon take the same course that the German rationalists had taken, and go "at last full length with the most liberal of them all." Thus Moses Stuart of Andover, himself a pioneer in America in the use of the grammatical interpretation of the Scriptures as promulgated by the Germans, nevertheless told the world, with more heat than logic, that the Unitarians, reasoning as they did, "must necessarily . . . come to the same conclusions with Eichhorn, and Paulus, and Eckermann, and Herder, and other distinguished men of the new German school." If, in a few years, the Unitarian tendency would not produce "the undisguised avowal of German divinity in all its latitude," said Stuart, he was prepared to swallow his own words (*Miscellanies*, pp. 182–88).

603. After Parker's sermon on *The Transient and Permanent in Christianity* it was seriously

urged, to escape the difficult choice and to remove the odium of Parker's attachment to Unitarianism, that the Association should be dissolved. In the end the majority took the less strenuous, if less logical, course: the Association was not dissolved, and Parker was not expelled; but he was vigorously denounced; and the refusal of his colleagues to exchange pulpits with him made their action virtual, if not actual, expulsion.

604. "Theodore Parker and Liberal Christianity," *New Englander*, II (Oct., 1844), 353–56.

605. O. B. Frothingham, *Theodore Parker* (Boston, 1874), p. 114.

606. "Theodore Parker and Liberal Christianity," *New Englander*, II (Oct., 1844), 556.

607. Frothingham, *Ripley*, pp. 80, 91.

608. *Ibid.*, pp. 84–87, 94–95; see also pp. 67–74.

609. *Christ. Exam.*, XI (Jan., 1832), 372.

610. Reproduced in Frothingham, *Ripley*, pp. 112–17.

611. *Ibid.*, p. 111.

612. He saw "as the key-stone of the system the important truth . . . that the amelioration of outward circumstances will be the *effect*, but can never be the *means* of mental and moral improvement." True progress, he saw, with Emerson, was inward progress; but he urged "more attention . . . to the philosophy of the system, so that teachers should not flatter themselves that they have caught the spirit, when they only imitate some of its mechanical details."—*Christ. Exam.*, XI (Jan., 1832), 355, 372.

613. The example of the Fourieristic disciples in Europe did not go unnoticed by the Brook Farmers. The *Harbinger* for April 4, 1846, contains an article by Ripley on "The Religious Movement in Germany," praising the "social character" of the movement commenced by Ronge in Germany. See esp. II, 190–191. Ripley's concept of the truly social character of Christianity was that it should "bring about a truer state of society, one in which human beings should stand in frank relations of true equality and fraternity, mutually helpful, respecting each other's occupation, and making one the helper of the other."—*Early Letters of Geo. Wm. Curtis to J. S. Dwight*, ed. by Geo. W. Cooke (N.Y., 1898), p. 45.

614. While reviewing Hedge's *Prose Writers of Germany* (1847), he asked concerning purely "philosophical speculation" and mere "literary culture" as illustrated in portions of that book, "to what does it amount?"—*Harbinger*, VI Feb. 5, 1848), 107. A scholar might take pleasure, he wrote about the same time, in the "remarkable thought processes" of Hegel and of Schel-

ling, the "great intellectual analyses" of Kant, or the "subtle speculations of the Oriental philosophers," but for him they had come to be merely" intellectual gymnastics"—"airy nothings."—Review of J. B. Stallo's *General Principles of the Philosophy of Nature* (Boston, 1848), in *Harbinger*, VI (Feb. 5, 1848), 110. While objecting to Stallo's book on the ground that the Hegel-Schelling-Oken thesis offers "no point of contact with the American mind," and attacking Strauss, Feuerbach, and mid–nineteenth-century materialists like Büchner, he was nonetheless interested in Eduard Hartmann's *Philosophy of the Unconscious* and usually took a positive attitude toward the advancements made in the sciences. See Frothingham, *Ripley*, pp. 229–30, 286.

615. Clarence Gohdes, *op. cit.*, p. 120.

616. See, for example, his article on George Bancroft in *Putnam's Magazine* for March, 1853.

617. Frothingham, *Ripley*, p. 210. Among the more important of his articles dealing with German subjects during his later years is a biographical sketch in *Putnam's* for November, 1856 (VIII, 517–27), of Heine's last years, based on Alfred M. Meissner's *Heinrich Heine: Erinnerungen* (Hamburg, 1856).

618. His growing social conservatism found some justification in the doctrine of evolution, in which he finally anchored his hopes for social betterment, and which he helped to popularize in America; for as he grew older, he became increasingly sure that the "increasing purpose" of the Creator was revealed less through sudden reform than through gradual change. On this head, see Howard A. Wilson's unpublished University of Wisconsin dissertation, "George Ripley: Social and Literary Critic," 1941. Not unnaturally he turned about 1870 with more than passing attention to Eduard von Hartmann and with increasing absorption to scientific books, notably books of physiology (Frothingham, *Ripley*, pp. 228–30, 235). In 1874 he spoke appreciatively of the tendency, "dating from the death of Hegel in 1831, and of Goethe the year following," of the "physical researches' rapidly . . . [taking] precedence of metaphysical speculation" (*ibid.*, p. 276). He still hoped, he said, for the "union of spiritual agencies and material conditions" (*ibid.*, p. 275); he professed to see in "the alleged materialism of Tyndall and Huxley . . . an unexpected support to the idealism of Berkeley" (*ibid.*, p. 277); and he foretold "a magnificent synthesis of the forces of material nature and the power of spiritual ideas" (*ibid.*, p. 275). But idealism had still to achieve its ends, and the achievements of science were already tangible. So, while continuing to revere Emersonian idealism and to

keep on friendly terms with the associates of his former idealistic endeavors, he wrote warningly to his sister Marianne, in Wisconsin, where she had become enthusiastic for the efforts of the Rev. W. Kimball to promote Liberal Christianity in the West: "I do not advise you to take Liberal Christianity as a drug. . . . [It] is evidently one of the offshoots of the great banian-tree planted by Theodore Parker" (ibid., p. 257). The tenor of the whole letter is that while Parkerism has born "an abundance of beautiful and wholesome fruit," it is not fruit for him and for those dear to him. Very revealing, also, is a comparison of Ripley's estimate of Emerson, written in 1869, with one written earlier. See ibid., pp. 266–72, where both are reproduced.

619. See his "Letter to a Theological Student," Dial, I, ii (Oct., 1840), 183–87.

620. Walter Elliott, The Life of Father Hecker (2nd ed., N.Y., 1894), p. 90. It is to be noted that in 1861 the funeral of his first wife (who had embraced Catholicism the year before) "was celebrated . . . in fullest accordance with the rite of the Roman Church."—Frothingham, Ripley, p. 239.

621. John Weiss, Life and Correspondence of Theodore Parker (2 vols., N.Y., 1864), I, 59, 160–62; Frothingham, Parker, p. 34; Commager, Parker, p. 24.

622. Commager, Parker, p. 26; Frothingham, Parker, p. 39.

623. Weiss, Parker, I, 72–75, 78, 95; Commager, Parker, pp. 30–32; Frothingham, Parker, 46–47: "Only by transcribing the journal, commenced in 1835, could any idea be obtained of the extent of his researches. The folio pages are crowded with lists of books read or to be read, —analyses, summaries, comments on writings of every description, in every tongue. Only to name them would be a fatigue,—Eichhorn, Herder, Ammon, De Wette, Paulus, Philo, the Greek historians, the fathers of the Church, the Greek and Latin poets, Plato, Spinoza, the Wolfenbüttel fragments . . . . In two months . . . the names of 65 volumes are given as having been read in German, English, Danish, Latin, Greek . . . ."

In the Spiritual Interpreter, a small magazine which he helped edit for a time in 1835, he published a number of papers reflecting the results of his studies in Biblical interpretation, —De Wette, Eichhorn, Astruc, and scholars of the moderate school of rationalism supplying the material. As yet he does not deny revelation in the Pentateuch, though he agrees with De Wette that the Psalms cannot be interpreted as Messianic prophecy.—Frothingham, Parker, pp. 55–56.

624. Weiss, Parker, I, 74, 82, 157; Commager, Parker, p. 30.

625. Weiss, Parker, I, 74, 75, 83, 85, 113; Frothingham, Parker, pp. 74–75.

626. For Parker's own account of the elaborate work that went into this book, see his "Experience as a Minister," Works (Cent. ed., 15 vols., Boston, 1910), XIII, 315. In the Preface (3rd ed., p. xxv) to the Introduction Parker gives a compendious bibliography of some two score of recent works of Biblical criticism and history (all but one or two of them by German authors) which he consulted in preparation of that work.

627. In March, 1858, shortly after the appearance of the third edition of the Introduction, Parker calculated his loss in these terms: "Nobody knows how much toil it cost me. I lived in a little country village, and had a plenty of time, health, and vigor. It must contain many errors, and I am sometimes astonished that I did the work as well as it is. It cost me 2000 dollars to stereotype it; I have received about 775 dollars back again! . . . But if I were to live my life over again I would do the same. I meant it for a labor of love. It has had no recognition nor welcome in America—it served the purpose of no sect." As a matter of fact, less than a year later the Christian Examiner for January, 1859 (LXVI, 125–27) noticed the work, if not in glowing terms, at least with some appreciation, notably of Parker's own contribution to the book. It has not been possible to ascertain the amount of the final loss or profit from the book, nor how many copies each of the three editions were printed. Considering the frequency with which copies of the third edition have turned up in recent years in bookseller's shops and in ministers' libraries (I have picked up two within a year in the remains of libraries of Unitarian ministers in Wisconsin), it would seem that the book had a fairly large circulation.

628. In the summer of 1837 he read Jacobi and Henry More, the ethical writings of De Wette, Fichte, Coleridge, and Descartes, Gesinius' Lectures on the Old Testament, Gabler, Paulus, and Bauer; later in that year he was seeking copies of Krummacher, Twesten, Tennemann, and Wegscheider. Then he read Bopp's Vergleichende Grammatik, which he pronounced "awfully written" but "doubtless valuable," Karcher's Analecta and Hobart's life of Swedenborg. "Spinoza . . . Ovid, Seneca are in prospect." "Hume, Gibbon, Robertson are trifles; Schleiermacher, Bouterwek, Baur, Hegel, Laplace, Leibnitz are more serious." "The absorbing study of this period is the literature of the Bible. The Egyptian and Phoenician alphabets have attractions for him; ancient inscriptions

and coins, Carthaginian, Persian, amuse him; the Orphic poems have a share of his time; Meiner's book 'On the Doctrine of the One God,' Stäudlin 'On the Morality of the Drama,' fall under his notice; but the Bible literature leads all the rest." While still in the Divinity School in 1835 he had acquired Herder's complete works in forty-five volumes, and on September 22, 1837, he wrote gleefully to his friend Wm. Silsbee, "I have got lots of new books—upwards of one hundred Germans! Come and see. Some of them are old friends, others are new—all sorts of creatures."—Weiss, *Parker*, I, 72, 99–104, 111–13; Frothingham, *Parker*, pp. 89, 91, 108.

629. Systematically, at great cost, and with all the love for bibliography of a true book-collector, Parker filled out each of the important branches of theological and philosophical learning, of modern science and literature, so that in these fields his library was as complete and up-to-date as his private means could make it. He had more modern theological material than the Harvard Divinity School; he absorbed in 1847 the entire library of Ripley into his own. His house in Boston was overrun by scholars who knew what treasures were to be found in his study.—Commager, *Parker*, pp. 123-29, *passim*.

There were over a hundred editions of the Bible, including a Nuremberg Bible of 1483, and several from the sixteenth century; Latin and Greek classics, many in rare sixteenth- and seventeenth-century editions; Renaissance geographies and books of travel, old chronicles and medieval histories; the huge sets of the *Monumenta Germanica Historica* and the *Bibliothek des litterarischen Vereins von Stuttgart*; a large section of old and new works on church history, Renaissance science and philosophy; another section on civil and canon law; "all the great names of Greece and Rome . . .; Burns as well as Dante, and Chaucer quite as well thumbed as Shakespeare, and many a Servian, Russian, Bohemian volume of provincial character"; and the hymns of all nations and all denominations.—Weiss, *Parker*, I, 4–8.

630. See *Journal*, Sept. 20, 1839; Weiss, *Parker*, II, 9.

631. *Christ. Exam.* XXV, iii (Jan., 1839), 367–84.

632. *Ibid.*, XXVIII, iii, 273–316. The first copy of Strauss had been brought to the vicinity by the Rev. Henry Walker of Charlestown about 1837. Walker was a graduate of the Divinity School who had been studying in Germany from 1833 to 1837. He lent the book to Parker upon his return from abroad.

633. See *Works*, XIII, 310.

634. *Works*, I, 122–23.

635. See Commager, *Parker*, p. 43.

636. See esp. *Works*, VIII, 472–73, 475–76, 477–79, 492.

637. Delivered in Waterville, Me., 1849, and printed in *Works*, VIII, 1–53.

638. See his letter to Dr. Francis of 1839 (Frothingham, *Parker*, p. 117), in which he argues, on the strength of De Wette's "Biblical Dogmatics," that eventually both the Old and New Testaments "will be dropped out from the Church." "I can't but wish," he adds, "that Jesus had written his own books; but even they must have contained some things local and temporary." The entering wedge made by Strauss and De Wette is here clearly discernible.

639. John W. Chadwick, *Theodore Parker* (Boston and N.Y., 1900), p. 92.

640. Frothingham, *Parker*, p. 152.

641. T. W. Higginson, editor of the work for the centenary edition, remarks in the Preface that he had to give up the attempt to verify the innumerable notes in his book. He failed to find all of the references in the Harvard Divinity School Library (comprising in 1842 some 1800 volumes), in Ripley's, Francis', and in Parker's libraries combined.

642. See *Works*, I, xx–xxi.

643. See *Works*, I, 34–36. While he adopts the distinction between speculative and practical religion, he goes beyond Kant in insisting that religion and morality are different in "type" and essentially "unlike." See *Works*, I, 34–36, notes.

644. *Works*, I, 12.

645. *Works*, I, 33.

646. *Works*, XIII, 301.

647. *Works*, VI, 1–38.

648. Weiss, *Parker*, I, 74.

649. *Ibid.*, I, 148; see also the review of Menzel's *German Literature* (*Works*, VIII, 489), where he takes Menzel to task for omitting mention of the *Monadology*.

650. See Weiss, *Parker*, I, 48, 150; also *Works*, II, 216.

651. See his letter of Oct. 3, 1853, quoted in Weiss, *Parker*, I, 149; also Chs. VIII, IX, and X of "Theism, Atheism and the Popular Theology," *Works*, II, 280–389, where he treats "Of Providence," "Of the Economy of Pain and Misery under the Universal Providence of God," and "Of the Economy of Moral Error under the Universal Providence of God" (published in 1853).

652. Weiss, *Parker*, I, 166, 169.

653. *Works*, II, 196.

654. He admired Goethe's precept of self-renunciation, but doubted that Goethe himself

lived up to it; he admired Goethe's diligence, but there was no getting round his being "a selfish rogue . . . a great pagan" (Weiss, *Parker*, II, 20–22). Goethe was too self-centered: he "would have been nobler had he *struggled* . . . . An excess of good fortune was his undoing." *Wilhelm Meister* was for Parker insufficiently moral, and especially the women of the work were objectionable, though well-drawn. He was strongly affected by the legendary story of Friederike Brion, and he censured Goethe for his part in that episode. Of all Goethe's works, Parker liked the *Wanderjahre* best: "I have a better opinion of the giant of Germany since reading this book than before. An enemy of Christianity could by no means have written that description of the School of the Three Reverences, which terminates in reverence of one's self. . . . Who can say that Goethe was ignorant of religion after having read 'The Confessions of a Fair Penitent' ?"—Frothingham, *Parker*, p. 58; see also pp. 108–9

655. For his remarks on Luther, see Weiss, *Parker*, I, 181; on Schiller, see *ibid.*, II, 23. He called Schiller "proud, inflated, stiff, diseasedly self-conscious."

656. Weiss, *Parker*, I, 306–7; Frothingham, *Parker*, p. 60. Heine heads the list of German poets translated into English by Parker. See Weiss, *Parker*, II, 30–38. Other German poets whom Parker translated at various times include Paul Gerhardt, Simon Dach, Opitz, Rückert, Körner, Geibel, and individual selections from *Des Knaben Wunderhorn*. While none are outstanding examples of the translator's art, his translations are a credit to Parker's poetic taste and his mastery of the German language. On the whole, they are better than his attempts at original poetry.

657. This could be so only because Parker insisted on seeing no difference between the moral foundation of Kant's practical reason and his own religious intuitions concerning God, moral law, and immortality.

658. *Works*, XIII, 300–302; Weiss, *Parker*, I, 454–55.

659. Consult Chadwick, *Parker*, pp. 92, 175–77; Frothingham, *Parker*, pp. 254–55.

660. Frothingham, *Parker*, pp. 149–50.

661. Chadwick, *Parker*, pp. 178–79.

662. See the review of Buckle's *History of Civilization* for a demonstration of Parker's phenomenal knowledge of the historical research of his time, *Works*, VIII, 364–418.

663. Chadwick, *Parker*, p. 186.

664. Weiss, *Parker*, I, 315, 376.

665. That Parker may have been influenced in his social and political views by Francis Lieber presents an interesting probability. Both held that a sound political system should have as its basis the moral law of the universe, and should treat the ethical nature of the individual as an end in itself, rather than as a means. Of course, Parker read very widely; and insofar as his political views were derived, they might have been drawn from many sources—among them Plato and Cousin. Moreover, in close contact as Parker was with the Transcendentalists of Boston and vicinity, among whom like ideas circulated freely, Parker could have come by his political views through association with them; though here again, it is worth remembering that Lieber's political theories were not unknown. Emerson, in 1854, recorded Lieber's theories as tallying with his own (*Journals*, VIII, 459); and after Lieber went to Columbia, Emerson spoke of his lectures as the outstanding academic performances to be heard in America (*Journals*, IX, 212; X, 55). The subject of Lieber's political influence merits exhaustive investigation.

666. It was a matter of some chagrin to Parker that despite the ease with which he read German and the facility he had in writing the language, his speaking knowledge of it was unequal to the establishment of unimpeded intercourse with the German savants.

667. Weiss, *Parker*, I, 214–44 *passim;* Frothingham, *Parker*, pp. 200–6.

668. See *Works*, XV, 13–14; Weiss, *Parker*, I, 430; also I, 269–71, 476ff.

In his later years Parker was active in aiding the political refugees who came to America in large numbers after the political defeat of 1848. Even as early as 1846 he was helping the Rev. Friedrich Münch to find a publisher in Boston. In 1851 he helped Dr. Fock, a professor of philosophy at Kiel, and Herr Edouard Pelz to find positions in New York and Boston. He went so far as to swallow his pride and ask his old enemy, Prof. C. C. Felton, to intercede for one of these refugees, Dr. Lobeck, a distinguished classicist of Königsberg. One of his closest friends was the Swiss natural scientist, Desor, who had visited America to help Agassiz in his Lake Superior explorations. During the summer of 1859—those last happy months in Switzerland before he went to Italy with his fatal illness—Parker enjoyed daily the companionship and intellectual stimulation of this generous host, still arguing, studying, discussing the literary, scientific, and theological questions of the day.—Frothingham, *Parker*, pp. 255–58; Commager, *Parker*, pp. 112ff.

669. See Clarke's essay, "The Two Carlyles, or Carlyle Past and Present," *Christ. Exam.*, LXXVII, ii (Sept., 1846), 206–31. "This new writer came opening up unknown worlds of

beauty and wonder. A strong influence, unlike any other, attracted us to his writing. Before we knew his name, we knew *him* . . . . We knew . . . young men and women who taught themselves German in order to read for themselves the authors made so luminous by this writer."—*Ibid.*, p. 212.

". . . The Unitarian reform had not gone deep enough. It had been a question of opinions, rather than principles and ideas. The common basis of both parties was the material philosophy of Locke, not the spiritual philosophy of earlier and later thinkers. . . . Now the first voice . . . to break this evil enchantment which held us all was, to many, the voice of Thomas Carlyle . . . a man capable of dispensing with the form . . . endowed with a high degree of intuitive faculty,—a born seer, a prophet, seeing the great realities of the universe . . . . The work of such a man is to break up the old formulas and introduce new light and life. This work was done for the Orthodox thirty years ago by . . . Coleridge; for the Unitarians in this vicinity, by . . . Carlyle. . . . Carlyle's 'Life of Schiller' opened the portals of German literature, and made an epoch in biography and criticism."—*Ibid.*, pp. 212–16, *passim*.

670. Edward E. Hale, (ed.), *James Freeman Clarke, Autobiography, Diary and Correspondence* (Boston and N.Y., 1892), pp. 39–40.

671. *Ibid.*, pp. 89–90.

672. *Ibid.*, p. 39.

673. Coleridge's *Aids to Reflection*, which he read in the Marsh edition during his senior year, confirmed (says Clarke) "my longing for a higher philosophy than that of John Locke and David Hartley. . . . Coleridge showed me from Kant that though knowledge begins *with* experience it does not come *from* experience. Then I discovered that I was born a transcendentalist; and smiled when I afterwards read, in one of Jacobi's works, that he had gone through exactly the same experience. Thus I became a great reader of Coleridge, and was quite ready to accept his distinction between the reason and the understanding judging according to sense." —*Ibid.*, p. 90.

In the phrase, "the understanding judging according to sense," we come again upon the damage done by Coleridge's having stated the distinction in these equivocal terms. We have already noted the trouble it gave Marsh and Emerson. Parker, it may be presumed, saw more clearly, though even he refused to go the full length with Kant in the applications of the distinctions between reason and understanding and between pure and practical reason. Clarke, on the other hand, appears never to have read Kant, or, indeed, entertained any

serious doubts about his understanding of Kant for he goes on blithely: "This distinction helped me much in my subsequent studies in theology. It enabled me to distinguish between truth as seen by the reason [precisely the 'truth' which Kant had demonstrated to be unascertainable], and its statement as formulated by the understanding. It enabled me to put logic in its proper place, and see that its function was not the discovery of truth, but that of arranging, methodizing, and harmonizing verbal propositions in regard to it. I could see that those who had the same spiritual experience, and who beheld the same truth, might differ in their statements concerning it, and that while truth was unchanging and eternal, theology might alter and improve from age to age . . . . According to the distinction of Coleridge, the vital truth perceived by the reason is not the same as the doctrinal statement enunciated by the understanding. The reason sees in Christ something divine, finds in him a visible manifestation of the invisible and eternal. In this intellectual vision both the Trinitarian and the Unitarian may be one, though when they come to express it as a doctrine they differ. The essential fact is the vision of truth as beheld by the reason, not as worked out by the understanding. Thus Coleridge's metaphysical statement has really put an end to much conscientious bigotry in the modern church."—*Ibid.*, pp. 39–40.

Here is involved what Kant specifically warned against, namely, the confusion of transcendental with transcendent knowledge.

674. *Ibid.*, p. 90.

675. Thomas W. Higginson, *Margaret Fuller Ossoli* (Boston, 1884), p. 144.

It is symbolic of his position that as late as 1845 he invited Parker, then in disgrace with the great majority of the Unitarian clergy, into his pulpit, and extended an invitation also to the Rev. Edward N. Kirk, who, for his part, admittedly would "not have received Mr. Clarke into his pulpit."—E. E. Hale, *op. cit.*, pp. 151–53.

Clarke always insisted that the term "Unitarian" had reference, not to a denial of the doctrine of the Trinity, but to the essential unity in organization and in the teaching of the Church Universal, which he hoped could be attained in the not too distant future. See *ibid.*, pp. 155, 295, note.

676. See Clarke's essay, "Are There Two Religions in the New Testament?" *Christ. Exam.*, LXXXVI, ii (Mar., 1869), 192–208; C. F. Thwing's statement in the *Boston Weekly Advertiser* for June 15, 1888; and Frothingham's in the *Radical* for Sept.–Dec., 1867, and Jan., 1868.

He was constantly answering both the orthodox and the liberals in an attempt to keep clearly defined his middle ground. He took the side of Emerson when Norton attacked the New School, less on the ground that the New School was entirely correct and the Old all wrong than on the ground that an acceptance, at all events, a sympathetic hearing of Carlyle, Schleiermacher, and Cousin would aid the much desired progress in religious thought. See his "New School in Literature and Religion," *Western Messenger*, VI, i (Nov., 1838), 42–47; and "German Theology" (excerpts from an article in the *Foreign Quar. Rev.*, with comments by Clarke) in the *Western Messenger*, VI, i (Nov., 1838), 57–60.

Yet he felt that both Emerson and Parker had gone too far. For his attitude toward Emerson, see his "Emerson and the New School," *Western Messenger*, VI, i (Nov., 1838), 37–42. His discourse, *Theodore Parker and His Theology* (Boston, 1859), delivered on September 25, 1859, illustrates the difference between him and Parker. He praises Parker the man but criticizes certain aspects of Parker the theologian, notably his too strong devotion to "pure, cold thought" (pp. 7–8) and his uncompromising championship of so-called "Absolute Religion," which, says Clarke, rests upon too great "a love of system." This love of system, together with the desire to simplify, has, in Clarke's opinion, driven Parker into rationalizations of religion which are too simple to include all of the soul's complexities. Thus Parker has come round, in his theology, to present a religion that is more negative than positive; he has been too strictly critical to be constructive. Clarke did not agree with Parker's denial of the divinity of Christ, and he affirmed a belief in an "actual revelation in Christianity, special in itself, of God" (pp. 17–18). Thus he held, in conformity with other Transcendentalists who were unwilling to abide in a purely critical philosophy, that "men are usually right in what they assert . . . and they are often wrong in what they deny" (p. 11). See also his "Essay on Miracles," *Western Messenger*, V, i (Apr., 1838), 36–44, for a statement of his belief in the miraculous acts of Jesus and their significance for Christian faith. His own preaching turned upon the message of God's love and upon forgiveness as one of the essentials of Christianity. His *Manual of Unitarian Belief* (12th ed., Boston, 1888) is an exposition of his essential doctrines, stated with exemplary simplicity and touching only the most vital concepts of Christian belief.

Clarke observed that while he and Parker had "known and loved each other for some twenty years . . . during all that time, he has never loved my opinions, nor I his." Nevertheless, he concluded, "If Christ be God the Son, second Person in the Trinity, I had rather stand before his bar with Theodore Parker, who denies him, but follows his steps, serving humanity, than with any Orthodox Doctor who writes Southside books to turn our sympathy for the oppressed into approbation for the oppressor."—*Theodore Parker and His Theology*, pp. 21–22.

677. Hale, *op. cit.*, pp. 85, 86, 90–91. For other indications of how fully Clarke entered into the "German craze" then regnant at Harvard, see *ibid.*, pp. 43, 47–48, 62–64, 115, 121, 125,174.

678. "Margaret," he said, "began the study of German early in 1832. Both she and I were attracted towards this literature, at the same time, by the wild bugle-call of Thomas Carlyle, in his romantic articles on Richter, Schiller, and Goethe. . . . Almost every evening I saw her, and heard an account of her studies."—*Memoirs of Margaret Fuller Ossoli*, by R. W. Emerson, W. H. Channing, and J. F. Clarke (2 vols., Boston, 1852), I, 114.

He taught her German pronunciation and exchanged German books with her for the better part of a year. They read Goethe's *Wahlverwandtschaften*, *Zweiter Römischer Aufenthalt*, and the *Campagne in Frankreich*, Lessing's *Miss Sara Sampson* and *Emilia Galotti*, Tieck, Richter, Novalis, and Körner.—*Ibid.*, I, 117, 118, 120–21; see also F. A. Braun, *Margaret Fuller and Goethe* (N.Y., 1910), p. 46.

Catching her enthusiasm for rendering the German masterpieces into English, he undertook a translation of Schiller's *Jungfrau von Orleans* and Goethe's *Hermann und Dorothea*, but never completed either, though he continued throughout his life to turn shorter poems from the German into English. During her lifetime, he sent many of his translations to Margaret Fuller for corrections and suggestions, and subsequently he chose his erstwhile classmate, Oliver Wendell Holmes, to perform the same services for him. Holmes, for his part, apparently enjoyed the relationship with Clarke and spoke of his translations from the German as "faithful, graceful and fluent," adding, in typically Holmesian fashion, that Clarke also wrote "good" original verses—"not as good as mine, but good."—J. W. Thomas, "J. F. Clarke as a Translator," *Amer.-Ger. Rev.*, X, ii (Dec., 1943), 31.

679. *Memoirs of Margaret Fuller Ossoli*, p.123.

680. W. H. Venable, *Beginnings of Literary Culture in the Ohio Valley* (Cincinnati, 1891), 80; Clarence C. F. Gohdes, *The Periodicals of American Transcendentalism*, p. 28.

681. Gohdes, *op. cit.*, pp. 17–35 *passim*.

682. In the numbers for February, April, May, June, and July, 1836, and January, March, May, and July, 1837.

683. January, and April, 1837.

684. March, 1839.

685. February, 1838.

686. February, 1839.

In addition to these contributions by Clarke, the *Messenger* printed several translations from theological writings, among them portions of *The Atonement* from the German of Wilhelm Traugott Krug, translated by Samuel Osgood (Sept., and Oct., 1836), and from Olshausen's *Commentary on the New Testament* (Feb., Mar., May, June, and July, 1837). Among thirty-four translations of various German poems (chiefly brief lyrics or epigrams) that are printed in the *Messenger*, Clarke contributed seven from Goethe and two from Schiller; Dwight, seven from Goethe and four from Schiller. The remaining fourteen, from Körner, Stolberg, Uhland, Goethe, and Rosengarten, are by various translators, including C. T. Brooks, Sarah Margaret Fuller, and C. P. Cranch. Important prose contributions dealing with German writers are Margaret Fuller's essay on "The Life of Körner" (Jan., and Feb., 1838) and a seventeen-page translation by "a friend of the editor" from Goethe's *Unterhaltungen deutscher Ausgewanderten* (Dec., 1837).

In general, the Germans are enthusiastically praised—notably Schiller and Goethe. But the editorial attitude is not entirely uncritical, as can be seen in Clarke's observation on his translation of Schiller's *Philosophical Letters*, that these letters are not entirely "recommended as to doctrine," but are for appreciation in the way that "a fine poem" is to be appreciated.

687. *Theodore*, p. xv. Even at that late date, Clarke felt himself under the necessity of defending the study of German theology before American skeptics, for both in the "orthodox shades of Princeton" and the "classic haunts of Cambridge" there are still those who scoff at it and attack it for infidelity (*ibid.*, pp. viii–ix). Clarke affirms that in Germany, "the land of light, the home of thought," the scholarly literature of theology is marked by the very opposite qualities; in it one finds impartial and profound investigation, systematic, complete treatises on doctrine, learned and accurate works on Church history, pioneer scholarship in criticism and philology— all showing "life, freedom, depth, and comprehensiveness" (p. x). If German theology is sometimes "extravagant and daring," it also shows "originality and freshness" (p. xiii). It is free from party spirit and sectarian rancor. From the time of Leibnitz

is has been marked by a dependence on the intuition, which has been overlooked in English theology since the days of the Cambridge Platonists (p. xiv). Kant was not the opponent but the successor of Leibnitz; the tendency of German philosophy has always been spiritual and profound (pp. xiv–xv).

688. In the Notes printed at the back of each volume, he included some explanatory aids to the interpretation of modern German philosophy, quoting Coleridge and German compilers as sources for his information; occasionally he draws on his knowledge of Schiller and Goethe to reinforce his points. He discusses the distinction between understanding and reason, citing the *Aids to Reflection* (I, 300–3). He quotes Furness, Sampson Reed, Hahn, Nitsch, and Bretschneider on the subject of miracles (I, 314); Schleiermacher on the subject of "ultimate Restoration" (II, 415–20); passages from *Tasso*, translated by "a friend," possibly Margaret Fuller (I, 308); Goethe's essay on the Strassburg Minster (II, 420); and Schiller's *Joan of Arc* (I, 303–4). He remarked later in life that the translation of *Theodore* had been little read (Hale, *op. cit.*, p. 380); yet his ardor for German literature and learning was not thereby diminished. Translating from the German remained a lifelong habit. In 1849, on a trip to Europe, he took particular care to visit the romantic scenes of the Rhineland made familiar to him by the German poets, and in Basel he did not neglect to pay a visit to the home of De Wette, only to learn that the author of *Theodor* had died a few months before. As late as 1851 he read German romance for recreation, and at various times he undertook to translate smaller works of German theology, among them Karl Hase's *Leben Jesu* (Boston, 1860). For other important details, consult John Wesley Thomas, *James Freeman, Clarke, Apostle of German Culture to America* (Boston, 1949).

689. For instance, he cites Gaussen, Gfrörer, Strauss, and Hase in his *Inspiration of the New Testament* (Boston, 1871).

690. Hale, *op. cit.*, pp. 295–300, 302, 307, 338, 380–81.

691. See, for example, his articles in the *Christ. Exam.*, LXXI, iii (Nov., 1861), 375–99, and LXXVII, ii (Sept., 1864), 206–31.

692. On the score of Quaker influence, see Odell Shepard, *Pedlar's Progress. The Life of Bronson Alcott* (Boston, 1937), pp. 69–70, 80, and F. B. Sanborn and Wm. T. Harris, *Amos Bronson Alcott. His Life and Philosophy* (2 vols., Boston, 1893), I, 155–58.

693. *The Journals of Bronson Alcott*, sel. and ed. by Odell Shepard (Boston, 1938), p. xxii.

694. *Ibid.*, p. 32 (Oct., 1832); also p. 67 (Sept. 27, 1835).

695. *Ibid.*, p. xxiii.

696. The excellent indexes which Professor Shepard supplied with both his edition of the *Journals* and his biography of Alcott afford a ready means for examining the extent of Alcott's acquaintance with books. The index to the *Journals* is, of course, little more than indicative of Alcott's reading, for the editor was able to select from the fifty-eight volumes of Alcott's manuscript journals something less than one-twentieth.

697. *Journals*, p. 67 (Sept. 27, 1835).

698. *Ibid.*, p. 230 (Mar. 28, 1850).

699. *Pedlar's Progress*, p. 50; Dorothy Mc-Cuskey, *Bronson Alcott, Teacher* (N.Y., 1940), p. 16.

700. *Pedlar's Progress*, p. 235; see also *Journals*, p. 218 (Jan. 1, 1850).

701. *Pedlar's Progress*, pp. 82–83.

702. Dr. Joseph Neef came to the United States about 1806. Two years later he published his *Sketch of a Plan and Method of Education, Founded on an Analysis of Human Faculties and Natural Reason, Suitable for the Offspring of a Free People and for all Rational Beings.* After three years of Pestalozzian educational activity in Philadelphia, he opened in 1809 the first Pestalozzi school in America at the falls of the Schuylkill in Pennsylvania. Four years later he published his second book, *Method of Instructing Children Rationally, in the Arts of Writing and Reading.* In the same year he moved his school to Village Green, Delaware County, near the town of Chester, Pa., remaining there until 1816, when he removed to Louisville, Ky., to engage in similar educational efforts there until about 1819. In 1825, at the request of Robert Owen, he moved his school again, this time to New Harmony, Ind., and remained there until the failure of the New Harmony project. He sought earnestly to spread and establish Pestalozzian ideals of education through publications, lectures, and practice. For details see Will S. Monroe, *History of the Pestalozzian Movement in the United States* (Syracuse, N.Y., 1907), pp. 29–108 *passim*; Oscar L. Bockstahler, "Contributions to American Literature by Hoosiers of German Ancestry," *Ind. Mag. of Hist.*, XXXVIII, iii (Sept., 1942), 231–50, notably p. 232; and Theodore Schreiber, "First Pestalozzian in the New World," *Amer.-Ger. Rev.*, IX, i (Oct., 1942), 25–27. It is said that many of the accomplishments of members of the Owen family were the outgrowth of Neef's ideas, and that in this respect his influence assumed national proportions. See R. F. Seyboldt, "Francis Joseph Nicolas Neef," *DAB*, XIII, 402; Meredith Nicholson, *The Hoosiers* (N.Y., 1915), pp. 105–7, 115; Robert D. Owen, *Threading My Way* (N.Y., 1874), pp. 283–84; and Charles H. Wood, "First Disciple of Pestalozzi in America," *Ind. School Journal*, XXXVII (1892), 659–65.

703. A cousin, who shared Amos Bronson's interest in the new theories of education.

704. For Maclure's discipleship of Pestalozzi, see W. S. Monroe, *op. cit.*, pp. 9–12.

705. *Pedlar's Progress*, pp. 84–85, 157. For the influence upon Alcott of William Russell's *American Journal of Education* and for Alcott's own account of how he endeavored to incorporate Pestalozzian principles into his methods in the Cheshire school, see W. S. Monroe, *op. cit.*, pp. 146–57. See also Dorothy McCuskey, *op. cit.*, pp. 181–85, for a list of books which Alcott bought for his pupils to read and another "for the Instructor's Use in conducting daily studies." Among the latter are (1) Russell's *Manual of Mutual Instruction*, (2) *Epitome of Pestalozzian Instruction*, (3) *Hints to Parents . . . in the Spirit of Pestalozzi's Method*, (4) Keagy's *Pestalozzian Primer*, and (5) Griscom's *Monitorial Instruction.*

706. For the history of Pestalozzian education in America (aside from the particulars already instanced concerning Maclure, Neef, and Alcott), see W. S. Monroe, *op. cit.*, pp. 158–223 *passim*; John B. Wilson, "The Antecedents of Brook Farm," *New Engl. Quar.*, XV, ii (June, 1942), 320–31.

707. *Pedlar's Progress*, p. 85; see also pp. 86–94; McCuskey, *op. cit.*; and George E. Haefner, *A Critical Estimate of the Educational Theories and Practices of Amos Bronson Alcott*, Columbia University Diss. (N.Y., 1937).

708. *Pedlar's Progress.* p. 141; Sanborn and Harris, *op. cit.*, I, 168–70.

709. *Pedlar's Progress*, pp. 151–57; *Journals*, pp. 32, 36.

710. *Pedlar's Progress*, p. 258.

711. Appearing serially in *Fraser's Magazine*, beginning February, 1833.

712. *Journals*, pp. 34–35 (1833); see also Sanborn and Harris, *op. cit.*, I, 165.

713. See *Journals*, pp. 61 (Aug. 7, 1835), 66–67 (Sept. 27, 1835), 471 (Dec. 4, 1876).

714. See *ibid.*, p. 29 (July 1, 1831), for Alcott's own statement regarding his deficiencies in the languages.

715. *Ibid.*, p. 39 (Apr. 22, 1834).

716. *Ibid.*, p. 39 (Apr. 29, 1834); see also p. 174 (Apr. 7, 1846), and *Pedlar's Progress*, pp. 158–61, esp. p. 160.

717. *Journals*, p. 39 (Apr. 29, 1834).

718. *Pedlar's Progress*, p. 160.

719. *Ibid.*

720. *Journals*, pp. 72, 73, 75, 122ff.

721. *Pedlar's Progress*, p. 196.

722. *Ibid.*, p. 258.

723. *Journals*, pp. 34–35 (1833).

724. His absorption in Berkeley during 1833 and frequent association with Dr. Channing at the same time represent other powerful influences that would need to be taken into account in any general treatment of Alcott's intellectual development.

725. On the head of particular Kantian ideas that appealed to Alcott, see Sanborn and Harris, *op. cit.*, II, 609–11.

726. *Journals*, pp. 31, 32, 39, 45, 61, 67, 109, 453, 464, 471.

727. *Ibid.*, p. 106 (Oct., 1838).

728. *Ibid.*, p. 136 (Dec. 5, 1838).

729. *Pedlar's Progress*, p. 440.

730. *Ibid.*, p. 294; see also *Journals*, p. 141.

731. *Ibid.*, pp. 340–41.

732. *Ibid.*, p. 149.

733. He was especially busy with his newly-acquired Platonic and neo-Platonic library, but found time also for the *Bhagavat-Gita*, Boehme's *Epistles*, Oken's *Physiophilosophy*, Swedenborg's *Animal Kingdom*, Ritter's *History of Philosophy*, Carlyle's *Cromwell, Miscellanies, Heroes and Hero-Worship*, and *Sartor*, Coleridge's *Friend* and *Church and State*, Fichte's *Destination of Man*, Goethe's *Faust* (both parts), *Wilhelm Meister, Essays on Art, Helena*, and the *Autobiography*, some unspecified works of Schiller and Richter, and the whole progression of neo-Platonists.—*Journals*, pp. 174, 175, 178–81, 282, 349; *Pedlar's Progress*, pp. 392–93.

734. *Journals*, pp. xxiii, 34, 136, 205, 211–12, 257, 263–64, 312; *Pedlar's Progress*, pp. 155, 157, 392, 439; Sanborn and Harris, *op. cit.*, I, 315; II, 401, 409, 426, 456, 553–54.

735. *Journals*, pp. 66–67 (Sept. 27, 1835).

736. *Ibid.*, pp. 34, 109, 332, 530; *Pedlar's Progress*, pp. 160, 341, 350, 416; Sanborn and Harris, *op. cit.*, I, 315; II, 370, 414, 426, 484, 604, 628.

737. *Tablets* (Boston, 1868), p. 189.

738. *Ibid.*, pp. 195–97; Sanborn and Harris, *op. cit.*, II, 401–2, 628.

739. *Tablets*, pp. 190–91.

740. *Concord Days* (Boston, 1872), p. 238.

741. *Journals*, p. 530.

742. *Pedlar's Progress*, pp. 350, 416–17.

743. *Journals*, p. 211; Sanborn and Harris, *op. cit.*, II, 455–56. The reference here, as subsequent entries indicate, is to Alcott's theory of Genesis as derived chiefly from Oken's *Elements of Physiophilosophy*, in a translation by Alfred Tulk (London, 1847). It seems that Alcott and Emerson discovered, or rediscovered, Oken

together. While Emerson says, in a letter dated August 4, 1842, "Oken, of whose speculations I have heard something, I take to be a scholar first, and then a continuator of Schelling's thought" (*Letters*, III, 77), he showed little further interest in Oken until 1849, when Alcott's enthusiasm and Stallo's book forcibly recalled his attention to Oken. On September 2, 1849, Alcott recorded another conversation with Emerson: "Of Swedenborg especially there was much said, and of the Goethe and Oken morphologies, with my late experiences and their fruits."—*Journals*, p. 212; Sanborn and Harris, *op. cit.*, p. 456.

744. On the same page of Alcott's journal that bears the passage just quoted regarding his "late revelation," there is pasted a slip of paper on which are written, in Emerson's hand, the six lines beginning "A subtle chain of countless rings" (*Journals*, p. 211; Sanborn and Harris, *op. cit.*, II, 456). These verses were used by Emerson as the motto for the 1849 edition of *Nature* (*Works*, I, 403–4) and were subsequently incorporated also in the poem "May Day" (*ibid.*, IX, 165–66). Emerson's theory of nature, in which the worm "mounts through all the spires of form" to man, is, of course, fundamentally opposed to his own earlier theory in *Nature*, and it is also at variance with Alcott's *de*volutionary theories of "Genesis" and "Lapse," not unlike the doctrines taught by the ancient Gnostics. But both theories derive, by opposing approaches, from the same source and particularly from the protracted discussions between Alcott and Emerson during August and September, 1849.

745. *Pedlar's Progress*, p. 437.

746. *Ibid.*, pp. 438–39.

747. *Ibid.*, p. 439.

748. *Journals*, p. 211.

749. *Works*, IV, 107. See also Emerson's *Journals*, III, 515.

750. Emerson's *Journals*, III, 505 (July 15, 1835).

751. *Ibid.*, pp. 512–15; see also pp. 505–6, 527.

752. *Works*, IV, 108.

753. London, 1847, p. 264. In Oken, the whole trunk with all its systems was repeated, with due modifications, in the hand.

754. *Tablets*, p. 192.

755. *Pedlar's Progress*, pp. 474–76. For details of Alcott's first visit to St. Louis, which turned out not altogether satisfactorily from Alcott's point of view, see *Journals*, pp. 303, 312–13, and my study, *New England Transcendentalism and St. Louis Hegelianism* (Phila., 1948), pp. 34–53.

756. *Pedlar's Progress*, pp. 476–77; *Journals*, p. 315.

757. George F. Hoar, *Autobiography of Seventy Years* (2 vols., N.Y., 1903), I, 74.

758. *Pedlar's Progress*, pp. 476, 481.

759. *Journals*, p. 340 (Aug. 6, 1861).

760. Harris came to Concord personally to invite him, and Alcott observed: "July 17 [1865] Harris comes and spends Tuesday and Wednesday. I find him a profound master of Hegel and the German thinkers, able to apply their dialectic to life, literature, art, society, and a man for whom a great future is opening. He gives hopeful accounts of Brockmeyer [*sic*], the German genius, and other members of his St. Louis circle; reads me papers of his own on philosophy, and hears many of my paragraphs, the oracles particularly, speaking of them all with enthusiasm . . . . The Personal Sketches also interest him deeply. I take great pleasure in this young man, now but thirty, a graduate [*sic*] of Yale, native of my state, and a successful teacher. My wife tells me that he reminds her of myself, at his age, when she first met me in Brooklyn, Conn. I take him to see Emerson, and they have sympathy about authors and opinions."—*Journals*, p. 373 (July 17, 1865).

761. *Pedlar's Progress*, pp. 477–80 *passim*.

762. *Ibid.*, p. 482.

763. *Ibid.*

764. *Journals*, p. 381 (Febr. 17, 1866). For details of this second visit, see *ibid.*, pp. 378–82, and see my *New England Transcendentalism and St. Louis Hegelianism*, pp. 34–53; for Emerson's visits to St. Louis, *ibid.*, pp. 53–65.

765. *Journals*, p. 379 (Feb. 9, 1866).

766. "If Harris finds a logic in it, calls it 'dialectic' or by any name known to philosophy, then I suppose I am entitled to the praise he bestows on my thinking."—*Journals*, p. 428; see also Sanborn and Harris, *op. cit.*, II, 613–17.

767. See *Journals* from 1866 on, esp. pp. 382, 388, 390, for the interesting concern expressed regarding "schools" and "systems."

768. *Ibid.*, p. 382 (Apr. 8, 1866).

769. *Ibid.*, p. 383 (July 20, 1866).

770. *Pedlar's Progress*, p. 483.

771. *Journals*, pp. 382, 386, 388, 390, 423, 424–25.

772. *Ibid.*, pp. 387–88 (Aug. 8, 1867).

773. *Ibid.*, pp. 384, 388 (1867).

774. *Ibid.*, p. 402 (1869).

775. *Ibid.*, p. 393 (1869).

776. *Ibid.*, p. 419 (May 7, 1871); also pp. 410–11, and *Pedlar's Progress*, p. 485.

777. *Pedlar's Progress*, p. 485.

778. *Ibid.*, p. 490.

779. *Journals*, p. 404 (1870).

780. *Ibid.*, p. 486.

781. *Ibid.*, p. 507; Denton J. Snider, *The St. Louis Movement* (St. Louis, 1920), p. 364;

Austin Warren, "The Concord School of Philosophy," *New Engl. Quar.*, II, ii (Apr., 1929), 199–233.

782. Snider, *op cit.*, pp. 307–8.

783. *Ibid.*, pp. 276–77.

784. *Ibid.*, pp. 332–37.

785. *Index*, XIII (Aug. 18, 1881), 78–79.

786. *Journals*, p. 420.

787. *Ibid.*, pp. 444–45, 466, 497, 498, 499, 502, 505, 505–6, 536.

788. *Ibid.*, pp. 428, 442, 444, 453–54, 497, 499–500, 525.

789. *Ibid.*, 428 (Nov. 16, 1872).

790. *Ibid.*, p. 497 (July 16, 1879).

791. *Ibid.*, p. 536 (Aug. 3, 1882).

792. *Ibid.*, p. 537 (Oct. 22, 1882). For Harris' explanation of the reason why he and Alcott could not agree on this point, see Sanborn and Harris, *op. cit.*, II, 629–32.

793. For a more detailed particularization of how Alcott's influence worked, through Harris and the Western Hegelians, to bring New England Transcendentalism of the thirties round full circle, as it were, and to redomesticate it in Concord during the eighties, and how this, in turn had its repercussions in the academic world, see my *New England Transcendentalism and St. Louis Hegelianism*, pp. 113–25.

794. Because he could not on authority alone accept the doctrine of damnation, he had rejected Calvinism and Presbyterianism and turned to Universalism. But the barren rationalistic principles of the Universalists, so calmly simple and reasonably reassuring on the surface, soon seemed to lead him to logical difficulties just as great, and he began to back away from that position when he perceived that it destroyed the very basis for public morality and neglected all higher authority. He was looking for some formulation which would make a place for religious feeling and yet explain it more satisfactorily than the Lockean philosophy did. Hence he was ready to accept one or another of the current teachings of intuitionism which were being propounded by the liberals in the Unitarian church.—Arthur M. Schlesinger, *Orestes A. Brownson A Pilgrim's Progress* (Boston, 1939), pp. 13–16ff.

795. Caroline Dall, *op. cit.*, p. 16.

796. Schlesinger, *op. cit.*, p. 33.

797. He continued as its minister until 1843.

798. Schlesinger, *op. cit.*, p. 54.

799. *Ibid.* See *The Convert* (N.Y., 1857), pp. 182–83: ". . . derived in part from Benjamin Constant, Victor Cousin, Heinrich Heine, and the publications of the Saint-Simonians." He adopted Heine's view of history as stated in *De l'Allemagne* (Paris, 1835), pp. 1–2, as a struggle between Nazarene spirituality and

Hellenic materialism. Brownson named the protagonists Catholicism and Protestantism, and contending against Heine and Saint-Simon, declared that true Christianity would be the social ideal of the future. For a later restatement of his position in *New Views* (1836), see *The Convert* of 1857, esp. pp. 185–87; also Schlesinger, *op. cit.*, pp. 55–56.

800. *Boston Quar. Rev.*, I, iv (Oct., 1838), 443.

801. The contributors were mainly writers with Transcendentalist sympathies, including Bancroft, Ripley, Alcott, Magaret Fuller, Sarah H. Whitman, Elizabeth P. Peabody, Parker, Brisbane, and W. H. Channing.

802. *Boston Quar. Rev.*, I, i (Jan., 1838), 2.

803. XXIII, ii (Nov., 1837), 170–94.

804. *Boston Quar. Rev.*, I, i (Jan., 1838), 101–2.

805. *Ibid.*, II, ii (Apr., 1839), 32. Brownson contended that the influence of German philosophy in America has been, on the whole, very small (I, i [Jan., 1838], 86); III, iii [July, 1840], 286). Yet he agreed with the Transcendentalists in their desire that French and German literature should become better known primarily because he believed it would bring in the right kind of democratic doctrine to counteract the overwhelming influence of aristocratic English literature (I, ii [Apr., 1838], 161–62; also iv [Oct., 1838], 435–41). In 1838 he was of the opinion that the best German literature had not yet been translated, and the next year he warmly welcomed Dwight's *Select Minor Poems of Goethe and Schiller* (I, iii [July, 1838], 434; II, ii [Apr., 1839], 187–205). The *Review* also carried, in January, 1840, a lengthy, appreciative review of Goethe by Mrs. Sarah H. Whitman, on the appearance of Goethe's *Conversations with Eckermann*, as translated by Margaret Fuller.

806. *Brownson's Quar. Rev.*, II, ii (Apr., 1845), 250, 252–53, 254–56; see also his review of her *Summer on the Lakes, ibid.*, I, iv (Oct., 1844), 546.

807. In his *Quarterly*, as early as January, 1844 (I, i, 136), he finds in Hedge traces of "miserable transcendentalism which has of late obtained amongst us, and which spins Truth, Good, Beauty, even God himself, out of the human soul, as the spider spins its web out of its own bowels."

808. Whatever virtue Brownson had seen in 1839 in Dwight's translations of Goethe and Schiller he rejected six years later as delusion and error, for Schiller has become in his mind the spokesman of Protestant liberalism, and his work is "false in its leading doctrines and unwholesome in its general tendency." In fact, he prefers the heathen Goethe on the ground

that at least Goethe never meddled with reform and, unlike Schiller, was not an "inbred radical. . . . *The Robbers* are not less reprehensible, to say the least, than the *Wahlverwandtschaften*." —II, iii (July, 1845), 383–84. His critique of the Weiss translation of the *Aesthetic Letters* is a penetrating study of Schiller's basic cultural theories. Brownson detects the Kantism of the work, but shows that Schiller's version of Kant's aesthetics is even less tenable than Kant's imperative in the realm of ethics. For when Schiller makes the play impulse (*Spieltrieb*)—an inclination of the soul—the determining factor of the aesthetic education of man, he is introducing a dangerous principle. In the final analysis, "his theory. . . practically reduces itself into the *Theory of Attraction*, the basis of Fourierism!" (p. 383). Schiller's error (and that of John Weiss, too, in his commentary on the work) is to define Christianity as "the moral imperative transfigured by love." This vague talk of "love" so common among the idealists and transcendentalists is evidence of a base naturalism in philosophy, the great single error of modern thought (p. 386).

809. *Ibid.*, pp. 387–88; see also I, iv (Oct., 1844), 546, and *The Convert*, Chs. XII and XIV.

810. Schlesinger, *op. cit.*, pp. 177–78.

811. Emerson, for example, was in 1832 enough the logician to repudiate the Unitarian church, and he was ever after an unwilling intuitionist. All his discontent with speculative philosophy stemmed from his inability to find the satisfactory logical and rational way and from an equal dissatisfaction with any purely intuitional theology or philosophy. Parker was, or thought he was, so far removed from the position of the intuitionist that in 1841, in *The Transient and Permanent in Christianity*, he willingly risked expulsion from the Unitarian Association by asserting the priority of reason over belief. Eventually he achieved a mediation, but again, as in Emerson's case, he was plagued all his life long by logical questions for which he found no complete answer and which made a botch of some of his writings—as, for example his review of Strauss. Ripley was led far enough by the critical spirit to leave his pulpit in 1840, but he found it less difficult than Emerson, for example, to espouse faith, and there are in his later life no such wrestlings with evolution, logic, and dialectics as in Emerson's case. Clarke came even earlier and more readily than Ripley to a mediate position, and from the first counseled both the orthodox and the liberals to steer a middle course between reason and intuition. But Hecker, before he definitely banned the strictly scientific from his religious thinking and made up his mind to become a

Catholic, went through a period when he found it hard to lay the spectre that his early reading of Kant had raised.

812. *New Views of Christianity* (1836), in *Collected Works*, ed. by H. F. Brownson (20 vols., Detroit, 1898–1908), IV, 44–45. After his conversion and his repudiation of reform, he was equally condemnatory of Schleiermacher for making religion purely subjective and for resolving the church "into general society," at the same time branding his "pantheistic spiritualism" as worse than rationalism, deism, and even the atheism of Baron d'Holbach (*Works*, III, 45; IV, 519; VIII, 424; IX, 480).

813. Actually he had begun to recommend eclecticism as a cure for what ailed America in his essay on "Recent Contributions to Philosophy" in the *Christian Examiner* for May, 1837 (XXII, 181–217). By October, 1838, he considered Cousin "if not the first, one of the first philosophers of the age."—*Boston Quar. Rev.*, I, iv (Oct., 1838), 443).

814. "Eclecticism—Ontology," *Boston Quar. Rev.*, II, ii (Apr., 1839), 179; see also "Eclectic Philosophy," *ibid.*, I, i (Jan., 1839), 27–53, esp. pp. 28, 32–34.

815. "Synthetic Philosophy," *Democratic Rev.*, XI (Dec., 1842), 567–78, esp. p. 571; and "Eclecticism—Ontology," *Boston Quar. Rev.*, II, ii (Apr., 1839), 178, 180–82. It is to be observed that Brownson interpreted Kant's analysis as purely empirical and therefore correct within its limits, and that he early defended Kant against the charge of "Transcendentalism" as the term was depreciatingly, popularly, and, as he pointed out, incorrectly used (*ibid.*, i [Jan., 1839], 27–28). On the contrary, says Brownson in 1839, Kant's method is "as truly experimental as Bacon's or Locke's" (*ibid.*, pp. 29, 30–31). If Kant is in error, it is not because he "leaves the path of experience or rushes off into speculation" but because he failed to make a thoroughgoing application of his method, for he conceived of experience too narrowly as merely experience of the senses. See *ibid.*, pp. 30–32, 38, 43, 47–49. It is at this point that he subsequently attacked Kant as the father of the new "sensist" and "materialist" schools.

816. *Boston Quar. Rev.*, II, i (Jan., 1839), 37–38, 42–45, 47–49.

817. *Ibid.*, II, ii (Apr., 1839), 178–79; see also V, ii (Apr., 1842), 176–77.

818. "Charles Elwood," *ibid.*, V, ii (Apr., 1842), 129–83, esp. pp. 175–76.

819. *Ibid.*, p. 176; *Works*, IV, 355.

820. This identification is repeated in 'Remarks on Universal History," *Dem. Rev.*, XII (May, 1843), 474; *Works*, IV, 391.

821. Henry F. Brownson, *Orestes Brownson's Early Life* (Detroit, 1898), p. 413.

822. "Critik der reinen Vernunft," *Brownson's Quar. Rev.*, I, iii (July, 1844), 282.

823. "Introduction," *ibid.*, I, i (Jan., 1844), 6, 8.

824. *Ibid.*, I, ii (Apr., 1844), 137–74; iii (July, 1844), 281–309; iv (Oct., 1844), 417–49. These essays, comprising a hundred pages, form the fullest and at the same time the most competent critical discussion which had appeared specifically of Kant's first Critique up to this time. In the course of it he shows a good deal of dialectical ability, and he drives home his points with a vengeance. He attacks what he calls the absurdity of Kant's asking the human mind to judge itself—to determine whether or not it has any right to form judgments at all.—*Ibid.*, I, iii (July, 1844), 288; *Works*, I, 162. Kant's subjective phenomenalism is completely misguided and out of focus because of his "fundamental error," which makes the effort as "impossible" as it is "absurd," in attempting "to find the object in the subject." If Kant had considered the truth of Fichte's simple equation that "me is me," he could never have fallen into his error. For Fichte's "simple truism is nothing but saying what *is*, is"; but simple as it is, it is enough "completely to refute the whole critical philosophy."—*Ibid.*, p. 283; *Works*, I, 163. In the final analysis, Kant has to be put down as an arch-skeptic who denied the possibility of human knowledge, and hence his *Critique* is in reality "the most masterly defence of Hume," whom he had set out to refute. Kantism leads to a soul-withering skepticism, "Universal Doubt and Nescience." —*Ibid.*, p. 308; *Works*, I, 184–85.

Brownson's later attacks upon Kant, which, while repeating his admiration for Kant's analytical powers, merely reiterate the arguments enunciated in the essays of 1844. See, for example, "An Old Quarrel," *Catholic World*, V (May, 1867), 145–59, esp. pp. 152–56. Other passages on Kant are to be found in *Works*, I, 222, 244–45; II, 295, 299, 520; V, 507; VI, 106; X, 263; XIX, 384.

825. See the article, "Charles Elwood," *Boston Quar. Rev.*, V, ii (Apr., 1842), 152–53, 156–60, 172–73, 175–78, 181–82, and "Remarks on Universal History," *Dem. Rev.* XII (May, 1843), 473–74. Henceforth Descartes is the arch-subjectivist, the father of all that is most vicious in modernity.

826. "Charles Elwood," *Boston Quar. Rev.*, V, ii (Apr., 1842), 176–77.

827. "The Giobertian Philosophy," *Brownson's Quar. Rev.*, XXI (Apr., 1864), 129–66, esp. pp. 149–54, and XXI (July, 1864), 293–315, esp.

pp. 294–95; see also "The Cartesian Doubt," *Catholic World*, VI (Nov., 1867), 234–51.

828. "Cousin's Philosophy," *Christ. Exam.*, XXI, i (Sept., 1836), 35–54, esp. p. 46.

829. "The Giobertian Philosophy," *Brownson's Quar. Rev.*, XXI (July, 1864), 295.

830. "Remarks on Universal History," *Dem. Rev.*, XII (May, 1843), 461.

831. *Ibid.*, pp. 461–62; see also p. 467.

832. *Ibid.*, p. 470.

833. "Introduction," *Brownson's Quar. Rev.*, I, i (Jan., 1844), 8; see also III (Oct., 1846), 409–39, esp. p. 425; XXI (July, 1864), 294–96; XXII (Oct., 1873), 433–65; XXIII (Jan., 1874), 1–37; XXIII (Apr., 1874), 145–79. Hegel's principles are "unreal and worthless," "really less genuine, less profound, and infinitely less worthy of confidence" than those of Reid. See *ibid.*, XXI (July, 1864), 295–96; and *Cath. World*, V (May, 1867), 153. Hegel's triads, by which he seeks to derive reality from possibility and existence from nothing, are simply ridiculous. See *Dem. Rev.*, XII (May, 1843), 461; also *Works*, I, 401; II, 38, 71, 268; VIII, 384; IX, 273; XI, 229. Far from being an ontologist, Hegel is a pure psychologist who has mistaken the method of the one for that of the other—"a subjective idealist who ends in atheism, like all followers of Kant." See *Brownson's Quar. Rev.*, I, i (Jan., 1844), 8, and René Wellek, "The Minor Transcendentalists and German Philosophy," *New Engl. Quar.*, XV, iv (Dec., 1942), 676. As Professor Wellek points out, Brownson's several mistaken references to Hegel's *Ideen* for *das Ideale* inspire no great confidence for Brownson's close reading of Hegel.

834. "Spiritual Despotism," *Brownson's Quar. Rev.*, XIV (Apr., 1857), 191–224, esp. p. 191.

835. "Holy Communion—Transubstantiation," *Brownson's Quar. Rev.*, XXIII (Jan., 1874), 55–77, esp. p. 59; see also "Refutation of Atheism," *ibid.*, p. 7; and "Catholicity and Naturalism," *Works*, VIII, 352.

836. Walter Elliott, *The Life of Father Hecker* (2nd ed., N.Y., 1894), 31; see also Henry D. Sedgwick, *Father Hecker* (Boston, 1900), pp. 5–6.

837. Elliott, *op. cit.*, pp. 15–22.

838. *Ibid.*, p. 32.

839. He was a "partial boarder," paying four dollars a week, at the same time undertaking the bread-making in partial payment for the instruction he received from Ripley, Bradford, Dana, and Dwight.—*Ibid.*, pp. 49–50.

840. "I loved him dearly," said Hecker in 1882. "But he was a complete failure. I loved him dearly, and he knew it, and he loved me; I know well he did. When I came back a Redemptorist from Europe, I went to see him at the *Tribune* office. He asked me, 'Can you do all that any Catholic priest can do?' 'Yes.' 'Then I will send for you when I am drawing towards my end.' . . . I am persuaded that the fear of facing his friends hindered George Ripley from becoming a Catholic. He sent for me when taken down by his last illness, but his message was not delivered. As soon as I heard that he was ill I hastened to his bedside, but his mind was gone and I could do nothing for him."—*Ibid.*, p. 90.

841. *Ibid.*, pp. 55–56.

842. *Ibid.*, pp. 55, 61; see also pp. 62, 63, 65, 76, and Sedgwick, *op. cit.*, pp. 18-19.

843. For details see Elliott, *op. cit.*, pp. 81–83, 84–88.

844. For his impassioned search at this time "among the philosophers" and "among the sects" for the truth, see Elliott, *op. cit.*, pp. 113–38, *passim*.

845. *Ibid.*, pp. 89, 151, 153–54.

846. *Ibid.*, p. 176.

847. *Ibid.*, p. 120.

848. "One day, however [says Hecker], I was walking along the road and Emerson joined me. Presently he said, 'Mr. Hecker, I suppose it was the art, the architecture, and so on of the Catholic Church which led you to her?' 'No,' said I; 'but it was what caused all that.'" Years later, after he had lectured in Concord on "Why I became a Catholic" (a lecture which Alcott came to hear, but not Emerson), he and Emerson met in the street—Hecker by now confident that he had the truth, Emerson still the transcendental philosopher seeking it. The encounter led Hecker to observe complacently that "none of these men are comfortable in conversation with an intelligent Catholic. . . . We had a little talk together. . . . He avoided my eyes until he quite turned round! Such men, confronted with actual, certain convictions are exceedingly uncomfortable. They feel in subjection to you. They cannot bear the steadfast glance of a man of certain principles any better than a dog can the look of his master. Like a dog, they turn away the head and show signs of uneasiness."—*Ibid.*, pp. 89–90.

Ernest the Seeker had long since ended his search, and had become sure of himself. As Professor Gabriel observes, what Hecker was not aware of was that when Emerson literally turned his back on Father Hecker, "he symbolized the rejection by the American people of the Paulist's argument. The golden day when the American democratic faith should for all Americans rest squarely upon Catholic theology did not dawn. Yet Hecker did not work in vain. If he failed to convert American democrats to Catholicism, he succeeded in converting an immigrant Catholic Church to New World democracy."—Ralph H. Gabriel, *The Course of American Democratic Thought. An Intellectual History since 1815* (N.Y.,1940), p. 65.

849. For a discussion of this aspect of Hecker's work and its effectiveness see Gabriel, *op. cit.*, pp. 62-66.

850. That he shared at this time the general enthusiasm for German literature is indicated by his contribution of seven translations to Dwight's *Select Minor Poems of Goethe and Schiller* and his composition of a prose parable on the subject of Moses Mendelssohn, "Evening Hours and Morning Hours," which appeared in the *Western Messenger*, VI, v (Mar., 1839), 342-44.

851. Jouffroy's book is a review of Scottish, German, and French contributions to ethics in the eighteenth and nineteenth centuries, in which he makes a judicious synthesis out of the three traditions on an eclectic basis. Channing added no notes, contributed nothing of his own to the subject, and in the Preface reaffirmed his trust in intuition and in "spiritualistic" religion. He disavowed any genuine interest in the Germans since Kant, for their energies are now absorbed, he says, by "ontology and logic."—Preface, p. xiv.

852. See O. B. Frothingham's review of Furness' *The Veil Partly Lifted and Jesus Becoming Visible* (Boston, 1864) in *Christ. Exam.*, LXXVI, iii (May, 1864), 374-92, esp. p. 375; also C. A. Bartol, "Dr. Furness and Dr. Bushnell: A Question of Words and Names," *ibid.*, LXVI, i (Jan., 1859), 112-24, esp. p. 116.

853. Taking issue with Parker and other advanced Transcendentalists on the historicity of Jesus, Furness yet felt he stood with them on other important questions. It was his desire always to give up fruitless theological argument in favor of evangelical preaching and practical reform. He was liberal enough to argue vigorously in favor of a recognition of Parker by the Unitarian Association when, in 1859, that body refused to send Parker an expression of sympathy at his illness.

Aside from his purely theological writings, Furness was a prolific translator of German verse. Reviewing Hedge's *Prose Writers of Germany* (which he helped to edit), he defended the Germans against the charge of "dreaming," and paid tribute to their art and music as well as poetry. See *Christ. Exam.*, XLIV, ii (Mar., 1848), 263-73. The next year he published a translation of G. H. Schubert's *The Mirror of Nature: A Book of [Popular Religious] Instruction and Entertainment* (Phila., 1849); and in

1856 appeared *Julius and Other Tales* from the German of Zschokke and Toepfer. His translation of Schiller's *Lied von der Glocke* (Phila., 1850) was regarded as one of the best versions of this much translated poem. In 1853 he published his immensely popular *Gems of German Verse*, poems of Goethe, Schiller, Uhland, Heine, Chamisso, and others, including what is still adjudged the best English version of Heine's "Zwei Grenadiere." At the Schiller anniversary celebration in the Academy of Music in Philadelphia, in 1859, Furness was the principal speaker. A final edition of his numerous translations, originally published in many of the liberal journals of the mid-century, appeared in 1886 under the title of *Verses, Translated from the German; and Hymns.*

THE LATER TRANSCENDENTALISTS

854. Lectures LIX-LXIX were printed under the title, *Transcendentalism with Preludes on Current Events*, by Joseph Cook, Boston, 1878. The Boston Monday Lectures, during 1875-1877, had the object "to present the results of the freshest German, English, and American scholarship" (Preface). They were stenographically reported in the *Boston Daily Advertiser*, and most of them were published in book form in Boston, New York, and London.

855. Joseph Cook, *Transcendentalism . . .*, p. 29.

856. *Ibid.*, p. 36.

857. *Ibid.*, p. 63; O. B. Frothingham, *Recollections and Impressions, 1822-1890* (N.Y., 1891), pp. 54-59, 134, 165-89.

858. Leading German universities, "through their great specialists in exegetical and historical research, have decisively given the opinion . . . that the Author of Christianity is historically only an idolized memory inwreathed with mythical fictions. . . . Tholuck, Julius Müller, Dorner, Twesten, Ullmann, Lange, Rothe, and Tischendorf, most of whom began their professorships . . . with great popularity, on account of their opposition to rationalistic views, are now particularly honoured on that very account."—*Ibid.*, pp. 29, 30, 37-38. See also Cook's essay on the "Decline of Rationalism in the German Universities," *Bibliotheca Sacra*, XXXII, cxxviii (Oct., 1875), 736-72, and a review of Immanuel H. Fichte's *Fragen und Bedenken über die nächste Fortbildung deutscher Speculation* (Leipzig, 1876) in the *North Amer. Rev.*, CXXIV, ccliv (Jan., 1877), 146-47.

859. Cook. *op. cit.*, p. 38. Only in America does this nonsense continue. Originally deriving inspiration from the rationalistic side of Ger-

man exegetical research, Free Religious Associationism soon developed an infidelity of its own—an apostasy which the Germans themselves would today be the first to denounce.

860. See, for example, the three volumes of collected lectures printed under the title of *Boston Lectures: Christianity aud Skepticism* (Boston, 1870, 1871, 1872).

861. The *Christian Examiner*, during the period from 1850 to 1880, continued to print more articles and reviews dealing with German theology than did any other American journal. After the *Massachusetts Quarterly Review* (1847–1850), none of the Transcendental organs put much emphasis on elucidating strictly foreign points of view; and the *Radical* (1865–1872) and the *Index* (1870–1886) differed markedly in this respect from the *Western Messenger* (1835–1841) and the *Dial* (1841–1844), both more typical of the earlier phase of Transcendentalism. No longer distinctly conscious of being evangels of German thought, writers in the later journals took German theology (as well as philosophy) for granted and no longer pointed to any revolutionary inspiration or novel instruction to be derived thence.

862. See the collection of addresses by Osgood, T. J. Sawyer, Frothingham, H. Blanchard, C. Miel, B. F. Barrett, E. H. Chapin, H. W. Bellows, A. D. Mayo, T. W. Higginson, B. Peters, D. Wasson, and Horace Greeley, delivered on the occasion of the first anniversary celebration of the Young Men's Christian Union of New York on May 13–14, 1858, and published under the title of *The Religious Aspects of Our Age, with a Glance at the Church of the Present and the Church of the Future* (N.Y., 1858).

863. For details, see Mrs. John T. Sargent (ed.), *Sketches and Reminiscences of the Radical Club of Chestnut Street, Boston* (Boston, 1880).

864. Recent general treatments of the free religious movements in the United States are Sidney Warren, *American Freethought, 1860–1914* (N.Y., 1843), and Stow Persons, *Free Religion, an American Faith* (New Haven, 1947). Both have appeared since this section was written; both add measurably to our knowledge of the free-thought movement but say very little about its relations with German religious and philosophical thought.

865. R. H. Gabriel, *op. cit.*, pp. 178–79.

866. Throughout the last decade of the Club's existence, scientific subjects were in the ascendancy. With O. W. Holmes's reasoned attack on Jonathan Edwards all could agree (Mrs. John T. Sargent [ed.], *op cit.*, pp. 362–75), but when Prof. Benj. Peirce explained the nebular theory in strictly evolutionary terms, it was observed that following his paper "there was less desire

than is generally the case to venture theories and criticisms," so that there followed a "period of unusual restraint" and the "reputation of the Club for rapid and brilliant conversation" was felt to be in danger (*ibid.*, pp. 250, 385). Again, when Edward S. Morse spoke on the subject of "Evolution," the membership "felt some delicacy" about venturing upon a discussion of the issues, beyond observing, as James F. Clarke did, that it was still difficult to tell on which side of the argument "the burden of proof rested" (pp. 184–85). Apparently the one person present on that occasion who thoroughly enjoyed Morse's discourse was Mark Twain. While he was obliged to leave at an early hour and was therefore unable to join much in the discussion, he became excited when the theory of metempsychosis was introduced, and came away convinced that "it's the passing off on a man of an old, damaged, second-hand soul that makes all the trouble" (pp. 186–87). Nathaniel S. Shaler's and Francis E. Abbot's papers on Darwinism again provoked a painful pause and then a restrained discussion (pp. 259–65, 265–70). Finally, when Professor Alpheus Hyatt's two discourses on "Heredity" and "Evolution" (pp. 315–28, 329–38) raised the issues still more insistently, the lines of cleavage began to be drawn sharply. The majority of the membership (which included people like Weiss, Wasson, and Bartol) were of the opinion that scientific men tend to make "the physical the basis of all things"; the smaller but no less determined group (including Abbot, Higginson, Frothingham, Peirce, Fiske, and Morse) declared that no true religion need fear anything from science or from men of science (p. 332).

In all these arguments, Leibnitz, Kant, Schelling, Hegel, Goethe, Helmholtz, Virchow, Haeckel, Schopenhauer, and a host of other Germans were referred to as authorities on one side or another. There was some justification for the remark made by a sympathetic journalist in Chicago, who, denying that the Radical Club had departed this life, expressed himself as pleased that "the harp that once through Sargent's halls the soul of Hegel shed" had not yet "sounded its last note" (p. 386). Indeed, the music was heard everywhere. Each month the New York *Tribune* carried to its national clientele one or two columns of description and comment concerning the latest meeting of the Club. Numerous other papers and magazines, some of them as far west as Chicago, more or less regularly devoted space to the Radical Club and either cheered it on or wished it dead. Through such agencies were disseminated the theological and scientific ideas of the new religion based on "human nature" or "humanity."

867. *Ibid.*, p. 310.

868. Consider, for example, the close association of Francis E. Abbot, editor of the *Index*, with Robert Ingersoll in the organization of the National Liberal League, of which association Abbot made the *Index* the official organ in 1877, at the same time that it was the mouthpiece, and was soon to become the property, of the Free Religious Association. The journal continued successfully under this joint sponsorship for nine years longer, except that Samuel Johnson, writing to Samuel Longfellow, on June 29, 1879, deplored the drift of "American radicalism into organization, reliance on numbers, utilities, forces, experience included, as contrasted with personal, interior, ideal values," and raised objections to Abbot's efforts at "organizing the Eternal Truth into Liberal Leagues."—Samuel Johnson, *Lectures, Essays, and Sermons* (Boston, 1883), pp. 127, 134; see also C. Gohdes, *op. cit.*, pp. 233–36, 240.

869. *Index*, VIII (Mar. 22, 1877), 134–35.

870. *Ibid.* (Apr. 19, 1877), pp. 186–87.

871. C. Gohdes *op. cit.*, pp. 247–53.

872. *Index*, XIV (Aug. 15, 1882), 78; Mead, *Influence of Emerson* (Boston, 1903), p. 111.

873. That these differences were real and recognized by Parker and Emerson themselves appears substantiated by Emerson, when, replying to Conway's request, shortly after Parker's death, for an article on Parker for the Cincinnati *Dial*, he wrote: "I have nothing to say of Parker. I know well what a calamity is the loss of his courage and patriotism to the country; but of his mind and genius, few are less accurately informed than I. . . . I have just written to his society, who have asked me to speak with Phillips in the funeral oration that I will come to hear, not to speak . . . . My relations to him are quite accidental and our differences of method and working such as really required all his catholicity and magnanimity to forgive in me."—M. D. Conway, *Autobiography* (2 vols., Boston and N.Y., 1904), I, 313.

874. *Index*, XIV (Oct. 5, 1882), 160–61.

875. *Ibid.* (Oct. 26, 1882), p. 195.

876. C. Gohdes, *op. cit.*, pp. 253–54.

877. Heinzen, who epitomized in one person most of the various German-American radicalisms, had in 1854 transferred his residence to Boston, where he continued through the columns of his *Pioneer* and his untiring personal efforts, to prosecute social, political, and religious revolution. Writing in the *Radical* for January, 1867 (II, v, 257–69), Samuel Johnson hailed the "German leaven" as a necessary "foil to grim Puritanism." He felt that the "speculative boldness" of the German mind has entered into American life "under admirable auspices" (pp. 168–69). Even their "courage in theological negation" is excused as "needful disintegrative work," and "Missouri is a monument of the Germans' fidelity to an abstract idea."

In the sixties and seventies such a point of view was not unusual, though in the middle of the century few were bold enough to espouse it. For example, in 1851, Samuel Osgood had taken a much less lenient attitude toward the German refugees of '48. He saw in their strong anti-Sabbatarianism a good tendency, but he denounced them as atheistical. He conceived their "sensual socialism" to be a definite American problem so long as they should remain unassimilated.—*Christ. Exam.*, LI, iii (Nov., 1851), 250–59.

878. *Index*, VII, cccv (May 25, 1876), 246–47.

879. See, for example, the communication from Milwaukee, dated December 20, 1875, in the *Index*, VII, cccxv (Jan. 6, 1876), 7.

880. *Ibid.*, cccxliv (July 27, 1876), 354.

881. Heinz Kloss, *Um die Einigung des Deutschamerikanertums . . .* (Berlin, 1937), pp. 224–28, *passim*.

882. I, xxxv (Aug. 27, 1870), 2–3.

883. See *Radical*, II, iii (Nov., 1866), 170–77, and ix (May, 1867), 543–49.

884. See, for instance, a letter on the St. Louis Hegelians by A. E. Kroeger in the *Radical*, I, x (May, 1866), 349–52; also the notice of Harris' articles in the *Journal of Speculative Philosophy*, written in a friendly, receptive tone, in the *Index*, VII, cccxlv (Aug. 3, 1876), 367; and the analytical discussions of Hegel, *ibid.*, XVI, dcclxxxvi (Jan. 15, 1885, 343–45, and dccciii (May 14, 1885), 551.

885. See Kroeger's critical articles on Goethe in the *Radical*, II, v (Jan., 1867), 273–82, and vi (Feb., 1867), 332–40, and his review of the *Life and Genius of Goethe: Lectures at the Concord School of Philosophy* (Boston, 1884) in *Index* XVII, dcccxlviii (Mar. 25, 1886), 466.

886. T. W. Higginson, *Cheerful Yesterdays* (Boston and N.Y., 1901), 169.

887. Most of these are popular expositions of the transcendentalist position, but occasionally Osgood wrote on literary topics, as for instance in his short piece entitled "The Love of the Tragic," *Western Messenger*, III, v (June, 1837), 749–53, where he reviewed the theories of Burke, Hume, and Schlegel. In an essay, "Religion in Prussia" (*ibid.*, iii [Apr. 1837], 635–37) he revealed his transcendental inclination to admire the German theologians, notably Schleiermacher.

888. II, ii (Sept., 1836), 73–91; iii (Oct., 1836), 185–90.

889. III, i (Feb., 1837), 433–51; ii (Mar., 1837), 505–19; iv (May, 1837), 647–61; v June, 1837), 719–32; vi (July, 1837), 791–803. This work by a conservative German Biblical critic had been acclaimed by some of the orthodox in America, though he was much more liberal than the average of those who were rated "conservative" in America.

890. *Christ. Exam.*, XXV, i (Sept., 1838), 1–23.

891. *The Holy Gospels, Illustrated by Overbeck*, ed. by Samuel Osgood (Boston, 1856).

892. Characteristic of his attitude is his address on "The Catholicity of the Church of the Future," given on the first anniversary celebration of the Young Men's Christian Union of New York, May 13, 1858. After complimenting the youthful Union upon its decision to avoid creed and dogma by adopting a broad catholicity, he urged them to follow their honest conviction though they remain a despised minority. But he also urged them to avoid the extreme of radicalism, as expressed by the "great Positivist of France, August Comte," who maintained that "the only way to destroy old institutions is by replacing them." For as "God never left Himself without a witness in any age," so High Church, Low Church, Broad Church, and No Church alike are to be searched and reverenced for the good each contains. True catholicity is to be achieved by a "reconciliation of science with faith, industry with spirituality, society with devotion, art with religion, and manliness with godliness."—*The Religious Aspects of the Age* (N.Y., 1858), pp. 13–14, 15, 17, 30.

893. *Christ. Exam.*, LXXXVI, ii (Mar., 1869), 171–91.

894. *Ibid.*, p. 172.

895. *Ibid.*, p. 176.

896. "Transcendentalism in New England," *Internat'l. Rev.*, III (Nov., 1876), 742–63.

897. *Ibid.*, pp. 757, 759–60

898. *Christ. Exam.*, XLII, ii (Mar., 1847), 255.

899. He paid tribute to German learning, but pointed also to its "weak passiveness and vagueness," its "flighty imagination." See his review of Clarke's *Theodore* in the *Christian Examiner*, XXXI, ii (Jan., 1842), 348–73, especially page 348. He felt that the new doctrine of the "soul's sufficiency" had no necessary connection with any historical antecedents, but could be found in all ages. It goes back to Hebrew and Greek times: "the Spring of wonder burst up in Teutonic soil, the same living water as in Indian bottles or Jewish jars." He criticizes Parker, "the deputy-sheriff of ideas," and other Transcendentalists for teaching the doctrine of "Divine impersonality," for personality properly understood is "no degradation or limitation" of God. See his *Radical Problems* (Boston, 1874), pp. 66, 76, 85. On the whole, Bartol uttered an effective protest against the growing materialist agnosticism of the sixties and seventies. The radicalism he preached consisted of a strong enunciation of the church's duties to further social progress and to strengthen the "bond between man and man."—*Ibid.*, p. 112.

900. Schiller, he feels, has been vastly overesteemed, and now "the moth and rust" are at work "on compositions which the schoolgirls thirty years ago were mad over,—Don Carlos, Maria Stuart, the Robbers, and Wilhelm Tell." —*The Life and Genius of Goethe*, ed. by F. B. Sanborn (Boston, 1886), p. 112. Bartol emphasizes what he considers Schiller's rigid conventionality, the hollow rhetoric of his lines, the lack of realism in his dramas, the comparative simplicity of his characters. Goethe, on the other hand, is the poet of life, with all its subtle shadings, its confusion of right and wrong. "Schiller is the poet of a section and season; Goethe, of ages and the world" (pp. 112, 128). Emerson was incapable of a complete understanding of Goethe's art, for Emerson is but "half-acquainted with this world; Goethe is native to the soil, and knows every mother's son and daughter by heart." Although indebted to Goethe for ideas and points of view, Emerson does an injustice to the author of *Faust* when he admits that to his "dainty mind" *Faust* is a disagreeable book, "as if a poem . . . could be made of the leavings when all the sad and dark passages of the world-tale should have been erased" (p. 115). Taking up the delicate question of the Goethean morality, Bartol pleads for the application of a relative standard. Even if Goethe did err, we cannot refuse to listen to his wisdom so dearly bought. "To say that Goethe gloated over the sin, while he gathered up the lesson, is a calumny. . . . Great men are too scarce to be thrown away, even for grievous faults. Consult proportion in what you judge" (pp. 117–18). On the whole, "Goethe's temper was goodness to every creature that breathes, from an instinctive piety with which the child of seven rears an altar to the Deity . . . He is religious [and] refuses, chief scientific genius as he was of his time, to admit a scientific basis for religion, it being his own; a naturalist, he sees in nature more than can be reduced to natural laws. He repents where he has been misled, and in 'Elective Affinities' deposits sad experiences, he says, as in a burial-urn. He judges that the sentiment of faith concerns us more than the object on which it is fixed" (pp. 122–23).

901. Emerson characterized N. L. Frothingham as "an excellent classical and German scholar" (*Works*, X, 335). He and his daughter Ellen, the sister of Octavius Brooks, were very active translators of German poetry during the thirties and forties. See O. B. Frothingham, *Recollections and Impressions*, pp. 3-5, for the large German content of his father's library.

902. *Ibid.*, pp. 22, 32-33, 53, 57-60, 74, 134. He mentions having read, already while at the Divinity School, De Wette, "the Strauss and Paulus Schools," Baur, Schwegler, Zeller, Schneckenburger, and the Theologische Jahrbücher"; but his real conversion to the new theology did not come until after 1847, when he went to Salem and met Theodore Parker, who appeared to him "a second Luther." "From a shelf in his library, I took Schwegler's 'Nachapostolisches Zeitalter' . . . which threw a flood of light on New-Testament criticism. This led to a study of F. C. Baur, the founder of the so-called 'Tübingen School.' A complete set of the *Theologische Jahrbücher*, the organ of his ideas was imported . . . and carefully perused."— *Ibid.*, pp. 29, 54, 57-59.

903. *Ibid.*, pp. 140-42, 144-45.

904. E.g., *Christ. Exam.*, LI, ii (Sept., 1851), 161-85.

905. In his article on Baur in the *Christian Examiner*, LXIV, i (Jan., 1858), 1-39, he demonstrated his high appreciation of German scholarship, though he remained unsympathetic toward certain of the doctrines of the Hegelian school.

906. *Recollections and Impressions*, p. 137.

907. "Essential human nature," wrote Frothingham in his *Religion of Humanity* (1872), "is the Messiah cradled in the bosom of every man." "Whether there shall be peace or war, rule or misrule, purity or corruption, justice or injustice . . . are questions that men must answer for themselves. There is no higher tribunal . . . there is no super-human or extra-human will by which they can be dealt with. If things go well or ill rests with those who are commissioned to make them go."—Second ed., N.Y., 1872, p. 109.

908. Infidels are not "the progressives" but those who make religion "a cloak of pride, selfishness, and cruelty" while punctiliously adhering to the letter of the Scriptures. The only infidelity that Frothingham fears is that following upon "ecclesiastical straight-jacketing," which is a "disbelief in the primary faculties of the human soul; disbelief in the capability of man's reason to discriminate between truth and error in all departments of knowledge sacred and profane. . . . They are infidels . . . who overlay their reason with heaps of anti-

quated traditions . . . and stand dumb before appalling iniquities in obedience to the ill-read letter of ancient record."—*Ibid.*, pp. 124, 126, 131-33.

909. Stedman left an appreciative appraisal of Frothingham in *Octavius Brooks Frothingham and the New Faith* (N.Y., 1876).

910. *Recollections and Impressions*, pp. 128, 134.

911. This periodical was founded by Francis E. Abbot, a professionally trained philosopher and one of Frothingham's ablest associates, who was supported by Emerson for the professorship of philosophy at Andrew D. White's new Cornell University. Failing of the appointment, he went to Toledo, Ohio, and founded the *Index* on January 1, 1870.—Francis E. Abbot, *Testimonials* (Boston, 1879), p. 32; *Proc. of the Third Annual Meeting of the Free Religious Assn. in Boston, May 26-27, 1870* (Boston, 1870), p. 8.

912. Ralph H. Gabriel, *op. cit.*, pp. 176-77; *Index*, I, i (Jan., 1870).

913. As Croly (*pseud.* C. G. David) understood positivism, it embraced the following tenets: "humanity is the supreme being; immortality exists, in objective and subjective forms, but not as conscious life of the mortal faculties; humanity should be paid service, love and worship, the latter being reverence for the noble qualities in man; wealth should be devoted to humanity . . . ; women should be worshipped as the example of all that is good in humanity. . . . Human conduct must be determined, not by rights, but by duties alone. These principles are valid and positive because they are proved by the discoveries of science."— Gabriel, *op. cit.*, p. 184.

914. Frothingham's *Recollections and Impressions*, full of references to Emerson, Parker, Kant, Strauss, Baur, and Schwegler as having influenced him, mentions Comte only once and positivism not at all.

915. Henry Edger, a British immigrant of 1851, was the chief earlier apostle in America of the Comtean philosophy. After spending six years energetically proselyting, he counted ten converts, among them his wife and three of his children. His disappointment and failure led him to abandon the United States about 1880, at the commencement of the decade that saw positivism sweep the country. For the origins of potisivism in America, as well as for the numerous causes that delayed its reception in the United States, see R. L. Hawkins, *Positivism in the United States 1853-1861*, (Cambridge, Mass., 1938), notably pp. 212-25; see also Hawkins, *Auguste Comte and the United States, 1816-1853* (Cambridge, Mass.,

1936), and W. I. Riley, *American Thought* (N.Y., 1915), pp. 397–408.

916. For evidence that Frothingham understood the uses to which New England Transcendentalists had tried to put German idealists from Kant to Hegel, see his history of *Transcendentalism in New England*, notably the section, "Germany," pp. 5–59.

917. See his long article, "The German Catholic Movement," *Christ. Exam.*, XLII, i (Jan., 1847), 55–81, a detailed review based on a thorough knowledge of recent history and religious movements, and of the significance of Ronge's revolt against the Roman church; see also "Germany, Religious and Political," *ibid.*, XLIII, iii (Nov., 1847), 394–427.

918. See Gohdes, *op. cit.*, p. 216. Parker rated him "certain and valuable" as a possible contributor to his *Massachusetts Quarterly Review.* —*Ibid.*, p. 165.

919. Frothingham, *Recollections and Impressions*, pp. 194–196.

920. See especially Ch. II, "America's Debt," and Ch. III, "The American Opportunity."

921. See his article in the *Radical*, II, i (Sept., 1866), 1–12, welcoming the new science as the means to fight the vestiges of supernaturalism still existing in New England; also his criticism of the position of Hedge, in the *Radical*, I, ii (Oct., 1865), 69–72.

922. Frothingham, *Recollections and Impressions*, p. 199; George W. Cooke, *Unitarianism in America*, p. 419. His manner of writing was always marked by ingenuity, recondite allusions, flights of wilfulness and fancy, but also exhibiting a cheerful independence. He was fond of music, full of special enthusiasms, never long devoted to one task, nervously going from one subject to another. His most important literary work, the biography of Parker, is marred by a lack of organization, though many passages in it are executed in dazzling colors. His bent toward poetry expressed itself in the great number of translations which he made from the German.

923. Weiss may have begun this book as early as 1837, for it appears likely that it was he who contributed the unsigned translation of Schiller's *Philosophic Letters* to the January and April numbers of the *Western Messenger*.

924. Weiss is incorrectly credited by Professor Morgan (*op. cit.*, No. 8242) with having translated Schiller's *Letters Prior to his Marriage* (Boston, 1841), and with the preparation of a book of *Moral and Religious Selections from . . . Jacobi, Shubart* [sic]*, Schiller, Ewald, Richter, Gellert, Haug, and Others* (Boston, 1841). See Morgan, *op. cit.*, No. C 560. Both are correctly ascribed by E. C. Parry (*Schiller*

in America, Phila., 1905), to Mrs. Jane Lee Weisse.

925. Frank P. Stearns, *Sketches from Concord and Appledore* (N.Y. and London, 1895), pp. 134–37, 146–51; T. W. Higginson, *Cheerful Yesterdays*, p. 112.

926. *Essays Religious, Social, Political* (Boston, 1889), p. 57.

927. E.g., see his series of letters analyzing and criticizing the Kantian position, in the *Radical*, I, iii (Nov., 1865), 102–5; X (June, 1866), 385, 393; and *Index*, XVII, dcccxliv (Feb. 25, 1886), 410–11; also "Buckle's Treatment of History," *Christ. Exam.*, LXXIV, ii (Jan., 1863), 51–76, and his "Character and Historical Position of Theodore Parker," *ibid.*, LXXVII, i (July, 1864), 1–41, one of the best pieces of characterization and appreciation of Parker ever written. Wasson's three-year residence at Stuttgart from 1870 to 1873 came too late to leave any noteworthy marks on his development beyond the notable essay, "Church and State in Germany," in the *Unitarian Review*, V, i (Jan., 1876), 1–28.

928. He wrote also a long analytical review of Goethe's *Meister* for the *Atlantic* of September and October, 1865, in which he professed an ever-growing admiration for this novel after repeated readings. The essay reveals a thorough knowledge of currents of thought in Germany since the early eighteenth century and, indeed, a great sympathy of feeling for the Kantian idealists and for Goethe. It is remarkably free of the current cant of criticism. It exhibits a beautiful clarity of feeling and expression and is, all in all, a fine appreciation based on a real understanding of Goethe.

929. Henry David Thoreau, Margaret Fuller, C. P. Cranch, J. S. Dwight, T. W. Higginson, C. T. Brooks, G. W. Curtis, and others more or less closely identified with the Transcendental movement are treated below, in the sections dealing with literary influences; they followed more the literary tradition of Margaret Fuller than Emerson and Parker's concern with philosophy and theology.

930. Samuel Johnson, *Lectures, Essays, and Sermons, with a Memoir by Samuel Longfellow* (Boston, 1883), pp. 29, 52.

931. *Ibid.*, pp. 416–60.

932. *Ibid.*, p. 434.

933. *Ibid.*, p. 439.

934. *Autobiography, Memories, and Experiences of M. D. Conway* (2 vols., Boston and N.Y., 1904), I, 137, 142–43, 147, 157.

935. Conway thought he saw something symbolic in a little episode which he witnessed in the Emerson household. Edith Emerson named her cat "Goethe." Emerson affected to

take it seriously, and once when the cat was in the library and scratched itself, he opened the door and politely said, "Goethe, you must retire; I don't like your manners."—*Ibid.*, I, 147.

936. *Ibid.*, pp. 199, 248.

937. *Ibid.*, pp. 306–15.

938. *Ibid.*, II, 13, 67–69, 155, 240–41, 308, 312–15, 400–1; for his sojourns in Germany during 1871 and 1884, see *ibid.*, pp. 245–53 and 416–17, respectively.

939. See "A Hunt after Devils," an anecdote after Auerbach's Keller, made famous by *Faust*, in *Harper's*, XXXVIII, iv (Mar., 1869), 540–48; "Christmas in Berlin," *Index*, XVI, dccxxxviii (Jan. 29, 1885), 363–64; "The Brothers Grimm," *Index*, XVI, dccxc (Feb. 12, 1885), 388–89; an article on Bismarck, *Radical*, I, xii (Aug., 1866), 486–90; a letter on Dr. Schliemann, *Index*, VIII, ccclxxv (Mar. 1, 1877), 99–100; and an article on Heine, *Internat'l Rev.*, VII, v (May, 1882), 425–38.

940. Boston born and bred, Cabot was at Harvard from 1836 to 1840. Early an admirer of Carlyle, he was further inspired by Longfellow's *Hyperion* to indulge his desire for a post-collegiate education at Heidelberg. He and two Harvard classmates spent the winter of 1840–1841 at Heidelberg and then migrated (after the fashion of German students) to Berlin, where they were welcomed and admitted to the University by Ranke, the great historian. Here Cabot enrolled in the course of Schelling, then delivering the famous series of lectures partially reported by Charles Stearns Wheeler and subsequently printed by Emerson in the *Dial* for January, 1843. After a semester at Berlin, Cabot went to Göttingen, where he concentrated upon Kant, though he also attended the courses in Rudolph Wagner's laboratory, at the same time that he engaged in the German student activities of the Liederkranz, fencing, dancing, and club life.

941. Higginson, who renewed his acquaintance with Cabot at this time, found in him then already what characterized Cabot during the remainder of his life—a "modest and reticent" nature, "bearing unconsciously a certain European prestige . . . which so much commanded the respect of a circle of young men that we gave him the sobriquet 'Jarno,' after the well-known philosophic leader in Goethe's 'Wilhelm Meister.' "—"J. E. Cabot," *Proc. Amer. Acad. of Arts and Sciences*, XXXIX (June, 1904), 652.

942. IV, iv (Apr., 1844), 409–15. Cabot told Higginson that he had read Kant's *Critique of Pure Reason* twice in the German and "thought he comprehended it, but that Meiklejohn's translation was beyond making out."—*Ibid.*, p. 652.

943. Emerson's *Letters*, III, 290 (June 26, 1844).

944. *Ibid.*, pp. 298–99 (Sept. 1, 1845).

945. *Ibid.*, p. 343 (Aug. 19, 1845).

946. Emerson's *Journals*, VII, 268–69; Higginson, *loc. cit.*, p. 652; John Weiss, *Parker*, I, 126; Gohdes, *op. cit.*, pp. 160–64. Parker's *Massachusetts Quarterly Review* maintained itself for three years, showing more of studious and systematic work than its predecessor but far less of freshness and originality, and then went under, as Parker explained in the last number, "because it became what its projectors designed it should be."—III, iv (Sept., 1850), 524. Higginson observed that while Parker's *Review* was designed to be "the *Dial* with a beard," it turned out rather to be "the beard without the *Dial*."

947. I, i (Dec., 1847), 140.

948. I, ii (Mar., 1848), 263–65.

949. If Stallo had met with more reviewers like Cabot, he might have had less occasion to regard his book as failing in its aim to arouse American thinkers to the importance of such Hegelian concepts as *Werden, Identitätslehre*, and the Absolute, and he might not have left his professorship of philosophy for the law and the bench.

950. Higginson, *loc. cit.*, p. 653; Emerson's *Letters*, VI, 73.

951. See his essay, "Hegel," in the *North Amer. Rev.*, CVI, ccxix (Apr., 1868), 447–83, in reality a review article on Hegel's *Werke*, 2nd ed., 15 vols., Berlin, 1840–1845; G. H. Lewes' *History of Philosophy from Thales to Comte*, Vol. I (London, 1867); and the *Journal of Speculative Philosophy*, Vol. I (St. Louis, 1867).

952. See esp. "Some Consideration on the Notion of Space," *Jour. of Spec. Philos.*, XII, iii (July, 1878), 225–36, an essay which Harris chose as the leading article for the number, followed immediately by William James's "Brute and Human Intellect," pp. 236–76. See also V, i (Jan., 1871), 38–48, and XIII, ii (Apr., 1879), 199–204.

953. He cites Goethe in support of his definition of a proper metaphysics and the conclusion that "Philosophy is idealism," not materialism; its methods are mental, not physical (CVI, ccxix, 447, 451–54). The facts of science, important as they are, must not be regarded as ends in themselves, but in relation to humanity. Their proper orientation is to be made, not in pursuing the strict method of physical science merely, but by relating them to the Hegelian concepts of *Werden* and *Identität*, in terms of the thesis-antithesis-synthesis movement of the Hegelian logic. This, and this method only, affords a means by which the

irresistible demands of science can be met, at the same time that the truths derived by the older method are preserved (pp. 455–59). The common tendency of inductive philosophers since Kant to oppose Hegelian idealism is a manifestation of a one-sided attention to the senses and the failure to recognize in the Hegelian system the full and adequate provision that it makes for science and natural law (pp. 462–66). The remaining portion of the essay is a vindication of Kantian idealism and of the Hegelian procedure. It is noteworthy that Harris thought it expedient to devote ten pages of the January, 1871, number of his *Journal* (V, i, 38–48) to call the attention of his readers to Cabot's essay.

THE SPREAD OF INTEREST IN GERMAN PHILOSOPHY

THE ST. LOUIS MOVEMENT

1. See D. H. Harris (ed.), *A Brief Report of the Meeting Commemorative of the Saint Louis Movement in Philosophy, Psychology, Literature, Art, and Education, in Honor of Dr. Denton J. Snider's Eightieth Birthday, Held January 14th and 15th, 1921* . . . (St. Louis, [1921]), pp. 15ff. Almost none of the speakers at this commemorative festival failed to pay reverence to the Transcendentalists. For the numerous points of association between the New England reformers and the St. Louis leaders, see Denton J. Snider, *The St. Louis Movement* . . . (St. Louis, 1921), and *A Writer of Books in His Genesis* (St. Louis, 1910), pp. 329–99 *passim*; Louis J. Block, "The Philosophic Schools of St. Louis, Jacksonville, Concord, and Chicago," in D. H. Harris (ed.), *op. cit.*, pp. 14–17; Cleon Forbes, "The St. Louis School of Thought," *Mo. Hist. Rev.*, XXVI, i (Oct., 1931), 69–70.

2. Snider, *The St. Louis Movement*, pp. 27–29.

3. Whereas the New England Transcendental movement had originated among discontented ministers who left the pulpit to spread their reforms through the lyceum lecture and the periodical column, the St. Louis Movement had its beginning chiefly among teachers who spread their doctrines through schools—private, public, elementary, collegiate, kindergarten, and communal. W. T. Harris was a teacher and administrator in the public school system of St. Louis, who rose eventually to the position of U.S. Commissioner of Education; Denton J. Snider, William McKendree Bryant, Thomas Davidson, Charles F. Childs, Louis J. Block, and Horace H. Morgan were high-school teachers; Francis E. Cook and B. V. Dixon were school principals; James K. Hosmer and George H. Howison taught at Washington University, and J. H. Watters taught in the St. Louis Medical School; the Misses Susan E. Blow, Amelia C. Fruchte, Susan V. Beeson, Mary E. Beedy, and Anna C. Brackett were all connected with the public or private schools of St. Louis. Among others prominent in the movement, A. E. Kroeger was a journalist by profession and for a time a city official; J. Z. Hall and J. H. Watters were physicians, and Britton A. Hill, J. G. Woerner, Horatio M. Jones, and H. C. Brokmeyer were lawyers.

4. Often spelled Brockmeyer. Brokmeyer's son tells us that while his father was about the business of advancing the life of pure thought, he utterly disdained to quibble over the spelling of names, even when his own name was involved. See Chas. M. Perry, *The St. Louis Movement in Philosophy: Some Source Material* (Norman, Okla., 1930), pp. 48–49. Brokmeyer's works were published under the name *Brokmeyer* (without the *c*). Although Harris and Snider generally used *Brockmeyer* and Alcott used both forms, *Brokmeyer* is adopted in this study. To his son Eugene, Brokmeyer often expressed his dissatisfaction with the English language as inadequate for reproducing the thought of Hegel. His impatience with language and other known traits of his personality offer clues why, when Louis J. Block undertook to revise Brokmeyer's translation of Hegel's *Logic*, he found the task "too much for him." The "professor of Philosophy" to whom the manuscript was next referred for editing professed it to be "too profound for him." However that may have been, something of the difficulty is suggested by W. F. Woerner's observation: "Brokmeyer was the worst speller I have ever known and absolutely indifferent to grammatical construction."—*Ibid.*, pp. 3,4 50.

5. See the bibliography in Perry, *op. cit.*, pp. 96–140.

6. See *JoSP*, XVI, iv (Oct., 1882), 433–39, for a bibliography, prepared by Harris, listing 111 titles by Kroeger.

7. Perry, *op. cit.*, p. 42.

8. Howison left Washington University in 1871 to teach in the Boston School of Technology (1871–1879). The following year he lectured on ethics at Harvard and spent 1880–1882 studying under Lotze, Paulsen, Michelet, Zeller, and others, chiefly at the University of Berlin. During 1883–1884 he occupied the post later held by John Dewey at the University of Michigan, and in 1884 went to the University

of California, where he remained as head of the Department of Philosophy until 1910 and as professor emeritus until his death in 1916.

During his St. Louis period, Howison concerned himself little with the more popular phases of the St. Louis Movement, but was an officer of the Philosophical Society and contributed articles to the avowedly Hegelian *Journal of Speculative Philosophy* (see especially his extended essay on German philosophy in the volume for 1883). He also participated in the fifth (1883) and seventh (1885) sessions of the Concord School of Philosophy. Eventually he demonstrated his individualism and originality by becoming virtually the founder of personalism, preferring a form of personal idealism or spiritual pluralism to the absolute idealism of Hegel. While he dissented at many points from Hegel, he was and remained a potent force in the advance of the speculative method of Hegel—directly through his teaching and his leadership in the "Philosophical Union" at Berkeley, and indirectly through the remarkable group of students who heard his message, learned his method, and, in their turn, promulgated both. Among the more prominent of his students were Charles Bakewell (1867–   ), head of the Department of Philosophy at Yale (1905–1933); Evander B. McGilvary (1864–1953), who taught at Cornell, 1899–1905, and at the University of Wisconsin, 1905–1934; Harry A. Overstreet (1875–   ), prominent at New York University from 1911 to 1939; Sidney Edward Mezes (1863–1931), professor at Texas from 1897 to 1908 and president from 1908 to 1914, and professor at the College of the City of New York (1914–1929) and president (1929–1931); and Arthur O. Lovejoy (1873–   ), active at Johns Hopkins from 1910 to 1938. While none of these taught a pure Hegelian doctrine, their tutelage and later prominence are enough to suggest that the speculative method as taught and exemplified by Howison (involving doctrines derived from Aristotle, Spinoza, Leibnitz, Fichte, Kant, Hegel, Lotze, and F. C. S. Schiller) received through them a powerful and widespread currency. To Howison as much as to any other man is attributable the American academic concern with speculative thought during the last decades of the nineteenth and the first of the twentieth centuries.

9. Twenty-one of those who formed the neucleus of the movement have 229 books to their credit, not counting the 111 titles that belong to Kroeger nor the 479 that belong to Harris.

Associated more or less closely with the movement were public men like Carl Schurz and Joseph Pulitzer and, among academicians,

George Sylvester Morris, a skillful teacher of philosophy at Michigan and Johns Hopkins (1870–1889), translator of Ueberweg's *History of Philosophy* (1871–1873), and editor of Griggs Philosophical Series to which he contributed *Kant's Critique of Pure Reason. A Critical Exposition* (1882) and *Hegel's Philosophy of the State and of History* (1887).

10. Edward L. Schaub (ed.), *William Torrey Harris, 1835–1935* (Chicago, 1936), p. 3. Bibliographies for the several members of the Movement are found in Perry, *op. cit.*, pp. 78–140. While the St. Louisans produced a veritable avalanche of books, not one of them wrote a book that can be called a literary success. The Transcendentalists, on the other hand, owed much of their force and permanence of influence to their literature.

11. However much the "multiracial, polyglotic" St. Louisans differed in religion, politics, and other matters, there was "one faith universal, that St. Louis could not help becoming the largest, richest, most influential city in the land." This "fanaticism" or "craze," as Snider called it, reached a kind of crest in a series of publications between 1869 and 1875 by Logan Uriah Reavis that culminated in his *St. Louis: The Future Great City of the World* (1875), a tome of some 900 pages. Reavis claimed that 150,000 copies of his several books passed into circulation. Concerning Reavis as the prophet of the "Illusion" see Snider, *op. cit.*, pp. 82–89.

12. Snider, *The St. Louis Movement*, p. 66.

13. Forbes, *loc. cit.*, XXV, i (Oct., 1930), 86; Snider, *The St. Louis Movement*, pp. 52–69.

14. Snider, *The St. Louis Movement*, p. 141.

15. "This upburst and domination of Germanism," says Snider (*The St. Louis Movement*, pp. 142–43), "I followed not from the outside but from the inside; I not only studied it as an object but felt it and appropriated it till it became a part of myself. And there were many natives here like me—and many who experienced it as the uplift of a new strange spirit ... as the revelation of the peculiar racial consciousness of old Teutonia welling forth just now on the banks of the Mississippi."

This period may be dated as beginning with the Great Camp Jackson Deed (1861) and ending with the retirement of Schurz from the U.S. Senate (1875), thus corresponding roughly with the Prussian surge toward unity from the conquest of Schleswig-Holstein in 1864 and the defeat of Austria in 1866 to the Franco-Prussian War of 1870, the annexation of Alsace-Lorraine, and the formation of the German Empire. American Teutonia sensed the rapid, gigantic upswing of ancient Teutonia—felt "the deep undercurrent of connection between German

St. Louis and the old, or rather, the new Fatherland in Europe." Snider speaks of the whole community being "borne along in the floodtide of German spirit." "The majority of the inhabitants were composed of Germans, German-Americans, and Germanizers, of which last class I was a right specimen. . . . Public manners and amusements . . . turned German; I joined a German club in which English was tabooed and in some cases unknown. The beer-house was then in its glory as a popular resort, especially Tony Niederwiesser's Valhalla, and George Wolbrecht's Tivoli. In the latter Gambrinus effloresced or rather effervesced with the highest overflow of his divine frothiness, melodiously attuned to the notes of the largest and best orchestra in town. . . . There was a triumphant swing in the crowd, a consciousness that it was on the time's top just now in St. Louis as well as on the other side of the globe." —*Ibid.*, pp. 144–45. See also Carl E. Schneider, "The Establishment of the First Prussian Consulate in the West," *Miss. Valley Hist. Rev.*, XXX, iv (Mar., 1944), 507–20, as well as Perry, *op. cit.*, pp. 27, 29–30.

16. Snider, *The St. Louis Movement*, pp. 146–47.

17. *Ibid.*, p. 36.

18. Both Woerner and Kroeger were born in Germany, but both came to America as boys aged 7 and 11, respectively.

19. In Targee Street, later the scene of the famous shooting chronicled in the ballad, "Frankie and Johnny."

20. See A. C. McGiffert, *Protestant Thought before Kant* (N.Y., 1911), p. 253. This conflict which the St. Louisans inherited and sought to arbitrate is, in a sense, the cumulative result of years of controversy. Dr. Channing's sermon at the ordination of Jared Sparks in 1819, Emerson's Divinity School address in 1838, the Norton-Ripley controversy of 1839–1840, and Parker's South Boston sermon in 1841 mark stages in that struggle. When the St. Louis Movement began, the differences between what Parker called the transient and the permanent elements in religion had not been as sharply drawn nor were they as clearly understood as they are now. The drawing of these distinctions between what has been called "religion itself, on the one hand, and the expression of religion in doctrines and rites, or the application of religion through institutions, on the other" is one of the great achievements of the nineteenth century—an achievement in which the St. Louis philosophers played no minor role.— E. C. Moore, *An Outline of the History of Christian Thought Since Kant* (N.Y., 1918), p. 6.

21. C. M. Perry, "W. T. Harris and the St. Louis Movement," *Monist*, XLVI, i (Jan., 1936), 61.

22. Snider, *The St. Louis Movement*, p. 100.

23. Snider could not recall that it held any meetings after 1885. Although he read hundreds of papers and lectures on innumerable occasions, he could not remember, when in 1919 he wrote the history of the Movement, that he "ever read a paper before the Philosophical Society." He remembered the Society as having had less an active or practical than a quiet or theoretical existence. Although Harris succeeded eminently in the "primal creative act of self-publication of the St. Louis Movement" by founding and editing twenty-two volumes of the *Journal*, that achievement was effected almost singlehandedly. It was Harris more than the co-operative movement who was responsible for the *Journal*. The Society itself never accomplished anything tangible. Says Snider, "The chief practical object . . . at its foundation was to publish its own generating book, the masterpiece of Hegel. But it never did its real task." In retrospect, the Society seemed to Snider to have existed primarily "to lead each member to give a rational account of his vocation" (an idea derived from *Wilhelm Meister*, which all the members studied intently at the time), and, secondarily, "to show famous visitors certain formal attentions," as when Julia Ward Howe, Emerson, Alcott, or some other luminary came to town. —*Ibid.*, pp. 32, 480–81.

24. There were really two Kant clubs, one going back to 1858–1859 and another founded by Harris in 1874. The latter was especially flourishing about 1877–1887. See W. T. Harris, *Hegel's Logic*, Preface, p. xv; D. H. Harris (ed.), *op. cit.*, pp. 89–93; Wm. Schuyler, "German Philosophy in St. Louis," *Bull. of the Washington Univ. Assn.*, No. 2 (Apr. 23, 1904), pp. 82–83; and Snider, *A Writer of Books*, p. 393.

25. There is a good deal of confusion regarding whether the Philosophical Society grew out of the first of these Kant clubs or the Hegel Club. Since the membership of both was largely the same and the organization of neither very close, it is likely that both were merged informally and gradually, as it were, into the Philosophical Society early in 1866.

26. Concerning the Aristotle Society, see the account given by Theodore Harris, the son of W. T. Harris, in a letter to Professor Cleon Forbes, printed in C. M Perry, *op. cit.*, p. 67.

27. Snider, *The St. Louis Movement*, p. 100.

28. A portion of it still reposes, a bulky manuscript, in the library of the Missouri Historical Society, and a number of manuscript

copies exist elsewhere; it has never appeared in print.

29. This is Harris' considered judgment, set down in his Preface to *Hegel's Logic*.

30. Snider, *The St. Louis Movement*, pp. 119–20, 204–5. Referring to those years when he wrestled with the Hegelian problem of "Being, Nothing, and Becoming," Snider felt himself whirled dizzily into the "vast Hegelian vortex . . . till I feared me I never would get out of that spiritual maelstrom. I would flee from my narrow rotating room into the steady open air, still my mind could not escape the whizzing wheel of Ixion, on which I seemed pinioned, and would keep careening around through its ever-repeating vortical triplicity. . . . I would wander through the streets for miles, seeking to walk off that logical vertigo . . . even in dreamland my brain's Flying Dutchman would start to whirl around. . . . So I would resolve to have nothing more to do with that infernal logic . . . I threw the book aside. . . . I even thought of burning it. . . . But the next Sunday afternoon I would speed to the philosophers' Academe . . . in Salisbury street and listen to . . . the master. He [Brokmeyer] could make all the fettered nomenclature of Hegel's philosophy dance freely in its heaviest chains—an astonishing feat of mental prestidigitation in seeming, and still at the same time most real. How did he do it? Logic. Again I would hurry home and take from its hiding place the same fatal book; again the brainwhirl would begin. . . . So I kept battling for weeks, months, years; finally came a certain mastery, or at least disentanglement from that vortical labyrinth of ever-spinning and interlacing triplets of categories; that is, I could now spin them better than they could spin me."— *Ibid.*, pp. 122–23.

Harris' experience was of a kind. Like Snider, he followed Brokmeyer's injunction to get at once Hegel's complete works; and like Snider, he suffered the torments of the damned, until Brokmeyer's "deep insights and his poetic power of setting them forth with symbols and imagery" enabled him to "seize the general thought, its trend as a whole, and gradually to descend to its details." See Harris' Preface to *Hegel's Logic*.

31. For Brokmeyer's own statement of the extreme importance of "self-determination," see his *A Mechanic's Diary* (Washington, D.C., 1910), p. 24.

32. Snider, *The St. Louis Movement*, pp. 123, 175.

33. See the significance attached to these phrases as used for chapter headings in his autobiography, *A Writer of Books in His*

Genesis and in *The St. Louis Movement*.

34. Snider, *The St. Louis Movement*, p. 174.

35. *Ibid.*, pp. 179, 212–17.

36. *Ibid.*, pp. 179, 268–69, 280, 479–86; E. L. Schaub (ed.), *op. cit.*, p. 35.

37. Snider, *The St. Louis Movement*, pp. 33, 236.

38. *Ibid.*, pp. 293–303, 577–85.

39. During his long term as president of the National Education Association he literally dominated the policies of the Association, but all his work was done from within. For the organization of the Association he was not responsible.

40. For example, Miss Blow described the rapture she felt at first awakening, under the influence of Harris' lecturing, to a vision of Hegel: "So vigorously had the lecturer wrestled with Kant, Fichte, Schelling, and Hegel that in two hours of what still seems to me miraculous explanation he had kindled in the mind of one eager listener a light which revealed idealism delivered from Solipsism. . . . The open secret was revealed and I knew that I stood upon the delectable mountains and discerned from afar the shining pinnacles of the Eternal City. . . . That afternoon was a solemn crisis in my life. I beheld eternal Reality. I was a novice admitted to a sacred fellowship."—Susan Blow, "The Service of Dr. Harris to the Kindergarten," *Kindergarten Review*, XX (June, 1910), 590.

41. Snider, *The St. Louis Movement*, p. 279.

42. *Ibid.*, p. 268.

43. *Ibid.*, pp. 269, 284ff.

44. *Ibid.*, pp. 267–68.

45. *Ibid.*, p. 445.

46. *Ibid.*, p. 270.

47. *Ibid.*, pp. 271–77, 285–86, 308.

48. *Ibid.*, pp. 326–38.

49. *Ibid.*, pp. 356–61.

50. *Ibid.*, pp. 359–61; *A Writer of Books*, p. 431.

51. Snider, *The St. Louis Movement*, p. 100.

52. *Ibid.*, pp. 347–50, 570–85.

53. *Ibid.*, pp. 267–69.

54. However, the *Journal of Speculative Philosophy* had a strong academic flavor from the beginning. It bears little evidence of the prodigious deeds performed in the Winning of the West, largely because Harris, an academician by nature, sought to say something above the ruck and circumstances of common life. Brokmeyer had little trouble convincing him that the theoretical explanation of all the momentous events compounded of disunion, war, and reconstruction lay in the Hegelian law of dialectical growth. Persuaded on this point, he readily followed Brokmeyer in subordinating even the ethico-political philosophy of Hegel

to his more speculative logic and metaphysics, the relative importance of which later generations have insisted on reversing. In ranking Hegel's works "in the order of their importance," Harris categorically put the *Logic* in first place and the ethical and political works in sixth and seventh, respectively. See *JoSP*, III, i (1869), v.

55. Harvey G. Townsend, "The Political Philosophy of Hegel in a Frontier Society," in E. L. Schaub, (ed.), *op. cit.*, pp. 70–71.

56. Re-examinations of Hegel's political philosophy have served to correct the view of Hegel as the propounder of political absolutism —have, in short, re-emphasized his political philosophy in precisely the terms in which Brokmeyer and his friends conceived it. Professor Townsend puts the matter thus:

"Hegel's continuous defense of the idea of a united Germany, though modified with the changing years, was neither at the beginning nor at the end a philosophy of isolated and irresponsible central authority and power. It was rather a studiously acquired and, in its total form, a very technical philosophy of the progressive integration of wills through the unfolding of reason. The dominant organicism of his theory, suggesting the modern totalitarian state, was nevertheless combined with the doctrine of free participation of individuals and groups, which should associate Hegel unmistakably with the rising tide of revolutionary liberalism."—*Ibid.*, pp. 72–73. Treitschke's view of Hegel, widely publicized as it was in his *History of Germany in the Nineteenth Century*, is largely responsible for the current misconceptions. To be contrasted with it is the interpretation of Hegel as given by Heinrich von Sybel in his *Founding of the German Empire* (tr. by M. L. Perrin, 5 vols., N.Y., 1890–1891), I, 14, and by Bernard Bosanquet in his *Germany in the Nineteenth Century* (3rd ed., London, 1915), XXV, 190–91.

57. VI, 263–79. This is a translation of Dr. Karl Rosenkranz's *Hegel as Publicist*, made by G. Stanley Hall. Harris himself secured the copyright for Rosenkranz' *Hegel as the National Philosopher of Germany* (tr. by G. Stanley Hall, repr. from the *JoSP*, N.Y., 1874), and prepared for it a sixteen-page "Introduction to Hegel's Philosophic Method."

58. *JoSP*, VI (1872), 268–69, 275.

59. *Ibid.*, p. 278. This view of Hegel as a political liberal was not at all uncommon at the time. It received especially widespread circulation in a series of essays by Emilio Castelar in *Harper's New Monthly Magazine* for July through November, 1873, entitled "The Republican Movement in Europe," in which Hegel is represented as the most conspicuous of the liberals, "the true philosopher of progress," "the philosopher *par excellence* of the only true political liberty, namely, the ethical." See XLVII, cclxxx (Sept., 1873), 579.

60. Snider, *The St. Louis Movement*, pp. 52–69.

61. *Ibid.*, pp. 94–116.

62. Harris, *Hegel's Logic*, Preface, p. xii. See also Snider, *A Writer of Books*, pp. 309–14.

63. For a key to the meaning of action and characters, see Perry, *op. cit.*, pp. 41–42, 44–45.

64. *JoSP*, II, ii (1863), 128.

65. A Columbia dissertation by Francis B. Harmon, *The Social Philosophy of the St. Louis Hegelians* (N.Y., 1943) traces the evolution of their social philosophy from Hegel's *Logic*, *Philosophy of Right*, and *Philosophy of History*, and then, in successive chapters, treats their theories of the Family, the Economic State, the State, and Religious and Educative Institutions.

66. Born on August 12, 1828, near Minden, Prussia, of a father who was a moderately wealthy Jewish businessman and a mother related to Bismarck, Brokmeyer received a common-school education in Germany. At sixteen, he rebelled against Prussian militarism and shipped for America, landing in New York with twenty-five cents in his pocket, three English words in his vocabulary, and a stock of independent ideas. Bootblack, currier, tanner, shoemaker, jack-of-all-trades, he pursued a vagrant way westward, traveling mainly afoot through Ohio and Indiana, thence south to Memphis and beyond, to Lowndes and Oktibbeha counties, Mississippi, where he amassed a small fortune operating a tannery and shoe factory, employing slave labor to manufacture shoes that cost him only a pittance. Tiring of money-grubbing, he resumed his interrupted educational career by entering Georgetown University in Kentucky, later literally arguing his way into and out of several institutions of higher learning. At Brown University he is said to have engaged in especially joyous disputation with President Wayland, picking up by the way solid kernels of Emersonian idealism and seemingly some of the eccentricities that accompanied the Transcendental ferment. Ever more dissatisfied with civilization, he abruptly headed west in 1854, settled in an abandoned cabin in Warren County, Missouri, and supporting himself by hunting and fishing, lived the life of a hermit, pondering questions "whence we come and whither we go."

The loss of his small fortune through the failure of an investment house was compensated for by his discovery of Hegel, in whom he seems to have found answers sufficient at least partially to reconcile himself to the ways of the world, for on May 1, 1856, he moved into St. Louis with his trunk full of books (Thucydides, Homer, Sophocles, Aristophanes, Plato's *Republic* and dialogues, Aristotle, Goethe, Hegel complete, Shakespeare, Molière, Calderon, Cervantes, and Sterne), and five days later he became an iron-molder.—*A Mechanic's Diary*, pp. 7, 8–9, 14. He prospered by his ingenuity and industry, indulged in land speculations, and became active on many fronts, meanwhile zealously consecrating his evenings to his precious books and permitting no interruptions except to frequent the haunts of small groups devoted to political and philosophical discussion.

At one of these informal meetings in 1858 he met Harris, the second in the triumvirate that was soon to be formed. Voluble, bewhiskered, wiry of build, agile of movement, eyes alert ("the quick, almost wild eye of the hunter"), he presented a striking figure as he stood up, not at all chagrined by his workingman's clothes, to defend his position against all comers. His most prominent feature was "an enormous nose, somewhat crooked, which had the power of flattening and bulging and curveting and crooking in a variety of ways expressive of what was going on within him."—Snider, *A Writer of Books*, p. 303. Eyes flashing and hands flailing, he boomed forth wisdom, wit, and profanity; then quite suddenly he would settle back at ease in a chair, cock high his heels, and with half-shut eyes ponder some profundity as he puffed at his "perpetual and vicious pipe."—Forbes, *Mo. Hist. Rev.*, XXV, i, (Oct., 1930), 91. Still unable to come to terms with the world, he suddenly bought a tract of land in the wilderness, built a log cabin, and resumed his solitary life. This idyl was brought to an abrupt end by a severe bilious fever, from the worst consequences of which he was saved by Harris, who found him and brought him back to St. Louis. Upon his recovery, he resumed his tutorship of Harris, who pooled his slender resources with those of two kindred "respectable vagabonds" and pensioned Brokmeyer to the extent of food and lodging while he made a literal translation of Hegel's monumental *Logic*. The first draft was completed during 1859–1860.

Shortly after his marriage in 1861, he enlisted in the militia, served with distinction, became a colonel, organized a regiment of his own, and found himself imprisoned for disloyalty on trumped-up charges. Speedily released, he was elected, six weeks later, as a "War Democrat" to the legislature, where during 1862–1864 he was prominant in opposing all measures aimed at disfranchising Southern sympathizers. In 1865 he opened a law office; the following year he was elected to the Board of Aldermen of St. Louis, and four years later to the state Senate. He took a prominent part in the constitutional convention of 1875. He was elected lieutenant-governor, and in 1876–1877 became acting governor during the illness of Governor Phelps. His ambition to represent Missouri in the U.S. Senate was frustrated by his defeat at the hands of a returned Confederate. His political decline coincided with the bursting of the St. Louis Bubble and the decadence of the St. Louis Movement in Philosophy.

His first wife died in 1864, and he married again in 1867. About 1880 he became an attorney for the Gould railroad, his explanation being that he had to make a living for his family, although it seems certain that the decision was prompted in a large measure by his disillusionment over political advancement and the failure to make Hegelianism prevail. His business often carried him into Oklahoma, where he became interested in the Indians. He reappeared in 1884 as elector-at-large on the Cleveland ticket, on this occasion receiving the largest popular vote ever cast in Missouri up to that time. But his half-melancholy sorties into the farther West combining fishing and hunting expeditions with a search for health, became more frequent and more prolonged. For some years he made his home among the Creek Indians, where Snider (whom he tried to draw away from his Homer classes to join him in the establishment of a kindergarten for the Indian children of Muscogee) found him "explaining the deeper philosophy of deer-stalking in a pow-wow with some Creek Indians" and trying to form a little philosophical society among them. They conferred upon him the title of "Great White Father" and offered him his choice of the fairest maiden of the tribe—an offer which his Hegelianism compelled him regretfully to decline. So he alternated between the wilderness and civilization, appearing occasionally to contribute a lecture to the courses arranged by Harris and Snider in Chicago, Milwaukee, and elsewhere, revising his translation of Hegel's *Logic*, shipping numerous mahogany and rosewood saplings back to St. Louis, where at his leisure he whittled out beautifully polished walking sticks for his friends, frugally utilizing the chips for equally aesthetic toothpicks, carefully cut in three different sizes and bottled with elaborately carved corks. The last ten years of his life were spent in St. Louis in quiet pursuits, chief of which was his retranslation of Hegel's *Logic*. He died July 26, 1906, in his seventy-eighth year, disappointed at the callous American unconcern with philosophy but believing that once the more insistent work of building a greater physical America were completed, his beloved Hegelianism would prevail and lead the nation to true cultural maturity.

67. Snider, *A Writer of Books*, p. 393.

68. *Ibid.*, pp. 373, 374–78, 395–98. A passage in Plato's *Parmenides*, read while still at Georgetown, regarding the necessity in philosophic speculation not only to examine the affirmation of any proposition but also to consider "what follows from a proposition" and particularly "what follows if we assume the opposite" led to a too literal application of this critical principle, which, in turn, soon led to his dismissal from Georgetown.—Schuyler, *loc. cit.*, pp. 64–65. Later, at Brown, his critical argumentativeness resulted in his "attacking before the whole class President Wayland's argument for the Higher Law."—Snider, *A Writer of Books*, p. 366.

69. Described in some detail in the latter sections of *A Mechanic's Diary*.

70. See *A Mechanic's Diary*, pp. 52, 55–56, 57–58, 59–60, 69 ff. Hegel's *Logic* became, says Snider, Brokmeyer's "anchor of life." "In his last days I found him reading it still, usually poring over his translation of it, with many retrospective reflections, one of which has stayed in my saddened memory on account of its melancholy implication of a lost career: 'If I had my life to live over again, I would devote it exclusively to Hegel— to his expansion and propagation.' Still I could never push him to the point of printing his dearest life-work, though he was at that time amply able to bear the expense." Snider felt that Brokmeyer's failure to get his translation in shape was owing to his having deserted his literary endeavors for three decades while he engaged in politics and consequently being unable, later, to resume his literary development, where, as a man of forty, he had left off. "The powers forbade him to do in the 90's what he might and ought to have done in the 60's."—Snider, *A Writer of Books*, pp. 384, 387.

71. *A Mechanic's Diary*, pp. 23, 52 ff. Among other authors and books mentioned in his diary between May 1 and November 8, 1856, are Alex. v. Humboldt's *Travels in South America* (pp. 63–64, 118–19), Darwin's *Naturalist's Voyage Around the World* (p. 65), Spinoza (p. 69), Rousseau (p. 121), Locke's *Essay on Human Understanding* (pp. 204–6, 220), the neo-Platonists from Ammonius Saccas to Plotinus and Proclus (pp. 229–36), Pythagoras, Heraclitus, Socrates, Plato, and Aristotle (pp. 231–32), the Church Fathers (pp. 231–33), Descartes (pp. 234–36), Kant (p. 235), and Goethe, who, of course, is prominently mentioned throughout the book.

72. Snider, *A Writer of Books*, pp. 387–88.

73. The year 1858 marks the time when he sloughed off his eccentricities bred of his earlier addiction to New England Transcendentalism. Applying his own logic, he now stood before his friends and declared that they too must transcend, "must rise out of and above Parker, Alcott, and Emerson." And when they asked how this was to be accomplished, he had ready the answer: "By following the precepts of Kant's criticism, Hegel's speculative logic, and Goethe's humanism as exemplified in *Faust* . . . the greatest literary embodiment of both and the greatest poem of all time."—*Ibid.*, pp. 390 ff.

74. *Ibid.*, pp. 389–90; *St. Louis Movement*, p. 279; Harris, *Hegel's Logic*, Preface, pp. viii–ix.

75. Snider says that Brokmeyer faltered only once during the trying two years that he devoted to his redoubtable task of "tracking and mapping that vast Sahara of Hegelian abstractions." He grew so image-thirsty that he took sudden flight one day from "anhydrous Philosophy to up-welling Poetry as the green oasis of salvation, from whose fountains everywhere began to bubble out" his fantastic drama, *A Foggy Night in Newport* (St. Louis, 1860)—"the whimsicalities of which," adds Snider, "he patched together in a rather crotchety whole."—*St. Louis Movement*, pp. 206–7.

76. Snider said that he himself never used Brokmeyer's version, "never needed it," because he had the original, which, he added, he could read "more easily than Brokmeyer's English" (*ibid.*, p. 13). Harris' account of how he struggled with Brokmeyer's translation offers further hints. He says it was made for "myself and two other friends (George Stedman and J. H. Watters) "at their expense," and he intimates that if he had considered it printable, he would have published it (*Hegel's Logic*, p. xi). He does not suggest, here or elsewhere, that he was under any obligation to print it, though the tacit assumption may well have been made by his associates then and later. Neither do his words suggest that he felt any sense of compunction, as Snider suggests he should have felt. The "callousness" of Harris in this matter may be attributed to what can be read between the lines that follow:

"I copied the work entire from the manuscript and am sure I read every word of it. I am equally sure that I did not understand at the most anything beyond the first volume and could not follow any of the discussions in the second and third volumes, or even remember the words from one page to another. It was all over my head, so to speak."—*Ibid.*, pp. xi–xii.

The last sentence may have been added

gratuitiously in deference to his friend Brokmeyer's feelings. What he might have said quite fairly is that he did not attain to an understanding of Hegel's logic until years later, when he had divested his mind of this orgy of literality and worked his way through histories and commentaries and, more especially, turned to Hegel himself. Indeed, he says what amounts to just that, but he took care to say it less bluntly; for Brokmeyer was just then setting to work to retranslate the whole, and Harris was never one to wound a friend's feelings. Concerning his failure to print Brokmeyer's translation Harris, in 1890, said simply: "The translation I copied still exists, but has never been printed, any portion of it." This statement implies neither excuse nor guilt. Harris then goes on to pay tribute to Brokmeyer's "deep insights" and his "power of setting them forth with symbols and imagery" in his conversations, thus corroborating Snider's testimony when he calls Brokmeyer an "unrealized, perchance unrealizable genius" who "would never smelt and turn into pure coin the crude but rich ore of his genius."—*St. Louis Movement*, pp. 204-5. All agree in testifying to Brokmeyer's ability as a talker, but when he sought to write, says Snider, it was as if "the cream of his genius . . . got quite skimmed off when he squeezed it through the pen-point into ink. It is too bad he never found or provided himself with a human phonograph, like the talk-recording Eckermann, as old Goethe did." —*Ibid.*, pp. 207-9; see also *A Writer of Books*, p. 324, and Brokmeyer's *Mechanic's Diary*, pp. 206, 216-17.

Brokmeyer's manuscript as it exists today, even after several hands have tried to make it readable, is a veritable tangle of English words trying, in the most literal fashion, to reproduce the thought of Hegel's involved sentences. So closely did Brokmeyer stick to the German text that often his sentences fall into the same syntactical divisions as the original, even to reproducing the punctuation. Lacking a glossary (such as W. H. Johnson and L. G. Struthers considered essential in both German-English and English-German when they published their translation in 1929), Brokmeyer's translation bogs down under its own weight of literality and the translator's ineptness with English idiom.

77. *JoSP*, I, iii (1867), 178-87; II, ii (1868), 114-20.

78. *A Writer of Books*, p. 327.

79. *Ibid.*, pp. 302-8. At this meeting Harris read from his translation of Hegel's *Introduction to the History of Philosophy*, stopping often to refer a word of doubtful meaning to Brok-

meyer's judgment, which the latter delivered "forcibly and undoubtingly." Ever watchful to find and test a new disciple, Harris gave Snider Hegel's *Philosophy of Nature* to translate—an assignment which Snider wrestled with throughout the autumn of 1865. On another occasion the hapless Snider, whose head by now was in a whirl, was assigned the preparation of a thesis on the History of the Doctrine of the Immortality of the Soul—a thesis that was never written and, to Snider's great relief, "never called for." Several times at these gatherings in Salisbury Street and on the way home (when Snider managed to get a seat alongside Brokmeyer on the streetcar) "a forthcoming Philosophical Society" was mentioned; and Brokmeyer spoke of it repeatedly when Snider visited him in his law office, whither he repaired henceforth, and where he oftener found a group of philosophers than litigants.—*Ibid.*, pp. 308, 312-13, 315, 316.

80. William Schuyler, a member of several of the associated clubs that operated in St. Louis, is the authority for the following data (*op. cit.*, pp. 72-73).

Directors: H. C. Brokmeyer, W. T. Harris, Britton A. Hill, G. H. Howison, J. Z. Hall, D. J. Snider, P. L. Tafel, J. H. Watters, C. F. Childs, A. E. Kroeger, T. J. Horner, J. G. Woerner, Nathan Hayward, Horatio M. Jones, J. A. Martling, C. L. Bernays, H. H. Morgan, and C. E. Michel.

Associates: G. V. Bailey, N. Meyers, D. V. Potter, A. Strothotte, E. C. Kehr, W. C. Lyman, A. Kukleham, J. F. Madison, Silas Bent, G. E. Goodson, H. Bryan, A. Lowry, W. Flint, J. E. Kimball, G. E. Seymour, D. R. Haynes, G. M. B. Maughs, J. A. Higgins, T. Kimball, Wm. Johnson, W. W. Stickney, T. D. Witt, F. M. Crunden, E. T. Merrick, E. L. Bynner, J. L. Pierce, Jno. Eysar, L. J. Block, F. C. Stone, Thomas Davidson, Wm. Berndt, W. C. Ball, F. E. Cook, and F. L. Soldan.

Auxiliaries: A. B. Alcott, R. W. Emerson, Jos. de Fonfride (Paris), E. A. Hitchcock (Washington, D.C.), N. B. Buford (Colorado), L. W. Reed (California), F. B. Sanborn (Concord, Mass.), John B. Stallo (Cincinnati), J. E. Cabot (Brookline, Mass.), Samuel Tyler (Maryland), Vincenzo Botta (New York City), Jos. C. G. Kennedy (Washington), Wm. Gilpin, Henry James (Swampscott, Mass.), E. H. Bowman (Illinois), D. A. Wasson (Boston), James H. Stirling (Scotland), A. Vera (Italy), Karl Rosenkranz (Prussia), I. Goddard (Ohio), August Willich (Cincinnati), F. H. Hedge (Massachusetts), C. W. Chapman (New Haven), R. T. Colburn (New York City), Friedrich Kapp, Ludwig Feuerbach, Moritz Carriere, Jacob Bernays (Germany), James B. Eads, Hy. T. Blow

Nath. Holmes, T. McWhorter, A. J. Dickerhoff, T. J. Sanders, J. H. Fichte (Germany), Charles Bernard (Paris), John Weiss (Massachusetts), C. B. D. Mills (New York), S. J. May (Syracuse), J. W. Albee, Charles C. Baldwin (Worcester), E. H. Bugbee (Connecticut), F. H. Peckham (Providence), R. R. Bishop (Boston), Benj. Szold (Baltimore), Franz Hoffmann (Germany), T. Collins Simon (England), and Wm. Clay (Detroit).

81. *A Mechanic's Diary*, pp. 229ff.

82. For other details of Alcott's visits to St. Louis, see my *New England Transcendentalism and St. Louis Hegelianism: Phases in the History of American Idealism* (Phila., 1948), pp. 34–53.

83. Snider did not learn until he went to Concord and more particularly when, more than a half-century later, he came to write his life of Emerson, "what an awful goblin" he had conjured up by his use of the word *system*. It is noteworthy that Emerson's journals and letters (or Alcott's, for that matter) are innocent of references to Snider. This silence is sufficiently conspicuous to suggest that Snider was in some measure *persona non grata* among the Concordians, as he himself sensed the situation whenever he was in Concord later. It may be noted, in palliation of Snider, that in his biography of Emerson (1921) he wrote sympathetically, and in some respects it is still the most illuminating account of Emerson's intellectual development.

84. Emerson's *Letters*, V, 500, 508, 545, 546. For other details regarding Emerson in St. Louis, see my *New England Transcendentalism and St. Louis Hegelianism*, pp. 53–65.

85. Among the subjects formally discussed by the Society were the following: *Faust*, Alcott's Lapse of the Soul, Religion, Friendship, Generation as a Psychological Fact, Memory, Politics, the Character of Emerson, of Thoreau, of Margaret Fuller, Hegel's Dialectic, Herbert Spencer, the Critiques of Hegel, J. F. T. Tafel's Philosophy, What is the True Actual? Motion —Pure Motion, Goethe's Philosophy of Colors, Shakespeare, The Substantiality of the Soul or Thinking Reason, The Infinite of the Imagination and that of the Reason, Personality as the Fundamental Principle, The Christ of Christianity, True Freedom, The Relation of the Individual to Society, The Correlation of Forces, The Permanent Principle of the Universe, *Generatio Equivoca*, and Schopenhauer's Fourfold Root of Sufficient Reason.—Wm. Schuyler, *op. cit.*, pp. 73–74.

86. *A Writer of Books*, pp. 310–11, 383–84. Brokmeyer felt (says Snider) "a world–creating demiurge" within him that he dared not resist —a genius that worked for both good and evil: "he could be a Faust and a Mephistopheles both in one, or each separately, with something else thrown in."—*Ibid.*, pp. 314, 363. Among Brokmeyer's shortcomings, whenever his negative daemon came over him, was the onesidedness of his institutionalism. Strongly motivated by the moral consciousness bred into him at Oberlin, Snider saw with alarm Brokmeyer's attitude toward the war, slavery, and reconstruction as less moral than abstract. Brokmeyer declared quite frankly that he was not interested in the slave; he was concerned chiefly with overthrowing evil institutions and with upholding or preserving good ones. This Snider considered an ethical deficiency in Brokmeyer, traceable to Hegel, whose section on morality in the *Philosophy of Right* Brokmeyer considered "weak and insufficient compared with the final sections, in which he treats of institutions." Snider was shocked beyond utterance when he heard Brokmeyer declare, "I would cut that *Morality* out of Hegel's book; it does not belong there; it is inconsistent with the rest."—*Ibid.*, p. 357.

Another defect that Snider saw in Brokmeyer's character was his glorification of metaphysics at the expense of aesthetics. This, Snider explained, resulted in Brokmeyer's inability to put into distinctive written form the eloquently spontaneous matter of his spoken word. Brokmeyer could not "form" his thoughts: his written word "never did or could express adequately the man's genius." "The moment he took to script and made his gigantesque conceptions flow into and out of a pen's point, there was an enormous shrinkage, as if they could not scrape through so small a vent. . . . He was aware of this collapse in his writing, and he usually upbraided the English language for it, as he often blamed somebody or something for shortcomings which lay in himself. . . ."—*Ibid.*, pp. 324–25.

87. Miss Harris lives on Prospect Road, Walpole, N.H., where she considerately set up a workshop for students interested in the wealth of manuscript materials in her possession. The first significant product is Kurt F. Leidecker's *Yankee Teacher. The Life of William Torrey Harris* (N.Y., 1946).

In a letter of February 10, 1944, Miss Harris writes: "I have just placed some of my father's papers in regard to the 'St. Louis Movement' . . . in the care of the Missouri Historical Society of St. Louis. Among those which I sent them last fall was the original notebook containing the translation of Hegel's Logic (referred to on p. xii in my father's preface [to *Hegel's Logic*, 1890]) by H. C. Brokmeyer, taken down in shorthand reporting style by my father in 1861; also there were other notebooks of my father's translation of Hegel's History of Philosophy, made by him in 1865–6 and written in longhand. In the collection, I included, too, Mr. Brokmeyer's letters to my father, covering the years 1861–1896; letters from S. H. Emery, Jr. (leader of the Quincy Movement), some from H. K. Jones of Jacksonville, and T. M. Johnson of Osceola."

Others of Miss Harris' materials have been placed in the Library of Congress.

88. The portion of the translation long in Miss Harris' keeping at Walpole, N. H., seems to be in Harris' handwriting, and is probably part of his first longhand transcription of the portions dictated to him by Brokmeyer. This copy appears to have been made during 1860–1861.

89. *A Writer of Books*, p. 319.

90. Emery's copy, presumably still in Quincy, has not yet been located. Most of these details were ascertained by Professor Paul R. Anderson, in the course of studying the various Platonic movements in the Midwest.

91. It is written in longhand on stamped paper bearing the name of Dayton & Arthur, Quincy, Ill. The sheets are abstract, legal cap size, number 16; 32 lines to the page, both sides used. Volume I contains 558, Volume II, 299, and Volume III, 509 pages. Possibly copies or parts of copies of Emery's and Jones's versions were made then or later. The only complete copy known today is Jones's in Jacksonville.

92. Brokmeyer's son Eugene tells me that when his father was asked on his deathbed what disposition was to be made of his manuscript, he replied, "Just leave it in the attic for the vermin; I have enjoyed every minute of my life devoted to it, in the hope that I might justify my existence by leaving something to posterity worth while, but apparently there is no demand for anything like that at this time."

Following Brokmeyer's death, David H. Harris, the brother of W. T. Harris, was placed in charge of a plan to secure the publication of Brokmeyer's works, W. T. Harris having agreed to get the manuscripts in shape and to write introductions (four in all). But Harris found himself in poor health, and in 1908 he returned the manuscripts; whereupon Louis J. Block, then in the Chicago public school system, was commissioned to make the revision, Harris still to write the introductions. At one time they considered publishing the whole of Brokmeyer's writings, but eventually they settled for the *Logic* only. W. T. Harris undertook the support of the project up to $75.00, and Snider subscribed $100. The St. Louis Society of

Psychology also agreed to help. D. H. Harris corresponded with Sonnenschein in London in 1909. Circulars were distributed early in 1909 announcing publication and soliciting subscriptions. Block completed his revisions as far as he could, but at W. T. Harris' death on November 5, 1909, his four introductions were still unwritten. Again the work languished, the removal of Harris' influence doubtless increasing the difficulties.

In 1920, D. H. Harris gave the manuscript of the *Logic* to the Missouri Historical Society of St. Louis. In March, 1923, he borrowed it and returned it in April. In October, 1925, he ordered it sent to Block. When he returned it in December, 1926, it was incomplete, and so it remains today. This activity during 1923–1926 reflects the efforts on the part of Harris and Block to have the Logic published in the London Allen & Unwin "Library of Philosophy," of which J. H. Muirhead was the general editor. When, in 1929, the W. H. Johnson and L. C. Struthers translation of Hegel's *Science of Logic* appeared in this series, Muirhead prefaced the text with the following note:

"Some years ago the Editor . . . was approached by the surviving friends of Henry Brockmeyer [*sic*] with a view to the publication . . . of the translation which he had left. It was to be accompanied by a short biography of the translator, and to partake of the character of a tribute to his memory both as a philosopher and a Governor of the State of Missouri. As it seemed inappropriate to have a volume of this kind included in a series devoted to the pure study of philosophy, it was impossible to accept this offer, and as there seemed no immediate prospect of the American translation coming out, the Editor felt himself free to make an arrangement with the present translators."

The fragment deposited in the Jefferson Memorial of the Missouri Historical Society, since it reproduces none of Hegel's elaborate "Observations" or "Notes" ("Anmerkungen") and because it breaks off at a point about one-fourth of the way through Book II, represents less than a fourth of Hegel's text. It consists of 217 yellow (copy), legal-cap sized sheets, typewritten on one side. The manuscript is in two batches, marked Volume I and Volume II. The sheets of Volume I are numbered 1–23, followed by a second series, numbered 1–222, of which pages 2–7 are missing. Volume II contains pages 1–78. The translation ends, in the Henning edition of Hegel's *Werke* (20 vols. in 22, 2nd ed., Berlin, 1834–1887) at the following point: Erster Theil: Die objective Logic; Zweite Abth.: Die Lehre vom Wesen; Zweites Buch: Das Wesen; Zweiter Abschnitt: Die

Erscheinung; Zweites Kapital: Die Erscheinung—A. Das Gesetz der Erscheinung (Vol. IV, p. 146 of *Werke*). The manuscript shows numerous corrections or revisions, made with pencil and pen by various hands; hence it is no longer an accurate or complete index to the Hegel that Brokmeyer taught from 1860 to 1880. The Jones manuscript, made in 1878 from Emery's copy, itself made two years earlier, appears to represent more accurately the Hegelian *Logic* current among the St. Louisans during the sixties.

93. Harris' *Hegel's Doctrine of Reflection, Being a Paraphrase and a Commentary Interpolated into the Text of the Second Volume of Hegel's Larger Logic, Treating of Essence* appeared in New York in 1881, and his *Hegel's Logic. A Book on the Genesis of the Categories of the Mind* was published by S. C. Griggs in Chicago in 1890.

94. Already at Andover he had begun to read "with avidity a class of literature whose chief interest . . . was its practical protest against some phase or other of orthodoxy." Among these were Locke's *Essay on Human Understanding* and Cousin's criticism of Locke— reading that inspired him to establish "both thought and action on solid foundations," and that ultimately led to his *Psychologic Foundations of Education. An Attempt to Show the Genesis of the Higher Faculties of the Mind* (N.Y., 1905). In the beginning, however, he stumbled around miserably among such pseudo-sciences as phrenology, hypnotism, and mesmerism. Although he devoted four terms of his preparatory education to Latin and Greek, he began, already at Andover, to disparage "the dead languages" and to demand to know more about nature as revealed by science. His desire appears to have originated in his reading, in 1835, Humboldt's *Kosmos* and shortly after such works as *Vestiges of Creation*. But during this "era of hobbies" he still found his interest diverted all too often to "spiritualism, the water cure, vegetarianism, socialism, and all manner of reforms."—Harris, "How I Was Educated," *Forum*, I (Aug., 1886), 552–61, and "Books That Have Helped Me," *ibid.*, III (Apr., 1887), 143–44.

95. It seems altogether likely that Alcott, who was volubly enthusiastic about his recent "Conversational Tours of the West" (despite the fact that so far they had netted him no more profit than a silver dollar) influenced Harris' decision to go west. But Alcott remained entirely unaware of the fact that his "Conversations" had provided for Harris the "turning point in his intellectual career" until years later, when Harris confessed as much to

him, and that by these talks (which had seemed a complete failure at the time) he had raised for himself the "most ardent, perhaps the most able, of all his interpreters and defenders."— Shepard, *Pedlars' Progress*, p. 467; *Journals of Alcott*, p. 295; Sanborn and Harris, *Alcott*, II 544–52.

96. "Books That Have Helped Me," *Forum*, III (Apr., 1887), 144–45. In 1887 Harris wrote: "I endeavor to re-read 'Wilhelm Meister' every year, and always find it more suggestive than before."

97. Harris proved an apt pupil. Soon he corralled a small group of kindred spirits, who, like himself, were willing to attend University Brokmeyer. In 1893 Harris recalled that this first class consisted, among others, of J. H. Watters, G. C. Stedman, S. D. Hayden, H. M. Jones, C. F. Childs, Brokmeyer, and himself. Others sometimes identified with this early group are Ira Divoll and Dr. R. A. Holland. The lessons began with Kant, although Brokmeyer's goal was to convert them all to Hegel, whose *Logic* he undertook to translate against the day when his fledglings should be ready to receive it.—Schuyler, *loc. cit.*, p. 66; Snider, *A Writer of Books*, pp. 342–62, 393–94; Harris, *Hegel's Logic*, p. viii.

98. For details, see "Books That Have Helped Me," *loc. cit.*, p. 147. By December, 1858, Kant's *Critique* had led him to make the "logical inference that the unity of time and space presupposes one absolute reason" and to obtain insight "into the true inference from Kant's 'Transcendental Aesthetic' regarding the demonstrability of God, freedom, and immortality." During 1859 he proceeded to the position of being able to refute "Sir William Hamilton's *Law of the Conditioned*, by proving the infinitude of space and showing that the supposed antinomy rests on confounding mental pictures with pure thought."—Harris, *Hegel's Logic*, pp. viii–ix.

99. The next step in his philosophical progress that Harris records came in 1866, when he arrived at "the first insight that is distinctively Hegelian,"—"the most important *apercu*" and "the highest thought" in Hegel's logic. This is the distinction between comprehension (*Begriff*) and idea (*Idee*). Harris ascribed to Hegel the honor of seeing "for the first time the pure-thought form of this doctrine." It became for Harris the basis of what he soon came to call "pure" or "speculative" philosophy.—Harris, *Hegel's Logic*, pp. ix–xi.

As he progressed, notably from 1866 onward, both in his grasp of Hegel and in his practice of "self-activity" and "self-publication" in the *Journal of Speculative Philosophy*, he felt convinced that he was advancing to Wilhelm Meister's second phase, his *Wanderjahre*. The third and final stage, the *Meisterschaft*, he did not attain until the formation of the Concord School about 1880 and the publication of his major philosophical works: (1) *Hegel's Doctrine of Reflection, Being a Paraphrase and Commentary Interpolated into the Text of the Second Volume of Hegel's Larger Logic* (N.Y., 1881); (2) *Hegel's Logic. A Book on the Genesis of the Categories of the Mind* (Chicago, 1890); and (3) *Psychologic Foundations of Education* (N.Y., 1905), which formed Volume XXXVII of the Appleton International Education Series, of which he was general editor. Thus Harris came to see his philosophical development as an illustration of the Hegelian dialectic—a life in three moments: the first, a phase of positivism (Harris called this his "saurian" period) up to 1858; second, a conversion to transcendentalism, from 1858 to 1866; and third, a transcending of transcendentalism, from 1866 onward. Insofar as Hegel was a factor in this development, Harris said in 1887:

"In reading his larger 'Logic,' I always feel myself ushered into a sort of high court of reason, in which all ideas of the mind are summoned to the bar and put on trial. . . . All the collisions and petty details of terrestrial affairs seem to fall away, and one gazes, as it were, into the eternal arch-types, and sees the essence of the conflict, the problem reduced to its lowest terms. In the concluding portions of this 'Logic' Hegel finds the highest idea of a Personal Being in whom will and intellect are one. This is the idea of God, whose knowing is creating. To me this appeared to be by far the most important thought reached by the German mind. . . . Indeed, Hegel's greatest merit seems to me to be that of interpreter of the deepest thought of all nations. This faculty of interpretation shines out pre-eminently in his 'Lectures on the Philosophy of History,' which I place by the side of his 'Logic' as the second of his greatest works. I believe that I have studied this book through nine times, with intervals of two years between my studies. . . . This work . . . comes nearer being a genuine theodicy, a justification of Providence in human history, than any other work I know. 'The world history,' says he, 'is the outward progress of man in consciousness of freedom.'"— "Books That Have Helped Me," *loc. cit.*, pp. 145–49; see also *Proc. Nat'l. Ed. Assn.* (1910), p. 92.

100. *JoSP*, XVII, iii (July, 1883), 310; and *Hegel's Logic*, pp. 1–5, 17, 18–21, 22–56 *passim*.

101. *JoSP*, VI, i (Jan., 1872), 3, 5.

102. *Ibid.*, XVII, iii (July, 1883), 297–99, 303–4.

103. *Ibid.*, p. 304.

104. *Ibid.*, p. 307.

105. *Ibid.*, pp. 307–10.

106. That is, materialists. See *ibid.*, VI, i (Jan., 1872), 1–4; also pp. 4–18.

107. Men on the order of Hume and Spencer. For Harris' refutation of these men's point of view, see his *Psychologic Foundations of Education*, pp. 218–19.

108. Typified by Kant and Hegel. See *ibid.*, pp. 220–28.

109. See esp. pp. 147–250.

110. Most succinctly stated by Harris in "Philosophy in Outline," *JoSP*, XVII, iii (July, 1883), 296–316; iv (Oct., 1883), 337–56, and much more elaborately in his *Hegel's Logic*, See also his "Introduction to Philosophy," *JoSP*, I i (1867), 57–60; ii, 114–20; iii, 187–90; iv, 236–40; II, i (1868), 51–55; ii, 176–81.

111. *JoSP*, I, i (1867), Preface. Already in the second number of the *Journal*, Harris felt obliged, in an editorial (for which he modestly reserved the last page of the number), to answer the questions of critics why the organ did not contain more original, "indigenous" material: "To prepare translations and commentary, together with original exposition, is our object. Originality will take care of itself. Once disciplined in Speculative thought, the new growth of our national life will furnish us objects whose comprehension shall constitute original philosophy without parallel." Harris contributed more pages of material to the *Journal* than any of his collaborators. The greater part of his work falls under classifications other than original— notably history of philosophy and commentary. Here, as elsewhere, it is apparent that his strength lay less in original thought than in clarifying and conserving what he considered best in the course of human thought. Professor Merle Curti very appropriately entitled his chapter on Harris in his *Social Ideas of American Educators* "William T. Harris, the Conservator."

112. See his "History of Philosophy in Outline," *JoSP*, X, iii (July, 1876), 225–70.

113. See the place which he accords to oriental thought, *ibid.*, pp. 231–37.

114. Including Colebrooke's translation of the *Sankhya Karika* (which he borrowed from Emerson), Wilkins' and Thompson's translations of the *Bhagavad Gita*, and Wilson's translation of the *Vishnu Purana*. He also drew upon the *Dial*, the *Massachusetts Quarterly*, and the works of Cousin, Sir William Jones, Max Müller, and Rhys Davids. See *JoSP*, IX, i (Jan., 1875), 104–5; "Books That Have Helped Me," *loc.*

cit., p. 150; *Hegel's Logic*, p. xiii; *Poet-Lore*, I (June, 1889), 253–59, esp. p. 254; and Kurt Leidecker, *loc. cit.*, p. 81.

115. For his writings on oriental philosophy and literature, see the bibliography in Charles M. Perry, *op. cit.*, pp. 96–140.

116. "Its value," he said, "is chiefly negative, aiding us in getting rid of sensuous conceptions in the realm of thought. It is a sort of cathartic for the imagination . . . a kind of prehistoric adumbration of European thought."—"The History of Philosophy in Outline," *JoSP*, X, iii (July, 1876), 233; "The Idea of the State and its Necessity," *The Western*, n.s., III (Apr., 1877), 211. The key word of his interpretation of Oriental philosophy is "negative unity." Thus "he sought to cover the many-hued and verdant growth of Hindu speculation by a Hegelian term that would grant it a modicum of right to exist, but show at the same time its transitory character." Orientalism could have little more than a "dialectical" value for him.— Leidecker, *loc. cit.*, pp. 85, 121.

117. Snider, *St. Louis Movement*, pp. 10–11. As early as October, 1865, on Snider's first meeting with the group and some months before the Society was founded, Harris put into his hands a copy of Hegel's *Philosophy of Nature* and "as my first discipline in philosophy," records Snider, "instructed me to make a translation of it." Snider adds: "Brokmeyer would never think of doing such a thing . . . but Harris . . . showed a touch of his pedagogical character by whipping me into line the first day."—*A Writer of Books*, p. 312.

118. Snider, *St. Louis Movement*, p. 480; *A Writer of Books*, p. 326. Thus was established the first definitely and significantly philosophical journal in the English language. It appeared regularly in quarterly numbers for twenty-one years, and it terminated only with the twenty-second volume, two of whose numbers bear the dates of January and April, 1888, the third, that of September, 1892, and the fourth, that of December, 1893. Without Harris' perseverance this achievement would hardly have been possible. The journal severely taxed his energies and was a constant drain on his purse. To William Schuyler he once confided, "I live to publish this Journal"; he did not abandon it until his duties as U.S. Commissioner of Education forced its discontinuance.

The first fourteen volumes were edited in St. Louis, the next seven in Concord, and the last in Washington, D.C. The first thirteen were printed in St. Louis, three different firms successively doing the work; the last nine bear the imprint of D. Appleton Co., of New York. While the paper used in the early volumes is not the best, its quality beginning with the third volume is noticeably better. Excellence of typography and of proofreading is uniform. The double-columned page was abandoned with the third volume, when the type size was also increased. Throughout the twenty-two volumes, severe economy of space is practiced, the materials being arranged so compactly that few blank spaces are left. The bulk of the volumes varied somewhat. Beginning with the ninth volume, the size of the quarterly numbers was increased from 96 to 112 pages each, though slight irregularities occur in several volumes. All volumes, with the exception of the seventh (three of whose issues number their pages from 1 to 96 and one from 1 to 92) number their pages consecutively for the four issues comprising each volume. Volume X contains a general index (ordered alphabetically) of the titles of the contents of the ten volumes; and Volume XV includes, in addition, a complete index, arranged alphabetically, of all subjects, contributors, book reviews, and correspondence in the fifteen volumes. No general index was ever made for the last volumes (XVI through XXII).

119. Snider felt that "Harris was a little heady in this matter; he precipitated his publication upon us before we or even he, were quite ready to support it with mature contributions. In my judgment Brokmeyer was the only man among us who had at that time anything vital and enduring to say, and the question then and ever afterwards in his case was, will he say it—formulate it with some degree of completeness? Still the Journal has vindicated its right to existence by more than twenty volumes . . . which have been read . . . the world over. I saw it in the public libraries at Rome and Athens, where nothing else from St. Louis could be seen . . . and very little from America. It is . . . the most famous and striking philosophical product of the movement, thanks to the tireless activity of its editor."—*A Writer of Books*, pp. 326–27.

120. Book reviews are distinguished from book notices arbitrarily by length; when longer than 500 words, they are classified as reviews.

121. This classification is again more or less arbitrary, for obviously the 1779 pages classified as original speculation vary considerably in quality. Compare, for example, C. S. Peirce's "Questions Concerning Certain Faculties Claimed for Man" (II, ii, 103–14) with A. B. Alcott's "Philosophemes" (VII, i 84–88); or compare the contributions of J. H. Stirling or William James or John Dewey or C. F. Goeschel with those of W. H. Kimball or Meeds Tuthill or

Elizabeth P. Peabody or J. G. Woerner. What is remarkable is that so large a portion of the 1779 pages is original (as distinct from translation, reprint, comment, analysis, criticism, or history of philosophy) and of a high order.

No distinction is made between (1) the more strictly technical philosophical contributions, such as belong to logic, epistemology, etc., and (2) contributions of a more-or-less applied nature, such as law, political science, religion, sociology, or economics, for two reasons: (1) it is very hard to make satisfactory distinctions of this sort, and (2) there is little of the latter type.

122. By and large there is perhaps less justification for labeling as original a considerable portion of Harris' 229 pages than for thus designating the work of any other of the more mportant contributors under this classification. As much as one half of the 229 pages represented partake of the nature of outlines of philosophy or aids to reflection and other types of writing, so that they are more nearly allied with the history and criticism of philosophy than with original speculation. Here, as elsewhere, is apparent Harris' equally great concern with the conservation of thought as with original thought.

123. As distinct from pure psychology, which is included under Philosophy.

124. Exclusive of Philosophy of Science and of Mathematics, of Editorials, Comments, etc., and of Original Speculation in the tabulation above. The 122 pages devoted to Philosophy of Science and the 58 pages given to Philosophy of Mathematics are not counted in this calculation. The 820 pages of editorial comment, correspondence, and book reviews, if broken down would not alter the percentages materially.

125. Including the General essay listed under German philosophy.

126. Blasche, Michelet, and Strauss, on the other hand, maintained that the pantheistic idea of God was the only true result of the Hegelian principle. They argued that the unity of Divinity and of Humanity was not to be realized in any one individual but in the whole of humanity, so that the latter became in reality a God–Man. Goeschel's attempts to justify the ecclesiastical idea of Christ as specifically the only God-Man and to demonstrate the idea of a personal immortality on the basis of Hegelian philosophy provide the reasons why he appealed to the St. Louisans. The same cause that led them to go to Goeschel repelled them from Spencer. The *Journal* reproduced the whole of Goeschel's *Proofs of the Immortality of the Human Soul in the Light of Speculative Philosophy*, tr. from the first Berlin edition of

1835. The first three installments (X, 1877) are by T. R. Vickery, the remaining seven (XVII–XX, 1883–1886) are by Susan E. Blow.

The same emphasis on the part of Rosenkranz to interpret Hegel's God theistically accounts for the 129 pages in the *Journal* devoted to the translations of Rosenkranz' commentaries on Hegel's *Phenomenology, Philosophy of History, Philosophy of Religion*, and the *Encyclopedia*. G. Stanley Hall is responsible for a large portion of these translations. Rosenkranz' name does not appear among the German philosophers above, because the St. Louisans' chief interest was in his exegesis of Hegel, rather than in Rosenkranz himself. The case of Goeschel is different, for he appeared (at least in the sections translated) more to build upon the Hegelian bases than merely to explain Hegel.

127. *JoSP*, I, i (1867), 133; V, ii (1871), 119.

128. The popular hue and cry about Schopenhauer being what it was, they had to defend Kant against this false disciple. That was easily done. One of the contributors disposed of him as one who is recognized only "in those circles which are unacquainted with scientific culture," and who believe "the more absurd a thought, the more truth must be contained in it."—Ella S. Morgan, "A. Schopenhauer's Philosophy," *JoSP*, IX, ii (Apr., 1875), 113, 138.

129. As early as 1865 Harris was elected president of the National Education Association, of which body he became a life director. In 1873 he became president of the National Association of School Superintendents. For fifteen years he was an officer of the American Social Science Association, and he was a member of the influential "Committee of Fifteen."

130. John S. Roberts, *William Torrey Harris. A Critical Study of His Educational and Related Philosophical Views* (Washington, D.C., 1924), esp. pp. 6–20, and Merle Curti, *Social Ideas of American Educators* (N. Y.,1935), pp. 310–47. See also Will S. Monroe, *op. cit.*, pp. 195–203.

131. *St. Louis Movement*, pp. 123, 174–75.

132. Here he conducted courses in (1) Mental Philosophy, i.e., psychology according to Hegel's logic, (2) Moral Philosophy, according to Hegel's philosophy of right, (3) Universal History, according to Hegel's philosophy of history, and (4) Natural Science, according to Hegel's philosophy of nature. His course in Moral Philosophy appears to have been especially successful. Although he used Hickok's *System of Moral Science* as a text, he subjected it to a "transformation" by spinning through it "many new threads" derived from Hegel's *Philosophy of Right*. This course, designed for high-school seniors, says Snider, became so

popular that some of his students, after graduating, asked him to offer "a postgraduate course in Mental and Moral Philosophy."—*A Writer of Books*, pp. 399–405, 407–8, 409–11.

133. *Ibid.*, pp. 415–18, 422–26; *St. Louis Movement*, p. 179.

134. *St. Louis Movement*, pp. 188–89.

135. *Ibid.*, pp. 191–94.

136. *Ibid.*, p. 195.

137. *A Writer of Books*, p. 415.

138. *St. Louis Movement*, pp. 195–96.

139. *Ibid.*, p. 196.

140. See especially the recapitulation of Snider's argument, *JoSP*, VI, iii (July, 1872), 250–51. It is interesting to observe that the idea is very similar to that expressed in Hedge's *Prose Writers of Germany* (3rd ed., N.Y. 1855), pp. 452–53.

In his next essay on Shakespeare, on *The Merchant of Venice*, Snider presents his argument even more baldly by dividing the "movement of the drama . . . into three parts: 1. Union; 2. The Separation; 3. The Return":

"Each of these parts is determined and complemented by the others. The Union, by which is meant the bringing together of the three pairs, has produced the collision between Antonio and Shylock, which then returns and dissolves itself. Hence the second step, the Separation, results necessarily from the first. But the parties must overcome this disruption, for they are rationally united, and the collision itself must be mediated; hence the obstacles are removed, and there follows the third stage of the movement, namely, the Return. This when completed is the same as the first Union, but with the collision which was involved in it harmonized. Here the play must end; no further action is possible. Or, to take more abstract terms, we may express these three stages as Thesis, Antithesis, Synthesis. That this movement is a type of the movement of Reason itself, needs not to be told to the Thinker. Every spiritual process involves the same moments, and a work of Art as the child of imaginative reason must bear the image of the parent."

141. VI–X (1872–1876). Others appeared in *The Western*, to which Snider bound himself to furnish an article for each number for one year, at the same time to pay into its ever-gaping treasury five to ten dollars for each contribution. In compensation for this patronage, he was called a "Stockholder," until at last, being chosen Editor, he was forced firmly to decline for fear that this honor would make a pauper of him.—*St. Louis Movement*, pp. 185–87.

142. *Ibid.*, p. 199.

143. *A Writer of Books*, p. 419.

144. *St. Louis Movement*, p. 200.

145. *A Writer of Books*, p. 423.

146. See also Snider's lecture, delivered at the Goethe School in Milwaukee in 1886, on "Mythology of the Second Part of Faust," in Marion V. Dudley (ed.), *Poetry and Philosophy of Goethe* (Chicago, 1887), pp. 138–79.

147. *St. Louis Movement*, pp. 302–5.

148. *Ibid.*, pp. 354–59.

149. *Ibid.*, pp. 280–81.

150. *Ibid.*, pp. 307, 354–55, 362–63.

151. *Ibid.*, pp. 261–62.

152. *Ibid.*, p. 430.

153. *Ibid.*, pp. 421–22.

154. He refused "emphatically to be entertained by any citizen" (as were the rest of the lecturers), and he "haughtily rejected all remuneration."—*Ibid.*, pp. 427–29.

155. *Ibid.*, pp. 430–31.

156. *Ibid.*, p. 419.

157. *Ibid.*, p. 394.

158. *Ibid.*, p. 447.

159. Charles M. Perry, *op. cit.*, p. 37.

160. Snider, *St. Louis Movement*, p. 444.

161. Among his allies and collaborators whom he particularly mentioned later were two well-known clergymen, Dr. David Swing and Dr. H. W. Thomas, as well as Professor Louis J. Block.—*Ibid.*, pp. 403–5; see also Perry, *op. cit.*, pp. 33–41.

162. Snider, *St. Louis Movement*, p. 447.

163. There were ten scheduled lectures during the week from Monday, December 26, to Saturday, December 31. In addition to his own discourses, which opened and concluded the program, Harris gave three, Tom Davidson three, and Frank L. Soldan and Miss Mary E. Beedy one each. Snider recorded with pardonable pride that he paid Harris and Davidson, who had come from a distance, each $150 plus expenses, and "the other speakers in proportion."—*Ibid.*, p. 535; see also Perry, *op. cit.*, pp. 36–37.

The newspapers reported the lectures "fairly," says Snider, and even the Eastern press "took note of the marvelous fact that Chicago had held a large and successful Dante School," and that this was to be followed the next year by a Goethe School as indeed it was. The New York *Sun* could not forego commenting editorially upon Chicago as the "reformed gambler," who, having been "converted from his maddest stock speculation to undertake the penitential journey through the Inferno," was thus viewing "a panorama of its sins."—*St. Louis Movement* pp. 539–42.

164. See *ibid.*, pp. 552–53, for the program of the 1888 Goethe School.

165. *Ibid.*, pp. 36–37. This was the only occasion for which Snider engaged "a regular

University Professor." Thomas, he said, was "a good man but a misfit for our work, in truth a double misfit—we did not fit him, nor he us who were studying Goethe as a Literary Bible, not so much philosophically or even historically, all of which methods have their due place in the University proper," but which had little place in Snider's curriculum. "Professor R. G. Moulton, who gave us excellent and sympathetic help in our later courses," says Snider, "belonged to the so-called University Extension Movement."—*St. Louis Movement*, pp. 555–56.

166. *Ibid.*, pp. 565–90, and Perry, *op. cit.*, pp. 33–41. The program of the 1892 Shakespeare School, in which Snider, Harris, R. G. Moulton, H. W. Mabie, and Dr. David Swing collaborated, announced that all profits (from the five-dollar enrollment fees) in excess of "actual expenses" would be donated to the work of "establishing and maintaining Kindergartens in the poorest districts of the city."

167. *St. Louis Movement*, pp. 571–73.

168. When, in 1880, shortly after his return from Europe, Snider returned to St. Louis, Mr. John Albee, then visiting St. Louis, remarked to him upon the extraordinary role played in that city by the women. "I never saw the like," he said. "I have not talked with any woman here who has not philosophized me beyond my depth. A day or two ago I went with Miss Blow to one of her kindergartens to see the children play, and she so overwhelmed me with her ponderous Hegelian nomenclature in explaining a little game of the babies that I heard my brain-pan crack like a pistol shot."—*Ibid.*, p. 291.

169. *Ibid.*, pp. 294–96, 300. Susan Blow studied under Mrs. Maria Kraus Boelte in New York during 1872–1873. Upon her return to St. Louis, she opened the first kindergarten, in the Des Peres School, in September, 1873. She spent 1877 in studying with Baroness Marenholz Bülow and visiting German Kindergartens, whereupon she was placed in charge of the Kindergarten Training School in St. Louis. Her first book, *Symbolic Education*, was published in 1894. About 1895 she began ranging throughout the country, expounding Froebel's philosophy and organizing kindergartens in many cities, but also lecturing on Homer, Dante, Shakespeare, and Goethe. When, in 1910, she returned to St. Louis for a meeting of the International Kindergarten Union, of which she was an officer, she had the satisfaction of seeing assembled a force of some six hundred kindergartners. See D. H. Harris (ed.), *op. cit.*, pp. 128–33.

170. *St. Louis Movement*, pp. 294, 301–2, 315–16.

171. *Ibid.*, pp. 319, 570–85.

172. Perry, *op. cit.*, pp. 34–35.

173. *Ibid.*, p. 39.

174. D. H. Harris (ed.), *op. cit.*, p. 43.

175. The more important contributions in psychology are to be found in *JoSP*, XIV, ii (Apr., 1880), 204–18, 225–39; XV, ii (Apr., 1881), 159–88; XXI ii (Apr., 1887), 189–221; and XXII, ii (Apr., 1888), 138–69.

176. *St. Louis Movement*, pp. 591–92.

177. Subsequently he added *Cosmos and Diacosmos* (1909) and *Biocosmos* (n.d.). William McKendree Bryant's Hegelian publications on education, psychology, and the philosophy of art, and his translation of the second part of Hegel's *Aesthetic* proved to be valuable supplementary books for Snider.

178. *St. Louis Movement*, p. 597; Perry, *op. cit.*, p. 37.

179. D. H. Harris (ed.) *op. cit.*, pp. 41–43; Snider, *St. Louis Movement*, p. 596. Miss May Whitcomb, a member of the Chicago Kindergarten College, put the number of students in the St. Louis Communal University who studied "Snider's Psychology" in 1908 at two hundred.—Perry, *op. cit.*, pp. 36, 37.

180. Weekly meetings, on Monday evenings, throughout the year were held, after 1910, usually in the assembly room of the Cabanne Branch Library. The Pedagogical Society, renamed the Society of Pedagogy and later the Society of Psychology, remained an active organization, and under the presidency of D. H. Harris maintained an active membership of several hundred, as late as 1929. When, upon Snider's death, in 1925, the Denton J Snider Association for Universal Culture was formed, it provided many of the members.

181. *St. Louis Movement*, pp. 523, 587.

182. *Ibid.*, 588; D. H. Harris (ed.), *op. cit.*, 31–47.

183. Perry, *op. cit.*, pp. 1–78 *passim*.

184. Snider appears to have been in complete charge, and on occasions a one-man faculty; but more often he was assisted, especially during his later period in Chicago, by Miss Elizabeth Harrison and Mrs. J. N. Crouse, the official heads of the kindergarten work in Chicago, as well as by Professor R. G. Moulton and Louis J. Block. The meetings were held principally on Saturday afternoons, ordinarily in the Lecture Hall of the Kindergarten College. For texts he used chiefly his own books, of which he distributed "thousands" to his students.—*Ibid.*, pp. 43, 70. In St. Louis he had the assistance principally of Miss Fruchte and Professor Cook.

185. *Ibid.*, pp. 8, 18, 23, 24, 32, 44, 70. Snider's system of psychology and its influence

through his several educational ventures, as well as through his published work, are matters that warrant closer study. His literary personality has recently been analyzed and appraised by Calvin V. Hueneman in "Denton J. Snider: A Critical Study" (diss., Univ. of Wis., 1953). Some of Snider's private papers, including unfinished manuscripts and voluminous notes, were presented by William H. Miner, his literary executor, to the library of the University of Oklahoma.

186. The meetings in South St. Louis were held at the home of Harris on Second Carondelet Avenue, and those in the north at Francis E. Cook's, then at the Rev. R. A. Holland's, and finally at William Schuyler's and James A. Garland's. The members were Cook, Harris, Snider, Henry W. Jameson, George B. McClellan, E. H. Long, William M. Bryant, Rev. R. A. Holland, George Lane, James A. Garland, T. R. Vickroy, Hugo Haenel, L. W. Allen, S. B. Blewett, William Schuyler, Miss Grace C. Bibb, and a few others.

The most important work that came out of this organization was the translation made during 1878–1881 by Harris (assisted by J. A. Garland) of the second volume of the *Logic*, published in 1881 as *Hegel's Doctrine of Reflection, Being a Paraphrase and a Commentary Interpolated into the Text of the Second Volume of Hegel's Larger Logic, Treating of "Essence."* —Wm. Schuyler, *op. cit.*, pp. 82–84; *JoSP*, XI, i (Jan., 1877), 109–10.

187. Snider's activity as a lecturer on Homer, Dante, Shakespeare, and Goethe prompted a series of small organizations, some of which attained the status of clubs. His singling out of his various classes his most adept pupil to become an instructor was a method of propagation that he employed wherever he held classes. Once a year, in a given locality, he would unify these classes into what he termed a "Literary School." Some of his lieutenants conducted classes that ran for years. In St. Louis, for example, Mrs. Thomas E. Ferguson had a Homer class continuously for ten years, and William F. Woerner conducted another. In Chicago he was especially fortunate in finding devoted assistants among his kindergartners.

188. The Rev. Dr. R. A. Holland's Literary Club, though its discussions often took a theological turn, was another active group. About 1881, when Holland went to Chicago, he wrote to Harris in Concord that he proposed "to remove the western headquarters of Hegelian study from St. Louis to Chicago." He founded Kant and Hegel clubs, allied himself with the Sniderian movement in Chicago, and found able allies in Meeds Tuthill, Austin Bierbower,

and Louis J. Block. Tuthill made a transcript of Brokmeyer's translation, which served in Chicago as other copies served in Jacksonville and Osceola.—Perry, *op. cit.*, p. 22; Snider, *St. Louis Movement*, pp. 304–5; Leidecker, *op. cit.*, p. 438.

189. Perry, *op. cit.*, p. 64. Another early club, with wider interests than Harris' musical group, was the Art Society. It originated during the war as an informal discussion group, meeting at the house of Mrs. Beverly Allen, but soon blossomed forth as the Art Society, holding semi-public lectures, exhibitions, and discussions on sculpture, painting, music, and literature. Bryant became, in time, the moving spirit of this club, and his publication, in 1879, of a translation of the second part of Hegels' *Æsthetik* provided the textbook for the Art Society.

Associated and interlaced with all these organizations were several educational institutions and federations: the St. Louis Froebel Society, organized by Mary C. McCulloch, long-time president of the Kindergarten Department of the National Education Association and a charter member and long the secretary of the International Kindergarten Union; the Society of Pedagogy; the Teachers' Fellowship Society; and the Wednesday Club. In the last three Amelia C. Fruchte was the guiding spirit. These latter groups appear to have made up most of Emerson's and Alcott's audiences when they spoke in St. Louis.

190. For a brief sketch of the institutional life of Jacksonville, see the excellent study by Prof. Paul R. Anderson, "Hiram K. Jones and Philosophy in Jacksonville," *Jour. Ill. State Hist. Soc.*, XXXIII, iv (Dec., 1940), 479–83.

191. Graduated B.A. from Illinois College in 1844, M.D., 1846, and M.S., 1847, co-founder of the Microscopic Society, a charter member of the Literary Society, acting superintendent of the Jacksonville Historical Society, lecturer on anatomy and physiology at the Illinois College, professor of philosophy there from 1886 to 1900, donor of some $70,000 to his alma mater, founder of the Plato Club in 1865, of the American Akademe about 1884, and the acknowledged leader of its numerous enterprises—Jones was for Jacksonville what Brokmeyer, Harris, and Snider combined were for St. Louis. His fame as a scientist declined after 1890, when he read before the local medical society a paper in which he rejected the germ theory.

192. For names of other prominent members, see *ibid.*, p. 494. "Harris at this time was not actively aligned with his brother's movement in St. Louis, although he knew about it and had natural sympathies with it. Block, on the other

hand, had been an associate of the group in St. Louis and provided a fresh approach, which he had acquired while there. As for the later inclinations of these men, Harris moved decidedly in the direction of Hegelianism and later became associated with Snider in the Communal University in St. Louis, while Block transferred his major allegiance from Hegel to Plato and became an important leader both in the Plato Club and the American Akademe. Harris left Jacksonville around 1880 . . . ; a little later Block moved to Chicago."—*Ibid.*, pp. 494–96. Here Block identified himself with Snider's efforts and, shifting his philosophical orientation back to Hegel, became closely associated with Dr. Holland's attempts to transfer the center of Hegelian studies from St. Louis to Chicago.

193. Sanborn and Harris, *Alcott*, II, 508; Alcott's *Journals*, p. 511 (Aug. 23, 1879).

194. Alcott's *Journals*, pp. 482–83; Sanborn and Harris, *Alcott*, II, 508–11.

195. It promptly enrolled thirty-three members, twenty-one of them from Jacksonville, and the remainder from all over the country, from Galveston to New York City. The membership included Louise M. Fuller (later the editor of the *Journal of the American Akademe*), Thomas M. Johnson (editor of the *Platonist* and the *Bibliotheca Platonica*), and Harris and Block, both of whom appeared later in the same summer on the Concord programs. Summers in Jacksonville not being deemed conducive to attracting people devoted to philosophical symposia, it was decided to make the Akademe a winter institution. On September 25, a constitution was adopted and eighteen new members inducted, including the publishers A. W. Wagnalls and Abner Doubleday of New York and others from Colorado to the Dutch West Indies. Before the year was out, Jones found it necessary to provide more commodious quarters than his office afforded. Accordingly he turned over to the Akademe a large upstairs room in his home, henceforth known as Akademe Hall. The first complete program was presented in 1883, the third Tuesday of each month being selected as the regular date of the meeting. Ten sessions were to be held each year, from September to June. By May, 1884, there were 180 members; in 1892, when the last meeting was held, 433 members were enrolled, although "probably no more than 200 were members at the time," for the roll was cumulative, and resignations were not recorded. The average attendance during the early years was around fifty; by 1890 it had begun to fall, and during the last years, the average fell to 30.—Paul R. Anderson, *loc. cit.*, pp. 507–8.

196. When he lectured in Jacksonville, though he chose usually a subject more or less identified with Plato, he managed to consider it from a Hegelian point of view. In his discourse on "Plato's Dialectic and Doctrine of Ideas" he emphasized the dialectical character of Plato's thought; in another lecture, on "Aristotle's Doctrine of Reason," his hearers again perceived an implied criticism of Platonic "ideas"; and in discussing "The Concrete and the Abstract in their Practical Relations to Life," he dwelt on the value of speculative philosophy after the manner of an orthodox Hegelian.—*Ibid.*, pp. 510–11.

Among others who contributed prominently to the meetings were Alex. Wilder, of Newark, N. J., the editor of the *Journal of the American Akademe* (1884–1888, 1889–1892), and Thomas M. Johnson of Osceola, Mo., editor of the *Platonist* (1881–1884, 1885–1888) and of the *Bibliotheca Platonica* (1889–1890). At a distance from Jacksonville (though both repeatedly came to the meetings) they maintained a greater degree of editorial independence than might have been possible had they been more closely affiliated with the Akademe. For a succinct characterization of these journals see Paul R. Anderson, *loc. cit.*, pp. 512–18.

197. See Paul R. Anderson, "Quincy, an Outpost of Philosophy," *Jour. Ill. State Hist. Soc.*, XXXIV, i, (Mar., 1941), 51.

198. Alcott visited in the home of Mrs. Sarah Denman and spoke to the Friends in Council, of whom Mrs. Denman was the organizer and leader; while Emerson visited in the Emery home in 1866 and returned to lecture in Quincy, later, in the year 1867, and in subsequent years. For interesting details regarding the East-West relationships in Quincy, see *ibid.*, pp. 54–57.

199. Born and reared in New Haven, Mrs. Denman had removed to Philadelphia shortly after her marriage, in 1826, to Mathew B. Denman (a land agent and man of means), and had gone to Quincy in 1842, where she became active in many philanthropic, civic, and political enterprises.

200. Sorosis of New York and of Jacksonville are listed as being older. The Quincy Friends in Council was the first club of its kind to own a building, a gift from Mr. Denman in 1878, and still on the grounds of the Historical Society of Quincy and Adams County. From Quincy, Friends in Council spread to Lawrence, Kans., Berlin, Wis., Marquette, Mich., Burlington and Rutland, Vt., and elsewhere.—*Ibid.*, p. 58.

201. They chose for their first book Lecky's *History of the Rise and Influence of the Spirit of Rationalism in Europe*. During the second and third years the club read Plato's dialogues.

Alcott appeared before its members on occasions when he visited the Lorenzo Bulls or the Denmans, and the club held special sessions in his honor. Hiram K. Jones often came to Quincy, sometimes for several weeks at a time, the guest of the Denmans. There were papers on Plato and neo-Platonism in its various forms. "Part of the program for two years was given over to the study of Cousin's *History of Modern Philosophy*. One year 'The Relation between Mind and Body' occupied its attention. In 1877–1878 the time was spent on the philosophy of history (presumably *à la* Hegel). One section in 1888–1889 was devoted to the study of English thinkers, and in 1889–1890, to evo-, lution as represented in the work of Haeckel, Darwin, Huxley, and Spencer. Somewhat characteristic was the program of 1879–1880, devoted to modern science, in which the following topics were considered: Method of Science (Mill, Whewell, Jevons), Definition and Object of Physics, Theories concerning the Ultimate Structure of Matter, The New Chemistry, Biology (Cook, Le Conte, Tyndall), The Descent of Life (Darwin, Haeckel, Galton, Huxley, Mivart), Mental Physiology (Lewis, Bain, Martineau, Lotze), Cosmogony (Spencer, Huxley), The Theistic Philosophy of Evolution (Gray)." Even while literary, scientific, and historical subjects were considered, philosophy remained the focal interest up to 1890 at least, after which date other interests began to intrude.—*Ibid.*, pp. 62–63.

An enlargement of the club's activities came through the ready and mutual interchange of contacts between Friends in Council and the Jacksonville Plato Club. They corresponded and exchanged papers, and when the American Akademe was formed in Jacksonville, Quincy provided one of the largest out-of-town membership lists.

The activities of Friends in Council were reported in the *Journal of the American Akademe*, while Platonic studies in Jacksonville were reported in detail by Mrs. J. O. King to Mrs. Denman throughout the sixties and seventies. These notes, mainly exegetical of Plato's dialogues, were painstakingly copied by Mrs. Denman. Four volumes of these, covering the years from 1873 to 1879, all in Mrs. Denman's handwriting, still exist and afford ample evidence to show that the ladies of Quincy pursued their philosophical studies seriously.—*Ibid.*, pp. 68–69.

202. Born in New England and reared in the home of a liberal Unitarian minister, who removed his family to Quincy when Samuel was fifteen, he enjoyed a year at Harvard and another at Amherst before entering the Comstock

Stove Foundry in Quincy and making a fortune. Already an Emerson enthusiast, he was further stimulated to philosophical pursuits by Emerson's visits to Quincy during the mid-sixties. Emerson advised him to study Plato's dialogues and recommended Stirling's *Secret of Hegel*. See *Journal of the American Akademe*, III (1887), 168–69. Plato did not hold Emery long; the first numbers of the *Journal of Speculative Philosophy* soon won him over to Hegel. A steady interchange of letters with Harris (whom, however, he did not meet until 1879, when both went East to organize the Concord School) and contributions to Harris' *Journal* led to an ever-increasing interest in Hegel, Harris, for his part, finding Emery "a young giant in philosophy."—Paul R. Anderson, "Quincy . . . ," *loc. cit.*, p. 72.

203. It kept no minutes and left no complete list of members, but it met regularly on Thursday evenings. The membership was never large, and the average attendance only eight or ten, but its members appear to have been well equipped for the study of philosophy. Among the more active members were Caroline and Mary Chapin (then in charge of the Quincy Female Academy, where the first meetings were held), Mrs. Emery, Mrs. C. H. Bull, Mrs. John McFadon, Mrs. Lorenzo Bull, Mrs. Ebenezer Baldwin, Dr. and Mrs. R. K. Rutherford, and Edward McClure, Emery's brother-in-law. Like Emery, McClure had made a fortune in business, and having retired, attended all the Concord sessions, and subsequently returned with the Emerys to the West. He was a great reader, especially of philosophical books. While his opinions were held in high regard, he steadfastly refused to write or publicly to discourse on philosophical subjects except in small, informal groups. Mrs. Ebenezer Baldwin was another who became an earnest student of Hegel, even to carrying a copy of Stirling's *Secret of Hegel* with her on a trip taken to restore her health.—*Ibid.*, p. 74.

204. D. H. Harris (ed.), *op. cit.*, p. 20.

205. Paul R. Anderson, "Quincy," *loc. cit.*, p. 81.

206. *Ibid.*, pp. 70–71.

207. As Professor Anderson points out, William James' memory was at fault when he intimated that this effort was made in 1872. It could not have been before 1879, as will appear from the following quotation and its reference to the "two young business men from Illinois," obviously a reference to Emery and McClure, who first journeyed East in 1879. Recollecting an informal philosophical club composed, among others, of himself, Tom Davidson, J. E. Cabot, and C. C. Everett, James wrote:

"The previous year we had gone over a good part of Hegel's larger Logic, under the self-constituted leadership of two young business man from Illinois, who had become enthusiastic Hegelians and, knowing almost no German, had actually possessed themselves of a manuscript translation of the entire three volumes of Logic, made by an extraordinary Pomeranian [sic] immigrant, named Brockmeyer [sic]. These disciples were leaving business for the law and studying at the Harvard law-school; but they saw the whole universe through Hegelian spectacles, and a more admirable *homo unis libri* than one of them, with his three big folios of Hegelian manuscript, I have never had the good fortune to know."

208. Emery was its most prolific writer. His first essay, an exegesis of the *Parmenides* (first printed in the *Journal of Speculative Philosophy* for July, 1872, read before the American Akademe in Jacksonville, and reprinted in an enlarged form in the *Journal of the American Akademe* for 1887), is inspired by a Hegelian interpretation of Plato, as Emery frankly admitted on the occasion of his oral presentation of the paper in Jacksonville. He sent three other contributions to the *Journal of Speculative Philosophy*: (1) a letter opposing, by the use of Hegelian principles, A. E. Kroeger's thesis that empirical knowledge is sufficient to establish immortality (VI, 90); (2) a brief article entitled "Does Formal Logic Explain Active Processes?" in which he argued that the Understanding has no way of establishing the existence of motion, and that reason alone can assure us of its certainty (XI, 410–11); and (3) an analysis of Lucretius, *On the Nature of Things* (XV, 198–200). He took an active part in the discussions at Concord and contributed several lectures, but of these only one (his discourse on "The Elective Affinities") has been preserved in print (*The Life and Genius of Goethe . . .* , ed. by F. B. Sanborn, Boston, 1886, 251–89).

209. Snider claims that Davidson forsook Hegel because after a "tussle" with the *Logic*, "he got badly thrown."—*St. Louis Movement*, p. 124.

210. Davidson turned up repeatedly for the programs arranged by Harris or Snider, notably in Chicago, where, according to Snider, he tried unsuccessfully to disarrange Snider's plans by setting up rival schools (*St. Louis Movement*, pp. 235–37, 540–43, 549–52). Brilliant, militant, mercurial, Davidson loved intellectual fencing and always succeeded in enlivening the programs in which he participated. After an extended sojourn (1878–1884) in Italy to study medieval commentaries of Aristotle and to write the life of Rosmini, he settled in London, where he participated in the activities of the Aristotelian Society, became the founder of "The Fellowship of the New Life," later "The New Fellowship," of which the Fabian Society is an offshoot. By 1887 he was living at St. Cloud, N.J., but spent much time in New York, lecturing, writing, and establishing a branch of the Fellowship and a Summer School for Cultural Sciences. In association with the People's Institute and the Educational Alliance of New York, and assisted by Joseph Pulitzer, he gathered a group of eager young men (chiefly Jewish socialists from the lower East Side) and organized the Bread-Winners' College, designed to help wage-earners share in the best culture of the ages and to raise them to " a higher level of mental and spiritual power."—D. H. Harris (ed.), *op. cit.*, pp. 59–60, 65; *DAB*, V, 96–97.

211. *Journal of the American Akademe*, V (1891), 252.

212. As Alcott freely acknowledged, *Journals*, p. 511 (Aug. 23, 1879).

THE CONCORD SCHOOL OF PHILOSOPHY

213. Sanborn and Harris, *Alcott*, II, 507–8.

214. Alcott's *Journals*, p. 483.

215. For details regarding fees, bequests, attendance records, length and dates of sessions and other pertinent data, see Sanborn and Harris, *Alcott*, I, 532–33; F. B. Sanborn (ed.), *The Genius and Character of Emerson. Lectures at the Concord School of Philosophy* (Boston, 1884), Preface; Snider, *St. Louis Movement*, pp. 350–75, 521–35; and my *New England Transcendentalism and St. Louis Hegelianism*, pp. 79–110, 136–43. The programs were regularly publicized in the *Journal of Speculative Philosophy*.

216. Alcott's *Journals*, pp. 496–98 (July 15–18, 1879).

217. See Lilian Whiting, *Boston Days . . .* (Boston, 1902), p. 175.

218. *Journals*, pp. 499, 500, 502, 503, 505.

219. See *JoSP*, XIV, i (Jan., 1880), 138; also ii (Apr., 1880), 251–53, and F. B. Sanborn (ed.), *op. cit.*, pp. xii–xiii.

220. The chief participants in this most distinctive feature of the third school were Mrs. Julia Ward Howe, the Rev. C. A. Bartol, Mr. J. E. Cabot, Presidents Noah Porter of Yale and John Bascom of Wisconsin, and Professors F. H. Hedge, George S. Morris, J. W. Means, and John Watson. For the program, see *JoSP*, XV, i (Jan., 1881), 76–77, and for Secretary Sanborn's reports, *ibid.*, iii (July, 1881), 303–20.

221. It is hard to imagine Harris sitting

through this perversion of Kantian terms without wincing. What might have happened if Brokmeyer had been present is interesting to speculate upon. But Harris and Snider had settled between them the question whether Brokmeyer should be invited to Concord by deciding emphatically, "It cannot be done, it cannot be done! . . . he would be sure to spill over in some diablery, or even profanity, which would shock all New England." The newspapers had already found enough to caricature without Brokmeyer's contributing any choice morsels. —Snider, *St. Louis Movement*, p. 282.

222. Here it may be observed (1) that Alcott paid scant attention to Kant's careful distinctions between *a posteriori* and *a priori* methods, and (2) that his easy identifications of Kant with Huxley in method and of practical reason with conscience and faith involve the same misconceptions that had persistently plagued the Transcendentalists in their efforts to cite Kant as authority for their affirmations.

Alcott went on to explain why Kant "merely shows the infirmity of reason by itself," and hence "settles nothing satisfactorily"; while the practical reason (identified with "the moral sentiment, conscience, the voice of God, and the Holy Spirit") "extends its horizon wider and wider under the illumination, the inspiration of faith."

At this point Harris might well have interrupted to remind Alcott of Kant's distinction between *"transcendental* knowledge" and *"transcendent* illusions," but Harris was not one to cross Alcott or to bring his Dean into ridicule.

223. *JoSP*, XV, iii (July, 1881), 305.

224. Alcott's *Journals*, pp. 497, 536.

225. *JoSP*, XV, iii (July, 1881), 306. The comment about Kant's supplying "the step that was . . . to take us out of our senses" was, of course, an unintentional witticism that probably went unmarked; but we may be sure that if either Brokmeyer or Snider had been present, one or the other would have improved the occasion to indulge in a little wordplay.

226. *Ibid.*, pp. 307–12.

227. *Ibid.*, pp. 312–14.

228. He went on to argue for catholicity, embracing (1) Kant, regarding whom, he said, we have "heard many things" throughout the week; (2) Fichte, "concerning whom we shall hear a paper next week by Mr. Edwin D. Mead"; (3) Schelling, whose influence Emerson had done something to spread through his reports in the *Dial*, supplied to him directly from Germany by Mr. Charles Stearns Wheeler and also by direct contact with J. E. Cabot, and (4) Hegel, of whom, "of course, we have heard much."—*Ibid.*, pp. 317–19.

229. *Ibid.*, pp. 319–20.

230. The Concordians missed, by precisely a month, the honor of being the first to hold a Kant celebration in America. Professor J. W. Mears of Hamilton College was responsible for arranging the first Kant centennial, observed in the parlor of the Temple Grove Hotel at Saratoga, N.Y., on July 6–7. For the names of the participants and other details see *JoSP*, XV, iii (July, 1881), 293–302.

The program comprised the following papers: (1) J. W. Mears, "Significance of the Centennial," (2) G. S. Morris, "The Higher Problems of Philosophy," (3) President John Bascom, "Kant's Distinction between Speculative and Practical Reason," (4) Josiah Royce, "A Critique of the *Critique*," (5) Lester F. Ward, of the U.S. Geological Survey, "The Antinomies of Kant in Relation to Modern Science," and (6) W. T. Harris, "The Relations of Kant's Kritik to Ancient and Modern Thought." The discussion the papers provoked was no less lively than at Concord. The report (in *JoSP*) reproduced twenty-five congratulatory letters elicited by the occasion from prominent professors, theologians, and other representative men. Only two were negative in spirit. Professor B. N. Martin of New York University felt that "the incompleteness of his [Kant's] work was so great a drawback upon its usefulness" that he "could never refer to it with enthusiasm" (*ibid.*, pp. 299–300); while the great McCosh, pleading a prior engagement, regretted his inability to show his "reverence for Kant . . . by attending," and closed with the profundity, "You know that I hold . . . that the American student should labor to take from Kant all that is natural and true, and reject all that is artificial and false."—*Ibid.*, p. 302.

231. Still greater diversity and breadth was sought by having Sanborn deliver three lectures on oracular philosophy; Watson, three on Kant, Schelling, and Fichte; and Kedney, four on the philosophy of aesthetics; while among the special lecturers who gave only one discourse at this session were Alex. Wilder of Newark (editor of the *Journal of the American Akademe*), who spoke on Alexandrian Platonism, Noah Porter on Kantian ethics, James McCosh on the Scottish philosophy, G. H. Howison on German philosophy since Hegel, R. A. Holland on Atomism, C. A. Bartol on the Nature of Knowledge, and R. G. Hazard on the Utility of the Metaphysical Pursuits.—F. B. Sanborn (ed.), *op cit.*, pp. xv–xvi. For other lecturers and their subjects at this session, see *ibid.*, pp. xvi–xviii. Several of the lectures of the fourth school (1882) were reproduced and others abstracted in an "unofficial" but "authorized"

publication prepared by R. L. Brightman, entitled *The Concord Lectures on Philosophy* (Cambridge, Mass., 1883). See also *JoSP.*, XVII, iii (July, 1883), 317.

232. *Journal*, p. 432 (Mar. 8, 1882).

233. For the subjects of "special" lectures in this session, see *JoSP*, XVII, ii (Apr., 1883), 214–15, and F. B. Sanborn (ed.), *op. cit.*, p. xviii.

234. This literary tendency was further accentuated in lectures by Miss Elizabeth P. Peabody on "Milton's *Paradise Lost*," John Albee on "The Norman Influence in English Language and Literature," Edwin D. Mead on "Carlyle and Emerson," Mrs. Julia W. Howe on "Margaret Fuller," Julian Hawthorne on "The Novel," Mrs. Cheney on "Hindu Literature," Dr. Kedney on "Art Appreciation" and on "The Higher Criticism," and H. G. O. Blake's customary readings from Thoreau's manuscripts.—Sanborn, *op. cit.*, p. xviii; *JoSP*, XVII, ii (Apr., 1883), 214–15; iii (July, 1883), 317–22.

235. What he refers to is that in 1881 "the two main threads of the School" were then most harmoniously "spun alongside of each other by those two ardent philosophic spinners, Dr. Harris and Dr. Jones." Even then he "often heard the whispered decision: 'Dr. Harris has taken intellectual possession of the School.'"—*St. Louis Movement*, pp. 307–8. As we have seen, Jones retired the next year.

236. The discourses on Emerson were edited by Sanborn under the title, *The Genius and Character of Emerson* (Boston, 1884).

237. For details, see *JoSP*, XIX, ii (Apr., 1885), 220–21; Sanborn (ed.), *The Life and Character of Goethe . . .* (Boston, 1886), pp. xxiii–xxiv. A similar volume grew out of the Goethe School in Milwaukee (1886): Marion V. Dudley (ed.), *Poetry and Philosophy of Goethe . . .* (Chicago, 1887). Unfortunately Brokmeyer's interesting but unexpected remarks on *Faust* were not deemed sufficiently canonical for publication.

238. Sanborn (ed.), *Emerson*, p. xxi.

239. Sanborn (ed.), *Goethe*, pp. v–xxiii; *JoSP*, XX, iv (Oct., 1886), 426–443.

240. Snider, *St. Louis Movement*, 272–73, 274–75, 521–22.

241. He also manifestly enjoyed the story about the romantic young couple, walking in the Walden woods, who became so entangled in their discussion of the philosophy of love that the young lady exclaimed to her suitor, "Pshaw! You are no philosopher, else you would understand the Yesness of my No!"— *Ibid.*, p. 275. Other choice bits of gossip are recorded *ibid.*, pp. 277, 287–89, 350–54, 522;

Austin Warren, "The Concord School of Philosophy," *New Engl. Quar.*, II, ii (Apr., 1929), 207–8, 211–12; and my *New England Transcendentalism and St. Louis Hegelianism*, p. 108.

242. In his own schools, where he was in sole charge, he educated his pupils during the off-season in smaller classes, which served also as recruiting stations for the larger annual schools. Snider felt that his Western schools were what the Eastern schools should have been.

243. Begun as a six-weeks school, the term was reduced to five weeks in 1880 and to four in 1882. Beginning in 1885 it varied from two to three weeks.

244. *JoSP*, II, i (1869), v.

245. Even while his personalism tended in the end to divert his Hegelianism into new channels, it is to be noted, as Odell Shepard has observed (*Pedlar's Progress*, 484, 494–95) that the doctrine of personalism had been given some development as well as currency by both Alcott and the St. Louisans long before Howison and Borden Parker Bowne gave it more precise form and application. There is enough similarity between the "personal idealism" of Howison and Bowne, on the one hand, and Alcott's doctrine of Personality and the theories current among the St. Louis philosophers, on the other, to suggest more than a casual relationship. All agreed upon a doctrine which regards ultimate reality of the world as incorporate in a Divine Person who "sustains the universe by a continuous act of creative will." Thus they achieved a mediate position between the absolutism of Hegelian idealism and its antithetical philosophies of agnosticism, positivism, materialism, and naturalism. The various ramifications are as yet far from clear, but as investigation into the origin and sources of personalism progresses, it is not improbable that what Whitman spoke of vaguely and Howison and Bowne more coherently as "Personalism" will be found to stem, at least in part, from Alcott's doctrine and from the theories of the St. Louis Hegelians. If that be true, we shall be able to point to another cyclic progression of thought and influence deriving basically from New England Transcendentalism, joining forces with elements of Western Hegelianism, given a new direction by Howison, eventually turning eastward, and, in individuals like Bowne, Royce, and even Creighton (each of whom had meanwhile drawn from sources in Germany), finding a new orientation and articulation in the East.

246. He wrote for the *Journal of Speculative Philosophy* and participated in the Concord and other schools. As a professor at Johns Hopkins and Michigan he became widely known as a

champion of Hegel and Kant, and he became an active co-worker with Harris in publishing the distinguished "Griggs Philosophical Series" of German philosophy. Besides Harris and Morris, John Dewey, C. C. Everett, Noah Porter, John Watson, and J. S. Kedney contributed to the series. Morris' translation of Ueberweg's *History of Philosophy* in 1873 marks an epoch in the history of philosophy in America.

247. *Collected Papers* (6 vols., Cambridge, Mass., 1931–1935), I, 18, 42.

248. All these relationships are discussed in more detail below.

249. Jean Wahl, *The Pluralist Philosophers of England and America* (London, 1925), p. 62, 192; *Letters of William James*, ed. by Henry James (2 vols., Boston, 1920), I 94–95, 208, 265.

250. Francis B. Harmon, *The Social Philosophy of the St. Louis Hegelians* (N.Y., 1943), p. 104.

251. *Writings of Walt Whitman* (10 vols., N.Y., 1902), IV, 322; IX, 170.

GERMAN PHILOSOPHY IN AMERICAN COLLEGES

252. For Locke's tremendous vogue, see Merle Curti, "The Great Mr. Locke: America's Philosopher, 1783–1861," *Huntington Lib. Quar.*, XI (1937), 107–51, and for the earlier period, Benjamin Rand, "Philosophical Instruction in Harvard University from 1636 to 1900," *Harvard Graduates' Mag.*, XXXVII (Sept., 1928), 35, 46–47ff.

253. Just when the influx of new texts by Scottish authors was at its height is not readily ascertainable, but the records of college curricula in the early decades of the century show that they were in general use by 1810, and that they held a dominant position until long after 1850. In 1827 at the College of Rhode Island (now Brown University, a Presbyterian establishment modeled after Princeton) the students read Kames's *Elements of Criticism*, Stewart's *Philosophy of the Mind*, Levi Hedge's *Logic*, Butler's *Analogy*, and Paley.—Louis F. Snow, *The College Curriculum in the United States* (Columbia Univ. Diss., N.Y., 1907), p. 122. At Hamilton College in 1813–1816, the course included Ferguson's *Civil Society*, Alex. Tytler's *Elements of History*, Duncan's *Logic*, Paley's *Moral Philosophy*, Kames's *Elements*, Paley's *Evidences of Natural and Revealed Religion*, and, again, Butler's *Analogy*.—*Documentary History of Hamilton College* (Clinton, N.Y., 1922), pp. 143–44. Washington and Lee, to pick another example from another section of the country, in 1842, required of its seniors Whately's *Logic*, Blair's *Rhetoric* and *Criticism*, Tytler's *History*,

Upham's *Abridgment of Mental Philosophy*, Paley on *Moral and Political Philosophy*, and Alexander's *Evidences of Natural and Revealed Religion.*—Wm. H. Ruffner, "The History of Washington College 1830–1848," *Wash. and Lee Univ. Hist. Papers*, VI (1904), 52–53. Professor Levi Hedge, who began teaching at Harvard in 1795, taught from 1820 to 1827 Stewart's *Philosophy of the Mind*, Paley's *Moral Philosophy*, Locke's *Essay*, and logic from his own textbook. At the same time Professor Frisbie gave a course to the seniors in intellectual philosophy and political economy and employed Brown's *Lectures on the Philosophy of the Mind*, Gay's *Political Economy*, and, in the course on natural religion, Paley's *Evidences* and Butler's *Analogy.*—Rand, *loc. cit.*, pp. 44–45.

The reasons for the ready acceptance of Reid, Stewart, Brown, and Hamilton lie in the American temperament and the nature of the compromise deemed necessary between theology and philosophy. Scottish "realism" was considered in harmony with the practical note of the country, and, more important, it was regarded an aid to faith and a safeguard to morality as against the skepticism of Hume and the atheism of the Voltairians. It accorded well with the needs of ecclesiastical orthodoxy, and its appeal to common sense made it easy to teach, putting it within the range of abilities of the busy college president who, besides discharging his many stated duties, was generally in charge also of the teaching of philosophy. The Scottish realism, as Riley has pointed out, was taught by men who took philosophy seriously but not speculatively. It was the one common ground on which the various protestant denominations that had established schools in America could best agree.—I. W. Riley, *American Thought from Puritanism to Pragmatism and Beyond* (N.Y., 1923), p. 119.

254. To be sure, early generations of students at Harvard and Yale studied Keckermann on logic, physics, and mathematics and consulted Wollebius' digest of theology, Alsted's encyclopedia, and Buxtorf's Hebrew grammer; but there was very little direct connection between the early use of these standard productions of German scholarship and the nineteenth-century concern with post-Kantian thought.

255. Alvin S. Haag suggests that men like John C. Kunze, John H. Dreyer, Will, Helmuth and Hendel, some of whom lived in New York, knew something about Kant.—"Some German Influences in American Philosophical Thought from 1800 to 1850" (Boston University Diss., 1939; typescript), pp. 8–9, 104–5, 193.

256. Educated at Marburg and Heidelberg,

Gros transmitted to America the system of scholastic philosophy then being taught by German theologians. His text, *Natural Principles of Rectitude* (1795), noteworthy as a "classic statement of scholastic psychology," was limited in its influence because it expounded an outmoded system. See Jay W. Fay, *American Psychology before William James* (New Brunswick, N. J., 1939), pp. 52, 53–58, 185n.; Snow, *op. cit.*, pp. 98–99; Anna Haddow, *Political Science in American Colleges and Universities, 1636–1900* (N.Y., 1939), pp. 65–67.

257. Cooper, an extreme rationalist and deist in 1812 argued before a college audience the necessity of physiology as a part of philosophic training, recommending among others the works of Albrecht von Haller, Blumenbach, and Leibnitz.—*Introductory Lecture of Thomas Cooper, Esq., Professor of Chemistry at Carlisle College* (Carlisle, Pa., 1934), pp. 176–77.

258. For an account of the investigation and its results, see Leonard Woods, *History of the Andover Theological Seminary* (Boston, 1885), pp. 152, 173–76. Not improbably, the formal investigation facilitated rather than suppressed the vogue of the Germans.

At the College of New Jersey (Princeton), long the stronghold of orthodoxy, Professors Alexander and Dod in 1840 wrote an account of New England Transcendentalism and its sources in support of Andrews Norton at the time of the Norton-Ripley controversy. Charles Hodge, of the Princeton Theological Seminary and founder and editor of the *Princeton Review*, who had studied in Paris, Halle, and Berlin, lent his support to the defenders of orthodoxy; on the other side appeared Andrew Preston Peabody and Theodore Parker. Characteristic of the stubborn resistance found in American colleges are the attack by I. N. Tarbox of Hamilton College on the Germans and the distrust voiced in 1848 by Noah Porter of the "foreign look" of Coleridge and the German "skeptics" back of him. See I. N. Tarbox, *An Address on the Origin, Progress, and Present Condition of Philosophy* (Utica, N.Y., 1845), and Porter's "Coleridge and His American Disciples," *Bibliotheca Sacra*, IV, i (Feb., 1847), 117–71.

259. For the influence of Woods and, to a lesser extent, of Moses Stuart in directing Smith to Germany, see Lewis F. Stearns, *Henry Boynton Smith* (Boston and N.Y., 1892), p. 20.

Woods's translation of George Christian Knapp's *Lectures on Christian Theology* was published in 1831, together with a thirteen-page preface presenting an appreciative account of the rise of the Halle school of theologians, with whom Knapp identified himself. The trans-

lation went through several British editions and was reprinted in Philadelphia as the "Second American Edition . . . from the last London edition" of 1854.

260. Remaining in Germany until 1840, Smith met many famous theological teachers, among them Tholuck of Halle, who helped stem the tide of rationalism then rife in the German universities. In Berlin he studied under Neander, Trendelenberg, Hengstenberg, and Schleiermacher. He became a close friend of Frau Hegel, widow of the philosopher, though he never subscribed entirely to the Hegelian system. On his return to America, he was much in the company of Moses Stuart and was on terms of familiarity with several of the New England Transcendentalists. However, he felt that some of the excesses and vagueness of Transcendentalism stood in need of correction, and he differed with them on ideological grounds, finding their theism inadequate.

261. See Elizabeth L. Smith, *Henry Boynton Smith, His Life and Work* (N.Y., 1881), p. 124.

262. *Bibliotheca Sacra*, II, ii (Apr., 1845), 260–90. His more important publications include *Textbooks of Church History* (5 vols., 1855–1879); a translation and revision of J. K. L. Gieseler's *Textbook of the History of Doctrine* (2 vols., 1861–1862); a revision and enlargement of a work by Karl R. Hagenbach; and his own *Relations of Faith and Philosophy* (1849) and *The Problem of the Philosophy of History* (1853).

263. See R. M. Wenley, *The Life and Work of George Sylvester Morris*, (N.Y., 1917), pp. 88, 91, 96, 153, 208, 213–23. Smith's career shows that the time had not yet come in seminaries like Union for the fullest reconciliation of German speculative thought and American Protestant tradition. While sufficiently well trained, Smith failed, or rather, abandoned the effort to reconcile "the present knowledge of nature and history with the religious faith handed down in the Church."—*Ibid.*, p. 209. Always dominated by a theological outlook, he labeled the thoroughgoing philosophical systems of theology as pantheistic. He regarded the "mediating theology" of Schleiermacher as the main phenomenon of German theology, and was stimulated by Neander and Twesten, both disciples of Schleiermacher, as well as by that "notable representative of the 'new orthodoxy' in Germany, Hengstenberg."—*Ibid.*, p. 195. He was also influenced by the theism of Trendelenberg and Ulrici, of Berlin and Halle; and with Tholuck, "perhaps the most representative member of the Conciliation or Mediating School of Theology," he was on terms of close personal friendship. Unlike Parker and the Transcendentalists,

he was "thoroughly scared" by developments in the Hegelian left wing, by Strauss particularly.—*Ibid.*, p. 212. See Haag, *op. cit.*, pp. 207–19, for the fullest treatment available of Smith's career.

264. *The Method and Influence of Theological Studies. A Discourse [at] the University of Vermont, August 5, 1845* (Burlington, 1845), p. 37.

265. *Orthodoxy and Heterodoxy* (N.Y., 1893), p. 159. See *ibid.*, pp. 154–61, for his later rejection *in toto* of the tendency to deny revelation and the miracles, as well as the fallibility and late origin of the Bible.

266. (1) *Eloquence and Virtue: Or, Outlines of a Systematic Rhetoric; from the German of Dr. Francis Theremin* (N.Y., 1850; Andover, 1854, 1859); (2) *A Manual of Church History, from the German of Dr. Henry E. F. Guericke* (Edinburgh, 1857; Andover, 1863); (3) "Introduction to the Christian Element in Plato and the Platonic Philosophy," translated from the German of D. C. Ackermann and included in Shedd's edition of Coleridge's works; (4) *The Gospel According to Mark*, by John Peter Lange, revised from the Edinburgh translation, with additions by Shedd (4th ed., N.Y., 1869).

267. The work of Dr. Kunze, Rev. John H. Dreyer, and Charles Rudolph Demme (an immigrant in 1818 and former student at Göttingen and Halle) was probably of minor influence in the English-speaking part of the country. Gettysburg, Hartwick, Union, and Newton among the seminaries were most notable for their early use of German scholarship.—Haag, *op. cit.*, pp. 112–13, 193.

268. A Prussian-born Zwinglian who studied at Heidelberg and Marburg, taking his Ph.D. degree at the latter university, he was called to Giessen as *Privatdozent* and was serving as Professor *Extraordinarius* when he decided to go to America. He first taught at Lafayette College at Mercersburg and served as president of Marshall College from 1836 to his death.

269. Harvey G. Townsend, *Philosophical Ideas in the United States* (N.Y., 1934), pp. 81–82.

270. Haag, *op. cit.*, pp. 172–73; *DAB*, XV, 389–90.

271. Haag, *op. cit.*, pp. 196, 200.

272. *Ibid.*, pp. 183–85.

273. See George L. Prentiss, *The Union Theological Seminary in the City of New York: Historical and Biographical Sketches* (N.Y., 1889), pp. 88–92; Haag, *op. cit.*, p. 31n.

274. Among the more important are the following: Henry N. Day's *Fundamental Philosophy from Krug* (1848); Emmanuel V. Gerhart's *Introduction to the Study of Philosophy* (1858); Louis Bautain's *Epitome of the History of Philosophy*, tr. by Caleb H. Sprague (1841); Wm. G. Tennemann's *Grundriss der Geschichte der Philosophie*, tr. by A. Johnson (Oxford, 1832), and a revised and enlarged translation by J. R. Morrell (Bohn Lib., London, 1852); Kant's *Religion within the Bounds of Pure Reason*, tr. by J. W. Semple (1838); Kant's *Kritik der reinen Vernunft*, tr. by F. Haywood (1838); Heeren's *Ancient Greece*, tr. by George Bancroft (1823); John B. Stallo's *General Principles of the Philosophy of Nature. Digest of Schelling, Hegel, Oken* (1848); De Wette's *Theodore; or, the Mystic's Conversion. History of the Conversion of a Protestant Clergyman*, tr. by J. F. Clarke (2 vols., 1841); and Samuel Osgood's translation of De Wette's *Human Life, or Practical Ethics* (2 vols., 1842).

Other works, chiefly of French derivation, which incorporated a great deal of German thought, sometimes in diluted form, include (1) Henning G. Linberg's translation of Cousin's *Introduction to the History of Philosophy* (1832); (2) Caleb S. Henry's translation of Cousin's *Elements of Psychology* (1834); (3) George Ripley's *Philosophical Miscellanies, Translated from the French of Cousin, Jouffroy, and Constant* (2 vols., 1838); (4) W. H. Channing's translation of Jouffroy's *Introduction to Ethics* (2 vols., 1841–1842); (5) J. C. Daniel's translation of Cousin's *Philosophy of the Beautiful* (1842); (6) O. W. Wight's rendition of Cousin's *Course of the History of Modern Philosophy* (2 vols., 1852; repr., 1854, 1861, 1866, 1869, 1877, 1879); (7) O. W. Wight's translation of Cousin's *Lectures of the True, the Beautiful, and the Good* (1854; enl. ed., 1861; repr., 1866, 1879); and (8) R. N. Tappan's translation of Jouffroy's *Moral Philosophy* (1862). To these might be added as books of reference in common use by the 1840's (1) De Gerando's *Histoire comparée des systèmes de Philosophie* and (2) Barchou de Penhoen's *Histoire de la Philosophie allemande depuis Leibnitz jusqu'à Hegel.*

W. H. Channing's translation of Jouffroy's *Introduction to Ethics* was used by James Walker as a text at Harvard from 1840 to 1850 (Rand, *loc. cit.*, pp. 190–91), and Bowen used Linberg's translation of Cousin's *Elements of Psychology* as early as 1845–1846 and as late as 1870–1871 (*ibid.*, pp. 194, 198–99). The latter became a favorite text in many other American colleges. It reached a fourth edition in 1856, the second (N.Y., 1838) having been especially prepared for use in colleges. Bowen, more than anybody else among the academicians of the time, was responsible for the vogue of the French eclectics and, through them, of the German transcendentalists, although he subsequently introduced students in his classes directly to German philosophical works in the original.

275. Of the two works that dominated the field during the earlier decades of the century, Hedge followed the Scottish realists and Whately was interested in restoring the Aristotelian *Organon*; but thereafter (as Townsend has observed, *op. cit.*, pp. 101–2) men like Walker, Bowen, Coppée, McCosh, Wayland, and Porter, even while still in the tradition of British thought, were all in varying degrees influenced by German romantic philosophy.

276. See Preface, pp. vi–vii. In his paper of 1837 on Locke and the Transcendentalists he had defended vigorously the achievements of Locke against the derogations of the New England idealists. He wrote then of the "diseased imagination" of everything stemming from Germany and of the "midsummer madness" and the "German mania" then manifested by American disciples. But by 1839 Bowen had undertaken to study the Germans, and his article on Kant in the *North American Review* for that year (XLIV, civ, 44–68) is a decidedly more moderate and profounder critique. It still reveals a disinclination to follow Kant, but it is designed to put his ideas in a fair light. Between 1839 and 1841 he visited Europe and devoted some time in Germany to the acquisition of firsthand information on the German philosophers (Rand, *loc. cit.*, p. 194). In the Preface to his *Logic* (1865) he still objects to Kant's "dogmatism and unbelief," but he is ready to admit that Kant's criticism "formed hardly less an era in the history of Logic than in that of Metaphysics" (Preface, pp. iv–v). Bowen's own book is eclectic, depending on Hamilton (himself a borrower from Kant and Lotze), Kiesewetter, Fries, Beneke, Dressler, and Drobisch, among others. Adjusting his courses to the principles of the elective system instituted by Eliot in 1869, Bowen, from 1870 to 1889, turned his attention more and more to continental philosophy, until in the end it received the larger share. Even in 1868–1869, an elective section of the senior class recited three times a week in Schwegler's *History of Philosophy*, translated by J. H. Seelye in 1856. In 1869–1870 the same class studied Schwegler and Kant's first *Critique*. Bowen became in reality the first professor to teach the history of philosophy at Harvard.

277. Attacking both idealism and materialism, Tappan, like Hickok a few years later, had recourse to the works of Coleridge and Kant, and finally attached to himself the label "Transcendentalist," by which he meant that he placed value on immediate intuition as opposed to Lockean sensationalism. He followed closely the Kantian distinction between synthetical and analytical, *a priori* and *a posteriori*, but defined Reason very loosely. See his *Elements of Logic*, (N.Y., 1844), 30–31, 42–49, 60, 66–67; also Fay, *op. cit.*, pp. 75–76, 110–11.

278. The odium attaching to Kant as tending toward skepticism did not attach to Lotze, who "tried to give a new turn to logic by urging that its object was not ultimately concerned with *a priori* noetic elements, or stoichiology," as Hamilton had charged. Instead of being analytic, he method was synthetic, his task being to work out and put together a system of coherent conclusions which would appear as self-evident by a criterion that was at bottom aesthetic and that would circumvent the idolatry of experience and skepticism.—G. S. Hall, *loc. cit.*, p. 150.

279. For an account of how the study of political science, law, and economics developed out of the common matrix of moral philosophy as taught in American colleges (under the aegis, first, of Grotius and Pufendorf and, later, of Locke and Hutcheson), see Anna Haddow, *Political Science in American Colleges, 1636–1900* (N.Y., 1939), pp. 1–82.

280. Eighteenth-century texts approached the study of ethics from the theological point of view, teaching that virtue consists in likeness to God. By a slow transition, lasting until the midnineteenth century, the concept of morality as a code revealed in Scripture was transformed into the concept that morality is best studied "in the innate intuitions and sentiments of men." This humanizing process, as Hall points out, was effected by the Scottish schools in conjunction with the teaching of Shaftesbury and the Cambridge Platonists. Jouffroy's *Introduction to Ethics* (translated by W.H. Channing in 1842), with its historical account of the English, French, and German schools, gave added impetus to the study of ethics and particularly to the more humanistic interpretation of it.

281. The ethical theories of the French and German writers were presented by Walker chiefly for the purpose of historical information. In the years 1850 to 1857, when ethics received his chief attention, he used Stewart as a text. In the above-mentioned list he included, however, Kant's *Grundlegung zur Metaphysik der Sitten* and *Kritik der praktischen Vernunft* (available in English translation by J. W. Semple, 1838), Schleiermacher's *Entwurf eines Systems der Sittenlehre*, and Hegel's *Grundlinien der Philosophie des Rechts*.—Rand, *Harv. Grad. Mag.* (Dec., 1928), pp. 190–91.

282. Hickok's system of ethics was widely influential in its day, being used at Mt. Holyoke

Seminary, Minnesota, and Wisconsin in the seventies and eighties.

283. Mark Hopkins, *Lectures on Moral Science* (Boston, 1862), p. viii.

284. George P. Schmidt, *The Old Time College President* (N.Y., 1930), pp. 122-23.

285. Just as in the fields of logic and ethics, the conservatives in the main did not quite ignore idealism but rather made their defense against it as best they could, so in the field of metaphysics. This important change took place about the middle of the nineteenth century— about the time when Transcendentalism was actively reaching beyond the confines of Boston and Concord and making converts wherever Emerson and Alcott spread the doctrine by lectures, and others like Clarke and Parker, carried it through their contributions in the periodicals.

286. Texts most generally used were Stewart's *Philosophy of Mind* (1828), Abercrombie's *Intellectual Powers* (1830), Upham's *Mental Philosophy* (1831), Rauch's *Psychology* (1840), Schmucker's *Psychology* (1842), Hickok's *Rational Psychology* (1848) and *Empirical Psychology* (1854), Wayland's *Elements of Intellectual Philosophy* (1854), Mahan's *System of Intellectual Philosophy* (1854), Haven's *Mental Philosophy* (1857), Porter's *On the Intellect* (1868), and Bascom's *Psychology* (1869). All these texts, except Stewart's and Abercrombie's, acknowledge a greater or lesser indebtedness to German speculation. In certain cases they adopt the Kantian terminology, and in the cases of Hickok and Mahan, go so far as to attempt a harmony of the German and Scottish points of view as well as terminology.

287. Widely read in ancient, British, and Continental sources, Upham was also a student of German scholarship, his first published work being a translation from Latin of Jahn's *Biblical Archaeology* (1823). Various stories are related of his early struggles with Kant, but it appears that his tripartite division of the faculties was derived not directly from Kant but from Asa Burton's *Essay on Some of the First Principles of Metaphysics* (1824).—Fay, *op. cit.*, pp. 91-109, 183, n. 57; *DAB*, XIX, 123-24.

288. Fay, *op. cit.*, pp. 125, 207, n. 159; Haag, *op. cit.*, p. 221.

289. A graduate of Union College, at Schenectady, he became Professor of Christian Theology at Western Reserve in 1836, moved thence to Auburn Theological Seminary, and finally in 1852 to Union College to become Professor of Mental and Moral Philosophy, and President in 1866.

290. *DAB*, IX, 5-6; Fay, *op. cit.*, pp. 120-25.

291. In this "super-Kantian transcendentalism" he stressed the "constructive" powers of the mind. See Fay, *op. cit.*, p. 91, and W. T. Harris' review of Hickok's *Creator and Creation* (1872) in the *Journal of Speculative Philosophy*, VI, iv (Oct., 1872), 383-84. "Accepting the current of distinction between the faculties of the sensibility, understanding, and reason, Hickok credited the reason with an intuitive insight of 'comprehension' altogether different from the discursive procedure of the understanding."—*DAB*, IX, 5-6.

292. First published, N.Y., 1854; 2nd ed., N.Y., 1857; rev. ed., Boston, 1882. It was used at Beloit College, for example, from 1866 to 1896, in the classes of Professor James J. Blaisdell, a man known as an absolute idealist, a "Christian philosopher," who rejected both realism and pragmatism. See Ed. D. Eaton, *Historical Sketches of Beloit College* (N.Y., 1928), p. 204. Hickok had other influential followers in the American academic tradition. His textbook in ethics was used as late as 1877 in Wisconsin in the classes of President Bascom. President J. H. Seelye, who held the chair of philosophy at Amherst from 1858 to 1895, was one of Hickok's staunchest allies. He believed "completely in the transcendental philosophy as presented by Dr. Hickok," and was himself a student of German as well as a translator. O. W. Wight, editor of philosophical books and in charge of philosophy at Hamilton College, dedicated one of his works to Hickok "as a token of the editor's admiration of one of the very ablest metaphysicians America has produced."—*The Philosophy of Sir William Hamilton*, arr. and ed. by O. W. Wight for Use in Schools and Colleges, (N.Y., 1853). It became customary to speak of Hickok as the "ablest dialectician of his day"—an opinion in which the Hegelian Harris, no mean dialectician himself, concurred. See his review of Hickok's *Logic of Reason, Universal and Eternal* (1875) in *JoSP*, IX, li (Apr., 1875), 222-23. Hickok and Harris exchanged letters in the next four numbers of the *Journal*, in which they set forth their differences in interpreting Kant's and Hegel's "Transcendental Logic," the conclusion of which was that while they differed on details, they agreed on essentials.

For an interesting statement of Hickok's plan for a comprehensive program of graduate study at Union College (which gave considerable emphasis to the idealist point of view), see his "The College Course and Its Enlargements for Graduates," *Bibliotheca Sacra*, X, i (Jan., 1853), 162.

293. Haven was by no means an idealist, but his tendency was to attempt the same bridging of the gap between contending philosophies

which was essayed by Hickok. His book is noteworthy for its clear, straightforward style and historical perspective, all of which made it a significant book not only in its own right but as offering a clear presentation of German idealism, including Kantian epistemology. Cf. Fay, *op. cit.*, pp. 126, 207, n. 162.

294. In the Preface to the edition of 1857 Mahan wrote: "The individuals for whom I feel most indebted as a philosopher are Coleridge, Cousin, and Kant—three luminaries of the first order." In later editions of *Intellectual Philosophy* (1854 and 1857), however, he described idealism as dangerous, because it builds on the "as if" basis and is therefore "subversive of all the principles of morality and religion."—Ed. of 1857, pp. 331–41, 388–90; see also the attack of Thomas C. Upham, Professor at Bowdoin, upon Transcendentalism, in his *Mental Philosophy* (1869), pp. 390–93.

In Mahan we have another case in which German thought colors an American philosophic point of view in certain particulars, but leaves him still unsympathetic to any total system of idealism. Toward the end of his career Mahan published a *Critical History of Philosophy* (2 vols., N.Y., 1883).

295. See Fay, *op. cit.*, pp. 146–47, 311, notes 26–29.

296. Symptomatic of what obtained in the larger schools is what took place at Harvard. In 1868–1869 Harvard had two professors of philosophy; twenty years later the corps of instructors was more than five times as large; for three courses in 1868–1869, there were twenty-four in 1896–1897. For schools like Brown, Williams, and Princeton, see their catalogs for the appropriate years; also A. C. Armstrong, Jr., "Philosophy in American Colleges," *Ed. Rev.*, XIII, i (Jan., 1897), 10–22; and George P. Adams and Wm. P. Montague (eds.), *Contemporary American Philosophy: Personal Statements* (2 vols., N.Y., 1930), I, 16, 20, 29–30.

297. Experimental psychology, which has since split off into an independent subject, accounted for a good part of the growth. Logic, now given less attention, if offered at all, became a part of the introductory course rather than a separate discipline for upperclassmen. Ethics as a subject gained in breadth and depth and occupied a relatively larger share of the student's time. Before 1900 there was only an insignificant amount of research in America in the history of philosophy, but it was recognized as a much needed development for the future. The course entitled Introduction to Philosophy came much into vogue. The material was ordinarily organized around special problems, and

the student was encouraged to work out his own belief after studying many different points of view. Courses in the Philosophy of Nature interpreting the meaning of evolutionary theory were sometimes offered; likewise a combination of ethics and the philosophy of religion. Some schools offered courses in rational psychology; in others the point of departure was the study of an epistemological or metaphysical problem; the larger schools treated psychology as a separate subject. It was introduced at Harvard in 1876, at Yale in 1881, at Princeton in 1883; Johns Hopkins established an experimental laboratory in 1881.—Armstrong, *loc. cit.*, pp. 15, 16–17, 19.

298. Rand, *loc. cit.*, pp. 195, 199.

299. In the Middle West such advocates of education reform as Calvin Stowe, Michael Frank, and the more enlightened German-American element (of Wisconsin, for instance), with their direct knowledge of the newest continental methods, had successfully pressed for the organization of elementary and secondary schools with modern features borrowed directly from Europe, and primarily from Prussia; but to President Tappan of Michigan goes the larger share of the credit for charting the plan of the future American university. In the years following his assumption of the presidency the successive calendars of Michigan carried the statement: "The system of Public Instruction adopted by the state of Michigan is copied from the Prussian, acknowledged to be the most perfect in the world."—Herbert Adams, "The Study of History in American Colleges and Universities," *Report of the Commissioner of Education for 1886–1887*, II, 89.

Tappan was an eastern-born Presbyterian clergyman of Dutch stock who had studied at Union College and Auburn Theological Seminary. Before coming to Michigan in 1852, he had made a name for himself as the author of speculative works on logic, the freedom of the will, the philosophy of university education. Between 1832 and 1839 he held the chair of intellectual philosophy at the University of the City of New York. From a firsthand acquaintance with continental higher schools, gained on a trip to Europe in 1852, he derived confirmation for the idea already made familiar to him through the writings of Cousin, Horace Mann, and a host of New England critics of the American college system, that American colleges, stagnating with their futile narrow perpetuation of the English organization and curriculum, needed to be shaken into a lively realization of the larger, broader cultural functions in the new age. Unlike so many critics of American colleges including, above all, Francis Wayland, who supported the idea that salvation lay in the direction of increased practicality (in the broadening of the curriculum to include science, modern languages, and professional schools), Tappan urged that the university should become the repository for the highest cultural and intellectual activity of the age, the refuge of men with the true scholarly spirit, an assemblage of disinterested, mature, disciplined students in every field of human endeavor; not a dispensary for that alone which is of immediate practical usefulness to the builders of Western commercial enterprise.

300. Henry P. Tappan, *University Education*, pp. 48–50, 68; Perry, *op. cit.*, pp. 222–23.

301. People ridiculed him for using the title of *Chancellor*, with its suggestion of the German *Kanzler*, instead of the term *President*, which to them seemed less foreign and arrogant. He drew to the faculty a number of German-trained men, probably no higher proportion than was to be found at Harvard at the time, but all of them chosen for broad humanistic capacities as inspiring teachers. As director of the Michigan observatory he called Dr. Brünnow from Berlin, a brilliant scientist, who shortly married Tappan's daughter. Beloved by his students, widely respected for his achievements in creating a foundation of such impressive solidarity and scope amidst the turmoil of frontier life, Tappan nevertheless had the defects of his greatness, and in his vision of an ideal failed to cope with petty but nonetheless important problems of day-by-day administration.

302. Jacob Gould Schurman (1854–1942), Cornell's third president, continued the policies of White. He spent two years in Berlin and Göttingen studying philosophy and later taught the subject in the newly founded Sage School of Philosophy at Ithaca, N.Y.

303. See Faust, *op. cit.*, II, 201–49; J. A. Walz, *German Influence in American Education and Culture* (Phila., 1936), pp. 43–56; C. F. Thwing, *The American and German University* (N.Y., 1928); B. A. Hinsdale, *loc. cit.*, I, 591–629; Herbert B. Adams, *loc. cit.*, II, 80ff. For acknowledgments of White's debt to continental models, see his *Autobiography* (2 vols., N.Y., 1905), I, 191, 272, 291.

304. G. S. Morris, "University Education," *Univ. of Mich. Philos. Papers*, 1st ser., No. 1 (Ann Arbor, 1886), pp. 38–39.

305. *JoSP*, XIII, iii (Oct., 1879), 398–99. It is to be noted, however, that Johns Hopkins under President Gilman appeared in the eyes of some to be "lukewarm towards philosophy"; that is to say, the school emphasized philology and laboratory sciences but appeared less in-

terested in supporting philosophy. See Fabian Franklin, *Life of Daniel Coit Gilman* (N.Y., 1910), p. 227. G. Stanley Hall, the herald of experimental psychology, and George S. Morris, representing speculative philosophy, were simultaneously invited to lecture at Johns Hopkins, both being "on trial for a chair" there. The decision went in favor of experimental psychology, and Hall was appointed, while Morris felt distinctly that the "times seemed against him," and not even Hopkins was sympathetic toward the idealism which Morris championed, and for which he subsequently labored at the University of Michigan. See R. W. Wenley, *op. cit.*, pp. 138–40, 147–53, for the influence of the conservative point of view on curricular reforms, and for the adoption of German educational practices, see Noah Porter, *The American Colleges and the American Public* (new ed., N.Y., 1878).

306. The progress made at Michigan and Hopkins is to be observed also at Columbia and Harvard. While in 1880–1881 Columbia had one professor of philosophy, ten years later there were four, sharing the fields of philosophy, psychology, ethics, and anthropology. The offerings in the graduate school were especially rich in the history of philosophy and were taught almost exclusively from texts by German authors. Among books used were Zeller's *Geschichte der griechischen Philosophie*, Ueberweg's *History of Philosophy* (Volume I of the Morris translation of 1871), Schwegler's *History of Philosophy*, Erdmann's *Geschichte der Philosophie*, and works of Harms, Kuno Fischer, Stöckl, Volkmann, Lotze, Hamilton, Sidgwick, Spencer, and von Hartmann. By 1894–1895 Columbia was using Zeller's *Outlines of Greek Philosophy*, Falckenberg's *History of Modern Philosophy*, and Windelband's *History of Philosophy* (in the Tufts translation of 1893). The graduate course was divided into three main divisions: The General History of Philosophy; the Philosophy of Kant and his Successors Fichte, Schelling, Hegel, Herbart, and Schopenhauer; and Contemporary Psychologists (using Wundt, Volkmann, Ribot, Münsterberg, James, and Baldwin as texts).—*A History of Columbia University, 1754–1904* (N.Y., 1904), pp. 278–99.

At Harvard in 1885–1886 the philosophical offerings were arranged in three groups according to degree of difficulty: (1) introductory courses; (2) advanced courses for undergraduates and graduates, including (a) Systematic courses, (b) Historical courses—including Indian, Greek, French, German, and British, and (c) courses on individual men—including Kant, Hegel, and Lotze; and (3) Research courses for graduates and specialists (seminaries). A staff of three full-time professors and one assistant professor in 1885–1886 offered the following: (1) History of Philosophy. Ferrier's *Lectures on Greek Philosophy*. Outlines of Modern Philosophy. (2) Psychology and Logic. Bain's *The Senses and the Intellect*. Jevon's *Elementary Lessons in Logic*. (3) Elementary Philosophy in Connection with Ethical and Regious Questions. Royce's *Religious Aspects of Philosophy*. (4) Ethics. Earlier English Ethics. Mill's Utilitarianism. Kant's Theory of Ethics. Lectures and Theses. (5) English Philosophy. Locke, Berkeley, Hume. (6) Earlier French Philosophy from Descartes to Leibnitz and German Philosophy from Kant to Hegel. (7) German Philosophy of the Present Day. Schopenhauer's *Die Welt als Wille und Vorstellung*, Hartmann's *Philosophie des Unbewussten*. Lotze's *Metaphysic* (omitted 1885–1886). (8) Hegel's *Phänomenologie* (omitted 1885–1886). (9) Special Advanced Study and Experimental Research in Psychology. (10) Philosophy of Religion. (11) Practical Ethics of Modern Society. Studies in Social Reforms, Temperance, Charity, Labor, etc. (12) Philosophical Theism. History of the Chief Philosophical Controversies about the Being and Nature of God. Discussions and Theses (omitted 1885–1886). (13) Modern Discussion of the Philosophy of Nature. Spinoza. Modern Monism. Spencer's Theory of Evolution.—G. S. Morris, "University Education," *loc. cit.*, pp. 37–38.

307. For a succinct description of the typical college curriculum (in this case Amherst), see James H. Tufts, "What I Believe," in G. P. Adams and W. P. Montague (eds.), *Contemporary American Philosophy*, II, 336.

308. Small colleges continued to teach Butler's *Analogy* and Evidences of Natural Theology (using usually Hopkins' *Evidences*) throughout the period. At Beloit, for instance, the course in Evidences was kept until 1900–1901. —Ed. D. Eaton, *op. cit.*, p. 204. The history of philosophy was not introduced into Luther College (Decorah, Ia.) until 1912–1913. At the University of North Carolina in 1889 the course consisted of Christian Evidences, with electives in the history of philosophy and natural theology; while at Mount Holyoke in 1887 the offerings were Hickok's *Psychology* and *Ethics*, Moral Science, the History of Art (using the *Outlines from Lübke*), Theism and Christian Evidences, Studies from Fischer's *Grounds of Theistic and Christian Belief*, Wright's *Logic of Christian Evidences*, Butler's *Analogy*, and four years of Bible study (see Mrs. Sarah D. Stow, *op. cit.*, pp. 150ff.). Even at the new University of Chicago, still dominated during the nineties by men

trained in American theological seminaries, Evidences of Christianity and Apologetics were offered regularly.—Joseph Dorfman, *Thorstein Veblen and His America* (N.Y., 1934) p. 43. For the religious atmosphere at Hopkins in the late eighties see *ibid.*, pp. 38–49, 55.

Resistance to evolutionist and materialist thinkers was as strong as that against idealism. So long as it was possible, some larger schools like Yale continued to measure every doctrine that claimed a right to enter into the philosophical courses by the yardstick of Christian orthodoxy. See President Porter's testimony in *Fifteen Years in the Chapel of Yale College*, p. 382. The question of permitting Professor Wm. G. Sumner to use Spencer's *Study of Sociology* in the classroom occasioned a two-year-long controversy, in which President Porter assailed the work for its assumption of evolutionism, its implied attacks on theism, and its offences against good taste and decency.—Dorfman, *op. cit.*, p. 43.

309. See H. G. Townsend, *op. cit.*, pp. 103–4. In 1887 the Princeton offerings in philosophical electives were the following: History of Philosophy, Metaphysics, Science and Religion, Comparative Politics, International and Constitutional Law, Physiology and Psychology, Pedagogics, Archaeology, and History of Art. Mental Philosophy was required in the Junior year.—V. L. Collins, *Princeton* (N.Y., 1914), pp. 321, 323.

310. "Materialism in Germany," *Presby. Quar. and Princeton Rev.*, IV, ii (Apr., 1875), 273–305, esp. p. 283.

311. "The Scottish Philosophy, as Contrasted with the German," *Princeton Rev.*, n.s., X, iv (Nov., 1882), 326–44, esp. p. 337. See also his *Realistic Philosophy Defended in a Philosophic Series* (N.Y., 1887), pp. 16–18.

312. *Problems of Philosophy and Principles of Epistemology and Metaphysics* (N.Y., 1905), pp. vii–viii, 333.

313. "Atheism in Colleges," *North Amer. Rev.*, CXXXII, i (Jan., 1881), 32–35. The course at Wisconsin in 1877 included Deductive and Inductive Logic, under Professor Carpenter, and Psychology, Ethics, Aesthetics, and Natural Theology, under President Bascom, who used Jevon's and Fowler's logics, Hickok's *Ethics*, Chadbourne on Natural Theology, and Bascom's *Psychology* and *Science of Beauty*.— *JoSP*, XI, ii (Apr., 1877), 217.

As G. Stanley Hall observed in 1900, the Scottish philosophy continued to recommend itself to American conditions because it "held to an immediate conviction of right and wrong, nonsuited the whole question of reality, which was ascribed to immediate sense, and discussed in the most lucid way practical matters of association, desire, will, feelings, raising no quarrel with religion, and not unsettling the young . . . . Under President McCosh . . . it developed an amiable *mod..s vivendi* with the new psychology and with religion; it has given to education in this country about all the philosophic basis yet popularly recognized; and it has been in wholesome and fructifying rapport with practical life at every point."—"College Philosophy...," *Forum*, XXIX (Mar.–Aug., 1900), 409–22, esp. pp. 413–14.

314. Most important among these are George S. Morris, professor at Michigan and Hopkins, who studied in Berlin for two years after 1864; Julius H. Seelye, president and professor of philosophy at Amherst from 1858 to 1895, studied at Halle in 1852–1853; Josiah Royce, professor at Harvard, studied at Göttingen in 1876 and heard Lotze in Berlin; James McKeen Cattel, professor of psychology at Columbia after 1890, studied at Göttingen; Benj. E. Smith, second translator of Schwegler's *History of Philosophy* and editor of the *Century Dictionary*, studied at Göttingen in 1880–1881; Borden P. Bowne, professor of philosophy in Boston University and dean of the Graduate School after 1876, studied at Göttingen in 1875; G. Stanley Hall, president of Clark University and professor of psychology and pedagogy, spent six years as a student in various German institutions between 1870 and 1882; George W. Howison, lecturer in philosophy at Michigan and head of the Department of Philosophy at the University of California from 1884 to 1909, studied in Europe in 1880–1882, chiefly at Berlin; Henry B. Smith, professor at Union Theological Seminary between 1850 and 1874, studied philosophy, theology, and church history at Halle and Berlin in 1837–1838; and George M. Duncan, professor at Yale from 1888, studied under Wundt, Zeller, and Ribot. In addition there were the German-American Charles P. Krauth, professor of Intellectual and Moral Philosophy at the University of Pennsylvania, and the prominent German-born Hugo Münsterberg at Harvard.

315. At Virginia were Georg Blättermann and Schele de Vere, European-trained teachers of foreign languages. At South Carolina was Francis Lieber, who raised political ethics to the status of an independent study. At Cincinnati, later Detroit and New York, was the Hegelian Johann B. Stallo. At Cornell, Bayard Taylor, famous as an authority on German life and literature, was employed from 1870 to 1877 to lecture on German literature. At Amherst was John F. Genung (Ph.D., Leipzig), who taught rhetoric and English literature, and also H. B.

Richardson, German-educated professor of modern languages from 1869 to 1878. For numerous others who fall within this category, see A. B. Faust, *op. cit.*, II, 201–49, 672–76.

316. Sarah D. Stow, *op. cit.*, p. 249. Cook took for his aim in this course to "present the results of the freshest German, English, and American scholarship on the most important and difficult topics concerning the relation of Religion and Science."—*Boston Monday Lectures. Transcendentalism with Preludes on Current Events* (Boston, 1878). According to Hall, it was Cook who first made Lotze popular in this country. Cook followed Lotze's solution of the conflict between faith and science; but he was no careful student of metaphysics, and his "representation of Lotzianism was most unfortunately misleading"; yet he succeeded for a time in convincing the young clergy that the most recent discoveries actually confirmed the Biblical story.—G. S. Hall, *Founders of Modern Psychology*, pp. 94–96.

317. Stow, *op. cit.*, p. 249.

318. *JoSP*, i (Jan., 1877), 103–7.

319. See White's *Some Practical Influences of German Thought upon the United States*, Address delivered at the Centennial Celebration of the German Society, Held in New York, October 4, 1884; also *Seven Great Statesmen* (N.Y., 1910); and *Methods of Teaching History* (Symposium of White, C. K. Adams, R. T. Ely, and others, Volume I of the *Pedagogical Library*, ed. by G. Stanley Hall; 2nd ed., Boston, 1885).

320. Peirce had three articles in Volume II, Howison appeared in Volumes V, XV, XVII, and XIX; Hall in VI, VII, and XI; Morris in X, XI, XV, and XVII; Hickok in X; James in XII and XIII; Royce in XII and XV; and Dewey in XVI, XVII, and XVIII.

321. *Principles of Philosophy* (forming Volume I of *Collected Papers*, ed. by Charles Hartshorne and Paul Weiss, Cambridge, 1931), Preface, p. xi, and p. 6.

322. *Collected Papers*, V, 274. Regarding the Germanic derivation of Peirce's pragmatism, see John Dewey, "The Development of American Pragmatism," in *Studies in the History of Ideas*, II (N.Y., 1925), 351–77, esp. pp. 351–54. A good discussion of Peirce's relation to Kant and Hegel on the one hand and to Emerson and James on the other is to be found in Frederic I. Carpenter, "Charles Peirce, Pragmatist," *New Engl. Quar.*, XIV, i (Mar., 1941), 34–48.

323. See *Collected Papers*, I, 6. In the articles printed in 1868 in the *Journal of Speculative Philosophy*, Peirce stood apart from the movement to which the journal owed its existence. Not Hegel, nor Kant, but mathematical

science, medieval logic, and Descartes at that time provided his starting point. Yet "what is remarkable in all this is . . . the sureness with which Peirce . . . arrived for himself at what is essential in the teaching of Kant, the doctrine that 'the real object of knowledge is determined by mind.'" See J. H. Muirhead, "Peirce's Place in American Philosophy," *Philosophical Rev.*, XXXVII, v (Sept., 1928), 446. On the basis of Duns Scotus he formulated an independent definition of the meaning and place of universals in the being of things (*ibid.*, p. 477). This, Professor Muirhead points out, is not to be identified with what Royce, in agreement with Hegel, called the abstract universal, though there is a clear similarity between Peirce's conception and Royce's "concrete universals."

324. *Ibid.*, pp. 477–78. Unlike Hegel, Peirce was not willing to reduce all experience to thought and immediacy. "There was feeling and there was will. Nevertheless experience through which there does not run a thread of thought like a strain of music through notes is a mere confusion and no true experience of anything."

325. "The place of the thing-in-itself has been taken once for all by the thing at the determination of which we arrive when the process, as just described, has been brought to completeness in an exhaustive and harmonious experience. This for us must remain an ideal; for its existence *as an ideal* witnesses to our belief in a community of minds or in a common mind (Peirce believed that the one implies the other) in which it will one day be realized."

Muirhead points out that Peirce, while not willing to use this argument as a proof for the existence of a universal mind, to which all truth was already present, thought that Royce's attempt to take this further step was well worthy of consideration. "But he himself could see his way no farther than to appeal to the harmony which the belief in it brings into life both from the side of theory and from practice. Like Coleridge he did not believe that the being of God was demonstrable in any strict sense of the word, but like Coleridge he was ready to say 'assume it and all becomes clear.'"—*Ibid.*, pp. 478–79.

326. *Principles of Philosophy*, pp. 18, 42.

327. *Ibid.*, Preface, p. vii.

328. Muirhead, *loc. cit.*, p. 478.

329. See especially his *Principles of Philosophy*.

330. See H. G. Townsend, "The Pragmatism of Peirce and Hegel," *Philosophical Rev.*, XXXVIII, iv (July, 1928), 297–303.

331. *Ibid.*, p. 298. In *The Simplest Mathematics* (*Collected Papers*, IV, 6), he declared:

"Hegel, so far as I knew him through a book by Vera [Aug. Vera, author of *Introduction à la philosophie de Hegel*, Paris, 1855, and a frequent contributor to the *Journal of Speculative Philosophy*], repelled me."

332. Royce received the doctorate at Hopkins in 1878 and Dewey in 1884. Much of Dewey's early interest in Hegel can be traced to the teaching of Morris. See R. M. Wenley, *George S. Morris* (N.Y., 1917), 313–21.

333. After graduating at Dartmouth, he entered Union Theological Seminary and came under the influence of Henry B. Smith, who determined Morris' choice of professors when he went to Germany. Smith also urged him to make the translation of Ueberweg and secured for him a position at Bowdoin.—Wenley, *op. cit.*, pp. 88, 91, 96, 120, 153, 218. Following two years of study in Europe, mainly at Berlin under Trendelenberg, the Aristotelian, Morris began in 1870 to teach modern languages and literatures at the University of Michigan, where he remained until his death, except for a period of lecturing at Hopkins during 1877–1880. In 1881 he became a member of the Department of Philosophy at Michigan, becoming head in 1885. For further details, see Wenley.

334. See his article, "University Education," *Univ. of Mich. Philos. Papers*, 1st ser., No. 1 (Ann Arbor, 1886); also Wenley, *op. cit.*, pp. 308–26.

335. Besides the two works by Morris, the series (known as "Griggs' Philosophical Classics" from the name of the publisher, S. C. Griggs & Co., of Chicago) included the following, all edited to a uniform plan: (1) *Schelling's Transcendental Idealism*, by John Watson, 1882; (2) Fichte's *Science of Knowledge*, by C. C. Everett, 1884; (3) *Hegel's Æsthetics*, by J. S. Kedney, 1885; (4) *Kant's Ethics*, by Noah Porter, 1886; (5) Leibnitz' *New Essays Concerning the Human Understanding*, by W. T. Harris, 1890. The aim of the series, stated in the prospectus, was "especially to show, as occasion may require, in what way German thought contains the natural complement of the much-needed corrective, of British speculation."— G. S. Morris, *Kant's Critique of Pure Reason*, Preface, p. v; see also his *British Thought and Thinkers* (Chicago, 1880), the introductory chapter, esp. pp. 19–22.

336. Professor Wenley (*op. cit.*, pp. 321–23) observed that Morris' residence in Germany brought him into contact with the same group of older conservative teachers of whom Smith himself was the disciple. Smith could not answer the questions that disturbed Morris; neither could Smith's mentors. For a time, in the seventies, Morris tried to fall back on a

theory of the relation between Thought and Being advanced by Trendelenberg, though soon afterward he found it insufficient and internally inconsistent because of its eclectic character.

337. *Ibid.*, pp. 254–56.

338. *Ibid.*, pp. 271–72.

339. In his undergraduate work at Marietta College, he had heard the president lecture "brilliantly in support of the Baconian method, which might have been called his hobby, and against German *a priorism* and its results." See J. W. Buckham and J. M. Stratton, eds., *George Holmes Howison* . . . (Berkeley, Calif., 1934). In St. Louis about 1865 the stimulation of Brokmeyer and Harris turned him seriously to study the German idealists. From 1872 to 1878 he was professor of logic and philosophy at the Massachusetts Institute of Technology. He lectured at Harvard on ethics during 1879–1880, and during the next two years studied in Europe, chiefly in Berlin, where he came under the influence of Dubois-Reymond, Ebbinghaus, Paulsen, Lasson, Zeller, and Michelet. In 1883–1884 he lectured at Michigan, and in 1884 was called to California, where he headed a strong and influential department until 1910.

340. Jean Wahl, *The Pluralist Philosophies of England and America*, tr. by Fred Rothwell (London, 1925), pp. 222–23.

341. "He seems not to have studied the philosophy of Lotze nor that of Renouvier [two men who stand at the source of pluralism]; the only predecessors of his pluralism that he quotes are Aristotle, Leibnitz, and Kant."— *Ibid.*, pp. 223–24. It was in Kant that he first found the conception of the ideal domain, the kingdom of ends, that is essential to his philosophy. He embraced the entire *a priori* theory of Kant, finding the Kantian distinction between noumenon and phenomenon basic. In his criticism of evolutionary philosophy he insisted that nature as studied by science must be treated as phenomenal and nothing more, while the real must be conceived as mental and plural. His debt to Leibnitz is apparent in his doctrine of the nature of souls. See *ibid.*, pp. 228–29, and H. G. Townsend, *op. cit.*, pp. 151–53.

342. G. Stanley Hall, in *Founders of Modern Psychology* (1895), has given English readers a detailed and sympathetic sketch of this best-known German psychologist among the post-Hegelians. Professor Cohen points out that Royce was profoundly influenced by Lotze in his general attitude to the importance of the "practical" in philosophy. Indeed, Royce himself frankly acknowledged his debt to Lotze.

See *Philosophical Rev.*, XXV, iii (May, 1916), 153, 282.

343. *Ibid.*, p. 153. John Dewey declared that "Royce gives a corrected restatement of the Kantian problem." He does away with the *Ding-an-sich*. See *Papers in Honor of Josiah Royce on his Sixtieth Birthday* (n.p., 1916), p. 22.

344. Jean Wahl, *op. cit.*, p. 38.

345. Howison, in *Papers in Honor of Josiah Royce*, p. 5.

346. *Ibid.*, p. 20.

347. For Royce's own statement of indebtedness to Schopenhauer, Kant, Hegel, and the Romantics, see *ibid.*, pp. 9, 282.

348. *Immanuel Kant 1724–1924*, Symposium ed. by E. C. Wilson (New Haven, 1925), p. 15; G. P. Adams and W. P. Montague, eds., *Contemporary American Philosophy, Personal Statements* (2 vols., N.Y., 1930), I, 23; see Palmer's *Autobiography of a Philosopher* (Boston and N.Y., 1930) for a fuller account of his life.

349. Adams and Montague, eds., *op. cit.*, I, 55.

350. See Katherine Gilbert, "James E. Creighton as Writer and Editor," *Journal of Philosophy*, XXII, x (May 7, 1925), 256–64.

351. Born in Vermont, Dewey studied at the University of Vermont and there came directly under the influence of the tradition of German philosophy instituted by James Marsh, then being actively promulgated by Marsh's successor, Professor Torrey. The latter introduced him to the German classical philosophers (see Adams and Montague, eds., *op. cit.*, II, 14–15). He entered the graduate school at Hopkins in 1884, where he heard Peirce, but was in closer sympathy with George S. Morris. At this time he sent some articles to W. T. Harris, which were published in the *Journal of Speculative Philosophy*, and he received encouragement from the editor. The teaching of Morris was perhaps the strongest influence in these years, and it ended by making Dewey an Hegelian for a period. See Dewey's testimony given in R. M. Wenley, *op. cit.*, p. 318.

352. Sidney Hook, *John Dewey, an Intellectual Portrait* (N.Y., 1939), pp. 10–15. Dewey expressed his relation to Hegel in these words: "I drifted away from Hegelianism [after 1884]. . . . Nevertheless I should never think of ignoring, much less denying . . . that acquaintance with Hegel has left a permanent deposit in my thinking. . . . In the content of his ideas there is often an extraordinary depth; in many of his analyses . . . an extraordinary acuteness. Were it possible for me to be a devotee of any system, I still should believe

that there is greater richness and . . . insight in Hegel than in any other single systematic philosophy . . . though when I say this I exclude Plato."—Adams and Montague (eds.), *op. cit.*, II, 20–21. For further details regarding Dewey's Hegelian background, see Morgan G. White's *The Origin of Dewey's Instrumentalism* (N. Y., 1943).

353. See Jean Wahl, *op. cit.*, pp. 29–33.

354. See *Letters of William James*, ed. by Henry James (2 vols., Boston, 1920), I, 142, 147.

355. *Ibid.*, I, 87, 117.

356. Jean Wahl, *op. cit.*, pp. 62, 192.

357. See James's direct testimony in *Letters*, I, 147, and Wahl, *op. cit.*, pp. 62, 192.

358. See his "Philosophical Conceptions and Practical Results," address before the Philosophical Union at the University of California, 1898, printed in P. R. Anderson and M. H. Fisch, eds., *Philosophy in America* (N.Y. and London, 1939), p. 541.

359. Jean Wahl, *op. cit.*, p. 72.

360. For details of Renouvier's debts to Kant, Berkeley, Hume, and others, see *ibid.*, pp. 63–71, 72–73, 87.

361. *Ibid.*, p. 88. His language in attacking the Hegelians was colorful and emphatic. He spoke of his "prejudice against all Hegelians, except Hegel himself . . . . Their sacerdotal airs! and their sterility! Contemplating their navels and the syllable oum!"—*Letters*, I, 265. See also I, 208.

"The way these cusses slip so fluently off into 'Ideal,' the 'Jenseitige,' the 'Inner,' etc., etc., etc., and undertake to give a *logical* explanation of everything which is so palpably trumped up *after* the facts, and the reasoning of which is so grotesquely incapable of going an inch into the future, is both disgusting and disheartening. You never saw such a mania for going deep into the bowels of truth, with such an absolute lack of intuition and perception of the skin thereof. . . . but the era of it may be past now [1867]—I don't know."—*Ibid.*, I, 94–95.

This passage was written five years before James came into active personal contact with the American Hegelians, when he participated in the fifth Concord School by delivering three lectures on psychology. But already there is evident in his remarks something of the attitude which he later assumed toward the St. Louisans, though he condescended meanwhile to print his first two published articles in Harris' *Journal* (XII and XIII for 1878 and 1879, respectively). He could not forbear poking sly fun at Emery and McClure of the West and their "self-constituted leadership" in trying to reform Boston and Cambridge by means of the Hegelian precepts contained in the three tomes

of Brokmeyer's translation of Hegel's *Logic* which they brought with them.

Snider, years later, observed that James sometimes showed "a streak of that peculiar psychological distemper known to outsiders as Bostonitis—not dangerous, hardly offensive, but symptomatic of some mighty local and possible personal superiority."—D. J. Snider, *St. Louis Movement*, pp. 334–35. While he credited James with "bringing to the fore the cardinal discipline of the age—Psychology," he resented James's attitude toward himself, Brokmeyer, Harris, and the Hegelians from Quincy and expressed his resentment unequivocally.—*Ibid.*, pp. 326–38.

362. *Letters*, II, 300.

363. Jean Wahl, *op. cit.*, pp. 183, 186. Fechner was an "immanent and phenomenal absolutist," who vigorously opposed the Hegelian "transcendent and noumenal pantheism." He was comparatively little known outside the Continent.—*Ibid.*, pp. 46–47; see also G. Stanley Hall, *Founders of Modern Psychology*, pp. 125–40, for a fuller treatment of Fechner.

364. For Lotze's pluralist and voluntarist interpretation of the real from the standpoint of ethical efficacy, and for his relation to Hegel, Herbart, and Fechner, see Wahl, *op. cit.*, pp. 50–55.

365. See the articles by Otto F. Kraushaar: "What James' Philosophical Orientation Owed to Lotze," *Philosophical Rev.*, XLVII, v (Sept., 1938), 517–26; "Lotze's Influence on the Psychology of William James," *ibid.*, XLIII, iii (May, 1936), 235–57; and "Lotze as a Factor in the Development of James's Radical Empiricism and Pluralism," *ibid.*, XLVIII, v (Sept., 1939), 455–71.

366. *Letters*, I, 127.

367. *Ibid.*, p. 120.

368. When in 1882 he made a tour of Europe, he went to the universities of Dresden, Berlin, Leipzig, Liège, Paris, and Prague expressly to inform himself on the progress of psychology. He made the acquaintance of Stumpf and Mach at Prague, Munck and Baginsky at Berlin, and Wundt and Ludwig at Leipzig. In 1893 Helmholtz paid a visit to James in Cambridge, and James kept up a correspondence with Stumpf for several years, as well as with Münsterberg before he came to America.—*Ibid.*, pp. 210, 230, 347.

369. Margaret Münsterberg, *Hugo Münsterberg. His Life and Work* (N.Y., 1922), pp. 29–51.

370. The son of a Norwegian immigrant farmer in the Middle West, Veblen became an observer of American life from the point of view of a critical, objective foreigner. Fully as important as his college courses in the tradition

of common-sense philosophy at Carleton College was his learning the German language at an early age and his subsequent study of the works of Kant, Spencer, and other philosophers borrowed from a learned German-American friend, Dr. Prentz.—Dorfman, *Thorstein Veblen and His America*, p. 30.

371. XVIII, iii (July, 1884), 260–74. Veblen was interested in tracing the development of Kant's ideas of determinism and moral freedom and interpreting the third *Critique* as an exposition of a method of inductive reasoning as an active, practical, or pragmatical element in the life process. Though the article was praised by men like Harris and Howison, its tendency is, of course, to establish a method of thought in harmony with Darwinian science and to clear away such romantic and idealistic structures as the various Hegelian systems.

372. The *Outlines of Metaphysics* is one of a series of six books edited by Ladd. See Dorfman *op. cit.*, pp. 53–54.

373. See Hall, *Founders of Modern Psychology*, p. 118; H. G. Townsend, *op. cit.*, pp. 153–54.

374. *Contemporary American Philosophy*, *Personal Statements*, II, 239–57. For his criticism of what he called Royce's resolution of all imperfection in the absolute, see *ibid.*, p. 246.

Among others whose effectiveness was felt in American lecture halls in favor of German philosophy before 1900 are to be mentioned the following:

James Hayden Tufts (1862–1942) and A. C. Armstrong (1860–1925) performed an important service in translating two important German histories of philosophy (*Windelband's History of Philosophy*, tr. by Tufts, 2nd ed., rev. and enl., N.Y., 1901; and *History of Philosophy* by Falckenberg, tr. by Armstrong, N. Y., 1903). Tufts was a student of President Seelye at Amherst; he studied in the Yale Divinity School, later taught at Michigan, and then spent a year at Berlin and Freiburg, where he received the doctorate. After 1892 he taught at the University of Chicago, where he worked in close sympathy with Dewey. Armstrong, professor of philosophy at Wesleyan University, was a realist devoted to the elucidation of the history of philosophy.

Professor Walter C. Everett (1860–1936), of Brown University, who studied in Germany (1895–1896) at Berlin and Strassburg, taught a system of realism which was in part constructed on the basis of Schopenhauer's statement of the doctrine of the grades of being. "Work under Windelband in Strassburg," said Everett, "greatly influenced my study and teaching of the history of philosophy. . . . Many years before one heard of emergent evolution or creative

synthesis, it affected my attitude to the problem of development, and also that of naturalism."—*Contemporary American Philosophy*, I, 332, 338.

Warner Fite (1867——), Professor of Ethics at Princeton, who elaborated a system of personalism, studied at Pennsylvania and the Philadelphia Divinity School before spending two years (1891–1893) in Germany.—*Ibid.*, I, 359.

E. V. McGilvary of Wisconsin (1864–1953) was a student of Howison at California. Though he moved far from Hegelian idealism, he stated that his acquaintance with Hegel "proved most useful." "Anyone who has studied Hegel sympathetically and thoroughly may violently revolt against his system; but rebels often carry away much that is positive from that against which they rebel."—*Ibid.*, II, 131.

The Scottish-born professor of the University of Michigan, Robert Mark Wenley (1861–1920), was largely influenced by the Hegelian Ed. Caird. Wenley's work was directed to the end of teaching a "synthesis such as the post-Kantians formulated, but freed from their soaring romanticism." Hearing Lotze in the eighties, Wenley was for a time attracted to his teachings.—*Ibid.*, II, 385–411.

Finally, George M. Duncan (1857–1928) enjoyed a long career of teaching at New York University. Educated at this school, he spent three years at Jena, Leipzig, and Berlin under Eucken, Paulsen, Wundt, and Fischer. His most important contribution to American appreciation of German thought was his translation, with notes and critical comments, of the *Philosophical Works of Leibnitz* (1890–1908).

375. Professor Townsend remarks of Dewey, for example: "His early training, like that of most of his generation . . . included a careful study of the Kantian and neo-Kantian philosophies. He retains many marks of an early Hegelianism. His revolt against idealism as a philosophy was neither a blind revolt nor a root-and-branch rejection. As a result of the range of his philosophical studies and the long period of his writing, there is scarcely an unqualified, or, one is tempted to add, an unambiguous dogma in his philosophy."—*Philosophical Ideas in the United States*, p. 235; see also Riley, *op. cit.*, pp. 323 ff.

Royce taught German Ethics in 1883–1884 and during 1890–1893 the Movement of German Thought from 1770 to 1830, in addition to a seminary in Metaphysics devoted to the discussion of the Hegelian system, and James taught a course in Kantian philosophy from 1896 to 1899. These examples can be multiplied manifold.

376. At Harvard, Bowen is credited with being the first to use German philosophical books in the original, in connection with his course in the history of philosophy. He conducted this course from its inception in 1868 until 1879, using as texts throughout the period Schwegler's *Geschichte der Philosophie im Umriss* and Kant's *Kritik der reinen Vernunft*. In his course in "Modern German Philosophy" offered by him from 1873–1874 until his retirement in 1889, the texts studied (in the original) were Hartmann's *Philosophie des Unbewussten* and Schopenhauer's *Die Welt als Wille und Vorstellung*.—Benj. Rand, "Philosophical Instruction at Harvard . . . ," *Harv. Grad. Mag.*, XXXVIII (Mar., 1929), 198–99; see also pp. 301, 308. A distinct course in Kantian philosophy, aside from Bowen's course which emphasized transcendentalism (but not exclusively) was introduced by Josiah Royce in 1890, and has since been taught regularly at Harvard.

377. A number of the titles listed below are from the compilation, made in 1895, by G. Stanley Hall, but many more are gathered from a number of other sources, notably from the descriptions of courses in college and university catalogs and from reports printed in the *Journal of Speculative Philosophy* of philosophical instruction in the larger universities.

Among the texts in most common use (with few exeptions before 1895) were the following: (1) Zeller's *Geschichte der griechischen Philosophie* (1844–1852), tr. by Alleyne in 1881, and used at Harvard under Palmer in the 80's; (2) Heeren's *Ancient Greece*, tr. by Bancroft (1823), used at Union as early as 1844; (3) J. J. Elmendorf's *Outlines of Lectures on the History of Philosophy* (1876); (4) Falckenberg's *History of Philosophy*, tr. by A. C. Armstrong (1893); (5) Kuno Fischer's *History of Modern Philosophy* (7 vols., 1887); (6) Fr. Ueberweg's *History of Philosophy*, tr. by G. S. Morris (1871–1873), used at Harvard by Bowen as early as 1872–1873; (7) Windelband's *History of Philosophy*, tr. by Tufts (1893); (8) Erdmann's *Geschichte der Philosophie* (3 vols., 1892–1897); (9) Harm's *Die Philosophie seit Kant* (1876); (10) F. Schlegel's *Philosophy of History*, tr. by J. B. Robertson (2 vols., 1835); (11) Hegel's *Philosophy of History*, tr. by J. Sibree (1857); (12) Wallace's *Prolegomena to Hegel's Logic* (1874); (13) Schopenhauer's *Die Welt als Wille und Vorstellung*, tr. by Haldane and Kemp (3 vols., 1883–1886), used in the original at Harvard, ca. 1873 to 1889; (14) Kant's *Religion within the Bounds of Reason*, tr. by J. W. Semple (1838); (15) John Watson's *Selections from Kant* (1888); (16) Kant's *Critique of Pure Reason*, tr. by J. M. D. Meiklejohn (1855) and again by Max

Müller, the earlier version being used by Bowen at Harvard from 1869 to 1889; (17) Mahaffy's rescript of Kant's *Æsthetic and Analytic* (1889); (18) Oswald Külpe's *Introduction to Philosophy*, tr. by Pillsbury and Titchener (1895; repr. 1907); (19) Schwegler's *History of Philosophy*, tr. by J. H. Seelye in 1856, but used by Bowen in the German edition from 1868 to 1879; (20) Deussen's *Elements of Metaphysics*, tr. by C. M. Duff (1894); (21) Deussen's *Outlines of Philosophy* (ca. 1900); (22) Lübke's *Aesthetics* (ca. 1878); (23) Ed. von Hartmann's *Philosophie des Unbewussten* (1868), used by Bowen from 1873 to 1889; (24) Hartmann's *Philosophie des Sittlichen* (1879); (25) G. V. Gizycki's *Student's Manual of Ethical Philosophy* (1889); (26) Volkmann's *Psychology* (1875); (27) Beneke's *Elements of Psychology* (1871); (28) H. Höffding's *Outline of Psychology* (1891); (29) T. A. Ribot's *German Psychology of To-day*, tr. by J. M. Baldwin (1886); (30) George T. Ladd's *Outlines of Lotze's Dictata in Psychology* (1886); (31) Lotze's *Metaphysics in Three Books—Ontology, Cosmology, and Psychology*, ed. by Bosanquet (1884); (32) Lotze's *System of Philosophy*, Part I: *Logic* (1884); (33) Lotze's *Microcosmos*, tr. by E. Hamilton and E. E. C. Jones (2 vols.); (34) Wundt's *Grundriss der Psychologie* (10th ed., 1896), tr. by Charles H. Judd; and (35) Wundt's *Vorlesungen über die Menschen- und Tierseele*, tr. by Creighton and Titchener (3 vols., 1863).

378. G. Stanley Hall, "On the History of American College Textbooks," *loc. cit.*, p. 160.

379. G. Stanley Hall (1844–1924) had studied at Williams in the class of 1867 under Mark Hopkins and John Bascom. On graduation, he entered Union Theological Seminary and enrolled in Henry B. Smith's courses in philosophy and theology. Encouraged by Henry Ward Beecher to go to Germany, he took up in 1868 (aged 22) residence at Bonn and later Berlin, and heard Meyer, Lange (famous author of the Biblical commentaries), and Dorner, "whose philosophical theory he [Hall] epitomized and which later appeared in a series of articles in the *Presbyterian Quarterly Review*," of which H. B. Smith was then editor. In the course of his philosophical studies at Union and later at Antioch, he became deeply interested in Hegel and made occasional Sunday trips to St. Louis to be instructed by W. T. Harris.— Louis N. Wilson, *G. Stanley Hall. A Sketch* (N.Y., 1914), p. 55. He translated Rosencranz's epitome of Hegel's doctrine for the *Journal of Speculative Philosophy*, Vols. VI, VII, and XI (1872, 1873, and 1877). Between intervals of teaching and study, he managed to return to Germany in the years 1870–1873, at

which time he read Zeller, Lotze, Fechner, and von Hartmann. Finally, in 1874, his reading of Wundt's *Grundzüge der physiologischen Psychologie* caused him to plan to go a third time to Germany and to enter Wundt's laboratory. In the meantime he took the Ph.D. degree at Harvard in 1878 under James, Everett, Palmer, Bowen, Bowditch, and Hedge; and between 1876 and 1878 he taught English at that school. During his third period in Germany (1878–1880) he devoted his attention to absorbing the techniques and principles of psychological research. He heard Helmholtz at Berlin and Wundt at Leipzig, and was in close contact with Fechner for a long period. Most important for his later development was the opportunity to become a co-worker in Wundt's psychological institute at Leipzig in the year of its founding. See Hall's own testimony regarding the unquestioned leadership taken by the German psychologists during the years (1870–1882) when he was repeatedly in Germany, as related in *Founders of Modern Psychology*, pp. v–vi, 42, 59.

380. Louis N. Wilson, *op cit.*, p. 59; see also Hall's two-volume autobiography, *Life and Confessions of a Psychologist* (London and N.Y., 1923).

381. Among other notable innovators in the new field are to be mentioned the following: George Trumbull Ladd, who studied at Andover in 1869 and became a professor at Yale in 1881, was interested in both German psychology and in supporting idealism. In 1892 he was one of the founders of the American Psychological Association and became its second president. Like Lotze, whom he helped to make known in this country, he sought to combat materialism, to reconcile the opposing claims of the realists and the idealists, and to attain a realistic spiritualism, monistic yet verging on personalism. One of his main efforts was to acquaint America with German thought as exhibited in the post-Kantian idealists, and he thoroughly indoctrinated his graduate students in the works of Hegel and Wundt. His translations of Lotze were widely used, and his *Elements of Physiological Psychology* (1887) was one of the first handbooks on the subject in the English language. See Riley, *op. cit.*, pp. 265–78.

James McKeen Cattell (1860–1944), son of the president of Lafayette College, rivaled Hall and James in his interest in transferring to America the new German methods of experimental psychology. Between 1880 and 1888 he studied at Geneva, Paris, Göttingen, Leipzig, and Cambridge. For a time he was an assistant in psychology in Wundt's laboratory at Leipzig, where in 1886 he took the doctorate. In 1888

he returned to America to begin a long career of teaching at Pennsylvania, where he held the first chair of psychology established in this country. His large and well-equipped laboratory at Columbia later, with its nineteen rooms and twenty instructors, was an outstanding establishment in its day.

At Princeton, James Mark Baldwin (1861–1934) established a famous department of psychology, which was similarly close to German precedents. A graduate of Princeton in 1884, Baldwin studied at Berlin, Leipzig, and Freiburg, under Paulsen, Delitzsch, Wundt, Heinze, Stumpf, and Riehl. He became "an enthusiast for the new psychology, and took back with him the full outfit of ideas—Fechner's and Weber's laws, the technique of reaction-time experiments, theories of mind and body, and cognate points of view as pronounced by Lotze, Fechner, and Wundt." Like Hall, he enjoyed the "freedom and range of graduate study" in Germany. Lotze he named as the "most sober and reasonable of the nineteenth century Germans," the "master who became a source of inspiration then and a means of intellectual discipline long afterwards." Baldwin's theoretical work "reached conclusions similar to those worked out by Münsterberg," and he elaborated a social theory of the self in agreement with that of Royce. In 1885 he translated Théodule Ribot's *German Psychology of Today*, an exposition of the work of Herbart, Lotze, Fechner, Wundt, and others. While he recognized the importance of German methods in raising psychology to the status of a separate discipline, in his later years, as Baldwin watched the development of German nationalism that led to World War I, he regretted the intense American emulation of German science in the eighties and nineties. "At that day, a German Ph.D. degree, or at least a residence in Germany for study, was almost indispensable to a young American teacher, wishing a post of college grade. In all the range of higher study—in philosophy, philology, physical science—German authorities were quoted, German methods adopted, and German approbation courted. The word 'seminar' came over with the thing, and studies became known as 'disciplines.' German governesses were placed in many American nurseries, and 'made in Germany' was as true of our education as of our children's toys and the cutlery of our kitchens. The real excellence of German microscopes and chronographs justified the state of mind which gave so uncritical a reception to German 'Idealismüsse' and German 'Weltanschauungen' in general." Like earlier critics, he found that many learned German writers displayed a "show of meretricious erudition," were interested in "dry-as-dust" minutiae of research, were blinded by "arrogant nationalism," and wrote in a style at once "heavy" and "obscure."—Baldwin, *Between Two Wars 1861–1921, Being Memoirs, Opinions and Letters Received* (2 vols., Boston, 1926), I, 35.

382. A course entitled History of Philosophy was listed as early as 1821 at Columbia College, but there is nothing to indicate that its history was continuous, or that other institutions generally had such a course at the time. Linberg's translation in 1832 of Cousin's *Introduction to the History of Philosophy* and Caleb S. Henry's version in 1841 of Bautain's *Epitome of the History of Philosophy* (repr. 1856, 1859, 1861) were in use at Pennsylvania and Harvard by the middle years of the century. Hickok used Heeren's *Ancient Greece* at Union College as early as 1844, and by 1866 lectures in the history of philosophy were given regularly. Henry B. Smith of Amherst in 1847 expressed a desire to give such a course, and in 1856 Julius H. Seelye of Amherst, the friend and student of Hickok, translated Schwegler's *History of Philosophy*, thus making available the first really usable history for college classes. Reaching its fifth edition within fifteen years, and written by a late Hegelian who emphasized Kant and the post-Kantians, and devoting more than one-third of the book to the Germans from Kant to Hegel, the book became a powerful force in turning academic attention to German critical idealism. A student of Seelye's, Benjamin Eli Smith (1857–1913), on the staff at Hopkins during 1880–1882 and fomerly a student at Göttingen and Leipzig, in 1880 prepared a revised, extended version of Schwegler's book. The book that came nearest rivaling Schwegler's was Francis Bowen's *Modern Philosophy from Descartes to Schopenhauer and Hartmann* (N.Y., 1877). Bowen's announced purpose was to call attention to earlier French and later German philosophers, "with whom comparatively few

English readers are at all familiar." Despite his former outspoken resistence to German idealism, Bowen recognized the value of thorough historical study of rival systems. In the meantime Princeton was offering an elective course in the history of philosophy. At the University of Minnesota, Professor Campbell devoted especial attention to Kant and Hegel in his historical course. At Johns Hopkins the course was given from the beginning of the institution; it was introduced at Indiana University in 1880, and at North Carolina in 1889. Small schools as a rule added the course as an elective, some waiting, however, until well into the new century.

383. On this head, see George H. Mead's essay, "The Philosophies of Royce, James, and Dewey in their American Setting," *Internat'l Jour. of Ethics*, XL (Jan., 1930), 211–31.

384. Charles Beard and Mary R. Beard, *The Rise of American Civilization* (N.Y., 1937), pp. 731–32.

385. Bancroft's ten-volume *History of the United States*, begun in 1834, is animated by this spirit, and the philosophical writings of Marsh, Hedge, Follen, Lieber, Murdock, Emerson, Rauch, Bowen, H. B. Smith, Philip Schaff, G. S. Morris, and especially the St. Louisans Brokmeyer, Harris, Snider, and Kroeger are imbued by the same principle. Rauch was one of the first in America to make the secret of Hegel his own; Lieber gave it wider currency in application by carrying the idea of *Entwicklung* into the area of American social experience and constitutional law. H. B. Smith and Philip Schaff lifted the implications of the Hegelian *Dialektik* into historical study, synthesizing the discordant incidents and the conflicting ideas of the young nation's life, thereby making a new chapter in the philosophy of history; while W. T. Harris, making a similar application to the school system, instituted a new era in American education.—Alvin S. Haag, *op. cit.*, p. 256.

SOME AREAS AND LINES OF INFLUENCE

1. The old chapbooks like the *Faustbuch*, the Fortunatus story, and the *Reynard the Fox* by Caxton (after the Low-German *Reynke de Vos*) were sold in Boston from 1680 on.

2. Jakob Boehme's treatise on the *Philosophically Divine* appeared in Philadelphia in 1688; Johann Beissel's *Mystische Sprüche* and other writings were issued from 1730; and Johannes Tauler's *Plain Path in Christian Perfection* in 1778 and thereafter. August Hermann Francke, the great pietistic leader, and Johann Kasper Lavater were well known. H. G. Zimmermann's reflections *On Solitude* were enormously popular. See Ed. Z. Davis, *Translations of German Poetry in American Magazines, 1741–1810* (Phila., 1905), pp. 194 ff.

3. *Ibid.*, pp. 96–125. In a similar way the struggle of Switzerland in her wars of liberation occasioned a good deal of American notice. See *ibid.*, pp. 134–81 *passim*, 197, 207.

4. *Ibid.*, pp. 21–61; Frederick H. Wilkens, *Early Influence of German Literature in America* (N.Y., 1900), p. 8; Bayard Q. Morgan, *A Critical Bibliography of German Literature in English Translation, 1481–1927, with Supplement... 1928–1935*, 2nd ed. (Stanford, Calif., 1938), pp. 143–45 (hereafter referred to as Morgan).

5. On Gellert and Herder see E. Z. Davis, *op. cit.*, pp. 27–31, 56–65, 195, and listings in Scott H. Goodnight, *German Literature in American Magazines Prior to 1846* (Madison, Wis., 1907), hereafter referred to as Goodnight. John Quincy Adams prepared a poetical rendering of *Oberon* in 1799–1801, but this was not published until 1940. See F. H. Wilkens, *op. cit.*, pp. 44, 47, and H.A. Pochmann's review of *Oberon* in *MLN*, LVI, iii (Mar., 1941), 225–27.

6. The Munchhausen tales by R. E. Raspe were introduced in 1787 and frequently reprinted throughout the next century. See Edwin G. Gudde, "An American Version of Munchhausen," *Amer. Lit.*, XIII, iv (Jan., 1942), 372–90. Other titles that lived far down the next century were Campe's *Robinson the Younger* (1790), Salzmann's *Elements of Morality for the Use of Children* (1795), and K. H. Bogatzky's *Golden Treasury* (1754, with seventy-seven printings

to 1925), a perpetual diary with Bible text commentary and verses.

7. *Lenore* was reprinted in America in 1798 and 1801, and a few of Bürger's other ballads appeared in the journals, as did also Goethe's "Erlkönig" and Herder's "Erlkönigs Tochter," in versions by "Monk" Lewis. On the whole, however, the runic and Gothic balladry gave rise as much to burlesque and parody as it did to serious translation. See E. Z. Davis, *op. cit.*, pp. 76, 85–93, 143–88 *passim*.

8. *Ibid.*, pp. 125–82 *passim*, and O. W. Long, "Werther in America," *Studies in Honor of John A. Walz* (Lancaster, Pa., 1941), pp. 86–116; Morgan, pp. 156–58.

9. For praises as well as attacks by reviewers, see Wilkens, *op. cit.*, pp. 36 ff.

10. See Morgan, pp. 417 f., and E. Z. Davis, *op. cit.*, p. 198.

11. Wilkens, *op. cit.*, pp. 20, 30–33.

12. *Miss Sara Sampson* was serialized in the *American Lady's Magazine* for 1799. Goethe's *Goetz von Berlichingen*, in many ways the companion-piece of the *Robbers*, was not played in America, and the Walter Scott translation did not appear here until 1814. British translations of *Iphigenie* (1793) and *Hermann und Dorothea* (1805) aroused virtually no notice at the time.

13. Wilkens, *op. cit.*, pp. 13–24.

14. *Ibid.*, p. 21.

15. See the numerous broadsides against the German drama in the *Port Folio* of Philadelphia in these years, cited in Davis, *op. cit.*, pp. 160 ff. Joseph Dennie, editor of *Port Folio*, fulminated against Kotzebue's Jacobin leanings; others found him a calumniator of Christianity, a threat to morality.

16. The data on periodical references can readily be located in Goodnight and in Martin H. Haertel, *German Literature in American Magazines 1846 to 1880* (Madison, Wis., 1908), herafter referred to as Haertel.

17. Note Adams' serialized *Journal of a Tour through Silesia*, in the *Port Folio*, Vol. I (1801) and "Letters from an American Resident Abroad, on Various Topics of Foreign Literature," *ibid.*, I (June 13 and 20, 1801). Other general views of German literature were published in the *Monthly Magazine and American*

Review (1800), the *Literary Miscellany* (1805), and the *Monthly Anthology and Boston Review* (1810).

18. She pointed out that the German romantics preserved, in an age of science and rationalism, a childlike innocence, a warmth of feeling, and purity of heart that she judged had virtually disappeared from other national cultures. Even while deploring certain wants or defects in him, she declared Goethe to be the greatest of the German poets, and she paid respect to his intellectual power. She strengthened the repute of Schiller immeasurably by celebrating his moral idealism, his impressive idealistic striving, and his noble work in the service of liberty. She drew attention to the Schlegels and others as serious students who supplied a firm philosophical and aesthetic grounding for the new movement. She revealed to the outside world the lyric genius of the Germans. Extended reviews of her book were carried within the year in the New York *Quarterly Review* and the Philadelphia *Analectic Magazine*.

19. By 1823 Bancroft was writing of German letters as one of the great national literatures. See Goodnight, p. 43. Bancroft's *Miscellanies* (1855) include reprints of his early articles on the subject.

20. Barnas Sears, president of the Newton Theological Institute at Andover and editor of the *Christian Review*, pointed out in 1841 the American debt to German scholars and the general interest in the study of German. He remarked that those who had "German works in their libraries . . . [are] not limited to theologians; the general scholar, the man of taste, the classical student, the man of science, the learned physician, the school teacher,— all are mastering the literature of Germany. "—*Christ. Rev.*, VI, xxii (June, 1841), 269-84.

21. For a comparison of attitudes see the article, "On the state of Polite Literature in Germany," by "S." in the *Portico* (Baltimore, 1816), where the view is that German taste is "hopelessly deficient." Bürger's *Lenore* has "absurdities and blemishes," and Goethe's *Hermann und Dorothea* is objectionable on moral grounds. —Goodnight, p. 39.

22. See John Weiss, *Life and Correspondence of Theodore Parker*, I, 63.

23. J. F. Clarke, in *Western Messenger*, II, i (Aug., 1836), 59.

24. With the founding of the *Western Messenger* in 1838 came the inception of a long line of Transcendentalist journals that extends to the *Open Court* of a much later period (1887-1936). Note the indexes to periodicals in Goodnight and Haertel for a list of journals that carried translations of German poetry and prose

together with reviews, notices, and criticism. A summation of these data is supplied in Table I, p. 343.

25. C. T. Brooks, J. H. Dwight, Herman Bokum, H. W. Longfellow, J. C. Mangan, Sarah Whitman, and Charles G. Leland are a few of the many who issued anthologies of German poetry. For the list of collections of German poetry in the period, see Morgan, pp. 577-628. A re-tabulation, broken down according to authors and periods, is to be found in Table II, below (pp. 344-45).

26. The studies by Goodnight and Haertel on German literature in American magazines to 1880 are an invaluable aid in examining the relative popularity of the German authors, and they are the principal source for the statistical data here presented.

27. The counts of periodical items for the period as a whole (1810-1864) are as follows: Goethe, 379; Schiller, 264; Jean Paul Richter, 101; Theodor Körner, 80; Uhland 73; Zschokke, 50; Heine, 46; Kotzebue, 43; Herder, 41; Luther, 36; Fouqué, 36; Rückert, 33; Lessing, 27; Tieck, 27; Krummacher (author of children's fables), 26; Bürger, 25; A. W. Schlegel, 24; Klopstock, 21; Wieland, 20. A number of the lesser Romantics follow next in order. See the full tabulation of these items as compiled from Goodnight and Haertel in Table I, below.

28. For the period 1810-1864, consult Table II, below; for the relative popularity of these lyric poets during the years 1865-1900, see the same table.

A check of the data on the number of books by individual authors translated and published in the English-speaking world (Britain as well as America) shows that juveniles and books of moral instruction bulked very large in the period. Note the prominence of Schmid, Barth, Wyss, and Bogatzky. Certain writers on history and on science (Niebuhr, Heeren, and the Humboldts) also ranked high. The literary figures with the greatest number of books in English translation (for the period 1810-1864) were Goethe, 216; Schiller, 187; Fouqué, 54; Kotzebue, 52; Zschokke, 52; Gerstäcker, 50; the Grimm brothers, 26; Klopstock, 26; Sealsfield, 25; Jean Paul, 24; and the Schlegel brothers, 24. In this count each edition and printing of a work was counted separately. The data are taken from Chart II, pp. 15-17, in Morgan. See Table III, below (pp. 346-41), where the tabulation is reproduced in fuller form.

29. The review, probably by the editor Robert Walsh, reflects no general growth of interest in Goethe's middle and later periods. The critic still errs in trying to approach this novel

as an example "of the sentimental species"; and like so many critics after him, he "is disposed to reprobate his [Goethe's] extravagancies." — (*Walsh's*) *Amer. Rev.*, III, i (Jan., 1812.) 51–69; cf. the article on this review by John C. Blankenagel, *JEGP*, XXXV, iii (July, 1936), 383–88.

30. No other German writer was as controversial a figure as Goethe. For details, see Goodnight, pp. 64–65, and Camillo von Klenze, "Das amerikanische Goethebild," *Mitteilungen der Akademie zur wissenschaftlichen Erforschung und zur Pflege des Deutschtums* (Munich, 1932), II, 191f., 198.

31. In Carlyle's writings, on the other hand, Goethe is placed above Schiller; and certain students of Goethe, especially Clarke and Margaret Fuller, followed Carlyle from the first. But, as von Klenze remarks, Carlyle left on the whole "but a negligible trace on the culture of the genteel tradition." — *Charles T. Brooks . . .*, MLA Monograph series, No. 7 (Boston, 1937), p. 21.

32. Bancroft's verdict was that "in everything that relates to firmness of principle, to love for truth itself, to humanity, to holiness, to love of freedom, he [Goethe] holds perhaps the lowest place." —*Miscellanies* (N.Y., 1855), pp. 173f., 180, 200, 203f.

33. *Christ. Exam. and Gen. Rev.*, VIII, ii (May, 1830), 187–200; *Christ. Exam.*, XXXII, iii (July, 1842), 398.

34. Felton's Preface (pp. xiv–xv) to the three-volume edition went far to mitigate the blackness of the picture that Menzel had drawn.

35. Norton published "Recent Publications Concerning Goethe," in *Sel. Jour. of Periodical Lit.*, I, ii (1833), 250–93. Bancroft's long review appeared unsigned in *Christ. Exam.*, XXVI, iii (July, 1839), 360–78. Wood's review of 1835, while repeating the complaint over Goethe's lack of moral conscience, showed independent scholarship and penetration in its treatment of *Meister* (see *Lit. and Theol. Rev.*, II, 282–307). Motley published a sketch of Goethe's life in the *N.Y. Rev.*, III, ii (Oct., 1838), 397–442. See Goodnight, pp. 74–81; also *N.Y.Rev.*, V (July, 1839), 1–48.

36. The temperate counsel of F. H. Hedge, an authority on German literature in close association with the Transcendentalists and the editor of the important anthology, *Prose Writers of Germany* (1847), is quoted by such a reviewer as A. P. Peabody in his review of Hedge's book in *North Amer. Rev.*, LXVII, ii (Oct., 1848), 464–85; see also Haertel, p. 66.

37. *Democratic Rev.*, XIX, vi (Dec., 1846), 443–46.

38. The dramas considered as productions for the stage never won much admiration.

39. See the review of Goethe's *Autobiography* in *Democratic Rev.* (1847); also *South. Quar. Rev.* (1847), and the review of Lewes' biography in the *Eclectic Magazine* for 1856. Lewes' biography stirred T. B. Holcombe, writing in the *Southern Literary Messenger* (XXII, ii, Mar., 1856, 180–88), to bring violent charges of "pantheistic infidelity" against Goethe.

40. Before 1814, when he was known chiefly for *The Robbers*, *The Ghostseer*, and occasional adaptations of other early plays, his youthful *Sturm-und-Drang* productions aroused attack in some quarters, particularly in the violently anti-Jacobin *Port Folio*, which in 1811 branded him as "sublimely mad." — *Port Folio*, n.s., VI, ii (Aug., 1811), 183–91; see also E. Z. Davis, *op. cit.*, pp. 160f.

41. In 1814 the *Quarterly Review* (X, xx, 359–409, esp. pp. 382–87), drew attention to *Don Carlos* and the *Bride of Messina*, calling the former "the finest play that Europe has seen for above a century," and recognizing in the latter a work "in the spirit of the ancient drama." A. H. Everett, in 1823, published in the *North American Review*, an important lengthy discussion of all the later dramas, and George Bancroft at this time drew attention to his shorter poems. Commending the poet's character so "as to establish him in the good graces of even the most pietistic critic," he enunciated what was soon to become the standard estimate of Schiller —a poet who believed in virtue, who had an "abhorrence of skepticism," and a "reverence for the sanctity of religion and the domestic affections." Bancroft was also among the first to sketch the contrast between the literary personalities of Goethe and Schiller. See *North Amer. Rev.*, XVI, ii (Apr., 1823), 397–425; XXII, ii (Oct., 1823), 268–87; and *Christ. Exam.*, XXVI, iii (July, 1839), 374. Carlyle's *Life of Schiller*, published anonymously, appeared in 1825 in London and was doubtless read before the Boston reprint of 1833 became available. Charles Follen, teaching German at Harvard, liked to play up the "moral" Schiller against the "licentious" Goethe. Metrical versions of *Don Carlos* and *Tell* were supplied in the 30's by George H. Calvert and Charles T. Brooks, respectively, and the *Wallenstein* trilogy was available in translations by Coleridge (1800) and Moir (1827; Boston reprint, 1837). Among the biographical studies perhaps none is so indicative of the poet's popular appeal as Mrs. E. F. Ellett's *Characters of Schiller* (1839; 2nd ed., 1842). The lyrics and ballads appeared in every manner of magazine, anthology, and gift annual, as well as in grammars and readers issued to aid the young in the study of the

language. See the lists in E. C. Parry, *op. cit.*, for detailed data on the widely scattered translations, imitations, and adaptations by Mrs. Hemans, Rufus Dawes, G. W. Haven, James G. Percival, and a host of others. The principal school texts then in use were those by Hermann Bokum, Carl Follen, George J. Adler, David Fosdick, and J. C. Oehlschlager. *Tell* was the favorite of all the plays, not only because it celebrated the theme of political liberty but also because it retold a story long popular in America. The long didactic poem, *The Song of the Bell*, was issued in several independent English versions and became the most popular poem of German origin after Körner's "Prayer during Battle." —C. von Klenze, *C. T. Brooks*, pp. 28 ff.; Goodnight, p. 103.

42. At the celebration in the Academy of Music in Philadelphia, W. H. Furness delivered an address which was widely printed and reviewed. In New York the exercises extended through several days, and *Tell*, *Wallensteins Lager*, and a play depicting the story of the poet's youth were performed. There was an exhibit of twelve *tableaux vivants* from his works. At the Cooper Institute, W. C. Bryant, Judge Charles P. Daly, Karl Schramm, and others addressed the gathering, and Reinhold Solger was awarded the prize for the best poem on the occasion. The Boston celebration was marked by an address in Music Hall delivered by F. H. Hedge, who called Schiller the "most eloquent," the "most national and cosmopolitan," the "most translatable" of poets—the "poet of Protestantism as Luther was its prophet." At Baltimore the Liederkranz performmed the *Song of the Bell* set to Romberg's music. Biographical essays by Godfrid Becker and Arnold Ruge were published in Cincinnati and St. Louis, respectively, to mark the anniversary. See E. C. Parry, *op. cit.*, pp. 327–41, 359–68. Two American sets of Schiller's *Works* were issued in 1860 and 1861. Among the many collections of his poems in translation, those by Furness and by Lord Bulwer Lytton were most notable. Among all the Schiller lyrics and ballads the particular American favorites were "Die Hoffnung", "Die Würde der Frauen," "Die Ideale," "Johanna's Farewell" in the *Jungfrau von Orleans*, and of course "Die Glocke." America had access to translations of the *Philosophische Briefe* (1837), the *Philosophical and Aesthetic Essays* (1844), the *Correspondence with Goethe* (1845), and the *History of the Thirty Years' War* (1828). For a characteristic tribute to Schiller as being for Germany what Shakespeare is for England, see *Natl. Quar. Rev.*, VI, xii (Mar., 1863), 207–39, esp. p. 208.

43. See the entries on Herder listed in Goodnight and Haertel, esp. the articles on "German Literature" in the *Ladies Magazine* for 1829; Bancroft's article in the *North Amer. Rev.* for 1825; and the study by George Ripley in the *Christ. Exam.* for 1835. On Lessing see the critique by G. H. Lewes in 1846; the survey of Lessing's writings in the *N.Y. Rev.* (1840); and the sketch of *Emilia Galotti* in 1840.

44. "German Literature," *South. Lit. Mess.*, II, vi (May, 1836), 373–80; see also *N.Y.Rev.* (1836–1837), pp. 263f., 277–79.

45. For details see Camillo von Klenze, *op. cit.*, pp. 33–35; Haertel, pp. 84–85.

46. For indications of this kind of influence see Henry A. Pochmann, "Irving's German Sources in the *Sketch Book*," *SP*, XXVII, ii (July, 1930) 477–507, and "Irving's German Tour and its Influence on His Tales," *PMLA*, XLV, iv (Dec., 1930), 1150–87.

47. Fouqué, virtually on the strength of *Undine* alone ranked third in the frequency of translations in the period 1810–1864. See Table III, below.

48. America did not completely overlook but certainly did not fully appreciate the stature of Novalis and Bettina; note in Morgan the American translations of *Heinrich von Ofterdingen* (1842, 1853) and of works by Bettina.

49. The *Struwwelpeter*, the fables of Krummacher, the vast number of little moral stories by Christoph von Schmid, and Wyss's *Swiss Family Robinson* were introduced. These bulked large in the totals of German prose made available in this country. Furthermore, books of religious instruction, like Bogatzky's *Golden Treasury*, Franz Hoffmann's many children's stories, and tales by Nieritz, went into many printings, often under the sponsorship of one of the Lutheran, Presbyterian, or other demonational societies.

50. For complete listings consult Morgan, Goodnight, Haertel, and Lillie V. Hathaway, *German Literature in the Mid-Nineteenth Century in England and America as Reflected in the Journals, 1840–1914* (Boston, 1935).

51. From *Engl. Lit. Gazette* (1857), quoted by L. V. Hathaway, *op. cit.*, pp. 99–100; see also *South. Quar. Rev.*, VI, ii (Oct., 1944), 428–45, and Haertel, pp. 12–14.

52. Note the enthusiasm expressed for Körner by the young Margaret Fuller in her essay in the *Western Messenger*, IV (1838), 306–9. Dr. Follen "rejoiced especially in several battle poems from Körner, the soldier and martyr of liberty."—A. P. Peabody, *Harvard Reminiscences* (Boston, 1881), p. 118.

53. The young Transcendentalist Wm. H.

Hurlbut, writing the earliest general critique of Heine and his times, branded the *Jung Deutschland* group as a "school of scoffers." Rückert's "oriental magnificence," Platen's "elegance and sincerity," Justinus Kerner's "spiritualism and quaintness," and Geibel's "gay materialism" he was inclined to rate somewhat lightly; but he looked on Heine as the leading contemporary writer, the greatest artist, even though he lacked "a great and noble purpose" and his macabre and satiric strain was "painful" and "lamentable".—*North Amer. Rev.*, LXIX, i (July, 1849), 216–49 *passim*. Other critics, E. I. Sears and George Ripley among them, deplored deficiencies in Heine's moral character; see Haertel, pp. 86–89, and H. B. Sachs, *Heine in America* (Phila., 1916), pp. 13–38.

54. George Eliot, "German Wit: Heinrich Heine" *Eclectic Mag.* (1856), and *Littell's Living Age* (1856); M. Arnold, "Heinrich Heine," *Littell's* (1863).

55. Charles Sealsfield (Karl Postl), Austrian-born traveler and chronicler of American frontier life, was much read in the 40's, when several of his "exotische Kulturromane" were translated, and Freytag's *Debit and Credit* (1858) was well received by both critics and the public. On Freytag see L. V. Hathaway, *op. cit.*, pp. 62f., 67–69, 92f.; and Haertel, p. 33. Other novelists are treated in the discussion of the period 1865–1899.

Of contemporary drama little need be said. Gutzkow's *Uriel Acosta* (1860) attracted some notice. Hebbel's dramas were not made available, and of Grillparzer's, only *Sappho*.

56. See *DNB*, VII, 43–44; and O. B. Frothingham, *Recollections and Impressions* (N.Y., 1891), pp. 3–8. The son, Octavius B., was later a member of the "radical" group and historian of the Transcendental movement; the daughter Ellen was a frequent translator from the German.

57. *Ibid.*, pp. 3, 8. He was opposed to extreme Romanticism, disliking Heine and Browning, too; but he approved of Anastasius Grün and Rückert, his only reservation being that the latter was (like most contemporary German writers) "too idealistic, too fluent" for his taste. See his essay on Rückert in *Christ. Exam.*, LI, iii (Nov., 1851), 436.

58. Praise of the Germans was neither unanimous nor uncritical. Francis Bowen, professor of philosophy at Harvard, denounced the German importations generally, especially their imputed dangerous effect on philosophic instruction. See *Christ. Exam.*, XXIII, ii (Nov., 1837), 170–94. Cornelius C. Felton, professor of Greek and later president of Harvard, was more conciliatory; his principal contribution to the study of the Germans was the translation of Menzel's *Deutsche Literatur* in 1840. If he damned Goethe's "licentiousness," he also penned praises of the Germans that have the ring of sincerity. In 1845 he was moved to call Germany "the luminous region in the literature of our age. "—*Christ. Exam.*, XXXII, ii (July, 1842), 398; see other reviews, *ibid.*, 1843, and *North Amer. Rev.*, 1842 and 1843. The Rev. Palmer Putnam (1814–1872) is remembered as the orator before the Phi Beta Kappa Society at Harvard in August, 1844, on which occasion Boston heard perhaps the most thunderous, indignant, and crushing blast against German "modernism", and against the "dissolute" Goethe that was ever uttered in that city; but there was no dearth of replies, among them those of George Calvert and Margaret Fuller.

The list of distinguished and able writers who had a part in the work of translating and interpreting the many German authors, old and new, is impressive, including a significantly wide range of professions and philosophic schools, and made up mostly of gifted amateurs in that day—men and women of varied and general interests: e.g., Andrews Norton, professor in the Harvard Divinity School; Nathaniel Greene, postmaster, politician, and gifted linguist; Eliza Buckminster Lee; Sarah H. Whitman of Providence; William Ware, editor of the *Christian Examiner*; Eliza Lee Cabot Follen, author and antislavery campaigner; Samuel Gray Ward, wealthy businessman and amateur painter and writer; Charles A. Dana, editor and journalist; George W. Haven, lawyer of Portsmouth; Alex. Hill Everett, reviewer and translator. For others, see the list of translators in Morgan.

59. Upon graduation from Harvard, Calvert resided at Göttingen from January, 1824, to September, 1825, acquiring the language and applying himself to studies and to social life. When, with youthful intrepidity, he called on the old master, he was pleasantly entertained and invited to return. During his stay at Göttingen, he visited A. W. Schlegel and the historian Niebuhr and formed a liking for the work of Lessing, Schiller, Jean Paul, and Goethe. At first it was Schiller whom he took up most enthusiastically, his first piece being a review in the *North American Review* of Carlyle's *Schiller*.

60. Even at this early date he was asserting that Goethe should be judged by his own admirable ideal of self-culture, and that when so understood he would appear "the most complete man of his time—the richest specimen of humanity since Shakespeare."—H. W. Pfund,

"George H. Calvert, Admirer of Goethe," *Studies in Honor of John A. Walz* (Lancaster, Pa., 1941), p. 135. On his travels in Europe in the 40's and 50's, Calvert visited Wordsworth, Carlyle, and Freiligrath in England, the old haunts of Goethe and Schiller at Weimar, the Rhine, and Wartburg. The color and atmosphere of these places, recorded by one whose enthusiasm for romantic landscapes could be compared only with that of Bayard Taylor, was reproduced in the two series of *Scenes and Thoughts in Europe* (1846, 1852). He made occasional poetic translations from *Faust* and from the dramas of Schiller during this time, and his later studies centered on the *Dichterpaar*. The principal work of his later years was *Goethe: His Life and Works. An Essay* (1872). This modest study, a work not designed to compete with Lewes' more detailed biography, presented the poet as intimately known to one who had made him the study of many years.

61. *South. Lit. Messenger*, II, vi (May, 1836), 373–80.

62. Other prominent critics and translators of the Middle States and the South were Mrs. E. F. Ellett of South Carolina, Mrs. Edward Robinson ("Talvj") of New York, Judge Beverly Tucker, C. G. Leland, and G. J. Adler. This list could be extended by a host of occasional contributors, professors, theologians, journalists, and lettered gentlemen who had a part in introducing the literature in our tongue and in explaining it in critical language not too remote from native habits of thought.

63. See Morgan, p. 8; also Charts A and B in L. V. Hathaway, *op. cit.*, pp. 126–27.

64. Virtually every periodical of consequence participated in the dissemination of critical opinion of German literature. Outstanding for high quality of editorship were the *Nation*, the *Atlantic*, the *New Englander* (to 1892), the *North American Review*, the *Critic* (from 1881), the *Century* (from 1881), *Harper's*, and the *Literary World*. Important journals in the South and West were the *Sewanee Review* (from 1892) and the *Dial* (1880–1895). Of those associated with religious bodies, the *Unitarian Review* (1871–1891) was outstanding for the abundance and broad toleration of its notices. Such more frankly journalistic media as *Appleton's*, *Baldwin's*, *Godey's*, the *New Eclectic* (*Southern Magazine*), *Putnam's*, *Scribner's*, and *Littell's Living Age* reprinted the favorite popular prose writers.

65. Among the host of writers and critics, in addition to those mentioned, who played a significant role in this work were Lowell, Howells, Henry James, Jr., C. E. Norton, A. S. Gibbs, T. S. Perry, Wm. Hand Bowne, B. W. Wells, and Wm. M. Paine. Among the professors of German were Kuno Francke of Harvard, Calvin Thomas and E. P. Evans of Michigan, H. H. Boyesen of Cornell, W. H. Carruth of Kansas, J. T. Hatfield of Northwestern, J. K. Hosmer of Washington University, and W. H. Rosenstengel of Wisconsin. Among foreign critics who were printed (or reprinted) in America were Ernst Haeckel, Richard Wagner, Fr. Spielhagen of Germany; and Edward Dowden, Matthew Arnold, David Masson, Algernon Swinburne, and John A. Symonds of England. For excellence of product and volume of work, the following American translators should be mentioned: C. T. Brooks, W. H. Furness, John Weiss, C. P. Cranch, and J. S. Dwight from New England; Bayard Taylor, C. G. Leland, Professor Schele de Vere, and Emma Lazarus; A. E. Kroeger, D. J. Snider, Susan Blow, W. T. Harris, Anna C. Brackett of the St. Louis school.

66. Of course, some of the *idées fixes* of criticism lingered on, e.g., the commonplace to the effect that German scholarship was "thorough" but lacked "esprit" and penetration, and the view that the language is "cumbersome and confused" when employed in prose. See Haertel, pp. 5f., and *Dial*, VI, lxxi (Mar., 1881), 296. Though at bottom there was agreement on the value of studying the literature, there was no unanimity over the question as to *which* writers were suited for wide currency in America. The main critical division developed over the status of romantic versus post-romantic writers, especially Heine. Thus Professor Hedge, holding to some of his early preferences, charged Hosmer with bad judgment when he limited the treatment of Jean Paul to four pages out of six hundred in his history, and when he gave the "un-German" Heine altogether too much prominence. He objected to Hosmer's quoting Heine's disrespectful remarks on Novalis and found the Romantics were slighted. See his review of Hosmer's *German Literature* in the *Unitarian Review* for March, 1879. Many critics continued to hold with Carlyle's romantic predilections and to disapprove of the Heine–*Jung Deutschland* and positivist reaction against romanticism. In general, the spokesmen for the religious section of opinion concurred. See R. M. Johnston's "Modern German Religious Poets," *Cath. World*, XXXVI (Mar., 1883), 764–78, and G. M. Hammell's article on Novalis in *Methodist Rev.*, LIII (Sept., 1893), 721–34.

67. There were John Weiss's complete *West-östlicher Divan* (1877), C. E. Norton's edition of the *Correspondence between Goethe and Carlyle* (1887), and a series of native studies on *Faust*.

Outstanding book-length studies of the life and writings were those by Calvert (1872), Boyesen (1879), Grimm (1880), Wm. M. Bryant (1893), Kuno Fischer (1895), and Mary H. Ford (1898), in addition to the volumes prepared for the students of the various Goethe schools under the auspices of the St. Louis Hegelians and the Concord School of Philosophy.

68. See the analysis in J. P. von Grueningen, "Goethe in American Periodicals from 1860 to 1900" (diss., Univ. of Wis., 1931), pp. 45–51.

69. The *Nation*, to take one example, mentioned the poem in 103 of the 332 references it made to Goethe.—*Ibid.*, pp. 131–49. *Faust* became the poet's established masterpiece, acclaimed by some "the masterwork of the century" (see E. C. Stedman's "The Nature of Poetry" in the *Century* for 1892). Bayard Taylor's pioneering rendering of Part II occasioned a good deal of comment on the conclusion of the story. Some critics thought all effort to interpret the second part futile, but there was a stronger tendency to insist that it had "in the highest sense simplicity of scope and plan," that "the poem is itself the victim of modern culture whose throes it represents." See the review of Boyesen's *Goethe and Schiller* in *Lit. World* for Mar. 15, 1879. Other noteworthy reviews include those by Professor John L. Lincoln in *Baptist Quar.* for July, 1869; W. W. Goodyear in *Lippincott's* for Feb., 1877; Professor Franklin Carter in *New Englander*, May, 1879; B. W. Wells in *Sewanee Rev.*, Aug., 1894; and J. Reinhard in *Sewanee Rev.*, Jan., 1897.

70. Von Grueningen, *op. cit.*, pp. 188 ff. Goethe days were observed by Chautauqua meetings. Prominent lecturers were Bayard Taylor, Anna C. Brackett, J. K. Hosmer, James MacAllister, Josiah Royce, Calvin Thomas, D. J. Snider, and W. T. Harris.

The main issues of controversy over Goethe, raised in the 30's were by no means settled out of hand. In the 90's he was mentioned in some quarters with that tone of reverence that implies his apotheosis to the very pinnacle of fame, in the company of Homer, Dante, and Shakespeare. He was if not a beloved, at least by nearly universal recognition a *great* writer. See, e.g., C. L. Moore's "Competitive Examination of Poets" in *Current Lit.* for Aug., 1897. Of the Transcendentalist champions of Goethe, the venerable F. H. Hedge was by far the most effective in carrying forward Margaret Fuller's defense of the master. He praised Goethe for wisdom, learning, and character, taking his stand on the proposition that though Goethe showed us nothing nobler than the realities of human nature, these would nonetheless be of great value. Hedge dismissed the caviling over

Goethean "selfishness" and "lack of patriotism," which continued to be heard. See the article by Hedge on Froude's *Carlyle* in the *Unitarian Rev.*, Feb., 1885; that by M. B. Anderson in the *Dial*, Mar., 1881; and the defense of Goethe's politics in the *Nation*, Sept. 16, 1875. The most perturbed and abusive of the all condemnations were those printed in the *Catholic World*, though other religious journals expressed comparable sentiments with more moderation of language. See von Grueningen, *op. cit.*, pp. 74–77, citing articles in the issues of May, 1887, April, 1879, and December, 1883, and an attack by Mary E. Nutting in the *Andover Review* for July, 1889. Goethe's relation to Friederike Brion was most often cited as a particularly reprehensible episode in his life (see *Amer. Church Rev.*, Jan., 1865, and articles by Frances A. Shaw in *Appleton's* for 1871 and by E. P. Sterns in *Lippincott's* for April, 1897); and the hue and cry over it continued until at least 1890, when Professor Calvin Thomas examined the matter and forcefully assaulted the structure compounded of hearsay and legend (*Open Court*, Jan. 30, 1890).

71. Only the circles of the St. Louisans made much of Goethe's relations to Indian mysticism, monism, and Buddhism, the majority of commentators stressing (with Matthew Arnold) Goethe's humanism and eclecticism. Goethe the critic was infrequently discussed; his scientific endeavors were treated chiefly in the *Open Court*, in connection with his place in the history of evolutionary theory.

72. Emma H. Nason, "The Loves of Goethe," *Cosmopolitan*, XXIV, ii (Dec., 1897), 172–81. Note O. B. Frothingham's warning against the irreligious character of *Meister*: "Were 'Wilhelm Meister' less admirable as a study of character, more engaging as a work of fiction, more heated or exaggerated in manner, it would be one of the most dangerous works ever published.... Neglect of moral judgment is absolute; ethical distinctions are calmly set aside; men and women whose conduct is reprehensible are praised for their elevation of character ... the authority of conscience is never admitted."— "The Morally Objectionable in Literature," *North Amer. Rev.*, CXXXV (Sept., 1882), 323–38, *passim*. On the other hand, Henry James, Jr., in discussing *Meister* as early as 1865, approached more closely to Goethe's spirit and artistic intent than did any other critic. See *North Amer. Rev.*, CI, i (July, 1865), 281–85.

73. The historians still paid respect to his high idealism, but nevertheless much of the glory shed on him was borrowed from Goethe, for the story of the Goethe-Schiller friendship was by now one of the best-known episodes in

German literary annals. Schiller's great later dramas were relatively neglected. The second printing of Hempel's edition of his works appeared in 1870; his poems, translated by Wireman (German and English), in 1871. The *Jungfrau von Orleans, Maria Stuart,* and *Tell* appeared in the 70's and the biography by Johannes Scherr had been available in English since 1860. Note also the translation of the *Jungfrau* by Calvert (1873 and 1874), the acting version of *Maria Stuart* as used by Mme Marie Seebach in New York in 1870, and the translation of *Tell* by Massie in 1878. After 1880 came reprintings of Lytton's version of the *Poems and Ballads,* the *Song of the Bell,* Carlyle's essays on Schiller, and W. H. Nevinson's *Life* (1896).

74. *Lit. World,* XV, xiv (July 12, 1884), 228; see also Haertel, pp. 79f.

75. In his review of Stahr's *Lessing* (*North Amer. Rev.,* Apr., 1768), Lowell pointed out Lessing's strong intelligence and critical acuity, his forthrightness and independence, all of which qualities Americans were quick to praise. He was, says Lowell, a type of the "great writer. . . the Valhalla of German letters can show one form [Lessing] in its simple manhood, statelier even than Goethe's." Lowell noted, too, his contribution to rational criticism in philosophy and theology: "At present the world has advanced to where Lessing stood, while the Church has done its best to stand stockstill." The *Laokoon* was received with enthusiasm as the outstanding document in literary criticism of the modern age. It was Lessing the critic and polemicist who was the subject of most of the articles; his dramas were usually dismissed as lacking fire and "poetical power." See W. L. Phelps, "Lessing and the German Drama," *New Englander,* LI, iii (Sept., 1889), 198–209. Other notable articles appeared in the *Nation,* L (Mar. 13, 1890), and LXII (Mar. 5, 1896); *Poet-Lore,* V (Dec., 1893); and *Meth. Quar. Rev.,* LIV,, v (Sept., 1894).

76. See articles in the *Atlantic,* XXXVI, i (July, 1875), 49–57, and XXXVII, v (May, 1876), 607–16.

77. See also *Poet-Lore,* V (Nov., 1893), 551–57; *Chautauquan,* XXIII, 610–14; and the essay, "Bayard Taylor on German Literature," *Penn Monthly,* XI (June, 1880), 449.

78. H. B. Sachs (*op. cit.,* p. 81) asserts that 10,000 copies were sold by 1891. Heine's prose was printed in collections by Newell Dunbar (1892) and S. L. Fleischmann (1876). Biographical studies available were those by G. Karpeles (N.Y., 1893), George Eliot (Girard, Kan., n.d.), and Wm. Sharp (N.Y., 1888).

79. *Littell's Living Age,* LXXIX, mx (Oct. 10, 1863), 51–62.

80. See the prefaces in Leland's edition, especially *Florentine Nights* (London, 1891) and *De l'Allemagne* (London, 1892); also his translation of von Embden's *Family Life of Heine* (London, 1893); Lowell's *Works* (1890), I, 364; II, 90, 167, 170, 229, 327, etc.; III, 259, 301; VI, 56, 116, 157, 164; and Howells' article, *Atlantic,* XXXII, ii (Aug., 1873), 237–39; also Sears's essay on Heine in *Natl. Quar. Rev.,* XIII, i (June, 1866), 56–77.

81. Sachs, *op. cit.,* pp. 52–54.

82. *Ibid.,* p. 61.

83. *Old and New,* V, vi (June, 1872), 730f. Even Professor Boyesen, writing for the *Atlantic* (XXXVI, vi, Dec., 1875, 689–98) regretted their unconventional lives and represented their striving as "extreme and largely futile." At most he had a condescending interest in Novalis, whose poems, he said, "possess a potent charm and even a kind of unity. . . . His early death shed a romantic halo over the incidents of his life, which were in themselves sufficiently pathetic" (p. 698). An article in the *Methodist Review* (LIII, v, Sept., 1893, 721–34), on other hand, was full of praise for the Christian mysticism of Novalis. See also Haertel, pp. 80–86.

84. The plays of Benedix were frequently played in the large theater centers and were published 1865–1880; those of Gustav von Moser (including his *Bibliothekar* as adapted and played by William Gillette in 1882) from 1875 to 1890; and of R. Voss, 1888–1900.

85. Schefer was a versatile minor poet of the post-classical period; Kortum, an eighteenth-century humorist. Busch's *Max und Moritz* (1871) elicited some response, but there was no general interest in this artist. After the middle 80's Frau Johanna Spyri, with *Heidi,* added yet another to the list of ever-popular and perennial children's stories from the German.

86. Note the articles on Sudermann in the *Atlantic* (1896) and the *Literary World* (1895, 1896), and on Gerhart Hauptmann in the *Literary World* (1895).

87. C. H. Brigham, "On the Study of German," *Christ. Exam.,* LXXXVII (July, 1869), 1–20.

88. Two of these were serialized in the *New Eclectic Magazine* and in *Littell's.* See Haertel for complete listings of reviews, and von Klenze, *C. T. Brooks,* pp. 36–38, for a discussion of Spielhagen.

89. *Auf der Höhe* (1875) was regarded as his masterpiece. His *Villa on the Rhine* drew widespread attention by discussing in its pages the writings of Spinoza, Goethe, Franklin, and Theodore Parker, and by dealing with current American public issues. Before 1880 Auerbach

was mentioned more frequently in the periodicals than any German author except Goethe, and doubtless his name was more widely known among casual readers than that of any classical author.

90. Quotation from article by Helen Zimmern, *Littell's*, CLXXVII (May 5, 1888), 561; see also *Eclectic Mag.*, LXXXV, ii (Aug., 1875), 250, and the review of T. S. Perry in the *Atlantic* for 1874, quoted at length by Haertel, pp. 49f.

91. W. D. Howells, *Criticism and Fiction* (N.Y., 1891), p. 128.

92. W. H. Browne in *New Eclectic*, VII (Aug., 1870), 210–19, and Professor Boyesen in *North American Review* for 1875 complained of his "morbidity" and "pantheism" in religion.

93. Others were "Eugenie Marlitt" (Eugenie John, 1825–1887), Elise Polko, Wilhelmine Hillern, "E. Werner" (Elisabeth Bürstenbinder, 1838–1918), Countess Hahn-Hahn, "W. Heimburg" (Bertha Behrens, 1850–1912), Nataly v. Eschstruth, and "Carl Detlef" (Klara Bauer). Male novelists entered the picture a little after the ladies and participated in the same endeavors, especially Felix Dahn, Adolf Streckfuss, Georg Ebers (romancer of far-away places and remote times), A. E. Brachvogel (historical novelist), K. A. Wildenhahn (historico-biographical novelist), Ernst Eckstein (historical romancer), and Karl Dingelstedt (exotic romancer).

94. See Hathaway, *op. cit.*, p. 108; Haertel, p. 60.

95. While in 1879 the *Literary World* had congratulated one of the translators, Mrs. A. L. (Furness) Wister, for her "eminent capacity . . . as a selector" of novels that are "well written, well bred, entertaining, and free from . . . ambiguous morality," the same magazine in 1895 expressed its boredom over these vapid, mediocre productions (X, vi, May 24, 1879, 166f., and XXVI, viii, Apr. 20, 1895, 120).

The sisterhood of fiction translators made a special category, for which the name of Clara Bell has become proverbial. Mary J. Safford, with ten of Ebers' works and a long list from other authors, exceeded even Clara Bell in volume of output. Mrs. J. W. Davis specialized in "Heimburg," and Mrs. Wister Englished a total of twenty-three novels of "Marlitt," "Werner," and others.

96. One novel of Sudermann's, *Frau Sorge*, was translated in the 90's, and his drama, *Die Heimat*, was produced and translated in 1896. Neither called forth much comment. Though Hauptmann's popularity was to rise soon after 1900, the *Atlantic* in 1896 denounced as "an-archism" his radical proletarian sympathies and labeled the heroes of his *Es War* as "radical" and "moral opportunists."—*Atlantic*, LXXVII, v (May, 1896), 697–702; also *Lit. World*, XXVI, viii (Apr. 20, 1895), 120, and XXVII, viii (Apr. 18, 1896), 120; Morgan, pp. 210–13. Schopenhauer's *Welt als Wille und Vorstellung* had been available in translation in England since 1883, and other writings in numerous printings were plentiful there before 1900, but there was no such welcome for this author in America. Except for a Milwaukee firm, which brought out his *Select Essays* in 1881 for its German-American trade, American publishers apparently subscribed to the common opinion that Schopenhauer, while consonant with the decadent European temper of the time, had no relevance for the optimistic progressivism of America. Only in the late 90's were his *Essays*, his *Aphorisms*, and his treatise on the will brought out in New York. As for Nietzsche, his *Unzeitgemässe Betrachtungen* had been reviewed in 1874 and 1875 (see Haertel, Nos. 1395 and 1478), and his works were available in a comprehensive (British) edition (1896, 1899), but the comment on him in the magazines was sparse indeed. But note the short article by the philosopher F. C. S. Schiller in the *Bookbuyer*, XXX, vii (Aug., 1896), 407–9.

From among the large volume of German scholarly, philosophical, and political writing made available in America, the following are especially significant: books of the socialist theorist Bebel (after 1896); Fr. Engels' *Anti-Dühring* (1892); Karl Marx's *Kapital* (1890) and *Manifesto* (1898); writings of Ernst Haeckel, Darwinist philosopher, 1879; writings of Ed. v. Hartmann; Ueberweg's *History of Philosophy*; writings of Pestalozzi, Froebel, and Rosenkranz on pedagogy; several books of social criticism by the popular publicist Max Nordau (after 1884); Winckelmann's treatise on *Ancient Art* (1880); and of Richard Wagner's writings, *Die Zukunftsmusik* (1873) and *Judentum* (1897),

The Wagnerian opera inspired not only extensive publishing of the opera texts but also discussions of Germanic mythology and the lore of the Minnesingers, notably A. E. Kroeger's book on *The Minnesingers of Germany* (1873). The fame of the German classical composers occasioned widespread treatment of the biographies of Mendelssohn, Schumann, the conductor von Bülow, and others.

Native Germans appeared occasionally in American journals in the capacity of reviewers and critics (often in reprints from English periodicals). Among these were Haeckel, R. Wagner, Spielhagen, and the literary historian Richard M. Meyer. Spielhagen had many acquaintances and correspondents here, and his criticism was well known.—Haertel, Nos. 400, 1793, 1797.

97. A unique article on Platen, detailed and appreciative, appeared in the *Southern Review* in 1868. Here and there a critic called attention to the *Novellen* of Keller, but not to his lyric poetry. See Helen Zimmern's article in *Appleton's*, XXIII, ii (June, 1880), 539–49. For full references to these authors, see the indexes to Haertel and Hathaway.

98. See Table III, below (pp. 346–47), listing translations in the period.

99. *Lit. World*, XVII, xii (June 12, 1886), 200f.

100. *Ibid.*, v (Mar. 6, 1886), 77f.; *Nation* for Apr. 22, 1886; Franklin Carter on *Faust*-literature in the *New Englander* for 1879. In 1893 the *Nation*, LVI (Feb., 16), 120, cited Spielhagen's observation that the scholarly and severely technical studies on Goethe and Schiller were no argument at all for these authors' vital contemporary influence, and the advent of the new naturalism seemed to him only to widen the gulf between the past and the present.

101. "The Decay of Earnestness," *Californian*, III, xiii (Jan., 1881), 18–25.

AMERICAN THEATER AND DRAMA

102. Virtually the only independent American effort was David Rittenhouse's translation of Lessing's bourgeois drama *Miss Sara Sampson* in 1789 or 1790.

103. Lessing's *Minna von Barnhelm* was translated and produced; Goethe's *Goetz* was translated by Scott, and his *Stella* and *Clavigo* appeared in 1798. *Werther* excited widespread imitation and adaptation in novel, opera, drama, and poetry. *The Robbers* also attained longterm popularity, and Kotzebue in 1798–1800 dominated the London stage, eight of his plays being performed there before 1800.

104. There were fifty-nine performances in New York in thirty-five seasons between 1794–1795 and 1828–1829; in Philadelphia it was played twenty-eight times in the same period. In the smaller centers we find occasional mention: Providence in 1805, New Orleans in 1806, and Albany in 1815. See C. F. Brede, *The German Drama in English on the Philadelphia Stage 1794–1830* (Phila., 1918); Louis C. Baker, *The German Drama in English on the New York Stage to 1830* (Phila., 1917); F. H. Wilkens, *op. cit.*; and George C. D. Odell, *Annals of the New York Stage* (14 vols., N.Y., 1927–1945). Whitman recalled seeing a performance in the Bowery after 1835, and audiences saw famous performers, such as Murdock, Edwin and Wilkes Booth, Edwin Adams, and John McCullough, in

the role of Carl Moor some thirty times between 1849 and 1875. See E. H. Dummer, "Schiller in English," *Monatshefte für deutschen Unterricht*, XXXV, vi (Oct., 1943), 334–37.

105. In 1795 the stages of Charleston, Philadelphia, and New York almost simultaneously presented works by Lessing and Schiller. Charleston led the way with the *première* of *Minna von Barnhelm (The Disbanded Officer, or the Baroness of Bruchsal)*, adapted by James Johnstone (London, 1786) on February 18, 1795. It was put on in Philadelphia the next year and then apparently forgotten. The season of 1795–1796 in New York saw the production of Reynolds' *Werther and Charlotte*, but there were only two performances. *Kabal and Love* was put on (in Lewis' translation) twice during the season of 1798–1799, thrice repeated by 1802, and revived in 1813–1815. Finally, 1795–1796 saw five performances in Philadelphia of an opera by Cobb, with music by Arnold, called *The Doctor and the Apothecary* (1788), based on a work by the Viennese composer Dittersdorf.

106. In Philadelphia, for example, the German church bodies fulminated against stage players quite as vigorously as did Presbyterians and Quakers. See C. F. Brede, *op. cit.* But German musicians supplying German music for theatrical entertainments became common early in the nineteenth century. See O. G. Sonneck, *Early Opera in America* (N.Y., 1915), pp. 72, 88. What few scattered performances in German were given are listed in L. C. Baker, *op. cit.*

107. The Count Maximilian von Moor ("de Moor" in English versions) has two sons, Karl and Franz. The former, a student at Leipzig, having been involved in madcap youthful adventures, is seized with remorse; he confesses his rashness to his father and begs forgiveness so that he may return home to his beloved Amalia. Moved by envy and hatred, the younger brother, Franz, causes an irreparable breach between Karl and his father. Karl reacts with feelings of hatred against mankind. He joins a band of outlaws with the intention of upsetting the moral balance of degenerate society by violence and hate. He frees his unhappy father, whom Franz has imprisoned and mistreated, but the Count dies before Karl can reveal himself. In the final act, Karl sobers and is horrified at his crimes against society. Deciding he must yield himself as a sacrifice for the restoration of a better moral order, he surrenders himself to the authorities after Amalia, who has remained loyal throughout, has died.

108. *A History of the American Theatre* (N.Y., 1832), p. 276. Born in 1766, in Perth Amboy,

and resident in New York during childhood, Dunlap spent three years in England after 1784, during which time his interest in the theater developed. Originally interested in painting, he led a dilettantish existence with artists and literati in New York. He was a member of the Friendly Club, and in 1793 formed a close friendship with Charles Brockden Brown. His earliest dramatic writings were *The Mysterious Monk* and *Fontainville Abbey*, about 1794–1796. When the Hodgkinsons accepted leading roles in the latter play, the connection was formed through which Dunlap assumed joint managership and, after 1797–1798, sole managership of the then leading stage of the country. The earliest evidence of Dunlap's contact with German literature is his translation of two idyls of Gessner (printed in the *N.Y. Mag.*, Dec., 1795). In 1796 he prepared an opera, *The Archers*, based on the Tell story, for presentation at the New York Theatre. For six years after 1797 his company took over the new Park Theatre, in a venture that was beset by grave financial difficulties. He introduced a total of twenty-four pieces from Kotzebue between 1798 and 1806, besides Zschokke's *Abaellino* (1800–1801) and Schiller's *Robbers* (1801–1802).

In introducing the Germans, Dunlap often went his way independently of English precedent, and it is owing largely to him that in America the Kotzebue fad went to much greater extremes than in England. He introduced eleven pieces from the German that were not produced in England at all, and a number of his pieces from Kotzebue and Zschokke were put on here before they were tried in England. He never showed any consuming enthusiasm for Kotzebue, but he recognized that his plays were financially promising, technically sound, and, when subjected to revision and skillful translation into good English idiom, better for his purposes than anything else available. See his *History of the American Theatre*, pp. 254, 256, 257 f. His merits as a translator were considerable. By applying his knowledge of stagecraft to another author's materials, he often constructed a play equalling or surpassing the original. See Oral A. Coad, *William Dunlap* (N.Y., 1917), p. 242. In revising, he excised phrases and expressions not consonant with American standards of manners, taste, morals, or religion. While he toned down Kotzebue's blatant Jacobinical and revolutionary sentiments when these intruded themselves into the plays, Dunlap tended also to play down the passages where traditional religious attitudes not consonant with his own deistical beliefs entered the play. See Charles M. Getchell, "The

Mind and Art of William Dunlap" (diss., Univ. of Wis., 1946). He promoted Gothicism vigorously, often under direct inspiration from German sources. *Fontainville Abbey* (1794) is significant as the first example of the Gothic in America, antedating C. B. Brown's first effort by two or three years. This work, based, according to Dunlap, on Mrs. Radcliffe's *Romance of the Forest*, has been called "more thoroughly Gothic than any of its dramatic precursors in England."—Coad, *op. cit.*, p. 154. *Ribbemont* (presented as *The Mysterious Monk* in 1796) belongs wholly in the Gothic category, and *The Knight's Adventure* (1797), in whose composition Dunlap had a hand, is closely related to *The Robbers*, via Godwin's *Caleb Williams.—Ibid.*, pp. 158–61. Had it not been for Dunlap, the account of German dramatic influence would be markedly different from what it is, though the final effect of Dunlap's close contacts with German drama of various schools and types was not so much to open new paths as to widen those barely established by his predecessors. It may be observed, however, that American sentimental drama from 1780 on developed generally independently of Kotzebue and other Germans. The American type, using the distressed-lover theme, is not paralleled in Kotzebue, whose pieces specialized rather in drawing affecting pictures of family life.

109. Dunlap, *History of the American Theatre*, pp. 253 f. *The Stranger* was first published in a free translation by August Schink in London in 1798; it ran through six editions that year.

110. The beautiful and mysterious Mrs. Haller lives as housekeeper on the estate of the Count of Wintersen. In the lodge lives the Stranger, a misanthrope, but one given to performing secret acts of charity. When the count's brother-in-law, Baron Steiner, falls in love with Mrs. Haller, we learn from her pitiful soliloquy that she is the Countess of Waldbourg, who three years earlier had left her husband and children to follow a false lover, and who has spent the interim in bitter repentance. The Baron discovers that the Stranger is an old and dear friend; he extracts from him promises to plead his (the Baron's) cause with Mrs. Haller. As the two are brought together, they recognize one another as estranged husband and wife. The latter will not ask forgiveness, for she feels it would prejudice her husband's honor to pardon her. He, however, brings in the children at a farewell meeting where the penitent wife and still loving husband are to part forever. Count and Countess "press the children in their arms with speechless

affections; then tear themselves away—gaze at each other—spread their arms, and rush into an embrace."

111. See Dunlap, *op. cit.*, pp. 203–5, for his account of how he acquired the language.

112. *Self-Immolation, or The Sacrifice of Love (Der Opfertod)*; *False Shame, or The American Orphan in Germany (Falsche Scham)*; *The Wild Goose Chace (Der Wildfang)*, equally successful as *Of Age Tomorrow*, farce with music, by Thos. Dibdin; *The Force of Calumny*, play in five acts *(Die Verläumder)*; *The Count of Burgundy*, comedy in four parts *(Der Graf von Burgund)*; *The Virgin of the Sun*, sometimes *Rolla, or The Virgin of the Sun*, heroic play in five acts *(Die Sonnenjungfrau)*; *Pizarro in Peru, or The Death of Rolla*, heroic spectacle tragedy in five acts *(Die Spanier in Peru)*; *Sighs, or the Daughter*, comedy in five acts *(Armut und Edelsinn)*; *The Corsicans, or The Dawning of Love*, drama in four acts *(Die Corsen)*; *The Stranger's Birthday*, sometimes *The Noble Lie*, sequel to *The Stranger (Die edle Lüge)*; *Joanna of Montfaucon*, dramatic romance in five acts *(Joanna von Montfaucon)*; *The Wise Man of the East*, play in five acts *(Das Schreibepult, oder Die Gefahren der Jugend)*; *The Happy Family*, five acts *(Die silberne Hochzeit)*. For data concerning publication of these plays, consult Morgan, pp. 280–89.

113. Meanwhile Philadelphia saw twenty-eight performances of nine different Kotzebue plays during the same season—two of them not previously put on in New York: *Reconciliation, or The Birthday (Versöhnung)* in the Dibdin version, and *Lovers' Vows*, as translated by Mrs. Inchbald for the London stage.

114. See the review in the *Commercial Advertiser* for December 11 and 17, 1798.

115. For *Pizarro*, the announcement promised: "Solemn Procession of Priests and Priestesses to be Sacrificed, with Hymns and Invocations before going to battle. . . . A wild retreat among stupendous Rocks. . . . Warriors returning from battle, with their prisoners. . . a Dungeon in the Rock," etc.—G. C. D. Odell, *op. cit.*, II, 85.

The plots of the dramas were well known in eighteenth-century fiction, opera, and drama, and were ultimately derived from Marmontel's *Incas*. In Dunlap's version, Alonzo, resisting the brutality of Pizarro on his march of conquest in Peru, is captured and sentenced to death. His friend Rolla frees him. As Rolla leaves the camp, he finds the child of Cora and Alonzo in the hands of the Spaniards. At the risk of his life he rescues the infant but is fatally wounded and lives only long enough to restore the child to its distracted parents.

116. *Commercial Advertiser*, Mar. 31, 1800; cf. G. C. D. Odell, *op. cit.*, II, 87.

117. See Coad, *William Dunlap*, p. 70. Though Dunlap's version was at first described as superior to that of R. B. Sheridan, the latter was often chosen in preference to Dunlap's more faithful rendition. Its great success in Charleston is described in Eola Willis, *The Charleston Stage in the XVIII Century* (Columbia, S.C., 1924), p. 456. The performances given in St. Louis from 1815 to 1839 are described in Wm. G. B. Carson, *The Theater on the Frontier. The Early Years of the St. Louis Stage* (Chicago, 1932), p. 90.

118. *Annals of the New York Stage*, II, 80–81.

119. For example, see *Port Folio*, I, xxxvi (Sept. 5, 1801), 283–86.

120. *Lovers' Vows* is the story of an erring Baron who in his youth led astray Theodosia. He later repented. Returning in misery to the scene of her early unhappiness, Theodosia accidentally meets her son, the illegitimate offspring of her union with the Baron. The amiable Frederick, in his endeavor to save his mother's life, encounters his natural father, robs him, but receives forgiveness. A tutor in the Baron's household assumes the role of moral advocate, persuades his employer to marry Theodosia and make Frederick his heir. Having thus repaired the evil of his youth, he further patronizes virtue by admitting Theodosia to the aristocracy, "and the audience, it is evident by the popularity of the play, was completely satisfied."—A. H. Quinn, *History of the American Drama from the Beginning to the Civil War* (2 vols., N.Y., 1923), I, 92.

121. G. C. D. Odell, *op. cit.*, II, 80–81. On the lighter side, *The Wild Goose Chace*, an artificial farce based on a device familiar from Molière's *L'Amour Médicin* and other eighteenth-century comedies, was one of Dunlap's most skillful and popular efforts. It is composed chiefly "of the tricks by which Frederick, an amorous youth of one and twenty, attempts to woo and win Nannette, daughter of an old dragon, Madam Brumbach. After a series of entertaining escapades, Frederick discovers that his tutor is the father of Nannette, and from him he gains permission to marry."—Coad, *op. cit.*, p. 218. Dunlap improved on the original by rounding out some sketchy characterization and brightening the dialogue, as well as by inserting several songs without warrant from Kotzebue —a practice then common on the English stage. In 1806–1807 Thomas Dibdin's version of the play, renamed *Of Age Tomorrow*, was substituted for Dunlap's rendition with equal success.

122. See G. C. D. Odell, *op. cit.*, pp. 99f.

123. C. F. Brede, *op. cit.*, p. 79.

124. *Gazette* for April 4, 1800.

125. *Port Folio*, I, xxxvi (Sept. 5, 1801), 287. Dennie's campaign had begun the year before. Typical of his line of attack is his printing of a British parody which expressed "contempt for *German* plays." See *ibid.*, I, n.s., vi (Feb. 15, 1806), 92. The controversy persisted for well over a decade and thoroughly aired both the conservative political views of the editor and the loyalty to Kotzebue of some of his correspondents.

126. Dunlap's version, generally recognized as one of his best efforts, was far superior to either of the two British versions (Ludger's and Dibdin's). Dunlap himself called it "perhaps the most meritorious of the many translations and alterations which came from his [Dunlap's] pen. . . . [It] was made more English, particularly in the *prominent characters* of Captain Bertram and his old brother sailor and boatswain, than any of the previous pieces from the same source."—Dunlap, *op. cit.*, p. 281. See also Coad, *Dunlap*, p. 228, and Quinn, *op. cit.*, p.100. The play tells the story of two elderly brothers, one ill and poor, the other choleric and rich, engaged for fifteen years in a lawsuit over a piece of land. The reconciliation is effected by Charlotte, the daughter of one brother, and her lover, a doctor. Comedy is provided by a number of well-drawn characters.

127. Originally a novelistic treatment of outlawry in Italy, *Abaellino* was cast into dramatic form by Zschokke in 1795. Its international career was long and brilliant, and it was acted throughout Europe in various languages and guises. See Coad, *Dunlap*, pp. 238f., and J. P. Hoskins, "Parke Godwin and Zschokke's Tales," *PMLA*, XX (1905), 265–95, esp. p. 283. Dunlap's translation proved a success from its *première* in 1801.

128. Dunlap's ascription of *Abaellino* to Schiller throws an interesting light on the popularity of *The Robbers*. The author claimed at the time he prepared the translation that he did not know who had written the original. Nothing daunted, he printed some copies of the play with the ascription, "translated from Schiller by William Dunlap," and in at least one town, Providence, it was billed as "the best dramatic work of the best drama-writer of the age, Schiller."—*Monthly Mag.*, III (1800), 456; C. F. Brede, *op. cit.*, pp. 102f. *Rugantino, or the Bravo of Venice*, a less successful version of *Abaellino* by M. G. Lewis, was produced in 1809–1810. It had a total of fifteen performances in Philadelphia and New York to 1827–1828.

129. Dunlap's search for successful stage materials went far and wide. His version of

Schiller's *Fiesco*, played on March 26, 1802, with Cooper in the title role was less than successful. See Coad, *Dunlap*, p. 238. *The Good Neighbor, an Interlude in One Act*, was concocted by Dunlap from a scene in some unidentified piece by the German actor-author August Wilhelm Iffland. Premiered as an afterpiece on February 28, 1803, it was a mild success that season (*ibid.*, p. 241). Another Iffland play, *Education*, a comedy prepared by Reynolds from *Das Gewissen*, was imported from England in 1813–1814, with little success. Another German play belonging to the period of Dunlap's managership was *The Tournament, a Tragedy*, "imitated by Marianna Starke from the *Agnes Bernauerin* (1780) of Count Jos. v. Toerring-Gutterzell. It had seven performances in 1803–1804 and the succeeding season. The story is a literal retelling of the incident involving the marriage of Albrecht, son of the Duke of Bavaria, with Agnes Bernauer, a commoner. The American adaptor "ventured to deviate from the truth by preserving the life of Agnes," and giving the "tragedy" a happy ending. See Baker, *op. cit.*, p. 50; Odell, *op. cit.*, p. 156; Coad, *op. cit.*, p. 240. The last play in which Dunlap had a hand was *Peter the Great, or the Russian Mother*, a translation from Jos. Marius Babo's *Die Strelitzen* (1790). This story from an incident in the reign of Czar Peter had five performances to 1815.

130. Kotzebue appears also as the source for the opera, *The Cossack and the Volunteer*. An unidentified translator adapted this from *Der Kosack und der Freiwillige, Liederspiel* (1813). Mr. Braun of the orchestra of the Chestnut Street Theater in Philadelphia is credited with arranging the music.—C. F. Brede, *op. cit.*, pp. 262f.

131. The following introductions were not successful: *The Devil's Elixir, or the Shadowless Man*, musical romance by E. Fitzball, founded on E. T. A. Hoffmann's tale, *Die Elixiere des Teufels*, put on in November, 1829, in New York; *Ugolino, or Blood for Blood*, tragedy attributed to J. B. Booth, presumably from Gerstenberg's *Sturm-und-Drang* tragedy *Ugolino* (1768), played in Philadelphia, 1825; *The Fortress of Sorrento*, petit historical drama, adapted by Mordecai M. Noah from Sonnlithner's text to Beethoven's *Fidelio*, put on by amateurs in New York and played three times from 1816–1817 to 1819–1820.

132. See Odell, *op. cit.*, II, 22, 171, on the Gothic plays put on under Dunlap's management in New York from 1798. On works echoing motifs from *The Robbers*, see Frederic Ewen, *The Prestige of Schiller in England 1788–1859* (N.Y., 1932), p. 42.

133. Another kind of dependency on German materials is to be found in the many pieces that employ Germanic historical events and traditional stories. Long before Schiller's *Tell*, British and particularly American audiences were applauding various dramatic treatments of the Tell story: *The Patriot, or Liberty Asserted* (1794), *The Archers, or Mountaineers of Switzerland* (1796), and a number of others culminating in Sheridan Knowles's *William Tell* (1825). See Baker, *op. cit.*, pp. 7–10, and Brede, *op. cit.*, pp. 64f. Coincident with these was the treatment of Frederick the Great between 1816 and 1829 in a number of plays and operatic works.

134. The numerous early nineteenth-century American productions in the Gothic-melodrama category are analyzed, season by season, with careful attention to probable sources, in the studies by Baker and Brede.

135. See O. S. Coad, "The Gothic Element in American Literature," *JEGP*, XXIV, i (Jan., 1925), 78.

136. In addition to sources already mentioned, the following works have been consulted: Arthur H. Wilson, *A History of the Philadelphia Theatre 1835–1855* (diss., Univ. of Pa., Phila., 1935); James D. Reese, *Old Drury of Philadelphia* (diss., Univ. of Pa., Phila., 1932); Frank R. Diffenderfer, "Early Lancaster Playbills and Playhouses," *Proc. Lancaster County Hist. Soc.*, VII (1902); Douglas L. Hunt, "The Nashville Theatre 1830–40," *Birmingham Southern College Bulletin*, XXVIII, iii (May, 1935); Jos. E. Schick, *The Early Theater in Eastern Iowa. Cultural Beginnings . . . 1836–1863* Chicago, 1939); Claire McGlinchee, *The First Decade of the Boston Museum, (1811–50)* (Boston, 1940); and Ed. G. Fletcher, *The Beginnings of the Professional Theatre in Texas* (Austin, 1936).

137. Schiller was particularly popular in Chicago. *Mary Stuart*, introduced in 1867, was given sixty-seven times before 1900, with Fanny Janauschek and Helen Modjeska, among others, in the title role. See *Monatshefte für deutschen Unterricht*, XXXV, vi (Oct., 1943), 334–37.

138. There is a certain parallelism in intention between Daly and Dunlap, though they differ in that Dunlap failed to realize his high hopes of exerting a long-continued influence on our stage, while Daly's company became the "standard of artistic achievement for this country," and even carried his practices abroad. See Quinn, *op. cit.*, I, 8f.

139. Daly did not translate directly from the German, but had close transcriptions made for him, which he then reworked with greater or lesser deviations in essential structure and characterization for his own purposes. Professor Boynton observed correctly that Daly was one who could say and believe that "plays are not written but re-written."

140. By 1865 there had been at least six performances in New York and twelve more by 1870. We find it in the playbills for Boston as late as the season of 1897–1898, with Margaret Mather in the title role. *Leah* was a profitable success, though in quality it was not among the greater productions of the German stage. Leah, a Jewess, is repudiated by her Christian lover, suffers great miseries, and rises in the end to a noble acceptance. The blank verse of the original was turned into pathetic prose, and Daly's treatment involved other considerable alterations. A part of the success of the play was owing to its novel presentation of a serious social problem in dramatic terms, and liberal American sentiment heartily approved its message.

141. Quinn, *op. cit.*, I, 10. "It is a powerful play in which a young girl, who, through her loss of natural protectors, has become the mistress of an Englishman, Lord Durley, and is forced to leave her lover, Count Julian Dalberg, who has offered to marry her." The final scene, in which the poor heroine goes mad at the sight of her lover about to marry another, provided the actress Clara Morris with special opportunities.

142. Daly's introductions from the German in later years (to 1899) are skillful adaptations from a number of lesser-known writers of comedy, who themselves borrowed heavily from the current French fashions of Sardou, Augier, and Dumas *fils*. These German authors form a group who (though they may be remembered as theater directors and contributers of a large number of erstwhile successes on the German stages) have not maintained any literary reputation beyond their own era.

143. In 1875 he produced *The Big Bonanza, or Bulls and Bears* from Gustav v. Moser's *Ultimo*, a comedy bordering on farce and dealing with the subject of high finance and speculation. The famous John Drew was introduced into New York to take the role of the young lover, Bob Ruggles. The play had its hundredth performance by June 28, 1875, and was seen as late as 1893 at the Columbus Theater. In 1879, again with Drew, New York saw *An Arabian Night, or Haroun al Raschid and his Mother-in-Law*, another farce-comedy by Moser. The next year Daly prepared *The Passing Regiment*, based on *Krieg im Frieden* by von Moser and Franz v. Schönthan and in 1881 produced this glorification of the Prussian officer class with great success. Although trans-

ferred to the American scene, the play retains greater fidelity to the structure of the original than is common in Daly's adaptations, though when read today, it has a foreign flavor. For details, see Quinn, *op. cit.*, I, 27. John Drew and Ada Rehan took the leads, and there were twenty-four performances during the season of 1881–1882.

Further from its original is Daly's version of the sequel to *Krieg im Frieden*, namely *Reif von Reiflingen*, played in November, 1882, as *Our English Friend*. It ran for fifty-eight nights during its first season. From the work of Franz v. Schönthan, Daly next adapted two clever farces, which, according to Professor Quinn, are today probably the best known of his plays: *Seven-Twenty-Eight, or Casting the Boomerang* from *Der Schwabenstreich*, and *A Night Off* from *Der Raub der Sabinerinnen* (by Franz in collaboration with Paul v. Schönthan). The former was introduced in 1883 and ran fifty-one times that season. It held its popularity to 1900 and beyond. *A Night Off* was first played in 1885. From *Goldfische* by Franz v. Schönthan and Gustav Kadelburg, Daly fashioned his well-known *Railroad of Love*, introduced in November, 1887. This satire of "Mitgiftjägerei," or pursuit of money, is recognized as one of his strongest and "daintiest" works. Notable later adaptations from Schönthan were *The Great Unknown* (from *Die berühmte Frau*), *The Last Word (Das letzte Wort)*, and *The Countess Gucki*. Several other comedy-farces of the same light and attractive cast were adaptations from Julius Rosen (pen name for N. Duffek, 1833–1892), Adolph L'Arronge (1838–1908), and Oscar Blumenthal (1852–1917). For others, see Quinn's valuable bibliographies.

144. For Daly's plans and purposes in this respect, see Montrose J. Moses, *The American Dramatist* (Boston, 1925), pp. 176–77.

145. See Edwin H. Zeydel, "The German Theatre in New York City, with Special Consideration of the Years 1878–1914," *Deutsch-Amerikanische Geschichtsblätter*, XV (1915), 255–309. See also the brief but suggestive study by Horst Frenz, "The German Drama in the Middle West," *Amer.-Ger. Rev.*, VIII, v (June, 1932), 15–17, 37, and the indispensable bibliographical notes by Adolf E. Zucker in *Monatshefte für deutschen Unterricht*, XXXV, v (May, 1943), 255–64, on the German-language theater in Baltimore, Chicago, Cincinnati, Davenport, Detroit, Indianapolis, Kansas City, Manitowoc, Milwaukee, New Orleans, New York, Philadelphia, San Francisco, and Toledo.

146. Actual beginnings appear to go back to 1837. See Fritz A. H. Leuchs, *Early German Theatre in New York, 1840–1872* (N.Y., 1928),

p. 228, and Odell, *op. cit.*, IV, 184, 295, 528.

147. Daniel Bandmann belonged in this latter category, playing Mephisto and Richard III very successfully in 1862. Later he had a long career on the English stage, and was a favorite in Boston and other cities. See Eugene Tompkins and Quincy Kilby, *History of the Boston Theatre 1854–1901* (Boston, 1908), pp. 104, 106, 354.

148. Leuchs, *op. cit.*, p. 202.

149. For a further discussion of the significance in the United States of the German theater, see the investigations of Professor Leuchs, and my bibliographical notes in Robert E. Spiller, *et al.* (eds.), *Literary History of the United States* (3 vols., N.Y., 1948), III, 289–90. German plays introduced after 1870 are listed in C. F. W. Scholz, "Bibliography of English Renditions of Modern German Drama," *Ger.-Amer. Annals*, n.s., XV, i–ii (Jan.-Apr., 1917), 3–27.

EARLY AMERICAN FICTION

150. Aside from the difficulties inherent in the problem of recognizing and establishing literary influence, as distinct from mere parallels or similarities, it is often hard to differentiate between philosophical and literary influence. At what point do the influences of a Kant or a Schelling cease to be philosophical and become literary? Philosophical concepts were assimilated and transmitted by Germans as various as Goethe, Schiller, the Schlegels, Novalis, and Heine, but their expression is often so charged with poetic qualities that we ordinarily think of their effect upon essentially literary men like Longfellow, Lowell, or Lanier as constituting literary influence. Often we apply the terms *philosophical* and *literary* with reference less to the source of the influence than to its object—less with respect to the originator than to the recipient. This broad distinction, or practice, is as nearly practicable as any other frame of reference that can readily be devised, and we shall not lose much of precision when we think of the type of influence which Germany exerted in seventeenth- and eighteenth-century America as being primarily "philosophical" (or theological), while during the nineteenth century, as our literary men turned to Germany, the "literary" influence came to be steadily stronger until the two ran along not merely complementarily but more nearly equally, and sometimes almost indistinguishably. Goethe's impact on Emerson is a case in point.

151. *The Choir Invisible* (N.Y., 1897), p. 30.

152. The Germanic quality of Brown's *Wie-*

land was noticed more than a hundred years ago by John Keats, who saw in Wieland "a domestic prototype of Schiller's Armenian [*Geisterseher*] . . . a strange American scion of the German trunk." See Amy Lowell's *John Keats* (2 vols., Boston, 1925), II, 336. Since then, attention has centered on Brown's dependence upon French and English rationalism, Godwinian and Richardsonian techniques, and various American ingredients, while the Germanic influence was largely overlooked until 1940, when Professor Harry R. Warfel re-examined the alleged connection in "Charles Brockden Brown's German Sources," *MLN*, I, ii (Sept., 1940), 357–65. Many of the motifs common to Richardson, Godwin, and Brown were current coin bearing the imprint of many mints—English, French, Spanish, Italian, and German. But Brown's Gothicism was one with a difference, just as his romanticism, embracing both faith in reason and neo-classical taste in letters, was distinguished from the narrower literary phases of romanticism. His Gothicism was no addiction to mere medievalism. As a disciple of the Enlightenment, he viewed the middle ages as rude and barbarous, and in the Preface to *Edgar Huntly* he described the common Gothic tales as "puerile." While he exploited the terror element of the Gothic, he laid his scene in America in modern times, and he gave a plausible, natural explanation for his mysteries, after the manner of the rational rather than the supernatural Gothic.

153. While Brown was proficient in Latin, Greek, and French, there is little to indicate that he mastered German, although there are numerous suggestions in his work that he had some knowledge of the language. Daily intimacy with Elihu H. Smith during 1795–1798, when Smith was enthusiastically studying German, and their common interest in all their literary ventures make the presumption strong that he was led by Smith to study German. It may be observed, however, that during the 90's a knowledge of German was not an absolute requirement for one bent on knowing the more sensational forms of German literature.

154. Among the more important and first of these were Karl F. Kahlert's (pseud. for Lorenz Flammenberg) *Der Geisterbanner*, translated as *The Necromancer; or, a Tale of the Black Forest*, by Peter Teuthold (2 vols., London, 1794), and Cajetan Tschink's *Geisterseher*, translated by Peter Will as *The Victim of Magical Delusion* 3 vols., London, 1795). Will's translation appeared serially in the *New York Weekly Magazine* during 1796–1797. Schiller's *Geisterseher* (1789), which appeared in London as *The Ghost-seer; or The Apparitionist* in 1795, re-

printed in the *New York Weekly Magazine* during 1795–1796 and twice the next year (in Charleston and New York), reinforced the same taste for the marvellous. Closely allied to these were tales that dealt with the secret societies such as the Illuminati, notably Christiane B. E. Naubert's *Hermann und Unna* (1788), translated anonymously and published in Dublin and London in 1794 and again in London in 1796. Feeding this same taste were Karlos Grosse's *Der Dolch*, appearing in London in 1795 as *The Dagger*, and Grosse's *Der Genius*, translated by James Trapp as *The Genius* (*London, 1796*) and also by Peter Will as *Horrid Mysteries* (London, 1797). This list is merely suggestive and may be greatly enlarged by searching B. Q. Morgan's bibliography. See also Dabney's *Additional Catalog* (Salem, 1794), which lists the following titles suggestive of the same type of sub-literary fare: *Baron of Manstow; Castle of Wolfenbach; Christiana, Princess of Swabia; Memoirs of Count Cronstadt; The Female Werther; The German Gil Blas, or The Adventures of Peter Klaus; History of Count Gleichen; Letters of Albert to Charlotte; Popular Tales of the Germans; Radizal, a Novel;* and *Rosenberg, a Legendary Tale.*

155. Professor David Lee Clark, who has had access to Brown's unpublished early diaries and letters, found in the books that occupied his mind at this time "the very essence for Wertherism and . . . world weariness," and concludes that his mind "was set before Godwin had published a word."—*Charles Brockden Brown. A Critical Biography* (N.Y., 1923), p. 21; *Edgar Huntly*, ed. by D. L. Clark (N.Y., 1928), p. viii. Considering that Brown's mind began to turn about 1787 to writing epics on such themes as Columbus, Pizarro, and Cortez, we understand why the German sentimentalists were, in Professor Clark's phrase, "his daily companions," and why it was that he served his literary apprenticeship in their workshop His interest in rationalists like Godwin appears to have begun about 1794–1795, or about the time he was introduced by Elihu H. Smith to the members of the Friendly Club of New York —among them William Dunlap, William Johnson, Dr. Edward Miller, the Rev. Dr. Samuel Miller, Dr. S. L. Mitchill, James Kent, Anthony Bleecker, Charles Adams, John Wills, and W W. Woolsey. See Wm. Dunlap, *Memoirs of Charles Brockden Brown* (Londen, 1822), pp. 10 46; Harry R. Warfel, *Charles Brockden Brown* (Gainesville, Fla., 1949), pp. 40 ff. Contact with this group broadened his interests to include the English and French rational radicals; but when it is recalled that among the membership of the Friendly Club, Smith, Dunlap, and

Samuel Miller were enthusiastic "Germanists," we comprehend why the new interest did not become one that would exclude his earlier addiction to German romance and sentiment. For their common interest in Bürger, Schiller, Kotzebue, and Zschokke, see Warfel, *op. cit.*, p. 110.

156. From Baron Johann K. Riesbeck's *Briefe eines reisenden Franzosen über Deutschland* (tr. by P. H. Maty as *Travels through Germany*, 2 vols., London, 1787, and often reprinted), Brown learned that Wieland, as poet and novelist, was "without doubt the first of all German writers" (II, 208). Baron Stolberg's *Reise in Deutschland* (tr. by Thos. Holcroft, 2 vols., London, 1796–1797, repr. 1797, 1801, 1806) and Dr. Charles Burney's *Musical Travels* (London, 1773) reinforced this opinion, as did numerous critical notices in American and British review periodicals. In a letter of 1793 Brown quoted from Wieland's *Oberon* (Canto VII, stanzas lii–liii) and added that he had read the whole, presumably in English. It is hard to see how this could have been so, since Sotheby's translation, considered the first, was not printed until 1798, unless Brown got hold of one of the earlier British versions that never appeared in print, or that he had indeed learned to read German. Cf. *Oberon* . . . , ed. by A. B. Faust (N.Y., 1940), pp. xvi–xvii; also *Wieland*, ed. by F. L. Pattee, p. 223; and Warfel, in *MLN*, I, ii (Sept., 1940), 359.

157. *Wieland*, Pattee ed., p. 7.

158. *Ibid.*, p. 63.

159. *Ibid.*, p. 88.

160. *Ibid.*, pp. 88, 90.

161. *Ibid.*, p. 47.

162. *Ibid.*, p. 13.

163. *Ibid.*, p. 88. Germanic notes occur in others of Brown's novels. *Ormond* is adressed to "I. E. Rosenberg, a native of Germany; Helena, Ormond's mistress, sings improvisations "not inferior to the happiest exertions of Handel and Arne"; and Mary Wilmot in *Clara Howard*, is the daughter of a German merchant and an English lady.

164. II (Apr., 1800), 284–87. As a general reader and later as an American editor who studied the British reviews with a professional eye, Brown realized the drawing power of the superscription "From the German," and became familiar with the editor's trick of making sometimes a German ascription for an American or a British work "to enhance the popularity and give a fashionable cachet" to it. Professor Warfel's discovery of a tale with a German title, in which Brown summarized one of his own stories, indicates that Brown himself used the trick. The practice was general enough to necessitate close scrutiny of everything in American periodical literature from 1780 to 1840 that is labeled "From the German" or that is otherwise alleged to be derived from Germanic sources. As an editor, Brown himself catered to this interest, and the *Monthly Magazine and American Review* (1799–1800) and the *Literary Magazine and American Register* (1803–1808) set a new high in America for the number of translations and intelligences from Germany. The former contains 17 and the latter 56 items, a number of them in three and four installments. For an itemization of these materials, see E. Z. Davis, *op. cit.*, pp. 202–3, 207–8.

165. Warfel, *loc. cit.*, p. 360.

166. See Christine Touaillon, *Der deutsche Frauenroman des 18. Jahrhunderts* (Vienna and Leipzig, 1919).

167. This theme is strongest in *Ormond*, where Constantia Dudley, achieving a "rational estimate" before every act, becomes the heroine exemplifying the new woman whose specifications Brown had previously drawn in *Alcuin*. *Edgar Huntly* demonstrates the folly of unconsidered rash attempts to do good. *Arthur Mervyn* illustrates the necessity for subduing unreasoning terror in the presence of pestilence and other adversities, presenting at the same time advanced ideas of women's rights and social laws.—Warfel, *loc. cit.*, p. 360.

168. *Ormond* (ed. by Ernest Marchand N.Y., 1937), p. 208.

169. *Ibid.*, p. 231. Constantia's father becomes an obstacle in the way of Ormond's goal. Ormond's murder of him becomes the benevolent act of a pre-Nietzschean superman. "For killing him [Ormond explains to the bereft daughter] I claim your gratitude. His death was a due and disinterested offering on the altar of your felicity and mine" (p. 231). All Ormond's acts are motivated by a high "experiment" in social revolution and reformation, the consummation of which he will allow no circumstance to circumvent or negate (p. 235; also pp. 207–8 and 231–34).

The German translation of *Ormond* in 1802 by F. von Oertel, the translator of Lewis' *Monk*, suggests that the "Germanic" quality of this novel was recognized. Brown, it should be added, had been apprised of the Illuminati "perfectibilians" that arose in Germany and spread over Europe not only through the great hubbub raised in America, at just the time when he wrote his novels, by John Robison's *Proofs of a Conspiracy* (1797), but by the numerous German novels which dealt with the ideas, schemes, activities, and symbolisms of the Illuminati and similar *Bünde*. These had prepared his mind long before Americans generally became excited and saw Illuminati lurking in every dark corner. Naubert's *Hermann und Unna: Eine Geschichte aus den Zeiten der Vehmgerichte* (tr. as *Hermann und Unna*, 3 vols., Dublin, 1794; London, 1796,) for example, told how "a hundred thousand individuals were held together by an invisible chain, known to each other, but indistinguishable to the rest of the world, whose sittings were covered with the most impenetrable secrecy; whose decrees were arbitrary and despotical, and were executed by assassins whose steel seldom failed to reach the heart of the unfortunate victim."—London ed., I, v–vi. To the Preface of the translation was added an "Essay on the Secret Tribunal and Its Judges" from the *Miscellaneous Works of Baron Bock*. Brown's friend, Elihu H. Smith, read *Hermann and Unna* in the Dublin edition of 1794 in 1795. See Warfel, *loc. cit.*, p. 361; C. Touaillon, *op. cit.*; Marianne Thalmann, *Der Trivialroman des 18. Jahrhunderts. Ein Beitrag zur Entwicklungsgeschichte der Geheimbundmystik* (Berlin, 1923), pp. 71–76; Vernon Stauffer, *New England and the Bavarian Illuminati* (N.Y., 1918); Agnes G. Murphy, *Banditry, Chivalry, and Terror in German Fiction, 1790–1831* (Chicago, 1935), and Edith Birkhead, *The Tale of Terror* (London, 1921).

170. *Early Influence of German Literature in America* (N.Y., 1900), p. 37.

171. *Die romantische Bewegung in der amerikanischen Literatur* (Weimar, 1910), p. 27.

172. Here, however, we must not lose sight of the fact that in the Preface to *Wieland* Brown specifically referred for confirmation of the idea of religious delusions leading to murder to an incident reported in the local papers (see *Wieland*, Pattee ed., p. 4, and Carl Van Doren's summary of the story in the *Nation* for Nov. 12, 1914). This report, relating how a farmer living near Tomhannock, N.Y., had killed his wife and four children in a fit of religious mania, was printed in the *New York Weekly Magazine* for July 20, 1796, the same periodical which was even then concluding its serialization of Schiller's *Geisterseher* (or "The Apparitionist," running in Volume I from May 9, 1795, to June 18, 1796), and was followed shortly after by Peter Will's version of Tschink's *Geisterseher* (or "The Victim of Magical Delusion," running from July 6, 1796, to June 28, 1797). Schiller's story presented many motifs Brown may have utilized, not only for the claptrap of secret societies and mysterious events but more especially for the arguments in which the relationship of reason, understanding, will, the senses, and the feelings to truth and morality are discussed, for both Schiller's and Brown's novels abound in such passages.

173. *Wieland*, p. 261.

174. *Ibid.*, p. 238; see also p. 257.

175. Uncritically assuming that strange voices which he heard are of heavenly origin, he interprets them as divine commands. He refuses to listen to all available sources of knowledge, brushing aside Pleyel's qualifying opinions and Carwin's explanation of ventriloquial phenomena.

While three important elements of *Wieland* (localities, characters, and atmosphere; the Illuminati theme; and the moral of the tale) appear to be derived from German sources, the two most sensational motifs of the novel—ventriloquism and internal spontaneous combustion—are drawn from other sources. Brown drew most of what he knew about ventriloquism from the *Encyclopaedia; or a Dictionary of the Arts and Sciences*, published in Philadelphia during the same year that *Wieland* appeared (see Pattee ed., pp. xxx–xxxiv). With regard to Brown's use of spontaneous combustion, of which so much is made in the early part of the novel, Brown himself referred (in a footnote) this phenomenon to accounts in "the Journals of Florence" and to "similar cases reported by Messrs. Merille and Muraire, in the Journal de Médicine for February and May, 1783," as well as the "researches of Maffei and Fontana." Pattee suggests that the possibilities of spontaneous combustion were discussed by Brown and his roommate, Dr. E. H. Smith, and with other physicians and scientifically-minded members of the Friendly Club. More recently Professor Warfel has undertaken to re-examine the *Selbstverbrennung* episode in *Wieland* with results suggesting that there was a Pennsylvania-German source and probably also German and English intermediary sources from which Brown derived the information originally printed in the Italian journals.

176. For indications of his influence on these authors, see David L. Clark (ed.), *Edgar Huntly* (N.Y., 1928), pp. xx–xxii, and *Ormond* (Marchand ed.), p. xxxviii.

177. For this information I am indebted to Professor Harry R. Warfel, who has transcribed and prepared for publication the extant diaries of Smith. It is to be desired that their publication will not be much longer delayed.

178. Long before Smith turned to learning German, he had been accustomed to read translations of German fictional and dramatic writing in British journals like the *Monthly Review*, the *Monthly Magazine*, the *English Review*, and the *Analytical Review*. But what is most suggestive among his wide talents and interests is that as early as 1796 his reading in the British reviews excited his interest in Kant, to whose

essay on world peace he made several references in his diary. Something of the extent of his concern with German literature can be gathered from his notations in the diary, which show that he read during 1795 Lavater's *Secret Journal of a Self-Observer* (doubtless in Peter Will's translation), the Dublin edition of *Hermann and Unna* (Sept. 14), Goethe's *Iphigenie auf Tauris*, apparently in the original (Sept. 28), a translation of Schiller's *Kabale und Liebe* (Dec. 2), Kalm's *Reise durch Nordamerika* (Apr. 2, 1796), and the translation of an unidentified German play, "The Negro Slave" (Nov. 19), that appeared in the London *Oracle* for October 10, 1796.

179. Preston A. Barba, "Cooper in Germany," *German-American Annals*, n.s., XII (Jan.-Feb., 1914), 3–60; also in *Ind. Univ. Studies*, II, xii (May 15, 1914), 49–104.

180. Thos. R. Lounsbury, *James Fenimore Cooper* (4th ed., Boston, 1884), p. 68.

181. From Berne he made a number of excursions into the surrounding country, including a trip to the Jungfrau, to Schaffhausen and Geneva, and a more extended tour through the central and eastern cantons, up the Rhine to its source, and back by the Grimsel Pass, Meiringen, and Thun to Berne.—R. E. Spiller, *Fenimore Cooper, Critic of His Times* (N.Y., 1931), pp. 141–45. In the journal of this period he recorded his daily travel experiences and took careful note of the past history as well as present details of each valley, town, or notable object that came under his observation, many of them later being transcribed to form letters that comprise the first volume of his *Sketches of Switzerland* (1836).

182. See *Excursions in Switzerland* (Paris, 1836), pp. 126–67.

183. See his tribute to Schiller in *A Residence in France* (Paris, 1836), pp. 173–74. The events associated with the affiliation of the cantons of Uri, Schwyz, and Unterwalden appealed to the defender of the principle of federal union; whereas the ruins of the castle of the Hapsburg family furnished inspiration for the paragraph on that "false policy that has endeavored to raise up, in the center of Europe, an Empire of discordant materials to counteract the power of Russia and France." On the other hand, "the castles of the Erlach family at Spietz and Hindelbank aroused only sympathetic thoughts in the mind of the American landed proprietor. The power of the latter family was economic, and in this sort of dominance Cooper believed," as he was later to demonstrate in the Littlepage trilogy.—Spiller, *op. cit.*, p, 146.

184. See the introduction to *The Heidenmauer*; Spiller, *op. cit.*, p. 195; *James Fenimore*

Cooper, Representative Selections, ed. by Spiller, (N.Y., 1936), p. 336, n. 70.

185. They proceeded from Paris by way of Cambrai, Brussels, and Aix-la-Chapelle, to Cologne on the Rhine, a stream which he called "an old acquaintance" in the introduction to *The Heidenmauer*. Thence they went by Koblenz, Mainz, Wiesbaden, Frankfurt-am-Main, Darmstadt, Mannheim, Heidelberg, and Ludwigsburg, to Stuttgart, again visiting Dürckheim, where he had laid the scene of *The Heidenmauer* (for details of the journey, see *Sketches*, Part II, Vol. I). Cooper himself wanted to turn eastward to Vienna, but was induced to continue southward out of consideration for the youngest of the children, whom he wanted to provide with an opportunity to form a memorable impression of Switzerland. Hence they proceeded to Zürich and Zug, thence westward to the Bernese Oberland and Berne to Vevey. Here, as he whiled away idle evenings on the lake, philosophizing with the boatman, he formed the outlines for his new book, *The Headsman* (1833). By October they were back in Paris, and by November of 1833 they all arrived in New York.

186. Appearing simultaneously with the Philadelphia edition of these two parts were the London and Paris editions, Part I being entitled *Excursions in Switzerland*, and Part II, *A Residence in France: With an Excursion up the Rhine, and a Second Visit to Switzerland*.

187. Although Cooper acquired what he called "a very respectable travelling German," it was "far from classical," as is indicated by various passages in the Swiss *Sketches*, among them the passage in *A Residence in France* (pp. 173–74) in which he expresses his preference for Schiller over Goethe. See also *Excursions*, pp. 96–97.

188. On the score of Cooper's archaeological prowess and his use of bookish sources for a traveler's information, see Spiller, *Fenimore Cooper*, pp. 159, 202, 324–25.

189. Following the first seven letters devoted to his residence in Paris, Letters VIII–XVI relate the journey via Belgium, up the Rhine, and through the Bernese Oberland; the remaining ones describe his summer residence at Vevey on Lake Geneva. In substance this volume covers roughly the fourth of his German-Swiss tours.

190. Although Cologne is the "dirtiest and most offensive [city] we have yet seen, or rather smelled in Europe," he proceeds in true tourist fashion to inspect the cathedral, to visit the birthplace of Rubens, to view the relics of the eleven thousand virgins, and to buy some Cologne water. He is especially profuse in

noting whatever of history or legend is worth recording at Rüdesheim, Ingelheim, Biebrich, Wiesbaden, Frankfurt-am-Main, Heidelberg, Ludwigsburg, Stuttgart, Tübingen, Tuttlingen, Schaffhausen, and Zürich.

191. As Cooper explains in the Introduction, the abbey, the castle, the devil's stone, the heathen wall, and the lore relating to them set in motion "the train of thought" and provided the locale for the novel—the destruction of the old orders in both church and state by the advent of Lutheranism. Further talks with the "philosophical" Kinzel and "a convocation held in the parlor of the Ox" clarified the theme of "the following pages," in which Cooper relates the past history of the schisms between church and state as emblematic of the six-teenth-century movement toward popular rights. These, as he saw it, had been given new meaning in terms of the advance of democratic principles in the Europe and America of his own day.

192. Spiller, *Fenimore Cooper*, pp. 218, 219-20.

193. The object of the book, which became also the guiding motive of much that he wrote later, is stated in the last paragraph in these terms: "Our object has been to show, by a rapidly-traced picture of life, the reluctant manner in which the mind of man abandons old to receive new impressions—the inconsistencies between profession and practice—the error of confounding the good with the bad, in any sect or persuasion—the common and governing principles that control the selfish, under every shade and degree of existence—and the high and immutable qualities of the good, the virtu-ous, and of the really noble." This is a heavy cargo for a novel to carry, and as a novel the book fell dead from Cooper's hand. But it remains an interesting examination into the causes for the decay, under the influence of Lutheranism, of feudalism and ancient tradi-tion in Europe, and an exposition of the signifi-cant social and religious heritage which the new world derived from the old.

194. He set himself to check the tendency to ape European models, and in *The Lay of the Scottish Fiddle* (1812), *Koningsmarke, the Long Finne* (1827), and in his several volumes on John Bull and Brother Jonathan he satirized the Englishman no less than the continental European. In his *Book of Vagaries* he ridiculed the vaunted German love of music and the ease with which Viennese society combines piety with profligacy. The vogue in America of phrenology and animal magnetism Paulding blamed on the Germans' addiction to the pseudo-scientific and mystical, and in *Merry Tales of Three Wise Men from Gotham* (1839) he made these "German vagaries" the special object of satire. In his telling, though essenti ally good-natured, ridicule of American readers who swallow "cheap imported goods" and of writers who imitate the "sentimental immo ralities of German authors" he aimed at keeping American literature within the limits of sanity.

195. Oral S. Coad, "The Gothic Element in American Literature before 1835," *JEGP* XXIV, i (1925), 72-93.

196. Odofriede, a deformed peasant, cast out by society, becomes a misanthrope. Evil spirits grant him beauty and riches in exchange for his soul. To avenge himself on mankind, he uses his wealth and charm to ruin the lives of his fellow men, until in the end he loses command over the spirits and is whisked away by the fearful one.

197. Thomas Roscoe, *The German Novelist* (4 vols., London, 1826), II, 60n. For other details, see Henry A. Pochmann, "Irving's German Sources in *The Sketch Book*," *Studies in Philol.*, XXVII, iii (July, 1930), 477-507, esp pp. 477-79.

198. *Blackwood's Edinburgh Mag.*, XI (June 1822), 689.

199. *Ibid.*, XVII (Jan., 1825), 66.

200. See the comment of editor R. W. White on Poe's "Berenice" in the *Southern Literary Messenger* for March, 1835.

201. Poe's Preface to *Tales of the Grotesque and Arabesque* (1839).

202. *Works of Edgar Allan Poe* (ed. by J. A. Harrison, 17 vols., N.Y., 1902), XIII, 144.

GERMANIC MATERIALS AND MOTIFS IN THE SHORT STORY

WASHINGTON IRVING

1. As editor, during 1812-1814, of the *Analectic Magazine*, he initiated a new policy by which the *Analectic* devoted during the first year of his command twenty-four pages to information about Germany, thus beginning a practice by which this periodical soon outdid all other native journals of the day in the dis-semination of German literary lore among American readers. See Goodnight, *op. cit* pp. 122-25.

2. Surfeited by this body of melodramatic murky, substandard literature from Germany he became predisposed to adopt what became his characteristically curious, quizzical, satiri cal attitude toward much of German literature The detachment with which he later handled typically German legendary motifs like that of Lenore in "The Spectre Bridegroom" or of Di

eisse Frau and similar German ghosts in tories like "The Adventure of My Uncle" and The Bold Dragoon" and the ease with which .e made the transition from the serious to the omic, or sportive Gothic, resulted in part at 2ast from this early conditioning.

3. For Scott's German interests at this time nd Scott's influence on Irving, see Pochmann, *c. cit.*, pp. 485–88, and Stanley T. Williams, *he Life of Washington Irving* (2 vols., N.Y. 935), I, 158–67.

4. P. M. Irving, *Life and Letters of Washing-m Irving* (4 vols., N.Y., 1862–1864), I, 282, 284, 85–86, and *Letters of Irving to Brevoort* (ed. by *. S. Hellman, 2 vols. in 1, N.Y., 1918), pp. 66–67.

He conjugated German verbs and scrawled ff pages of declensions: "Gute Milch, gutes lier, guter Wein." He had trouble with the pelling of "Erzalungen" *(Erzählungen)*, with enitives and neuters. Discouraged by the 1sufferable difficulties of the language, he metimes turned to his fragment of a novel, *?osalie*, and other old or abortive literary rojects, only to return to "that awful language" 'hich barred his ready access to such delightful its of lore as he extracted and jotted down, in is notebook of 1818, from Johann Kaspar Ries-eck's *Travels in Germany* (tr. by P. H. Maty; vols., London, 1787), I, 140–42: "Watzman lountain in Bavaria where it is said the uropean Charles the great and all his army re confined until Doomsday—near Sallzburg *ic*]—a cleft of the mountain from whence you ear a dull rumbling like distant thunder." In ermany, four years later, he visited the scene here these marvelous events had reputedly ·anspired, and standing in the ravine, strained is ears, half credulous, half amused, for sounds f the phantom army. See Williams, *Life*, I, 56, and *Journals of Washington Irving*, ed. by *.* P. Trent and G. S. Hellman (3 vols, Boston, 919), I, 90ff. In a note appended to "Rip Van 'inkle," Irving facetiously (or mistakenly) ·ted this old legend as the source of his ·ory.

5. *Letters of Irving to Brevoort*, pp. 286–87.

6. His "scribbling" pleased him so much that 2 would not stop to accept any other employ-.ent, however needed, certain, or lucrative. he essays and stories that comprise *The Sketch* ·ook bolstered his faltering confidence to re-2dicate himself to a writing career. As the 1ccess of *The Sketch Book* seems to prove, he as right in trusting to his genius. But it may 2 added that *Tales of a Traveller* (1824) need t have been the comparative failure that it as if Irving had adhered more closely to the .ethod in *The Sketch Book* of adapting German

sources that made "Rip Van Winkle," "The Legend of Sleepy Hollow," and "The Spectre Bridegroom" such decided hits. But by 1823–1824 "the buzzards of criticism," with their cries of "Stolen!" and "Plagiarized!" had made Irving timid about reworking old German legends and myths. Consequently *Tales of a Traveller* became another salmagundi of titbits and counterfeit anecdotes of spurious or dis-guised origin, while the legends and fairy lore of Salzburg and of Rübezahl, carefully gathered though they had been during Irving's Dresden sojourn, reposed in his notebooks, whence his timidity prevented his drawing them forth.

7. Apparently Irving had proceeded far enough by 1819 in his study of German (barring the possibility that he found someone to trans-late the tale for him) to read the story of Peter Klaus in the original, because no translation of it had yet appeared in English or, as far as I have been able to discover, in any language that Irving could read at the time. The story as told in Büsching's *Volks-Sagen* (1812), where Irving could have found his source as readily as in Otmar, appears to have received its first English translation in the *London Magazine* for March, 1822—too late for Irving's purposes.

8. What makes Irving's story classic is his elaborations upon Otmar's bare narrative, the embroidery, and the inimitable style which Irving added. He translated the locale from the Harz to his own beloved shadowy Catskills, beside the azure Hudson. He substituted for Otmar's *Rittermänner* of the Kyffhäuser a company of odd-looking personages whom we recognize as the characters of one of his earliest works—Hendrick Hudson and his men, legend-ary shades of the Catskills like the phantom army of Friedrich der Rotbart. He changed the goatherd to a ne'er-do-well but lovable Dutchman, thus providing for those felicitous scenes of Van Winkle domesticity, marred by termagancy on the one side and shiftlessness on the other. He contrasted the tranquil atmos-phere of the colonial inn under whose sign loll the contented Dutch wiseacres with the bustling contentiousness of the mob that intro-duces Rip to the new era. All this is touched by Irving's poignant feeling of mutability, his love for the old Federalistic certitudes, his distrust of the untried promises of Jeffersonian republi-canism. For the political significance of the little scene that is enacted before Doolittle's hotel upon Rip's return, see my selected edition of *Washington Irving* (American Writers Series, N.Y., 1934), Introduction, pp. xlii–lx, esp. p. xlv. Finally, Irving stretched out the story after Rip's return from his long sleep to relate, in his leisurely way, Rip's changed condition,

person, and character after he got from under "petticoat government."

9. For the happy manner in which Irving combined something of his own with something borrowed from bookish or legendary materials for a dozen other pieces in *The Sketch Book*, see Williams, *Life*, I, 182–83, and for others of Irving's writings, *ibid.*, pp. 263–325.

10. The fact that the story of "der verzauberte Kaiser Friedrich" immediately follows "Peter Klaus" in Otmar's book suggests that Otmar rather than Grässe, Büsching, or some other, supplied Irving's source. In the other collections the stories are separated.

11. *Works of Washington Irving* (3 vols., N.Y.: P. F. Collier, n.d.), III, 571 n.

12. The subterfuge involved in these notes is probably little more than a reflection of his dislike for ungenerous critics who harped upon the derivative nature of his best offerings. To reveal the sources of his stories was to bait the track and turn the pack loose upon himself. However, his use of unacknowledged materials in *The Sketch Book* was not his least offense of this kind. Later he angered the Spaniards by offering translations from obscure books as original stories. See Williams, *Life*, pp. 183–84.

13. Besides knowing the oral tradition current in Sleepy Hollow of "the ghost of a Hessian trooper, whose head had been carried away by a cannon-ball, in some nameless battle during the revolutionary war," Irving was familiar with what he called "the favorite goblin of German tales" in several versions, including Scott's translation of "Der wilde Jäger" and Otmar's "Wild Huntsman of Hacklenburg." In the latter the wild rider hurls a shank of meat at his victim's head. Before writing his adaptation of the libretto of Weber's *Freischütz*, entitled *The Wild Huntsman* (1824), Irving familiarized himself with many of the German variants of the story. Burns's "Tam O'Shanter," too, was something to his purpose. Tam and Ichabod encounter a number of similar experiences on their luckless rides, but unlike Ichabod, Tam himself escapes bodily injury, while his nag loses her tail. Moreover, Burns does not use what is central in Irving's story—the rivalry-in-love motif, nor what is even more important, the climactic head-hurling incident. The latter Irving found in no English or German tradition until he happened upon the *Rübezahl* legends as told by Johann K. A. Musaeus in *Volksmärchen der Deutschen* (1782).

14. The legends of Rübezahl ("Number-Nip" in the English version) were available in a translation ascribed to William Beckford, published in two volumes in London by Murray in 1791 under the title of *Popular Tales of the*

Germans. Whether Irving used the original or the translation is immaterial. Beckford follows the original so closely that his version serves as well as that of Musaeus for purposes of comparison. Since the parallel passages are given in extenso in my essay in *Studies in Philology* (XXVII, 500–503), they are merely summarized here. All references to Irving's writings, except where otherwise indicated, are to the "Spuyten Duyvil" edition (12 vols., N.Y., 1881).

15. Compare *Popular Tales of the Germans*, II, 143–44, and *The Sketch Book*, 417; see also pp. 425, 442, 446.

16. *Popular Tales*, II, 145–46, and *The Sketch Book*, p. 446; also pp. 423–24.

17. *PT*, II, 146; *TSB*, pp. 447, 448, 449.

18. *PT*, III, 147; *TSB*, pp. 448–49.

19. *PT*, II, 147; *TSB*, pp. 449–50.

20. *PT*, II, 147; *TSB*, p. 450.

21. *PT*, II, 149–50; *TSB*, p. 450.

22. *PT*, II, 151; *TSB*, pp. 451–52.

23. *PT*, II, 165; *TSB*, p. 452.

24. In Germany later Irving made a tour of the Riesengebirge, the scene of Rübezahl's activities; his off-hand references (*Journals*, I 192, 206, 219) to the Rübezahl lore indicate prior familiarity. An interesting point in this connection is that one of the names by which Rübezahl went was "Rip," a variant for "Nip."

25. P. M. Irving, *op. cit.*, I, 335–36.

26. *The Sketch Book*, p. 202. To give the story an authentic German atmosphere (despite Irving's burlesque overtones), he laid the scene in "the heights of the Odenwald, a wild and romantic tract in Upper Germany"; the characters are given significant names like Count von Altenburg, Herman von Starkenfaust, and Baron von Landshort, "a dry branch of the great family of Katzellenbogen," which name Irving took the pains to translate in a footnote; words like *Rhein-wein*, *Ferne-wein*, *Saus und Braus* are scattered throughout; and the heroine is said to know all the "chivalric wonders of the Heldenbuch" and the "tender ballads of the Minne-lieders by heart."

27. *Journals*, I, 225.

28. Precisely what Irving's primary motive in visiting Germany was is hard to determine but it is certain that Scott's strong championship of German literature bore weight with him. Also, the remarkable success of his first short stories, which had drawn so heavily upon Teutonic legends, made him eager to know more of Germany and her literature. After basking for a while in the public favor occasioned by the success of *The Sketch Book*, and following a vacation in Paris, the necessity of earning a livelihood recalled him to the realities of an author's life. But the projected work on

'Buckthorne," once called tentatively "The History of an Author," and originally based on his observations of what transpired at literary dinners like those of Longman's, eventually underwent a dozen transformations before finally appearing as Part II in *Tales of a Traveller*. The other manuscripts he worked on at the time simply would not jell. None was committed to paper as readily as "Rip Van Winkle," for instance. He was sorely in need of stimulation. In Paris he saw a good deal of George Bancroft, just turned 21, fresh from his studies under Heeren and Schlosser, and what he learned from Bancroft about Germany as a paradise for the literary antiquarian played its part in the decision that finally took him there in 1822. In the meantime, *Bracebridge Hall* had been completed and published in 1822; and while it got him a handsome check from Murray, the book was a letdown after *The Sketch Book* (for details, see Williams, *Life*, I, 207–12). No one knew better than Irving that the book was too pale and buccolic for the romance-hungry readers of 1822. The one robust story between the two covers—"The Stout Gentleman"—the critics chose to damn as "indelicate," "indecent." Obviously he had worked the English countryside and antiquarian materials to the limit of the readers' endurance. Here begins Irving's practice of changing his habitat in search of new matter when old themes begin to run thin. Everything pointed to Germany as the land where his stock-in-trade might find most ready replenishment. When finally his physician advised him to try the baths in Germany, his mind was easily made up, and on July 17, 1822, he entered the Rhineland at Aix-la-Chapelle. From here his itinerary lay by way of Wiesbaden to Mainz, down the Rhine to Koblenz, thence to Frankfurt, Darmstadt, via the Bergstrasse, through the Odenwald, to Heidelberg, then to Karlsruhe, Kehl, Strassburg, thence eastward to Ulm, Augsburg, Munich, Salzburg to Vienna and finally to Dresden for the winter.

From the date of his departure from Aix (Aug. 6, 1822) until he reached Paris a year later, Irving wrote little that survives in print. Though he had gone to Germany with the intention of doing a German Sketch Book (sometimes he spoke of it as "a book on Germany" or "my German book") he worked only in a desultory fashion on such narratives as 'Buckthorne." In the midst of excursions into the country surrounding Dresden (where he settled longest), the social whirl of the capital, a none-too-promising love affair, amateur theatricals, visits to art galleries, and struggles with a recalcitrant language, his pen did little

more than make notes in his journals of the stuff that eventually supplied some of the fodder for *Tales of a Traveller*, the actual composition of the bulk of which took place in Paris during the winter of 1823–1824. See the *Journals* for the Dresden period and Williams, *Life*, pp. 218, 272–74.

29. P. M. Irving, *op. cit.*, II, 101; also *Journals*, I, 55, n. 3.

30. On the first day of his arrival on German soil he made note of two superstitious beliefs held by the natives (*Journals*, I, 49); just below Bingen he observed the Mouse Tower and on a height opposite the ruins of the castle of Ehrenfels. In the Odenwald, where he had laid the scene of his "Spectre Bridegroom," he was interested in the medieval castles "famous in German song and story," and at Heidelberg he inquired after "legend and goblin tale" clustering round its castles. At Erbach he remarked on the "chateau of Erbach—Rittershalle, or Knight Hall—armour of Goetz von Berlichingen—Gustav Adolph—Wallenstein." Goetz, as the hero of Goethe's play, had been familiar to him since his youth, when it had been popular on the New York stage. *Wallenstein* had been available in English since 1800. Near Baden he entered a note about the medieval Westphalian court of justice, the *Fehmgericht*, which had been called to his attention by Scott, and much earlier, by the New York plays of the Dunlap-Kotzebue era.

31. Intent on the picturesque, romantic past, he missed completely the political drama gradually unfolding itself in Germany in the post-Napoleonic era, apparently unaware of what Fichte's popular works had done for the disunited states. To Hegel's declaration that the era of roughhewing Teutonia was over, and that she was now free to turn to the inward kingdom of the intellect and the spirit—to these subtler forces Irving remained oblivious. To the new economic thought, the radical theological speculations, and the revolutionary philosophy of Germany he was as insensible as he had been (and as he remained to the end) about such matters, even in his native land. The Germany that interested him was not of the present or future, but of the fabled past.

32. For instance, at Munich, "one part rubbish the other fine," while he met royalty, his repeated visits to the library with its "500,000 volumes" most absorbed his attention. During his month at Vienna, he regularly patronized the Imperial Library.—*Journals*, I, 79, 81, 104–5.

33. One of them contains the supernatural sleep motif, already used in "Rip Van Winkle." Repeatedly he notes in his diary, as he did at

the Golden Eagle in Ober Hollabrun, "sit up until near eleven . . . read'g and writing. Read old legends after going to bed." To his sister he wrote: "I have some wonderful tales told me which I shall keep in mind against I have another match at story-telling with the children." —P. M. Irving, *op. cit.*, I, 114; II, 119. At Salzburg he "inscrolled page after page of fable," some in his journals, others in his letters to the Van Warts and the Storrows, who (he knew) would preserve every scrap that came from Geoffrey Crayon, and where all might be borrowed later if needed for a first draft of some tale.

"Put me in mind [he wrote to Susan Storrow] . . . of the Emperor and his army shut up in the enchanted mountain—which mountain I have absolutely seen with my own eyes. Put me in mind of the little dwarf woman. . . . Put me in mind of the Black Huntsman and the enchanted Bullets. Put me in mind. . . ."— Williams, *Life*, I, 225; *Journals*, Oct. 19, 1822. Unfortunately he never made literary use of any of these except the story of the Black Huntsman and the enchanted Bullets.

34. *Journals*, I, 101 (Nov. 2, 1922).

35. P. M. Irving, *op. cit.*, II, 124. Leaving Vienna on November 18, he arrived at Prague on November 22 for a stop of four days. Here he assembled odds and ends for romances that were vaguely germinating in his mind. But soon he was off again, across the broad Bohemian plain, through Schan, Laun, Teplitz, to Peterswald, where he entered Saxony. Throughout his tour he jotted down bits of folklore and German words, phrases, and savings: for example, "trinkgeld," "amtsmann," "landwehr," "hausknecht," "elegant schöne," "lusthaus," "landkutscher." For many phrases he added a translation; thus, "Bei dem hängt der Himmel voller Geigen" he rendered "with him the heaven hangs full of fiddles," adding, "German saying of a merry fellow who lives joyously"; and "*Gleich*, says the valet de place, is an hour, and *gleich, gleich*—two hours." Other examples, with references, are recorded in my essay on "Irving's German Tour and Its Influence on His Tales," *PMLA*, XLV, iv (Dec., 1930), 1150–87, esp. pp. 1157–58.

36. The romantic lore of Germany now took on added meaning. In May, in preparation for a tour of the Riesengebirge, the legendary haunt of Rübezahl (whose exploits he had already turned to good use), he read the entire Rübezahl saga with the Fosters.—*Journals*, I, 192, 219.

37. See *Journals*, I, 137–38, 139, 144, 168, 170, 184, 217.

38. For information regarding this elusive,

interesting individual, see Walter A. Reichart, "Washington Irving's Friend and Collaborator: Barham John Livius, Esq.," *PMLA*, LVI, ii (June, 1941), 513–31.

39. The evenings that Irving was not at court or at the Fosters he spent at the theater, often devoting three evenings a week to playgoing. For German operas and plays seen while in Germany, see my essay in *PMLA*, XLV, 1154– 55. Irving's vocation (for it amounted to that) as opera- and play-goer and his work as playwright and libretto writer are not sufficiently recognized. During the seventeen years that he spent in Europe he saw a vast number of plays and operas, whose titles, recorded in his diaries, constitute a list—English, French, Italian, German, Spanish—unequalled in the record of any other American man of letters.

Following his participation in amateur theatricals at the Foster house, Irving renewed his contacts with John Howard Payne, then engaged in the selection and revision of French plays for the London stage. Irving gave advice, often more than advice, in connection with the plays on which Payne worked during 1823– 1824. Two of them, *Charles II* and *Richelieu*, are largely the handiwork of Irving. With these, we may consider *Abu Hassan* and *The Wild Huntsman*—adapted by Irving from the German—as the four finished pieces of Irving the playwright.

Early in 1823, Irving decided to write an English libretto—part translation, part adaptation, from the then most popular German opera of Carl Maria von Weber, a man with whom he was soon on terms of intimacy. He set to work on April 20, with the libretto of *Abu Hassan* by Karl Franz Heimers before him. That evening he heard Weber play his own music. Irving wrote steadily and finished the rough draft on April 25. The next day his friend Colonel Livius played the music for him; and notations in the diary for the first half of May indicate how rapidly the writing proceeded, Irving working with Livius on the songs until May 28, when the alterations were finished.

On May 30 he began work translating and adapting from the German of Friedrich Kind the libretto of Weber's most famous opera, *Der Freischütz*. (Irving had first seen it performed in Darmstadt on September 20 and again on October 12, 1822.) By June 4 he was revising. We hear no more of it until we come to the Paris journals, October 8 and 11, 1823, when Irving together with Livius, finally retouched the libretto. It was first produced on the English stage under the title of *The Wild Huntsman* in London on July 22, 1824. In this connection Irving and Livius deserve credit that has no been given them by the bibliographers of the opera and drama. "One may stress the fact," says Hellman, "that the first version in English of a libretto of the first German opera was written by the first famous American man of letters." See George S. Hellman, *Washington Irving, Esq.* (N.Y., 1925), pp. 148ff.; also Williams, *Life*, I, 234-35, 236, 255-72.

40. See Irving's humorous comments on this meeting, *Journals*, I, 145. Among things purchased at this time is "Jean Paul's work," and thereafter he frequently mentions reading his writings.—*Journals*, I, 187, 198.

41. *Ibid.*, p. 189; see also pp. 151, 173-74, 198.

42. As a constant theater-goer and busy with amateur theatricals, operatic and dramatic compositions of his own, Irving could hardly have missed meeting Tieck, the leading dramatic critic in Dresden. Indeed, a careful reading of the manuscript notebooks from which G. S. Hellman and W. P. Trent selected and edited the three volumes of the *Journals* shows that the editors consistently misread *Tieck* as *Treck* in making the transcription, so that the references which Irving made later in "Buckthorne" to Tieck's *Phantasus* and his (Irving's) "Fancy" take on added meaning in the light of their close association in Dresden. I surmised that this relationship existed in my 1930 essay in *PMLA*, XLV, 1170. The hunch was substantiated the following year by Professor Edwin H. Zeydel in a note, "Washington Irving and Ludwig Tieck," *PMLA*, XLVI, 946-47. See also *The Correspondence of John Lothrop Motley* (ed. by G.W. Curtis; 2 vols., N.Y., 1889), I, 36, in which Motley reports meeting Tieck in 1834 and Tieck's speaking appreciatively of Irving. Tieck possessed not only the 1831 edition of Irving's writings but a number of individual titles, in both English and German.

Throughout the period of his German residence Irving added to the knowledge he had acquired earlier of Bürger's poems, Schiller's and Kotzebue's plays, the translations of Hoffmann in *Blackwood's*, and tales of other German romancers appearing in other periodicals, a familiarity with Chamisso's "Peter Schlemihl," a tale based on the old German folk story of the man who sold his shadow to the devil; and he read Jean Paul, Tieck, Friedrich Laun, Arndt's *Märchen*, the Grimms' *Märchen*, much of Goethe and some of Schiller's historical and dramatic works, while Mrs. Foster entertained him by reading from the multi-volume edition of Musaeus and from other collections. See *Journals*, II, ii; Williams, *Life*, I, 179, 213, 223, 272, 446-47; II, 287; *Journal of 1823-1824* (ed. by Williams, Cambridge, 1931), pp. 72-73, 243.

Other literary associations are detailed in *PMLA*, XLV, iv (Dec., 1930), 1158-60.

43. Williams, *Life*, I, 235.

44. This was regular procedure beginning early in December, when he engaged the first tutor, until May 16, 1823, when he noted in his diary, "Lesson in morning—paid Schott forty dollars for ninety-six hours of German teaching," and the next day he added, "Pay off Mr. Keysler for five and one-half months German tuition at eight dollars the month. Forty-four doll[ars]" (*Journals*, I, 194, 195). Early in January, when he met Tieck, Irving still carried on his part of the conversation in English, though this probably means no more than that Tieck's mastery of English invited Irving to use his native tongue in order to facilitate communication. Also, the princes and other members of the Dresden court, being as eager to display their command of English as their distinguished guest was desirous of concealing his halting German, invited Irving, during his early months among them, to speak English. While he never acquired the same facility for speaking German (or French, for that matter) that he subsequently achieved in Spanish, he could make himself understood in both German and French, and he made steady progress during the Dresden period in his ability to handle the language. The Dresden *Abendzeitung* proudly reported on Jan. 22, 1823: "Herr Washington Irving . . . busies himself tirelessly with our language which he himself speaks, and with whose characteristics he has been acquainted since his earlier sojourn on the Rhine, at Mainz and Vienna."

45. *Journals*, II, 9-10, 11, 19, 47, 50, 86, 107, 156; III, 190; and Williams, *Life*, I, 222, 230-32, 443, n. 36.

46. Even during his last days in Germany, while accompanying the Fosters to Rotterdam, he was in a frenzy of activity not to miss anything of importance by the wayside. Together they visited notable spots ranging from the site of the Leipzig Battle of Nations to Auerbach's Keller of Faustian fame, and he made a special effort to trace the wanderings of "The White Woman" of Germany, later turned to good advantage in Part I of *Tales of a Traveller*. On every possible occasion he urged Mrs. Foster to read, as she had done so often in Dresden, tales of German witches and goblins from Musaeus and other collections, while he busily entered notations in his journal like a miser adding pennies to his hoard.—Williams, *Life*, I, 243; P. M. Irving, *op. cit.*, IV, 369.

47. *Ibid.*, II, 137-38.

48. During 1823-1824 Irving projected a number of literary undertakings that came to

little. One of them appears to owe its inception to Goethe's *Faust*. On September 11, 1824, Kemble asked Irving to write a play for him. His diaries reveal neither assent nor refusal, but during the following month Irving conceived the plan of a play to be entitled *The Cavalier*. Though nothing came of it, there remain certain notes of a play called *El Embozado*, based on a suggestion given to Irving the preceding March by Byron's friend, Medwin. *El Embozado: The Cloaked Figure* was to be a drama of the dual nature of man—a story of crime and seduction in which the young offender is finally saved by the intervention of his better self (Irving later treated a similar theme in his "Don Juan: a Spectral Research"). Hellman connects Irving's *El Embozado* with Goethe's *Faust*, for which (Irving remarks) Goethe apparently got suggestions from the *Magico Prodigioso* of Calderón. Irving had long been familiar with the story of Faust and had read Goethe's version in the original. See Williams, *Life*, I, 443, n. 36; *Journals*, I, 173; II, 156; Hellman, *op cit.*, pp. 166–67.

49. Having been sent for, on April 27, 1823, by the Queen of Saxony, who intimated that she expected "he would write something about Dresden, etc.," he felt himself in a measure commissioned and committed to write about Germany.—*Journals*, I, 185.

50. One suspects that the reference is to books mentioned on December 15, 1823: "Return home, and find parcel from Mrs. Foster, with German books." In Paris he read indefatigably and counted himself particularly fortunate at having "within five minutes' walk . . . the great national library."—*Ibid.*, II, 168–69, 181–83.

51. P. M. Irving, *op. cit.*, II, 166.

52. *Ibid.*, p. 164

53. *Ibid.*, pp. 20, 55.

54. "Wrote a little at 'History of an Author'" is one passage in his diary at the time. "Tried to commence work on Germany, but could do nothing" is another. Then follows: "Toward twelve o'clock, an idea of a plan dawned on me—made it out a little, and minuted down heads of it." This was a plan "to mingle up the legendary superstitions of Germany in the form of tales and local descriptions and a little bit of the cream of travelling incidents." On December 17, 1823, he wrote: "Woke early—felt depressed and desponding—suddenly a thought struck me how to arrange the MSS on hand, so as to make two more volumes of 'Sketch Book' ready . . . in the spring." By January 3, 1824, he finished "Wolfert Webber," but then he wrote no more until February (*ibid.*, II, 178–79). On February 8 he complained of "a fit of

sterility for this month past" so that he despaired of "the hope of getting ready for a spring appearance." He also reported that he had "determined to introduce my 'History of an Author,' breaking it into parts and distributing it through the two volumes," explaining that it had "grown stale" and that he would never be able to finish it "as a separate work" (*ibid.*, II, 185–86). Then he wrote "The Bold Dragoon," "The Adventure of My Uncle," "The Adventure of My Aunt," "The Mysterious Picture," and the Italian banditti tales at the rate of ten to thirty pages a day (*ibid.*, II, 187–91), but by March 25, he had again changed everything. Writing to Murray he said he had given up the idea of a second *Sketch Book*—instead, he had "run into a plan and thrown off writings which will be more novel and attractive," that after some "rewriting and filling up" the whole would be ready in six weeks, and that the title would be "Tales of a Traveller, by Geoffrey Crayon, Gent."—*Ibid.*, II, 191.

55. At the last moment the manuscripts were found to be too few for two octavo volumes. He was obliged to pad by writing introductions, conclusions, links, and interpolated passages for "Buckthorne," and he dashed off another robber tale (which it is impossible to say). *Tales of a Traveller* appeared in four parts: Part I. Strange Stories of a Nervous Gentleman; Part II. Buckthorne and his Friends; Part III. The Italian Banditti; and Part IV. Money Diggers.

56. See *Memoirs, Journal, and Correspondence of Thomas Moore*, ed. by Lord John Russell (8 vols., London, 1853), III, 252–53. Actually certain autobiographical portions of the story, or stories, had been put in the first draft even earlier.

57. That is, the sections entitled "The Young Man of Great Expectations," "Grave Reflections of a Disappointed Man," "The Booby Squire," and "The Strolling Manager." Irving worked on the second half of Buckthorne intermittently from December 23, 1822, to June 14, 1823. The last parts appear to have been composed chiefly during this period when he was engaged in private theatricals at the Foster's, reading *Faust* and discussing *Egmont* with Emily, talking with Baron Lutzerode about the English and German theaters, and regularly attending the Dresden theater. Very likely his theatrical interests led him to *Wilhelm Meister's Lehrjahre*, Goethe's story of the apprentice who follows a theatrical career to prepare for life.

58. Compare *Tales of a Traveller*, p. 182, and *Wilhelm Meisters Lehrjahre*, Bk. I, Chaps. IV and VI, *Goethes Werke* (Weimar ed., 102 vols., 1887–1918), XXI, 18–24.

59. *Tales*, pp. 184–85, and *Werke*, XXI, 88.

60. *Tales*, 187–88, and *Werke*, XXI, 122–23, 211–16.

61. *Tales*, p. 92, and *Werke*, XXII, 238–39.

62. *Tales*, pp. 253, 255, and *Werke*, XXII, 238.

63. *Tales*, esp. pp. 253–61, and *Werke*, XXII 230–56.

64. A group of bachelors have gathered on a baronet's estate for a great hunt. The weather turning inclement, they assemble in the baronial hall, an idyllic setting for the ghost stories which they proceed to relate.

65. That Irving read some of Tieck's works we know, although we do not know precisely which; but considering Tieck's reputation in Dresden and the cordial relations which existed between him and Irving, it is not likely that Irving overlooked Tieck's popular tales. Moreover, "Buckthorne" contains a direct allusion to *Phantasus*. We read that Buckthorne "fell in company with a special knot of fellows, of lively parts and ready wits, who had lived occasionally upon town, and became initiated into the Fancy," a club similar to Tieck's Phantasus. See *Tales*, p. 214, and compare Tieck's *Phantasus*, Vol. IV of *Schriften* (28 vols., Berlin, 1828–1854), esp. the "Einleitung" and the links.

66. Grässe, J. T. G. *Sagenbuch des Preussischen Staates* (2 vols., Glogau, 1868–1871), I, 15, 224, 267, 283, 521, 765, 783; II, 76, 366, 479, 664, 779.

67. *Ibid.*, I, 572–75. "Die Edelfrau von Scharzfeld" was included in the collections of Büsching, Gottschalck, Grässe, and Roscoe. Very likely Irving read the tale in Büsching, though it is not impossible that the story came to him by word of mouth, as Professor Williams conjectures (*Life*, I, 288). Another possibility is that he received a hint for his tale from Jean Paul's *Des Feldpredigers Schmelzle Reise nach Flätz* (*Werke*, 2nd ed., 33 vols., Berlin, 1840–1842, XXIX, 241–319, esp. pp. 296–307), in which there is a nocturnal visit of much the same kind as Irving's "Uncle" experiences. The fact that Irving, after meeting Jean Paul, bought his works and read some of them lends plausibility to the conjecture (see *Journals*, I, 187). But whether the source is Büsching or Jean Paul and possibly an anecdote current in Paris does not matter so much as that the subject matter is common legendary material, nowhere more than in Germany, and that Irving used it, along with materials gathered elsewhere, to spin another of his characteristic gruesomely ludicrous tales.

68. For "The Adventure of My Aunt," the next story, no specific source seems to exist, at least not in German. Common to many literatures, of course, is the motif of the movable eye which the disconsolate widow sees in the portrait of her departed husband, but which belongs to a flesh-and-blood person, a servant, who, secreting himself behind the picture, cuts out an eye of the portrait to observe the lady and take her unawares—to "violate her purse and rifle her strong box."

69. For Irving's familiarity with Schiller, see P. M. Irving, *op. cit.*, II, 155; *Journals*, II, 156, 166, 190, 203; Williams, *Life*, I, 38, 294, 443, 446; II, 288, 357.

70. See E. Parry, "Schiller in America," *Americana Germanica* (Phila., 1905); and consult the Index (under Schiller in America) of the Pochmann-Schultz *Bibliography of German Culture in America*.

71. Another influence of *Die Räuber* is found in *Tales of a Traveller*, the episode in "The Story of the Young Robber," in which the bride, falling into the clutches of the gang, is raffled off by the members of the band. Like Carl Moor, the young robber kills her to keep her from becoming common property. Compare *Die Räuber*, V, ii, and *Tales*, pp. 358–63.

72. The dragoon, a roistering blade, rides jollily into the old Flemish town of Bruges, demands lodging of an old innkeeper, and though the house is full, will not take No for an answer. With many loud oaths and claps on the thigh, he cajoles the landlord into a good humor, kisses the landlord's wife, tickles his daughter, chucks the barmaid under the chin, does the honors to the house generally, and so ingratiates himself with the burghers that they agree to let him sleep in the garret. He is warned that the room is haunted, but a bold dragoon fears no ghosts. Becoming uncomfortable under the warmth of a double featherbed, he gets up and strolls about the house. When he returns to his room, he finds a most uncommon hubbub. By the light of the fire he sees a pale weazen-faced fellow, in a long flannel gown and a tall white-tasseled night-cap, sitting by the fire with a bellows under his arm by way of a bagpipe, from which he forces asthmatical music. The musician's performance grows fiercer and fiercer, and his head and night-cap bob about like mad. Gradually the pieces of furniture in the room get into motion, and a wild dance begins, in which a long-backed, bandy-legged chair thrusts out a claw-foot, then a crooked arm, and making a leg, slides gracefully up to an easy chair of tarnished brocade and leads it gallantly out in a ghostly minuet. By degrees the dancing mania seizes other pieces of furniture. The antique, long-bodied chairs pair off in couples and perform a country dance; a three-legged

stool dances a hornpipe, though badly encumbered by its supernumerary leg; while the
amorous tongs seize the shovel and whirl it
about the room in a German dance. Suddenly
the musician strikes up "Paddy O'Rafferty,"
whereupon the dragoon goes into action, seizes
two handles of the clothes-press to lead her off
in an Irish dance when—whir!—the whole
revel is at an end, and the bold dragoon finds
himself seated in the middle of the floor, the
clothes-press sprawling before him, the two
handles in his hands.

73. *Journals*, I, 135.

74. The next story, "The Adventure of the
German Student," is written in a different key,
striking a real note of horror. A German student
in Paris falls in love with an imaginary lady,
woven of his dreams. Meeting her in distress one
night in the streets of Paris, he takes her to his
quarters, only to find her a corpse the next
morning. A police officer informs him that the
lady had been guillotined the day before, and
the truth of the statement is confirmed when
the student undoes a band about the lady's
neck and her head falls to the floor. The young
man is tormented by the belief that an evil
angel had reanimated the dead body to ensnare
him.

The story is pitched in the vein of Hoffmann
and has all the earmarks of a German horror
story; yet there appears to be no specific German source for it. By Irving's own statement
in the mock-acknowledgment of sources that
he made in the preface for the pieces comprising
the book, it is "founded on an anecdote related
to me as existing somewhere in French." He
might gracefully have added that he got it from
Tom Moore, who had it from Horace Smith
(Williams, *Life*, II, 288); but it was not Irving's
way to make such an explicit statement when
he could do little gentle spoofing. The tricks of
Dietrich Knickerbocker never forsook him.

75. See Williams, *Life*, II, 293–94.

76. Oral S. Coad, "The Gothic Element in
American Literature before 1835," *JEGP*,
XXIV (1925), 85.

77. More than half of the pieces employ German legendary materials, but they are adulter-
ated with other elements. For such concoctions
a search of printed sources would have sufficed,
and his trip to Germany to gather legendary
material and to absorb atmosphere was largely
wasted effort. Of the real literary treasures that
he dug up in Germany he made little use: the
Märchen that he wrote so carefully into his
notebooks remained between the covers of
those books. Instead, he snatched his materials
from vicarious sources—his haphazard reading,
anecdotes related to him, travel experiences,

memories. The book does not owe to Germany,
as *The Alhambra* owes to Spain, a solid body of
authentic, indigenous material.

78. Irving's journals from 1820 to 1825 exhibit a painful consciousness of the hostile
critics and the necessity under which he felt
himself to give them no more cause to charge
him with plagiarism, even if he had to resort to
subterfuge. Equally distressing was the realization that his good friend John Howard Payne
had felt himself called to say to him, as early
as the summer of 1822, "I want to see you
swimming without corks—throwing by translations and reconstructions and writing something from your own brain."—Williams, *Life*,
I, 268. What was worse was the gnawing
awareness, as he reshuffled the manuscripts for
Tales of a Traveller, that he could not swim
without corks. His mind could transcribe, but
it could not draw something out of thin air;
it needed to have something substantial—a
legend, a ruined castle, an anecdote, or an
experience—to work on. Lacking a creative
mind, Irving had to resort to books and to
travel. As for travel, he was fast coming to
realize what Emerson was soon to state classi-
cally: "Travelling is a fool's paradise," an
attempt "to get somewhat which he does not
carry." Yet he must go on stuffing his books
with secondhand gewgaws, scraps dropped at
dinner tables, tags picked up in museums,
fragments from travelers' chats, memoranda
made in the theater, recollections from random
experiences. This having to content himself
with ragtags and the skulking involved in
dressing them up to make them pass for coin of
the realm was melancholy, dubious business.
And when, after many false starts and prodigious labor, the book was finally done, the reviewers paid him off in precisely the coin he hated
most.

79. *Blackwood's* charged him with "pillaging
the Germans," "working up old stories"; another
Edinburgh reviewer said he had "no inven-
tive faculties at all"; even American friends
could no longer be relied on. The *New York
Mirror* for September 25, 1824, added its bit:
"Take away his *Dutchman with his pipe, his old
mansion with his Ghosts, his Uncle Trim*, and
his Aunt Tabitha—and perhaps a clown of an
Old Bachelor, and Mr. Irving is like the *one-
hundredth copy* of a digusting original." *Tales of
a Traveller* should be retitled "Stories for Children by *a Baby Six Feet High*."

80. His supernaturalism was always tinged
with either humor or irony; he preserved an air
of detachment and dished up a whimsical medley of the gruesomely ludicrous. No reader is
frightened by a ghost that appears in the castle

of a baron named Landshort of the family of Katzenellenbogen, or by a headless horseman who serves only to introduce the story of a pumpkin shattering on the cranium of Ichabod Crane. Even "The German Student," Irving's best-sustained story of horror, ends in a characteristic Knickerbocker caper.

81. Fred L. Pattee, *The Development of the American Short Story* (N.Y., 1923), p. 17.

82. *Letters of Irving to Brevoort*, pp. 425–28; see also pp. 432–34; for his method of writing the book, combining the antiquarian's search for book lore with the romanticist's immersion in atmosphere, see *The Alhambra*, pp. vii, 30, 40, 47, 56–58, 163–64, 351, 385, 405; P. M. Irving, *op. cit.*, II, 95–96, 100–104, 134–37; and compare *Journals*, III, 97–100, with *Alhambra*, pp. 42–44.

83. His Spanish lessons began December 10, 1824. On January 15, 1825, he said he was reading Spanish "satisfactorily"; yet the lessons continued for some time longer.

84. Grimm's story in summary form is as follows: An innkeeper, accompanied by two companions, is returning from a journey. They pass by some gibbets on which hang three unlucky wights who had been executed some time ago. One of the innkeeper's companions remarks that the dangling corpses were men who had frequently been the guests of the innkeeper. In grim jest, the innkeeper compliments the dead men on their nimbleness, as they swing to and fro in the wind, and derisively asks them to be his guests at his house that evening. Arrived at home, the innkeeper goes to his room, where, to his horror, he finds the three dead men waiting for him. They are seated about the table and beckon him to join them. His frantic calls summon attendants, to whom he relates what has happened. He takes to his bed, and in three days he is dead.

In Irving's "Guests from Gibbet Island," Yan Yost Vanderscamp, proprietor of "Die Wilde Gans," runs a riotous, uproarious tavern, "a complete rendezvous for boisterous men of the seas," in reality a pirates' den. The government suddenly takes rigorous measures to eradicate piracy, and several of the most noted freebooters are caught and executed. Among them are three of Vanderscamp's comrades, who are hanged on Gibbet Island, in full view of their favorite resort. One evening, as Vanderscamp returns from a sail in a boat manned by Pluto, his surly Negro slave, the Negro rows the boat near Gibbet Island. They behold "the bodies of his three companions and brothers in iniquity dangling in the moonlight, their rags fluttering, and their chains clanging, as they were slowly swung backward and forward by the rising breeze." Prompted by his companion, Vanderscamp says, "Come, my lads in the wind! I will be happy if you will drop in to supper." The only reply is a dismal creaking of chains. But on reaching home, Vanderscamp is told that three guests are awaiting him in his room. "Vanderscamp made a desperate effort, scrambled up to the room, and threw open the door. Sure enough, there at a table, sat the three guests from Gibbet Island, with halters round their necks, and bobbing their cups together. . . . Vanderscamp saw and heard no more. Starting back with horror, he missed his footing on the landing place, and fell from the top of the stairs to the bottom. He was taken up speechless, and, either from the fall or the fright, was buried . . . on the following Saturday."

85. Gottschalck's tale (as well as Grimm's just mentioned) was translated and published in 1826 in Thomas Roscoe's *German Novelists*, a collection well known to Irving.

86. Compare the characterizations of the villain as found in Irving's tale (*Wolfert's Roost*, pp. 327–28) and Gottschalck's in Roscoe's *German Novelists*, pp. 228–33.

87. If, as I believe, this tale of Gottschalck's served as a suggestion for Irving's story, it is very likely that Irving consciously avoided the theme of incest as incompatible with American taste. He had once drawn the charge that "The Stout Gentleman" was "coarse," and was loath to take unnecessary risks.

88. Finally, in this last volume of short tales, Irving used an anecdote which he had long saved "against another fit of scribbling." On his tour from Aix to Dresden, some one told him of a "couple who prayed continuously for children, but in spite of their prayers, they never got any, which was tho[ugh]t very remarkable" (*Journals*, II, III). Many years later he turned it to advantage in "The Widow's Ordeal" by making it the pivot of the story. The little anecdote may or may not be of German origin, but it does illustrate how Irving would seize upon this or that scrap of lore in the course of his rambles, and how he might eventually turn it to use.

89. Letter to Scott, quoted by Irving in *The Sketch Book*, Preface, p. 9.

90. *Letters of Irving to Brevoort*, pp. 400–401.

NATHANIEL HAWTHORNE

91. The passage in which this judgment is made was reprinted in *Littell's Living Age* for October, 1844 (II, 654), and quoted again in a critique on Hawthorne in the *Democratic Review* for April, 1845 (XVI, 384), though the

latter critic professed to find echoes of Hoffmann also in Hawthorne (*ibid.*, p. 378).

92. First printed in *Godey's Lady's Book* for November, 1847; reproduced in *The Complete Works of Edgar Allan Poe* (ed. by James A. Harrison, Virginia ed., 17 vols., N.Y., 1902), XIII, 144. This edition is hereafter cited as *Works.* It is to be observed that this is a guarded statement. While nothing in the way of implication could be stronger, the charge of plagiarism is not expressly made. The qualifying phrase, "in *some* of his work," seems calculated.

93. On April 3, 1852, *Littell's* (XXXIII, 19) all but repeated the words of the *Athenaeum* five years earlier, and an article in the *Revue des Deux Mondes* for April, 1852 (XIV, 365), pointed out a resemblance of Hawthorne's style to that of Toepfer, but substituted Nordier's name for Tieck's; while the *National Magazine* for January, 1853, observed: "Saving certain shadowy resemblances to some of the Germans, his manner of working out a sketch is unlike that of any other author." Lowell's characterization of Hawthorne in *A Fable for Critics* as "a John Bunyan Fouqué, a Puritan Tieck" is, of course, part banter.

94. Prof. H. M. Belden's purpose in "Poe's Criticism of Hawthorne," *Anglia,* XXIII (1901), 376–404, is "to establish Poe's sincerity as a critic." More favorable to Hawthorne are the conclusions reached in Anton Schönbach, "Beiträge zur Charakteristik Nathaniel Hawthornes," *Englische Studien,* VII (1884), 301–2; Pattee, *Development of the American Short Story,* pp. 105–6; and Myrtle J. Joseph, "Tieck and Hawthorne," Columbia Univ. Master's thesis, 1911.

95. *The Complete Works of Nathaniel Hawthorne* (Fireside ed., 13 vols., Boston, 1896), IX, 332–33; herafter cited as *Works.*

While the three Peabody sisters were assiduous students of the German language and literature, they failed to transfer their enthusiasm to him. They did succeed in arousing his interest in some aspects of the "Newness," particularly Brook Farm, which Hawthorne joined in 1841. While there, he lived in an infectious atmosphere, but he appears not to have joined any of the several classes at Brook Farm that studied German language, literature, philosophy, or music.—Moncure D. Conway, *Life of Nathaniel Hawthorne* (London, 1890), pp. 65–66, 84; Julian Hawthorne, *Nathaniel Hawthorne and His Wife* (2 vols., Boston, 1885), I, 40, 183, 185–87, 251, 263. That he was not then or later an accomplished linguist appears from the doubt he expressed in 1853 regarding his qualifications for a post as "Translator to the State Department," which his friends sought to secure for him.

However, J. P. Lathrop's argument (*op. cit.,* p. 207) that Hawthorne did not know Tieck and never would have looked into him if Poe had not nosed out a scent of plagiarism, and that Hawthorne made an effort to get hold of Tieck's tale mentioned in the *Note-Books* only after reading Poe's criticism (and so, of course, after writing the tales in question) is invalid for reasons of chronology. Hawthorne read Tieck's tale on April 8–11, 1843; *Mosses* was published in 1846; Poe's criticism was first printed in November, 1846.

96. Among the more important collections of translations that included tales of Tieck, B. Q. Morgan (*op cit.,* p. 483) lists seven before 1846. Although Hawthorne was not a close follower of British periodicals, he could have come upon several of Tieck's tales translated there. These are easily identified by turning to the Roloff-Mix-Nicolai bibliographies edited by B. Q. Morgan and A. R. Hohlfeld, *German Literature in British Magazines, 1750–1860* (Madison, Wis., 1949), and Lilie V. Hathaway, *German literature . . . in England and America as Reflected in the Journals, 1840–1914* (Boston, 1935). From 1825 to 1850 only six of Tieck's tales appeared in American periodicals, but there were many more reviews and critical notices, all of which are identified in the bibliographies of Goodnight and Haertel.

97. In "The Virtuoso's Collection," when the illusions of fancy tempt the visitor with marvelous fruits, he says: "I might desire a cottage, but I would have it founded on sure and stable truth, not on dreams and fantasies. I have learned to look for the real and the true."— *Works,* II, 543. "My destiny is linked with the realities of earth; but give you are welcome to your visions and shadows of a future state; but give me what I can see, and touch, and understand, and I ask no more."—*Ibid.,* p. 559. In another place Hawthorne rejects the *elixir vitae* because "it would produce death while bestowing the shadow of life."—*Ibid.,* pp. 551–52. In "The Birthmark" Aylmer comes to ruin because he failed "to find the perfect future in the present."—*Ibid.,* p. 69. See also II, 210–11. Again and again Hawthorne returns to this idea. "Dr. Heidegger's Experiment," "Young Goodman Brown," "The Virtuoso's Collection," "The Birthmark," "The Great Carbuncle," "Drowne's Wooden Image," "The Ambitious Guest," "The Bosom Serpent," "The Artist of the Beautiful," "Monsieur du Miroir," "Feathertop," "The Lily's Quest," "The Hall of Fantasy"—what are they but repetitions of the moral enforcing his humanistic warning?

98. Poe, *Works*, XI, 113.

99. The December, 1844, number of the *Review* contained his article on Amelia Webly, and the very number that made the Tieck-Hawthorne allegation contained two articles by Poe—one entitled "Plagiarism" and the other "Mr. Poe Lectures on the Poets." In the issue for May, 1845, appeared the translation of Tieck's "Die Freunde," summarized above. Poe's "Power of Words" was published in the next number.

100. Poe had kept up carefully with Hawthorne's growing reputation. In his 1847 article he lists (giving magazine titles and exact dates) the reviews of Hawthorne's tales which had appeared before *Mosses*, indicating at the same time that he knew such reviews of *Mosses* as had appeared since 1846. That being so, he was familiar with the comparisons that had been made between Tieck and Hawthorne.

101. Not that Poe was necessarily fooled. His statement is carefully worded. He does not directly make the charge of plagiarism: he says "whose manner, in *some* of his works, is absolutely identical with that *habitual* to Hawthorne." He italicized "habitual" because he had noted Hawthorne's fondness for the particular kind of allegory contained in Tieck's tale, and he emphasized "some" because he knew very well that "Die Freunde" was not a typical tale of Tieck's. It is, in fact, one of the least characteristic of his shorter pieces and represents, according to Rudolf Haym, *Die romantische Schule* (3rd ed., Berlin, 1914) pp. 74–76, the transition from his earlier imitative to the romantic style with which Tieck's characteristic manner is customarily associated. How or why the translator chose this piece, so different from the *Märchen*, for which critics praised Tieck most highly, is not readily explicable; but in so doing, he chanced on a piece that bears unmistakable likenesses to Hawthorne's moralized stories that Poe was reviewing.

H. M. Belden, working on the dubious assumption that Poe knew no German (*Anglia*, XXIII, 389, 404), cites contemporary British reviews of Tieck and comes to the odd conclusion that Poe, seeing in them a characterization of Tieck's work similar to what he observed in Hawthorne's tales, honestly believed Hawthorne to have derived from Tieck. The truth of the matter is that it was Hawthorne, not Poe, who knew little German. What is more, Poe's sincerity as a critic in this case is questionable for the simple reason that the charge brought against Hawthorne is calculatingly phrased. His use of, and special emphasis upon, the word *some* smacks of the species of literary chicanery

that Poe indulged in on other occasions and suggests that Poe, knowing full well that Tieck's "Die Freunde" was far from characteristic of Tieck's manner, yet chose it as serving to hang on his strongest American competitor the charge of plagiarism. Compare this performance with Poe's calculated demolition of Drake and Halleck's poetic reputations.

102. *Works*, II, 213.

103. *Ibid.*, p. 224.

104. H. A. Beers, *A History of English Romanticism in the Nineteenth Century* (N.Y., 1901), p. 163.

105. *Works*, III, 381–83; IX, 42.

106. *Ibid.*, I, 153.

107. *Ibid.*, IX, 43, 83, 159

108. For numerous examples, see John Erskine, *Leading American Novelists* (N.Y., 1910), p. 193; Randall Stewart (ed.), *The American Notebooks of Nathaniel Hawthorne* (New Haven, 1932).

109. See W. C. Brownell, *American Prose Masters* (N.Y., 1909), 115; P. E. More, *Shelburne Essays*, First Series (N.Y., 1907), pp. 45, 53, 70.

110. Erskine, *op. cit.*, pp. 211–13, 233–34; P. E. More, *op. cit.*, pp. 47–49, 53; and appropriate chapters in Randall Stewart, *Nathaniel Hawthorne* (New Haven, 1948).

111. For illustrations of how Hawthorne expanded suggestions jotted down in his notebooks into stories, compare *Works*, IX, 22, with "Mrs. Bullfrog"; IX, 37, with "The Vision of the Fountain"; IX, 106, 110, with "The Birthmark"; and IX, 38, with "The Lily's Quest." For further glimpses into his workshop, see Anton Schönbach, *loc. cit.*, pp. 292–96; Myrtle J. Joseph, *op. cit.*, pp. 44–49; Eliz. L. Chandler, *A Study of the Sources of the Tales and Romances Written by Nathaniel Hawthorne before 1853* (Northampton, Mass., 1926); Randall Stewart, "Hawthorne and *The Faerie Queene*," *Phil. Quar.*, XII, ii (Apr., 1933), 196–206; Stewart's edition of the *American Notebooks*; Alice L. Cooke, "Some Evidences of Hawthorne's Indebtedness to Swift," *Univ. of Texas Studies in English*, XVIII (1928), 140–62; Neal F. Doubleday, "Hawthorne's Satirical Allegory," *College English*, III, iv (Jan., 1942), 325–37; three essays by Prof. Arlin Turner: "Autobiographical Elements in Hawthorne's *Blithedale Romance*," *Univ. of Texas Studies in English*, XV (1935), 39–62; "Hawthorne's Literary Borrowings," *PMLA*, LI, ii (June, 1936), 543–62; "Hawthorne's Methods of Using his Source Materials," *Studies for William A. Read* (Baton Rouge, La., 1940), 301–12; and Spiller *et al.*, *Lit. Hist. of the U.S.*, III, 548–51.

112. Cited by H. A. Beers (*op. cit.*, p. 164) as

evidence of Hawthorne's borrowing from Tieck. Hawthorne treated the same general theme also in "The Wedding Knell."

113. *Works*, I, 164.

114. *Ibid.*, p. 153.

115. Poe's *Works*, XI, 111. Two other tales of Tieck's that have been suggested as influencing Hawthorne (see Turner, "Hawthorne's Literary Borrowings," *PMLA*, LI, 559) were both available in Carlyle's translation of 1827. The first is "The Fair-Haired Eckbert," which is the history of a man who, like Arthur Dimmesdale, dwells in solitude and is persecuted by a guilty conscience. The other is "The Runenberg," which relates the story of a man whose heart, like that of Hawthorne's Man of Adamant or Ethan Brand, has been so far hardened that he finally goes insane. But obviously these are common motifs not necessarily betokening literary dependence.

116. See Alfred A. Kern, "The Sources of Hawthorne's Feathertop," *PMLA*, XLVI, iv (Dec., 1931), 1253–59; M. D. Conway, *op. cit.*, pp. 71–72; Alex. Jessup and H. S. Canby, *The Book of the Short Story* (N.Y., 1903), pp. 10–11; Anton Schönbach, *loc. cit.*, pp. 295, 301–2; Eliz. A. Chandler, *op. cit.*; and F. L. Pattee, *op. cit.*, p. 106.

In Tieck's satire a figure of Robin Hood, made of burnished leather, but exceedingly smart, is used as a scarecrow. Becoming vitalized by a shooting star, it appears as Baron Ledebrinna and becomes a great authority on literary matters. Like Hawthorne's Feathertop, he is only a scarecrow, but his impositions on the people, blinded by vanity and false standards, hoodwink them into accepting him as a literary dictator. Throughout the story there are hints of his true nature, just as in Hawthorne's story; he talks of scarecrows and compares himself and others to them; he waves his arms, shrugs his shoulders, and gesticulates. In Tieck's story a good deal is made of Ledebrinna's amorous ambitions, and the later portions of the novel recount his adventures as a lover.

117. *Works* XI, 211.

118. Omitted from the collected edition of Hawthorne's works, this entry first appeared in print in "Passages from Hawthorne's Note-Books," *Atl. Monthly* (Dec., 1866), p. 692.

119. Chronologically, it is possible that the "tale of Tieck" over which Hawthorne labored in 1843 was Tieck's "Vogelscheuche," for though he could hardly have seen it in the *Novellenkranz* version of 1835, it had become available in Volume XIV of Tieck's *Gesammelte Novellen* of 1842 and in Volume XXVII of his *Schriften* of the same year.

The note of 1840, in comparison with that of 1849, is so remotely related to "Feathertop" that is can hardly be regarded as the primary source of the tale. Indeed, the earlier note is of significance mainly as showing that Hawthorne had already conceived the idea of writing a story on a scarecrow as the model of various types of men, and that alone may be accountable for his being drawn to Tieck's story in 1843. There may well have been a direct connection between Hawthorne's note of 1840 and his reading Tieck's tale in 1843, and between both of these and the note of 1849, as well as "Feathertop" itself. Following his dismissal from the surveyorship of the Salem Custom House in 1849, Hawthorne had the further incentive of "immolating one or two" of the Salem gentry who he believed were responsible. His satire therefore had a most immediate political and personal motivation. For details, see Alfred A. Kern, "Hawthorne's *Feathertop* and R. L. R.," *PMLA*, LII, ii (June, 1937), 508.

120. Consult E. G. Gudde, "E. Th. A. Hoffmann's Reception in England," *PMLA*, XLI, iv (Dec., 1926), 1005–10, and the bibliographies by Morgan, Morgan and Hohlfeld (eds.), Hathaway, Goodnight, and Haertel.

121. *Peter Schlemihls wundersame Geschichte* (1814), translated in 1824, was available in seven editions or reprints—1824, 1838, 1843 (2), 1844 (2)—by the time Hawthorne's *Mosses* appeared, so that Hawthorne had ample opportunities for knowing the story. In "The Virtuoso's Collection" the virtuoso calls "Peter Schlemihl's shadow . . . one of my most valuable possessions" (*Works*, II, 556). However, the reference is one that Hawthorne might have made without ever having read Chamisso's tale, for Peter Schlemihl had become the common butt of jokes leveled at the extravagancies of German romanticists. Hawthorne's passage, in its context, is in the nature of a sneer. What's more, in Hawthorne's story there is no loss of shadow: the author merely holds a conversation with his double (himself, as he fancies) in the mirror. The idea is a common possession. Hawthorne himself wrote on his blotter, as early as October 17, 1835: "To make one's reflection in a mirror the subject of a story."

122. Hawthorne's knowledge of books has not yet been exhaustively studied, but Professor Austin Warren's essay, "Hawthorne's Reading," *New Engl. Quar.*, VIII, iv (Dec., 1935), 480–97, is very informative. After *Pilgrim's Progress*, he was influenced most profoundly by the Bible, Spenser, Shakespeare, and the New England historians (in the order named). But he was not a bookish author; and, as Professor Warren points out, when Hawthorne

sat down to write, "it was—literally and meta-
phorically—in a bare room populated primarily
by the creations of his own imagination" (ibid.,
p. 497). The composition of his stories, particularly of his novels, was always an intense and
exhausting experience. Books did not contribute much to the process. The modern literatures barely touched him—German no more
than the others. German transcendentalism,
hailed by Emerson, Ripley, and others of his
associates in Concord and at Brook Farm, left
him cold. Except for his satirical comments in
his diaries and letters, "The Celestial Railroad,"
and his less pointed references in The Blithedale
Romance and "Earth's Holocaust," he had
little to say about German thought.

EDGAR ALLAN POE

123. For notable examples, see Works, XII,
41–106; XIII, 141–55. All references, unless
otherwise indicated, are to the Virginia-Harri-
son edition.

124. Works, I, 150–51. Compare Poe's statement in his letter to Thomas W. White, April
30, 1835, printed in Mod. Phil., XXV (1927),
101–5.

125. Richard H. Stoddard, for example, expressed the guarded and uncertain opinion: "If
Hawthorne's master was Tieck, as Poe declared,
the master of Poe, as far as he had one, was
Hoffmann."—Works of Edgar Allan Poe (London, 1884), I, xiv. In 1881 E. C. Stedman
remarked: "He [Poe] was no disciple of Beckford, Godwin, Maturin, Hoffmann or Fouqué."
—Edgar Allan Poe (Boston, 1881), p. 63. But in
1894, in the Stedman-Woodberry edition of
Poe's writings, Stedman expressed another
view: "There is a pseudo-horror to be found in
certain of his pieces, and enough of Ernest
Hoffmann's method to suggest that the
brilliant author of the Fantasiestücke, whether
a secondary name or not, was one of Poe's
early teachers. . . . Hoffmann's spell was unquestionable."—Complete Works of Edgar Allan
Poe (Chicago, 1894–1895), i, 96, 98. Meanwhile,
Stedman's co-editor, G. E. Woodberry, in his
biography of Poe in 1885 said not a word
about German sources, but declared of the very
tales in which Stedman saw convincing evidence of Hoffmann's unquestionable spell that
"Bulwer and Disraeli, the popular writers of his
time, gave direction to his genius, both in subject and style."—Edgar Allan Poe (Boston,
1885), p. 65; also p. 85. In his later biography of
Poe (2 vols., Boston, 1909), I, 132–34, and
notes, 379–81, à propos of Palmer Cobb's work
on Poe's indebtedness to Hoffmann, Woodberry admitted the influence. His vacillation of

opinion is similar to Stedman's; neither is sure
of his stand. Nor is James A. Harrison very
positive or precise (Works, I, 153–54): "Where
or how, precisely, Poe became at first inoculated
with this spirit of occult Germany . . . is not
clear. . . . That somehow—somewhere—he became saturated with the doctrines of Schelling
and founded some of his finest tales and 'dialogues of the dead' ('Monos and Una' and 'Eiros
and Charmion,' for example) on their poetic
mysticism, there can be no doubt. . . . His
dreams were his most vivid realities, and he was
of the dreaming race—the Germanic—the race
of Novalis and Schelling, his masters across the
sea."

Later biographers and critics of Poe—
among them Arthur Ransome, John W. Rob-
ertson, Mary E. Phillips, Hervey Allen, Una
Pope-Hennessy, Arthur H. Quinn, and N.
Bryllion Fagin—are occupied more with ex-
plaining what Poe's mind put forth than with
how it was formed. Noteworthy exceptions are
Killis Campbell, "Poe's Reading," Univ. of
Texas Studies in English, V (1925), 166–96, and
The Mind of Poe and Other Studies (Cambridge,
Mass., 1933); Margaret Alterton, The Origins of
Poe's Critical Theory (Iowa City, Ia., 1925);
Floyd Stovall, "Poe's Debt to Coleridge,"
Univ. of Texas Studies in English, X (1930), 70–
127, and his "Poe as a Poet of Ideas," ibid., XI
(1931, 56–62.) Among studies dealing specifically
with the question of Poe's debt to Germany,
the first, in point of time, are Gustav Gruener's
articles: "Notes on the Influence of E. T. A.
Hoffmann upon E. A. Poe," PMLA, XIX, i
(Mar., 1904), 1–25, and "Poe's Knowledge of
German," Mod. Philol., II, i (June, 1904),
125–40. A broader investigation is Palmer
Cobb's "The Influence of E. T. A. Hoffmann
on the Tales of E. A. Poe," Studies in Philol.,
III (1908), 1–105. Cobb's emphasis falls
upon four of Poe's stories, "William Wilson,"
"A Tale of the Ragged Mountains," "The
Oval Portrait," and "The Assignation," as
deriving from "Die Elixiere des Teufels," "Der
Magnetiseur," "Die Jesuiterkirche in G——,"
"Doge und Dogaressa," respectively. In the
first three cases the debt is obvious; the last is
doubtful. The treatise by Paul Wächtler,
Edgar Allan Poe und die deutsche Romantik
(Leipzig, 1911), primarily concerned with
biographical and psychological matters, including Poe's peculiar mental and physical
similarities with Fichte, Schelling, Novalis,
Tieck, Arnim, Hoffmann, and others, does not
deal with literary relations either exhaustively
or conclusively.

126. The late Professor Killis Campbell, our
most cautious and best informed Poe scholar,

often expressed to his students his belief that Poe had "a good reading knowledge of German." I have a letter from him confirming this opinion.

127. *The Life of E. A. Poe*, I, 379.

128. *The Development of the Short Story in the South* (Charlottesville, 1911), pp. 17–24.

129. "Poe's Criticism of Hawthorne," *Anglia* XXIII (1901), pp. 376, 389.

130. For specimens, see *Works*, XIV, Introduction, p. vi; also pp. 38–72.

131. At Stoke-Newington, as well as under Masters Clarke and Burke in Richmond, he showed unusual skill in Latin.—Charles Kent (ed.), *The Unveiling of the Bust of Edgar Allan Poe: Poe Memorial, 1899* (Lynchburg, Va., 1901), pp. 13–14. He learned to speak French with "marked facility."—J. H. Ingram, *Edgar Allan Poe* (2 vols., London, 1880), I, 20, 25. At the University of Virginia, where he studied from January 19 to December 15, 1826, he excelled in Latin and French and was accounted "a successful student of Italian and Spanish."—Kent, *op. cit.*, pp. 14, 20, 21. A circumstance not without significance is the fact that Poe's library cards were signed by the irascible but gifted Professor Blaettermann. See A. H. Quinn, *Edgar Allan Poe: A Critical Biography* (N.Y., 1941), p. 103. No German titles are included, but since most of Poe's work was done under the supervision of Blaettermann, who shared with Follen the honor of introducing German as a subject of collegiate instruction in America, it is not impossible that some of Blaettermann's enthusiasm for his native language and literature was imparted to his impressionable student. Indeed, J. A. Harrison professed to find a "perceptible influence" of Blaettermann "all through Poe's humorous, imaginative work." See Gruener, *loc. cit.*, p. 127. The "School of Ancient and Modern Languages," in which Poe was enrolled, included "Latin and Greek languages, the Hebrew, rhetoric, belles lettres, ancient history and ancient geography . . . French, Spanish, Italian, German, and the English language, in its Anglo-Saxon form; also modern history, and modern geography." —Kent, *op. cit.*, p. 14. Here was more than even a Poe could acquire in a year. Indeed, it were well not to add to the seminal influences supposedly exerted on Poe by his year in Charlottesville. But it may be observed that Jefferson's School of Ancient and Modern Languages did develop some polyglots. Henry Tutwiller, at the end of the session, was reported excelling in Greek, Latin, French, Italian, German, Spanish, and mathematics; while Gessner Harrison, who is mentioned along with Tutwiller as among the "hard students," excelled

in Greek, Latin, French, Italian, German, and medicine" (*ibid.*, p. 14). It may be that Poe, besides enrolling in the classes of Latin, French, Italian, and Spanish, also studied German. Certainly he was better prepared than most of the students for the study of languages. See *Works*, I, 45–47; Quinn, *op. cit.*, pp. 97–117.

132. Kent, *op. cit.*, p. 14; Gruener, *loc. cit.*, p. 128.

133. *Works*, VII, 28; also used as a motto for the title-page of *Tales of the Grotesque and Arabesque;* see *Works*, I, 150.

134. *Works*, II, 1.

135. *Ibid.*, pp. 27–28.

136. See Stedman-Woodberry ed. of *Works*, I, 114–16, and Homer E. Woodbridge, "The Supernatural in Hawthorne and Poe," *Colo. College Lang. Ser.*, II (Nov., 1911), 147.

137. See *Works*, II, 28–29; for Leibnitz, II, 126, IX, 65, XIV, 217, XVI, 25, 223; for Kant, II, 126, 276, VI, 201; for Schelling, II, 29, 348, 390, XI, 5; for Fichte, II, 28, 359, 392; and for Hegel, XVI, 164.

138. Poe was also familiar with Locke's definition of personal identity as "the sameness of a rational being," and Locke's phrase "principium individuationis." See Works, II, 20, and Locke's *Essay concerning Human Understanding*, Bk. II, ch. xxvii, par. 9.

139. *Works*, II, 128–29, 131. See Campbell, "Poe's Reading," *loc. cit.*, p. 190.

140. His critics have questioned his knowledge of all foreign languages, including French (see Arvede Barine, *Revue des Deux Mondes*, CXLII, 566), and ridiculed even his English. The extent to which they went in their indiscriminate charges is seen in the accusations made by Thomas Dunn English:

"He professes to know every language and to be proficient in every art and science under the sun—when, except that half Choctaw, half Winnebago he habitually uses . . . he is ignorant of all. If he really understands the English language, the sooner he translates his notices of the New York literati into it, the better. . . .

". . . His frequent quotations from languages of which he is entirely ignorant, and his constant blunders expose him to ridicule, while his cool plagiarisms from known or forgotten writers, excite the public amazement."—*N.Y. Mirror*, June 23, 1846.

The persistent reiteration of such charges, corroborated by Poe's first biographer, Griswold, did not fail to make its impression, so that even T. W. Higginson said:

"Poe's [work] is broken and disfigured by all sorts of inequalities and imitations; he not disdaining, for want of true integrity, to disguise and falsify, to claim knowledge that he did not possess, to invent quotations and references, and even, as Griswold showed, to manipulate and exaggerate puffs for himself. I remember the chagrin with which I looked through Tieck, in my student-days, to find the 'Journey into the Blue Distance' to which Poe refers in the 'House of Usher' [*Works*, III, 287] and how one of the poet's intimates laughed me to scorn for being deceived by any of Poe's citations, saying that he hardly knew a word of German."—Higginson, *Short Studies in American Authors* (Boston, 1880), p. 17.

Higginson's remarks serve merely to convict him of precisely the sin which he imputes to Poe, for, as Henry A. Beers has pointed out: "Colonel Higginson, *a propos* of Poe's sham learning and his habit of mystifying the reader by imaginary citations, confesses to have hunted in vain for this fascinatingly entitled 'Journey into the Blue Distance'; and to having been laughed at for his pains by a friend who assured him that Poe could scarcely read a word of German. But Tieck really did write this story, 'Das alte Buch; oder Reise ins Blaue hinein,' which Poe misleadingly refers to under its alternate title."—*A History of English Romanticism in the Nineteenth Century* (N.Y., 1901), p. 163.

It is time that the evidence for making these broad charges be gathered and the testimony weighed.

141. For instance, in his review of *Thiodolf, the Icelander and Aslauga's Knight*, he goes easily from Fouqué's book into a general though brief survey of German literature and literary criticism, and is rather happy in his generalizations. See *Graham's Mag.*, Dec., 1846; also *Works*, XVI, 115–17.

142. "The German *Schwärmerei*—not exactly humbug, but sky-rocketing seems to be the only term by which we can conveniently designate the peculiar style of criticism which has lately come into fashion through the influence of certain members of the Fabian family—people who live (upon beans) about Boston."—*Works*, XVI, 166.

143. *Ibid.*, VIII, 163.

144. *Ibid.*, XV, 266–70, exp. p. 270.

145. After using the saying, "Er hat grosse Augen gemacht," he adds: "Here Mr. Crabb again made great eyes (as we say in Germany)." —*Works*, VI, 20. In the Marginalia he distinguishes between *edelgeboren* and *wohlgeboren*: "Nothing, to the true taste, is so offensive as mere hyperism. In Germany *wohlgeboren* is a loftier title than *edelgeboren*."—*Works*, XVI, 8. In the *Marginalia*, also, he distinguished between *Dichtkunst* and *Dichten*: "The Germans have two words . . . the terms *Dichtkunst*, the

art of fiction, and *Dichten*, to feign—which are generally used for poetry and to make verses" (*Works*, XVI, 91); and in reviewing Longfellow's *Ballads and Other Poems*, he made use of the distinction (*Works*, XI, 74). He also notes that "art" in German has an "extensive signification" which the English does not possess (*Works*, IX, 200).

146. He quotes several lines from Schiller's "Nadowessisches Totenlied" (which Poe, probably following the book before him, calls *Nadowessische Todenklage*), his purpose being to show that a few of the lines from Mrs. Hemans had been suggested by the passage from Schiller (*Works*, IX, 200). In the same article he asserts that her "Lays of Many Lands" were suggested by Herder's *Stimmen der Völker in Liedern*, and he quotes this troublesome title correctly. Professor Campbell suggests (*Poems*, p. 296) that just as Poe was quick to pick up telling German phrases, such as "phantasy-pieces," so he recognized good German titles, as when he adapted Uhland's "The Castle by the Sea" to his "a kingdom by the sea." Poe knew two of O. L. B. Wolff's collections of songs and ballads, including his *Sammlung vorzüglicher Volkslieder der bekanntesten Nationen, grösstentheils zum ersten Male metrisch in das Deutsche übertragen*, Frankfurt, 1837 (*Works*, XII, 95–96,) and he cited two other long German titles correctly (*Works*, II, 276). The motto selected from Goethe for the title-page of *Tales of the Grotesque and Arabesque* is aptly chosen (*Works*, II, 149–50).

In only one instance is there the suggestion that Poe's German was faulty, but even here the evidence is inconclusive and may be interpreted to argue the contrary. In "How to Write a Blackwood's Article" (*Works*, II, 279), after quoting some "piquant expressions" from French, Spanish, and Italian to be used by the magazine writer who wishes to give his piece a *recherché* tone, Poe quotes also the following German lines:

"Und sterb' ich doch, so sterb' ich denn
Durch sie — durch sie."

"That's German—from Schiller. 'And if I die, at least, I die—for thee—for thee!'"

Now these lines are not from Schiller, but from Goethe, occurring in the ballad "Das Veilchen." Furthermore, they are incorrectly quoted. The first line reads: "Und sterb' ich denn, so sterb' ich doch." Moreover, *durch sie* is not equivalent to "for thee." But the fact that Poe assigns the lines to Schiller and makes a mistake also in quoting them may be an indication that he was quoting from memory, and that he forgot the author as well as the exact wording of the passage.

In "A Predicament" (*Works*, II, 295), Poe parodies these same lines as follows:

"Und stubby duck, so stubby dun
Duk she! duk she!"

Professor Gruener (*loc. cit.*, p. 133) argues from this parody that Poe knew at least two facts about German pronunciation: namely, that the final *d* in *und* is pronounced like a *t*, and that the German *ch* in *durch* is pronounced more like a *k* than the English *ch* in *church*. These distinctions a person only superficially acquainted with the German would hardly make.

147. *Works*, V, 259.

148. Possibly *Deutsche Zeitschrift für die Chirurgie*, which dates back to the early 30's of the nineteenth century.

149. *Works*, V, i; first published in *Snowdon's Lady's Companion*, December, 1842.

150. Confirmed by the statement made in Mrs. Austin's book (p. 314) and by a search of the British Museum and of American libraries.

151. See Goodnight, *op. cit.*, pp. 208, 211, 213, 220. None of these reviews contained the passage either in the original or in translation.

152. Poe had reviewed (in 1836) Mrs. Austin's translation of Fr. von Raumer's *England in 1835* (*Works*, IX, 53–64); doubtless he knew also others of Mrs. Austin's books.

153. *Novalis Schriften* (ed. by J. Minor; 4 vols., Jena, 1907), II, 315.

154. Poe has *gowönulich*, evidently a misprint (*Works*, V, 21).

155. Poe has a colon instead of a period.

156. *Fragments of German Prose Writers* (N.Y., 1841), p. 97; Poe, *Works*, V, 1.

157. Both translators follow the original rather closely. Poe is closer in line 4, where Mrs. Austin translates *die* as *every*; in lines 7–8 where Mrs. Austin inserts *it was;* in the slight matter of the semicolon; and in Poe's more literal translation of *kam* in the last sentence where, however, he disregards *hervor*. It is a fine point whether Poe or Mrs. Austin translated *Begebenheit* and *Zufälle* more exactly.

Evidence such as this would be conclusive in almost any case but Poe's. Some of his more severe critics see in his translation a duplication of the method he employed in compiling *The Conchologist's First Book*, that is, a deliberate attempt to cover up plagiarism by making slight modifications of the model before him— not important enough to change the sense materially, but sufficient to give his version the appearance of originality. Both translators make *idealischer* modify the wrong noun, and

both render *gleichfalls* somewhat inexactly as *equally*. But if Poe followed this procedure, he had, in the first place, somehow to find the original passage in Novalis, for he quotes the German for it. Whoever has looked for a passage in Novalis' *Fragmente*, especially in such an edition as Poe used in the forties (i.e., lacking the elaborate tables and indexes of more recent editions) will agree that Poe exhibited some facility in the use of German in the mere matter of running down the passage. Of course, there is the possibility that he asked a second person to look up the passage for him; but that seems unlikely when we consider how often Poe would have required the services of such a second person. Moreover, why should he have gone to all the trouble and, in this case, committed a deliberate deception for the mere motto of a tale, when he had so little to gain? He would have achieved virtually the same effect if he had simply quoted Mrs. Austin or given his own translation, without indicating, in addition, the common source—"Novalis. *Moralische Ansichten*." On the other hand, if he ran across the German passage in his reading of Novalis and jotted it down, what was more natural than that he would cite the German and supply his own translations?

There is evidence that Poe knew and admired the writings of Novalis. Harrison and Woodberry both think Poe was influenced by Novalis. The former speaks of Novalis as one of "Poe's masters across the German sea" (*Works* I, 134), and the latter regards Poe's "prose poem" *Eureka* as growing out of a "single phrase of Novalis" (*Poe*, I, 93). Since there was no complete translation of Novalis in Poe's day, and the fragments translated by Mrs. Austin cover only seven small pages of her booklet, it seems reasonable to assume that Poe knew Novalis in the original, and that he translated the passage in question independently, though his attention may have been directed to Novalis by Mrs. Austin in the first instance. While all three of Poe's quotations from Novalis are taken from the *Fragmente*, they are taken from widely separated sections of the book. It would seem that Poe not only had access to a copy of at least this one work of Novalis but read it.

158. Quoted, *Works*, VIII, 44, 47; mentioned VIII, 43–44, 47, 126; X, viii, 65, 116; XI, 5, 250; XII, 131; XIII, 43; XVI, 115–17; Woodberry, *Poe*, I, 177–78; and below.

159. Killis Campbell, "Poe's Reading," *loc. cit.*, p. 189.

160. *Works*, I, 150, VII, 28; and II, 279, 295. Both of these poems of Goethe were available to Poe in the original and in translation in

Bancroft's article, "The Life and Genius of Goethe," *N. Amer. Rev.*, XIV (Oct., 1824), 303–25. On the other hand, Poe's references and quotations are too numerous and various to make tenable the assumption that he relied solely on translations in magazine articles and anthologies. The passage in *Politian*, scene iv, line 65, beginning "Knowest thou the land," may be nothing more than an unconscious echo of Mignon's song, "Kennst du das Land"; for this lyric from *Wilhelm Meister* was already a common possession by 1835 when it is thought Poe wrote this dramatic poem.

161. Campbell, *loc. cit.*, p. 189.

162. *Works*, IX, 200; Quoted, mentioned, II, 279, VII, 155, VIII, 138, IX, 200, 202.

163. See, for Bürger, *Works*, esp. IX, 173, 202; for Herder, IX, 200, 202, XI, 65; for Körner, XI, 65, 80; for F. Schlegel, XI, 5, XVI, 117.

164. For Musaeus, see *Works*, XVI, 117; for Wieland, XVI, 161; for Winckelmann, XI, 5; and for Uhland, XI, 65.

165. *Works*, IX, 202.

166. The appropriated passage occurs in an installment of the *Marginalia* in the *Democratic Rev.*, XIV (July, 1846), 30, that is not included in the Virginia edition. Poe's subterfuge was first uncovered by Professor Carl F. Schreiber in an essay entitled "Mr. Poe at his Conjurations Again," *Colophon*, II (May, 1930), 2. Pückler-Muskau's book, translated by Mrs. Austin (London, *ca.* 1831) and reprinted in Philadelphia in 1833, in a pirated edition, under the title, *Tour of a Prince*, was known to Poe; he reviewed it and used it as one of those "quaint and curious" volumes of forgotten lore from which to extract, when the occasion seemed to call for it, some odd reference or recondite allusion.

167. *Works*, XI, 67.

168. *Ibid.*, p. 69.

169. *Ibid.*, XVI, 42.

170. *Ibid.*, III, 287; IV, 102; XIII, 144, 145; IX, 202.

171. *Ibid.*, X, 30–39; XVI, 48–51.

172. *Ibid.*, XVI, 117.

173. *Ibid.*, X, 39.

174. See Quinn, *Poe*, pp. 336–40. Poe discusses and criticizes the German *Kunstroman* as a "mad—or perhaps a profound idea" (*Works* VIII, 232). He translates three passages from Novalis. One is used as a motto for "The Mystery of Marie Rogêt" (*Works*, V, 1). Another of the *Fragmente* is utilized in the *Marginalia*: "The artist belongs to his work, not the work to the artist"—following which Poe adds his own ideas about the matter (compare *Works*, XVI, 98–99, and Novalis, *Schriften*, II, 298). In "The Tale of the Ragged Mountains"

(*Works*, V, 171) he quotes possibly from Carlyle's essay on Novalis, apothegm no. 121 from Novalis' "Paralipomena zum Blütenstaub" (*Schriften*, II, 141); "We are near waking when we dream that we dream." "The Man of the Crowd" begins with "It was well said of a certain German book that '*es lässt sich nicht lesen.*'" This Poe translates literally: "it does not permit itself to be read" (*Works*, IV, 134). He is familiar with the legends of the Wandering Jew, "known to German writers as Ahasuerus" (*Works*, XIV, 217), and in *Pinakidia* there is a note about "German epic poems composed in metre of sixteen and seventeen syllables" (*Works*, XIV, 186–87). In the *Marginalia* he comments on the "epidemic of history writing" current in Germany (*Works*, XVI, 12), and in another note cites "an old German chronicle about Reynard the Fox" to illustrate a point (*Works*, XVI, 173). Here, too, he criticizes an assertion of Hegel's, which he considers jargon and not original with Hegel in the first place (*Works*, XVI, 164). Besides his references to Leibnitz, Kant, Fichte, Schelling, and Hegel, Poe is interested in the German scientists, historians, and scholars. Alex. v. Humboldt, to whom he dedicated *Eureka*, is mentioned a number of times and quoted once (*Works*, XVI, 186–87, 299). Kepler, whom he considered an "immortal," he mentioned ten times (*Works*, VI, 209, XVI, 196–97, 352). Johann H. Schroeter, Johann F. Encke, and F. W. Beissel are each mentioned once (*Works*, XVI, 352–53, II, 49), Helvetius twice (*Works*, XVI, 351, 352), and Mädler a number of times. See *Works*, XVI, 294–99, for Poe's discussion of Mädler's *Die Centralsonne* (1846) and *Über das Fixstern System* (1847), neither of which had been translated by 1847, though Poe may have relied on contemporary British discussions of the theories advanced by Mädler. Among German historians, Poe praises Niebuhr above all others in his review of Niebuhr's *Roman History* (*Works*, VIII, 227). Von Raumer, whose *America and the American People* he reviewed for the *Broadway Journal* for November 29, 1845, he condemns vigorously (*Works*, XIII, 13–16; see also IX, 53–64). To argue, in the face of this cumulative evidence, that Poe knew no German seems like trying to beat Poe at his own little game of perverseness.

175. See Harrison's statement on this head (*Works*, I, 153–54) and especially Paul Wächtler's *E. A. Poe und die deutsche Romantik*, pp. 7–43, esp. pp. 18–43. Besides the direct avenue, there were the British and American translators and before them the French. The path of German literature to America, if it is traced chronologically, lies through France, whence it was

introduced into England; Americans derived it from both intermediaries. Thus Hoffmann, for instance, might well have attracted Poe's attention by way of French translations. In 1829 François Loevè-Veimars, who had made a name for himself as translator of Heine and Schiller and by his articles on German literature generally, began an edition of Hoffmann in French. Though never completed, it contained Hoffmann's most characteristic works. The last volume of the French edition appeared in 1833, the year Poe published his first tale. "France," wrote Champfleury, "was unanimous in welcoming the tales of Hoffmann and ranking them among the *chef-d'oeuvres* of romancers." See Gustav Thurau, *E. T. A. Hoffmanns Erzählungen in Frankreich* (Königsberg, 1896), p. 245. Hoffmann was considered a "German classic . . . more popular in France than in Germany. His tales were read by everybody. . . . Hoffmann was the most popular author of the day in France."—Theo. Süpfle, *Geschichte des deutschen Kultureinflusses auf Frankreich* (3 vols., Gotha, 1886–1890), II, 154.

But since Poe shows himself familiar with books and selections from the German which in his day were not translated into French, or any other language of which he was master, we may conclude that he generally had sufficient means for learning what he wanted to know of German belles-lettres without depending on French or other translators.

176. Gruener, *loc. cit.*, p. 140.

177. In this area Defoe and Swift were Poe's prototypes. We recognize their influence in the journalistic instinct, sardonic humor, love for hoaxing the public, genius for seizing upon the latest discovery or scientific inference and pressing it to its conclusion, and mastery of verisimilitude by the use of minutiae.

178. Campbell says of the sources of these stories: "A good many of the books and periodicals to which he [Poe] went for his subjects were publications of his own time. Much of the detail, for instance, that appears in 'The Mystery of Marie Rogêt' was either quoted or adapted from the New York and Philadelphia newspapers of the eighteen-forties."—*Poe's Short Stories* (N.Y., 1927), p. xxi.

179. For an example of this kind of reasoning, see *Works*, IV, 153–56.

180. *Ibid.*, p. 179. The idea is elaborated *ibid.*, V, 2, 38–39.

181. *Ibid.*, V, 171, XVI, 98–99.

182. For examples see *Schriften*, II, 124, 195, 202, 262, 274; III, 3–4, 26, 339, 374; compare Poe's *Works*, IV, 153–56, 166. The idea occurs also in Tieck's *Schriften*, (28 vols., Berlin 1828–1854), IV, 51.

183. Palmer Cobb, in *Studies in Philology*, III (1908), 48–70, has pointed out in detail the similarities between Poe's "Tale of the Ragged Mountains" and Hoffmann's "Der Magnetiseur," and Paul Wächtler (*op.cit.*, pp. 47–55) has drawn parallels between Hoffmann's tales of mesmerism and those of Poe.

184. E. T. A. Hoffmann, *Sämmtliche Werke*, ed. by Eduard Griesebach (15 vols., Leipzig, n.d.), I, 139–75; VIII, 92–130; hereafter cited as *Werke*.

185. *Ibid.*, VIII, 131. The parallelisms between Poe's "Tale of the Ragged Mountains" and Hoffmann's "Magnetiseur" are obvious, though there are marked differences which Cobb does not sufficiently recognize. Moreover, he appears not to take sufficiently into account the similarities which Poe's story has with "Der unheimliche Gast," the companion-piece of "Der Magnetiseur."

Before Poe wrote "The Tale of the Ragged Mountains," he had become interested in the doctrine of metempsychosis, as "Berenice" (1835), "Morella" (1835), "Ligeia" (1838), and "Eleonora" (1842) illustrate. Already fascinated by this doctrine, and hitting upon it in some of Hoffmann's tales, Poe would naturally read on, especially when he found the German romancer combining hypnotism or mesmerism with metempsychosis. Since Poe had written before 1844 four stories dealing with metempsychosis, in none of which there is a hint of hypnosis or mesmerism, it is significant that, beginning in 1844, he wrote three more stories in which he combined metempsychosis and mesmerism in precisely the manner of Hoffmann.

Poe's use of the term "fantasy-piece" in describing his stories gives us some intimation about the time when he became acquainted with Hoffmann. In the preface to *Tales of the Grotesque and Arabesque*, he says, "Let us admit, for the moment, that the 'fantasy-pieces' now given *are* Germanic" (*Works*, I, 150). To be observed here is that "fantasy-piece" is inclosed in quotation marks and written as one word, as in the German term of Hoffmann's *Fantasie-stücke*. Poe's preface was written in 1839. The collection of tales appeared in 1840. Two years later he planned a new edition of his tales, to be entitled *Phantasy-Pieces*, the title-page of which Poe prepared, and a copy of which is reproduced in Quinn's *Poe*, p. 338. In a letter to Professor Anthon of New York, Poe wrote in June, 1844: "My tales, a great number of which might be called fantasy-pieces, are in number thirty-six" (*Works*, XVII, 179).

It may be that Poe first saw Hoffmann's title, *Fantasie-stücke in Callots Manier* (4 vols., Bamberg, 1814–1815) in the original; but more probably, he saw it first in Carlyle's appendix to *German Romance* (1827), where Carlyle speaks of Hoffmann's "Golden Pot" as belonging to "a strange sort (the Fantasy-piece) of which he himself is the originator. Carlyle later translates the title literally as "Fantasy-pieces in Callot's Manner," and refers to "Prinzessin Brambilla" as "properly another Fantasy-piece." See Carlyle's *Works*, Centenary ed. (30 vols., London, 1898–1899), XXI, 4, XXII, 12–13, 16.

The title, *Tales of the Grotesque and Arabesque*, supplies another link connecting Poe with Hoffmann. It has been argued plausibly, especially by Gruener, that Poe's title was suggested by an essay of Scott's "On the Supernatural in Fictional Composition; and particularly on the Works of Ernest Theodore Hoffmann" in the *Foreign Quart. Rev.*, I, i (July, 1827), 60–98. Scott's essay was the most carefully thought-out and best-written review of Hoffmann yet to appear in English. Even in Germany it was recommended by Goethe to the German public, and in France it furnished material for two articles on Hoffmann: (1) "Du Marveilleux dans le Roman," a free translation of the first fourteen pages of Scott's article, published in *Revue de Paris*, I (1829), 25 ff.; and (2) the introduction to François A. Loevè-Veimars' French edition of Hoffmann's writings (Paris, 1829–1833)—a free and condensed translation of the last twenty-six pages of Scott's article. See Gruener's "Notes," *loc. cit.*, p. 8. Poe was obliged by his duties as editor, if for no other reason, to follow British and American periodical literature. If he saw this particular number of the *Foreign Quarterly Rev.*—and the first number of a new magazine is likely to be more widely distributed and read than later issues—he must have been impressed by Scott's article dealing with a man whose works were so strikingly like his own, and who has accordingly been called his "Doppelgänger".

In his detailed characterization of Hoffmann's "Fantasic mode of writing," Scott said, "In fact, the grotesque in his composition partly resembles the arabesque in painting" (*loc. cit.*, pp. 81–82). Poe's eye for striking phrases would be sure to note "grotesque" and "arabesque", found in near juxtaposition and used to describe "weird tales" of the type that interested him—designations which, as he put it in the Preface to his own collection of 1840, "indicate with sufficient precision the prevalent tenor of these tales." It seems altogether likely that if anything was lacking, after Poe read Carlyle's *German Romance*, Scott's article would have supplied whatever was needed to send him to Hoffmann's writings.

Turning now to Poe's own stories, we may note that his first productions in prose are sixteen tales known as the *Tales of the Folio Club*, later incorporated into his first published collection, *Tales of the Grotesque and Arabesque*. These tales are the first 16 printed in vol. II of *Works* (see intro., xxxv). Three of them suggest German influence. "Metzengerstein" is avowedly imitative of the German manner. "The Visionary" suggests Schiller's "Der Geisterseher," and "Some Passages in the Life of a Lion" is the kind of title made popular by the German romancers—e.g., Jean Paul's "Auswahl aus des Teufels Papieren" and Hoffmann's "Blätter aus dem Tagebuch eines reisenden Enthusiasten." The introduction to the *Tales of the Folio Club* is satirical of dilettante, philistine literary clubs (see *Works*, II, xxxv–xxxix), and was intended to be printed with the tales, but finally withheld by the author. The suppressed introduction details the origin and nature of the Folio Club, for, says Poe, "I like to begin at the beginning." This is probably a take-off on Hoffmann, who likewise begins (and grows tedious in the process) at the beginning (see *Werke*, VI, 9–30). He proceeds to describe the eleven members, who are required to be "erudite and witty" and to prepare every month a "Short Prose Tale . . . to be read to the company assembled over a glass of wine."

Now, the best-known collection of Hoffmann's tales is *Die Serapionsbrüder*, purporting to be the tales read before the *Serapions-Klubb*, a club of young fellows who take the name from the story of an insane hermit monk named Serapion, who believes he is the martyred monk Serapion whose death occurred 400 years before. The members style themselves Serapionsbrüder, and *das echt Serapionische* is the standard of excellence set up for their literary productions. They meet once a month at the house of one of the brethern, and over a glass of wine each individual, in turn, reads his prose tale. The solemn pledge of each member is to show himself as "geistreich, lebendig, gemüthlich, anregbar, und witzig" as it lies in his power to be (*Werke*, VI, 9–17, 145). Poe's and Hoffmann's devices are strikingly similar, despite the wide difference in tone between the two sketches, and it may well be that Poe's realization of the parallelism led him finally to suppress his introduction. It was first printed in the Virginia edition.

186. Cobb, *loc. cit.*, p. 51. It is noteworthy in this connection that Morella's reading, in the tale entitled "Morella," consists of "those mystical writings which are usually considered the mere dross of German literature" (*Works*, II, 27–28). In the same tale Poe speaks of "the wild pantheism of Fichte" and the "doctrines

of Identity urged by Schelling," which "formed, for a long time, almost the sole conversation of Morella and myself" (*ibid.*, pp. 28–29). In the Preface to *Tales of the Grotesque and Arabesque* he denies that his stories express that "Germanism" and "pseudo horror" associated with "some of the secondary names of German literature" (*ibid.*, I, 150–51)—a phrase, by the way, used by Scott in his essay on Hoffmann. At one time or another, he mentioned a considerable number of German writers who would fall under this classification, but Hoffmann, the most characteristic of the lot, is not named. The omission was doubtless intentional; for an inveterate pursuer of plagiarism in others, Poe would hardly discuss or mention prominently a writer whose works bore any striking resemblance to his own.

187. *Werke*, I, 141.
188. *Ibid.*, pp. 142–44.
189. *Works*, V, 163–65.
190. *Ibid.*, p. 169.
191. *Ibid.*, pp. 171–73.

192. Among other striking points of similarity is the fact that both writers employ the device of having the characters introduced through the reminiscences of an older man. Hoffmann uses the Baron to tell of the Major-Alban relationship, and Poe employs Dr. Templeton to relate the Oldeb-Bedloe affair. Furthermore, both are military figures. In Hoffmann's "Der unheimliche Gast," where the "Sizilianischer Graf-Graf S—i" is the exact counterpart of the Danish Major-Alban of "Der Magnetiseur," Hoffmann goes back for the beginnings of the story to the military campaign of Wellington in Spain (*Werke*, VIII, 94). Poe's Oldeb-Bedloe is a young officer under Hastings in India.

The procedure of the hypnotists' getting the mastery over the minds of their patients is the same in Hoffmann and Poe (compare *Werke*, I, 157, 163, VIII, 110, 113, 117–18, and *Works*, V, 164–65, 175). Unlike modern hypnotists, Poe's and Hoffmann's *magnetiseurs* proceed slowly, and after many failures, by repeated psychic suggestions on their dreams, to direct suggestion, and finally to complete control through a mere glance.

Bedloe's dream contains certain elements the suggestions for which Poe may have derived from a dream of Medardus in *Die Elixiere des Teufels*. Bedloe's vision of seeing himself struck by a poisoned arrow and his sensations while he still sees with his eyes yet feels his soul leave his body are strikingly like the dream of Medardus, in which he sees himself stabbed to the heart and sees his soul separated from his body. Once the soul is dissolved into the ether,

the body with its gaping wounds becomes plainly visible. A comparison of Hoffmann and Poe (*Werke*, II, 250; *Works*, V, 172–73) shows similarities in these self-contemplative passages extending to verbal identities. Finally, a reunion of body and soul takes place, and the martyrs come to their original selves: in Hoffmann's tale, "durch einen elektrischen Schlag"; in Poe's story, by the "shock of a galvanic battery."

It is possible that Hoffmann was responsible, also, for something in Poe's "Conversation of Eiros and Charmion" (1829) and "Colloquy of Monos and Una" (1841), although Jean Paul's speculations on the states of mind in the transition from life to death may be chiefly responsible for Poe's conceptions in these two dialogues.

Palmer Cobb points out (*op. cit.*, pp. 68–69) another similarity in Poe's and Hoffmann's treatment of dreams generally. Compare Hoffmann, *Werke*, II, 250, and I, 46, with Poe, *Marginalia* in *Works*, XVI, 88–89.

193. He goes on to state his own beliefs in the matter (*Works*, X, 241).

194. *Works*, V, 254. Poe's professed belief that a mesmerized person is endowed with heightened perception and intelligence, enabling him to see the relation of all things, is put in the mouth of Mr. Vankirk. See *Works*, V, 243–44.

195. The explanation for this clairvoyant state the German romanticists sought, says Wächtler, "in der Annahme eines inneren Körpers, des Astralleibes, der unmittelbar mit der Natur in Verbindung stände, dessen Wahrnehmungen übertäubt würden. Der Astraleib sei der unsterbliche Teil des Menschen" (*op. cit.*, p. 48). Poe has Vankirk propound the same theory in identical terms (*Works*, V, 250).

196. *Works*, VI, 163.
197. *Ibid.*, p. 165.
198. *Ibid.*, p. 166. It has been suggested with some plausibility by T. T. Watts (*Rambles and Reveries of an Art Student in Europe*, Phila., 1855, pp. 37–38) that a partial source for the conclusion of this story (and of "Mesmeric Revelation") is Justinus Kerner's *Seherin von Prevorst*, a book of the fantastic order which had considerable vogue in America about this time, and that would have appealed to Poe. Poe's attention could easily have been directed to it by Mrs. Catherine Crowe's translation which was printed simultaneously in London and New York, where it was published by Harpers in 1845 and advertised in the *Broadway Journal*, II (Aug. 2, 1845), 63—a periodical with which Poe was officially connected at the time. While this book may have contributed something towards Poe's "Facts in the Case of M. Valdemar," it obviously came too late to have

any influence on "Mesmeric Revelation," published in 1844, a year before Mrs. Crowe's translation appeared. Of course, Poe may have known Kerner's book in the original; it is certain that he was familiar with Margaret Fuller's *Summer on the Lakes*, which included (pp. 126–64) a lengthy account of Kerner's *Seherin von Prevorst*.

199. There come to mind Calderon's *Magico Prodigioso* and Goethe's *Faust*, Irving's "Don Juan: A Spectral Research," Hawthorne's "Howe's Masquerade," Stevenson's "Dr. Jekyll and Mr. Hyde," and Boaden's "The Man with Two Lives." Only the last named (Boston, 1829) is sufficiently close to Poe's "William Wilson" to suggest the possibility of influence, and that has been effectively disposed of by Stedman in *Works of E. A. Poe* (Stedman-Woodberry ed., IV, 295–96) and Woodberry's *Life* (I, 232 n.).

200. See Wächtler, *op. cit.*, p. 73, and Ricarda Huch, *Blütezeit der Romantik*, Chs. XIV and XV.

201. Georg Ellinger, *E. T. A. Hoffmann* (Hamburg, 1884), 92.

202. For the narrative parallels between the two stories—the growth of evil in the hero (or villain) as he progresses in his criminal career, the evocation of his double (or better self), and the fierce struggles between the dual personalities until the double is slain—see Palmer Cobb's circumstantial account.

203. *Works*, III, 325.

204. A secondary motif in Hoffmann's story—Medardus' play at faro in the Prince's palace—Poe elaborates and makes into his more effective, because focal, gambling scene at Oxford. Compare *Werke*, II, 124–25, and *Works*, III, 316–18.

205. Ellinger, *op. cit.*, pp. 120–21.

206. *Works*, XIV, 193–202; also XI, 106–9.

207. *Ibid.*, XIV, 194.

208. *Works*, VI, 147. According to Novalis, it lies in the very nature of man; it is part and parcel of his hankering after liberty (see Novalis, *Schriften*, II, 211). Tieck, also, knew what Poe meant by this impulse toward perversity. See, for example, his feelings when standing on the edge of an abyss, in Tieck's *Schriften* (28 vols., Berlin, 1828–1854), V, 138–39, VI, 350–31. Compare Poe's *Works*, VI, 149–50.

209. *Works*, VI, 151–53.

210. Ellinger, *op. cit.*, p. 92, and Scott in the *Foreign Quar. Rev.*, I (1827), 81.

211. *Werke*, VIII, 183–84. In the ingenious detection of Cardillac as a murderer we have a striking anticipation of the analytic method which Poe was to apply so effectively in his detective and ratiocinative stories.

212. *Werke*, III, 15.

213. Compare *Werke*, II, 158–59, 165, 176, 214, and *Works*, V, 93, 94.

214. Cf. Wächtler, *op. cit.*, p. 68, and Stephan Hoch, *Die Vampyrsagen und ihre Verwendung in der deutschen Literatur* (Berlin, 1896).

216. They expressed their ideas about the relation of Love and Death, of Blood and Lust, not only in their writings but in their personal lives. Thus Brentano wrote to Karoline von Günderode: "Öffne alle Adern deines weissen Leibes, dass sich das heisse schäumende Blut aus tausend wonnigen Springbrunnen spritze. So will ich dich sehen und trinken aus den tausend Quellen, trinken bis ich berauscht bin und deinen Tod mit jauchzender Raserei beweinen kann."—Geiger, Ludwig, *Karoline von Günderode und ihre Freunde* (Stuttgart, 1895), 108.

Novalis repeatedly dwelt on the theme. See "Hymnen an die Nacht," *Schriften*, I, 27, and "Das Lied der Toten," *Schriften*, I, 114–18, as well as the *Fragmente* in *Schriften*, II, 281, III, 66, 299. Ludwig Tieck commented at length on "geheimnisvolle Gelüste, aus Furcht, Grauen und Mitleid gemischt," "Blut und Mord," "Schauer und Graus," and the "Wollust . . . oder magische Wunsch, zu schaffen und zu vernichten, in der höchsten Liebe zu verderben und in der Blutgier mit den reinsten Herzensfibern zu schwelgen."—*Schriften*, XIII, 60. The folk songs of von Arnim-Brentano in *Des Knaben Wunderhorn* (1818), which Poe knew, include two songs handling similar themes: "Der Pfalzgraf" and "Der Scheintot" (see *Des Knaben Wunderhorn*, 2nd ed., 2 vols., Berlin, 1876, II, 87–88, and I, 307–9). In the former, two lovers, one of whom dies, are married in the grave; and the latter is the story of a young wife who gives birth to a child after she is buried. She is disinterred by her husband; her death had been only a form of asphyxiation.

Achim von Arnim treated a similar theme at least twice (see Arnim's *Werke*, ed. by Bettina von Arnim, 26 vols., Berlin, 1833–1836, XV, 162, XX, 106), and Heinrich von Kleist relates the story of how the Amazon Penthesilea, believing herself insulted by Achilles, her lover, sets her dogs on him and herself tears his body with hands and teeth (Kleist's *Sämmtliche Werke und Briefe*, ed. by Wm. Herzog, 6 vols., Leipzig, 1909, II, 441, 462–463). In his story, "Die Marquise von O" (*ibid.*, IV, 143–203), a young officer despoils the marquise, whom he holds for dead, but who only lies in a trance. A child is the fruit of the deed.

Other notable examples are found in Zacharias Werner (*Ausgewählte Schriften*, hrsg. von seinen Freunden, 13 vols., Grimma, 1841, II,

77) and Adolf Müllner (*Dramatische Werke*, 7 vols., Braunschweig, 1828, III, 160), and Müllner's *Die Schuld*, I, ix, 462–83). Finally, there is Heine, who knew that Love and Death are often closely allied. He sang of Love as of a Sphinx who kisses the beloved with its lips and with its claws tears the object of its love to pieces (Heine's *Sämmtliche Werke*, ed. by E. Elster, 7 vols., Leipzig, n.d., I, 9). Love for the dead he mentions several times. Two poems especially treat the theme. In the one a Franciscan conjures up from the grave the corpse of a beautiful woman (*ibid.*, I, 268; see also "Salon III," *ibid.*, IV, 328); and in the other, "Helena," the poet calls his beloved to him from the grave. The insatiable woman kills him by drawing the breath from his breast (*ibid.*, I, 9).

217. *Werke*, IX, 171–91, esp. p. 187.

218. It need not be assumed, of course, that Poe had no other possible sources; there were reported a number of cases from life concerning which Poe might have had information. Wächtler (*op. cit.*, pp. 71–72) cites three, and there were others. Pitaval tells, in his *Causes célèbres*, how a young man, watching by the corpse of a young girl, is so affected by her beauty as to violate her. After several years, he returns to the community and learns that the girl had awakened from what had been only a trance, and had given birth to a child. Madame de Gomez, in *Les Cent Nouvelles* (à la Haye, 1739, XIX, 184), relates a parallel case. Finally, there is the case, often reported in newspapers and magazines (where Poe may have chanced upon the story), of Sergeant François of Paris, who, in the 1740's, dug up corpses in the graveyards and horribly mutilated them. With him the erotic impulse played no role. See *Der Vampyr in den Pariser Friedhöfen. Ein höchst interessanter Kriminalfall der neuesten Zeit; zunächst für Psychologen und Ärzte. Aus dem Französischen der* "Gazette des Tribunaux," Stuttgart, 1849.

219. Compare *Werke*, III, 23–24, and *Works*, II, 250–52.

220. *Works*, II, 252.

221. *Ibid.*, pp. 250–52.

222. James T. Shotwell, "Edgar Allan Poe, as Poet and Romancer," *Univ. of Toronto Quar.*, II, iv (June, 1896), 267.

223. Nathanael, in his fancy, sees Clara's eyes dissolving into ruddy and glowing drops and falling upon his bared breast (*Werke*, III, 23–24). In Poe the drops are by implication connected with the soulful eyes of Ligeia, and they appear to contribute toward Rowena's transformation in the end.

224. Shotwell, *loc. cit.*, pp. 267–68.

225. Hoffmann made a similar observation

concerning his story; see *Werke*, III, 36.

226. *Works*, XVII, 49–51.

227. *Ibid.*, p. 52.

228. *Ibid.*, II, 33–34.

229. *Ibid.*, p. 29.

230. Wächtler, *op. cit.*, p. 93.

231. See *Schriften*, I, lxi; II, 115, 178, 190, 193, 198; III, 29, 83, 163–64, 168, 273, 321, 353. The whole conception of Poe's theory of the power of the will and of the transformation of the body of his dead beloved into a living one could have derived from Novalis's *Heinrich von Ofterdingen*, and perhaps also from the facts of Novalis' life, which were well known in Poe's day. Novalis believed, as his biographer Just remarks, that he could keep Sophie von Kühn alive through his mere *will* to do so (*ibid.*, I, lxi). His love of Sophie, like the love of Poe's character for Ligeia, Morella, Berenice, and Eleonora, is not the love of Eros, but the love of the intellect, or of the embodiment of the idea in Beauty (*ibid.*, I, lix, lxxi–lxxii). When Sophie died, Novalis formed the will to follow her; he willed to die (*ibid.*, I, lxv). But the preoccupations of his aesthetic and philosophical studies kept him alive in spite of himself and gave him an interest in living. When he met Julie von Carpentier a year later (*ibid.*, I, lxxi–lxxii), he saw in her Sophie—the embodiment of his abstract ideal of womanly beauty. *Heinrich von Ofterdingen*, loosely based on the story of his own life, contains these elements highly poetized. In rough outline *Heinrich von Ofterdingen* parallels "Ligeia" and "Morella."

232. Emile Lauviere, *Edgar Poe, sa vie et son oeuvre* (Paris, 1904), 595; Stedman, *Works of Poe* (Stedman-Woodberry ed.), I, 98; Cobb, *op. cit.*, pp. 81–90; Campbell, *The Mind of Poe*, p. 171; Quinn, *op. cit.*, p. 214.

233. Cobb, *op. cit.*, pp. 81–90.

234. *Works*, IV, 249.

235. Hoffmann is especially fond of such fantasies as he treats in "Der goldene Topf," where the student Anselmus sees in the doorknocker of Archivarius Lindhorst's house the head of an old applewoman (*Werke*, I, 176), and in "Der Kampf der Sänger," where peculiar roots in the hands of Klingsohr appear to be meek men and woman (*Werke*, II, 7). Tieck's "Blaubart" contains a passage in which the figures on the tapestry become alive very much like the horse in the tapestry on the wall of Metzengerstein, and step out into the room from the walls, but there is no hint of metempsychosis; moreover, the figures return to their places (*Schriften*, IX, 170–71). Heine's poem, "Geoffrey Rudel and Melisande von Tripoli," describes a scene in which figures from the tapestries of Castle Bloy become alive (*Sämmtliche Werke*, I,

362). The feud between the two houses, Berlifitzing and Metzengerstein, remind Wächtler (*op. cit.*, p. 80) of Arnim's "Die Gleichen" and of Kleist's "Familie Schroffenstein," a German version of the Romeo-and-Juliet theme. Stedman finds certain common properties between "Metzengerstein" and Hoffmann's "Das Majorat," but these, like the others, are generalities on which one cannot put a finger with assurance.

236. *Sämmtliche Werke*, III, 179–339.

237. *Schriften*, IV, 245–83. The horrible masqueradings and the bizarre costuming represent the chief similarities.

238. *Werke*, III, 7–39.

239. *Ibid.*, V, 1–98. The wizard in "Klein Zaches" is named Prosper Alpanus; Poe's hero is Prince Prosper. The oriental splendor behind heavy walls is another common feature. Other similarities have been pointed out between Poe's "Masque of the Red Death" and Eichendorff's "Ahnung und Gegenwart" by J. Wesley Thomas (*Amerikanische Dichter und die deutsche Literatur*, Goslar, 1950, p. 81), but they do not appear to constitute influence.

240. See Stedman, Poe's *Works* (Stedman-Woodberry ed.), I, 97.

241. First observed by Gruener, *loc. cit.*, p. 16.

242. Scott, *loc, cit.*, p. 91.

243. Compare *ibid.*, p. 87, and Poe's *Works*, III, 277–78.

244. *Works*, III, 277, 297.

245. While Scott's translated passages from Hoffmann's tales are faithful, the passage in which he describes the castle R——sitten differs in a number of respects from the original. In the German story the deep chasm itself is only mentioned in passing. Scott emphasized and thus heightened its descriptive effect and allegorical significance. The fact that Poe seized upon this detail and re-emphasized it, that his description (external and internal) of the House of Usher are markedly like Scott's, and that he seems to have appropriated other features from the article (as noted earlier), all suggest that Poe owes more to Scott's article than to a first-hand reading of "Das Majorat." It may well be that Scott's essay aroused, or accentuated Poe's, interest in Hoffmann and subsequently led him to become better acquainted with the German romantics; for in other and later stories of Poe (as we have seen) there are more significant and striking resemblances which could not have been gleaned from Scott's article or other intermediary sources.

246. *Die Majoratsherren* (ed. by J. Cerny, Vienna, n.d.), pp. 75–78, 81.

247. *Ibid.*, pp. 93, 94.

248. *Ibid.*, pp. 73–75.

249. *Ibid.*, p. 90.

250. *Ibid.*, p. 94.

251. Wächtler, *op. cit.*, pp. 96–97.

252. *Sämmtliche Werke* (2. Ausg., 33 Bde., Berlin, 1840–1842), XXIV, 345.

253. *Ibid.* Jean Paul's *Quintus Fixlein* contains another sketch, "Der Tod eines Engels" (*ibid.*, III, 4), which treats a related subject and suggests Poe's pieces; but the similarities are best explained on the ground of *Geistes-* or *Gesinnungsverwandtschaft* between the two authors.

254. *Werke*, XII, 5–16.

255. See *Works*, XVI, 160.

256. Bon-Bon is a *restaurateur* of uncommon qualifications; he is skillful in an equal degree as a philosopher. His metaphysical *dicta*, while not always clear to his auditors, are nevertheless profound: Kant himself is indebted to Bon-Bon for his metaphysics. Bon-Bon is also a connoisseur of fine drinks and a special master in the art of tippling. He takes his drinks according to code, with a flourish and *éclat*, each brand at a particular time; and he rounds his philosophical *essais* with a sip from a bottle calculated to give him powers of discrimination and profundity that aid in the spinning of his next syllogism. But his tippling propensities result in tinging his mind with a "strange intensity and mysticism" so that he appears to have been "deeply tinctured with the *diablerie* of his favorite German studies" (*Works*, II, 129). On the eve of the story, the Devil himself appears and leads Bon-Bon from one metaphysical subtlety to another until the wine overpowers him, and even the Devil refuses to have his soul.

257. *Works*, XVII, 28.

258. "Lionizing" finds an interesting parallel in Jean Paul's chapter in *Auswahl aus des Teufels Papieren* entitled "Physiognomische Postskript über die Nasen der Menschen" (*Werke*, IV, 247–54). In both of the stories, a mountebank becomes a literary lion by virtue of his extraordinarily long nose. In both stories the hero's lionship suddenly ends, the caprice of his admirers having turned to a new fad.

259. *Works*, XVII, 30.

260. There is plenty of evidence that Poe read *Blackwood's* as well as the *Foreign Quarterly*, the *Westminster*, and the *Edinburgh*. See *Works*, II, 35–41; VIII, 82, 111; XI, 11; Woodberry, *Poe*, I, 220; II, 61, 71, 408–9; and Campbell, *The Mind of Poe*, p. 180. Poe read William Mudford's "Iron Shroud" in the January, 1831, number of *Blackwood's* and later made use of its idea and atmosphere in "The Pit and the Pendulum" (see Pattee, *op. cit.*, p. 123; Woodberry, *Poe*, I, 382). In one of his later stories he showed himself familiar with the gruesome

series entitled "Passages from the Diary of a Late Physician" (*Works*, II, 274). The nature of this kind of tale is apparent in the following representative titles: "The Murder Hole," "The Murderer's Last Night," "The Dance of Death. From the German," "The Pandour and His Highness. A Hungarian Sketch," and "Bracelets. A Sketch from the German." Many of these *melanges* of sensation and horror—"flamboyant with adjectives and tremulous with sentimentality"—appeared in American annuals, souvenir books, gift-books, and ladies' books, which were themselves derived from German examples.

"In Germany the annual had had a long history. At first it had been a miscellany of poetic and elegant extracts, but after Schiller had used it for his *Maid of Orleans* and Goethe for his *Hermann und Dorothea*, it had become so favorite a vehicle for original articles that H. Payne in 1836, in the *North American Review*, could say, 'An author whose subject is within the intellectual reach of general readers, and who wishes to be soon and widely read, is more sure of being so in Germany, by contributing to a *Taschenbuch* than by any other mode in which he can give his works to the world.' . . . Hoffmann in Germany made use of it constantly for his weird tales. . . . In England the annual dates back to 1821. . . . Very probably the early American annuals were copied from these English predecessors, though the editors of the first 'annual proper' published in America, *The Atlantic Souvenir, a Christmas and New Years' Offering* (Phila., 1825), acknowledged their indebtedness for the idea to Germany and France: 'On the continent of Europe such a volume has long been the attendant of the season, and the shops of Germany and France abound every winter with those which are suited to every age and taste.'"—Pattee, *op. cit.*, p. 123; see also pp. 27–31, 69–90, and for more extended studies, Ralph Thompson, *American Literary Annuals and Gift Books, 1835-1865* (N.Y., 1936), and P. A. Shelley, "The German Heritage of the American Annuals and Gift-Book" (diss., Harvard, 1938).

261. Pattee, *op. cit.*, p. 124.

262. For variations see the Harrison-Virginia ed., II, 356–67.

263. In 1926, when I first considered the question of possible Germanic influence on Poe's critical theories, the subject had received only cursory attention, in F. C. Prescott's *Selections from the Critical Writings of Edgar Allan Poe* (N.Y., 1909), and in greater detail in Margaret Alterton's *Origins of Poe's Critical Theories* (Iowa City, Ia., 1925). In the latter, a chapter on "Unity in the Drama and the Fine

Arts" is devoted to what Poe derived from A. W. Schlegel for his dramatic criticism. In my earlier study I was chiefly interested in the matter of Poe's adaptation of Schlegel's principle of unity to Poe's theory and technique of the short story. Since then Professor James S. Wilson has published his essay, "Poe's Philosophy of Composition," *North Amer. Rev.*, CCXXIII (Dec., 1927), 675–84, and three years later appeared the illuminating inquiry by Professor Floyd Stovall into "Poe's Debt to Coleridge," *Univ. of Texas Studies in English*, No. 10 (1930), pp. 70–127.

264. G. F. Richardson, "Poe's Doctrine of Effect," *The Charles Mills Gayley Anniversary Papers* (Berkeley, Calif., 1902), pp. 177–86. Poe's criticisms of Hawthorne's tales (*Works*, XI, 102–13, XIII, 141–55), for instance, have all the earmarks of being pieces of literary joinery, composed of none-too-well digested hints derived from his reading, involving him in anomalies and contradictions. Poe's critical theories, like his philosophical speculations, were an eclectic product, sometimes imperfectly assimilated matter borrowed from many sources—mostly from Coleridge, but also from the British reviews, A. W. Schlegel, Plato, Aristotle, Horace, and Christian philosophers, the German romantics, Justice Wm. Wirt and his own reading in the law, Kames and Blair, Dryden and Pope, Locke, Stewart, and Tennemann, among others. Woodberry speaks of Poe's "constant parroting of Coleridge," and at one time called Coleridge "the guiding genius of Poe's entire intellectual life," but subsequently changed *entire* to *early* in concession of the greater importance which A. W. Schlegel assumed in Poe's later development as critic and thinker. See his *Poe*, I, 177–78, and the one-volume edition (Boston, 1885), pp. 93–94. Whether Poe first came to know Schlegel through Coleridge, or whether he read both about the same time, or Schlegel even before Coleridge, are questions that seem to be of some importance, although a conclusive answer is not easily given.

265. Campbell ("Poe's Reading," *loc. cit.*, pp. 169–70) counts thirty references to Coleridge and five quotations, together with important influences of Coleridge on Poe's prose and verse. See also Poe's *Works*, IX, 51–52.

266. *The Mind of Poe*, p. 139.

267. It has been suggested that Poe's characterization in his "Letter to B——" of Sophocles as "the bee" indicates that Poe was familiar with Schlegel's *Lectures on Dramatic Art and Poetry* as early as 1831, but it is to be remembered that Schlegel was not the first to call Sophocles "the Attic bee."

268. *Works*, VIII, 43–47.

269. Compare *Works*, VIII, 44–47, with *Course of Lectures on Dramatic Art and Literature by Augustus Wilhelm Schlegel*, tr. by John Black, rev. according to the latest German ed. by the Rev. A. J. W. Morrison (London, 1845), pp. 121, 66–68, 70–71, 54–59, 114–15, 66–67, 115.

270. Compare Poe's *Works*, VIII, 44, 46, 47, with Schlegel's *Lectures* (Black trans.), pp. 66, 113 ff., 121.

271. *Works*, VIII, 282; see also pp. 285, 293, 295, 296, 299, 302, 306, 309.

272. *Ibid.*, pp. 125–26. It is noteworthy that the sense of form is the quality in which Poe's early verse is most defective and his latest most marked. It is also significant that of the thirteen tales published by Poe before 1835 only three are so-called "tales of effect." It would appear that the idea gleaned from Schlegel was an important one for Poe's development as poet as well as story writer.

273. From his review of Hawthorne's *Twice-Told Tales* (2nd ed., 1842), printed in *Graham's Mag.* for May, 1842, and reprinted in *Works*, XI, 108.

274. These editions are so inaccessible that the 1845 Bohn edition (Black trans.) is used for all references.

275. See J. F. Ferrier, "The Plagiarisms of S. T. Coleridge," *Edinburgh Rev.*, XLII (Mar., 1840), 287–99; Sara Coleridge's edition of her father's lectures, prefixed to the Shedd edition of the *Biographia Literaria*; J. L. Haney, *The German Influence on S. T. Coleridge* (Phila., 1902); Emma G. Jaeck, *op. cit.*, 160–62; Anna A. Helmholtz, *The Indebtedness of S. T. Coleridge to A. W. Schlegel* (Madison, Wis., 1907); G. Herzfeld, "A. W. Schlegel und seine Beziehungen zu englischen Dichtern und Kritikern," *Archiv für das Studium der neueren Sprachen*, CXXXIX (1919), 149–62.

276. Poe quotes Schlegel's *Lectures* twice: once in a passage containing ninety-three words (*Works*, VIII, 44, from *Lectures*, p. 121), and again in a passage of fifty-three words (*Works*, VIII, 47, from *Lectures*, p. 115). The former is referred to "a German critic"; the latter is attributed directly to "Augustus William [*sic*] Schlegel." The rest of the essay is a rehash of what Schlegel has to say in Lectures IV, V, and VII on the Greek stage and on Euripides, the most notable borrowings being from pages 54–59, 66–71, 114–15, and 121 in the Black translation. Poe mentions Schlegel oftener than any other German writer.

277. The numerous encomiums heaped on the German critic alone would have been sufficient provocation for Poe, just setting out as *litterateur* and critic, to make closer inquiries

and to provide himself with Black's translation of the *Lectures*, readily available since 1815 and republished in Philadelphia in 1833. See also Alterton, *op. cit.*, pp. 7–45, esp. pp. 30–35.

278. "Poe's Debt to Coleridge," *loc. cit.*, pp. 80–100, esp. pp. 80–83.

279. In the "Letter to B——," *Works*, VII, xliii.

280. For a lucid discussion of the evolution of Poe's mature thought in terms of "oneness" or "unity," see the introduction to the Alterton-Craig edition of Poe, American Writers Series (N.Y., 1935), pp. xiii–cxviii.

281. As the context indicates, Schlegel here means "effect," for the passage occurs in the part of Lecture II entitled "Effect." He often uses the terms "impression" and "effect" interchangeably. See *ibid.*, pp. 38, 39, 41, 243, 244. Poe, in his earlier formulation of the unity-of-effect theory uses "impression." See *Works*, XI, 106–7. In his later criticism (1847), when he repeated his theory, he still used the term "impression," but he italicized *"effect"*—evidently a deliberate choice of Poe's to emphasize the term (*Works*, XIII, 150, 152). Professor Wilson's remarks (*loc. cit.*, p. 683) are pertinent here: "In the original, the phrase from Schlegel is '*Einheit der Interesse*' and . . . '*Gesammteindruck auf das Gemüth*.' Poe's 'totality of impression' seems a truer translation than Black's 'joint impression,' even if Poe never saw the original."

In any case, it is easy enough to see how Poe derived from Schlegel's "Einheit der Interesse" (unity of interest), his unity of interest and singleness of effect; and how from "Gesammt Eindruck" (totality of impression), he got his totality or singleness of impression.

282. Precisely the means he emphasized in "The Philosophy of Composition" (*Works*, XIV, 193–208) and "The Poetic Principle" (*ibid.*, pp. 266–92).

283. From this point it was no long step to Poe's conclusion about the brevity of a good poem or prose tale. See *ibid.*, XI, 106–7, XIII, 150–53.

284. This bears a strong resemblance to Poe's statement that "if the writer's very first sentence tend not to the outbringing of this effect, then in his very first step has he committed a blunder."—*Ibid.*, VIII, 108; XIII, 153.

285. Compare *ibid.*, VIII, 108, X, 153: "In the whole composition there should be no word written of which the tendency, direct or indirect, is not to the one pre-established design. And by such means, with such care and skill, a picture is at length painted which leaves the mind of him who contemplates it with a kindred art, a sense of the fullest satisfaction."

286. Schlegel, *Lectures*, pp. 37–38.

287. *Works*, X, 114–33, esp. p. 122.

288. *Works*, XIV, 196–97. Poe seems also to have taken a hint from Schlegel for his theory concerning the assistance of rhythm, musical tone, and harmony in the production of the pre-established effect. Compare Schlegel, *op. cit.*, p. 38, and Poe, *Works*, XIV, 275. In good poetry, according to Poe, the writer's object is the "Rhythmical Creation of Beauty." Compare *Works*, XIV, 275, and Schlegel, *op. cit.*, p. 18: "Poetry is . . . the power of creating what is beautiful, and representing it to the eye or the ear." In prose, it is to create "an elevating excitement of the Soul," which, Poe goes on to say, "is quite independent of that passion which is the intoxication of the Heart—or of the Truth which is the satisfaction of Reason. For, in regard to Passion, alas! its tendency is to degrade, rather than to elevate the Soul. Love, on the contrary—Love—the true, the Divine Eros—the Uranian, as distinguished from the Dionaean Venus—is unquestionably the truest of all themes."—*Works*, XIV, 90; compare R. M. Waerner, *Romanticism and the Romantic School in Germany* (N.Y., 1910), pp. 28–29. This is but a restatement of Schlegel's idea plus a touch of Poesque terminology; compare Schlegel, *op. cit.*, 244; also pp. 37–38, and *Works*, XIV, 205.

Just here enters the interesting question whether Poe's theorizing on the relation of poetry to music derived anything from the German *Romantiker*, for his concept of poetry as reaching its consummation in music appears to be little more than a recapitulation of German romantic theory as exemplified by Schleiermacher, Wackenroder, the Schlegels, and especially Novalis. The idea of music as the realization of Poetry is implied by Schleiermacher's declaration that the feeling of man should accompany all his doings "as if it were a holy music; he should do all *with* religion, nothing *through* religion." Wackenroder said

that poetry lay conquered at the feet of music. Tieck sought to make tones and notes themselves into "pure poetry," and in *Sternbald* (1798) tried to resolve both life and poetry in music. Hoffmann is another who tried to make the transition from romantic authorship to musical composition. Novalis carried the doctrine to its extreme by seeing the consummation of art in "poems which would sound melodiously and are full of beautiful words, but without any sense or connection"; see P. E. More, "A Note on Poe's Method," *Studies in Philol.*, XX, iii (July, 1923) 204; Campbell, *The Mind of Poe*, p. 185. Evidence, external and internal, is too meager definitely to prove that Poe derived this theory from the Germans, but the presumption is strong that he did, or at least, that he drew confirmation from them for his views.

289. It is odd that a critic of Poe's perspicuity, while being so solicitous of the reader's state of mental concentration, should have overlooked the effect of the time element on the creative process itself within the poet's mind.

290. Compare Schlegel, *op. cit.*, pp. 75–76, and Poe's *Works*, XIV, 267. Compare further Schlegel, p. 38, and Poe, XIII, 149, 151, for a parallelism in the idea that an artist is to be judged by the degree of his success in producing what he sets out to produce. Compare also Poe's and Schlegel's attitudes toward the public: *Works*, XIII, 149–50, and Schlegel, *op. cit.*, p. 38.

291. Poe's authorship of these three essays in the *Messenger* has been established by Margaret Alterton, *op. cit.*, pp. 107–10.

292. *Southern Lit. Messenger*, III, i (Dec., 1836), 158.

293. Compare *ibid.*, II, xii (Nov., 1836), 739, and Wm. G. Tennemann, *A Manual of the History of Philosophy*, tr. by the Rev. Arthur Johnson, 2nd ed. (after the first Oxford ed., 1832), London, 1852, p. 55. See Alterton, *op. cit.*, pp. 109, 111.

NINETHEENTH-CENTURY POETS, NOVELISTS, AND CRITICS

EARLY POETS

1. John Quincy Adams' verse translation of Wieland's *Oberon*, made during 1799–1801, exerted no influence at the time, for it remained in manuscript until 1940. Philip Freneau (1752–1832), even while he held the post of translator in Jefferson's Department of State, appears not to have found a knowledge of German necessary, nor did his poetry, then or later, concern itself with anything respecting Germany beyond references to Hessian soldiers and to William

Tell as the deliverer of Switzerland. The startling coincidences between Schiller's "Indian Death Dirge" of about 1793 and Freneau's "Indian Burying Ground" (1788) is explicable on the ground that both poets found their source in Jonathan Carver's *Travels* (London, 1778), p. 399.

2. In his poem "To Ennui" the reference to Altorf is probably a reflection of Fanny Wright's play on the subject of William Tell rather than of any direct knowledge of any German literary treatment of the theme.

3. *South. Lit. Messenger*, XIII (Dec., 1847), 762.

4. The precise extent of Halleck's knowledge of the German language and literature remains in doubt. He made a brief tour "from Lausanne, through Switzerland to Basle and thence down the Rhine to Strasburg" (James G. Wilson, *Life and Letters of Fitz-Greene Halleck*, N.Y., 1869, p. 252); he associated with people like Eugene MacCarthy and Lorenzo Da Ponte, who were accomplished German students, and was himself rated by Poe as "a good linguist" (N. F. Adkins, *Fitz-Greene Halleck*, New Haven, 1930, pp. 134, 142; Poe's *Works*, XV, 55); but when his books were sold in 1868, the auction catalogue listed as the sole German content of his library three volumes of Goetheana, all of them in translation. Except for his much admired version of the "Zueignung" of *Faust I* (first printed in the *New York Mirror* for June 29, 1839), which appears to be a faithful translation, the other three pieces of his bearing superscriptions "From the German" or "Translated from Goethe" (one from Hoffmann von Fallersleben, another ascribed to Goethe, and a third not yet identified) appear less translations than free adaptations—so free that the sources of two of them have never been fixed. The presumption is strong that he relied on existing French or English versions.

5. Adkins, *op. cit.*, pp. 187–88; J. G. Wilson, *op. cit.*, pp. 228–29.

6. Profoundly impressed by *Der arme Heinrich*, he translated a large portion of it. Subsequently he composed three Minnesongs based on Walther von der Vogelweide and other Middle High German poets, and a number of other poems on such German and Scandinavian models as A. W. Schlegel ("Life's a Dream"), Johann Peter Hebel ("The Little Witch"), and Christian Hendricksen Pram ("The Power of Song"), as well as lesser poets. Another group of his poems, published under the rubric "Teutonia," is inspired in manner and structure by poems of Herder, Schiller, and Goethe. In addition, he wrote a great many songs to the music of various foreign national airs. Eighteen of these were written for German melodies, on the models of J. H. Voss, Mathias Claudius, Ludwig Hölty, Jens Baggesen (who wrote in both Danish and German), and Friedrich von Matthisson. Among his posthumous poems is one entitled "Midnight Music," which imitates the measure and structure of Goethe's "Nachtgesang." He liked to experiment with versification and prosodic effects, particularly to test meters that were little known or foreign to the English tongue. *The Dream of a Day and Other Poems* (1843) includes some 150 forms or modifications of stanzas, many of them based on German models. His *Studies in Verse*, in which he imitated "all accessible" cultivated dialects, remains an unpublished curiosity. For further details see Adolph B. Benson, "James Gates Percival, Student of German Culture," *New Engl. Quar.*, II, iv (Oct., 1929), 603–24.

7. His sonnet on William Tell, composed in 1827 and published in *The Talisman* for 1828, was merely a literary exercise on a theme made popular by the *Tell* literature in the periodicals of the day.

In his *Lectures on Poetry* (delivered in 1826 but not printed until 1884) there is a remarkable parallelism between the Kantian tripartition of mental faculties and Bryant's theory that poetry addresses itself to the passions, the understanding, and the intellect. But the terms as employed in these lectures (notably the first two) are used loosely, and the parallelism is only suggestive; for there is nothing to indicate that Bryant knew much about Kant at this time, or that he learned much about him later.

8. At Munich he spent three months, and subsequently four months in Heidelberg, whence he was recalled to New York by the illness of a colleague, Leggett, of the *New York Evening Post*. At Heidelberg he met Longfellow, who, in an effort to conquer his grief over the death of his young wife and to prepare himself for his Harvard professorship, was deeply immersed in a systematic study of German literature. Whether led by Longfellow or by his own inclination, or both, Bryant undertook, at the age of 41, to add German to his knowledge of French, Italian, Spanish, and the classical languages. He appears to have made fair progress and gained a degree of initiation into the works of Goethe, Schiller, Rückert, and Heine. Two days before his departure from Heidelberg (January 23, 1836), his translation of Uhland's ballad, "Der Graf von Breiers," appeared in the *New York Mirror*. Upon his return to America, the infectious atmosphere of German balladry remained sufficiently sustained for him to translate and publish, in July of the same year, in the *New York Evening Post*, another Teutonic poem which has not yet been identified, but which unquestionably belongs to the type represented by Körner's *Leier und Schwert*. At the same time he turned old nursery rhymes and popular songs of the day into the idiom of France, Germany, Spain, and Italy, and tried to arouse his daughter's interest in foreign languages, especially recommending to her the German language and literature.—Parke Godwin, *A Biography of William Cullen Bryant* (2 vols., N.Y., 1883), I, 308, 315, 358.

9. Besides the two poems already mentioned, he translated "Das Lied vom Mägdlein und dem Ringe" from Uhland in 1842; "Nähe der Geliebten," Goethe, 1844; "The Paradise of Tears," an unidentified poem of N. Müller, 1844; "Der Wanderer in der Sägemühle," Kerner, 1844; "Burgfräulein von Windeck," Chamisso, 1850; "Die Worte des Koran," Zedlitz, 1865; and "Das erste Lied," Houwald, 1876.

10. The lectures of Dr. Follen on the German poets "quickened his zeal," and "more decidedly the singular enthusiasm of his teacher, the Baron Ludwig von Mendelsloe," for German balladry stimulated Bryant's fondness for the poetry of tradition and superstition, for the grotesque and the horrific. See, for example, his "The Murdered Traveller," *U.S. Gazette*, I (Jan. 1, 1825), 286, and "The Robber," *N.Y. Mirror*, XI (July 6, 1834), 4.

11. T. McDowell (ed.), *William Cullen Bryant Representative Selections* . . . (N.Y., 1935), p. li.

12. "The Strange Lady," written while he was still in Heidelberg, and based on a typical German legend, that of the handsome Albert, who is led into the forest and to his doom by a dark-haired enchantress, is seriously conceived and without any thought of burlesque. "The Hunter's Vision," also written in Germany, derives from the same general sources, but seems more immediately inspired by Goethe's ballad, "Der Fischer," in which a fisherman, entranced by a mermaid, glides into the water to join her. In Bryant's poem the same motif is adapted to a hunter, who is drawn by a feminine vision (or forest sprite) to join her. "A Presentiment," too, belongs to this first period of Bryant's enthusiasm for German balladry. As in Goethe's "Erlkönig," which turns on the ghostly ride of a father and his son through the night, so Bryant's poem describes a similar ride, relates the same progressively portentous interchange of question and answer between father and son, and finally presents the same tragic conclusion, although the precise manner of the boy's death is more specifically indicated in Bryant's poem than in his model. See A. H. Herrick, "W. C. Bryant's Bezeihungen zur deutschen Dichtung," *Mod. Lang. Notes* XXXII, vi (June, 1917), 344–51.

13. During his second trip to Europe (1845), after a leisurely trip up the Rhine, he fell in, at Düsseldorf, with the artists Hunt and Leutze. They took him to the studios of Schroeter, of Köhler, and of Lessing, just then sketching out his now famous "Martyrdom of John Huss." Later, his friends Henry Wheaton and Theo. S. Fay introduced him to all that was "rare and notable . . . in Berlin." His third trip to Germany (1849) was spoiled for him by the presence of soldiers everywhere; but in 1857–1858 and again in 1867 he visited Germany. His journeyings on these five occasions were in the nature of a tourist's.

He seldom strayed far from the beaten paths of the sight-seers. He appraised the lands he traversed with a journalist-traveler's eye; and while he wrote and printed in the *New York Evening Post* running accounts of his experiences and observations, there is little to indicate that he peered very far below the surface or, so far as concerns Germany, carefully appraised her spiritual achievements. However, the *Evening Post* regularly printed German notices and often lengthy extracts from foreign journals.

14. For the Schiller Festival, November 11, 1859, at the Cooper Institute, he delivered an address on Schiller as a moral idealist and a poet of freedom particularly worthy of wholehearted American attention. In 1870 he spoke as a pro-German at a German fair on the Franco-Prussian war, and on May 7 of the next year he delivered an address on "The Progress of German Literature" at a banquet given in honor of the German ambassador, Baron von Gerolt. On the occasion of the "Jahrhundertfeier" of the New York Goethe Club, of which he was a member, Bryant, despite his 80 years, delivered on August 27, 1875, a vigorous address honoring Goethe. In the last year of his life he spoke at a dinner given by the German Social Science Association, April 8, 1878, in honor of Bayard Taylor as the translator of *Faust* and the newly appointed Minister to Germany. At the conclusion of his address Bryant was toasted as "the Nestor of American poets," to which he replied in a brief German speech.

HENRY WADSWORTH LONGFELLOW

15. Longfellow's interest in Germany is treated in detail in James T. Hatfield, *New Light on Longfellow, with Special Reference to His Relations to Germany* (Boston, 1933), and in Lawrance Thompson, *Young Longfellow (1807–1843)* (N.Y., 1938). My indebtedness to these studies is indicated in the notes.

16. On his way to New York City, whence he sailed on May 15, 1826, he called on Ticknor, who gave him letters to Irving, Southey, and Professor Eichhorn. Passing through Northampton, he stopped at the Round Hill School to consult George Cogswell and George Bancroft, both of whom urged him to spend a year at Göttingen.

17. Experiences along his route of travel whetted his appetite for German literature. While in Vienna, he had been intrigued by the

Nachtwächterlied ("Hört, ihr Herren") and had painstakingly copied in German script five lines of it. Dresden, where he arrived on January 13, 1829, offered many advantages. Irving's letters provided easy access to the cosmopolitan society of the Saxon capital, and he soon found a round of court balls, tableaux, concerts, plays, and operas competing with his studies. He engaged a tutor and made some progress in his study of German, even to interlarding the lines of his diary with German phrases. Böttiger, who had known Wieland, Herder, Schiller, and Goethe, conversed agreeably on German literary men and lent him books from his own library; and Longfellow availed himself of other academic and social opportunities which men like Baron von Löwenstein could provide. See *New Light*, pp. 13–15; *Young Longfellow*, pp. 175, 375 n. 8, and Samuel Longfellow, *Life of Henry Wadsworth Longfellow* (3 vols., N.Y., 1891), I, 163–64 (hereafter cited as *Life*).

18. His first visit to Preble's rooms in "Jew Alley" immediately transported him into the gay, romantic atmosphere of student life in a German university town. His delight on meeting his old Portland friend he commemorated in a sprightly prose account in the first six numbers of a manuscript newspaper, *"Old Dominion Zeitung,"* which they prepared for their own amusement, and which became the repository of sketches, stories, news items, songs, jokes, quotations, pen drawings, satirical sketches of the Bowdoin Trustees, and all kinds of nonsense. They also kept a quarto "Journal" (still preserved in Craigie House), filled with drawings, satirical sketches of persons and happenings, and the general *pot pourri* of a student's random experiences, all plentifully besprinkled with snatches of German. For these records, see *Young Longfellow*, pp. 137–39, and *New Light*, pp. 15–18, also frontispieces.

Preble gave up his quarters and settled with Longfellow on the Weenderstrasse, just opposite the old town hall. Here they lived and ate together and attended the same classes. Longfellow proceeded immediately to present his letters from Bancroft and Ticknor and was "well received" by the professors. To allay any fears that his parents might have respecting distractions, he reported that "there are no amusements here whatever: so there is no alternative but study"; neither need they fear that he or Preble would become involved in duelling: "Pray set your mind perfectly at rest." Finding Göttingen everyway as good as represented, he asked permission to spend at least the summer: "The Library here is the largest in Germany and full of choise [*sic*] rare works and the advantages for a student of my particular

pursuits are certainly not overrated in the universal fame of the University of Göttingen." —*Young Longfellow*, pp. 139–40.

19. *New Light*, pp. 18–19; see also *Life*, I, 168, and *Young Longfellow*, p. 142.

20. For one thing, there was no course of lectures on modern literature at the moment. He attended two courses given by Hofrat Heeren on ancient and modern European history and another by Professor Wendt on Natural Law. He could not have assimilated much of the lectures, but he doubtless learned a good deal of German by his attendance three hours daily upon these German discourses. Much of his time (he wrote) was occupied studying German "under the guidance of an able professor," Benecke, in whose house he also took his meals —an arrangement conducive to his learning to speak the language. He also made the acquaintance of Blumenbach, and with Dr. Bode, a one-time associate of Bancroft's in the Round Hill School at Northampton, he made a short walking tour. For the rest, he pursued "other branches of modern literature"; that is, he read in Spanish and French literature, and he undertook what he described to his father as "a kind of Sketch-Book of scenes in France, Spain and Italy"—the beginning of what was ultimately published in book form as *Outre-Mer* in 1835. "By it [he added] I hope to prove that I *have not* wasted my time. . . . But the German language is beyond measure difficult; not to read,—that is not so hard—but to write. And one must write, and write correctly, in order to teach. I can only promise to do my best. I can assuredly lay a good foundation, and much more I cannot expect to do. If I can have the Professorship at Bow. Coll.—I should like it—but I must have it on fair grounds:—with the same privileges as the other professors. No state of probation— and no calling me boy—and retrenching of salary" (May 15, 1829. See *Life*, I, 174–75; *Young Longfellow*, pp. 143–44; *New Light*, p. 19).

Shortly before leaving on his Easter vacation tour of Belgium, England, and France of a month's duration, he asked permission to remain in Göttingen throughout the summer; however, late in May, when he received the letter from his father granting the request, but urging him to return by the end of September, he was ready to quit Germany. Homesickness and alarm at his father's report of his sister Elizabeth's illness caused him to leave Göttingen on June 6. Traveling *via* Paris, where he heard of his sister's death, he passed through London, Oxford, and Stratford, and on July 1 sailed from Liverpool, arriving in New York on August 11, 1829, thus bringing to a close a journey that had been planned for a year, but that had been lengthened into three years and three months.—*New Light*, pp. 22–23; *Life*, I, 176.

21. For examples, see *Life*, I, 172, and *New Light*, pp. 15–16. His Göttingen notebook contains a page of translation from Luther, another from Heine's *Reisebilder*, and a shorter passage from Voss's *Luise*. His extracts from German poetry are of "painstaking, but by no means impeccable, accuracy." There are slips and solecisms aplenty, and he refers to Löwenstein as "Livingstern" and "Livingstein," to Böttiger as "Böticher," and to "the celebrated Naturalist, Blumingbach."—*New Light*, p. 23.

During his first stay in Germany he was still a good deal the youthful romantic seeker after the picturesque. This characteristic appears in the several pen drawings which he made of himself, clothed in conventional student garb, seated at a table, a long German pipe in his mouth, a *Stein* before him on the table, and in his hand a book labeled "Goethe." It bears the title, in Longfellow's handwriting, "H. W. L. 'in the clouds' at Göttingen. April 3, 1829." (The sketch is reproduced as the frontispiece in *New Light*. A similar sketch of himself and Preble is to be found in *Life*, I, opposite p. 166.) The picture is more a pose (or romantically imaginative conception of himself) than a realistic portrait of the kind of student he knew himself to be. The volume of Goethe in his hands would have been appropriate in a picture of Longfellow at Heidelberg in 1835–1836, but there is little to suggest that at Göttingen in 1829 he got much beyond the phrase book and grammar.

22. Where French had been the only language offered, it now became a required subject for all students through the Sophomore year, and Juniors were permitted to elect either Spanish or Italian. In 1831 German was added as an elective for Juniors. In 1834, the Juniors were required to take two terms of Spanish or Greek, and Seniors could elect, during their two terms, Italian, German, or Hebrew. During his second and third years at Bowdoin Longfellow taught single-handedly French, Spanish, Italian, and German, and he complained of the excessive routine chores of correcting exercises daily.—*Young Longfellow*, pp. 150, 153, 180.

He was enabled to add considerably to the meager stock of German books in the Bowdoin library (for details, see *New Light*, p. 25), and occasionally he tried his hand at translating as well as composing in German. The Bowdoin notebook for 1833 contains several transcriptions and two original poems in German which Professor Hatfield calls properly "laudable,

though halting attempts." Both are printed in *New Light*, pp. 25–26.

23. The youthful author speaks of having "trimmed" his "midnight lamp in a German university" (*Works*, 16 vols., Standard Library ed., Boston and N.Y., 1891, VII, 21). Quotations from A. W. Schlegel's comments on the *Nibelungenlied* and the *Hofbuch* indicate that he knew something of current German literary theory regarding popular or folk literature (pp. 91–92). A night journey, in a French diligence prompts the young man to make a translation of a stanza of Bürger's "Lenore" (p. 112). The "German moralist" who is quoted in the chapter entitled "A Tailor's Drawer" has been identified by T. M. Campbell as Jean Paul Friedrich Richter—Longfellow's first reference to an author who came to hold a warm place in his esteem; and Hatfield finds the "German allegory" mentioned in the same chapter akin to Jean Paul; while the thesis that "music is the universal language of mankind—poetry their universal pastime and delight" (p .154) suggests Herder. More definite and important are three quotations from Goethe—one from *Werther* and two from *Faust*. The first (p. 176) is a translation of a passage from the second letter in *Werther*. The second—"What I catch is at present only sketch-ways, as it were; but I prepare myself betimes for the Italian journey" —is a translation of lines 4275–78 of *Faust I*. It stands fittingly at the head of the chapter entitled "The Journey into Italy." The third occurs in a passage in which, observing "in the shadow of a column . . . a young man wrapped in a cloak, earnestly conversing in a low whisper with a female figure," Longfelllow is prompted to comment, "Beware, poor girl, lest thy gentle nature prove thy undoing! Perhaps, alas, thou art already undone! And I almost heard the evil spirit whisper, as in Faust, 'How different was it with thee, Margaret, when still full of innocence, thou camest to the altar here,—out of the well-worn little book lispedst prayers, half child-sport, half God in the heart! Margaret, where is thy head? What crime in thy heart!'" Compare *Works*, VII, 231, and *Faust I*, lines 3776–87. At the close of the book Longfellow devotes four pages to a rapid sketch of his German tour, following roughly the route he had traveled in 1829: from Trieste *via* Gratz and the Steiermark to Vienna, a visit to the ancient castle of Greifenstein, thence to Prague, Dresden, Leipzig, Göttingen, Cassel, Frankfurt-am-Main, Mainz, and on down the Rhine. For the elaboration of these travel experiences, he added, he had not time. They were reserved for his next book, *Hyperion* (1839).

24. The controversy over the terms of his

appointment was never forgotten, and his impatience with the narrow religionism, the petty gossip, and the isolation of Brunswick are reflected in a satirical tale entitled "The Wonderful Tale of a Little Man in Gosling Green," which he had the foresight to publish anonymously in Greeley's *New-Yorker* for November 1, 1834. The tale, together with explanatory details, is reprinted in *Amer. Lit.*, III, ii (May, 1931), 136–48. Hatfield has observed that the style of the "Tale," in its digressiveness, quaint turns, unexpected similes, far-fetched allusions, and whimsical mystifications, while deriving ultimately from Sterne, seems more immediately influenced by Jean Paul, to whom Longfellow accorded, especially during the Bowdoin and early Cambridge periods, a high and unique place.—*New Light*, p. 138; see also *Young Longfellow*, pp. 147–209.

The young man who had traveled widely and breathed the enlightened atmosphere of some of the most famous European universities found Bowdoin provincial. His ideas of educational reforms and teaching techniques found little favor among the Bowdoin authorities. How advanced these ideas were appears from a letter to his father, written from Göttingen on March 10, 1829, when, the Bowdoin offer still hanging fire, he proposed an educational venture which must have seemed wild to his practical-minded father.

European universities, he writes, are as yet undreamed of in the U.S., where "the idea of a University" remains still "Two or three large brick buildings—with a chapel and a President to pray in it!" Even Mr. Jefferson's "bold attempt" is a failure, for he began "where everybody in *our* country would have begun—by building college halls and then trying to stock them with students. . . . European universities were never founded in this manner." One begins properly with "professors in whom the spirit moves," who are "well enough known to attract students to themselves, and . . . capable of teaching them something they did not know before." Next, capital must be expended for libraries, and books must be made freely available to students. If the Bowdoin affair should terminate badly, he proposed to take the University of Paris and "the German Universities" for a model—to "let two or three Professors begin the work—let them deliver lectures in some town (Portland seems to me better adapted for it than any other place in our part of the country)." "Yes," he concluded, "let Portland set an example to the whole U. States. Let us begin forth-with: As soon as I return—If the matter seems at all plausible— I mean to proffer my humble endeavors to the execution of such a plan—and

put my shoulder to the wheel. The present is just the moment: we must take the tide there is in the affairs of men."—*New Light*, pp. 20–22.

Just attained to the maturity of twenty-two, but already up to establishing a university of his own, he found Bowdoin short of his ideal; and though he found domestic happiness and a busy career as professor, poet, critic, and scholar during his six years there, he privately expressed, as early as January 4, 1831, his impatience with "this land of Barbarism—this miserable Down East," and longed for release from his "exile." When, in the summer of 1832, he received an inquiry whether he would consider a translation to New York University, he frankly expressed "a strong desire to tread a stage on which I can take longer strides and spout to a larger audience." But the New York invitation failed to materialize, and efforts to secure a diplomatic post in Spain, a plan to take over Cogswell's Round Hill School at Northampton, and the prospect of taking a position in the department of languages and literatures at the University of Virginia, all came to naught. For details see *Young Longfellow*, pp. 167, 175, 182–83, 188–89, 194–97, 199, 205–7.

25. Longfellow met Leigh Hunt, the Lockharts and Babbages, Sir John Bowring, the translator of Chamisso's *Peter Schlemihl*, August Hayward, translator of *Faust*, and the Carlyles. During his repeated visits to the Carlyles there was much talk of Goethe and Schiller. The persuasive "pistol bullets" of Carlyle's talk while dwelling on the idealism of Schiller and the deep moral purposefulness of *Wilhelm Meister* (which Longfellow had examined only cursorily) opened up to the young American an entirely new approach to an area of these Germans whom he had hardly considered except as lyric poets. Carlyle's opinion of Goethe as "the greatest man that ever lived, excepting only Jesus Christ" set him to thinking and inspired a desire to learn more of the deeper import of Goethe, whom he had neglected during his first stay in Germany.—*Young Longfellow*, pp. 211–16; *New Light*, pp. 33–34.

26. Although he was disappointed at finding Professor Berzelius and other notables to whom he had brought letters of introduction away for the summer, Longfellow set forthwith to work (under the direction of Professor Lignel of the University of Upsala, who was in Stockholm at the time) "picking up crumbs in the Swedish language." He also made some elementary explorations into the Finnish language. Meanwhile the delicate condition of his wife's health made travel difficult, and the itinerary by which the party had planned to reach Heidelberg was rearranged several times. By early

September they were in Copenhagen, where Longfellow took lessons in Danish from Professor Bolling, fraternized with the learned gentlemen there as he had in Stockholm, and continued his search for books for the Harvard Library which the Harvard authorities had commissioned him to buy to the extent of 200 pounds sterling.—*Life*, I, 210, 214–16; *New Light*, pp. 34–35; *Young Longfellow*, p. 219

27. For details see *New Light*, pp. 35–36, and *Young Longfellow*, pp. 222–23.

28. In Bonn Longfellow paid his respects to A. W. v. Schlegel, the first of the notable German literary men whose acquaintance he made. He was, he said, "much gratified to see the translator of Shakespeare," whose version of the *Merchant of Venice* he had seen enacted in the City Theater of Hamburg, but his account, detailed though it is, deals largely with externalities and in no way suggests that he recognized Schlegel at the time as much more than the translator of Shakespeare.

29. Her home, only two doors west of the Karlstor, housed also the Russian German-speaking Baron von Ramm, who became his companion on many a ramble in the vicinity. Not far away, Clara Crowninshield found shelter with the romantic-minded Hepp family, where a group of cultivated and socially-inclined boarders arranged almost daily whist parties or musical entertainments, and where Longfellow was known as "Wilhelm Meister." —*New Light*, p. 37.

30. He presented a letter from Dr. Lieber to Mittermeier, the famed law professor, and found a ready welcome. He became acquainted with Gervinus, the Shakespeare scholar, who unfortunately left Heidelberg for Göttingen early in 1836; with Reichlin-Meldegg, who was lecturing on Shakespeare and Schiller; with Thibaut, whose discourses on the Pandects he heard; with Paulus, the rationalist theologian; with Bertrand and Schlosser. He heard with especial interest Schlosser's "long discourse upon German literature at the present day," including the "Romantic School" and "Young Germany" whose chief apostle Longfellow learned was Heine. Schlosser closed by castigating Wolfgang Menzel, the latest historian of German literature, as a swash-buckling critic who handled matters "*ganz* burschikos." Dr. Umbreit, the librarian, showed him the MSS in the University Library and offered him the use of his own books, while Prorektor Bähr gave him free access to the library shelves.—*Life*, I, 220–21; *New Light*, p. 38; Long, *Literary Pioneers*, pp. 172–73.

31. He undertook also the superintendence of Clara Crowninshield's German studies, and with his assistance she prepared a manuscript album of thirty-seven songs (sixteen of them from Goethe) with full musical accompaniment. This manuscript together with Clara's diaries, is preserved at Craigie House.—*New Light*, pp. 38–39.

32. Like Paul Fleming in *Hyperion*, he "buried himself in books,—in old, dusty books. He worked his way diligently through the ancient poetic lore of Germany . . . into the bright sunny land of harvests, where, amid the golden grain and the blue corn-flowers, walk the modern bards, and sing."—*Hyperion* (*Works*, VIII), p. 70.

33. This work, a running chronological list, with comments and detailed references to sources, originally prepared for printing, remains a bound MS volume stored in Craigie House, of interest today chiefly as indicating the thoroughness and industry with which Longfellow worked at Heidelberg.—*New Light*, p. 39; I, 227.

34. He worked through the five volumes of Wackernagel's *Altdeutsches Lesebuch* and considered it "the best book of the kind" he had ever seen. He studied Grimm's *Deutsche Grammatik* in three volumes, the *Ludwigslied*, the *Annolied*, some of the *Minnelieder*, and parts of the *Nibelungenlied*, which he thought "deserves an entire translation in English." He read Flögel's *Geschichte der komischen Literatur*, Rosenkranz' *Geschichte der Poesie* (turned to good use in *Hyperion*, esp. in Bk. I, Ch. VII), and Schubert's *History of the Soul*. In folk literature, he read the *Märchen* of Grimm and Musaeus, Görres' *Volksbücher*, Erlach's *Volkslieder*, and *Till Eulenspiegel* and *Des Knaben Wunderhorn*. He read in and about Herder; he consulted the text of *Nathan der Weise* after seeing the piece performed in Mannheim; and he commented on the dramatic action of *Emilia Galotti*. Of Schiller, he read *Don Carlos*, *Wallenstein*, and *The Thirty Years' War*. Bürger's ballads induced him to read also a life of Bürger, and he reread Uhland, Salis, and Matthisson, already begun at Rotterdom. With Clara Crowninshield he perused Novalis' *Heinrich von Ofterdingen*, and among representative prose tales of the later romantics, a number of tales by Hoffmann, Tieck, and Carové, Chamisso's *Peter Schlemihl*, and Fouqué's *Undine*. Besides Heine's *Romantische Schule*, he found the poetry of Klopstock, the Stolbergs, Hebel, M. Frey, Zedlitz, and Salis-Seewis to his taste; and he laid the foundation for his apostrophes in *Hyperion* to Jean Paul as the "eagle of German literature" by reading *Campaner-Tal*, *Flegeljahre*, and *Titan*. —*New Light*, pp. 39–40, 42; *Literary Pioneers*, pp. 173–75, 253 n. 35.

35. See his penetrating observations, *New Light*, pp. 40–41, substantially the same sentiments that animate Chapter VII in Book II of *Hyperion*: "Mill-Wheels and Other Wheels," esp. p. 114. Among his prized possessions, still preserved in Craigie House, is a fine copy of *Des Knaben Wunderhorn*, acquired at Heidelberg during the winter of 1835–1836. He also owned and frequently used Erlach's collection of *Volkslieder der Deutschen* in five volumes and Meinert's *Alte deutsche Volkslieder*. His close attention to these collections largely accounts for his fine appreciation of the German *Volkslied* and his success in rendering it in translation and imitation.

36. *New Light*, p. 40. For his comments on Goethe's works at the time he read them in Heidelberg, see *Literary Pioneers*, pp. 174–77.

37. *New Light*, p. 41.

38. Mary's last words, as he recorded them in his diary, had been, "I will be with you." Sitting alone in his study, he mused: "The clock is now striking ten. I am sitting alone in my new home; and yet not alone—for the spirit of her, who loved me, and who I trust still loves me— is with me. Not many days before her death she said to me: 'We shall be so happy in Heidelberg!' I feel assured of her presence—and am happy in knowing that she is so. O my beloved Mary—teach me to be good, and kind, and gentle as thou wert here on earth."—*Young Longfellow*, p. 230.

39. He found satisfaction in the company of Bryant, who, however, was called away from Heidelberg late in January; and he sought the modest social diversions that Heidelberg afforded. But a cheerfulness momentarily evoked by his first participation in German Christmas festivities ended abruptly with the arrival, on Christmas eve, of a letter telling him of the death of his brother-in-law and dearest friend, George W. Pierce. What helped him conquer an overpowering mood of loneliness and dejection was a bracing letter from Ticknor, who, having been crushed the year before by the loss of his only son, expressed the hope that Longfellow would find that inner "support without which all external consolation is idle and unavailing," and counseled him to devote himself "to constant and interesting intellectual labor; you will find it will go further than any other merely human means; at least such is my experience" (*Life*. I, 223). Resolving henceforth to "bear upon my shield the holy cross," he returned to his books; but his first sustained bout with German scholarship in the University library, while preparing the elaborate syllabus of ten centuries of German literature, soon showed him that arid fact-gathering and

source-hunting were not much to his taste. He told himself that as a professor at Harvard he must be proficient in the realm of literary history, but he soon put by the desire to follow strictly in the path of scientific German scholarship or to emulate the intellectual feats of Ticknor, his predecessor. Immersion in the romantic literature of Germany directed the main emphasis of his life into the language of sentiment and emotion (see *Young Longfellow*, p. 231). The resolution and calm required for the composition of poetry was still lacking; he was still too close to his sorrow for that. But the foundations for a poetic career were laid during the winter of 1835–1836 at Heidelberg.

40. See his judgments on *Werther* in his diary for December 29, 1835, printed in O. W. Long. "Goethe and Longfellow," *Germanic Rev.*, VII, ii (Apr., 1932), 153; other criticisms of *Werther* appear in *New Light*, pp. 41–42, and *Literary Pioneers*, pp. 174–76.

41. Under the combined influence of Goethe, who advised renunciation and resolution, and of Ticknor, who counseled faith and perseverance, Longfellow became himself the moral counsellor and spiritual comforter of George W. Greene, who wrote to him from Florence in a mood of ill health and spiritual despair. See the Goethean precepts propounded by Longfellow in his letter to Greene on January 22, 1836, in *Life*, I, 224–25, also pp. 227–28. He paused little in his own labors unless it were to make a translation of such bits as Salis' "Song of the Silent Land" (*Life*, I, 224) and Aloys Schreiber's "An die Glocke" (*New Light*, p. 43) or to seek diversion during the gloomy winter in the company of Clara Crowninshield and Julie Hepp, ever ready to arrange evenings devoted to cards or music or literary discussions, which always grew spirited when they considered the relative merits of Goethe and Schiller (*Young Longfellow*, p. 232). He undertook for the *North American Review* an elaborate article on the German drama that he never completed.

42. In April he made a four-day trip in the company of three friends to Frankfurt, where he saw the annual fair, viewed Dannecker's statue of Ariadne, inspected Goethe's house, and heard *Don Giovanni*, his favorite opera. A few weeks later he went to Mannheim to see *Nathan der Weise* enacted by the celebrated Esslaer, then 70 years old. By May 14, he was again "growing tired of being cooped up in Heidelberg—beautiful as it is," and felt "a strong desire to be once more on the wing" (*New Light*, p. 43). In June he made a brief excursion to the baths of Ems and saw at Mainz the cathedral, the cloisters of Saint Willigis, and the tomb of Frauenlob the Minne-

singer (*Life*, I, 229–31). Returned to Heidelberg, he still found himself restless. He began to discover certain provincialisms in Heidelberg that he had not previously noticed. "The people in general" and "the professors' wives" in particular were "rather limited in their notions, especially affecting America." "Verily," he mused, "the inhabitants of Heidelberg are not a very cleanly and sweet-scented race! Every front entry smells worse than a stable.... The Hauptstrasse is but a mile long;—there are all kinds of utter abominations on the sidewalks. . . . The English are by far the most cleanly and decent people on the face of the earth;—including ourselves under the name of English" (*New Light*, p. 43; see also *Literary Pioneers*, p. 177).

43. Finding solitary travel as an "experiment of moral alchemy" unsatisfactory, he sought such amusement as scenery and notebook afforded. At various stages in his journey he recorded his observations and feelings in very tolerable German (one such passage, consisting of three paragraphs, correct and idiomatic in all but one phrase, is reproduced in *New Light*, p. 44). The Journey from Munich to Salzburg was made by coach, in the company of three others, one of whom was "Grilparzer [*sic*], a poet from Vienna, an insignificant man in appearance; but a very pleasant one in reality" (*New Light*, p. 44). At Ischl he had for his companion, a Mr. K., the intelligent, good-hearted, and eccentric Englishman who figures in *Hyperion* as Mr. Berkeley, and who really ate his breakfast at St. Gilgen in the hydropathic fashion there described (*Hyperion*, p. 247; *Life*, I, 235). And it was at St. Gilgen, on July 5, that he copied from the wall of the little chapel the inscription which he afterwards translated and used as the motto for *Hyperion*, and which is highly characteristic of many of his later didactic lyrics:

> Blicke nicht trauernd in die Vergangenheit,
> sie kommt nicht wieder; nütze weise die
> Gegenwart,
> sie ist dein; der düstern Zukunft geh' ohne
> Furcht mit männlichem Sinne entgegen.

From St. Gilgen he proceeded by way of Innsbruck, Constance, Zürich, Brunnen, the Furca and Grimsel passes, and Interlaken to Thun, where on July 20, his path crossed that of the Appletons of Boston. Eleven days later, after he had gone to Geneva and back, he rejoined them at Interlaken and was promptly struck by Frances, the younger of the Appleton sisters.

44. *New Light*, pp. 45–46; *Young Longfellow*, pp. 235–37.

45. While they drove along the lake at Zürich, Longfellow translated Uhland's ballad of the "Castle by the Sea," with the assistance of Lady Fanny, who was scribe on the occasion, and made "some of the best lines," as he reminded her years later. Then they "got out of the carriage and walked," and after a boat ride, resumed their attempt to capture Uhland's elusive mood in English words. At Schaffhausen, while trying to cheer the failing invalid in the Appleton party, Longfellow read *Modern Characteristics*, a work on contemporary German men of letters. In it he found a sketch of Hoffmann von Fallersleben, which he considered "capital," a judgment that is reflected in the relatively large proportion of space devoted to that German poet ten years later in his *Poets and Poetry of Europe.*—*New Light*, p. 46; *Young Longfellow*, pp. 236–37.

46. Back at Interlaken, Frances Appleton wrote a brief confession: "Miss Mr. L. considerably." And it may be that she dispatched a message that softened the rebuff which she had given him earlier; for in Paris, on September 28, the young widower made an unexpected transcription in his journal of a well-known German *Volkslied* intimating as much— "Kommt a Vogel geflogen . . ."—*Young Longfellow*, 237–38.

47. Upon retiring, Ticknor had urged that the Smith Professor should be relieved of all routine teaching, that he should lecture only and supervise the department, leaving the class drill in French, Spanish, Italian, and German to the foreign-born instructors, Sales, Bachi. Surault, and Bokum. The new professor was pleased with his new position and the payment of his salary for the first quarter "without any ado," as he reported the matter to his father, adding, "I think I shall have nothing to do but lecture.... I have no classes to hear ... and in all probability shall never be required to hear any." This last surmise turned out to be overoptimistic. Before many months passed, he found his position entailed both responsibilities and trials. The four instructors were "all pulling the wrong way except one." He supervised the individual classes; sometimes he took a class, and almost invariably enjoyed doing so, because he did so by choice. But there were times when a tutor left suddenly and when, no substitute being available, he was required to hear recitations.—*Young Longfellow*, p. 241; *New Light*, pp. 48, 52; *Life*, I, 257.

48. *New Light*, p. 49; *Life*, I, 256; *Young Longfellow*, p. 243.

49. By May 12, the plan was taking definite shape. To his father he wrote: "I have a class in German, and shall soon commence my lectures

I give you a sketch of my course: 1. Introduction. History of the French Language. 2. The Other Languages of the South of Europe. 3. History of the Northern, or Gothic, Languages. 4. Anglo-Saxon Literature. 5 and 6. Swedish Literature. 7. Sketch of German Literature. 8, 9, 10. Life and Writings of Goethe. 11 and 12. Life and Writings of Jean Paul Richter."— *Life*, pp. 261–62. It is to be observed that six of the twelve lectures are devoted to modern German literature, three of them to Goethe. The omission of Schiller is noteworthy in view of the emphasis which Follen had given to him. It has been said that Longfellow never properly evaluated Goethe in comparison with other German figures, and that Jean Paul received always the greater share of his veneration. That he was powerfully drawn to Jean Paul appears both from the outline of this first course of lectures and from statements that he made at various times, chiefly one of 1837, wherein he calls him "the most magnificent of the German prose writers" (*Life*, I, 259). But this apostrophe, and Book I, Chapter V of *Hyperion* (entitled "Jean Paul, the Only-One"), where Richter is referred to as "a comet among the bright stars of German literature," comprise the more significant references to him (I count twenty in all). They belong principally to the young Longfellow, the author of the romantic *Hyperion*—a book expressive of many sentiments not representative of the mature Longfellow. By contrast, he refers to Goethe no less than 200 times, including thirty quotations or translations of his own. His admiration of Richter is a youthful enthusiasm; his love of Goethe, while never completely unqualified, grew deeper as the years passed, serving him, especially after he passed the *mezzo cammin* of his life, often as a personal comforter, as well as a source of poetic inspiration.

50. For further details regarding the contents of these lectures see *New Light*, pp. 53–54, 56–62, and *Literary Pioneers*, pp. 179–80, 182–88.

· The number of Harvard undergraduates pursuing the study of modern languages had grown steadily under Ticknor's administration. When Longfellow took charge, a modern language was a required study for Sophomores and Juniors, throughout both years, and for Seniors during the first and second terms. Longfellow viewed his position as challenging his best efforts to be both instructive and interesting. He counted strongly and correctly on his ability as a reader and as a translator of interesting passages for illustrative purposes; and his innovation of courteously addressing each student as "Mister" won approval. He was fortunate, also, in the room assigned to him for

his first class—"Corporation Room No. 5," which provided the right atmosphere. Young Edward Everett Hale, a member of the new professor's first regular class, recalled: "We met in a sort of parlor, carpeted, hung with pictures, and otherwise handsomely furnished. . . . We sat round a mahogany table . . . and the whole affair had the aspect of a friendly gathering in a private house, in which the study of German was the amusement of the occasion. He began with familiar ballads,—read them to us, and made us read them to him. Of course, we soon committed them to memory without meaning to, and I think this was probably part of his theory. At the same time we were learning the paradigms by rote."—*New Light*, pp. 52–53.

Here were innovations, indeed, and the fourteen-year-old Hale could not escape noting the difference between the average tutor's method of "setting lessons and exercises, and hearing and receiving them" and this newer procedure, which, as he noted at the time, he believed he would "like very much." When Longfellow gave his next course of lectures, at the opening of the new academic year (Sept. 1837), Hale was again present , and again he set down, with the characteristic temerity of a fifteen-year-old Junior, his impressions: "The lectures are to be extemporaneous translations of the German with explanations; as he called it, recitations in which he recites and we hear. He made a long introduction to the matter in hand, very flowery and bombastical indeed, which appeared to me very much out of taste. I believe, however, that it was entirely extemporaneous and that he was carried away by the current of his thoughts. In fact, he appeared to say just what came uppermost. The regular translation and explanation part of the lecture was very good."—*Ibid.*, p. 55.

Hale went to hear the second lecture, which he "liked a good deal better than the first." But when, on October 27, Longfellow concluded his discourses on *Faust I*, and offered to continue with *Faust II* for a volunteer section, Hale decided, "I shall not go. The lectures are tolerably interesting, but not good enough to compensate for the time taken up by them."—*Literary Pioneers*, p. 181.

In the meantime Longfellow's duties had been more clearly defined: "He was to give one lecture a week [actually he gave two a week]; to superintend studies and instructors, being present at least once a month in each course; to give two lectures a week during the summer term on 'Belles Lettres, or Literary History.'" He altered the program of his lectures, and to emphasize more recent German literature, began with Goethe's *Faust* on September 18,

1837. As during the preceding spring, he spoke from notes.—*New Light*, p. 55; *Life*, I, 276–77.

51. The success of his first series of lectures was such that he told his father in August, 1837, he would "probably have an edition printed . . . not at my expense—which is something unusual."—*Literary Pioneers*, pp. 180–81.

52. During his early months in Heidelberg he engaged in joyous disputation with Fräulein Julie Hepp, upholding the "noble idealism" of Schiller against her championship of Goethe's "realism." "I told her I thought the moral impression of Goethe's works was not good, to which she replied, 'Das ist das allgemeine Irrthum.'" As he went on to read Goethe's later works, he modified his views, but he was not yet ready to agree that all the condemnation of Goethe constituted merely "universal error" or "common misconception." In his journal for June 4, 1836, he recorded the judgment of a "fat man" whom he met at the hotel a few days earlier, "Goethe desecrates everything he touches. It is as if you should take a beautiful rose, and trample it in the dirt and then say, 'There's your rose— your beautiful rose.'"—*Literary Pioneers*, pp. 175, 254, n. 53. At another time he said, "There is enough misery in the world to make our hearts heavy; in books let us have something more than this —something to strengthen and elevate and purify us. Schiller, the beautiful Schiller, does this. He is the prophet of the ideal, Goethe the prophet of the real."—*Ibid.*, p. 177.

53. These sentiments are echoed in the portion of his lectures where he outlined for his students the three epochs in Goethe's life (see below).

54. *New Light*, pp. 61–62.

55. The passage appears to have been suggested by Menzel's *German Literature* (Felton's translation, 3 vols., Boston, 1840), II, 27; also pp. 24–26, 40, 89–92.

56. *Ibid.*, p. 62. It is to be noted, too, that his strictures on *Werther*, as set down in his Heidelberg diary, are tempered in his Harvard lectures: "As for the moral effect of the book, I cannot think it bad, unless upon minds weak and willing to err." See *Literary Pioneers*, pp. 185–86, and *Germanic* Rev., VII, ii (Apr., 1932), 163.

57. The reference reflects Menzel's *German Literature*, III, 21 ff.

Obviously this is Longfellow's own feeling about the incontinent defamation of Goethe's character. Before his classes he quoted Menzel's charges that Goethe was "not patriotic," that he was "aristocratical and conservative," that he possessed a "base soul," that he "deemed

weakness beauty," that he was "selfish," that he was an "enthusiast only for *himself*," and that he was "always *perfecting* himself." These accusations, coming from Menzel, Goethe's countryman, he represented as doubly vicious: "If ever a man was . . . misunderstood and calumniated out of his own country, that man was Goethe." And by way of refutation, he pointed out that Goethe was not responsible for his egoism—that the ever-present coterie of worshippers made him an egoist. In exonerating Goethe of the charge of selfishness, he offered what he called "my own impressions." He accounts the singleness of Goethe's purpose in making self culture his main study from youth to old age a great honor to the man—this endeavor to develop and improve what nature had given him, going steadily forward "perfecting himself into a complete man." All the accusations fall flat before the fact that Goethe was a great philosopher: "This was his religion, to busy himself with the present, fulfilling his destiny. . . . This was his idea of human perfectibility, and he seems almost to have realized it in his own person." Such men are not to be bound by the conventions imposed by lesser men on ordinary men (here he cited his own translation of Venetian Epigram, No. 10). So much for the charge of indifference and self-culture. As for his aloofness from political issues and lack of patriotic fervor, we have the "wise and true" testimony of Eckermann to the contrary. Of Goethe's moral and religious character Professor Longfellow found it "difficult to say anything definite," beyond quoting the famous passage in which Faust makes his pantheistic confession of faith to Margaret in the garden. He translated, and presumably read to his students at this point lines 3432–58. He also adduced pertinent passages from Mrs. Austin's *Characteristics*, I, 100–103, to show that the subject of religion and immortality occupied Goethe's mind from childhood to the end of his life. Longfellow steadily regarded *Faust* as largely autobiographical and read much of the autobiographical into others of Goethe's writings.

Having concluded his biographical account and having presented a general estimate of the man and his philosophical outlook, Longfellow concluded in a manner apparently designed to be disarming:

"I will now state my estimate of that character in the fewest possible words: This man, then, was a man of comprehensive and commanding intellect; of rich imagination; and strong, simple, healthy common sense. In character he was calm and dignified; of great gentleness and benignity in his judgments of other men; of great sensibility to all forms of beauty; and great love for all forms of truth. He seems to me, indeed, to be strikingly like Franklin, though with more imagination. The practical tendency of his mind was the same; his love of science was the same; his benignant philosophic soothsayings seem nothing more than this worldly wisdom of Poor Richard versified and idealized."—*Literary Pioneers*, p. 184.

Here is to be noted another bodily transfer of matter from his lectures to *Hyperion*. The Baron, referring to the various appellations conferred on Goethe by his admirers and detractors, says, "Well, call him Old Humbug, or Old Heathen, or what you please; I maintain that, with all his errors and shortcomings, he was a glorious specimen of a man." "He certainly was," admits Fleming. "Did it ever occur to you that he was in some points like Ben Franklin,—a kind of rhymed Ben Franklin? The practical tendency of his mind was the same; his love of science was the same; his benignant, philosophic spirit was the same; and a vast number of his poetic maxims and soothsayings seem nothing more than the worldly wisdom of Poor Richard, versified."—*Hyperion*, p. 123.

The quotations from Longfellow's notes are transcriptions made by Professor Hatfield while he worked in Craigie House and graciously sent to me at the time. See also *New Light*, pp. 59–62. and *Literary Pioneers*, pp. 182–84.

58. See *New Light*, pp. 50–51, for his letter to Mary Appleton expressing his difficulty while writing lectures in turning from "Christian Dante" back to "Heathen Goethe."

59. While he doubtless revised and altered these notes in later years, their general conformity to passages in *Hyperion* and the precise dates written on some of them suggest that they survive substantially in the form first written in 1837–1838.

60. For example, in the lecture on Goethe's life and character, he practically ignored the "Lili" episode and devoted too much space to such minor characters as Hofrat Hüsgen.—*New Light*, p. 59.

61. *Ibid.*, p. 59; *Life*, I, 284.

62. *New Light*, pp. 59–60.

63. Of special interest as indicating what the successive generations of Longfellow's students heard regarding *Faust* is his teaching-copy of Part I, bought in 1837, and interleaved for manuscript notations, including assignments, outlines of scenes, translations of key passages, comments on and elucidations of the text, the chronology of the play, the prevalence of popular superstitions, illustrated by numerous instances of compacts with the devil, the histor-

ical Doctor Faustus, the first Faust book, the puppet plays, the treatment of the legend in the drama, beginning with Marlowe, and references to the translations made by Gower, Hayward, Blackie, Syme, Anster, Birch, Talbot, and Bernays. He calls attention to some "desperate blunders" made by Gower and Hayward. Annotations of the text include the observation that "Auerbach's Cellar" is "perhaps the very best" scene in the entire play, the Cathedral scene is "grand," and the Prison scene is "dreadful." Unable completely to forego making a display of his learning, he draws literary parallels—some illuminating, some veering on the pedantic—to individual passages in the text, drawing upon Sanskrit, the Bible, Old English, Rabbinical literature, the Eddas, saints' legends, and the modern literatures in many languages. The archangel's song in the "Prologue in Heaven" reminds him of Bryant's "Song of the Stars," and of two stanzas in Milton's hymn, "On the Morning of Christ's Nativity." Faust, as he appears in the first monologue (ll. 354–61), is compared to Marlowe's Faustus, Byron's Manfred, and Goethe's own restless life and aspirations. Faust's second monologue (ll. 602–736), as well as the one in "Forest and Cavern" (ll. 3217–50), suggests certain lines in Wordsworth's *Excursion* (IV, 130–45, 513–39). Mephistopheles is to be studied in relation to the satanic figures of Dante, Milton, Calderon, Byron, and Bailey; the character of Margaret, a composite of Goethe's Gretchen, Frederica, and Lili, may be compared with the Margaret in the Old English play of *The Countrie Girl*. Opposite "Haupt- und Staatsaktion" (l. 583) he cites Wieland: "Shakespeare's Stücke sind grössten Theils Haupt- und-Staatsaktionen, oder dramatische Novellen und Märchen." "Das dreimal glühende Licht" (l. 1318) led him to investigate its symbolic meaning and to record: "Picture of a three-fold candlestick, used in some churches in the M[iddle] A[ges]. From *Ancient Mysteries Described*." The "Pentagramma" (l. 1396) is elucidated by a quotation from John Holland's *Cruciana*: "Employed all over Asia in ancient times as a charm against witchcraft. Bishop Kennet reports opinion [that] if [the sign is] placed against body, the angles will point to the places where Christ was wounded." Laid into the book at this point is a loose sheet of paper illustrating the pentagram. Longfellow's inscription reads: "Drawn by Agassiz to explain the pentagraph. Jan. 17, 1871." (See *New Light*, opposite p. 132; Longfellow introduced the pentagram into *Christus: The Divine Tragedy*, *Works*, V, 93.) The song of the Spirits (ll. 1446–1505) reminds him of Ariel's song in *The*

Tempest (I, ii, 376); and the magic mantle which Mephistopheles supplies for his own and Faust's convenience suggests several literary parallels of similar cloaks put to equally evil uses. The magic mirror of the "Hexenküche" (l.2430) is a common device found in the *Gesta Romanorum*, in Cervantes, and elsewhere. Two idiomatic expressions are happily explained: "Ja, wenn man's nicht ein bisschen tiefer wüsste" (l. 3051) is translated, "Yes, if I did not know a trick worth two of that!" and "in allen Ehren" (l. 3052) is rendered "Honor bright." Opposite Mephistopheles' mocking observation, "Ich hab' euch oft beneidet/ Um's Zwillingspaar, das unter Rosen weidet" (ll. 3337–38), Longfellow wrote the rhapsodic word "Exquisite!" The passage in which Margaret, expressing her fear of Mephistopheles, of his cynicism, and of his cross-marked brow, concludes "Dass er nicht mag eine Seele leiden" (l. 3490), Longfellow finds paralleled in St. Theresa's characterization of Satan as one who is incapable of loving —"Poor wretch! He does not love." A bit of independent research appears in his note, line 3569— "Im Sünderhemdchen Kirchbuss' thun"—where he cites, from the *Collections of the Maine Historical Society*, I (1831), 272, a parallel case of public penance for adultery as exacted by New England law in York, Me., in 1640. He refers to Shelley's translations from the "Walpurgis Night," adds a number of notes explanatory of allusions in the "Walpurgis-Night's Dream" and calls attention to Heine's description of the Brocken. Finally, he questionably derives Margaret's "Lass mich nur erst das Kind noch tränken" (l. 4443) from the old Spanish ballad of *Conde Alarcor*.

64. While Emerson and his fellow-Transcendentalists were assiduous in introducing German transcendental patterns of thought, and Ripley and Parker were upsetting the orthodox by proclaiming a disturbing brand of German theological criticism, Longfellow was most influential in transforming American critical opinion of German literature (especially of Goethe's relative rank in the German literary hierarchy) in academic circles, while Margaret Fuller did the same work among the more general reading public.

65. *Life*, I, 330, 331, (Apr. 19 and 21, 1839).

66. *Hyperion*, p. 123.

67. *Ibid.*; *Life*, I, 330.

68. *Poets and Poetry of Europe* (1847), p. 281.

69. *Life*, II, 47 (June 21, 1846).

70. *Literary Pioneers*, p. 196. Highly important in this development was the infectious pro-German atmosphere of the Cambridge-Boston community that enveloped and ab-

sorbed Longfellow. There was Carl Follen, the first professor of German at Harvard, whose death in 1840 Longfellow mourned as a personal loss; George Ticknor, who carried on between Follen's dismissal in 1835 and Longfellow's inaugural; George Bancroft, whom Longfellow consulted regarding his first European tour, and whose numerous articles on German literature in general and Goethe in particular he read; J. G. Cogswell, co-founder with Bancroft of the Round Hill School, which Longfellow had once considered taking over; Edward Everett, who had brought from Germany the books that formed the nucleus of Harvard's German library, who lectured in Boston on Goethe, Schelling, and Hegel, and who served as president of Harvard from 1846 to 1849; and F. H. Hedge, an early member of the Transcendental Club, translator of Leibnitz, Fichte, Chamisso, Tieck, and Hoffmann, editor of *Prose Writers of Germany*—all of them men who like himself, had studied in Germany and got their inspiration at first hand.

Then there were several informal groups to which he belonged—for example, the Five of Clubs, composed of C. C. Felton, Charles Sumner, G. S. Hillard, H. R. Cleveland, and himself, and the "Young Faculty Meeting," including some of the same group, plus Benjamin Pierce. In both groups the members went by Germanized names; their Socratic *gaudiola*, complete with German songs and full accompaniment of *Studenten* conviviality, were held on Monday evenings after they had dutifully attended the more decorous sessions of the Harvard faculty. There were also individuals like C. T. Brooks, indefatigible translator from the German, and, somewhat later, Bayard Taylor, translator of *Faust*.

Next, a great number of native Germans came to make Craigie House a kind of second home—people like Tellkampf, who passed the winter of 1838–1839 in Boston lecturing on "the various schools of German philosophy," Franz Lieber, Carl Schurz, Nikolaus Heinrich Julius, Gustav Pfizer, Knut J. Clement, Abbe Liszt, and Dr. J. G. Karl of Bremen. Freiligrath, though he never came to America, elicited much sympathy, and his welfare engrossed much of Longfellow's time. Longfellow's sympathy for German exiles was well known, and he paid the price of seeking shelter or careers for a host of expatriated artists and intellectuals. He was expected to get up concerts and lectures for "invading foreign talent," to make subscriptions for foreign monuments, and to write memorial verses for American Goethe societies.—*New Light*, pp. 66–67, 81. As the years passed, demands upon his time multiplied manifold (see *Life*, II, 59, 175). On March 29, 1850, he observed: "To-day a new class in college wanting to read Faust. And I cannot in conscience say No. Inclination to do everything for the young men prompts me to say Yes; and accordingly I say Yes. It is only one impediment more between me and the real work I have to do."—*Life*, II, 175. The "seventy lectures" to which he felt "doomed" for 1850–1851 hung over him "like a dark curtain."—*Ibid.*, p. 177. After repeated "six hours in the lecture room" he felt "like a schoolmaster," "a playmate for boys," "a fat mill-horse, grinding round with blinkers on."—*Ibid.*, I, 307, 342; II, 259. Remembering that "Art is long and life is short," he resolved to retire, and on April 19, 1854, he delivered his last lecture.—*Ibid.*, II, 259–60, 268. Throughout all the trials and vexations of the years when he tried to combine an academic with a poetic career, there was one professional association that, far from wearisome, lightened his burden—his long friendship with Bernard Rölker, who came to his assistance as instructor in German in August, 1838, and remained, at the same rank, for eighteen years. Rölker's fine *German Reader* was long used at Harvard; his complete translation of *Wahlverwandtschaften* appears to have introduced Longfellow to that work of Goethe's; and his excellent prose version of Hartmann von Aue's *Der arme Heinrich* was put to good use while Longfellow was engaged in writing *The Golden Legend*. For a good, though brief sketch of Rölker, see *New Light*, pp. 64–65.

71. *New Light*, p. 71.

72. *Young Longfellow*, p. 267; *ibid.*, p. 268; compare *Wilhelm Meister's Apprenticeship* (tr. by Carlyle, 2 vols., London, 1899), I, 17, II, 232; also II, 2.

73. *Outre-Mer*, p. 235.

74. *Young Longfellow*, p. 268. A passage copied into his notebook in the churchyard of St. Gilgen, and soon to be used as the motto for *Hyperion*, reinforced the same principle: "Look not mournfully into the Past. It comes not back again. Wisely improve the Present. It is thine. Go forth and meet the shadowy Future, without fear, and with a manly heart." He recurred to the idea of living in the present repeatedly; see *Life*, I, 252, 258–59, 263, 303, 314.

75. *Young Longfellow*, p. 405, n. 7. The poem was given its final form on July 26, a month after he wrote the first six stanzas.

76. *Works*, I, 20.

77. See also *Faust I*, l. 1787: "Die Zeit ist kurz, die Kunst ist lang," as well as *Wilhelm Meister*, vii, 9, and compare Longfellow's "Quatrain": "Why waste the hours in idle talk, When life is short, and time is flying?"—*Life*, III, 415.

78. The thought and expression are not, of course, original with Goethe, as Longfellow well knew, for he had quoted Hippocrates to the same effect in 1834. What he did not know in 1838, when he wrote "A Psalm of Life," was that other notable anticipations were to be found in Horace, Chaucer, and Franklin's "Ephemera." But it was not until the next year—April 19, 1839, to be exact—that Felton called his attention to "the great similarity between his [Horace's] morality and Goethe's." Two days later, he called Horace "the Latin Goethe—or rather (Spirit of the past forgive me!) Goethe is the German Horace." "He is my favorite classic . . . and half of what we now cry up as so wonderfully said by the German, was quite as well said two thousand years ago by Horace." But he goes on to add, in the next paragraph, what after all shows that Goethe was very much more on his mind than Horace ever was:

"There—the church bells begin to ring. Shall I go, or stay? Do you know I seldom stay at home from church without thinking of that pretty little poem of Goethe, where he says that a truant boy was chased over field and through forest by a church-bell!"—*Life*, I, 330.

Previous to this time (that is, while he was engaged on his several Psalms of Life) he had felt secure in attributing the mandate to live in the present and related ideas to Goethe, as when he wrote in his diary for September 11, 1838: "'Was heute nicht geschieht, ist morgen nicht gethan' [*Faust I*, l. 225] says Goethe. What to-day is not a-doing / Is to-morrow still undone." —*Life*, I, 307. And less than a month prior to his discovery that these sentiments were not entirely original with Goethe he closed a letter to his friend Samuel Ward with the quatrain from Goethe's *Zahme Xenien*, iv, seemingly under the impression that its expression was peculiar to Goethe: "Liegt dir Gestern klar und offen / Wirkst du heute kräftig frei, / Kannst auch auf ein Morgen hoffen / Das nicht minder glücklich sei."—*Life*, I, 327.

The influence on "A Psalm of Life," to whatever ultimate source it may be traced, was, in Longfellow's case, one that derived most directly from Goethe.

79. The release which he sought from the pangs of unrequited love needed frequent reaffirmation. Another expression of his purposefulness and of his resolve to build strength into his every thought and action was put into a poem now entitled "The Light of Stars," also written in the summer of 1838 and published six months later in the *Knickerbocker* as "A Second Psalm of Life" (*Works*, I, 23–25; *Young Longfellow*, pp. 270–71). The third Psalm, "The

Village Blacksmith," repeats the same injunction (see the prefatory note, *Works*, I, 64).

80. *Life*, I, 303–5.

81. *New Light*, p. 68; see also *Young Longfellow*, pp. 282, 411–14, n. 20.

82. *Life*, I, 391.

83. For portions of his lectures emphasizing this "growth of character" in Goethe's works, see *Young Longfellow*, pp. 273–74; *Literary Pioneers*, pp. 182–84.

84. *Young Longfellow*, p. 274.

85. *Hyperion*, p. 78. His admiration of *Wilhelm Meister* was never unqualified. See *Life*, II, 230–31. He reread the book in 1852 and again in 1870.

86. *Life*, I, 256, 273–74; *New Light*, p. 49; *Young Longfellow*, pp. 243, 250.

87. This letter, here printed for the first time, from a photostatic copy graciously supplied by the Rosenbach Company of New York, in whose possession the original remains, has led to interesting findings, for which I am indebted to the late Professor James T. Hatfield, who learned of the existence in Herischdorf, Silesia, of Clara von Jordan, a granddaughter of Clara Crowninshield. This contact led to Clara von Jordan's sending to Prof. H. W. L. Dana the diaries of her grandmother, together with the MS collection of 36 songs set to music, which Longfellow helped Clara Crowninshield prepare during their Heidelberg winter. Sixteen of the 36 poems are from Goethe: (1) Lied der Nacht: "Im Windsgeräusch," (2) Wonne der Wehmut: "Trocknet nicht," (3) Klärchens Lied: "Freudvoll und leidvoll," (4) Wechsel: "Auf Kieseln im Bache," (5) Erster Verlust: "Ach wer bringt," (6) Geistesgruss: "Hoch auf dem alten," (7) Trost in Tränen: "Wie kommt's," (8) Nachgefühl: "Wenn die Reben," (9) Mignon: "Kennst du das Land," (10) Sehnsucht: "Was zieht mir," (11) Der Fischer: "Das Wasser rauscht," (12) Der Junggesell und der Mühlbach: "Wo willst du," (13) Wanderers Nachtlied: "Der du von dem Himmel," (14) Gretchens Lied: "Meine Ruh' ist hin," and the harper's two songs: (15) "An die Türen will ich schleichen," and (16) "Nur wer die Sehnsucht kennt."

88. *Young Longfellow*, p. 284.

89. The action of *Hyperion* follows closely enough Longfellow's own steps as he journeyed sorrowfully up the Rhine in December, 1835, with, as Professor Hatfield observed, "a curious back–turn from Mayence to Bingen" (see *Hyperion*, Bk. I, Ch. V). Then followed, in regular order, an excursion to Frankfurt with Baron von Ramm, Julie, and Clara (Apr. 10–14, 1836); a tour of the German baths with Mrs. Bryant, her daughters, and Clara (June 11–19);

and finally his own solitary pilgrimage through South Germany, the Tyrol, and Switzerland (June 25–August 20), except that the Swiss experiences (which came last in his travels) are put first, and the real order of travel from Stuttgart to the Tyrol is reversed, the better to introduce the "romance" with Mary Ashburton (Frances Appleton). "Persons and events step freely from the diary into the romance: the 'Baron' corresponds to Baron Jacques von Ramm, a German-speaking lord of landed estates in Russian Esthonia, who also lived in the Himmelhahn *pension*, and took frequent walks with the young American" during which they discussed German literature in general and Goethe in particular, very much in the manner described in *Hyperion.—New Light*, p. 71. The man from Bayreuth, "with large intellectual eyes," who "knew Jean Paul" actually held forth on Richter at a Heidelberg hotel dinner on June 4, 1836, very much as Longfellow reports in Book I, Chapter V. The account of Fleming's journey in the company of the refreshing Englishman named "Mr. Berkley" is authentic enough, except that the Englishman's name in reality was Kinsley. The visit to the sculptor Dannecker (*Hyperion*, pp. 282–83), the gossip of Frau Himmelauen (p. 78), and the Latin conversations (p. 259) are literal transcriptions of reality; even the episode of the Polish count who seduced "Emma of Ilmenau" is based on the story of a Pole who did seduce a young lady in Heidelberg—though she was not from Ilmenau (pp. 135– 36; cf. *New Light*, pp. 71–72). Similarly, Mary Ashburton's sketchbook, the scenes of student life (which seem to owe something to Auerbach's Cellar scene in *Faust*) and the inscription that stands at the head of *Hyperion* were drawn from the traveler's notebook.

90. *Hyperion*, p. 70.

91. *Ibid.*, p. 45.

92. *Ibid.*, pp. 95–96. He took particular pains to quote in full the lines of Uhland's "Castle by the Sea" that he had translated, with the help of Frances Appleton at Zürich (*ibid.*, pp. 184–85). A ramble which the Baron and Fleming took along the banks of a brook inspired the long passage in which Longfellow succeeds admirably in describing the essential spirit of German song (*ibid.*, p. 114). This passage, in which he uses Goethe's "Junggesell und der Mühlbach" for illustrative purposes, is typical of the kind of material that fills page upon page of the book, and explains why in his own songs later he fell so easily into the vein of the German lyric.

93. See O. Deiml, *Der Einfluss von Jean Paul auf Longfellows Prosastil* (Erlangen, 1927). Built

as the book is on the general pattern of *Outre-Mer*, it was easy to modify the sketchbook technique by extending the episodic materials, after the manner of Jean Paul, to make numerous sallies away from the main plot in search of decorative elements in both prose and verse, touching legends, quixotic or romantic adventures, sentimental or moral meditations, and anecdotes, all heightened by tricks learned from "Jean Paul, the *Only-One*," as Longfellow calls him. This designation means, of course, not that Richter is the only German writer worth considering, nor that he is the greatest of them all, but that he is "the only one of his kind." That Longfellow agreed with the Franconian champion of Jean Paul is patent in his adoption of many of Jean Paul's stylistic turns in *Hyperion*: the "wild imagination" and "bold flights" of fancy, his "reckless, multitudinous prodigality" of detail, the "extravagances" and eccentric turns of wit and whimsey, the incongruous comparisons, the "magic coloring," and his "serious playfulness." —*Hyperion*, pp. 37–40; *New Light*, pp. 72–73, 76.

94. In the chapter entitled "Glimpses into Cloud-Land," the Professor instucts Fleming in the doctrines of "Fichte's Destiny of Man and Schubert's History of the Soul" and, to elucidate his opinions on the conflicting Past, Present, and Future, illustrates his meaning by an elaborate explanation of the Walpurgis Night scene on the Pharsalian Plains in *Faust II*. Just as the mocking Mephistopheles sits down between the solemn antique Sphinxes and questions them, "even thus does a scoffing and unbelieving Present sit down between the unknown Future and a too believing Past, and question and challenge the gigantic forms of Faith" (*Hyperion*, pp. 99, 102). At the end of the book Fleming, having been properly instructed, resolves, "Henceforth be mine a life of action and reality! I will work in my own sphere, nor wish it other than it is. This alone is health and happiness. This alone is Life,—

Life that shall send
A challenge to its end,
And when it comes, say, Welcome, friend!

Why had I not made these sage reflections, this wise resolve, sooner? Can such a simple result spring only from the long and intricate process of experience?" (pp. 276–77).

95. Diary, Mar. 23, 1838, quoted in *Young Longfellow*, p. 278.

96. *Hyperion*, p. 222.

97. Letter to Greene, July 23, 1839; *Young Longfellow*, p. 282.

98. The self-possessed Fanny, who had once before checked the too ardent widower, almost ten years older then herself, did not appreciate the warmth of sentiment expressed in some of the episodes. Though he betrayed no confidence and left out the details of all *real* scenes, the whole was an indiscretion which the clacking of tongues did nothing to alleviate. She doubtless interpreted the book as a public insult to her, an express wish to triumph over his weak passion by obliterating her from his mind and memory, thus freeing himself to pursue nobler, holier purposes. When she gave no sign, he saw the enormity of his *faux pas*; but rationalizing his purposes as best he could, feebly reaffirming the doubtful virtue of renunciation, and clutching desperately at what was left of resolution, he wrote to Greene on January 2, 1840, in a tone at once confessional, apologetic, resigned, but also partially in the vein of self-justification:

"No matter; I had the glorious satisfaction of writing it; and thereby gained a great victory, *not* over the 'dark ladie' but over myself. I now once more rejoice in my freedom; and am no longer the thrall of anyone. I have great faith in one's writing himself clear from a passion—giving vent to pent-up fire. But George, George! It was a horrible thing. . . . But it was all sincere. My mind was morbid. I have portrayed it all in the book; and how is a man to come out of it; not by shooting himself like Werther; but in a better way. . . . If I had called the book 'Heart's Ease, or the Cure of a morbid mind' it would have been better understood" (*ibid.*, p. 284).

99. Apr. 24, 1840, quoted in *New Light*, p. 70. The allusion to Dante is to the *Inferno*, iii, 51: "Let us not speak of them, but look, and pass."

100. *Young Longfellow*, pp. 336–37.

101. *Ibid.*, p. 342; *New Light*, p. 70.

102. The chapter on "The Landlady's Daughter" may have some connection with a similar episode in the *Harzreise;* see *New Light*, pp. 74–75. During 1839 he exchanged opinions on Heine's style with Mary Appleton. In his Harvard lectures on Goethe (also printed in *Hyperion*, p. 124) and in the lecture on "German Tales and Traditions" he quoted a considerable passage regarding German legends from the *Harzreise*. Marginal notes in this lecture show that the passage was "worked up" for insertion in *Hyperion*, where it was to have stood after the remarks on Müller's "Wohin?" (*Hyperion*, pp. 115–16; see *New Light*, p. 87). He continued to be interested in Heine, and he published an essay on him in *Graham's Magazine* for March, 1842. In this article he accused Heine of seeking to establish a religion of sensu-

ality based on a philosophy of pleasure of the type cultivated by young ladies and young men in America who maintain that "nature must not be interferred with in any way" (XX, iii, 134). While admitting that Heine possessed an abundance of wit, vigor, and brilliance, Longfellow found him lacking in taste and refinement; he resembles Byron in recklessness and Sterne in sentimentality. Cf. *New Light*, p. 88.

103. *New Light*, p. 78.

104. The Germanic content of *Hyperion* led some to conclude that Longfellow belonged to the Transcendentalist group, and an anonymous reviewer charge him with writing in that "Germanico-metaphysical style in which small ideas are now-a-days clothed and magnified, much as small-waisted boys are stuffed out with cushions and pillows, when they would enact Falstaff."—*Mercantile Journal* (Boston), Sept. 27, 1839. But Felton replied to the charge of "Germanism"; and Longfellow, while he explained that he had no apologies to make for his sympathetic treatment of German literature, wished it understood that he knew little about the doctrines of Kant and Schleiermacher or of Baur and De Wette, and cared less; for the American Transcendentalists, he cared not at all. When Ripley urged him to contribute to the Dwight volume of German translations in the *Specimens of Standard Foreign Literature*, he politely refused, even after his name had been printed as a prospective collaborator. Much of what he saw and heard of the "German craze" seemed to him superficial, and writing to Greene on September 17, 1841, he said as much: "Everybody talks about German literature and philosophy, as if they knew something of them."—*Life*, I, 368; *Young Longfellow*, pp. 311–12.

105. After being refused by Cogswell (for the *N.Y. Rev.*), the essay appeared in the *New World*, VII (Oct., 1840), 522–24. See also *New Light*, p. 86.

106. So does stanza 6 of the "Prelude" in *Voices*.

107. *Hyperion*, p. 76.

108. *New Light*, pp. 84–85.

109. The four new ones are Wilhelm Müller's "The Bird and the Ship," Tiedge's "Die Welle" (both admirably rendered), Stockmann's "Wie sie so sanft ruhn" (an unrhymed "graveyard" product), and an unidentified poem entitled "The Happiest Land." The "Hymn of the Moravian Nuns of Bethlehem at the Consecration of Pulaski's Banner" was suggested by an account in the *North American Review* for April, 1825.—*Works.*, I, 39.

110. *Young Longfellow*, p. 309.

111. *Works*, I, 50–51.

112. What Poe was saying about the derivative nature of his poems could be discounted, but not so easily ignored was the warning of his friend Theophilus Eaton against the danger of seeking to escape the hard path of life's duty and the implications of what he said when commenting on the *Voices* and the "newer" note of the "ballads":

"I think your residence abroad, and your thorough acquintance with foreign literature, has affected your style, sometimes injuriously. But you are now one of us, I hope for good—and every year and every new effort will make you more entirely our own. Your ballad about the Fisherman's Daughter . . . is the best thing of its kind our country has produced." — *Young Longfellow*, 310 p.

113. The same volume included also a translation of Bishop Tegnér's long poem in hexameters, *The Children of the Lord's Supper*. Longfellow's first attempt in this measure (the 44 lines of *Frithiof's Homestead*, 1837) was also a translation of the same Swedish author. "The new production. . . does not only show a mastery of Swedish, but marks a praiseworthy advance in technique, indicating an approach to the style of *Evangeline*." — *New Light*, p. 87.

During 1840 Longfellow wrote *The Spanish Student* (1843), described by himself as "a beaker full of the warm South; no German fogs or Scandinavian sea-weed about it — but music, sunshine and odours manifold." Ironically enough, its one performance was in a German version by Carl Böttiger of Dessau, given on the stage of the Court Theater in Dessau on January 28, 1855. Thoroughly Spanish though it be, it nevertheless contains several Germanic touches. The lines —

I can remember still . . .
As in a dream or in some former life
Gardens and palace walls—

appear to be reminiscent of Goethe's "Mignon," and Preciosa's "And this from thee" recalls a similar remark of Luise to Ferdinand in Schiller's *Kabale und Liebe*—*New Light*, p. 86.

114. For details see *Young Longfellow*, pp. 314–26.

115. *New Light*, p. 92. Professor Hatfield's exhaustive account of Longfellow's third visit to Germany (*ibid.*, pp. 88–109) and of the Longfellow-Freiligrath relationship (*ibid.*, pp. 90–105) obviates the need for a detailed rehearsal here. Most of the fifty-odd letters that passed between the two poets are printed by Hatfield in *PMLA*, XLVIII, iv (Dec., 1933), 1223–91.

Longfellow was often at the Freiligraths' apartment, where he met Louise von Gall, a poetess from Darmstadt, whose ability as a singer won her the title of "Nachtigal" in this group. From the fact that the owner of the apartment was named Ihl, they coined, by easy derivation the house-name of "Ihlium". Freiligrath was "Hector," his wife "Andromache," and Fräulein von Gall "Helena" of "Gallina." Longfellow was initiated, with proper ceremonies, as "Nestor." During July, when they attempted to promote a romance between the American widower and the lovely poetess, the matchmaking friends playfully called Longfellow "Paris", and even after Longfellow's marriage Freiligrath and Heuberger rallied him for having disdained the German beauty, who by that time was also happily married, to Levin Schücking. — *New Light*, pp. 91–92, 96–97.

116. A four-day trip down the Rhine, in company with the Freiligraths and other literati, and later an *Ausflug* to the lovely Wispertal, added variety and fun to the already rich program of entertainment of dances, parties, ingenious charades, and tableaux that the Marienberg circle provided for their American friend. An exploration of Nuremberg fixed in his mind the quaint charm of the old city—its musical bells, the dialect, and its historic, artistic, and poetic associations—so that months later he could memorialize them in his well-known poem. He added a large boxfull of books (German, Flemish, and French) to his already considerable library of European literature, and he greatly enlarged his knowledge of more recent as well as of older German books. See *New Light*, pp. 104–5, for details.

117. The most obvious parallel exists between "The Slave's Dream" and "Der Mohrenfürst," though it is not a case of servile imitation. "The slave, who 'started in his sleep and smiled,'" as Hatfield observes, "has not much in common with the Moorish prince who battered his drumhead to pieces," while Longfellow's meter and tone give an entirely different coloration to his poem. Again, there appear to be parallels between Longfellow's lines in the poem "Witness"—"In Ocean's wide domains / Half buried in the sands / Lie skeletons in chains / With shackled feet and hands" —and these verses from Freiligrath's "Die Toten im Meere": "Tief unter grüne Meereswell' / Auf Muschelbank und Kies / Da schlummert mancher Schiffsgesell, / Der frisch vom Lande stiess." But the tendency of the two pieces is altogether different. Finally, "To the Driving Cloud" turns, like Freiligrath's "Negro on Skates," on the contrast between a savage in his native environment and the same individual transformed into a slave, in modern surroundings, and there is more than a casual relationship between the two poems, though Longfellow's hexameters lend an individual character to his poem. For the rest, there is no dearth of similarities between individual poems of the two writers, but none of them is close enough to constitute what can properly be called influence. See *New Light*, pp. 102–4, 106–8. Freiligrath made masterful versions of ten of Longfellow's poems, and he translated *Hiawatha* entire (Stuttgart, 1857); and Longfellow made a number of Freiligrath's poems available to English readers. From first to last Freiligrath introduced, either personally or by letter, virtually all of his more notable contemporary German men of letters to Longfellow, kept him posted on German literary developments, and attended to his requests for books, while Longfellow exhausted every means at his command for bringing his exiled friend to "the freest country in the world" and settling him in a professorial post, first at Columbia and later at Harvard as his own successor, meanwhile sending several considerable gifts of money during the period of Freiligrath's exile in England.—*New Light*, pp. 98–100.

118. There were long evenings when "the divine Fanny" read to him from the *Heldenbuch* or the *American Sketches* of "our favorite Sealsfield," or Jean Paul's *Flegeljahre*, or Heine's *Buch der Lieder*, or Fichte's lecture on *The Nature of the Scholar* and Smith's biography of Fichte. His Goethe lectures at the University went better than ever, and on Mar. 15, 1844, Pres. Quincy asked him to change the hour to accommodate "many, if not all, of the Juniors" who "wish to attend." Even Fanny was tempted to disguise herself "à la Portia," go to College, and "be a listener." She entered fully into his activities; she suggested the poem on the Springfield arsenal and applauded the one on Nuremberg. Together, they went on "bravely with the book of translations," the volume of *Poets and Poetry of Europe*. They read Goethe's *Italienische Reise* and, two days later, "Dickens' Letters from Italy, now published in a volume . . . striking to read in connection with Goethe on the same theme—one all drollery, the other all wisdom." One day they read Zschokke's tales, on another they heard Emerson lecture on Goethe, and on still another they had a small musical party at Craigie House— "Chopin, Schubert, De Meyer, Liszt, and some German songs." He read widely in other foreign literatures, but fully half his reading time was devoted to German, and perhaps as much as half of that to Goethe. On June 21, 1846, he observed: "I dreamed last night that Goethe was alive and in Cambridge. I gave him a supper at Willard's tavern. He had a beautiful face,

but his body was like the Belgian giant's, with an immeasurable coat. I told him I thought Clärchen's song in Egmont was one of his best lyrics. The god smiled." Goethe was being domesticated indeed when he could be wined and dined at Willard's.—*Life*, II, 18, 29–30, 33, 35–36, 41–44, 77; *New Light*, pp. 110–11.

Longfellow's German library, steadily added to from the time of his first visit to Germany, is far too extensive to be catalogued here. The Goetheana were especially extensive. As German professor at Harvard, he was steadily on the alert for new translations of Goethe's works for the College library as well as for his own study. He possessed three versions of *Werther*, four of *Wilhelm Meister*, four of *Dichtung und Wahrheit*, and fourteen of *Faust*, besides individual editions in German, the fifty-six-volume Cotta edition of 1827–1835 and several less comprehensive collected editions in translation. These books he acquired with something more than a mere collector's pride, for his notes show that he made comparisons of at least nine different translations of *Faust*. In 1839 he thought all existing poetic translations "heartily poor," Hayward's prose one being "incomparably the best." For his own perusal he always preferred the original, and he was often severely critical of the translators' errors and stupidities, in several cases going to the trouble to refer to the original and to make comparisons and improvements. See *Life*, I, 348, 364, 401; II, 30, 175; III 162, 195.

Other German writers had less extensive but proportionate representation in his library.

119. Fourteen of the German poems were in Longfellow's own translation, seven of them especially prepared for this anthology: (1) the anonymous "Silent Love" from Erlach's *Volkslieder*, (2) the evergreen folksong, "O Tannenbaum," (3) Simon Dach's "Anke von Tharau," (4) Dach's "Blessed are the Dead," (5) Mosen's "Statue over the Cathedral Door," (6) Dach's "Legend of the Cross-Bill," and (7) Heine's "The Sea hath its Pearls"—all impeccably rendered.

His next volume of poetry, *The Belfry of Bruges and Other Poems* (1845), contains several German notes, including allusions and translations. "Walter von der Vogelweide" relates the legend of the feeding of the birds on Walter's tomb and refers to the Wartburgkrieg; and the sonnet "Autumn" contains a felicitous allusion to the legend of Charlemagne's "golden bridge" over the Rhine at Bingen (doubtless inspired by Geibel's "Goldene Brücke" in Simrock's *Rheinsagen*). There are also six translations, five of them reprinted from *Poets and Poetry of Europe*, the new offering being a group of a dozen short

"Poetic Aphorisms" from the epigrammatic poet Fr. von Logau translated from Wm. Müller's *Dichter des XVII. Jahrhunderts*.

120. A notable exception is J. P. Worden (*Über Longfellows Beziehungen zur deutschen Literatur*, Halle, 1900), whose findings are incorporated below. Professor T. M. Campbell likewise (in *Longfellows Wechselbeziehungen zu der deutschen Literatur*, Leipzig, 1907), fails to find influence.

121. *Life*, II, 117.

122. *New Light*, p. 114.

123. See Wm. Scherer, *Geschichte der deutschen Literatur* (Berlin, 1883), p. 569, for a brief summation; also G. H. Lewes, *Life and Works of Goethe* (Everyman ed., N.Y., 1916), p. 423.

124. Aside from the facts, (1) that both stories deal with the trials of a banished folk, whose fate is bound up with that of two lovers, (2) that both heroines are beautiful young women (and what heroine is not?), and (3) that both are industrious and helpful in tending the sick and reviving the faint, there are certain striking dissimilarities. Dorothea, an exile, marries Hermann, a good solid and established burgher, and lives the life of a happy woman in the management of Hermann's substantial home; while Evangeline, emerging from a position of social security, becomes an exiled wanderer who ends finally as a sister of mercy. Dorothea becomes the very embodiment of matronly contentment; Evangeline spends her life in a fruitless search for her lover, once narrowly missing him. Longfellow chose to end his story with the lovers' meeting in a hospital in Philadelphia, there to die in each other's arms, rather than to follow the events as more-or-less authenticated history relates them, namely, that Gabriel married, that Evangeline eventually lost her mind, and after disconsolate wanderings up and down the Teche country in lower Louisiana, died, and was buried near the wall of the old Capuchin church in St. Martinsville, in southwest Louisiana. Evangeline is the central figure of the American poem, while in the German idyl Hermann occupies that position: Dorothea is kept in the background and does not make her appearance before the seventh of Goethe's nine sections. In Longfellow's poem, Gabriel, after his first introduction at the beginning of the story, hardly reappears until the last lines of the poem, and then only to die. In Goethe's poem, Hermann seeks Dorothea; in Longfellow's it is Evangeline who conducts the search. Evangeline and Gabriel learned their ABC's "out of the selfsame book," while Hermann and Dorothea are utter strangers until they meet quite by chance. Evangeline and Gabriel had long been desig-

nated by their parents as meant for each other; their love is of long standing, and their betrothal is a matter of course; in Goethe's poem, love is depicted as love at first sight. Dorothea appears at first in straitened circumstances— willing to become a maidservant in Hermann's home, Hermann meanwhile being the heir apparent of wealthy people. In *Evangeline*, lover and beloved are presented as living in equally easy circumstances and as of equal social standing. Moreover, Dorothea has loved before, her lover having been guillotined in Paris as a result of his patriotic fervor; Evangeline's love is her first. In both stories a betrothal is consummated in the presence of parents and friends, but while in Goethe's story not only father and mother are present (though the girl's parents are both absent), and the mother plays a particularly prominent role, in Longfellow's tale only the two fathers play a part, neither mother being mentioned. Finally, as a result of the different termination of events immediately following the betrothal, Longfellow's work develops a tragic tone, while Goethe's has been described as "beseelt von der innigsten Herzenswärme."

The structure of the two poems of almost equal length is markedly different: Longfellow begins at the beginning and proceeds in simple chronological order, Goethe *in medias res.* Goethe divides his story into nine *Gesänge;* Longfellow has two parts—the first leading up to the banishment and separation, and the second relating the wanderings of the lovers. Goethe's poem observes strictly the unities; Longfellow's embraces a lifetime and a continent. In the German story, the characters speak in their own persons and relate their own experiences; the American story is presented from the point of view of the third person. While these variations appear superficial, their results are important, for they make impossible in the one precisely what constitutes the strength of the other. In *Hermann und Dorothea* the emphasis is on the unfolding of human nature; in *Evangeline* natural nature is given relatively greater prominence. In the German poem the characters develop plastically, as it were; in *Evangeline* they are merely presented, full-bodied. In the former full use is made of every situation; in the latter one scene is broken off before yielding its potentialities for character portrayal, and another begun. The one is as economical as the other is prodigal in descriptive details and character portrayal. Goethe's every stroke adds a contributory detail toward the unified, complete painting; Longfellow draws his story in bold, decisive strokes and for the rest, while he devotes

enough time and skill to setting, makes little effort to fuse scene with character. Goethe's is a descriptive technique; Longfellow's, the narrative. In *Hermann und Dorothea* much space is devoted to what the characters say and more to how they react to the various situations; little is devoted to links by which continuity of narrative is maintained; everything is subordinated to bringing out the human values of the story. In *Evangeline* the opposite procedure is used: Longfellow, not his characters, relates the events and describes the scenes— with resulting loss in character portrayal. The reason for this difference lies, of course, in Longfellow's realization of his limitations in the technique of dramatic (or direct) presentation, which he had tried in *The Spanish Student* and found essentially unsuited to his abilities. This basic difference is illustrated in Longfellow's relatively skimpy characterization in the betrothal scene and the fullness with which Goethe drew it, or in Longfellow's loose introduction of essentially foreign elements and Goethe's close motivation throughout. Concerning Evangeline little is said except in general terms: she is beautiful, and she is a good housekeeper; Gabriel is repeatedly mentioned, but he speaks never a word until he is discovered on his deathbed. Contrast the fullness and richness in which not only Hermann and Dorothea but also the father and mother, the pastor and even the apothecary, are drawn. Details in *Hermann und Dorothea* derive from an inner, organic necessity; in *Evangeline* they are embellishments. It is not to our purpose to call one technique better than the other. The significant thing is that they are markedly different. Goethe drew upon his own observations of life; Longfellow derived many of his richest descriptions from books and from Banvard's diorama of the Mississippi Valley, an area of the country he had never seen, and phases of life he never experienced.

125. However, his three English versions were acquired after he had written *Evangeline*.

126. *Life,* I, 301.

127. *New Light,* p. 115.

128. *Life,* III, 147.

129. Evidently Goethe's poem did not in 1838 suggest anything that he might utilize. Seven years later, when he heard Conolly relate the Acadian story, he may have recalled the German idyl, and he may have hit on the idea of adopting a similar plan as well as Goethe's meter, but there is no evidence to show that he did either.

130. The latter possibility is most plausible in view of the number of references in Longfellow's diaries between November 28, 1845,

when *Evangeline* was begun, and February 27, 1847 when it was completed, to hexameters and to Homer. See *Life*, II, 26, 36, 66, 67, 68, 76–77. As early as 1835 (three years before he read *Hermann und Dorothea*) he had been struck by the effectiveness of the hexameter in Tegnér's *Frithiof's Saga*. Between 1837 and 1845 (when he decided to use the measure for *Evangeline* despite its alleged unfitness for the English idiom) he busied himself much rendering various ones of Tegnér's poems into English hexameters and with other experiments in classical forms. (Relevant passages are to be found in *Life*, I, 401–2, 404, 434, II, 23, 77, 80; *Works*, I, 219–21; *Poetical Works*, Cambridge ed., pp. 598, 675; and *New Light*, p. 118.) These experiments convinced him of the applicability of hexameters to his purpose.

131. He read Ida von Hahn-Hahn in 1847 and Gost[w]ick's *Spirit of German Poetry* in 1848 (*Life*, II, 32; *New Light*, p. 113). In 1848, also, he received a considerable shipment of German books, including Börne's *Schriften* and Heine's *Atta Troll*. He enjoyed Jean Paul's *Levana* and *Campaner-Tal* and Schefer's *Albrecht Dürer* (*New Light*, p. 118; *Life*, II, 120, 123). It was in this year, too, that Immanuel Vitalis Scherb, the German poet from Basel, came to Cambridge armed with a letter of introduction and an unfinished tragedy on the *Bauernkrieg*. They had much talk together (as Scherb had wherever he went, and he went everywhere) about the German poets (*Life*, II, 120, 162, 163, 197, 307, 312, 395). During 1849 he revised his translation of Schelling's essay on Dante for publication the next year in *Graham's Magazine* (*Life*, II, 162). He stayed away from the Commencement exercises of 1850 to read Goethe's *Campagne in Frankreich* (*Life*, II, 184), and in the same year he acquired the formidable set of publications of the *Literaturverein* of Stuttgart (*New Light*, p. 120).

132. *Kavanagh*, p. 369.

133. *Life*, I, 346.

134. *Ibid.*, p. 405 (Nov. 8, 1841); also I, 423.

135. It is about four times as long as the original, panoramic in its scope, encyclopedic in its grasp of human history—a symphony of many modes and phases of life. It is full of episodes and sidelights, sometimes numerous and prominent enough to obscure the main story, a miracle play with all its accompanying éclat, including a wild *gaudiolum* of the monks at midnight, a sermon in the street, a dispute and a fight among scholastics of Salerno, a copyist in his *scriptorium* glorying in his art, a pious abbot, a carousing friar, a cocksure traveling scholar, a contrite monk, a sneaking friar; Walter von der Vogelweide is introduced;

a crusade is thrust into the medley; the Abbess Irmingard relates the story of her love for Walter before her entrance into the cloister; and a picture of simple peasant life is drawn— all these besides the main story of Prince Henry of Hoheneck and Elsie, the young girl who volunteers to offer her life in order to effect the cure of Prince Henry. Added to this multifarious scene is the struggle between the good and evil angels who strive against each other, or for and against Poor Prince Henry, and finally, the Mephistophelean figure of Lucifer, who directs the forces of evil and assumes the same role that Mephistopheles plays in *Faust*.

136. Longfellow's copy, preserved in Craigie House, shows significant marginal notes.

137. Unlike Heinrich, he has not been driven to hopelessness by nameless bodily ills; his trials are more mental than physical. His inconclusive faith, uncertainty of desires, lack of knowledge, and arrogance of will are further complicated by the disconcerting influence of Lucifer, who seeks to disintegrate completely Prince Henry's already torn mind. In these respects, Longfellow's poem bears closer analogies to Goethe's *Faust* than to Hartmann's poem.

Cast into a complex dramatic form, Longfellow's poem is divided into prologue, epilogue, and six "parts" rather than "acts." Three of the parts—the first, second, and sixth—are concerned primarily with the story of Prince Henry and Elsie; the other three find few parallels in Hartmann's tale; they contain the digressions and sidelights by means of which Longfellow aimed to present the multiform aspects of medieval life—"to introduce some portion of the darkness and corruption of the Middle Ages" against which the "bright stream of faith" could be high-lighted (*Works*, V, 12). For such a portrayal of contrasts and interplay of conflicting forces, Goethe's *Faust* was a more adaptable model than the rigidly economical pattern of Hartmann's poem.

The Promethean theme of *Faust* had long interested Longfellow. In *Hyperion* (p. 140) the Baron says to Fleming, "There is something Faust-like in you"—an observation that is interesting but obviously questionable, for there is little of the Promethean Faust-fire in the sentimental Fleming and less of the Titan blood in his model, the Harvard professor of modern languages and literatures. To realize the difference one needs only to compare Goethe's "Prometheus" with Longfellow's tame poem by the same title. But Longfellow's attraction to the Lucifer or Mephistopheles motif and the applicability of the elastic form of *Faust* for his purposes prompted a departure from Hartmann's model and a reworking of the subject on Faustian lines. This departure is already apparent in the cantata-like prologue which Longfellow chose to add, and which suggests various scenes in *Faust*. The struggle represented in the prologue, in which the good angels contend with the evil angels (who, led by Lucifer, attempt to tear down the cross of the Strassburg cathedral) is reminiscent of Mephistopheles' part in the struggle between the angelic forces fighting for Faust's soul. In the first scene of the drama proper the analogies become even clearer, extending to similarities in setting and stage directions. In the manner of Faust's monologue, Prince Henry bewails his lot as one who has lost all friends, and who (as the sequel explains) is suffering from some nameless ailment. At the conclusion of the monologue there is "a flash of lightning, out of which Lucifer appears, in the garb of a travelling physician" (*Works*, V, 143). This is recognizable as a reworking of Goethe's stage direction: "Es zuckt eine Flamme. . . . Mephistopheles tritt, indem der Nebel fällt, gekleidet wie ein fahrender Scholastikus, hinter dem Ofen hervor" (ll. 481, 1320). Compare also the phial and drinking episodes and the accompanying angels' warnings, *Faust*, ll. 690, 720, 726, and *Works*, V, 148, 150–53. Lucifer's sudden appearance in disguise, his hatred of sacred objects and symbols, his fear that he may finally be cheated of Henry's soul, his sneers at academic learning, his disguise as a priest, all appear to be derived from Goethe's Mephisto. The accompanying *diablerie* owes nothing to Hartmann but much to Goethe.

Prince Henry's review of the learning of his age and his comments on its inadequacy suggest the opening scenes in *Faust* and the colloquy between Faust and Wagner. Having found all other remedies ineffectual, Prince Henry turns to black arts and, like Faust, becomes adept in magic, alchemy, and necromancy. He pursues these studies in his search for a remedy of his bodily ailments, but he has also the philosophical turn of mind that seeks a solution of the deep mysteries of the universe. In Faustian desperation he leaps "Headlong into the mysteries / Of life and death" (p. 150). While this skeptical cast of mind appears only fitfully in Prince Henry, it is nonetheless a motivating force in his life, and shows Longfellow digressing from Hartmann's example while following Goethe's lead. In reply to Friar Cuthbert's invitation to visit "the image of the Virgin Mary that moves its holy eye," he, a prince, who flourished "about 1230," replies: "Oh, had I faith as in the days gone by / That knew no doubt, and feared no mystery" (p. 264). This

typifies more the skeptical temperament of the nineteenth century than the simple faith of the thirteenth.

Lucifer has all of Mephisto's craftiness, for every situation a solution and for every question an answer, couched in typically satanic paradox, equivocal double talk, or sardonic irony (pp. 144–49). His most notable departure from Goethe's model is that he is not the playful *Schalk* that Goethe portrays. But he is from the first the agent of negation and destruction. His first act is to tempt the Prince to suicide; next, he encourages the monks to unseemly conduct; and he curses whatever and whoever impedes his nihilistic course of action. Yet in the end, his fate is the same as that of Mephistopheles. Like Goethe's Satan who "stets das Böse will und stets das Gute schafft" (l.1336), so Lucifer "is God's minister, / And labors for some good / By us not understood" (p. 292). Lucifer is also the pessimist who scorns and belittles all human endeavor, rejecting all belief in human integrity and progress, while professing pity for man and his lot (compare *Faust I*, ll. 280–82, 294–96, and *Works*, V, 146, 147, 151, 180–81, 185–86, 262–63). Another Mephistophelean attitude appears in Lucifer's seating himself in the confessional chair and mockingly, hypocritically re-enacting the many scenes that have been acted there. Again, just as Mephistopheles scoffs at the learning of the scholastics, so Lucifer laughs up his sleeve when he sees the contentiousness of the scholars at Salerno. Both laugh derisively at man's misuse of his rational faculties (*Faust I*, ll. 282–86, 292; *Works*, V, 277). And, just as Mephistopheles becomes agitated in the presence of Margaret's purity, or whenever the conversation turns upon God or sacred matters, so Lucifer grows uncomfortable in the presence of Elsie or expressions of faith and piety. In the end Lucifer has to admit his impotency where Elsie is concerned, just as Mephisto finds himself unable to triumph over Margaret (*Faust I*, ll. 2625–27; *Works*, V, 277); but both are sure the men are theirs—body and soul; yet in both cases, they underrate their man, as both underrate mankind in general; and both are, in the end, cheated of their victims.

138. Like Tennyson in his *Idylls*, Longfellow adapted his characters to Victorian demands. The result is a variety of inconsistencies and anachronisms: the story of Little Red Riding Hood was hardly current in Germany during the early thirteenth century; Erwin von Steinbach flourished approximately a century after 1230, the year of Longfellow's story; Saint John Nepomuck died in 1393; and Fra Gabriella Bartella, who furnished Friar Cuthbert's sermon, lived in the fifteenth century (*Works*,

V, 13; *New Light*, p. 127). While slips of this kind are perhaps inevitable in so compendious a panorama, even Freiligrath found the "old, homely, simple story of our *Arme Heinrich*" treated with "too much brilliancy."—*PMLA*, XLVIII, iv (Dec., 1933), 1276.

The wealth of medieval lore which Longfellow drew from Germanic sources is too various to be accounted for in detail. Much of it he gathered as a traveler in Germany. Some came from Scheible's *Kloster*, which he imported in 1848. The adventures of Monk Felix are taken directly from Mailáth's *Altdeutsche Geschichte*. The Fastrada legend he found in Mossmann, as well as in Müller's ballad, "Die Sage vom Frankenburger See." The story of Christ and the Sultan's daughter is virtually a translation from *Des Knaben Wunderhorn*. The Easter Play is in the best tradition of older German miracles and mysteries, though Longfellow read widely also in English models and in the apocryphal Gospels. The midnight *gaudiolum* of the monks owes something to the wild scenes in Auerbach's Celler. The line "Still is the night" may be an "unconscious memory" of Heine, and the allusion to the Jews of Bacharach may stem from the same source, while the phrase "with lyre and sword" suggests Körner, whose *Leier und Schwert* Longfellow owned and studied.

139. Some amounting virtually to translations appear in *Faust I*, ll. 1–10, and *Works*, V, 142; I, 27–28, and V, 142; I, 18–20, and V, 143; I, 690–94, and V, 148–49; I, 1607–9, and V, 150. This note represents the irreducible minimum to which the limitations of space forced me to condense the section of my manuscript in which parallels between the texts of Longfellow and von Hartmann were cited. Fortunately for those who desire a fuller presentation of these data, there has recently appeared a thirty-five–page brochure in which these borrowings and parallels are presented: Carl Hammer, Jr., *Longfellow's "Golden Legend" and Goethe's "Faust,"* Louisiana State Univ. Studies, Humanities series No. 2 (Baton Rouge, 1952).

140. The year following the resignation of his professorship, Longfellow published *Hiawatha*, which is so patently indigenous as hardly to admit of foreign influences; though even here it has been suggested that in the "Famine" scene, for example, the dialogue between Minnehaha and old Nokomis may owe its structure and coloration to Goethe's "Erlkönig" (*New Light*, p. 129). In 1856 he followed the suggestion of his German friend Scherb to write on the subject of the Puritans and the Quakers, a suggestion that led to *The New England Tragedies*. Hatfield has suggested

that the point-blank "No!" which Longfellow had noted earlier in *Hermann und Dorothea* VIII, 64) may have offered a suggestion for *Miles Standish* (1858). The story of "Bertha," the beautiful spinner, the queen of Helvetia," derived from Old Germanic mythology, which Longfellow first "read at a stall in the streets of Southampton" (*Works*, II, 339); and the last two lines of the eighth canto appear to derive from a similar passage by Fr. Gotter in the *Göttinger Musen-Almanach* (1771, p. 4), which Longfellow could have read at Göttingen, Heidelberg, or elsewhere.

141. A major disappointment of this trip was his failure to see once again Freiligrath, whose removal from London to Cannstadt at just this time prevented their meeting.

142. For the most pertinent references, see *Life*, II, 182, 209, 282, 299, 333, 341, 347, 378, 392, 395; III, 8, 10, 19–20, 136, 142, 147, 153, 162, 167, 172, 175, 176, 185, 186, 196, 197, 199, 206, 207–8, 211, 218, 236, 237, 263, 273, 276, 280, 283, 298; *New Light*, 129–36.

143. Platen's "Mut und Unmut" was translated for the same work. In 1870, also, he made an uninspired version of "Ein' feste Burg" for the Interlude "Martin Luther" in *The Christus*, in 1879 he published his translation of "Forsaken," the first stanza of which had already been used as the heading for Book II of *Hyperion;* and Mahlmann's "Allah" seems also to belong to this period.

144. In Part II of *Tales of a Wayside Inn* (1872) "The Cobbler of Hagenau" is a tale with a German background, based on the story of Tetzel and his indulgences and containing references to *Reineke Fuchs*, the Meistersingers, Brant, and Eulenspiegel. In the Interlude following "Elizabeth," that story is spoken of as "worthy of some German bard / Hebel, or Voss, or Eberhard" (*Works*, IV, 226). "Vox Populi," written in 1870, and forming a part of the Third Flight in *Birds of Passage*, is suggestive of Heine's manner, as is also "The Brook and the Wave" in the same section. "The Hanging of the Crane," first printed in the *New York Ledger* for March 28, 1874, owes its form and structure, as did the earlier "Building of the Ship," to Schiller's *Song of the Bell*. *Keramos* (1878) appears to derive from the same source. "Morituri Salutamus," written for the fiftieth anniversary of the Bowdoin class of 1825, lists among examples of productive old age "Goethe at Weimar, toiling to the last" and completing *Faust* "when eighty years were past" (*Works*, III, 195). *The Masque* of *Pandora* (1875), inspired mainly by Greek drama contains suggestions of the Second Part of *Faust*, notably in the chorus of the Oreades,

Waters, Winds, and Forests; and the "Chorus of the Eumenides" suggests Goethe's *Iphigenie*. "The Children's Crusade," a fragment written in 1879, owes some of its lines to Heine's "Wallfahrt nach Kevlaar," while "Mad River" (1882) in both form and sentiment seems to go back to Goethe's "Der Junggesell und der Mühlbach," which, as we have observed, fascinated Longfellow many years before (*Hyperion*, pp. 113–16).

145. O. W. Long, "Goethe and Longfellow," *Germanic Rev.*, VIII, ii (Apr., 1932), 175.

JAMES RUSSELL LOWELL

146. *Selected Literary Essays of James Russell Lowell*, ed. by Will D. Howe and Norman Foerster (Boston, 1914), Introduction, pp. xv–xvi. So it is that often, instead of his essays' developing in a straightforward, organic manner, they seem rather to proceed as if his line of thought had been suggested by some word or passage, until the next cleverly turned phrase set him off on another tack.

147. *Works* (Elmwood ed., 16 vols., Boston, 1904), XI, 132.

148. On October 9, 1835, he professed to getting on "astonishingly" well with the German language, but found *Faust* hard going in comparison with what he had read of Schiller. In 1838 he contributed to *The Harvardan* two verse translations from Uhland: "The Serenade" and "The White Stag."—George Wurfl, *Lowell's Debt to Goethe* (State College, Pa., 1936), pp. 11–12.

149. *Works*, XIV, 59.

150. *Ibid.*, p. 54.

151. Wurfl, *op. cit.*, pp. 13–14. Maria White, soon to become Lowell's betrothed, was fond of German literature. Her enthusiasm doubtless played its part in developing his sympathetic attitude toward the romantic literature of Germany. See, for example, *Works*, XII, 79. After she read him some extracts from Goethe's correspondence with Bettina Brentano, he eagerly read the book and considered it "beautiful" but thought it "mournful that all this love should have been given to the cold, hard Goethe."

152. "Lessing," *Works*, II, 194–95.

153. Exceptions occur in a familiar essay, "On Getting Up," contributed to the *Boston Miscellany* for 1842, which contains a number of scattered German literary references (see *Early Prose Writings*, London, 1903, pp. 40–48), and in a series of essays written during the later 40's for the *North American Review* (see *The Round Table*, Boston, 1913, pp. 10, 20, 23, 92, 94, 139, 169, 202, 213). In *A Fable for Critics* (1848) he refers to Hawthorne as "a John Bunyan Fouqué, a Puritan Tieck," and in the same year he records his impatience with German refugees of 1848 who flock to Boston and try to capitalize on their sufferings.—*Works*, IX, 90; see also XV, 5, and "On a Certain Condescension in Foreigners" (1869).

154. *The Round Table*, pp. 21, 172.

155. *Lectures on English Poets* (Cleveland, 1897), pp. 4, 7, 8, 13, 27, 123, 128–29, 156.

156. Lowell never developed any affection for the German language. In his essay on Lessing (1866) he wrote: "I have sometimes thought the German tongue at least an accessory before the fact, if nothing more, in the offenses of German literature. The language has such a fatal genius for going stern-foremost, for yawing, and for not minding the helm . . . that he must be a great sailor indeed who can safely make it the vehicle for anything but imperishable commodities."—*Works*, II, 164.

Writing to Miss Loring from Dresden, October 3, 1855, he reported: "I get up *um sieben Uhr*, and das Mädchen brings me my coffee and Butterbrod at 8. Then I begin to study. I am reading for my own amusement (du lieber Gott!) the *aesthetische Forschungen von Adolf Zeising*, pp. 568, large octavo! Then I overset something aus German into English. Then comes dinner at 1 o'clock, with ungeheuer German dishes. Nachmittag I study Spanish . . . *Um sechs Uhr ich gehe spazieren*, and at 7 come home, and Dr. R[eichenbach] dictates and I write. Aber potztausend Donnerwetter! what a language it is to be sure! with nominatives sending out as many roots as . . . witchgrass. . . . The confounded genders! If I die I will have engraved on my tombstone that I died of *der, die, das*, not because I caught 'em, but because I couldn't."—*Works*, XIV, 318–19

157. *New Letters of James Russell Lowell*, ed. by M. A. DeWolfe Howe (N.Y., 1932), pp. 77, 117.

158. *Works*, XIV, 332, 336.

159. When Lowell set out for Europe, he had hoped that travel and study might bring him solace and refreshment of spirit. The two years since his wife's death had been both sad and trying. Abroad he hoped his thoughts might turn into new directions. Instead, they constantly turned homeward, and he found himself oppressed by a sense of loss and loneliness. In such a state of mind he could plod dutifully through books and labor to acquire language skills, but he could not respond to the beauties of a foreign literature, or rouse his mind to a spontaneous play with new ideas. His letters are full of German phrases, but hardly any author except Goethe gets any real attention.

160. *Works*, XII, 385.

161. Wurfl, *op. cit.*, p. 19.

162. A long article on Grant White's edition of Shakespeare in 1859 and a review of Max Müller's *Lectures on the Science of Language* in 1862 contain references that make it clear he was keeping up with German contributions to learning. The 1866 essays on Carlyle and on Swinburne's tragedies contain extended references to Carlyle's German sources and to German dramatic criticism, respectively. That on Lessing followed in 1866, and the essay on Chaucer (1870) listed two German studies of Chaucer.

163. Few of his comments reveal deep penetration or real appreciation. The eighteenth century as a whole is a "dead waste" (*Works*, II, 139, 146, 169, 175–76, 187, 208, 217–19, 222; IV, 379). Goethe excepted, the writers of the *Sturm-und-Drang* period are a lowly lot. Even Schiller, whom he had once regarded as morally superior to Goethe, is now named with Wieland, Goethe, and Jean Paul as requiring "biographical chemistry" to bleach the spots from his reputation (*Works*, II, 187). Richter's humor, fine though it be, would be better if Richter had not dealt out "his wine by beer measure" (*Works*, II, 165). Heine's "battle against *Philisterei*" is laudable, but he lacks "a refined perception" and often shocks us with a certain "*Unfläthigkeit*, as at the end of his *Deutschland*, which, if it makes Germans laugh, as we should be sorry to believe, makes other people hold their noses" (*Works*, II, 170). As for German humor in general, it is dreary stuff. Even Goethe, with his "mixture of sentimentalism and sausages" and his "absurd Werthermontirung," shows himself "insensitive to the ridiculous." Herr Hub's *Deutsche komische und humoristische Dichtung* is almost enough to convince readers that no German has even a suspicion of what humor is, unless the book itself "be a joke in three volumes, the *want* of fun being the real point thereof" (*Works*, II, 168–69). Among the romanticists, Tieck is discussed as a dramatist (*Works*, II, 130) and as a critic of Shakespeare (*Works*, III, 70; *Atl. Monthly*, III, Feb., 1859, 246), and Novalis, Fouqué, Bürger, Marx, and Schopenhauer are mentioned (*Works*, I, 381; IV, 32, 380; XI, 181, 312).

Lowell's knowledge of German literature was not altogether confined to the eighteenth and nineteenth centuries. Besides lecturing on Middle High German literature, on the *Nibelungenlied*, and Wolfram, Lowell discussed the German folk epic and the *Parzival* in his essay on Dante. The Minnesingers seemed to him wearisomely artificial, he knew the tenth century nun Hroswitha's drama of Theophilus,

and he properly appraised Luther's significance (*Works*, I, 125, 171; II, 363, 367; III, 318). But the number and variety of references is no real indication that Lowell turned as spontaneously or naturally for inspiration to German as he turned to English literature. A high proportion of his German references occur in the essays on Lessing and on Carlyle. The one name that occurs most often is, of course, Goethe. The mature Lowell never feels that Goethe's supremacy among the Germans is to be doubted; he habitually expresses his opinion of other Germans by equating them, in this or that particular, with Goethe; and he repeatedly lists Goethe with Homer, Plato, Virgil, Dante, Cervantes, and Shakespeare (*Works*, II, 157, III, 301, 381; XIV, 320; *The Function of the Poet and Other Essays*, Boston, 1920, p. 61). Yet few of Goethe's individual works received Lowell's expression of unqualified approval. Goethe's (as well as Schiller's) "striving after a Grecian instead of a purely human ideal" is deplored. Goethe "wasted his time and thwarted his energy on the mechanical mock-antique of an unreadable 'Achilleïs.'" It does not disturb Lowell to know that Goethe always bought his classicisms cheap, at second hand, and that for the "purposes of mere aesthetic nourishment [he] always milked other minds," and he does not suggest that the product might have been more authentic if Goethe had done the foraging himself. He calls Goethe "The man of widest acquirement in modern times" and heartily approves his method of levying contribution on lesser minds when it is successful, as it is in *Hermann und Dorothea* (*Works*, II, 127, 129; III, 46–47, 133; XI, 142; Wurfl, *op. cit.*, p. 49). Nor was it only the "mock-antique" dramas that Lowell would willingly have given up to oblivion. He used the phrase "dull as a comedy of Goethe" in contexts which indicate that he placed Goethe's comedies at the nadir (*Works*, II, 146; XI, 202). No German drama really satisfied him: they are all too much contrived, "constructed a priori," and therefore "tedious" (*Works*, XI, 209, XIV, 337; Wurfl, *op. cit.*, 38). Far more reprehensible, however, is the "innate weakness and futile tendency of the 'storm and thrust'" productions, "the egotistical-superman" tendency of *Goetz*, and the "spiritual hypochondriacs" in *Werther*, whose heartbreaks are "audibly prolonged through life" (*Works*, II 93–94, 222, 251, 267; III, 63). He responded more favorably to the Gothic spirit in *Faust*, esteeming it "the only immortal production of the greatest of recent poets, because, despite its Hellenic overtones, it is truly Gothic in execution" (*Works*, II, 139, IV, 235). In it Goethe gave supreme embodiment to one of the two or three myths which seem to be rooted in human consciousness. The figure of Faust is an integral, authentic part of "the natural history of intellect, Mephistopheles being merely the projected impersonation of that scepticism which is the invariable result of a purely intellectual culture" (*The Function of the Poet . . .* pp. 64–66; *Works*, III, 90). Thus Goethe is at once of his age and above it, transcending both the provincial and the national (*Works*, II, 84, 121, 150; III, 25, 101; IV, 234, 380; VI, 103, 108). But his serene impartiality is too detached, too conscious, too profound; and although Lowell himself never came within miles of a battlefield, he repeats the hackneyed criticism when he expresses the wish that Goethe might have "smelt hostile powder from a less aesthetic distance" (*Works*, II, 286). A subject of more serious reproach, which the Puritan Lowell shared with Longfellow, Emerson, and the great host of American critics, is the cold morality with which Goethe pursued his ideal of self-culture. Although Lowell observed that such matters are irrelevant to the evaluation of Goethe's poetry, he held that the world has every right to take them into account in estimating the worth of Goethe the man (*Works*, II, 194–95, 241–42). That Goethe as an individual greatly interested Lowell appears from his wide reading in Goethe's correspondence with Bettina Brentano (*Works*, XII, 78–79), with Frau von Stein (*Works*, II, 168), with Auguste Stolberg (*Works*, II, 251), with Zelter (Wurfl, *op. cit.*, p. 58), and with Knebel (*ibid.*, p. 28; *Works*, II, 111). He early read Eckermann's *Conversations*, referred familiarly to *Dichtung und Wahrheit* (*Works*, I, 357), and praised G. H. Lewes' *Life of Goethe* (Wurfl, *op. cit.*, p. 36). Thus he familiarized himself so thoroughly with Goethe's life that in 1881, when he visited various German localities rich in Goethe associations, he had trouble persuading himself that he had not personally known some of the leading actors in these scenes (*Works*, XII, 271; XVI, 89).

164. For examples see *Works*, I, 352; II, 86, 108, 139; III, 123; IV, 140; XI, 176.

165. *Works*, II, 85. Lowell regrets that as Carlyle grew older he turned for a hero from the moderate and wise Goethe to an "asserter of the divine legitimacy of *Faustrecht*" like Frederick the Great and glorified this ideal in his "*Fritziad.*"

166. *Works*, III, 57–58.

167. *Ibid.*, pp. 66–67.

168. *Ibid.*, p. 87.

169. As early as 1848 Lowell recognized the importance of German Shakespeare criticism by observing "we owe to the Germans . . . the first thorough study, criticism, and consequent appreciation" of Shakespeare (*The Round Table*, p. 21). Ten years later, while reviewing Grant White's edition of Shakespeare, he introduced some humorous remarks on the extravagancies of German aestheticians, but again credited them with "the first philosophical appreciation" of Shakespeare. In the same article he referred a bit condescendingly to P. H. Sillig's *Die Shakespeare-Literatur bis Mitte 1854* (Leipzig, 1858), and remarked that he was tolerably familiar with many of Herr Sillig's 500 bibliographical items, adding "Among which (setting aside a few remarks by Goethe) we are inclined to value as highly as anything Tieck's essay on the Element of the Wonderful in Shakespeare" (*Atl. Monthly*, III, Feb., 1859, 245–46). When he incorporated much of this article in the essay "Shakespeare Once More" (1868), he omitted the passage just quoted, and added this observation on German contributions to "productive" criticism: "Lessing, as might have been expected, opened the first glimpse in the new direction; Goethe followed with his famous exposition of Hamlet; A. W. Schlegel took a more comprehensive view in his Lectures, which Coleridge worked over into English, adding many fine criticisms of his own on single passages; and finally Gervinus has devoted four volumes to a comment on the plays, full of excellent matter, though pushing the moral exegesis beyond all reasonable bounds." He added that he merely mentioned Ulrici's book because it seemed "unwieldy and dull,—zeal without knowledge."—*Works*, III, 67–68. For a revision of his view of Coleridge's debt to the Germans, compare *Works*, XIII, 134, and his essay on "Coleridge" (1885).

170. *Works*, II, 171, 224. Lessing's minor poems are dismissed with a few sentences, and the plays are considered striking proof that critical insight alone is not sufficient for great creative work, though both *Minna* and *Emilia* act better than anything by Goethe or Schiller. In *Nathan the Wise* he finds "a sober luster of reflection" that makes good reading but a tiresome play (*Works*, II, 227). But in prose Lessing is supreme. "Never was there a better example of the discourse of reason" than the *Laocoon*, and the *Dramaturgie* stands a close second (*Works*, II, 229).

171. Judging from what he says in "Shakespeare Once More," one concludes that the following aspects of his Shakespeare criticism were derived from Germany: (1) the historical approach with its interest in the age and circumstances surrounding the poet; (2) the attack on the view of Shakespeare as an inspired idiot, lacking judgment and a knowledge of the rules; (3) the organic theory of an inner unity as

distinguished from such mechanical conceptions as the three unities and the "laws" of verisimilitude, decorum, and propriety; (4) the interpretation of Shakespeare as placing the central idea or moral of his plays within his main characters; and (5) the distinction between classic and romantic drama as found in the shifting of Destiny to a place within man rather than, as in the Greek, outside or above his control. These, in the main, are the conclusion reached by Prof. Robert P. Falk in a seminar study which he undertook at my suggestion in 1938–1939.

172. While expressing surprise in his essay on Dante at the late beginning of German interest in the great Florentine, he paid tribute to Kopisch, Witte, Wegele, and Ruth as Dante scholars and to the translators, Bachenschwanz, Kannegiesser, Streckfuss, Kopisch, and Prince John of Saxony (*Works*, IV, 22, 145–46, 149, 150, 157, 169, 181, 190, 228).

173. On Chaucer, he singled out Alfons Kissner's *Chaucer in seinen Beziehungen zur italienischen Literatur* (1867) and Wilhelm Hertzberg's translation (1866), at the same time labeling Hertzberg's introduction "one of the best essays on Chaucer yet written" (*Works*, III, 298).

174. In his appreciative review of Max Müller's *Lectures on the Science of Language* (*Atl. Monthly*, Jan., 1862), he voiced his impatience with the productions of "Teutonic Gelehrte" like Bopp, Popp, Zeuss, Lasser, and Diefenbach, whose "works are terrors to the uninitiated," but in a later essay he remarked that it was long our shame that we had to go to the Germans to be taught the elements of our mother tongue (*Works*, XI, 155). His sense of obligation to, and impatience with, German scholarship, which "supplied the raw material in almost every branch of science for the defter wits of other nations to work on," received definitive expression in his essay on Lessing (*Works*, II, 165–67). In it he acknowledged a definite personal obligation, as he did still more pointedly 20 years later in the Harvard Anniversary address, in which, even while he warned against the danger of the Germans' "misleading us in some directions into pedantry," he said, "We owe a great debt to the Germans . No one is more indebted to them than I" (*Works*, V, 152).

175. *Works*, II, 164; XIV, 318.

176. The confusion wrought by Coleridge alone is sufficiently puzzling, although it may be presumed that in Lowell's day it was less so. At all events, Lowell was fully aware of Coleridge's borrowings and once remarked that Coleridge's acknowledgment of general indebtedness to the Germans was "wholly inadequate, and his evasions in regard to Schlegel leave a very painful impression on the mind."—*Works*, XIII, 134.

177. For instance, he never occupied himself as closely with English critical writings as he did with Adolf Zeising's *Aesthetische Forschungen* (*Works*, XIV, 318), Vischer's *Aesthetik*, which he called the "best treatise on the subject, ancient or modern" (*Works*, II, 164), Goethe's numerous but scattered critical pronouncements, Schlegel's *Vorlesungen*, and the entire school of German Shakespeareans. His attitude toward Coleridge, Lamb, and Hazlitt is hardly comparable, partly because much of it is of a piece with German criticism, partly because it is less considerable.

178. If we limit the term "literature" so as to exclude criticism and scholarship, J. J. Reilly appears justified in remarking on "the comparatively slight impression which German literature seems to have made on Lowell (*J. R. Lowell as Critic*, N.Y., 1915, p. 48), and J. M. Hart is essentially right in observing that though "no one would be so ill-advised as to suggest that Lowell did not know German literature well," his sympathy with it, particularly with Goethe, showed rather surprising limitations."—*PMLA*, VI (1892), 25–31.

OLIVER WENDELL HOLMES

179. For the Genteel writers from Longfellow, through Brooks, Taylor, and Stedman, to Higginson, Germany provided the staple of romance and sentiment; German ways of thought, poetry, educational methods were admittedly superior; facility in the German language was the necessary accomplishment of a cultivated man; and to make some specimens of German literature available in English was a bounden duty. Despite his Victorian taste and manners, Holmes was as much the child of the eighteenth as of the nineteenth century, who turned for inspiration oftener to the Queen Anne writers than to the romantic transcendentalists of Germany.

His education abroad was pursued in Paris, and he never admitted having lost anything by failing to make the rounds of the German universities. Born and bred to enjoy all the requisites of what the Autocrat prescribed as the necessary accoutrements of a gentleman, he had, as a child, "tumbled about" in his father's library, which contained "between one and two thousand books," but it contained almost no German books. Later, at Harvard, he studied "French and Italian, and some Spanish," but if he attended the classes of Karl

Follen, he forgot to mention it. During his two years in Paris, where he completed his medical education, French became "a second mother tongue," but the two brief German excursions which he made—the conventional Rhine outing in 1834 and a more extended journey through Germany and Switzerland in 1835—left him with only a slight appreciation of German literary lore and probably less of the language. —*Works* (Standard Library ed., 15 vols., Boston, 1892), I, 23; XIV, 42, 60, 97, 102, 148.

180. *Works*, XIV, 217.

181. *Ibid.*, I, 125–27; II, 3–4, 15–16, 78, 85–86, 281–82, 301.

182. *Ibid.*, I, 204.

183. *Ibid.*, p. 23.

184. *Ibid.*, p. 262.

185. *Ibid.*, p. 131.

186. *Ibid.*, p. 14. In writing the biography of Emerson, Holmes found it hard to treat sympathetically Emerson's mystical idealism, particularly his excursions into Oriental and German philosophies. Temperamentally and professionally conditioned to laboratory methods and inductive processes, the intuitional and *a priori* thought processes of the Transcendentalists seemed to him "vagaries." To deal with "the incommunicable, the inconceivable, the absolute, and the antinomies," said the Autocrat, is like playing "with a bundle of jackstraws."—*Works*, XI, 306.

187. Leibnitz and Goethe each are referred to five times, Kant and Jean Paul each four times, and Schopenhauer and A. v. Humboldt each once. Luther is credited with having hatched "the egg of the reformation" which Erasmus laid (*Works*, I, 87–88). Schlegel's reading of Shakespeare is properly evaluated (I, 33); Zimmermann's *Treatise on Solitude* is recalled as something that he saw "lying about on library tables . . . in our younger days" (I, 6); Ranke is mentioned as a foremost German historian (IV, 27); and at the suggestion of George Bancroft, Holmes wrote the verses "To Christian Gottfried Ehrenberg, for his 'Jubilaeum' at Berlin, Nov. 5, 1868" (XIII, 105–6). For the rest, a few German scientists are mentioned in the *Autocrat* (I, 281), the *Professor* (II, 11–12), and *Elsie Venner* (V, 221). Only in his medical essays did Holmes really use the Germans to good advantage. In his essay on "Homeopathy and Its Kindred Delusions," he singled out Samuel Hahnemann for attack, and in the course of the essay cited sixteen other German medical authorities for or against Hahnemann's doctrines. In others of the medical essays, six more German physicians and specialists are mentioned, and several scientific periodicals are cited. But here, as in the essay on homeopathy, a number of the references are admittedly derived from translations, manuals, and encyclopedias; and it may be presumed that most of his sources involving German authorities were secondary. For, says his biographer, in describing the Doctor's method of work, "His hand was always on the Cyclopaedias, the Dictionaries of biography, and the innumerable works of reference of every conceivable kind which stood in serried ranks beside his table."—*Works*, XV, 11.

JOHN GREENLEAF WHITTIER

188. In February, 1837, he went to Harrisburg, Pa., as a delegate to the State Anti-Slavery Convention, visited in the home of Governor Ritner, and in *The Liberator* for March 1837, published his "Lines," later entitled "Ritner," praising the Governor's courageous single stand against the slave power in politics and referring to the proud history of the liberty-loving Pennsylvania-German Friends who had been the first religious body in this country to issue a protest against slavery. See *Whittier Correspondence from the Oak Knoll Collection, 1830–1892* (ed. by John Albree, Salem, Mass., 1911), p. 46, and *Works* (Standard Lib. ed., 9 vols., Boston and N.Y., 1892–1894), VI, 128–29. The next year Whittier became the editor of the *Pennsylvania Freeman*. From it pages during the two years of Whittier's editorship, Professor Iola K. Eastburn (*Whittier's Relation to German Thought*, Americana Germanica, No. 20, Phila., 1915) cites a dozen references to German-American antislavery activities. Among the more notable are (1) the tribute to the early German settlers in the poem "Pennsylvania Hall," in the number for May 31, 1838; (2) references to the pamphlets *What is Abolition?* and *The Moral Condition of the Slaves*, published in the German language by the Philadelphia press of C. F. Stollmeyer, editor of the *German-American National Gazette* and active propagandist for abolition; and (3) the translation of Stollmeyer's editorial "A Voice from Germany. G. Seidensticker's Views of American Slavery" (in the number for Feb. 28, 1839), in which German-Americans are exhorted to use their influence and voting power to wipe out the institution that brings down on their adopted land the derision of despotic Europe.

189. The *Essex Gazette* for September 27, 1828, contained a long synopsis by Whittier of "Der Freischütz, or The Magic Ball, from the German of A. Apel," with a headnote explaining that the scene is laid "in a wild and romantic district of Germany" and calling attention to "the wildness of conception" and "the awful

grandeur" of the tale. The translation used by Whittier had appeared in *Tales of the Wild and the Wonderful* (London and Phila., 1826), pp. 97 ff. In the *New England Review* for October 11, 1830, Whittier published "The Skeptic," a tale of a German university student and his wicked companion Faustendorff, with a prefatory note describing it as "a thrilling development of the horrible effects of infidelity on the human heart." In the same magazine for September 5, 1831, appeared Whittier's story, "The Everlasting Taper," which (says the author) "is an old narration, and would figure well in an improved edition of Faust's Mephistopheles." The story has several things in common with the Faust legend, but the scene is France, not Germany. Another reference to heartless wickedness as Whittier associated it with Mephistopheles occurs in his article, "Thomas Carlyle on the Slavery Question" (1850), *Works*, VII, 133. For further details, see Eastburn, *op. cit.*, pp. 79–82, 149–52.

190. H. H. Clark, (ed.), *Major Americna Poets* (N.Y., 1936), p. 802. In the poem "The Demon of the Study" (1835) he mentioned, among other hobgoblins, the fiend of Faust, Agrippa's demon, and the devil of Martin Luther (*Works*, I, 25). Agrippa's name also appears several times in "The Pennsylvania Pilgrim." In 1840 Whittier prepared a version of Goethe's "Erlkönig," based on an earlier translation by A. Geohegan (see Eastburn, *op. cit.*, 87–90). Between 1844 and 1878 he referred seven times to Fouqué's *Undine* (*ibid.*, pp. 35, 93–94), which had been translated by his friend, the Rev. Thomas Tracey in his *Miniature Romances from Germany* (Boston, 1841). He mentioned also Fouqué's "Die Kohlerfamilie" in "The Agency of Evil" (*Works*, VII, 263), and Novalis' belief "that the Christian religion is the root of all democracy and the highest fact in the rights of man" (*Works*, VI, 185). He knew something about Jean Paul and thought Auerbach's story of Gellert "touching and beautiful" (Eastburn, *op. cit.*, pp. 140–41). In "The Haschisch" (1854) there is a reference to "the wizard lights and demon play" of Walpurgis night (*Works*, III, 173), and the lines, "She weaves her golden hair, she sings / Her spell-song low and faint," from "The Witch of Wenham" (1877) doubtless involve an echo of Heine's "Lorelei" (*Works*, I, 361).

191. See, e.g., "The Vale of the Merrimac" (1825), *Works*, IV, 335; "Pennsylvania Hall" (1835), III, 62; and "To a Friend" (1841), IV, 24.

192. In "Cobbler Keezar's Vision" (1861) Whittier pictures the old man mending shoes on a Connecticut hillside, recalling the German countryside, the merry grape-stained maidens of his native land, the clowns, puppets, imps, and Rhenish flagons of a Frankfurt fair, while he looks into the future through a magic lapstone wrought by Agrippa of Nettesheim and given by him to a cobbler Minnesinger, who in turn gave it to Keezar (*Works*, I, 241–47). In "The Sycamores" (1857) Keezar is described "singing, as he draws his stitches, songs his German masters taught" him (*Works*, I, 182). In "The Pennsylvania Pilgrim" (1871) the memories of Pastorius turn to the German mystics and scholars who had been his friends (*Works*, I, 322, 325, 330, 335) or upon his youthful experiences in Germany comprising "Old World flowers," "Altdorf Burschensong," or Christmas observances, all still vivid in his memory (*Works*, I, 338, 340–41). For similar allusions in "The Vision of Echard," see *Works*, II, 315–16.

No traveler himself, Whittier wrote, in 1850, to Bayard Taylor thanking him for his tales of travel and adventure—reading which, he said, enabled him to spend "a merry Christmas in Berlin." Ten years later, when they had become fast friends, he confessed that Taylor was his most valued proxy by whom to travel far while sitting quietly in his study at Amesbury. —Eastburn, *op. cit.*, pp. 35, 40.

193. Follen's eloquent question, "Shall the U.S.—the free U.S., which could not bear the bonds of a king—cradle the bondage which a king is abolishing?" inspired Whittier's widely known and quoted poem originally entitled "Stanzas," later "Follen," and finally "Expostulation."—*Works*, III, 24–28; VIII, 141–42.

194. Eastburn, *op. cit.*, 12–15. Whittier's memorial poem, "Follen, on Reading His Essay on 'The Future State'" (*Works*, IV, 29–34), celebrates the sweet serenity and benignity of Follen's spirit as the prototype of a soulful humanitarianism incarnate in Tauler, Echard, Spener, Eleanora Johanna von Merlau, Rahel, Woolman, and Pastorius. See *Works*, I, 141–44, 322, 325, 330, 334–35; II, 315–22; IV, 20.

195. Luther the reformer served Whittier as a model, not only for virtues to be emulated but also for shortcomings to be avoided (*Works*, I, 249; IV, 42; VI, 74; Eastburn, *op. cit.*, p. 120) One of Whittier's ringing war poems, "Ein' feste Burg ist unser Gott," exhorting the nation to recognize slavery as the real issue, was set to the rhythm and tune of Luther's hymn by the same title (*Works*, III, 219–22).

The name of Melanchthon appears several times in Whittier's essays and letters, usually in conjunction with that of Luther (*Works*, VI, 128–29). The tribute "To Ronge," a young German

Catholic priest of Whittier's own time, who had been excommunicated because of his protest against the "pious fraud" of the Bishop of Treves, is, like many of Whittier's references to Luther, evidence of his sympathy with the iconoclastic reform that characterized the poet's middle years (cf. *Works*, IV, 41; Eastburn, *op. cit.*, pp. 101–2). Another contemporary voice from Germany, that of Freiligrath, encouraged him, as it did Longfellow, when he wrote his *Poems of Slavery*.

On July 6, 1848, Whittier published in the *National Era* an editorial entitled "Our Diplomacy Trouble Abroad," in which he spoke of "Germany, fermenting like its beer, with new republicanism," and described with approval a "society of abolition propagandism, composed of learned professors, statesmen and divines, just established for the avowed purpose of acting upon the slave system of the U.S. through the German emigrants, who are fast filling up our new States and Territories" (Eastburn, *op. cit.*, p. 103). In the poem "Yorktown" (*Works*, III, 131) and the article "Democracy and Slavery" (*Works*, IV, 114), both published in the same journal, he spoke of Prussia's ironic laughter at the existence of slavery in the Land of Freedom, and compared the slaveowner's prating of liberty to Frederick the Great's apostrophizing Cato and Brutus. For other references, see Eastburn, *op. cit.*, pp. 73–74, 104, 122–24, 141–45.

196. See "The Proselytes," *Works*, V, 205–12. The introductory paragraphs, in which the weary student is depicted poring over books of bitter and vituperative theological controversy, reveal Whittier's conception of the German intellectual seeker after spiritual truth as far from sympathetic with the so-called German critical study of the Scriptures. That Whittier was aware of the materialistic, as well as the mystical, strain in German thought is evident from his description, in *The Stranger in Lowell* (1841), of a Pennsylvania-German named J. A. Etzler, who "was possessed by the belief that the world was to be restored to its paradisiacal state by the sole agency of mechanics" (*Works*, V, 353). Whittier's judgment of Etzler's *Paradise within the Reach of Man, without Labor, by the Powers of Nature and Machinery*, recalls Thoreau's longer castigation of the same work for similar reasons.

197. *Complete Works of John Greenleaf Whittier* (Student's Cambridge ed., Boston, 1894), p. 519. For evidence that Pastorius belonged to the Society of Friends, though there seems to be no record of his joining, see Eastburn, *op cit.*, p. 50.

In his Preface to John Woolman's journal (1871), Whittier repeated the story how, "in 1688, a meeting of Quakers, who had emigrated from Kriesheim and settled at Germantown, Pa., addressed a memorial against" the buying and keeping of Negroes "to the Yearly Meeting for the Pennsylvania and New Jersey colonies."—*Works*, VII, 321. Sewall's *Selling of Joseph* was first printed in 1700.

Whittier's principal sources for "The Pennsylvania Pilgrim" were articles by Oswald Seidensticker in *Der deutsche Pionier* for 1870 and 1871 and the *Penn Monthly* for January and February, 1872, as well as essays by Robert Ellis Thompson in the *Penn Monthly* for August, September, and October, 1871. Besides the details of Pastorius' life in Germany, Whittier's poem presents a wealth of descriptive and narrative documentary material, all indicating that Whittier worked hard to make the picture both detailed and authentic. The mystics Philipp Jacob Spener and Eleanora von Merlau are sympathetically portrayed, though they were probably less closely associated with Pastorius than Whittier represents them. There are also allusions to the seventeenth-century shoemaker-mystic Jacob Boehme, whose doctrines, as presented in *Morgenröthe*, had long been familiar to Whittier (Eastburn, *op. cit.*, 116–17). Agrippa of Nettesheim is mentioned, and there is a tolerant description of "painful Kelpius ... maddest of good men," who, "weird as a wizard" in his "den by Wissahickon ... read what man ne'er read before, and saw the visions man shall see no more" until the trump of the Apocalypse shall sound.—*Works*, I, 330. Whittier's poem on Pastorius contains minor inaccuracies, chiefly in regard to names and religious affiliations, which students of Pennsylvania history and sectarian controversialists have pointed out (see esp. *The Penn Monthly*, III [Nov., 1872], 636–37). Some of Whittier's errors are owing to his lack of facility in German. While he speaks in his preface to the poem of his sources, chiefly Seidensticker's articles in *Der deutsche Pionier*, he confessed, in a letter of May 17, 1875, to Julius Kirschbaum (who had sent him a copy of his German translation of Whittier's "Clerical Oppressors") that he lacked fluency in the language.—Eastburn, *op cit.*, pp. 76–77.

198. For an account of the factual basis of the story, see Howard M. Chapin, "Whittier's 'Palatine' Discovered," *Amer. Collector*, III (1927), 118–22.

199. Three decades earlier Whittier had found in C. J. P. Spitta's *Geduld* an expression of the religious peace which was so important an element in his conception of the spirit of German mysticism, and had made "a free

paraphrase" for his "Angel of Patience" (*Works*, II, 216) from an unidentified German poem celebrating this quality. A translation by the eminent German orientalist, Max Müller, inspired "The Brewing of Soma" (1872), perhaps Whittier's best known hymn and containing his beautiful prayer for spiritual peace, beginning "Dear Lord and Father of mankind / Forgive our foolish ways!"

200. The other Elizabeth is the thirteenth century Saint Elizabeth of Hungary.

201. Among the poets represented are Rückert, Chamisso, Grimm, Carové, and Jean Paul. Whittier's continued interest in German *Märchen* and folk materials appears in these collections, as well as in his ballad, "The Brown Dwarf of Ruegen" (1880), written for *St. Nicholas* and based on Arndt's "Die neun Berge bei Rambin." He probably used the close translation contained in Thomas Knightly's *Fairy Mythology of Various Countries* (London, 1850), a copy of which was in his library at Amesbury, but he did not follow Knightly closely. Elsewhere we find allusions to the tales of Münchhausen (*Essex Mag.*, Jan. 5, 1825; *Works*, VIII, 378), the songs of Hans Sachs (*Works*, III, 292), the coal burner in Hauff's *Kaltes Herz* who traded his heart of flesh for a cobblestone (*Works*, VII, 144), Bürger's *Lenore* (*Works*, V, 411), Walther von der Vogelweide's bequest to the birds (*Works*, VII, 243), and the "Blue-Cap of German fable" (*Poetical Works*, Student's Cambridge ed., p. 513). Other German literary figures prominently mentioned are Nicolai (1831), Schiller (1836, 1848), Logau (1844), Krummacher (1844, 1853), Holthaus (1844), Lessing (twice in 1853), and Herder (1853). For details, see Eastburn, *op. cit.*, pp. 135–41.

The German content of Whittier's library at Amesbury was relatively slight: a dozen books translated from the German, including Goethe's *Werther*, *Hermann und Dorothea*, and *Faust*, two collections of Jean Paul's writings, and the *Theologia Germanica* (which he mentioned in 1862 as the book Luther "loved next to his Bible."—*Works*, VII, 284–85). He owned also a dozen other books on German subjects, such as Lewes' *Life of Goethe*, Eliz. Buckingham's *Life of Jean Paul*, and *William Penn in Germany*, the journal of Penn's visit to Germany in 1677. In his study at Oak Knoll, where he spent much of his time after 1876, are preserved three translations from the German, including A. W. Schlegel's *Lectures on Dramatic Art and Literature*, and *The Pennsylvania Dutch and Other Essays* by Phoebe Earle Gibbons, published in the same year as "The Pennsylvania Pilgrim." For further details, see Eastburn, *op. cit.*, pp. 152–54.

HENRY DAVID THOREAU

202. After graduating from Harvard College, he insisted upon and secured unrestricted borrowing privileges from the College library. As Mr. Canby observes, "Harvard library stands behind his books. It overpacked the Journal and the 'Week' with reading . . . it is difficult to conceive 'Walden' without a background of an easy familiarity with the world's best books."—*Thoreau* (Boston, 1939), p. 50. During 1841–1843 he had Emerson's rich library to browse in; in 1843 he read "deeply, if briefly" in the libraries of New York City; and throughout life he kept adding to his own very carefully selected library until it contained, at his death, some four hundred volumes. He read less widely than did many of his contemporaries; he lacked the Transcendentalists' pride in catholicity that sometimes ran to dilettantism; he selected his books as carefully as he chose what he must do; and choosing thus deliberately, he became an example of whom it may be said that "what he read he became."

203. Wm. E. Channing, *Thoreau: The Poet Naturalist* (Boston, 1873), p, 41.

204. His purpose was (as he said it was Goethe's in the *Italienische Reise*) simply to give "an exact description of things as they appeared to him, and their effect upon him."—*Writings* (Walden ed., 20 vols., Boston, 1906), I, 347; see also II, 347–48; *Journal* (Walden ed., I, 15; and Canby, *op. cit.*, p. 272.

205. *Writings*, I, 350.

206. *Ibid.*, 347–40, 351–53, 400–401.

207. See the extensive extracts from Goethe chiefly from the *Italienische Reise*, in *Journal*, I, 9–10, 11, 15.

208. *Writings*, I, 348–30.

209. "Books," he said, "must be read as deliberately as they are written."—*Journal*, I, 369. "How many a man has not dated a new era in his life from the reading of a book."—*Writings*, II, 114; see also pp. 112, 120; Channing, *op. cit.*, p. 40.

210. *Writings*, VI, 296.

211. B. V. Crawford (ed.), *Henry David Thoreau. Representative Selections . . .* (N.Y., 1934), p. xxix.

212. Channing, *op. cit.*, pp. 41, 203. For Thoreau's favorite reading, as well as his abysmal gaps in taste and knowledge of books, see Crawford, *op. cit.*, pp. xvii–xxx; Norman Foerster, "The Intellectual Heritage of Thoreau," *Texas Review*, II, iii (Jan, 1917), 192–212; Channing, *op. cit.*, pp. 40, 58; F. B. Sanborn, *The Personality of Thoreau* (Boston, 1901), p. 36; Mark Van Doren, *Henry David Thoreau. A Critical Study* (Boston, 1916), pp. 97–98; *Writings*, II, 117, 119.

In 1836, during his senior year, Thoreau attended some of Longfellow's initial lectures on German literature (Canby, *op. cit.*, pp. 43–44). The winter before, when he boarded at O. A. Brownson's house in Canton, Mass., he and Brownson "stuck heartily to studying German" (Channing, *op. cit.*, p. 32). When Thoreau left Cambridge in 1837, he was "more or less qualified to read and write Greek, Latin, French, German, Italian, and Spanish"; and somewhat later in Concord, he carried forward his German studies "enthusiastically" with Sarah Ripley. In 1845, when Sanborn first met him, he had improved his knowledge of French to read it "as readily as English"; he continued to read Latin and Greek "without difficulty"; but of German, Italian, and Spanish he seemed to Sanborn to have retained only "a little."— Sanborn, *op. cit.*, pp. 36–37, 105.

213. *Journals*, I, 4–6, 8–10, 11. The translations appear to be Thoreau's own; they do not correspond to any known printed versions. They were subsequently used in the *Week* (*Writings*, I, 348, 352). Compare also *Journals*, I, 15, and *Writings*, I, 347–38.

214. Among the several inventories that Thoreau made of his library, one hurriedly penciled list includes "Goethe" and "De Staël's Germany." See Van Doren, *op. cit.*, pp. 88-90. De Staël's *Germany* was first noticed in his *Journal* on March 4, 1838. Another list, reproduced in the appendix to Sanborn's biography, includes the following items: (1) "Ein Schauspiel von Goethe [title not indicated]"; (2) "Schiller's Dreysigjähriger Krieg. Leipzig ed. 2 v." (3) "Life of Schiller. By Carlyle. New York 1 v." (4) "Marie Stuart. Stuttgart und Tübingen ed. 1 v. [German]"; (5) [J. F.] Grund's Geometry. 1 v." (6) [Leonhard] Euler's Algebra. Boston. 1 v." (7) "Zimmermann on Solitude. Albany. 1 v." (8) "German Dictionary. Philad. 1 v." (9) "German Reader. By Follen. Boston. 1 v." (10) "German Grammar. By Follen. Boston. 1 v." (11) "Goethe's Wilhelm Meister. Boston. 5 v." (12) [Johann M.] Bechstein's Cage Birds and Sweet Warblers. 1 v." and (13) "Günderode. From the German. 1 v." The last is doubtless Margaret Fuller's translation of the *Correspondence of Fräulein Günderode and Bettina von Arnim*, a booklet of 106 pages appearing in 1842, and containing about a fourth of the complete text, subsequently completed and published in 1861.

215. For example, *Journal*, IX, 242–43 (Feb. 6, 1857), and *Writings*, V, 318.

216. Channing, *op. cit.*, p. 41.

217. "Thoreau's Journal," *Shelburne Essays, Fifth Series*, (N.Y., 1908), p. 118.

218. Again, while there is in Thoreau little concern, in the usual religious sense, with God and the soul, there is "a strong sense of individualism, or sublime egoism, reaching out to embrace the world in ecstatic communion," which is on the surface very much like Schleiermacher's contemplation of the universe. This reverie, or contemplation, that spurns all limitations, Paul Elmer More reminds us, passed easily into the romantic ideal of music—and that in a very literal sense. A music box was for Thoreau a means of consolation for the loss of a brother; a hand organ was an instrument of the gods; and the humming of telegraph wires seemed to speak to his soul of the secret harmony of the universe. (Consult the index to the *Journal* for illustrative passages.) In the many cases in which Thoreau pays rhapsodical homage to the droning telegraph wires there is often something vacillating from the sublime to the ludicrous. Nor was Thoreau unaware, as More again reminds us, of this intrusion of humor, or irony, into his ecstasy. Like Friedrich Schlegel, Thoreau indulged in the romantic irony of smiling down upon himself and walking through life a *Doppelgänger*. See *Journal*, IV, 291 (Aug. 8, 1852), though it does not necessarily follow that he learned about romantic irony from the German *Romantiker*.

Other characteristic motifs in Thoreau's books seem to have the mark of German romanticism and suggest either Tieck or Novalis. Such are his observations on childhood, on sleep, and on nighttime, on the all-enveloping sacrament of silence, and on the new mythology which is to be the end of our study and our art: "all the phenomena of nature need to be seen from the point of view of wonder and awe. . . . Men are probably nearer to the essential truth in their superstitions than in their reason" (*Journal*, IV, 158; see also II, 279–80), and other passages as indicated under appropriate rubrics in the index to the *Journal*.

These parallelisms, says P. E. More (*op. cit.*, p. 121), are not cases of translation or plagiarism, but rather of that "larger and vague migration of thought from one land to another," a part of the atmosphere or climate in which romanticism thrives, and they show how thoroughly the transcendental philosophy of New England had absorbed, or appropriated, the ideas and language of German romanticism, if not its inmost spirit—however circuitous the line by which they passed from one to the other. However, Thoreau's insistence on moral idealism and "character" is not to be confused with the *Gemüt* and *Gefühlsphilosophie* of the *romantische Schule*. For a succinct statement of this divergence, see *ibid.*, pp. 121-31, and for an even stronger statement, Van Doren, *op. cit.*, pp. 54-55.

219. *Writings*, I, 347–52 (including transcriptions and elaborations from *Journal*, I, 15), 401; VI, 62, 168, 301, 383; and *Journal*, I, 19. While he confessed in the *Week* that he was "not much acquainted with the works of Goethe" (*Writings*, I, 347), he urged B. B. Wiley to read the *Autobiography* "by all means" (*ibid.*, VI, 301, Apr. 26, 1857). The only other works of Goethe's that Thoreau mentions are *Tasso*, *Italienische Reise*, *Iphigenie*, *Faust*, and *Meister*, though it may be presumed that he also knew Margaret Fuller's translation of *Eckermanns Gespräche* (Vol. IV of Ripley's *Specimens of Foreign Standard Literature*). *Tasso* and *Italienische Reise* he obviously read in the German, but there is nothing to suggest that he read more of Goethe in the original. He appears to have known enough about Goethe to warrant his drawing a contrast between Carlyle's "titanic" style and the "more lasting style of Goethe," and expressing the wish that Carlyle had "cultivated the style of Goethe more, that of Richter less."—*Writings*, IV, 331–32. While he admired the truthfulness of Goethe's descriptions, notably in the *Italian Travels* (even suggesting that he sought in his own writing to emulate Goethe's descriptive techniques; see *Journal*, I, 11, 15, and *Writings*, I, 347–48), yet the very care with which Goethe wrote led him to censure Goethe, who, instead of fulfilling the stature of the Man of Genius, was only the Artisan. See *Writings*, I, 348–49, as well as pp. 250–51. There is a hint (although it is nowhere stated in so many words) that Puritan Thoreau agreed with Puritan Emerson in being unable to excuse moral laxity in "such as he." Finally, despite all of Goethe's cultivation, he lacked universality—the assertions of Thoreau's fellow-Transcendentalists notwithstanding (*Writings*, I, 148–49). In short, Goethe lacked the savage, primitive virtues and was not, after all, Thoreau's man.

220. He mentions Schiller only cursorily in his essay on Carlyle (*Writings*, IV, 330, 340, 351), either in pointing out obvious connections and comparisons with Goethe or in referring to Carlyle's biography of Schiller. He repeatedly draws a parallel between John Brown and Wilhelm Tell (*Writings*, IV, 441; *Journal*, I, 196; XII, 412; and *Writings*, IV, 426, 441); but his knowledge of the Swiss hero could easily have come from other sources than Schiller's play. He possessed, by 1840, a two-volume, Leipzig edition of Schiller's *Geschichte des Dreissigjährigen Kriegs*. Though he normally acquired books for the purpose of reading them, it may, in the absence of any references to Schiller's history, be doubted that he waded through these volumes.

Jean Paul F. Richter naturally comes in for a good deal of attention in his essay on Carlyle (*Writings*, IV, 331, 332, 338, 351), but he is not mentioned elsewhere, and Thoreau probably knew no more of him than what could be gleaned from Carlyle's essays.

221. *Writings*, IV, 353.

222. The extent of Coleridge's influence on Thoreau has not yet been studied exhaustively, but there are significant suggestions in Crawford, *op. cit.*, p. xxviii, and especially in Raymond W. Adams, "Thoreau's Literary Theory and Criticism," unpublished Ph.D. diss., Univ. of North Carolina, 1928.

223. *Journal*, I, 466.

224. For details see Fred W. Lorch, "Thoreau and the Organic Principle in Poetry," *PMLA*, LIII, i (Mar., 1938), 286–302, esp. pp. 290–97. Here it may be observed that Thoreau drew from the Harvard library on September 5, 1836, "Schlegel's Hist. Litt. [vol.] 1," and on October 3, 1836, "Schlegel's Hist. Litt. [vol.] 2," and the list of charges for 1836–1837 repeats the same entries. The library had at the time both "F. Schlegel's *Geschichte der alten und neuen Litt.* 2. Th., Wien, 1815, and *Lectures on the Hist. of Lit.*, 2 vols., Phila., 1818." It is not clear whether Thoreau borrowed the German or the English edition.

One important respect in which Thoreau's theory of poetic expression differs from that of the German romanticists derives from the insistence that poetry speaks a higher truth than does the prose of science, and that it adopts a more general and universal language. Poetry, he said, has no antiquity; it is timeless (*Writings*, I, 98). "A fact truly stated . . . acquires a mythological or universal significance" (*Journal*, III, 65), and requires a more than local, individual, or particular expression: "Say it and have done with it. Express it without expressing yourself" (*Journal*, III, 85). In thus emphasizing impersonality and objectivity as the mark of great writing, he distinguished himself sharply from the typical *Gefühlsmensch* among the Germans who dwelt long and lovingly on his emotional uniqueness.

225. It had twelve American printings between 1793 and 1819, and was very popular during Thoreau's younger years. It may be recalled that the Autocrat of the Breakfast Table remembered seeing it often lying about in libraries or adorning parlor tables.

226. Thoreau's copy, published in Albany, was doubtless the one printed there in 1796.

227. It is believed that Thoreau not only helped Wheeler build his cabin but later spent six weeks with him in his retreat (*Writings*, VI, 58–59 n.; Crawford, *op. cit.*, p. xxxi; Canby,

op. cit., p. 206). His friend Channing also lived on the prairie, and in March, 1845, wrote urging Thoreau to "go out upon that field which I once christened 'Briars' . . . build yourself a hut, and there begin the grand process of devouring yourself alive" (*Writings*, VI, 121). Emerson, in *Nature* and elsewhere, had recommended solitude, and had, at least in poetry if not in actuality, said good-bye to a proud world. Wordsworth and Coleridge had sought the wild places of the British Isles; Germans like Novalis, of whom a good deal was made in the *Dial*, had apostrophized night and solitude in much the same manner in which Thoreau came to glorify them; and finally Zimmermann had popularized the idea of solitary reflection as a cure for souls by presenting a whole programme in a work of two volumes.

228. See *Journal*, I, 244 (Apr. 5, 1841), 299 (Dec. 24, 1841).

229. Zimmermann's and Thoreau's ideas diverge at several points. Zimmermann is less copious in his observations on the effect of natural solitude upon the mind than is Thoreau, who found the woods and fields a more satisfactory retiring room than a book-lined study. Although Zimmermann pointed out that solitude and simplicity are natural companions, Thoreau put more emphasis on the code of simplicity, especially on renouncing the so-called conveniences of housekeeping. But both sought solitude as an antidote for the frivolity of society and as a proper sphere for the cultivation of liberty and independence; both recommended solitude as nourishing the mind and feeding the imagination; finally, they agreed in identifying solitude with bravery and both with music—an identification and parallelism all the more striking because unusual. Compare Zimmermann's *Solitude*, Vol. I, Ch. IV, with Thoreau's *Journal*, I, 102–6. For other parallels between the two see Grant Loomis, "Thoreau and Zimmermann," *New Engl. Quar.*, X, iv (Dec., 1937), 789–92; and Canby, *op. cit.*, p. 206, 470–71, n. 3.

230. *Writings*, I, 389; V, 318; *Journal*, III, 118–19 (Nov. 15, 1851); XIII, 153 (Feb. 17, 1860). On February 6, 1860, Thoreau drew "Gesner" from the Harvard library. There is no indication whether this was the *Historia Animalum* (4 vols., Tiguri, 1551–1560) or Edward Topsell's translation, *The Historie of Foure-footed Beastes . . . Collected out of the volumes of Conradus Gesner, and all other Writers* (London, 1607). When he had occasion to quote Gesner in his books or in the *Journal*, he used Topsell. See, e.g., *Writings*, V, 318. Since these references extend from 1846 to 1860, the presumption is strong

that Topsell's *Gesner* was in his own library.

231. *Writings*, IV, 121; V, 92–93; *Journal*, II, 11; V, 117, 120–21. Several of these quotations were transferred bodily from the journals to the works, as were some from Topsell's *Gesner*. Most of the quotations from Humboldt are drawn from his *Personal Narrative of Travels on the New Continent*. I have not been able to identify the particular translation of Humboldt that Thoreau used.

232. *Journal*, III, 200 (Jan. 17, 1852). The passage is quoted later in *Walden* (*Writings*, II, 25). Madame Pfeiffer was an adventuresome German traveler who published in 1850 *Eine Frauenfahrt um die Welt*. In July, 1854, the Harvard library acquired the second English edition of this work, entitled *A Woman's Journey Round the World*. Thoreau's quotation is derived from Chapter XXII, page 301, of this edition. Quite possibly Thoreau knew also the translation made by William Hazlitt (London, 1852).

233. Crantz's *History of Greenland* is quoted four times in *Cape Cod* (*Writings*, IV, 60, 60–61, 149–50). I have not found the passages in Thoreau's *Journal*. He withdrew "Crantz's Greenland 1. 2." from the Harvard library on February 6, 1860. Although the library possessed also several copies of Crantz in German, the one used by Thoreau was doubtless the *History of Greenland: from the High-Dutch* (2 vols., London, 1767).

For information regarding Thoreau's withdrawals at Cambridge I am indebted to Professor Francis L. Utley. It seems that Thoreau borrowed only one other German work from the Harvard library. On December 10, 1855, he took out "Loskiel Mission . . . America 1796 [1794 ?]." The library had at the time Georg H. Loskiel's *Geschichte der Mission der Ev. Brüder unter den Indianern in Nordamerika* (Leipzig, 1789), and the *History of the Missions of the United Brethren among the Indians in North America*, (tr. by C. I. La Trobe, London, 1794). I have not noted any use that Thoreau made of this work in either the original or the translation.

234. Channing, *op. cit.* (1873), p. 40. Other occasional references occur to the *Nibelungenlied* (*Journal*, I, 57), to Luther (*Writings*, IV, 333), Barthold G. Niebuhr (*ibid.*, V, 290), and Johann J. Winckelmann's *History of Ancient Art* (*Journal*, IX, 242–43), but the sum of their combined significance is slight.

HERMAN MELVILLE

235. *Moby-Dick*, I, 139, 167. All references are to the Standard edition, 16 vols., London, 1922–1924.

236. The extraordinary range of literary and historical allusion in his "Fragments from a Writing Desk," composed seven years before *Typee*, suggests that the young man was no stranger to books. His brief subjection to the classical curriculum of the Albany Academy laid the foundation for the knowledge of the classics which his later writings reveal, and it may be presumed that he read somewhat during the years from 1837 to 1841, when he taught school in New York and Massachusetts. It has been suggested that books, among them Otto von Kotzebue's *New Voyage Round the World* (1830), first aroused what Melville called his "everlasting itch for things remote" which sent him a-whaling in the first place, thus preparing him for his writing career. While the whaling adventure was primarily an education by experience, his signing on the *Lucy Ann* on the return voyage threw him much in the company of Dr. Long Ghost (John B. Troy?), a colorful adventurer and "a capital fellow to finish Melville's education."—R. M. Weaver, *Herman Melville, Mariner and Mystic* (N.Y., 1921), p. 218. Dr. Long Ghost was an educated man who had enjoyed having and spending money, had cultivated a fine taste for wines, and had associated with gentlemen. During the long hours of the night, Melville found him a boon companion; he could quote Vergil, talk learnedly of Hobbes of Malmesbury, and repeat poetry by the canto (see *Omoo*, pp. 13–15). "He was himself a picaresque library, and he who ran with him had much to read." —Weaver, *op. cit.*, p. 53. Later, aboard the U.S. frigate *United States*, Melville found not only the raw materials for *White-Jacket* but a man named "Nord," in whose eyes Melville recognized at once "a reader of good books . . . an earnest thinker," who had "been bolted in the mill of adversity." With Nord, he "scoured all the prairies of reading, dived into the bosom of authors, and tore out their hearts."—*White-Jacket*, p. 63. For a suggestive account of how Melville came, even during his experience on the *United States*, to appreciate philosophical books in a manner to learn to do a little "prancing" of his own "on Coleridge's High German horse," see Ch. XLI of *White-Jacket*, pp. 207–9. Thus was born the writer Melville who described himself as "a pondering man," and who professed, "I have swam through libraries and sailed through oceans."—Weaver, *op. cit.*, p. 339; *Moby-Dick*, I, 167.

237. *Journal up the Straits* . . . ed. by R. M. Weaver (N.Y., 1935), Introduction, p. v.

238. Evert Duyckinck's choice collection of 17,000 volumes and the lists of "Books Lent" that Duyckinck kept give us some insight into the use Melville made of his opportunities. For suggestive details regarding his reading, see Willard Thorp (ed.), *Melville. Representative Selections* . . . (N.Y., 1938), pp. xxv–xxviii; Luther S. Mansfield, *Herman Melville, Author and New Yorker 1844–1851* (Chicago, 1938), pp. 189–208; Wm. Braswell, *Melville's Religious Thought* . . . (Durham, N.C., 1943), pp. 3–18; K. H. Sundermann, *Herman Melvilles Gedankengut* . . . (Berlin, 1937); and esp. Jay Leyda, *The Melville Log* (2 vols., N.Y., 1951), I, 193 ff. It requires no great effort to gauge the impact of his rapidly widening familiarity with books as it is manifested in the greater allusiveness and the tendency toward philosophical allegory in *Mardi* of 1849 and *White-Jacket* of 1850. It is this quickening of his philosophical perceptions that Melville referred to when he told Hawthorne: "From my twenty-fifth year I date my life. Three weeks have scarcely passed, at any time between then [1844] and now, that I have not unfolded within myself."—Julian Hawthorne, *Nathaniel Hawthorne and His Wife* (2 vols., Boston, 1884), I, 405.

239. Leyda, *op. cit.*, I, 319–23; Weaver, *Melville*, pp. 285, 286–89. With Adler he sketched "a plan for going down the Danube from Vienna to Constantinople; thence to Athens by the steamer; to Beyrout and Jerusalem—Alexandria and the Pyramids." While these plans came to naught for lack of money, they stuck together throughout Melville's stay in England, and subsequently Adler turned up in Paris to help Melville over his difficulties with French and to resume their talks of "high German metaphysics." Melville's brief Rhineland tour was rendered cheerless after Adler's departure and of little profit to him so far as acquiring much of the German spirit goes; but back in London his haunting the bookshops may be presumed to have been inspired partly by a desire to provide himself with the materials more expertly to "ride the high German horse." Among books acquired were no German titles, for Melville knew no German; but it may well be that his purchase in London of Goethe's *Autobiography* and his *Letters from Italy* (both in the Bohn edition), coupled with his meeting Bayard Taylor soon after his return, stimulated his interest in Goethe. Another German book purchased at the time was Lavater's *Essays on Physiognomy*, subsequently referred to a number of times in his writings.—Weaver, *Melville*, pp. 298–99, 301–2, 304; Mansfield, *op. cit.*, p. 199.

In the spring of 1857, on the return trip from the Holy Land, Melville made a leisurely and more enjoyable tour of Germany. He crossed Switzerland from Lake Maggiore and entered

Germany at Basel, proceeded to Heidelberg and Frankfurt (where the places of Goethe interest fascinated him), and thence down the Rhine to Amsterdam.—*Journal up the Straits*, pp. 166–71.

240. Weaver, *Melville*, p. 308.

241. For his reading of German authors he appears to have relied largely upon the Duyckinck, the New York Library Society, and other New York collections. Something, we may be sure, came to him by way of Carlyle, several of whose books he owned and several others of which he borrowed from Duyckinck, but whom he does not mention in his writings, though the marks of Carlyle's influence are everywhere, especially in *Pierre*. See R. S. Forsythe (ed.), *Pierre* (N.Y., 1941), pp. xxxvi-xxxvii. He learned still more about German thought from Coleridge, whom he repeatedly mentions. See *White-Jacket*, pp. 63, 193, 207; *Moby-Dick*, I, 236–37; *Billy Budd*, p. 389; and the diary, quoted by Weaver, *Melville*, p. 285; also Braswell, *op. cit.*, pp. 20, 108. In London, in 1849, he acquired the Bulwer Lytton translation of *The Poems and Ballads of Schiller*, and shortly after his return from abroad, borrowed Evert Duyckinck's two-volume (London, 1845) edition of Jean Paul's *Flower, Fruit, and Thorn Pieces;* also *Sartor Resartus, Heroes and Hero-Worship* and Carlyle's versions of *Wilhelm Meister* and *German Romance*. In 1862 he bought and read Madame de Staël's *Germany* in a New York edition of 1859, underscoring (and commenting upon) various passages in her discussion of Goethe's *Elective Affinities* that confirmed his own doubts about human intellectual profundity.—Mansfield, *op. cit.*, pp. 199, 206; Braswell, *op. cit.*, p. 15; Leyda, *op. cit.*, II, 651. During the last years of his life he acquired seven volumes of Schopenhauer's works (then being made available in English) and marked numerous passages apparently consonant with his own views, but they came too late to exert any influence on his more characteristic writings. For details, see Braswell, *op. cit.*, pp., 117, 144, n. 49.

242. *Journal up the Straits*, pp. 79–80.

243. Strauss's *Life of Jesus*, says Melville, has robbed the pilgrim to the Holy Land of much that was formerly sacred.—*Ibid.*, pp. 107–8. *Clarel*, which represents his mature deliberations on the conflict between knowledge and faith, science and religion, often returns to the same theme. See *Clarel*, I, 136; also *Moby-Dick*, II, 106; Weaver, *Melville*, p. 360; and Wm. E. Sedgwick, *Herman Melville. The Tragedy of Mind* (Cambridge, Mass., 1945), pp. 208–14.

244. It was this torn state of mind that Hawthorne came to know well in his friend while they lived near each other in the Berkshires, and when they sometimes "talked ontological heroics together" and argued "about time and eternity, things of this world and the next, and books, and publishers, and all possible and impossible matters . . . deep into the night."—Julian Hawthorne, *op. cit.*, I, 400, 415. And it was this same perplexity of mind that Hawthorne commented on sadly five years later when Melville visited him in Liverpool, just before embarking for the Near East, as the result of Melville's long wandering over the deserts of speculation and his inability either to believe or to "be comfortable in his unbelief."—*Ibid.*, II, 135.

245. Miss Nathalia Wright has counted some 600 Biblical references in Melville's prose writings. See *Amer. Lit.*, XII, ii (May, 1940), 185. He referred to St. Augustine on original guilt; he was brought up on Calvin; he wrote familiarly of Luther and Melanchthon, he read John and Jeremy Taylor, Fuller, Burton, Browne, Massillon, Tillotson, Bayle, Montaigne, Voltaire, Paine, Volney, Herbert of Cherbury, Edwards, and Ethan Allen; and he searched Dante and Milton for their contributions to his problems. He had some knowledge of Polynesian, Hindu, Buddhist, and Persian religions, and he avowed a special interest in the position of evil in Zoroastrianism, Manichaeism, and Parseeism. There are also references to the early Christian heretics, the Gnostics, and the Marcionites. He wrote familiarly of Mohammed and the Koran years before he went to the Holy Land, and there are "incidental references to Egyptian, Assyrian, Chinese, and Norse beliefs and an abundance of references to Greek and Roman mythologies."—Braswell, *op. cit.*, pp. 11–14, 18.

246. He knew something of Baconian utilitarianism and Spinoza's pantheism. He wrote of Hobbes as if he knew a great deal about him; he commented at length on the Lockean rejection of innate ideas; he referred to Berkeley on matter, Edwards on will, and Priestley on necessity; he praised Hume's skepticism, and in his copy of Schopenhauer's *World as Will and Idea* he heavily underscored a passage which reads: "From every page of David Hume there is more to be learned than from the collected philosophical works of Hegel, Herbart, and Schleiermacher together."—Braswell, *op. cit.*, pp. 14, 15, and notes.

247. In his copy of *World as Will and Idea*, (I, xi), he marked Schopenhauer's passage on the significance of Kant, and opposite a passage in his copy of *Literature and Dogma*, in which Arnold spoke of "something *splay*, some-

thing blunt-edged, unhandy, and infelicitous" in the German mind as well as in the language, he wrote "True" (*ibid.*, p. 15), whence we conclude that he was not overfond of German ways of thought, though he knew too little German to have formed an intelligent opinion based on his own reading of the German philosophers in their own language.

248. *Redburn*, p. 254; *Mardi*, I, 14.

249. *Mardi*, I, 230, 244, 325, 339, 366–69; II, 37, 86–87, 104, 140–42, 160–61, 189, 212, 255, 298–303, 309–11, 329. Other notable references to Kant, aside from the satirical passages on the post-Kantians and the British and American disciples, occur in *Moby-Dick*, II, 59; *Pierre*, pp. 372, 390–92, 409, 418; and in his diary, quoted in Weaver, *Melville*, pp. 285, 288.

250. Thus it would appear that Melville knew something about Kantian thought some time before he met Professor Adler and Dr. Taylor. The tone of dissatisfaction with German metaphysics and the satirical note that characterizes several of his references to the Transcendentalists is doubtless indicative less of disrespect for Kant or critical transcendentalism than of impatience with abstruse philosophy of whatever kind that leads to no positive conclusion or that pretends to more than it achieves. Although he had come to suspect, when he wrote *Mardi*, that the question "What is Truth? is more final than any answer" (*Mardi*, I, 329), as a voyager in the "World of Mind" he dared not overlook any readings or bearings by which he might steer a safe course among the Mardian Isles.

251. *Moby-Dick*, I, 234–44 *passim*.

252. *Ibid.*, I, 222.

253. *Ibid.*, I, 204.

254. *Pierre*, p. 233.

255. At least, Melville's outburst (*ibid.*, p. 421) against "practical unreason" seems to indicate as much.

256. *Ibid.*, p. 231; see also pp. 384, 473, 499.

257. Pierre's experiences serve but to confirm what Melville had said to Hawthorne: "Perhaps, after all, there is *no* secret . . . [and] the Problem of the Universe is like the Freemason's mighty secret, so terrible to all children. It turns out, at last, to consist of a triangle, a mallet, and an apron, —nothing more."—Julian Hawthorne, *op. cit.*, I, 388. Truth, Melville concluded, lies at the bottom of an endless spiral staircase, concealed by the endlessness of the spirals and the blackness of the shaft. See *Pierre*, p. 402; also pp. 397, 421, 472.

258. After coming to another impasse in *Pierre*, Melville shrank within himself. While he continued, as Hawthorne observed, to wander to and fro in the "dismal and monotonous" metaphysical regions, and on occasions to regale his friends and visitors with philosophical monologues in the Coleridgean manner, his will to believe appears to have effected at least a partial triumph by the time he wrote *Clarel* (1876), in which he heaps scorn upon Jewish Margoth, a shallow scientist, who, in his insensibility to spiritual values, declares that "All's mere geology," while an ass brays confirmation (*Clarel*, I, 310; see also p. 329; Julian Hawthorne, *op. cit.*, II, 135; Braswell, *op. cit.*, pp. 108, 110–20; and Weaver, *Melville*, pp. 16, 351). At all events, when, during the last year of his life, he wrote *Billy Budd*, he penned what has been called his "testament of acceptance." See E. L. G. Watson, "Melville's Testament of Acceptance," *New Engl. Quar.*, VI (June, 1933). 319–27. The daemonic titanism of Ahab has given way before a sense of resignation to the inscrutable laws of the universe and acquiescence in the wisdom of God that remains still past man's finding out, but that is no longer hateful. In what degree this change of heart is attributable to the growing influence upon him of the Christian tradition, the mediating and humanizing experiencing of life and old age, a re-examination of and a pondering upon Kantian ethics, or other influences is conjectural.

What can be asserted with fair assurance is that his heaping of abuse upon the "new Apostles . . . muttering Kantian categories through teeth and lips dry and dusty as any miller's, with the crumbs of Graham crackers" (*Pierre*, p. 418) proceeds less from any dissatisfaction with Kant than from the persistence of certain "reconcilers" of the "Optimist" or "Compensation" school (*ibid.*, p. 385)—that is, philosophers who pretend to have found the talismanic secret. The group includes all those from Plato and Spinoza to Goethe and Emerson "and many more" who belong to "this guild of self-imposters," together with "a preposterous rabble of Muggletonian Scots and Yankees, whose vile brogue still the more bespeaks the stripedness of their Greek and German Neoplatonic originals" (*ibid.*, p. 290). It is noteworthy that Kant is never mentioned in this company. He probably had in mind men like Fichte, Schelling, and Schleiermacher among the Germans, and Carlyle and Emerson among Scotch and Yankee disciples. The transcendentalist philosopher Plotinus Plinlimnon in *Pierre*, the spineless Rev. Mr. Falsgrave in the same book, and the chaplain in *White-Jacket*, who is genial, well bred, and learned in Plato and in the German philosophers, but who preaches sermons wholly unsuited to the crew—these are not attacks on Kant but on false disciples and traducers of honest divers after the truth like Kant. But even Emerson, whose optimism Melville could not stomach, and whose reputation for expounding unintelligible "transcendentalisms, myths and oracular gibberish" had predisposed Melville to question his sincerity— even this Emerson, granted that he be a humbug, seemed to Melville "no common humbug". For the sake of argument (he wrote to Evert Duyckinck) let us call Emerson a fool: "Then had I rather be a fool than a wise man.—I love all men who *dive*. Any fish can swim near the surface, but it takes a great whale to go down stairs five miles or more...." He does not credit Emerson precisely with this ability, but he improves the occasion to honor "the whole corps of thought-divers, that have been diving and coming up again with blood-shot eyes since the world began." (See Thorp, *op. cit.*, pp. 371–72). For Melville, Kant was one of those thought-divers, and there is not an instance among the dozens of passages that belittle his disciples of all kinds which impugns Kant's sincerity or depreciates his philosophic abilities. The passage in *Moby-Dick* (II, 59), in which Melville recommends that Ahab, rather than balance Locke against Kant, throw both overboard if he wishes the *Pequod* to "float light and right," is not so much a condemnation of either Locke or Kant, or both, as an expression of discontent with all philosophy. It is of the same order as Emerson's asking, "Who has not looked into a metaphysical book? And what sensible man ever looked twice?"—*Works*, II, 438.

259. *Pierre*, p. 233.
260. Of the German post-Kantians Melville appears to have known little beyond what he learned from his conversations with Taylor and Adler respecting them. Schleiermacher and the Schlegels are mentioned once, and Schelling not at all; there are in *Moby-Dick* (II, 190) and notably in *Mardi* (I, 268; II, 279; see also Julian Hawthorne, *op. cit.*, I, 387–88) passages emphasizing the Ego in a manner suggesting Fichte, but the ideas need not have come directly from Fichte. A single reference to Hegel is made *en passant* in *Clarel* (I, 246) and has no particular significance. Herder is passed over altogether. Zimmermann on solitude is twice mentioned in *The Confidence Man*—pp. 75, 180.

There is some concern with pseudo-scientists like Lavater, whose *Physiognomy* Melville purchased in 1850. Lavater is directly mentioned several times (*Mardi*, I, 294; II, 227; *Moby-Dick*, II, 81, 83; *Redburn*, p. 351), and there are some allusions to his characteristic ideas (*Mardi*, I, 113; *Moby-Dick*, II, 83; *Pierre*, p. 109; *The Confidence Man*, p. 309; *Clarel*, II,

56). The same is true of Gall, Spurzheim, and Mesmer) *Mardi*, II, 227; *Moby-Dick*, II, 81; *Billy Budd*, pp. 72–73; Meade Minnigerode, *Some Personal Letters of Herman Melville*, N.Y., 1922, p. 71), but concern with phrenology, physiognomy, and mesmerism in the periodical literature of the day and popular interest in them was so widespread that no special importance attaches to such references as Melville makes to them.

261. Julian Hawthorne, *op. cit.*, I, 401. In 1856, in Constantinople, he recalled Schiller's *Ghostseer* (*Journal up the Straits*, p. 32), and four years later he reread some of Schiller's ballads (Sundermann, *op. cit.*, p. 111). In *The Confidence Man* (p. 251) he expressed some doubt about Schiller's tenet that "beauty is at bottom incompatible with ill." A final reference occurs in his lecture on "Travelling." See also Leon Howard, *Herman Melville. A Biography* (N.Y., 1951), p. 333. Obviously Schiller did not provide a vitally inspiring force for Melville.

262. Julian Hawthorne, *op. cit.*, I, 406. Professor Leon Howard (*op. cit.*, pp. 171, 179, 194; also p. 299) finds unmistakable evidence that Melville read Goethe's *Autobiography* with special reference to his own inner unfolding while he pondered the allegorical ambiguities of *Mardi*, *Moby-Dick*, and *Pierre*. He alludes to Eckermann's *Gespräche* several times (*Mardi*, I, 204; *Moby-Dick*, I, xix; II, 119; *Pierre*, p. 284); he mentions *Werther* twice (*Clarel*, p. 284; *The Confidence Man*, p. 22); and he appears thoroughly familiar with *Faust* (*Mardi*, I, 45; *White-Jacket*, p. 23; *Moby-Dick*, I, 174; *Irsael Potter*, p. 163; *The Confidence Man*, p. 223; *Billy Budd*, p. 315). He repeats Goethe's "See Naples, and—then die!" from the Italian letters (*Poems*, p. 384), and Dr. Sundermann has discovered a similarity between Goethe's "Mohamets Gesang" and Melville's poem "The Muster" (*Poems*, pp. 108–9), written in 1865. Following an argument in *Clarel* (II, 12–13) turning upon the Christian concept of Heaven as a haven for the oppressed, the theme of love as presented in the Sermon on the Mount, and evil in human nature, Melville remarks: "We've touched a theme / From which the club and lyceum swerve, / Nor Herr von Goethe would esteem." Here is reflected the popular American conception of Goethe as a worldly, hedonistic pagan, characterized by Pierre as a "gold-laced virtuoso" and an "inconceivable coxcomb" (*Pierre*, pp. 421–22; but see *Moby-Dick*, II, 119).

Goethe's claim that he found the "Talismanic Secret" but proves Goethe a pretentious quack who belongs, with Plato and Spinoza, to the "guild of self-imposters" (*Pierre*, p. 290).

Hateful as he found Goethe's "pantheism," he found even more detestable his optimism: "Goethe's 'Live in the all'" leads himd to expostulate, "What nonesense!" Yet he added this postscript: "This 'all' feeling, though, there is some truth in it. You must often have felt it, lying on the grass on a warm summer's day. Your legs seem to send out shoots into the earth. . . . This is the *all* feeling. But what plays the mischief with the truth is that men will insist upon the universal application of a temporary feeling or opinion."—Julian Hawthorne, *op. cit.*, I, 406. Here speaks Melville the intellectual skeptic who has come to see truth as so partial or many-sided that he regards the assertion of its pretensions and even the search for it ridiculous.

263. *Op. cit.*, pp. 113 ff.

264. *Pierre*, p. 74; see also pp. 57, 235–39.

265. *Ibid.*, p. 297.

MARGARET FULLER

266. R. W. Emerson, W. H. Channing, and J. F. Clarke, *Memoirs of Margaret Fuller Ossoli* (2 vols., Boston, 1881), I, 114. Apparently no one impelled her more than the younger Carlyle to a study of the German writers, though F. H. Hedge, who had known her since 1823, encouraged her to study German and lent her books from his library. Even when she was only 13, Hedge had been impressed by her energetic, robust personality—her mind of "mighty force" and her "independent spirit full of extravagant enthusiasms for great literature." —*Ibid.*, I, 90–93. Except for her periods of residence at Groton, Mass., in 1824–1826 and 1833–1836, she moved in the social and intellectual circles of Cambridge throughout the formative years of her life. She was virtually a member of the famous Class of 1829, for she knew personally the students and professors identified with the new spirit at Harvard at that period. Besides Hedge, W. H. Channing, and J. F. Clarke among the students, Professors Everett, Ticknor, Beck, Follen, and Gräter were her friends and mentors. See Thos. W. Higginson, *Margaret Fuller Ossoli* (2nd ed., Boston, 1884), pp. 33, 44–45.

About 1832 there was a crystallization of the slowly developing tendencies toward the study of German. In that year Ripley, Parker, and Clarke were first attracted to it, and Margaret's mind was ready to approach the Germans sympathetically. As yet she had found no sphere of activity fully to engage her active mind and well-trained talents. Her first period of study of the language proved a welcome release from the confines of what she considered her circumscribed existence, compounded of what she called "a heavy weight of deceived friendship" and "a great burden of family cares." She likened her progress in German to "the rebound of a string pressed almost to bursting."— *Woman in the Nineteenth Century*, ed. by Arthur B. Fuller (new ed., Boston, 1893), pp. 358–59. She occupied herself with the masterpieces of French, Italian, Latin, and Spanish literatures as well as with the German, but to her passionate, essentially romantic nature it soon became evident that the recent German literature spoke more directly than any other.—*Memoirs*, I, 112–13. Though self-taught, she gained proficiency in German in a remarkably short time. Clarke reports in detail on her studies in 1832: within the year she has read Goethe's *Faust*, *Tasso*, *Iphigenie*, *Hermann und Dorothea*, *Die Wahlverwandtschaften*, and *Dichtung und Wahrheit*, as well as substantial portions of the works of Tieck, Körner, Novalis, Jean Paul, and Schiller. Even during 1833–1836, while living at Groton, cut off from the intellectual atmosphere of Cambridge, she went on with her studies uninterruptedly, Hedge and Clarke sending her books from their own libraries. Thus she added to her knowledge the dramas of Lessing, the poetry of Heine, Klopstock, and Uhland, and other writings of Goethe, Jean Paul, Novalis, and Schiller's chief plays, as well as the historical and critical works of Goethe and Schiller. For details see *Memoirs*, I, 108, 121–22, 130, 147–48, 150, 160, 169–70, 174, 242–44; Higginson, *op. cit.*, pp. 89–90; and Harold C. Goddard, *Studies in New England Transcendentalism* (N.Y., 1908), pp. 93–97.

267. *Memoirs*, I, 55, 127, 123—24. She got Fichte and Jacobi, but found she "could not understand [Fichte] at all, though the treatise . . . . was one intended to be popular," while Jacobi she could understand only "in details, but not in system." Even "consulting Buhle's and Tennemann's histories of philosophy and dipping into Brown, Stewart, and that class of books" proved unsatisfactory.—*Ibid.*, pp. 127–28, 165. She took up the study of De Wette and Herder as early as 1833, but she quickly learned that neither provided the "system" that answered her needs. During her residence at Groton, too, she dipped into German theology and read Eichhorn and Jahn in the original. She was attempting to study the "evidences of Christianity" at a time when, as she wrote Dr. Hedge, she "doubted the providence of God, but not the immortality of the soul." Her translating the German theologians, chiefly De Wette and Herder, for Dr. Channing one evening a week during 1836 and her reading of De Wette's *Theodore* (which she put aside without

finishing) likewise left no permanent impression on her mind.—*Ibid.*, pp. 175, 245–46; Higginson, *op. cit.*, p. 45.

268. *Memoirs*, I, 234; also pp. 236–38.

269. The instrumentality of Coleridge, as well as of her Transcendentalist friends, notably Emerson, in the formulation of her private creed is apparent. Never systematically formulating her philosophy, she did adumbrate a philosophical position that has points in common with German idealism in general and with Fichte's social ethics and Schelling's pantheistic *Identitätsphilosophie* in particular. Hers was a view which saw the universe as a continuous process, with gradations of being ranging from "nature" at the bottom through "man" to "Spirit," or" higher existence," at the summit. This universe was a kind of idealist absolute under the aspect of eternity, but from the temporal aspect it was in process of becoming. The human will was the agency that carried forward the movement from nature to Spirit, and it is Spirit that ascends through, though "not superseding nature." Margaret placed strong emphasis on the organic unity, the oneness and interdependence of parts, with which she viewed the life process. Phrases to the effect that "life and thought" are man's "means of interpreting nature and aspiring to God" point up her conception of the duty of effort and discipline in the struggle toward perfection. Nature is a system whose laws demand man's active work of "interpreting," and God, together with other "intelligences," is a transcendent principle, to which man aspires, but which is hardly encompassed by human understanding. This basically Emersonian metaphysical stucture underlies her thought throughout the period of her work in New England. See her "Credo" in *Memoirs*, I, 88–89; also pp. 77, 123, and the summary of her argument in *Woman in the Nineteenth Century*, given in Mason Wade, *Margaret Fuller, Whetstone of Genius* (N.Y., 1940), p. 289.

270. *Memoirs*, II, 85.

271. *Ibid.*, p. 74.

272. *Ibid.*, I, 342.

273. *Ibid.*, II, 133.

274. *Ibid.*, I, 340–41, 342. Changes wrought on this theme are to be found in all that Margaret wrote, especially in *Woman in the Nineteenth Century*, where the passages are too numerous to list. Poesy was "the always baffled, always reaspiring hope of the finite to compass the infinite," the "Sehnsucht of music."—*Ibid.*, p. 175. It found expression in "External Nature; the Life of Man; Literature; The Fine Arts."—*Ibid.*, I, 327. Again, in another formulation, she wrote of "Religion, in

the two modulations of poetry and music," which "descends through an infinity of waves to the lowest abysses of human nature."—*Art, Literature, and the Drama* (Boston, 1889), p. 16.

275. *Memoirs*, II, 134; see also I, 120; II, 39.

276. *Ibid.*, I, 189–91, 265, 278, 319–20.

277. *Ibid.*, p. 186.

278. One of the concrete results was her translation, made about 1841, of Schelling's famous lecture *Über das Verhältnis der bildenden Künste zur Natur*, the effect of which can be traced in the fragmentary accounts and snatches from her Conversations that we have in her memoirs (*ibid.*, I, 319–51, esp. pp. 324–27, 324–27, 340–45). Ironically enough, as Dr. Wellek observes, she might have saved herself the labor if she had recalled, from her reading of Coleridge's *Literary Remains* in 1837, that Coleridge's paraphrase in his lecture, "Poesy or Art" already made this treatise available.— René Wellek, "The Minor Transcendentalists and German Philosophy," *New Engl. Quar.*, XV, iv (Dec., 1942), 678–79. Sara Coleridge's edition of Coleridge's *Notes and Lectures* (1849) lists the parallels between Schelling and Coleridge. It is worth observing that Coleridge's "Poesy or Art" offers one of the few instances, if not the only one, where he employs the word "poesy," and insofar as Schelling stood close to the forefront of his mind at the time when he wrote the lecture, the German origin of the term seems as inescapable in his case as in Margaret's. In 1847, when Dr. Hedge published his *Prose Writers of Germany*, he used J. E. Cabot's translation of Schelling's lecture, and Margaret's remains still unpublished.

279. *Memoirs*, I, 171. In her journalistic work in New York, after the autumn of 1844, she wrote very little on philosophy, theology, or science. There is a review by her of A. v. Humboldt's *Kosmos* in the *Tribune* for July 11, 1845; a brief biographical notice of William Smith's *Memoir of J. G. Fichte*, for July 9, 1846; and in reviewing new editions of C. B. Brown's *Ormond* and *Wieland* (*Tribune*, July 25, 1846) she wrote with disarming innocence of Brown and Godwin as "born Hegelians, without the pretensions of science." Apparently she never got much beyond her earlier difficulties with Jacobi and Fichte.

280. *Memoirs*, I, 204–5.

281. Her class of beginners could read, at the end of three weeks, thirty pages at a lesson. "With more advanced pupils," she reported, "I read, in twenty-four weeks, Schiller's Don Carlos, Artists, and Song of the Bell . . . Goethe's Hermann and Dorothea, Goetz . . . Iphigenia, first part of Faust,—3 weeks of thorough study . . . as valuable to me as to them,—and

Clavigo . . . Lessing's Nathan, Minna, Emilia Galeotti [sic]; parts of Tieck's Phantasus, and nearly the whole of Richter's Titan."—*Ibid.*, I, 174.

We may be sure that this remarkable list of books was covered in twenty-four weeks ony by dint of hard work and superior stimulatioln from the teacher. Her choiçe of works, especially her emphasis on Goethe, when Goethe was widely suspect, and when the teaching of German literature was in its formative stages, is testimony to her discrimination. Her choice of Tieck and Jean Paul betrays a leaning toward romanticism which is a significant portent of later developments.

282. It was observed by many who heard her Conversations later that they were based essentially on the principles and methods of the classroom.

283. Her experiences in the liberal atmosphere of Alcott's Temple School gave her decided and advanced opinions on the teaching of foreign languages to children. She was convinced that the modern European tongues, "by familiar instruction and an *intelligent method*," might be taught "with perfect ease during the years of childhood." She felt that "much of the most precious part of short human lives is now wasted from an ignorance of what might easily be done for children, and without taking from them time they need for common life, play, and bodily growth, more than at present."—*Life Without and Life Within*, pp. 95–96, 103. It was to be several decades before the principles here enunciated got as much as recognition, much less practical introduction, in the educational system of our country.

284. For her detailed plans, see *Memoirs*, I, 168–69.

285. Higginson relates an anecdote to the effect that when Margaret's successor in Alcott's school was confronted by one of Margaret's admirers who claimed, "Miss Fuller says she *thinks* in German; do you believe it ?" the reply was, "Oh, yes! I do not doubt it; I myself dream in Cherokee."—*Op. cit.*, pp. 92–93.

Horace Greeley, writing after Margaret's death, seriously put forth the theory that her knowledge of German hampered her expression in English. The so-called German influence on her expression is not so much the result as the evidence of her sympathy for the writers of the German Romantic School. She admired Novalis and Jean Paul despite— or perhaps because of —their fondness for far-fetched metaphors, symbolism, dark allegory, and discursiveness. But readers who have trouble with her writing are oftener struggling with her thought than with her mode of expressing it. She was a subtle psychologist; her mind moved suddenly, sometimes brilliantly, from a central theme to tangential matters, and she had little gift for shaping her thoughts into any kind of external orderliness. She was often careless about grammatical structure and wrote too hastily to make the successive steps of her thought clear; she seldom revised and was too impatient to polish her expression. Poe, always a severe critic of expression, while calling her an "ill-tempered" and "detestable old maid," yet admitted his admiration for her style (*Works*, Harrison ed., XV, 79; XVII, 290, 333).

Margaret's fervent desire to visit the German scenes made vivid by her reading was frustrated first by family complications and later by her overwhelming disappointment over the sad termination of her romance with James Nathan (Gotendorf), the Hamburg merchant, whom she had met in New York. When she finally went to Europe, many things prevented her visit to Germany, among them a shift in her interests away from Germany to contemporary France, England, and Italy. So "Germanico" never set foot on German soil.

286. See her statement in the *Dial*, II, i (July, 1841), 134; also *Art, Literature, and the Drama*, p. 7; *Life Without and Life Within*, p. 96; and *Memoirs*, I, 169. It is not recorded how many of her "Conversations" were on the subject of German literature. The only indication is that "Goethe" is named as one of the topics, but undoubtedly she drew largely upon her favorite reading, even when the announced topic was "Mythology" or "Nature."—*Memoirs* I, 351.

287. Higginson, *op. cit.*, p. 141. She supported the venture with characteristic generosity and idealistic enthusiasm. She received little, if any, of the promised compensation for her work as editor of the *Dial* during its first two years or for her translation of Eckermann's *Conversations with Goethe*, published in Ripley's series.

Though German literature had found champions before Margaret Fuller wrote for the *Dial*, the proportion of material on the subject was nowhere so high as in that magazine. Roughly classifying the contents of the *Dial* as literature (including literary criticisms and book reviews), philosophy, theology, social criticism, education, the arts, and the sciences, an analysis of its four volumes shows that literature absorbed 56.3 per cent of the total space, or 317 items, aggregating 1142 pages. A breakdown of the latter, according to nationalities, reveals the following percentages of space: American, 53 per cent, or 255 items totaling 607 pages; German, 18.4 per cent (21 items, 210 pages); Greek, 5 per cent (4 items, 57 pages);

French, 4.3 per cent (3 items, 48 pages); Italian, 1.9 per cent (4 items, 21 pages); all others (Chinese, Latin, Indian, Egyptian, Spanish, etc.) receiving less than 1 per cent each.

288. *Art, Literature, and the Drama*, pp. 353–449. An excerpt (Act II, sc. 1–2) appeared in the *Dial*, II, iii (Jan., 1842), 399–407. In the Preface she made abundant apologies for the shortcomings of her translation: inexact metrical pattern, broken lines, slight omissions, condensations of thought, and a few misconstructions of idiomatic expressions; yet the work is rendered in clear, simple verse and, on the whole does justice to the structure and tone of the original. She took Coleridge's treatment of *Wallenstein* for her ideal of translation, preserving a tender conscience about the liberties permissible in the translator's art. See *Life Without and Life Within*, p. 96, and *Art, Literature, and the Drama*, pp. 355–56; also the Preface to her translation of *Günderode* (Boston, 1861), p. vi: "The exact transmission of thought seems to me the one important thing in a translation; if grace and purity of style come of themselves, it is so much gained."

289. *Memoirs*, I, 287.

290. He fidgeted under her attentions, and she smarted at his rebuffs. She tried the art of pleasing, cajolery, and what she termed "shocking familiarity"; but Emerson maintained his reserve toward the woman who asked him archly, "Who would be a goody that could be a genius?" Finally they came to an understanding: Margaret recorded having "an excellent talk: we agreed that my God was love, his truth." Thereafter she was content to accept his friendship on his, not her, terms. Wistfully she wrote, "My expectations are moderate now!"—H. R. Warfel, "Margaret Fuller and Ralph Waldo Emerson," *PMLA*, L (June, 1935), 577–78, 581–82, 589–83.

291. Higginson, *op. cit.*, p. 189.

292. As a girl, Bettina (1785–1859) had been closely associated with the Heidelberg school of romantics. In many ways she carried to an extreme the idiosyncrasies, the hyperemotionality, the pose of spiritual flirtatiousness of that group. In America she became known through her sensational, partly fictional *Goethes Briefwechsel mit einem Kinde* (1835–1837), wherein she styled herself as the admiring "child" who basked in the radiance of Goethe's company. Emerson was fond of Bettina's "pure and poetic" nature, "her wit, humor, will, and pure aspirations," and encouraged the appearance of the first American edition of *Goethe's Correspondence with a Child* in 1841 (See *Journals*, V, 145, 237–38; VI, 229; IX, 212; *Letters*, II, 208–9, 210 n., 220, 236. 254 n.; III, 77); but Mar-

garet was the first to notice Bettina, for she owned, or at least was reading, the book in May, 1838 (Emerson's *Letters*, II, 135–36). There was formed quickly a little Bettina-cult among such adherents of Transcendentalism as Lydia Maria Child, Caroline Sturgis, J. S. Dwight, G. W. Curtis, Louisa May Alcott, Mrs. Eliza Buckminster Lee, and Albert Brisbane.

293. *Die Günderode* (2 vols., Grünberg, 1840; published in America as *Günderode* (Boston, 1842); reprinted as *Günderode. Correspondence of Fräulein Günderode and Bettina von Arnim* (Boston, 1861). The first eighty-six pages are essentially the same text as that of the 1842 edition; the remainder, together with minor revisions of the first part, was translated by Mrs. Minna Wesselhoeft.

294. See Margaret's "Bettina Brentano and her Friend Günderode," *Dial*, II, iii (Jan., 1842), 351; also p. 316; *Memoirs*, II, 51–52, 58, 140.

295. *Günderode* (Boston, 1842), pp. vi–ix.

296. Margaret's life as a case history of pathological repression and sublimation is perhaps overemphasized in Katherine Anthony's *Margaret Fuller. A Psychological Biography* (N. Y., 1920), p. 37; but her translation of *Günderode* shows how strong was her predilection for the society of admiring young girls, and the overtones of homosexual attraction appear plainly in her description of Karoline. However, the formation of cults of friendship is so important a part of romantic *Weltanschauung* that Margaret's views must be examined for their literary and philosophical ramifications just as carefully as for their purely psychological significance.

297. *William Wetmore Story and his Friends* (2 vols., Boston, 1903), I 103.

298. See *Dial*, I, iv (Apr., 1841), 494–96; *Life Without and Life Within*, pp. 21–24.

299. Many of her critics emphasized her pose of literary dictator as the mark of her work. This impression gained currency because of a mannerism of hers resulting from a strong confidence in her own powers—an evidence merely that she had the courage to speak her convictions in conformity with her principles. In a time when the sensitive feelings of a Cooper or a Longfellow were distinctly discouraging to any kind of objective criticism, and when Poe was lashing out in personal pique against the objects of his irrational animus, Margaret stoutly affirmed her determination to criticize justly and fairly in the light of universal, ideal principles which she recognized.—*Life Without and Life Within*, p. 88.

300. Helen C. McMaster, *Margaret Fuller as a Literary Critic*, Univ. of Buffalo Studies, VII, iii (Dec., 1928), 42.

301. *Art, Literature, and the Drama*, p. 357.

302. *Ibid.*, p. 179. See also her "Short Essay on Critics," *Dial*, I, i (July, 1840), 5–11, a remarkably sane yet penetrating statement of the critic's function.

303. See *Memoirs*, I, 30.

304. *Ibid.*, pp. 146, 160–61. Many of her translations from Goethe were made without thought of publication, but for her pleasure or profit. They reveal much about her struggles over the fundamental questions of religion at the time when she was looking for guidance from Goethe. See F. A. Braun, *Margaret Fuller and Goethe* (N.Y., 1910), pp. 216–41, for a full discussion of her translations from Goethe; also the bibliography in Mason Wade, *The Writings of Margaret Fuller*, pp. 595–600.

In her work of introducing the masters of German literature, she could contribute little to the fame of Lessing and Schiller, already relatively well known in America. She accepted both as established classics and devoted to them a large portion of the time in her classes at Alcott's school. Of Lessing she had little to say in her critical works, though Schiller is mentioned frequently as an example of the "classical" mode of dramatic composition, linked in her mind with Sophocles and Shakespeare.— *Memoirs*, I, 121; *Art, Literature, and the Drama*, pp. 111, 210. She admired Schiller's historical writings, as well as his poetry and dramas.— *Memoirs*, I, 148, 244. His high idealism and moral fervor spoke directly to the strain of New England idealism in her, and there was much less of a struggle between her nature and his than between the more complex, worldly Goethe and herself. In 1833 she said: "I don't like Goethe as well as Schiller now. I mean, I am not so happy in reading him. That perfect wisdom and *merciless* nature seems cold, after those seducing pictures of forms more beautiful than truth."—*Memoirs*, I, 117. However, in the years following, as she trained herself in the Goethean point of view, the interest in Schiller was eclipsed by admiration for the author of *Faust* and *Meister*. See *Woman in the Nineteenth Century*, pp. 30, 44–45, 232, 342; *Art, Literature, and the Drama*, p. 90; *Life Without and Life Within*, pp. 134–135.

305. Parker and Ripley both started from a supposition that they could show him to be devout, even Christian, at heart; but they censured him on the score of morality for his personal conduct toward Friederike and Lili and for bringing Christine Vulpius into his house as his unwedded wife.

306. *Memoirs*, I, 197.

307. Other pieces of Goethe criticism include a review of *Egmont*, translated anonymously (Boston, 1841), in *Dial*, II, iii (Jan., 1842), 394; a short notice of a new translation of *Faust*, in *Dial*, II, i (July, 1841), 134; a review of George Calvert's translation of the *Correspondence between Schiller and Goethe*, in the *New York Daily Tribune* for March 14, 1845; a review of S. G. Ward's translation of Goethe's *Essays on Art* (Boston, 1845), in the *Tribune* for May 29, 1845. The last two contain ringing answers to the attacks upon Goethe by Palmer Putnam in the 1844 Phi Beta Kappa address at Harvard.

308. In the Preface to the *Conversations* she made a brilliant attack on all classes of Goethe's critics and met the charges arranged under four heads: "(1) He is not a Christian. (2) He is not an Idealist. (3) He is not a Democrat. (4) He is not Schiller." Unlike Parker, who took recourse to the "Bekenntnisse einer schönen Seele" to argue that Goethe was a Christian, Margaret readily admitted that he was a "Greek" in spirit, and as such was not to be judged by conventional Christian standards. She pointed out that this is at the bottom of his aversion "for the worship of sorrow," and that his creed is one of self-reliance and calm acceptance— hence not moralistic at all in the usual sense of the word. He is not a spiritual writer as commonly conceived; he leaves his readers to draw the moral for themselves. As to the second charge, she pointed out that his plan was never to "alter or exalt Nature," and implied that this, too, is a justifiable way of looking at the universe. As to his being aristocratic, she was not much alarmed at the appearance of acquiescence to tradition in the old sage; she explained it on the ground that an artist needs repose to do his work, and that by nature Goethe was reflective not active, and conservative because his study was the world as it is, not as he would dream it should be. For those who wanted the other there was Schiller; but one Schiller, she felt, was enough.

Margaret pleaded for "habits of more liberal criticism" and urged Goethe's detractors to "leave this way of judging from comparison or personal prejudice." Admitting that her own tastes are "often displeased by German writers, even by Goethe," she attempted an honest assessment of his achievements. She saw that he stood for perfection of the few, for a belief in man's continual effort, for thought rather than reformist action, for nature rather than providence. He was the best German stylist, an admirable critic of art and literature, an acute observer of human beings and of external nature. His mind saw well the individuality of character and the universality of thought. On the negative side, she admitted she was disturbed— as were many—by his aversion to pain and by the isolation of his heart. And on the point of structure, she admitted that some of his later works fell short of the masterly handling shown in the works of his classical period (pp. xviii–xxi).

309. *Dial*, I, iii (Jan., 1841), 240–74; also *Life Without and Life Within*, pp. 13–22.

310. *Ibid.*, p. 14.

311. *Ibid.*, p. 20. Though "he did not in one short life complete his circle," we cannot in this world where so few men have in any degree redeemed their inheritance, "neglect a nature so rich and so manifestly progressive" (p. 15). She admits that in the "Lili-Episode" he was "'right as a genius, but wrong as a character.'" She disposes of the oft-repeated charge of his Epicureanism by showing the difference between "calm self-trust" and the imputed "selfish indifference." Thus she sets the question of his importance quite apart from the question of his spiritualism. Thus she taught Emerson and the Transcendentalists (and eventually the more sensitive or squeamish moralistic critics in the ranks of the conservatives) a point of view which would take them out of their parochialism into the full current of modern life.

Her point of view is elaborated in subsequent discussions, notably the essay "Goethe" in the *Dial*, II, i (July, 1841), 1–41, which is perhaps the most impressive of them all. She moved through his several periods with the assurance that results from thorough study, able to explain the significance of each work for the life of the author and his age. Werther represents a phase of his youth that he soon overcame; Faust of *Faust I* represents the highest idealistic striving that Goethe ever showed; *Meister* is a continuation of *Faust*; the *Wanderjahre* is an indispensable second part of the *Lehrjahre*, wherein the analysis of Wilhelm is completed. The portraits of Marianne, Philine, Theresa, Natalie, and Makarie are symbolical of the stages of education through which the hero must pass. Makarie emerges as the outstandingly spiritual figure, the one who touches most closely the high idealism of Margaret's nature and the one where Goethe's "simple soberness" is abandoned for a time to "glow with the central fire" (*ibid.*, p. 43). In a few paragraphs she absolves the *Wahlverwandtschaften* of charges of coldness and immorality; she reads this work as one that is "moral in its outward effect, and religious even to piety in its spirit." "Holy" Ottilie is a person of "saintly sweetness" (*ibid.*, pp. 48, 49), and the work is so carefully executed, so richly and delicately wrought, as to command the highest praise: "It is a work of art! At last I understand that world

within a world, that ripest fruit of human nature, which is called art."—*Ibid.*, p. 50. Following a similar analysis of *Iphigenie auf Tauris*, she begs her reader to "enter into his higher tendency, thank him for such angels as Iphigenie, whose simple truth mocks at all his wise 'Beschränkungen.'"

In this spirit of enthusiastic enjoyment of his poetic art she presented Goethe in her "Conversations" in Boston and her essays in the *Dial*. Thus she helped Emerson to read Goethe with a less clouded vision and brought him round from an attitude of disdain to the point where he could make Goethe the writer-type in his *Representative Men*. See *Carlyle-Emerson Correspondence*, II, 114; *Memoirs*, I, 242–43.

312. She was, of course, familiar with Emerson's preachments on this score; but his self-reliance, as she interpreted what he said regarding woman's proper sphere in general and how he conducted himself with respect to her in particular, did not appear to extend equally to men and women. See Warfel, *loc. cit.*, pp. 592–93.

313. *Life Without and Life Within*, esp. pp. 298–99.

314. *Memoirs*, I, 149, 266.

315. See Higgenson, *op. cit.*, p. 289; also p. 284; *Memoirs*, I, 167.

316. *Memoirs*, I, 160–61.

317. On the matter of her appreciation of nature, for example, she stood nearer to the romantics than to Goethe. Though Goethe taught her much in the way of careful observation of nature, and his Spinozistic pantheism had something in common with her feeling for the God immanent in nature, his *Farbenlehre* appealed to her not because it was a scientific, empirical study but because she could interpret it in its "mystical significance."—Higginson, *op. cit.*, p. 101. Like Novalis, she looked on the forms of nature symbolically and mystically, and had no sympathy with the "botanizing, geologizing, and dissecting" of the natural scientist.—*Memoirs*, I, 263.

318. The period of her greatest enthusiasm for Richter was her years at Groton. She prescribed his *Titan*, a most difficult and obscure book for school children, to be read by her advanced class in Alcott's school. The reading of Jean Paul let loose the torrents of sentiment within her, and she loved him deeply.—*Ibid.*, I, 130. *Titan*, she said, is a "noble work, and fit to raise a reader into that high serene of thought where pedants cannot enter."—*Ibid.*, pp. 169–70. By 1833 she had written the poems on Richter that she published in the *Dial* in 1840. In them she celebrated him as the "Poet of Nature," a fanciful, delicate painter of scenes in

the gorgeous style of Titian, a man "with Raphael's dignity" and "celestial love." Is there in Richter "a want of order," as his critics say? No, "not of *system* in its highest sense," for he has the order and plan of the universe itself, being coequal to it and its perfect mirror. "Nature's wise temple and the azure dome / Have plan enough for the free spirit's home!" This is the effusive, girlish language with which she praised the romantic subjectivity, sublime striving, and moral earnestness of an archromantic.

319. See Mason Wade, *op. cit.*, pp. 215–17, and K. Anthony, *op. cit.*, p. 155.

320. *Memoirs*, I, 118–19; also pp. 120–21, 123.

321. Note her mystical flower-fantasies, with their peculiar hints at a doctrine of the transmigration of souls: "Yuca Filamentosa," *Dial*, II, iii (Jan., 1842), 286–88; "Magnolia of Lake Pontchartrain," *ibid.*, I, iii (Jan., 1841), 299–305; also her poems on the passionflower (*Memoirs*, I, 111), the "Dahlia, rose and heliotrope" (*Life Without and Life Within*, p. 367), "The flower and the Pearl" (*ibid.*, p. 351), and "Lines" (*ibid.*, p. 375). They are filled with symbolism derived mainly from Novalis ("die blaue Blume"), from *Faust* ("the mothers"), and from remoter neo-Platonic sources. See Higginson, *op. cit.*, pp. 96–97, 99, 305; *Memoirs*, II, 95. She was especially fond of the symbol of the carbuncle of *Heinrich von Ofterdingen*. See *Woman in the Nineteenth Century*, p. 343, and *Memoirs*, II, 95.

322. She explained these phenomena as evidences of the overdevelopment of the spiritual faculties. By no means unduly obsessed with the subject, she took the common-sense attitude that the material and spiritual parts of man's nature "should be in equipoise." She sought a rationale for the phenomena of second sight and prophecy, which, to a woman of her unusal gifts and intuitive powers, seemed an undeniable fact of her existence. In a poet with thorough training and artistic organization, she felt that these gifts of clairvoyance could be transformed into true prophetic power, but she doubted that there was much of higher meaning in the life of the seeress described by Kerner.— *Summer on the Lakes*, p. 164.

323. See her poem, "Sub Rosa Crux," *Memoirs*, II, 114.

324. She understood well what Goethe meant by "das Dämonische"; indeed, she divined that she was more under the power of the "magnetic fluid" than he—that she was better fitted than he for the role of prophet of the spiritual kingdom. "With me, for weeks and months, the daemon works his will."—*Memoirs*, I, 224–26;

see also pp. 218, 222, 284, and K. Anthony, *op. cit.*, pp. 52–53.

325. "Romaic and Rhine Ballads," *Dial*, III, ii (Oct., 1842), 137–80.

326. See *Woman in the Nineteenth Century*, pp. 58–59.

327. *Dial*, III, ii (Oct., 1842), 179; *Art, Literature, and the Drama*, p. 333; Higginson, *op. cit.*, pp. 131, 294.

328. Among other Germans that occupied her attention, Theodor Körner appealed to her romantic interest in medievalism and nationalism. See her essay on Körner in the *Western Messenger*, IV, v (Jan., 1838), 306–11, 369–75, and *Memoirs*, II, 252. She admired Ferdinand Freiligrath, the exiled poet of political liberty (see *At Home and Abroad*, p. 180). Uhland and Heine figure little in her writings; her projected papers on Novalis and on Tieck never appeared in print. On the subject of Fouqué, she wrote a review of the *Undine* for the *Tribune* (Apr. 4, 1845). Klopstock, whom she studied early, is the subject of a sentimental sketch "Meta" (*Dial*, Jan., 1841), one of her weakest performances—one in which she gave a falsely sentimental impression of Klopstock.

329. Her first response went out to Haydn and Handel, well represented in the great choral concerts of the 30's. After 1838, when she came within easy reach of Boston, she heard many performances of classical works by Beethoven, Mozart, and others, and the realization broke upon her that a great new cultural force was opening up for her in the musical art. When, in 1841, the epoch-making Boston Academy music series presented the Beethoven symphonies, the Boston community felt that Beethoven was attuned to the currents of idealism then stirring New England. Some of the younger Transcendentalists, notably J. S. Dwight, supported the vogue vigorously and became converts to the kind of faith that seemed to speak out of Beethoven's great measures. Margaret devoted space in the *Dial* to urging public support of the concerts. The Beethoven vogue coincided with the high point of the Transcendentalist enthusiasm; after 1844 the Beethoven symphonies were dropped from the programs.

330. *Woman in the Nineteenth Century*, pp. 190–91; *Memoirs*, I, 343. In her article on Goethe (*Dial*, July, 1841) she cited Beethoven as the example of the artist who succeeded where the poet failed—the one figure with whom she dared to reproach Goethe: "We pardon thee, Goethe,—but thee, Beethoven, we revere, for thou hast maintained the worship of the Manly, the Permanent, the True!"—

Life Without and Life Within, pp. 45–47. See also *Art, Literature, and the Drama*, 224–25, for her statement of how the "spiral and undulatory movements of the beautiful creation" are best expressed in music, and how the listener finds in music "thought most clearly, because most mystically, perceived." See *Memoirs*, I, 186, 309–10, and her poem "The Land of Music," *At Home and Abroad*, p. 107. Margaret came to the hearing of Beethoven with her curiosity aroused from her reading of Bettina's *Correspondence with a Child*. Even in Germany, Bettina's sympathetic appreciation did much for the recognition of Beethoven; in America there was formed something like a Beethoven cult among Margaret's friends, including Dwight, Lydia Maria Child, and the poet Cranch. In private correspondence these enthusiasts fell into the jargon of musical terminology which they playfully employed to describe emotions and feelings: the "flat seventh," "the diapason of the soul," etc., in obvious imitation of Bettina. As for Margaret, she had always been fond of such words as "harmony," "dissonance," "rhythm," "chord," and "melody." Now she yielded more and more to the temptation to write in musical metaphors and thus to becloud still further her none too clear style. For examples, see *Woman in the Nineteenth Century*; Mason Wade, *op. cit.*, pp. 289–90; *Memoirs*, II, 59–60, 99–100; Emerson's *Letters*, I, 280.

331. *Memoirs*, I, 275.

332. Emerson showed a sharp perception of the way in which her partly frustrated and thwarted impulses found their "compensation" and their "solace" in art, poetry, and especially music. See her letter, written one evening on returning from the symphony, addressed to Beethoven, confiding her desperate longing— reminiscent of Bettina's adulatory letters (*Memoirs*, I, 232–34).

333. See Emerson's *Letters*, II, 239 (Nov. 24, 1839).

334. In her earlier career she had been relatively indifferent to the organized reform movements of the day, especially toward the slavery issues and the question of socialism, though she was active in the cause of women's rights from the first. It was traditional in her family to stand for democratic Jeffersonianism against Bostonian Federalism, and she was too strong an individualist to entertain the thought of residing at Brook Farm. Like Emerson, she wished the reformers well, but was not convinced that the time was ripe for building a Utopia. After 1844, she began to devote more space in her columns to articles on political developments and social experiments, here and abroad, and especially in Germany; and she welcomed the advent of the New York *Deutsche Schnellpost* as the organ of the German-Americans in this country. When she saw at first hand the turmoil of Italy and the evils there of oppression, she was stirred to take an active part in political affairs.

335. *Memoirs*, I, 213.

336. However important Goethe and the Romantic School were to her, still she recognized that the enthusiasm of regenerate Unitarianism which went by the Transcendental name was basically of New England origin, and she kept throughout her characteristic American faith in heroic, unbending idealism. But insofar as American Transcendentalism is a part of the broader movement toward romanticism that characterizes the early decades of the nineteenth century, it was inevitable that some American thinkers would become aware of the universal nature of the movement. Margaret was one of those.

337. This inheritance originated in the occasional visits that she made to Brook Farm, where the young Transcendentalists gathered to sing, read poetry, enact plays, and hold discussions. Here she often led the conversation, heard the amateur musical performances of Cranch and Dwight, and encouraged their translating the lyrics of Goethe and Schiller. In this carefree, sociable, irrepressibly joyous group of talented and congenial spirits there was engendered a new romantic approach toward life and art which in several cases dominated these men for the better part of the century and in some cases fed directly into the forces that culminated in the Genteel Tradition. In the beginning, it was the *Romantische Schule* transplanted to America, isolated and scorned for the most part by the average citizen as well as by the theological and social stalwarts of New England. Yet it was the starting-point for an important tradition in American art and music as well as in literature and criticism. The communal character of so many of the translation projects carried out by these men is noteworthy. Ripley, John Weiss, J. E. Cabot, C. T. Brooks, and others were represented in Hedge's *Prose Writers of Germany*, while Bancroft, Margaret Fuller, Clarke, G. W. Haven, N. L. Frothingham, Hedge, and C. P. Cranch, W. H. Channing contributed to Dwight's *Select Minor Poems*. Goethe's *Autobiography* was prepared principally by Godwin, but parts were completed by Dwight and Dana. Three men collaborated in the *Memoirs* of Margaret Fuller. The *Dial*, the *Western Messenger*, and Dwight's *Journal of Music* were essentially co-operative undertakings. Collaboration continued un-

abated among the St. Louis Hegelians and the later school of Concord philosophers.

MINOR MOVEMENTS AND GROUPS

338. Among others to be mentioned was Charles A. Dana, another member of the Brook Farm community, later editor of the New York *Sun*. His contribution to the excitement for German was his teaching the language (as well as Greek) in the Brook Farm school. He translated Part III of Goethe's *Autobiography*. James Elliot Cabot (1821–1903), editor, author, and biographer of Emerson, studied in Germany, wrote a notable article on Kant for the last number of the *Dial*, and provided selections from Kant and Schelling for Hedge's *Prose Writers*. J. M. Mackie, not properly a Transcendentalist, was a great admirer of Emerson and Parker. After studying at Berlin, he lived in New York as journalist and author, and in 1845 published a biography of Leibnitz, based on a German work by Guhrauer, besides writing many reviews and notices of translations and of current German publications. William Batchelder Greene, a brilliant, dashing youth, translated some German tales for the *Dial*. Jones Very (1813–1880) was acquainted with portions of the writings of Goethe and Schiller, but there is little to suggest any direct influence of German writers upon him. Similarly, W. E. Channing the younger (1818–1901), though much in the company of Emerson, S. G. Ward, Thoreau, and later, Sanborn, one of the leading contributors to the *Dial*, the *Present*, and the *Harbinger*, and inevitably subjected to a variety of German influences, remained on the periphery of the German furor.

339. In a portion of her journal labeled "My Sentimental Period," she describes how she was caught up in the Bettina fad, Bettina's book inducing in many girls of Louisa May's generation a desire to form secret ideal attachments with men far older than themselves. As Bettina had worshipped Goethe, so she adored Emerson, writing letters to him that were never sent, leaving flowers on his doorstep, and singing Mignon's song under his window "in very bad German."—Ednah D. Cheney, *Louisa May Alcott. Her Life, Letters, and Journals* (Boston, 1890), pp. 57–59, 345.

340. Late in life she wrote, "R. W. E. gave me Goethe's works at fifteen, and they have been my delight ever since."—*Ibid.*, p. 398; see also pp. 208, 351.

341. *Ibid.*, pp. 101–2, 104, 122, 123, 160, 162.
342. *Ibid.*, pp. 104–5.
343. *Ibid.*, pp. 157, 165.
344. *Ibid.*, p. 166.

345. See Katherine Anthony, *Louisa May Alcott* (N.Y., 1938), p. 156. While reading proof on *Moods*, she planned "a story of two men something like Jean Paul and Goethe, only more every-day people," but the fate of *Moods* dashed her hopes of utilizing such material, and the book as planned was never written.— Cheney, *op. cit.*, pp. 160, 162, 265. Although she tried to teach herself, so that she could say, "I nearly died of German," she made little headway. In 1865 she missed an opportunity to go to Europe because she "spoke neither French nor German"; but before the year was out another opportunity came to attend an invalid on a tour abroad. She visited Germany, and in her journal she described the "lovely voyage up the Rhine" from Cologne to Mainz, filling her head with pictures, she said, to "last all my life." At Frankfurt she gloried in the literary associations of that city, particularly those touching Goethe.—*Ibid.*, pp. 160, 162, 167, 173, 175, 182, 262.

346. *Ibid.*, pp. 196–98, 201, 261, 268, 273, 275, 314, 320–21, 336, 346, 347, 352, 357, 359.

347. For examples see *Little Women* (Boston, 1904), pp. 150, 347–49, 365, 373, 384, 386; *Little Men* (Boston, 1903), pp. 19, 29; *Work* (Boston, 1904), p. 225; *Jo's Boys* (Boston, 1886), pp. 324–25; and the titlepage of *Morning Glories*.

348. Cheney, *op. cit.*, p. 296.
349. *Ibid.*, pp. 289–90, 379.

350. Even before he arrived in Cambridge, he had studied "some German" with an old Swiss gentleman "who taught a very bad pronunciation."—*The Life and Letters of C. P. Cranch*, by Leonora Cranch Scott (Boston and N.Y., 1917), p. 19.

351. *Ibid.*, pp. 24–46 *passim*.

352 Frederick DeWolfe Miller, *Christopher P. Cranch and His Caricatures of New England Transcendentalism* (Cambridge, Mass., 1951).

353. *Life and Letters*, p. 60. Cranch never was able to achieve settled religious convictions. He wrote much poetry for the *Western Messenger* but contributed little to the discussion of theological questions; such essays as he wrote were more poetical than controversial. See his "False Reasoning of the Trinitarians," *Western Messenger*, May, 1837; "Every Child a Unitarian," *ibid.*, Dec., 1837; "Modern Platonism," *ibid.*, Dec., 1838; "Dreams," *ibid.*, June, 1839. Inspired by a reading of Carlyle and Jouffroy and by the personal influence of Emerson and W. H. Channing, he was vaguely determined to stand with them; but when, in 1840, his father inquired to know whether his son were turning Transcendentalist, Cranch replied that he was little interested in the "cold, barren"

system of idealism as propounded by Kant and Fichte, adding that the "quite opposite" philosophy constructed by Cousin and Jouffroy seemed to him to have "far greater recommendations."—*Life and Letters*, p. 50.

354. *Ibid.*, p. 76. Several of his poems echo the characteristic Transcendentalist attitude toward music. See especially his ode read at the annual dinner of the Harvard Musical Association, Boston, January 27, 1874, and his ode to the memory of Margaret Fuller, wherein he shows a complete sympathy for her theories of music; also the sonnet "Beethoven's Fifth Symphony."—*The Bird and the Bell* (Boston, 1875), pp. 235–37, 163–73, and *Ariel and Caliban* (Boston and N.Y., 1887), p. 154.

355. *Life and Letters*, p. 300.

356. Dwight included one in his *Select Minor Poems*, and Brooks printed two from Goethe in *German Songs and Ballads* (1842). His version of Heine's "Lorelei" appeared in *Folk Songs*, edited by Palmer in 1861. He published a good deal in contemporary journals, where a careful search would probably bring to light others of his widely scattered publications. See, for example, H. M. Haertel, *op. cit.*, nos. 33 and 1215, and B. Q. Morgan, *op. cit.*, C47.

357. "He was intimately identified with almost every movement made in behalf of music for nearly a half-century in [Boston]. . . . His work was unique and was never likely to be repeated on the part of any interpreter of music."—George W. Cooke, *J. S. Dwight, Brook Farmer, Editor, and Critic of Music. A Biography* (Boston, 1898), Preface, p. xi.

The son of a free-thinking Boston physician, Dwight went through the Boston Latin School and Harvard College, graduating in 1832. While studying in the Divinity School, he was active in the Pierian Sodality and practiced in instrumental ensembles with Cranch and other young musicians. That music was equally strong as theology in his interests is suggested by his choice of a topic for his dissertation, "The Proper Character of Poetry and Music for Public Worship" (1836). He took a leading part in the formation of the Harvard Musical Association in 1837. From small beginnings, the Association was destined to grow into one of great influence in the cultural life of New England. Since 1815 Boston had had its Handel and Haydn Society, inspired and organized by Gottlieb Graupner, a German-born music teacher and publisher. Between 1839 and 1841 the city had a full-fledged *Musical Magazine*, edited by Theodore Hach, a German cellist. Yet before 1841, despite the founding of the Academy of Music in 1833, there had been little development of orchestral music, and the great

symphonic literature of the German school was unknown. By 1841 the Academy, which up to that time had devoted itself primarily to sacred vocal music, oratorios and choruses, was prevailed upon to perform the larger symphonic works of Beethoven, Mendelssohn, Mozart, Haydn, and Weber. These are the concerts to which the Brook Farmers, according to their own reports, responded with ready and receptive enthusiasm. In Beethoven they heard a spiritual message of soaring idealism that found no adequate statement in other music. It spoke of the deepest convictions and insights within them—of "ideas of spiritual freedom, of self-reliance, of the dignity of human nature, of social justice, equal opportunities for all, [of] a common birthright in the beautiful." See Dwight's article, "Music as a Means of Culture," *Atl. Monthly*, XXVI, clv (Sept., 1870), 321–22; see also p. 323. Thus the growth of interest in Beethoven's music went parallel with the most outspoken expression of idealistic striving.

Boston became an important musical center, visited by many famous European soloists—among them Ole Bull, Vieuxtemps, and Jenny Lind. For a time after 1849 the Germania Musical Society, a "miniature but model orchestra from Germany," performed with a standard of excellence unknown in America up to that time. The Harvard Musical Association sponsored chamber music performances in 1844–1850. One important event was the performance of Schiller's *Song of the Bell*, set to music by Romberg and provided with English text by S. A. Eliot.—J. S. Dwight, "History of Music in Boston," in Justin Winsor (ed.), *Memorial History of Boston* (Boston, 1880–1881), IV, 424, 428–31.

358. George Bancroft, Margaret Fuller, J. F. Clarke, W. H. Channing, F. H. Hedge, N. L. Frothingham, G. W. Haven, C. P. Cranch, and C. T. Brooks together provided 35 of the 120 poems in the volume. Of the other translation projects which Dwight planned, he published only Part IV of Goethe's *Dichtung und Wahrheit* for the Godwin-Dana volume of 1846, but he assisted Mrs. Eliza B. Lee in her work of translating Jean Paul.

359. Though his friends Lowell and Curtis did their best to find a publisher for his lectures, no editor could be found who would risk bringing out so strange and incomprehensible a book. Yet his Transcendental friends were as enthusiastic as the rest of the world was cool. They saw him as a prophet inspired and listened to his mystical interpretations of the symbolic values in tones and voices. The New York *Tribune*, as might be expected, welcomed his lectures warmly, but some of his audience

thought him a little naive and ineffectual, albeit most lovable and earnest. "His whole life," said Amelia Russell, "seemed one dream of music; and I do not think that he was ever fully awake to all the harsh grating of this outer world."—Cooke, *op. cit.*, pp. 61-62, 74, 78-80, 106, 118-19.

360. *Ibid.*, pp. 103-8.

361. He fought for a radical change in the selection of music to be used in church services. Strongly committed to the principle that music is a universal language free of the fetters of doctrine or dogma, he sought to break down the artifical distinctions between "sacred" and "profane" music, between hymn and song, and between chant (or mass) and hymn. He and Cranch waged a sharp battle with the Unitarians over the propriety of introducing portions of the mass, on the one hand, and secular music, on the other, into Protestant services. As early as 1839 Cranch had published in the *Western Messenger* a defense of introducing a hymn to the Virgin Mary at a concert held in the Cincinnati Presbyterian Church. Cranch argued that the words of the hymn were not used with any intent to insult the Protestant who objected to ritualistic forms, but that as *art* the words with their appropriate music might still be worth listening to.—*West. Mess.*, VI, v (Mar., 1839), 339-41. Dwight introduced masses and secular music into the services of Channing's Religious Union of Associationists. When some members objected, he defended the practice on the ground that music as such ought not to be associated with any particular set of doctrines, "for music is more catholic than all the churches,—the faithful, many-sided servant of the human heart; and whatsoever is good music is a harmony and help to what is most religious, loving, and profound in human souls, whether it was born on Catholic on heretic or even on heathen soil."—Cooke, *op. cit.*, p. 133.

362. He felt that "music must have some most intimate connection with the social destiny of man," that it is the popular art *par excellence*, and therefore especially adapted to American society. It is "a true conservative element, in which Liberty and Order are both fully typed and made beautifully perfect in each other. A free people must be rhythmically educated in the whole tone and temper of their daily life . . . to be fit for freedom. . . . This artistic sentiment allies itself with our progressive energies. . . ."—*Ibid.*, pp. 151-52.

363. He published articles in translation by the outstanding authorities of the day, such as Schumann, Liszt, and Wagner. One important feature was the European correspondence

written by Alex. W. Thayer, the biographer of Beethoven. In 1840-1851 he prepared a translation of Oulibicheff's biography of Mozart, for which he found no publisher. After 1859 his translations from the German were almost wholly limited to musical publications. He translated the words of Bach's St. Matthew Passion music, the *Lieder* of Schubert, Schumann, and many others, including Heine's *Buch der Lieder* as set to music by Schumann. A longer task was the translation of M. Wohlfahrt's *Guide to Musical Composition.*—*Ibid.*, pp. 155-56, 189, 227.

364. A recent study of Higginson is Howard W. Hintz's "T. W. Higginson: Disciple of the Newness," diss., New York University, 1939.

365. He got into all the reform movements, including Frothingham's Free Religious Association, vigorously upheld the antislavery tradition of his family, ran for Congress, resisted the Fugitive Slave Law, gained prominence in the Civil War as the first commander of a Negro regiment for the North, and in his later years settled down to a comfortable existence as author, historian, and essayist.—*Cheerful Yesterdays* (Boston and N.Y., 1900), pp. 85-128 *passim.*

366. See his "Decline of the Sentimental," in *The New World and the New Book* (Boston, 1892), pp. 178ff.

367. "An American Temperament," *ibid.*, p. 25.

368. *Ibid.*, pp. 8-9; "Literature as an Art," *Atlantic Essays* (Boston, 1871), pp. 25ff., 32, 35; and *Cheerful Yesterdays*, pp. 188-89.

369. Brooks came from a family of old Massachusetts Puritan stock. He entered Harvard in 1828, having as classmates John Dwight and Samuel Osgood and as collegemates Charles Sumner, J. L. Motley, O. W. Holmes, and others of the famous class of '29. Follen and Beck initiated him into the German language. Follen's influence, among the many factors that go to explain his interest in German, was paramount. A distinguished student of languages, Brooks was offered a tutorship in Greek, but he entered the Divinity school instead and studied along with such later Transcendentalists as Bartol, Osgood, Cranch, and Dwight. In this company he continued his German alongside his theological studies. The best treatments of Brooks are C. W. Wendte, *Poems, Original and Translated by C. T. Brooks. With a Memoir by C. W. Wendte*, selected and edited by W. P. Andrews (Boston, 1885) and Camillo von Klenze, *C. T. Brooks, Translator from the German, and The Genteel Tradition* (Boston and London, 1937).

370. Including Bürger, Hölty, Schiller,

Goethe, Rückert, and Klopstock. A few of the poems included were contributed by Dwight, Frothingham, Cranch, Sarah Whitman, and Longfellow.

371. Brooks's work was well received by students of German literature on both sides of the Atlantic. Carlyle congratulated him for his "perfect accuracy" in rendering Jean Paul. Among the Germans who praised his efforts were Freiligrath and Auersperg, with both of whom he exchanged occasional letters. In 1865–1866 he traveled to Europe, met scholars and writers in many European countries, including Germany, and was pleased to find that in many instances his fame as a translator had preceded him.—Wendte, *op. cit.*, pp. 55, 79, 87; von Klenze, *op. cit.*, pp. 102–14.

Among translation projects undertaken in his later years were works of lesser authors whose fame on the whole has not persisted beyond their own time (for details see von Klenze's excellent study). There were two works of fiction by Berthold Auerbach—a portion of *Dorfgeschichten* (1877) and *Dichter und Kaufmann* (1877), Rückert's long, intricate, and obscure poem *Die Weisheit des Brahmanen* (1882); Leopold Schefer's *Laienbrevier* (1875); and several works from the field of humorous literature, for the appreciation and translation of which Brooks possessed special aptitudes. For a list of translations that still remain in manuscript, see von Klenze, pp. 100–101.

372. He found European life much to his liking; the thought of returning to "naked America" became repugnant to him, and for a time he made frequent trips across the Atlantic. He traversed Germany, Austria, and Switzerland several times, studied French, Italian, and German. The last he considered "the most unmusical language of Babel" and the most difficult. See H. A. Beers, *Nathaniel Parker Willis* (Boston, 1885), pp. 122–23; *Pencillings by the Way* (2nd ed., London, 1839), pp. 138–63 *passim*.

373. *Famous Persons and Places* (N.Y., 1854), pp. 385–91. The titles of *Fun-Jottings or Laughs I have Taken a Pen To* (1853) and *The Rag-Bag, a Collection of Ephemera* (1859) are indicative of their contents.

374. See Richmond C. Beatty, *Bayard Taylor, Laureate of the Gilded Age* (Norman, Okla., 1936). An illuminating but, unfortunately, still unpublished study is Professor John T. Krumpelmann's dissertation, "Bayard Taylor as Literary Mediator between Germany and America," Harvard University, 1924.

An American in point of view, tastes, and opinions, Taylor was also an adopted citizen of Germany. Gotha was his second home, for which he exhibited a deep and abiding love just as German was his second tongue. His second wife was the daughter of the famous astronomer Hansen; he lived for long periods among the German people, knew intimately the German landscape from the Baltic to the Rhine; and finally he was chosen to fill the post of American Minister in Berlin in 1878.

Reared outside the orbit of the New England tradition, he stood halfway between the "Bohemianism" of New York and the "Brahminism" of Boston. As one who took his origin in Chester County, Pennsylvania, in the Middle Atlantic region, it was perhaps all the easier for Taylor to become the spokesman for the America of the postwar decades. Nor did he undergo the normalizing process of attending college, but forced his way upward through hack-writing and reporting, relying on his ample natural gifts and hard work. He trained his sensitive mind in observation and careful, even photographic, reporting, thus absorbing immediately the American scene developing around him.

Little in Taylor's ancestry or early life points to either his enthusiasm for authorship or his interest in Germany. Though both grandmothers were of South German descent—typical representatives of the race of Pennsylvania-Dutch—the English Quaker element in the family predominated. As a child he was quick to learn and to compose verses. He read all the popular magazines and devoured all the novels, histories, geographies, travel books, and volumes of poetry which the circulating library of Kennett Square afforded.—Marie Hansen Taylor and H. E. Scudder, *Life and Letters of Bayard Taylor* (2 vols., Boston, 1885), I, 5, 9–10; R. C. Beatty, *op. cit.*, pp. 2–4. Irving's sketches and tales, Willis' letters, and Howitt's *Rural Life in Germany* whetted his appetite for travel abroad, particularly Germany. Thus early, authorship and travel were linked in his mind. As a youth he took a printer's apprenticeship for the dual purpose of learning the literary business and laying up money for a jaunt to Europe. At the age of 19 he made his plans, consulted travelers and friends, and set off on a twenty-four–dollar passage to Europe. Additional funds came partly from the proceeds of a volume of poems he had printed and partly from advances granted by publishers and editors, notably Horace Greeley, of the *Tribune*, in return for which he contracted to send travel letters from the continent. He accompanied his cousin Franklin Taylor, going to Germany to study, and he hoped to remain abroad a year, possibly two.

Taylor knew practically no German when he

embarked, but certain initial factors inclined him to Germany. Greeley's assignment, rather indefinite, to be sure, called for letters on German life and society: "If the letters are good," promised the editor, "you shall be paid for them, but don't write until you know something."—*Life and Letters*, I, 38. He decided to settle down in Germany and really live among the people. Greeley, he knew, was exacting.

375. As early as November, 1844, in a letter to his mother, he reported good progress in the "glorious" language and a determination to master it and its literature. By the following May he could say: "I was so good a German that I was often not suspected of being a foreigner."—John R. Schultz (ed.), *The Unpublished Letters of Bayard Taylor in the Huntington Library* (San Marino, Calif., 1937), pp. 8–9; *Life and Letters*, I, 44. His first reading was in Hauff, Uhland, and Schiller; he took pleasure in visiting the tombs, literary shrines, and former homes of Germany's famous authors; he called on Mendelssohn, Freiligrath, Rückert, and Gerstäcker, traveled through the Harz mountains in Goethe's footsteps, and saw Schiller's room in Gohlis.—Beatty, *op. cit.*, p. 38; *Views Afoot* (Phila., 1889), p. 149.

376. For details see *Life and Letters*, I, 222, 342; *Critical Essays and Literary Notes* (N.Y., 1880), pp. 92–111; *At Home and Abroad, First Series*, pp. 340–41.

377. The book contains a detailed account of a trip from Heidelberg to Nuremberg through the Odenwald, a picture of the "panorama of the Upper Danube," and a "walk through the Thuringian Forest." Taylor tarried at the Wartburg to recall the literary associations of Heinrich von Ofterdingen, Walther von der Vogelweide, Wolfram von Eschenbach, Martin Luther, and the brothers Grimm. Here as much as in the earlier book, he indulged in flights of lyrical landscape description, handling his themes in a masterly manner. He saw his beloved Thuringia and the Black Forest through the eyes of an ardent lover of nature, and was poet enough to find phrases adequate to convey his sense of the natural beauty of this "green region of mountains and meadows, of tinkling herds and fairy lore."—*Life and Letters*, II, 478. There were also sketches of such literary personages as Rückert, Gutzkow, the Dresden Circle, Alex. von Humboldt, and finally of literary Weimar, with its memories of Goethe and Schiller.

378. Other notable sketches are "The Little Land of Appenzell" (German Switzerland), "In the Teutoburger Forest," partly reminiscent of his earlier visit to Freiligrath, and "The Kyffhäuser and its Legends," the story of the sleeping Barbarossa.

379. The feeling expressed is of a piece with the general ambition among the genteel poets to prepare translations of the world's masterpieces and thereby to instruct and elevate a nation of cultural sluggards. Taylor's *Faust* is one of a series that includes Longfellow's Dante, Bryant's Homer, Cranch's Virgil, Higginson's Epictetus, and G. H. Palmer's *Odyssey*.

380. *Life and Letters*, II, 517. His remarkable memory was a serviceable aid in the work and so was his unexcelled facility in the German language. Once started, he neglected nothing to make his work *the* authoritative English *Faust*. He studied all the scholarship on the poem and spent much time in Europe gathering materials on Goethe's life and personality at first hand (see *Life and Letters*, II, 464, 493, 506). He carefully studied the methods and shortcomings of his predecessors, and set himself a high standard of fidelity in translating (see his letter to W. H. Furness, *ibid.*, II, 493). Despite his feeling that he was equal to the task, he was to discover sometimes that he had to "break his head in the hunt for words." It was a "heart-rending yet intensely fascinating labor."—*Ibid.*, II, 537.

On completing the first draft, he sent the manuscript to Longfellow and Lowell for criticism and received their heartiest encouragement. The launching of the poem was a great *coup* for the publisher, and simultaneous publication was arranged in America, England, and Germany. The numerous reviews were almost uniformly full of congratulation and praise. In honor of the publication Fields fêted Taylor with an elaborate dinner, attended by all the notables; only Emerson and Whittier sent regrets, but congratulated the author by letter. The newly won honors were so exhilarating that he immediately determined upon another great work devoted to German literature—lives of Goethe and Schiller. But the sale of *Faust* did not reach expectations. Though "accepted in England, Germany, and America as much the best," as Taylor said, at the end of two years the book returned the writer only $500.

381. Differences over problems of interpretation arose as soon as the work appeared. See Taylor's correspondence with R. H. Chittenden in *Life and Letters*, II, 517–20. Taylor's performance has been subjected to severe criticism in the study by Mrs. J. C. S. Haskell, *Bayard Taylor's Translation of Goethe's Faust*, Columbia diss. (N. Y., 1908). See also Morgan, *op. cit.*, p. 166.

382. For details see A. H. Smyth, *Bayard Taylor* (Boston, 1896), p. 195; *Life and Letters*, II, 567, 697–98, 701. The entire series was

published posthumously as *Studies in German Literature* (N.Y., 1879).

Judged from the position of historical or critical scholarship, none of the series is to be rated very high, for the material that Taylor used was a digest of readily available German commentaries and histories; but considered as popular lectures they were successful and of no little cultural value. He brought a lively enthusiasm to his subjects. The lectures on Goethe and on *Faust* were a wholesome corrective to the prejudice against the Goethean morality and the "incomprehensibility" of *Faust II*. Though he may have oversimplified, Taylor did succeed in conveying the idea that *Faust* was to be studied as a whole, that the second part could not be dismissed in the way that Carlyle, Lamb, Hayward, and Lewes rejected it.

383. The chapter on Hebel, "the German Burns," is one of his best studies of a German writer, and incorporates amusing and skillful translations of Hebel's poems in the Alemannic dialect. Friedrich Rückert is treated in another essay. Two others, "Autumn Days in Weimar" and "Weimar in June," are devoted to the story of Taylor's study of Goethe's life and are filled with the literary associations of the town, the history of the duchy and court, and accounts of meetings with descendants of the old literary families.

384. He made use of every personal and official connection he could muster to get at his sources. In 1874 he returned to America with his notebooks and his lively mind filled with the subject; he also had aquired a large new library of scholarly works on the two authors. He expected he would require fully three years for the writing of his "dear, unpaying work," but the months and years ran on, and he was busy with lesser employments—newspaper work, his own long poems, lecturing, and translating *Don Carlos* for Lawrence Barrett, the tragedian, in 1877—the text of which has never been published.

385. *Life and Letters*, II, 572.

386. In 1874 Hjalmar H. Boyesen found that Taylor could repeat the whole of *Faust I* from memory. Taylor's reverence for Goethe at this time is best revealed in the solemn and earnest, if somewhat fulsome, lines of his "Ode to Goethe," read on the occasion of the presentation by the Goethe Club of a bust to be set up in Central Park, New York City, August 25, 1875. His *Masque of the Gods* and *Prince Deukalion* are heavily burdened with allegorical figures reminiscent of the characters of *Pandora* and *Faust II*. The hexameters of "Home Pastorals" (1875) were used in conscious imitation of

Goethe and Gregorovius.—*Life and Letters*, II, 520. Occasionally he turned to other German poems, as in the case of the free-rhymed *ottava rima* form of the *Picture of St. John*, which Taylor himself compared to Wieland's stanza form in *Oberon*.—Smyth, *op. cit.*, p. 220; Haskell, *op. cit.*, 9 n.

387. Though cast in a large mold, he aspired too highly and in too many directions for his intrinsic abilities. His whole career, his poetic achievement most of all, was only an approximation to high distinction. His buoyant enthusiasm, coupled with abundant industry, tended to deploy in the void because he lacked true harmony and concentration. "Aside from his experiments in prose, Taylor wrote lyrics, pastorals, idyls, odes, dramatic lyrics, lyrical dramas, translations, poems in German, poems in every mood and every metre, poems conspicuously or unconsciously imitative of a host of poets (he had a remarkable but ill-controlled memory), poems on themes Oriental, Greek, Norse, American from coast to coast, poems classical, sentimental, romantic, realistic, poems of love, of nature, of art."—*Cambridge Hist. of Amer. Lit.*, III, 42. He sought what he liked to call "cosmical experience," but in his eagerness for universality he lost himself.

388. For indications of American and German appraisals of his importance as a mediator between the two peoples, see *Life and Letters*, II, 531, 661, 697, 731–32, 768.

389. One of his most vivid recollections was his mother's reading to him the ballad-legend of the ruined castle of the Weibertreu, and his memorizing it. His early attachment to everything Germanic, Leland himself used to explain, was owing to an ancestress who had married a "High German Doctor with a reputation for sorcery. . . . My mother's opinion was that this was a very strong case of atavism, and that the mysterious ancestor had through the ages cropped out in me." Leland fancied that this ancestor was Washington Irving's High German doctor who laid the mystic spell on Sleepy Hollow.—Elizabeth R. Pennell, *Charles Godfrey Leland. A Biography* (2 vols., Boston, 1906), I, 19, 34. As a child of nine he came under the tutelage of Bronson Alcott, who encouraged the lad's interest in German literature. By 1839–1840, while preparing for Princeton, he considered himself a Transcendentalist, and he read "every scrap of everything about Germany" that he could lay his hands on: "I was very far gone and used to go home from school and . . . study the beloved 'Critic of Pure Reason' and Carlyle's 'Miscellanies.'" During his college years he extended his knowledge to include a thorough reading of Schelling's *Transcendental*

Idealism (in a French version), Fichte's *Destiny of Man*, a handbook on German philosophy, an English version of Spinoza's *Tractatus Theologico-Politicus*, Kant's *Aesthetik*, and something of Schleiermacher, Justinus Kerner, and Jacob Boehme. He felt himself so well versed in philosophy that he could pass judgment on the Germanism of Carlyle and Emerson: "They dabbled or trifled with freethought and 'immortality,' crying Goethe up as the Light of Lights, while all their inner souls were bound in the most Puritanical and petty goody-goodyism."—*Ibid.*, I, 250; Charles G. Leland, *Memoirs* (N.Y., 1893), pp. 47, 55, 78–79, 82, 96, 146, 156–57.

390. Upon his return from Germany in 1848 to his native Philadelphia, he turned journalist and worked as editor under P. T. Barnum and R. W. Griswold. He was active as artist, poet, critic, folklorist, philologist, archeologist, humorist, columnist, lawyer, soldier, editor, reformer, and educator. He turned out some fifty books on the most varied subjects, not to mention uncounted contributions to periodicals. Although he wished to be remembered for his services to education, especially his successful efforts to establish industrial art as a branch of public education, his translation of Heine was among his most notable achievements, and his creation of the comic Hans Breitmann was no less. Aside from the numerous series of Breitmann ballads, several volumes of German travel sketches and impressions, and his translation of Heine, there is a long list of translations from German literature. Many of these are individual pieces, usually as contributions to periodicals; others are complete volumes of one or several German authors. From 1842 on, when he contributed his first renditions from the German to the *Nassau Literary Monthly*, until 1893, when he brought out an eight-volume edition of the *Works of Heinrich Heine*, together with a translation of von Embden's biography, he exercised his talents as a translator of Lessing, Joseph von Eichendorff, Josef von Scheffel, and C. H. Neumann, not to mention shorter pieces from a great many other German authors. The 1893 edition of Heine was a thorough revision of earlier translations—*Pictures of Travel* (*Reisebilder*), 1855, and the *Book of Songs* (*Buch der Lieder*), 1864. For details see Joseph Jackson's "Bibliography of the Works of C. G. Leland," *Pa. Mag. of Hist. and Biog.*, Vols. XLIX–LI (1925–1927).

391. Pennell, *op. cit.*, I, 154–55, 163, 178.

392. *Memoirs*, pp. 140, 145.

393. His admiration did not blind him to Heine's defects, as he made clear in the Preface to his *Pictures of Travel*. To appreciate Heine

required, he felt, taking him all in all as he is; he aimed at making his translation "strictly true to the original." Occasionally he failed to capture Heine's deft and delicate play of wit, but he succeeded in producing a literally accurate version.

394. Pennell, *op. cit.*, I, 343–44.

395. See *Hans Breitmann Ballads* (Complete ed., Phila., 1897), pp. 3–5. Edward S. Bradley, *George H. Boker, Poet and Patriot* (Phila., 1927), pp. 261–62.

396. Lowell called Leland's parody of the *Hildebrandslied* "wonderfully good." "The ingenuity with which you have managed the German pronunciation (especially in choosing words where the transposition of p and b, d and t, is comic) adds a new chord to the lyre of humour."—Pennell, *op. cit.*, I, 290.

397. E. S. Bradley, "Hans Breitmann in England and America," *The Colophon*, n.s., II, i (Autumn, 1936), 67.

398. Pennell, *op. cit.*, I, 353.

399. *Memoirs*, p. 336.

400. *Ibid.*, pp. 340–41.

401. See Stoddard's *Recollections* (ed. by R. Hitchcock, N.Y., 1903), pp. 50–67.

402. *Ibid.*, p. 97.

403. A few of his poems contain German allusions: "Drachenfels" has a German locale, "The Helmet" relates a legend concerning a young German warrior, and "The Wine Cup" is vaguely reminiscent of Uhland's "Glück von Edenhall."

404. His parents spoke and read German, his mother having acquired her facility about the time her brother Edward Everett returned from Germany. Her translations from French and German appeared in the periodicals for years. Hale was a member of Longfellow's earliest classes in German at Harvard.

405. *Ralph Waldo Emerson* (Boston, 1902), pp. 33–34, 37–38.

406. It was their ambition to be able to read Strauss's *Leben Jesu*, a book which was then on the proscribed list at the college.—E. S. Bradley, *George Henry Boker*, p. 16. Later, even while at work in a law office, Boker read widely "in English . . . German, French and the classics."—*Ibid.*, p. 35. Two of Boker's five critical essays reflect an early enthusiasm for ancient Germanic literature.—*Ibid.*, p. 25. He followed the trail of his friend "Charlie" Leland on a tour of Europe shortly afterward, and declared the tour through Paris to Heidelberg "the greatest experience of his life."—*Ibid.*, p. 41.

407. *Ibid.*, p. 246.

408. These letters are printed in his *Writings* (15 vols., Hartford, Conn., 1904), II, 61–209.

His account of the trip up the Rhine and his description of old Heidelberg are worthy of Taylor's best efforts. In Germany Warner made good use of his opportunities to get an insight into the life of the people. He was especially attached to Munich, "the dear old city," in which he felt himself "firmly planted."—*Writings*, II, 209.

409. Unlike most of them, however, he was no linguist. He went on only one foreign tour, from which, uncharacteristically, Germany was excluded. When in 1871 Taylor sent him a copy of his *Faust*, Stedman admitted his "great misfortune not to read German," and added, "since the receipt of your 'Faust,' I have more understanding of Brooks [the latter's translation of 1856]."—Laura Stedman and George M. Gould, *Life and Letters of Edmund C. Stedman* (2 vols., N.Y., 1910), I, 445–49, 488. But it is obvious from his facility in handling German phrases and titles in his essay on Bayard Taylor and elsewhere that he was not entirely ignorant of the language. Moreover, he had read to good purpose such common sources of information as Carlyle's essays, Taylor's complete literary output, and a surprisingly large proportion (for a man who held a seat on the New York Stock Exchange for forty years) of the vast body of German literature that was available in English. Among Germans whom he mentions most frequently are Goethe, Schiller, Heine, von Arnim, Novalis, the Schlegels, Lessing, Eduard v. Hartmann, Schopenhauer, Richter, Voss, Fouqué, Freiligrath, Strodtmann, E. T. A. Hoffmann, Hans Sachs, Boehme, Eckermann, Haydn, Liszt, Bach, Beethoven, von Bülow, and Kepler.

410. Goethe, of course, stood pre-eminent in his estimation, and he appears to have been especially fond of the *Conversations* with Eckermann and the *Goethe-Schiller Correspondence*. Other important books for him were Lessing's *Laokoon* and the *Hamburgische Dramaturgie* and Heine's *Romantische Schule*. See *The Nature and Elements of Poetry* (N.Y., 1892), pp. 18–19, 54, 66, 71, 118–19, 125–27, 237; *Genius and Other Essays* (N.Y., 1911), pp. 7–8, 42; and *Poets of America* (N.Y., 1885), p. 372. He devoted much attention to the analysis of genius. In *Genius and Other Essays* he begins his discussion by citing the preromantic position of Lessing. He quotes several passages from the *Dramaturgie*, discusses the effect of Lessing's theories on Goethe, Schiller, and Heine, and obviously derives his ideas on the limits of poetry and painting from the *Laokoon* (*ibid.*, pp. 7–8, 71; *Poets of America*, p. 449). He proceeds next to cite Schopenhauer as one who "dispassionately considered

the nature of talent and genius" (*Genius and Other Essays*, p. 21) and concludes that talent lies more in the greater skill and acuteness of the discursive than in the intuitive cognition, while genius "exhibits a development of the intuitive faculty greater than is needed for the service of the Will. . . . Genius is a man who knows without learning, and teaches the world what he never learned."—*Ibid.*, pp. 21, 24. Finally, he draws upon Schopenhauer's successor, Eduard von Hartmann, for his theory of the Unconscious as the explanation of the creative faculty.—*Ibid.*, p. 22; see also *The Nature and Elements of Poetry*, pp. 46, 156–57, 282. On other occasions in his studies of the poetic faculties he cited Boehme's description of his mystic communion with the spirit (*Genius and Other Essays*, p. 6); Fr. Schlegel's definition in terms of "almost unconscious choice of the highest degree of excellence, and... taste as its highest activity" (*The Nature and Elements of Poetry*, p. 47); and Goethe's doctrine of the daemonic (*Genius and Other Essays*, pp. 8–9). In *The Nature and Elements of Poetry* (pp. 26, 47, 92, 134, 143) he adopts Schlegel's idea of personality in literature and Schopenhauer's identification of music and poetry (*Genius and Other Essays*, pp. 8–9, 21, 24). He was familiar with Fr. Schlegel's *Philosophy of History* in the Robertson translation, as well as A. W. Schlegel's *Lectures*; of Schopenhauer he knew the Saunders translation of *The Art of Literature* and *The Art of Controversy*.

411. His own "Ballad of Lager Bier" remains a testimony to the popular appeal of certain standard concepts about Germany. It celebrates the happy conviviality fostered by the good plebeian brew, which, for Stedman, conjures up a world of Teutonic associations—Göttingen, Munich, Nuremberg, Hans Sachs, Goethe, Faust, the Brocken and Walpurgisnacht revelry, gentle Margaret, Mephisto, Mignon, and Undine. All this obviously had a deeper inspiration than Pfaff's and other *Bierstuben* which he and his colleagues frequented. One other poem of Stedman's shows some evidence of German associations. It is entitled "Kennst du?" and begins "Do you know the blue of the Carib Sea?" See *Poems of Edmund Clarence Stedman* (Boston and N.Y., 1908), pp. 85–90, 325–27.

412. *Poets of America*, pp. 180–224 *passim*.

413. *The Nature and Elements of Poetry*, pp. 21, 65, 130.

414. *Poets of America*, p. 373.

415. *Ibid.*, p. 147.

416. Slason Thompson, *The Life of Eugene Field* (N.Y., 1927), pp. 59–60; *Writings* (12 vols., N.Y., 1901–1903), III, 117–21, and XII, 198–99.

417. *Writings*, III, 102–3; XII, 9–14.

418. As his brother observed, it was a trait of Field's "that no matter where he wandered, he speedily became imbued with the spirit of his surroundings, and his quickly gathered impressions found vent through his pen, whether he was in 'St. Martin's Lane' in London, with 'Mynheer Van Der Bloom' in Amsterdam, or on the 'Schnellzug' from Hanover to Leipzig."—*Ibid.*, I, xxxvi, 200–204.

419. *Ibid.*, III, 9–11.

420. *Ibid.*, pp. 161–63.

421. *Ibid.*, pp. 145–46; IX, 37–39, 44–45, 46 47.

422. *Ibid.*, XII, 125–26.

423. *Life*, pp. 192–93.

424. For example, poems like "The Three Kings of Cologne" (*Writings*, III, 135–36), "Ben Apfelgarten" (IX, 67–70), "Twin Idols" (IX, 56–57), or tales like "Ludwig and Eloise" (II, 187–94), "The Werewolf" (X, 259–65), and "The Fairies of Pesth" (II, 273–90). The last relates the strange event that inspired Volkmann's *Fairy Waltz*. "Franz Abt" (V, 167–72) is another story occasioned by Field's love for German music. With all his love for music, he did not hesitate to ridicule it, as in "The Platonic Bassoon" (V, 195–213) and in "'Die Walküre' und der Boonerangelungen" (X, 296–303).

425. The paraphrases from Heine are "Widow or Daughter?" (*ibid.*, I, 62) and "A Heine Love Song" (IX, 71). "A Paraphrase of Heine" (IX, 194) is not a paraphrase but a translation of No. 65 of Heine's *Lyrisches Intermezzo*, "Es fällt ein Stern herunter." He translated Uhland's "Der weisse Hirsch" (IX, 212–13), "Der Wirthin Töchterlein" (I, 90–91), and "Die Kapelle" (IX, 72).

426. A journalist, contributor to many periodicals, and long an editor, he surveyed a great variety of periodicals and books, and quantities of German stories and poems in translation passed over his editorial desk. Among his intimate friends in Charleston was the Rev. James W. Miles, who was steeped in German metaphysics, but of this little seems to have been imparted to Simms. With German literature he had more acquaintance, and his translations included selections from Italian, French, Latin, and German. In one of the short paragraphs of *Egeria: Voices of Thought and Counsel* (Phila., 1853, pp. 285–86) he discussed Goethe's song of Margaret in *Faust* and appended a translation of his own. The same volume (pp. 245–46) includes his rendition of one of Schiller's epigrams. In *Confession, or the Blind Heart* (1841) he quoted nine lines from the scene between Faust and Wagner, and for

one of the chapter headings (most of which are drawn from Shakespeare) he used another brief passage from *Faust*. Fouqué's romance of the waternymph seems to have exercised the same fascination on him that Poe confessed; Undine appears in four separate poems of Simms.

427. Aubrey Starke, *Sidney Lanier* (Chapel Hill, N.C., 1933), p. 430.

428. About this time Carlyle's essays powerfully reinforced his interest in German romanticism, "a territory," says Aubrey Starke, "that was forever afterwards Lanier's spiritual home." —*Ibid.*, pp. 29, 39; see also Philip Graham, "Lanier's Reading," *Univ. of Texas Studies in English*, XI (Sept. 1, 1931), 63–89. In *Thorn Fruit*, by Lanier's brother Clifford, Sidney, who is thinly disguised as Mark Wilton, translates for Lucy Pegram (Ginna Hankins) "some of the beautiful German poems her old library furnished in the original" and wins her love thereby. We read: "Schiller's 'Des Mädchens Klage,' Heine's 'Du bist wie eine Blume,' and 'Die Nähe der Geliebten' of Goethe's were rapturously applauded by his fair auditor."

429. During the first years of service he spent his abundant leisure in the study of music and of German, French, and Spanish. In 1863, while stationed at St. Petersburg, he had access to a small local library, and here he translated parts of Heine, Herder, Goethe, and Schiller. After a raid on his camp by the enemy, he reported a German glossary among the "lost treasures," and to his father he wrote urging that he secure for him "at any price, editions of the German poets Uhland, Lessing, and Tieck." While a prisoner at Point Lookout in 1864, he made translations of Heine's "Ein Fichtenbaum steht einsam" and Herder's "Frühlings Gruss," versions which have the virtue of being literal if not smooth.—Graham, *loc. cit.*, pp. 66–67.

430. Starke, *op. cit.*, pp. 118–19. Manhood is "morn-clear"; Ginna Hankins is called "all Heaven sweet"; night, in Germanic verbal fashion, "oncometh." However, Morgan Callaway (*Select Poems of Sidney Lanier*, N.Y., 1900, pp. xli–xlii) suggests plausibly that the frequent use of compounds is a habit that Lanier could have acquired from his study of Old English, in which, as in German, such compounds abound.

431. Graham, *loc. cit.*, p. 69.

432. Starke, *op. cit.*, p. 483, n. 2.

433. *Ibid.*, p. 92.

434. *Works of Sidney Lanier* (Centennial ed., 10 vols., Baltimore, 1945), V, 38.

435. We do not know how well Lanier mastered the language, and the extent of his acquaintance with German literature is hard to

determine. For the sources from which he acquired his knowledge, see Graham, *loc. cit.*, pp. 76–87, and Starke, *op. cit.*, p. 97. He often engaged himself to do more than he could accomplish, and frequently he had to be content with haphazard attainment of his numerous goals. It is doubtful that he ever achieved facility in his handling of German, although he was able to render German poems in smooth translation and to write at least one poem in good German. His sonnet "An Frau Falk-Auerbach" (1878) is, as Bayard Taylor said, "quite remarkable for a neophyte in the language," but, while it is "informed with a distinct idea, which is German in its nature," it moves "stiffly and somewhat awkwardly."

Lanier was acquainted with many Germans in this country. In 1872, in San Antonio, whither he went in search of health, he enjoyed the hospitality of Germans of that city, moving in the circle of people bearing names like Thielepape, Mahucke, Herff, Scheidemantel, and Duerber. He went with Scheidemantel to the meetings of the Männerchor and, as he reported to his wife, found the singing of "the old German lieder . . . under the leadership of the venerable Herr Thielepape" so beautiful that "imperious tears" rushed to his eyes. When he performed for them on his flute, "Herr Thielepape arose and ran to me and grasped my hand and declared that he hat never heert de flude accompany itself pefore."— Starke, *op. cit.*, p. 162.

In New York the next year, by which time he had decided to devote himself to music, he made an ever-widening circle of friends among the German musicians, a circle soon extended to include also those of Philadelphia and Baltimore. Among them were Gottlieb, Seifert, and Frau Falk-Auerbach of the Peabody Conservatory, Theodore Thomas and Leopold Damrosch (conductor of the Philharmonic Society of New York), Carl Wehner of Philadelphia, and members of the Philadelphia and Baltimore Männerchor orchestras and Liederkranz societies.—*Ibid.*, p. 95; see also Gay W. Allen, "Lanier as a Literary Critic," *Philol. Quar.*, XVII, ii (Apr., 1938), 125. To his wife Lanier wrote on May 25, 1876: "I had an invitation from Wehner to . . . spend the morning with him. I went . . . flute in hand. His knowledge of English is less than mine of German, and we wasted not a word in talk beyond the usual salutations. . . . At the end of each movement, as we played straight through the book, my big, phlegmatic, square-built German cried 'Gut!', and looked meaningly upon me; I said, 'Wunderschön,' and looked meaningly upon him."—*Letters of Sidney Lanier* (N.Y., 1899),

pp. 115–16. Lanier's knowledge of German, never that of the expert, was equal to his making a translation of Wagner's *Rheingold.*—Starke, *op. cit.*, pp. 106–7.

436. *Letters*, pp. 103–4; see also his poems on Wagner and Beethoven in *Poems*, pp. 95–96 and 98–100, respectively.

437. Starke, *op. cit.*, p. 209.

438. See Gay W. Allen, *loc. cit.*, pp. 125–26; also his *American Prosody* (N.Y., 1938), pp. 277–301, and Georg Brandes, *Main Currents in the Nineteenth Century* (N.Y., 1923), II, 115–16.

WALT WHITMAN

439. *Complete Writings*, ed. by his Literary Executors, Paumanok ed. (N. Y., 1902), I, 108 (hereafter referred to as *Writings*).

440. *Ibid.*, I, 73.

441. *Ibid.*, p. 18.

442. *Ibid.*, V, 296; III, 53–54.

443. *Ibid.*, IX, 4.

444. See the elaborate notes made by Whitman on his reading, covering all ages, Oriental and Occidental, *ibid.*, IX, 1–230, X, 1–134. Cf. Norman Foerster, *American Criticism*, pp. 160–71, and H. S. Canby, *Walt Whitman* (Boston, 1943), p. 68.

445. For his borrowings from scientific writers see Alice L. Cooke, "Whitman's Indebtedness to the Scientific Thought of His Day," *Univ. of Texas Studies in English*, XIV (July, 1934), 89–115, and Joseph Beaver, *Walt Whitman: Poet of Science* (N.Y., 1951); for his relations to Emersonian, Coleridgean, and Carlylean transcendentalism, see J. B. Moore, "The Master of Whitman," *Studies in Philol.*, XXIII (Jan., 1926), 77–89; C. Gohdes, "Whitman and Emerson," *Sewanee Rev.*, XXXVII (Jan., 1929), 79–83; Wm. S. Kennedy, "Identities of Thought and Phrase in Emerson and Whitman," *Conservator*, VIII, vi (Aug., 1897), 88–91; Leon Howard, "For a Critique of Whitman's Transcendentalism," *Mod. Lang. Notes*, XLII (Feb., 1932), 79–85; Fred M. Smith, "Whitman's Poet-Prophet and Carlyle's Hero," *PMLA*, LV (Dec., 1940), 1146–64; Wm. S. Kennedy, *Reminiscences of Walt Whitman* (London, 1896), pp. 76–84; J. T. Trowbridge, *My Own Story* (Boston and N.Y., 1903), pp. 365–68; for his borrowings from George Sand see Esther Shepard, *Walt Whitman's Pose* (N.Y. 1938); for his Hegelianism see M. C. Boatright, "Whitman and Hegel," *Univ. of Texas Studies in English*, IX (July, 1929), 134–50; R. P. Falk, "Walt Whitman and German Thought," *Jour. Engl. Germ. Philol.*, XL (July, 1941), 315–30; W. B. Fulgham, "Whitman's Debt to Joseph Gostwick," *Amer. Lit.*, XII, iv (Jan., 1941),

491–96; Newton Arvin, *Whitman* (N. Y., 1938), pp. 191–97; and Gay W. Allen, *Walt Whitman Handbook* (Chicago, 1946), Ch. III; for his parallels with Herder, Goethe, the Schlegels, Heine, Zschokke, and other German poets and philosophers, see R. P. Falk, *loc. cit.*; Charles Glicksberg, "Walt Whitman and Heinrich Zschokke," *Notes and Queries*, CLXVI (June 22, 1934), 382–84; Florence B. Freedman, "Walt Whitman and Heinrich Zschokke: A Further Note," *Amer. Lit.*, XV, ii (May, 1943), 181–82; Richard Riethmueller, *Walt Whitman and the Germans* (Phila., 1906).

446. *Specimen Days* (1882), in *Writings*, IV, 322.

447. *Writings*, IX, 70.

448. *November Boughs* (1888), in *Writings*, III, 66; see also *Writings*, V, 55–56.

449. His polyglotism (which included words gleaned from Latin, Italian, Spanish, and French phrase books, from the streets of New Orleans and New York, and from various other sources) did not include German. Late in life, referring to the elder Traubel's recitation of some German verses to him, he said, "I couldn't understand a word."—Horace Traubel, *With Walt Whitman in Camden* (3 vols., N.Y., 1915), I, 217; see also II, 2, 5, 53, 191–92; III, 159–60, 495 (hereafter referred to as *Camden*). He never traveled outside his native country, but he did come in contact with Germans, German-Americans, and others who could impart to him a good deal of information about Germany. From first to last, in New York, New Orleans, Brooklyn, Washington, Boston, Philadelphia, Camden, St. Louis, and elsewhere, he was actually conscious of many racial, or national, elements, including the German. He had not Thoreau's "great fault of disdain—disdain of men (for Tom, Dick, and Harry)," but constantly cultivated what he called his gregarious amativeness for men. In later life he came to know well a number of Germans. Of primary importance among these was Maurice Henry Traubel, the father of Horace Traubel, who Boswellized Whitman's late years. Their frequent meetings resolved themselves largely into the senior Traubel's reading German poetry to Whitman (in both the original and translation) and generally familiarizing him with the writings of "Goethe, Schiller, Heine, Lessing." Whitman respected Traubel's knowledge, called him "a great man," and acknowledged that he learned much from him.—*Camden*, I, 146, 217; II, 252–53; III, 173; see also Falk, in *JEGP*, LX, 316. Among some notes left by Whitman that date presumably to 1856–1857 (*Writings*, IX, 111–12) there is a reference to a "Conversation with

Mr. Held about German poets . . . Freiligrath, Rückert, Uhland, Kinkel, Hoffmann, Heine, and Xavier." Among prominent citizens of Brooklyn and New York, Whitman recorded the names of a number of Germans. In 1857 he encouraged Friedrich Huene, a young poet, orator, exile of 48, and co-worker with Whitman on the Brooklyn *Daily Times*, to undertake a translation of *Leaves of Grass* into German. Later he maintained an anxious correspondence with Karl Knortz and Thomas W. Rolleston, co-translators into German of *Leaves of Grass* (Zürich, 1889), occasionally received clippings from German newspapers (which Traubel read for him), and remained constantly desirous that his poems should have a good reception in Germany. The subscribers for the 1876 edition of *Leaves of Grass* included Hubert Herkimer, the painter, and Franz Hueffer, the musical writer.

Whitman frequented Pfaff's restaurant for years and knew intimately both the host and the Bohemian society of the place. His editorials and columns in the Brooklyn *Daily Eagle* for 1857–1859 contain a number of appreciative references to "Schneiders," the German theater near by, and to the social and convivial entertainments of the large German element in Brooklyn. In Camden the primitive printing office of his friend William Kurtz was one of his favorite lounging places. On visiting St. Louis in 1879, he observed the perfect fusion of native and foreign elements in that city: "its American electricity goes well with its German phlegm."—*Writings*, IV, 282. He celebrated the "polyglot construction stamp" of America (*ibid.*, V, 209), constantly opposed what he called "Yankeedoodledom," nativists, and the Know-Nothing Party, and said that if he had his way, he would banish the word *foreigner*. See his editorials in *The Gathering of the Forces* (ed. by C. Rogers and J. Black, 2 vols., N.Y., 1920), I, 14–22, 159–65; II, 15–17.

450. Whenever he mentions prominent national strains, the German is always ranked alongside the English and French. Germany, equally with Homer's Greece and Shakespeare's Britain, comes constantly to his mind. His globe-circling survey of the world, past and present, singles out "the German intellect" as one "from which American students may well derive profit," and he advises the young men and women of the United States "to overhaul . . . the literatures of Italy, Spain, France, and Germany . . . needed for the future of the United States," and he hopes for the day when "really good translations" will be available.— *Writings*, V, 274–75, 277; also III, 52–54. His identifications of Germany with "intellec-

tual" progress occur so often that there can be no doubt about the pre-eminence he attached tot he Germans as philosophers, just as he ascribed courtesy to the French, manliness to the Scandinavians, art to the Italians, and mysticism to the Orientals.—*Ibid.*, V, 228. Despite his hatred of American emulation of Europe, in the realm of philosophy, he said in *Specimen Days* (*ibid.*, IV, 322–23), "the contribution which German Kant and Fichte and Schelling and Hegel have bequeath'd to humanity . . . are indispensable to the erudition of America's future."

In that orgy of Whitmanesque cosmopolitanism, "Salut au Monde," he sees "the Syrian Alps and the Karnac Alps," he beholds mariners "traverse the Zuyder Zee or the Scheld," while other steamers lie in Hamburg and Bremen harbors; he sees the windings of the Danube and the Oder; he imagines himself an "inhabitant of Berlin, Berne, Frankfort, Stuttgart"; he delivers a message of good will from America to the "workingmen of the Rhine, the Elbe, or the Weser . . . the Bavarian, Swabian, Saxon." For comparisons he constantly recurs to Germany. The significance of Carlyle, Burns, and Elias Hicks is equated against the achievements of Goethe, of "Haydn, Beethoven, Mozart, and Weber," of "Kant, Fichte, and Hegel." He bemoans the fact that America has not developed "any characteristic music, the finest tie of nationality, such as the German Volkslied, the German airs of friendship, wine and love," a more powerful cement amongst Germans than all racial, linguistic, and institutional forces. In "Proud Music of the Storm," a passionate paean in praise of music comparable to Schiller's "Die Macht des Gesanges," he hears to the accompaniment of the "German organ majestic," the symphonies and oratorios of "Beethoven, Handel, or Haydn," the *Creation* laving him "in billows of Godhead." For the powerful impact upon him of German music and drama, see *Writings*, IV, 26, 185, 216–17, 287–88, 290–91; VI, 50, 184–95; VII, 49; Trowbridge, *My Own Story*, p. 369.

451. Professor Emory Holloway concludes, on the basis of his identification of nearly a hundred quotations from more or less well known authors and of more than a hundred book reviews that Whitman wrote for the *Eagle*, that "Whitman reviewed more books and knew more about books than any contemporary editor in Brooklyn, if not New York, exclusive of the editors of literary periodicals." —*Uncollected Poetry and Prose* (ed. by Emory Holloway, 2 vols., Garden City, N.Y., 1921), I, 126. Among the books Whitman reviewed were John v. Müller's *History of the World* (tr. by

Alex. H. Everett), Leonard Schmitz's *History of Rome*, J. F. Spurzheim's *Phrenology*, J. J. v. Tschudi's *Travels in Peru*, Theo. Dwight's *Summer Tours*, Bayard Taylor's *Views Afoot*, Fr. L. G. v. Raumer's *Amerika*, Fr. v. Schlegel's *Philosophy of Life and Philosophy of Language* (tr. by A. J. W. Morrison), Goethe's *Autobiography*, and Schiller's *Homage of the Arts and other Translations* (tr. by C. T. Brooks). He wrote reviews also of Coleridge's *Aids*, *Biographia Literaria*, and *Letters*, Carlyle's *Heroes*, *French Revolution*, and *Past and Present*, W. E. Channing's *Self-Culture*, Emerson's *Spiritual Laws*, Margaret Fuller's *Papers on Literature and Art*, and Lydia M. Child's *Memoirs of Madame de Staël and Madame Roland*. He also quoted (sometimes briefly, sometimes to the length of a column or two) from the following Germans in either his Miscellany or his Sunday Reading columns: Goethe, Herder (2), Karl T. Körner, F. W. Krummacher, Jean Paul, Schiller, Uhland (2), Heinrich Voss, and Zschokke (2).

452. *Camden*, II, 244; see also I, 141, and Richard Maurice Bucke, *Walt Whitman* (Phila., 1883), p. 52.

453. The Old German *Nibelungenlied*, "an integral sign or landmark," he said he "went over thoroughly."—*Writings*, II, 55. Whether he meant by this statement that he secured a translation and really prepared (as one of his memoranda suggests) "a running sketch" of the poem, or whether he contented himself here, as elsewhere, with what he found on the subject in Gostick's *German Literature* (Phila., 1854) and more especially in Carlyle's essay on "The Nibelungen Lied" remains problematical. His longest note on the subject follows the latter closely, point for point (compare *Writings*, IX, 83, and Carlyle's *Essays*, Centenary ed., II, 221–22, 239–64 *passim*, 265–66, 267, 268, 270); although Gostick's *German Literature* seems to have supplied supplementary data, especially of the narrative (compare Gostick, pp. 18–31, and *Writings*, IX, 117, 187, 228; X, 14). He concluded that the *Nibelungenlied*, like the Scandinavian eddas or the Charlemagne cycle and all" archetypal poems," had their origin "in the great historic perturbations, which they came in to sum up and confirm."—*Writings*, V, 55–56, 96 n., 292; VI, 124; IX, 83, 117, 187, 216, 228; *Camden*, I, 241. Great authors, or "literatuses" (says Whitman), in fashioning types of "Siegfried and Hagen," of "Brunhelde and Chriemhelde," first formed the standards of society, politics, religion, and personality of early Germanic times; they subsequently became "the main support of chivalry, the feudal, ecclesiastical, dynastic world . . . forming its osseous structure, holding it together for hun-

dreds, thousands of years, preserving its flesh and bloom, giving it form, decision, rounding it out, and so saturating it in the conscious and unconscious blood, breed, belief, and intuitions of man, that it still prevails powerful to this day, in defiance to the mighty changes of time."— *Writings*, V, 55–56; see also 58–59, 96–97. Here is a concept of literature and of the "literatus" sufficiently grand even for Whitman.

454. On the scope of his reading, see his reading notes in the last two volumes of *Writings*, as well as Professor Norman Foerster's appraisal of Whitman's general knowledge of books: "As far as reading prepares a writer for critical speculation . . . Whitman was far better equipped for his task than has ordinarily been realized. He was far better equipped than Poe, probably in quantity of reading, quite certainly in quality."—*American Criticism*, pp. 169–70. Speaking of the pre-1855 period, Canby (*Walt Whitman*, p. 68) estimates that "it is doubtful if many American writers or editors (the Concord and Boston group excepted) were reading more widely and with as earnest a search for values."

455. *Camden*, III, 160–61; see also *Writings*, IX, 111.

456. For other notable examples, see *Camden*, I, 152, 200, 215, 223; *Writings*, I, 108.

457. Clifton J. Furness, "Walt Whitman's Estimate of Shakespeare," *Harvard Studies and Notes in Philol. and Lit.* XIV (1932), 1.

458. *Writings*, VI, 293.

459. *Prose Writers of Germany*, p. 265. All references to this book are to the third edition (N.Y., 1855). Whitman owned a copy of this book.

460. In this case, since Whitman was preparing notes which presumably he alone would see, he was less circumspect about covering his tracks than in his published writings, though even here he sometimes slipped, as we have observed. Another notable instance in which he dropped his guard is his reference, in a footnote in *Specimen Days* (*Writings*, IV, 321; see also IX, 171), to Gostick as an authority on Hegel. This hint provoked researches into Gostick's book as the source of Whitman's Hegelianism (notably by M. C. Boatright, R. P. Falk, and W. B. Fulgham), but the extent of his pilferings from this source for his information on Hegel has been only roughly indicated and his borrowings in other respects from Gostick have gone entirely unnoticed.

For example, Whitman's information on Niebuhr (whom he valued as the "Founder of a New Theory of History") came from Gostick. At the end of one of his passages on the German historian, he wrote: "See pages 249–50–51

German Literature" (*Writings*, IX, 116). The passages indicated present the following parallelism:

GOSTICK (p. 249): "In Roman history Barthold Niebuhr, who was born at Copenhagen in 1776, stands alone as the founder of the new school of research, by which the fictions which were mingled with the early history of Rome, and copied from book to book, and from one century to another, have been finally exploded. . . . During his youth he visited London and Edinburgh. . . . Niebuhr was employed in several political offices during the remainder of his life, until 1823, when he retired to Bonn, and there devoted himself to the task of arranging the copious materials of his Roman history. The French Revolution of July 1830 had such an effect on the mind of Niebuhr, that it hastened his death, which took place at Bonn, January 2, 1831." [Here follows an extract from the Introduction to Niebuhr's *Roman History*.]

WHITMAN (IX, 116): "Barthold Niebuhr— 1776–1831—55 years. Born at Copenhagen, during youth visited London and Edinburgh. Was an occupant of political offices for the younger manhood years of his life—but in 1823 (aged 47) retired to Bonn and became the great reformer of Roman history (and ancient History generally). Was much excited by the French Revolution of July 1830, said to have hastened his death, Jan. 1831—See pages 249–50–51 German Literature."

Another such note appears in Whitman's memoranda (*Writings*, X, 16): "Hegel, German literature, prose writers of Germany." The meaning of this memorandum is obviously this: "For Hegel, consult Gostick's *German Literature* and Hedge's *Prose Writers of Germany.*"

Still another note, on Lessing, is drawn from the same source:

GOSTICK (pp. 116–17): "We . . . find a preparation for a new era in literature in the writings of Gotthold Ephraim Lessing (1729–1787), who was equally eminent as a dramatist and a critic. . . . His life was characterized by remarkable activity. He lived at various times in Berlin, Leipsic, Breslau, Hamburg, and Wolfenbüttel. . . . He ably exposed the pedantry of Gottsched, the failure of Klopstock as an epic poet, the false imitations of the ancient classics which had been fashionable, the unpoetic fables of Gellert and others, and the falsity of that style of descriptive poetry which had attempted to do with the pen the work of the painter. This last error was fully criticized in his 'Laokoon,' which appeared in 1766. . . . it was in the drama that his services were most remarkable. . . . He produced a didactic drama entitled 'Nathan the Wise' . . . in this work the action is suspended for the sake of the doctrine of universal religious toleration which Nathan inculcates. . . . It reminds us of a very important change in the tone of German literature from the national and Christian character which we find in Klopstock, to the cosmopolitan character which prevails in the writings of Goethe, Schiller, and other modern poets."

WHITMAN (IX, 155): "Gotthold Ephraim Lessing—1729–87—contemporary of Voltaire —very active—lived in Berlin Leipsic, Breslau, Hamburg, etc. Was a severe and almost perfect critic—exposed Klopstock's deficiencies as a poet and the false imitations of the classics— author of Laocoön (1766)—and of good dramas —also a didactic drama, *Nathan the Wise*, inculcating Kosmos religious notions. He was the R.W. Emerson of his age and paved the way for Goethe and Schiller—Lessing was a Jew."

Whitman's spelling of Gost[w]ick's name has occasioned some confusion and comment, but there is no mystery involved here. Whitman used the 1854 edition of Joseph Gostick's *German Literature* (Phila.: Lippincott, Gambro & Co., 1854, vii + 324 pp.). In the second, revised, and greatly enlarged edition the name is spelled Gostwick: Joseph Gostwick and Robert Harrison, *Outlines of German Literature* (London: Williams & Norgate; Boston: Schönhof & Möller; N.Y.: Henry Holt & Co., 1873, xii + 588 pp.). A reprint of the latter came out in 1883. Whitman knew neither of these much improved editions.

461. *Writings*, IX, 110.

462. *Essays* (Centenary ed.), I, 198–257. The passages which Whitman paraphrased, or copied, are found in I, 202, 208, 210–11, 211–42 *passim*, 243, 248.

463. A good portion of the last two pages of Goethe memoranda is devoted to a kind of running argument with Carlyle regarding Goethe's stature as a poet. Revealing comments appear in his remarks on Carlyle's calling Goethe an "antique worthy":

"Carlyle vaunts him as showing that a man can live even these days as an 'Antique Worthy'. This vaunt Goethe deserves—he is indeed a cultivated German aristocrat, physically inextricable from his age and position, but morally bent to the Attic spirit and its occasions two thousand and more years ago. That is he, such are his productions. The assumption that

Goethe passed through the first stage of darkness and complaint to the second stage of consideration and knowledge and thence to the third stage of triumph and faith—this assumption cannot pass, cannot stand amid the judgments of the soul. Goethe's was the faith of physical well being, a good digestion and appetite, it was not the faith of the masters, poets, prophets, divine persons. Such faith he perhaps came near and saw the artistical beauty of— perhaps fancied he had it—but he never had it." —*Writings*, IX, 112–13. The stages in Goethe's development here enumerated reflect Carlyle's *Essays*, II, 430–35, and I, 210–11; also II, 440.

One point of Carlyle's particularly bothered him. Forced to admit Carlyle's observations about Goethe's universal appeal to the cultivated and uncultivated alike, Whitman still found inexplicable his question, "Why do uneducated minds also receive pleasure from Goethe? . . . To the little court at Weimar, to the poetical world, to the learned and literary worlds, Goethe has a deserved greatness. To the genius of America he is neither dear nor the reverse of dear. He passes with the general crowd upon whom the American glance descends with indifference. Our road is our own." —*Writings*, I, 202, 208; IX, 113–14.

This judgment, like that on Shakespeare, who represented for Whitman another modern living in an atmosphere of feudalism and aristocracy, is his characteristic and, in some respects, final attitude toward Goethe; and this, we must conclude, was based less on a firsthand knowledge of a large portion of Goethe's writings than upon a rummaging about among such books as Longfellow's anthology, Gostick's handbook, Lewis' biography, and above all, Carlyle's essays.

Carlyle's essays, it may be observed, served Whitman on a number of other occasions. In 1857 he took cognizance of Carlyle's emphasis in his essay on "Schiller" (1831) on the *Briefwechsel zwischen Schiller und Goethe in den Jahren 1794–1805*, and some years later, in Camden, he busied himself with *The Correspondence of Goethe and Schiller*, available since 1845 in the Calvert, and since 1877–1879 in the Schmitz translation. See *Camden*, I, 57. Another striking instance of close borrowing from Carlyle is Whitman's two-page memorandum of Jean Paul (see *Writings*, IX, 121–23), all taken almost verbatim from Carlyle's essay of 1830 on Richter (*Essays*, II, 96–159). Whitman's transcriptions are from pages 97, 99, 104, 105, 114, 115–19, 120, 123, 124–25, 135, 137, 139, 141, 142–43, 153–58 *passim*. A few supplementary details are drawn from Carlyle's earlier article on Jean Paul (*Essays*, I, 1–25), the particular passages supplying Whitman with data being from pages 6, 7, 8–9, 10, 11, 11–14, 25. Professor Emory Holloway points to another, much later, instance of borrowing in his "Notes from a Whitman Student's Scrapbook," *American Scholar*, II (1933), 277–78.

464. The review is reprinted in *Uncollected Poetry and Prose*, I, 139–41, and in *Gathering of the Forces*, II, 294–95.

465. *Uncollected Poetry and Prose*, I, 140 n.

466. *Ibid.*, I, 140.

467. See *Writings*, V, 218–22; also III, 44–45, 63, 65; VII, 60. On the score of Whitman's avowed purpose of writing an autobiographical book, consider his remark, "This is no book, / Who touches this touches a man" (*Writings*, II, 289); also "The book is autobiographic at bottom" (*ibid.*, VI, 285); his observation in "Good-Bye My Fancy" (*ibid.*, VII, 60) that his "chief work" has the aim "to utter the same old human *critter* —but . . . in Democratic American modern and scientific conditions." See also *ibid.*, III, 44–45, 63–65, and *Walt Whitman's Workshop*, pp. 9, 131, 174. In a letter written in 1882 to Edward Dowden, Whitman reiterated what he had said at greater length in the 1855 Preface and repeated substantially in the 1876 Preface: "The principle of my book is a model or ideal . . . of a complete healthy, heroic, practical modern *Man*. . . . I seek to typify a living Human Personality."—Bliss Perry, *Walt Whitman* (Boston, 1906), pp. 199–200. During his last years he spoke with satisfaction of his tenacity of purpose "from first to last, to put *a Person*, a human being (myself, in the latter part of the nineteenth century, in America,) fully and truly on record" (*Writings*, III, 65) and of creating an autobiographic "Epic of Man" (*ibid.*, IX, 110–11).

468. *Uncollected Poetry and Prose*, I, 140 n.

469. Emory Holloway, *Whitman: An Interpretation in Narrative* (N.Y., 1926) p. 17. A hint of how directly vital Goethe's autobiography was to Whitman and how he found in it a model for his glorification of "Personality" appears in his statement to Horace Traubel on November 23, 1888: "Goethe impresses me as above all to stand for essential literature, art, life—in perfect persons—perfect you, me: to force the real into the abstract ideal: to make himself, Goethe, the supremest example of personal identity: everything making for it: in us, in Goethe; every man repeating the same experience. . . . Goethe would ask: 'What are your forty, fifty, hundred, social, national, phantasms? This only is real—this person. . . .'"—*Camden*, III, 159.

470. See Esther Shepherd, *Walt Whitman's Pose*.

471. Fred M. Smith, "Whitman's Poet-Prophet and Carlyle's Hero," *PMLA*, LV, iv (Dec., 1940), 1146–64.

472. See Whitman's letter to Emerson, August, 1856; *Writings*, V, 270; John Burroughs, *Notes on Walt Whitman as Poet and Person* (N.Y., 1867), pp. 16–17; Richard M. Bucke, *Walt Whitman* (Phila., 1883), p. 83; and the detailed record of Whitman's daily talk during his late years in Camden, which serve to show that he "longed more for the approbation of Emerson than for that of any other man."

473. Emerson's essay on Goethe in *Representative Men* seems not to have made much of an impression on Whitman; there appears to be no carry-over from this essay into Whitman's extended note on Goethe written in January-February, 1856. It does not follow, however, because Whitman claimed he had not read Emerson's essays before 1855 (see Wm. S. Kennedy, *Reminiscences*, p. 76, and R. M. Bucke, *Walt Whitman*, pp. 73–98, esp. p. 82) that therefore he had not become indoctrinated with some Emersonian ideas; for while he may not have read the Essays, first or second series, before 1855, he could readily have acquired much knowledge about Emerson through the reviews. For instance, the *Democratic Review*, for which Whitman himself wrote between 1841 and 1847, published between 1839 and 1845 five long essays (itemized by Kennedy, *op. cit.*, pp. 80–81) on Emerson and Emersonianism.

474. A singular gap in Whitman's knowledge of Goethe's writings occurs in the case of *Wilhelm Meister*, which Whitman nowhere mentions except in a passing reference, obviously based on Carlyle's essay on "Goethe" (1832). See *Writings*, IX, 112–113; compare Carlyle's *Essays*, I, 232–42. Readily available in Carlyle's translation, this work might have served equally well with the *Autobiography* and *Faust* during the gestation period of *Leaves of Grass* as a biographical and autobiographical model. There is the possibility, of course, that his failure to mention *Wilhelm Meister* prominently was studied.

In 1888 he said that he knew little of Goethe at first hand beyond a reading of *Faust* and a "looking into" this or that translation, picking up "a poem, a glint, here and there"; yet he insisted on his right to "an opinion of Goethe" (*Camden*, III, 159–60). His admiration of Goethe was qualified: Goethe's aloofness from his contemporary world—his failure to play a decisive role in the turbulent Europe of his later life—was antithetical to his own democratic-nationalistic creed. "The Goethean theory and lesson (if I may briefly state it so) of the exclusive sufficiency of artistic, scientific, literary equipment to the character, irrespective of any strong claim of the political ties of nation, state, or city, could have answer'd under the conventionality and pettiness of Weimar, or of Germany, or even Europe, of those times; but it will not do for America at all."—*Writings*, VI, 6; see also III, 49; V, 223; IX, 110–14; *Camden*, II, 2–5; III, 159–60. This charge of aloofness was, of course, a stock criticism, and is not necessarily a reflection of much firsthand knowledge of Goethe.

475. *Camden*, I, 56.
476. *Ibid.*, III, 159.
477. *Ibid.*, I, 291.
478. *Ibid.*, II, 378.
479. See *ibid.*, II, 159, for Traubel's report of another instance of Bucke's linking *Faust* with *Leaves of Grass*, on which occasion Whitman took particular pains to say that he had never read *Faust* very attentively. At another time, while admitting that he had known Bayard Taylor for years (*ibid.*, I, 55), he declared that he had never read Taylor's translation (*ibid.*, I, 126)—a declaration that is a little hard to swallow in view of Taylor's general position and the great reputation of his *Faust*. See also *I Sit and Look Out*, pp. 69, 215 n. 18, and *Uncollected Poetry and Prose*, I, 136.

480. Richard Riethmüller, *loc. cit.*, p. 37.

481. As in Goethe's Prologue in Heaven, "the evil spirit that eternally denies" (*Faust I*, l. 1338) is acknowledged by the Lord to be an indispensable ally in preserving mankind from false security and enervation; so Satan is included, together with Father, Son, and Santa Spirita, in the "Square Deific." In *Faust*, God says:

"Ever too prone is man activity to shirk,
In unconditioned rest he fain would live;
Hence this companion purposely I give,
Who stirs, excites, and must, as devil work."
                                        (ll. 340–43)

Whitman repeatedly expresses a similar idea in stressing the strenuous life: the man who has never imperiled his life but has retained it to old age, in ease and riches, has not lived—has not achieved anything worth while. In "Song of Myself" Whitman says:

"Evil propels me and reform of evil propels me. . . .
I am not the poet of goodness only, I do not decline to be the poet of wickedness also."   (*Writings*, I, 60).

482. Among his memoranda is this notation:

"Theories of Evil—*Festus, Faust, Manfred, Paradise Lost, Book of Job.*"—*Ibid.*, IX, 154.

483. In the poem "Roaming in Thought (After reading Hegel)," he wrote in 1881:

"Roaming in thought over the Universe, I saw the little that was good steadily hastening towards Immortality,
And the vast all that is call'd Evil I saw hastening to merge itself and become lost and dead."   (*Ibid.*, II, 35).

Riethmüller suggests evidence of dependence in the parallelism between Goethe's "Alles Vergängliche / Ist nur ein Gleichnis" (*Faust II*, ll. 12104–5) and Whitman's oft-repeated expression that "Nothing is ever really lost, or can be lost" (*Writings*, II, 309). But in view of Whitman's prefatory note to these lines to the effect that they were suggested by a talk he had "lately [1888] with a German spiritualist," it seems gratuitous to seek the source in Goethe or Boehme.

Similarly, it has been suggested that Whitman's feminism may owe something to Goethe's "Ewig-Weibliche" which draws men ever onward and upward, and that his assigning the feminine gender to "Santa Spirita" in "Chanting the Square Deific" is evidence of a lingering reminiscence in Whitman's mind of the closing words of *Faust*. Whitman's Santa Spirita, "including all life on earth, touching, including God, including Saviour and Satan, ethereal, pervading all" and completing the "square deific," is akin to the hardly definable but inviolable feminine power that brings final harmony in Goethe's spirit-world. But again the relationship, in the absence of stronger external evidence, is not supported by internal evidence strong enough to warrant the conclusion that anything more than a parallelism is involved.

484. See Charles I. Glicksberg, in *Notes and Queries*, CLXVI, 382–84. We cannot be positive regarding when Whitman's attention was first directed to Zschokke, but opportunites were not lacking during the late 30's and early 40's, when the periodicals contained much information about him. The publication of Parke Godwin's translation of *Selbstschau* (*Autobiography*) in 1845 was widely noticed. During the period of Whitman's editorship of the Brooklyn *Daily Eagle*, the paper serialized Zschokke's "Journal of a Poor Vicar in Wiltshire," and there is good reason for believing that Whitman himself was responsible for the notice of *Zschokke's Tales* (tr. by Parke Godwin, N.Y., 1845) that appeared in the Brooklyn *Evening Star* for February 9, 1845.

485. Glicksberg, *loc. cit.*, p. 383.

486. Especially those of 1846–1847, collected in *The Gathering of the Forces*; see also H. S. Canby, *Walt Whitman*, pp. 88–99.

487. The passage, in Godwin's translation, reads: "The Life of Man is striking and interesting enough to stand by itself, unrecommended by the merit or celebrity of the Statesman and Author" (p. iv).

488. One paragraph which Whitman copied from page 10 of Godwin's translation reads thus:

"I thought that I was alone with God in the World, and that He was educating me in the School of Life, until I should be fit to live at home in Heaven with Him. For me he had built this wonderful place, (the Earth), and all which I saw, men, women, children, animals, were all moved about solely for me and in my presence, being without life or motion when I was away. Whenever I came God hastened to continue the wonderful spectacle for me, to teach and educate the child."

These sentiments, suggestive as they are of passages in "There was a Child Went Forth," in "Song of Myself," and in others of Whitman's poems, where his subjective egoism enables him to see in the visible universe "for me an audience interminable," are yet presented with a difference.

489. *November Boughs* (Phila., 1888), p. 18; *Writings*, III, 66; see also V, 55–56. Unfortunately in Whitman's estimation Goethe forgot this lesson all too soon, and lived too exclusively a literary existence. Even Schiller, whose arduous idealism he admired, seemed deficient on the score of literary exclusiveness. See *Camden*, I, 57, 58, 146, 217, 357; II, 188–89, 407, 436; *Writings*, III, 157; IV, 285; IX, 114. Bucke tells us that Schiller's "Diver" was one of the poems that Whitman loved to recite (*Walt Whitman*, p. 53; see also *Walt Whitman's Workshop*, p. 205), and Traubel records Whitman's quoting, on September 30, 1888, "something from Schiller on the background of art," possibly something that had lodged in his memory since 1846 when he reviewed C. T. Brooks's translation of Schiller's *Homage of the Arts*.

490. It is not necessary to speculate on whether Whitman read Herder in translation or relied on criticism and commentary. He had access to both, in books and periodicals, American as well as British. See the bibliographies of B. Q. Morgan, S. H. Goodnight, and H. M. Haertel.

Herder had begun with Hamann's proposition that poetry is the mother tongue of the human race. The first language of a people is only a collection of the elements of poetry. The origin of poetry and of language being intimately related, poetry cannot be, says Herder, the privilege of a few cultivated men: it must be a gift for the peoples of the world. Poetry ranks the higher the nearer the nation (or the individual who helps compose it) stands to nature. Hence the most glorious poetic productions are those of the oldest peoples and of children of nature, like Moses and Homer. For culture is dangerous to poetry. Culture weakens; it destroys the pregnancy of thought and simplicity of expression, the naiveté and sincerity of sentiment—all of which the old heroes of literature possessed. While attention to their methods may teach modern poets how to write, mere imitation of the great masters will not raise modern poetry to a higher or nobler plane. "The old poets knew how to absorb and reflect their own nature and history, the current thoughts and the language. We must become imitators of ourselves—we must become original." See R. Riethmüller, *loc. cit.*, p. 42. For Herder's "intuitive grasp of the organic unity of all mankind, of the inevitable interdependence of the individual, the nation, and the race, which made him the father of the modern evolutionary view of history," see Kuno Francke, *Social Forces in German Literature* (3rd. ed., N.Y., 1893), p. 319.

491. *Writings*, V, 54–57, 165–68; VI, 101–2, 105–7.

492. *Ibid.*, V, 205; VI, 11, 284–86. Whitman's conclusions regarding the stature of the bards who composed the *Nibelungenlied* and F. Schlegel's theories of literature both appear to have contributed toward the formulation of these views.

493. A comparison of the basic ideas in Whitman's essay, "The Bible as Poetry," with Herder's *Vom Geist der ebräischen Poesie* serves to clarify the close parallelism.

494. Leading references to Heine are found in *Uncollected Poetry and Prose*, II, 94; *Writings*, VII, 11, 70–71; IX, 88; *Camden*, I, 95, 106, 217, 461; II, 53, 324, 336, 474, 546, 553, 554, 560–62; III, 9, 184, 190, 355. He especially emphasized Heine's contemporaneity, his freedom and fearlessness in applying ideas to life, his attack of "humbuggeries," his "superb fusion of culture and native elemental genius," the "primal quality, the direct off-throwing of nature" which he embodied in his writings. He identified himself with Heine as bridging a gap between romanticism and realism and as insisting on the necessity for embodying and actually living the theories of the nineteenth century. The attempt to link *Faust* with *Leaves of Grass* repeatedly elicited protestations from

Whitman; but when Traubel mentioned the autobiographical nature of Heine as identical with *Leaves of Grass*—as fulfilling Whitman's requirement that true autobiography must flow spontaneously from personality—Whitman did not demur but observed that Heine's work met the requirements of "great autobiography . . . pre-eminently above all others." In short, he found in Heine that spirit of revolt, "an appeal to nature, an appeal to final meanings . . . a primal quality not to be named or described," which he himself sought to incorporate in his own work.—*Camden*, II, 562.

495. *Writings*, IX, 181.

496. *Ibid.*, pp. 166–186.

497. See below. He also followed the course of the Baconian theory as espoused by Germans like Kuno Fischer and Karl Müller.—*Camden*, I, 30–32.

498. *Writings*, VI, 152.

499. *Ibid.*, V, 6.

500. *Ibid.*, IX, 116.

501. This attitude is of a piece with his alternately claiming consistency for his philosophy and denying it, of inviting disciples and disclaiming any intention of founding a school. See *Writings*, I, 70, 108, 140, 290.

502. *Camden*, I, 156.

503. *Writings*, II, 168.

504. *Ibid.*, I, 68.

505. *Ibid.*, II, 15.

506. *Ibid.*, I, 181–82.

507. *Ibid.*, p. 64.

508. *Ibid.*, II, 107.

509. *Ibid.*, I, 294. On May 5, 1888, he said to Traubel: "I doubt if anybody includes more than I do: I have room for them all: I am a great accepter."—*Camden*, II, 436.

510. *Writings*, I, 156.

511. *Ibid.*, p. 154.

512. *Ibid.*, pp. 146–47. In "I Hear It Charged Against Me" he said: "I will establish . . . the institution of the dear love of comrades."

513. "What we see," he added, "is superior to what we reason about—what establishes itself in the age, in the heart, is finally the only logic—can boast of the only real verification." —*Camden*, I, 149. Again, he said, "I believe in immortality, and by that I mean *identity*. I known I have arrived at this result more by what may be called feeling than formal reason— but I believe it: yes I know it. I am easily put to flight . . . when attacked, but I return to the faith, inevitably—believe it, and stick to it, to the end. Emerson somewhere speaks of encountering irresistible logic yet standing fast to his conviction. There is a judgment back of judgment. . . . Logic does very little for me: my enemies say it, meaning one thing—I say

it, meaning another thing."—*Ibid.*, I, 110–11. "I am more likely to be governed by my intuitive than by my critical self, anyhow."— *Ibid.*, II, 199. Once he went so far in his anti-intellectualism to declare, "Intellect is a fiend." —*Walt Whitman's Workshop*, pp. 19, 187.

514. *Writings*, V, 279.

515. *Ibid.*, p. 119. The "invaluable contributions of Leibnitz, Kant, and Hegel" are in the same category with the sacred poems, exhibiting "the religious tone, the consciousness of mystery, the recognition of the unknown, the Deity over and under all, and of the divine purpose" and illustrating "literature's [not philosophy's] real heights and elevations."— *Ibid.*, V, 136 n.

516. "I resist anything better than my own diversity."—"Song of Myself," l. 349.

517. The inconclusiveness and dissatisfaction which Whitman felt is first distinctly enunciated in the third edition (1860–1861) of *Leaves of Grass*, especially in "Bardic Symbols," subsequently called "As I Ebb'd with the Ocean of Life," and "Out of the Cradle Endlessly Rocking." Consult H. S. Canby, *Whitman*, pp. 180–81.

518. *Camden*, I, 156. The necessity under which his disciples placed him of acting always "in character" conspired to develop and accentuate a pose beyond his natural inclination. One of the characteristics of this pose was the false position into which it drove him of denying indebtedness in cases where the debt was most obvious. See the contradictory evidence he gave at various times regarding his debt to Emerson as stated in John T. Trowbridge, *op. cit.*, pp. 367–39, and in W. S. Kennedy, *op. cit.*, pp. 76–85; also his later references to Emerson as recorded in *Camden, passim*. Whitman was one of those complex individuals in whom the pose became so powerful that the man who was Whitman became so nearly identified with the poseur as to make the two indistinguishable. The pose was so long and constantly cultivated and the myth so completely embellished, especially in that atmosphere of adoration and discipleship with which Traubel and other admirers surrounded him, that Whitman came near being the man they told him he was and the poet-philosopher he wished to be.

519. This tendency will be recognized in a comparison of such key poems as "Song of Myself" (1855), "Out of the Cradle Endlessly Rocking" (1859), "When Lilacs Last in the Dooryard Bloom'd" (1865), and "Passage to India" (1871). Compare also the uncompromising and raucous notes in the early prefaces with

the more mediate position expressed in his later prose essays.

520. *Writings*, IX, 170–71. Coleridge's doctrine of opposites (which Whitman encountered during the 40's when he read the *Biographia* and the *Aids*) and Emerson's pronouncements on polarity may well have conditioned him to accept the Hegelian principle.

521. See F. O. Matthiessen, *American Renaissance*, pp. 538–39.

522. *Writings*, IX, 170–71. Whitman goes on to say that all the "variegated, countless objects, the perplexing ideas of immortality," the seeming contradictions between "the fact of death, chemical dissolution, and segregation" and all the conviction of "Identity's continuance, despite of death"—the whole "long train of baffling contradictory events"—become under the "absolute logic" of Hegelian reason, "only so many steps on one eternal process of creative thought."—*Ibid.*, IX, 172.

523. *Writings*, I, 146.

524. "The Base of All Metaphysics," in which he first made his broad assertion of familiarity with all systems of philosophy, is dated 1871. Among the notes reprinted by Dr. Bucke are several that belong to 1856 and 1857 (*Writings*, IX, 88, 111–12, 120), but they deal with literary figures; while the passages dealing with philosophers belong, according to Dr. Bucke, to "the late sixties or very early seventies."—*Ibid.*, IX, 166 n. Except for these notations, designed as outlines for a series of "Sunday evening lectures" on "the great German metaphysicians," Whitman's notes are nonphilosophical in character. The manuscripts from which Dr. Bucke printed these notes were "simply a series of fragments," but they form a unit and have all the earmarks of having been made at one time or very nearly consecutively. The coherence which they exhibit is not necessarily an indication that they were written in close sequence, but the fact that the order of subjects treated is very close to that of Gostick suggests that they were the result of concentrated attention. It is entirely possible that Whitman read scatteringly about German transcendental philosophy before becoming absorbed in it, but in view of the general cohesion and tone of the lecture notes it is more likely that the period of writing these notes and the period of concentrated interest in German thought were nearly coincident. His reference in the midst of his notations on the German idealists (*Writings*, IX, 184) to his *Vistas*, published in 1871, is suggestive. Although Gostick's book became available to him in 1854, there is no evidence to show that he read it at that time.

525. While ascribed to Burroughs, the passage is in reality a reproduction from a section called "Supplementary Notes" at the back of the second 1871 edition of *Leaves of Grass*. There can be no doubt that it was written by Whitman. In old age Burroughs himself, in telling about the share that Whitman had in writing Bucke's book, said: "If I remember rightly the Supplementary Notes to the last edition were entirely written by him."—Clara Barrus, *Life and Letters of John Burroughs* (2 vols., Boston and N.Y., 1925), I, 128; see also *As a Strong Bird on Pinions Free* (Washington, D.C., 1872), Advertisement, pp. 2–3; and Bucke, *op. cit.*, pp. 210–11.

526. *As a Strong Bird*, Advertisement, p. 4. The passage is reprinted as part of the "Notice of 1873" which Dr. Bucke included in the second appendix of his biography, pp. 210–13. The same advertisement continues with a blurb for *Democratic Vistas*. In it Whitmann is quoted as having said in a letter to Burroughs, "I wish to put on record [*in Democratic Vistas*] the rough sketch or outline, if not more, of a new breed of authors, poets, artists for America—comprehensive, Hegelian, Democratic, sacerdotal."

527. The letter is printed in Bucke, *op. cit.*, pp. 73–98; see esp. p. 82.

528. *As a Strong Bird*, Advertisement, p. 4. The title poem of this little volume, now entitled "Thou Mother with Thy Equal Brood," read in the light of Hegelian identities, takes on a special meaning and significance.

529. *Writings*, I, 167–68.

530. *Ibid.*, pp. 168–69. Final and paramount to all, says Whitman, is man's idea of his own position in the world of time and space, his faith in the scheme of things, the destinies which he necessitates, his clue to the relations between himself and the outside world, and his ability in intellect and spirit to cope and be equal with them and with Time and Space. These, and thoughts upon these, come to the soul and touch all human beings and form "the greatest themes." For these supreme subjects only Hegel "is large enough and free enough" for America.—*Ibid.*, IX, 169–70.

Hereupon follow the paragraphs already quoted which terminate in the passage adapted from Gostick in which Hegel is said to view all things in the universe—past, present, and future—as but "a succession of steps in the one eternal process of creative thought." The passage concludes: "Without depreciating poets, patriots, saints, statesmen, inventors and the like, I rate Hegel as Humanity's chiefest teacher and the choicest loved physician of my mind and soul."—*Ibid.*, IX, 172–73.

531. This last remark refers directly to the selection from Hegel's *Introduction to the Philosophy of History* printed in Hedge's anthology (pp. 451–52) and there entitled "History as the Manifestation of Spirit." It is to be noted that Whitman nowhere quotes Hegel directly, and that he mentions only two of Hegel's works by title: the *Encyclopaedia* and the *Introduction to the Philosophy of History* (*ibid.*, IX, 167, 173). On the basis of the remaining sections of Hegel's *Introduction to the Philosophy of History* (as reproduced in Hedge's anthology), Whitman credits Hegel with having given "the same clue to the fitness of things and unending progress, to the universe of moral purposes that the sciences, in their spheres . . . have established in the material purposes. . . . The last and crowning proof of each is the same, that they fit the mind, and the idea of all, and are necessary to be so in the nature of things."— *Ibid.*, IX, 173. Then he proceeds to draw "a great distinction" between the pagans and the Christians. The former, led by Greek theology, "appreciated and expressed the sense of nature, life, beauty, the objective world," but the problems of "fate, immutable law, the sense of power and precedence" left them in a state of "mystery and baffling unknowness"; while the latter, adopting the principle of "the Christian cultus," in "which the moral dominates," were enabled to approximate the Hegelian ideal of viewing the history of the world as a progression in the consciousness of freedom. Compare *Writings*, IX, 173–74, and Hedge's *Prose Writers*, pp. 450–52.

532. The source of this portion of his notes is indicated in a manuscript scrap in the Whitman Collection at the Library of Congress (Division of Manuscripts) referring to an article on Schelling in Volume XIV of the *New American Cyclopedia*, edited by Ripley and Dana and first published in 1862. The same note also refers to articles on Fichte and Kant in Volumes IX and XII of the seventh edition of the *Encyclopedia Britannica*, published 1830–1842 (see Newton Arvin, *Whitman*, pp. 308–9). Obviously the dates of publication of these encyclopedias are of little help in determining the time when Whitman made these notes. Whitman himself gives no indication of date.

533. Some of the facts and critical comments regarding Kant which Whitman records (*Writings*, IX, 174–75) could readily have been derived from Hedge (p. 57), Gostick (p. 266), and De Staël (I, 156); but since all are, without exception, in the article in the seventh edition of the *Britannica*, it would seem that the last named was his chief, if not sole, source on Kant's life.

534. While Kant's arduous labors represent, says Whitman, "in some respects, probably the most illustrious service ever rendered to the human mind" (*Writings*, IX, 177), it is clear that he was not vitally interested in Kant or his epistemological problems.

535. *Writings*, IX, 178–79. For all these memoranda on Fichte, Whitman merely made an abbreviated transcription of what lay open before him in Volume IX of the *Britannica* (7th ed.).

536. *Writings*, IX, 180. Besides applauding Schelling for checking Fichte's "all-devouring egoism," Whitman approves Schelling's identification of the material and ideal realms, and especially Schelling's argument that the "same universal spirit manifests itself in the individual Man, in aggregates, in concrete Nature, and in Historic Progress." While this part of Schelling's philosophy "elevates Man's reason" and "claims for it the comprehension of divine things," it demands, unfortunately, "a sort of Platonic ecstasy or inebriation as the fountain of utterance." At all events, Schelling's "palace of idealistic pantheism," while one of the "most beautiful and majestic structures ever achieved by the intellect or imagination of man (for in Schelling's philosophy there is at least as much imagination as intellect)," was "never completed" and remained "more or less deficient and fragmentary."—*Ibid.*, pp. 180–81. In this attempted summary and estimate of Schelling Whitman followed closely the *New American Cyclopedia*, first edition, 1862.

537. This opinion is a common one, but Whitman's phraseology suggests Hedge, *op. cit.*, p. 57.

538. Another phrase doubtless borrowed from Hedge, *op. cit.*, p. 383.

539. *Writings*, IX, 181, 182.

540. *Ibid.*, pp. 168, 169, 170, 172, 173, 174, 175–76, 178, 179, 181, 182, 185.

541. *Ibid.*, p. 183. The notes conclude (following some general remarks on Leibnitz as "starting German metaphysics," gleaned, in all likelihood, from an essay in the *Atlantic Monthly* for June, 1858) with another passage of fulsome praise for Hegel, who, aided by Kant, Fichte, and Schelling, performed "the most signal service to humanity" by "carrying Democracy . . . into the highest region."—*Ibid.*, p. 184.

542. Although neither Carlyle nor Hegel considered the United States worthy of serious attention, Whitman fancifully suggests that the principal works of both might not inappropriately be collected and bound together under the title, "*Speculations for the use of North America, and Democracy there with the*

relations of the same to Metaphysics, including Lessons and Warnings (encouragements too, and of the vastest,) from the Old World to the New."—*Writings,* IV, 311.

543. *Ibid,* IV, 313.

544. *Ibid.,* p. 316.

545. *Ibid.,* IV, 318-19.

546. *Ibid.,* pp. 319-20.

547. He explains that Hegel regards the whole earth, in its infinite variety and contrariety as but necessary unfoldings in the endless process of creative thought, "which, amid numberless apparent failures and contradictions is held together by central and never-broken unity—not contradictions . . . at all, but radiations of one consistent and eternal purpose."—*Ibid.,* IV, 320.

548. "Not any one part, or any one form of government, is absolutely or exclusively true," for "truth consists in the just relation of objects to each other. . . . The specious, the unjust, the cruel, and what is called the unnatural," whether in democracy, oligarchy, or despotism, are not only permitted but in a certain sense inevitable in the divine scheme; but they are, "by the whole constitution of the scheme, partial, inconsistent, temporary, and though ever so great an ostensible majority, are destined to failures" in the one all-enfolding purpose.—*Ibid.,* p. 321. This portion of Whitman's presentation is simply a restatement of Gostick, *op. cit.,* p. 270. Compare also Gostick's remark, "A majority of democracy in any country may rule as oppressively as on oligarchy" (*ibid.,* p. 270), with Whitman's observation in *Specimen Days* (*Writings,* IV, 321): "A majority or democracy may rule as outrageously and do as great harm as an oligarchy or despotism—though far less likely to do so."

549. In the theology, Hegel "translates into science" all apparent contradictions and makes them "fractional and imperfect expressions of one essential unity."—*Writings,* IV, 321.

550. *Ibid.,* pp. 323-24.

551. "There is that about them," adds Whitman, "which only the vastness, the multiplicity and the vitality of America would seem able to comprehend, to give scope and illustration to, or to be fit for, or even originate. It is strange to me that they were born in Germany, or in the old world at all."—*Writings,* IV, 322 n.

Regarding the uses to which Hegelian philosophy was put in imperialistic Germany, if the matter came to his attention, Whitman apparently troubled his head not at all. Like the St. Louisans, he took at face value Hegel's definition of the history of the world as "the progress in the consciousness of freedom" and

concluded, *ipso facto,* that Hegel was the philosopher of and for democracy.

552. See his notes, *Writings,* IX, 168-85 *passim,* esp. p. 185.

553. Consider his "Roaming in Thought (After Reading Hegel)," a poem of 1881.

554. *Writings,* IV, 320. Finding in Hegel both warrant and voucher for his own large faith in freedom, he adopted the Hegelian philosophy in the lump, or *en masse,* as he might have said, without inquiring into the epistemological bases on which it stood or the dialectical method by which it was built. For his distrust of cold logic, as against his fondness for intuition, see *Leaves of Grass* (inclusive edition, ed. by Emory Holloway, Garden City, 1925), p. 504; *Writings,* II, 149; V, 322-23; *Workshop,* p. 49.

It goes without saying that there are important points of difference between Hegel and Whitman. At opposite poles in their philosophical methodology, Hegel dwelt in the realm of the general and universal in about the same proportion in which Whitman concentrated on the individual and particular. Hegel saw the world and mankind through macroscopic eyes; Whitman, through microscopic eyes. For details, see Olive W. Parsons, "Whitman the Non-Hegelian," *PMLA,* LVIII, iv (Dec., 1943), 1073-93, esp. pp. 1083-92. There is little use laboring the point, or demanding of Whitman methods and processes of thought which he specifically disdained or denounced. His high praise of Hegel originated from an admiration for the conclusions which Hegel reached, not from any critical appreciation of the methods employed. Whitman had no opportunities to consult Hegel in the original, and he availed himself of few of the more reliable secondary sources that could have led him to a better understanding of the more technical aspects of German idealism. For example, he appears not to have known Stirling's *Secret of Hegel* (available since 1865) or William Wallace's shorter *Logic* (which appeared in 1874). Neither did he learn much from W. T. Harris, on whom he called in Concord in 1881. There were pleasant relations with others of the Concord School of Philosophy, and Whitman was pleased when the Morse bust of himself, on being refused in Boston, found a home in the Hegelian shrine in Concord. But he found little in their type of Hegelianism that struck a responsive chord and regarded the *Journal of Speculative Philosophy* as entirely too abstruse (see *Writings,* V, 26; *Camden,* I, 191, 284-85; II, 542). For one thing, the contacts came too late. If he had made the acquaintance of Harris a decade earlier, while he was actively engaged in puzzling out Hegel à la Gostick, Hedge, Carlyle, and the encyclopedias, the contact might have been more fruitful. But by 1881 Hegel had rendered up what was renderable to Whitman, and apparently he felt no need for reconsidering a subject into which he had gone as deeply as he cared too, and which had served and was still serving him admirably.

555. *As a Strong Bird*, Advertisement, p. 4.

556. For a neat summation of this relationship, see Newton Arvin, *Whitman*, pp. 196–97; also Clifton J. Furness, *Walt Whitman's Workshop*, pp. 149, 236.

LATER NINETEENTH-CENTURY WRITERS

557. See *Writings* (23 vols., Boston, 1904–1922), XII, 87; XIII, 149; XIV, 7, 25, 235; XV, 50, 58; XVII, 95; XXI, 203; XXII, 169–70, 172–75; XXIII, 257; and index to Vol. XVIII.

558. See *ibid.*, III, 6; XXI, 77.

559. His comments about Germany are often of a general nature—usually to criticize her militarism as destructive of her renowned culture. See *ibid.*, XXIII, 3–4, and Clara Barrus, *Life and Letters of John Burroughs*, II, 213.

560. It would seem that he kept Eckermann constantly near, for the great majority of his references to Goethe, early and late, are traceable to that book. The number of Goethe's works to which he refers is significantly small. Besides Eckermann, he mentioned only the *Autobiography*, *Werther*, the Goethe-Bettina letters, and *Wilhelm Meister*—all available in translation. For the rest he seems to have depended on Lewes' *Life of Goethe*, Carlyle, Tyndall's criticism of Goethe as a man of science, Hermann Grimm's life, and Matthew Arnold's critiques.

561. Barrus, *Life and Letters*, II, 173.

562. *Writings*, XVI, 238–39.

563. *Ibid.*, IV, 76.

564. *Ibid.*, X, 102.

565. *Ibid.*, pp. 154–55, 182.

566. *Ibid.*, XXI, 30.

567. *Ibid.*, III, 58.

568. *Ibid.*, X, 68.

569. *Ibid.*, p. 172.

570. *Ibid.*, XXI, 28–29.

571. *Ibid.*, XVII, 77; see also *Heart of Burroughs' Journal* (Boston, 1928), pp. 134–35, 145.

572. One would expect that Burroughs closely examined Goethe as a man of science, but there is little to suggest that he knew at first hand Goethe's more technical scientific treatises—doubtless because they were not available in translation. There are references to Goethe's discussions of the phenomena of the weather (*Writings*, III, 66; IV, 88), his relation to other scientists (*ibid.*, II, 64; XV, 73, 91), his opinions on scientific methodology (*ibid.*, VIII, 49–50, 54), and his remarks on matter. Finding Goethe's definition of matter as "the living garment of God" consonant with his own reverential view of the Cosmic, he quoted Goethe's phrase four times (*ibid.*, XVIII, 111, 260, 280; XIX, 134). Knowing little of Goethe's more special studies, Burroughs followed and repeated the conventional opinion that while "certain branches of scientific inquiry drew Goethe sharply . . . his aptitude in them was clearly less than in his chosen field," where he was supreme, even above Shakespeare and Milton.—*Ibid.*, VIII, 73, 151.

573. *Ibid.*, VI, 245.

574. *Ibid.*, X, 203–4.

575. *Ibid.*, XVIII, 98.

576. *Ibid.*, VIII, 254.

577. *Ibid.*, X, 140.

578. Much of the same criticism applies to what Burroughs has to say about other German writers. His comparison of the stylistic elements of Strauss's *Leben Jesu* with those of Renan's work, in the absence of a real knowledge of German, is a case in point (*ibid.*, X, 64, 79). His friendship for Whitman led him to make inquiries about Freiligrath, who had translated some of Whitman's poems (*ibid.*, III, 213). He cited Lessing's *Laokoon* in defense of Whitman (*ibid.*, p. 235), and he considered Heine's sympathetic theory of criticism as the only one properly applicable to Whitman's poetry (*ibid.*, II, 179, 233; X, 89; XVI, 97). Schiller is mentioned a half-dozen times; he knew F. v. Schlegel's *Philosophy of History*, and he read Carlyle's essays to good purpose.

579. *Ibid.*, XV, 91; XVIII, 221; XIX, 198.

580. *Ibid.*, XVI, 160. He was also a good deal interested in Schopenhauer. See *ibid.*, X, 67, 261–72; XVII, 198.

581. The title is as symptomatic of his approach to literature as its contents are various. Among his "literary passions" are 18 English writers, 7 American, 4 German, 4 Spanish, 2 French, 2 Russian, and one Norwegian.

582. *Years of My Youth* (N.Y., 1916), p. 90.

583. His study of German was not pursued with the idea of mastering the language but chiefly to read the poetry of Heine. Years later he confessed: "To this day I could not frame a proper letter in Spanish, German, French, or Italian, but I have a literary sense of them all. I wished to taste the fruit of my study before I had climbed the tree where it grew, and in a manner I did begin to gather the fruit without the interposition of the tree. Without clear knowledge of their grammatical forms, I

imitated their literary forms."—*Ibid.*, p. 100. However, in *My Literary Passions* (N.Y., 1895), p. 170, he observed: "I could once write a passable literary German . . . and I have still what I think I may call a fair German vocabulary."

His interest in German was immediately reflected in his insertion into the *Ashtabula Sentinel* of several stories from Heine, a biographical sketch of Goethe in 1855, and, two years later, a serialization of several of Zschokke's longer tales and shorter pieces from Goethe and others.

584. Germans were so numerous and the craze for Germanism so prevalent that he carried his "zeal for everything German" even to taking his lunch in one of the German beer saloons, only to find that the diet of cheese, mustard, sauerkraut, and lager beer made him "very sick," so that he was obliged to forego it as an expression of his love for German poetry. —*Years of My Youth*, p. 136; see also pp. 135, 178, 210; and Mildred Howells (ed.), *Life and Letters of William Dean Howells* (2 vols., Garden City, 1928), I, 20, 23.

585. When, in 1860, Howells was appointed consul to Rome (subsequently changed to Venice), he was disappointed that he did not get the post in Munich, for which he had specifically asked. Four years in Munich instead of Venice, and the opportunity to study at one of the German universities might have materially altered his literary outlook; but he went to Italy, and "for the present," he wrote, I went no further into German literature, and I recurred to it in later years only for deeper and fuller knowledge of Heine."—*My Literary Passions*, pp. 218, 233.

586. *Ibid.*, p. 148.

587. At fifteen he read "a great deal" of Goethe's prose and "somewhat of his poetry"—notably *Wilhelm Meister*, the *Wahlverwandtschaften*, and *Faust*—with little enthusiasm. Not until ten years later did he "go faithfully through Faust and come to know his power." Part of his earlier dissatisfaction with Goethe's prose he later ascribed to the "unwisdom of the critics" who led him to expect too much.—*Ibid.*, pp. 178, 188.

588. *Criticism and Fiction* (N.Y., 1891), pp. 22–24.

589. "Editor's Easy Chair," *Harper's Mag.*, CII, dcx (Mar., 1901), 643.

590. *Criticism and Fiction*, pp. 86–87.

591. *My Literary Passions*, pp. 169–70.

592. *Ibid.*, p. 172.

593. *Years of My Youth*, pp. 178–79; D. G. Cooke, *William Dean Howells* (N.Y., 1922), p. 27.

594. *Literary Friends and Acquaintance* (N.Y. 1900), p. 216.

595. H. B. Sachs, *Heine in America* (Phila., 1916), pp. 171–72.

596. Howells professed to have found great pleasure in some of Auerbach's stories, notably *Edelweiss*, but in the end he felt that Auerbach's work affected him "as if it dealt with pigmies." —*My Literary Passions*, p. 233. During his youth he "felt the romantic beauty of Uhland and was aware of something of Schiller's grandeur" (*ibid.*, p. 179), but he did not afterwards often refer to either. His "Movers" is a narrative poem in hexameters faintly reminiscent of *Hermann und Dorothea*, which he says he studied, along with Kingsley's *Andromeda* and Longfellow's *Evangeline*, in preparation for another narrative poem written about the same time—"The Pilot's Story." Except for a lingering interest in Goethe and an enduring love for Heine, Howells' early infatuation with German literature subsided about the time he went to Italy.

597. See *Notes of a Son and Brother* (N.Y., 1914)), pp. 23–24, 28–34.

598. *Letters of Henry James*, ed. by Percy Lubbock (N.Y., 1920), I, 32; Pelham Edgar, *Henry James, Man and Author* (London, 1927), pp. 19–20.

599. See his discussion of *Wilhelm Meister* in *Notes and Reviews* (Cambridge, Mass., 1921) and his comparison of Dumas and Goethe in the *Nation* for October 30, 1874.

It has recently been pointed out by Professor J. Wesley Thomas (*Amerikanische Dichter und die deutsche Literatur*, Goslar, 1950, pp. 133–37) that while James's first reading of *Wilhelm Meister* left him bewildered, because the book seemed to violate every idea he then entertained regarding a well-constructed novel, he eventually came to understand why Goethe succeeded so well in character delineation despite his inattention to externalities and the usual novel technique. Dr. Thomas points to the wide difference between James's objections to *Wilhelm Meister* in 1865 and his appraisal of Goethe as the consummate artist in 1873 (while reviewing Victor Cherbulliez' *Meta Holdenis*), and argues that as James grew ever more wary of the cramping effect of plot, he found in, and eventually adopted from, Goethe's method some of his later techniques for his own basically psychological approach that permitted a "continuous revelation" of character. The suggestion deserves to be weighed along with the numerous claims made for the influence upon James by Mérimée, Daudet, Gautier, Flaubert, Balzac, Zola, Turgenev, George Sand, George Eliot, Hawthorne, and the rest.

600. *My Mark Twain* (N.Y., 1919), p. 17.

601. He said as much himself: "The self-taught man seldom knows anything accurately." —*What Is Man? and Other Essays*, p. 290. All references are to the Harper's Author's National Edition of Mark Twain's *Works*. "To me the most important feature of my life is its literary feature. I have been professionally literary something more than fifty years."—*Ibid.*, p. 130. "One isn't a printer ten years without setting up acres of good and bad literature, and learning unconsciously at first, consciously later—to discriminate between the two, within his mental limitations, and meantime he is unconsciously acquiring what is called a style."—*Ibid.*, p. 136. A typesetter in New York in 1853, he answered his sister's inquiry about how he spent his leisure hours: "Where would you suppose, with a free printer's library containing more than 4,000 volumes within a quarter of a mile of me, and nobody at home to talk to?"—*Mark Twain's Letters*, ed. by A. B. Paine (2 vols., N.Y., 1917), II, 543; Minnie M. Brashear, *Mark Twain Son of Missouri* (Chapel Hill, 1934), p. 157. Later, on the river, his fellow-pilots regarded him as "a great reader—a student of history, travel, literature, and the sciences."—A. B. Paine, *Mark Twain. A Biography* (Centenary ed., 4 vols. in 2, N.Y., 1935), p. 151.

602. Notably Vol. I, Chs. IX–XI, and Vol. II, Ch. XXI.

603. *What is Man?*, p. 227; see A. B. Paine, *op. cit.*, p. 624.

604. His remarks about not knowing anything about books, at least, "not enough to hurt . . . only a few languages and a little history" are part of his studied banter (*Letters*, II, 543). He particularly enjoyed his wife's "torture" when she had to admit to a distinguished visitor from abroad that her husband was unacquainted with the several foreign authors who came up for discussion.—Paine, *op. cit.*, p. 1350. "It was part of the legend he deliberately created about himself, either because it pleased his vanity to believe that what he had read had been of small value in his development, or because he knew that he was more interesting to his American public in the role of an original."—Brashear, *op. cit.*, p. 197.

605. Howells, *My Mark Twain*, p. 18.

606. The simple truth is that Mark Twain read early and late, in books of many kinds, and in certain types of books almost constantly. "I like," he said, "history, biography, travels, curious facts and strange happenings, and science. And I detest novels, poetry, and theology."—Paine, *op. cit.*, p. 1536. The books he liked above all others were the Bible, *Don Quixote, Morte d'Arthur*, Lecky's *History of European Morals*, Suetonius' *Lives*, Carlyle's *French Revolution*, Greville's *Journal*, Saint-Simon's *Memoirs*, and Pepys' *Diary*. These he kept on a table at his bedside or on a handy shelf in the billiard room; he read them again and again, and Paine observed that he always had something new to say about them following each rereading.—*Op. cit.*, pp. 6–7, 511, 1536.

For *Innocents Abroad* he borrowed passages from literary sources totaling some 9,000 words by my count. *A propos* of his method of writing this, his first full-length book, he observed that "it wears a man out to have to read up a hundred pages of history every two or three miles"—meaning, every two or three pages.—*Innocents Abroad*, II, 232. Aside from guide books and historical works, the Bible was his main source for this book; and Chapters XV and XXI of Volume II illustrate how diligently he "read up on the Bible" while writing the book. *Roughing It* and *Life on the Mississippi*, usually considered books in which he drew most directly upon personal experience, contain, each, some 11,000 words of quoted matter exclusive of the appendices; and in *Following the Equator* he quoted passages aggregating 25,000 words. *Joan of Arc*, the book which Mark Twain himself held in higher esteem than anything else that he wrote, is based, by his own statement, on "five French sources and five English ones" (*Letters*, II, 624), while in preparation for *A Connecticut Yankee* he studied Malory, Lecky, and other books treating of the period until he could say, "I have saturated myself with the atmosphere of the day and the subject and got myself into the swing of the work."—Paine, *op. cit.*, p. 840; see also p. 790 and *A Connecticut Yankee*, pp. 2–3. *The Prince and the Pauper* was inspired by Yonge's *The Prince and the Page;* while *Tom Sawyer* and *Huckleberry Finn* without the episodes derived from his reading in Cervantes, Casanova, Baron Trenck, Cellini, and Dumas would be emasculated, indeed. The indebtedness of these last books is discussed briefly in O. H. Moore, "Mark Twain and Don Quixote," *PMLA*, XXXVII (June, 1922), 324–46, and in greater detail in my Master's thesis, "The Mind of Mark Twain" (typescript and microfilm, Univ. of Texas Library, 1924), pp. 1–46 and Appendix A.

607. Of German authors, he mentions Heine five times, Goethe and Schiller each three times, and Fritz Reuter once. Most of these references occur in the sections of *A Tramp Abroad* which record his excursions in Germany and Switzerland. He speaks of Schiller only in connection with Wilhelm Tell, and then only

because his travels took him to places associated with Tell. There is nothing to suggest that he read Schiller's play, though he may well have seen it acted in the course of his frequent attendance upon the German theater. Heine's lyrics he appears to have known at first hand. He was interested in Goetz, that "fine old German Robin Hood," and he claimed on one occasion to have bettered the existing translations of a disputed passage in *Faust*, with the aid of "a family pow-wow . . . and a heap of dictionaries."— H. W. Fisher, *Abroad with Mark Twain and Eugene Field* (N.Y., 1922), pp. 192–93. These, except for a long review of Adolf von Wilbrandt's play, *Der Meister von Palmyra* (in *The Man That Corrupted Hadleyburg*, pp. 202–15) and occasional references to such Germanic figures as Baron Münchausen, comprise all his significant allusions to German literature. His literary tastes were neither catholic nor exquisite. But he read a great deal, often whatever he happened upon, seldom with either system or plan. Appendix A, pp. 126–206 of "The Mind of Mark Twain" (cited above) brings together the important passages in Mark Twain's writings that bear on his knowledge of books and authors.

608. *My Mark Twain*, p. 17.

609. Paine, *op. cit.*, p. 616.

610. John R. Schultz, "New Letters of Mark Twain," *Amer. Lit.*, VIII, i (Mar., 1936), 47–48.

611. Paine, *op. cit.*, p. 623; the speech is reprinted in *A Tramp Abroad*, II, 305–7. During the late summer and early fall the whole party made a leisurely trip through Switzerland and Italy and back to Munich, where they spent the following winter. This journey was undertaken partly to gather materials for a book on Germany in the manner of *Innocents Abroad*. Clemens, accompanied by Twitchell, often struck off afoot for a jaunt of a day or more while the family followed by rail to rejoin them at some predetermined point along the way. It was a perfect holiday, undertaken in the spirit reflected in *A Tramp Abroad* (1880), a book which serves still as a delightful guide to the Neckar Valley, the Black Forest region, and the Swiss Alps. On the alert for fact and fable, literary and historical, and appreciative of the charm of scenery, he produced a German sketch book incorporating a wealth of custom and legend, all invested in the rare poetical quality that is equalled only by his recollections of boyhood and of pilot life on the Mississippi. For Mark Twain's attitude toward Germany as reflected in *A Tramp Abroad*, see V. R. West, "Mark Twain in Germany," *Amer.-Ger. Rev.*, II, iv (June, 1936), 32–37, esp. pp. 32–33, 36–37. A. Hüppy has handled the subject of Mark

Twain's travels in Switzerland in *Mark Twain und die Schweiz*, Zürich, 1935.

612. Paine, *op. cit.*, p. 638; J. R. Schultz, *loc. cit.*, p. 49.

613. *Ibid.*, p. 50; *A Tramp Abroad*, I, 98, 212.

614. In this connection, see his account of the German maid's impieties as recorded in *Mark Twain's Autobiography* (ed. by A. B. Paine, 2 vols., N. Y., 1914), II, 167–69.

615. Paine, *op. cit.*, p. 848.

616. Dixon Wecter, "Mark Twain as Translator from the German," *Amer. Lit.*, XIII, iii (Nov., 1941), 255.

617. Also in *The American Claimant*, pp. 308–38. Mark Twain claimed in a prefatory note that it was "a valuable invention" and guaranteed to teach French or any other tongue as well as German by the simple expedient of substituting for the German passages the desired language. He called it "the Patent Universally-Applicable Automatically-Adjustable Language Drama." The plot is simple. Two sisters, required by their father to speak only German for three months, in order to learn the language and to keep them from communicating with their lovers, contrive to meet the young men, who have been put under similar duress. Circumventing the father, landlady, and maid, they succeed in carrying on a lively exchange of ideas and sentiments, exclusively in the inane and stereotyped phrases of their Meisterschaft texts.

In characteristic manner Mark Twain added a note to the effect that if the reader discovered "some tolerably rancid German here and there in the piece," the fault was "attributable to the proof-reader." But that worthy, or someone else responsible for correcting Mark Twain's worst and sometimes most felicitous errors, struck out this blanket disclaimer.—Paine, *op. cit.*, p. 849. There occur many bad spellings and misprints in the printed version, although whoever "corrected" the manuscript took seriously his job of "purifying" the "rancid" state of the manuscript, now preserved in the Huntington Library. The handwriting of the reviser is not Mark Twain's. It need hardly be observed that the manuscript form is incomparably more funny than the published text. A reprinting of portions of the Huntington manuscript by Ada M. Klett in the *American German Review*, VII, ii (Dec., 1940), 10–11, makes it clear that Mark Twain had not attained full "Meisterschaft" of the German language in 1887, but it is equally clear that many of his atrocities are studied, for even in the passages which he had merely to copy verbatim from the type, or specimen, sentences in the text of Meisterschaft or Ollendorff's books, he preferred to make "improvements" of his own.

618. After a rapid tour of France and Switzerland, they rested for a time at Aix, proceeded thence to Beyreuth for the Wagner festival (commemorated in an appreciative essay, "At the Shrine of St. Wagner"), and after various side trips they went to Heidelberg, shortly afterward settling in Berlin for the winter.

619. Paine, *op. cit.*, p. 936.

620. *Ibid.*, p. 933. Earlier than this he had produced a compound of eighty letters (*A Tramp Abroad*, p. 306). He persisted in trying to break this record, but as late as 1898 he had come no nearer than "Hottentotenstrottelmutterattentäterlattengitterwetterkotterbeutelratte" (a mere seventy). However, the next year he produced what is probably "the last word in monstrosities": "Personaleinkommensteuerschätzungskommissionsmitgliedreisekostenrechnungsergänzungsrevisionsfund"(ninety-five). He added: "If I could get a similar word engraved upon my tombstone I should sleep beneath it in peace."—John T. Krumpelmann, *Mark Twain and the German Language* (Baton Rouge, La., 1953), p. 16.

As for learning German the regular way, he again resolved, during this second period of residence in Germany, as he had earlier, that he would abandon altogether the German grammar as "outrageous and impossible," for "only the dead have time to learn it."—*A Tramp Abroad*, II, 305; Paine, *op. cit.*, p. 623. With or without benefit of grammar, however, the study of German continued until (as Professor Krumpelmann's detailed inquiries show) he could read journalistic German easily, could write German almost flawlessly, could understand even rapid conversational German, and could, "if in the mood to try and given time to shape his phrases," speak acceptably but never fluently.

621. *In The American Claimant and Other Stories and Sketches*, pp. 502–17.

622. For a discussion of this racy translation, see the essay by Dixon Wecter, *loc. cit.*, pp. 257–63. The manuscript of twenty-six pages remained unpublished until the centennial year of 1935, when Harper brought it out as *Slovenly's Peter*, with a preface by Clara C. Gabrilowitsch.

623. Again the family were with him—all but Susy, who had died in 1896. There were journeyings in Germany and Switzerland, but much time was spent in Vienna. Here they met the same courtly reception which Berlin had accorded them earlier.

624. *Mark Twain's Speeches* (ed. by A. B. Paine, N.Y., 1910), pp. 168–75. Averring himself the truest friend of the German language, he asked for a number of reformations, among

them the banning of parentheses, separable verbs, and the use of more than thirteen subjects to the sentence. A few months later, reverting to the use of compound words in German, he wrote on the "Beauties of the German Language" (*Autobiography*, II, 164–66.) While preparing for an audience later with Emperor Franz Joseph, he compacted a speech that would cover all emergencies into a single German sentence of eighteen words, but he found the Emperor so cordially informal that he forgot to deliver it.—Paine, *op. cit.*, 1078–79.

625. During the winter of 1897–1898 he translated several German plays which remained unproduced and unpublished, and during the next year he undertook several plays for the Burgtheater in collaboration with a Vienna journalist and playwright, Siegmund Schlesinger. The plan was for Mark Twain to provide the plots based on American themes. The opening scenes of one of them, to be called "Die Goldgräberin," were actually written, but it developed that Schlesinger's lack of English and Mark Twain's difficulties with rapid-fire German made a bad combination, so that the plans had to be abandoned. But Director-General Herr Schlenther, head of the Burgtheater, never doubted that a play by Clemens and Schlesinger, with Frau Kati Schratt (later the favorite of Emperor Franz Joseph), would have been a great success.—Paine, *op. cit.*, pp. 1682, 1071, 1075.

626. *Letters*, II, 671. In an essay entitled "About Play-Acting," written in Vienna and first printed in the *Forum* for October of that year, he said that he had found the play "deeply fascinating," and that he believed it would turn out to be Wilbrandt's "masterpiece . . . and make his name permanent in German literature."—*The Man Who Corrupted Hadleyburg*, p. 202. The rest of the eulogistic critique is an elaboration of the "dark metempsychosis" in the play, which he said constituted "the strength of the piece." It gave him an overpowering sense of "the passage of a dimly connected procession of dream pictures."—*Ibid.*, p. 203.

627. While his interpretation doubtless goes beyond Wilbrandt's intention, the important thing is Mark Twain's analysis of it as a pessimistic commentary on life. It may be no more than a coincidence, but it seems more likely that Wilbrandt's "majestic drama of depth and seriousness" (*ibid.*, pp. 208, 215) set his mind, already in a responsive mood, to work on the ideas that underlie *What is Man?* and *The Mysterious Stranger*, especially the latter. (Compare *The Man Who Corrupted Hadleyburg*, pp. 208–9, with the last long speech of *The Myste-*

rious Stranger.) Mark Twain's mysterious stranger, Philip Traum, is made of the same stuff that Wilbrandt's mysterious stranger, Pausanias, is made of, and the imaginary medieval Austrian village, Eseldorf, and its spiritual atmosphere are not unlike those of Palmyra in Wilbrandt's drama.

The connection between Mark Twain and Wilbrandt was suggested as early as 1919 (*MLN*, VI, 372–73), and more recently it has been argued (by J. Wesley Thomas, *op. cit.*, pp. 131–32) that there is a similar relationship between the monistic determinism of Ernst Haeckel and the pessimism of Arthur Schopenhauer, on the one hand, and Mark Twain's mechanistic fatalism of his later years, as well as his expression of it in *What is Man?* and *The Mysterious Stranger*, on the other. This influence, while possible, is hard to substantiate, the evidence being almost exclusively internal and by no means conclusive. A series of personal disasters, coupled with the direct influences upon him of mechanistically-minded men like Macfarlane and Ingersoll and his early familiarity with various forms of scientific rationalism, were sufficient to set his mind in the direction of misanthropy long before he encountered Haeckel and Schopenhauer.

628. During all his years as a journalist he appears to have reviewed only one German book, Berthold Auerbach's *Black Forest Village Stories*, for the *Overland Monthly*, September, 1869. For the preceding number he had reviewed Bayard Taylor's *By-Ways of Europe*.

629. *Letters of Bret Harte* (N.Y., 1926), pp. 73–178; *Writings* (22 vols., Boston and N.Y., 1902–1914), XI, 143; T. D. Pemberton, *Life of Bret Harte*, (N.Y., 1903).

630. His fame as a writer had preceded him. Some of his poems had been translated into German by Freiligrath; three volumes of stories had appeared in 1873–1874; the novel *Gabriel Conroy* went through fourteen printings; and while *The Two Men of Sandy Bar* turned out a failure on the American stage, the German version was a fair success.—George R. Stewart, *Bret Harte, Argonaut and Exile* (Boston, 1931), pp. 224, 227, 232.

631. *Letters*, pp. 117–18, 120, 139.

632. Several later stories touch upon German themes in a superficial way. In "The Indiscretion of Elizabeth" he makes a good deal of the red tape of German petty officialdom, and in "Unser Karl," a tale belonging to the espionage class, he turns to good account his experiences in the consular service. Altogether the best of his German yarns are those embodying German-American characters. "Peter Schroeder" is the story of a Civil War veteran who distin-guished himself under Schurz only to find that Anglo-Americans ridicule his dialect and his patriotism. Having yearned for Germany for fifteen years, he goes thither, only to find himself a stranger there as much as in the United States. "The Man and the Mountain" is a variation upon the same theme of repatriation, except that the main character is a Swiss gardener. The dialect in both stories is convincing. Finally, there are three poems that touch German matters. The first, in the form of an ironic preface to Wallace's romantic opera *Lurline* (1830), is really a parody on the opera and on Heine's "Lorelei." The second, included among the Civil War poems and entitled "Schalk!" is an ironic poem advising Americans to fight in the German way as prescribed by Emil Schalk. The last, "Schimmelpfennig," commemorates the German-American general of that name who fought in the Civil War.

633. An Easterner by birth, and a graduate of Yale, he sailed round the Horn, spent 1862–1866 in California, went back to New England intending to study theology, but soon turned back, taught school in Ohio, then in Oakland High School (1871–1873), and thereafter became professor of English at the University of California. A teacher, poet, critic, contributor to magazines, and translator all his life, he was a wide reader, especially of English, but hardly less so of French and German, literature.

634. W. B. Parker, *Edward Rowland Sill* (N.Y., 1915), pp. 99, 104.

635. Possessed of a fine feeling for French and German lyrics (see *Prose of Edward Rowland Sill*, Boston, 1900, pp. 93–94, 117–22), he found existing English translations of German lyrics generally "abominable" and offered a few of his own from Schubert, Goethe, and Rückert. See *Poetical Works* (Household ed., Boston, 1906), pp. 252–54, 355, 356; also *Poems* (Boston, 1889), pp. 80–81.

636. See *Prose*, pp. 24, 33–34, 107.

637. *Prose*, pp. xlv, 181.

638. *Prose*, p. 141.

639. Walter Neale, *Life of Ambrose Bierce* (N.Y., 1929), pp. 40–41, 386. His biographer relates a story of how, in 1872, a group of American writers exposed him at a London dinner in honor of Mark Twain. They gave him one of his own stories to read. Flattered but forgetful of his youthful fondness for foreign phrases, Bierce read without a qualm through the first page; but on turning the page, he came upon phrases in four different languages which he could neither pronounce nor translate.—*Ibid.*, pp. 42–43.

640. Gustav A. Danziger's translation appeared serially in the Sunday magazine section

of the *San Francisco Examiner* beginning September 18, 1891. *The Monk and the Hangman's Daughter* appeared under the joint authorship of Bierce and Danziger in 1892. How large a hand Bierce had in this adaptation, or new rendition, is an open question.

641. Goethe's *Erlkönig* he says was known "two thousand years ago in Greece as 'The Demos and the Infant Industry'" (*The Devil's Dictionary*, N.Y., 1926, p. 201). He professes to be familiar with the archaeological investigations of Dr. Schliemann (*ibid.*, p. 110) and with the *Monadology* of Leibnitz (*ibid.*, p. 221). He defines *Understanding* as "a cerebral secretion that enables one having it to know a horse from a horse by the roof on the house," and, he adds, that its nature and laws have been exhaustively expounded by Locke, "who rode a house, and by Kant, who lives in a horse."—*Ibid.*, p. 356. In the case of Nietzsche and Schopenhauer there are indications that he possessed more than a passing familiarity with their works. His two essays on the position of woman in *The Shadow of the Dial* (1909) appear to be influenced by his reading of Nietzsche's and Schopenhauer's views of women. See *The Shadow of the Dial* (San Francisco, 1909), pp. 79–186, 187–203; also Neale, *op. cit.*, pp. 29, 114, 241.

642. German characters appear also in *The Faith Doctor* (1891), and Swiss-Americans play a prominent role in *Roxy* (1879).

643. It will be recalled that Lanier had used German characters in a German-American setting in his *Tiger-Lilies* as early as 1867.

644. For bibliographical documentation of this shift, see Richard Mönnig, *Amerika und England im deutschen, österreichischen und schweizerischen Schrifttum der Jahre 1945–1949: Eine Bibliographie* (Stuttgart, 1951).

AMERICAN LITERARY CRITICISM

645. See Wm. Charvat, *The Origins of American Critical Thought 1810–1835* (Phila., 1936).

646. It was denominated the "New School" by Carlyle (*Crit. and Misc. Essays*, Cent. ed., I, 54), whose influence can be traced from 1827, when his first articles on German literature appeared, until past the middle of the century, when Whitman, for example, extracted pages of memoranda from these essays.

647. German criticism of Shakespeare comes nearest to forming a coherent body of thought, and therefore its impact on American writers can be traced more readily and more surely than the influence of the individual German critic or the particular critical principle.

Ideas and techniques first applied by Germans to Shakespeare were capable of indefinite expansion and application. For example, the Schlegelian interpretation of Aristotelian organic unity, first applied to Shakespeare, soon received a wider application, and in the thought of an Emerson or a Thoreau became the basis of all art and life. Where individual German critics or particular criteria (apart from Shakespeare criticism) made themselves felt in America—as they did in the cases of Poe, Longfellow, and Lanier—these influences are treated in the preceding sections on these writers.

648. The German discovery of Shakespeare was the third in what may be termed a series of three waves of English influence upon German literature of the eighteenth century. The first involved such classicists as Addison, Pope, and Defoe; the second introduced Milton, Richardson, and Edward Young; and the third (*ca.* 1760–1780) coincides roughly with the *Sturm-und-Drang* agitation and brought in, besides Shakespeare, Ossian and English balladry, Sterne, Fielding, and Young's *Conjectures*.

Lessing's first notice of Shakespeare occurred in *Beyträge zur Historie und Aufnahme des Theaters* (1750), where he recommended the study of Shakespeare and the Restoration dramatists. By 1759 he was calling for a German translation and pointing out (in the famous seventeenth *Literaturbrief*) that Shakespearean sublimity, terror, and melancholy were more consonant with German taste than the over-refinement of manners, the delicate sensibilities, and the romantic heroics that characterized the French drama. In the 1760's a number of dramas were produced on German stages, and *Sturm-und-Drang* critics (Gerstenberg, Herder, and Hamann), following Young's *Conjectures on Original Composition* (1760), hailed him às "der grosse Wilde," an original genius. The young Goethe's enthusiasm produced the famous address *Zum Shakespeares Tag* (1771), and the activity of translating, adapting, playing, and criticizing Shakespeare went on in ever-increasing tempo.

649. These first three tendencies were instituted chiefly by Lessing in the *Hamburgische Dramaturgie* (1767–1768). He was seconded by many others, notably by Herder, who sharply differentiated between Shakespearean and Greek drama and emphasized the dominant ideas of *Hamlet, Macbeth*, and *Othello*, and by Schiller, who drew very sharply the distinction (based on the differing conditions and different epochs) between classic and romantic poetry. See T. M. Raysor (ed.), *Coleridge's Shakespeare Criticism* (2 vols., Cambridge, Mass., 1930), I, xxvii–xxix.

The Schlegels popularized Shakespeare by their translations, their periodical criticism, their lectures, and their control over stage productions (see L. M. Price, *The Reception of English Literature in Germany*, Berkeley, 1932, pp. 322–23). Friedrich Schlegel insisted that an all-pervading unity of theme transfuses the plays of Shakespeare, and he defended the romantic belief that art proceeds from the soul of genius and obeys no external laws.— Augustus Ralli, *A History of Shakespeare Criticism* (London, 1932), p. 115. A. W. Schlegel's *Vorlesungen* synthesized the romantic attitudes: He attacked the neoclassical position once again, describing Shakespeare not as a wildly luxuriant genius but as a consummate artist, whose very puns and plays on words have their ground in nature. He popularized the historicist position by urging the difference in conditions under which ancient and modern dramas were produced. He clarified the distinction between classical and romantic drama; he encouraged the study of the literatures of all countries, arguing that even barbarous literatures have a claim on our aesthetic appreciation when they are viewed in relation to the times in which they were produced; and he established as a basic principle the idea that the unity of art, proceeding organically from within, applies as much to Shakespeare's plays as to nature itself.—Ralli, *op. cit.*, pp. 117–23; A. A. Helmholtz, *The Indebtedness of S. T. Coleridge to A. W. Schlegel* (Madison, Wis., 1907)' p. 355; Raysor, *op. cit.*, I, xxx; and especially R. P. Falk, "Representative American Criticism of Shakespeare, 1830–1885," unpublished diss., Univ. of Wisconsin, 1940, pp. 10–11.

650. Coleridge gave expression to all these principles. "While the remains of his 1808 lectures show less similarity to Schlegel, the 1811 and 1818 lectures become progressively more dependent . . . so that the ultimate effect of his work on Shakespeare is closely parallel to that of the German critic."—Helmholtz, *op. cit.*, pp. 355–57. However, Coleridge's best criticism is his aesthetic analysis of specific plays and his study of individual characters. If he was Schlegel's debtor in general principles of aesthetics, much of his practical or applied criticism was either his own or derived from British roots. He left his most profound impress on American critics like Hudson and Giles precisely in these respects. See Raysor, *op. cit.*, pp. xxxii–xxxiii, liii; R. W. Babcock, *The Genesis of Shakespeare Idolatry* (Chapel Hill, 1931); and R. P. Falk, *op. cit.*, p. 12.

651. XI, 202–4.

652. Wm. Charvat *op. cit.*, pp. 127, 180–82.

653. See his essay comparing French and English tragedy, *North Amer. Rev.*, XVI (Jan,. 1823), 132; also *ibid.*, XLIX (Oct., 1839), 324.

654. *Ibid.*, (VIII Mar., 1819), 320; Charvat, *op. cit.*, p. 179. These unpublished lectures, on subjects ranging from general literary theory to careful analyses of character, are made available in part in G. M. Weimar's unprinted dissertation, "Richard Henry Dana the Elder, Critic," New York Univ., 1920. Excellent summaries are provided by Falk, *op. cit.*, pp. 29–39. Professor Falk (p. 36) finds Dana closest to the "new" critics in his interpretation of Hamlet as a sensitive, delicate student and thinker who is unable to cope with a difficult practical situation.

655. Hudson lectured in the South and West during the 40's. The friend of such men as Dana, Parker, Emerson, and Ticknor, he was a respected member of the Boston literary circle and after 1849 a priest in the Protestant Episcopal Church. Convinced that "the Bible apart, Shakespeare's dramas are . . . the greatest classic and literary treasures of the world," Hudson clothed his interpretations in a rhapsodic and at the same time highly moral tone calculated to bring Shakespeare within the comprehension of the "average American." To the same end he published between 1851 and 1856 and eleven-volume edition of the dramas— an edition that is rich in the kind of aesthetic interpretation that characterizes his highly successful *Lectures*. Instead of supplying textual criticism, he consciously followed the paths laid out in the writings of Coleridge, Schlegel, Lamb, and Hazlitt.—A. J. George, *Essays on English Studies by Henry N. Hudson* (Boston, 1906), pp. 7, 104. The "Hudson" Shakespeare, revised by various hands and still published today, remains a popular and influential college edition.

656. Karl Knortz, *Shakespeare in Amerika* (Berlin, 1882), p. 58.

657. *Lectures on Shakespeare* (2 vols., N.Y., 1848), I, 134, 169.

658. For a more detailed consideration of his critical opinions and their Germanic parallels, see Falk, *op. cit.*, pp. 45–78.

659. A professional reviewer and essayist, literary editor of the *Boston Daily Globe*, and a free-lance lecturer in the lyceum movement, he was master of a richly epigrammatic style. Versed equally in English, American, and German criticism, he placed Schlegel "among the greatest critics of the world" and Schlegel and Coleridge together as "the originators of the school of philosophical criticism." See "Shakespeare's Critics," *North Amer. Rev.*, July, 1848; repr. in *Essays and Reviews* (2 vols., Boston, 1848–1849; 7th ed., Boston, 1878), II, 217, 220.

660. See "Shakespeare, the Man and the Dramatist," *Atl. Monthly*, June, 1867, p. 719.

661. Ulrici's book, for example, seemed to him, as it did to Lowell, "German in the worst sense of the word," built on the theory that Shakespeare wrote to illustrate the five points of Calvinism. Ulrici is "as far from Shakespeare in spirit as old Rhymer himself."—*Essays and Reviews*, II, 225. Schlegel himself shared in this Teutonic error, and "even Goethe, the most comprehensive intelligence since Shakespeare, failed to 'pluck out the heart' of Hamlet's mystery."—*Atl. Monthly*, XIX (June, 1867), 722.

662. Falk, *op. cit.*, p. 152.

663. *Works*, II, 68. Despite his avowal of "principles," Lowell's criticism was variously derived and often impressionistic in practice. Basically humanistic, or antiromantic, in his more mature professions, and desirous of judging objectively on the basis of standards, he lacked the intellectual vigor needed to lift him above impressionism. See Norman Foerster *American Criticism* (N.Y., 1928), pp. 111–56; H. H. Clark, "Lowell's Criticism of Romantic Literature," *PMLA*, XLI (Mar., 1926), 209–28; H. H. Clark, "Lowell—Humanitarian, Nationalist, or Humanist ?" *Studies in Philol.*, XXVII, iii (July, 1930), 411–41, esp. pp. 430–41. Lowell stood out among his contemporaries because of his accomplished versatility. Bookish and academic, well—though more widely than deeply or systematically—read in English, Spanish, French, German, and classical literatures, an epicurean browser blessed with a retentive memory, Lowell was understandably an eclectic whose theory and practice would be widely at variance. His knowledge of the classics was important in forming his literary creed, but he could not avoid judging the Greeks by the presuppositions of the nineteenth century. See *Works*, III, 29, 34; J. P. Pritchard, "Lowell's Debt to Horace's *Ars Poetica*," *Amer. Lit.*, III (Nov., 1931), 259–76, and "Aristotle's Poetics and Certain American Literary Critics," *Classical Weekly*, XXVII (Jan. 15, 1934), 89–93.

Concluding that Lowell's critical methodology involved sensitivity to impressions, historical understanding, and an aesthetical judgment, Professor Foerster suggests that "it remained for Lowell to state more clearly [than his predecessors] the nature of historical criticism, to exemplify it in studies of a series of great writers, and to demonstrate its value as a preparation for literary criticism in its highest form." While Lowell considered the principles of art to be "immutable," he felt that their application must accommodate itself to

the material supplied to them by the time and by the national character and traditions. "Behind this conception lies, as Lowell knew, the idea of the organic—the idea that literature is not a manufacture but a growth. . . . The critic who does not seek to understand the genetic principle in the writers of the past is incapable of a complete criticism."—Foerster, *op. cit.*, pp. 120,124.

664. It appeared in the *Atlantic* for January and February, 1859, as a review of R. G. White's edition of Shakespeare.

665. This approach was no less important in Schlegel and Coleridge, and Lowell might have derived it thence, or, for that matter, from Sainte-Beuve or H. A. Taine, except that he thrice refers the historical method specifically to Goethe.

666. *Works*, III, 63.

667. For details, see Falk, *op. cit.*, pp. 26–28.

668. Goethe had taken his criticism lightly and had what appeared to be a subjective or impressionistic view of the critical function. In mature life, he said, "I am more and more convinced that whenever one has to express an opinion on the actions or on the writings of others, unless this be done from a certain one-sided enthusiasm, or from a loving interest in the person or the work, the result is hardly worth considering."—*Goethe's Literary Essays*, ed. by J. E. Spingarn (N.Y., 1921), pp. 141–42. As editor of the *North American Review* and the *Atlantic*, Lowell was required to undertake a great deal of formal criticism and saw the task before him as far more serious than Goethe in his detachment viewed it. Still, he called upon Goethe for support whenever the opportunity offered, as when, starting from Coleridge's "primary" and "secondary" imagination, he developed his threefold theory of imagination (Foerster, *op. cit.*, pp. 133–40); he elected to omit much of the "Coleridgean moonshine" and tried "to lay hold of the term [imagination] with his understanding," in order "den Gegenstand fest zu halten," in the words of Goethe.—*Works*, II, 86.

669. For details, see Falk, *op. cit.*, pp. 88, 89–93, 124–36.

670. She defined the critic's function as a supplement to that of the creative artist, in which both strive together to realize the ideal standard that lies outside or beyond both. Literature is but one of the many evidences in the life of the universe (along with art, religion, and science) that there is a progressive tendency working all things up from Nature, through Man, to Spirit or Ideality. Literature is to be brought before the bar of reason, where critic and writer can settle their differences on equal

terms. When she set about to judge, she applied her principles with conviction and energy; and while she was charged with being a "lean old maid" or "Dr. Johnson in Petticoats," she spoke her convictions, as she believed, fairly and in the light of the high ideal principles that she recognized. Her practice, at a time when a Longfellow or a Cooper nursed their sensitive feelings and a Poe slashed about him in personal pique, was salutary to the development of a sane, responsible criticism.

671. *Life Without and Life Within*, p. 88.

672. See *Art, Literature, and the Drama*, pp. 13–20, 119, 357; and "Short Essay on Critics," *Dial*, I, i (July, 1840), 5–11.

673. In *Art, Literature, and the Drama* (p. 179) she distinguished between the one mode of criticism which tries "by the highest standard of literary perfection . . . each work that comes in its way, rejecting all that is possible to reject, and receiving with toleration only what is capable of standing the severest test," and the other, which "enters into the natural history of everything . . . believes no impulse to be entirely vain . . . and believes there is beauty in each natural form, if its law and progress be understood."

674. *Letters*, I, 153, n. 62.

675. *Ibid.*, II, 248, n. 2.

676. *Ibid.*, pp. 424–26.

677. Emerson's reading of Coleridge from 1829 onward seems not to have inspired him to formulate any clear-cut idea of organic unity until after his more active concern with Schlegel's lectures provided the stimulus; as a definite principle of art the idea finds its first notable expression in "The Poet."

678. "The Poet," *Works*, III, 5.

679. *Ibid.*, p. 8.

680. The importance which Emerson attached to expression appears to be in some measure attributable to Goethe, although the notion is already implicit in the section on "Language" in *Nature* and in *The American Scholar*. Emerson had been familiar since 1829 with Coleridge's remarks on the subject in the Preface to *Aids to Reflection*. But in the journal of 1837 he definitely linked the idea with quotations transcribed into his diaries out of Eckermann's conversations and the correspondence of Goethe and Zelter:

"Lively feeling of the circumstance, and faculty to express it makes the poet.—Goethe.

"They say much of the study of the Ancients, but what else does that signify than, direct your attention to the real world and seek to express it, *since that did the ancients* whilst they lived.—Goethe."—*Journals*, IV, 194 (Mar. 18, 1837). The italics are Emerson's and the

phraseology suggests that these notations are Emerson's own literal translations.

Another point of contact between Emerson and Goethe is in the view of the ancients *versus* the moderns, the classic *versus* the romantic. He cites (as Lowell was to do later) the dictum: "'*Should*,' says Goethe, "was the genius of the antique drama; *Would* of the modern, but *should* is always great and stern; *would* is weak and small.'"—*Journals*, IV, 90 (Sept. 23, 1836). The observation harmonized with his own humanistic conception of the ethical values of art based on universally valid spiritual truths or eternal laws; it supported the arguments for his concept of nature in its symbolic role as means to an end, of art as means to the achievement of the ideal.

In his applied criticism Emerson looked down upon poets from this empyrean height and accordingly found even Shakespeare wanting—a "half-man," only "a master of revels to mankind."—*Works*, IV, 217. For this reason, despite his tributes to Goethe's mind, he never materially changed his early view of Goethe the man, when he remarked in 1834, "the Puritan in me accepts no apology for bad morals in such as he."—*Carlyle-Emerson Correspondence*, I, 30. If he did not completely reject art in favor of religion, he was concerned with raising it to the level of religion.

681. In Poe, to be sure, it was used in the concoction of a technic for the short story and short poem; but despite Poe's effort to invest the concept with a mathematical-philosophical aura, it remains somewhat artificial and mechanical. In Poe beauty reputedly has nothing to do with the didactic or moral; in Emerson Beauty, Truth, and Goodness are one. Emerson identifies beauty and virtue; Poe persits in damning the "heresy of the didactic."

682. *Works*, IV, 204.

683. See *ibid.*, pp. 189, 194, 195–96.

684. Emerson was inclined to rate Very's essay on Shakespeare "with those of Coleridge, Lamb, and Goethe."—Wm. I. Bartlett, *Jones Very. Emerson's "Brave Saint"* (Durham, N. C., 1942), p. 60.

685. *Studies in Shakespeare* (Boston, 1886; 4th ed., 1889), p. 52.

686. "The Anatomizing of William Shakespeare," *Atl. Monthly*, LIII (May, 1884), 596, 603.

687. *Ibid.*, p. 604.

688. *Ibid.*, p. 602; see also "King Lear," *Atl. Monthly*, XLVI (July, 1880), 113.

689. Horace Traubel, *Walt Whitman in Camden*, I, 240–41.

690. Whitman's praise and censure of Shakespeare is treated by C. J. Furness, "Walt Whit-

man's Estimate of Shakespeare," *Harvard Studies and Notes in Philol. and Lit.*, XIV 1932), 1–33; R. C. Harrison, "Walt Whitman and Shakespeare," *PMLA*, XLIV (Dec., 1929), 1201–38; J. O. Johnson, "Walt Whitman as a Critic of Literature," *Univ. of Nebraska Studies in Lang., Lit., and Criticism*, No. 16 (1938), pp. 35–50; Falk, *op. cit.*, pp. 310–39; and Falk, "Shakespeare's Place in Walt Whitman's America," *Shakespeare Assn. Bulletin*, XVII, ii (Apr., 1942), 86–96, esp. pp. 89–91.

691. He echoed the St. Louis Hegelians in declaring that "the formulas of Hegel are an essential and crowning justification of New World Democracy in the creative realms of time and space."—*Specimen Days* (1882), in *Complete Prose Works* (N.Y., 1914), p. 169. He welcomed Hegel's concept of historical progress in which conflicting ideas are reconciled in a higher synthesis—the doctine of a cosmic consciousness that unfolds through conflict and contradiction to divine ends. The seeds of the present are contained in the past, and a close reading of the past, even of feudal society, reveals latent germs of the future democratic order of things. For Whitman the societies that bred Homer and Shakespeare were alike "feudal" (*Writings*, VI, 136), and he significantly drew the dividing line just at the close of the Elizabethan age, Shakespeare's work marking at once the sunset of feudalism and its "last gorgeous effort before the advance of the new day."—*Prose Works*, p. 475.

692. Falk, *loc. cit.*, p. 90.

693. *Writings*, VI, 120–23, 125; III, 59; V, 96, 207–8.

694. *November Boughs*, ed. by David McKay (Phila., 1888), p. 18.

695. *Writings*, V, 55, 130.

696. See Floyd Stovall (ed.), *Walt Whitman…* (N.Y., 1934), p. xv.

697. See Alice L. Cooke, "Whitman's Indebtedness to the Scientific Thought of His Day," *Univ. of Texas Studies in English*, XIV (July, 1934), 89–115.

698. *Writings*, VI, 136; C. J. Furness, *loc. cit.*, p. 9.

699. *Shakespeare from an American Point of View* (3rd ed., N.Y., 1882), p. 466.

700. Falk, *op. cit.*, p. 352.

701. For a statement of the esteem in which the German system of higher education came to be regarded, see James M. Hart, *German Universities: A Narrative of Personal Experiences, with Statistical Information … and a Comparison of the German, English, and American Systems …* (N.Y., 1874; 2nd ed., 1878).

INDEX

Index